the SAILOR'S

WORD BOOK

the SAILOR'S WORD BOOK

The classic source for over 14,000 nautical and naval terms

including some more especially military
and scientific, but useful to the seamen;
as well as archaisms of early voyages, etc.

By the late
Admiral **W. H. Smyth** KSF, DCL, &c.

Revised for the press by
Vice-Admiral Sir E. Belcher KCB, &c

CONWAY

Volume © Conway 1991

This edition published in 2005 by
Conway
An imprint of Anova Books Ltd
10 Southcombe Street
London W14 0RA
www.anovabooks.com

Distributed in the U.S. and Canada by:
Sterling Publishing Co., Inc.
387 Park Avenue South
New York, NY 10016-8810

Reprinted 2009

British Library Cataloguing in Publication Data
A catalogue record for this book is available from the British Library

ISBN 9780851779720

Printed and bound at SNP Leefung Printers Ltd, China.

To receive regular email updates on forthcoming Conway titles, email
conway@anovabooks.com with Conway Update in the subject field.

THE EDITOR'S PREFACE.

THE recent loss of Admiral William Henry Smyth, noticed as it was by the leading periodicals, will have recalled to many, not only the social character and amiable qualities of the compiler of this Work, but also his distinguished professional career and high reputation as an officer, a navigator, and a seaman, which will be a guarantee for the details of this posthumous publication.

When, in 1858, the Admiral reached the allotted term of three-score years and ten, yet in perfect health, he executed his resolution of resigning to younger men the posts he held in the active scientific world, and concentrated his attention, at his quiet and literary retreat of St. John's Lodge, near Aylesbury, on reducing for the press the vast amount of professional as well as general information which he had amassed during a long, active, and earnest life: the material for this "Digest" outstanding as the last, largest, and most important part of it. Had he survived but a few months more, a preface in his own terse and peculiar style, containing his last ideas, would have rendered these remarks unnecessary; but he was cut off on the 8th of September, 1865, leaving this favourite manuscript to the affectionate care of his family and friends. By them it has been most carefully revised; and is now presented to the public, especially to his honoured profession, for the benefit of which he thought and worked during the long period which elapsed between his leaving the quarter-deck and his death; as his Charts (constructed from his numerous surveys), his twenty years' Essays in the *United Service Journal,* his efforts to render his astronomical researches accessible to seamen,—all testify.

Admiral Smyth was what has been called a *commonplacer.* He had the habit of methodically storing up, through a long series of years, all that could profit the seaman, whether scientific or practical. A collector of coins, and in various ways an antiquary, he knew well, not merely that "many mickles make a muckle," but that it will sometimes chance that the turning up of one little thing makes another little thing into a great one. And he culled from the intelligent friends with whom he associated many points of critical definition which cannot be found elsewhere. Thus, in addition to naval terms, he has introduced others relating to fortification; to ancient and modern arms and armour; to objects of natural history occurring at sea, in travel, &c.: the whole forming such an assemblage of interesting and instructive matter as will prove valuable to both seaman and landsman.

This "Digest" may engage the attention of the naval officer, not merely for the information it conveys, but for the doubts it may raise in matters deserving further research. Independently of the variety of subjects treated, the author's characteristic manner of handling them will make it to his former brother officers a reminiscence of one of the true tars of the old school—the rising generation will find here old terms (often misunderstood by younger writers) interpreted by one who was never content with a definition until he had confirmed it satisfactorily by the aid of the most accomplished of his cotemporaries; the landsman will discover the meaning or derivation of words either obsolete or which are not elsewhere to be traced, though occurring in general literature. To all it is the legacy of an officer highly appreciated by men of science, who on shore as well as afloat fought his way to eminence in every department, and always deemed it his pride that no aim was dearer to him than the advancement of his noble profession.

LONDON, *May, 1867.*

CAPTN W.H.SMYTH R.N. KSF. FRS FSA. IRAS

1842

INTRODUCTION.

WHAT'S in a word? is a question which it is held clever to quote and wise to think unanswerable: and yet there is a very good answer, and it is—a meaning, if you know it. But there is another question, and it is, What's a word in? There is never a poor fellow in this world but must ask it now and then with a blank face, when aground for want of a meaning. And the answer is—a dictionary, if you have it. Unfortunately, there may be a dictionary, and one may have it, and yet the word may not be there. It may be an old dictionary, and the word a new one; or a new dictionary, and the word an old one; a grave dictionary, and the word a slang one; a slang dictionary, and the word a grave one; and so on through a double line of battle of antitheses. Such is assuredly matter for serious cogitation: and voluntarily to encounter those anomalous perplexities requires no small amount of endurance, for the task is equally crabbed and onerous, without a ray of hope to the pioneer beyond that of making himself humbly useful. This brings me to my story.

Many years ago, I harboured thoughts of compiling a kind of detailed nautical vade mecum; but a lot of other irons already in the fire marred the project. Still the scheme was backing and filling, when the late

Major Shadwell Clerke—opening the year 1836 in the *United Service Journal*—fired off the following, to me, unexpected announcement:—

"A Nautical Dictionary, or Cyclopædia of Naval Science and Nomenclature, is still a desideratum. That of Falconer is imperfect and out of date. We have heard that the design of such a work has been entertained, and materials for its execution collected, by Captain W. H. Smyth, whom we earnestly recommend to prosecute an undertaking of such promise to the service of which he is so experienced and distinguished a member—it could not be in more competent hands."

This broad hint must have been signalled by the gallant Major in the way of a stimulating fillip, and accordingly it aroused considerable attention. Among those who were excited by the notification was my friend Captain Basil Hall, who wrote to me from Paris a few days afterwards —13th of January, 1836—in these words:

"I read a day or two ago, in the *United Service Journal*, that you had some thoughts of preparing a Nautical Dictionary for publication; and from your connection with that journal, or at least your acquaintance with our friend the editor, I am led to fear that the report may be true. You will understand the use of the word *fear* when I tell you that, for nearly three years, *my* own thoughts have turned in the same direction, and I have been busily preparing for a task to which I meant to buckle to with a will, and to which I meant to devote some four or five years of exclusive diligence. What I am anxious to know, as soon as may be, is the fact of your having undertaken a similar work, *or not*. For I assure you I am not so foolish, nor so insensible either to my own peace of mind or my own reputation; nor am I so careless of your good opinion and regard, as to enter the lists with you. I repeat, neither my feelings nor my judgment would permit me in any way to cross your hawse, if indeed, as I too much fear, you have got before me. There is one other man in the service besides yourself, and only one, with whom no consideration would induce me to enter into competition—and that is Beaufort—but his hands, I presume, are full enough, and I had somehow imagined yours were too. So much so, that you were one of the first men I meant to consult on my return to England, and to beg assistance from. I should not have minded the competition of any one else, but I am not so vain as to suppose that I could do the thing as well as either of you—and therefore, even if I were not restrained by motives of personal friendship, I should never dream of risking my reputation for professional, scientific, or literary attainments by a struggle in which I should certainly be worsted."

To this hearty and laudatory interpellation, an immediate reply was returned, stating that I had long held the subject in view, but that other weighty avocations occasioned its hanging fire, and had compelled me to suspend it *sine die.* Still I considered such a work necessary to the current wants, as well those of seafarers as of the landsmen who evince a taste for nautical matters; and that, from his profession and literary prowess, I knew of no one better fitted for the task than himself—adding that, under the emergency, my papers were at his service, and I would occasionally give him such personal aid as might lie in my power. This was acknowledged in a long explicatory letter, of which the following are extracts:—

"I trust I know the value of a compliment as well as any man, and I can say, with perfect truth, that in the whole of my career (such as it has been), professional, scientific, or literary, no compliment—I may say no circumstance—has occurred which has given me so much honest gratification as your letter of the 3d. I know you are a man not to say what you do not truly think, nor to express yourself strongly where you have not observed carefully. I shall therefore not disclaim your compliment, but rather seek, in a kindred spirit, to work up to the mark which you assign me—and which I know but too well how far I am short of.

"I do hope, indeed, that as you say, 'we may row in the same boat without catching crabs;' but of this I am quite resolved, not to cross your hawse, nor to interfere with your project, which you have alluded to as having already commenced. That is to say, I shall not interfere unless I can be of use to it and to you, and with your full concurrence, and, as I hope, your companionship. * * * *

"What I should propose would be, that you should furnish the professional technicalities in all the different branches, and that I should endeavour to popularize them. Here and there—as in the matter of Navigation—I also might intrude with some few technicalities. But generally speaking it would be you who should provide the real solid stuff, and I who should attempt to dress it up so as to be intelligible *beyond* the limits of the sea-service; and also to be intelligible to those young persons whom it is very important to instruct in general and even popular views, but for whom it would be needless to write a new elementary treatise. * * * *

"This is a sketch of my plan. What think you of it? I must add one thing, however, that you must be the senior officer on the occasion. I shall act in all this matter, and in the most perfect good faith, as your subordinate."

In responding to this full and frank overture, I entered into a few more particulars respecting my progress and purpose in the projected work; and invited him—on his return from France—to come at once to Bedford and ransack my papers.

Accordingly, in the autumn of 1836, Captain Basil Hall and his family—the whole of the Schloss Handfeldt party—arrived at my house, where he was located in a quiet library, with all my materials for the Naval Dictionary before him. Here he remained in close examination of them during two days, when he promised to send me his ultimatum in writing after due deliberation. He required time for this, seeing I had fairly warned him that my onerous undertakings would necessarily throw the heavier share of our performance upon his shoulders. On the 27th of November I received a letter from Edinburgh, in which he made this statement:—

"With respect to the Marine Dictionary I think we have come to a clear understanding—namely, that for the present it is standing fast. *I* certainly had a notion that I was an interloper, and as soon as I saw the vast deal you had done in the way of preparation, that it became me as a man of fair dealing, to back out. This does not, however, appear to have been your wish, but on the contrary that we may still make a joint work of it by-and-by, when we have leisure, both of us, to engage in it heartily—tooth and nail. I shall therefore keep it in my thoughts, and endeavour to shape my future plans so as to meet this view, and, should I see occasion, I can write to you about it. My present notion is, that if ever we do set about it, I must come to Bedford for a season, and give myself entirely up to the work, under your direction. The work, to be worth a straw, or at all what would be expected from you and me, would require no small labour on our parts, for a considerable length of time."

We consequently lay upon our oars for some time, but occasionally pulling a stroke or two to keep to the station, and be ready for headway when required. While thus prepared, in 1842 my excellent and highly accomplished friend was most unexpectedly assailed by an afflicting malady, which at once reduced a brilliant mind to a distressing fatuity, which—after two lingering years—closed his valuable life, and clued up our arrangements.

Meantime our plan had oozed out, and too great an expectation was evoked in certain quarters, the inquiries from whence were frequent reminders. At length in 1865, most of my undertakings having been completed, and out of the way, I made an overhaul of the bulky ribs and trucks of the scheme in question. Both my judgment and feelings united in showing that it is now too late in the day for me to think of setting about such a work as was contemplated thirty years ago; yet finding myself still capable of application, and fully knowing all the bearings of the case, I feel assured that a comprehensive and useful "word-book" may be made from the shakings. On the whole, therefore, the foregoing particulars seem to be a necessary prelude to this introduction.

Doubtless a well-digested marine dictionary would be equally beneficial to the country and to the service, for the utility of such a work in assisting those who are engaged in carrying on practical sea duties is so generally admitted, that it is allowable here to dilate upon its importance, especially when it is considered how much information a youth has to acquire, on his first going afloat, in order to qualify him for a position so totally different from what he had hitherto been familiar with. In this case such a volume might justly be deemed one of the most useful of his companions, as it would at all times answer his questions, and aid that ardour of inquiry which some of his shipmates might not find it easy to satisfy. It would quicken the slow progress of experience, and aid those who take a pleasure in the knowledge and discharge of their duties. But a work of this description must necessarily require constant additions, and revised explanations, to enable it to keep pace with the wondrous alterations and innovations which are now taking place in every department of the naval service. The future of all this is utterly inscrutable!

Nor has this province been neglected, as the efforts of Captain John Smith (of mine own clan), Maynwaring, Boteler, Blanckley, Falconer, Young, and many others, testify; and however they may fall short of what naval science demands, they are full of initiative training. Indeed they may all be advantageously consulted, for honey is not the less sweet because it is gathered from many flowers; and I have freely availed myself of their various works, as far as they go, though I have adopted no term without holding myself responsible for its actuality. Such a vaunt may be considered to savour of the *parturiunt montes* apothegm, but the reader may confidently rest assured that whatever shortcomings he may detect they are not the result of negligence.

It has been pronounced that such lexicography may be too diffuse; that to describe the track of every particular rope through its different channels, however requisite for seamen, would be useless and unintelligible to a landsman. But surely nothing can be considered useless which tends directly to information, nor can that be unintelligible which is clearly defined. Moreover, such a work may be so carried out as not only to be instructive in professional minutiæ, but also to be a vehicle for making us acquainted with the rules which guided the seamen of former times, thereby affording an insight into those which are likely to direct them in their own.

From the causes already stated, my project of a full sailor's dictionary fell to the ground; yet in course of time, and at the age of seventy-seven, finding leisure at last on hand, I thought it feasible to work my materials into a sort of maritime glossary. The objects of such a digest are to afford a ready reference to young or old, professional or non-professional, persons, who by consulting it may obtain an instant answer to a given question. Now although many of the explanations may be superfluous to some seamen, still they may lead others to a right understanding of various brackish expressions and phrases, without having to put crude queries, many of which those inquired of might be unable to solve. Nor is it only those afloat who are to be thus considered; all the empire is more or less connected with its navy and its commerce, and nautical phraseology is thereby daily becoming more habitual with all classes of the lieges than of erst. Even our parliamentary orators, with a proper national bias, talk of swamping a measure, danger ahead, taking the wind out of an antagonist's sails, drifting into war, steering a bill through the shoals of opposition or throwing it overboard, following in the wake of a leader, trimming to the breeze, tiding a question over the session, opinions above or below the gangway, and the like, so rife of late in St. Stephen's; even when a member "rats" on seeing that the pumps cannot keep his party from falling to leeward, he is but imitating the vermin that quit a sinking ship.

This predeliction for sea idiom is assuredly proper in a maritime people, especially as many of the phrases are at once graphic, terse, and perspicuous. How could the whereabouts of an aching tooth be better pointed out to an operative dentist than Jack's "'Tis the aftermost grinder aloft, on the starboard quarter." The ship expressions preserve many British and Anglo-Saxon words, with their quaint old preterites and telling colloquialisms; and such may require explanation, as well for the youthful aspirant as for the cocoa-nut-headed prelector in nautic lore. It is indeed remarkable how largely that foundation of the English language has been preserved by means of our sailors.

This phraseology has necessarily been added to from time to time, and consequently bears the stamp of our successive ages of sea-life. In the "ancient and fishlike" terms that brave Raleigh derived from his predecessors, many epithets must have resulted from ardent recollections of home and those at home, for in a ship we find—

Apeak,	Cat's-paw,	Driver,	Hound,	Rabbit,	Stays,
Apron,	Cot,	Earings,	Jewel,	Ribband,	Stirrup,
Astay,	Cradle,	Eyes,	Lacings,	Saddle,	Tiller,
Bonnet,	Crib,	Fox,	Martingale,	Sheaves,	Truck,
Braces,	Crowfoot,	Garnet,	Mouse,	Sheets,	Truss,
Bridle,	Crow's nest,	Goose-neck,	Nettle,	Sheep-shank,	Watch,
Cap,	Crown,	Goose-wing,	Pins,	Shoe,	Whip,
Catharpins,	Diamond,	Horse,	Puddings,	Sister,	Yard.
Catheads,	Dog,	Hose,			

Most of the real sea-terms are pregnant with meaning; but those who undertake to expound them ought to be tolerably versed in the topic. Thus perhaps there was no great harm in Dr. Johnson's being utterly ignorant of maritime language, but it was temerariously vain in that sturdy lexicographer to assert that *belay* is a sea-phrase for splicing a rope; *main sheet*, for the largest sail in a ship; and *bight*, for the circumference of a coil of rope; and we long had him on the hip respecting the *purser*, a personage whom he—misled by Burser—at once pronounced to be the paymaster of a ship; as the then purser was, in fact, more familiar with slops, tobacco, pork, dips, biscuit, and the like, than with cash payments—for, excepting short-allowance dues, he had very little meddling with money matters. But the Admiralty have recently swamped the well-known and distinctive nautical title—despite of its time-honoured claims to repute—and introduced the army appellative, PAY-MASTER, in its stead.

The pithy conciseness of the brackish tongue renders it eminently useful on duty. In some of their sea-phrases the French, our great rivals, use a heap of words more than we are wont to do. An instance is given —supposing a ship of the former met with one of ours, and they should desire to salute each other, the English commander would sing out, "Man ship!" but the French captain would have to exclaim, "Rangez du monde sur les vergues pour donner des cris de salut!" By the way, there is a *ben trovato* respecting the difficulty of doing our naval tidings into French: a translator of note made quite a mull of a ship being *brought up* by her anchors, and of another which was stranded from *borrowing* too much; while "a man-of-war riding easily in the road at Spithead" was rendered "Un homme de guerre se promenait à cheval à son aise sur le chemin de Spithead." Some of the French terms, however, are recommended by their Parisian stamp, as in calling iron bilboes "bas de soie"—the waist-netting "Saint Aubinet"—the quarter-gallery a "jardin d'amour:" but similar elegance was not manifested in dubbing the open-hearted thorough-bred tar "un loup de mer."

In the work before us, the nautical import of the terms is duly considered, and the orthography, as far as feasible, is ruled by authority and custom, with an occasional slight glance at the probable etymology of the words—slight, because derivation is a seductive and frequently illusory pilot. Our language is said to have been arraigned by foreigners for its hissing enunciation; but, regardless of the rebuke, our pundits have, of late, unnecessarily increased the whistling by substituting the sibilant *s* for the vocal *z*, in all sorts of cases. Happily this same *s* not being yet acclimatized to the galley, Jack will continue to give tongue to an enterprizing cruize after Portugueze merchandize, and there anent.

The plan of our work may be said to comprise the treating *de omnibus rebus nauticis,* for many branches of knowledge are demanded of the intelligent seaman. Thus in Naval Architecture, the terms used in the construction of ships, the plans and sections, and the mechanical means of the builders, are undoubted requirements of a sea word-book. So also in Astronomy, or that portion of nautical science constituting observations which are necessary to the determinations of the navigator. In Mathematics, especially the branch distinguished as practical, the doctrine which teaches whatever is capable of being numbered or measured, requires verbal elucidation, not so much for the educated youth, as for him who labours under difficulties—who is

> "In canvass'd berth, profoundly deep in thought,
> His busy mind with sines and tangents fraught."

Many of the words in our columns are not *de facto* sea-terms, but as they are in rife and familiar use on ship-board, they obtained a lodgment;

whence it becomes rather a difficult matter to mark a boundary for nautic language. Various expressions are also retained which, though now unused or all but obsolete, occur so frequently in professional treatises and antiquated journals, that their exposition may often be welcomed by a general reader: they are here introduced, not as worthy of revival, yet as necessary to be understood when fallen in with. And it should be remembered, that—especially during our last conflict with France—so many combined enterprises occurred, that the most general naval and military phrases pertained, in a manner, to both arms of the service.

What may be termed mere galley-slang also demands explanation, since even officers are sometimes ashore—I was going to say at sea—respecting its purport; and I recollect at a court-martial holden on a seaman for insolence to his superior, the lingo used by the shrewd culprit was liable to be thought respectful or otherwise according to the manner of utterance, and he was admitted to the benefit of the doubtful meaning. Still it must be admitted that all vulgarisms, as far as practicable, should be indignantly spurned from our noble English language—a language unequalled for excellence in fluency, capacity, and strength. A stern critic may also, and in truth, aver that terms are included on our roll the which are not altogether of maritime usage. This we have admitted, but the allegation will be greatly weakened on scrutiny, for they are here given in the sense entertained of them in nautic parlance. Such are generally illustrative of some of the lingual or local peculiarities of sea-life, or borne on its literature, and therefore are necessarily admitted as having a footing in maritime philology. Some of our misused words and archaic phrases are, by influence of the newspaper magnates, brought across the Atlantic, and re-appear among us under the style and title of Americanisms: after which fashion, in the lapse of time and the mutation of dialect, vocables once differing in origin and meaning may become identical in sense and sound.*

Finally, Natural History, a taste for which is a substantial blessing to the sailor, is too vast a department for our professional pages. However, a few requisite definitions of the familiar products of the air, earth, and water are introduced. Numbers of marine birds and many fishes—so often misnamed—are entered upon the muster; and especially those

* As for example the word *alarm*, *alarum*, a bell, from the German *lärm;* but the military *alarm* on a drum is the Italian *all'arme.*

which the blue-jackets vote to be very good eating; yet, as a reverend
author has well observed, we should, in such cases, recur to the probable
state of their appetites at the time of experiment. The most general
nautic dishes and refections are likewise cited, to the making of which
most of our sea-cooks are competent—there being no purée, entremet, or
fricandeau to trouble them. But though they are at times libelled as
being sent from the infernal regions, they are pretty fair in their way;
and though no great shakes in domestic chemistry, they can enter the
lists against any white-aproned *artiste* at pea-soup, beef-steak, lobscouse,
pillau, curried shark, twice-laid, or savoury sea-pie. Still, a more
luxurious tendency in this department is casting its shadow before; and
there are Sybarites invading the ocean to whom the taste of junk is all
but unknown.

A DIGEST

OF

SEA TERMS AND PHRASES.

A. The highest class of the excellence of merchant ships on Lloyd's books, subdivided into A 1 and A 2, after which they descend by the vowels: A 1 being the very best of the first class. Formerly a river-built (Thames) ship took the first rate for 12 years, a Bristol one for 11, and those of the northern ports 10. Some of the outport built ships keep their rating 6 to 8 years, and inferior ones only 4. But improvements in ship-building, and the large introduction of iron, are now claiming longer life.

A is an Anglo-Saxonism for *in* or *on;* as *a'*board, *a'*going, &c.

A.B. The rating of *Able Seamen* on the ship's books: these two letters are often used as an epithet for the person so rated. He must be equal to all the duties required of a seaman in a ship—not only as regards the saying to "hand, reef, and steer," but also to strop a block, splice, knot, turn in rigging, raise a mouse on the mainstay, and be an example to the *ordinary seamen* and *landsmen*.

ABAB. A Turkish sailor who plies in coasting craft.

ABACK. The situation of a ship's sails when the wind bears against their front surfaces. They are *laid aback*, when this is purposely effected to deaden her way by rounding in the weather-braces; and *taken aback*, when brought to by an unexpected change of wind, or by inattention in the helmsman.—*All aback forward*, the notice given from the forecastle, when the head-sails are pressed aback by a sudden change in the wind. (*See* WORK ABACK.)—*Taken aback*, a colloquialism for being suddenly surprised or found out.

ABACUS. A board with balls sliding on small rods, used in China, Russia, &c., for calculating bills, &c.

ABAFT. This word, generally speaking, means behind, inferred relatively, beginning from the stem and continuing towards the stern, that is, the hinder part of the ship.—*Abaft the beam* implies any direction between a supposed transverse line amidships and the stern, whether in or out of the ship. It is the relative situation of an object with the ship, when that object is placed in the arc of the horizon contained between a line at right angles with the keel and the point of the compass which is directly opposite the ship's course. An object—as a man overboard—is described by the look-out man at the mast-head as abeam, before, or abaft the beam, by so many points of the compass. As a vessel seen may be "three points before the beam," &c.

ABAKA. A fine vegetable fibre, with which the white Manila rope, so much used on the India station, is made. This rope floats in water, and is not subject to rot, nor does it require tarring. A frigate on the China station in 1805 had nearly the whole of her running rigging of this cordage.

ABANDONMENT of a vessel. Deserting and abandoning her by reason of unseaworthiness or danger of remaining in her, also when grounded and cannot be saved. This never occurs but in imminent cases; therefore, before the insured can demand recompense from the underwriter, they must cede or *abandon* to him the right of all property which may be recovered from shipwreck, capture, or any other peril stated in the policy. Other parties entering and bringing the vessel into port obtain salvage. (*Vide* DERELICT.)

ABASE, To. An old word signifying to lower a flag or sail. *Abaisser* is in use in the French marine, and both may be derived from the still older *abeigh*. *Abase* literally means to cast down, to humble.

ABATE, To. An old Anglo-Norman word from *abattre*, to beat down or destroy; as, to *abate* a castle or fort, is to beat it down; and a gale is said to *abate* when it decreases. The term is still used in law.

ABATEMENT. A plea by which a reduction of freight is demanded, when unforeseen causes have delayed or hindered the performance of a stipulated charter-party.

ABATIS. An obstruction used in temporary fortification, composed of felled trees deprived of their smaller branches, and secured to the ground side by side with their tops towards the enemy; applicable to the front of posts, works, or positions, and occasionally to the bars of rivers.

ABBEY-LUBBER. This is an old term of reproach for idleness, and is here quoted only as bearing upon the nautical lubber. In the "*Burnynge of Paule's Church*, 1563," it is thus explained—"An Abbey-lubber, that was idle, well-fed, a long lewd lither loiterer, that might worke, and would not."

ABBLAST. Cross-bow; hence,

ABBLASTER. Cross-bow man.

ABBROCHYN. The old term for beginning or broaching a barrel, cask, or any "vesselle of drynke."

ABEAM. In a line at right angles to the vessel's length; opposite the centre of a ship's side.

ABEAM-ARM. For this curved timber, *see* FORK-BEAM.

ABER. An ancient British word for the mouth of a river—as Aber-brothick, Aber-avon, Aberystwith, and Aber-conway, &c. It also means the confluence of two or more streams.

ABERRATION. An apparent change of place, or alteration of their mean position, in the fixed stars, caused by the earth's orbital move-ment.—*Aberration of a planet* signifies its progressive geocentric motion, or the space through which it appears to move, as seen from the earth, during the time which light occupies in passing from the planet to us.—*Crown of aberration* is a spurious circle surrounding the proper disc of the sun.—*Constant of aberration*, or amount of displace-ment in the sun's longitude, arising from the progressive motion of light, is established at $20''{\cdot}45$.

ABET, To. To excite or encourage—a common word, greatly in use at boat-racings, and other competitive acts.

ABITED. A provincial term for *mildewed*.

ABJURATION. The oath taken till lately by all officers on receiving their commission, by which they abjured any claim of the Stuarts to the throne, the power of the Pope, and the Romish religion.

ABLE. A term not simply expressive of strong faculties, but as acquainted with and equal to perform the expected duty.—*Able sea-man*, a thorough or regular bred sailor. (*See* A.B.)—*Able-bodied*, sound, healthy, and fit for the Royal service.

ABLE-WHACKETS. A popular sea-game with cards, wherein the loser is beaten over the palms of the hands with a handkerchief tightly twisted like a rope. Very popular with horny-fisted salts.

ABOARD. Inside or upon a ship; the act of residing afloat; to hug the land in approaching the shore.—*To fall aboard of*, is for one vessel to run foul of another.—*To haul the tacks aboard*, is to bring their weather clues down to the chess-tree, or literally, to set the courses. —*To lay an enemy aboard*, to run into or alongside.

ABODE. Waited for; as, ship ran to the appointed place of rendezvous and *abode* there for her consort.

ABORD. An Anglo-Saxon term, meaning across, from shore to shore, of a port or river.

ABOUT. Circularly; the situation of a ship after she has gone round, and trimmed sails on the opposite tack.—*Ready about!* and *About-ship!* are orders to the ship's company to prepare for tacking by being at their stations.

ABOVE-BOARD. Over the deck; a term used for open fair dealing, without artifice or trick.

ABOX. A word used in veering for *aback*, alluding to the situation of the head-yards in paying off. (*See* BRACE-ABOX.)—*Lay the head-yards abox*—in former times, and even at present, many good seamen prefer to lay the head-yards square, or abox, to heave-to. It brings the vessel more under command for sudden evolution, wearing, or staying.

ABRAHAM-MEN. A cant term for vagabonds, who formerly begged about under pretence of having been discharged destitute from ships and hospitals; whence an idle malingerer wanting to enter the doctor's list is said to "sham Abraham." From a ward in Bedlam which was appropriated for the reception of idiots, which was named Abraham: it is a very old term, and was cited by Burton in the *Anatomy of Melancholy* so far back as 1621.

ABRASE, To. To dubb or smooth planks.

ABRASION. The rubbing off or wearing away of the parts of a rock, or of the soil, by the impinging and friction of other bodies.

ABREAST. Side by side, parallel, or opposite to; generally used in opposition to *abaft* or *afore.*—*Line abreast* means a fleet advancing or retreating uniformly on a line parallel with the beam.—*Abreast of a place*, is directly off it; a direction at right angles with the keel or ship's length. In the army the term was formerly used for any number of men in front; but at present they are determined by files. —*Abreast.* Within-board, signifies on a parallel with the beam.

ABRID. A pintle-plate.

ABROACH. On tap, in use; spoken of barrels of beer or other liquors.

ABROAD. Synonymous with foreign, or being on a foreign station. Also an old word for *spread;* as, all sail *abroad.*

ABRUPT. A word applied to steep, broken, or craggy cliffs and headlands, especially such as are bold-to and precipitous.

ABSCISS. A part either of the diameter or the transverse axis of a conic section, intercepted between the vertex or any other fixed point and a semi-ordinate.—*Abscission of a planet*, its being outstripped by another, which joins a third one before it.

ABSENCE. A permission occasionally obtained, on urgent affairs, by officers to quit their duties.

ABSOLUTE. Anything free from conditions.—*Absolute equations*, the sum of the optic and eccentric equation, or the anomalies arising from a planet's not being equally distant from the earth at all times, and its motion not being uniform.—*Absolute gravity* is the whole force with which a body tends downwards.

ABSORPTION. A term formerly used for the sinking of islands and tracts of land, instead of *subsidence.*

ABSQUATULATE. *See* SQUATTER.

ABSTRACT. A brief register of the warrant officer's stores, by which the supplies, expenses, and remains are duly balanced. An *abstract log* contains the most important subjects of a ship's log.

ABSTRACT MATHEMATICS, or Pure. The branch which investigates and demonstrates the properties of magnitude, figure, or quantity, absolutely and generally considered, without restriction to any species in particular; such as arithmetic and geometry.

A-BURTON. The situation of casks when they are stowed in the hold athwart ship, or in a line with the beam.

ABUT. When two timbers or planks are united end-ways, they are said to *butt* or *abut* against each other. (*See* BUTT.)

ABYME. Places supposed to be the site of constant whirlpools, such as Charybdis, the Maelstrom, and others. It means generally an abyss.

ABYSS. A deep mass of waters; in hydrography it was synonymous with *gulf.*

ACADEMITE. An old term for an officer brought up at the Royal Navy Academy at Portsmouth, afterwards named the Royal Naval College.

ACAIR-PHUILL. Compounded of the British *acair* or anchor, and *phuill*, a pill, or harbour, and means a safe anchorage.

ACALEPHÆ. A class of marine animals of low organization, having a translucent jelly-like structure, and frequently possessing the property of stinging, whence their name (ἀκαλήφη, a nettle). The common jelly-fish (*Medusa*) and the Portuguese man-of-war (*Physalia*) are the best-known examples.

ACAST. The old word for *lost* or *cast-away.* In weighing anchor the head-yards are generally braced *acast*, to cause the vessel to cast in the direction. " Does she take *acast?*" is frequently the question of the officer abaft.

ACATER. An old word for purveyor of victuals, whence *caterer*, or superintendent and provider of a mess. Thus in Ben Jonson's "Devil of an Ass "—

> " He is my wardrobe-man, my *acater*,
> Cook, butler, and steward."

ACATES. Victuals; provisions purchased; delicious food; dainties.

ACATIUM. A word used in Roman naval affairs for a small boat, and also the main-mast of a ship.

ACCELERATION. The increase of velocity in a moving body by the force of gravity. A planet is said to be accelerated when its actual diurnal motion exceeds its mean. In fixed stars the acceleration is the mean time by which they anticipate the sun's diurnal revolution, which is 3′ 56″ nearly.—*Acceleration of the moon* is the increase of her mean motion, caused by a slow change in the excentricity of the terrestrial orbit, and which has sensibly diminished the length of the moon's revolution since the time of the earliest observations.

ACCESS. Means of entry on board.

ACCESSIBLE. A place which can be approached by land or sea.

ACCLIVITY. The upward slope of an inclined cliff.

ACCOIL, To. To coil together, by folding round. (*See* COIL.)

ACCOLADE [*ad* and *collum*, Lat.] The ceremony of dubbing a knight, and the consequent embrace formerly customary on the occasion.

ACCOMMODATIONS. Cabins fitted for passengers.—*Accommodation ladder*, a convenient flight of steps fixed at the gangway, by which officers and visitors enter the ship. — *Accommodation*, the physical application of one thing to another by analogy.

ACCOMPANY, To. To sail together; to sail in convoy.

ACCOST, To. To pass within hail of a ship; to sail coastwise; to approach, to draw near, or come side by side.

ACCOUNT, GOING UPON. A phrase for buccaneering.

ACCOUNTANT-GENERAL OF THE NAVY. Superintendent of pay and general accounts of the navy.

ACCOUNTS. The several books and registers of stores, provisions, slops, and contingents of a ship or fleet; and they are strictly enjoined to be correct, real, and precise, both in receipt and expenditure.— *Account sales*, a form of book-keeping in commerce.

ACCOUTREMENT. An old term for an habiliment, or part of the trappings and furniture of a soldier or knight; now generally used for the belts, pouches, and equipments of soldiers or marines.

ACCUL. A word used by old voyagers for the end of a deep bay; it is corrupted from *cul de sac*.

ACHATOUR. The old word for caterer of a mess.

ACHERNAR. A star of the first magnitude in the constellation Eridanus, called by navigators the "Spring of the River." It is invisible in our latitude. (α Eridani.) Properly should be *acher nahr*.

ACHIEVEMENT. A signal exploit; escutcheon; armorial bearings granted for achievement.

ACHROMATIC. An optical term applied to those telescopes in which aberration of the rays of light, and the colours dependent thereon, are partially corrected. (*See* APLANATIC.)

ACHRONICAL. An ancient term, signifying the rising of the heavenly bodies at sunset, or setting at sunrise.

ACKER. *See* EAGRE or EAGOR. Also, an eddying ripple on the surface of flooded waters. A tide swelling above another tide, as in the Severn. (*See* BORE.)

ACK-MEN, OR ACK-PIRATES. Fresh-water thieves; those who steal on navigable rivers.

A COCKBILL (*see* COCK-BILL). The anchor hangs by its ring at the cat-head, in a position for dropping.

ACOLYTE. A term sometimes used to distinguish the smaller component of a double star. A subordinate officer in the ancient church.

ACON. A flat-bottomed Mediterranean boat or lump, for carrying cargoes over shoals.

ACQUITTANCE. A commercial term, more generally called *quittance* (which see).

ACRE, OR ACRE-FIGHT. An old duel fought by warriors between the frontiers of England and Scotland, with sword and lance. This duelling was also called *camp-fight.*

ACROSS THE TIDE. A ship riding across tide, with the wind in the direction of the tide, would tend to leeward of her anchor; but with a weather tide, or that running against the wind, if the tide be strong, would tend to windward. A ship under sail should prefer the tack that stems the tide, with the wind *across the stream,* when the anchor is let go.

ACROSTOLIUM. A buckler, helmet, or other symbolical ornament on the prow of ancient ships; the origin of the modern figure-head.

ACT AND INTENTION. Must be united in admiralty law.

ACTE. A peninsula; the term was particularly applied by the ancients to the sea-coast around Mount Athos.

ACT OF COURT. The decision of the court or judge on the verdict, or the overruling of the court on a point of law.

ACT OF GOD. This comprehends all sudden accidents arising from physical causes, as distinguished from *human* agency, such as from lightning, earthquakes, hurricanes, plagues, and epidemic contagion amongst the crew. For none of these are ship-owners responsible.

ACT OF GRACE. An act of parliament for a general and free pardon to deserters from the service and others.

ACTING COMMISSION. When a commissioned officer is invalided, his vacancy is filled up pending the pleasure of the admiralty by an acting order. But when an officer dies on a station, where the admiralty delegates the power to the admiral commanding in chief, the vacancy is filled by an acting commission. Thus also rear-admirals now act on acting commissions as vice-admirals during command on their station, but return to their proper position on the navy list when it ceases.

ACTION. Synonymous with *battle.* Also a term in mechanics for the effort which one body exerts against another, or the effects resulting therefrom.—*Action and reaction,* the mutual, successive, contrary impulses of two bodies.

ACTIVE SERVICE. Duty against an enemy; operations in his presence. Or in the present day it denotes serving on full-pay, on the active list, in contradistinction to those who are virtually retired, and placed on separate lists.

ACTIVITY.   The virtue of acting.   The sphere of *activity* is the surrounding space to which the efficacy of a body extends, as the attraction of the magnet.

ACTO, or Acton.   A kind of defensive tunic, made of quilted leather, or other strong material, formerly worn under the outer dress, and even under a coat of mail.

ACTUARIÆ.   Long light vessels of the ancients, especially contrived for swiftness; propelled both by sails and oars; of the latter never less than twenty.

ACUMBA.   Oakum.   The Anglo-Saxon term for the *hards*, or the coarse part, of flax or unplucked wool.

ACUTE.   Terminating in a point, and opposed to *obtuse*.   An *acute* angle is less than a right one, or within 90°.

ACUTE-ANGLED TRIANGLE.   That which has all its angles acute.

ADAMANT.   The load-stone; the magnet—the sense in which it was held by early voyagers; but others considered it a "precyowse stone," or gem.

ADAMAS.   The moon in nautic horoscopes.

ADAPTER.   A brass tube to fit the eye-end of a telescope, into which all the eye-pieces will screw.

ADARRIS.   A word which Howell explains as the flower of sea-water.

ADDEL, or Addle.   An old term for the putrid water in casks.

ADDICE, an adze.   Also the addled eggs of gulls and other sea-fowl.

ADDLINGS.   Accumulated pay or wages.

ADELANTADO.   A lieutenant of the king of Spain, but used by old English writers for "admiral."

ADHESION.   Consent to a proposal.   Union or temporary cohesion; as, two vessels forced into *adhesion* by the pressure of the tide on their beam.

ADIT.   A space in ancient ships, in the upper and broadest part, at which people entered.   The *adit* of a military mine, is the aperture by which it is dug and charged: the name is also applied to an air-hole or drift.

ADJACENT.   Lying close to another object; a word applied to the relative situations of capes or bays from the ship.—*Adjacent angle* is one immediately contiguous to another, so that they have one common side.

ADJOURN, To.   To put off till another day.   *Adjournments* can be made in courts-martial from day to day, Sundays excepted, until sentence is passed.

ADJUDICATION.   The act of adjudging prizes by legal decree. Captors are compelled to submit the adjudication of their captures to a competent tribunal.

ADJUST, To. To arrange an instrument for use and observation; as, to adjust a sextant, or the escapement of a chronometer. To set the frame of a ship.

ADJUSTMENT. In marine insurance, the ascertaining and finally settling the amount of indemnity—whether of average or of salvage —which the insured (after all proper deductions have been made) is entitled to receive under the policy, when the ship is lost.

ADJUSTMENT OF THE COMPASS. Swinging a ship to every point of bearing, to note the variation or error of the needle upon each rhumb, due to the local attraction of the iron, or the mass, on each separate compass bearing. Thus, in lat. 76° N. it was found to be + 22° 30′ with the head W.S.W., and − 56° 30′ on the opposite bearing, or E.N.E.

ADJUTANT. [From Lat. *adjuvo*, to help.] A military assistant to field-officers. The term has been applied to an assistant captain of a fleet. It is indeed the duty performed by first lieutenants.

ADMEASUREMENT. The calculation of proportions according to assumed rules, often ignorantly practised in estimating the tonnage of a ship.

ADMIRAL. The derivation of this noble title from the Greek *almyros*, from the Latin *admirabilis*, from the Saxon *aenmereeal*, and from the French *aumer*, appear all fanciful. It is extensively received that the Sicilians first adopted it from *emir*, the sea, of their Saracen masters; but it presents a kind of unusual etymological inversion. The term is most frequent in old Romance; but the style and title was not used by us until 1286; and in 1294, William de Leybourne was designated "Amiral de la Mer du Roy d'Angleterre;" six years afterwards Viscount Narbonne was constituted Admiral of France; which dates nearly fix the commencement of the two states as maritime powers.

The *admiral* is the chief commander of a fleet, but of this rank there are three degrees, distinguished by a flag at the fore, main, or mizen mast, according to the title of *admiral, vice-admiral,* or *rear-admiral*. These were again subdivided according to their colour of red, white, or blue, which had to be likewise borne by the squadrons they respectively commanded. (*See* FLAG.) In 1865 the colours were omitted, and the only flag now hoisted by ships of war is the white St. George's ensign, and for admirals the white St. George's cross at the main, fore, or mizen.

The *admiral of the fleet* is the highest officer under the admiralty of Great Britain; it is rather an honorary distinction, and usually attained by seniority and service: when this officer serves afloat, he hoists the proud distinction of the Union flag at the main.

The *lord high-admiral* was one of the principal officers of the state, who formerly decided all cases relating to the sea: he wore a gold call and chain, similar in form to that which has descended to the boatswain and his mate. This dignity has been extinct for many years, and the duty merged into that of the lords-commissioners and admiralty court; in 1827, it was revived for a short time in the person of His Royal Highness the Duke of Clarence.

The epithet of *admiral* was also formerly applied to any large or leading ship, without reference to flag; and is still used for the principal vessel in the cod and whale fisheries. That which arrives first in any port of Newfoundland retains this title during the season, with certain rights of beach in flakes. The master of the second ship becomes the vice-admiral, and the master of the third the rear-admiral.

ADMIRAL. A beautiful and rare shell of the genus *Conus;* the varieties are designated the grand-admiral, the vice-admiral, the orange-admiral, and the extra-admiral.

ADMIRALTY. An office for the administration of naval affairs, presided over by a lord high-admiral, whether the duty be discharged by one person, or by commissioners under the royal patent, who are styled lords, and during our former wars generally consisted of seven. The present constitution of the Board of Admiralty comprises—the first lord, a minister and civilian as to office; four naval lords; one civil lord attending to accounts, &c.; one chief secretary; one second secretary. Two lords and one secretary form a legal Board of Admiralty wherever they may be assembled, under the authority of the board or its chief.

ADMIRALTY BLACK-BOOK. See BLACK-BOOK.

ADMIRALTY COURT. The constitution of this court relatively to the legislative power of the king in council, is analogous to that of the courts of common law relatively to the parliament of the kingdom.— *High Court of Admiralty*, a supreme court of law, in which the authority of the lord high-admiral is ostensibly exercised in his *judicial* capacity for the trial of maritime causes of a civil nature. Although termed the High Court of Admiralty, more properly this is the Court of Vice-Admiralty, and relates solely to civil and military matters of the sea, and sea boundaries, prizes, collisions, vessels or goods cast on the shore where the vice-admirals have civil jurisdiction, but no naval power, as the lord-lieutenants of counties are named in their patents " vice-admirals of the same;" in like manner all governors of colonies. All cases in connection are tried by the Admiralty Court in London, or by our " courts of vice-admiralty and prize jurisdictions abroad." Admirable as some of the decisions of this expensive tribunal have been, it has all the powers of the Inquisition in its practice, and has thereby been an instrument of persecution to some innocent navigators, while it has befriended notorious villains. Besides this we have the Admiralty Court of Oyer and Terminer, for the trial of all murders, piracies, or criminal acts which occur within the limits of the country, on the coast-lines, at sea, or wherever the admiralty jurisdiction extends—the deck of a British ship included.

ADMIRALTY MIDSHIPMAN. Formerly one who, having served the appointed time, and passed his examination for lieutenant, was appointed to a ship by the admiralty, and thus named in contradistinction to those who used to be rated by the captain; he generally had precedence for promotion to "acting orders."

ADONIS. An anguilliform fish, about six inches long: it is of a golden colour, with a greenish tint, and has a white line from its very small gills to the tail.

ADORNINGS. The carved work on the quarter and stern-galleries of men-of-war.

ADOWN. The bawl of privateersmen for the crew of a captured vessel to go below. Saxon, *adoun*.

ADREAMT. Dozing; the sensation so often combatted with towards the end of a first or a middle watch, it being the state, as an old author has it, "between sleeping and waking."

ADRENT, or ADREYNTE. An old term for *drowned*.

ADRIFT. Floating at random; the state of a boat or vessel broken from her moorings, and driven to and fro without control by the winds and waves. Cast loose; cut adrift.

ADSCRIPTS. Sometimes used for the tangents of arcs.

AD VALOREM. Duties levied on commercial goods, according to their value.

ADVANCE, To. An old word, meaning to raise to honour.

ADVANCED POST. A spot of ground seized by a party to secure their front. A piquet or outpost.

ADVANCED SQUADRON. One on the look-out.—*Advance*, or *vanguard*, that division of a force which is next the enemy, or which marches before a body.—*Advance fosse*, a ditch of water round the esplanade or glacis of a fortification.—*Advance!* the order to marines and small-arm men to move forward.

ADVANCE-LIST. The register by which two months' wages to the crew are paid, on first commission, and a quarter's to officers.

ADVANCEMENT. Promotion to higher rank.

ADVANCE MONEY. In men-of-war and most merchant ships the advance of two months' wages is given to the crew, previous to going to sea; the clearing off of which is called *working up the dead horse*.

ADVANCE NOTE. A document issued by owners of a ship or their agents, promising to pay a seaman, or to his order, a sum of money in part of his wages, within a certain number of days after he has sailed in the ship. Advance notes are quite negotiable before a seaman has taken his departure.

ADVANTAGE, or VANTAGE-GROUND. That which gives superiority of attack on, or defence against, an enemy; affording means of annoyance or resistance.

ADVENTURE. An enterprise in which something is left to hazard. —*A bill of adventure* is one signed by the merchant, by which he takes the chances of the voyage.

ADVERSARY. Generally applied to an enemy, but strictly an opponent in single combat.

ADVERSE. The opposite of favourable; as, an *adverse* wind.

ADVICE-BOAT. A small fast-sailing vessel in advance of a fleet, employed to carry intelligence with all possible despatch. They were first used in 1692, to gain tidings of what was transacting in Brest, previous to the battle of La Hogue.

ADVOCATE GENERAL. An officer of the High Court of Admiralty, whose duty it is to appear for the lord high-admiral in that court, the court of delegates, or any other wherein his rights are concerned.— *Judge-advocate of the navy*, a law officer appointed to watch over and direct proceedings connected with courts-martial.—*Deputy judge-advocate*, an appointment made by the sudden selection of some secretary, or captain's clerk, to perform the duty at a court-martial (where no legal person is empowered), utterly ignorant of the law or the customs of the naval service.

ADZE, or ADDICE. A cutting tool of the axe kind, for dubbing flat and circular work, much used by shipwrights, especially by the Parsee builders in India, with whom it serves for axe, plane, and chisel. It is a curious fact that from the polar regions to the equator, and southerly throughout Polynesia, this instrument and its peculiar adaptations, whether made of iron, basalt, nephrite, &c., all preserve the same idea or identity of conception.

ÆINAUTÆ. Senators of Miletus, who held their deliberations on board ship.

ÆRATÆ. Ancient ships fitted with brazen prows.

AEROLITES. One of the many names given to those solid masses or stones which occasionally fall from the atmosphere to the surface of the earth. The assumption of their periodicity cannot, as yet, be considered as confirmed.

AEROLOGY. The rational doctrine or science of the air and its phenomena.

AEROMANCY. Formerly the art of divining by the air, but now used for foretelling the changes in the weather, either by experience or by instruments.

AEROMETRY. The science of measuring the air, its powers, pressure, and properties.

ÆSTIVAL. Belonging to summer; the solstitial point whereby the sun's ascent above the equator is determined.

ÆSTUARY. *See* ESTUARY.

ÆWUL. An Anglo-Saxon term for a twig basket for catching fish.

AFEARD. This is a very common expression for *afraid*, and though thought low, is a true archaism of our language, as seen in Chaucer, Shakspeare, and Ben Jonson. Major Moor terms it an old and good word.

AFER. The south-west wind of the Latins, and used by some of the early voyagers.

AFFAIR. An indecisive engagement; a duel.

AFFECTED. An algebraic term for an equation in which the unknown quantity rises to two or more several powers.

AFFECTIONATE FRIENDS. An official inconsistent subscription, even to letters of reproof and imprest, used by the former Board of Commissioners of the Navy to such officers as were not of noble families or bore titles; the only British board that ever made so mean a distinction, equally kind with the regrets of the clergy on burning a heretic, or those of Walton in cutting a live fish *tenderly*. It was probably adopted from James, Duke of York, who, when lord high-admiral, always so subscribed his official letters. It is said that this practice was discontinued in consequence of a distinguished naval captain—a knight—adding, "your affectionate friend." He was thereupon desired to "discontinue such an expression," when he replied, "I am, gentlemen, no longer your affectionate friend, J. Phil . . more."

AFFIDAVIT. A declaration upon oath, weakened in importance by its too frequent administration at custom-houses, lazarettos, &c. Declarations are now substituted in the case of naval officers.

AFFIRMATIVE. The positive sign or quantity in algebra; also the signal flag or pendant by which a request or order is answered.

AFFLUENT. A stream flowing directly into another stream; a more specific term than tributary.

AFFORCIAMENT. An old term for a fortress or stronghold.

AFFREIGHTMENT. A contract for the letting the vessel, or a part of her, for freight. (*See* CONTRACT OF AFFREIGHTMENT.)

AFLOAT. Borne up and supported by the water; buoyed clear of the ground; also used for being on board ship.

AFORE. A Saxon word opposed to abaft, and signifying that part of the ship which lies forward or near the stem. It also means farther forward; as, the galley is *afore* the bitts.—*Afore*, the same as *before* the mast.—*Afore the beam*, all the field of view from amidship in a right angle to the ship's keel to the horizon forward.

AFORE THE MAST. *See* BEFORE THE MAST.

AFOUNDRIT. An archaism of *sunk* or *foundered*.

AFRAID. One of the most reproachful sea-epithets, as not only conveying the meaning being struck with fear, but also implies rank cowardice. (*See* AFEARD.)

AFT—a Saxon word contradistinctive of *fore*, and an abbreviation of *abaft*—the hinder part of the ship, or that nearest the stern.—*Right aft* is in a direct line with the keel from the stern.—*To haul aft a sheet* is to pull on the rope which brings the clue or corner of the sails more in the direction of the stern.—The mast *rakes aft* when it inclines towards the stern.

AFT-CASTLE. An elevation on the after-part of our ships of war, opposed to forecastle, for the purpose of fighting.

AFTER. A comparative adjective, applied to any object in the hind part of a ship or boat; as, the *after*-cabin, the *after*-hatchway, &c. —*After* sails, yards, and braces—those attached to the main and mizzen masts. Opposed to *fore*.

AFTER-BODY. That part of the ship's hull which is abaft the midships or dead-flat, as seen from astern. The term is, however, more particularly used in expressing the *figure* or *shape* of that part of the ship. (*See* DEAD-FLAT.)

AFTER-CLAP. Whatever disagreeable occurrence takes place after the consequences of the cause were thought at an end; a principal application being when a ship, supposed to have struck, opens her fire again. This is a very old English word, alluding to unexpected events happening after the seeming end of an affair; thus Spenser, in "Mother Hubbard's Tale"—

> "And bad next day that all should readie be,
> But they more subtill meaning had than he:
> For the next morrowes mede they closely ment,
> For feare of *after-claps*, for to prevent."

AFTER-END. The stern of a ship, or anything in her which has that end towards the stern.

AFTER-FACE. *See* BACK OF THE STERN-POST.

AFTER-GUARD. The men who are stationed on the quarter-deck and poop, to work the after-sails. It was generally composed of ordinary seamen and landsmen, constituting with waisters the largest part of the crew, on whom the principal drudgery of the ship devolved. At present the crews of ships-of-war are composed chiefly of able and ordinary seamen—landsmen are omitted.

AFTER-LADDER leads to captain's and officers' quarters, and only used by officers.

AFTERMOST. The last objects in a ship, reckoned from forwards; as, the *aftermost* mast, *aftermost* guns, &c.

AFTERNOON-WATCH. The men on deck-duty from noon till 4 P.M.

AFTER-ORDERS. Those which are given out after the regular issue of the daily orders.

AFTER-PART. The locality towards the stern, from dead-flat; as, in the *after-part* of the fore-hold.

AFTER-PEAK. The contracted part of a vessel's hold, which lies in the run, or aftermost portion of the hold, in contradistinction to *fore-peak*. Both are the sharp ends of the ship.

AFTER-RAKE. That part of the hull which overhangs the after-end of keel.

AFTER-SAILS. All those on the after-masts, as well as on the stays between the main and mizen masts. Their effect is to balance the head-sails, in the manner that a weather-cock or vane is moved, of which the main-mast must be considered the pivot or centre. The reverse of *head-sails*. " Square the after-yards," refers to the yards on the main and mizen masts.

AFTER-TIMBERS. All those timbers abaft the midship section or bearing part of a vessel.

AFTMOST. The same as *aftermost*.

AFTWARD. In the direction of the stern.

AGA. A superior Turkish officer.

AGAINST THE SUN. Coiling a rope in the direction from the right hand towards the left—the contrary of *with the sun*. This term applies to a position north of the sun; south of the sun it would be reversed.

AGAL-AGAL. One of the sea fuci, forming a commercial article from the Malay Isles to China, where it is made into a strong cement. The best is the *Gracilaria spinosa*. Agal-agal derives its name from Tanjong Agal on the north coast of Borneo; where it was originally collected. It is now found in great abundance throughout the Polynesian Islands, Mauritius, &c. It is soluble, and forms a clear jelly—used by consumptive patients. It fetches a high price in China. It is supposed that the sea-swallow derives his materials for the edible bird's nests at Borneo from this fucus.

AGATE. The cap for the pivots of the compass-cards, formed of hard siliceous stone, a chalcedony or carnelian, &c.

AGAVE. The American aloe, from which cordage is made; similar to the piña of Manila. The fruit also, when expressed, affords the refreshing drink " pulque."

AGE. In chronology, a period of a hundred years.—*Ship's age,* one of the stipulations of contracts at Lloyd's.—*Age of the moon,* is the interval of time or number of days elapsed since the previous conjunction or new moon.

AGENCY. Payment *pro operâ et labore,* fixed by the prize act at five per cent. as a fair average, but it gives nothing where the property is restored; in such cases it is usual for the agent to charge a gross sum.

AGENCY, NAVAL. A useful class of persons, who transact the monetary affairs of officers, and frequently help them to the top branches of the profession. They are paid for their services by a percentage of $2\frac{1}{2}$.

AGENT. In physics, expresses that by which a thing is done or effected. —*Navy agent* is a deputy employed to pass accounts, transact business, and receive pay or other monies, in behoof of the officers and crew, and to apply the proceeds as directed by them.—*Agent victuallers,* officers appointed to the charge of provisions at our foreign ports and stations, to contract for, buy, and regulate, under the authority of the commissioners of the navy. (*See* NEGLIGENCE.)—*Prize agent,* one appointed for the sale of prizes, and nominated in equal numbers by the commander, the officers, and the ship's company.

AGENTS TO LLOYD'S. *See* LLOYD'S AGENTS.

AGGRESSION. The first act of injury in provoking warfare.

AGIO. An Italian word, applied to denote the profit arising from discounting bills; also the difference between the value of bank-stock and currency.

AGISTMENT. An embankment against the sea or rivers, or one thrown up to fence out a stream.

AGON. A Chinese kind of metal cymbal. (*See* GONG.) It is singular that Gower, *circa* 1395, using this old word for *gone,* thus metallicizes—

> "Of brasse, of silver, and of golde,
> The world is passed, and *agon.*"

AGONIST. A champion; prize-fighter.

AGREEMENT. Except vessels of less than eighty tons register, the master of a ship must enter into an agreement with every seaman whom he carries from any port in Great Britain as one of his crew; and that agreement must be in the form sanctioned by the Board of Trade. (*See* RUNNING AGREEMENT.)

AGROUND. The situation of a ship or other vessel whose bottom touches or rests upon the ground. It also signifies stranded, and is used figuratively for being disabled or hindered.

AGUA-ARDIENTE [Sp.] Corrupted into *aguardiente,*—the adulterated brandy of Spain supplied to ships.

AGUADA. The Spanish and Portuguese term for a watering-place.

AGUGLIA. A common name for sharp-pointed rocks. From the Italian for needle; written *agulha* in Spanish and Portuguese charts.

AHEAD. A term especially referable to any object farther onward, or immediately before the ship, or in the course steered, and therefore opposed to *astern.*—*Ahead of the reckoning*, is sailing beyond the estimated position of the ship.—*Ahead* is also used for progress; as, *cannot get ahead*, and is generally applied to forward, in advance.

AHOLD. A term of our early navigators, for bringing a ship close to the wind, so as to hold or keep to it.

AHOO, OR ALL AHOO, as our Saxon forefathers had it; awry, aslant, lopsided. (*See* ASKEW.)

AHOY! *See* Ho!

AHULL. A ship under bare poles and her helm alee, driving from wind and sea, stern foremost. Also a ship deserted, and exposed to the tempestuous winds.

AID, To. To succour; to supply with provisions or stores.

AID-DE-CAMP. A military staff officer, who carries and circulates the general's orders; and another class selected as expert at carving and dancing. In a ship, flag-lieutenant to an admiral, or, in action, the quarter-deck midshipmen to a captain.

AIGRE. The sudden flowing of the sea, called in the fens of Lincolnshire, *acker.* (*See* BORE.)

AIGUADE [Fr.] AGUADA [Sp.] Water as provision for ships.

AIGUADES. Watering-places on French coasts.

AIGUILLE *aimantee*, magnetic needle. — *de carène*, outrigger. — *d'inclinaison*, dipping needle. — *de tré*, or *à ralingue*, a bolt-rope needle.

AIGUILLES. The peculiar small fishing-boats in the Garonne and other rivers of Guienne.

AIGULETS [Fr. *aiguillettes*]. Tagged points or cords worn across the breast in some uniforms of generals, staff-officers, and special mounted corps.

AILETTES. Small plates of steel placed on the shoulders in mediæval armour.

AIM. The direction of a musket, cannon, or any other fire-arm or missile weapon towards its object.—*To take aim*, directing the piece to the object.

AIR. The elastic, compressible, and dilatable fluid encompassing the terraqueous globe. It penetrates and pervades other bodies, and thus animates and excites all nature.—*Air* means also a gentle breath of wind gliding over the surface of the water.—*To air*, to dry or ventilate.

AIR-BLADDER. A vesicle containing gas, situated immediately beneath the spinal column in most fish, and often communicating by a tube with the gullet. It is the homologue of the lungs of air-breathing vertebrates.

AIR-BRAVING. Defying the winds.

AIR-CONE, in the marine engine, is to receive the gases which enter the hot-well from the air-pump, where, after ascending, they escape through a pipe at the top.

AIRE. A name in our northern islands for a bank of sand.

AIR-FUNNEL. A cavity formed by omission of a timber in the upper works of a vessel, to admit fresh air into the hold of a ship and convey the foul out of it.

AIR-GUN. A silent weapon, which propels bullets by the expansive force of air only.

AIRING-STAGE. A wooden platform, on which gunpowder is aired and dried.

AIR-JACKET. A leathern garment furnished with inflated bladders, to buoy the wearer up in the water. (*See*-AYR.)

AIR-PIPES. Funnels for clearing ships' holds of foul air, on the principle of the rarefying power of heat.

AIR-PORTS. Large scuttles in ships' bows for the admission of air, when the other ports are down. The Americans also call their side-ports by that name.

AIR-PUMP. An apparatus to remove the water and gases accumulating in the condenser while the engine is at work.

AIR-SCUTTLES. The same as *air-ports.*

AIR-SHAFTS. Vertical holes made in mining, to supply the adits with fresh air. Wooden shafts are sometimes adopted on board ship for a similar purpose.

AIRT, or ART. A north-country word for a bearing point of the compass or quarter of the heavens. Thus the song—

> "Of a' the *airts* the wind can blaw,
> I dearly love the west."

AIRY. Breezy.

AKEDOWN. A form of the term *acton*, as a defensive dress.

ALABLASTER. An arbalist or cross-bow man; also the corruption of *alabaster.*

ALAMAK. The name given in nautical astronomy to that beautiful double star *Anak al ard* of the Arabians, or γ Andromedæ.

ALAMOTTIE. The *Procellaria pelagica*, or Storm-finch; Mother Cary's chicken, or stormy petrel.

ALAND. A term formerly used for to the shore, on shore, or to land.

ALARM, ALARUM [from the Italian *all'armi!*] An apprehension from sudden noise or report. The drum or signal by which men are summoned to stand on their guard in time of danger.—*False alarm* is sometimes occasioned by a timid or negligent sentry, and at others designedly by an officer, to ascertain the promptness of his men. Sometimes false alarms are given by the enemy to harass the adversary. Old Rider defines *alarm* as a "watch-word shewing the neernesse of the enemies."

ALARM-POST. A place appointed for troops to assemble, in case of a sudden alarm.

ALBACORE. A fish of the family *Scomberidæ*, found in shoals in the ocean; it is about 5 or 6 feet long, with an average weight of nearly 100 lbs. when fine.

ALBANY BEEF. A name for the sturgeon of the Hudson River, where it is taken in quantity for commerce.

ALBATROSS. A large, voracious, long-winged sea-bird, belonging to the genus *Diomedea;* very abundant in the Southern Ocean and the Northern Pacific, though said to be rarely met with within the tropics.

ALBION. An early name of England, from the whiteness of the eastern coast cliffs.

ALBURNUM. The sapwood of timber, commonly termed the slab-cuts.

ALCAID. A governor, or officer of justice, amongst the Moors, Spaniards, and Portuguese.

ALCATRAZ. The pelican. Alcatraz Island is situated in the mouth of the river San Francisco, in California, so named from its being covered with these birds. Also Alcatraz on the coast of Africa, from *Pelecanus sula*—booby. Columbus mentions the alcatraz when nearing America, and Drayton says—

> "Most like to that sharp-sighted *alcatras*,
> That beats the air above the liquid glass."

ALDEBARAN. The lucida of Taurus, the well-known nautical star, popularly called Bull's-eye.

A-LEE. The contrary of *a-weather:* the position of the helm when its tiller is borne over to the lee-side of the ship, in order to go about or put her head to windward.—*Hard a-lee!* or *luff a-lee!* is said to the steersman to put the helm down.—*Helm's a-lee!* the word of command given on putting the helm down, and causing the head-sails to shake in the wind.

ALEMAYNE. The early name for Germany.

ALERT. On the look-out, and ready for any sudden duty. Nearly synonymous with *alarm*. *Alerto* — called frequently by Spanish sentinels.

ALEWIFE. The *Clupea alosa*, a fish of the herring kind, which appears in the *Philosophical Transactions* for 1678, as the *aloofe;* the corruption therefore was a ready one.

ALEXIACUS. The appellation under which Neptune was implored to protect the nets of the tunny fisheries from the sword-fish.

ALFERE, or ALFEREZ [*alfier*, Fr.; *alferez*, Span.] Standard-bearer; ensign; cornet. The old English term for ensign; it was in use in our forces till the civil wars of Charles I.

ALFONDIZA. The custom-house at Lisbon.

ALGA. A species of millepora.

ALGÆ. Sea-weeds, and the floating scum-like substances on fresh water; they deserve to be more studied, for some, as dulse, laver, badderlocks, &c., are eatable, and others are useful for manure.

ALGEBRA. A general method of resolving mathematical problems, by means of equations, or rather computing abstract quantities by symbols or signs; a literal arithmetic.

ALGENIB. A principal star (γ) in Pegasus.

ALGERE. A spear used by fishermen in olden times.

ALGIER DUTY. An imposition laid on merchants' goods by the Long Parliament, for the redemption of captives in the Mediterranean.

ALGOL. A wonderful variable star in Perseus, which goes through its changes in about two days and twenty-one hours.

ALGOLOGY. Scientific researches into the nature of sea-plants.

ALGORAB. A star taking rank as the a of Corvus, but its brightness of late is rivalled by β Corvi.

ALHIDADE. An Arabic name for the index or fiducial of an astronomical or geometrical instrument, carrying sight or telescope; used by early navigators. A rule on the back of a common astrolabe, to measure heights, &c.

ALIEN. Generally speaking, one born in a foreign country, out of the king's allegiance; but if the parents be of the king's obedience, the child is no alien. An alien enemy, or person under the allegiance of the state at war with us, is not *generally* disabled from being a witness in admiralty courts; nor are debts due to him forfeited, but only suspended.—*Alien's duty*, the impost laid on all goods imported into England in foreign bottoms, over and above the regular customs.

ALIGNMENT. An imaginary line, drawn to regulate the order of a squadron.

ALIQUOT PART. That which will exactly divide a number, leaving no remainder.

ALL. The total quantity; quite; wholly.—*All aback*, when all the sails are taken aback by the winds.—*All ahoo*, or *all-a-ugh*, confused; hanging over; crooked.—*All-a-taunt-o*, a ship fully rigged, with masts in and yards crossed.—*All hands*, the whole ship's company.—*All* *hands ahoy,* the boatswain's summons for the whole crew to repair on deck, in distinction from the watch.—*All hands make sail!* the cheering order when about to chase a strange vessel.—*All hands to quarters!* the call in armed merchantmen, answering to the *Beat to quarters* in a man-of-war.—*All in the wind,* when a vessel's head is too close to the wind, so that all her sails are shivering.—*All over,* resemblance to a particular object, as a ship in bad kelter: "she's a privateer *all over.*"—*All overish,* the state of feeling when a man is neither ill nor well, restless in bed and indifferent to meals. In the tropics this is considered as the premonitory symptom of disease, and a warning which should be looked to.—*All ready,* the answer from the tops when the sails are cast loose, and ready to be dropped.—*All standing,* fully equipped, or with clothes on. To be brought up *all standing,* is to be suddenly checked or stopped, without any preparation.—*Paid off all standing,* without unrigging or waiting to return stores; perhaps recommissioned the next day or hour.—*All's well,* the sentry's call at each bell struck (or half hour) between the periods of broad daylight, or from 8 P.M. to 4 A.M.—*All to pieces,* a phrase used for out-and-out, extremely, or excessively; as, "we beat her in sailing *all to pieces.*"— *All weathers,* any time or season; continually.

ALLAN. A word from the Saxon, still used in the north to denote a piece of land nearly surrounded by a stream.

ALLEGE. A French ballast-boat.

ALLEGIANCE. The legal obedience of a subject to his sovereign in return for the protection afforded; a debt which, in a natural-born subject, cannot be cancelled by any change of time, or place, or circumstance, without the united consent of the legislature.

ALLER-FLOAT, OR ALLER-TROUT. A species of fine trout frequenting the shady holes under the roots of the *aller* or alder tree, on the banks of rivers and brooks.

ALLIANCE. A league or confederacy between sovereigns or states, for mutual safety and defence. Subjects of allies cannot trade with the common enemy, on pain of the property being confiscated as prize to the captors.

ALLICIENCY. The attractive power of the magnet.

ALLIGATOR [from the Spanish *lagarto*]. The crocodile of America. The head of this voracious animal is flat and imbricate; several of the under teeth enter into and pass through the upper jaw; the nape is naked; on the tail are two rough lateral lines.

ALLIGATOR WATER. The brackish water inside the mouths of tropical rivers, with white and muddy surface running into the sea.

ALLISION. Synonymous in marine law with *collision,* though the jurists of Holland introduce it to mark a distinction between one vessel running against another and two vessels striking each other.

ALLOCUTION. The harangue anciently made by the Roman generals
to exhort their forces.

ALLOTMENT. A part of the pay apportioned monthly to the wives,
children, mothers, or destitute fathers of the warrant and petty officers,
seamen, and marines of ships of war on foreign stations. In the
merchant service all such stipulations for allotting any portion of a
seaman's wages during his absence must be inserted in the agreement.

ALLOTMENT-LIST. A document containing the requisite details, attested by the four signing officers, to be transmitted to the Navy Office.

ALLOTTING. Persons agreeing to buy a ship's cargo appoint a disin-
terested person to allot a share to each by affixing their respective names.

ALLOW, To. To concede a destined portion of stores, &c.

ALLOWANCE. The ration or allotted quantum of provisions which
each individual receives; and it is either double, full, two-thirds, half,
or short, according to incidents.

ALLUVION. An accretion formed along sea-shores and the banks of
rivers by the deposition of the various substances held in solution or
washed by the waters. Sea alluvions differ from those of rivers, in
that they form a slope *towards* the land.

ALLY. A friendly or confederated state.

ALMACANTARS. Circles parallel to the horizon, and supposed to
pass through every degree of the meridian. An Arabic term, synonymous with *parallels of latitude*.

ALMACANTARS STAFF. An instrument formerly used at sea for
observing the sun's amplitude, formed of an arc of about 15 degrees.

ALMADIA. A small African canoe, made of the bark of trees. Some
of the larger square-sterned negro-boats are also thus designated.

ALMAFADAS. Large dunnage cut on the coast of Portugal.

ALMAGEST. The celebrated work of Ptolemy on geometry and
astronomy. Ricciolus adopted the term in 1651 for his *Body of
Mathematical Science*. It became general, whence Chaucer—

> "His *Almagiste* and bookes, grete and small."

ALMANAC. A record of the days, feasts, and celestial phenomena of
the year. Though confounded with calendar, it is essentially different
—the latter relating to time in general, and the almanac to that of a
year; but the term calendar can be properly used for a particular
year. (*See* EPHEMERIS.)

ALMURY. The upright part of an astrolabe.

ALMATH [*Hamal*]. The star in Aries whence the first mansion of
the moon takes its name. The Frankeleine in Chaucer says:—

> "And by his eighte speres in his werking,
> He knew ful wel how far *Alnath* was shove
> Fro the hed of thilke fix Aries above,
> That in the ninthe spere considered is."

ALMIRANTE. A great sea-officer or high-admiral in Spain.

ALMIRANTESA. The wife of an admiral.

ALMURY. The upright part of an astrolabe.

ALNUS CAVER. Transport-ships of the early English, so called from the wood of which they were constructed.

ALOFT [Anglo-Saxon, *alofte*, on high]. Above; over-head; on high. Synonymous with up above the tops, at the mast-head, or anywhere about the higher yards, masts, and rigging of ships.—*Aloft there!* the hailing of people in the tops.—*Away aloft!* the command to the people in the rigging to climb to their stations. Also, heaven: "Poor Tom is gone *aloft*."

ALONDE. An old English word for ashore, on land.

ALONG [Saxon]. Lengthwise.—*Alongside*, by the side of a ship; side by side.—*Lying along*, when the wind, being on the beam, presses the ship over to leeward with the press of sail; or, *lying along* the land.

ALONGSHORE. A common nautical phrase signifying along the coast, or a course which is in sight of the shore, and nearly parallel to it. (*See* 'LONGSHORE.)

ALONGST. In the middle of a stream; moored head and stern.

ALOOF. The old word for "keep your luff," in the act of sailing to the wind. (*See* LUFF.)—*Keep aloof*, at a distance.

ALOOFE. *See* ALEWIFE.

ALOW. Synonymous with *below;* as *alow* and *aloft*, though more properly *low* and *aloft*. Carrying all sail *alow and aloft* is when the reefs are shaken out, and all the studding-sails set.

ALPHABETICAL LIST. This is a list which accompanies the ship's books; it contains the names and number of every person in the pay-book.

ALTAIR. The bright nautical star α Aquilæ, binary.

ALTAR. A platform in the upper part of a dock.

ALTEMETRIE. The old term for trigonometry among navigators.

ALTERNATE. Reciprocal.—*Alternate angles* are the internal angles formed by a line cutting two parallels, and lying on the opposite side of the cutting line; the one below the first parallel, and the other above.—*Alternate ratio* is that of which the antecedents and consequents bear respectively to each other in any proportion which has the quantities of the same kind.

ALTERNATING WINDS. Peculiar winds blowing at stated times one way, and then, from a sudden alteration in the temperature of the elements, setting in the contrary direction. A remarkable instance is that of the Gulf of Arta in the Ionian Sea, where the effect is promoted by local causes. All land and sea breezes are strictly alternating winds. These however are mostly inter-tropical; the solar heat causing the sea-breeze to blow on the land by day, and condensation and greater heat of the sea causing a reaction when the land has cooled to a lower temperature.

ALTERNATION or PERMUTATION OF QUANTITIES, is the varying or changing their order, and is easily found by a continual multiplication of all numbers.

ALTIMETRY. Trigonometry; the art of measuring heights or depressions of land, whether accessible or not.

ALTITUDE. The elevation of any of the heavenly bodies above the plane of the horizon, or its angular distance from the horizon, measured in the direction of a great circle passing through the zenith. Also the third dimension of a body, considered with regard to its elevation above the ground.—*Apparent altitude* is that which appears by sensible observations made on the surface of the globe.—*Altitude of the pole.* The arc of the meridian between the pole of the heavens and the horizon of any place, and therefore equal to its geographical latitude.—*Altitude of the cone of the earth's and moon's shadow,* is the height of the one or the other during an eclipse, and is measured from the centre of the body.—*Altitude of a shot or shell.* The perpendicular height of the vertex of the curve in which it moves above the horizon.—*Meridian altitude.* The arc of the meridian,—or greater or less altitude, measured from the horizon, of a celestial object in its passage over the meridian, above or below the pole, of the place of the observer. In Polar regions two such transits of the sun, and in England similarly, circumpolar stars afford double observations for the determination of time or latitude. The general term is understood by seamen to denote mid-day, when the passage and meridian altitude of the sun affords the latitude.—*True altitude* is that produced by correcting the apparent one for parallax and refraction.

ALTMIKLEC. A silver Turkish coin of 60 paras, or 2s. 9½d. sterling.

ALUFFE, OR ALOOF. Nearer to the wind. This is a very old form of *luff;* being noticed by Matthew Paris, and other writers, as a sea-term. (*See* LUFF.)

ALURE. An old term for the gutter or drain along a battlement or parapet wall.

ALVEUS. A very small ancient boat, made from the single trunk of a tree. A monoxylon, or canoe.

A.M. The uncials for *ante-meridian,* or in the forenoon. (*See* MERIDIAN.)

AMAIN [Saxon *a,* and *mœgn,* force, strength]. This was the old word to an enemy for "yield," and was written *amayne* and *almayne.* Its literal signification is, with force or vigour, all at once, suddenly; and it is generally used to anything which is moved by a tackle-fall, as "lower amain!" let run at once. When we used to demand the salute in the narrow seas, the lowering of the topsail was called *striking amain* (*see* STRIKING), and it was demanded by the *wave amain* (*see* WAVE), or brandishing a bright sword to and fro.

AMALPHITAN CODE, the oldest code of modern sea-laws, compiled, during the first Crusade, by the people of Amalfi in Italy, who then possessed considerable commerce and maritime power.

AMAYE. Sea-marks on the French coast.

AMBASSADOR. A practical joke performed on board ship in warm climates, in which the dupes are unmercifully ducked in the wash-deck tub:—

> "And he was wash'd, who ne'er was wash'd before."

AMBER. A hard resinous substance of vegetable origin, generally of a bright yellow colour, and translucent. It is chiefly obtained from the southern shores of the Baltic, and those of Sicily, where it is thrown up by the sea, but it also occurs in beds of lignite.

AMBERGRIS. A fragrant drug found floating on sea-coasts, the origin and production of which was long a matter of dispute, although now known to be a morbid product developed in the intestines of the spermaceti whale (*Physeter macrocephalus*). It is of a grayish colour, very light, easily fusible, and is used both as a perfume and a cordial, in various extracts, essences, and tinctures.

AMBIENT [from *ambio*, Lat., to go round]. Surrounding, or investing; whence the atmosphere is designated ambient, because it encompasses the earth.

AMBIGENAL. One of the triple hyperboles of the second order.

AMBIT of a geometrical figure is the perimeter, or the line, or sum or all the lines, by which it is bounded.

AMBITION is usually denominated a virtue or a vice according to its direction; but assuredly more of the former, as it is a grand stimulus to officers to avoid reproach, and aspire to eminence and honour.

AMBLYGON. Obtuse angular.

AMBRY. *See* AUMBREY.

AMBUSCADE [Span. *emboscada*]. A body of men lying in wait to surprise an enemy, or cut off his supplies; also the site where they lurk. This, as well as *ambush*, obviously arose from woods having afforded the hiding-places.

AMBUSH. Signifies an attempt to lie in concealment for the purpose of surprising an enemy without his perceiving the intention until he is attacked.

AMELIORATION. An allowance made to the neutral purchaser, on reclaiming a ship irregularly condemned, for repairs she has undergone in his service.

AMICABLE NUMBERS are such as are mutually equal to the sum of each other's aliquot parts.

AMIDSHIPS. The middle of the ship, whether in regard to her length between stem and stern, or in breadth between the two sides. To put the helm *amidships* is to place it in a line with the keel. The term, however, has a more general bearing to the axis of the ship; as guns, or stores, or place amidships has reference to that line, fore and aft. Externally the term "amidships" as to striking, boarding, &c., would be about the mainmast, or half the length of the ship. (*See* MIDSHIPS.)

AMIDWARD. Towards the 'midship or middle section of the vessel.

AMLAGH. A Manx or Gaelic term denoting to manure with sea-weed.

AMLEE. A Manx or Gaelic term for sea-weed.

AMMUNITION. This word had an infinite variety of meanings. It includes every description of warlike stores, comprehending not only the ordnance, but the powder, balls, bullets, cartridges, and equipments.— *Ammunition bread*, that which is for the supply of armies or garrisons. —*Ammunition chest*, a box placed abaft near the stern or in the tops of men-of-war, to contain ammunition, for the arms therein placed, in readiness for immediate action.—*Ammunition shoes*, those made for soldiers and sailors, and particularly for use by those frequenting the magazine, being soft and free from metal.—*Ammunition waggon*, a close cart for conveying military effects.—*Ammunition wife*, a name applied to women of doubtful character.

AMNESTY. An act of oblivion, by which, in a professional view, pardon is granted to those who have rebelled or deserted their colours; also to deserters who return to their ships.

AMOK. A term signifying slaughter, but denoting the practice of the Malays, when infuriated to madness with bang (a preparation from a species of hemp), of sallying into the streets, or decks, to murder any whom they may chance to meet, until they are either slain or fall from exhaustion.—*To run a-muck.* To run madly and attack all we meet (*Pope, Dryden*). As in the case of mad dogs, certain death awaited them, for if not killed in being taken, torture and impalement followed.

AMORAYLE. An archaism of *admiral*.

AMORCE [Fr.] A word sometimes used to signify priming-powder.

AMPERES. An ancient vessel, in which the rowers used an oar on each side at once.

AMPHIBIA. A class of animals which, from a peculiar arrangement of breathing organs, can live either in water or on land. [Gr. *amphibios*, having a double manner of life.] Hence *amphibious*.

AMPHIPRORÆ. Ancient vessels, both ends of which were prow-shaped, so that in narrow channels they need not turn.

AMPHISCII. The inhabitants of the torrid zone are thus denominated from their shadow being turned one part of the year to the north and the other to the south.

AMPHOTEROPLON. *See* HETOROPLON.

AMPLITUDE. As a general term, implies extent. In astronomy, it is an arc of the horizon intercepted between the true east or west points thereof, and the centre of the sun, star, or planet, at its rising or setting. In other words, it is the horizontal angular distance of a star from the east or west points. It is eastern or ortive when the heavenly object rises, and western or occiduous when it sets, and is moreover northern or southern according to its quarter of the horizon. —*Amplitude*, in gunnery, is the range or whole distance of a projectile, or the right horizontal line subtending the curvilineal path in which it moved.—*Amplitude*, in magnetism, is the difference between the rising and setting of the sun from the east and west points, as indicated by the mariner's or magnetic compass—which subtracted from the true amplitude, constitutes the error of the compass, which is the combined effect of variation and local deviation.

AMPOTIS. The recess or ebb of the tide.

AMRELL. An archaic orthography for *admiral.*

AMULET. A small relic or sacred sentence, preservative against disaster and disease, appended to the neck by superstitious people: few Italian or Spanish seamen are without them.

AMUSETTE. A kind of gun on a stock, like that of a musket, but mounted as a swivel, carrying a ball from half a pound to two pounds weight.

AMY. A foreigner serving on board, subject to some prince in friendship with us.

ANACLASTICS, OR ANACLATICS. The ancient doctrine of refracted light or dioptrics.—*Anaclastic curves,* the apparent curves formed at the bottom of a vessel full of water, or anything at great depths overboard to an eye placed in the air; also the heavenly vault as seen through the atmosphere.

ANADROMOUS. A term applied to migratory fishes, which have their stated times of ascending rivers from the sea, and returning again, as the salmon and others.

ANALEM. A mathematical instrument for finding the course and elevation of the sun.

ANALEMMA. A projection of the sphere on the plane of the meridian, taken in a lateral point of view, so that the colours become circles, whilst those whose planes pass through the eye become right lines, and the oblique circles ellipses. On globes it is represented by a narrow double-looped formed figure, the length of which is equal to the breadth of the torrid zone, and is divided into months and days, to show approximately the solar declination and the equation of time.

ANALOGY. Resemblance, relation, or equality; a similitude of ratios or proportions.

ANALYSIS. The resolution of anything into its constituent parts: mathematically, it is the method of resolving problems by reducing them to equations.—*Analysis of curves* is that which shows their properties, points of inflection, station, variation, &c.—*Analysis of finite quantities* is termed specious arithmetic or algebra.—*Analysis of infinites* is a modern introduction, and used for fluxions or the differential calculus.—*Analysis of powers* is the evolution or resolving them into their roots.—*Analysis of metals*, fluids, solids, earths, manures, &c.

ANALYTIC. That which partakes of the property of analysis, and is reducible thereby.

ANAN. A word going out of use, uttered when an order was not understood, equal to "What do you say, sir,?" It is also used by corruption for *anon*, immediately.

ANANAS. (*Bromelia*). Pine-apple.

ANAPHORA. A term sometimes applied to the oblique ascensions of the stars.

ANAS. A genus of water-birds of the order *Natatores*. Now restricted to the typical ducks.

ANASTROUS. *See* DODECATIMORIA.

ANAUMACHION. The crime amongst the ancients of refusing to serve in the fleet—the punishment affixed to which was infamy.

ANCHIROMACHUS.—A kind of vessel of the middle ages used for transporting anchors and naval stores.

ANCHOR. A large and heavy instrument in use from the earliest times for holding and retaining ships, which it executes with admirable force. With few exceptions it consists of a long iron shank, having at one end a ring, to which the cable is attached, and the other branching out into two arms, with flukes or palms at their bill or extremity. A stock of timber or iron is fixed at right angles to the arms, and serves to guide the flukes perpendicularly to the surface of the ground. According to their various form and size, anchors obtain the epithets of the *sheet, best bower, small bower, spare, stream, kedge,* and *grappling* (which see under their respective heads).

Anchor floating, see FLOATING ANCHOR.—*At anchor*, the situation of a ship which rides by its anchor.—*To anchor*, to cast or to let go the anchor, so that it falls into the ground for the ship to ride thereby.—*To anchor* with a spring on the cable, *see* SPRING. *Anchor* is also used figuratively for anything which confers security or stability.

ANCHORABLE. Fit for anchorage.

ANCHORAGE. Ground which is suitable, and neither too deep, shallow, or exposed for ships to ride in safety upon; also the set of anchors belonging to a ship; also a royal duty levied from vessels coming to a port or roadstead for the use of its advantages. It is generally marked on the charts by an anchor, and described according to its attributes of good, snug, open, or exposed.

ANCHOR-BALL. A pyrotechnical combustible attached to a grapnel for adhering to and setting fire to ships.

ANCHOR-CHOCKS. Pieces indented into a wooden anchor-stock where it has become worn or defective in the way of the shank; also pieces of wood or iron on which an anchor rests when it is stowed.

ANCHOR-DAVIT. *See* DAVIT.

ANCHORED. Held by the anchor; also the act of having cast anchor.

ANCHOR-HOLD. The fastness of the flukes on the ground; also the act of having cast anchor, and taken the ground. (*See* HOME.)

ANCHOR-HOOPS. Strong iron hoops, binding the stock to the end of the shank and over the nuts of the anchor.

ANCHOR-ICE. The ice which is formed on and incrustates the beds of lakes and rivers: the *ground-gru* of the eastern counties of England. (*See* ICE-ANCHOR.)

ANCHORING. The act of casting anchor.—*Anchoring ground* is that where anchors will find bottom, fix themselves, and hold ships securely: free from rocks, wrecks, or other matters which would break or foul the anchor or injure the cable. In legal points it is not admitted as either port, creek, road, or roadstead, unless it be *statio tutissima nautis*. A vessel dropping anchor in known foul ground, or where any danger is incurred by inability to recover the anchor, or by being there detained until driven off by stress of weather, is not legally anchored.

ANCHOR-LINING. The short pieces of plank fastened to the sides of the ship, under the fore-channels, to prevent the bill of the anchor from tearing the ship's side when fishing or drawing it up. (*See also* BILL-BOARDS.)

ANCHOR-RING. Formerly the great ring welded into the hole for it. Recent anchors have Jew's-harp shackles, easily replaced, and not so liable to be destroyed by chain-cables.

ANCHOR-SEAT. An old term for the prow of a ship, still in use with eastern nations—Chinese, Japanese, &c.

ANCHOR-SHACKLE. An open link of iron which connects the chain with the anchor—a "Jew's-harp" shackle.

ANCHOR-SMITH. A forger of anchors.

ANCHOR-STOCK. A bar at the upper end of the shank, crossing the direction of the flukes transversely, to steady their proper direction.

In small anchors it is made of iron, but in large ones it is composed of two long cheeks or beams of oak, strongly bolted and tree-nailed together, secured with four iron hoops. It is now generally superseded by the iron stock.

ANCHOR-STOCK-FASHION. The method of placing the butt of one wale-plank nearly over the middle of the other; and the planks being broadest in the middle, and tapered to the ends, they resemble an anchor-stock, with which it is more in keeping than is the method called *top-and-butt;* also pursued in fishing spars, making false rudder-heads, &c.

ANCHOR-STOCKING is a mode of securing and working planks in general with tapered butts.

ANCHOR-STOCK TACKLE. A small tackle attached to the upper part of the anchor-stock when stowing the anchor, its object being to bring it perpendicular and closer to the ship.

ANCHOR-WATCH. A sub-division of the watch kept constantly on deck during the time the ship lies at single anchor, to be in readiness to hoist jib or stay-sails, to keep the ship clear of her anchor; or in readiness to veer more cable or let go another anchor in case the ship should drive or part her anchor. This watch is also in readiness to avoid collision in close rivers by veering cable, setting sail, using the helm, &c., which formerly involved the essence of seamanship.

ANCHOVY. The *Engraulis encrasicholus.* A small fish of the family *Clupeidæ*, about four inches in length, much used in sauces and seasoning when cured. It is migratory, but principally taken in the Mediterranean, where those of Gorgona are most esteemed in commerce.

ANCIENT. A term formerly used for the colours and their bearer, as ensign is now. Shakspeare's Nym was only a corporal, but Pistol was an ancient.

ANCON. A corner or angle of a knee-timber.—*Ancon* [Sp.] Harbour, bay, or anchorage.

ANCOR-STRENG. A very old designation of a cable.

ANCYLE. A kind of dart thrown with a leathern thong.

ANDREA-FERRARA. *See* FERRARA.

ANDREW, OR ANDREW MILLAR. A cant name for a man-of-war, and also for government and government authorities.

ANDROMEDA. A hemispherical medusa found in the Indian and Red Seas. The body is transparent and brownish, with a black cross in the middle, and has foliaceous white arms on the under part.

ANDROMEDÆ a. (Alpheratz.) A star of the first magnitude in the constellation of Andromeda.

ANELACE. The early name for a dirk or dagger usually worn at the girdle.

ANEMOMACHIA. A whirlwind or hurricane in old writers.

ANEMOMETER, or Wind-gauge. An instrument wherewith to measure the direction and velocity of wind under its varying forces—a desideratum at sea.

ANEMONE. *See* Sea-anemone.

ANEMOSCOPE. A vane index with pointers to tell the changes of the wind without referring to the weather-cock.

AN-END. The position of any spar when erected perpendicularly to the deck. The top-masts are said to be *an-end* when swayed up to their usual stations and fidded. To strike a spar or plank *an-end* is to drive it in the direction of its length. (*See* Every Rope an-end.)

ANENT, or Anenst. Opposite to; over against.

ANEROID. A portable barometer or instrument for showing variations of the weather by the pressure of the atmosphere upon a metallic box hermetically sealed.

ANEROST. A coast-word of the western counties for *nigh* or *almost.*

ANEW. Enough, as relating to number.

ANGEL-FISH. The *Squatina angelus,* of the shark family. It inhabits the northern seas, is six or eight feet long, with a cinereous rough back and white smooth belly; the mouth is beneath the anterior part of the head, and the pectoral fins are very large. (Also, *Chœtodon.*)

ANGEL-HEAD. The hook or barb of an arrow; probably *angle-head.*

ANGEL-SHOT. A ball cut in two, and the halves joined by a chain.

ANGIL. An old term for a fishing-hook [from the Anglo-Saxon *ongul,* for the same]. It means also a red worm used for a bait in angling or fishing.

ANGLE. The space or aperture intersected by the natural inclination of two lines or planes meeting each other, the place of intersection being called the vertex or angular point, and the lines legs. Angles are distinguished by the number of degrees they subtend, to 360°, or the whole circumference of a circle. Angles are acute, obtuse, right, curvilinear, rectilinear, &c. (all of which see).

ANGLE-DOG, or Angle-twitch. A large earth-worm, sought for bait.

ANGLE-IRONS. Certain strips of iron having their edges turned up at an angle to each other; they are of various sizes, and used for the ribs and knees of the framing of iron vessels.

ANGLE OF COMMUTATION. The difference between the heliocentric longitudes of the earth and a planet or comet, the latter being reduced to the ecliptic.

ANGLE OF ECCENTRICITY. An astronomical term denoting the angle whose sine is equal to the eccentricity of an orbit.

ANGLE OF ELEVATION. *See* Elevation.

ANGLE OF INCIDENCE. *See* Incidence.

ANGLE OF LEE-WAY. The difference between the apparent compass-course and the true one—arising from lateral pressure and the effect of sea when close-hauled. It is not applicable to courses when the wind and sea are fair.

ANGLE OF POSITION. A term usually confined to double stars, to distinguish the line of bearing between them when they are apparently very near to each other.

ANGLE OF REFLECTION. See REFLECTION.

ANGLE OF SITUATION. This was formerly called the *angle of position*, and is also termed the *parallactic angle* (which see).

ANGLE OF THE CENTRE. In fortification, the angle formed at the centre of the polygon by lines drawn from thence to the points of two adjacent bastions.

ANGLE OF THE SHOULDER. See EPAULE.

ANGLE OF THE VERTICAL. The difference between the geographical and geocentric latitudes of a place upon the earth's surface.

ANGLER. A fisherman, or one who angles for recreation rather than profit. Also a species of *Lophius* or toad-fish; from its ugliness and habits called also the *sea-devil*. It throws out feelers by which small fry are enticed within its power.

ANGLES OF TIMBERS. See BEVELLINGS.

ANGLING. The practice of catching fish by means of a rod, line, hook, and bait, which by its mixture of idleness and chance forms recreation; but however simple the art appears, it requires much nicety.

ANGON. A javelin formerly used by the French, the point of which resembled a *fleur-de-lis:* it is also generally applied to the half-pike or javelin.

ANGOSIADE. An astronomical falsehood; a term originating from the pretended observations of D'Angos at Malta.

ANGRA [Sp.] Bay or inlet.—*Angra grande, pequena,* &c., on the coasts of Spanish and Portuguese settlements.

ANGUILLIFORM. Applied to fishes having the shape, softness, and appearance of eels.

ANGULAR CRAB. An ugly long-armed crustacean—the *Gonophlex angulatus*—with eyes on remarkably long stalks.

ANGULAR DISTANCE. This term, when applied to celestial bodies, implies that the sun and moon, or moon and stars, are within measuring distance for lunars.

ANGULAR MOTION is that which describes an angle, or moves circularly round a point, as planets revolving about the sun.

ANGULAR VELOCITY. This is a term used in the orbits of double stars, and implies the motion in a certain time of one star round the other.

ANILLA. A commercial term for indigo, derived from the plant whence it is prepared. [Sp. *anil*, indigo, Indigofera; *alnyl*, Arab.]

ANIMAL FLOWERS. *Actiniæ*, or sea-anemones and similar animals, which project a circle of tentacula resembling flowers. Formerly they were all classed under zoophytes.

ANIMATE. The giving power or encouragement.—*To animate a battery*, to place guns in its embrasures.—*To animate a needle*, to magnetize it.—*To animate the crew* in various ways for any special duty.

ANKER. An anker of brandy contains ten gallons. The kegs in which Hollands is mostly exported are ankers and half-ankers.

ANKER-FISH. A name of a kind of cuttle-fish.

ANKLE-BONE. An old seaman's term for the crawfish.

ANNELIDS. A class of worm-like animals, of which the body is composed of a series of rings.

ANNET. A sea-gull, well known in Northumberland and on the northern coasts.

ANNIVERSARY WINDS. Those which blow constantly at certain seasons of the year, as monsoon, trade, and etesian winds.

ANNONA. An ancient tax for the yearly supply of corn or provisions for the army and capital: still in use in Italy.

ANNOTINÆ. The ancient Roman victuallers or provision vessels.

ANNOTTO (*Bixa orellana*). The plant from the dried pulp of the seed-vessels of which a delicate red dye is obtained, used to give a rich colour to milk, butter, and cheese.

ANNUAL. Those astronomical motions which return or terminate every year.

ANNUAL ACCOUNTS. The ship's books and papers for the year.

ANNUAL EQUATION. An inequality in the moon's march, arising from the eccentricity of the earth's orbit, whereby the diurnal motion is sometimes quicker and at other times slower than her mean motion.

ANNUAL PARALLAX. *See* PARALLAX.

ANNUAL RETURNS. In addition to the general accounts of the year, there are three returns to be transmitted to the admiral or senior officer for the Admiralty. They are, a report of the sailing and other qualities of the ship; state of the ship as to men; and progress of the young gentlemen in navigation.

ANNUAL VARIATION. The change produced in the right ascension or declination of a star by the precession of the equinoxes and proper motion of the star taken together. Also, the annual variation of the compass.

ANNUL, To. To nullify a signal.

ANNULAR. Resembling an annulus or ring. An *annular* eclipse takes place when the apparent diameter of the moon is less than that of the sun, and a zone of light surrounds the moon while central.

ANNULAR SCUPPER. A contrivance for fitting scuppers so that

the whole can be enlarged by a movable concentric ring, in order that a surcharge of water can be freely delivered; invented by Captain Downes, R.N.

ANNULUS. A geometrical figure. (*See* RING.)

ANNULUS ASTRONOMICUS. A ring of brass used formerly in navigation. In 1575 Martin Frobisher, when fitting out on his first voyage for the discovery of a north-west passage, was supplied with one which cost thirty shillings.

ANOMALISTIC MONTH. *See* ANOMALISTIC PERIOD.

ANOMALISTIC PERIOD. The time of revolution of a primary or secondary planet in reference to its line of apsides; that is, from one perigee or apogee to another.

ANOMALISTIC YEAR. The space of time in which the earth passes through her orbit—distinct from and longer than the tropical year, owing to the precession of the equinoxes.

ANOMALY. Deviation from common rule. An irregularity in the motion of a planet by which it deviates from the aphelion or apogee. —*Mean anomaly* formerly signified the distance of a planet's mean place from the apogee: it is the angular distance of a planet or comet from perihelion supposing it to have moved with its mean velocity.— *True anomaly*, the true angular distance of a planet or comet from perihelion. (*See* EXCENTRIC and EQUATED.)

ANON. Quickly, directly, immediately.

ANONYMOUS PARTNERSHIPS. Those not carried on under a special name, and the particulars known only to the parties themselves. This is much practised in France, and often occasions trouble in prize-courts.

ANSÆ. The dolphins or handles of brass ordnance. Also the projections or arms of the ring on each side of Saturn's globe, in certain situations relative to the earth.

ANSERES. Birds of the goose tribe.

ANSWER, To. To reply, to succeed; as, the frigate has *answered* the signal. This boat will not *answer*.

ANSWERS HER HELM. When a ship obeys the rudder or steers.

ANTARCTIC. Opposite to the Arctic—abbreviated from *anti-arctic*.

ANTARCTIC CIRCLE. One of the lesser circles of the sphere, on the south parallel of the equator, and $23\frac{1}{2}°$ from the south pole.

ANTARCTIC OCEAN. That which surrounds the south pole, within the imaginary circle so called.

ANTARCTIC POLE. The south end of the earth's axis.

ANTARES. A star of the first magnitude, popularly known as the *scorpion's heart* (a Scorpio): it is one of those called "nautical" stars, used for determining the latitude and longitude at night.

ANTECEDENTAL METHOD. A branch of general geometrical proportion, or universal comparison of ratios.

ANTECEDENTIA. A planet's apparent motion to the westward, contrary to the order of the signs.

ANTECEDENT OF A RATIO. The first of the two terms.

ANTECIANS. Those inhabitants of the earth who live under the same meridian, but in opposite hemispheres. (*See* ANTISCII.)

ANTE LUCAN. Before daylight.

ANTE MERIDIAN. Before noon.

ANTE MURAL. *See* OUTWORK.

ANTHELION. A mock or spurious sun; a luminous meteor, resembling, but usually larger than, the solar disc.

ANTHRACITE. [Gr. *anthrax* and *lithos*.] A stone coal demanding great draught to burn, affording great heat, little smoke, and peculiarly adapted for steamers.

ANTICTHONES. The inhabitants of countries diametrically opposite to each other.

ANTI-GALLICANS. A pair of extra backstays, sometimes used by merchantmen, to support the masts when running before the trades.

ANTI-GUGGLER. A straw, or crooked tube, introduced into a spirit cask or neck of a bottle, to suck out the contents; commonly used in 1800 to rob the captain's steward's hanging safe in hot climates. Is to be found in old dictionaries.

ANTILOGARITHM. The complement of the logarithm of a sine, tangent, or secant.

ANTIPARALLELS. Those lines which make equal angles with two other lines, but contrary ways.

ANTIPATHES. A kind of coral having a black horny stem.

ANTIPODES. Such inhabitants of the earth as are diametrically opposite to each other. From the people, the term has passed to the places themselves, which are situated at the two extremities of any diameter of the earth.

ANTISCII. The people who dwell in opposite hemispheres of the earth, and whose shadows at noon fall in contrary directions.

ANT ISLANDS. Generally found on Spanish charts as *Hormigas*.

ANVIL. The massive block of iron on which armourers hammer forge-work. It is also an archaism for the handle or hilt of a sword: thus Coriolanus—

> "Here I clip
> The anvil of my sword."

It is moreover a little narrow flag at the end of a lance.

ANYHOW. Do the duty by all means, and at any rate or risk: as Nelson, impatient for getting to Copenhagen in 1801, exclaimed—

"Let it be by the Sound, by the Belt, or anyhow, only lose not an hour."

ANY PORT IN A STORM signifies contentment with whatever may betide.

APAGOG. A mathematical progress from one proposition to another.

APE, or SEA-APE. The long-tailed shark. Also, an active American seal.

APEEK. A ship drawn directly over the anchor is *apeek:* when the fore-stay and cable form a line, it is *short stay apeek;* when in a line with the main-stay, *long stay apeek.* The anchor is *apeek* when the cable has been sufficiently hove in to bring the ship over it.—*Yards apeek.* When they are topped up by contrary lifts. (*See* PEAK.)

APERTÆ. Ancient deep-waisted ships, with high-decked forecastle and poop.

APERTURE, in astronomy. The opening of a telescope tube next the object-glass, through which the rays of light and image of the object are conveyed to the eye. It is usually estimated by the clear diameter of the object-glass.

APEX. The summit or vertex of anything; as the upper point of a triangle.

APHELION. That point in the orbit of a planet or comet which is most remote from the sun, and at which the angular motion is slowest; being the end of the greater elliptic axis. The opposite of *perihelion.*

APHELLAN. The name of the double star *a* Geminorum, better known as Castor.

APHRACTI. Ancient vessels with open waists, resembling the present Torbay-boats.

APLANATIC. That refraction which entirely corrects the aberration and colour of the rays of light.

APLETS. Nets for the herring-fishery.

APLUSTRE. A word applied in ancient vessels both to the ornament on the prow and to the streamer or ensign on the stern. Here, as in the rudder-head of Dutch vessels frequently, the dog-vane was carried to denote the direction of the wind.

APOBATHRÆ. Ancient gang-boards from the ship to the quays.

APOCATASTASIS. The time in which a planet returns to the same point of the zodiac whence it departed.

APOGEE. That point of the moon's orbit which is furthest from the earth; the opposite of *perigee.* The *apogee* of the sun is synonymous with the *aphelion* of the earth. The word is also used as a general term to express the greatest distance of any heavenly body from the earth.

A-POISE. Said of a vessel properly trimmed.

APOSTLES. The knight-heads or bollard timbers, where hawsers or heavy ropes are belayed.

APOTOME. The difference of two incommensurable mathematical quantities.

APPALTO. The commercial term for a monopoly in Mediterranean ports.

APPARATUS. Ammunition and equipage for war.

APPAREL. In marine insurance, means the *furniture* or appurtenances of a ship, as masts, yards, sails, ground gear, guns, &c. More comprehensive than *apparatus*.

APPARELLED. Fully equipped for service.

APPARENT. In appearance, as visible to the eye, or evident to the mind, which in the case of astronomical motions, distances, altitudes, and magnitudes, will be found to differ materially from their real state, and require correcting to find the true place.

APPARENT EQUINOX. The position of the equinox as affected by nutation.

APPARENT HORIZON. *See* HORIZON.

APPARENT MOTION. The motion of celestial bodies as viewed from the earth.

APPARENT NOON. The instant that the sun's centre is on the meridian of a place.

APPARENT OBLIQUITY. The obliquity of the ecliptic affected with nutation.

APPARENT PLACE OF A STAR. This is the position for any day which it seems to occupy in the heavens, as affected with aberration and nutation.

APPARENT TIME. The time resulting from an observation of the sun—an expression *per contractionem* for apparent solar time.

APPARITION. A star or planet becoming visible after occultation. *Perpetual apparition* of the lesser northern circles, wherein the stars being above the horizon, never set.

APPEARANCE. The first making of a land-fall: formerly astronomically used for phenomenon and phase. The day of an officer's first joining a ship after his being appointed.

APPLE-PIE ORDER. A strange but not uncommon term for a ship in excellent condition and well looked to. Neat and orderly. Absurdly said to be a corruption of *du pol au pied*.

APPLICATE. The ordinate, or right line drawn across a curve, so as to be bisected by its diameter.

APPLICATION. A word of extensive use, for the principles of adjusting, augmenting, and perfecting the relations between sciences.

APPOINTED. Commissioned—named for a special duty.

APPOINTMENT. The equipment, ordnance, furniture, and necessaries of a ship. Also an officer's commission. In the Army, *appointments* usually imply military accoutrements, such as belts, sashes, gorgets, &c.

APPORTER. A bringer into the realm.

APPRAISEMENT. A law instrument taken out by the captors of a vessel, who are primarily answerable for the expense.

APPRENTICE. One who is covenanted to serve another on condition of being instructed in an art, and ships' apprentices are to the same effect. Boys under eighteen years of age bound to masters of merchant ships were exempted from impressment for three years from the date of their indentures; which documents were in duplicate, and exempt from stamp duty.

APPROACHES. The trenches, zig-zags, saps, and other works, by which a besieger makes good his way up to a fortified place. (*See* Trenches.)

APPROVAL. The senior officer's signature to a demand or application.

APPROXIMATION. A continual approach to a quantity sought, where there is no possibility of arriving at it exactly.

APPULSE. A near approach of one heavenly body to another, so as to form an apparent contact: the term is principally used with reference to stars or planets when the moon passes close to them without causing occultation.

APRON, or Stomach-piece. A strengthening compass timber fayed abaft the lower part of the stem, and above the foremost end of the keel; that is, from the head down to the fore dead-wood knee, to which it is scarfed. It is sided to receive the fastenings of the fore-hoods or planking of the bow.—*Apron of a gun*, a square piece of sheet-lead laid over the touch-hole for protecting the vent from damp; also over the gun-lock.—*Apron of a dock*, the platform rising where the gates are closed, and on which the sill is fastened down.

APSIDES, Line of. The imaginary line joining the aphelion and perihelion points in the orbit of a planet.

APSIS. Either of the two points in planetary orbits where they are at the greatest and the least distance from the sun, and are termed *higher* or *lower* accordingly. The two are joined by a diameter called the *line of the apsides*.

AQUAGE. The old law-term denoting the toll paid for water-carriage.

AQUARIUS. The eleventh sign in the zodiac (α Aquarius Sadalmelik).

AQUATIC. Inhabiting or relating to the water.

AQUATILE. An archaism for *aquatic;* thus Howell's lexicon describes the crocodile as "partly aquatil, partly terrestrial."

AQUATITES. The law-term for everything living in the water.

AQUE. Wall-sided flat-floored boats, which navigate the Rhine.

AQUEDUCT. Conduits or canals built for the conveyance of water.

AQUILA. The constellation Aquila, in which *a* Aquilæ is an important star of the first magnitude: used by seamen in determining the latitude and longitude; also in lunar distances. (*See* ALTAIR.)

AQUILON. The north-east wind, formerly much dreaded by mariners.

ARAMECH. The Arabic name for the star Arcturus.

ARBALIST [from *arcus* and *balista*]. An engine to throw stones, or the cross-bow used for bullets, darts, arrows, &c.: formerly arbalisters formed part of a naval force.

ARBITER. The judge to whom two persons refer their differences; not always judicial, but the arbiter, in his own person, of the fate of empires and peoples.

ARBITRAGE. The referring commercial disputes to the arbitration of two or more indifferent persons.

ARBITRATION. The settlement of disputes out of court.

ARBOR. In chronometry, a shaft, spindle, or axis.

ARBY. A northern name for the thrift or sea-lavender.

ARC, OR ARCH. The segment of a circle or any curved line, by which all angles are measured.

ARC DIURNAL. *See* DIURNAL ARC.

ARC NOCTURNAL. *See* NOCTURNAL ARC.

ARC OF DIRECTION OR PROGRESSION. The arc which a planet appears to describe when its motion is direct or progressive in the order of the signs.

ARC OF VISION. The sun's depth below the horizon when the planets and stars begin to appear.

ARCH-BOARD. The part of the stern over the counter, immediately under the knuckles of the stern-timbers.

ARCH OF THE COVE. An elliptical moulding sprung over the cove of a ship, at the lower part of the taffrail.

ARCHED SQUALL. A violent gust of wind, usually distinguished by the arched form of the clouds near the horizon, whence they rise rapidly towards the zenith, leaving the sky visible through it.

ARCHEL, ARCHIL, ORCHILL. *Rocella tinctorum fucus*, a lichen found on the rocks of the Canary and Cape de Verde groups; it yields a rich purple. Litmus, largely used in chemistry, is derived from it.

ARCHES. A common term among seamen for the Archipelago. (*See* also GALLEY-ARCHES.)

ARCHI-GUBERNUS. The commander of the imperial ship in ancient times.

ARCHIMEDES' SCREW. An ingenious spiral pump for draining docks or raising water to any proposed height,—the invention of that wonderful man. It is also used to remove grain in breweries from a lower to a higher level. The name has been recently applied to the very important introduction in steam navigation—the propelling screw. (*See* SCREW-PROPELLER.)

ARCHING. When a vessel is not strongly built there is always a tendency in the greater section to lift, and the lower sections to fall; hence the fore and after ends droop, producing arching, or *hogging* (which see).

ARCHIPELAGO. A corruption of Aegeopelagus, now applied to clusters of islands in general. Originally the Ægean Sea. An archipelago has a great number of islands of varous sizes, disposed without order; but often contains several subordinate groups. Such are the Ægean, the Corean, the Caribbean, Indian, Polynesian, and others.

ARCHITECTURE. *See* NAVAL ARCHITECTURE.

ARCTIC. Northern, or lying under *arktos*, the Bear; an epithet given to the north polar regions comprised within the *arctic circle*, a lesser circle of the sphere, very nearly 23° 28′ distant from the north pole.

ARCTIC OCEAN. So called from surrounding the pole within the imaginary circle of that name.

ARCTIC POLE. The north pole of the globe.

ARCTURUS. α Boötis. A star of the first magnitude, close to the knee of Arctophylax, or Boötes. One of the nautical stars.

ARD, OR AIRD. A British or Gaelic term for a rocky eminence, or rocks on a wash: hence the word *hard*, in present use. It is also an enunciation.

ARDENT. Said of a vessel when she gripes, or comes to the wind quickly.

ARE. The archaism for *oar* (which see). A measure of land in France containing 100 square metres.

AREA. The plane or surface contained between any boundary lines. The superficial contents of any figure or work; as, the *area* of any square or triangle.

ARENACEOUS. Sandy; partaking of the qualities of sand; brittle; as, *arenaceous* limestone, quartz, &c.

ARENAL. In meteorology, a cloud of dust, often so thick as to prevent seeing a stone's-throw off. It is common in South America, being raised by the wind from adjoining shores. Also off the coast of Africa at the termination of the desert of Zahara.

ARENATION. The burying of scorbutic patients up to the neck in holes in a sandy beach, for cure; also spreading hot sand over a diseased person.

AREOMETER. An instrument for measuring the specific gravity of fluids.

ARGIN. An old word for an *embankment*.

ARGO. A name famous from Jason's romantic expedition, but absurdly quoted as the first ship, for the fleets of Danaus and Minos are mentioned long before, and the *Argo* herself was chased by a squadron under Æetes.

ARGO NAVIS. The southern constellation of the Ship, containing 9 clusters, 3 nebulæ, 13 double and 540 single stars, of which about 64 are easily visible. As most of these were invisible to the Greeks, the name was probably given by the Egyptians.

ARGOL. The tartaric acid or lees adhering to the sides of wine-casks, particularly of port-wine; an article of commerce; supertartrate of potass.

ARGOLET. A light horseman of the middle ages.

ARGONAUTA. The paper-nautilus. The sail which it was supposed to spread to catch the wind, is merely a modified arm which invests the outer surface of the shell.

ARGONAUTS. A company of forty-four heroes who sailed in the *Argo* to obtain the golden fleece; an expedition which fixes one of the most memorable epochs in history. Also a Geographical Society instituted at Venice, to whom we owe the publication of all the charts, maps, and directories of Coronelli.

ARGOSY. A merchant ship or carrack of burden, principally of the Levant; the name is by some derived from Ragusa, but by others with more probability from the *Argo*. Shakspeare mentions "argosies with portly sail." Those of the Frescobaldi were the richest and most adventurous of those times.

ARGOZIN, or ARGNESYN. The person whose office it was to attend to the shackles of the galley-slaves, over whom he had especial charge.

ARGUMENT. An astronomical quantity upon which an equation depends,—or any known number by which an unknown one proportional to the first may be found.

ARGUMENT OF LATITUDE. The distance of a celestial body from one of the nodes of its orbit, upon which the latitude depends.

ARIES. The most important point of departure in astronomy. A northern constellation forming the first of the twelve signs of the zodiac, into which the sun enters about the 20th of March. With Musca, Aries contains 22 nebulæ, 8 double and 148 single stars, but not above 50 are visible to the unassisted eye. The commencement of this sign, called the first point of Aries, is the origin from which the right ascensions of the heavenly bodies are reckoned upon the equator, and their longitudes upon the ecliptic.

ARIS. Sharp corner of stones in piers and docks.

ARIS PIECES. Those parts of a made mast which are under the hoops.

ARITHMETIC. The art of computation by numbers; or that branch which considers their powers and properties.

ARK. The sacred and capacious vessel built by Noah for preservation against the flood. It was 300 cubits in length, 50 in breadth, and 30 in height; and of whatever materials it was constructed, it was pitched over or pay'd with bitumen. *Ark* is also the name of a mare's-tail cloud, or cirrhus, when it forms a streak across the sky.

ARLOUP. An archaism for the deck, now called *orlop* (which see).

ARM. A deep and comparatively narrow inlet of the sea. That part of an anchor on which the palm is shut. The extremity of the bibbs which support the tressel-trees. Each extremity or end of a yard, beam, or bracket.—*To arm*, to fit, furnish, and provide for war; to cap and set a loadstone; to apply putty or tallow to the lower end of the lead previous to sounding, in order to draw up a specimen of the bottom.—*To arm a shot*, is to roll rope-yarns about a cross-bar shot, in order to facilitate ramming it home, and also to prevent the ends catching any accidental inequalities in the bore.

ARMADA. A Spanish term signifying a royal fleet; it comes from the same root as army. The word *armado* is used by Shakspeare.

ARMADILLA. A squadron of guarda-costas, which formerly cruized on the coasts of South America, to prevent smuggling.

ARMADOR. A Spanish privateer.

ARMAMENT. A naval or military force equipped for an expedition. The arming of a vessel or place.

ARMAMENTA. The rigging and tackling of an ancient ship. It included shipmen and all the necessary furniture of war.

ARMATÆ. Ancient ships fitted with sails and oars, but which fought under the latter only.

ARM-CHEST. A portable locker on the upper deck or tops for holding arms, and affording a ready supply of cutlasses, pistols, muskets or other weapons.

ARMED. Completely equipped for war.—*Armed at all points*, covered with armour.—*Armed "en flute,"* see FLUTE.—*Armed mast*, made of more than one tree.—*Armed ship*, a vessel fitted out by merchants to annoy the enemy, and furnished with letters of marque, and bearing a commission from the Admiralty to carry on warlike proceedings.

ARMED STEM. *See* BEAK.

ARMILLARY SPHERE. An instrument composed of various circles, to assist the student in gaining a knowledge of the arrangement and motions of the heavenly bodies. A brass *armilla tolomœi* was one of the instruments supplied to Martin Frobisher in 1576, price £4, 6s. 8d.

ARMING. A piece of tallow placed in the cavity and over the bottom of a sounding lead, to which any objects at the bottom of the sea become attached, and are brought with the lead to the surface.

ARMINGS. Red dress cloths which were formerly hung fore and aft, outside the upper works on holidays; still used by foreigners. (*See* TOP-ARMINGS.) It was also the name of a kind of boarding-net.

ARMIPOTENT. Powerful in war.

ARMISTICE. A cessation of arms for a given time; a short truce for the suspension of hostilities.

ARMLET. A narrow inlet of the sea; a smaller branch than the arm. Also the name of a piece of armour for the arm, to protect it from the jar of the bow-string.

ARMOGAN. An old term for good opportunity or season for navigation, which, if neglected, was liable to costs of demurrage. It is a Mediterranean word for fine weather.

ARMORIC. The language of Brittany, Cornwall, and Wales: the word in its original signification meant *maritime*.

ARMOUR. A defensive habit to protect the wearer from his enemy; also defensive arms. In old statutes this is frequently called *harness*.

ARMOUR-CLAD. A ship of war fitted with iron plates on the outside to render her shot-proof.

ARMOURER. In a man-of-war, is a person appointed by warrant to keep the small arms in complete condition for service. As he is also the ship's blacksmith, a mate is allowed to assist at the forge.

ARMOURY. A place appropriated for the keeping of small arms.

ARM-RACK. A frame or fitting for the stowage of arms (usually vertical) out of harm's way, but in readiness for immediate use. In the conveyance of troops by sea arm-racks form a part of the proper accommodation.

ARMS. The munitions of war,—all kinds of weapons whether for offence or defence. Those in a ship are cannons, carronades, mortars, howitzers, muskets, pistols, tomahawks, cutlasses, bayonets, and boarding-pikes.

ARMS OF A GREAT GUN. The trunnions.

ARMSTRONG GUN. Invented by Sir William Armstrong. In its most familiar form, a rifled breech-loading gun of wrought iron, constructed principally of spirally coiled bars, and occasionally having an inner tube or core of steel; ranging in size from the smallest field-piece up to the 100 pounder; rifled with numerous shallow grooves, which are taken by the expansion of the leaden coating of its projectile. Late experiments however, connected with iron-plated ships are developing muzzle-loading Armstrong guns, constructed on somewhat similar principles, but with simpler rifling, ranging in size up to the 600 pounder weighing 23 tons.

ARMY. A large body of disciplined men, with appropriate sub-divisions, commanded by a general. A fleet is sometimes called a naval army.—*Flying army*, a small body sent to harass a country, intercept convoys, and alarm the enemy.

ARMYE. A early term for a naval armament.

ARNOT. A northern name for the shrimp.

ARONDEL. A light and swift tartan: probably a corruption of *hirondelle* (swallow).

ARPENT. A French measure of land, equal to 100 square rods or perches, each of 18 feet. It is about ⅐th less than the English acre.

ARQUEBUSS. A word sometimes used for carbine, but formerly meant a garrison-piece, carrying a ball of $3\frac{1}{2}$ ounces; it was generally placed in loop-holes. (*See* HAGBUT.)

ARRACK. An Indian term for all ardent liquors, but that which we designate thus is obtained by the fermentation of toddy (a juice pro-cured from palm-trees), of rice, and of sugar. In Turkey arrack is extracted from vine-stalks taken out of wine-presses.

ARRAIER. The officer who formerly had the care of the men's armour, and whose business it was to see them duly accoutred.

ARRAY. The order of battle.—*To array*. To equip, dress, or arm for battle.

ARREARS. The difference between the full pay of a commissioned officer, and what he is empowered to draw for till his accounts are passed.

ARREST. The suspension of an officer's duty, and restraint of his person, previous to trying him by a court-martial. Seamen in her Majesty service cannot be *arrested* for debts under twenty pounds, and that contracted before they entered the navy. Yet it is held in law, that this affords no exemption from *arrests* either in civil or criminal suits.

ARRIBA. [Sp. pronounced *arriva*]. Aloft, quickly.—*Agir contre son gré, montar arriba*, to mount aloft, which has passed into seamen's lingo as *areevo*, up, aloft, quickly:—mount *areevo*, or go on deck.

ARRIBAR, To. To land, to attain the bank, to arrive.

ARRIVE, To. In the most nautical sense, is to come to any place by water, to reach the shore.

ARROBA. A Portuguese commercial weight of 32 lbs. Also, a Spanish general wine measure of $4\frac{1}{4}$ English gallons. The lesser *arroba*, used for oil, is only $3\frac{1}{3}$ English gallons. A Spanish weight of 25 lbs. avoirdupois; one-fourth of a quintal. Also, a rough country cart in Southern Russia.

ARROW. A missive weapon of offence, and whether ancient or modern, in the rudest form among savages or refined by art, is always

a slender stick, armed at one end, and occasionally feathered at the
other. The natives of Tropical Africa feather the metal barb.

ARROW. In fortification, a work placed at the salient angles of the
glacis, communicating with the covert way.—*Broad arrow.* The
royal mark for stores of every kind. (*See* BROAD ARROW.)

ARSENAL. A repository of the munitions of war. Some combine
both magazines of naval and military stores, and docks for the construction and repair of ships.

ARSHEEN. A Russian measure of 2 feet 4 in. = 2·333—also Chinese,
four of which make 3 yards English.

ART. A spelling of *airt* (which see). Also, practice as distinguished
from theory.

ARTEMON. The mainsail of ancient ships.

ARTHUR. A well-known sea game, alluded to by Grose, Smollet, and
other writers.

ARTICLES. The express stipulations to which seamen bind themselves by signature, on joining a merchant ship.

ARTICLES OF WAR. A code of rules and orders based on the act
of parliament for the regulation and government of her Majesty's
ships, vessels, and forces by sea: and as they are frequently read to all
hands, no individual can plead ignorance of them. It is now termed
the New Naval Code.—The *articles of war* for the land forces have a
similar foundation and relation to their service; the act in this case, however, is passed annually, the army itself having, in law, no more than
one year's permanence unless so periodically renewed by act of
parliament.

ARTIFICER. One who works by hand in wood or metal; generally
termed an *idler on board,* from his not keeping night-watch, and only
appearing on deck duty when the hands are turned up.

ARTIFICIAL EYE. An eye worked in the end of rope, which is
neater but not so strong as a spliced eye.

ARTIFICIAL HORIZON. An artificial means of catching the
altitude of a celestial body when the sea horizon is obscured by fog,
darkness, or the intervention of land; a simple one is still the greatest
desideratum of navigators. Also a trough filled with pure mercury,
used on land, wherein the double altitude of a celestial body is
reflected.

ARTIFICIAL LINES. The ingenious contrivances for representing
logarithmic sines and tangents, so useful in navigation, on a scale.

ARTILLERY was formerly synonymous with archery, but now comprehends every description of ordnance, guns, mortars, fire-arms, and
all their appurtenances. The term is also applied to the noble corps
destined to that service: as also to the theory and practice of the

science of projectiles: it was moreover given to all kinds of missile weapons, and the translators of the Bible make Jonathan give his "artillery unto his lad."

ARTILLERY, ROYAL MARINE. Formerly a select branch of the *R. Marines*, specially instructed in gunnery and the care of artillery stores; assigned in due proportion to all ships of war. It is now separate from the other branch (to whose original title the denomination of Light Infantry has been added), and rests on its own official basis; its relation to ships of war, however, remaining the same as before, although while on shore the Royal Marine forces are regulated by an annual act of parliament. (*See* ROYAL MARINE ARTILLERY.)

ARTIST. A name formerly applied to those mariners who were also expert navigators.

ARTIZAN. A mechanic or operative workman. (*See* ARTIFICER.)

ARX. A fort or castle for the defence of a place.

ASCENDANT. The part of the ecliptic above the horizon.

ASCENDING NODE. *See* NODE.

ASCENDING SIGNS. Those in which the sun appears to ascend towards the north pole, or in which his motion in declination is towards the north.

ASCENSION. The act of mounting or rising upwards. (*See* RIGHT ASCENSION.)

ASCENSIONAL DIFFERENCE. The equinoctial arc intercepted between the *right* and *oblique* ascensions (which see).

ASCENSION OBLIQUE. *See* OBLIQUE ASCENSION.

ASCENSION RIGHT. *See* RIGHT ASCENSION.

ASCII. The inhabitants of the torrid zone, who twice a year, being under a vertical sun, have no shadow.

AS DEAF AS THE MAINMAST. Said of one who does not readily catch an order given. Thus at sea the mainmast is synonymous with the door-post on shore.

ASHES. *See* WINDWARD.

ASHLAR. Blocks of stone masonry fronting docks, piers, and other erections; this term is applied to common or free-stone as they come of various lengths, breadths, and thicknesses from the quarry.

ASHORE. Aground, on land.—To *go ashore*, to disembark from a boat. Opposed to *aboard*.

ASH-PIT. A receptacle for ashes before the fire-bars in a steamer, or under them in most fire-places.

ASIENTO [Sp.] A sitting, contract, or convention; such as that between Spain and other powers in relation to the supply of stores for South America.

ASK, or Asker. A name of the water-newt.

ASKEW. Awry, crooked, oblique.

ASLANT. Formed or placed in an oblique line, as with dagger-knees, &c.—*To sail aslant*, turning to windward.

ASLEEP. The sail filled with wind just enough for swelling or bellying out,—as contrasted with its flapping.

ASPECT. The looming of the land from sea-ward.

ASPER. A minute Turkish coin in accounts, of which three go to a para.

ASPIC. An ancient 12-pounder piece of ordnance, about 11 feet long.

ASPIRANT DE MARINE. Midshipman in the French navy.

ASPORTATION. The carrying of a vessel or goods illegally.

ASSAIL, To. To attack, leap upon, board, &c.

ASSAULT. A hostile attack. The effort to storm a place, and gain possession of a post by main force.

ASSEGAI. The spear used by the Kaffirs in South Africa; it is frequently feather-bent to revolve in its flight.

ASSEGUAY. The knife-dagger used in the Levant.

ASSEMBLY. That long roll beat of the drum by which soldiers, or armed parties, are ordered to repair to their stations. It is sometimes called the *fall-in*.

ASSES'-BRIDGE. The well-known name of prop. 5, b. i. of Euclid, the difficulty of which makes many give in.

ASSIEGE, To. To besiege, to invest or beset with an armed force.

ASSIGNABLE. Any finite geometrical ratio, or magnitude that can be marked out or denoted.

ASSILAG. The name given in the Hebrides to a small sea-bird with a black bill. The stormy petrel.

ASSISTANCE. Aid or help: strongly enjoined to be given whenever a signal is made requiring it.

ASSISTANT-SURGEON. The designation given some years ago to those formerly called "surgeon's mates," and considered a boon by the corps.

ASSORTMENT. The arrangement of goods, tools, &c., in a series.

ASSURANCE. (*See* Marine Insurance.) Conveyance or deed: in which light Shakspeare makes Tranio say that his father will "pass assurance."

ASSURGENT. A heraldic term for a man or beast rising out of the sea.

ASSUROR. He who makes out the policy of assurance for a ship: he is not answerable for the neglect of the master or seamen.

A-STARBOARD. The opposite to *a-port*.

A-STAY. Said of the anchor when, in heaving in, the cable forms such an angle with the surface as to appear in a line with the stays of the ship.—*A long stay* apeek is when the cable forms an acute angle with the water's surface, or coincides with the main-stay—*short stay* when it coincides with the forestay.

ASTELLABRE. The same as *astrolabe*.

ASTERIA. *See* SEA-STAR.

ASTERISM. Synonymous with *constellation*, a group of stars.

ASTERN. Any distance behind a vessel; in the after-part of the ship; in the direction of the stern, and therefore the opposite of *ahead*.—*To drop astern*, is to be left behind,—when abaft a right angle to the keel at the mainmast, she drops astern.

ASTEROIDS. The name by which the minor planets between the orbits of Jupiter and Mars were proposed to be distinguished by Sir W. Herschel. They are very small bodies, which have all been discovered since the commencement of the present century; yet their present number is over eighty.

ASTRAGAL. A moulding formerly round a cannon, at a little distance from its breech, the *cascabel*, and another near the muzzle. It is a half round on a flat moulding.

ASTRAL. Sidereal, relating to the stars.

ASTROLABE. An armillary sphere.—*Sea-astrolabe*, a useful graduated brass ring, with a movable index, for taking the altitude of stars and planets: it derived its name from the armillary sphere of Hipparchus, at Alexandria.

ASTROMETRY. The numerical expression of the apparent magnitudes of the so-called fixed stars.

ASTRONOMICAL CLOCK. A capital bit of horology, the pendulum of which is usually compensated to sidereal time, for astronomical purposes. (*See* SIDEREAL TIME.)

ASTRONOMICAL HOURS. Those which are reckoned from noon or midnight of one natural day, to noon or midnight of another.

ASTRONOMICAL OBSERVATIONS. There have been occasional slight records of celestial phenomena from the remotest times, but the most useful ones are those collected and preserved by Ptolemy. Since 1672, science has been enriched with a continued series of astronomical observations of accuracy and value never dreamed of by the ancients.

ASTRONOMICAL PLACE OF A STAR OR PLANET. Its longitude or place in the ecliptic, reckoned from the first point of Aries, according to the natural order of the signs.

ASTRONOMICAL TABLES. Tables for facilitating the calculation of the apparent places of the sun, moon, and planets.

ASTRONOMICALS. The sexagesimal fractions.

ASTRONOMY. The splendid department of the mixed sciences which teaches the laws and phenomena of the universal system. It is *practical* when it treats of the magnitudes, periods, and distances of the heavenly bodies; and *physical* when it investigates the causes. In the first division the more useful adaptation *nautical* is included (which see).

ASTROSCOPIA. Skill in examining the nature and properties of stars with a telescope.

ASTRUM, or Astron. Sirius, or the Dog-star. Sometimes applied to a cluster of stars.

ASWIM. Afloat, borne on the waters.

ASYLUM. A sanctuary or refuge; a name given to a benevolent institution at Greenwich, for 800 boys and 200 girls, orphans of seamen and marines. The Royal Military Asylum is also an excellent establishment of a similar nature at Chelsea, besides numerous others.

ASYMMETRY. A mathematical disproportion. The relation of two quantities which have no measure in common.

ASYMPTOTES. Lines which continually approximate each other, but can never meet.

ATABAL. A Moorish kettle-drum.

ATAGAN. *See* Yatagan.

AT ANCHOR. The situation of a vessel riding in a road or port by her anchor.

ATAR. A perfume of commerce, well known as atar-of-roses; atar being the Arabic word for fragrance, corrupted into *otto*.

A'TAUNTO, or All-a-Taunt-o. Every mast an-end and fully rigged.

ATEGAR. The old English hand-dart, named from the Saxon *aeton* to fling, and *gar*, a weapon.

ATHERINE. A silvery fish used in the manufacture of artificial pearls; it is 4 or 5 inches long, inhabits various seas, but is taken in great numbers in the Mediterranean. It is also called *argentine*.

ATHILLEDA. The rule and sights of an astrolabe.

ATHWART. The transverse direction; anything extending or across the line of a ship's course.—*Athwart hawse*, a vessel, boat, or floating lumber accidentally drifted across the stem of a ship, the transverse position of the drift being understood.—*Athwart the forefoot*, just before the stem; ships fire a shot in this direction to arrest a stranger, and make her bring-to.—*Athwart ships*, in the direction of the beam; from side to side: in opposition to *fore-and-aft*.

ATHWART THE TIDE. *See* Across the Tide.

ATLANTIC. The sea which separates Europe and Africa from the Americas, so named from the elevated range called the Atlas Mountains in Marocco.

ATLANTIDES. The daughters of Atlas; a name of the Pleiades.

ATLAS. A large book of maps or charts; so called from the character of that name in ancient mythology, son of Uranus, and represented as bearing the world on his back. Also the Indian satin of commerce.

ATMOSPHERE. The ambient air, or thin elastic fluid which surrounds the globe, and gradually diminishing in gravity rises to an unknown height, yet by gravitation partakes of all its motions.

ATMOSPHERIC or Single-action Steam-engine. A condensing machine, in which the downward stroke of the piston is performed by the pressure of the atmosphere acting against a vacuum.

ATMOSPHERICAL TIDES. The motions generated by the joint influence of the sun and moon; and by the rotatory and orbital course of the earth,—as developed in trade-winds, equinoctial gales, &c.

ATOLLS. An Indian name for those singular coral formations known as lagoon-islands, such as the Maldive cluster, those in the Pacific, and in other parts within the tropics, where the apparently insignificant reef-building zoophytes reside.

ATRIE. To bring the ship to in a gale.

A-TRIP. The anchor is *a-trip*, or a-weigh, when the purchase has just made it break ground, or raised it clear. Sails are *a-trip* when they are hoisted from the cap, sheeted home, and ready for trimming. Yards are *a-trip* when swayed up, ready to have the stops cut for crossing: so an upper-mast is said to be *a-trip*, when the fid is loosened preparatory to lowering it.

ATTACHED. Belongs to; in military parlance an officer or soldier is attached to any regiment or company with which he is ordered to do duty.

ATTACK. A general assault or onset upon an enemy. Also the arrangement for investment or battle. (*See* False Attack.)

ATTEMPT, To. To endeavour to carry a vessel or place by surprise; to venture at some risk, as in trying a new channel, &c.

ATTENDANT MASTER. A dock-yard official. (*See* Master Attendant.)

ATTENTION. A military word of command, calling the soldier from the quiescent position of "at ease" into readiness for any exercise or evolution. Also the erect posture due to that word of command, and which is assumed by a private soldier in the presence of an officer. The attending to signals.

ATTERRAGE. The land-fall, or making the land. Usually marked on French charts and plans to show the landing-place.

ATTESTATION. In Admiralty courts the attestation of a deed signifies the testifying to the signing or execution of it.

ATTESTED. Legally certified; proved by evidence.

ATTILE. An old law term for the rigging or furniture of a ship.

ATTORNEY. *See* SEA-ATTORNEY.

ATTRACTION. The power of drawing, or the principle by which all bodies mutually tend towards each other; the great agent in nature's wonderful operations.—*Attraction of mountains,* the deviating influence exercised on the plumb-line by the vicinity of high land. But exerting also a marvellous effect on all floating bodies, for every seaman knows that a ship stands inshore faster than she stands out, the distances being similar.

ATWEEN, OR ATWIXT. Betwixt or between, shortened into *'tween,* that is, in the intermediate space. The word *'tween decks* is usually applied to the lower deck of a frigate, and *orlop* to that of a line-of-battle ship.

AUBERK, OR HAUBERK. One who held land to be ready with a coat of mail and attend his lord when called upon so to do. Thus the old poet:—

"Auberk, sketoun, and scheld
Was mani to-broken in that feld."

AUDIT. The final passing of accounts.

AUDITORS OF THE IMPREST. Officers who had the charge of the great accounts of the royal customs, naval and military expenses, &c.; they are now superseded by the commissioners for auditing the public accounts.

AUGES. An astronomical term, synonymous with *apsides.*

AUGET. A tube filled with powder for firing a mine.

AUGMENTATION OF THE MOON'S DIAMETER. The increase of her apparent diameter occasioned by an increase of altitude: or that which is due to the difference between her distance from the observer and the centre of the earth.

AUGRE, OR AUGER. A wimble, or instrument for boring holes for bolts, tree-nails, and other purposes.

AUK, OR AWK. A sea-bird with short wings. The great auk or gair-fowl (*Alca impennis*) was formerly common on all the northern coasts, where they laid their eggs, ingeniously poised, on the bare rocks. They were very good eating, and having been taken in great numbers by the Esquimaux, and by European sailors on whaling voyages, the species is now supposed to be exterminated.

AULIN. An arctic gull (*Cataractes parasiticus*), given to make other sea-birds mute through fear, and then eat their discharge—whence it is termed *dirty aulin* by the northern boatmen.

AUMBREY. An old north-country term for a bread and cheese locker.

AUNE. Contraction of *ulna.* French cloth measure: at Rouen it is equal to the English ell—at Paris 0·95—at Calais 1·52 of that measure.

AURIGA. A northern constellation, and one of the old 48 asterisms; it is popularly known as the *Waggoner*: α Auriga, Capella.

AURORA. The faint light which precedes sunrising. Also the mythological mother of the winds and stars.

AURORA AUSTRALIS or **BOREALIS.** The extraordinary and luminous meteoric phenomenon which by its streaming effulgence cheers the dreary nights of polar regions. It is singular that these beautiful appearances are nowhere mentioned by the ancients. They seem to be governed by electricity, are most frequent in frosty weather, and are proved to be many miles above the surface of the earth, from some of them being visible over 30° of longitude and 20° of latitude at the same instant! In colour they vary from yellow to deep red; in form they are Proteus-like, assuming that of streamers, columns, fans, or arches, with a quick flitting, and sometimes whizzing noises. The aurora is not vivid above the 76th degree of north latitude, and is seldom seen before the end of August. Cook was the first navigator who recorded the southern lights.

AUSTER. The south wind of the ancients, gusts from which quarter are called *autan*.

AUSTRAL. Relating to the south.—*Austral signs*, those on the south side of the equator, or the last six of the zodiac.

AUTHORITY. The legal power or right of commanding.

AUTOMIC BLOW-OFF APPARATUS. *See* BLOWING-OFF.

AUTUMNAL EQUINOX. The time when the sun crosses the equator, under a southerly motion, and the days and nights are then everywhere equal in length. (*See* LIBRA.)

AUTUMNAL POINT. That part of the ecliptic whence the sun descends southward.

AUTUMNAL SIGNS. Libra, Scorpio, and Sagittarius.

AUXILIARIES. Confederates, an assisting body of allies; or, physically speaking, vessels using steam as an auxiliary to wind.

AUXILIARY SCREW. A vessel in which the screw is used as an auxiliary force. Such a vessel is usually fully masted for sailing purposes.

AVANIA. The fine or imposition imposed on Christians residing under Turkish governors, when they break the laws.

AVANT-FOSSE. In fortification, an advanced ditch without the counterscarp, and stretching along the foot of the glacis.

AVAST. The order to stop, hold, cease, or stay, in any operation: its derivation from the Italian *basta* is more plausible than *have fast*.

AVAST HEAVING! The cry to arrest the capstan when nippers are jammed, or any other impediment occurs in heaving in the cable, not unfrequently when a hand, foot, or finger, is jammed;—stop!

AVENTAILE. The movable part of a helmet.

AVENUE. The inlet into a port.

AVERAGE. Whether *general* or *particular*, is a term of ambiguous construction, meaning the damage incurred for the safety of the ship and cargo; the contribution made by the owners in general, apportioned to their respective investments, to repair any particular loss or expense sustained; and a small duty paid to the master for his care of the whole. Goods thrown overboard for the purpose of lightening the ship, are so thrown for the good of all, and the loss thus sustained must be made up by a general average or contribution from all the parties interested. (*See* GENERAL AVERAGE.)

AVERAGE-ADJUSTER. A qualified person engaged in making statements to show the proper application of loss, damage, or expenses in consequence of the accidents of a sea adventure.

AVERAGE-AGREEMENT. A written document signed by the consignees of a cargo, binding themselves to pay a certain proportion of general average that may from accident arise against them.

AVERAGE-STATER. *See* AVERAGE-ADJUSTER.

AVIST. A west country term for "a fishing."

AVVISO. An Italian advice-boat. [*Aviso*, Sp.] Despatch-boat or tender.

AWAFT, OR AWHEFT. The displaying of a stopped flag. (*See* WHEFT.)

AWAIT. Ambush; cutting off vessels by means of boats hidden in coves which they must pass in their course.

AWARD. A judgment, in maritime cases, by arbitration; and the decision or sentence of a court-martial.

A-WASH. Reefs even with the surface. The anchor just rising to the water's edge, in heaving up.

AWAY ALOFT. The order to the men in the rigging to start up.

AWAY OFF. At a distance, but in sight.

AWAY SHE GOES. The order to step out with the tackle fall. The cry when a vessel starts on the ways launching; also when a ship, having stowed her anchor, fills and makes sail.

AWAY THERE. The call for a boat's crew; as, "*away there!* bargemen."

AWAY WITH IT. The order to walk along briskly with a tackle fall, as catting the anchor, &c.

AWBLAST. The arbalest, or cross-bow.

AWBLASTER. The designation of a crossbow-man.

A-WEATHER. The position of the helm when its tiller is moved to the windward side of the ship, in the direction from which the wind blows. The opposite of *a-lee*.

AWEIGH. The anchor being *atrip*, or after breaking out of the ground.

AWK. *See* AUK.

AWKWARD SQUAD. A division formed of those men who are backward in gaining dexterity. (*See* SQUAD.)

AWL. A tool of a carpenter, sail-maker, and cobbler.

AWME. A tierce of 39 gallons. A Dutch liquid measure.

AWNING. A cover or canvas canopy suspended by a crow-foot and spread over a ship, boat, or other vessel, to protect the decks and crew from the sun and weather. (*See* EUPHRÆ.) Also that part of the poop-deck which is continued forward beyond the bulk-head of the cabin.

AWNING-ROPES. The ridge and side ropes for securing the awning.

AXE. A large flat edge-tool, for trimming and reducing timber. Also an Anglo-Saxon word for *ask*, which seamen still adhere to, and it is difficult to say why a word should be thought improper which has descended from our earliest poets; it may have become obsolete, but without absolutely being vulgar or incorrect.

AXIOM. A self-evident truth or proposition, that cannot be made plainer by demonstration.

AXIS. The imaginary line upon which a planet revolves, the extremities of which are termed the poles,—therefore a line joining the north and south poles. The real or imaginary line that passes through the centre of any cylindrical or spherical body on which it may revolve. Also a right line proceeding from the vertex of a cone to the middle of its base. Also, an imaginary right line passing through the middle of a ship perpendicularly to its base, and equally distant from its sides;— an imaginary line passing through the centre of a gun's bore, parallel with its position.—*Axis of a telescope.* (*See* COLLIMATION, LINE OF.)

AXLE-TREES. The two cross-pieces of a gun-carriage, fixed across and under the fore and hinder parts of the cheeks. The cylindrical iron which goes through the wheel of the chain-pump, and bears the weight of it.

AYE, AYE, SIR. A prompt reply on receiving an order. Also the answer on comprehending an order. *Aye-aye*, the answer to a sentinel's hail, from a boat which has a commissioned officer on board below the rank of captain. The name of the ship in reply from the boat indicates the presence of a captain. The word "flag," indicates the presence of an admiral.

AYLET. The sea-swallow.

AYONT. Beyond.

AYR. An open sea-beach, and also a bank of sand. (*See* AIRE.) The mediæval term for *oar*.

AYT. *See* EYGHT.

AZIMUTH. A word borrowed from the Arabic. The complement of the amplitude, or an arc between the meridian of a place and any given vertical line.

AZIMUTHAL ERROR. *See* MERIDIAN ERROR.

AZIMUTH CIRCLES. *See* VERTICAL CIRCLES.

AZIMUTH COMPASS. A superior graduated compass for ascertaining the amount of magnetic variation, by amplitude or azimuth, when the sun is from 8° to 15° high, either after its rising or before its setting. (*See* MAGNETIC AZIMUTH.) It is fitted with vertical sight vanes for the purpose of observing objects elevated above the horizon.

AZOGUE. [Sp.] Quicksilver.

AZOGUES. Spanish ships fitted expressly for carrying quicksilver.

AZUMBRE. A Spanish wine-measure, eight of which make an arroba.

AZURE. The deep blue colour of the sky, when perfectly cloudless.

B.

BAARD. A mediæval transport.

BAARE-Y-LANE. The Manx or Gaelic term for high-water.

BAAS. An old term for the skipper of a Dutch trader.

BAB. The Arabic for *mouth* or *gate;* especially used by seamen for the entrance of the Red Sea, *Bab-el-mandeb.*

BABBING. An east-country method of catching crabs, by enticing them to the surface of the water with baited lines, and then taking them with a landing net.

BABBLING. The sound made by shallow rivers flowing over stony beds.

BAC. A large flat-bottomed French ferry-boat. In local names it denotes a ferry or place of boating.

BACALLAO [Sp.] A name given to Newfoundland and its adjacent islands, whence the epithet is also applied to the cod-fish salted there.

BACCHI. Two ancient warlike machines; the one resembled a battering-ram, the other cast out fire.

BACK. *To back an anchor.* To carry a small anchor ahead of the one by which the ship rides, to partake of the strain, and check the latter from coming home.—*To back a ship at anchor.* For this purpose the mizen topsail is generally used; a hawser should be kept ready to wind her, and if the wind falls she must be hove apeak.—*To back and fill.* To get to windward in very narrow channels, by a series of

smart alternate boards and backing, with weather tides.—*To back a sail.*
To brace its yard so that the wind may blow directly on the front of
the sail, and thus retard the ship's course. A sailing vessel is backed
by means of the sails, a steamer by reversing the paddles or screw-
propeller.—*To back astern.* To impel the water with the oars contrary
to the usual mode, or towards the head of the boat, so that she shall
recede.—*To back the larboard* or *starboard oars.* To back with the
right or left oars only, so as to round suddenly.—*To back out.* (*See
Back a Sail.*) The term is also familiarly used for retreating out of
a difficulty.—*To back a rope or chain,* is to put on a preventer when
it is thought likely to break from age or extra strain.—*To back water.*
To impel a boat astern, so as to recede in a direction opposite to the
former course.—*Backing the worming.* The act of passing small yarn
in the holi-days, or crevices left between the worming and edges of
the rope, to prevent the admission of wet, or to render all parts of equal
diameter, so that the service may be smooth.—*Wind backing.* The
wind is said to back when it changes contrary to its usual circuit. In
the northern hemisphere on the polar side of the trades, the wind
usually changes from east, by the south, to west, and so on to north.
In the same latitudes in the southern hemisphere the reverse usually
takes place. When it backs, it is generally supposed to be a sign of
a freshening breeze.

BACK. The outside or convex part of compass-timber. Also a wharf.

BACK, OF A SHIP. The keel and kelson are figuratively thus termed.

BACK, OF THE POST. An additional timber bolted to the after-part of
the stern-post, and forming its after-face.

BACK-BOARD. A board across the stern sheets of a boat to support
the back of passengers; and also to form the *box* in which the coxswain
sits.

BACK-CUTTING. When the water-level is such that the excavation
of a canal, or other channel, does not furnish earth enough for its own
banks, recourse is had to *back-cutting,* or the nearest earth behind the
base of the banks.

BACK-FRAME. A vertical wheel for turning the three whirlers of a
small rope-machine.

BACK-HER. The order, in steam-navigation, directing the engineer
to reverse the movement of the cranks and urge the vessel astern.

BACKING. The timber behind the armour-plates of a ship.

BACK-O'-BEYOND. Said of an unknown distance.

BACK OFF ALL. The order when the harpooner has thrown his
harpoon into the whale. Also, to back off a sudden danger.

BACK-ROPE. The rope-pendant, or small chain for staying the dolphin-
striker. Also a piece long enough to reach from the cat-block to the

stem, and up to the forecastle, to haul the cat-block forward to hook the ring of the anchor—similarly also for hooking the fish-tackle. (*See* GAUB-LINE.)

BACKS. The outermost boards of a sawn tree.

BACK-STAFF. A name formerly given to a peculiar sea-quadrant, because the back of the observer was turned towards the sun at the time of observing its zenith distance. The inventor was Captain Davis, the Welsh navigator, about 1590. It consists of a graduated arc of 30° united to a centre by two radii, with a second arc of smaller radius, but measuring 6° on the side of it. To the first arc a vane is attached for sight,—to the second one for shade,—and at the vertex the horizontal vane has a slit in it.

BACKSTAY-PLATES. Used to support the backstays.

BACKSTAYS. Long ropes extending from all mast-heads above a lower-mast to both sides of the ship or chain-wales; they are extended and set up with dead eyes and laniards to the backstay-plates. Their use is to second the shrouds in supporting the mast when strained by a weight of sail in a fresh wind. They are usually distinguished into breast and after backstays; the first being intended to sustain the mast when the ship sails upon a wind; or, in other terms, when the wind acts upon a ship obliquely from forwards; the second is to enable her to carry sail when the wind is abaft the beam; a third, or shifting backstay, is temporary, and used where great strain is demanded when chasing, chased, or carrying on a heavy pressure of canvas: they are fitted either with lashing eyes, or hook and thimble with salvigee strop, so as to be instantly removed.

BACKSTAY-STOOLS. Detached small channels, or chain-wales, fixed abaft the principal ones. They are introduced in preference to extending the length of the channels.

BACKSTERS. Flat pieces of wood or cork, strapped on the feet in order to walk over loose beach.

BACK-STRAPPED. As a ship carried round to the back of Gibraltar by a counter-current and eddies of wind, the strong currents detaining her there.

BACK-SWEEP. That which forms the hollow of the top-timber of a frame.

BACK-WATER. The swell of the sea thrown back, or rebounded by its contact with any solid body. Also the loss of power occasioned by it to paddles of steamboats, &c. The water in a mill-race which cannot get away in consequence of the swelling of the river below. Also, an artificial accumulation of water reserved for clearing channel-beds and tide-ways. Also, a creek or arm of the sea which runs parallel to the coast, having only a narrow strip of land between it and the sea, and communicating with the latter by barred entrances. The west coast of India is remarkable for its back-waters, which give a most useful smooth water communication from one place to another, such as from Cochin to Quilon, a distance of nearly 70 miles.

BACON, To SAVE. This is an old shore-saw, adopted in nautical phraseology for expressing "to escape," but generally used in *pejus ruere;* as in Gray's *Long Story*. (*See* FOUL HAWSE.)

BAD-BERTH. A foul or rocky anchorage.

BADDERLOCK. The *Fucus esculentus*, a kind of eatable sea-weed on our northern shores. Also called *pursill*.

BADDOCK. A name from the Gaelic for the fry of the *Gadus carbonarius*, or coal-fish.

BADGE. Quarter badges. False quarter-galleries in imitation of frigate-built ships. Also, in naval architecture, a carved ornament placed on the outside of small ships, very near the stern, containing either a window, or the representation of one, with marine decorations.

BADGE, SEAMAN'S. *See* GOOD-CONDUCT BADGE.

BADGER, To. To tease or confound by frivolous orders.

BADGER-BAG. The fictitious Neptune who visits the ship on her crossing the line.

BAD-NAME. This should be avoided by a ship, for once acquired for inefficiency or privateer habits, it requires time and reformation to get rid of it again. "Give a dog a bad name" most forcibly exemplified. Ships have endured it even under repeated changes of captains— one ship had her name changed, but she became worse.

BAD-RELIEF. One who turns out sluggishly to relieve the watch on deck. (*See* ONE-BELL.)

BAESSY. The old orthography of the gun since called *base*.

BAFFLING. Is said of the wind when it frequently shifts from one point to another.

BAG. A commercial term of quantity; as, a bread or biscuit *bag*, a sand-*bag*, &c. An empty purse.—*To bag on a bowline*, to be leewardly, to drop from a course.

BAG, OF THE HEAD-RAILS. The lowest part of the head-rails, or that part which forms the sweep of the rail.

BAG, THE. Allowed for the men to keep their clothes in. The *ditty bag* included needles and needfuls, love-tokens, jewels, &c.

BAGALA. A rude description of high-sterned vessel of various burdens, from 50 to 300 tons, employed at Muskat and on the shores of Oman: the word signifying *mule* among the Arabs, and therefore indicative of carrying rather than sailing.

BAG AND BAGGAGE. The whole movable property.

BAGGAGE. The necessaries, utensils, and apparel of troops.

BAGGAGE-GUARD. A small proportion of any body of troops on the march, to whom the care of the whole baggage is assigned.

BAGGETY. The fish otherwise called the lump or sea-owl (*Cyclopterus lumpus*).

BAGGONET. The old term for bayonet, and not a vulgarism.

BAGNIO. A sort of barrack in Mediterranean sea-ports, where the galley-slaves and convicts are confined.

BAGPIPE. *To bagpipe the mizen* is to lay it aback, by bringing the sheet to the mizen-shrouds.

BAG-REEF. A fourth or lower reef of fore-and-aft sails, often used in the royal navy.—*Bag-reef of topsails*, first reef (of five in American navy); a short reef, usually taken in to prevent a large sail from bagging when on a wind.

BAGREL. A minnow or baggie.

BAGUIO. A rare but dreadfully violent wind among the Philippine Isles.

BAHAR. A commercial weight of a quarter of a ton in the Molucca Islands.

BAIDAR. A swift open canoe of the Arctic tribes and Kurile Isles, used in pursuing otters and even whales; a slender frame from 18 to 25 feet long, covered with hides. They are impelled by six or twelve paddles. (*See* KAIACK.)

BAIKIE. A northern name for the *Larus marinus*, or black-backed gull.

BAIKY. The ballium, or inclosed plot of ground in an ancient fort.

BAIL. A surety. The cargo of a captured or detained vessel is not allowed to be taken on bail before adjudication without mutual consent. It was also a northern term for a beacon or signal.

BAIL-BOND. The obligation entered into by sureties. Also when a person appears as proxy for the master of a vessel, or, on obtaining letters of marque, he makes himself personally responsible. In prize matters, however, the bail-bond is not a mere personal security given to the individual captors, but an assurance to abide by the adjudication of the court.

BAIL'D. This phrase "I'll be bail'd" is considered as an equivalent to "I'll be bound;" but it is probably an old enunciation for "I'll be poisoned," or "I'll be tormented," if what I utter is not true.

BAILO. A Levantine term for consul.

BAILS, OR BAILES. The hoops which bear up the tilt of a boat.

BAIOCCO. An Italian copper coin, about equal to our halfpenny. Also a generic term for copper money or small coin.

BAIRLINN. A Gaelic term for a high rolling billow.

BAIT. The natural or artificial charge of a hook, to allure fish.

BAITLAND. An old word, formerly used to signify a port where refreshments could be procured.

BALÆNA. The zoological name for the right whale.

BALANCE. One of the simple mechanical powers, used in determining the weights and masses of different bodies. Also, one of the twelve signs of the zodiac, called Libra. Balance-wheel of a chronometer—*see* COMPENSATION.

BALANCE, To. To contract a sail into a narrower compass;—this is peculiar to the mizen of a ship, and to the mainsail of those vessels wherein it is extended by a boom. The operation of balancing the mizen is performed by lowering the yard or gaff a little, then rolling up a small portion of the sail at the peak or upper corner, and lashing it about one-fifth down towards the mast. A boom main-sail is balanced by rolling up a portion of the clew, or lower aftermost corner, and fastening it strongly to the boom.—N.B. It is requisite in both cases to wrap a piece of old canvas round the sail, under the lashing, to prevent its being fretted by the latter.

BALANCE-FISH. The hammer-headed shark (which see).

BALANCE-FRAMES. Those frames or bends of timber, of an equal capacity or area, which are equally distant from the ship's centre of gravity.

BALANCE OF TRADE. A computation of the value of all commodities which we import or export, showing the difference in amount.

BALANCE-REEF. A reef-band that crosses a sail from the outer head-earing to the tack diagonally, making it nearly triangular, and is used to contract it in very blowing weather. (2) A balance reef-band is generally placed in all gaff-sails; the band runs from the throat to the clew, so that it may be reefed either way—by lacing the foot or lower half; or by lacing the gaff drooped to the band: the latter is only done in the worst weather.—This is a point on which seamen may select—but the old plan, as first given, affords more power; (2) is applicable to the severest weather.

BALANCING-POINT. A familiar term for centre of gravity. (*See* GRAVITY.)

BALANDRA. A Spanish pleasure-boat. A lighter, a species of schooner.

BALANUS. The acorn-shell. A sessile cirriped.

BALCAR. *See* BALKAR.

BALCONY. The projecting open galleries of old line-of-battle ships' sterns, now disused. They were convenient and ornamental in hot climates, but were afterwards inclosed within sash windows.

BALDRICK. A leathern girdle or sword-belt. Also the zodiac.

BALE. A pack. This word appears in the statute Richard II. c. 3, and is still in common use.

BALE, To. To lade water out of a ship or vessel with buckets (which were of old called *bayles*), cans, or the like, when the pumps are ineffective or choked.

BALEEN. The scientific term for the whalebone of commerce, derived from *balæna*, a whale. It consists of a series of long horny plates growing from each side of the palate in place of teeth.

BALE GOODS. Merchandise packed in large bundles, not in cases or casks.

BALENOT. A porpoise or small whale which frequents the river St. Lawrence.

BALESTILHA. The cross-staff of the early Portuguese navigators.

BALINGER, OR BALANGHA. A kind of small sloop or barge; small vessels of war formerly without forecastles. The name was also given by some of the early voyagers to a large trading-boat of the Philippines and Moluccas.

BALISTES. A fish with mailed skin. File-fish.

BALIZAS. Land and sea marks on Portuguese coasts.

BALK. Straight young trees after they are felled and squared; a beam or timber used for temporary purposes, and under 8 inches square. Balks, of timber of any squared size, as mahogany, intended for planks, or, when very large, for booms or rafts.

BALKAR. A man placed on an eminence, like the ancient Olpis, to watch the movements of shoals of fish. In our early statutes he is called *balcor*.

BALL. In a general sense, implies a spherical and round body, whether naturally so or formed into that figure by art. In a military view it comprehends all sorts of bullets for fire-arms, from the cannon to the pistol: also those pyrotechnic projectiles for guns or mortars, whether intended to destroy, or only to give light, smoke, or stench.

BALLAHOU. A sharp-floored fast-sailing schooner, with taunt fore-and-aft sails, and no topsails, common in Bermuda and the West Indies. The foremast of the ballahou rakes forward, the mainmast aft.

BALL-AND-SOCKET. A clever adaptation to give astronomical or surveying instruments full play and motion every way by a brass ball fitted into a spherical cell, and usually carried by an endless screw.

BALLARAG, To. To abuse or bully. Thus Warton of the French king—

"You surely thought to *ballarag* us
With your fine squadron off Cape Lagos."

BALLAST. A certain portion of stone, pig-iron, gravel, water, or such like materials, deposited in a ship's hold when she either has no cargo or too little to bring her sufficiently low in the water. It is used to counterbalance the effect of the wind upon the masts, and give the ship a proper stability, that she may be enabled to carry sail without danger of overturning. The art of ballasting consists in placing the centre of gravity, so as neither to be too high nor too low, too far forward nor too far aft, and that the surface of the water may nearly rise to the extreme breadth amidships, and thus the ship will be enabled to carry a good sail, incline but little, and ply well to windward. A want of true knowledge in this department has led to putting too great a weight in ships' bottoms, which impedes their sailing and endangers their masts by excessive rolling, the consequence of bringing the centre of gravity too low. It should be trimmed with due regard to the capacity, gravity, and flooring, and to the nature of whatever is to be deposited thereon. (*See* TRIM.)

BALLAST. As a verb, signifies to steady;—as a substantive, a comprehensive mind. A man is said to "lose his ballast" when his judgment fails him, or he becomes top-heavy from conceit.

BALLASTAGE. An old right of the Admiralty in all our royal rivers, of levying a rate for supplying ships with ballast.

BALLAST-BASKET. Usually made of osier, for the transport and measure of shingle-ballast. Supplied to the gunner for transport of loose ammunition.

BALLAST-LIGHTER. A large flat-floored barge, for heaving up and carrying ballast.

BALLAST-MARK. The horizontal line described by the surface of the water on the body of a ship, when she is immersed with her usual weight of ballast on board.

BALLAST-MASTER. A person appointed to see the port-regulations in respect to ballast carried out.

BALLAST-PORTS. Square holes cut in the sides of merchantmen for taking in ballast. But should be securely barred and caulked in before proceeding to sea.

BALLAST-SHIFTING. When by heavy rolling the ballast shifts in the hold.

BALLAST-SHINGLE. Composed of coarse gravel.

BALLAST-SHOOTING. (*See* SHOOT.) In England, and indeed in most frequented ports, the throwing of ballast overboard is strictly prohibited and subject to fine.

BALLAST-SHOVEL. A peculiar square and spoon-pointed iron shovel.

BALLAST-TRIM. When a vessel has only ballast on board.

BALLATOON. A sort of long heavy luggage-vessel of upwards of a hundred tons, employed on the river between Moscow and the Caspian Sea.

BALL-CARTRIDGE. For small arms.

BALL-CLAY. Adhesive strong bottom, brought up by the flukes of the anchors in massy lumps.

BALLISTA. An ancient military engine, like an enormous cross-bow, for throwing stones, darts, and javelins against the enemy with rapidity and violence. Also, the name of the geometrical cross called Jacob's staff.

BALLISTER. A cross-bow man.

BALLISTIC PENDULUM. An instrument for determining the velocity of projectiles. The original pendulum was of very massive construction, the arc through which it receded when impinged on by the projectile, taking into account their respective weights, afforded, with considerable calculation, a measure of the velocity of impact. Latterly the electro-ballistic pendulum, which by means of electric currents is made to register with very great accuracy the time occupied by the projectile in passing over a measured space, has superseded it, as being more accurate, less cumbrous, and less laborious in its accompanying calculations.

BALLIUM. A plot of ground in ancient fortifications: called also *baiky.*

BALLOCH. Gaelic for the discharge of a river into a lake.

BALLOEN. A Siamese decorated state-galley, imitating a sea-monster, with from seventy to a hundred oars of a side.

BALL-OFF, To. To twist rope-yarns into balls, with a running end in the heart for making spun-yarn.

BALLOON-FISH (*Tetraodon*). A plectognathous fish, covered with spines, which has the power of inflating its body till it becomes almost globular.

BALLOW. Deep water inside a shoal or bar.

BALL-STELL. The geometrical instrument named *della stella.*

BALLY. A Teutonic word for inclosure, now prefixed to many sea-ports in Ireland, as Bally-castle, Bally-haven, Bally-shannon, and Bally-water.

BALSA, OR BALZA. A South American tree, very porous, which grows to an immense height in a few years, and is almost as light as cork. Hence the balsa-wood is used for the surf-boat called *balsa.* (*See* JANGADA.)

BALTHEUS ORIONIS. The three bright stars constituting Orion's Belt.

BALUSTERS. The ornamental pillars or pilasters of the balcony or galleries in the sterns of ships, dividing the ward-room deck from the one above.

BAMBA. A commercial shell of value on the Gold Coast of Africa and below it.

BAMBO. An East Indian measure of five English pints.

BAMBOO (*Bambusa arundinacea*). A magnificent articulated cane, which holds a conspicuous rank in the tropics from its rapid growth and almost universal properties:—the succulent buds are eaten fresh and the young stems make excellent preserves. The large stems are useful in agricultural and domestic implements; also in building both houses and ships; in making baskets, cages, hats, and furniture, besides sails, paper, and in various departments of the Indian *materia medica.*

BAMBOOZLE, To. To decoy the enemy by hoisting false colours.

BANANA (*Musa paradisaica*). A valuable species of plantain, the fruit of which is much used in tropical climates, both fresh and made into bread. Gerarde named it Adam's apple from a notion that it was the forbidden fruit of Eden; whilst others supposed it to be the grapes brought out of the Promised Land by the spies of Moses. The spikes of fruit often weigh forty pounds.

BANCO [Sp.] Seat for rowers.

BAND. The musicians of a band are called idlers in large ships. Also a small body of armed men or retainers, as the band of gentlemen pensioners; also an iron hoop round a gun-carriage, mast, &c.; also a slip of canvas stitched across a sail, to strengthen the parts most liable to pressure.—*Reef-bands*, rope-bands or robands; rudder-bands (which see).

BANDAGE. A fillet or swathe, of the utmost importance in surgery. Also, formerly, parcelling to ropes.

BANDALEERS, OR BANDOLEERS. A wide leathern belt for the carriage of small cases of wood, covered with leather, each containing a charge for a firelock; in use before the modern cartouche-boxes were introduced.

BANDECOOT. A large species of fierce rat in India, which infests the drains, &c.

BANDED-DRUM. *See* GRUNTER.

BANDED-MAIL. A kind of armour which consisted of alternate rows of leather or cotton and single chain-mail.

BANDEROLD, OR BANDEROLE. A small streamer or banner, usually fixed on a pike: from *banderola*, Sp. diminutive of *bandera*, the flag or ensign.

BAND-FISH, OR RIBBON-FISHES. A popular name of the *Gymnetrus* genus.

BANDLE. An Irish measure of two feet in length.

BANG. A mixture of opium, hemp-leaves, and tobacco, of an intoxicating quality, chewed and smoked by the Malays and other people in the East, who, being mostly prohibited the use of wine, double upon Mahomet by indulging in other intoxicating matter, as if the manner of doing it cleared off the crime of drunkenness. This horrid stuff gives the maddening excitement which makes a Malay run *amuk* (which see).—*To bang* is colloquially used to express excelling or beating rivals. (*See* SUFFOLK-BANG.)

BANGE. Light fine rain.

BANGLES. The hoops of a spar. Also, the rings on the wrists and ankles of Oriental people, chiefly used by females.

BANIAN. A sailor's coloured frock-shirt.

BANIAN or BANYAN DAYS. Those in which no flesh-meat is issued to the messes. It is obvious that they are a remnant of the maigre days of the Roman Catholics, who deem it a mortal sin to eat flesh on certain days. Stock-fish used to be served out, till it was found to promote scurvy. The term is derived from a religious sect in the East, who, believing in metempsychosis, eat of no creature endued with life.

BANIAN-TREE. *Ficus indica* of India and Polynesia. The tendrils from high branches extend 60 to 80 feet, take root on reaching the ground, and form a cover over some acres. Religious rites from which women are excluded are there performed.

BANJO. The brass frame in which the screw-propeller of a steamer works, and is hung for hoisting the screw on deck. This frame fits between slides fixed on the inner and outer stern-posts; resting in large carriages firmly secured thereto. The banjo is essential to lifting the screw.—Also, the rude instrument used in negro concerts.

BANK. The right or left boundary of a river, in looking from its source towards the sea, and the immediate margin or border of a lake. Also, a thwart, *banco*, or bench, for the rowers in a galley. Also, a rising ground in the sea, differing from a shoal, because not rocky but composed of sand, mud, or gravel. Also, mural elevations constructed of clay, stones, or any materials at hand, to prevent inundations.

BANK, To. Also, an old word meaning to sail along the margins or banks of river-ports: thus Shakspeare in "King John" makes Lewis the Dauphin demand—

> "Have I not heard these islanders shout out
> *Vive le Roy!* as I have *bank'd* their towns?"

BANKA. A canoe of the Philippines, consisting of a single piece.

BANKER. A vessel employed in the deep-sea cod-fishery on the great banks of Newfoundland. Also, a man who works on the sides of a canal, or on an embankment; a navvy.

BANK-FIRES. In steamers, taking advantage of a breeze by allowing the fires to burn down low, and then pulling them down to a side of the bridge of the fire-place, and there covering them up with ashes taken from the ash-pit, at the same time nearly closing the dampers in the funnel and ash-pit doors. This, with attention on the part of the engineers, will maintain the water hot, and a slight pressure of steam in the boilers. When fuel is added and draught induced the fires are said to be "drawn forward," and steam is speedily generated.

BANK-HARBOUR. That which is protected from the violence of the sea by banks of mud, gravel, sand, shingle, or silt.

BANK-HOOK. A large fish-hook laid baited in running water, attached by a line to the bank.

BANKING. A general term applied to fishing on the great bank of Newfoundland.

BANK OF OARS [*banco*, Sp.] A seat or bench for rowers in the happily all but extinct galley: these are properly called the athwarts, but thwarts by seamen. The common galleys have 25 banks on each side, with one oar to each bank, and four men to each oar. The galeasses have 32 banks on a side, and 6 or 7 rowers to each bank. (*See* DOUBLE-BANK, when two men pull separate oars on the same thwart.)

BANKSAL, OR BANKSAUL, and in Calcutta spelled *bankshall*. A shop, office, or other place, for transacting business. Also, a square inclosure at the pearl-fishery. Also, a beach store-house wherein ships deposit their rigging and furniture while undergoing repair. Also, where small commercial courts and arbitrations are held.

BANN. A proclamation made in the army by beat of drum, sound of trumpet, &c., requiring the strict observance of discipline, either for the declaring of a new officer, the punishing an offender, or the like.

BANNAG. A northern name for a white trout, a sea-trout.

BANNAK-FLUKE. A name of the turbot, as distinguished from the halibut.

BANNER. A small square flag edged with fringe.

BANNERER. The bearer of a banner.

BANNERET. A knight made on the field of battle.

BANNEROL. A little banner or streamer.

BANNOCK. A name given to a certain hard ship-biscuit.

BANQUETTE. In fortification, a small terrace, properly of earth, on the inside of the parapet, of such height that the defenders standing on it may conveniently fire over the top.

BANSTICKLE. A diminutive fish, called also the three-spined stickleback (*Gasterosteus aculeatus*).

BAPTISM. A ceremony practised on passengers on their first passing the equinoctial line: a riotous and ludicrous custom, which from the violence of its ducking, shaving, and other practical jokes, is becoming annually less in vogue. It is esteemed a usurpation of privilege to baptize on crossing the tropics.

BAR, OF A PORT OR HARBOUR. An accumulated shoal or bank of sand, shingle, gravel, or other uliginous substances, thrown up by the sea to the mouth of a river or harbour, so as to endanger, and sometimes totally prevent, the navigation into it.—*Bars of rivers* are some shifting and some permanent. The position of the bar of any river may commonly be guessed by attending to the form of the shores at the embouchure. The shore on which the deposition of sediment is going on will be flat, whilst the opposite one is steep. It is along the side of the latter that the deepest channel of the river lies; and in the line of this channel, but without the points that form the mouth of the river, will be the *bar*. If both the shores are of the same nature, which seldom happens, the bar will lie opposite the middle of the channel. Rivers in general have what may be deemed a bar, in respect of the depth of the channel within, although it may not rise high enough to impede the navigation—for the increased deposition that takes place when the current slackens, through the want of declivity, and of shores to retain it, must necessarily form a bank. Bars of small rivers may be deepened by means of stockades to confine the river current, and prolong it beyond the natural points of the river's mouth. They operate to remove the place of deposition further out, and into deeper water. Bars, however, act as breakwaters in most instances, and consequently secure smooth water within them. The deposit in all curvilinear or serpentine rivers will always be found at the point opposite to the curve into which the ebb strikes and rebounds, deepening the hollow and depositing on the tongue. Therefore if it be deemed advisable to change the position of a bar, it may be in some cases aided by works projected on the last curve seaward. By such means a parallel canal may be forced which will admit vessels under the cover of the bar.—*Bar*, a boom formed of huge trees, or spars lashed together, moored transversely across a port, to prevent entrance or egress.—*Bar*, the short bits of bar-iron, about half a pound each, used as the medium of traffic on the Negro coast.—*Bar-harbour*, one which, from a bar at its entrance, cannot admit ships of great burden, or can only do so at high-water.—*Capstan-bars*, large thick bars put into the holes of the drum-head of the capstan, by which it is turned round, they working as horizontal radial levers.—*Hatch-bars*, flat iron bars to lock over the hatches for security from theft, &c.— *Port-bar*, a piece of wood or iron variously fitted to secure a gun-port when shut.—*Bar-shallow*, a term sometimes applied to a portion of a bar with less water on it than on other parts of the bar.—*Bar-shot*, two half balls joined together by a bar of iron, for cutting and destroying spars and rigging. When whole balls are thus fitted they are more properly double-headed shot.—*To bar*. To secure the lower-deck ports, as above.

BARACOOTA. A tropical fish (*Sphyræna baracuda*), considered in the West Indies to be dangerously poisonous at times, nevertheless eaten, and deemed the sea-salmon.

BARBACAN. In fortification, an outer defence.

BARBADOES-TAR. A mineral fluid bitumen resembling petroleum, of nauseous taste and offensive smell.

BARBALOT. The barbel. Also, a puffin.

BARB-BOLTS. Those which have their points jagged or barbed to make them hold securely, where those commonly in use cannot be clinched. The same as *rag-bolt*. Those of copper used for the false keel.

BARBECUE. A tropical custom of dressing a pig whole.

BARBEL (*Barbus vulgaris*). An English river-fish of the carp family, distinguished by the four appendant beards, whence its name is derived. It is between 2 and 3 feet in length, and coarse. Also, *barbel* is a small piece of armour which protects part of the bassenet.

BARBER. A rating on the ships' books for one who shaves the people, for which he receives the pay of an ordinary seaman. In meteorology, *barber* is a singular vapour rising in streams from the sea surface,— owing probably to exhalations being condensed into a visible form, on entering a cold atmosphere. It is well known on the shores of Nova Scotia. Also, the condensed breath in frosty weather on beard or moustaches in Arctic travelling.

BARBETTE. A mode of mounting guns to fire over the parapet, so as to have free range, instead of through embrasures.

BARCA-LONGA. A large Spanish undecked coasting-vessel, navigated with pole-masts, *i.e.* single-masts, without any topmast or upper part; and high square sails, called lugsails. Propelled with sweeps as well. The name is also applied to Spanish gun-boats by our seamen.

BARCES. Short guns with a large bore formerly used in ships.

BARCHETTA. A small bark for transporting water, provisions, &c.

BARCONE. A short Mediterranean lighter.

BAREKA. A small barrel: spelled also *barika* (Sp. *baréca*). Hence the nautical name *breaker* for a small cask or keg.

BARE-POLES. The condition of a ship having no sails set when out at sea, and either scudding or lying-to by stress of weather. (*See* UNDER BARE-POLES.)

BARE-ROOM. An old phrase for *bore-down*.

BARGE. A boat of a long, slight, and spacious construction, generally carvel-built, double-banked, for the use of admirals and captains of ships of war.—*Barge*, in boat attacks, is next in strength to the launch. It is likewise a vessel or boat of state, furnished and equipped in the most sumptuous style;—and of this sort we may naturally suppose to have been the famous barge or galley of Cleopatra, which, according to the beautiful description of Shakspeare—

> "Like a burnished throne
> Burnt on the water: the poop was beaten gold,
> Purple her sails; and so perfumed, that
> The winds were love-sick with them; the oars were silver.

Which to the tune of flutes kept time, and made
The water which they beat to follow faster
As amorous of their strokes."

The barges of the lord-mayor, civic companies, &c., and the coal-barges of the Thames are varieties. Also, an early man-of-war, of about 100 tons. Also, an east-country vessel of peculiar construction. Also, a flat-bottomed vessel of burden, used on rivers for conveying goods from one place to another, and loading and unloading ships: it has various names, as a Ware barge, a west-country barge, a sand barge, a row-barge, a Severn trough, a light horseman, &c. They are usually fitted with a large sprit-sail to a mast, which, working upon a hinge, is easily struck for passing under bridges. Also, the bread-barge or tray or basket, for containing biscuit at meals.

BARGEES. The crews of canal-boats and barges.

BARGE-MATE. The officer who steers when a high personage is to visit the ship.

BARGE-MEN. The crew of the barge, who are usually picked men. Also, the large maggots with black heads that infest biscuit.

BARGET. An old term for a small barge.

BARILLA. An alkali procured by burning salsola, kali, and other sea-shore plants. It forms a profitable article of Mediterranean commerce. (See KELP.)

BARK. The exterior covering of vegetable bodies, many of which are useful in making paper, cordage, cloth, dyes, and medicines.

BARK, OR BARQUE [from *barca*, Low Latin]. A general name given to small ships, square-sterned, without head-rails; it is, however, peculiarly appropriated by seamen to a three-masted vessel with only fore-and-aft sails on her mizen-mast.—*Bark-rigged*. Rigged as a bark, with no square sails on the mizen-mast.

BARKANTINE, OR BARQUANTINE. A name applied on the great lakes of North America to a vessel square-rigged on the foremast, and fore-and-aft rigged on the main and mizen masts. They are not three-masted schooners, as they have a regular brigantine's foremast. They are long in proportion to their other dimensions, to suit the navigation of the canals which connect some of these lakes.

BARKERS. An old term for lower-deck guns and pistols.

BARKEY. A sailor's term for the pet ship to which he belongs.

BARKING-IRONS. Large duelling pistols.

BARLING. An old term for the lamprey.—*Barling-spars*, fit for any smaller masts or yards.

BARNACLE (*Lepas anatifera*). A species of shell-fish, often found sticking by its pedicle to the bottom of ships, doing no other injury than deadening the way a little:

> "*Barnacles*, termed *soland geese*
> In th' islands of the Orcades."—*Hudibras.*

They were formerly supposed to produce the barnacle-goose! (vide old cyclopedias): the poet, however, was too good a naturalist to believe this, but here, as in many other places, he means to banter some of the papers which were published by the first establishers of the Royal Society. The shell is compressed and multivalve. The tentacula are long and pectinated like a feather, whence arose the fable of their becoming geese. They belong to the order of *Cirripeds.*

BARNAGH. The Manx or Gaelic term for a limpet.

BAROMETER. A glass tube of 36 inches in length, filled with the open end upwards with refined mercury—thus boiled and suddenly inverted into a cistern, which is furnished with a leathern bag, on which the atmosphere, acting by its varying weight, presses the fluid metal up to corresponding heights in the tube, easily read off by an external scale attached thereto. By attentive observations on this simple prophet, practised seamen are enabled to foretel many approaching changes of wind or weather, and thus by shortening sail in time, save hull, spars, and lives. This instrument also affords the means of accurately determining the heights or depressions of mountains and valleys. This is the *mercurial* barometer; another, the *aneroid* barometer, invented by Monsr. Vidi, measures approximately, but not with the permanence of the mercurial. It is constructed to measure the weight of a column of air or pressure of the atmosphere, by pressure on a very delicate metallic box hermetically sealed. It is more sensible to passing changes, but not so reliable as the mercurial barometer. 29·60 is taken as the mean pressure in England; as it rises or falls below this mark, fine weather or strong winds may be looked for:—30·60 is very high, and 29·00 very low. The barometer is affected by the direction of the wind, thus N.N.E. is the highest, and S.S.W. the lowest—therefore these matters govern the decision of men of science, who are not led astray by the change of reading alone. The seaman pilot notes the heavens; the direction of the wind—and the pressure due to that direction—not forgetting sudden changes of temperature. Attention is due to the surface, whether convex or concave.

BARQUE. The same as *bark* (which see).

BARR. A peremptory exception to a proposition.

BARRA-BOATS. Vessels of the Western Isles of Scotland, carrying ten or twelve men. They are extremely sharp fore and aft, having no floor, but with sides rising straight from the keel, so that a transverse section resembles the letter V. They are swift and safe, for in proportion as they heel to a breeze their bearings are increased, while from their lightness they are as buoyant as Norway skiffs.

BARRACAN. A strong undiapered camblet, used for garments in the Levant and in Barbary; anciently it formed the Roman toga.

BARRACK-MASTER. The officer placed in charge of a barrack.

BARRACKS. Originally mere log-huts, but of late extensive houses built for the accommodation and quartering of troops. Also, the portion of the lower deck where the marines mess. Also, little cabins made by Spanish fishermen on the sea-shore, called *barracas*, whence our name.

BARRACK SMACK. A corruption of *Berwick smack;* a word applied to small Scotch traders. The masters were nicknamed *barrack-masters.*

BARRATRY. Any fraudulent act of the master or mariners committed to the prejudice of the ship's owners or underwriters, whether by fraudulently losing the vessel, deserting her, selling her, or committing any other embezzlement. The diverting a ship from her right course, with evil intent, is barratry.

BARRED KILLIFISH. A small fish from two to four inches in length, which frequents salt-water creeks, floats, and the vicinity of wharves.

BARREL. A cylindrical vessel for holding both liquid and dry goods. Also, a commercial measure of $31\frac{1}{2}$ gallons.

BARREL OF A CAPSTAN. The cylinder between the whelps and the paul rim, constituting the main-piece.

BARREL OF A PUMP. The wooden tube which forms the body of the engine.

BARREL OF SMALL ARMS. The tube through which the bullets are discharged. In artillery the term belongs to the construction of certain guns, and signifies the inner tube, as distinguished from the breech-piece, trunnion-piece, and hoops or outer coils, the other essential parts of "built-up guns" (which see).

BARREL OF THE WHEEL. The cylinder round which the tiller-ropes are wound.

BARREL-BUILDER. The old rating for a cooper.

BARREL-BULK. A measure of capacity for freight in a ship, equal to five cubic feet: so that eight barrel-bulk are equal to one ton measurement.

BARREL-SCREW. A powerful machine, consisting of two large poppets, or male screws, moved by levers in their heads, upon a bank of plank, with a female screw at each end. It is of great use in starting a launch.

BARRICADE. A strong wooden rail, supported by stanchions extending as a fence across the foremost part of the quarter-deck, on the top of which some of the seamen's hammocks are usually stowed in time of battle. In a vessel of war the vacant spaces between the stanchions are commonly filled with rope-mats, cork, or pieces of old cable; and the upper part, which contains a double rope-netting above the sail, is stuffed with full hammocks to intercept small shot in the time of battle. Also, a temporary fortification or fence made with abatis, palisades, or any obstacles, to bar the approach of an enemy by a given avenue.

BARRIER OF ICE. Ice stretching from the land-ice to the sea or main ice, or across a channel, so as to render it impassable.

BARRIER REEFS. . Coral reefs that either extend in straight lines in front of the shores of a continent or large island, or encircle smaller isles, in both cases being separated from the land by a channel of water. Barrier reefs in New South Wales, the Bermudas, Laccadives, Maldives, &c.

BARRIERS. A martial exercise of men armed with short swords, within certain railings which separated them from the spectators. It has long been discontinued in England.

BARROW. A hillock, a tumulus.

BARSE. The common river-perch.

BARTIZAN. The overhanging turrets on a battlement.

BARUTH. An Indian measure, with a corresponding weight of $3\frac{1}{2}$ lbs. avoirdupois.

BASE. The breech of a gun. Also, the lowest part of the perimeter of a geometrical figure. When applied to a delta it is that edge of it which is washed by the sea, or recipient of the deltic branches. Also, the lowest part of a mountain or chain of mountains. Also, the level line on which any work stands, as the foot of a pillar. Also, an old boat-gun; a wall-piece on the musketoon principle, carrying a five-ounce ball.

BASE-LINE. In strategy, the line joining the various points of a base of operations. In surveying, the base on which the triangulation is founded.

BASE OF OPERATIONS. In strategy, one or a series of strategic points at which are established the magazines and means of supply necessary for an army in the field.

BASE-RING. In guns of cast-metal, the flat moulding round the breech at that part where the longitudinal surface ends and the vertical termination or cascable begins. The length of the gun is reckoned from the after-edge of the base-ring to the face of the muzzle : but in built-up guns, there being generally no base-ring moulded, and the breech assuming various forms, the length is measured from the after-extreme of the breech, exclusive of any button or other adjunct.

BASHAW. A Turkish title of honour and command; more properly *pacha.*

BASIL. The angle to which the edge of shipwrights' cutting tools is ground away.

BASILICON. An ointment composed of wax, resin, pitch, black resin, and olive oil. *Yellow basilicon,* of olive oil, yellow resin, Burgundy pitch, and turpentine.

BASILICUS. A name of Regulus or the Lion's Heart, a Leonis; a star of the first magnitude.

BASILISK. An old name for a long 48-pounder, the gun next in size to the carthoun: called basilisk from the snakes or dragons sculptured in the place of dolphins. According to Sir William Monson its random range was 3000 paces. Also, in still earlier times, a gun throwing an iron ball of 200 lbs. weight.

BASILLARD. An old term for a poniard.

BASIN. A wet-dock provided with flood-gates for restraining the water, in which shipping may be kept afloat in all times of tide. Also, all those sheltered spaces of water which are nearly surrounded with slopes from which waters are received; these receptacles have a circular shape and narrow entrance. Geographically basins may be divided, as upper, lower, lacustrine, fluvial, mediterranean, &c.

BASIS. *See* BASE.

BASKET. In field-works, baskets or corbeilles are used, to be filled with earth, and placed by one another, to cover the men from the enemy's shot.

BASKET-FISH. A name for several species of *Euryale;* a kind of starfish, the arms of which divide and subdivide many times, and curl up and intertwine at the ends, giving the whole animal something of the appearance of a round basket.

BASKET-HILT. The guard continued up the hilt of a cutlass, so as to protect the whole hand from injury.

BASKING SHARK. So called from being often seen lying still in the sunshine. A large cartilaginous fish, the *Squalus maximus* of Linnæus, inhabiting the Northern Ocean. It attains a length of 30 feet, but is neither fierce nor voracious. Its liver yields from eight to twelve barrels of oil.

BASS, OR BAST. A soft sedge or rush (*Juncus lævis*), of which coarse kinds of rope and matting are made. A Gaelic term for the blade of an oar.

BASSE. A species of perch (*Perca labrax*), found on the coast and in estuaries, commonly about 18 inches long.

BASSOS. A name in old charts for shoals; whence bas-fond and basso-fondo. Rocks awash, or below water.

BAST. Lime-tree, linden (*Tilia europea*). Bast is made also from the bark of various other trees, macerated in water till the fibrous layers separate. In the Pacific Isles it is very fine and strong, from *Hibiscus tiliaceus.*

BASTA. A word in former use for *enough*, from the Italian.

BASTARD. A term applied to all pieces of ordnance which are of unusual or irregular proportions : the government bastard-cannon had a 7-inch bore, and sent a 40-lb. shot. Also, a fair-weather square sail in some Mediterranean craft, and occasionally used for an awning.

BASTARD-MACKEREL, or Horse-Mackerel. The *Caranx trachurus*, a dry, coarse, and unwholesome fish, of the family *Scomberidæ*, very common in the Mediterranean.

BASTARD-PITCH. A mixture of colophony, black pitch, and tar. They are boiled down together, and put into barrels of pine-wood, forming, when the ingredients are mixed in equal portions, a substance of a very liquid consistence, called in France *bray gras*. If a thicker consistence is desired, a greater proportion of colophony is added, and it is cast in moulds. It is then called *bastard-pitch.*

BASTE, To. To beat in punition. A mode of sewing in sail-making.

BASTILE. A temporary wooden tower, used formerly in naval and military warfare.

BASTIONS. Projecting portions of a rampart, so disposed that the bottom of the escarp of each part of the whole rampart may be defended from the parapet of some other part. Their form and dimensions are influenced by many considerations, especially by the effect and range of fire-arms; but it is essential to them to have two faces and two flanks; the former having an average length, according to present systems, of 130 yards, the latter of 40 yards.

BASTON, or Baton. A club used of old by authority. (*See* Batoon.)

BASTONADO. Beating a criminal with sticks [from *bastone*, a cudgel]. A punishment common among Jews, Greeks, and Romans, and still practised in the Levant, China, and Russia.

BAT, or Sea-bat. An Anglo-Saxon term for boat or vessel. Also a broad-bodied thoracic fish, with a small head, and distinguished by its large triangular dorsal and anal fins, which exceed the length of the body. It is the *Chætodon vespertilio* of naturalists.

BAT AND FORAGE. A regulated allowance in money and forage to officers in the field.

BATARDATES. Square-stemmed row-galleys.

BATARDEAU. In fortification, a dam of masonry crossing the ditch : its top is constructed of such a form as to afford no passage along it.

BATARDELLES. Galleys less strong than the capitana, and placed on each side of her.

BATEAU. A flat-bottomed, sharp-ended clumsy boat, used on the rivers and lakes of Canada; some of them are large. Also a peculiar army pontoon.

BATED. A plump, full-roed fish is said to be bated.

BATELLA. A small plying-boat.

BATH. (*See* WASHING-PLACE.) An order of knighthood instituted in 1339, revived in 1725, and enlarged as a national reward of naval and military merit in January, 1815. Henry IV. gave this name, because the forty-six esquires on whom he conferred this honour at his coronation had watched all the previous night, and then *bathed* as typical of their pure virtue. The order was supposed to belong to men who distinguished themselves by valour as regards the navy, but it is now deemed an inferior representation of court favour.

BATILLAGE. An old term for boat-hire.

BATMAN. A Turkish weight of 6 okes, or about 18 lbs. English. There is also a smaller batman in Turkey, of about 4 lbs. 10 oz. English. In Persia there are also two batmans—the larger equal to 12 lbs. English, and the other is of about half that weight. Also, a soldier assigned to a mounted officer as groom.

BATOON, BASTON, OR BATON. A staff, truncheon, or badge of military honour for field-marshals. A term in heraldry. Also, *batoons of St. Paul*, the fossil spines of echini, found in Malta and elsewhere.

BAT-SWAIN. An Anglo-Saxon expression for boatswain.

BATTA. Extra allowance of pay granted to troops in India, varying somewhat with the nature of the service they are employed upon, and their distance from the capital of the presidency.

BATTALIA. The order of battle.

BATTALION. A force of soldiers, complete in staff and officers, of such strength as will allow of its manœuvres on the field of battle being intimately regulated by one superior officer. The term is now proper to infantry only, and represents from 500 to 1000 men. It is the ordinary unit made use of in estimating the infantry strength of an army.

BATTARD. An early cannon of small size.

BATTELOE. A lateen-rigged vessel of India.

BATTENING THE HATCHES. Securing the tarpaulins over them. (*See* BATTENS.)

BATTENS. In general, scantlings of wood from 1 inch to 3 inches broad. Long slips of fir used for setting fair the sheer lines of a ship, or drawing the lines by in the moulding loft, and setting off distances.

BATTENS FOR HAMMOCKS. *See* HAMMOCK-BATTENS.

BATTENS of the Hatches.   Long narrow laths, or straightened hoops of casks, serving by the help of nailing to confine the edges of the tarpaulins, and keep them close down to the sides of the hatchways, in bad weather.   Also, thin strips of wood put upon rigging, to keep it from chafing, by those who dislike mats: when large these are designated *Scotchmen.*

BATTERING GUNS.   Properly guns whose weight and power fit them for demolishing by direct force the works of the enemy; hence all heavy, as distinguished from field or light, guns come under the term.   (*See* Siege Artillery and Garrison Artillery.)

BATTERING RAM.   *See* Ram.

BATTERING TRAIN.   The train of heavy ordnance necessary for a siege, which, since the copious introduction of vertical and other shell fire, is more correctly rendered by the term siege-train (which see).

BATTERY.   A place whereon cannon, mortars, &c., are or may be mounted for action.   It generally has a parapet for the protection of the gunners, and other defences and conveniences according to its importance and objects.   (*See also* Floating Battery.)   Also, a company of artillery.   In field-artillery it includes men, guns (usually six in the British service), horses, carriages, &c., complete for service.

BATTLE.   An engagement between two fleets, or even single ships, usually called a sea-fight or engagement.   The conflict between the forces of two contending armies.

BATTLE LANTERNS (American).   *See* Fighting Lanterns.

BATTLEMENTS.   The vertical notches or openings made in the parapet walls of old castles and fortified buildings, to serve for embrasures to the bowmen, arquebusiers, &c., of former days.

BATTLE-ROYAL.   A term derived from cock-fighting, but generally applied to a noisy confused row.

BATTLE THE WATCH, To.   To shift as well as we can; to contend with a difficulty.   To depend on one's own exertions.

BATTLING-STONE.   A large stone with a smooth surface by the side of a stream, on which washers beat their linen.

BATTS.   A north-country term for flat grounds adjoining islands in rivers, sometimes used for the islands themselves.

BAT-WARD.   An old term for a boat-keeper.

BAUN.   *See* Bore.

BAVIER.   The beaver of a helmet.

BAVIN.   Brushwood bound up with only one withe: a faggot is tied with two.   It is often spelled *baven,* but Shakspeare has

"Rash bavin wits,
Soon kindled and soon burned."

This underwood is sometimes procurable by ships where none other can be got. Bavin in war applies to fascines.

BAW-BURD. An old expression of larboard.

BAWDRICK. Corrupted from *baldrick*. A girdle or sword-belt.

BAWE. A species of worm, formerly used as a bait for fishing.

BAWGIE. One of the names given to the great black and white gull (*Larus marinus*) in the Shetlands.

BAWKIE. A northern term for the auk, or razor-bill.

BAXIOS. [Sp.] Rocks or sandbanks covered with water. Scopuli.

BAY. The fore-part of a ship between decks, before the bitts (*see* SICK BAY). Foremost messing-places between decks in ships of war.

BAY. An inlet of the sea formed by the curvature of the land between two capes or headlands, often used synonymously with gulf; though, in strict accuracy, the term should be applied only to those large recesses which are wider from cape to cape than they are deep. Exposed to sea-winds, a bay is mostly insecure. A bay is distinguished from a bend, as that a vessel may not be able to fetch out on either tack, and is embayed. A bay has proportionably a wider entrance than either a gulf or haven; a creek has usually a small inlet, and is always much less than a bay.

BAY. Laurel; hence crowned with bays.

BAYAMOS. Violent blasts of wind blowing from the land, on the south side of Cuba, and especially from the Bight of Bayamo, by which some of our cruisers have been damaged. They are accompanied by vivid lightning, and generally terminate in rain.

BAY-GULF. A branch of the sea, of which the entrance is the widest part, as contradistinguished from the strait-gulf. The Bay of Biscay is a well-known example of the semi-circular gulf.

BAY-ICE. Ice newly formed on the surface of the sea, and having the colour of the water; it is then in the first stage of consolidation. The epithet is, however, also applied to ice a foot or two in thickness in bays.

BAYLE. An old term for bucket.

BAYONET [Sp. *bayoneta*]. A pike-dagger to fit on the muzzle of a musket, so as not to interfere with its firing.

BAZAR, or BAZAAR. A market, or market-place. An oriental term.

BAZARAS. A large flat-bottomed pleasure-boat of the Ganges, moved with both sails and oars.

BEACH. A littoral margin, or line of coast along the sea-shore, composed of sand, gravel, shingle, broken shells, or a mixture of them all: any gently sloping part of the coast alternately dry and covered by the tide. The same as *strand*.

BEACH, To.   Sudden landing—to run a boat on the shore, to land a person with intent to desert him—an old buccaneer custom.   To land a boat on a beach before a dangerous sea, this demands practical skill, for which the Dover and Deal men are famed.

BEACH-COMBERS.   Loiterers around a bay or harbour.

BEACH-COMBING.   Loafing about a port to filch small things.

BEACH - FLEA.   A small crustacean (*Talitra*) frequenting sandy shores.

BEACH-GRASS.   *Alga marina* thrown up by the surf or tide.

BEACHING A VESSEL.   *See under* VOLUNTARY STRANDING.   Also, the act of running a vessel up on the beach for various purposes where there is no other accommodation.

BEACH-MAN.   A person on the coast of Africa who acts as interpreter to shipmasters, and assists them in conducting the trade.

BEACH-MASTER.   A superior officer, captain, appointed to superintend disembarkation of an attacking force, who holds plenary powers, and generally leads the storming party.   His acts when in the heat of action, if he summarily shoot a coward, are unquestioned—poor Falconer, to wit!

BEACH-MEN.   A name applied to boatmen and those who land people through a heavy surf.

BEACH-RANGERS.   Men hanging about sea-ports, who have been turned out of vessels for bad conduct.

BEACH-TRAMPERS.   A name applied to the coast-guard.

BEACON.   [Anglo-Saxon, *béacn*.]   A post or stake erected over a shoal or sandbank, as a warning to seamen to keep at a distance; also a signal-mark placed on the top of hills, eminences, or buildings near the shore for the safe guidance of shipping.

BEACONAGE.   A payment levied for the maintenance of beacons.

BEAFT.   Often used by east-country men for abaft.

BEAK, OR BEAK-HEAD.   A piece of brass like a beak, fixed at the head of the ancient galleys, with which they pierced their enemies.   Pisæus is said to have first added the rostrum or beak-head.   Later it was a small platform at the fore part of the upper deck, but the term is now applied to that part without the ship before the forecastle, or knee of the head, which is fastened to the stem and is supported by the main knee.   Latterly, to meet steam propulsion, the whole of this is enlarged, strengthened, and armed with iron plates, and thus the armed stem revives the ancient strategy in sea-fights.   Shakspeare makes Ariel thus allude to the beak in the "Tempest:"—

> "I boarded the king's ship; now on the beak,
> Now in the waist, the deck, in every cabin,
> I flam'd amazement."

BEAKER. A flat drinking tumbler or cup, from the German *becher*. (*See* BICKER.)

BEAK-HEAD BEAM. For this important timber *see* CAT-BEAM.

BEAK-HEAD BULKHEAD. The old termination aft of the space called *beak-head*, which inclosed the fore part of the ship.

BEAL. A word of Gaelic derivation for an opening or narrow pass between two hills.

BEAM. A long double stratum of murky clouds generally observed over the surface of the Mediterranean previous to a violent storm or an earthquake. The French call it *trave*.

BEAM. (*See* ABEAM.)—*Before the beam* is an arc of the horizon, comprehended between a line that crosses the ship's length at right angles and some object at a distance before it; or between the line of the beam and that point of the compass which she stems. On the *weather* or *lee* beam is in a direction to windward or leeward at right angles with the keel.

BEAM-ARM. Synonymous with *crow-foot* (which see).

BEAM-ENDS. A ship is said to be on her beam-ends when she has heeled over so much on one side that her beams approach to a vertical position; hence also a person lying down is metaphorically said to be on his beam-ends.

BEAM-FILLINGS. Short lengths of wood cut to fit in between the beams to complete the cargo of a timber ship.

BEAM-LINE. A line raised along the inside of the ship fore and aft, showing the upper sides of the beams at her side.

BEAM OF THE ANCHOR. Synonymous with *anchor-stock*.

BEAMS. Strong transverse pieces of timber stretching across the ship from one side to the other, to support the decks and retain the sides at their proper distance, with which they are firmly connected by means of strong knees, and sometimes of standards. They are sustained at each end by thick stringers on the ship's side, called shelf-pieces, upon which they rest. The main-beam is next abaft the main-mast, which is stepped between two beams with transverse supports termed partners; the foremost of these is generally termed the main-beam, or the after-beam of the main-hatchway. The greatest beam of all is called the midship-beam.

BEAN-COD. A small fishing-vessel, or pilot-boat, common on the sea-coasts and in the rivers of Spain and Portugal; extremely sharp forward, having its stem bent inward above in a considerable curve; it is commonly navigated with a large lateen sail, which extends the whole length of the deck, and sometimes of an outrigger over the stern, and is accordingly well fitted to ply to windward. They frequently set as many as twenty different sails, alow and aloft, by every possible contrivance, so as to puzzle seamen who are not familiar with the rig.

BEAR. A large block of stone, matted, loaded with shot, and fitted with ropes, by which it is rowsed or pulled to and fro to grind the decks withal. Also, a coir-mat filled with sand similarly used.

BEAR, THE CONSTELLATIONS OF THE. Ursa Major and Minor, most important to seamen, as instantly indicating by the pointers and pole-star the true north at night, much more correctly than any compass bearing.

BEAR, To. The direction of an object from the viewer; it is used in the following different phrases: The land's end bore E.N.E.; *i.e.* it was seen from the ship in a line with the E.N.E. point of the compass. We bore down upon the enemy; *i.e.* having the advantage of the wind, or being to windward, we approached the enemy by sailing large, or from the wind. When a ship that was to windward comes under another ship's stern, and so gives her the wind, she is said to bear under the lee; often as a mark of respect. She bears in with the land, is said of a ship when she runs towards the shore. We bore off the land; *i.e.* we increased our distance from the land.—*To bear down* upon a ship, is to approach her from the windward.—*To bear ordnance*, to carry her guns well.—*To bear sail*, stiff under canvas.— *To bear up*, to put the helm up, and keep a vessel off her course, letting her recede from the wind and move to leeward; this is synony-mous with *to bear away*, but is applied to the ship instead of the helm. —*Bear up*, one who has duly served for a commission, but from want of interest bears up broken-hearted and accepts an inferior warrant, or quits the profession, seeking some less important vocation; some middies have borne up and yet become bishops, lord-chancellors, judges, surgeons, &c.—*To bear up round*, is to put a ship right before the wind.—*To bring a cannon to bear*, signifies that it now lies right with the mark.—*To bear off from* and *in with* the land, signifies standing off or going towards the coast.

BEAR A BOB, OR A FIST. Jocular for "lend a hand."

BEAR A HAND. Hasten.

BEARD. The silky filaments or byssus by which some testacea adhere to rocks. Of an oyster, the gills.

BEARDIE. A northern name of the three-spined stickleback.

BEARDING. The angular fore-part of the rudder, in juxtaposition with the stern-post. Also, the corresponding bevel of the stern-post. Also, the bevelling of any piece of timber or plank to any required angle: as the bearding of dead wood, clamps, &c.

BEARDING-LINE. In shipbuilding, is a curved line made by beard-ing the dead-wood to the shape of the ship's body.

BEARERS. Pieces of plank placed on the bolts which are driven through the standards or posts for the carpenters' stages to rest upon.

BEARING. An arc of the horizon intercepted between the nearest meridian and any distant object, either discovered by the eye and referred to a point on the compass, or resulting from finical proportion. There is the *true* or astronomical bearing, and the *magnetic* bearing. It is also the situation of any distant object, estimated with regard to the ship's position; and in this sense the object must bear either ahead, astern, abreast, on the bow, or on the quarter; if a ship sails with a side wind, a distant object is said to bear to leeward or to windward, on the lee quarter or bow, or on the weather quarter or bow.

BEARING BACKSTAYS AFT. To throw the breast backstays out of the cross-tree horns or outriggers and bear them aft. If not done, when suddenly bracing up, the cross-tree horn is frequently sprung or broken off.

BEARING BINNACLE. A small binnacle with a single compass, usually placed before the other. In line-of-battle ships it is generally placed on the fife-rail in the centre and foremost part of the poop.

BEARINGS. The widest part of a vessel below the plank-shear. The line of flotation which is formed by the water upon her sides when she sits upright with her provisions, stores, and ballast, on board in proper trim.

BEARINGS, To BRING TO HIS. Used in conversation for "to bring to reason." To bring an unruly subject to his senses, to know he is under control, to reduce to order.

BEAT. The verb means to excel, surpass, or overcome.

> "And then their ships could only follow,
> For we had beat them all dead hollow."

BEATEN BACK. Returning into port from stress of foul weather.

BEATING, or TURNING TO WINDWARD. The operation of making progress by alternate tacks at sea against the wind, in a zig-zag line, or transverse courses; beating, however, is generally understood to be turning to windward in a storm or fresh wind.

BEATING THE BOOBY. The beating of the hands from side to side in cold weather to create artificial warmth.

BEATING WIND. That which requires the ship to make her way by tacks; a baffling or contrary wind.

BEATSTER. One who *beats* or mends the Yarmouth herring-nets.

BEAT TO ARMS. The signal by drum to summon the men to their quarters.

BEAT TO QUARTERS. The order for the drummer to summon every one to his respective station.

BEAVER. A helmet in general, but particularly that part which lets down to allow of the wearer's drinking.

BECALM, To. To intercept the current of the wind in its passage to a ship, by means of any contiguous object, as a high shore, some other ship to windward, &c. At this time the sails remain in a sort of rest, and consequently deprived of their power to govern the motion of the ship. Thus one sail becalms another.

BECALMED. Implies that from the weather being calm, and not a breath of wind blowing, the sails hang loose against the mast.

BECHE DE MER. *See* TREPANG.

BECK [the Anglo-Saxon *becca*]. A small mountain-brook or rivulet, common to all northern dialects. A Gaelic or Manx term for a thwart or bench in the boat.

BECKET. A piece of rope placed so as to confine a spar or another rope; anything used to keep loose ropes, tackles, or spars in a convenient place; hence, beckets are either large hooks or short pieces of rope with a knot at one end and an eye in the other; or formed like a circular wreath for handles; as with cutlass hilts, boarding pikes, tomahawks, &c.; or they are wooden brackets, and probably from a corruption and misapplication of this last term arose the word becket, which seems often to be confounded with bracket. Also, a grummet either of rope or iron, fixed to the bottom of a block, for making fast the standing end of the fall.

BECKET, THE TACKS AND SHEETS IN THE. The order to hang up the weather-main and fore-sheet, and the lee-main and fore-tack, to the small knot and eye becket on the foremost-main and fore-shrouds, when the ship is close hauled, to prevent them from hanging in the water. A kind of large cleat seized on a vessel's fore or main rigging for the sheets and tacks to lie in when not required. Cant term for pockets—"Hands out of beckets, sir."

BED. Flat thick pieces of wood, lodged under the quarters of casks containing any liquid, and stowed in a ship's hold, in order to keep them bilge-free; being steadied upon the beds by means of wedges called quoins. The impression made by a ship's bottom on the mud on having been left by an ebb-tide. The bite made in the ground by the fluke of an anchor. A kind of false deck, or platform, placed on those decks where the guns were too low for the ports.—*Bed of a gun-carriage*, or *stool-bed*. The piece of wood between the cheeks or brackets which, with the intervention of the quoin, supports the breech of the gun. It is itself supported, forward, on the bed-bolt, and aft, generally with the intervention of an elevating-screw, on the rear axle-tree.

BED OR BARREL SCREWS. A powerful machine for lifting large

bodies, and placed against the gripe of a ship to be launched for starting her.

BED-BOLT. A horizontal bolt passing through both brackets of a gun-carriage near their centres, and on which the forward end of the stool-bed rests.

BEDDING A CASK. Placing dunnage round it.

BEDLAMERS. Young Labrador seals, which set up a dismal cry when they cannot escape their pursuers—and go madly after each other in the sea.

BED OF A MORTAR. The solid frame on which a mortar is mounted for firing. For sea-service it is generally made of wood; for land-service, of iron, except in the smaller natures. In mortar vessels as latterly fitted, the bed traverses on a central pivot over a large table or platform of wood, having under it massive india-rubber buffers, to moderate the jar from the discharge.—*Bed of a river*, that part of the channel of a stream over which the water generally flows, as also that part of the basin of a sea or lake on which the water lies.

BED-OF-GUNS. A nautical phrase implying ordnance too heavy for a ship's scantling, or a fort over-gunned.

BE-DUNDERED. Stupified with noise.

BEE. A ring or hoop of metal.—*Bees of the bowsprit.* (*See* BEE-BLOCKS.)

BEE-BLOCKS. Pieces of hard wood bolted to the outer end of the bowsprit, to reeve the fore-topmast stays through, the bolt, serving as a pin, commonly called bees.

BEEF. A figurative term for strength.—*More beef!* more men on.

BEEF-KID. A mess utensil for carrying meat from the coppers.

BEETLE. A shipwright's heavy mallet for driving the wedges called reeming irons, so as to open the seams in order to caulk. (*See* REEMING.)

BEETLE-HEAD. A large beetle, weighing 1000 lbs., swayed up by a crabwinch to a height, and dropped by a pincer-shaped hook; it is used in pile-driving.

BEFORE or ABAFT THE BEAM. The bearing of any object which is before or abaft a right line to the keel, at the midship section of a ship.

BEFORE THE MAST. The station of the working seamen, as distinguishing them from the officers.

BEGGAR-BOLTS. A contemptuous term for the missiles which were thrown by the galley-slaves at an approaching enemy.

BEHAVIOUR. The action and qualities of a ship under different impulses. Seamen speak of the manner in which she behaves, as if she acted by her own instinct.

BEIKAT. *See* BYKAT.

BEILED. A sea-term in the old law-books, apparently for moored.

BEING. *See* BING.

BELAY, To. To fasten a rope when it has been sufficiently hauled upon, by twining it several times round a cleat, belaying pin, or kevel, without hitching or seizing; this is chiefly applied to the running rigging, which needs to be so secured that it may be quickly let go in case of a squall or change of wind; there being several other expressions used for securing large ropes, as bitting, making fast, stoppering, &c.—*Belay there*, stop! that is enough!—*Belay that yarn*, we have had enough of it. Stand fast, secure all, when a hawser has been sufficiently hauled. When the topsails, or other sails have been hoisted taut up, or " belay the main-tack," &c.

BELAYING PINS. Small wooden or iron cylinders, fixed in racks in different parts of the ship, for belaying running ropes to.

BELEAGUER. To invest or closely surround an enemy's post, in such manner as to prevent all relief or communication.

BELFRY. An ornamental frame or shelter, under which the ship's bell is suspended.

BELL. *Strike the bell.* The order to strike the clapper against the bell as many times as there are half hours of the watch elapsed; hence we say it is two bells, three bells, &c., meaning there are two or three half-hours past. The watch of four hours is eight bells.

BELLA STELLA. A name used by old seamen for the cross-staff.

BELLATRIX. γ Orionis.

BELL-BUOY. A large can-buoy on which is placed, in wicker-work, a bell, which is sounded by the heaving and setting of the sea.

BELLIGERENT. An epithet applied to any country which is in a state of warfare.

BELLOWS. An old hand at the bellows. A colloquialism for a man up to his duty. "A fresh hand at the *bellows*" is said when a gale increases.

BELL-ROPE. A short rope spliced round a thimble in the eye of the bell-crank, with a double wall-knot crowned at its end.

BELLS. *See* WATCH.

BELL-TOP. A name applied to the top of a quarter-gallery, when the upper stool is hollowed away, or made like a rim.

BELL-WARE. A name of the *Zostera marina* (which see).

BELLY. The swell of a sail. The inner or hollow part of compass timber; the outside is called the *back*. To belly a sail is to inflate or fill it with the wind, so as to give a taut leech.—*Bellying canvas* is generally applied to a vessel going free, as when the belly and foot reefs which will not stand on a wind, are shaken out.—*Bellying to the breeze*, the sails filling or being inflated by the wind.—*Bellying to leeward*, when too much sail is injudiciously carried.

BELLY-BAND. A strip of canvas, half way between the close-reef and the foot of square sails, to strengthen them. Also applied to an army officer's sash.

BELLY-GUY. A tackle applied half-way up sheers, or long spars that require support in the middle. Frequently applied to masts that have been crippled by injudiciously setting up the rigging too taut.

BELLY-MAT. *See* PAUNCH-MAT.

BELLY-STAY. Used half-mast down when a mast requires support; as belly-guy, above.

BELOW. The opposite of *on* or *'pon deck*. Generally used to distinguish the watch on deck, and those off the watch.

BELT. A metaphorical term in geography for long and proportionally narrow encircling strips of land having any particular feature; as a belt of sand, a belt of hills, &c. It is, in use, nearly synonymous with zone. Also, to beat with a colt or rope's end.

BELTING. A beating; formerly given by a belt.

BELTS. The dusky streaks crossing the surface of the planet Jupiter, and supposed to be openings in his atmosphere.

BENCHES OF BOATS. The seats in the after-part whereon the passengers sit; properly stern-sheets, the others are athwarts, whereon the rowers sit.

BEND, To. To fasten one rope to another, or to an anchor. The term is also applied to any sudden or remarkable change in the direction of a river, and is then synonymous with bight or loop.—*Bend a sail* is to extend or make it fast to its proper yard or stay. (*See* GRANNY'S BEND.) Also, *bend to your oars*, throw them well forward.

BEND. The chock of the bowsprit.

BENDER. A contrivance to bend small cross-bows, formerly used in the navy. Also, "look out for a *bender*," or "strike out for a bend," applied to coiling the hempen cables.

BENDING ROPES, is to join them together with a bowline knot, and then make their own ends fast upon themselves; not so secure as splicing, but sooner done, and readiest, when it is designed to take them asunder again. There are several bends, as *Carrick-bend*, *hawser-bend*, *sheet-bend*, *bowline-bend*, &c.

BENDING THE CABLE. The operation of clinching, or tying the cable to the ring of its anchor. The term is still used for shackling chain-cables to their anchors.

BEND-MOULD. A mould made to form the futtocks in the square body, assisted by the *rising-square* and *floor-hollow*.

BEND ON THE TACK. In hoisting signals, that piece of rope called the distant line—which keeps the flags so far asunder that they are not confused. Also, in setting free sails, the studding-sail tack, &c.

BEND-ROLL. A rest formerly used for a heavy musket.

BENDS. The thickest and strongest planks on the outward part of a ship's side, between the plank-streaks on which men set their feet in climbing up. They are more properly called wales, or wails. They are reckoned from the water, and are distinguished by the titles of *first, second,* or *third bend.* They are the chief strength of a ship's sides, and have the beams, knees, and foot-hooks bolted to them. Bends are also the frames or ribs that form the ship's body from the keel to the top of the side, individualized by each particular station. That at the broadest part of the ship is denominated the *midship-bend* or *dead-flat.*

BE-NEAPED. The situation of a vessel when she is aground at the height of spring-tides. (*See* NEAPED.)

BENGAL-LIGHT. *See* BLUE-LIGHT.

BENJY. A low-crowned straw-hat, with a very broad brim.

BENK. A north-country term for a low bank, or ledge of rock; probably the origin of *bunk,* or sleeping-places in merchant vessels. (*See* BUNK.)

BENN. A small kind of salmon; the earliest in the Solway Frith.

BENT. The trivial name of the *Arundo arenaria,* or coarse unprofitable grass growing on the sea-shore.

BENTINCK-BOOM. That which stretches the foot of the fore-sail in many small square-rigged merchantmen; particularly used in whalers among the ice, with a reefed fore-sail to see clearly ahead. The tack and sheet are thus dispensed with, a spar with tackle amidships brings the leeches taut on a wind. It is principally worked by its bowline.

BENTINCKS. Triangular courses, so named after Captain Bentinck, by whom they were invented, but which have since been superseded by storm stay-sails. They are still used by the Americans as try-sails.

BENTINCK-SHROUDS. Formerly used; extending from the weather-futtock staves to the opposite lee-channels.

BENT ON A SPLICE. Going to be married.

BERG. A word adopted from the German, and applied to the features of land distinguished as steppes, banquettes, shelves, terraces, and parallel roads. (*See* ICEBERG.)

BERGLE. A northern name for the wrasse.

BERM. In fortification, a narrow space of level ground, averaging about a foot and a half in width, generally left between the foot of the exterior slope of the parapet and the top of the escarp; in permanent fortification its principal purpose is to retain the earth of the parapet, which, when the latter is deformed by fire or by weather, would otherwise fall into the ditch; in field fortification it also serves to protect the escarp from the pressure of a too imminent parapet.

BERMUDA SAILS. *See* 'MUGIAN.

BERMUDA SQUALL. A sudden and strong wintry tempest experienced in the Atlantic Ocean, near the Bermudas; it is preceded by heavy clouds, thunder, and lightning. It belongs to the Gulf Stream, and is felt, throughout its course, up to the banks of Newfoundland.

BERMUDIANS. Three-masted schooners, built at Bermuda during the war of 1814; they went through the waves without rising to them, and consequently were too ticklish for northern stations.

BERNAK. The barnacle goose (*Anser bernicla*).

BERSIS. A species of cannon formerly much used at sea.

BERTH. The station in which a ship rides at anchor, either alone, or in a fleet; as, she lies in a good berth, *i.e.* in good anchoring ground, well sheltered from the wind and sea, and at a proper distance from the shore and other vessels.—*Snug berth*, a place, situation, or establishment. A sleeping berth.—*To berth a vessel*, is to fix upon, and put her into the place she is to occupy.—*To berth a ship's company*, to allot to each man the space in which his hammock is to be hung, giving the customary 14 inches in width.—*To give a berth*, to keep clear of, as to give a point of land a wide berth, is to keep at a due distance from it.

BERTH. The room or apartment where any number of the officers, or ship's company, mess and reside; in a ship of war there is commonly one of these between every two guns as the mess-places of the crew.

BERTH AND SPACE. In shipbuilding, the distance from the moulding edge of one timber to the moulding edge of the next timber. Same as room and space, or timber and space.

BERTH-DECK. The 'tween decks.

BERTHER. He who assigns places for the respective hammocks to hang in.

BERTHING. The rising or working up of the planks of a ship's sides; as berthing up a bulkhead, or bringing up in general. Berthing also denotes the planking outside, above the sheer-strake, and is called the berthing of the quarter-deck, of the poop, or of the forecastle, as the case may be.

BERTHING OF THE HEAD. *See* HEAD-BOARDS.

BERVIE. A haddock split and half-dried.

BERWICK SMACK. The old and well-found packets of former days, until superseded by steamers. (*See* BARRACK SMACK.)

BESET IN ICE. Surrounded with ice, and no opening for advance or retreat, so as to be obliged to remain immovable.

BESIEGE, To. To endeavour to gain possession of a fortified place defended by an enemy, by directing against it a connected series of offensive military operations.

BESSY-LORCH. A northern name of the *Gobio fluviatilis* or gudgeon.

BEST BOWER. *See* BOWER-ANCHOR.

BETELGUESE. The lucida of Orion, α Orionis, and a standard Greenwich star of the first magnitude.

BETHEL. *See* FLOATING-BETHEL.

BETTY MARTIN. *See* MARTIN.

BETWEEN DECKS. The space contained between any two whole decks of a ship.

BETWIXT WIND AND WATER. About the line of load immersion of the ship's hull; or that part of the vessel which is at the surface of the water.

BEVEL. An instrument by which bevelling angles are taken. Also a sloped surface.

BEVELLING. Any alteration from a square in hewing timber, as taken by the bevel, bevelling rule, or bevelling boards.—*A standing bevelling* is that made without, or outside a square; an *under-bevelling* within; and the angle is optionally acute or obtuse. In shipbuilding, it is the art of hewing a timber with a proper and regular curve, according to a mould which is laid on one side of its surface.

BEVELLING-BOARD. A piece of board on which the bevellings or angles of the timbers are described.

BEVERAGE. A West India drink, made of sugar-cane juice and water.

BEWPAR. The old name for buntin, still used in navy office documents.

BEWTER. A northern name for the black-wak, or bittern.

BEZANT. An early gold coin, so called from having been first coined at Byzantium.

BIBBS. Pieces of timber bolted to the hounds of a mast, to support the tressel-trees.

BIBLE. A hand-axe. Also, a squared piece of freestone to grind the deck with sand in cleaning it; a small holystone, so called from seamen using them kneeling.

BIBLE-PRESS. A hand rolling-board for cartridges, rocket, and port-fire cases.

BICKER, OR BEAKER. A flat bowl or basin for containing liquors, formerly made of wood, but in later times of other substances. Thus Butler:

> "And into pikes, and musqueteers,
> Stamp beakers, cups, and porringers."

BID-HOOK. A small kind of boat-hook.

BIEL-BRIEF. The bottomry contract in Denmark, Sweden, and the north of Germany.

BIERLING. An old name for a small galley.

BIFURCATE. A river is said to bifurcate, or to form a fork, when it divides into two distinct branches, as at the heads of deltas and in fluvial basins.

BIGHT. A substantive made from the preterperfect tense of *bend*. The space lying between two promontories or headlands, being wider and smaller than a gulf, but larger than a bay. It is also used generally for any coast-bend or indentation, and is mostly held as a synonym of shallow bay.

BIGHT. The loop of a rope when it is folded, in contradistinction to the end; as, her anchor hooked the bight of our cable, *i.e.* caught any part of it between the ends. The bight of his cable has swept our anchor, *i.e.* the bight of the cable of another ship as she ranged about has entangled itself about the flukes of our anchor. Any part of the chord or curvature of a rope between the ends may be called a bight.

BIG-WIGS. A cant term for the higher officers.

BILANCELLA. A destructive mode of fishing in the Mediterranean, by means of two vessels towing a large net stretched between them.

BILANCIIS DEFERENDIS. A writ directed to a corporation, for the carrying of weights to such a haven, there to weigh the wool that persons, by our ancient laws, were licensed to transport.

BILANDER. A small merchant vessel with two masts, particularly distinguished from other vessels with two masts by the form of her main-sail, which is bent to the whole length of her yard, hanging fore and aft, and inclined to the horizon at an angle of about 45°. Few vessels are now rigged in this manner, and the name is rather indiscriminately used.

BILBO. An old term for a flexible kind of cutlass, from Bilboa, where the best Spanish sword-blades were made. Shakspeare humorously describes Falstaff in the buck-basket, like a good bilbo, coiled hilt to point.

BILBOES. Long bars or bolts, on which iron shackles slid, with a padlock at the end; used to confine the legs of prisoners in a manner similar to the punishment of the stocks. The offender was condemned to irons, more or less ponderous according to the nature of the offence of which he was guilty. Several of them are yet to be seen in the Tower of London, taken in the Spanish Armada. Shakspeare mentions Hamlet thinking of a kind of fighting,

> "That would not let me sleep: methought, I lay
> Worse than the mutines in the bilboes."

BILCOCK. The northern name for the water-rail.

BILGE, OR BULGE. That part of the floor in a ship—on either side of the keel—which approaches nearer to a horizontal than to a perpendicular direction, and begins to round upwards. It is where the floors and second futtocks unite, and upon which the ship would rest if laid on the ground; hence, when a ship receives a fracture in this part, she is said to be bilged or bulged.—*Bilge* is also the largest circumference of a cask, or that which extends round by the bung-hole.

BILGE-BLOCKS.   *See* SLIDING BILGE-BLOCKS.

BILGE-COADS.   In launching a ship, same with sliding-planks.

BILGE-FEVER.   The illness occasioned by a foul hold.

BILGE-FREE.   A cask so stowed as to rest entirely on its beds, keeping the lower part of the bilge at least the thickness of the hand clear of the bottom of the ship, or other place on which it is stowed.

BILGE-KEELS.   Used for vessels of very light draught and flattish bottoms, to make them hold a better wind, also to support them upright when grounded.   The *Warrior* and other iron-clads are fitted with bilge-keels.

BILGE-KEELSONS.   These are fitted inside of the bilge, to afford strength where iron, ores, and other heavy cargo are shipped.   Otherwise they are the same as sister-keelsons.

BILGE-PIECES.   Synonymous with *bilge-keels.*

BILGE-PLANKS.   Certain thick strengthenings on the inner and outer lines of the bilge, to secure the *shiftings* as well as bilge-keels.

BILGE-PUMP.   A small pump used for carrying off the water which may lodge about the lee-bilge, so as not to be under the action of the main pumps.   In a steamer it is worked by a single link off one of the levers.

BILGE-TREES.   Another name for bilge-coads.

BILGE-WATER.   The rain or sea-water which occasionally enters a vessel, and running down to her floor, remains in the bilge of the ship till pumped out, by reason of her flat bottom, which prevents it from going to the well of the pump; it is always (especially if the ship does not leak) of a dirty colour and disgusting penetrating smell.   It seems to have been a sad nuisance in early voyages; and in the earliest sea-ballad known (*temp.* Hen. VI.) it is thus grumbled at:—

> "A sak of strawe were there ryght good,
>   For som must lyg theym in theyr hood,
>   I had as lefe be in the wood
>   W'out mete or drynk.
>   For when that we shall go to bedde,
>   The pumpe was nygh our bedde's hedde;
>   A man were as good to be dede
>   As smell thereof ye stynk."

The mixture of tar-water and the drainings of sugar cargo is about the worst perfume known.

BILL.   A weapon or implement of war, a pike or halbert of the English infantry.   It was formerly carried by sentinels, whence Shakspeare humorously made Dogberry tell the sleepy watchmen to have a care that their bills be not stolen. Also, the point or tapered extremity of the fluke at the arm of an anchor. Also a point of land, of which a familiar instance may be cited in the Bill of Portland.

BILLAT. A name on the coast of Yorkshire for the piltock or coal-fish, when it is a year old.

BILL-BOARDS. Doubling under the fore-channels to the water-line, to protect the planking from the bill of the anchor.

BILLET. The allowance to landlords for quartering men in the royal service; the lodging-money charged by consuls for the same.

BILLET-HEAD. A carved prow bending in and out, contrariwise to the fiddle-head (scroll-head). Also, a round piece of wood fixed in the bow or stern of a whale-boat, about which the line is veered when the whale is struck. Synonymous with bollard.

BILLET-WOOD. Small wood mostly used for dunnage in stowing ships' cargoes, also for fuel, usually sold by the fathom; it is 3 feet 4 inches long, and 7½ inches in compass.

BILL-FISH. *See* GAR-FISH.

BILL-HOOK. A species of hatchet used in wooding a ship, similar to that used by hedgers.

BILL OF EXCHANGE. A means of remitting money from one country to another. The receiver must present it for acceptance to the parties on whom it is drawn without loss of time, he may then claim the money after the date specified on the bill has elapsed.

BILL OF FREEDOM. A full pass for a neutral in time of war.

BILL OF HEALTH. A certificate properly authenticated by the consul, or other proper authority at any port, that the ship comes from a place where no contagious disorder prevails, and that none of the crew, at the time of her departure, were infected with any such dis-temper. Such constitutes a *clean* bill of health, in contradistinction to a *foul* bill.

BILL OF LADING. A memorandum by which the master of a ship acknowledges the receipt of the goods specified therein, and promises to deliver them, in like good condition, to the consignee, or his order. It differs from a charter-party insomuch as it is given only for a single article or more, laden amongst the sundries of a ship's cargo.

BILL OF SALE. A written document by which the property of a vessel, or shares thereof, are transferred to a purchaser.

BILL OF SIGHT, OR OF VIEW. A warrant for a custom-house officer to examine goods which had been shipped for foreign parts, but not sold there.

BILL OF STORE. A kind of license, or custom-house permission, for re-importing unsold goods from foreign ports duty free, within a speci-fied limit of time.

BILLOWS. The surges of the sea, or waves raised by the wind; a term more in use among poets than seamen.

BILLS. The ends of compass or knee timber.

BILLY BOY or BOAT. A Humber or east-coast boat, of river-barge build, and a try-sail; a bluff-bowed north-country trader, or large one-masted vessel of burden.

BINARY SYSTEM. When two stars forming a double-star are found to revolve about each other.

BIND. A quantity of eels, containing 10 sticks of 25 each.

BINDINGS. In shipbuilding, a general name for the beams, knees, clamps, waterways, transoms, and other connecting parts of a ship or vessel.

BINDING-STRAKES. Thick planks on the decks, in midships, between the hatchways. Also the principal strakes of plank in a vessel, especially the sheer-strake and wales, which are bolted to the knees and shelf-pieces.

BING. A heap; an old north-country word for the sea-shore, and sometimes spelled *being*.

BINGE, To. To rinse, or bull, a cask.

BINGID. An old term for locker.

BINK. *See* BENK.

BINN. A sort of large locker, with a lid on the top, for containing a vessel's stores: bread-binn, sail-binn, flour-binn, &c.

BINNACLE (formerly BITTACLE). It appears evidently to be derived from the French term *habittacle*, a small habitation, which is now used for the same purpose by the seamen of that nation. The binnacle is a wooden case or box, which contains the compass, and a light to illuminate the compass at night; there are usually three binnacles on the deck of a ship-of-war, two near the helm being designed for the man who steers, weather and lee, and the other amidships, 10 or 12 feet before these, where the quarter-master, who conns the ship, stands when *steering*, or going with a free wind. (*See* CONN.)

BINNACLE-LIGHT. The lamp throwing light upon the compass-card.

BINOCLE. A small binocular or two-eyed telescope.

BIOR-LINN. Perhaps the oldest of our terms for boat. (*See* BIRLIN.)

BIRD-BOLT. A species of arrow, short and thick, used to kill birds without piercing their skins.

BIRD'S-FOOT SEA-STAR. The *Palmipes membranaceus*, one of the *Arteriadœ*, with a flat thin pentagonal body, of a bright scarlet colour.

BIRD'S NEST. A round top at a mast-head for a look-out station. A smaller crow's-nest. Chiefly used in whalers, where a constant look-out is kept for whales. (*See* EDIBLE BIRD'S-NEST.)

BIREMIS. In Roman antiquity, a vessel with two rows of oars.

BIRLIN. A sort of small vessel or galley-boat of the Hebrides; it is fitted with four to eight long oars, but is seldom furnished with sails.

BIRT. A kind of turbot.

BIRTH-MARKS. A ship must not be loaded above her birth-marks, for, says a maritime proverb, a master must know the capacity of his vessel, as well as a rider the strength of his horse.

BISCUIT [*i.e. bis coctus*, or Fr. *bis-cuit*]. Bread intended for naval or military expeditions is now simply flour well kneaded, with the least possible quantity of water, into flat cakes, and slowly baked. Pliny calls it *panis nauticus;* and of the *panis militaris*, he says that it was heavier by one-third than the grain from which it was made.

BISHOP. A name of the great northern diver (*Colymbus glacialis*).

BISMER. A name of the stickleback (*Gasterosteus spinachia*).

BIT. A West Indian silver coin, varying from 4*d.* to 6*d.* In America it is 12½ cents, and in the Spanish settlements is equal with the real, or one-eighth of a dollar. It was, in fact, Spanish money cut into bits, and known as "cut-money."

BITE. Is said of the anchor when it holds fast in the ground on reaching it. Also, the hold which the short end of a lever has upon the thing to be lifted. Also, to bite off the top of small-arm cartridges.

BITTER. Any turn of a cable about the bitts is called a bitter. Hence a ship is "brought up to a bitter" when the cable is allowed to run out to that stop.

BITTER-BUMP. A north-country name for the bittern.

BITTER-END. That part of the cable which is abaft the bitts, and therefore within board when the ship rides at anchor. They say, "Bend to the bitter-end" when they would have that end bent to the anchor, and when a chain or rope is paid out to the bitter-end, no more remains to be let go. The bitter-end is the clinching end—sometimes that end is bent to the anchor, because it has never been used, and is more trustworthy. The first 40 fathoms of a cable of 115 fathoms is generally worn out when the inner end is comparatively new.

BITT-HEADS. The upright pieces of oak-timber let in and bolted to the beams of two decks at least, and to which the cross-pieces are let on and bolted. (*See* BITTS.)

BITT-PINS. Similar to belaying-pins, but larger. Used to prevent the cable from slipping off the cross-piece of the bitts, also to confine the cable and messenger there, in heaving in the cable.

BITTS. A frame composed of two strong pieces of straight oak timber, fixed upright in the fore-part of a ship, and bolted securely to the beams, whereon to fasten the cables as she rides at anchor; in ships of war there are usually two pairs of cable-bitts, and when they are both used at once the cable is said to be double-bitted. Since the introduction of chain-cables, bitts are coated with iron, and vary in their shapes. There are several other smaller bitts; as, the topsail-sheet bitts, paul-bitts, carrick-bitts, windlass-bitts, winch-bitts, jear-bitts, riding-bitts, gallows-bitts, and fore-brace bitts.

BITT-STOPPER. One rove through the knee of the bitts, which nips the cable on the bight: it consists of four or five fathoms of rope tailed out nipper fashion at one end, and clench-knotted at the other. The old bitt-stopper, by its running loop on a standing end, bound the cable down in a bight abaft the bitts—the tail twisted round the fore part helped to draw it still closer. It is now disused—chain cables having superseded hemp.

BITT THE CABLE, To. To put it round the bitts, in order to fasten it, or slacken it out gradually, which last is called veering away.

BIVOUAC. The resting for the night in the open-air by an armed party, instead of encamping.

BIZE. A piercing cold wind from the frozen summits of the Pyrenees.

BLACKAMOOR. A thoroughly black negro.

BLACK-BIRD CATCHING. The slave-trade.

BLACK-BIRDS. A slang term on the coast of Africa for a cargo of slaves.

BLACK-BOOK OF THE ADMIRALTY. An imaginary record of offences. Also, a document of great authority in naval law, as it contains the ancient admiralty statutes and ordinances.

BLACK-FISH. A common name applied by sailors to many different species of cetaceans. The animal so called in the south seas belongs to the genus *Globiocephalus*. It is from 15 to 20 feet long, and occurs in countless shoals.

BLACK-FISHER. A water-poacher: one who kills salmon in close-time.

BLACK-FISHING. The illegally taking of salmon, under night, by means of torches and spears with barbed prongs.

BLACK-HEAD. The pewitt-gull (*Larus ridibundus*).

BLACK-HOLE. A place of solitary confinement for soldiers, and tried in some large ships.

BLACK-INDIES. Newcastle, Sunderland, and Shields.

BLACKING. For the ship's bends and yards. A good mixture is made of coal-tar, vegetable-tar, and salt-water, boiled together, and laid on hot.

BLACKING DOWN. The tarring and blacking of rigging; or the operation of blacking the ship's sides with tar or mineral blacking.

BLACK-JACK. The ensign of a pirate. Also, a capacious tin can for beer, which was formerly made of waxed leather. In 1630 Taylor wrote—

> "Nor or of blacke-jacks at gentle buttry-bars,
> Whose liquor oftentimes breeds household wars."

BLACK-LIST. A record of misdemeanours impolitically kept by some officers for their private use—the very essence of private tyranny, now forbidden.

BLACK-LOCK. A trout thought to be peculiar to Lough Melvin, on the west of Ireland.

BLACK SHIPS. The name by which the English builders designate those constructed of teak in India.

BLACK SOUTH-EASTER. The well-known violent wind at the Cape of Good Hope, in which the vapoury clouds called the Devil's Table-cloth appear on Table Mountain.

BLACK SQUALL. This squall, although generally ascribed to the West Indies, as well as the white squall, may be principally ascribed to a peculiar heated state of the atmosphere near land. As blackey, when interrogated about weather, generally observes, "Massa, look to leeward," it may be easily understood that it is the condensed air repelled by a colder medium to leeward, and driven back with condensed electricity and danger. So it is sudden to Johnny Newcomes, who lose sails, spars, and ships, by capsizing.

BLACK'S THE WHITE OF MY EYE. When Jack avers that no one can say this or that of him. It is an indignant expression of innocence of a charge.

BLACK-STRAKE. The range of plank immediately above the wales in a ship's side; they are always covered with a mixture of tar and lamp-black, which not only preserves them from the heat of the sun and the weather, but forms an agreeable variety with the painted or varnished parts above them. Vessels with no ports have frequently two such strakes—one above, the other below the wales, the latter being also called the diminishing strake.

BLACK-STRAP. The dark country wines of the Mediterranean. Also, bad port, such as was served for the sick in former times.

BLACK-TANG. The sea-weed *Fucus vesicolosus*, or tangle.

BLACKWALL-HITCH. A sort of tackle-hook guy, made by putting the bight of a rope over the back of the hook, and there jamming it by the standing part. A mode of hooking on the bare end of a rope where no length remains to make a cat's-paw.

BLACK WHALE. The name by which the right whale of the south seas (*Balœna australis*) is often known to whalemen.

BLAD. A term on our northern coasts for a squall with rain.

BLADDER-FISH. A term for the tetrodon. (*See* BALLOON-FISH.)

BLADE OF AN ANCHOR. That part of the arm prepared to receive the palm.

BLADE or WASH OF AN OAR. Is the flat part of it which is plunged into the water in rowing. The force and effect in a great measure depends on the length of this part, when adequate force is applied. When long oars are used, the boat is generally single-banked, so that the fulcrum is removed further from the rower. Also, the motive part of the screw-propeller.

BLAE, or BLEA. The alburnum or sap-wood of timber.

BLAKE. Yellow. North of England.

BLANK. Level line mark for cannon, as point-blank, equal to 800 yards. It was also the term for the white mark in the centre of a butt, at which the arrow was aimed.

BLANKET. The coat of fat or blubber under the skin of a whale.

BLARE, To. To bellow or roar vehemently.—*Blare*, a mixture of hair and tar made into a kind of paste, used for tightening the seams of boats.

BLARNEY. Idle discourse; obsequious flattery.

BLASHY. Watery or dirty; applied to weather, as "a blashy day," a wet day. In parlance, trifling or flimsy.

BLAST. A sudden and violent gust of wind: it is generally of short duration, and succeeded by a fine breeze.—*To blast*, to blow up with gunpowder.

BLAST-ENGINE. A ventilating machine to draw off the foul air from the hold of a ship, and induce a current of fresh air into it.

BLATHER. Thin mud or puddle. Also, idle nonsense.

BLAY. A name of the bleak.

BLAZE, To. To fire away as briskly as possible. To blaze away is to keep up a running discharge of fire-arms. Also, to spear salmon. Also, in the woods, to mark a tree by cutting away a portion of its outer surface, thus leaving a patch of whiter internal surface exposed, to call attention or mark a track.

BLAZERS. Applied to mortar or bomb vessels, from the great emission of flame to throw a 13-inch shell.

BLAZING STARS. The popular name of comets.

BLEAK. The *Leuciscus alburnus* of naturalists, and the fresh-water sprat of Isaak Walton. The name of this fish is from the Anglo-Saxon *blican*, owing to its shining whiteness—its lustrous scales having long been used in the manufacture of false pearls.

BLEEDING THE MONKEY. The monkey is a tall pyramidal kid or bucket, which conveys the grog from the grog-tub to the mess—stealing from this *in transitu* is so termed.

BLEED THE BUOYS. To let the water out.

BLENNY. A small acanthopterygious fish (*Blennius*).

BLETHER-HEAD. A blockhead.

BLETHERING. Talking idle nonsense; insolent prate.

BLIND. A name on the west coast of Scotland for the pogge, or miller's-thumb (*Cottus cataphractus*).

BLIND. Everything that covers besiegers from the enemy. (*See* ORILLON.)

BLINDAGE. A temporary wooden shelter faced with earth, both in siege works and in fortified places, against splinters of shells and the like.

BLIND-BUCKLERS. Those fitted for the hawse-holes, which have no aperture for the cable, and therefore used at sea to prevent the water coming in.

BLIND-HARBOUR. One, the entrance of which is so shut in as not readily to be perceived.

BLIND-ROCK. One lying just under the surface of the water, so as not to be visible in calms.

BLIND-SHELL. One which, from accident or bad fuze, has fallen without exploding, or one purposely filled with lead, as at the siege of Cadiz. Also used at night filled with fuze composition, and enlarged fuze-hole, to indicate the range.

BLIND-STAKES. A sort of river-weir.

BLINK OF THE ICE. A bright appearance or looming (the iceberg reflected in the atmosphere above it), often assuming an arched form; so called by the Greenlanders, and by which reflection they always know when they are approaching ice long before they see it. In Greenland blink means iceberg.

BLIRT. A gust of wind and rain.

BLOAT, To. To dry by smoke; a method latterly applied almost exclusively to cure herrings or bloaters.—*Bloated* is also applied to any half-dried fish.

BLOCCO. Paper and hair used in paying a vessel's bottom.

BLOCK. (In mechanics termed a pulley.) Blocks are flattish oval pieces of wood, with sheaves in them, for all the running ropes to run in. They are used for various purposes in a ship, either to increase the mechanical power of the ropes, or to arrange the ends of them in certain places on the deck, that they may be readily found when wanted; they are consequently of various sizes and powers, and obtain various names, according to their form or situation, thus:—A single block contains only one sheave or wheel. A double block has two sheaves. A treble or threefold block, three, and so on. A long-tackle or fiddle-block has two sheaves—one below the other, like a fiddle. Cistern or sister block for topsail lifts and reef tackles. Every block is composed of three, and generally four, parts:—(1.) The shell, or outside wooden part. (2.) The sheave, or wheel, on which the rope runs. (3.) The pin, or axle, on which the sheave turns. (4.) The strop, or part by which the block is made fast to any particular station, and is usually made either of rope or of iron. Blocks are named and distinguished by the ropes which they carry, and the uses they serve for, as bowlines, braces, clue-lines, halliards, &c. &c. They are either made or morticed (which see).

BLOCK. The large piece of elm out of which the figure is carved at the head of the ship.

BLOCKADE. The investment of a town or fortress by sea and land; shutting up all the avenues, so that it can receive no relief.—*To blockade a port* is to prevent any communication therewith by sea, and cut off supplies, in order to compel a surrender when the provisions and ammunition are exhausted.—*To raise a blockade* is to discontinue it.—Blockade is violated by egress as well as by ingress. Warning on the spot is sufficient notice of a blockade *de facto*. Declaration is useless without actual investment. If a ship break a blockade, though she escape the blockading force, she is, if taken in any part of her future voyage, captured *in delicto*, and subject to confiscation. The absence of the blockading force removes liability, and *might* (in such cases) overrules *right*.

BLOCK AND BLOCK. The situation of a tackle when the blocks are drawn close together, so that the mechanical power becomes arrested until the tackle is again overhauled by drawing the blocks asunder. Synonymous with chock-a-block.

BLOCKHOUSE. A small work, generally built of logs, to protect adjacent ports. Blockhouses were primarily constructed in our American colonies, because they could be immediately built from the heavy timber felled to clear away the spot, and open the lines of fire. The ends were simply crossed alternately and pinned. Two such structures, with a space of 6 feet for clay, formed, on an elevated position, a very formidable casemated work. The slanting overhanging roof furnished excellent cover in lieu of loop-holes for musketry.

BLOCK-MAKER. A manufacturer of blocks.

BLOCKS. The several transverse pieces or logs of timber, piled in plane, on which a ship is built, or to place her on for repair: they consist of solid pieces of oak laid on the ground-ways.

BLOCKS, FIXED. *See* FIXED BLOCKS.

BLOOD-SUCKERS. Lazy fellows, who, by skulking, throw their proportion of labour on the shoulders of their shipmates.

BLOODY FLAG. A large red flag.

BLOOM. A peculiar warm blast of wind; a term used in iron-foundries.

BLORE. An old word for a stiff gale.

BLOUT. A northern term for the sudden breaking-up of a storm. Blout has been misused for blirt.

BLOW. Applied to the breathing of whales and other cetaceans. The expired air from the lungs being highly charged with moisture, which condenses at the temperature of the atmosphere, appears like a column of steam.

BLOW. A gale of wind.

BLOWE. A very old English word for scold or revile, still in use, as when a man receives a good blowing-up.

BLOW-HOLES. The nostrils of the cetaceans, situated on the highest part of the head. In the whalebone whales they form two longitudinal slits, placed side by side. In the porpoises, grampuses, &c., they are united into a single crescentic opening.

BLOW HOME. The wind does not cease or moderate till it comes past that place, blowing continuously over the land and sea with equal velocity. In a naval sense, it does not blow home when a sea-wind is interrupted by a mountainous range along shore.

BLOWING GREAT GUNS AND SMALL ARMS. Heavy gales; a hurricane.

BLOWING HARD. Said of the wind when it is strong and steady.

BLOWING THE GRAMPUS. Throwing water over a sleeper on watch.

BLOWING WEATHER. A nautical term for a continuance of strong gales. (*See* GALE.)

BLOWN COD. A split cod, half dried by exposure to the wind. *Blown* is also frequently applied to bloated herrings, when only partly cured. Also, a cod-fish rises to the surface, and is easily taken, if blown. By being hauled nearly up, and the hook breaking, it loses the power for some time of contracting the air-bladder, and thus dies head out of water.

BLOWN ITSELF OUT. Said of a falling gale of wind.

BLOW OFF, To. To clear up in the clouds.

BLOW-OFF-PIPE, in a steamer, is a pipe at the foot of each boiler, communicating with the sea, and furnished with a cock to open and shut it.—*Blowing-off* is the act or operation of using the blow-off-pipe to cleanse a marine steam-engine of its brine deposit; also, to clear the boilers of water, to lighten a ship if grounded.

BLOW-OUT. Extravagant feasting regardless of consequences.

BLOW OVER, (IT WILL). Said of a gale which is expected to pass away quickly.

BLOW-PIPE. An engine of offence used by the Araucanians and Borneans, and with the latter termed *sumpitan :* the poisoned arrow, *sumpit,* will wound at the distance of 140 or more yards. The arrow is forced through (like boys' pea-shooters) by the forcible and sudden exertion of the lungs. A wafer can be hit at 30 yards to a certainty, and small birds are unerringly stunned at 30 yards by pellets of clay.

BLOW THE GAFF. To reveal a secret; to expose or inform against a person.

BLOW-THROUGH VALVE. A valve admitting steam into the condenser, in order to clear it of air and water before starting the engine.

BLOW UP, To. To abuse angrily.

BLOW-VALVE. A valve by which the first vacuum necessary for starting a steam-engine is produced.

BLUBBER. The layer of fat in whales between the skin and the flesh, which is flinched or peeled off, and boiled for oil, varying from 10 to 20 inches in thickness. (*See* SEA-BLUBBER.)

BLUBBER FORKS AND CHOPPERS. The implements with which blubber is "made off," or cut for stowing away.

BLUBBER-GUY. A large rope stretched from the main to the fore mast head of whalers, to which the speck-falls are attached for the operation of flensing.

BLUE. *Till all's blue :* carried to the utmost—a phrase borrowed from the idea of a vessel making out of port, and getting into blue water. —*To look blue,* to be surprised, disappointed, or taken aback, with a countenance expressive of displeasure.

BLUE-JACKETS. The seamen as distinguished from the marines.

BLUE LIGHT. A pyrotechnical preparation for signals by night. Also called Bengal light.

BLUE-LIGHTISM. Affected sanctimoniousness.

BLUE MOON. An indefinite period.

BLUE-NOSE. A general term for a native of Nova Scotia.

BLUE PETER. The signal for sailing when hoisted at the fore-top-mast head; this well-known flag has a blue ground with a white square in the centre.

BLUE PIGEON. A nickname for the sounding lead.

BLUE WATER. The open ocean.

BLUFF. An abrupt high land, projecting almost perpendicularly into the sea, and presenting a bold front, rather rounded than cliffy in outline, as with the headland.

BLUFF-BOWED. Applied to a vessel that has broad and flat bows —that is, full and square formed : the opposite of lean.

BLUFF-HEADED. When a ship has but a small rake forward on, being built with her stem too straight up.

BLUNDERBUSS. A short fire-arm, with a large bore and wide mouth, to scatter a number of musket or pistol bullets or slugs.

BLUNK. A sudden squall, or stormy weather.

BLUSTROUS. Stormy: also said of a braggadocio.

BO. Abbreviation of *boy*. A familiar epithet for a comrade, derived probably from the negro.

BOADNASH. Buckhemshein coins of Barbary.

BOANGA. A Malay piratical vessel, impelled by oars.

BOARD. Certain offices under the control of the executive government, where the business of any particular department is carried on : as the Board of Admiralty, the Navy Board, Board of Ordnance, India Board, Board of Trade, &c. Also, timber sawn to a less thickness than plank : all broad stuff of under $1\frac{1}{2}$ inch in thickness. (*See* PLANK.) Also, the space comprehended between any two places when the ship changes her course by tacking; or, it is the line over which she runs between tack and tack when working to windward, or sailing against the direction of the wind.—*To make a good board.* To sail in a straight line when close-hauled, without deviating to leeward. —*To make short boards,* is to tack frequently before the ship has run any great length of way.—*To make a stern board,* is when by a current, or any other accident, the vessel comes head to wind, the helm is shifted, and she has fallen back on the opposite tack, losing what she had gained, instead of having advanced beyond it. To make a stern board is frequently a very critical as well as seamanlike operation, as in very close channels. The vessel is allowed to run up into the wind until she has shot up to the weather danger; the helm is then shifted, and with all aback forward, she falls short off on the opposite tack. Such is also achieved at anchor in club-hauling (which see).—*To board a ship,* is to enter her in a hostile manner in order to take forcible possession of her, either from the attacking ship or by armed boats. The word *board* has various other applications among seamen :—*To go aboard* signifies to go into the ship.—*To slip by the board,* is to slip down a ship's side.—*To board it up,* is to beat up, sometimes on one tack and sometimes on another.—*The weather-board* is the side of the ship which is to windward.—*By the board,* close to a ship's deck.

BOARD AND BOARD. Alongside, as when two ships touch each other.

BOARDERS. Sailors appointed to make an attack by boarding, or to repel such attempt from the enemy. Four men selected from each gun were generally allotted as boarders, also to trim sails, tend pumps, repair rigging, &c.

BOARD HIM. A colloquialism for I'll ask, demand, or accost him. Hence Shakspeare makes Polonius say of Hamlet,
"I'll board him presently."
To make acquaintance with; to fasten on.

BOARD HIM IN THE SMOKE. To take a person by surprise, as by firing a broadside, and boarding in the smoke.

BOARDING. An assault made by one vessel on another, by entering her in battle with a detachment of armed men.

BOARDING-BOOK. A register which has for its object the recording all particulars relative to every ship boarded, a copy of which is transmitted to the admiral under whose orders the ship is employed. (*See* GUARD-BOOK.)

BOARDING-NETTINGS. A framework of stout rope-netting placed where necessary, to obstruct an enemy's boarders.

BOARDING-PIKE. A defensive lance against boarders.

BOARDLINGS. Flippant understrappers of the admiralty and navy-boards.

BOARD OF TRADE. A committee of the Privy Council appointed for the consideration of commercial matters.

BOAT. A small open vessel, conducted on the water by rowing or sailing. The construction, machinery, and even the names of boats, are very different, according to the various purposes for which they are calculated, and the services on which they are employed. Thus we have the long-boat and the jolly-boat, life-boat and gun-boat, but they will appear under their respective appellations.—*A bold boat*, one that will endure a rough sea well.—*Man the boat*, send the crew in to row and manage it.

BOATABLE. Water navigable for boats and small river-craft.

BOAT-BUOYS. Means added to increase the buoyancy of life-boats, &c.

BOAT-CHOCKS. Clamps of wood upon which a boat rests when stowed on a vessel's deck.

BOAT-CLOAK. A mantle for the officer going on duty; when left in the boat it is in the coxswain's charge.

BOAT-DAVIT. A curved piece of timber with a sheave at its outer end, which projects over the boat's stern, while the inner end is shipped into a cleat on each side of the bottom of the boat, for weighing anchors when needed. (*See* DAVIT.)

BOAT-FAST. *See* PAINTER.

BOAT-GEER. A general name for the rigging and furniture of a boat.

BOAT-HIRE. Expenses for the use of shore-boats.

BOAT-HOOK. An iron hook with a straight prong at its hinder part; it is fixed upon a pole, by the help of which a boat is either pulled to, or pushed off from, any place, and is capable of holding on by anything.

BOATILA. A narrow-sterned, flat-bottomed boat of the Gulf of Manar.

BOATING. Transporting men, munitions, or goods, in boats.

BOAT-KEEPER. One of the boat's crew who remains in charge of her during the absence of the others. In small vessels he is sometimes called the boatman.

BOAT-NAILS. Those supplied for the carpenter's use are of various lengths, generally rose-headed, square at the points, and made both of copper and iron. (*See* NAILS.)

BOAT-ROPE. A separate rope veered to the boat to be towed at the ship's stern.

BOAT'S CREW. The men appointed as the crew of any particular boat, as the barge's crew, cutter's crew, &c.

BOAT'S-GRIPES. Lashings for the secure stowage of boats. (*See* GRIPES.)

BOAT-SKIDS. Portable pieces of plank used to prevent chafing when a boat is hoisted or lowered. (*See* SKIDS.)

BOATSWAIN. The officer who superintends the boat-sails, ship's-sails, rigging, canvas, colours, anchors, cables and cordage, committed to his charge. He ought also to take care that the blocks and running ropes are regularly placed to answer the purposes for which they are intended, and that the sails are properly fitted to their yards and stays, and well-furled or reefed when occasion requires. He pipes the hands to their several duties, seeing that they attend his call, and ought to be in every way a thorough seaman. Although termed boatswain, the boats are not in his charge. They, with the spars, &c., and stores for repair, belong to the carpenter. The boatswain is the officer of the first lieutenant; he gives no order, but reports defects, and carries out the will of his superior.

BOATSWAIN-BIRD. *Phaeton œthereus,* a tropical bird, so called from its sort of whistle. It is distinguished by two long feathers in the tail, called the marling-spike.

BOATSWAIN-CAPTAIN. An epithet given by certain popinjays in the service to such of their betters as fully understand the various duties of their station.

BOATSWAIN'S MATE. Is an assistant to the boatswain, who had the peculiar command of the long-boat. He summons the watch or crew by his whistle, and during his watch looks to the decks, and has peculiar calls for "grog," "'bout ship," "pipe to breakfast," "sweepers," &c.

BOATSWAIN'S STORE-ROOM. Built expressly for boatswain's stores, on a platform or light deck.

BOATSWAIN'S YEOMAN. *See* YEOMAN.

BOAT THE ANCHOR. Place the anchor inboard in the boat.

BOAT THE OARS. Put them in their proper places fore and aft on the thwarts ready for use.

BOB. A knot of worms on a string, used in fishing for eels; also colloquially, it means a berth.—*Shift your bob*, to move about, to dodge, to fish.—*Bear a bob*, make haste, be brisk.

BOB. The ball or balance-weight of a clock's pendulum; the weight attached to the plumb-line.

BOBBERY. A disturbance, row, or squabble; a term much used in the East Indies and China.

BOBBING. A particular method of fishing for eels—

> "His hook he bated with a dragon's tail,
> And sat upon a rock, and bobb'd for whale."

BOBBING ABOUT. Heaving and setting without making any way.

BOBBLE. The state of waves when dashing about without any regular set or direction, as in cross tides or currents.

BOBSTAY-COLLARS. These are made with large rope, and an eye spliced in each end; they are secured round the bowsprit, on the upper side, with a rose lashing. They are almost entirely superseded by iron bands.

BOBSTAY-HOLES. Those cut through the fore-part of the knee of the head, between the cheeks, for the admission of the bobstay; they are not much used now, as chain bobstays are almost universal, which are secured to plates by shackles.

BOBSTAY-PLATES. Iron plates by which the lower end of the bobstay is attached to the stem.

BOBSTAYS. Ropes or chains used to confine the bowsprit downward to the stem or cut-water. They are fitted in various ways. Their use is to counteract the strain of the foremast-stays, which draw it upwards. The bowsprit is also fortified by shrouds from the bows on each side, which are all very necessary, as the fore-mast and the upper spars on the main-mast are stayed and greatly supported by the bowsprit.

BOCCA. [Sp. *boca*, mouth.] Is a term used both in the Levant, and on the north coast of South America, or the Spanish Main, for a mouth or channel into any port or harbour, or the entrance into a sound which has a passage out by a contrary way.—*Bocca Tigris*, Canton River.

BODIES. The figure of a ship, abstractedly considered, is divided into different parts or figures, each of which has the appellation body, as fore-body, midship-body, square-body, &c.

BODKIN. A dirk or dagger, a word still in use, though Johnson says it is the oldest acceptation of it. It is the *bodekin* of Chaucer; and Shakspeare makes Hamlet ask who would bear the ills of life,

> "When he himself might his quietus make
> With a bare bodkin?"

BODY. The principal corps of an army, or the main strength of a fleet.

BODY, OF A PLACE. In fortification, the space inclosed by the enceinte, or line of bastions and curtains.

BODY-HOOPS. Those which secure the aris pieces of a made mast.

BODY-PLAN. The draught of a proposed ship, showing the breadth and timbers; it is a section supposed to cut the vessel through the broadest part; it is otherwise called the plan of projection.

BODY-POST. An additional stern-post introduced at the fore-part of an aperture cut in the dead-wood in a ship fitted with a screw-propeller.

BOG. A marsh, or a tract of land, which from its form and impermeable bottom retains stagnant water. (*See* QUAGMIRE.)

BOG-BLUTER. A northern name for the bittern, from its habit of thrusting its bill into marshy places.

BOG-TROTTER. Any one who lives among marshy moors, but generally applied to the Emeralders.

BOGUE, To. To drop off from the wind. To edge away to leeward with the wind; not holding a good wind, and driving very much to leeward. Used only to clumsy inferior craft.

BOGUE. Mouth of a river; hence disembogue. Bogue forts, China.

BOHEMIAN. A conceited dawdler in his duties. Shakspeare ridicules Simple as a Bohemian Tartar; both of which terms were applied to gipsies.

BOILER. Of a steam-engine, made of wrought iron, or copper-plates, which being partly filled with water, and having fire applied to the outside, generates steam to supply the engine.

BOILERS. Termed coppers; the ship's cooking utensils, of iron or copper.

BOILING. The "whole boiling" means the entire quantity, or whole party; applied to number or quantity. A contemptuous epithet.

BOLD-BOW. A broad bluff bow.

BOLDERING WEATHER. Cloudy and thundery.

BOLD-SHORE. A steep coast where the water, deepening rapidly, admits the near approach of shipping without the danger of grounding.

BOLD-TO. Applied to land; the same as steep-to.

BOLE. A small boat.

BOLIDE. A name for aërolite (which see).

BOLINE. *See* BOWLINE. *Clavus in navi.*

BOLLAN. The Manx or Gaelic term for the fish old-wife.

BOLLARD. A thick piece of wood on the head of a whale-boat, round which the harpooner gives the line a turn, in order to veer it steadily, and check the animal's velocity. Also a strong timber fixed vertically into the ground, part being left above it, on which to fasten ropes.

Also a lighter sort of dolphin for attaching vessels to. Wharves have bollards to which vessels are secured when alongside.

BOLLARD-TIMBERS. Two pieces of oak, usually called knight-heads (which see).

BOLLING or BOWLING AWAY. Going with a free wind.

BOLME. An old term for a waterman's pole or boom.

BOLOTO. A small boat of the Philippines and Moluccas.

BOLSTERS. Small cushions or bags of tarred canvas, used to preserve the stays from being chafed by the motion of the masts, when the ship pitches at sea. Pieces of soft wood covered with canvas, placed on the tressel-trees, for the eyes of the rigging to rest upon, and prevent a sharp nip. Also pieces of oak timber fayed to the curvature of the bow, under the hawse-holes, and down upon the upper cheek, to prevent the cable from rubbing against the cheeks.—*Bolsters* for sheets, tacks, &c., are small pieces of fir or oak, fayed under the gunwale, or other part, with the outer surface rounded to prevent chafing.— *Bolsters*, for the anchor lining. Solid pieces of oak bolted to the ship's side at the fore part of the fore-chains on which the stanchions are fixed that receive the anchor lining.

BOLT. A cylindrical pin of iron or copper to unite the different parts of a vessel, varied in form according to the places where they are required. In shipbuilding square ones are used in frame-fastening; the heads of all bolts are round, saucer, or collared.—*Bolt of the irons*, which runs through three pairs of shackles.—*Drift* or *drive-bolts* are used to drive out others. —*Bay-bolts*, have jags or barbs on each side, to keep them from flying out of their holes.—*Clench-bolts* are clenched with rivetting hammers.— *Fend* or *fender bolts*, made with long and thick heads, and struck into the outermost bends of the ship, to save her sides from bruises.—*Forelock-bolts* have at the end a forelock of iron driven in, to keep them from starting back.—*Set-bolts* are used for forcing the planks, and bringing them close together.—*Ring-bolts* are used for the bringing to of the planks, and those parts whereto are fastened the breeches and tackle of the guns.—*Scarp-bolts* and *keel-bolts*, pointed, not clinched, used for false keel or temporary purposes.—*Bringing-to bolts*, fitted with an eye at one end, and a nut and screw at the other, for bringing to the ends at the stem, &c.—*To bolt*, to start off, to run away.

BOLT-BOAT. An old term for a boat which makes good weather in a rough sea.

BOLTING TIMBERS. Those on each side of the stem, continued up for the security of the bowsprit. (*See* KNIGHT-HEADS.)

BOLT OF CANVAS. The piece or roll of 39 yards in which it is supplied, but which usually measure about 40 yards in length; it is generally from 22 to 30 inches wide.

BOLT-ROPE. A rope sewed all round the edge of the sail, to prevent the canvas from tearing. The bottom part of it is called the foot-rope, the sides leech-ropes, and if the sail be oblong or square the upper part is called the head-rope; the stay or weather rope of fore-and-aft sails is termed the luff.

BOLTROPE-NEEDLE. A strong needle for stitching the sail to the bolt-ropes.

BOLT-SPRIT. *See* Bowsprit.

BOLT-STRAKE. Certain strakes of plank which the beam fastenings pass through.

BOLT-TOE. The cock of a gun-lock.

BOMB [formerly *bomber*, from *bomba*]. The mortar of bomb-vessels.

BOMB or MORTAR VESSELS. Small ships fortified for throwing bombs into a fortress; said to be the invention of M. Reyneau, and to have been first used at the bombardment of Algiers in 1682. Until then it had been judged impracticable to bombard a place from the sea.

BOMBALO. A delicate kind of sand-eel taken in quantities at Bombay.

BOMBARD. A piece of ordnance, anciently in use before the introduction of more complete cannon with improved gunpowder, propelling iron balls. Its bore, for the projection of stone shot, sometimes exceeded 20 inches in diameter, but was short; its chamber, for containing the powder-charge, being about as long, but much narrower both within and without. There were also very diminutive varieties of it. It has been vaguely called by some writers *basilisk*, and by the Dutch *donderbass*. Used to assail a town, fortress, or fleet, by the projection of shells from mortars. It was also the name of a barrel, or large vessel for liquids; hence, among other choice epithets, Prince Henry calls that "tun of man," Falstaff, a "huge bombard of sack." Also, a Mediterranean vessel, with two masts like the English ketch.

BOMB-BED BEAMS. The beams which support the bomb-bed in bomb-vessels.

BOMB-BEDS. *See* Bed of a Mortar.

BOMBO. Weak cold punch.

BOMB-SHELL. A large hollow ball of cast-iron, for throwing from mortars (distinguished by having ears or lugs, by which to lift it with the shell-hooks into the mortar), and having a hole to receive the fuze, which communicates ignition to the charge contained in the shell. (*See* Fuze.)

BOME-SPAR [a corruption of *boom*]. A spar of a larger kind.

BOMKIN. *See* Bumkin.

BONA FIDE. In good faith; without subterfuge—*Bona fides* is a condition necessary to entitle to the privilege of pre-emption in our admiralty courts.

BONAVENTURE. The old outer mizen, long disused.

BONDING. *See* WAREHOUSING-SYSTEM.

BONDING-POND. An inclosed space of water where the tide flows, for keeping timber in.

BOND-MAN. A harsh method in some ships, in keeping one man bound for the good behaviour of another on leave.

BOND OF BOTTOMRY. An authority to borrow money, by pledging the keel or bottom of the ship. (*See* BOTTOMRY.)

BONE, To. To seize, take, or apprehend. A ship is said to carry a bone in her mouth and cut a feather, when she makes the water foam before her.

BON GRACE. Junk-fenders; for booming off obstacles from a ship's sides or bows. (*See* BOW-GRACE.)

BONITO. The *Thynnus pelamys*, a fish of the scomber family, commonly about 2 feet long, with a sharp head, small mouth, full eyes, and a regular semi-lunar tail.

BONI-VOCHIL. The Hebridean name for the great northern diver (*Colymbus glacialis*).

BONNET. An additional part laced to the foot of the jibs, or other fore-and-aft sails, in small vessels in moderate weather, to gather more wind. They are commonly one-third of the depth of the sails they belong to. Thus we say, "Lace on the bonnet," or "Shake off the bonnet." Bonnets have lately been introduced to secure the foot of an upper-topsail to a lower-topsail yard. The unbonnetted sail is for storm service. Bonnet, in fortification, is a raised portion of the works at any salient angle, having the same plan, but 10 or 12 feet more command than the work on which it is based. It assists in protecting from enfilade, and affords a plunging fire.

BONNET-FLOOK. A name of the well-known flat-fish, brill, pearl, or mouse-dab; the *Pleuronectes rhombus*.

BONXIE. The Shetland name for the skua-gull (*Cataractes vulgaris*). Also a very general northern term for sea-birds.

BONY-FISH. One of the names of the hard-head (which see).

BOOBY. A well-known tropical sea-bird, *Sula fusca*, of the family *Pelecanidæ*. It is fond of resting out of the water at night, even preferring an unstable perch on the yard of a ship. The name is derived from the way in which it allows itself to be caught immediately after settling. The direction in which they fly as evening comes on often shows where land may be found.

BOOBY-HATCH. A smaller kind of companion, but readily removable; it is in use for merchantmen's half decks, and lifts off in one piece.

BOOK. A commercial term for a peculiar packing of muslins, bastas, and other stuffs.—*Brought to book*, made to account.

BOOKING. A reprimand.

BOOKS. (*See* SHIP'S BOOKS.) Official documents.

BOOM. A long spar run out from different places in the ship, to extend or boom out the foot of a particular sail; as, jib-boom, flying jib-boom, studding-sail booms, driver or spanker boom, ringtail-boom, main-boom, square-sail boom, &c. A ship is said to come booming forwards when she comes with all the sail she can make. Boom also denotes a cable stretched athwart the mouth of a river or harbour, with yards, top-masts, or stout spars of wood lashed to it, to prevent the entrance of an enemy.—*To top one's boom*, is to start off.—*To boom off*, to shove a boat or vessel away with spars.

BOOMAGE. A duty levied to compound for harbour dues, anchorage, and soundage.

BOOM-BOATS. Those stowed on the booms.

BOOM-BRACE PENDANT. A rope attached to the extremity of a studding-sail boom, and leading down on deck; it is used to counteract the pressure of the sail upon the boom.

BOOM-COVER. The tarpaulin, or painted, cover over the spars.

BOOMING. Sound of distant guns; it is often, but wrongly, applied to the hissing or whistling of shot.

BOOM-IRONS. Are metal rings fitted on the yard-arms, through which the studding-sail booms traverse; there is one on each top-sail yard-arm, but on the lower yards a second, which opens to allow the boom to be triced up; it is one-fourth from the yard-arms, and holds down the heel of the boom when it is rigged out.

BOOM-JIGGER. A tackle used in large ships, for rigging out or running in the top-mast studding-sail booms.

BOOMKIN. *See* BUMKIN.

BOOM-MAINSAIL. *See* MAINSAIL.

BOOMS. A space where the spare spars are stowed; the launch being generally stowed between them.

BOOPAH. A Tongatabou canoe with a single outrigger.

BOOTHYR. An old term, denoting a small river vessel.

BOOT-TOPPING. The old operation of scraping off the grass, slime, shells, &c., which adhere to the bottom, near the surface of the water, and daubing it over with a mixture of tallow, sulphur, and resin, as a temporary protection against worms. This is chiefly performed where there is no dock or other commodious situation for breaming or careening, or when the hurry of a voyage renders it inconvenient to have the whole bottom properly trimmed and cleansed. The term is now applied to sheathing a vessel with planking over felt.

BOOTY. That sort of prize which may be distributed at the capstan-head, or at once.

BOOZE. A carouse; hence, *boozy*, elevated by liquor.

BORA. A very violent wind experienced in the upper part of the Adriatic Sea, but which fortunately is of no great duration.

BORACCHIO [Sp. *borracho*, drunk]. A skin for holding wine or water, usually a goat's. Used in the Levant. A skin-full; literally, gorged with wine.

BORASCA. A storm, with thunder and lightning.

BORD. The sea-coast, an old term. Formerly meant the side, edge, or brim; hence, as applied to a ship, to throw overboard, is to cast anything over the side of the vessel.

BORDELS. An old word for houses built along a strand. In the old play called the "Ladies' Privilege," it is said:—"These gentlemen know better to cut a caper than a cable, or board a pink in the bordels than a pinnace."

BORDER. A term referring to the nature of the vegetation on the margin of a stream or lake, or to artificial works constructed along the banks.

BORD YOU. A saying of a man waiting, to one who is drinking, meaning that he claims the next turn.

BORE. A sudden and rapid flow of tide in certain inlets of the sea; as the monstrous wave in the river Hoogley, called *bahu* by the natives, which rolls in with the noise of distant thunder at flood-tide. It occurs from February to November, at the new and full moon. Its cause has not been clearly defined, although it probably arises from the currents during spring-tides, acting on a peculiar conformation of the banks and bed of the river; it strikes invariably on the same part of the banks, majestically rolling over to one side, and passing on diagonally to the other with impetuous violence. The bore also occurs in England, near Bristol; and in America, in several rivers, but especially in the Bay of Fundy, where at the river Petticodiac the tide rises 76 feet. It also occurs in Borneo and several rivers in the East. (*See* HYGRE.) Also, the interior cavity of a piece of ordnance, generally cylindrical in shape, except when a part of it is modified into a chamber.

BOREAS. A classical name for the north wind, still in use; indeed a brackish proverb for extreme severity of weather says—"Cold and chilly, like Boreas with an iceberg in each pocket."

BORE DOWN. Sailed down from to windward.

BORHAME. A northern term for the flounder.

BORING. In Arctic seas, the operation of forcing the ship through loose ice under a heavy press of sail; at least attempting the chance of advantage of cracks or openings in the pack.

BORN WITH A SILVER SPOON IN HIS MOUTH. Said of a person who, by birth or connection, has all the usual obstacles to advancement cleared away for him. Those who toil unceasingly for preferment, and toil in vain, are said to have been born with a wooden ladle. Again, the silver-spoon gentry are said to come on board through the cabin windows; those less favoured, over the bows, or through the hawse-holes.

BORNE. Placed on the books for victuals and wages; also supernumerary and "for rank."

BORROW, To. To approach closely either to land or wind; to hug a shoal or coast in order to avoid adverse tide.

BORT. The name given to a long fishing-line in the Shetland Isles.

BOSS. A head of water, or reservoir. Also the apex of a shield.

BOTARGA. The roe of the mullet pressed flat and dried; that of commerce, however, is from the tunny, a large fish of passage which is common in the Mediterranean. The best kind comes from Tunis; it must be chosen dry and reddish. The usual way of eating it is with olive-oil and lemon-juice.

BOTCH, To. To make bungling work.

BOTE'S-CARLE. An old term for the coxswain of a boat.

BOTHERED. Getting among adverse currents, with shifting winds.

BOTH SHEETS AFT. The situation of a square-rigged ship that sails before the wind, or with the wind right astern. It is said also of a half-drunken sailor rolling along with his hands in his pockets and elbows square.

BOTTE. An old English term for boat, and assuredly the damaged boat into which Prospero is turned adrift by Shakspeare.

BOTTLE-BUMP. The bittern, so called on our east coast.

BOTTLE-CHARTS. Those on which the set of surface currents are exhibited, derived from papers found in bottles which have been thrown overboard for that purpose, and washed up on the beach, or picked up by other ships.

BOTTLE-NOSE, OR BOTTLE-NOSED WHALE. A name applied to several of the smaller cetaceans of the northern seas, more especially to the *Hyperoodon rostratus.*

BOTTOM. A name for rich low land formed by alluvial deposits: but in a general sense it denotes the lowest part of a thing, in contradistinction to the top or uppermost part. In navigation, it is used to denote as well the channel of rivers and harbours as the body or hull of a ship. Thus, in the former sense we say "a gravelly bottom, clayey bottom," &c., and in the latter sense "a British bottom, a Dutch bottom," &c. By statute, certain commodities imported in foreign bottoms pay a duty called "petty customs," over and above what they are liable to if imported in British bottoms. Bottom of a ship or boat is that part which is below the wales.

BOTTOM-CLEAN. Thoroughly clean, free from weeds, &c.

BOTTOM-PLANK. That which is placed between the garboard strake and lower back-strake.

BOTTOMREE, or BOTTOMRY-BOND. The contract of bottomry is a negotiable instrument, which may be put in suit by the person to whom it is transferred : it is in use in all countries of maritime commerce and interests. A contract in the nature of a mortgage of a ship, when the owner of it borrows money to enable him to carry on the voyage, and pledge the keel, or bottom of the ship, as a security for the repayment. If the ship be lost the lender also loses his whole money ; but if it return in safety then he shall receive back his principal, and also the premium stipulated to be paid, however it may exceed the usual or legal rate of interest. The affair is, however, only regarded as valid upon the ground of necessity; and thus exacting more than the interest allowed by law is not deemed usury.

BOTTOMRY PREMIUM. A high rate of interest charged on the safety of the ship—the lender losing his whole money if she be lost.

BOTTOM-WIND. A phenomenon that occurs on the lakes in the north of England, especially Derwent Water, which is often agitated by swelling waves without any apparent cause.

BOUCHE. *See* BUSH.

BOUGE or BOWGE AND CHINE, or BILGE AND CHIMB. The end of one cask stowed against the bilge of another. To prepare a ship for the purpose of sinking it.

BOUILLI. Termed by seamen bully-beef; disliked because all the substance is boiled away to enrich the cook's grease-tub, and the meat is useless as food; rejected even by dogs. In one ship of war it produced mutiny; vide Adams' account of the *Bounty* miseries. It is also the name given to highly cooked meat in hermetically sealed tin canisters.

BOULDER-HEAD. A work against the encroachment of the sea, made of wooden stakes.

BOULDERS. Stones worn and rounded by the attrition of the waves of the sea: the word, on the authority of Hunter, was considered a technical term in the fourteenth century, as appears in a warrant of John of Gaunt for the repair of Pontefract Castle—" De peres, appelés buldres, a n're dit chastel come nous semblerez resonables pur la defense de meisme."

BOULEPONGES. A drink to which many of the deaths of Europeans in India were ascribed; but in Bernier's " Travels," in the train of Aurungzebe, in 1664, we are informed that " bouleponge is a beverage made of arrack, sugar, lemon-juice, and a little muscadine." Probably a corruption of bowls of punch. (*See* PUNCH.)

BOUNCE. The larger dog-fish.

BOUNCER. A gun which kicks violently when fired.

BOUND. Destined for a particular service. Intended voyage to a place.—*Ice-bound.* Totally surrounded with ice.—*Tide-bound,* or beneaped. (*See* NEAP.)—*Wind-bound.* Prevented from sailing by contrary wind.—*Where are you bound to?*—*i.e.* To what place are you going?—*Bound on a cruise.* A corruption of the old word *bowne,* which is still in use on the northern coasts, and means to make ready, to prepare.

BOUNTY. A sum of money given by government, authorized by act of parliament or royal proclamation, to men who voluntarily enter into the army or navy; and the widow of such volunteer seaman killed or drowned in the service was entitled to a bounty equal to a year's pay.

BOUNTY-BOATS. Those which fished under the encouragement of a bounty from government.

BOUNTY-LIST. A register of all persons who have received the bounty to which they are entitled after having passed three musters in the service.

BOURN. *See* BURN.

BOURSE. A place where merchants congregate. An exchange.

BOUSE. *See* BOWSE.

BOUT. A turn, trial, or round. An attack of illness; a convivial meeting.—*'Bout ship,* the brief order for "about ship."

BOW. The fore-end of a ship or boat; being the rounding part of a vessel forward, beginning on both sides where the planks arch inwards, and terminating where they close, at the rabbet of the stem or prow, being larboard or starboard from that division. A bold bow is broad and round; a lean bow, narrow and thin.—*On the bow.* An arc of the horizon (not exceeding 45°) comprehended between some distant object and that point of the compass which is right ahead. Four points on either bow is met by four points before the beam.

BOW. An astronomical instrument formerly used at sea, consisting of only one large graduated arc of 90°, three vanes, and a shank or staff. Also the bow of yew, a weapon of our early fleets.

BOW. *She bows to the breeze;* when the sails belly out full, and the ship inclines and goes ahead, pitching or bowing over the blue waves.

BOW-BYE. The situation of a ship when, in stays, she falls back off the wind again, and gets into irons, which demands practical seamanship for her extrication. This was deemed a lubberly act in our fleets of old.

BOW-CHASERS. Two long chase-guns placed forward in the bow-ports to fire directly ahead, and being of small bore for their length, carry shot to a great distance.

BOWD-EATEN. An old expression for eaten by weevils.

BOWER-ANCHORS. Those at the bows and in constant working use. They are called best and small, not from a difference of size, but as to the bow on which they are placed; starboard being the best bower, and port the small bower. The appropriated cables assume the respective names. (*See also* SPARE-ANCHOR, SHEET, STREAM, COASTING, KEDGE, &c.)

BOW-FAST. A rope or chain for securing a vessel by the bow. (*See* FAST.)

BOWGE, OR BOUGE. An old term for bilge.

BOWGER. A name given in the Hebrides to the coulter-neb, or puffin (*Fratercula arctica*).

BOWGRACE. A kind of frame or fender of old junk, placed round the bows and sides of a ship to prevent her receiving injury from floating ice or timbers. (*See* BONGRACE.)

BOWING. An injury done to yards by too much topping, and letting their weights hang by the lifts. The state of a top-sail yard when it arches in the centre from hoisting it too tautly. Also of the mast when it bellies or is crippled by injudiciously setting up the rigging too taut.

BOWING THE SEA. Meeting a turbulent swell in coming to the wind.

BOWLINE. A rope leading forward which is fastened to a space connected by bridles to cringles on the leech or perpendicular edge of the square sails: it is used to keep the weather-edge of the sail tight forward and steady when the ship is close hauled to the wind; and which, indeed, being hauled taut, enables the ship to come nearer to the wind. Hence the ship sails on a bowline, or stands on a taut bowline.—*To check or come up a bowline* is to slacken it when the wind becomes large or free.—*To sharp or set taut a bowline* is to pull it as taut as it can well bear.

BOWLINE-BEND. The mode of bending warps or hawsers together by taking a bowline in the end of one rope, and passing the end of the other through the bight, and making a bowline upon it.

BOWLINE-BRIDLE. The span attached to the cringles on the leech of a square sail to which the bowline is toggled or clinched.

BOWLINE-CRINGLE. An eye worked into the leech-rope of a sail; usually in that of a foresail two, a mainsail three, and the fore-topsails three, but the main-topsail four. By these the sails are found in the dark, by feeling alone.

BOWLINE HAUL. A hearty and simultaneous bowse. (*See* ONE! TWO!! THREE!!!) In hauling the bowline it is customary for the leading man to veer, and then haul, three times in succession, singing out one, two, three—at the last the weight of all the men is thrown in together: this is followed by "belay, oh!" When the bowlines are reported "bowlines hauled, sir," by the officer in command of the fore-part of the ship, the hands, or the watch, return to their duties.

BOWLINE-KNOT. That by which the bowline-bridles were fastened to the cringles: the bowline-knot is made by an involution of the end and a bight upon the standing part of a rope. A further involution makes what is termed a bowline on a bight. It is very difficult to explain by words:—holding the rope some distance from the end by the left hand, the end held in the right is laid on the main part, and by a twist given. screw-fashion to the right, a loop or kink is formed inclosing this end, which is then passed behind, and back in the same direction with the former, and then jammed home. It is rapidly done, easily undone, and one of the most seamanlike acts, exhibiting grace as well as power. It can be made by a man with but one arm.

BOW-LINES. In shipbuilding, longitudinal curves representing the ship's fore-body cut in a vertical section.

BOWLING-ALONG. Going with a free wind.

BOW-LOG TIMBERS. A provincial name for hawse-wood.

BOWMAN. In a single-banked boat he who rows the foremost oar and manages the boat-hook; called by the French "brigadier de l'embarcation." In double-banked boats there are always two bowmen. Also an archer, differently pronounced.

BOW-OAR. The foremost oar or oars, in pulling a boat.

BOW-PIECES. The ordnance in the bows; also in building.

BOW-RAIL. · A rail round the bows.

BOWSE, To. To pull upon any body with a tackle, or complication of pullies, in order to remove it, &c. Hauling upon a tack is called "bowsing upon a tack," and when they would have the men pull all together, they cry, "Bowse away." Also used in setting up rigging, as "Bowse away, starboard;" "Bowse away, port." It is, however, mostly a gun-tackle term.—*Bowse up the jib*, a colloquialism to denote the act of tippling: it is an old phrase, and was probably derived from the Dutch *buyzen*, to booze.

BOWSPRIT, OR BOLTSPRIT. A large spar, ranking with a lower-mast, projecting over the stem; beyond it extends the jib-boom, and beyond that again the flying jib-boom. To these spars are secured the stays of the fore-mast and of the spars above it; on these stays are set the fore and fore-topmast stay-sails, the jib, and flying-jib, which have a most useful influence in counterbalancing the pressure of the after-sails, thereby tending to force the ship ahead instead of merely turning her round. In former times underneath these spars were set a sprit-sail, sprit-topsail, &c.

BOWSPRIT, RUNNING. In cutter-rigged vessels. (*See* CUTTER.)

BOWSPRIT-BITTS. Are strong upright timbers secured to the beams below the deck; they have a cross-piece bolted to them, the inner end of the bowsprit steps between them, and is thus prevented from slipping in. The cross-piece prevents it from canting up.

BOWSPRIT-CAP. The crance or cap on the outer end of the bowsprit, through which the jib-boom traverses.

BOWSPRIT-GEAR. A term denoting the ropes, blocks, &c., belonging to the bowsprit.

BOWSPRIT-HEART. The heart or block of wood used to secure the lower end of the fore-stay, through which the inner end of the jib-boom is inserted. It is seldom, if ever, used now, an iron band round the bowsprit, with an eye on each side for the fore-stays, being preferred.

BOWSPRIT-HORSES. The ridge-ropes which extend from the bowsprit-cap to the knight-heads.

BOWSPRIT-LADDER. Skids over the bowsprit from the beak-head in some ships, to enable men to run out upon the bowsprit.

BOWSPRIT-NETTING. The netting placed just above a vessel's bowsprit, for stowing away the fore-topmast stay-sail; it is usually lashed between the ridge-ropes.

BOWSPRIT-SHROUDS. Strong ropes or chains leading from nearly the outer end of the bowsprit to the luff of the bow, giving lateral support to that spar.

BOW-STAVES. Early supplied to our men-of-war.

BOW-TIMBERS. Those which form the bow of the ship.

BOX. The space between the back-board and the stern-post of a boat, where the coxswain sits.

BOXES OF THE PUMPS. Each ordinary pump has an upper and lower box, the one a fixture in the lower part of its chamber, the other attached to the end of the spear or piston-rod; in the centre of each box is a valve opening upwards.

BOXHAULING. Is an evolution by which a ship is veered sharp round on her heel, when the object is to avoid making a great sweep. The helm is put a-lee, the head-yards braced flat aback, the after-yards squared, the driver taken in, and the head-sheets hauled to windward; when she begins to gather stern-way the helm is shifted and sails trimmed. It is only resorted to in emergencies, as a seaman never likes to see his ship have sternway. With much wind and sea this evolution would be dangerous.

BOXING. A square piece of dry hard wood, used in connecting the frame timbers. Also, the projection formerly left at the hawse-pieces, in the wake of the hawse-holes, where the planks do not run through; now disused. The stem is said to be boxed when it is joined to the fore end of the keel by a side scarph. (*See* BOXING OF RUDDER.)

BOXING OFF. Is performed by hauling the head-sheets to windward, and laying the head-yards flat aback, to pay the ship's head out of the wind, when the action of the helm alone is not sufficient for that purpose; as when she is got "in irons."

BOX THE COMPASS, To. Not only to repeat the names of the thirty-two points in order and backwards, but also to be able to answer any and all questions respecting its divisions.

BOYART. An old term for a hoy.

BOYAUX. The zig-zags or tortuous trenches in the approach of a besieger.

BOYER. A sloop of Flemish construction, with a raised work at each end.

BRAB. The sheaf of the young leaves of the Palmyra palm (and also of the cocoa-nut), from which sinnot or plait for hats is made.

BRAB-TREE. The Palmyra palm.

BRACE. The braces are ropes belonging to all the yards of a ship; two to each yard, rove through blocks that are stropped to the yards, or fastened to pendants, seized to the yard-arms. Their use is either to square or traverse the yards horizontally; hence, *to brace the yard*, is to bring it to either side by means of the braces. In shipbuilding, braces are plates of iron, copper, or mixed metal, which are used to bind efficiently a weakness in a vessel; as also to receive the pintles by which the rudder is hung.

BRACE ABACK. To brace the yards in, so as to lay the sails aback. —*To brace about*, to turn the yards round for the contrary tack, or in consequence of a change of wind.—*To brace abox*, a manœuvre to insure casting the right way, by bracing the head-yards flat aback (not square).—*To brace by*, to brace the yards in contrary directions to each other on the different masts, to effect the stopping of the vessel. (*See* COUNTER-BRACING.)—*To brace in*, to lay the yard less oblique, as for a free wind, or nearly square.—*To brace round*, synonymous with brace about.—*To brace sharp*, to cause the yards to have the smallest possible angle with the keel, for the ship to have head-way: deemed generally to form an angle of 20° with the keel.—*To brace to*, is to check or ease off the lee braces, and round in the weather ones, to assist in the manœuvre of tacking or wearing.—*To brace up*, or *brace sharp up*, to lay the yards more obliquely fore and aft, by easing off the weather-braces and hauling in the lee ones, which enables a ship to lie as close to the wind as possible.

BRACE OF SHAKES. A moment: taken from the flapping of a sail. I will be with you before it shakes thrice.

BRACE PENDANTS. Are lengths of rope, or now more generally chain, into which the yard-arm brace-blocks are spliced. They are used in the merchant service to save rope, to give the blocks more freedom for slewing to their work, but chiefly because when the brace is let go, the falling chain will overhaul it, making it easier to haul in the other brace.

BRACE UP AND HAUL AFT! The order usually given after being hove-to, with fore or main topsail square or aback, and jib-sheet flowing, *i.e.* haul aft jib-sheet, brace up the yards which had been squared, for the purpose of heaving to.

BRACK. The Manx or Gaelic name for mackerel.

BRACKETS. Short crooked timbers resembling knees, fixed in the frame of a ship's head to support the gratings; they likewise served to support and ornament the gallery. Also, the two vertical side-pieces of the carriage of any piece of ordnance, which support it by the trunnions. Called also cheeks. Also, triangular supports to miscellaneous things.

BRACKISH. Water not fresh; from the Icelandic *breke*, the sea.

BRADS. Small nails.

BRAE. A declivity or precipice.

BRAGGIR. The name given in the Western Islands of Scotland to the broad leaves growing on the top of the *Alga marina*, or sea-grass.

BRAILS. Ropes passing through leading blocks on the hoops of the mizen-mast and gaff, and fastened to the outermost leech of the sail, in different places, to truss it close up as occasion requires; all try-sails and several of the stay-sails also have brails.

BRAIL UP! The order to pull upon the brails, and thereby spill and haul in the sail. The mizen, or spanker, or driver, or any of the gaff-sails, as they may be termed, when brailed up, are deemed furled; unless it blows hard, when they are farther secured by gaskets.

BRAKE. The handle or lever by which a common ship-pump is usually worked. It operates by means of two iron bolts, one thrust through the inner hole of it, which bolted through forms the lever axis in the iron crutch of the pump, and serves as the fulcrum for the brake, supporting it between the cheeks. The other bolt connects the extremity of the brake to the pump-spear, which draws up the spear box or piston, charged with the water in the tube; derived from *brachium*, an arm or lever. Also, used to check the speed of machinery by frictional force pressing on the circumference of the largest wheel acted on by leverage of the brake.

BRAN, To. To go on; to lie under a floe edge, in foggy weather, in a boat in Arctic seas, to watch the approach of whales.

BRANCH. The diploma of those pilots who have passed at the Trinity House, as competent to navigate vessels in particular places. The word branch is also metaphorically used for river divergents, but its application to affluents is improper. Any branch or ramification, as in estuaries, where they traverse, river-like, miles of territory, in labyrinthine mazes.

BRANCH-PILOT. One approved by the Trinity House, and holding a branch, for a particular navigation.

BRAND. The Anglo-Saxon for a burnished sword. A burned device or character, especially that of the broad arrow on government stores, to deface or erase which is felony.

BRANDED TICKET. A discharge given to an infamous man, on which his character is written, and the reason he is turned out of the service. In the army, deserters are branded with D; also B for bad character. In the navy, a corner of the ticket is cut off.

BRANDLING. A supposed fry of the salmon species, found on the north of England coasts. Also, the angler's dew-worm.

BRANDY-PAWNEE. A cant term for brandy and water in India.

BRANLAIG. The Manx or Gaelic term for a cove or creek on a shore between rocks.

BRANLIE, OR BRANLIN. A northern name for the samlet or par.

BRAN-NEW. Quite new: said of a sail which has never been bent.

BRASH. Small fragments of crushed ice, collected by wind or currents, near the shore; or such that the ship can easily force through.

BRASS. Impudent assurance.

BRASSARTS. Pieces between the elbow and the top of the shoulder in ancient armour.

BRASSER. A defensive bit of armour for the arm.

BRAT. A northern name for a turbot.

BRAVE. This word was not only used to express courage by our early seamen, but was also applied to strength; as, "we had a brave wind."

BRAWET. A kind of eel in the north.

BRAY, To. To beat and bruise in a mortar.

BREACH. Formerly, what is made by the breaking in of the sea, now applied also to the openings or gaps made in the works of fortified places battered by an enemy's cannon. Also, an old term for a heavy surf or broken water on a sea-coast; by some called *brist*.

BREACHING. The act of leaping out of the water; applied to whales.

BREACH OF THE SEA. Waves breaking over the hull of a vessel in bad weather, or when stranded.—*A clear breach* implies the waves rolling clean over without breaking. Shakspeare in "Twelfth Night" uses the term for the breaking of the waves.—*Clean-breach*, when masts and every object on deck is swept away.

BREACHY. Brackish, as applied to water, probably originating in the sea breaking in.

BREAD. The usual name given to biscuit.

BREAD-BARGE. The tray in which biscuit is handed round.

BREAD-FRUIT (*Artocarpus incisa*). This most useful tree has a wide range of growth, but the seedless variety produced in Tahiti and some of the South Sea Islands is superior to others; it has an historical interest from its connection with the voyage of the *Bounty* in 1787.

BREAD-ROOM. The lowest and aftermost part of the orlop deck, where the biscuit is kept, separated by a bulk-head from the rest; but any place parted off from below deck for containing the bread is so designated.

BREAD-ROOM JACK. The purser's steward's help.

BREADTH. The measure of a vessel from side to side in any particular place athwart-ships. (*See* STRAIGHT OF BREADTH, HEIGHT OF BREADTH, TOP BREADTH, &c.)—*Breadth of beam*, extreme breadth of a ship.

BREADTH EXTREME. *See* EXTREME BREADTH or BEAM.

BREADTH LINE. A curved line of the ship lengthwise, intersecting the timbers at their greatest extent from the middle line of the ship.

BREADTH-MOULDED. *See* MOULDED-BREADTH.

BREADTH-RIDERS. Timbers placed nearly in the broadest part of the ship, and diagonally, so as to strengthen two or more timbers.

BREAK, To. To deprive of commission, warrant, or rating, by court-martial.

BREAK. The sudden rise of a deck when not flush; when the aft, and sometimes the fore part, of a vessel's deck is kept up to give more height below, and at the drifts.—*Break of the poop*, where it ends at the foremost part.

BREAKAGE. The leaving of empty spaces in stowing the hold. In marine insurance, the term alludes to damage occurring to goods.

BREAK-BEAMS. Beams introduced at the break of a deck, or any sudden termination of planking.

BREAK-BULK. To open the hold, to begin unloading and disposing of the goods therein, under legal provisions.

BREAKERS. Small barrels for containing water or other liquids; they are also used in watering the ship as gang-casks. (*See* BARECA.) Also, those billows which break violently over reefs, rocks, or shallows, lying immediately at, or under, the surface of the sea. They are distinguished both by their appearance and sound, as they cover that part of the sea with a perpetual foam, and produce loud roaring, very different from what the waves usually have over a deeper bottom. Also, a name given to those rocks which occasion the waves to break over them.—*Breakers ahead!* the common password to warn the officer of broken water in the direction of the course. (*See also* SHIP-BREAKER.)

BREAK-GROUND. Beginning to weigh, or to lift the anchor from the bottom. On shore it means to begin the works for besieging a place, or opening the trenches.

BREAKING. Breaking out stores or cargo in the hold. The act of extricating casks or other objects from the hold-stowage.

BREAKING LIBERTY. Not returning at the appointed time.

BREAKING OF A GALE. Indications of a return of fine weather; short gusts at intervals; moaning or whistling of the wind through the rigging.

BREAKING-PLATE DISTANCE. The point within which iron-plated ships, under concentrated fire, may be damaged.

BREAKING THE EY. See EYGHT.

BREAKING-UP OF THE MONSOON. A nautical term for the violent storms that attend the shifting of periodical winds.

BREAK-OFF. (See BROKEN-OFF). "She breaks off from her course," applied only when the wind will not allow of keeping the course; applies only to "close-hauled" or "on a wind."—*Break-off!* an order to quit one department of duty, to clap on to another.

BREAK-SHEER, To. When a ship at anchor is laid in a proper position to keep clear of her anchor, but is forced by the wind or current out of that position, she is said to break her sheer. Also, for a vessel to break her sheer, or her back, means destroying the gradual sweep lengthways.

BREAK-UP, To. To take a ship to pieces when she becomes old and unserviceable.

BREAK-WATER. Any erection or object so placed as to prevent the sea from rolling inwards. Where there is no mole or jetty the hull of an old ship may be sunk at the entrance of a small harbour, to break off or diminish the force of the waves as they advance towards the vessels moored within. Every bar to a river or harbour, intended to secure smooth water within, acts as a break-water.

BREAM. A common fresh as well as salt water fish (*Abramis brama*), little esteemed as food.

BREAMING. Cleaning a ship's bottom by burning off the grass, ooze, shells, or sea-weed, which it has contracted by lying long in harbour; it is performed by holding kindled furze, faggots, or reeds to the bottom, which, by melting the pitch that formerly covered it, loosens whatever filth may have adhered to the planks; the bottom is then covered anew with a composition of sulphur, tallow, &c., which not only makes it smooth and slippery, so as to divide the fluid more readily, but also poisons and destroys those worms which eat through the planks in the course of a voyage. This operation may be performed either by laying the ship aground after the tide has ebbed from her or by docking or careening.

BREAST, To. To run abeam of a cape or object. To cut through a sea, the surface of which is poetically termed breast.—*To breast the sea* to meet it by the bow on a wind.—*To breast the surf*, to brave it, and overcome it swimming.—*To breast a bar*, to heave at the capstan.—*To breast to*, the act of giving a sheer to a boat.

BREAST-BACKSTAYS. They extend from the head of an upper-mast, through an outrigger, down to the channels before the standing backstays, for supporting the upper spars from to windward. When to leeward, they are borne abaft the top-rim. (*See* BACKSTAY.)

BREAST-BEAMS. Those beams at the fore-part of the quarter-deck, and the after-part of the forecastle, in those vessels which have a poop and a top-gallant forecastle.

BREAST-FAST. A large rope or chain, used to confine a ship's broadside to a wharf or quay, or to some other ship, as the head-fast confines her forward, and the stern-fast abaft.

BREAST-GASKETS. An old term for bunt-gaskets.

BREAST-HOOKS. Thick pieces of timber, incurvated into the form of knees, and used to strengthen the fore-part of a ship, where they are placed at different heights, directly across the stem internally, so as to unite it with the bows on each side, and form the principal security, supporting the hawse-pieces and strain of the cables. The breast-hooks are strongly connected to the stem and hawse-pieces by tree-nails, and by bolts driven from without through all, and fore-locked or clinched upon rings inside.

BREAST-RAIL. The upper rail of the balcony; formerly it was applied to a railing in front of the quarter-deck, and at the after-part of the forecastle-deck. Also, fife-rail.

BREAST-ROPE. The lashing or laniard of the yard-parrels. (*See also* HORSE.) Also, the bight of a mat-worked band fastened between the shrouds for the safety of the lad's-man in the chains, when sounding, so that he may hang over the water, and let the lead swing clear.

BREAST-WORK. A sort of balustrade of rails, mouldings, or stanchions, which terminates the quarter-deck and poop at the fore ends, and also incloses the forecastles both before and behind. (*See* PARAPET.) Now applicable to the poop-rails only. In fortification, it signifies a parapet thrown up as high as the breasts of the men defending it.

BREATHER. A tropical squall.

BREATH OF WIND. All but a dead calm.

BREECHING. A strong rope passing through at the cascable of a gun, used to secure it to the ship's side, and prevent it recoiling too much in time of battle, also to secure it when the ship labours; it is fixed by reeving it through a thimble stropped upon the cascable or knob at the breech of the gun; one end is rove and clinched, and the other is passed through the ring-bolt in the ship's side, and seized back. The breeching is of sufficient length to let the muzzle of the cannon come within the ship's side to be charged, or to be housed and lashed. Clinch-shackles have superseded the ring-bolts, so that guns may be instantly unshackled and shifted.

BREECHING-BOLT. Applies to the above.

BREECH-LOADER. A gun, large or small, charged at the breech. The method is a very old one revived, but with such scientific modifications as to have enormously increased the effectiveness of small-arms; with cannon its successful practical application to the larger natures has not yet been arrived at, but with field-guns it has added largely to accuracy of practice and facility of loading.

BREECH OF A CANNON. The after-end, next the vent or touch-hole. It is the most massive part of a gun; strictly speaking, it is all the solid metal behind the bottom of the bore. Also, the outside angle formed by the knee-timber, the inside of which is the throat.

BREECH-SIGHT. The notch cut on the base ring of a gun.

BREEZE. This word is widely understood as a pleasant zephyr; but among seamen it is usually applied as synonymous with wind in general, whether weak or strong.

BREEZE, Sea or Land. A shifting wind blowing from sea and land alternately at certain hours, and sensibly only near the coasts; they are occasioned by the action of the sun raising the temperature of the land so as to draw an aërial current from seaward by day, which is returned as the earth cools at night.

BREEZE, To kick up a. To excite disturbance, and promote a quarrel-some row.

BREEZING UP. The gale freshening.

BREEZO. A toast given by the presiding person at a mess-table; derived from *brisée générale.*

BREVET. A rank in the army higher than the regimental commission held by an officer, affording him a precedence in garrison and brigade duties. Something approaching this has been attempted afloat, under the term "staff."

BREWING. The appearance of a collection of black and tempestuous clouds, rising gradually from a particular part of the hemisphere, as the forerunner of a storm.

BRICKLAYER'S CLERK. A contemptuous expression for lubberly pretenders to having seen "better days," but who were forced to betake themselves to sea-life.

BRIDGE. A narrow gangway between two hatchways, sometimes termed a bridge. Military bridges to afford a passage across a river for troops, are constructed with boats, pontoons, casks, trusses, trestles, &c.

Bridge in steam-vessels is the connection between the paddle-boxes, from which the officer in charge directs the motion of the vessel. Also, the middle part of the fire-bars in a marine boiler, on either side of which the fires are banked. Also, a narrow ridge of rock, sand, or shingle, across the bottom of a channel, so as to occasion a shoal over which the tide ripples. That between Mount Edgecombe and St. Nicholas' Isle, at Plymouth, has occasioned much loss of life.

BRIDGE-ISLET. A portion of land which becomes insular at high-water—as Old Woman's Isle at Bombay, and among others, the celebrated Lindisfarne, thus *tidally* sung by Scott:—

> "The tide did now his flood-mark gain,
> And girdled in the saint's domain:
> For, with the flow and ebb, its style
> Varies from continent to isle;
> Dry-shod, o'er sands, twice ev'ry day
> The pilgrims to the shrine find way;
> Twice every day the waves efface
> Of staves and sandall'd feet the trace."

BRIDGE-TRAIN. An equipment for insuring the passage of troops over a river. Pontooners. (*See* PONTOON.)

BRIDLE. *See* MOORING BRIDLE and BOWLINE BRIDLE.

BRIDLE-PORT. A square port in the bows of a ship, for taking in mooring bridles. They are also used for guns removed from the port abaft, and required to fire as near a line ahead as possible. They are main-deck chase-ports.

BRIDLES. The upper part of the moorings laid in the queen's harbours, to ride ships or vessels of war. (*See* MOORINGS.)

BRIG. A two-masted square-rigged vessel, without a square main-sail, or a trysail-mast abaft the main-mast. This properly constituted the snow, but both classes are latterly blended, and the terms therefore synonymous.

BRIGADE. A party or body of men detached for a special service. A division of troops under the command of a general officer. In artillery organization on land, a brigade is a force usually composed of more than a battery; in the field it commonly consists of two or three batteries; on paper, and for administrative purposes, of eight.

BRIGADE-MAJOR. A staff officer attached to a brigade, and is the channel through which all orders are received from the general and communicated to the troops.

BRIGADE-ORDERS. Those issued by the general officer commanding troops which are brigaded.

BRIGADIER. An officer commanding a brigade, and somewhat the same as commodore for a squadron of ships.

BRIGANDINE. A pliant scale-like coat of mail.

BRIGANTINE. A square-rigged vessel with two masts. A term variously applied by the mariners of different European nations to a peculiar sort of vessel of their own marine. Amongst British seamen this vessel is distinguished by having her main-sail set nearly in the plane of her keel, whereas the main-sails of larger ships are spread athwart the ship's length, and made fast to a yard which hangs parallel to the deck; but in a brig, the foremost side of the main-sail is fastened at different heights to hoops which encircle the main-mast, and slide up and down it as the sail is hoisted or lowered: it is extended by a gaff above and a boom below. Brigantine is a derivative from brig, first applied to passage-boats; in the Celtic meaning "passage over the water." (*See* HERMAPHRODITE or BRIG-SCHOONER.)

BRIGANTS. Formerly, natives of the northern parts of England.

BRIGDIE. A northern name for the basking shark (*Squalus maximus*).

BRIGHT LOOK-OUT. A vigilant one.

BRIG-SCHOONER. (*See* HERMAPHRODITE and BRIGANTINE, by which term she is at present classed in law.) Square-rigged on the foremast, schooner on the mainmast.

BRILL. The *Pleuronectes rhombus*, a common fish, allied to, but rather smaller than, the turbot.

BRIM. The margin or bank of a stream, lake, or river.

BRIMSTONE. *See* SULPHUR.

BRINE, OR PICKLE. Water replete with saline particles, as brine-pickle for salt meat. The briny wave.

BRINE-GAUGE. *See* SALINOMETER.

BRINE-PUMPS. When inconvenient to blow off the brine which collects at the bottom of a steamer's boilers, the brine-pump is used for clearing away the deposit.

BRING BY THE LEE, To. To incline so rapidly to leeward of the course when the ship sails large, or nearly before the wind, as in scudding before a gale, that the lee-side is unexpectedly brought to windward, and by laying the sails all aback, exposes her to the danger of oversetting. (*See* BROACH-TO.)

BRING 'EM NEAR. The day-and-night telescope.

BRINGERS UP. The last men in a boarding or small-arm party. Among soldiers, it means the whole last rank of a battalion drawn up, being the hindmost men of every file.

BRING HOME THE ANCHOR, To, is to weigh it. It applies also when the flukes slip or will not hold; a ship then brings home her anchor.—*Bring home the log.* When the pin slips out of the log ship and it slides through the water.

BRINGING IN. The detention of a vessel on the high seas, and bringing her into port for adjudication.

BRINGING-TO THE YARD.   Hoisting up a sail, and bending it to
its yard.

BRING-TO, To.   To bend, as to bring-to a sail to the yard.   Also, to
check the course of a ship by trimming the sails so that they shall
counteract each other, and keep her nearly stationary, when she is said
to lie by, or lie-to, or heave-to.—*Bring to!* The order from one
ship to another to put herself in that situation in order to her being
boarded, spoken to, or examined.   Firing a blank gun across the bows
of a ship is the forcible signal to shorten sail and bring-to until further
pleasure.—*Bring-to* is also used in applying a rope to the capstan, as
" bring-to the messenger."

BRING-TO AN ANCHOR, To.   To let go the anchor in the intended
port.   "All hands bring ship to an anchor!"   The order by which the
people are summoned for that duty, by the pipes of the boatswain and
his mates.

BRING UP, To.   To cast anchor.

BRING UP WITH A ROUND TURN.   Suddenly arresting a running rope by taking a round turn round a bollard, bitt-head, or cleat.
Said of doing a thing effectually though abruptly.   It is used to bring
one up to his senses by a severe rating.

BRISAS.   A north-east wind which blows on the coast of South America
during the trades.

BRISMAK.   A name among the Shetlanders for the excellent fish
called tusk or torsk, the best of the cod kind (*Brosmus vulgaris*).

BRISTOL FASHION AND SHIPSHAPE.   Said when Bristol was
in its palmy commercial days, unannoyed by Liverpool, and its shipping was all in proper good order.

BRITISH-BUILT SHIP.   Such as has been built in Great Britain or
Ireland, Guernsey, Jersey, the Isle of Man, or some of the colonies,
plantations, islands, or territories in Asia, Africa, or America, which,
at the time of building the ship, belonged to or were in possession of
her Majesty; or any ship whatsoever which has been taken and condemned as lawful prize.

BRITISH SEAS.   *See* QUATUOR MARIA.

BRITISH SHIP.   May be foreign built, or rebuilt on a foreign keel
which belonged to any of the people of Great Britain and Ireland,
Guernsey, Jersey, or the Isle of Man, or of any colony, island, or
territory in Asia, Africa, or America, or was registered before the 1st
of May, 1786.

BRITISH SUBJECT.   Settled in an enemy's country, may not trade
in any contraband goods.

BRITTLE-STAR.   The common name of a long-rayed starfish (*Ophio-
coma rosula*).

BROACH A BUSINESS, To. To begin it.

BROACH-TO, To. To fly up into the wind. It generally happens when a ship is carrying a press of canvas with the wind on the quarter, and a good deal of after-sail set. The masts are endangered by the course being so altered, as to bring it more in opposition to, and thereby increasing the pressure of the wind. In extreme cases the sails are caught flat aback, when the masts would be likely to give way, or the ship might go down stern foremost.

BROAD ARROW. The royal mark for government stores of every description. To obliterate, deface, or remove this mark is felony; or even to be in possession of any goods so marked without sufficient grounds. It is no doubt one of the Ditmarsh runes.

BROAD AXE. Formerly a warlike instrument; also for beheading; specially applied to the axe of carpenters for mast-making, and sometimes cutting away the masts or cable.

BROAD CLOTH. Square sails.

BROAD OF WATER. An extensive lake with a channel communicating with the sea, or a wide opening of a river after passing a narrow entrance.

BROAD PENNANT. A swallow-tailed piece of buntin at the masthead of a man-of-war; the distinctive mark of a commodore. The term is frequently used for the officer himself. It tapers, in contradistinction to a cornet, which has only the triangle cut out of it.

BROAD R. See BROAD ARROW.

BROADS. Fresh-water lakes, in contradistinction to rivers or narrow waters.

BROADSIDE. The whole array, or the simultaneous discharge of the artillery on one side of a ship of war above and below. It also implies the whole of that side of a ship above the water which is situate between the bow and quarter, and is in a position nearly perpendicular to the horizon. Also, a name given to the old folio sheets whereon ballads and proclamations were printed of old (broad-sheet).

BROADSIDE-ON. The whole side of a vessel; the opposite of *end-on*.

BROADSIDE WEIGHT OF METAL. The weight of iron which the guns of a ship can project, when single-shotted, from one side. (*See* WEIGHT OF METAL.)

BROADSWORD. *See* CUTLAS.

BROCAGE. The same with *brokerage* (which see).

BROCLES. *See* STRAKE-NAILS.

BRODIE. The fry of the rock-tangle, or Hettle-codling, a fish caught on the Hettle Bank, in the Firth of Forth.

BROGGING. A north-country method of catching eels, by means of small sticks called brogs.

BROGUES. Among seamen, coarse sandals made of green hide; but Shakspeare makes Arviragus put "his clouted brogues from off his feet," for "answering his steps too loud." This would rather refer to shoes strengthened with hob-nails.

BROKE. Sentence of a court-martial, depriving an officer of his commission.

BROKEN. An old army word, used for *reduced;* as, a broken lieutenant, &c. The word is also applied to troops in line when not dressed. The heart of a gale is said to be broken; parole is broken; also, leave, bulk, &c. (which see).

BROKEN-BACKED. The state of a ship so loosened in her frame, either by age, weakness, or some great strain from grounding amidships, as to droop at each end, causing the lines of her sheer to be interrupted, and termed *hogged.* It may result from fault of construction, in the midship portions having more buoyancy, and the extreme ends too much weight, as anchors, boats, guns, &c., to sustain.

BROKEN-OFF. Fallen off, in azimuth, from the course. Also, men taken from one duty to be put on another.

BROKEN SQUALL. When the clouds separate in divisions, passing ahead and astern of a ship, and affecting her but little, if at all.

BROKEN WATER. The contention of currents in a narrow channel. Also, the waves breaking on and near shallows, occasionally the result of vast shoals of fish, as porpoise, skipjacks, &c., which worry untutored seamen.

BROKER. Originally a broken tradesman, from the Anglo-Saxon *broc,* a misfortune; but, in later times, a person who usually transacts the business of negotiating between the merchants and shipowners respecting cargoes and clearances: he also effects insurances with the underwriters; and while on the one hand he is looked to as to the regularity of the contract, on the other he is expected to make a candid disclosure of all the circumstances which may affect the risk.

BROKET. A small brook; the sea-lark is so called at the Farne Islands.

BROKE-UP. Said of a gale of wind passing away; or a ship which has gone to pieces on a reef, &c.

BROND. An old spelling of *brand,* a sword.

BRONGIE. A name given to the cormorant in the Shetland Islands.

BROOD. Oysters of about two years old, which are dredged up at sea, for placing on the oyster-beds.

BROOD-HEN STAR. The cluster of the Pleiades.

BROOK, OR BROOKLET. Streams of fresh or salt water, less than a rivulet, creeping through narrow and shallow passages. The clouds *brook-up,* when they draw together and threaten rain.

BROOM. A besom at the mast-head signifies that the ship is to be sold: derived probably from the old practice of displaying boughs at shops and taverns. Also, a sort of *spartium*, of which ropes are made.

BROOMING. *See* BREAMING.

BROTHER-OFFICERS. Those of the same ship or regiment.

BROTH OF A BOY. An excellent, though roystering fellow.

BROUGHT BY THE LEE. *See* BRING BY THE LEE.

BROUGHT-TO. A chase made to stop, and heave-to. Also, the cable is brought-to when fastened to the messenger by nippers. The messenger is brought to the capstan, or the cable to the windlass.

BROUGHT TO HIS BEARINGS. Reduced to obedience.

BROUGHT TO THE GANGWAY. Punished.

BROW. An inclined plane of planks, on one or both sides of a ship, to communicate internally; a stage-gangway for the accommodation of the shipwrights, in conveying plank, timber, and weighty articles on board. Also, the face of a rising ground. An old term for a gang-board.

BROWN BESS. A nickname for the old government regulation bronzed musket, although till recently it was brightly burnished.

BROWN BILL. The old weapon of the English infantry: hence, perhaps the expression "Brown Bess" for a musket.

BROWN GEORGE. A hard and coarse biscuit.

BROWNIE. The Polar bear, so called by the whalers. It is also a northern term for goblin.

BROWN JANET. A cant phrase for a knapsack.

BROWN-PAPER WARRANT. *See* WARRANT.

BROWSE. A light kind of dunnage.

BRUISE-WATER. A ship with very bluff bows, built more for carrying than sailing.

BRUISING WATER. Pitching heavily to a head-sea, and making but little head-way.

BRUN-SWYNE. An early name for a seal.

BRUSH. A move; a skirmish.

BRYDPORT. An old word signifying cable. The best hemp grew at Bridport, in Dorsetshire; and there was a statute, that the cables and hawsers for the Royal Navy were to be made thereabouts.

BUB. A liquor or drink. *Bub* and *grub* meaning inversely meat and drink.

BUBBLE. Another term for spirit-level, used for astronomical instruments.

BUBBLER. A fish found in the waters of the Ohio, thus named from the bubbling noise it makes.

BUCCANEER. A name given to certain piratical rovers, of various

European nations, who formerly infested the coasts of Spanish America. They were originally inoffensive settlers in Hispaniola, but were inhumanly driven from their habitations by the jealous policy of the Spaniards; whence originated their implacable hatred to that nation. Also, a large musketoon, about 8 feet in length, so called from having been used by those marauders.

BUCENTAUR. A large and splendid galley of the doge of Venice, in which he received the great lords and persons of quality who went there, accompanied by the ambassadors and councillors of state, and all the senators seated on benches by him. The same vessel served also in the magnificent ceremony on Ascension-day, when the doge threw a ring into the sea to espouse it, and to denote his dominion over the Gulf of Venice.

BUCHAN BOILERS. The heavy breaking billows among the rocks on the coast of Buchan.

BUCHT. A Shetland term for lines of 55 fathoms.

BUCK, To. To wash a sail.

BUCKALL. An earthen wine-cup used in the sea-ports of Portugal, Spain, and Italy. [from *bocale*, It.]

BUCKER. A name for the grampus in the Hebrides. It is also applied, on some of our northern coasts, to the porpoise.

BUCKET. A small globe of hoops, covered with canvas, used as a recall for the boats of whalers.

BUCKET-ROPE. That which is tied to a bucket for drawing water up from alongside.

BUCKETS. Are made either of canvas, of leather, or of wood; the latter are used principally for washing the decks, and therefore answer the purposes of pails.

BUCKET-VALVE. In a steamer's engine, is a flat metal plate filling up the passage between the air-pump and the condenser, and acted upon by both in admitting or repressing the passage of water.

BUCKHORN. Whitings, haddocks, thornbacks, gurnet, and other fish, cleaned, gently salted, and dried in the sun.

BUCKIE. A northern name for the whelk.

BUCKIE-INGRAM. A name for the hermit-crab.

BUCKIE-PRINS. A northern designation for a periwinkle.

BUCKLE. A mast buckles when it suffers by compression, so that the fibre takes a sinuous form, and the grain is *upset*. Also, in Polar regions, the bending or arching of the ice upwards, preceding a nip.

BUCKLERS. Two blocks of wood fitted together to stop the hawse-holes, leaving only sufficient space between them for the cable to pass, and thereby preventing the ship taking in much water in a heavy head-sea. They are either *riding* or *blind bucklers* (which see).

BUCKRA. A term for white man, used by the blacks in the West Indies, Southern States of America, and the African coast.

BUCK-WEEL. A bow-net for fish.

BUDE. An old name for the biscuit-weevil.

BUDGE-BARREL. A small cask with copper and wooden hoops, and one head formed by a leather hose or bag, drawing close by a string, for carrying powder in safety from sparks. In heraldry, the common bucket is called a water bouget or budget.

BUDGEROW. A cabined passage-boat of the Ganges and Hooghly.

BUFFET A BILLOW, To. To work against wind and tide.

BUG. An old term for a vessel more remarkable in size than efficiency. Thus, when Drake fell upon Cadiz, his sailors regarded the huge galleys opposed to them as mere "great bugges."

BUGALILO. A large trading-boat of the Gulf of Persia; the *buglo* of our seamen.

BUGAZEENS. An old commercial term for calicoes.

BUILD. A vessel's form or construction.

BUILD A CHAPEL, To. To turn a ship suddenly by negligent steerage.

BUILDER'S CERTIFICATE. A necessary document in admiralty courts, containing a true account of a ship's denomination, tonnage, trim, where built, and for whom.

BUILDING. The work of constructing ships, as distinguished from naval architecture, which may rather be considered as the art or theory of delineating ships on a plane. The pieces by which this complicated machine is framed, are joined together in various places by scarfing, rabetting, tenanting, and scoring.

BUILT. A prefix to denote the construction of a vessel, as carvel or clinker-built, bluff-built, frigate-built, sharp-built, &c.; English, French, or American built, &c.

BUILT-BLOCK. Synonymous with *made-block* (which see). The lower masts of large ships are built or made.

BUILT-UP GUNS. Recently invented guns of great strength, specially adapted to meet the requirements of rifled artillery and of the attack of iron plating. They are usually composed of an inner core or barrel (which may be of coiled and welded iron, but is now generally preferred of tough steel), with a breech-piece, trunnion-piece, and various outer strengthening hoops or coils of wrought iron, shrunk or otherwise forced on; having their parts put together at such predetermined relative tensions, as to support one another under the shock of explosion, and thereby avoiding the faults of solid cast or forged guns, whereof the inner parts are liable to be destroyed before the outer can take their share of the strain. The first practical example of the method was afforded by the Armstrong gun, the "building up" which obtained in ancient days, before the casting of solid guns, having been apparently resorted to as an easy means of producing large masses of metal, without realizing the principle of the mutual support of the various parts.

BUIRAN. A Gaelic word signifying the sea coming in, with a noise as of the roar of a bull.

BULCH, To. To bilge a ship.

BULGE. (*See* BILGE.) That part of the ship she bears upon when on the ground.

BULGE-WAYS. Otherwise *bilge-ways* (which see).

BULK. In bulk; things stowed without cases or packages. (*See* BULK-HEAD and LADEN IN BULK.)

BULKER. A person employed to measure goods, and ascertain the amount of freight with which they are chargeable.

BULK-HEAD, THE. Afore, is the partition between the forecastle and gratings in the head, and in which are the chase-ports.

BULK-HEADS. Partitions built up in several parts of a ship, to form and separate the various cabins from each other. Some are particularly strong, as those in the hold, which are mostly built with rabetted or cyphered plank; others are light, and removable at pleasure. Indeed the word is applied to any division made with boards, to separate one portion of the 'tween decks from another.

BULK OF A SHIP. Implies the whole cargo when stowed in the hold.

BULL. An old male whale. Also, a small keg; also the weak grog made by pouring water into a spirit-cask nearly empty.

BULL-DANCE. At sea it is performed by men only, when without women. It is sometimes called a stag-dance.

BULL-DOG, OR MUZZLED BULL-DOG. The great gun which stands "housed" in the officer's ward-room cabin. General term for main-deck guns.

BULLETIN. Any official account of a public transaction.

BULLET-MOULD. An implement for casting bullets.

BULLETS. Leaden balls with which all kinds of firearms are loaded.

BULLHEAD, OR BULL-JUB. A name of the fish called miller's-thumb (*Cottus gobio*).

BULLOCK-BLOCKS. Blocks secured under the top-mast trestle-trees, which receive the top-sail ties through them, in order to increase the mechanical power used in hoisting them up.

BULLOCK-SLINGS. Used to hoist in live bullocks.

BULL'S-EYE. A sort of block without a sheave, for a rope to reeve through; it is grooved for stropping. Also, the central mark of a target. Also, a hemispherical piece of ground glass of great thickness, inserted into small openings in the decks, port-lids, and scuttle-hatches, for the admission of light below.

BULL'S-EYE CRINGLE. A piece of wood in the form of a ring, which answers the purpose of an iron thimble; it is seldom used by English seamen, and then only for the fore and main bowline-bridles.

BULL-TROUT. The salmon-trout of the Tweed. A large species of trout taken in the waters of Northumberland.

BULLYRAG, To. To reproach contemptuously, and in a hectoring manner; to bluster, to abuse, and to insult noisily. Shakspeare makes mine host of the Garter dub Falstaff a bully-rook.

BULWARK. The planking or wood-work round a vessel above her deck, and fastened externally to the stanchions and timber-heads. In this form it is a synonym of berthing. Also, the old name for a bastion.

BULWARK-NETTING. An ornamental frame of netting answering the purpose of a bulwark.

BUMBARD. A cask or large vessel for liquids. (*See* BOMBARD.) Trinculo, in the "Tempest," thinks an impending storm-cloud "looks like a foul bumbard."

BUM-BOAT. A boat employed to carry provisions, vegetables, and small merchandise for sale to ships, either in port or lying at a distance from the shore; thus serving to communicate with the adjacent town. The name is corrupted from bombard, the vessels in which beer was formerly carried to soldiers on duty.

BUMKIN, BUMPKIN, OR BOOMKIN. A short boom or beam of timber projecting from each bow of a ship, where it is fayed down upon the false rail. Its use is to extend the clue or lower corner of the fore-sail to windward, for which purpose there is a large block fixed on its outer end, through which the tack is passed, and when hauled tight down is said to be aboard. The name is also applied to the pieces on each quarter, for the main-brace blocks.

BUMKIN. A small outrigger over the stern of a boat, usually serving to extend the mizen.

BUMMAREE. A word synonymous with *bottomry*, in maritime law. It is also a name given to a class of speculating salesmen of fish, not recognized as regular tradesmen.

BUMP, To. To bump a boat, is to pull astern of her in another, and insultingly or inimically give her the stem; a practice in rivers and narrow channels.

BUMP-ASHORE. Running stem-on to a beach or bank. A ship bumps by the action of the waves lifting and dropping her on the bottom when she is aground.

BUMPERS. Logs of wood placed over a ship's side to keep off ice.

BUND. In India, an embankment; whence, Bunda head, and Bunda boat.

BUNDLE-UP! The call to the men below to hurry up on deck.

BUNDLING Things into a Boat. Loading it in a slovenly way.

BUNGLE, To. To perform a duty in a slovenly manner.

BUNGO, or Bonga. A sort of boat used in the Southern States of America, made of the bonga-tree hollowed out.

BUNG-STARTER. A stave shaped like a bat, which, applied to either side of the bung, causes it to start out. Also, a soubriquet for the captain of the hold. Also, a name given to the master's assistant serving his apprenticeship for hold duties.

BUNG-UP and BILGE-FREE. A cask so placed that its bung-stave is uppermost, and it rests entirely on its beds.

BUNK. A sleeping-place in the fore-peak of merchantmen; standing bed-places fixed on the sides between decks.

BUNKER. For stowing coal in steamers. Cellular spaces on each side which deliver the coal to the engine-room.—*Wing-bunkers* below the decks, cutting off the angular side-spaces of the hold, and hatched over, are usually filled with sand, holystones, brooms, junk-blocks, &c., saving stowage.

BUNT of a Sail. The middle part of it, formed designedly into a bag or cavity, that the sail may gather more wind. It is used mostly in top-sails, because courses are generally cut square, or with but small allowance for bunt or compass. "The bunt holds much leeward wind;" that is, it hangs much to leeward. In "handed" or "furled" sails, the bunt is the middle gathering which is tossed up on the centre of the yard.—*To bunt a sail* is to haul up the middle part of it in furling, and secure it by the bunt-gasket.

BUNTERS. The men on the yard who gather in the bunt when furling sails.

BUNT-FAIR. Before the wind.

BUNT-GASKET. *See* Gasket.

BUNTING. A name on our southern shores for the shrimp.

BUNTING, or Buntin. A thin woollen stuff, of which the ship's colours, flags, and signals are usually made.

BUNT-JIGGER. A small gun-tackle purchase, of two single blocks, one fitted with two tails, used in large vessels for bowsing up the bunt of a sail when furling: a peculiar combination of two points, fitted to a spar to which it is hooked.

BUNTLINE-CLOTH. The lining sewed up the fore-part of the sail in the direction of the buntline to prevent that rope from chafing the sail.

BUNTLINE-CRINGLE. An eye worked into the bolt-rope of a sail, to receive a buntline. This is only in top-gallant sails, and is seldom used now. In the merchant service all buntlines are generally passed through an eyelet-hole in the sail, and clinched round its own part.

BUNTLINES. Ropes attached to the foot-ropes of top-sails and courses, which, passing over and before the canvas, turn it up forward, and thus disarm the force of the wind; at one-third from each clue, eyelet-holes are worked in the canvas, and by grummets passed through, a toggle is secured on both bights : to this buntline-toggle the buntline attaches by an eye or loop. When the sails are loosed to dry, the bowlines, unbent from the bridles, are attached to these toggles, and haul out the sails by the foot-ropes like table-cloths. The buntline is rove through a block at the mast-head, passes through the buntline span attached to the tye-blocks on the yard to retain them in the bunt, or amidships, down before all, and looped to the toggles afore-said. By aid of the clue-lines, reef-tackles, and buntlines, a top-sail is taken in or quieted if the sheets carry away, but more especially by the buntlines, as the wind has no hold then to belly the canvas.

BUNTLINE-SPANS. Short pieces of rope with a thimble in one end, the other whipped; the buntlines are rove through these thimbles : they are attached to the tie-blocks to keep the sail in the bunt when hauled up.

BUNTLINE-TOGGLES. *See* BUNTLINES and TOGGLE.

BUNT SLAB-LINES. Reeve through a block on the slings of the yard or under the top, and pass abaft the sail, making fast to its foot. Their object is to lift the foot of a course so as to see underneath it, or to prevent it from chafing. Something of the same kind is used for top-sails, to keep them from rubbing on the stays when flapping in a calm.

BUOY. A sort of close cask, or block of wood, fastened by a rope to the anchor, to show its situation after being cast, that the ship may not come so near it as to entangle her cable about its stock or flukes.—*To buoy a cable* is to make fast a spar, cask, or the like, to the bight of the cable, in order to prevent its galling or rubbing on the bottom. When a buoy floats on the water it is said to watch. When a vessel slips her cable she attaches a buoy to it in order afterwards to recover it. Thus the blockading squadrons off Brest and in Basque Roads fre-quently slipped, by signal, and each in beautiful order returned and picked up their cables.—*To stream the buoy* is to let it fall from the ship's side into the water, which is always done before the anchor is let go, that it may not be fouled by the buoy-rope as it sinks to the bottom.—*Buoys* of various kinds are also placed upon rocks or sand-banks to direct mariners where to avoid danger.

BUOYANCY. Capacity for floating lightly.—*Centre of buoyancy*, in naval architecture, the mean centre of that part of the vessel which is immersed in the water. (*See* CENTRE OF CAVITY.)

BUOYANT. The property of floating lightly on the water.

BUOY-ROPE. The rope which attaches the buoy to the anchor, which should always be of sufficient strength to lift the anchor should the cable part; it should also be little more in length than equal to the depth of the water (at high-water) where the anchor lies.—*To bend the buoy-rope*, pass the running eye over one fluke, take a hitch over the other arm, and seize. Or, take a clove-hitch over the crown on each arm or fluke, stopping the end to its own part, or to the shank.

BUOY-ROPE KNOT. Used where the end is lashed to the shank. A knot made by unlaying the strands of a cable-laid rope, and also the small strand of each large strand; and after single and double walling them, as for a stopper-knot, worm the divisions, and round the rope.

BURBOT. A fresh-water fish (*Molva lota*) in esteem with fishermen.

BURDEN. Is the quantity of contents or number of tons weight of goods or munitions which a ship will carry, when loaded to a proper sea-trim: and this is ascertained by certain fixed rules of measurement. The precise burden or burthen is about twice the tonnage, but then a vessel would be deemed deeply laden.

BURG [the Anglo-Saxon *burh*]. A word connected with fortification in German, as in almost all the Teutonic languages of Europe. In Arabic the same term, with the alteration of a letter, *burj*, signifies primarily a bastion, and by extension any fortified place on a rising ground. This meaning has been retained by all northern nations who have borrowed the word; and we, with the rest, name our towns, once fortified, burghs or boroughs.

BURGALL. A fish of the American coasts, from 6 to 12 inches long: it is also called the blue-perch, the chogset, and the nibbler—the last from its habit of nibbling off the bait thrown for other fishes.

BURGEE. A swallow-tailed or tapered broad pendant; in the merchant service it generally has the ship's name on it.

BURGOMASTER. In the Arctic Sea, a large species of gull (*Larus glaucus*).

BURGONET. A steel head-piece, or kind of helmet. Shakspeare makes Cleopatra, alluding to Antony, exclaim—

> "The demi-Atlas of this earth, the arm
> And burgonet of men."

In the second part of "Henry VI." Clifford threatens Warwick—

> "And from thy burgonet I'll rend thy bear,
> And tread it underfoot with all contempt."

BURGOO. A seafaring dish made of boiled oat-meal seasoned with salt, butter, and sugar. (*See* LOBLOLLY and SKILLAGALEE.)

BURLEY. The butt-end of a lance.

BURLEY-TWINE. A strong and coarse twine or small string.

BURN, OR BOURNE. The Anglo-Saxon term for a small stream or brook, originating from springs, and winding through meadows, thus differing from a beck. Shakspeare makes Edgar say in "King Lear"—

> " Come o'er the bourn, Bessy, to me."

The word also signifies a boundary.

BURNETIZE, To. To impregnate canvas, timber, or cordage with Sir William Burnett's fluid, a solution of chloride of zinc.

BURN THE WATER. A phrase denoting the act of killing salmon in the night, with a lister and lighted torch in the boat.

BURN-TROUT. A northern term for a small species of river-trout.

BURR. The iris or hazy circle which appears round the moon before rain. Also, a Manx or Gaelic term for the wind blowing across on the tide. Also, the sound made by the Newcastle men in pronouncing the letter R.

BURREL. A langrage shot, consisting of bits of iron, bullets, nails, and other matters, got together in haste for a sudden emergency.

BURROCK. A small weir over a river, where weals are laid for taking fish.

BURR-PUMP. A name of the bilge-pump.

BURSER. *See* PURSER.

BURST. The explosion of a shell or any gun.

BURTHEN. *See* BURDEN.

BURTON. A small tackle rove in a particular manner; it is formed by two blocks or pullies, with a hook-block in the bight of the running part; it is generally used to set up or tighten the shrouds, whence it is frequently termed a top-burton tackle; but it is equally useful to move or draw along any weighty body in the hold or on the deck, as anchors, bales of goods, large casks, &c. (*See* SPANISH BURTON.) The burton purchase, also *runner purchase* (which see).

BUSH, OR BOUCHE. A circular shouldered piece of metal, usually of brass, let into the lignum vitæ sheaves of such blocks as have iron pins, thereby preventing the sheave from wearing, without adding much to its weight. The operation of placing it in the wood is called bushing or coaking, though the last name is usually given to smaller bushes of a square shape. Brass bushes are also extensively applied in the marine steam-engine work. Also, in artillery, the plug (generally of copper, on account of the superior resistance of that metal to the flame of exploded gunpowder), having a diameter of about an inch, and a length equal to the intended length of the vent, screwed into the metal of the gun at the place of the vent, which is then drilled in it. Guns may be re-bushed when the vent has worn too large, by the substitution of a new bush.

BUSH. The forests in the West Indies, Australia, &c.

BUSHED. Cased with harder metal, as that inserted into the holes of some rudder braces or sheaves in general, to prevent their wearing.

BUSHED-BLOCK. *See* COAK.

BUSKING. Piratical cruising; also, used generally, for beating to windward along a coast, or cruising off and on.

BUSS. A small strong-built Dutch vessel with two masts, used in the herring and mackerel fisheries, being generally of 50 to 70 tons burden.

BUST-HEAD. *See* HEAD.

BUSY AS THE DEVIL IN A GALE OF WIND. Fidgetty restlessness, or double diligence in a bad cause; the imp being supposed to be mischievous in hard gales.

BUT. A northern name for a flounder or plaice. Also, a conical basket for catching fish.

BUTCHER'S BILL. A nickname for the official return of killed and wounded which follows an action.

BUTESCARLI. The early name for the sea-officers in the British Navy (*see the* EQUIPMENT OF).

BUTT. The joining of two timbers or planks endways. Also, the opening between the ends of two planks when worked. Also, the extremities of the planks themselves when they are united, or abut against each other. The word likewise is used to denote the largest end of all timber. Planks under water as they rise are joined one end to another. In large ships butt-ends are most carefully bolted, for if any one of them should spring, or give way, the leak would be very dangerous and difficult to stop.—*To start* or *spring a butt* is to loosen the end of a plank by the ship's weakness or labouring.—*Butt-heads* are the same with butt-ends.—*Butt* is also a mark for shooting at, and the hind part of a musket or pistol. Also, a wine-measure of 126 gallons.

BUTT-AND-BUTT. A term denoting that the butt ends of two planks come together, but do not overlay each other. (*See* HOOK AND BUTT and HOOK-SCARPH.)

BUTT-END. The shoulder part of a firelock.

BUTTER-BOX. A name given to the brig-traders of lumpy form, from London, Bristol, and other English ports. A cant term for a Dutchman.

BUTTER-BUMP. A name of the bittern in the north.

BUTTER-FINGERED. Having a careless habit of allowing things to drop through the fingers.

BUTTLE. An eastern-county name for the bittern.

BUTTOCK. The breadth of the ship astern from the tuck upwards : it is terminated by the counter above, by the bilge below, by the stern-post in the middle, and by the quarter on the side. That part abaft the after body, which is bounded by the fashion pieces, and by the wing transom, and the upper or second water-line. A ship is said to have a broad, or narrow, buttock according to her transom convexity under the stern.

BUTTOCK-LINES. In shipbuilding, the longitudinal curves at the rounding part of the after body in a vertical section.

BUTTON. The knob of metal which terminates the breech end of most guns, and which affords a convenient bearing for the application of handspikes, breechings, &c.

BUTTONS, To MAKE. A common time-honoured, but strange expression for sudden apprehension or misgiving.

BUTTRESS. In fortification. (See COUNTER-FORT.)

BUTT-SHAFT, OR BUTT-BOLT. An arrow without a barb, used for shooting at a butt.

BUTT-SLINGING A BOWSPRIT. See SLINGS.

BUXSISH. A gratuity, in oriental trading.

BUZZING. Sometimes used for booming (which see).

BY. On or close to the wind.—Full and by, not to lift or shiver the sails; rap-full.

BY AND LARGE. To the wind and off it; within six points.

BYKAT. A northern term for a male salmon of a certain age, because of the beak which then grows on its under-jaw.

BYLLIS. An old spelling for bill (which see).

BYRNIE. Early English for body-armour.

BYRTH. The old expression for tonnage. (See BIRTH or BERTH.)

BYSSA. An ancient gun for discharging stones at the enemy.

BYSSUS. The silken filaments of any of the bivalved molluscs which adhere to rocks, as the Pinna, Mytilus, &c. The silken byssus of the great pinna, or wing-shell, is woven into dresses. In the Chama gigas it will sustain 1000 lbs. Also, the woolly substance found in damp parts of a ship.

BY THE BOARD. Over the ship's side. When a mast is carried away near the deck it is said to go by the board.

BY THE HEAD. When a ship is deeper forward than abaft.

BY THE LEE. The situation of a vessel going free, when she has fallen off so much as to bring the wind round her stern, and to take her sails aback on the other side.

BY THE STERN. When the ship draws more water abaft than forward. (*See* BY THE HEAD.)

BY THE WIND. Is when a ship sails as nearly to the direction of the wind as possible. (*See* FULL and BY.) In general terms, within six points; or the axis of the ship is 67½ degrees from the direction of the wind.

BY-WASH. The outlet of water from a dam or discharge channel.

C.

CAAG. *See* KAAG.

CABANE. A flat-bottomed passage-boat of the Loire.

CABBAGE. Those principally useful to the seaman are the esculent cabbage-tree (*Areca oleracea*), which attains to a great height in the W. Indies. The sheaths of the leaves are very close, and form the green top of the trunk a foot and a half in length; this is cut off, and its white heart eaten. Also, the *Crambe maritima*, sea-kail, or marine cabbage, growing in the west of England.

CABIN. A room or compartment partitioned off in a ship, where the officers and passengers reside. In a man-of-war, the principal cabin, in which the captain or admiral lives, is the upper after-part of the vessel.

CABIN-BOY. A boy whose duty is to attend and serve the officers and passengers in the cabin.

CABIN-LECTURE. *See* JOBATION.

CABIN-MATE. A companion, when two occupy a cabin furnished with two bed-places.

CABLE. A thick, strong rope or chain which serves to keep a ship at anchor; the rope is cable-laid, 10 inches in circumference and upwards (those below this size being hawsers), commonly of hemp or coir, which latter is still used by the Calcutta pilot-brigs on account of its lightness and elasticity. But cables have recently, and all but exclusively, been superseded by iron chain.—*A shot of cable*, two cables spliced together.

CABLE, To COIL A. To lay it in fakes and tiers one over the other.—*To lay a-cable*. (*See* LAYING.)—*To pay cheap the cable*, to hand it out apace; to throw it over.—*To pay out more cable*, to let more out of the ship.—*To serve or plait the cable*, to bind it about with ropes, canvas, &c.; to keep it from galling in the hawse-pipe. (*See* ROUNDING,

CACKLING, KECKLING, &c.)—*To splice a cable*, to make two pieces fast together, by working the several yarns of the rope into each other; with chain it is done by means of shackles.—*To veer more cable*, to let more out.

CABLE-BENDS. Two small ropes for lashing the end of a hempen cable to its own part, in order to secure the clinch by which it is fastened to the anchor-ring.

CABLE-BITTED. So bitted as to enable the cable to be nipped or rendered with ease.

CABLE-BITTS. *See* BITTS.

CABLE-BUOYS. Peculiar casks employed to buoy up rope cables in a rocky anchorage, to prevent their rubbing against the rocks; they are also attached to the end of a cable when it is slipped, with the object of finding it again.

CABLE-ENOUGH. The call when cable enough is veered to permit of the anchor being brought to the cat-head.

CABLE-HANGER. A term applied to any person catching oysters in the river Medway, not free of the fishery, and who is liable to such penalty as the mayor and citizens of Rochester shall impose upon him.

CABLE-LAID ROPE. Is a rope of which each strand is a hawser-laid rope. Hawser-laid ropes are simple three-strand ropes, and range up to the same size as cablets, as from $\frac{3}{4}$ to 9 inches. (*See* ROPE.)

CABLE-SHEET, SHEET-CABLE. The spare bower cable belonging to a ship. Sheet is deemed stand-by, and is also applied to its anchor.

CABLE'S LENGTH. A measure of about 100 fathoms, by which the distances of ships in a fleet are frequently estimated. This term is frequently misunderstood. In all marine charts a cable is deemed 607·56 feet, or one-tenth of a sea mile. In ropemaking the cable varies from 100 to 115 fathoms; cablet, 120 fathoms; hawser-laid, 130 fathoms, as determined by the admiralty in 1830.

CABLE-STAGE. A place constructed in the hold, or cable-tier, for coiling cables and hawsers on.

CABLE-STREAM, STREAM-CABLE. A hawser or rope something smaller than the bower, used to move or hold the ship temporarily during a calm in a river or haven, sheltered from the wind and sea, &c.

CABLE-TIER. The place in a hold, or between decks, where the cables are coiled away.

CABOBBLED. Confused or puzzled.

CABOBS, OR KEBAUB. The Turkish name for small fillets of meat broiled on wooden spits; the use of the term has been extended eastward, and in India signifies a hot spiced dish of fish, flesh, or fowl.

CABONS. *See* KABURUS.

CABOOSE, OR CAMBOOSE. The cook-room or kitchen of merchantmen on deck; a diminutive substitute for the galley of a man-of-war. It is generally furnished with cast-iron apparatus for cooking.

CABOTAGE [Ital.] Sailing from cape to cape along a coast; or the details of coast pilotage.

CABURNS. Spun rope-yarn lines, for worming a cable, seizing, winding tacks, and the like.

CACAO [Sp.] The plant *Theobroma*, from which what is commonly termed cocoa is derived.

CACCLE, or Keccle. To apply a particular kind of service to the cable. (*See* Keckling.)

CACHE. A hidden reservoir of provision (to secure it from bears) in Arctic travel. Also, a deposit of despatches, &c.

CADE. A small barrel of about 500 herrings, or 1000 sprats.

CADENCE. The uniform time and space for marching, more indispensable to large bodies of troops than to parties of small-arm men; yet an important part even of their drill. The regularity requisite in pulling.

CADET. A volunteer, who, serving at his own charge, to learn experience, waits for preferment; a designation, recently introduced, for young gentlemen formerly rated volunteers of the first class. Properly, the younger son in French.

CADGE, To. To carry.—*Cadger*, a carrier. Kedge may be a corruption, as being carriable.

CÆSAR'S PENNY. The tip given by a recruiting sergeant.

CAFFILA. *See* Kafila.

CAGE. An iron cage formed of hoops on the top of a pole, and filled with combustibles to blaze for two hours. It is lighted one hour before high-water, and marks an intricate channel navigable for the period it burns; much used formerly by fishermen.

CAGE-WROCK. An old term for a ship's upper works.

CAIQUE, or Kaique. A small Levantine vessel. Also, a graceful skiff seen in perfection at Constantinople, where it almost monopolizes the boat traffic. It is fast, but crank, being so narrow that the oars or sculls have their looms enlarged into ball-shaped masses to counterbalance their out-board length. It has borne for ages the wave-line now brought out in England as the highest result of marine architecture. It may have from one to ten or twelve rowers.

CAIRBAN. A name in the Hebrides for the basking-shark.

CAIRN. Piles of stones used as marks in surveying.

CAISSON, or Caissoon. An adopted term for a sort of float sunk to a required depth by letting water into it, when it is hauled under the ship's bottom, receives her steadily, and on pumping out the water floats her. These were long used in Holland, afterwards at Venice, and in Russia, where they were known as *camels* (which see). Caisson is also a vessel fitted with valves, to act instead of gates for a dry dock. Used also in *pontoons* (which see).

CAKE-ICE. Ice formed in the early part of the season.

CALABASH. *Cucurbita*, a gourd abundant within the tropics, furnishing drinking and washing utensils. At Tahiti and the Sandwich Islands they attain a diameter of 2 feet. There is also a calabash-tree, the fruit not exceeding the size of oranges.

CALABASS. An early kind of light musket with a wheel-lock. Bourne mentions it in 1578.

CALALOO. A dish of fish and vegetables.

CALAMUS. *See* RATTAN.

CALANCA. A creek or cove on Italian and Spanish coasts.

CALAVANCES [*Phaseolus vulgaris. Haricot*, Fr.] Small beans sometimes used for soup, instead of pease.

CALCULATE, To. This word, though disrated from respectability by American misuse, signified to foretell or prophesy; it is thus used by Shakspeare in the first act of "Julius Cæsar." To calculate the ship's position, either from astronomical observations or rate of the log.

CALENDAR. A distribution of time. (*See* ALMANAC.)

CALENDAR-TIME. On which officers' bills are drawn.

CALF. A word generally applied to the young of marine mammalia, as the whale.—*Calf*, in the Arctic regions, a mass of floe ice breaking from under a floe, which when disengaged rises with violence to the surface of the water; it differs from a tongue, which is the same body kept fixed beneath the main floe. The iceberg is formed by the repeated freezing of thawed snow running down over the slopes, until at length the wave from beneath and weight above causes it to break off and fall into the sea, or, as termed in Greenland, to calve. Thus, berg, is fresh-water ice, the work of years. The floe, is salt water frozen suddenly each winter, and dissolving in the summer.

CALF, OR CALVA. A Norwegian name, also used in the Hebrides, for islets lying off islands, and bearing a similar relation to them in size that a calf does to a cow. As the Calf at Mull and the Calf of Man.

CALFAT. The old word for caulking. [*Calfater*, Fr.; probably from *cale*, wedge, and *faire*, to make.] To wedge up an opening with any soft material, as oakum. [*Calafatear*, Sp.]

CALIBER, OR CALIBRE. The diameter of the bore of a gun, cannon, shot, or bullet. A ship's caliber means the known weight her armament represents.

CALIPASH. The upper shell of a turtle.

CALIPEE. The under shell of a turtle.

CALIVER. A hand-gun or arquebuss; probably the old name of the

matchlock or carabine, precursors of the modern firelock, or Enfield
rifle. (*See* CALABASS.)

CALL. A peculiar silver pipe or whistle, used by the boatswain and his
mates to attract attention, and summon the sailors to their meals or
duties by various strains, each of them appropriated to some particular
purpose, such as hoisting, heaving, lowering, veering away, belaying,
letting go a tackle-fall, sweeping, &c. This piping is as attentively
observed by sailors, as the bugle or beat of drum is obeyed by soldiers.
The coxswains of the boats of French ships of war are supplied with
calls to "in bow oar," or "of all," "oars," &c.

CALLIPERS. Bow-legged compasses, used to measure the girth of
timber, the external diameter of masts, shot, and other circular or
cylindrical substances. Also, an instrument with a sliding leg, used
for measuring the packages constituting a ship's cargo, which is paid
for by its cubical contents.

CALL THE WATCH. This is done every four hours, except at the
dog-watches, to relieve those on deck, also by pipe. "All the watch,"
or all the starboard, or the port, first, second, third, or fourth watches.

CALM. There being no wind stirring it is designated flat, dead, or
stark, under each of which the surface of the sea is unruffled.

CALM LATITUDES. That tropical tract of ocean which lies between
the north-east and south-east trade-winds; its situation varies several
degrees, depending upon the season of the year. The term is also
applied to a part of the sea on the Polar side of the trades, between
them and the westerly winds.

CALVERED SALMON. Salmon prepared in a peculiar manner in
early times.

CALVE'S TONGUE. A sort of moulding usually made at the caps
and bases of round pillars, to taper or hance the round part to the
square.

CAMBER. The part of a dockyard where cambering is performed, and
timber kept. Also, a small dock in the royal yards, for the convenience of loading and discharging timber. Also, anything that curves
upwards.—*To camber*, to curve ship-planks.

CAMBER-KEELED. Keel slightly arched upwards in the middle of
the length, but not actually hogged.

CAMBOOSE. A form of *caboose* (which see).

CAMELS. All large ships are built, at St. Petersburg, in a dockyard
off the Granite Quay, where the water is shallow; therefore a number
of camels or caissons are kept at Cronstadt, for the purpose of carrying
them down the river. Camels are hollow cases of wood, constructed
in two halves, so as to embrace the keel, and lay hold of the hull of a
ship on both sides. They are first filled with water and sunk, in order

to be fixed on. The water is then pumped out, when the vessel gradually rises, and the process is continued until the ship is enabled to pass over the shoal. Similar camels were used at Rotterdam about 1690.

CAME-TO. Brought to an anchor.

CAMFER. *See* CHAMFER.

CAMISADO. A sudden surprise or assault of the enemy.

CAMOCK. A very early term for crooked timber.

CAMP. The whole extent of ground on which an army pitches its tents and lodges. (*See* LEAVING THE CAMP.)

CAMP, OR CAMP-OUT, TO. In American travel, to rest for the night without a standing roof; whether under a light tent, a screen of boughs, or any make-shift that the neighbourhood may afford.

CAMPAIGN. A series of connected operations by an army in the field, unbroken by its retiring into quarters.

CAMPAIGNER. A veteran soldier.

CAMP-EQUIPAGE. *See* EQUIPAGE.

CAMPER. *See* KEMP.

CAMPESON. *See* GAMBISON.

CAMP-FIGHT. *See* ACRE.

CAN. A tin vessel used by sailors to drink out of.

CANAICHE, OR CANASH. An inner port, as at Granada in the West Indies.

CANAL-BOAT. A barge generally towed by horses, but furnished with a large square-sail for occasional use.

CAN-BODIES. The old term for anchor-buoys, now can-buoys.

CAN-BUOYS. Are in the form of a cone, and therefore would countenance the term cone-buoys. They are floated over sands and other obstructions in navigation, as marks to be avoided; they are made very large, to be seen at a distance; where there are several, they are distinguished by their colour, as black, red, white, or chequered, &c.

CANCELLED TICKET. One rendered useless by some subsequent arrangement or clerk's error. In either case the word "cancelled" is to be written across in large characters, and due record made. The corner cut off cancels good character, yet they are a certificate for time.

CANCER. The Crab; the fourth sign of the zodiac, which the sun enters about the 21st of June, and commences the summer solstice.

CANDLE-BARK. A cylindrical tin box for candles.

CANE. The rattan (*Calamus rudentum*), is extensively used in the East for rigging, rope, and cables. The latter have remained for years at the bottom of the sea uninjured by teredo, or any destructive crustacea. The cables, too, resist any but the sharpest axes, when used to connect logs as booms, to stop the navigation of rivers.

CANEVAS. The old word for hempen canvas; but many races, even the Chinese, make sails entirely of cane. The Americans frequently use cotton, and term that cloth duck. In the islands of the South Pacific it is made from the bark of various trees, grasses, &c.

CAN-HOOKS. They are used to sling a cask by the chimes, or ends of its staves, and are formed by reeving the two ends of a piece of rope or chain through the eyes of two flat hooks, and there making them fast. The tackle is then hooked to the middle of the bight.

CANISTER SHOT. *See* CASE-SHOT.

CANNIKIN. A small drinking-vessel.

CANNON. The well-known piece of artillery, mounted in battery on board or on shore, and made either of brass or iron. The principal parts are:—1st. The breech, together with the cascable and its button, called by seamen the pomelion. The breech is of solid metal, from the bottom of the concave cylinder or chamber to the cascable. 2d. The trunnions, which project on each side, and serve to support the cannon, hold it almost in equilibrio. 3d. The bore or caliber, is the interior of the cylinder, wherein the powder and shot are lodged when the cannon is loaded. The entrance of the bore is called the mouth or muzzle. It may be generally described as gradually tapering, with the various modifications of first and second reinforce and swell, to the muzzle or forward end. (*See* GUN.)

CANNONADE. The opening and continuance of the fire of artillery on any object attacked. Battering with cannon-shot.

CANNON-PERER. An ancient piece of ordnance used in ships of war for throwing stone shot.

CANNON-PETRONEL. A piece of ordnance with a 6-inch bore which carried a 24 lb. ball.

CANNON, RIFLED. Introduced by Captain Blakely, Sir W. Armstrong, and others.

CANNON ROYAL. A 60-pounder of eight and a half inches bore. (*See* CARTHOUN.)

CANNON-SERPENTINE. An old name for a gun of 7-inches bore.

CANOE. A peculiar boat used by several uncivilized nations, formed of the trunk of a tree hollowed out, and sometimes of several pieces of bark joined together, and again of hide. They are of various sizes, according to the uses for which they are designed, or the countries to which they belong. Some carry sail, but they are commonly rowed with paddles, somewhat resembling a corn-shovel; and instead of rowing with it horizontally, as with an oar, they manage it perpendicularly. In Greenland and Hudson Bay, the Esquimaux limits of America, skin-boats are chiefly in use, under the name of kaiack, oomiak, baidar, &c.

CANOPUS. The lucida of Argo Navis, and a Greenwich star. Also, a city of classical importance, visited by the heroes of the Trojan war, the reputed burial-place of the pilot of Menelaus, &c. But, as some ancient places have been so fortunate as to renew their classical importance in modern times, so this, under the modern name of Abukeir, has received a new "stamp of fate," by its overlooking, like Salamis, the scene of a naval battle, which also led to a decision of the fate of nations. In this bay Nelson, at one blow, destroyed the fleet of the enemy, and cut off the veteran army of France from the shores of Egypt. The Canopian mouth of the Nile was the most westerly of all the branches of that celebrated river.

CANOPY. A light awning over the stern-sheets of a boat.

CANT, To. To turn anything about, or so that it does not stand square. To diverge from a central right line. Cant the boat or ship; *i.e.* for careening her.

CANT. A cut made in a whale between the neck and the fins, to which the cant-purchase is made fast, for turning the animal round in the operation of flensing.

CANTARA. A watering-place.

CANT-BLOCKS. The large purchase-blocks used by whalers to cant the whales round under the process of flensing.

CANT-BODY. An imaginary figure of that part of a ship's body which forms the shape forward and aft, and whose planes make obtuse angles with the midship line of the ship.

CANTEEN. A small tin vessel for men on service to carry liquids. Also, a small chest containing utensils for an officer's messing. Also, a kind of suttling-house in garrisons.

CANTERA. A Spanish fishing-boat.

CANT-FALLS. *See* SPIKE-TACKLE.

CANT-HOOK. A lever with a hook at one end for heavy articles.

CANTICK-QUOINS. Short three-edged pieces of wood to steady casks from labouring against each other.

CANTING BALLAST. Is when by a sudden gust or stress of weather a ship is thrown so far over that the ballast settles to leeward, and prevents the ship from righting.

CANTING-LIVRE. *See* CONSOLE-BRACKET.

CANT-LINE. Synonymous with *girt-line*, as to cant the top over the lowermast-head.

CANTONMENTS. Troops detached and quartered in different towns and villages near each other.

CANT-PURCHASE. This is formed by a block suspended from the mainmast-head, and another block made fast to the cant cut in the whale. (*See* CANT-BLOCKS.)

CANT-RIBBONS. Those ribbons that do not lie in a horizontal or level direction.

CANT-ROPE. *See* FOUR CANT.

CANT-SPAR. A hand-mast pole, fit for making small masts or yards, booms, &c.

CANT-TIMBERS. They derive their name from being canted or raised obliquely from the keel. The upper ends of those on the bow are inclined to the stem, as those in the after-part incline to the stern-post above. In a word, cant-timbers are those which do not stand square with the middle line of the ship. They may be deemed radial bow or stern-timbers.

CANVAS [from *cannabis*, hemp]. A cloth made of hemp, and used for the sails of ships. It is purchased in bolts, and numbered from 1 to 8, rarely to 9 and 10. Number 1 being the coarsest and strongest, is used for the lower sails, as fore-sail and main-sail in large ships. When a vessel is in motion by means of her sails she is said to be under canvas.

CANVAS-BACK DUCK. An American wild duck (*Fuligula valisneria*), which takes this name from the colour of the back feathers; much esteemed as a delicacy.

CANVAS-CLIMBER. A word used by Marston for a sailor who goes aloft; hence Marina tells Leonine—

> "And, clasping to a mast, endur'd a sea
> That almost burst the deck, and from the ladder-tackle
> Wash'd off a canvas-climber."

CAP. A strong thick block of wood having two large holes through it, the one square, the other round, used to confine two masts together, when one is erected at the head of the other, in order to lengthen it. The principal caps of a ship are those of the lower masts, which are fitted with a strong eye-bolt on each side, wherein to hook the block by which the top-mast is drawn up through the cap. In the same manner as the top mast slides up through the cap of the lower mast, the topgallant-mast slides up through the cap of the top-masts. When made of iron the cap used to be called a crance.—*To cap* a mast-head is placing tarpaulin guards against weather. The term is applied to any covering such as lead put over iron bolts to prevent corrosion by sea-water, canvas covers over the ends of rigging, &c. &c. Also, pieces of oak laid on the upper blocks on which a vessel is built, to receive the keel. They are split out for the addition of the false keel, and therefore should be of the most free-grained timber. Also, the coating which guards the top of a quill tube. Also, the percussion priming for firearms.—*Cap-a-pied*, armed from head to foot.

CAP, To. To puzzle or beat in argument. To salute by touching the head-covering, as Shakspeare makes Iago's friends act to Othello. It is now more an academic than a sea-term.

CAPABARRE. An old term for misappropriating government stores. (*See* Marryat's *Novels*.)

CAPACISE. A corrupt form of *capsize*.

CAPACITY. Burden, tonnage, fitness for the service, rating.

CAPE. A projecting point of land jutting out from the coast-line; the extremity of a promontory, of which last it is the secondary rank. It differs from a headland, since a cape may be low. The Cape of Good Hope is always familiarly known as "The Cape." *Cape* was also used for a rhumb-line.

CAPE, To. To keep a course. How does she cape? how does she lie her course?

CAPE FLY-AWAY. A cloud-bank on the horizon, mistaken for land, which disappears as the ship advances. (*See* Fog.)

CAPE-HEN. *See* Molly-mok.

CAPELLA. The lucida of Auriga, and a nautical star.

CAPE-MERCHANT [*capo*]. An old name for super-cargo in early voyages, as also the head merchant in a factory.

CAPE-PIGEON, or Cape-petrel. A sea-bird which follows a ship in her passage round the cape; the *Procellaria capensis*. (*See* Pintado.)

CAPER. A light-armed vessel of the 17th century, used by the Dutch for privateering.

CAPER CORNER-WAY. Diagonally.

CAPFUL OF WIND. A light flaw, which suddenly careens a vessel and passes off.

CAPITAL of a Work. In fortification, an imaginary line bisecting its most prominent salient angle.

CAPITANA. Formerly the principal galley in a Mediterranean fleet: the admiral's ship.

CAPITULATION. The conditions on which a subdued force surrenders, agreed upon between the contending parties.

CAPLIN, or Capelin. A fish of the family Clupeidæ, very similar to a smelt; frequently imported from Newfoundland dried. It is the general bait for codfish there.

CAP'N. The way in which some address the commanders of merchant vessels.

CAPON. A jeering name for the red-herring.

CAPONNIERE. In fortification, a passage across the bottom of the ditch, covered, at the least, by a parapet on each side, and very generally also with a bomb-proof roof, when it may be furnished with many guns, which are of great importance in the defence of a fortress, as the besieger can hardly silence them till he has constructed batteries on the brink of the ditch.

CAPOTE. A good storm-coat with a hood, much worn in the Levant, and made of a special manufacture.

CAPPANUS. The worm which adheres to, and gnaws the bottom of a ship, to prevent which all ships should be sheathed with copper.

CAPPED. A ship making against a race or very strong currents.

CAPRICORNUS. The tenth sign of the zodiac, which the sun enters about the 21st of December, and opens the winter solstice.

CAP-SCUTTLE. A framing composed of coamings and head-ledges raised above the deck, with a top which shuts closely over into a rabbet.

CAP-SHORE. A supporting spar between the cap and the tressle-tree.

CAPSIZE, To. To upset or overturn anything.

CAP-SQUARE. The clamp of iron which shuts over the trunnions of a gun to secure them to the carriage, having a curve to receive one-third part of the trunnion, the other two being sunk in the carriage; it is closed by forelocks.

CAPSTAN, Cabestan, Capstern, Capston, &c. A mechanical arrangement for lifting great weights. There is a variety of capsterns, but they agree in having a horizontal circular head, which has square holes around its edge, and in these long bars are shipped, and are said to be "swifted" when their outer ends are traced together; beneath is a perpendicular barrel, round which is wrapped the rope or chain used to lift the anchor or other great weight, even to the heaving a ship off a shoal. Now, in most ships where a capstern is used to lift the anchor, the chain cable is itself brought to the capstern. The purchase or lifting power is gained by the great sweep of the bars. A perpendicular iron spindle passes through the whole capstern, and is stepped into a socket on the deck below the one on which it stands. In some cases capsterns are double in height, so that bars may be worked on two decks, giving more room for the men.

CAPSTAN, To Come up the. In one sense is to lift the pauls and walk back, or turn the capstan the contrary way, thereby slackening, or letting out some of the rope on which they have been heaving. The sudden order would be obeyed by surging, or letting go any rope on which they were heaving. Synonymous to "Come up the purchase."

CAPSTAN, To heave at the. To urge it round, by pushing against the bars, as already described.

CAPSTAN, To man the. To place the sailors at it in readiness to heave.

CAPSTAN, To paul the. To drop all the pauls into their sockets, to prevent the capstan from recoiling during any pause of heaving.

CAPSTAN, To rig the. To fix the bars in their respective holes, thrust in the pins to confine them, and reeve the swifter through the ends.

CAPSTAN, Surge the. Is the order to slacken the rope which is wound round the barrel while heaving, to prevent it from riding or fouling. This term specially applies to surging the messenger when it rides, or when the two lashing eyes foul on the whelps or the barrel.

CAPSTAN-BAR PINS. Pins inserted through their ends to prevent their unshipping.

CAPSTAN-BARRING. An obsolete sea-punishment, in which the offender was sentenced to carry a capstan-bar during a watch.

CAPSTAN-BARS. Long pieces of wood of the best ash or hiccory, one end of which is thrust into the square holes in the drum-head, like the spokes of a wheel. They are used to heave the capstan round, by the men setting their hands and chests against them, and walking round. They are also held in their places in the drumhead holes, by little iron bolts called capstan or safety pins, to prevent their flying out when the surging overcomes the force of the men. Many men have been killed by this action, and more by the omission to "pin and swift."

CAPSTAN-ROOM. *See* Room.

CAPSTAN-STEP. (*See* Step of the Capstan.) The men march round to the tune of a fiddle or fife, and the phrase of excitement is, "Step out, lads, make your feet tell."

CAPSTAN-SWIFTER. A rope passed horizontally through notches in the outer ends of the bars, and drawn very tight: the intent is to steady the men as they walk round when the ship rolls, and to give room for a greater number to assist, by manning the swifters both within and without.

CAPTAIN. This title is said to be derived from the eastern military magistrate *katapan*, meaning "over everything;" but the term *capitano* was in use among the Italians nearly 200 years before Basilius II. appointed his katapan of Apulia and Calabria, A.D. 984. Hence, the corruption of the Apulian province into *capitanata*. Among the Anglo-Saxons the captain was *schipp-hláford*, or ship's lord. The captain, strictly speaking, is the officer commanding a line-of-battle ship, or a frigate carrying twenty or more cannon. A captain in the royal navy is answerable for any bad conduct in the military government, navigation, and equipment of his ship; also for any neglect of duty in his inferior officers, whose several charges he is appointed to regulate. It is also a title, though incorrectly, given to the masters of all vessels whatever, they having no commissions. It is also applied in the navy itself to the chief sailor of particular gangs of men; in rank, captain of the forecastle, admiral's coxswain, captain's coxswain, captain of the hold, captain of maintop, captain of foretop, &c.

CAPTAIN. A name given to the crooner, crowner, or gray gurnard (*Trigla gurnardus*).

CAPTAIN OF A MERCHANT SHIP. Is a certificated officer in the mercantile marine, intrusted with the entire charge of a ship, both as regards life and property. He is in no way invested with special powers to meet his peculiar circumstances, but has chiefly to depend upon moral influence for maintaining order amongst his passengers and crew during the many weeks or even months that he is cut off from appeal to the laws of his country, only resorting to force on extreme occasions. Great tact and judgment is required to fulfil this duty properly.

CAPTAIN OF A SHIP OF WAR. Is the commanding officer; as well the post-captain (a title now disused) as those whose proper title is commander.

CAPTAIN OF THE FLEET. Is a temporary admiralty appointment; he is entitled to be considered as a flag-officer, and to a share in the prize-money accordingly. He carries out all orders issued by the commander-in-chief, but his special duty is to keep up the discipline of the fleet, in which he is supreme. He is the adjutant-general of the force, hoisting the flag and wearing the uniform of rear-admiral.

CAPTAIN OF THE HEAD. Not a recognized rating, but an ordinary man appointed to attend to the swabs, and to keep the ship's head clean.

CAPTAIN OF THE HOLD. The last of the captains in rank, as a first-class petty officer.

CAPTAIN OF THE PORT. The captain of the port is probably better explained by referring to that situation at Gibraltar. He belongs to the Board of Health; he controls the entries and departures, the berthing at the anchorage, and general marine duties, but possesses no naval authority. Hence, the port-captain is quite another officer. (*See* PORT-CAPTAIN.)

CAPTAIN-GENERAL. The highest army rank.

CAPTAIN'S CLERK. One whose duty is strictly to keep all books and official papers necessary for passing the captain's accounts at the admiralty.

CAPTAIN'S CLOAK. The jocose name given to the last sweeping clause, the thirty-sixth article of war :—"All other crimes not capital, and for which no punishment is hereby directed to be inflicted, shall be punished according to the laws and customs in such cases used at sea."

CAPTAIN'S GIG. *See* GIG.

CAPTAIN'S STORE-ROOM. A place of reserve on the platform deck, for the captain's wines and sea-stores.

CAPTIVE. A prisoner of war.

CAPTORS. The conquerors of and sharers in the proceeds of a prize. Captors are not at liberty to release prisoners belonging to the ships of the enemy. The last survivor is in law the only captor.

CAPTURE. A prize taken by a ship of war at sea; is the taking forcible possession of vessels or goods belonging to one nation by those of a hostile nation. Vessels are looked on as prizes if they fight under any other standard than that of the state from which they have their commission; if they have no charty-party, manifest, or bill of lading, or if loaded with effects belonging to the king's enemies, or even contraband goods. Whether the capture be lawful or unlawful, the insurer is rendered liable to the loss.

CAR. A north-country word, denoting any swampy land surrounded by inclosures, and occasionally under water.

CARABINEER. One who uses the carbine.

CARACK, Carrak, or Carrick. A large ship of burden, the same with those called galleons. Hippus, the Tyrian, is said to have first devised caracks, and onerary vessels of prodigious bulk for traffic or offence.

CARACORA. A proa of Borneo, Ternate, and the Eastern Isles; also called caracol by early voyagers.

CARAMOUSSAL. A Turkish merchant ship with a pink-stern.

CARAVEL, or Caravela. A Portuguese despatch boat, lateen-rigged, formerly in use; it had square sails only on the fore-mast, though dignified as a caravela.

CARAVELAO. A light pink-sterned vessel of the Azores.

CARBASSE. *See* Karbatz.

CARBIN. A name in our northern isles for the basking shark.

CARBINE, or Carabine. A fire-arm of less length and weight than a musket, originally carrying a smaller ball, though latterly, for the convenience of the supply of ammunition, throwing the same bullet as the musket, though with a smaller charge. It has been proper to mounted troops since about A.D. 1556, and has been preferred to the musket as a weapon for the tops of ships as well as boats.

CARCASS. An iron shell for incendiary purposes, filled with a very fiercely flaming composition of saltpetre, sulphur, resin, turpentine, antimony, and tallow. It has three vents for the flame, and sometimes is equipped with pistol barrels, so fitted in its interior as to discharge their bullets at various times.

CARCASS OF A SHIP. The ribs, with keel, stem, and stern-post, after the planks are stripped off.

CARCATUS [from *caricato*, It.] A law-term for a freighted ship.

CARD. The dial or face of the magnetic compass-card.

"Reason the card, but passion is the gale."—*Pope.*

Probably derived from *cardinal.*

CARDINAL POINTS. The general name by which the north, east, south, and west rhumbs of the horizon are distinguished.

CARDINAL POINTS OF THE ECLIPTIC. The equinoctial and solstitial points; namely, the commencement of Aries and Libra, and of Cancer and Capricornus.

CARDINAL SIGNS. The zodiacal signs which the sun enters at the equinoxes and solstices.

CARDINAL WINDS. Those from the due north, east, south, and west points of the compass.

CAREEN, To. A ship is said to careen when she inclines to one side, or lies over when sailing on a wind; off her keel or carina.

CAREENING. The operation of heaving the ship down on one side, by arranging the ballast, or the application of a strong purchase to her masts, which require to be expressly supported for the occasion to prevent their springing; by these means one side of the bottom, elevated above the surface of the water, may be cleansed or repaired. (*See* BREAMING.) But this operation is now nearly superseded by sheathing ships with copper, whereby they keep a clean bottom for several years.

CAREENING BEACH. A part of the strand prepared for the purpose of a ship's being grounded on a list or careen, to repair defects.

CARFINDO. One of the carpenter's crew.

CARGO. The merchandise a ship is freighted with.

CARGO-BOOK. The master of every coasting-vessel is required to keep a cargo-book, stating the name of the ship, of the master, of the port to which she belongs, and that to which she is bound; with a roll of all goods, shippers, and consignees. In all other merchant ships the cargo-book is a clean copy of all cargo entered in the gangway-book, and shows the mark, number, quality, and (if measurement goods) the dimensions of such packages of a ship's cargo.

CARICATORE. Places where the traders of Sicily take in their goods, from *caricare*, to load.

CARINA. An old term, from the Latin, for the keel, or a ship's bottom. The north-country term keel means an entire vessel: "So many keels touched the strand." (*See* KEEL.)

CARL, OR MALE HEMP. *See* FIMBLE or FEMBLE HEMP.

CARLE-CRAB. The male of the black-clawed crab, *Cancer pagurus;* also of the partan or common crab.

CARLINE-KNEES. Timbers going athwart the ship, from the sides to the hatchway, serving to sustain the deck on both sides.

CARLINES, or CARLINGS. Pieces of timber about five inches square, lying fore and aft, along from one beam to another. On and athwart these the ledges rest, whereon the planks of the deck and other portions of carpentry are made fast. The carlines have their end let into the beams, called "culver-tail-wise," or scored in pigeon-fashion. There are other carlines of a subordinate character.

CARLINO, or CAROLINE. A small silver coin of Naples, value 4d. English. Ten carlini make a ducat in commerce.

CARN-TANGLE. A long and large fucus, thrown on our northern beaches after a gale of wind in the offing.

CAROUS. A sort of gallery in ancient ships, which turned on a pivot. It was hoisted to a given height by tackles, and thus brought to project over, or into, the vessel of an adversary, furnishing a bridge for boarding.

CARP. A well-known fresh-water fish of the Cyprinidæ family, considered to have been introduced into England in the time of Henry VIII.; but in Dame Berner's book on angling, published in 1486, it is described as the "daynteous fysshe" in England.

CARPENTER, SHIP. A ship-builder. An officer appointed to examine and keep in order the hull of a ship, and all her appurtenances, likewise the stores committed to him by indenture from the store-keeper of the dockyard. The absence of other tradesmen whilst a ship is at sea, and the numerous emergencies in which ships are placed requiring invention, render a good ship's carpenter one of the most valuable artizans on board.

CARPENTER'S CREW. Consists of a portion of the crew, provided for ship-carpentry and ship-building. In ships of war there are two carpenter's mates and one caulker, one blacksmith, and a carpenter's crew, according to the size of the ship.

CARPENTER'S STORE-ROOM. An apartment built below, on the platform-deck, for keeping the carpenter's stores and spare tools in.

CARPENTER'S YEOMAN. See YEOMAN.

CARPET-KNIGHT. A man who obtains knighthood on a pretence for services in which he never participated.

CARPET-MEN. Those officers who, without services or merit, obtain rapid promotion through political or other interest, and are yet declared "highly meritorious and distinguished."

CARR. See KARR.

CARRAC, CARRACA, CARRACK, OR CARRICKE. A name given by the Spaniards and Portuguese to the vessels they sent to Brazil and the East Indies; large, round built, and fitted for fight as well as burden. Their capacity lay in their depth, which was extraordinary. English vessels of size and value were sometimes also so called.

CARRARA. The great northern diver, *Colymbus glacialis*.

CARREE. A Manx or Gaelic term for the scud or small clouds that drive with the wind.

CARRIAGE of a Gun. The frame on which it is mounted for firing, constructed either exclusively for this purpose, or also for travelling in the field. Carriages for its transport only, are not included under this term. The first kind only is in general use afloat, where it usually consists of two thick planks (called brackets or cheeks) laid on edge to support the trunnions, and resting, besides other transverse connections, on two axle-trees, which are borne on low solid wooden wheels called trucks, or sometimes, to diminish the recoil, on flat blocks called chocks. The hind axle-tree takes, with the intervention of various elevating arrangements, the preponderance of the breech. The second kind is adapted for field and siege work: the shallow brackets are raised in front on high wheels, but unite behind into a solid beam called the trail, which tapers downwards, and rests on the ground when in action, but for travel is connected to a two-wheeled carriage called a *limber* (which see). Gun-carriages are chiefly made of elm for ship-board, as less given to splinter from shot, and of oak on shore; wrought-iron, however, is being applied for the carriages of the large guns recently introduced, and even cast-iron is economically used in some fortresses little liable to sudden counter-battery.

CARRICK. An old Gaelic term for a castle or fortress, as well as for a rock in the sea.

CARRICK-BEND. A kind of knot, formed on a bight by putting the end of a rope over its standing part, and then passing it.

CARRICK-BITTS. The bitts which support the ends or spindles of the windlass, whence they are also called windlass-bitts.

CARRIED. Taken, applied to the capture of forts and ships.

CARRONADE. A short gun, capable of carrying a large ball, and useful in close engagements at sea. It takes its name from the large iron-foundry on the banks of the Carron, near Falkirk, in Scotland, where this sort of ordnance was first made, or the principle applied to an improved construction. Shorter and lighter than the common cannon, and having a chamber for the powder like a mortar, they are generally of large calibre, and carried on the upper works, as the poop and forecastle.

CARRONADE SLIDE. Composed of two wide balks of elm on which the carronade carriage slides. As the slide is bolted to the ship's side, and is a radius from that bolt or pivot, carronades were once the only guns which could be truly concentrated on a given object.

CARRY, To. To subdue a vessel by boarding her. To move anything along the decks. (*See* Lash and Carry, as relating to hammocks.)

Also, to obtain possession of a fort or place by force. Also, the direction or movement of the clouds. Also, a gun is said to carry its shot so many yards. Also, a ship carries her canvas, and her cargo.

CARRY AWAY, To. To break; as, "That ship has carried away her fore-topmast," *i.e.* has broken it off. It is customary to say, we carried away this or that, when knocked, shot, or blown away. It is also used when a rope has been parted by violence.

CARRYING ON DUTY. The operations of the officer in charge of the deck or watch.

CARRYING ON THE WAR. Making suitable arrangements for carrying on the lark or amusement.

CARRY ON, To. To spread all sail; also, beyond discretion, or at all hazards. In galley-slang, to joke a person even to anger; also riotous frolicking.

CARRY THE KEG. *See* KEG.

CARTE BLANCHE. In the service sense of the term, implies an authority to act at discretion.

CARTEL. A ship commissioned in time of war to exchange the prisoners of any two hostile powers, or to carry a proposal from one to the other; for this reason she has only one gun, for the purpose of firing signals, as the officer who commands her is particularly ordered to carry no cargo, ammunition, or implements of war. Cartel also signifies an agreement between two hostile powers for a mutual exchange of prisoners. In late wars, ships of war fully armed, but under cartel, carried commissions for settling peace, as flags of truce. Cartel-ships, by trading in any way, are liable to confiscation.

CARTHOUN. The ancient cannon royal, carrying a 66 lb. ball, with a point blank range of 185 paces, and an extreme one of about 2000. It was 12 feet long and of $8\frac{1}{2}$ inches diameter of bore.

CARTOUCH-BOX. The accoutrement which contains the musket-cartridges: now generally called a pouch.

CARTOW. *See* CART-PIECE.

CART-PIECE. An early battering cannon mounted on a peculiar cart.

CARTRIDGE. The case in which the exact charge of powder for fire-arms is made up—of paper for small-arms, of flannel for great guns, or of sheet metal for breech-loading muskets. For small-arms generally the cartridge contains the bullet as well as the powder, and in the case of most breech-loaders, the percussion priming also; in the case of some very light pieces the shot is included, and then named a round of "fixed ammunition;" and for breech-loading guns some sort of lubricator is generally inclosed in the forward end of the cartridge.

CARTRIDGE-BOX. A cylindrical wooden box with a lid sliding upon a handle of small rope, just containing one cartridge, and used for its safe conveyance from the magazine to the gun—borne to and fro by powder-monkeys (boys) of old. The term is loosely applied to the ammunition pouch.

CARUEL. *See* CARVEL.

CARVED WORK. The ornaments of a ship which are wrought by the carver.

CARVEL. A light lateen-rigged vessel of small burden, formerly used by the Spaniards and Portuguese. Also, a coarse sea-blubber, on which turtles are said to feed.

CARVEL-BUILT. A vessel or boat, the planks of which are all flush and smooth, the edges laid close to each other, and caulked to make them water-tight: in contradistinction to clinker-built, where they overlap each other.

CARY. *See* MOTHER CARY'S CHICKEN. *Procellaria pelagica.*

CASCABLE. That generally convex part of a gun which terminates the breech end of it. The term includes the usual button which is connected to it by the neck of the cascable.

CASCADE. A fall of water from a considerable height, rather by successive stages than in a single mass, as with a cataract.

CASCO. A rubbish-lighter of the Philippine Islands.

CASE. The outside planking of the ship.

CASE-BOOK. A register or journal in which the surgeon records the cases of all the sick and wounded, who are placed under medical treatment.

CASEMATE. In fortification, a chamber having a vaulted roof capable of resisting vertical fire, and affording embrasures or loopholes to contribute to the defence of the place: without these it would be merely a bomb-proof.

CASERNES. Often considered as synonymous with *barracks;* but more correctly small lodgments erected between the ramparts and houses of a fortified town, to ease the inhabitants by quartering soldiers there, who are also in better condition for duty than if living in various parts.

CASE-SHOT, COMMON. Called also canister-shot. Adapted for close quarters if the enemy be uncovered. It consists of a number of small iron balls, varying in weight and number, packed in a cylindrical tin case fitting the bore of the gun from which it is to be fired. Burrel, langrage, and other irregular substitutes, may be included under the term. Spherical case-shot are officially called *shrapnel-shell* (which see).

CASHIERED. Sentenced by a court-martial to be dismissed the service. By such sentence an officer is rendered ever after incapable of serving the sovereign in any position, naval or military.

CASING. The lining, veneering, or planking over a ship's timbers, especially for the cabin-beams; the sheathing of her. Also a bulk-head round a mast to prevent the interference of cargo, or shifting materials.

CASING-COVER. In the marine steam-engine is a steam-tight open-ing for the slide-valve rod to pass through.

CASK. A barrel for fluid or solid provisions. (*See* STOWAGE.)

CASKETS (properly GASKETS). Small ropes made of sinnet, and fastened to grummets or little rings upon the yards. Their use is to make the sail fast to the yard when it is to be furled.

CASSAVA, OR CASSADA. A species of the genus *Jatropha janipha*, well known to seamen as the cassava bread of the West Indies. Tapioca is produced from the *Jatropha manihot*. Caution is necessary in the use of these roots, as the juice is poisonous. The root used as chewsticks, to cleanse the teeth and gums, by the negroes, produces a copious flow of frothy saliva.

CAST. A coast term meaning four, as applied to haddocks, herrings, &c. Also, the appearance of the sky when day begins to break. A cast of pots, &c.—*A'cast*, when a ship's yards are braced a'cast pre-paratory to weighing. Also condemned, cast by survey, &c.

CAST, To. To fall off, so as to bring the direction of the wind on one side of the ship, which before was right ahead. This term is particu-larly applied to a ship riding head to wind, when her anchor first loosens from the ground. To pay a vessel's head off, or turn it, is getting under weigh on the tack she is to sail upon, and it is casting to starboard, or port, according to the intention.—*To cast anchor.* To drop or let go the anchor for riding by—synonymous with to anchor. —*To cast a traverse.* To calculate and lay off the courses and dis-tances run over upon a chart.—*To cast off.* To let go at once. To loosen from.

CAST. A short boat passage.

CAST-AWAY. Shipwrecked.

CAST-AWAYS. People belonging to vessels stranded by stress of weather. Men who have hidden themselves, or are purposely left behind, when their vessel quits port.

CASTING ACCOUNTS. Sea-sickness.

CAST-KNEES. Those hanging knees which compass or arch over the angle of a man-of-war's ports, rider, &c.

CASTLE. A place strong by art or nature, or by both. A sort of little citadel. (*See* FORECASTLE, AFTER-CASTLE, &c.)

CASTLE-WRIGHTS. Particular artificers employed in the erection of the early ship's castles.

CAST-OFFS. Landsmen's clothes.

CAST OF THE LEAD. The act of heaving the lead into the sea to ascertain what depth of water there is. (*See also* HEAVE and SOUND.) The result is a cast—"Get a cast of the lead."

CASTOR. α Gemini, a well-known nautical star in the zodiac, which has proved to be a double star.

CASTOR AND POLLUX. Fiery balls which appear at the mast-heads, yard-arms, or sticking to the rigging of vessels in a gale at sea. (*See* COMPOSANT and CORPO SANTO.)

CASTRAMETATION. The art of planning camps, and selecting an appropriate position, in which the main requirement is that the troops of all arms should be so planted in camp as immediately to cover their proper positions in the line of battle.

CAST THE WRONG WAY. *See* WRONG WAY.

CASUALTIES. In a military sense, comprehends all men who die, are wounded, desert, or are discharged as unfit for service.

CAT. A ship formed on the Norwegian model, and usually employed in the coal and timber trade. These vessels are generally built remarkably strong, and may carry six hundred tons; or in the language of their own mariners, from 20 to 30 keels of coals. A cat is distinguished by a narrow stern, projecting quarters, a deep waist, and no ornamental figure on the prow.

CATALAN. A small Spanish fishing-boat.

CATAMARAN. A sort of raft used in the East Indies, Brazils, and elsewhere: those of the island of Ceylon, like those of Madras and other parts of that coast, are formed of three logs; the timber preferred for their construction is the *Dup* wood, or *Cherne-Maram*, the pine varnish-tree. Their length is from 20 to 25 feet, and breadth $2\frac{1}{2}$ to $3\frac{1}{2}$ feet, secured together by means of three spreaders and cross lashings, through small holes; the centre log is much the largest, with a curved surface at the fore-end, which tends and finishes upwards to a point. The side logs are very similar in form, and fitted to the centre log. These floats are navigated with great skill by one or two men, in a kneeling position; they think nothing of passing through the surf which lashes the beach at Madras and at other parts of these coasts, when even the boats of the country could not live upon the waves; they are also propelled out to the shipping at anchor when boats of the best construction and form would be swamped. In the monsoons, when a sail can be got on them, a small outrigger is placed at the end of two poles, as a balance, with a bamboo mast and yard, and a mat or cotton-cloth sail, all three parts of which are connected; and when the tack and sheet of the sail are let go, it all falls fore and aft alongside, and being light, is easily managed. In carrying a press of sail, they are trimmed by the balance-lever, by going out on the poles so as to keep the log on the surface of the water, and not impede its velocity, which, in a strong wind, is very great.

CATANADROMI. Migratory fishes, which have their stated times of going from fresh-water to salt and returning, as the salmon, &c.

CATAPULT. A military engine used by the ancients for throwing stones, spears, &c.

CATARACT. The sudden fall of a large body of water from a higher to a lower level, and rather in a single sheet than by successive leaps, as in a cascade.

CATASCOPIA. Small vessels anciently used for reconnoitring and carrying despatches.

CAT-BEAM. This, called also the beakhead-beam, is the broadest beam in the ship, and is generally made of two beams tabled and bolted together.

CAT-BLOCK. A two or three fold block, with an iron strop and large hook to it, which is employed to cat or draw the anchor up to the cat-head, which is also fitted with three great sheaves to correspond.

CATCH. A term used among fishermen to denote a quantity of fish taken at one time.

CATCH A CRAB. In rowing, when an oar gets so far beneath the surface of the water, that the rower cannot recover it in time to prevent his being knocked backwards.

CATCH A TURN THERE. Belay quickly.

CATCH-FAKE. An unseemly doubling in a badly coiled rope.

CATERER. A purveyor and provider of provisions: now used for the person who takes charge of and regulates the economy of a mess. (*See* ACATER.)

CAT-FALL. The rope rove for the cat-purchase, by which the anchor is raised to the cat-head or catted.

CAT-FISH. A name for the sea-wolf (*Anarrhicas lupus*).

CAT-GUT. A term applied to the sea-laces or *Fucus filum*. (*See* SEA CAT-GUT.

CAT-HARPINGS, OR CATHARPIN LEGS. Ropes under the tops at the lower end of the futtock-shrouds, serving to brace in the shrouds tighter, and affording room to brace the yards more obliquely when the ship is close-hauled. They keep the shrouds taut for the better ease and safety of the mast.

CAT-HEAD. The cat-head passes through the bow-bulwark obliquely forward on a radial line from the fore-mast, rests on the timbers even with the water-way, passes through the deck, and is secured to the side-timbers. It is selected from curved timber. Its upper head is on a level with the upper rail; it is furnished with three great sheaves, and externally strengthened by a cat-head knee. It not only is used to lift the anchor from the surface of the water, but as it "looks forward," the cat-block is frequently lashed to the cable to aid by its powerful purchase when the capstan fails to make an impression. The cat-fall rove through the sheaves, and the cat-block furnish the cat-purchase. The cat-head thus serves to suspend the anchor clear of the bow, when it is necessary to let it go: the knee by which it is supported is generally ornamented with carving. Termed also *cat-head bracket*.

CAT-HOLES. Places or spaces made in the quarter, for carrying out fasts or springs for steadying or heaving astern.

CAT-HOOK. A strong hook which is a continuation of the iron strop of the cat-block, used to hook the ring of the anchor when it is to be drawn up or catted.

CAT-LAP. A common phrase for tea or weak drink.

CAT O' NINE TAILS. An instrument of punishment used on board ships in the navy; it is commonly of nine pieces of line or cord, about half a yard long, fixed upon a piece of thick rope for a handle, and having three knots on each, at small intervals, nearest one end; with this the seamen who transgress are flogged upon the bare back.

CATRAIA. The catraia of Lisbon and Oporto, or pilot surf-boats, are about 56 feet long, by 15 feet beam, impelled by sixteen oars.

CAT-RIG. A rig which in smooth water surpasses every other, but, being utterly unsuited for sea or heavy weather, is only applicable to pleasure-boats who can choose their weather. It allows one sail only —an enormous fore-and-aft main-sail, spread by a gaff at the head and a boom at the foot, hoisted on a stout mast, which is stepped close to the stem.

CAT-ROPE. A line for hauling the cat-hook about: also cat-back-rope, which hauls the block to the ring of the anchor in order to hook it.

CAT'S-PAW. A light air perceived at a distance in a calm, by the impressions made on the surface of the sea, which it sweeps very gently, and then passes away, being equally partial and transitory. Old superstitious seamen are seen to scratch the backstays with their nails, and whistle to invoke even these cat's-paws, the general forerunner of the steadier breeze. Cat's-paw is also a name given to a particular twisting hitch, made in the bight of a rope, so as to induce two small bights, in order to hook a tackle on them both. Also, good-looking seamen employed to entice volunteers.

CAT'S-SKIN. A light partial current of air, as with the cat's-paw.

CAT'S-TAIL. The inner part of the cat-head, that fays down upon the cat-beam.

CAT-STOPPER, or CATHEAD-STOPPER. A piece of rope or chain rove through the ring of an anchor, to secure it for sea, or singled before letting it go.

CAT-TACKLE. A strong tackle, used to draw the anchor perpendicularly up to the cat-head, which latter is sometimes called cat.

CATTAN. *See* KATAN.

CAT THE ANCHOR. When the cat is hooked and "cable enough" veered and stoppered, the anchor hangs below the cat-head, swings beneath it; it is then hauled close up to the cat-head by the purchase called the cat-fall. The cat-stopper is then passed, and the cat-block unhooked.

CATTING. The act of heaving the anchor by the cat-tackle. Also, sea-sickness.

CATTY. A Chinese commercial weight of 18 ozs. English. Tea is packed in one or two or more catty boxes, hence most likely our word tea-caddy.

CAUDAL FIN. The vertical median fin terminating the tail of fishes.

CAUDICARIÆ. A kind of lighter used by the Romans on the Tiber.

CAUL. The membrane encompassing the head of some infants when born, and from early antiquity esteemed an omen of good fortune, and a preservative against drowning; it was sought by the Roman lawyers with as much avidity as by modern voyagers. Also, a northern name for a dam-dike. Also, an oriental license. (*See* KAULE.)

CAULK, To. (*See* CAULKING.) To lie down on deck and sleep, with clothes on.

CAULKER. He who caulks and pays the seams. This word is mistaken by many for *cawker* (which see).

CAULKER'S SEAT. A box slung to a ship's side whereon a caulker can sit and use his irons; it contains his tools and oakum.

CAULKING OF A SHIP. Forcing a quantity of oakum, or old ropes untwisted and drawn asunder, into the seams of the planks, or into the intervals where the planks are joined together in the ship's decks or sides, or rends in the planks, in order to prevent the entrance of water. After the oakum is driven in very hard, hot melted pitch or rosin is poured into the groove, to keep the water from rotting it. Among the ancients the first who made use of pitch in caulking were the inhabitants of Phæacia, afterwards called Corfu. Wax and rosin appear to have been commonly used before that period; and the Poles still substitute an unctuous clay for the same purpose for the vessels on their navigable rivers.

CAULKING-BUTT. The opening between ends or joints of the planks when worked for caulking.

CAULKING-IRONS. The peculiar chisels used for the purpose of caulking: they are the caulking-iron, the making-iron, the reeming-iron, and the rasing-iron.

CAULKING-MALLET. The wooden beetle or instrument with which the caulking-irons are driven.

CAURY. Worm-eaten.

CAVALIER. In fortification, a work raised considerably higher than its neighbours, but generally of similar plan. Its object is to afford a plunging fire, especially into the near approaches of a besieger, and to shelter adjacent faces from enfilade. Its most frequent position in fortresses is at the salient of the ravelin, or within the bastion; and in siege-works in the advanced trenches, for the purpose of enabling the musketry of the attack to drive the defenders out of the covered way.

CAVALLO, by some CARVALHAS. An oceanic fish, well-known as the bonito or horse-mackerel.

CAVALOT. A gun carrying a ball of one pound.

CAVALRY. That body of soldiers which serves and fights on horseback.

CAVER. See KAVER.

CAVIARE. A preparation of the roe of sturgeons and other fish salted. It forms a lucrative branch of commerce in Italy and Russia.

CAVIL. A large cleat for belaying the fore and main tacks, sheets, and braces to. (See KEVEL.)

CAVITY. In naval architecture signifies the displacement formed in the water by the immersed bottom and sides of the vessel.

CAWE, OR CAWFE. An east-country eel-box, or a floating perforated cage in which lobsters are kept.

CAWKER. An old term signifying a glass of strong spirits taken in the morning.

CAY, OR CAYOS. Little insulated sandy spots and rocks. The Spaniards in the West Indies called the Bahamas *Los Cayos*, which we wrote *Lucayos*. (See KEY.)

CAZE-MATTE. See CASEMATE.

CAZERNS. See CASERNES.

C.B. The uncials of Companion of the most honourable Order of the Bath. This grade was recently distributed so profusely that an undecorated veteran testily remarked that if government went on thus there would soon be more C.B.'s than A.B.'s in the navy.

CEASE FIRING. The order to leave off.

CEILING. The lining or planks on the inside of a ship's frame: these are placed on the flat of the floor, and carried up to the hold-beams. The term is a synonym of *foot-waling* (which see).

CELLS. See SILLS.

CELOCES, OR CELETES. Light row-boats, formerly used in piracy, and also for conveying advice.

CEMENT, ROMAN. For docks, piers, &c. See POZZOLANA.

CENTIME. See FRANC.

CENTINEL. See SENTRY.

CENTRAL ECLIPSE. See ECLIPSE.

CENTRE (usually CENTER). The division of a fleet between the van and the rear of the line of battle, and between the weather and lee divisions in the order of sailing.

CENTRE OF CAVITY, OF DISPLACEMENT, OF IMMERSION, AND OF BUOYANCY, are synonymous terms in naval architecture for the mean centre of that part of a vessel which is immersed in the water.

CENTRE OF GRAVITY, OR BALANCING POINT. *See* GRAVITY.

CENTRE OF MOTION. *See* MOTION (CENTRE OF).

CENTURION. A military officer who commanded one hundred men, in the Roman armies.

CEOLA. A very old term for a large ship.

CERADENE. A large fresh-water mussel.

CERCURI. Ancient ships of burden fitted with both sails and oars.

CERTIFICATE. A voucher or written testimony to the truth of any statement. An attestation of servitude, signed by the captain, is given with all discharges of men in the navy.

CERTIFY, To. To bear official testimony.

CESSATION OF ARMS. A discontinuation or suspension of hostilities.

CETINE. An ancient large float, says Heyschius, "in bulk like a whale;" derived from cetus, which applied both to whale and ship.

C.G. Coast-guard (which see).

CHAD. A fish like a small bream, abundant on the south-west coasts of England.

CHAFE, To. To rub or fret the surface of a cable, mast, or yard, by the motion of the ship or otherwise, against anything that is too hard for it.—*Chafing-gear*, is the stuff put upon the rigging and spars to prevent their being chafed.

CHAFFER. A name for a whale or grampus of the northern seas.

CHAFING-CHEEKS. A name given by old sailors to the sheaves instead of blocks on the yards in light-rigged vessels.

CHAFING-GEAR. Mats, sinnet, spun-yarn, strands, battens, scotchmen, and the like.

CHAIN. When mountains, hills, lakes, and islands are linked together, or follow each other in succession, so that their whole length greatly exceeds their breadth, they form what is termed a chain. A measuring chain is divided into links, &c., made of stout wire, because line is apt to shrink on wet ground and give way. The chain measure is 66 feet.

CHAINAGE OF SHIP. An old right of the admiral.

CHAIN-BOLT. A large bolt to secure the chains of the dead-eyes through the toe-link, for the purpose of securing the masts by the shrouds. Also, the bolts which fasten the channel-plates to the ship's side.

CHAIN-CABLE COMPRESSOR. A curved arm of iron which

revolves on a bolt through an eye at one end, at the other is a larger eye in which a tackle is hooked; it is used to bind the cable against the pipe through which it is passing, and check it from running out too quickly.

CHAIN-CABLE CONTROLLER. A contrivance for the prevention of one part of the chain riding on another while heaving in.

CHAIN-CABLES. Are not new; Cæsar found them on the shores of the British Channel. In 1818 I saw upwards of eighty sail of vessels with them at Desenzano, on the Lago di Garda. They have all but superseded hemp cables in recent times; they are divided into parts 15 fathoms in length, which are connected by shackles, any one of which may be slipped in emergency; at each $7\frac{1}{2}$ fathoms a swivel used to be inserted, but in many cases they are now dispensed with.

CHAIN-CABLE SHACKLES. Used for coupling the parts of a chain-cable at various lengths, so that they may be disconnected when circumstance demands it.

CHAIN-HOOK. An iron rod with a handling-eye at one end, and a hook at the other, for hauling the chain-cables about.

CHAIN-PIPE. An aperture through which a chain-cable passes from the chain-well to the deck above.

CHAIN-PLATES. Plates of iron with their lower ends bolted to the ship's sides under the channels, and to these plates the dead-eyes are fastened; other plates lap over and secure them below. Formerly, and still in great ships, the dead-eyes were linked to chain-pieces, and from their being occasionally made in one plate they have obtained this appellation.

CHAIN-PUMP. This is composed of two long metal tubes let down through the decks somewhat apart from each other, but joined at their lower ends, which are pierced with holes for the admission of water. Above the upper part of the tubes is a sprocket-wheel worked by crank handles; over this wheel, and passing through both tubes, is an endless chain, furnished at certain distances with bucket valves or pistons, turning round a friction roller. The whole, when set in motion by means of the crank handles, passing down one tube and up the other, raises the water very rapidly.

CHAINS, properly CHAIN-WALES, or CHANNELS. Broad and thick planks projecting horizontally from the ship's outside, to which they are fayed and bolted, abreast of and somewhat behind the masts. They are formed to project the chain-plate, and give the lower rigging greater outrig or spread, free from the topsides of the ship, thus affording greater security and support to the masts, as well as to prevent the shrouds from damaging the gunwale, or being hurt by rubbing against it. Of course they are respectively designated fore, main, and mizen.

They are now discontinued in many ships, the eyes being secured to the timber-heads, and frequently within the gunwale to the stringers or lower shelf-pieces above the water-way.—*In the chains*, applies to the leadsman who stands on the channels between two shrouds to heave the hand-lead.

CHAIN-SHOT. Two balls connected either by a bar or chain, for cutting and destroying the spars and rigging of an enemy's ship.

CHAIN-SLINGS. Chains attached to the sling-hoop and mast-head, by which a lower yard is hung. Used for boat or any other slings demanded.

CHAIN-STOPPER. There are various kinds of stoppers for chain-cables, mostly acting by clamping or compression.

CHAIN, TOP. A chain to sling the lower yards in time of battle, to prevent them from falling down when the ropes by which they are hung are shot away.

CHAIN-WELL, OR LOCKER. A receptacle below deck for containing the chain-cable, which is passed thither through the deck-pipe.

CHALAND. A large flat-bottomed boat of the Loire.

CHALDERS. Synonymous with *gudgeons* of the rudder.

CHALDRICK. An Orkney name for the sea-pie (*Hæmantopus ostralegus*).

CHALDRON. A measure of coals, consisting of 36 bushels; a cubic yard = 19 cwts. 19 lbs.

CHALINK. A kind of Massoolah boat.

CHALK, TO. To cut.—*To walk one's chalks*, to run off; also, an ordeal for drunkenness, to see whether the suspected person can move along the line. "Walking a deck-seam" is to the same purpose, as the man is to proceed without overstepping it on either side.

CHALKS. Marks. "Better by chalks:" wagers were sometimes determined by he who could reach furthest or highest, and there make a chalk-mark.—*Long chalks*, great odds.

CHALLENGE. The demand of a sentinel to any one who approaches his post. Also, the defiance to fight.

CHAMADE. To challenge attention. A signal made by beat of drum when a conference is desired by the enemy on having matter to propose. It is also termed beating a parley.

CHAMBER, OR CHAMBER-PIECE. A charge piece in old ordnance, like a *paterero*, to put into the breech of a gun prepared for it. (*See* MURTHERER.) Used by the Chinese, as in *gingals* (which see).

CHAMBER OF A MINE. The seat or receptacle prepared for the powder-charge, usually at the end of the gallery, and out of the direct line of it; and, if possible, tamped or buried with tight packing of earth, &c., to increase the force of explosion.

CHAMBER OF A PIECE OF ORDNANCE. The end of the bore modified to receive the charge of powder. In mortars, howitzers, and shell-guns, they are of smaller diameter than the bore, for the charges being comparatively small, more effect is thus expected. The gomer chamber (which see) is generally adopted in our service. In rifled guns the powder-chamber is not rifled; it and the bullet-chamber differ in other minute respects from the rest of the bore. Patereroes for festive occasions are sometimes called chambers; as the small mortars, formerly used for firing salutes in the parks, termed also pint-pots from their shape and handles.

CHAMBERS. Clear spaces between the riders, in those vessels which have floor and futtock riders.

CHAMPFER. The cutting or taking off a sharp edge or angle from a plank or timber. It is also called camfering.

CHAMPION. The great champion of England, who at the coronation of the sovereign throws down his gauntlet, and defies all comers. Held at the coronations of George IV., William IV., and Victoria, by a naval officer, a middy in 1821.

CHANCERY, In. When a ship gets into irons. (*See* Irons.)

CHANCY. Dangerous.

CHANDLER, Ship. Dealer in general stores for ships.

CHANGE. In warrantry, is the voluntary substitution of a different voyage for a merchant ship than the one originally specified or agreed upon, an act which discharges the insurers. (*See* Deviation.)

CHANGEY-FOR-CHANGEY. A rude barter among men-of-war's men, as bread for vegetables, or any "swap."

CHANNEL. In hydrography, the fairway, or deepest part of a river, harbour, or strait, which is most convenient for the track of shipping. Also, an arm of the sea, or water communication running between an island or islands and the main or continent, as the British Channel. In an extended sense it implies any passage which separates lands, and leads from one ocean into another, without distinction as to shape.

CHANNEL-BOLTS. The long bolts which pass through all the planks, and connect the channel to the side.

CHANNEL-GROPERS. The home-station ships cruising in the Channel; usually small vessels to watch the coast in former times, and to arrest smugglers.

CHANNEL-GROPING. The carrying despatches, and cruising from port to port in soundings.

CHANNEL-PLATES. *See* Chain-plates.

CHANNEL-WALES. Strakes worked between the gun-deck and the upper deck ports of large ships. Also, the outside plank which receives the bolts of the chain-plates. The wale-plank extends fore and aft to support the channels.

CHANTICLEER. A name in the Frith of Forth for the dragonet or gowdie (*Callionymus lyra*). The early or vigilant cock, from which several English vessels of war have derived their names.

CHAP. A general term for a man of any age after boyhood; but it is not generally meant as a compliment.

CHAPE. The top locket of a sword scabbard.

CHAPELLING A SHIP. The act of turning her round in a light breeze, when she is close hauled, without bracing the head-yards, so that she will lie the same way that she did before. This is commonly occasioned by the negligence of the steersman, or by a sudden change of the wind.

CHAPLAIN. The priest appointed to perform divine service on board ships in the royal navy.

CHAPMAN. A small merchant or trader; a ship's supercargo.

CHAR. A fine species of trout taken in our northern lakes.

CHARACTERS. Certain marks invented for shortening the expression of mathematical calculations, as $+$, $-$, $\times$, $\div$, $=$, $:$ $::$ $:$, $\sqrt{}$, &c.

CHARGE. The proportional quantity of powder and ball wherewith a gun is loaded for execution. The rules for loading large ordnance are: that the piece be first cleaned or scoured inside; that the proper quantity of powder be next driven in and rammed down, care however being taken that the powder in ramming be not bruised, because that weakens its effect; that a little quantity of paper, lint, or the like, be rammed over it, and then the ball be intruded. If the ball be red hot, a tompion, or trencher of green wood, is to be driven in before it. Also, in martial law, an indictment or specification of the crime of which a prisoner stands accused. Also, in evolutions, the brisk advance of a body to attack an enemy, with bayonets fixed at the charge, or firmly held at the hip. Also, the command on duty, every man's office.—*A ship of charge*, is one so deeply immersed as to steer badly. —*To charge a piece*, is to put in the proper quantity of ammunition.

CHARGER. The horse ridden by an officer in action; a term loosely applied to any war-horse.

CHARITY-SLOOPS. Certain 10-gun brigs built towards the end of Napoleon's war, something smaller than the 18-gun brigs; these were rated sloops, and scandal whispers "in order that so many commanders might charitably be employed."

CHARLES'S WAIN. The seven conspicuous stars in Ursa Major, of which two are called the pointers, from showing a line to the pole-star.

CHART, OR SEA-CHART. A hydrographical map, or a projection of some part of the earth's superficies *in plano*, for the use of navigators, further distinguished as plane charts, Mercator charts, globular charts, and the bottle or current chart, to aid in the investigation of surface currents (all which see). A selenographic chart represents the moon, especially as seen by the aid of photography and Mr. De la Rue's arrangement.

CHARTER. To charter a vessel is to take her to freight, under a charter-party. The charter or written instrument by which she is hired to carry freight.

CHARTERED SHIP. One let to hire to one or more, or to a company. A *general* ship is where persons, unconnected, load goods.

CHARTERER. The person hiring or chartering a ship, or the government or a company by their agents.

CHARTER-PARTY. The deed or written contract between the owners and the merchants for the hire of a ship, and safe delivery of the cargo; thus differing from a bill of lading, which relates only to a portion of the cargo. It is the same in civil law with an indenture at the common law. It ought to contain the name and burden of the vessel, the names of the master and freighters, the place and time of lading and unlading, and stipulations as to demurrage. The charter-party is dissolved by a complete embargo, though not by the temporary stopping of a port. It is thus colloquially termed a pair of indentures.

CHASE, To. To pursue a ship, which is also called giving chase.—*A stern chase* is when the chaser follows the chased astern, directly upon the same point of the compass.—*To lie with a ship's fore-foot in a chase*, is to sail and meet with her by the nearest distance, and so to cross her in her way, as to come across her fore-foot. A ship is said to have a good chase when she is so built forward or astern that she can carry many guns to shoot forwards or backwards; according to which she is said to have a good forward or good stern chase. Chasing to windward, is often termed chasing in the wind's eye.

CHASE. The vessel pursued by some other, that pursuing being the chaser. This word is also applied to a receptacle for deer and game, between a forest and a park in size, and stored with a larger stock of timber than the latter.

CHASE, Bow. Cannon situated in the fore part of the ship to fire upon any object ahead of her. Chasing ahead, or varying on either bow.

CHASE OF A GUN. That part of the conical external surface extending from the moulding in front of the trunnions to that which marks the commencement of the muzzle; that is, in old pattern guns, from the ogee of the second reinforce, to the neck or muzzle astragal.

CHASE-GUNS. Such guns as are removed to the chase-ports ahead or astern, if not pivot-guns.

CHASE-PORTS. The gun-ports at the bows and through the stern of a war-ship.

CHASER. The ship which is pursuing another.

CHASE-SIGHT. Where the sight is usually placed.

CHASE-STERN. The cannon which are placed in the after-part of a ship, pointing astern.

CHASSE MAREES. The coasting vessels of the French shores of the Channel; generally lugger-rigged; either with two or three masts, and sometimes a topsail; the hull being bluffer when used for burden only, are thus distinguished from luggers. They seldom venture off shore, but coast it.

CHATHAM. *See* CHEST OF CHATHAM.

CHATS. Lice. Also lazy fellows.

CHATTA, OR CHATTY. An Indian term for an earthen vessel sometimes used for cooking.

CHAW. *See* QUID.

CHEATING THE DEVIL. Softenings of very profane phrases, the mere euphuisms of hard swearing, as *od rot it, od's blood, dash it, dang you, see you blowed first, deuce take it, by gosh, be darned*, and the like profane preludes, such as boatswains and their mates are wont to use.

CHEAT THE GLASS. *See* FLOGGING THE GLASS.

CHEBACCO BOAT. A description of fishing-vessel employed in the Newfoundland fisheries. It is probably named from Chebucto Bay.

CHECK. (*See* BOWLINE.) To slack off a little upon it, and belay it again. Usually done when the wind is by, or as long as she can lay her course without the aid of the bowline.—*To check* is to slacken or ease off a brace, which is found to be too stiffly extended, or when the wind is drawing aft. It is also used in a contrary sense when applied to the cable running out, and then implies to stopper the cable.— *Check her*, stop her way.

CHECKERS. A game much used by seamen, especially in the tops, where usually a checker-board will be found carved.

CHECKING-LINES. These are rove through thimbles at the eyes of the top-mast and top-gallant rigging, one end bent to the lift and brace, the other into the top. They are used to haul them in to the mast-head, instead of sending men aloft.

CHEEK. Insolent language.—*Own cheek*, one's self.—*Cheeky*, flippant.

CHEEK-BLOCKS. Usually fitted to the fore-topmast head, for the purpose of leading the jib-stay, halliards, &c.

CHEEKS. A general term among mechanics for those pieces of timber in any machine which are double, and perfectly corresponding to each other. The projections at the throat-end of a gaff which embrace the mast are termed jaws. Also, the sides of a gun-carriage. (*See* BRACKETS.) Also, the sides of a block. Also, an old soubriquet for a marine, derived from a rough pun on his uniform in olden days.

CHEEKS, OR CHEEK-KNEES. Pieces of compass-timber on the ship's bows, for the security of the beak-head, or knee of the head, whence the term *head-knee*. Two pieces of timber fitted on each side of a mast, from beneath the hounds and its uppermost end. Also, the circular pieces on the aft-side of the carrick-bitts.

CHEEKS OF AN EMBRASURE. The interior faces or sides of an embrasure.

CHEEKS OF THE MAST. The faces or projecting parts on each side of the masts, formed to sustain the trestle-trees upon which the frame of the top, together with the top-mast, immediately rest. (*See* HOUNDS and TRESTLE-TREE BIBS.)

CHEER, To. To salute a ship *en passant*, by the people all coming on deck and huzzahing three times; it also implies to encourage or animate. (*See also* HEARTY and MAN SHIP!)

CHEERING. The result of an animated excitement in action, which often incites to valour. Also, practised on ships parting at sea, on joining an admiral, &c. In piratical vessels, to frighten their prey with a semblance of valour.

CHEERLY. Quickly; with a hearty will. "Cheerly, boys, cheerly," when the rope comes in slowly, or hoisting a sail with a few hands.

CHEESE. A circle of wads covered with painted canvas.

CHELYNGE. An early name of the cod-fish.

CHEQUE, OR CHECK. An office in dockyards. Cheque for muster, pay, provision, desertion, discharged, or dead—under DDD. or DSq^d.

CHEQUE, CLERK OF THE. An officer in the royal dockyards, who goes on board to muster the ship's company, of whom he keeps a register, thereby to check false musters, the penalty of which is cashiering.

CHEQUERED SIDES. Those painted so as to show all the ports; more particularly applicable to two or more rows.

CHERIMERI. In the East, a bribe in making a contract or bargain.

CHERRY. A species of smelt or spurling, taken in the Frith of Tay.

CHESIL. From the Anglo-Saxon word *ceosl*, still used for a bank of shingle, as that remarkable one connecting the Isle of Portland with the mainland, called the Chesil Beach.

CHESS-TREE. A piece of oak fastened with iron bolts on each topside of the ship. Used for boarding the main-tack to, or hauling home the clues of the main-sail, for which purpose there is a hole in the upper part, through which the tack passes, that extends the clue of the sail to windward. Where chain has been substituted of late for rope, iron plates with thimble-eyes are used for chess-trees.

CHEST OF CHATHAM. An ancient institution, restored and established by an order in council of Queen Elizabeth, in 1590, supported by a contribution from each seaman and apprentice, according to the amount of his wages, for the wounded and hurt seamen of the royal navy, under the name of smart-money.

CHEST-ROPE. The same with the guest or gift rope, and is added to the boat-rope when the boat is towed astern of the ship, to keep her from sheering, *i.e.* from swinging to and fro. (*See* GUEST-ROPE.)

CHEVAUX DE FRISE. An adopted term for pickets pointed with iron, and standing through beams, to stop an enemy: this defence is also called a turn-pike or pike-turn.

CHEVENDER. An old name for the chevin or chub.

CHEVILS. *See* KEVELS.

CHEVIN. An old name for the chub.

CHEVRON. The distinguishing mark on the sleeves of sergeants and corporals' coats, the insignia of a non-commissioned officer. Also, a mark recently instituted as a testimony of good conduct in a private. Further, now worn by seamen getting good-service pay.

CHEWING OF OAKUM OR PITCH. When a ship suffers leakage from inefficient caulking. (*See* SPACE.)

CHEZ-VOUS. A kind of "All Souls" night in Bengal, when meats and fruits are placed in every corner of a native's house. Hence *shevoe*, for a ship-gala.

CHICO [Sp. for small].—*Boca-chica*, small mouth of a river.

CHIEF. *See* COMMANDER-IN-CHIEF. A common abbreviation.

CHIEF MATE, OR CHIEF OFFICER. The next to a commander in a merchantman, and who, in the absence of the latter, acts as his deputy.

CHIGRE, CHAGOE, CHIGGRE, OR JIGGER. A very minute insect of tropical countries, which pierces the thick skin of the foot, and breeds there, producing great pain. It is neatly extricated with its sac entire by clever negroes.

CHILLED SHOT. Shot of very rapidly cooled cast-iron, *i.e.* cast in iron moulds, and thus found to acquire a hardness which renders them of nearly equal efficiency with steel shot for penetrating iron plates, yet produced at about one-quarter the price. They invariably break up on passing through the plates, and their fragments are very destructive on crowded decks; though in the attack of iron war vessels, where the demolishment of guns, carriages, machinery, turrets, &c., is required, the palm must still be awarded to steel shot and shell.

CHIMBE [Anglo-Saxon]. The prominent part or end of the staves, where they project beyond the head of a cask.

CHIME. *See* CHINE.

CHIME IN, To. To join a mess meal or treat. To chime in to a chorus or song.

CHINCKLE. A small bight in a line.

CHINE. The backbone of a cliff, from the backbones of animals; a name given in the Isle of Wight, as Black Gang Chine, and along the coasts of Hampshire. Also, that part of the waterway which is left the thickest, so as to project above the deck-plank; and it is notched or gouged hollow in front, to let the water run free.

CHINE AND CHINE. Casks stowed end to end.

CHINED. Timber or plank slightly hollowed out.

CHINGLE. Gravel. (*See* SHINGLE.)

CHINGUERITO. A hot and dangerous sort of white corn brandy, made in Spanish America.

CHINSE, To. To stop small seams, by working in oakum with a knife or chisel—a temporary expedient. To caulk slightly those openings that will not bear the force required for caulking.

CHINSING-IRON. A caulker's tool for chinsing seams with.

CHIP, To. To trim a gun when first taken from the mould or castings.

CHIPS. The familiar soubriquet of the carpenter on board ship. The fragments of timber and the planings of plank are included among chips.—*Chip of the old block*, a son like his father.

CHIRURGEON. [Fr.] The old name for surgeon.

CHISEL. A well-known edged tool for cutting away wood, iron, &c.

CHIT. A note. Formerly the note for slops given by the officer of a division to be presented to the purser.

CHIULES. The Saxon ships so called.

CHIVEY. A knife.

CHLET. An old Manx term for a rock in the sea.

CHOCK. A sort of wedge used to rest or confine any weighty body, and prevent it from fetching way when the ship is in motion. Also, pieces fitted to supply a deficiency or defect after the manner of filling. Also, blocks of timber latterly substituted beneath the beams for knees, and wedged by iron keys. (*See* BOAT-CHOCKS.)—*Chock of the bowsprit. See* BEND.—*Chocks of the rudder*, large accurately adapted pieces of timber kept in readiness to choak the rudder, by filling up the excavation on the side of the rudder hole, in case of any accident. It is also choaked or chocked, when a ship is likely to get strong stern-way, when tiller-ropes break, &c.—*To chock*, is to put a wedge under anything to prevent its rolling. (*See* CHUCKS.)

CHOCK-A-BLOCK, OR CHOCK AND BLOCK. Is the same with *block-a-block* and *two-blocks* (which see). When the lower block of a tackle is run close up to the upper one, so that you can hoist no higher, the blocks being together.

CHOCK-AFT, CHOCK-FULL, CHOCK-HOME, CHOCK-UP, &c. Denote as far aft, full, home, up, &c., as possible, or that which fits closely to one another.

CHOCK-CHANNELS. Those filled in with wood between the chain-plates, according to a plan introduced by Captain Couch, R.N.

CHOCOLATE-GALE. A brisk N.W. wind of the West Indies and Spanish main.

CHOGSET. *See* BURGALL.

CHOKE. The nip of a rocket.

CHOKED. When a running rope sticks in a block, either by slipping between the cheeks and the shiver, or any other accident, so that it cannot run.

CHOKE-FULL. Entirely full; top full.

CHOKE THE LUFF. To place suddenly the fall of a tackle close to the block across the jaw of the next turn of the rope in the block, so as to prevent the leading part from rendering. Familiarly said of having a meal to assuage hunger; to be silenced.

CHOKEY. An East Indian guard-house and prison.

CHOMMERY. *See* CHASSE-MARÉE, for which this is the men's term.

CHOP. A permit or license of departure for merchant ships in the China trade. A Chinese word signifying quality. Also, an imperial chop or mandate; a proclamation.

CHOP, OR CHAPP. The entrance of a channel, as the Chops of the English Channel.

CHOP-ABOUT, To. Is applied to the wind when it varies and changes suddenly, and at short intervals of time.

CHOPPING-SEA. A synonym of *cockling-sea* (which see).

CHOPT. Done suddenly in exigence; as, *chopt* to an anchor.

CHORD. In geometry, is a line which joins the extremities of any arc of a circle.

CHOW-CHOW. Eatables; a word borrowed from the Chinese. It is supposed to be derived from *chou-chou*, the tender parts of cabbage-tree, bamboo, &c., preserved.

CHOWDER. The principal food in the Newfoundland bankers, or stationary fishing vessels; it consists of a stew of fresh codfish, rashers of salt pork or bacon, biscuit, and lots of pepper. Also, a buccaneer's savoury dish, and a favourite dish in North America. (*See* COD-FISHER'S CREW.) Chowder is a fish-seller in the western counties.

CHOWDER-HEADED. Stupid, or batter-brained.

CHRISTIAN. A gold Danish coin, value in England from 16*s.* to 16*s.* 4*d.*

CHRISTIAN'S GALES. The tremendous storms in 1795-6, which desolated the fleet proceeding to attack the French West India Islands, under Admiral Christian.

CHROCKLE. A tangle or *thoro'put* (which see).

CHRODANE. The Manx and Gaelic term for gurnet.

CHRONOMETER. A valuable time-piece fitted with a compensation-balance, adjusted for the accurate measurement of time in all climates, and used by navigators for the determination of the longitude.

CHRONOMETER RATE. The number of seconds or parts of seconds which it loses or gains per diem. (*See* RATING.)

CHRUIN. A Gaelic term for masts.—*Chruin-spreie*, the bowsprit.

CHUB. The *Leuciscus cephalus*, a fresh-water fish.

CHUCK. A sea-shell. Nickname for a boatswain, "Old chucks." Also, an old word signifying large chips of wood.

CHUCKLE-HEADED. Clownishly stupid; lubberly.

CHULLERS. A northern name for the gills of a fish.

CHUNAM. Lime made of burned shells, and much used in India for the naval store-houses. That made at Madras is of peculiarly fine quality, and easily takes a polish like white marble.

CHUNK. A coarse slice of meat or bread; more properly *junk*. Also, the negro term for lumps of firewood.

CHUNTOCK. A powerful dignitary among the Chinese. (*See* JANTOOK.)

CHURCH. The part of the ship arranged on Sunday for divine service.

CHURCH-WARDEN. A name given on the coast of Sussex to the shag or cormorant. Why, deponent sayeth not.

CHUTE. A fall of water or rapid; the word is much used in North America, wherever the nomenclature of the country retains traces of the early French settlers. (*See* SHOOT.)

CILLS. Horizontal pieces of timber to ports or scuttles; mostly spelled *sills* (which see). Generally pronounced by sailors *sell*, as the port-sell.

CINGLE [from *cir-cingle*, a horse's belt]. A belt worn by seamen.

CINQUE-PORT. A kind of fishing-net, having five entrances.

CINQUE PORTS, THE. These are five highly privileged stations, the once great emporiums of British commerce and maritime greatness; they are Dover, Hastings, Sandwich, Romney, and Hythe, which, lying opposite to France, were considered of the utmost importance. To these were afterwards added Winchelsea, Rye, and Seaford. These places were honoured with peculiar immunities and privileges, on condition of their providing a certain number of ships at their own charge for forty days. Being exempted from the jurisdiction of the Admiralty court, the Lord Warden of the Cinque Ports is authorized to make rules for the government of pilots within his jurisdiction, and in many other general acts exceptions are provided to save the franchises of the Cinque Ports unimpeached. It is a singular fact that it has never been legally determined whether the Downs and adjacent roadsteads are included in the limits of the Cinque Ports. All derelicts found without the limits by Cinque Port vessels are droits of admiralty. This organization was nearly broken up in the late state reforms, but the Lord Warden still possesses some power and jurisdiction.

CIPHERING. A term in carpentry. (*See* SYPHERING.)

CIRCLE. A plane figure bounded by a line called the circumference, everywhere equally distant from a point within it, called the centre.

CIRCLE OF PERPETUAL APPARITION. A circle of the heavens parallel to the equator, and at a distance from the pole of any place equal to the latitude: within this circle the stars never set.

CIRCLES, GREAT, LESS, AZIMUTH, VERTICAL (which see).

CIRCLES OF LONGITUDE. These are great circles passing through the poles of the ecliptic, and so cutting it at right angles.

CIRCULARS. Certain official letters which are sent to several persons, and convey the same information.

CIRCUMNAVIGATION. The term for making a voyage round the world.

CIRCUMPOLAR. A region which includes that portion of the starry sphere which remains constantly above the horizon of any place.

CIRCUMVALLATION, LINES OF. Intrenchments thrown up by a besieging army, outside itself, and round the besieged place, but fronting towards the country, to prevent interference from outside. This continuous method has gone out of favour, though some covering works of concentrated strength are still considered essential.

CIRRIPEDIA. A group of marine animals, allied to the crustacea. They are free and natatory when young, but in the adult state attached to rocks or some floating substance. They are protected by a multivalve shell, and have long ciliated curled tentacles, whence their name (*curl-footed*). The barnacles (*Lepas*) and the acorn-shells (*Balanus*) are familiar examples.

CIRRO-CUMULUS. This, the *sonder-cloud*, or system of small roundish clouds in the upper regions of the atmosphere, commonly moves in a different current of air from that which is blowing at the earth's surface. It forms the mackerel sky alluded to in the following distich:—

"A mack'rel sky and mares'-tails
Make lofty ships carry low sails."

CIRRO-STRATUS. Is the stratus of the upper regions of the atmosphere, heavier looking than the cirrus, but not so heavy as the stratus.

CIRRUS. The elegant modification of elevated clouds, usually termed mares'-tails (see the distich given at CIRRO-CUMULUS); otherwise the curl-cloud.

CISCO. A fish of the herring kind, of which thousands of barrels are annually taken and salted in Lake Ontario.

CISTERN. A reservoir for water placed in different parts of a ship, where a constant supply may be required. Also furnished with a leaden pipe, which goes through the ship's side, whereby it is occasionally filled with sea-water, and which is thence pumped up to wash the decks, &c.

CITADEL. A fortified work of superior strength, and dominating everything else, generally separated therefrom by an open space of glacis or esplanade; often useful against domestic as well as foreign enemies.

CIVIL BRANCH. That department executed by civilians, as contradistinguished from the army or navy branch.

CIVILIANS. The surgeon, chaplain, purser or paymaster, assistant surgeons, secretary, and ship clerks, on board men-of-war.

CIVIL LORD. The lay or junior member of the admiralty board.

CIVIL WAR. That between subjects of the same realm, or between factions of the same state.

CLAIMANTS. Persons appealing to the jurisdiction of the admiralty court. They are denominated colourable, or fair, according to the informality, or justice, of their claims.

CLAKE. A name for the barnacle-goose (*Anser bernicla*). Also, for the *Lepas anatifera*, a cirriped often found attached to vessels or timber by a long fleshy peduncle, sometimes 4 or 5 feet in length.

CLAM. A well-known bivalve shell-fish. "As happy as a clam at high-water," a figurative expression for otiose comfort.

CLAMBER. To climb; to ascend quickly.

CLAMPING. Applying a cross-head, or stirrup-piece, in a socket.

CLAMP-NAILS. Such nails as are used to fasten clamps; they are short and stout, with large heads.

CLAMPS. Pieces of timber applied to a mast or yard, to prevent the wood from bursting. Also, thick planks lying fore and aft under the beams of the first orlop or second deck, the same as the rising-timbers are to the deck. They are securely fayed to all the timbers, to which they are fastened by nails through the clamp, and penetrating two-thirds of the thickness of the timbers. Also, substantial strakes, worked inside, on which the ends of the beams rest. Also, smooth crooked plates of iron fore-locked upon the trunnions of cannon; these, however, are more properly termed cap-squares. (*See* CARRIAGE.) Also, any plate of iron made to open and shut, so as to confine a spar. A one-cheeked block; the spar to which it is fastened being the other cheek.—*To clamp*, is to unite two bodies by surfaces or circular plates.—*Clamped*, is when a piece of board is fitted with the grain to the end of another piece of board across the grain.

CLAMS. Strong pieces used by shipwrights for drawing bolts, &c.

Also, a kind of forceps used for bringing up specimens of the bottom in sounding; a drag. (*See* DEEP-SEA CLAM.)

CLANG. The rattling or clashing of arms.

CLAP-BOARD [German, *klapp-bord*]. An east-country commercial plank, which ought to be upwards of 13 feet in length; cask-staves are also clap-boards. Clap-board, in the colonies, is the covering the side of a house with narrow boards, "lapping fashion," in contradistinction to shingling, or tiling, or clench-built.

CLAP-MATCH. A sort of seal, distinct from the fur-seal.

CLAP ON! The order to lay hold of any rope, in order to haul upon it. Also, to "Clap on the stoppers before the bitts," *i.e.* fasten the stoppers; or, "Clap on the cat-fall," *i.e.* lay hold of the cat-fall.—*To clap a stopper over all*, to stop a thing effectually; to clap on the stopper before the bits next to the manger or hawse-hole; to order silence.— *To clap in irons*, to order an offender into the bilboes.—*To clap on canvas*, to make more sail.

CLAPPER. A name for the valve of a pump-box. Also, a plank or foot-bridge across a running stream; also, the clapper of a bell.

CLAP-SILL. The lockage of a flood-gate.

CLARTY. In north-country whalers, used for *wet, slippery*.

CLASHY. Showery weather.

CLASP-HOOK. An iron clasp, in two parts, moving upon the same pivot, and overlapping one another. Used for bending chain-sheets to the clues of sails, jib-halliards, &c. (*See* SPAR-HOOK.)

CLASS. Order or rank; specially relating to dockyard men.

CLASSIFICATION OF SHIPS. A register made of vessels according to the report rendered in by special surveyors. (*See* NAVY AND LLOYD'S REGISTER.)

CLAW, OR CLAW OFF, TO. To beat, or turn to windward from a lee-shore, so as to be at sufficient distance from it to avoid shipwreck. It is generally used when getting to windward is difficult.

CLAYMORE. Anciently a two-handed sword of the Highlanders, but latterly applied to their basket-hilted sword.

CLEACHING NET. A hand-net with a hoop and bar, used by fishermen on the banks of the Severn.

CLEAN. Free from danger, as clean coast, clean harbour; in general parlance means quite, entirely. So Shakspeare represents Ægeon

"Roaming clean through the bounds of Asia."

Also, applied to a ship's hull with a fine run fore and aft.—*Clean entrance*, clean run.—*To clean a ship's bottom*. (*See* BREAMING and HOG.)

CLEAN BILL. (*See* BILL OF HEALTH.) When all are in health.

CLEAN DONE. Quite. In a seamanlike manner; purpose well effected; adroitly tricked. (*See* WEATHERED.)

CLEAN-FISH. On the northern coasts, a salmon perfectly in season.

CLEAN-FULL. Keeping the sail full, bellying, off the wind.

CLEAN OFF THE REEL. When the ship by her rapidity pulls the line off the log-reel, without its being assisted. Also, upright conduct. Also, any performance without stop or hindrance, off-hand.

CLEAN SHIP. A whale-ship unfortunate in her trip, having no fish or oil.

CLEAR. Is variously applied, to weather, sea-coasts, cordage, navigation, &c., as opposed to foggy, to dangerous, to entangled. It is usually opposed to *foul* in all these senses.

CLEAR, To. Has several significations, particularly to escape from, to unload, to empty, to prepare, &c., as:—*To clear for action.* To prepare for action.—*To clear away* for this or that, is to get obstructions out of the way.—*To clear the decks.* To remove lumber, put things in their places, and coil down the ropes. Also, to take the things off a table after a meal.—*To clear goods.* To pay the custom-house dues and duties.—*To clear the land.* To escape from the land.—*To clear a lighter, or the hold.* To empty either.

CLEARANCE. The document from the customs, by which a vessel and her cargo, by entering all particulars at the custom-house, and paying the dues, is permitted to clear out or sail.

CLEAR FOR GOING ABOUT. Every man to his station, and every rope an end.

CLEARING LIGHTERS. All vessels pertaining to public departments should be cleared with the utmost despatch.

CLEAR THE PENDANT. *See* Up and Clear the Pendant.

CLEAR WATER. A term in Polar seas implying no ice to obstruct navigation, well off the land, having sea-room.

CLEAT A GUN, To. To nail large cleats under the trucks of the lower-deckers in bad weather, to insure their not fetching way.

CLEATS, or Cleets. Pieces of wood of different shapes used to fasten ropes upon: some have one and some two arms. They are called belaying cleat, deck-cleat, and a thumb-cleat. Also, small wedges of wood fastened on the yards, to keep ropes or the earing of the sail from slipping off the yard. Mostly made of elm or oak.

CLEAVAGE. The splitting of any body having a structure or line of cleavage: as fir cleaves longitudinally, slates horizontally, stones roughly, smoothly, conchoidal, or stratified, &c.

CLEFTS. Wood sawn lengthways into pieces less in thickness than in breadth. (*See* Plank.)

CLENCH, To. To secure the end of a bolt by burring the point with a hammer. Also, a mode of securing the end of one rope to another. (*See* Clinch.)

CLENCHED BOLTS. Those fastened by means of a ring, or an iron plate, with a rivetting hammer at the end where they protrude through the wood, to prevent their drawing.

CLENCH-NAILS. They are much used in boat-building, being such as can be driven without splitting the boards, and drawn without breaking. (*See* ROVE AND CLENCH.)

CLEP. A north-country name for a small grapnel.

CLERK. Any naval officer doing the duty of a clerk.

CLETT. A northern or Erse word to express a rock broken from a cliff, as the holm in Orkney and Shetland.

CLEUGH. A precipice, a cliff. Also, a ravine or cleft.

CLEW. Of a hammock or cot. (*See* CLUE.)

CLICKS. Small pieces of iron falling into a notched wheel attached to the winches in cutters, &c., and thereby serving the office of pauls. (*See* RATCHET, or RATCHET-PAUL, in machinery.) It more peculiarly belongs to inferior clock-work, hence click.

CLIFF [from the Anglo-Saxon *cleof*]. A precipitous termination of the land, whatever be the soil. (*See* CRAG.)

CLIMATE. Formerly meant a zone of the earth parallel to the equator, in which the days are of a certain length at the summer solstice. The term has now passed to the physical branch of geography, and means the general character of the weather.

CLINCH. A particular method of fastening large ropes by a half hitch, with the end stopped back to its own part by seizings; it is chiefly to fasten the hawsers suddenly to the rings of the kedges or small anchors; and the breechings of guns to the ring-bolts in the ship's side. Those parts of a rope or cable which are clinched. Thus the outer end is "bent" by the clinch to the ring of the anchor. The inner or tier-clinch in the good old times was clinched to the main-mast, passing under the tier beams (where it was unlawfully, as regards the custom of the navy, clinched). Thus "the cable runs out to the clinch," means, there is no more to veer.—*To clinch* is to batter or rivet a bolt's end upon a ring or piece of plate iron; or to turn back the point of a nail that it may hold fast. (*See* CLENCH.)

CLINCH A BUSINESS, To. To finish it; to settle it beyond further dispute, as the recruit taking the shilling.

CLINCH-BUILT. Clinker, or overlapping edges.

CLINCHER. An incontrovertible and smart reply; but sometimes the confirmation of a story by a lie, or by some still more improbable yarn: synonymous with *capping*.

CLINCHER OR CLINKER BUILT. Made of clincher-work, by the planks lapping one over the other. The contrary of *carvel-work*. Iron ships after this fashion are distinguished as being *lap-jointed*.

CLINCHER-NAILS. Those which are of malleable metal, as copper, wrought iron, &c., which clinch by turning back the points in rough-built fir boats where roofs and clinching are thus avoided.

CLINCHER-WORK. The disposition of the planks in the side of any boat or vessel, when the lower edge of every plank overlaps that next below it. This is sometimes written as pronounced, *clinker-work.*

CLIPHOOK. A hook employed for some of the ends of the running rigging.

CLIPPER. A fast sailer, formerly chiefly applied to the sharp-built raking schooners of America, and latterly to Australian passenger-ships. Larger vessels now built after their model are termed clipper-built: sharp and fast; low in the water; rakish.

CLIVE. An old spelling of *cliff.*

CLOCK-CALM. When not a breath of wind ruffles the water.

CLOCK-STARS. A name for the nautical stars, which, from their positions having been very exactly ascertained, are used for determining time.

CLOD-HOPPER. A clownish lubberly landsman.

CLOKIE-DOO. A west of Scotland name for the horse-mackerel.

CLOSE-ABOARD. Near or alongside; too close to be safe. "The boat is close aboard," a caution to the officer in command to receive his visitor. "The land is close aboard," danger inferred.

CLOSE-BUTT. Where caulking is not used, the butts or joints of the planks are sometimes rabbetted, and fayed close, whence they are thus denominated.

CLOSE CONTRACT. One not advertised.

CLOSED PORT. One interdicted.

CLOSE-FIST. One who drives a hard bargain in petty traffic.

CLOSE HARBOUR. That is one gained by labour from the element, formed by encircling a portion of water with walls and quays, except at the entrance, or by excavating the land adjacent to the sea or river, and then letting in the water.

CLOSE-HAULED. The general arrangement or trim of a ship's sails when she endeavours to progress in the nearest direction possible contrary to the wind; in this manner of sailing the keel of square-rigged vessels commonly makes an angle of six points with the line of the wind, but cutters, luggers, and other fore-and-aft rigged vessels will sail even nearer. This point of sailing is synonymous with *on a taut bowline* and *on a wind.*

CLOSE PACK. The ice floes so jammed together that boring is impossible, and present efforts useless. (*See* PACK.)

CLOSE PORTS. Those which lie up rivers; a term in contradistinction to *out-ports.*

CLOSE-QUARTERS, OR CLOSE-FIGHTS. Certain strong bulkheads or barriers of wood, formerly stretching across a merchant ship in several places; they were used for retreat and shelter when a ship was boarded by an adversary, and were therefore fitted with loopholes. Powder-chests were also fixed upon the deck, containing missiles which might be fired from the close quarters upon the boarders. The old slave-ships were thus fitted in case of the negroes rising, and flat-headed nails were cast along the deck to prevent their walking with naked feet. In the navy, yard-arm and yard-arm, sides touching.

CLOSE-REEFED. The last reefs of the top-sails, or other sails set, being taken in.

CLOSE-SIGHT. The notch in the base-ring of a cannon, to place the eye in a line with the top-sight.

CLOSE THE WIND, To. To haul to it.—*Close upon a tack or bow-line*, or *close by a wind*, is when the wind is on either bow, and the tacks or bowlines are hauled forwards that they may take the wind to make the best of their way.—*Close to the wind*, when her head is just so near the wind as to fill the sails without shaking them.

CLOSE WITH THE LAND, To. To approach near to it.

CLOSH [from the Danish *klos*]. A sobriquet for east-country seamen.

CLOTHED. A mast is said to be clothed when the sail is so long as to reach the deck-gratings. Also, well clothed with canvas; sails well cut, well set, and plenty of them.

CLOTHES-LINES. A complete system of parallel lines, hoisted between the main and mizen masts twice a week to dry the washed clothes of the seamen.

CLOTHING. The rigging of the bowsprit.—*Clothing the bowsprit* is rigging it. Also, the purser's slops for the men.

CLOTH IN THE WIND. Too near to the wind, and sails shivering. Also, groggy.

CLOTHS. In a sail, are the breadths of canvas in its whole width. When a ship has broad sails they say she spreads much cloth.

CLOTTING. A west-country method of catching eels with worsted thread.

CLOUD. A collection of vapours suspended in the atmosphere. Also, under a cloud of canvas.

CLOUGH. A word derived from the verb *to cleave*, and signifying a narrow valley between two hills. (*See* CLEUGH.) Also, in commerce, an allowance on the turn of the beam in weighing.

CLOUT. From the Teutonic *kotzen*, a blow. Also, a gore of blood.

CLOUT-NAILS [Fr. *clouter*]. To stud with nails, as ships' bottoms and piles were before the introduction of sheet copper.

CLOUTS. Thin plates of iron nailed on that part of the axle-tree of a gun-carriage that comes through the nave, and through which the linch-pin goes.

CLOVE-HITCH. A knot or noose by which one rope is fastened to another. (*See* HITCH.) Two half hitches round a spar or rope.

CLOVE-HOOK. Synonymous with *clasp-hook.*

CLOVES. Planks made by cleaving. Certain weights for wool, butter, &c. Also, long spike-nails [derived from *clou,* Fr.]

CLOW. A kind of sluice in which the aperture is regulated by a board sliding in a frame and groove.

CLOY, To. To drive an iron spike by main force into the vent or touch-hole of a gun, which renders it unserviceable till the spike be either worked out, or a new vent drilled. (*See* NAIL and SPIKE.)

CLUBBED. A fashion which obtained in the time of pig-tails of doubling them up while at sea.

CLUBBING. Drifting down a current with an anchor out.

CLUBBING A FLEET. Manœuvring so as to place the first division on the windward side.

CLUBBOCK. The spotted blenny or gunnel (*Gunellus vulgaris*).

CLUB-HAUL, To. A method of tacking a ship by letting go the lee-anchor as soon as the wind is out of the sails, which brings her head to wind, and as soon as she pays off, the cable is cut and the sails trimmed; this is never had recourse to but in perilous situations, and when it is expected that the ship would otherwise miss stays. The most gallant example was performed by Captain Hayes in H.M.S. *Magnificent,* 74, in Basque Roads, in 1814, when with lower-yards and topmasts struck, he escaped between two reefs from the enemy at Oleron. He bore the name of *Magnificent Hayes* to the day of his death, for the style in which he executed it.

CLUB-LAW. The rule of violence and strength.

CLUE. Of a square sail, either of the lower corners reaching down to where the tacks and sheets are made fast to it; and is that part which comes goring out from the square of the sail.

CLUE-GARNETS. A sort of tackle rove through a garnet block, attached to the clues of the main and fore sails to haul up and truss them to the yard; which is termed clueing up those sails as for goose-wings, or for furling. (*See* BLOCKS.)

CLUE-LINES. Are for the same purpose as clue-garnets, only that the latter term is solely appropriated to the courses, while the word clue-line is applied to those ropes on all the other square sails; they come down from the quarters of the yards to the clues, or lower corners of the sails, and by which the sails are hauled or clued up for furling.

CLUE OF A HAMMOCK. The combination of small lines by which it is suspended, being formed of knittles, grommets, and laniards;

they are termed double or single clues, according as there are one or two at each end. Latterly iron grommets or rings were introduced, but did not afford the required spread, and in some cases triangular irons, or span-shackles were substituted, called *Spanish clues*, formed by fixing the knittles at equal distances upon a piece of rope instead of a grommet, which having an eye spliced, and a laniard placed at each end, extends the hammock in the same way as a double clue.— *From clue to earing.* A phrase implying from the bottom to the top, or synonymous with "from top to toe." Or literally the diagonal of a square sail. Also, every portion, as in shifting dress; removing every article. Also, cleaning a ship from clue to earing; every crevice.—*A clue up.* A case of despair. In readiness for death.

CLUE-ROPE. In large sails, the eye or loop at the clues is made of a rope larger than the bolt-rope into which it is spliced.

CLUE UP! The order to clue up the square sails.

CLUMP. A circular plantation of trees.

CLUMP-BLOCKS. Those that are made thicker or stronger than ordinary blocks. (*See* BLOCK, TACK-AND-SHEET.)

CLUSTER. *See* GROUP.

CLUTCH. The oyster spawn adhering to stones, oyster shells, &c.

CLUTCH. Forked stanchions of iron or wood. The same as crutch, clutch, or clamp block. (*See* SNATCH-BLOCK.)

CLUTTERY. Weather inclining to stormy.

COACH, OR COUCH. A sort of chamber or apartment in a large ship of war, just before the great cabin. The floor of it is formed by the aftmost part of the quarter-deck, and the roof of it by the poop: it is generally the habitation of the flag-captain.

COACH-HORSES. The crew of the state barge; usually fifteen selected men, to support the captain in any daring exploits.

COACH-WHIP. The pendant.

COAD. In ship-building, the fayed piece called *bilge-keel*.

COAK. A small perforated triangular bit of brass inserted into the middle of the shiver (now called *sheave*) of a block, to keep it from splitting and galling by the pin, whereon it turns. Called also *bush*, *cock* or *cogg*, and *dowel*.

COAKING. Uniting pieces of spar by means of tabular projections formed by cutting away the solid of one piece into a hollow, so as to make a projection in the other fit in correctly, the butts preventing the pieces from drawing asunder. Coaks, or dowels, are fitted into the beams and knees of vessels, to prevent their slipping.

COAL-FISH. The *Gadus carbonarius*. Called *gerrack* in its first year, *cuth* or *queth* in its second, *sayth* in its third, *lythe* in its fourth, and *colmie* in its fifth, when it is full grown.

COALING. Taking in a supply of coals for a cruise or voyage.

COALS. To be hauled over the coals, is to be brought to strict account.

COAL-SACKS. An early name of some dark patches of sky in the Milky Way, nearly void of stars visible to the naked eye. The largest patch is near the Southern Cross, and called the Black Magellanic Cloud.

COAL-SAY. The coal-fish.

COAL-TAR. Tar extracted from bituminous coal.

COAL-TRIMMER. One employed in a steamer to stow and trim the fuel. This duty and that of the stoker are generally combined.

COAMING-CARLINGS. Those timbers that inclose the mortar-beds of bomb-vessels, and which are called carlings, because they are shifted occasionally. Short beams where a hatchway is cut.

COAMINGS OF THE HATCHES OR GRATINGS. Certain raised work rather higher than the decks, about the edges of the hatch-openings of a ship, to prevent the water on deck from running down. Loop-holes were made in the coamings for firing muskets from below, in order to clear the deck of an enemy when a ship is boarded. There is a rabbet in their inside upper edge, to receive the hatches or gratings.

COAST. The sea-shore and the adjoining country; in fact, the sea-front of the land. (*See* SHORE.)

COAST-BLOCKADE. A body of men formerly under the jurisdiction of the Customs, termed Preventive Service, offering a disposable force in emergency; but which has been turned over to the control of the Admiralty, and now become the Coast-guard, over which a commodore, as controller-general, presides. (*See* SEA FENCIBLES.)

COASTER. *See* COASTING.

COASTING, OR TO COAST ALONG. The act of making a progress along the sea-coast of any country, for which purpose it is necessary to observe the time and direction of the tide, to know the reigning winds, the roads and havens, the different depths of water, and the qualities of the ground. As these vessels are not fitted for distant sea voyages, they are termed coasters.

COASTING PILOT. A pilot who has become sufficiently acquainted with the nature of any particular coast, to conduct a ship or fleet from one part of it to another; but only within his limits. He may be superseded by the first branch-pilot he meets after passing his bounds.

COASTING TRADE. The commerce of one port of the United Kingdom with another port thereof. A trade confined by law to British ships and vessels.

COAST-WAITER. Custom-house superintendents of the landing and shipping of goods coastways.

COAST-WARNING. Synonymous with *storm-signal;* formerly fire-beacons were used to give warning of the approach of an enemy.

COAT. A piece of tarred canvas nailed round above the partners, or that part where the mast or bowsprit enters the deck. Its use is to prevent the water from running down between decks. There is sometimes a coat for the rudder, nailed round the hole where the rudder traverses in the ship's counter. It also implies the stuff with which the ship's sides or masts are varnished, to defend them from the sun and weather, as turpentine, pitch, varnish, or paint; in this sense we say, "Give her a coat of tar or paint." By neglecting the scraper this may become a crust of coatings.

COAT OF MAIL. The chiton shell.

COAT-TACKS. The peculiar nails with which the mast coats are fastened.

COB. A young herring. Also, a sea-gull. Also, a sort of short break-water—so called in our early statutes: such was that which forms the harbour of Lyme Regis, originally composed of piles and timber, lined with heaps of rock; but now constructed of stone compacted with cement.

COBB. A Gibraltar term for a Spanish dollar.

COBBING. An old punishment sometimes inflicted at sea for breach of certain regulations—chiefly for those quitting their station during the night. The offender was struck a certain number of times on the breech with a flat piece of wood called the *cobbing-board*. Also, when *watch* was cried, all persons were expected to take off their hats on pain of being cobbed.

COBBLE, To. To mend or repair hastily. Also, the coggle or cog (which see).—*Cobble or coggle stones*, pebbly shingle, ballast-stones rounded by attrition, boulders, &c.

COBBLER. An armourer's rasp.

COBBO. The small fish known as the miller's-thumb.

COBLE. A low flat-floored boat with a square stern, used in the cod and turbot fishery, 20 feet long and 5 feet broad; of about one ton burden, rowed with three pairs of oars, and furnished with a lug-sail; it is admirably constructed for encountering a heavy swell. Its stability is secured by the rudder extending 4 or 5 feet under her bottom. It belonged originally to the stormy coast of Yorkshire. There is also a small boat under the same name used by salmon fishers.

COBOOSE. *See* CABOOSE.

COCK. That curved arm affixed to the lock of small arms, which, when released by the touch of the trigger, flies forward and discharges the piece by percussion, whether of flint and steel, fulminating priming, needles abutting on the latter, &c.

COCKADE. First worn by St. Louis on his unfortunate crusade.

COCK-A-HOOP. In full confidence, and high spirits.

COCKANDY.   A name on our northern shores for the puffin, otherwise called *Tom Noddy* (*Fratercula arctica*).

COCK-BILL.   The situation of the anchor when suspended from the cat-head ready for letting go.   Also said of a cable when it hangs right up and down.   To put the yards a-cock-bill is to top them up by one lift to an angle with the deck.   The symbol of mourning.

COCK-BOAT.   A very small boat used on rivers or near the shore. Formerly the cock was the general name of a yawl: it is derived from *coggle* or *cog* (which see).

COCKETS, or COQUETS.   An official custom-house warrant descriptive of certain goods which the searcher is to allow to pass and be shipped. Also, a galley term for counterfeit ship-papers.—*Cocket bread.*   Hard sea-biscuit.

COCK-PADDLE.   A name of the paddle or lump-fish (*Cyclopterus lumpus*).

COCKLE.   A common bivalve mollusc (*Cardium edule*), often used as food.

COCKLING SEA.   Tumbling waves dashing against each other with a short and quick motion.

COCKPIT.   The place where the wounded men are attended to, situated near the after hatch-way, and under the lower gun-deck.   The midshipmen alone inhabited the cockpit in former times, but in later days commission and warrant officers, civilians, &c., have their cabins there. —*Fore cockpit.*   A place leading to the magazine passage, and the boatswain's, gunner's, and carpenter's store-rooms; in large ships, and during war time, the boatswain and carpenter generally had their cabins in the fore cockpit, instead of being under the forecastle.

COCKPITARIAN.   A midshipman or master's mate; so called from messing in the cockpit of a line-of-battle ship.

COCKSETUS.   An old law-term for a boatman or coxswain.

COCKSWAIN, or COXSWAIN.   The person who steers a boat; after the officer in command he has charge of the crew, and all things belonging to it.   He must be ready with his crew to man the boat on all occasions.

COCOA, or CHOCOLATE NUTS, commonly so termed.   (*See* CACAO.)   It is the breakfast food of the navy.

COCOA-NUT TREE.   The *Palma cocos* yields *toddy;* the nut a valuable oil and milky juice; the stem, bark, branches, &c., also serve numerous purposes.   (*See* PALMA.)

COD.   The centre of a deep bay.   The bay of a trawl or seine.   Also, the *Gadus morrhua*, one of the most important of oceanic fishes.   The cod is always found on the submerged hills known as banks; as the Dogger Bank, and banks of Newfoundland.   (*See* LING.)

COD-BAIT. The large sea-worm or lug, dug from the wet sands. The squid or cuttle, herrings, caplin, any meat, or even a false fish of bright tin or pewter. (*See* JIG.)

CODDY-MODDY. A gull in its first year's plumage.

CODE OF SIGNALS. Series of flags, &c., for communicating at sea.

COD-FISHER'S CREW. The crew of a banker, or fishing-vessel, which anchors in 60 or 70 fathoms on the Great Bank of Newfoundland, and remains fishing until full, or driven off by stress of weather. Season from June until October. (*See* FISHERIES.)

CODGER. An easy-going man of regularity. Also, a knowing and eccentric hanger-on; one who will not move faster than he pleases.

COD-LINE. An eighteen-thread line.

COD-SOUNDS. The swim-bladders of the cod-fish, cured and packed for the market; the palates also of the fish are included as "tongues and sounds."

COEHORN. A brass mortar, named after the Dutch engineer who invented it. It is the smallest piece of ordnance in the service, having a bore of $4\frac{1}{2}$ inches diameter, a length of 1 foot, and a weight of $\frac{3}{4}$ cwt. They throw their 12-pounder shells with much precision to moderate distances, and being fixed to wooden beds, are very handy for ships' gangways, launches, &c., afloat, and for advanced trenches, the attack of stockades, &c., ashore.

COFFER, OR COFFRE. A depth sunk in the bottom of a dry ditch, to baffle besiegers when they attempt to cross it.

COFFER-DAM. A coffer-dam consists of two rows of piles, each row boarded strongly inside, and being filled with clay within well rammed, thereby resists outward pressure, and is impenetrable by the surrounding water. (*See* CAISSON.)

COGGE. An Anglo-Saxon word for a cock-boat or light yawl, being thus mentioned in *Morte Arthure*—

"Then he covers his cogge, and caches one ankere."

But coggo, as enumerated in an ordinance of parliament (*temp.* Rich. II.), seems to have been a vessel of burden used to carry troops.

COGGE-WARE. Goods carried in a cogge.

COGGLE, OR COG. A small fishing-boat upon the coasts of Yorkshire, and in the rivers Ouse and Humber. Hence the *cogmen*, who after shipwreck or losses by sea, wandered about to defraud people by begging and stealing, until they were restrained by proper laws.

COGGS. The same with *coaks* or *dowels* (which see).

COGS OF A WHEEL; applies to all wheel machinery now used at sea or on shore: thus *windlass-cogs, capstan-cogs,* &c.

COGUING THE NOSE. Making comfortable over hot negus or grog.

COIGN. *See* QUOIN.

COIL. A certain quantity of rope laid up in ring fashion. The manner in which all ropes are disposed of on board ship for convenience of stowage. They are laid up round, one fake over another, or by concentric turns, termed *Flemish coil*, forming but one tier, and lying flat on the deck, the end being in the middle of it, as a snake or worm coils itself.

COILING. A sort of serpentine winding of a cable or other rope, that it may occupy a small space in the ship. Each of the windings of this sort is called a *fake*, and one range of *fakes* upon the same line is called a *tier*. There are generally from five to seven fakes in a tier, and three or four tiers in the whole length of the cable. The smaller ropes employed about the sails are coiled upon cleats at sea, to prevent their being entangled.

COIR. Cordage made from the fibrous husks of the cocoa-nut; though cables made of it are disgreeable to handle and coil away, they have the advantage of floating in water, so that vessels ride easily by them; they are still used by the Calcutta pilot-brigs. True coir is from the *Borassus gomutus*, the long fibrous black cloth-like covering of the stem. It is from this that the black cables in the East are made; the cocoa-nut fibre being of a reddish hue. It is used for strong brushes, being cylindrical and smooth, with a natural gloss.

COKERS. The old name for cocoa-nut trees.

CO-LATITUDE. The abbreviation for complement of latitude, or what it is short of 90°.

COLD-CHISEL. A stout chisel made of steel, used for cutting iron when it is cold.

COLD-EEL. The *Gymnotus electricus*.

COLE [from the German *kohl*]. Colewort or sea-kale; a plant in its wild state peculiar to the sea-coast.

COLE-GOOSE. A name for the cormorant (*Phalacrocorax carbo*).

COLLAR. An eye in the end or bight of a shroud or stay, to go over the mast-head. The upper part of a stay. Also, a rope formed into a wreath, with a heart or dead-eye seized in the bight, to which the stay is confined at the lower part. Also, the neck of a bolt.

COLLAR-BEAM. The beam upon which the stanchions of the beak-head bulk-head stand.

COLLECTOR OF CUSTOMS. An officer who takes the general superintendence of the customs at any port.

COLLIERS. Vessels employed exclusively to carry coals from the northern ports of England. This trade has immemorially been an excellent nursery for seamen. But Shakspeare, in *Twelfth Night*, makes Sir Toby exclaim, "Hang him, foul collier!" The evil genius has lately introduced steam screw-vessels into this invaluable school.

COLLIMATION, Line of. The optical axis of a telescope, or an imaginary line passing through the centre of the tube.

COLLISION. The case of one ship running foul of another; the injuries arising from which, where no blame is imputable to the master of either, is generally borne by the owners of both in equal parts. (*See* Allision.)

COLLISION-CLAUSE. *See* Running-down Clause.

COLLOP. A cut from a joint of meat. "Scotch collops."

COLMIE. A fifth-year or full-grown coal-fish; sometimes called *comb*.

COLMOW. An old word for the sea-mew, derived from the Anglo-Saxon.

COLONEL. The commander of a regiment, either of horse or foot.

COLONNATI. The Spanish pillared dollar.

COLOURABLE. Ships' papers so drawn up as to be available for more purposes than one. In admiralty law, a probable plea.

COLOUR-CHESTS. Chests appropriated to the reception of flags for making signals.

COLOURS. The flags or banners which distinguish the ships of different nations. Also, the regimental flags of the army. Hauling down colours in token of submission, and the use of signals, are mentioned by Plutarch in *Themistocles*.

COLOUR-SERGEANT. The senior sergeant of a company of infantry; he acts as a kind of sergeant-major, and generally as pay-sergeant also to the company. From amongst these trustworthy men, the sergeants for attendance on the colours in the field were originally detailed.

COLT. A short piece of rope with a large knot at one end, kept in the pocket for starting skulkers.

COLUMBIAD. A name given in the United States to a peculiar pattern of gun in their service, principally adapted to the firing of heavy shells: its external form does not appear to have been the result of much science, and it is now generally superseded by the Dahlgren pattern.

COLUMN. A body of troops in deep files and narrow front, so disposed as to move in regular succession.

COLURES. Great circles passing through the equinoctial and solstitial points, and the poles of the earth.

COMB. A small piece of timber under the lower part of the beak-head, for the fore-tack to be hauled to, in some vessels, instead of a bumkin: it has the same use in bringing the fore-tack on board that the chess-tree has to the main-tack. Also, the notched scale of a wire-micrometer. Also, that projecting piece on the top of the cock of a gun-lock, which affords the thumb a convenient hold for drawing it back.

COMBATANTS. Men, or bodies of troops, engaged in battle with each other.

COMBE. *See* Coomb and Cwm.

COMBERS. Heavy surges breaking on a beach.

COMBERS, Grass. Men who volunteer from the plough-tail, and often prove valuable seamen.

COMBING THE CAT. The boatswain, or other operator, running his fingers through the cat-o'-nine tails, to separate them.

COMBINGS. *See* Coamings.

COMBING SEA. A rolling and crested wave.

COMBUSTION. Burning, &c. (*See* Spontaneous Combustion.)

COME NO NEAR! The order to the helmsman to steer the ship on the course indicated, and not closer to the wind, while going "full and by."—*Come on board, sir.* An officer reporting himself to his superior on returning from duty or leave.—*Come to.* To bring the ship close to the wind.—*Come to an anchor.* To let go the anchor.—*Come up!* with a rope or tackle, is to slack it off.—*Comes up*, with the helm. A close-hauled ship comes up (to her course) as the wind changes in her favour. To *come up with* or overhaul a vessel chased.—*Come up the capstan.* Is to turn it the contrary way to that which it was heaving, so as to take the strain off, or slacken or let out some of the cablet or rope which is about it.—*Come up the tackle-fall.* Is to let go.—*To come up*, in ship-building, is to cast loose the fore-locks or lashings of a sett, in order to take in closer to the plank.

COMING-HOME. Said of the anchor when it has been dropped on bad holding ground, or is dislodged from its bed by the violence of the wind and sea, and is dragged along by the vessel, or is tripped by insufficient length of cable.—*Coming round on her heel.* Turning in the same spot.—*Coming the old soldier.* Petty manœuvring.—*Coming-up glass.* (*See* Double-image Micrometer.)

COMITY. A certain *comitas gentium*, or judgment of tribunals, having competent jurisdiction in any one state, are regarded in the courts of all other civilized powers as conclusive. Especially binding in all prize matters, however manifestly unjust may be the decision. (*See* Judgment.)

COMMAND. The words of command are the terms used by officers in exercise or upon service. All commands belong to the senior officer. Also, in fortification, the height of the top of the parapet of a work above the level of the country, or above that of another work. Generally, one position is said to be commanded by another when it can be seen into from the latter.

COMMANDANT. The officer in command of a squadron, ship, garrison, fort, or regiment.

COMMANDER. An officer in the royal navy, commanding a ship of war of under twenty guns, a sloop of war, armed ship, or bomb-vessel. He was entitled master and commander, and ranked with a major of the army: now simply termed commander, and ranking with lieutenant-colonel, but junior of that rank. The act of the commander is binding upon the interests of all under him, and he is alone responsible for costs and damages: he may act erroneously, and abandon what might have turned out good prize to himself and crew.—*Commander* is also the name of a large wooden mallet used specially in the sail and rigging lofts, as anything of metal would injure the ropes or canvas.

COMMANDER-IN-CHIEF. The senior officer in any port or station appointed to hold command over all other vessels within the limits assigned to him. Thus the commodore on the coast of Africa is, *de facto*, commander-in-chief, free from the interference of any other authority afloat.

COMMAND-OF-MIND MEN. Steady officers, who command coolly.

COMMEATUS, or Provisions, going to the enemy's ports, subject only to *pre*-emption, a right of purchase upon reasonable terms, but previously liable to confiscation (Robinson). *Commeatus*, in admiralty law, is a general term, signifying drink as well as eatables.

COMMERCE. Was not much practised by the Romans. The principal objects of their water-carriage were the supply of corn, still termed *annona*, and the tribute and spoils of conquered countries.

COMMERCIAL CODE OF SIGNALS. As Marryat's and others.

COMMISSARIAT. The department of supplies to the army.

COMMISSARY. The principal officer in charge of the commissariat.

COMMISSION. The authority by which an officer officiates in his post. Also, an allowance paid to agents or factors for transacting the business of others.

COMMISSIONED OFFICERS. Those appointed by commissions. Such are admirals, down to lieutenants, in the royal navy; and in the army, all from the general to the ensign inclusive.

COMMISSIONERS, Lords, of the Admiralty. In general the crown appoints five or seven commissioners for executing the office of lord high-admiral, &c.; for this important and high office has seldom been intrusted to any single person. The admiralty jurisdiction extends to all offences mentioned in the articles of war, or new naval code, as regards places beyond the powers of the law courts, or outside the bounds of a county. But all criminal acts committed within the limits of a county, or within a line drawn from one headland to the next, are specially liable to be tried by the common law courts. The high court of admiralty civil court takes cognizance of salvage, prize-derelict, collision, &c., at sea beyond the county limits, even as relates to ships of war if in fault.

COMMISSIONERS OF CUSTOMS. The board of management of the customs department of the public revenue.

COMMISSIONERS OF THE NAVY. Certain officers formerly appointed to superintend the affairs of the navy, under the direction of the lords-commissioners of the Admiralty. Their duty was more immediately concerned in the building, docking, and repairing of ships in the dock-yards; they had also the appointment of some of the officers, as surgeons, masters, &c., and the transport, victualling, and medical departments were controlled by that board. It was abolished in 1831.

COMMIT ONE'S SELF, To. To break through regulations. To incur responsibility without regard to results.

COMMODORE. A senior officer in command of a detached squadron. A captain finding five or six ships assembled, was formerly permitted to hoist his pennant, and command as commodore; and a necessity arising for holding a court-martial, he ordered the said court to assemble. Again, where an admiral dies in command, the senior captain hoists a first-class broad pennant, and appoints a captain, secretary, and flag-lieutenant, fulfils the duties of a rear-admiral, and wears the uniform. Commodores of the second class have no captain or pennant-lieutenant. A commodore rates with brigadier-generals, according to dates of commission (being of full colonel's rank). He is next in command to a rear-admiral, but cannot hoist his broad pennant in the presence of an admiral, or superior captain, without permission. The broad pennant is a swallow-tailed tapered burgee. The second-class commodore is to hoist his broad pennant, white at the fore. It is a title given by courtesy to the senior captain, where three or more ships of war are cruising in company. It was also imported into the East India Company's vessels, the senior being so termed, *inter se.* It moreover denotes the convoy ship, which carries a light in her top. The epithet is corrupted from the Spanish *comendador.*

COMMUNICATION. Corresponding by letter, hail, or signal. (*See* LINE OF COMMUNICATION and BOYAUX.)

COMMUTE, To. To lighten the sentence of a court-martial, on a recommendation of the court to the commander-in-chief.

COMPANION. The framing and sash-lights upon the quarter-deck or round-house, through which light passes to the cabins and decks below; and a sort of wooden hood placed over the entrance or staircase of the master's cabin in small ships. Flush-decked vessels are generally fitted with movable companions, to keep the rain or water from descending, which are unshipped when the capstan is required.

COMPANION-LADDER. Denotes the ladder by which the officers ascend to, and descend from, the quarter-deck.

COMPANION-WAY. The staircase, porch, or berthing of the ladder-way to the cabin.

COMPANY. The whole crew of any ship, including her officers, men, and boys. In the army, a small body of foot, or subdivision of a regiment, commanded by a captain.

COMPARATIVE RANK. *See* RANK.

COMPARISON WATCH. The job-watch for taking an observation, compared before and after with the chronometer.

COMPARTMENT BULKHEADS. Some of the iron ships have adopted the admirable Chinese plan of dividing the hold athwart-ship by strong water-tight bulk-heads, into compartments, so that a leak in any one of them does not communicate with the others—thus strengthening a vessel, besides adding to its security. Compartment bulkheads were first directed to be fitted under the superintendence of Commander Belcher in H.M. ships *Erebus* and *Terror* at Chatham, for Arctic service in 1835. H.M.S. *Terror*, Commander Back, was saved entirely owing to this fitment, the after section being full of water all the passage home; and lately the mail packet *Samphire* was similarly saved.

COMPASANT. A corruption of *corpo santo*, a ball of electric light observed flickering about the masts, yard-arms, and rigging, during heavy rain, thunder, and lightning.

COMPASS. An instrument employed by navigators to guide the ship's course at sea. It consists of a circular box, containing a fly or paper card, which represents the horizon, and is suspended by two concentric rings called gimbals. The fly is divided into thirty-two equal parts, by lines drawn from the centre to the circumference, called points or rhumbs; the interval between the points is subdivided into 360 degrees—consequently, the distance or angle comprehended between any two rhumbs is equal to 11 degrees and 15 minutes. The four cardinal points lie opposite to each other; the north and south points form top and bottom, leaving the east on the right hand, and the west on the left; the names of all the inferior points are compounded of these according to their situation. This card is attached to a magnetic needle, which, carrying the card round with it, points north, excepting for the local annual variation and the deviation caused by the iron in the ship; the angle which the course makes with that meridian is shown by the lubber's point, a dark line inside the box. (*See* ADJUSTMENT OF THE COMPASS.)

COMPASS, To. To curve; also to obtain one's object.

COMPASSING. (*See* COMPASS TIMBERS.)

COMPASSIONATE ALLOWANCES. Grants are made on the compassionate fund to the legitimate children of deceased officers, on its being shown to the Admiralty that they deserve them.

COMPASS-SAW. A narrow saw, which, inserted in a hole bored by a centre-bit, follows out required curves.

COMPASS-TIMBERS. Such as are curved, crooked, or arched, for ship-building.

COMPENSATION. If a detained vessel is lost by the negligence and misconduct of the prizemaster, compensation must be rendered, and the actual captors are responsible. The principal being answerable in law for the agent's acts.

COMPENSATOR OF THE COMPASS. See MAGNETIC COMPENSATOR.

COMPLAIN, To. The creaking of masts, or timbers, when overpressed, without any apparent external defect. One man threatening to complain of another, is saying that he will report misconduct to the officer in charge of the quarter-deck.

COMPLEMENT. The proper number of men employed in any ship, either for navigation or battle. In navigation the complement of the course is what it wants of eight points; of latitude, what it is short of 90°. (See CO-LATITUDE.)

COMPLEMENT OF LONGITUDE. See SUPPLEMENT OF LONGITUDE.

COMPLETE BOOK. A book which contains the names and particulars of every person borne for wages on board, as age, place of birth, rating, times of entry and discharge, &c.

COMPLIMENT, To. To render naval or military honour where due.

COMPO. The monthly portion of wages paid to the ship's company.

COMPOSITION NAILS. Those which are made of mixed metal, and which, being largely used for nailing on copper sheathing, are erroneously called *copper nails*.

COMPOUND. A term used in India for a lawn garden, or inclosed ground round a house.

COMPRADOR [Sp]. A Chinese contractor in shipping concerns, or in purchasing present supplies.

COMPRESS. A pad of soft linen used by the surgeon for the dressing of a wound.

COMPRESSION OF THE POLES. The amount of flattening at the polar regions of a planet, by which the polar diameter is less than the equatorial.

COMPRESSOR. A mechanism generally adopted afloat for facilitating the working of the large guns recently introduced; the gun-carriage is thus compressed to its slide or platform during the recoil, and set free again by the turn of a handle for running up. It is of various forms; one of the simpler kind used to be always applied to carronade slides.

COMPRESSOR-STOPPER. A contrivance for holding the chain-cable by compression.

COMPROMISE. The mutual agreement of a party or parties at difference, to refer to arbitration, or make an end of the matter.

COMPTROLLER OF THE CUSTOMS. The officer who controls and has a check on the collectors of customs. (*See* CONTROLLER.)

COMPTROLLER OF THE NAVY. Formerly the chief commissioner of the navy board, at which he presided.

COMRADE. A barrack term for a fellow-soldier, serving in the same company.

CONCEALMENT, OR SUPPRESSIO VERI. Consists in the suppression of any fact or circumstance as to the state of the ship, the nature of her employ, and the time of sailing or expected arrival, material to the risk of insurance, and is fatal to the insured. But it is held immaterial to disclose the secret destination of privateers, the usages of trade, or matters equally open to both parties.

CONCENTRATED FIRE. The bringing the whole or several guns to bear on a single point.

CONCH. A large univalve, used as a horn by pilots, fishermen, &c., in fogs: a *strombus, triton,* or sometimes a *murex.*

CONCHS. A name for the wreckers of the Bahama reefs, in allusion to the shells on those shores. Though plunder is their object, the *Conchs* are very serviceable to humanity, and evince both courage and address in saving the lives of the wrecked.

CONCLUDING-LINE. A small rope hitched to the middle of the steps of the stern-ladders. Also, a small line leading through the centre of the steps of a Jacob's ladder.

CONDEMNATION. A captured ship declared by sentence of the admiralty court to be lawful prize. But the transfer of a prize vessel carried into a neutral port, and sold without a condemnation, or the authority of any judicial proceedings, is null and void.

CONDEMNED. Unserviceable, as bad provisions, old stores, &c.

CONDENSER. The chamber of a marine engine, where the steam, after having performed its duty, is instantly reduced to water. Sailing ships frequently carry condensers, for the purpose of making fresh from salt water.

CONDER. A watcher of fishes, the same as balker, huer, and olpis. See statute (1 Jac. cap. 23) relating to his employment, which was to give notice to the fishermen from an eminence which way the herring shoals were going.

CONDITIONS. The terms of surrender.

CONDUCT-LIST. A roll to accompany the tickets of all persons sent to a hospital for medical treatment; it details their names, numbers on the ship's books, the date of their being sent, and the nature of their ailment.

CONDUCT-MONEY. A sum advanced to defray the travelling expenses of volunteers, and of soldiers and sailors to their quarters and ships. (*See* SAFE-CONDUCT.)

CONDUCTOR. A thick metal wire, generally of copper, extending from above the main truck downwards into the water, or in the form of a chain with long links. Its use is to defend the ship from the effects of lightning, by conveying the electric fluid into the sea.

CONE. A solid figure having a circle for its base, and produced by the entire revolution of a right-angled triangle about its perpendicular side, which is termed the axis of the cone.

CONE-BUOY. *See* CAN-BUOY.

CONEY-FISH. A name of the burbot.

CONFIGURATION. The relative positions of celestial bodies, as for instance those of Jupiter's satellites, with respect to the primary at any one time.

CONFINEMENT. Inflicted restraint; an arrest.

CONFIRMED RANK. When an officer is placed in a vacancy by "acting order," he only holds temporary rank until "confirmed" therein by the Admiralty. An acting order given by competent authority is not disturbed by any casual superior.

CONFLICT. An indecisive action.

CONFLUENTS. Those streams which join and flow together. The confluence is the point of junction of an affluent river with its recipient.

CONGER. A large species of sea-eel, furnishing a somewhat vile viand, but eatable when strongly curried. Not at all despised by the people of Cornwall in "fishy pie."

CONGREVE-ROCKET. A very powerful form of rocket, invented by the late Sir William Congreve, R.A., and intended to do the work of artillery without the inconvenience of its weight. In its present form, however, the rocket is so uncertain, that it is in little favour save for exceptional occasions.

CONICAL TOPS OF MOUNTAINS not unfrequently indicate their nature: the truncated sugar-loaf form is generally assumed by volcanoes, though the same is occasionally met with in other mountains.

CONIC SECTIONS. The curved lines and plane figures which are produced by the intersection of a plane with a cone.

CONJEE. Gruel made of rice.

CONJUGATE AXIS. The secondary diameter of an ellipse, perpendicular to the transverse axis.

CONJUNCTION, in nautical astronomy, is when two bodies have the same longitude or right ascension.

CONN, Con, or Cun, as pronounced by seamen. This word is derived from the Anglo-Saxon *conne, connan,* to know, or be skilful. The pilot of old was skilful, and later the master was selected to conn the ship in action, that is, direct the helmsman. The quarter-master during ordinary watches conns the ship, and stands beside the wheel at the conn, unless close-hauled, when his station is at the weather-side, where he can see the weather-leeches of the sails.

CONNECTING-ROD. In the marine engine, the part which connects the side-levers and the crank together.

CONNINGS. Reckonings.

CONQUER, To. To overcome decidedly.

CONSCRIPTION. Not only furnishes conscripts for the French army, but also levies a number of men who are compelled to serve afloat.

CONSECRATION OF COLOURS. A rite practised in the army, but not in the navy.

CONSIGN, To. To send a consignment of goods to an agent or factor for sale or disposal.

CONSIGNEE. The party to whose care a ship or a consignment of goods is intrusted.

CONSIGNMENT. Goods assigned from beyond sea, or elsewhere, to a factor.

CONSOLE-BRACKET. A light piece of ornament at the fore-part of the quarter-gallery, otherwise called a *canting-livre.*

CONSORT. Any vessel keeping company with another.—*In consort,* ships sailing together in partnership.

CONSORTSHIP. The practice of two or more ships agreeing to join in adventure, under which a strict division of all prizes must be made. (*See* Ton for Ton.)

CONSTRUCTION. In naval architecture, is to give the ship such a form as may be most suitable for the service for which she is designed. In navigation, it is the method of ascertaining a ship's course by trigonometrical diagrams. (*See* Inspection.)

CONSTRUCTIVE TOTAL LOSS. When the repair of damage sustained by the perils of the sea would cost more than the ship would be worth after being repaired.

CONSUL. An officer established by a commission from the crown, in all foreign countries of any considerable trade, to facilitate business, and represent the merchants of his nation. They take rank with captains, but are to wait on them if a boat be sent. Commanders wait on consuls, but vice-consuls wait on commanders (*in Etiquette*). Ministers and *chargés d'affaires* retire in case of hostilities, but consuls are permitted to remain to watch the interests of their countrymen. When commerce began to flourish in modern Europe, occasion soon arose for the institution of a kind of court-merchant, to determine commercial affairs in a summary way. Their authority depends very much on their commission, and on the words of the treaty on which it is founded. The consuls are to take care of the affairs of the trade, and of the rights, interests, and privileges of their countrymen in foreign ports. Not being public ministers, they are liable to the *lex loci* both civil and criminal, and their exemption from certain taxes depends upon treaty and custom.

CONTACT. Brought in contact with, as touching the sides of a ship. In astronomy, bringing a reflected body, as the sun, in contact with the moon or with a star. (*See* LUNAR DISTANCES, MEASUREMENT BY SEXTANT, &c.)

CONTENTS. A document which the master of a merchantman must deliver to the custom-house searcher, before he can clear outwards; it describes the vessel's destination, cargo, and all necessary particulars.

CONTINENT. In geography, a large extent of land which is not entirely surrounded by water, or separated from other lands by the sea, as Europe, Asia, and Africa. It is also used in contradistinction to *island*, though America seems insulated.

CONTINGENT. The quota of armed men, or pecuniary subsidy, which one state gives to another. Also, certain allowances made to commanding officers to defray necessary expenses.

CONTINUED LINES. In field-works, means a succession of fronts without any interruption, save the necessary passages; differing thus from *interrupted lines*.

CONTINUOUS SERVICE MEN. Those seamen who, having entered for a period, on being paid off, are permitted to have leave, and return to the flag-ship at the port for general service.

CONT-LINE. The space between the bilges of two casks stowed side by side.

CONTOUR. The sweep of a ship's shape.

CONTRABAND. The ship is involved in the legal fate of the cargo; the master should therefore be careful not to take any goods on board without all custom-house duties being paid up, and see that they be not prohibited by parliament or public proclamation. Contraband is simply defined, "merchandise forbidden by the law of nations to be supplied to an enemy;" but it affords fat dodges to the admiralty court sharks.

CONTRABAND OF WAR. Arms, ammunition, and all stores which may aid hostilities; masts, ship-timber going to an enemy's port, hemp, provisions, and even money under stipulations, pitch and tar, sail-cloth. They must, however, be taken *in delicto*, in the actual prosecution of a voyage to the enemy's port.

CONTRACT OF AFFREIGHTMENT. The agreement for the letting to freight the whole or any part of a vessel for one or more voyages; the *charter-party*.

CONTRACT TICKET. A printed form of agreement with every passenger in a passenger-ship, prescribed by the legislature.

CONTRARY. The wind when opposed to a vessel's course.

> "Cruel was the stately ship that bore her love from Mary,
> And cruel was the fair wind that wouldn't blow contrary."

CONTRAVALLATION, Lines of. Continuous lines of intrenchment round the besieged fortress, and fronting towards it, to guard against any sorties from the place. (*See* Circumvallation.)

CONTRIBUTION. Money paid in order to save a place from being plundered by a hostile force. (*See* Ransom.) Also, a sum raised among merchants, where goods have been thrown overboard in stress of weather, towards the loss of the owners thereof.

CONTROLLER. Differs from *comptroller*, which applies chiefly to the duties of an *accompt*. But the controller of the navy controls naval matters in ship-building, fitting, &c. There is also the controller of victualling, and the controller-general of the coast-guard.

CONTUMACY. The not appearing to the three calls of the admiralty court, after the allegation has been presented to the judge, with a schedule of expenses to be taxed, and an oath of their necessity.

CONVALESCENT. Those men who are recovering health, but not sufficiently recovered to perform their duties, are reported by the surgeon "convalescent." Convalescents are *amused* by picking oakum!

CONVENIENT PORT. A general law-term in cases of capture, within a certain latitude of discretion; a place where a vessel can lie in safety, and holding ready communication with the tribunals which have to decide the question of capture.

CONVENTION. An agreement made between hostile troops, for the evacuation of a post, or the suspension of hostilities.

CONVERGENT. In geography, a stream which comes into another stream, but whose course is unknown, is simply a convergent.

CONVERSION. Reducing a vessel by a deck, thereby converting a line-of-battle ship into a frigate, or a crank three-decker into a good two-decker; or a serviceable vessel into a hulk, resembling a prison or dungeon, internally and externally, as much as possible.

CONVERSION OF STORES. Adapting the sails, ropes, or timbers from one purpose to another, with the least possible waste.

CONVEXITY. The curved limb of the moon; an outward curve.

CONVICT-SHIP. A vessel appropriated to the convicts of a dock-yard; also one hired to carry out convicts to their destination.

CONVOY. A fleet of merchant ships similarly bound, protected by an armed force. Also, the ship or ships appointed to conduct and defend them on their passage. Also, a guard of troops to escort a supply of stores to a detached force.

CONVOY-INSTRUCTIONS. The printed regulations supplied by the senior officer to each ship of the convoy.

CONVOY-LIST. A return of the merchantmen placed under the protection of men-of-war, for safe conduct to their destination.

COOK. A man of each mess who is caterer for the day, and answerable too, wherefore he is allowed the surplus grog, termed *plush* (which see). The cook, *par excellence*, in the navy, was a man of importance, responsible for the proper cooking of the food, yet not overboiling the meat to extract the fat—his perquisite. The coppers were closely inspected daily by the captain, and if they soiled a cambric handkerchief the cook's allowance was stopped. Now, the ship's cook is a first-class petty officer, and cannot be punished as heretofore. In a merchant-man the cook is, *ex officio*, the hero of the fore-sheet, as the steward is of the main one.

COOKING A DAY'S WORK. To save the officer in charge. Reckoning too is cooked, as in a certain Antarctic discovery of land, which James Ross afterwards sailed over.

COOK-ROOM, OR COOK-HOUSE. The galley or caboose containing the cooking apparatus, and where victuals are dressed.

COOLIE, COULEY, KOULI, OR CHULIAH. A person who carries a load; a porter or day-labourer in India and China.

COOMB. The Anglo-Saxon *comb;* a low place inclosed with hills; a valley. (*See* CWM.)

COOMINGS, OR COMBINGS. The rim of the hatchways. (*See* COAMINGS.)

COOM OF A WAVE. The comb or crest. The white summit when it breaks.

COON-TRAIE. A Manx and Erse term for the neap-tide.

COOP, OR FISH-COOP. A hollow vessel made with twigs, with which fish are taken in the Humber. (*See* HEN-COOP.)

COOPER. A rating for a first-class petty officer, who repairs casks, &c.

COOT. A water-fowl common on lakes and rivers (*Fulica atra*). The toes are long and not webbed, but bordered by a scalloped membrane. The name is sometimes used for the guillemot (*Uria troile*), and often applied to a stupid person.

COOTH. *See* CUTH.

COP, OR COPT. The top of a conical hill.

COPE. An old English word for cape.

COPECK. *See* KOPEK.

COPERNICAN SYSTEM. The Pythagorean system of the universe, revived by Copernicus in the sixteenth century, and now confirmed; in which the sun occupies the central space, and the planets with their attendant satellites revolve about him.

COPILL. An old term for a variety of the coble.

COPING. In ship-building, turning the ends of iron lodging-knees, so that they may hook into the beams.

COPPER, To. To cover the ship's bottom with prepared copper.

COPPER-BOLTS. *See* COPPER-FASTENED.

COPPERED, OR COPPER-BOTTOMED. Sheathed with thin sheets of copper, which prevents the teredo eating into the planks, or shell and weed accumulating on the surface, whereby a ship is retarded in her sailing.

COPPER-FASTENED. The bolts and other metal work in the bottom of ships, made of copper instead of iron, so that the vessel may afterwards be

coppered without danger of its corroding the heads of the bolts by gal-
vanic action, as ensues when copper and iron are in contact with sea-water.

COPPER-NAILS. These are chiefly used in boat-building, and for plank
nails in the vicinity of the binnacle, as iron affects the compass-needle.
They are not to be confounded with *composition nails,* which are cast.
(*See* ROOF, or ROVE AND CLINCH.)

COPPERS. The ship's boilers for cooking; the name is generally used,
even where the apparatus may be made of iron.

COQUILLAGE. Shell-fish in general. It applies to anchorages where
oysters abound, or where fish are plentiful, and shell-fish for bait easily
obtainable. It is specially a term belonging to French and Spanish
fishermen.

CORAB. A sort of boat, otherwise called *coracle.*

CORACLE. An ancient British truckle or boat, constructed of wicker-
work, and still in use amongst Welsh fishermen and on the Irish lakes.
It is covered by skins, oil-cloth, &c., which are removed when out of use;
it is of an oval form; contains one man, who, on reaching the shore,
shoulders his coracle, deposits it in safety, and covers it with dried rushes
or heather. The Arctic *baidar* is of similar construction. It is probably
of the like primitive fabric with the *cymba sutiles* of Herodotus.

CORACORA. *See* KORACORA.

CORAL. A name applied to the hard calcareous support or skeleton of
many species of marine zoophytes. The coral-producing animals abound
chiefly in tropical seas, sometimes forming, by the aggregated growth of
countless generations, reefs, barriers, and islands of vast extent. The
"red coral" (*Corallium rubrum*) of the Mediterranean is highly prized for
ornamental purposes.

CORALAN. A small open boat for the Mediterranean coral fishery.

CORAL-BAND. *See* SAND AND CORAL BANK or ISLETS.

CORBEILLE [Fr. basket]. Miner's basket; small gabion used temporarily for shelter to riflemen, and placed on the parapet, either to fire
through, or for protection from a force placed on a higher level.

CORBILLARD [Fr.] A large boat of transport.

CORD. Small rope; that of an inch or less in circumference.

CORD OR CHURD OF WOOD; as firewood. A statute stack is 8 feet long,
4 feet broad, and 4 feet high.

CORDAGE. A general term for the running-rigging of a ship, as also for
rope of any size which is kept in reserve, and for all stuff to make ropes.
—*Cable-laid cordage.* Ropes, the three strands of which are composed
of three other strands, as are cables and cablets. (*See* ROPE.)

CORDILLA. The coarse German hemp, otherwise called *torse.*

CORDLIE. A name for the tunny fish.

CORDON. In fortification, the horizontal moulding of masonry along the
top of the true escarp. Also, sometimes used for lines of circumvallation
or blockade, or any connected chain of troops or even sentries. Also, the
riband of an order of knighthood or honour, and hence used by the

French as signifying a member thereof, as Cordon bleu, Knight of the order of the Holy Ghost, &c.

CORDOVAN. Leather made from seal-skin; the term is derived from the superior leather prepared at Cordova in Spain.

CORDUROY. Applied to roads formed in new settlements, of trees laid roughly on sleepers transverse to the direction of the road: as suddenly for artillery.

CORKIR, or CUDBEAR. The *Lecanora tartarea*, a lichen producing a purple dye, growing on the stones of the Western Isles, and in Norway.

CORMORANT. A well-known sea-bird (*Phalacrocorax carbo*) of the family *Pelecanidæ*.

CORN, To. A remainder of the Anglo-Saxon *ge-cyrned*, salted. To preserve meat for a time by salting it slightly.

CORNED. Slightly intoxicated. In Chaucer's *Canterbury Tales*, mention is made of " corny ale."

CORNED POWDER. Powder granulated from the mill-cakes and sifted.

CORNET. A commissioned officer who carries the colours belonging to a cavalry troop, equivalent to an ensign in the infantry; the junior subaltern rank in the horse.

CORNISH RING. The astragal of the muzzle or neck of a gun; it is the next ring from the mouth backwards. (Now disused.)

CORN-SALAD. A species of Valerianella. The top-leaves are used for salad, a good anti-scorbutic with vinegar.

CORNS OF POWDER. The small grains that gunpowder consists of. The powder reduced for fire-works, quill-tubes, &c.; sometimes by alcohol.

COROMONTINES. A peculiar race of negroes, brought from the interior of Africa, and sold; but so ferocious as to be greatly dreaded in the West Indies.

CORONA. In timber, consists of rows of microscopic cylinders, situated between the wood and the pith; it is that part from which all the branches take their rise, and from it all the wood-threads grow.—*Corona* astronomically means the luminous ring or glory which surrounds the sun or moon during an eclipse, or the intervention of a thin cloud. They are generally faintly coloured at their edges. Frequently when there is a halo encircling the moon, there is a small corona more immediately around it. Coronæ, as well as halos, have been observed to prognosticate rain, hail, or snow, being the result of snow or dense vapours nearer the earth, through which the object becomes hazy.

CORONER. An important officer. Seamen should understand that his duties embrace all acts within a line drawn from one headland to another; or within the body of the county. His duty is to investigate, on the part of the crown, all accidents, deaths, wrecks, &c.; and his warrant is not to be contemned or avoided.

COROUSE. The ancient weapon invented by Duilius for boarding. An attempt was made in 1798 to re-introduce it in French privateers.

COROWNEL. The old word for colonel.

CORPHOUN. An out-of-the-way name for a herring.

CORPORAL, Ship's. In a ship of war was, under the master-at-arms, employed to teach the sailors the use of small arms; to attend at the gangways when entering ports, and see that no spirituous liquors were brought on board without leave. Also, to extinguish the fire and candles at eight o'clock in winter, and nine o'clock in summer, when the evening gun was fired; and to see that there were no lights below, but such as were under the charge of the proper sentinels. In the marines or army in general the corporal is a non-commissioned officer next below the sergeant in the scale of authority. The ship's corporal of the present day is the superior of the first-class working petty officers, and solely attends to police matters under the master-at-arms or superintendent-in-chief.

CORPORAL OATH. So called because the witness when he swears lays his right hand on the holy evangelists, or New Testament.

CORPOSANT. [*Corpo santo*, Ital.] *See* COMPASANT.

CORPS. Any body of troops acting under one commander.

CORPSE. Jack's term for the party of marines embarked; the corps.

CORRECTIONS. Reductions of observations of the sun, moon, or stars.

CORRIDOR. *See* COVERT-WAY.

CORRYNE POWDER. Corn-powder, a fine kind of gunpowder.

CORSAIR. A name commonly given to the piratical cruisers of Barbary, who frequently plundered the merchant ships indiscriminately.

CORSELET. The old name for a piece of armour used to cover the body of a fighting-man.

CORTEGE. The official staff, civil or military.

CORUSCATIONS. Atmospheric flashes of light, as in auroras.

CORVETTES. Flush-decked ships, equipped with one tier of guns: fine vessels for warm climates, from admitting a free circulation of air. The Bermuda-built corvettes were deemed superior vessels, swift, weatherly, "lie to" well, and carry sail in a stiff breeze. The cedar of which they are chiefly built is very buoyant, but also brittle.

CORVORANT. An old mode of spelling *cormorant*.

COSIER. A lubber, a botcher, a tailoring fellow [*coser*, Sp. to sew?]

COSMICAL RISING AND SETTING OF THE HEAVENLY BODIES. Their rising and setting with the sun.

COSMOGRAPHER. Formerly applied to "too clever by half." Now, one who describes the world or universe in all its parts.

COSS. A measure of distance in India, varying in different districts from one mile and a half to two miles.

COSTAL. Relating to the coast.

COSTEIE. An old English word for going by the coast.

COSTERA. A law archaism for the sea-coast.

COSTS AND DAMAGE. Demurrage is generally given against a captor for unjustifiable detention. Where English merchants provoke expense by using false papers, the court decrees the captors their expenses on restitution. (*See* EXPENSES.)

COT. A wooden bed-frame suspended from the beams of a ship for the officers, between decks. It is inclosed in canvas, sewed in the form of a chest, about 6 feet long, 1 foot deep, and 2 or 3 feet wide, in which the mattress is laid.

COTT. An old term for a little boat.

COTTON, GUN. *See* GUN-COTTON.

COTTONINA. The thick sail-cloth of the Levant.

COUBAIS. An ornamented Japanese barge of forty oars.

COUD. An old term used for *conn* or *cunn*.

COULTER-NEB. A name of the puffin (*Fratercula arctica*).

COUNCIL-OF-WAR. The assemblage of officers for concerting measures of moment, too often deemed the symbol of irresolution in the commander-in-chief.

COUNTER. A term which enters into the composition of divers words of our language, and generally implies opposition, as *counter-brace, counter-current*, &c.—*Counter of a ship,* refers to her after-seat on the water: the counter above extends from the gun-deck line, or lower ribbon moulding of the cabin windows, to the water-line (or seat of water); the lower counter is arched below that line, and constitutes the hollow run. It is formed on the transom-buttocks.

COUNTER-APPROACHES. Works effected outside the place by the garrison during a siege, to enfilade, command, or otherwise check the approaches of the besieger.

COUNTER-BALANCE WEIGHT, in the marine engine. (*See* LEVER.) Also in many marine barometers, where it slides and is fixed by adjusting screws, so as to produce an even-balanced swing, free from jerk.

COUNTER-BRACE, To. Is bracing the head-yards one way, and the after-yards another. The counter-brace is the lee-brace of the fore-topsail-yard, but is only distinguished by this name at the time of the ship's going about (called tacking), when the sail begins to shiver in the wind, this brace is hauled in to flatten the sail against the lee-side of the top-mast, and increase the effect of the wind in forcing her round. Counter-bracing becomes necessary to render the vessel stationary when sounding, lowering a boat, or speaking a stranger. It is now an obsolete term, and the manœuvre is called *heaving-to.*

COUNTER-CURRENT. That portion of water diverted from the main stream of a current by the particular formation of the coast or other obstruction, and which therefore runs in a contrary direction. There is also a current formed under the lee-counter of a ship when going through the water, which retains floating objects there, and is fatal to a man, by sucking him under.

COUNTERFORTS. Masonry adjuncts, advantageous to all retaining walls, but especially to those which, like the escarps of fortresses, are liable to be battered. They are attached at regular intervals to the hinder face of the wall, and perpendicular to it; having various proportions, but generally the same height as the wall; they hold it from being

thrust forward from behind, and, even when it is battered away, retain
the earth at the back at such a steep slope that the formation of a practicable breach remains very difficult. When arches are turned between
the counterforts, the strength of the whole structure is much increased:
it is then called a *counter-arched revetement*.

COUNTERGUARD. In fortification, a smaller rampart raised in front
of a larger one, principally with the intention of delaying for a period
the besieger's·attack. Other means, however, are generally preferred in
modern times, except when a rapid fall in the ground renders it difficult
to cover the main escarp by ordinary resources.

COUNTER-LINE. A word often used for *contravallation*.

COUNTERMARCH. To change the direction of a march to its exact
opposite. In some military movements this involves the changing of
front and wings.

COUNTERMINES. Military defensive mines: they may be arranged on
a system for the protection of the whole of a front of fortification by the
discovering and blowing up not only the subterranean approaches of the
besieger, but also his more important lodgments above.

COUNTER-MOULD. The converse of mould (which see).

COUNTER-RAILS. The balustrade work, or ornamental moulding across
a square stern, where the counter terminates.

COUNTERSCARP. In fortification, the outer side of the ditch next the
country; it is usually of less height, and less strongly revetted than the
escarp, the side which forms the face of the rampart.

COUNTER-SEA. The disturbed state of the sea after a gale, when, the
wind having changed, the sea still runs in its old direction.

COUNTERSIGN. A particular word or number which is exchanged
between sentinels, and intrusted to those on duty. (*See* PAROLE.)

COUNTER-SUNK. Those holes which are made for the heads of bolts or
nails to be sunk in, so as to be even with the general surface.

COUNTER-TIMBERS. Short right-aft timbers for the purpose of
strengthening the counter, and forming the stern.

COUNTER-TRENCHES. *See* COUNTER-APPROACHES.

COUNTRY. A term synonymous with *station*. The place whither a
ship happens to be ordered.

COUP DE GRACE. The finishing shot which brings an enemy to surrender; or the wound which deprives an adversary of life or resistance.

COUP DE MAIN. A sudden and vigorous attack.

COUP D'ŒIL. The skill of distinguishing, at first sight, the weakness of
an enemy's position, as Nelson did at the Nile.

COUPLE, To. To bend two hawsers together; coupling links of a cable;
coupling shackles.

COUREAU. A small yawl of the Garonne. Also, a narrow strait or
channel.

COURSE. The direction taken by anything in motion, shown by the point
of the compass *towards* which they run, as water in a river, tides, and cur-

rents; but of the wind, as similarly indicated by the compass-point *from* which it blows. Course is also the ship's way. In common parlance, it is the point of the compass upon which the ship sails, the direction in which she proceeds, or is intended to go. When the wind is foul, she cannot "lie her course;" if free, she "steers her course."

COURSES. A name by which the sails hanging from the lower yards of a ship are usually distinguished, viz. the main-sail, fore-sail, and mizen: the stay-sails upon the lower masts are sometimes also comprehended in this denomination, as are the main stay-sails of all brigs and schooners. A ship is under her courses when she has no sail set but the fore-sail, main-sail, and mizen. Try-sails are courses (which see), sometimes termed *bentincks.*

COURSET. The paper on which the night's course is set for the officer in charge of the watch.

COURT-MARTIAL. A tribunal held under an act of parliament, of the year 1749, and not, like the mutiny act, requiring yearly re-enactment. It has lately, 6th August, 1861, been changed to the "Naval Discipline Act." At present a court may be composed of five, but must not exceed nine, members. No officer shall sit who is under twenty-one years of age. No flag-officer can be tried unless the president also be a flag-officer, and the others flag, or captains. No captain shall be tried unless the president be of higher rank, and the others captains and commanders. No court for the trial of any officer, or person below the rank of captain, shall be legal, unless the president is a captain, or of higher rank, nor unless, in addition, there be two other officers of the rank of commander, or of higher rank. Any witness summoned—civil, naval, or military—by the judge-advocate, refusing to attend or give evidence, to be punished as for same in civil courts. The admiralty can issue commissions to officers to hold courts-martial on foreign stations, without which they cannot be convened. A commander-in-chief on a foreign station, holding such a commission, may under his hand authorize an officer in command of a detached portion to hold courts-martial. Formerly all officers composing the court, attendants, witnesses, &c., were compelled to appear in their full-dress uniforms; but by recent orders, the undress uniform, with cocked hat and sword, is to be worn.

COUTEL. A military implement which served both for a knife and a dagger.

COUTERE. A piece of armour which covered the elbow.

COVE. An inlet in a coast, sometimes extensive, as the Cove of Cork. In naval architecture, the arched moulding sunk in at the foot or lower part of the taffrail.—*My cove,* a familiar friendly term.

COVER. Security from attack or interruption, as under cover of the ship's guns, under cover of the parapet. In the field exercise and drill of troops, one body is said to cover another exactly in rear of it. Covers for sails when furled (to protect them from the weather when loosing and airing them is precluded), are made of strong canvas painted.

COVERED WAY. In fortification, a space running along the outside of the ditch for the convenient passage of troops and guns, covered from the country by a palisading and the parapet of the glacis. It is of importance to an active defence, as besides enabling a powerful musketry fire to be poured on thè near approaches of the besieger, it affords to the garrison a secure base from which to sally in force at any hour of the day or night.

COVERING-BOARD. *See* PLANK-SHEERS.

COVERING-PARTY. A force detached to protect a party sent on especial duty.

COVERT-WAY. *See* COVERED WAY.

COW. Applied by whalers to the female whale.—*To cow*. To depress with fear.

COWARDICE, AND DESERTION OF DUTY IN FIGHT. Are criminal by law, even in the crew of a merchant-ship. Such poltroonery is very rare.

COWD. To float slowly. A Scotch term, as "the boat cowds braely awa."

COW-HITCH. A slippery or lubberly hitch.

COWHORN. The seaman's appellation of the coehorn.

COWIE. A name among Scotch fishermen for the porpoise.

COWL. The cover of a funnel.

COWRIE. Small shells, *Cyprœa moneta*, used for money or barter in Africa and the East Indies.

COXSON, OR COXON. *See* COCKSWAIN.

COX'S TRAVERSE. Up one hatchway and down another, to elude duty. (*See* TOM COX.)

C.P. Mark for men sent by civil power.

CRAB. A wooden pillar, the lower end of which being let down through a ship's decks, rests upon a socket like the capstan, and having in its upper end three or four holes at different heights, long oars are thrust through them, each acting like two levers. It is employed to wind in the cable, or any other weighty matter. Also, a portable wooden or cast-iron machine, fitted with wheels and pinions similar to those of a winch, of use in loading and discharging timber-vessels, &c.—*The crab with three claws*, is used to launch ships, and to heave them into the dock, or off the key.—*To catch a crab*. To pull an oar too light or too deep in the water; to miss time in rowing. This derisive phrase for a false stroke may have been derived from the Italian *chiappar un gragno*, to express the same action.

CRABBING TO IT. Carrying an overpress of sail in a fresh gale, by which a ship crabs or drifts sideways to leeward.

CRABBLER. *See* KRABLA.

CRAB-BOAT. Resembles a large jolly-boat.

CRAB-CAPSTAN. *See* CRAB.

CRAB-WINDLASS. A light windlass for barges.

CRAB-YAWS. *See* YAWS.

CRACK. "In a crack," immediately.

CRACKER. So named from the noise it makes in exploding; it is applied to a small pistol. Also, to a little hard cabin biscuit, so called from its noise in breaking.

CRACKNEL. A small bark. Also, biscuits (see 1 Ki. xiv. 3).

CRACK OFFICER. One of the best class.

CRACK ON, To. To carry all sail.

CRACK-ORDER. High regularity.

CRACK-SHIP. One uncommonly smart in her evolutions and discipline, perhaps from the old English word for a fine boy. Crack is generally used for first-rate or excellent.

CRADLE. A frame consisting of bilgeways, poppets, &c., on the principle of the wedge, placed under the bottom of a ship, and resting on the ways on which it slips, thus launching her steadily into the water, at which time it supports her weight while she slides down the greased ways. The cradle being the support of the ship, she carries it with her into the water, when, becoming buoyant, the frame separates from the hull, floats on the surface, and is again collected for similar purposes.

CRADLES. Standing bedsteads made up for wounded seamen, that they may be more comfortable than is possible in a hammock. Boats' chocks are sometimes called cradles.

CRAFT [from the Anglo-Saxon word *craft*, a trading vessel]. It is now a general name for lighters, hoys, barges, &c., employed to load or land any goods or stores.—*Small craft*. The small vessels of war attendant on a fleet, such as cutters, schooners, gun-boats, &c., generally commanded by lieutenants. Craft is also a term in sea-phraseology for every kind of vessel, especially for a favourite ship. Also, all manner of nets, lines, hooks, &c., used in fishing.

CRAG. A precipitous cliff whose strata if vertical, or nearly so, subdivide into points.

CRAGER. A small river lighter, mentioned in our early statutes.

CRAGSMAN. One who climbs cliffs overhanging the sea to procure sea-fowls, or their eggs.

CRAIG-FLOOK. The smear-dab, or rock-flounder.

CRAIK, or CRAKE. A ship; a diminutive corrupted from *carrack*.

CRAIL. *See* KREEL.

CRAIL-CAPON. A haddock dried without being split.

CRAKERS. Choice soldiers (*temp.* Henry VIII.) Perhaps managers of the crakys, and therefore early artillery.

CRAKYS. An old term for great guns.

CRAMP. A machine to facilitate the screwing of two pieces of timber together.

CRAMPER. A yarn or twine worn round the leg as a remedy against cramp.

CRAMPETS. The cramp rings of a sword scabbard. Ferrule to a staff.

CRAMPINGS. A nautical phrase to express the fetters and bolts for offenders.

CRAMPOON. *See* CREEPER.

CRANAGE. The money paid for the use of a wharf crane. Also, the permission to use a crane at any wharf or pier.

CRANCE. A sort of iron cap on the outer end of the bowsprit, through which the jib-boom traverses. The name is not unfrequently applied to any boom-iron.

CRANE. A machine for raising and lowering great weights, by which timber and stores are hoisted upon wharfs, &c. Also, a kind of catapult for casting stones in ancient warfare. Also, pieces of iron or timber at a vessel's sides, used to stow boats or spars upon. Also, as many fresh or green unsalted herrings as would fill a barrel.

CRANE-BARGE. A low flat-floored lump, fitted for the purpose of carrying a crane, in aid of marine works.

CRANE-LINES. Those which formerly went from the spritsail-topmast to the middle of the forestay, serving to steady the former. Also, small lines for keeping the lee backstays from chafing against the yards.

CRANG. The carcass of a whale after being flinched or the blubber stripped off.

CRANK, or CRANK-SIDED. A vessel, by her construction or her stowage, inclined to lean over a great deal, or from insufficient ballast or cargo incapable of carrying sail, without danger of overturning. The opposite term is *stiff*, or the quality of standing well up to her canvas.—*Cranky* expresses a foolish capriciousness. Ships built too deep in proportion to their breadth are notoriously crank.—*Crank by the ground*, is a ship whose floor is so narrow that she cannot be brought on the ground without danger.

CRANK-HATCHES. Are raised coamings on a steamer's deck, to form coverings for the cranks of the engines below.

CRANK-PIN. In steam machinery, it goes through both arms of the crank at their extremities; to this pin the connecting-rod is attached.

CRANKS of a MARINE ENGINE; eccentric, as in a turning-lathe. The bend or knee pinned on the shafts, by which they are moved round with a circular motion. Also, iron handles for working pumps, windlasses, &c. Also, erect iron forks on the quarter-deck for the capstan-bars, or other things, to be stowed thereon. Also, the axis and handle of a grindstone. Also, an old term for the sudden or frequent involutions of the planets in their orbits.

CRANK-SHAFT. In a steamer. (*See* INTERMEDIATE SHAFT.)

CRAPPO, or GENERAL CRAPAUD. Jack's name for a Frenchman, one whom he thinks would be a better sailor if he would but talk English instead of French.

CRARE, or CRAYER. A slow unwieldy trading vessel of olden times. Thus Shakspeare, in *Cymbeline*, with hydrographic parlance:—

> "Who ever yet could sound thy bottom? Find
> The ooze, to show what coast thy sluggish crare
> Might easiliest harbour in?"

CRATER of a MINE. Synonymous with *funnel* (which see).

CRAVAISE. An Anglo-Norman word for cray-fish.

CRAVEN. An old term synonymous with *recreant* (which see).

CRAWL. A sort of pen, formed by a barrier of stakes and hurdles on the sea-coast, to contain fish or turtle. On the coast of Africa, a pen for slaves awaiting shipment.

CRAWLING OFF. Working off a lee-shore by slow degrees.

CRAY-FISH. A lobster-like crustacean (*Astacus fluviatilis*) found in fresh-water.

CRAZY. Said of a ship in a bad state.

CREAK. The straining noise made by timbers, cabin bulk-heads, and spars in rolling.

CREAR. A kind of Scotch lighter. (*See* CRARE.)

CREEK. A narrow inlet of the sea shoaling suddenly. Also, the channels connecting the several branches of a river and lake islands, and one lake or lagoon with another. It differs from a cove, in being proportionately deeper and narrower. In law, it is part of a haven where anything is landed from the sea.

CREEL, OR CRUE, for fishing. *See* KREEL.

CREENGAL. *See* CRINGLE.

CREEPER. A small grapnel (iron instrument with four claws) for dragging for articles dropped overboard in harbour. When anything falls, a dish or other white object thrown immediately after it will greatly guide the creeping.

CREES. *See* KRIS.

CREMAILLEE. More commonly called *indented* (which see), with regard to lines or parapets.

CRENELLE. A loop-hole in a fortress.

CRENG. *See* KRANG.

CREOLE. This term applies in the West Indies and Spanish America, &c., to a person of European and unmixed origin, but colonial born.

CREPUSCULUM. *See* TWILIGHT.

CRESPIE. A northern term for a small whale or a grampus.

CRESSET. A beacon light set on a watch-tower.

CRESSIT. A small crease or dagger.

CREST. The highest part of a mountain, or range of mountains, and the summit of a sea-wave.

CREW. Comprehends every officer and man on board-ship, borne as complement on the books. There are in ships of war several particular crews or gangs, as the gunner's, carpenter's, sailmaker's, blacksmith's, armourer's, and cooper's crews.

CRIB. A small berth in a packet.

CRICK. A small jack-screw.

CRIMPS. Detested agents who trepan seamen, by treating, advancing money, &c., by which the dupes become indebted, and when well plied with liquor are induced to sign articles, and are shipped off, only discovering their mistake on finding themselves at sea robbed of all they possessed.

CRINGLE. A short piece of rope worked grommet fashion into the bolt-rope of a sail, and containing a metal ring or thimble. The use of the cringle is generally to hold the end of some rope, which is fastened thereto for the purpose of drawing up the sail to its yard, or extending the skirts or leech by means of bowline *bridles*, to stand upon a side-wind. The word seems to be derived from the old English *crencled*, or circularly formed. Cringles should be made of the strands of new bolt-rope. Those for the reef and reef-tackle pendant are stuck through holes made in the tablings.

CRINKYL. The cringle or loop in the leech of a sail.

CRIPPLE, To. To disable an enemy's ship by wounding his masts, yards, and steerage gear, thereby placing him *hors de combat*.

CRISS-CROSS. The mark of a man who cannot write his name.

CROAKER. A tropical fish which makes a *cris-cris* noise.

CROAKY. A term applied to plank when it curves much in short lengths.

CROCHERT. A hagbut or hand cannon, anciently in use.

CROCK [Anglo-Saxon, *croca*]. An earthen mess-vessel, and the usual vegetables were called crock-herbs. In the *Faerie Queene* Spenser cites the utensil:—

> "Therefore the vulgar did aboute him flocke,
> Like foolish flies about an honey-crocke."

CROCODILES. A designation for those who served in Egypt under Lord Keith.

CROJEK. The mode of pronouncing *cross-jack* (which see).

CRONNAG. In the Manx and Erse, signifies a rock that can be seen before low-water.

CROOKED-CATCH. An iron implement bent in the form of the letter S.

CROOKS. *Crooked timbers.* Short arms or branches of trees.

CROONER. The gray gurnard (*Trigla gurnardus*), so called on account of the creaking noise it makes after being taken.

CROSS-BARS. Round bars of iron, bent at each end, used as levers to turn the shank of an anchor.

CROSS-BAR-SHOT. The famed cross-bar-shot, or properly *bar-shot*, used by the Americans: when folded it presented a bar or complete shot, and could thus be placed in the gun. But as it left the muzzle it expanded to a cross, with four quarters of a shot at its radial points. It was used to destroy the rigging as well as do execution amongst men.

CROSS-BITT. The same as *cross-piece* (which see).

CROSS-BORED. Bored with holes alternately on the edges of planks, to separate the fastenings, so as to avoid splitting the timbers or beams.

CROSS-BOW. An ancient weapon of our fleet, when also in use on shore.

CROSS-CHOCKS. Large pieces of timber fayed across the dead-wood amidships, to make good the deficiency of the heels of the lower futtocks.

CROSS-FISH. A northern name for the *asterias* or star-fish; so called from the Norwegian *kors-fisk*. Also, the *Uraster rubens*.

CROSS-GRAINED. Not straight-grained as in good wood; hence the perverse and vexatious disposition of the ne'er-do-wells. As Cotton's *Juno*—

"That cross-grained, peevish, scolding queen."

CROSS-HEAD. In a steamer's engine, is on the top of the piston-rod athwart the cylinder; and there is another fitted to the air pump, both having side-rods. (*See* CYLINDER CROSS-HEAD.)

CROSSING A SHIP'S WAKE. When a ship sails over the transient track which another has just passed, *i.e.* passes close astern of her.

CROSSING THE CABLES IN THE HATCHWAY. A method by which the operation of coiling is facilitated; it alludes to hempen cables, which are now seldom used.

CROSS IN THE HAWSE. Is when a ship moored with two anchors from the bows has swung the wrong way once, whereby the two cables lie across each other.—*To cross a vessel's hawse* is to sail across the line of her course, a little ahead of her.

CROSSJACK-YARD [pronounced *crojeck-yard*]. The lower yard on the mizen-mast, to the arms of which the clues of the mizen top-sail are extended. The term is applied to any fore-and-aft vessels setting a square-sail, flying, below the lower cross-trees. It is now very common in merchant ships to set a sail called a cross-jack upon this yard.

CROSS-PAWLS. *See* CROSS-SPALES.

CROSS-PIECE. The transverse timber of the bitts. Also, a rail of timber extending over the windlass of some merchant-ships from the knight-heads to the belfry. It is furnished with wooden pins to fasten the running-rigging to, as occasion requires.—*Cross-pieces.* Short pieces laid across the keel of a line-of-battle ship, and scarphed to the lower ends of the first futtocks, as strengtheners.

CROSS-SEA. A sea not caused by the wind then blowing. During a heavy gale which changes quickly (a cyclone, for instance), each change of wind produces a direction of the sea, which lasts for some hours after the wind which caused it has changed, so that in a part of the sea which has experienced all the changes of one of these gales, the sea runs up in pyramids, sending the tops of the waves perpendicularly into the air, which are then spread by the prevailing wind; the effect is awfully grand and dangerous, for it generally renders a ship ungovernable until it abates.

CROSS-SOMER. A beam of timber.

CROSS-SPALES OR SPALLS. Temporary beams nailed across a vessel to keep the sides together, and support the ship in frame, until the deck-knees are fastened.

CROSS-STAFF. *See* FORE-STAFF.

CROSS-SWELL. This is similar to a cross-sea, except that it undulates without breaking violently.

CROSS-TAIL. In a steam-engine, is of the same form as the cylinder cross-head: it has iron straps catching the pins in the ends of the side-levers.

CROSS-TIDE. The varying directions of the flow amongst shoals that are under water. (*See* CURRENT.)

CROSS-TIMBERS. *See* CROSS-PIECES.

CROSS-TREES. Certain timbers supported by the cheeks and trestle-trees at the upper ends of the lower and top masts, athwart which they are laid to sustain the frame of the tops on the one, and to extend the top-gallant shrouds on the other.

CROTCHED-YARD. The old orthography for *cross-jack-yard* (which see).

CROTCHES. *See* CRUTCHES.

CROW, OR CROW-BAR. An iron lever furnished with a sharp point at one end, and two claws on a slight bevel bend at the other, to prize or remove weighty bodies, like pieces of timber, to draw spike-nails, &c. Also, to direct and manage the great guns.

CROWDIE. Meal and milk mixed in a cold state; but sometimes a mere composition of oatmeal and boiled water, eaten with treacle, or butter and sugar, as condiment.

CROWD SAIL, To. To carry an extraordinary press of canvas on a ship, as in pursuit of, or flight from, an enemy, &c.

CROW-FOOT. A number of small lines spreading out from an uvrow or long block, used to suspend the awnings by, or to keep the top-sails from striking violently, and fretting against the top-rims. (*See* EUPHROE.) Also, a kind of stand, attached to the end of mess-tables, and hooked to a beam above.—*Crow-foot* or *beam-arm* is also a crooked timber, extended from the side of a beam to the ship's side, in the wake of the hatchway, supplying the place of a beam.—*Crow's-foot* is the name of the four-pointed irons thrown in front of a position, to hamper the advance of cavalry, and other assailants, for in whatsoever way they fall one point is upwards. The phrase of *crow's-feet* is also jocularly applied to the wrinkles spreading from the outer corner of the eyes—a joke used both by Chaucer and Spenser.

CROWN. A common denomination in most parts of Europe for a silver coin, varying in local value from 2s. 6d. sterling to 8s. (*See also* PREROGATIVE.)—*Crown of an anchor.* The place where the arms are joined to the shank, and unite at the throat.—*Crown of a gale.* Its extreme violence.—In fortification, to crown is to effect a lodgment on the top of; thus, the besieger *crowns* the covered way when he occupies with his trenches the crest of the glacis.

CROWN, OR DOUBLE CROWN. A knot; is to pass the strands of a rope over and under each other above the knot by way of finish. (*See* KNOT.)

CROWNING. The finishing part of some knots on the end of a rope, to prevent the ends of the strands becoming loose. They are more particularly useful in all kinds of stoppers. (*See* WALL AND CROWN.)

CROWN-WORK. In fortification, the largest definite form of out-work, having for its head two contiguous bastioned fronts, and for its sides two long strait faces, flanked by the artillery fire of the place. Or a detached work, according to the circumstances of the ground, requiring such advanced occupation.

CROW-PURSE. The egg-capsule of a skate.

CROW-SHELL. A fresh-water mussel.

CROW'S NEST. A small shelter for the look-out man : sometimes made with a cask, at the top-gallant mast-head of whalers, whence fish are espied. Also, for the ice-master to note the lanes or open spaces in the ice.

CROY. An inclosure on the sea-beach in the north for catching fish. When the tide flows the fishes swim over the wattles, but are left by the ebbing of the water.

CRUE. *See* KREEL.

CRUE-HERRING. The shad (*Clupea alosa*).

CRUER. *See* CRARE.

CRUISE, OR CRUIZE. A voyage in quest of an enemy expected to sail through any particular tract of the sea at a certain season,—the seeker traversing the cruising latitude under easy sail, backward and forward. The parts of seas frequented by whales are called the cruising grounds of whalers.

CRUISERS. Small men-of-war, made use of in the Channel and elsewhere to secure our merchant ships from the enemy's small frigates and privateers. They were generally such as sailed well, and were well manned.

CRUIVES. Inclosed spaces in a dam or weir for taking salmon.

CRUMMY. Fleshy or corpulent.

CRUPPER. The train tackle ring-bolt in a gun-carriage.

CRUSADO. *See* CRUZADO.

CRUTCH, OR CROTCH. A support fixed upon the taffrail for the main boom of a sloop, brig, cutter, &c., and a chock for the driver-boom of a ship when their respective sails are furled. Also, crooked timber inside the after-peak of a vessel, for securing the heels of the cant or half-timbers : they are fayed and bolted on the foot-waling. Also, stanchions of wood or iron whose upper parts are forked to receive masts, yards, and other spars, and which are fixed along the sides and gangways. Crutches are used instead of rowlocks, and also on the sides of large boats to support the oars and spars.

CRUZADO. A Portuguese coin of 480 reis, value 2s. 7¼d. sterling in Portugal; in England, 2s. to 2s. 2d.

CUBBRIDGE HEADS. The old bulkheads of the forecastle and half-decks, wherein were placed the "murderers," or guns for clearing the decks in emergency.

CUBE. A solid body inclosed by six square sides or faces. A cubical foot is 12 inches square every way, of any solid substance.

CUB-HOUSE, OR CUBBOOS. *See* CABOOSE.

CUBICULATÆ. Roman ships furnished with cabins.

CUCKOLD'S-KNOT OR NECK. A knot by which a rope is secured to a spar—the two parts of the rope crossing each other, and seized together.

CUDBEAR. (*See* CORKIR.) A violet dye—archil, a test.

CUDBERDUCE. The cuthbert-duck, a bird of the Farn Isles, off Northumberland.

CUDDIC, Cuddy, or Cudle. All derived from cuttle-fish varieties of sepia used for baits.

CUDDIE, or Cuddin. One of the many names for the coal-fish, a staple article of the coast of Scotland. The *Gadus carbonarius* is taken nearly all the year round by fishing from the rocks, and by means of landing nets. If this fish be not delicate, it is at least nutritious, and as it contains much oil, it furnishes light as well as food.

CUDDING. A northern name for the char.

CUDDY. A sort of cabin or cook-room, generally in the fore-part, but sometimes near the stern of lighters and barges of burden. In the oceanic traders it is a cabin abaft, under the round-house or poop-deck, for the commander and his passengers. Also, the little cabin of a boat.

CUDDY-LEGS. A name in the north for large herrings.

CUIRASS. Armour or covering for the breast, anciently made of hide.

CUIRASSIERS. Horse soldiers who wear the cuirass, a piece of defensive armour, covering the body from the neck to the waist.

CUISSES. Armour to protect the thighs.

CULAGIUM. An archaic law-term for the laying up of a ship in the dock to be repaired.

CULCH. *See* Oyster-bed.

CULLOCK. A species of bivalved mollusc on our northern shores, the *Tellina rhomboides.*

CULMINATION, in nautical astronomy, is the transit or passage of any celestial body over the meridian of a place.

CULRING. An old corruption of *culverin.*

CULTELLUS. *See* Coutel.

CULVER. A Saxon word for pigeon, whence Culver-cliff, Reculvers, &c., from being resorted to by those birds. [Latin, *columba; b* and *v* are often interchanged.]

CULVERIN. An ancient cannon of about $5\frac{1}{4}$ inches bore, and from 9 to 12 feet long, carrying a ball of 18 pounds, with a first graze at 180 paces. Formerly a favourite sea-gun, its random range being 2500 paces. The name is derived from a snake (*coluber*), or a dragon, being sculptured upon it, thus forming handles.

CULVER-TAIL. The fastenings of a ship's carlings into the beams.

CULVER-TAILED. Fastened by dove-tailing—a way of letting one timber into another, so that they cannot slip asunder.

CULWARD. The archaic term for a coward.

CUMULO-CIRRUS-STRATUS. A horizontal sheet of cloud, with cirrus above and cumulus beneath; it is better known as the *nimbus* or *rain-cloud.*

CUMULO-STRATUS. This is the twain-cloud, so called because the stratus blends with the cumulus; it is most frequent during a changeable state of the barometer.

CUMULUS. A cloud indicative of fair weather, when it is small: it is sometimes seen in dense heaps, whence it obtained the name of *stacken cloud.* It is then a forerunner of change.

CUND, To. To give notice which way a shoal of fish is gone.

CUNETTE. *See* **CUVETTE.**

CUNN, or Con. *See* **CONN.**

CUNNENG. A northern name for the lamprey.

CUP. A solid piece of cast-iron let into the step of the capstan, and in which the iron spindle at the heel of the capstan works. Also, colloquially used for come, as, "Cup, let me alone."

CUPOLA-SHIP. Captain Coles's; the cupola being discontinued, now called *turret-ship* (which see).

CUR. An east-country term for the bull-head.

CURE, To. To salt meat or fish.

CUR-FISH. A small kind of dog-fish.

CURIET. A breast-plate made of leather.

CURL. The bending over or disruption of the ice, causing it to pile. Also, the curl of the surf on the shore.

CURL-CLOUD. The same as *cirrus* (which see).

CURLEW. A well-known coast bird, with a long curved bill, the *Numenius arquatus.*

CURRACH. A skiff, formerly used on the Scottish coasts.

CURRA-CURRA. A peculiarly fast boat among the Malay Islands.

CURRENT. A certain progressive flowing of the sea in one direction, by which all bodies floating therein are compelled more or less to submit to the stream. The *setting* of the current, is that point of the compass towards which the waters run; and the *drift* of the current is the rate it runs at in an hour. Currents are general and particular, the former depending on causes in constant action, the latter on occasional circumstances. (*See* DIRECTION.)

CURRENT SAILING. The method of determining the true motion of a ship, when, besides being acted upon by the wind, she is drifting by the effect of a current. A due allowance must therefore be made by the navigator.

CURRIER. A small musketoon with a swivel mounting.

CURSOR. The moving wire in a reading microscope.

CURTAIN. In fortification, that part of the rampart which is between the flanks of two opposite bastions, which are thereby connected.

CURTALL, or CURTALD. An ancient piece of ordnance used in our early fleets, apparently a short one.

CURTATE DISTANCE. An astronomical term, denoting the distance of a body from the sun or earth projected upon the ecliptic.

CURTLE-AXE. The old term for cutlass or cutlace.

CURVED FIRE. A name coming into use with the increasing application of the fire of heavy and elongated shells to long-range bombardment and cannonade. It is intermediate between horizontal and vertical fire, possessing much of the accuracy and direct force of the former, as well as of the searching properties of the latter.

CURVE OF THE COAST. When the shore alternately recedes and projects gradually, so as to trend towards a curve shape.

CUSEFORNE. A long open whale-boat of Japan.

CUSHIES. Armour for the thighs. The same as *cuisses.*

CUSK. A fine table-fish taken in cod-schools. *See* TUSK or TORSK.

CUSPS. The extremities of a crescent moon, or inferior planet.

CUSSELS. The green-bone, or viviparous blenny.

CUSTOM. The toll paid by merchants to the crown for goods exported or imported; otherwise called duty.—*Custom of the country,* a small present to certain authorities in the less frequented ports, being equally gift and bribe.

CUSTOM-HOUSE. An office established on the frontiers of a state, or in some chief city or port, for the receipt of customs and duties imposed by authority of the sovereign, and regulated by writs or books of rates.

CUSTOM-HOUSE AGENT. He who transacts the relative business of passing goods, as to the entries required for the ship's clearance.

CUSTOM-HOUSE OFFICERS. A term comprehending all the officials employed in enforcing the customs.

CUT. A narrow boat channel; a canal.—*To cut,* to renounce acquaintance with any one.

CUT AND RUN, To. To cut the cable for an escape. Also, to move off quickly; to quit occupation; to be gone.

CUT AND THRUST. To give point with a sword after striking a slash.

CUT A STICK, To. To make off clandestinely.—*Cut your stick,* be off, or go away.

CUTE. Sharp, crafty, apparently from *acute;* but some insist that it is the Anglo-Saxon word *cuth,* rather meaning certain, known, or familiar.

CUTH. A name given in Orkney and Shetland to the coal-fish before it is fully grown; perhaps the same as *piltock* (which see).

CUTLAS, OR COUTELAS. A sabre which was slightly curved, but recently applied to the small-handled swords supplied to the navy—the *cutlash* of Jack. By Shakspeare called a curtle-axe; thus Rosalind, preparing to disguise herself as a man, is made to say

"A gallant curtle-ax upon my thigh."

CUT-LINE. The space between the bilges of two casks stowed end to end.

CUT OFF. A term used to denote a vessel's being seized by stratagem by the natives, and the crew being murdered. Also, to intercept a retreat.

CUT OF THE JIB. A phrase for the aspect of a vessel, or person.

CUT OUT, To. To attack and carry a vessel by a boat force; one of the most dashing and desperate services practised by Nelson and Cochrane, of which latter that of cutting out the *Esmeralda* at Callao stands unequalled.

CUTTER. A small single-masted, sharp-built broad vessel, commonly navigated in the English Channel, furnished with a straight running bowsprit, occasionally run in horizontally on the deck; except for which, and the largeness of the sails, they are rigged much like sloops. Either clincher or carvel-built, no jib-stay, the jib hoisting and hanging by the halliards alone. She carries a fore-and-aft main-sail, gaff-topsail, stay-foresail, and jib. The name is derived from their fast sailing. The cutter (as H.M.S. *Dwarf*) has been made to set every sail, even royal studding-sails, sky-scrapers, moon-rakers, star-gazers, water and below-water sails, that could be set by any vessel on one mast. One of the largest which has answered effectually, was the *Viper*, of 460 tons and 28 guns; this vessel was very useful during the American war, particularly by getting into Gibraltar at a critical period of the siege.

CUTTER-BRIG. A vessel with square sails, a fore-and-aft main-sail, and a jigger-mast with a smaller one. (*See* KETCH.)

CUTTERS of a ship are broader for their length, deeper and shorter in proportion than the barge or pinnace; are fitter for sailing, and commonly employed in carrying light stores, passengers, &c., to and from the ships; some are clench-built. They generally row ten oars; others of similar build only four, which last are termed jolly-boats. The cutters for ships of the line are carvel-built of 25 feet, and fit for anchor work.

CUTTER-STAY FASHION. The turning-in of a dead-eye with the end of the shroud down.

CUT THE CABLE, To. A manœuvre sometimes necessary for making a ship cast the right way, or when the anchor cannot be weighed.

CUTTIE. A name on our northern coasts for the black guillemot (*Uria grille*).

CUTTING. The adjusting of a cask or spar, or turning it round.

CUTTING A FEATHER. It is common when a ship has too broad a bow to say, "She will not cut a feather," meaning that she will not pass through the water so swift as to make less foam or froth.

CUTTING DOWN. Taking a deck off a ship; as ships of the line are converted into frigates, the *Royal Sovereign* into a turret ship, &c.— *Cutting down* is also a dangerous midshipman's trick, and sometimes practised by the men: it consists in cutting the laniard of a cot or hammock in which a person is then asleep, and letting him fall—*lumpus* —either by the head or the feet.

CUTTING-DOWN LINE. An elliptical curve line used by ship-wrights in the delineation of ships; it determines the depth of all the floor timbers, and likewise the height of the dead-wood fore and aft. It is limited in the middle of the ship by the thickness of the floor timbers, and abaft by the breadth of the keelson, and must be carried up so high upon the stern as to leave sufficient substance for the breeches of the rising timbers.

CUTTING HIS PAINTER. Making off suddenly or clandestinely, or "departed this life."

CUTTING IN. Making the special directions for taking the blubber off a whale, which is flinched by taking off circularly ribbons of the skin with blubber attached; the animal being made to turn in the water as the purchases at the mast-heads heave it upwards.

CUTTING-OUT. A night-meal or forage in the officer's pantry.

CUTTING OUT or In. In polar phraseology, is performed by sawing canals in a floe of ice, to enable a ship to regain open water.

CUTTING RIGGING. This includes the act of measuring it.

CUTTLE-FISH. A common marine animal of the genus *Sepia*, and class *Cephalopoda*. It has ten tentacles or arms ranged around the mouth, two being of much greater length than the others. When in danger it ejects a black inky substance, darkening the water for some distance around. The oval internal calcareous shell, "cuttle-bone," often found lying on the beach, was formerly much used in pharmacy.

CUTTS. Flat-bottomed horse-ferry boats of a former day.

CUTTY-GUN. A northern term for a short pipe.

CUT-WATER. The foremost part of a vessel's prow, or the sharp part of the knee of a ship's head below the beak. It cuts or divides the water before reaching the bow, which would retard progress. It is fayed to the fore-part of the main stem. (*See* KNEE OF THE HEAD.)

CUVETTE, called also CUNETTE. A deeper trench cut along the middle of a dry moat; a ditch within a ditch, generally carried down till there be water to fill it.

CWM, or COMB. A British word signifying an inlet, valley, or low place, where the hilly sides round together in a concave form; the sides of a *glyn* being, on the contrary, convex.

CYCLE. A term generally applied to an interval of time in which the same phenomena recur.

CYCLE OF ECLIPSES. A period of about 6586 days, which is the time of a revolution of the moon's node; after the lapse of this period the eclipses recur in the same order as before, with few exceptions. This cycle was known to the ancients under the name of Saros.

CYCLOID. A geometrical curve of the higher kind.

CYCLONE. *See* TYPHOON.

CYLINDER. The body of a pump; any tubular part of an engine.— *Charge cylinder* of a gun, is the part which receives the powder and ball, the remaining portion being styled the *vacant cylinder*. Especially in marine steam-engines, the cylindrical metal tube, with a diameter proportionate to the power of the engine, of which it may be termed the chief part, since it contains the active steam. Also, a cartridge box for the service of artillery. (*See* CARTRIDGE-BOX.)

CYLINDER-COVER. In the steam-engine, is a metal lid with a hole in the centre for the piston-rod to work through.

CYLINDER CROSS-HEAD. An adaptation on the top of the piston-rod, stretching out athwart the cylinder, from the ends of which the side-rods hang.

CYLINDER ESCAPE-VALVES. Small conical valves at each end of

the cylinder, for the purpose of letting off any water that may collect above or below the piston.

CYLINDER POWDER. That made upon the improved method of charring the wood to be used as charcoal in iron cylinders. All British government gunpowder is now made thus.

CYPHERING. A term in carpentry. (*See* SYPHERING.)

D.

D. In the *Complete Book*, D means dead or deserted; Dsq., discharged from the service, or into another ship.

DAB. The sea-flounder. An old general term for a pleuronect or flat fish of any kind, but usually appropriated to the *Platessa limanda*. The word is familiarly applied to one who is expert in anything.

DABBERLACK. A kind of long sea-weed on our northern coasts.

DAB-CHICK. The little grebe, *Podiceps minor*. A small diving bird common in lakes and rivers.

DACOITS. *See* DEKOYTS.

.DADDICK. A west-country term for rotten-wood, touch-wood, &c.

DAGEN. A peculiar dirk or poignard.

DAGGAR. An old term for a dog-fish.

DAGGER-KNEE. A substitute for the hanging-knee, applied to the under side of the lodging-knee; it is placed out of the perpendicular to avoid a port-hole. Anything placed aslant or obliquely, now generally termed diagonal, of which, indeed, it is a corruption.

DAGGER-PIECE, OR DAGGER-WOOD. A timber or plank that faces on to the poppets of the bilge-ways, and crosses them diagonally, to keep them together. The plank securing the head is called the daggerplank.

DAGGES. An old term for pistols or hand-guns.

DAHLGREN GUN. A modification of the Paixhan gun, introduced into the United States service by Lieut., now Admiral, Dahlgren, of that navy; having, in obedience to the results of ingenious experiment on the varying force of explosion on different parts of a gun, what has been called the soda-water bottle or pear-shaped form.

DAHM. An Arab or Indian decked boat.

DAILY PROGRESS. A daily return when in port of all particulars relative to the progress of a ship's equipment.

DAIRS. Small unsaleable fish.

DALE. A trough or spout to carry off water, usually named from the office it has to perform, as a pump-dale, &c. Also, a place forward, to save the decks from being wetted, now almost abolished.

DALLOP. A heap or lump in a clumsy state. A large quantity of anything.

DAM. A barrier of stones, stakes, or rubble, constructed to stop or impede the course of a stream. (*See* INUNDATION and FLOATING DAM.)

DAMASCENED. The mixing of various metals in the Damascus blades, the kris, or other weapons; sometimes by adding silver, to produce a watered effect.

DAMASCUS BLADE. Swords famed for the quality and temper of the metal, as well as the beauty of the *jowhir*, or watering of the blades.

DAMASK. Steel worked in the Damascus style, showing the wavy lines of the different metals; usually termed watered or twisted.

DAMBER. An old word for lubberly rogue.

DAMELOPRE. An ancient flat-floored vessel belonging to Holland, and intended to carry heavy cargoes over their shallow waters.

DAMMAH. A kind of turpentine or resin from a species of pine, which is used in the East Indies for the same purposes to which turpentine and pitch are applied. It is exported in large quantities from Sumatra to Bengal and other places, where it is much used for paying seams and the bottoms of vessels, for which latter purpose it is often mixed with sulphur, and answers admirably in warm climates.

DAMPER. The means by which the furnace of each boiler in a steamer can be regulated independently, by increasing or diminishing the draught to the fire.

DAMSEL. A coast name for the skate-fish.

DANCERS. The coruscations of the aurora. (*See* MERRY DANCERS.)

DANDIES. Rowers of the budgerow boats on the Ganges.

DANDY. A sloop or cutter with a jigger-mast abaft, on which a mizen-lug-sail is set.

DANGER. Perils and hazard of the sea. Any rock or shoal which interferes with navigation.

DANK. Moist, mouldy: a sense in which Shakspeare uses it; also Tusser—
"*Dank* ling forgot will quickly rot."

DANKER. A north-country term for a dark cloud.

DANSKERS. Natives of Denmark.

DARBIES. An old cant word for irons or hand-cuffs; it is still retained.

DARE. An old word for to challenge, or incite to emulation; still in full use.

DARE-DEVIL. One who fears nothing, and will attempt anything.

DARKENING. Closing of the evening twilight.

DARK GLASSES. Shades fitted to instruments of reflection for preventing the bright rays of the sun from hurting the eye of the observer.

DARKS. Nights on which the moon does not shine,—much looked to by smugglers.

DARKY. A common term for a negro.

DARNING THE WATER. A term applied to the action of a fleet cruising to and fro before a blockaded port.

DARRAG. A Manx or Erse term for a strong fishing-line made of black hair snoods.

DARSENA. An inner harbour or wet dock in the Mediterranean.

DARTS. Weapons used in our early fleets from the round-tops.

DASH. The present with which bargains are sealed on the coast of Africa.

DASHING. The rolling and breaking of the sea.

DATOO. West wind in the Straits of Gibraltar: very healthy. Also, a Malay term of rank, and four of whom form the council of the sultan of the Malayu Islands.

DATUM. The base level.

DAVID'S-STAFF. A kind of quadrant formerly used in navigation.

DAVIE. An old term for davit.

DAVIT. A piece of timber or iron, with sheaves or blocks at its end, projecting over a vessel's quarter or stern, to hoist up and suspend one end of a boat.—*Fish-davit*, is a beam of timber, with a roller or sheave at its end, used as a crane, whereby to hoist the flukes of the anchor to the top of the bow, without injuring the planks of the ship's side as it ascends, and called fishing the anchor; the lower end of this davit rests on the fore-chains, the upper end being properly secured by a tackle from the mast-head; to which end is hung a large block, and through it a strong rope is rove, called the fish-pendant, to the outer end of which is fitted a large hook, and to its inner end a tackle; the former is called the fish-hook, the latter the fish-tackle. There is also a davit of a smaller kind, occasionally fixed in the long-boat, and with the assistance of a small windlass, used to weigh the anchor by the buoy-rope, &c.

DAVIT-GUYS. Ropes used to steady boats' davits.

DAVIT-ROPE. The lashing which secures the davit to the shrouds when out of use.

DAVIT-TOPPING-LIFT. A rope made fast to the outer end of a davit, and rove through a block made fast to a vessel's mast aloft, with a tackle attached. Usually employed for bringing the anchor inboard.

DAVY JONES. The spirit of the sea; a nikker; a sea-devil.

DAVY JONES'S LOCKER. The ocean; the common receptacle for all things thrown overboard; it is a phrase for death or the other world, when speaking of a person who has been buried at sea.

DAW-FISH. The *Scyllium catulus*, a small dog-fish.

DAWK-BOAT. A boat for the conveyance of letters in India; *dawk* being the Hindostanee for *mail*.

DAY. The astronomical day is reckoned from noon to noon, continuously through the twenty-four hours, like the other days. It commences at noon, twelve hours after the civil day, which itself begins twelve hours after the nautical day, so that the *noon* of the civil day, the *beginning* of the astronomical day, and the *end* of the nautical day, occur at the same moment. (*See the words* SOLAR *and* SIDEREAL.)

DAY-BOOK. An old and better name for the log-book; a journal [Fr.]

DAY-MATES. Formerly the mates of the several decks—now abolished. (*See* Sub-lieutenant.)

DAY-SKY. The aspect of the sky at day-break, or at twilight.

DAY'S WORK. In navigation, the reckoning or reduction of the ship's courses and distances made good during twenty-four hours, or from noon to noon, according to the rules of trigonometry, and thence ascertaining her latitude and longitude by *dead reckoning* (which see).

D-BLOCK. A lump of oak in the shape of a D, bolted to the ship's side in the channels to reeve the lifts through.

DEAD-ANGLE. In fortification, is an angle receiving no defence, either by its own fire or that of any other works.

DEAD-CALM. A total cessation of wind; the same as *flat-calm*.

DEAD-DOORS. Those fitted in a rabbet to the outside of the quarter-gallery doors, with the object of keeping out the sea, in case of the gallery being carried away.

DEADEN A SHIP'S WAY, To. To retard a vessel's progress by bracing in the yards, so as to reduce the effect of the sails, or by backing minor sails. Also, when sounding to luff up and shake all, to obtain a cast of the deep-sea lead.

DEAD-EYE, or Dead Man's Eye. A sort of round flattish wooden block, or oblate piece of elm, encircled, and fixed to the channels by the chain-plate: it is pierced with three holes through the flat part, in order to receive a rope called the laniard, which, corresponding with three holes in another dead-eye on the shroud end, creates a purchase to set up and extend the shrouds and stays, backstays, &c., of the standing and top-mast rigging. The term *dead* seems to have been used because there is no revolving sheave to lessen the friction. In merchant-ships they are generally fitted with iron-plates, in the room of chains, extending from the vessel's side to the top of the rail, where they are connected with the rigging. The dead-eyes used for the stays have only one hole, which, however, is large enough to receive ten or twelve turns of the laniard—these are generally termed *hearts*, on account of their shape. The *crowfeet dead-eyes* are long cylindrical blocks with a number of small holes in them, to receive the legs or lines composing the crowfoot. Also called *uvrows*.

DEAD-FLAT. The timber or frame possessing the greatest breadth and capacity in the ship: where several timbers are thrown in, of the same area, the middle one is reckoned a dead-flat, about one third of the length of the ship from the head. It is generally distinguished as the midship-bend.

DEAD-FREIGHT. The sum to which a merchant is liable for goods which he has failed to ship.

DEAD-HEAD. A kind of *dolphin* (which see). Also, a rough block of wood used as an anchor-buoy.

DEAD-HEADED. Timber trees which have ceased growing.

DEAD-HORSE. A term applied by seamen to labour which has been paid for in advance. When they commence earning money again, there is in some merchant ships a ceremony performed of dragging round the decks an effigy of their fruitless labour in the shape of a horse, running him up to the yard-arm, and cutting him adrift to fall into the sea amidst loud cheers.

DEAD-LIFT. The moving of a very inert body.

DEAD-LIGHTS. Strong wooden shutters made exactly to fit the cabin windows externally; they are fixed on the approach of bad weather. Also, luminous appearances sometimes seen over putrescent bodies.

DEAD-LOWN. A completely still atmosphere.

DEAD-MEN. The reef or gasket-ends carelessly left dangling under the yard when the sail is furled, instead of being tucked in.

DEAD-MEN'S EFFECTS. When a seaman dies on board, or is drowned, his effects are sold at the mast by auction, and the produce charged against the purchasers' names on the ship's books.

DEAD-MONTHS. A term for winter.

DEAD-ON-END. The wind blowing directly adverse to the vessel's intended course.

DEAD-PAY. That given formerly in shares, or for names borne, but for which no one appears, as was formerly practised with *widows' men*.

DEAD-RECKONING. The estimation of the ship's place without any observation of the heavenly bodies; it is discovered from the distance she has run by the log, and the courses steered by the compass, then rectifying these data by the usual allowance for current, leeway, &c., according to the ship's known trim. This reckoning, however, should be corrected by astronomical observations of the sun, moon, and stars, whenever available, proving the importance of practical astronomy.

DEAD-RISING. In ship-building, is that part of a ship which lies aft between the keel and her floor-timbers towards the stern-post; generally it is applied to those parts of the bottom, throughout the ship's length, where the sweep or curve at the head of the floor-timber terminates, or inflects to join the keel. (*See* RISING-LINE.)

DEAD-ROPES. Those which do not run in any block.

DEAD-SHARES. An allowance formerly made to officers of the fleet, from fictitious numbers borne on the complement (*temp.* Henry VIII.), varying from fifty shares for an admiral, to half a share for the cook's mate.

DEAD-SHEAVE. A scored aperture in the heel of a top-mast, through which a second top-tackle pendant can be rove. It is usually a section of a lignum-vitæ sheave let in, so as to avoid chafe.

DEAD-TICKET. Persons dying on board, those discharged from the service, and all officers promoted, are cleared from the ship's books by a dead-ticket, which must be filled up in a similar manner to the *sick-ticket* (which see).

DEAD UPON A WIND. Braced sharp up and bowlines hauled.

DEAD-WATER. The eddy-water under the counter of a ship under way; so called because passing away slower than the water alongside. A ship is said to *make much dead-water* when she has a great eddy following her stern, often occasioned by her having a square tuck. A vessel with a round buttock at her line of floatation can have but little dead-water, the rounding abaft allowing the fluid soon to recover its state of rest.

DEAD WEIGHT. A vessel's lading when it consists of heavy goods, but particularly such as pay freight according to their weight and not their *stowage*.

DEAD WOOD. Certain blocks of timber, generally oak, fayed on the upper side of the keel, particularly at the extremities before and abaft, where these pieces are placed upon each other to a considerable height, because the ship is there so narrow as not to admit of the two half timbers, which are therefore scored into this dead wood, where the angle of the floor-timbers gradually diminishes on approaching the stem and stern-post. In the fore-part of the ship the dead wood generally extends from the stemson, upon which it is scarphed, to the loof-frame; and in the after-end, from the stern-post, where it is confined by the knee, to the after balance frame. It is connected to the keel by strong spike nails. The dead wood afore and abaft is equal in depth to two-thirds of the depth of the keel, and as broad as can be procured, not exceeding the breadth of the keel, *i.e.* continued as high as the *cutting-down* line in both bodies, to afford a stepping for the heels of the cant timbers.

DEAD-WOOD KNEES. The upper foremost and aftermost pieces of dead wood; being crooked pieces of timber, the bolting of which connects the keel with the stem and stern posts.

DEAD WORKS. All that part of the ship which is above water when she is laden. The same as *upper work*, or *supernatant* (which see).

DEAL BEACH. This coast consists of gravelly shingle; and a man who is pock-marked, or in galley-cant cribbage-faced, is figuratively said to have been rolled on Deal beach.

DEAL-ENDS. Applied to deal-planks when under 6 feet in length.

DEATH or Money Boats. So termed from the risk in such frail craft. They were very long, very narrow, and as thin as the skiffs of our rivers. During the war of 1800-14 they carried gold between Dover and Calais, and defied the custom-house officers.

DEATH-WOUND. A law-term for the starting of a butt end, or spring-ing a fatal leak. A ship had received her death-wound, but by pumping was kept afloat till three days after the time she was insured for: it was determined that the risk was at an end before the loss happened, and that the insurer was not liable.

DEBARK, To. To land; to go on shore.

DEBENTURE. A custom-house certificate given to the exporter of goods, on which a bounty or drawback is allowed. Also, a general term for a bill or bond.

DEBOUCHE. The mouth of a river, outlet of a wood, defile, or narrow pass. In military language, troops defile or march out from.

DECAGON. A plane geometrical figure that has ten equal sides, and as many equal angles.

DECAMP, To. To raise the camp; the breaking up from a place where an army has been encamped.

DECEPTIO VISUS. Any extraordinary instance of deception to the sight, occasioned by the effects of atmospheric media. (*See* TERRESTRIAL REFRACTION and MIRAGE.)

DECIMATION. The punishing every tenth soldier by lot, was truly *decimatio legionis.*

DECIME. A small copper coin of France, equal to two sous, or one-tenth of a franc.

DECK, To. A word formerly in use for to trim, as "we deckt up our sails."

DECK-BEAM KNEES. The same as *lodging-knees.*

DECK-BEAMS. *See* BEAMS.

DECK-CARGO, otherwise *deck-load* (which see).

DECK-CLEATS. Pieces of wood temporarily nailed to the deck to secure objects in bad weather, as guns, deck-load, &c.

DECK-HOOK. The compass timber bolted horizontally athwart a ship's bow, connecting the stem, timbers, and deck-planks of the fore-part; it is part and parcel of the *breast-hooks.*

DECK-HOUSE. An oblong-house on the deck of some merchantmen, especially east-country vessels, and latterly in passenger steamers, with a gangway on each side of it. (Sometimes termed *round-house.*)

DECK-LOAD. Timber, casks, or other cargo not liable to damage from wet, stowed on the deck of merchant vessels. This, with the exception of carboys of vitriol, is not included in a general policy of insurance on goods, unless it be specially stipulated.

DECK-NAILS. A kind of spike with a snug head, commonly made in a diamond form; they are single or double deck-nails, and from 4 to 12 inches long.

DECK-PIPE. An iron pipe through which the chain cable is paid into the chain-locker.

DECK-PUMPS. In a steamer, are at the side of the vessel, worked with a lever by manual power, to supply additional water. In a ship-of-war, used for washing decks (one of the mid-ship pumps).

DECKS. The platforms laid longitudinally over the transverse beams; in ships of war they support the guns. The terms in use for these decks are, assuming the largest ship of the line:—*Poop*, the deck which includes from the mizen-mast to the taffrail. The *upper* or *spar-deck*, from stem to stern, having conventional divisions; as, *quarter-deck*, which is, when clear for action, the space abaft the mainmast, including the cabin; next, *the waist*, between the fore and main masts, on which the spars and booms are secured. In some ships guns are continued (always in flush-decked ships) along the gangway; then *the forecastle*, which commences on the gangway, from the main-tack chock forward to the bows. Small craft, as brigs and corvettes, are sometimes fitted with top-gallant forecastles, to shelter the men from heavy seas which wash over. Next, the *main or gun-deck*, the entire length of the ship. It is also divided conventionally into the various cabins, the waist (under the gangway), the galley, from the fore-hatchway to the sick bay, and bows. Next below, is the *middle deck* of a three-decker, or *lower* of a two-decker, succeeded by lower deck and the orlop-deck, which carries no guns. The guns on these several decks increase in size and number from the poop downwards. Thus, although a vessel termed a three-decker was rated 120 guns, the fact stood thus:—

	Guns.	Pounders.	lbs.
Poop, ...	10	24	240
Quarter-deck, . . .	22	24 long	
Forecastle, ...	10	32 cans. }	848
Main-deck, . . .	34	24	816
Middle, ...	36	24	864
Lower, ...	36	32	1152
	148		3960

Broadside of 1980

But latterly, 56 and 84 pounders on the lower, and 32 on the middle, afforded a heavier weight of broadside. The *Santissima Trinidada*, taken from the Spaniards, carried four whole tiers of guns. Now, the tonnage of the largest of these would be insignificant. "Deckers" are exploded, and a *Pallas* of the same tonnage (2372) carries 8 guns, a *Bellerophon* (4272) carries 18 guns, ranging in size, however, from the 64-pounder up to the 300-pounder.—*Flush-deck*, or deck flush fore and aft, implies a continued floor laid from stem to stern, upon one line, without any stops or intervals.—*Half-deck.* In the Northumberland colliers the steerage itself is called the half-deck, and is usually the habitation of the ship's crew.

DECK-SEAM. The interstices between the planks.

DECK-SHEET. That sheet of a studding-sail which leads directly to the deck, by which it is steadied until set; it is also useful in taking it in, should the downhaul be carried away.

DECK-STANDARD-KNEES. Iron knees having two tails, the one going on the bottom of a deck-beam, the other on the top of a hold-beam, while the middle part is bolted to the ship's side.

DECK-STOPPER. (*See* STOPPER.) A strong stopper used for securing the cable forward of the capstan or windlass while it is overhauled. Also abaft the windlass or bitts to prevent more cable from running out.

DECK-TACKLE. A purchase led along the decks.

DECLARATION OF WAR. A ceremonial frequently omitted, and esteemed by the greatest authorities rather a proof of magnanimity than a duty. The Romans proclaimed it; but except Achaia, none of the Grecian states did. It would be to the interests of humanity and courtesy were it made indispensable. It has been held (especially in the case of the *Leopard* and *Chesapeake*) that without a declaration of war, no hostile act at the order of an admiral is legal.

DECLINATION, of a celestial object, is the arc between its centre and the equinoctial: with the sun, it is its angular distance from the equator, either north or south, and is named accordingly.

DECLINATION, To Correct. A cant phrase for taking a glass of grog at noon, when the day's works are being reduced.

DECOY. So to change the aspect of a ship-of-war by striking a top-gallant-mast, setting ragged sails, disfiguring the sides by whitewash or gunpowder, yellow, &c., as to induce a vessel of inferior force to chase; when, getting within gunshot range, she becomes an easy capture. Similar manœuvres are sometimes used by a single ship to induce an enemy's squadron to follow her into the view of her own fleet.

DEEP. A word figuratively applied to the ocean. On the coast of Germany, to the northward of Friesland, it is of the same import as gulf on the coasts of France, Spain, Italy, &c. Also, any depth over 20 fathoms.—*Deep-sea fishing.* In contradistinction to coast, or when the hand-lead reaches bottom at 20 fathoms.—*Hand deeps.* Out of ordinary leadsman's sounding.—A vessel is deep as regards her lading, and is also said to sail deep when her expenses run high.

DEEPENING. Running from shoal water by the lead.

DEEPSEA-LINE. Usually a strong and water-laid line. It is used with a lead of 28 lbs., and adapted to find bottom in 200 fathoms or more. It is marked by knots every ten fathoms, and by a small knot every five. The marks are now nearly superseded by Massey's patent sounding-machine.—*Marks and Deeps,* &c., *see* Lead and Line.

DEEP-WAIST. That part of the open skids between the main and fore drifts in men-of-war. It also relates to the remaining part of a ship's deck, when the quarter-deck and forecastle are much elevated above the level of the main-deck, so as to leave a vacant space, called the waist, on the middle of the upper deck, as in many packets.

DEESE. An east-country term for a place where herrings are dried.

DEFAULTER'S BOOK. Where men's offences are registered against them, and may be magnified without appeal.

DEFECTS. An official return of the state of a ship as to what is required for her hull and equipment, and what repairs she stands in need of. Upon this return a ship is ordered to sea, into harbour, into dock, or paid out of commission.

DEFICIENCY. What is wanting of a ship's cargo at the time of delivery.

DEFILADE. In fortification, is the art of so disposing defensive works, *on irregular or commanded sites*, that the troops within them shall be covered from the direct fire of the enemy.

DEFILE. A narrow pass between two heights, which obliges a force marching through to narrow its front. This may prove disastrous if attacked, on account of the difficulty of receiving aid from the rear.

DEFILING. Filing off, marching past.

DEFINITIVE. Conclusive; decisive.

DEFLECTION. The tendency of a ship from her true course; the departure of the magnetic needle from its true bearing, when influenced by iron or the local attraction of the mass. In artillery, the deviation of a shot from the direction in which it is fired. The term is usually reserved to lateral deviations, especially those resulting from irregular causes — those constant ones due to the regular motion of rifled projectiles coming under either of the designations "constant deflection," "derivation," borrowed from the French, or "drift," from the Americans. These latter, according to the direction usually given to the rifling in the present day, all tend away to the right, though they include some subordinate curves not yet distinctly determined.

DEFORMED BASTION. One out of shape from the irregularity of its lines and angles.

DEGRADATION. Debasement and disgrace. The suspension of a petty officer from his station; and also the depriving an officer or soldier of his arms previous to his being delivered over to the civil power for execution.

DEGREE. A degree of longitude is the 1-360th part of the great equatorial circle, or any circle parallel to it. A degree of latitude is the 90th part of the quadrant, or quarter of a great meridional circle. Each degree is divided into 60 minutes, and each minute into 60 seconds, according to the sexagesimal division of the circle. Also, rank or condition.

DEKOYTS, or DACOITS. Robbers in India, and also pirates who infested the rivers between Calcutta and Burhampore, but now suppressed by the improved system of river police, and the establishment of fast rowing boats of light draught.

DEL. Saxon for part.—*Del a bit*, not a bit, a phrase much altered for the worse by those not aware of its antiquity.

DEL CREDERE. A percentage on a cargo, under particular circumstances of trust. Also, the commission under which brokers sometimes guarantee to the insured the solvency of the underwriters.

DELEGATES. Not heard of in the navy since the mutiny at the Nore.

DELFYN. The old form of spelling *dolphin*.

DELICTUM. To be actual, must unite intention and act.

DELIVER. To yield, to rescue, to deliver battle, to deliver a broadside, a shot, or a blow. Also, to take goods from the ship to the shore. To discharge a cargo from a vessel into the keeping of its consignees.

DELIVERED. The state of the harpoon when imbedded in the body of a fish, so that the barbs hold fast.

DELIVERERS. Particular artificers employed in our early ships of war, in constructing the castles.

DELL. A narrow valley, ravine, or small dale.

DELTA. A name given by the Greeks to the alluvial tract inclosed between the bifurcating branches of the Nile and the sea-line. It is well known that rivers which deposit great quantities of matter, do also very often separate into two or more branches, previous to their discharge into the sea; thus forming triangular spaces, aptly called *deltas* from their resemblance to the Greek letter Δ.

All deltas appear by their section to be formed of matter totally different from that of the adjacent country. They are the creation of the rivers themselves, which, having brought down with their floods vast quantities of mud and sand from the upper lands, deposit them in the lowest place, the sea; at whose margin, the current which has hitherto impelled them ceasing, they are deposited by the mere action of gravity. This is particularly illustrated on the western coast of Africa by the shoals off the Rio Grande, Rio Nunez, and others. The coast, as well as the embouchures of the rivers, exhibit a deposit of deep mud, and yet far at sea banks of clean siliceous sand arise.

DEMAND. The official paper by which stores are desired for a ship, the making out of which is the duty of the officer in whose charge the stores will be placed: they must be approved by the captain and admiral before being presented to the dockyard authorities. Also, whence from? where bound?

DEMI-BASTION. In fortification, a bastion which has a flank on one side only.

DEMI-CANNON. An ancient name for a gun carrying a ball of 33 pounds weight, with a length of from 12 to 14 feet, and a diameter of bore of 6½ inches; its point-blank range was estimated at 162 paces, and its random one at 2000.

DEMI-CULVERIN. An ancient cannon which threw a ball of 9 pounds weight, was about 9 feet long, and 4 inches in diameter of bore; its point-blank range was called 174 paces, and its random one about 1800.

DEMIHAG. A long pistol, much used in the sixteenth century.

DEMILANCE. A light horseman, who carried a light lance.

DEMILUNE. In fortification, the outwork, more properly called a *ravelin* (which see).

DEMI-REVETMENT. In fortification, that form of retaining wall for the face of a rampart which is only carried up as high as cover exists in front of it, leaving above it the remaining height, in the form of an earthen mound at its natural slope, exposed to, but invulnerable by shot.

DEMONSTRATION-SHIPS. Those kept in a certain state of preparation for war, though on a peace establishment.

DEMURRAGE. The compensation due to a ship-owner from a freighter for unduly delaying his vessel in port beyond the time specified in the charter-party or bill of lading. It is in fact an extended freight. A ship unjustly detained, as a prize, is entitled to demurrage. Vessels chartered to convey government stores have a term given for discharge by government aid. If not delivered within that period, demurrage, as stated in the document, is paid per diem for any "unavoidable delay."

DEN. A sandy tract near the sea, as at Exmouth and other places.

DEN AND STROND. A liberty for ships or vessels to run or come ashore. Edward I. granted this privilege to the barons of the Cinque Ports.

DE NAUTICO FŒNORE. Of nautical usury; bottomry.

DENE. The Anglo-Saxon *dœne;* implying a kind of hollow or ravine through which a rivulet runs, the banks on either side being studded with trees.

DENEB. The bright star in the constellation Cygnus, well known as a standard nautical star.

DENSITY. The weight of a body in comparison with its bulk.

DENTICE. An excellent fish, so named from being well furnished with teeth. It is of the *Sparidæ* family, and frequents the Adriatic.

DEPARTMENT. A term by which the divisions in the public services are distinguished, as the civil, the commissariat, the military, the naval, the victualling, &c.

DEPARTURE. The bearing of an object on the coast from which a vessel commences her dead reckoning and takes her departure. The distance of any two places lying on the same parallel counted in miles of the equator.

DEPOT. A magazine in which military stores are deposited. Also, a company left in England for the purpose of recruiting when regiments are ordered abroad.

DEPRESS. The order to adjust the quoin in great-gun exercise; to depress the muzzle to point at an object below the level, in contradistinction to elevate.

DEPRESSED POLE. That end of the earth's axis which is below the horizon of the spectator according to his being in the northern or southern hemisphere. Also applied to the stars. (*See* POLAR DISTANCES.)

DEPRESSION, OF THE HORIZON. (*See* DIP.) In artillery, the angle below the horizon at which the axis of a gun is laid in order to strike an object on a lower level. The depression required in batteries of very elevated site (those of Gibraltar for example), for the laying the guns on near vessels, is so great as to necessitate a peculiar carriage.

DEPTH OF A SAIL. The extent of the square sails from the head-rope to the foot-rope, or the length of the after-leech of a stay-sail or boom-sail; in other words, it is the extent of the longest cloth of canvas in any sail.

DEPTH OF HOLD. The height between the floor and the lower-deck; it is therefore one of the principal dimensions given for the construction of a ship. It varies, of course, according to the end for which she is designed, trade or war.

DERELICT [Lat. *derelictus*, abandoned]. Anything abandoned at sea. A ship is derelict either by consent or by compulsion, stress of weather, &c., and yet, to save the owner's rights, if any cat, dog, or other domestic animal be found on board alive, it is not forfeited. The owner may yet recover, on payment of salvage, within a year and a day—otherwise the whole may be awarded. (*See* SALVAGE.)

DERIVATION. In artillery, the constant deflection of a rifled projectile. (*See* DEFLECTION.)

DERRICK. A single spar, supported by stays and guys, to which a purchase is attached, used in loading and unloading vessels. Also, a small crane either inside or outside of a ship.

DERRICK, To.   A cant term for setting out on a small not over-creditable enterprise.   The act is said to be named from a Tyburn executioner.

DERRING-DO.   A Spenserian term for deeds of arms.

DESCENDING NODE.   *See* Node.

DESCENDING SIGNS.   Those in which the sun appears to descend from the north pole, or in which his motion in declination is towards the south.

DESCENDING SQUALL.   A fitful gust of wind issuing from clouds which are formed in the lower parts of the atmosphere.   It is usually accompanied with heavy showers, and the weatherwise observe that the squall is seldom so violent when it is followed as when it is preceded by rain.   (*See* White Squall as a forerunner.)

DESCENSION.   The same as *oblique ascension* (which see).

DESCENT.   The landing of troops for the purpose of invading a country.   The passage down a river.

DESCRIPTION-BOOK.   A register in which the age, place of birth, and personal description of the crew are recorded.

DESERT.   An extensive tract, either absolutely sterile, or having no other vegetation than small patches of grass or shrubs.   Many portions of the present deserts seem to be reclaimable.

DESERTER.   One that quits his ship or the service without leave.   He is marked R (*run*) on the books, and any clothes or other effects he may have left on board are sold by auction at the mast, and the produce borne to account.

DESERTION.   The act of quitting the Army or Navy without leave, with intention not to return.

DESERTION-MONEY.   The sum of three pounds paid to him who apprehends a deserter, which is charged against the offender's growing pay—his wages for previous service having become forfeited from his having *run*.

DESTROYING PAPERS.   A ground of condemnation in the Admiralty court.

DETACHED.   On detached service.   A squadron may be detached under a commodore or senior officer.

DETACHED BASTION.   A bastion cut off by a ditch about its gorge from the body of the place, which latter is thus rendered in a degree independent of the fall of the former.

DETACHED ESCARP.   An escarp wall, originally invented by Carnot, and revived by the Prussians, removed some distance to the front of the rampart; which latter, being finished exteriorly at the natural slope of the earth, remains effective after the destruction of the wall by a besieger. It was at first intended, being kept low and covered by a near counterguard, to offer extraordinary difficulties to the besieger's breaching batteries; but improved artillery has nullified that supposed advantage.

DETACHED WORKS.   Works included in the scheme of defence of a fortress, but separated from it, and beyond the glacis.

DETACHMENT. A force detached from the main body for employment on any particular service.

DETAIL OF DUTY. The captain's night orders.

DETENTION OF A VESSEL: on just ground, as supposed war, suspicious papers, undue number of men, found hovering, or cargo not in conformity with papers or law.

DETONATING HAMMER. A modern introduction into the Royal Navy for firing the guns. With the aid of an attached laniard, it is made to descend forcibly upon the percussion arm of the tube, and fires the piece instantaneously. It is, however, already generally superseded by the use of the *friction tube* (which see).

DEVIATION. A voluntary departure from the usual course of the voyage, without any necessary or justifiable cause : a step which discharges the insurers from further responsibility. Liberty to touch, stay, or trade in any particular place not in the usual course of the voyage must be expressly specified in the contract, and even this is subordinate to the voyage. The cases of necessity which justify deviation are—1, stress of weather; 2, urgent want of repairs; 3, to join convoy; 4, succouring ships in distress; 5, avoiding capture or detention; 6, sickness; 7, mutiny of the crew. It differs from a *change* of voyage, which must have been resolved upon before the sailing of the ship. (*See* CHANGE.)—*Deviation* is also the attraction of a ship's iron on the needle. It is a term recently introduced to distinguish a sort of second variation to be allowed for in iron vessels.

DEVIL. A sort of priming made by damping and bruising gunpowder.

DEVIL-BOLTS. Those with false clenches, often introduced into contract-built ships.

DEVIL-FISH. The *Lophius piscatorius*, a hideous creature, which has also obtained the name of fish-frog, monk-fish, bellows-fish, sea-devil, and other appellatives significant of its ugliness and bad manners. There is also a powerful *Raia*, which grows to an immense size in the tropics, known as the devil-fish, the terror of the pearl-divers. *Manta* of Spaniards.

DEVILRY. Spirited roguery; wanton mischief, short of crime.

DEVIL'S CLAW. A very strong kind of split hook made to grasp a link of a chain cable, and used as a stopper.

DEVIL'S SMILES. Gleams of sunshine among dark clouds, either in the heavens or captain's face!

DEVIL'S TABLE-CLOTH. *See* TABLE-CLOTH.

DEVIL TO PAY AND NO PITCH HOT. The seam which margins the water-ways was called the "devil," why only caulkers can tell, who perhaps found it sometimes difficult for their tools. The phrase, however, means service expected, and no one ready to perform it. Impatience, and naught to satisfy it.

DEW-POINT. A meteorological term for the degree of temperature at which the moisture of the atmosphere would begin to precipitate; it may be readily ascertained by means of the hygrometer.

DHOLL. A kind of dried split pea supplied in India to the navy.

DHONY, or Dhoney. A country trading-craft of India from 50 to 150 tons; mostly flat-bottomed. (*See* Doney.)

DHOW. The Arab dhow is a vessel of about 150 to 250 tons burden by measurement—grab-built, with ten or twelve ports; about 85 feet long from stem to stern, 20 feet 9 inches broad, and 11 feet 6 inches deep. Of late years this description of vessel has been well built at Cochin, on the Malabar coast, in the European style. They have a great rise of floor; are calculated for sailing with small cargoes; and are fully prepared, by internal equipment, for defence—many of them are sheathed on 2½-inch plank bottoms, with 1-inch board, and the preparation of chunam and oil, called *galgal*, put between; causing the vessel to be very dry and durable, and preventing the encroachments of the worm or *Teredo navalis*. The worm is one of the greatest enemies in India to timber *in* the water, as the white ant (*termites*) is out of it. On the outside of the sheathing board there is a coat of whitewash, made from the same materials as that between the sheathing and planks, and renewed every season they put to sea. They have generally one mast and a lateen sail. The yard is the length of the vessel aloft, and the mast rakes forward, for the purpose of keeping this ponderous weight clear in raising and lowering. The tack of the sail is brought to the stem-head, and sheets aft in the usual way. The halyards lead to the taffrail, having a pendant and treble purchase block, which becomes the backstay, to support the mast when the sail is set. This, with three pairs of shrouds, completes the rigging, the whole made of *coir* rope. Several of these vessels were fitted as brigs, after their arrival in Arabia, and armed by the Arabs for cruising in the Red Sea and Arabian Gulf, as piratical vessels. It was of this class of vessel that Tippoo Sultan's navy at Onore consisted. The large dhows generally make one voyage in the season, to the southward of Arabia; taking advantage of the north-east monsoon to come down, and the south-west to return with an exchange cargo. The Arabs who man them are a powerful well-grown people, and very acute and intelligent in trade. They usually navigate their ships to Bengal in perfect safety, and with great skill. This was well known to Captain Collier and his officers of the *Liverpool* frigate, when they had the trial cruise with the Imam of Muscat's fine frigate in 1820.

DIACLE. An old term for a boat-compass.

DIAGONAL BRACES, knees, planks, &c., are such as cross a vessel's timbers obliquely. (*See* Trussing.)

DIAGONAL RIBBAND. A narrow plank made to a line formed on the half-breadth plan, by taking the intersections of the diagonal line with the timbers. (*See* Ribbands.)

DIAGONALS. A line cutting the body-plan diagonally from the timbers to the middle line. Diagonals are the several lines on the draughts, delineating the station of the harpings and ribs, to form the body by.

DIAGONAL TRUSSING. A particular method of binding and strengthening a vessel internally by a series of riders and truss-pieces placed diagonally.

DIAMETER. In geometry, a right line passing through the centre of any circular figure from one point of its circumference to another.

DIAMETER, APPARENT. The angle which the diameter of a heavenly body subtends at any time, varying inversely with its distance. The true is the real diameter, commonly expressed in miles.

DIAMOND-CUT. *See* RHOMBUS.

DIAMOND-KNOT. An ornamental knot worked with the strands of a rope, sometimes used for bucket-strops, on the foot-ropes of jib-booms, man-ropes, &c.

DIBBS. A galley term for ready money. Also, a small pool of water.

DICE. *See* DYCE.

DICHOTOMIZED. A term applied to the moon, when her longitude differs 90° from that of the sun, in which position only half her disc is illuminated.

DICKADEE. A northern name for the sand-piper.

DICK-A-DILVER. A name for the periwinkle on our eastern coasts.

DICKER-WORK. The timbering of tide-harbours in the Channel. Wattling between piles.

DICKEY. An officer acting in commission.—*It's all dickey with him.* It's all up with him.

DIDDLE, To. To deceive.

DIEGO. A very strong and heavy sword.

DIE ON THE FIN, To. An expression applied to whales, which when dying rise to the surface, after the final dive, with one side uppermost.

DIET. The regulated food for patients in sick-bays and hospitals.

DIFFERENCE. An important army term, meaning firstly the sum to be paid by officers when exchanging from the half to full pay; and, secondly, the price or difference in value of the several commissions.

DIFFERENCE OF LATITUDE. The distance between any two places on the same meridian, or the difference between the parallels of latitude of any two places expressed in miles of the equator.

DIFFERENCE OF LONGITUDE. The difference of any place from another eastward or westward, counted in degrees of the equator: that is, the difference between two places is an arc of the equator contained between their meridians, but measured in space on the parallel. Thus the difference of a degree of longitude in miles of the meridian would be—

At 20° lat.	56·4 miles
„ 40 „	38·6 „
„ 60 „	30·0 „
„ 80 „	10·4 „

DIFFERENTIAL OBSERVATION. Taking the differences of right ascension and declination between a comet and a star, the position of which has been already determined.

DIFFICULTY. A word unknown to true salts.

DIGHT [from the Anglo-Saxon *diht*, arranging or disposing]. Now applied to dressing or preparing for muster; setting things in order.

DIGIT. A twelfth part of the diameter; a term employed to denote the magnitude of an eclipse; as, so many *digits eclipsed*.

DIKE. *See* DYKE.

DILL. An edible dark brown sea-weed, torn from the rocks at low-water.

DILLOSK. The dried leaves of an edible sea-weed. (*See* DULSE and PEPPER DULSE.)

DILLY-WRECK. A common corruption of *derelict* (which see).

DIME. An American silver coin, in value the tenth of a dollar.

DIMINISHED ANGLE. In fortification, that formed by the exterior side and the line of defence.

DIMINISHING PLANK. The same as *diminishing stuff* (which see).

DIMINISHING STRAKES. *See* BLACK STRAKE.

DIMINISHING STUFF. In ship-building, the planking wrought under the wales, where it is thinned progressively to the thickness of the bottom plank.

DIMINUTION OF OBLIQUITY. A slow approximation of the planes of the ecliptic and the equator, at the present rate of 0·485″ annually.

DIMSEL. A piece of stagnant water, larger than a pond and less than a lake.

DING, To. To dash down or throw with violence.

DING-DONG. Ships firing into each other in good earnest.

DINGHEY. A small boat of Bombay, propelled by paddles, and fitted with a settee sail, the mast raking forwards; also, the boats in use on the Hooghly; also, a small extra boat in men-of-war and merchant ships.

DINGLE. A hollow vale-like space between two hills. A clough; also, a sort of boat used in Ireland, a coracle.

DINNAGE. *See* DUNNAGE.

DIP. The inclination of the magnetic needle towards the earth. (*See* DIPPING-NEEDLE.) Also, the smallest candle formerly issued by the purser.

DIP, To. To lower. An object is said to be dipping when by refraction it is visible just above the horizon. Also, to quit the deck suddenly.

DIP OF THE HORIZON. The angle contained between the sensible and apparent horizons, the angular point being the eye of the observer; or it is an allowance made in all astronomical observations of altitude for the height of the eye above the level of the sea.

DIPPED. The limb of the sun or moon as it instantly dips below the horizon.

DIPPER. A name for the water-ousel (*Cinclus aquaticus*). A bird of the Passerine order, but an expert diver, frequenting running streams in mountainous countries.

DIPPING-LADLE. A metal ladle for taking boiling pitch from the cauldron.

DIPPING-NEEDLE. An instrument for ascertaining the amount of the magnet's inclination towards the earth; it is so delicately suspended, that, instead of vibrating horizontally, one end *dips* or yields to the vertical force. This instrument has been so perfected by Mr. R. W. Fox of Falmouth, that even at sea in the heaviest gales of wind the dip could instantly, by magnetic deflectors, be ascertained to *minutes*, far beyond what heretofore could be elicited from the most expensive instruments, observed over 365 days on shore.

DIPPING-NET. A small net used for taking shad and other fish out of the water.

DIPS. *See* LEAD-LINE.

DIP-SECTOR. An ingenious instrument for measuring the true dip of the horizon, invented by Dr. Wollaston, and very important, not only where the nature and quantity of the atmospherical refraction are to be examined, but for ascertaining the rates of chronometers, and the exact latitude in those particular regions where accidental refractions are very great, for the difference between the calculated dip and that observed by the sector may exceed three minutes. It is a reflecting instrument, of small compass, but requiring patience and practice in its use.

DIPSY. The float of a fishing-line.

DIRECT-ACTING ENGINE. A steam engine in which the connecting rod is led at once from the head of the piston to the crank, thus communicating the rotatory motion without the intervention of side-levers.

DIRECT FIRE. One of the five varieties into which artillerists usually divide *horizontal fire* (which see).

DIRECTION OR SET OF THE WIND AND CURRENT. These are opposite terms; the direction of the winds and waves being named from the point of the compass *whence* they come; but the direction of a current is the point *towards* which it runs. A current running to leeward is said to have a *leeward set*, the opposite is a *windward set*.

DIRECTION. *See* ARC OF DIRECTION.

DIRECT MOTION. *See* MOTION.

DIRK. A small *do-little* sword or dagger, formerly worn by junior naval officers on duty.

DIRT-GABARD. A large ballast-lighter.

DIRTY AULIN. A name for the arctic skua (*Cataractes parasiticus*), a sea-bird, allied to the gulls.

DIRTY DOG AND NO SAILOR OR SOLDIER. A mean, spiritless, and utterly useless rascal.

DISABLED. To be placed *hors de combat* by the weather or an enemy.

DISAPPOINT. To counterwork an enemy's operations in mining.

DISARM. To deprive people of their weapons and ammunition.

DISBANDED. When the officers and men of a regiment are dismissed, on a reduction of the army.

DISC, OR DISK. In nautical astronomy, the circular visible surface presented by any celestial body to the eye of the observer.

DISCARCARE. [Ital.] An old term meaning to unlade a vessel.

DISCHARGED. When applied to a ship, signifies when she is unladen. When expressed of the officers or crew, it implies that they are disbanded from immediate service; and in individual cases, that the person is dismissed in consequence of long service, disability, or at his own request. When spoken of cannon, it means that it is fired off.

DISCHARGE-TICKET. On all foreign stations men are discharged by *foreign remove-tickets,* and in other cases by *dead, sick,* or *unserviceable ticket,* whether at home or abroad.

DISCHARGE-VALVE. In the marine engine, is a valve covering the top of the barrel of the air-pump, opening when pressed from below.

DISCIPLINARIAN. An officer who maintains strict dicipline and obedience to the laws of the navy, and himself setting an example.

DISCOURSE, To. An old sea term to traverse to and fro off the proper course.

DISCOVERY SHIP. A vessel fitted for the purpose of exploring un-known seas and coasts. Discovery vessels were formerly taken from the merchant service; they have latterly been replaced by ships of war, furnished with every improved instrument, and acting, on occasion, as active pilots leading in war service.

DISCRETION. To surrender at discretion, implies an unconditional yielding to the mercy of the conquerors.

DISEMBARK. The opposite of embark; the landing of troops from any vessel or transport.

DISEMBAY. To work clear out of a gulf or bay.

DISEMBOGUE. The fall of a river into the sea; it has also been used for the passage of vessels across the mouth of a river and out of one.

DISGUISE. Ships in all times have been permitted to assume disguise to impose upon enemies, and obtain from countries in their possession com-modities of which they stand in need.

DISH, To. To supplant, ruin, or frustrate.

DISLODGE. To drive an enemy from any post or station.

DI-SLYNG. *See* SLYNG.

DISMANTLED. The state of a ship unrigged, and all her stores, guns, &c., taken out, in readiness for her being laid up in ordinary, or going into dock, &c. &c. To dismantle a gun is to render it unfit for service. The same applies to a fort.

DISMASTED. State of a ship deprived of her masts, by gales or by design.

DISMISS. Pipe down the people. To dismiss a drill from parade is to break the ranks.

DISMISSION. A summary discharge from the service; which a court-martial is empowered to inflict on any officer convicted of a breach of special laws, though it cannot for minor offences which formerly carried death!

DISMOUNT, To. To break the carriages of guns, and thereby render them unfit for service. Also, in gun exercise, to lift a gun from its carriage and deposit it elsewhere.

DISMOUNTED. The state of a cannon taken off a carriage, or when, by the enemy's shot, it is rendered unmanageable. Also, cavalry on foot acting as infantry.

DISOBEDIENCE. An infraction of the orders of a superior; punishable by a court-martial, according to the nature and degree of the offence.

DISORDER. The confusion occasioned by a heavy fire from an enemy.

DISORGANIZE, To. To degrade a man-of-war to a privateer by irregularity.

DISPART, or Throw of the Shot. The difference between the semi-diameter of the base-ring at the breech of a gun, and that of the ring at the swell of the muzzle. On account of the dispart, the line of aim makes a small angle with the axis; so that the elevation of the latter above the horizon is greater than that of the line of aim: an allowance for the dispart is consequently necessary in determining the commencement of the graduations on the tangent scale, by which the required elevation is given to the gun.

DISPARTING A GUN. To bring the line of sight and line of metal to be parallel by setting up a mark on the muzzle-ring of a cannon, so that a sight-line, taken from the top of the base-ring behind the touch-hole, to the mark set near the muzzle, may be parallel to the axis of the bore. (See Gun.)

DISPART-SIGHT. A gun-sight fixed on the top of the second reinforce-ring—about the middle of the piece—for point-blank or horizontal firing, to eliminate the difference of the diameters between the breech and the mouth of the cannon.

DISPATCH. All duty is required to be performed with diligence.

DISPATCHES. Not simply letters, but such documents as demand every effort for their immediate delivery. "Charged with dispatches" overrides all signals of hindrance on a voyage.

DISPLACEMENT. The centre of gravity of the displacement relates to the part of the ship under water, considered as homogeneous. The weight of water which a vessel displaces when floating is the same as the weight of the ship. (See Centre of Cavity.)

DISPOSED QUARTERS. The distribution when the camp is marked about a place besieged.

DISPOSITION. A draught representing the several timbers that compose a ship's frame properly disposed with respect to ports and other parts. Also, the arrangement of a ship's company for watches, quarters, reefing, furling, and other duties. In a military sense it means the placing of a body of troops upon the most advantageous ground.

DISRANK, or Disrate. To degrade in rank or station.

DISREPAIR. A bar to any claim on account of sea-unworthiness in a warranty.

DISTANCE. The run which a ship has made upon the log-board. In speaking of double stars, it is the space separating the centres of the two stars, expressed in seconds of arc. (See Lunar Distance.)

DISTILLING SEA-WATER. Apparatus for the conversion of sea-water into potable fresh water have long been invented, though little used; but of late the larger ships are effectively fitted with adaptations for the purpose.

DISTINCTION. Flags of distinction, badges, honourable note of superiority.

DISTINGUISHING PENDANT. In fleets and squadrons, instead of hoisting several flags to denote the number of the ship on the list of the Navy, pendants are used. Thus ten ships may be signalled separately. If more, then, as one answers, her pendant is hauled down, and then two pendants succeed. (*See* SIGNALLING.)

DISTRESS. A term used when a ship requires immediate assistance from unlooked-for damage or danger. (*See* SIGNAL OF DISTRESS.)

DISTRICT ORDERS. Those issued by a general commanding a district.

DISTURBANCE. *See* SPANISH DISTURBANCE.

DITCH. In fortification the excavation in front of the parapet of any work, ranging in width from a few feet in field fortification to thirty or forty yards in permanent works, having its steep side next the rampart called the escarp: the opposite one is the counterscarp. Its principal use is to secure the escarp as long as possible. There are wet ditches and dry ones, the former being less in favour than the latter, since a dry ditch so much facilitates sorties, counter-approaches, and the like. That kind which may be made wet or dry at pleasure is most useful.

DITTY-BAG. Derives its name from the *dittis* or Manchester stuff of which it was once made. It is in use among seamen for holding their smaller necessaries. The ditty-bag of old, when a seaman prided himself on his rig, as the result of his own ability to fit himself from clue to earing, was a treasured article, probably worked in exquisite device by his lady-love. Well can we recollect the pride exhibited in its display when "on end clothes" was a joyful sound to the old pig-tailed tar.

DITTY-BOX. A small caddy for holding a seaman's stock of *valuables*.

DIURNAL ARC. That part of a circle, parallel to the equator, which is described by a celestial body from its rising to its setting.

DIURNAL PARALLAX. *See* PARALLAX.

DIVE, To. To descend or plunge voluntarily head-foremost under the water. To go off deck in the watch. A ship is said to be "*diving into it*" when she pitches heavily against a head-sea.

DIVER. One versed in the art of descending under water to considerable depths and abiding there a competent time for several purposes, as to recover wrecks of ships, fish for pearls, sponges, corals, &c. The diver is now a rating in H.M. ships; he may be of any rank of seaman, but he receives £1, 10s. 5d. per annum additional pay—one penny a-day for risking life! Also, a common web-footed sea-bird of the genus *Colymbus*.

DIVERGENT. A stream flowing laterally out of a river, contradistinguished from convergent.

DIVERSION. A manœuvre to attract, wholly or partially, the enemy's attention away from some other part of the operations.

DIVIE-GOO. A northern term for the *Larus marinus* or black-backed gull.

DIVINE SERVICE. Ordered by the articles of war, whenever the weather on a Sunday will allow of it.

DIVING-APPARATUS. Supplied to the flag-ship, and also a man with the title of diver, to examine defects below water.

DIVING-BELL. Used in under-water operations for recovering treasure, raising ships, anchors, &c.

DIVING-DRESS. India-rubber habiliments, the head-piece is of light metal fitted with strong glass eyes, and an attached pliable pipe to maintain a supply of air. The shoes are weighted.

DIVISION. A select number of ships in a fleet or squadron of men-of-war, distinguished by a particular flag, pendant, or vane. A squadron may be ranged into two or three divisions, the commanding officer of which is always stationed in the centre. In a fleet the admiral divides it into three squadrons, each of which is commanded by an admiral, and is again divided into divisions; each squadron had its proper colours (now distinguishing mark) according to the rank of the admiral who commanded it, and each division its proper mast. The private ships carried pendants of the same colour with their respective squadrons at the masts of their particular divisions, so that the ships in the last division of the blue squadron carried a blue pendant at their main top-gallant-mast head, the vane at the mizen. All these are superseded by the abolition of the Red and Blue. The St. George's white ensign flag and pendant alone are used.

DIVISIONS. The sub-classification of a ship's company under the lieutenants. Also, a muster of the crew. Also, of an army, a force generally complete in itself, commanded by a major-general, of an average strength of eight or ten thousand men: it is itself composed of several brigades, each of which again is composed of several battalions, besides the complement of artillery, transport-corps, and generally also of cavalry, for the whole. Of a battalion, a term sometimes used in exercise, when the companies of a battalion have been equalized as to strength, for one of such companies.

DJERME. *See* JERME.

DOA. A Persian trading vessel.

DOASTA. An inferior spirit, often drugged or doctored for unwary sailors in the pestiferous dens of filthy Calcutta and other sea-ports in India.

DOB. The animal inhabiting the razor-shell (*solen*), used as a bait by fishermen.

DOBBER. The float of a fishing-line.

DOBBIN. A phrase on our southern coasts for sea-gravel mixed with sand.

DOCK. An artificial receptacle for shipping, in which they can discharge or take in cargo, and refit.—A *dry dock* is a broad and deep trench, formed on the side of a harbour, or on the banks of a river, and commodiously fitted either to build ships in or to receive them to be repaired or breamed. They have strong flood-gates, to prevent the flux of the tide from entering while the ship is under repair. There are likewise docks where a ship can only be cleaned during the recess of the tide, as she floats again on the return of the flood. Docks of the latter kind are not furnished with the usual flood-gates; but the term is also used for what is more appropriately called a *float* (which see). Also, in polar parlance, an opening cut out of an ice-floe, into which a ship is warped for security.

DOCK-DUES. The charges made upon shipping for the use of docks.

DOCKERS. Inhabitants of the town which sprang up between the docks and the town of Plymouth. Dock solicited and obtained the royal license, in 1823, to be called Devonport—a very inappropriate name, Plymouth being wholly within the county of Devon, while Hamoaze is equally in Devon and Cornwall.

DOCK HERSELF, To. When a ship is on the ooze, and swaddles a bed, she is said to dock herself.

DOCKING A SHIP. The act of drawing her into dock, and placing her properly on blocks, in order to give her the required repair, cleanse the bottom, and cover it anew. (*See* BREAMING.)

DOCK UP, OR DUCK UP. To clue up a corner of a sail that hinders the helmsman from seeing.

DOCKYARD DUTY. The attendance of a lieutenant and party in the arsenal, for stowing, procuring stores, &c.

DOCKYARD MATIES. The artificers in a dockyard. In former times an established declaration of war between the mates and midshipmen *versus* the maties was hotly kept up. Many deaths and injuries never disclosed were hushed up or patiently borne. It terminated about 1830.

DOCK-YARDS. Arsenals containing all sorts of naval stores and timber for ship-building. In England the royal dock-yards are at Deptford, Woolwich, Chatham, Sheerness, Portsmouth, Devonport, Pembroke. Those in our colonies are at the Cape of Good Hope, Gibraltar, Malta, Bermuda, Halifax, Jamaica, Antigua, Trincomalee, and Hong Kong. There Her Majesty's ships and vessels of war are generally moored during peace, and such as want repairing are taken into the docks, examined, and refitted for service. These yards are generally supplied from the north with hemp, pitch, tar, rosin, canvas, oak-plank, and several other species of stores. The largest masts are usually imported from New England. Until 1831 these yards were governed by a commissioner resident at the port, who superintended all the musters of the officers, artificers, and labourers employed in the dockyard and ordinary; he also controlled their payment, examined their accounts, contracted and drew bills on the Navy Office to supply the deficiency of stores, and, finally, regulated whatever belonged to the dockyard. In 1831 the commissioners of the Navy were abolished, and admirals and captains superintendent command the dockyards under the controller of the Navy and the Admiralty.

DOCTOR. A name which seamen apply to every medical officer. Also, a jocular name for the ship's cook.

DOCTOR'S LIST. The roll of those excused from duty by reason of illness.

DODD. A round-topped hill, generally an offshoot from a higher mountain.

DODECAGON. A regular polygon, having twelve sides and as many angles.

DODECATIMORIA. The anastrous signs, or twelve portions of the ecliptic which the signs anciently occupied, but have since deserted by the precession of the equinoxes.

DODGE. A homely but expressive phrase for shuffling conduct, or cunning of purpose. Also, to watch or follow a ship from place to place.

DODMAN. A shell-fish with a hod-like lump. A sea-snail, otherwise called *hodmandod.*

DOFF, To. To put aside.

DO FOR, To. A double-barrelled expression, meaning alike to take care of or provide for an individual, or to ruin or kill him.

DOG. The hammer of a firelock or pistol; that which holds the flint, called also *dog-head.* Also, a sort of iron hook or bar with a sharp fang at one end, so as to be easily driven into a piece of timber, and drag it along by means of a rope fastened to it, upon which a number of men can pull. *Dog* is also an iron implement with a fang at each end, to be driven into two pieces of timber, to support and steady one of them while being dubbed, hewn, or sawn.—*Span-dogs.* Used to lift timber. A pair of dogs linked together, and being hooked at an extended angle, press home with greater strain.

DOG-BITCH-THIMBLE. An excellent contrivance by which the topsail-sheet-block is prevented making the half cant or turn so frequently seen in the clue when the block is secured there.

DOG-BOLT. A cap square bolt.

DOG-DRAVE. A kind of sea-fish mentioned in early charters.

DOG-FISH. A name commonly applied to several small species of the shark family.

DOGG. A small silver coin of the West Indies, six of which make a bitt. Also, in meteorology, *see* STUBB.

DOGGED. A mode of attaching a rope to a spar or cable, in contradistinction to racking, by which slipping is prevented; half-hitched and end stopped back, is one mode.

DOGGER. A Dutch smack of about 150 tons, navigated in the German Ocean. It is mostly equipped with a main and a mizen mast, and somewhat resembles a ketch or a galliot. It is principally used for fishing on the Dogger Bank.

DOGGER-FISH. Fish bought out of the Dutch doggers.

DOGGER-MEN. The seafaring fishermen belonging to doggers.

DOGS. The last supports knocked away at the launching of a ship.

DOG'S-BODY. Dried pease boiled in a cloth.

DOG-SHORES. Two long square blocks of timber, resting diagonally with their heads to the cleats. They are placed forward to support the bilge-ways on the ground-ways, thereby preventing the ship from starting off the slips while the keel-blocks are being taken out.

DOG-SLEEP. The uncomfortable fitful naps taken when all hands are kept up by stress.

DOG'S TAIL. A name for the constellation Ursa Minor or Little Bear.

DOG-STOPPER. Put on before all to enable the men to bit the cable, sometimes to fleet the messenger.

DOG-TONGUE. A name assigned to a kind of sole.

DOG-VANE. A small vane made of thread, cork, and feathers, or buntin, fastened on the end of a half-pike, and placed on the weather gunwale, so as to be readily seen, and show the direction of the wind. The term is also familiarly applied to a cockade.

DOG-WATCH. The half-watches of two hours each, from 4 to 6, and from 6 to 8, in the evening. By this arrangement an uneven number of watches is made—seven instead of six in the twenty-four hours; otherwise there would be a succession of the same watches at the same hours throughout the voyage or cruise. Theodore Hook explained them as *cur-tailed*. (*See* WATCH.)

DOIT. A small Dutch coin, valued at about half a farthing; formerly current on our eastern shores.

DOLDRUMS. Those parts of the sea where calms are known to prevail. They exist between and on the polar sides of the trade-winds, but vary their position many degrees of latitude in the course of the year, depending upon the sun's declination. Also applied to a person in low spirits.

DOLE. A stated allowance; but applied to a scanty share or portion.

DOLE-FISH. The share of fish that was given to our northern fishermen as part payment for their labour.

DOLING. A fishing-boat with two masts, on the coasts of Sussex and Kent; each of the masts carries a sprit-sail.

DO-LITTLE, or DO-LITTLE SWORD. The old term for a dirk.

DOLLAR. For this universally known coin, see PIECE OF EIGHT.

DOLLOP. An old word for a lump, portion, or share. From the Gaelic *diolab*.

DOLPHIN. Naturalists understand by this word numerous species of small cetaceous animals of the genus *Delphinus*, found in nearly all seas. They greatly resemble porpoises, and are often called by this name by sailors; but they are distinguished by having a longer and more slender snout. The word is also generally, but less correctly, applied to a fish, the dorado (*Coryphæna hippuris*), celebrated for the changing hues of its surface when dying. Also, a small light ancient boat, which gave rise to Pliny's story of the boy going daily to school across the Lucrine lake on a dolphin. Also, in ordnance, especially brass guns, two handles nearly over the trunnions for lifting the guns by. Also, a French gold coin (*dauphine*), formerly in great currency. Also, a stout post on a quay-head, or in a beach, to make hawsers fast to. The name is also given to a spar or block of wood, with a ring-bolt at each end, through which a hawser can be rove, for vessels to ride by; the same as *wooden buoys*.

DOLPHIN OF THE MAST. A kind of wreath or strap formed of plaited cordage, to be fastened occasionally round the lower yards to prevent nip, or as a support to the puddening, where the lower yards rest in the sling, the use of which is to sustain the fore and main yards by the jeers, in case the rigging or chains, by which those yards are suspended, should be shot away in action. (*See* PUDDENING.)

DOLPHIN-STRIKER. A short perpendicular gaff spar, under the bow-sprit-end, for guying down the jib-boom, of which indeed it is the chief support, by means of the martingales. (*See* MARTINGALE.)

DOLVER. The reclaimed fen-grounds of our eastern coasts.

DOMESTIC NAVIGATION. A term applied to coasting trade.

DOMINIONS. It is a settled point that a conquered country forms immediately a part of the king's dominions; and a condemnation of ships within its harbours as droits of admiralty, is valid, although the conquest may not yet have been confirmed by treaty.

DON. A general name for Spaniards. One of the "perfumed" terms of its time.—*To don.* To put on.

DONDERBASS. *See* BOMBARD.

DONEY. The doney of the Coromandel coast is about 70 feet long, 20 feet broad, and 12 feet deep; with a flat bottom or keel part, which at the broadest place is 7 feet, and diminishes to 10 inches in the siding of the stem and stern-post. The fore and after bodies are similar in form from midships. Their light draught of water is about 4 feet, and when loaded about 9 feet. These unshapely vessels in the fine season trade from Madras and Ceylon, and many of them to the Gulf of Manar, as the water is shoal between Ceylon and the southern part of the continent. They have only one mast, and are navigated by the natives in the rudest way; their means for finding the latitude being a little square board, with a string fast to the centre, at the other end of which are certain knots. The upper edge of the board is held by one hand so as to touch the north star, and the lower edge the horizon. Then the string is brought with the other hand to touch the tip of the nose, and the knot which comes in contact with the tip of the nose tells the latitude.

DONJON. The keep, or place of retreat, in old fortifications. A redoubt of a fortress; the highest and strongest tower.

DONKEY-ENGINE. An auxiliary steam-engine for feeding the boilers of the principal engine when they are stopped; or for any other duties independent of the ship's propelling engines.

DONKEY-FRIGATE. Those of 28 guns, frigate-built; that is, having guns protected by an upper deck, with guns on the quarter-deck and forecastle; ship-sloops, in contradistinction to corvettes and sloops.

DONNY. A small fishing-net.

DOOLAH. A passage-boat on the Canton river.

DOOTED. Timber rendered unsound by fissures.

DORADO. The *Coryphœna hippuris*, an oceanic fish; often called "dolphin."

DOREY. A flat-floored cargo-boat in the West Indies, named after the fish John Dory.

DORNICLE. A northern name for the vivaparous blenny.

DORRA. From the Gaelic *dorga;* a crab-net.

DORSAL FIN. The median fin placed upon the back of fishes.

DORY. A fish, *Zeus faber*, commonly known as "John Dory," or truly *jaune dorée*, from its golden hues.

DOTTLE. The small portion of tobacco remaining unsmoked in the pipe.

DOUBLE, To. To cover a ship with an extra planking, usually of 4 inches, either internally or externally, when through age or otherwise she has become loosened; the process strengthens her without driving out the former fastenings. Doubling, however, is a term applied only where the plank thus used is not less than 2 inches thick.—To *double* a cape. (*See* DOUBLING A CAPE.)

DOUBLE-ACTING ENGINE. One in which the steam acts upon the piston against a vacuum, both in the upward and downward movement.

DOUBLE-BANK A ROPE, To. To clap men on both sides.

DOUBLE-BANKED. When two opposite oars are pulled by rowers seated on the same thwart; or when there are two men labouring upon each oar. Also, 60-gun frigates which carry guns along the gangway, as was the custom with Indiamen, are usually styled *double-bankers*.

DOUBLE-BITTED. Two turns of the cable round the bitts instead of one.

DOUBLE-BLOCK. One fitted with a couple of sheaves, in holes side by side.

DOUBLE-BREECHING. Additional breeching on the non-recoil system, or security for guns in heavy weather.

DOUBLE-CAPSTAN. One shaft so constructed as to be worked both on an upper and lower deck, as in ships of the line, or in Phillips' patent capstan.

DOUBLE-CROWN. A name given to a plait made with the strands of a rope, which forms part of several useful and ornamental knots.

DOUBLE DECK-NAILS. *See* DECK-NAILS.

DOUBLE DUTCH COILED AGAINST THE SUN. Gibberish, or any unintelligible or difficult language.

DOUBLE EAGLE. A gold coin of the United States, of 10 dollars; value £2, 1s. 8d., at the average rate of exchange.

DOUBLE-FUTTOCKS. Timbers in the cant-bodies, extending from the dead-wood to the run of the second futtock-head.

DOUBLE-HEADED MAUL. One with double faces; top-mauls in contradistinction to pin-mauls.

DOUBLE-HEADED SHOT. Differing from bar-shot by being similar to dumb-bells, only the shot are hemispherical.

DOUBLE-IMAGE MICROMETER. Has one of its lenses divided, and separable to a certain distance by a screw, which at the same time moves an index upon a graduated scale. When fitted to a telescope for sea use, as in chase, it is called a *coming-up glass.*

DOUBLE INSURANCE. Where the insured makes two insurances on the same risks and the same interest.

DOUBLE-IRONED. Both legs shackled to the bilboe-bolts.

DOUBLE-JACK. *See* JACK-SCREW.

DOUBLE-LAND. That appearance of a coast when the sea-line is bounded by parallel ranges of hills, rising inland one above the other.

DOUBLE-SIDED. A line-of-battle ship painted so as to show the ports of both decks; or a vessel painted to resemble one, as used to be frequent in the Indian marine.

DOUBLE-STAR. Two stars so close together as to be separable only with a telescope. They are either optically so owing to their accidental situation in the heavens, or physically near each other in space, and one of them revolving round the other.

DOUBLE-TIDE. Working double-tides is doing extra duty. (*See* WORK DOUBLE-TIDES.)

DOUBLE UPON, To. *See* DOUBLING UPON.

DOUBLE WALL-KNOT. With or without a crown, or a double crown, is made by intertwisting the unlaid ends of a rope in a peculiar manner.

DOUBLE-WHIP. A whip is simply a rope rove through a single block; a double whip is when it passes through a lower tail or hook-block, and the standing end is secured to the upper block, or where it is attached.

DOUBLING. (*See* RANK.) Putting two ranks into one.

DOUBLING A CAPE. In navigation, is to sail round or pass beyond it, so that the point of land separates the ship from her former situation.

DOUBLING-NAILS. The nails commonly used in doubling.

DOUBLING UPON. In a naval engagement, the act of inclosing any part of a hostile fleet between two fires, as Nelson did at the Nile. The van or rear of one fleet, taking advantage of the wind or other circumstances, runs round the van or rear of the enemy, who will thereby be exposed to great danger and confusion.

DOUBLOON. A Spanish gold coin, value 16 dollars: £3, 3s. to £3, 6s. English.

DOUGH-BOYS. Hard dumplings boiled in salt water. A corruption of *dough-balls.*

DOUSE, To. To lower or slacken down suddenly; expressed of a sail in a squall of wind, an extended hawser, &c. Douse the glim, your colours, &c., to knock down.

DOUT, To. To put out a light; to extinguish; *do out.* Shakspeare makes the dauphin of France say in "King Henry V.:"—

> "That their hot blood may spin in English eyes,
> And dout them."

DOUTER, OR DOUSER. An extinguisher.

D'OUTRE MER. From beyond the sea.

DOVER COURT BEETLE. A heavy mallet. There is an old proverb: "A Dover court; all speakers and no hearers."

> "A Dover court beetle, and wedges with steel,
> Strong lever to raise up the block from the wheel."—*Tusser.*

DOVE-TAIL. The fastening or letting in of one timber into another by a dove-tailed end and score, so that they hold firmly together, and cannot come asunder endwise. The operation of cutting the mortise is called dove-tailing.

DOVE-TAIL PLATES. Metal plates resembling dove-tails in form, let into the heel of the stern-post and the keel, to bind them together; and also those used for connecting the stem-foot with the fore end of the keel.

DOWAL. A coak of metal in a sheave.

DOWBREK. A northern term for the fish also called spärling or smelt.

DOWEL. A cylindrical piece of hard wood about three inches in diameter, and the same in length, used as an additional security in scarphing two pieces of timber together. Dowels are also used to secure the joinings of the felloes, or circumferential parts of wheels; and by coopers in joining together the contiguous boards forming the heads of casks.—*Dowel*, or *dowel-bit*, is the tool used to cut the holes for the dowels.

DOWELLING. The method of uniting the butts of the frame-timbers together with a cylindrical piece or tenon let in at each end.

DOWN ALL CHESTS! The order to get all the officers' and seamen's chests down below from off the gun-decks when clearing the ship for an engagement.

DOWN ALL HAMMOCKS! The order for all the sailors to carry their hammocks down, and hang them up in their respective berths in readiness to go to bed, or to lessen top-weight and resistance to wind in chase.

DOWN ALONG. Sailing coastways down Channel.

DOWN EAST. Far away in that bearing. This term, as *down west*, &c., is an Americanism, recently adopted into our vernacular.

DOWNFALLS. The descending waters of rivers and creeks.

DOWN-HAUL. A rope passing up along a stay, leading through cringles of the stay-sails or jib, and made fast to the upper corner of the sail to pull it down when shortening sail. Also, through blocks on the outer clues to the outer yard-arms of studding-sails, to take them in securely. Also, the cock-pit term for a great-coat.

DOWN-HAUL TACKLES. Employed when lower yards are struck in bad weather to prevent them from swaying about after the trusses are unrove.

DOWN IN THE MOUTH. Low-spirited or disheartened.

DOWN KILLOCK! Let go the grapnel; the corruption of keel-hook or anchor.

DOWN OARS! The order on shoving off a boat when the men have had them "tossed up."

DOWNS. An accumulation of drifted sand, which the sea gathers along its shores. The name is also applied to the anchorage or sea-space between the eastern coast of Kent and the Goodwin Sands, the well-known roadstead for ships, stretching from the South to the North Foreland, where both outward and homeward-bound ships frequently make some stay, and squadrons of men-of-war rendezvous in time of war. It is defended by the castles of Sandwich, Deal, and Dover.

DOWN WIND, DOWN SEA. A proverbial expression among seamen between the tropics, where the sea is soon raised by the wind, and when that abates is soon smooth again.

DOWN WITH THE HELM! An order to put the helm alee.

DOWSING CHOCK. A breast-hook or piece fayed athwart the apron and lapped on the knight-heads, or inside stuff, above the upper deck; otherwise termed *hawse-hook*.

DOYLT. Lazy or stupid.

DO YOU HEAR THERE? An inquiry following an order, but very often needlessly.

DRABLER. A piece of canvas laced on the bonnet of a sail to give it more drop, or as Captain Boteler says—" As the bonnet is to the course, so in all respects is the drabler to the bonnet." It is only used when both course and bonnet are not deep enough to clothe the mast.

DRACHMA. A Greek coin, value sevenpence three farthings sterling; 14 cents. American or Spanish real.

DRAFT, or DRAUGHT. A small allowance for waste on goods sold by weight.

DRAFT OF HANDS. A certain number of men appointed to serve on board a particular man-of-war, who are then said to be *drafted*. A transfer of hands from one ship to complete the complement of another.

DRAG. A machine consisting of a sharp square frame of iron encircled with a net, and commonly used to rake the mud off from the platform or bottom of the docks, or to clean rivers, or for dragging on the bottom for anything lost. Also, a creeper.

DRAG FOR THE ANCHOR, To. The same as *creep* or *sweep*.

DRAGGING. An old word for dredging.

DRAGGING ON HER. Said of a vessel in chase, or rounding a point, when she is obliged to carry more canvas to a fresh wind than she otherwise would.

DRAG-NET. A trawl or net to draw on the bottom for flat-fish.

DRAGOMAN. The name for a Turkish interpreter; it is corrupted from *tarij-mán*.

DRAGON. An old name for a musketoon.

DRAGON BEAM or PIECE. A strut or abutment.

DRAGONET. A sea-fish, the gowdie, or *Callionymus lyra*.

DRAGON-VOLANT. The old name for a gun of large calibre used in the French navy, whence the term was adopted into ours.

DRAGOON. Originally a soldier trained to serve alike on horse or foot, or as Dr. Johnson equivocally explains it, "who fights indifferently on foot or on horseback." (*See* TROOPER.) The term is now applied to all cavalry soldiers who have no other special designation.

DRAG-ROPES. Those used in the artillery by the men in pulling the gun backwards and forwards in practice and in action.

DRAGS. Whatever hangs over the ship into the sea, as shirts, coats, or the like; and boats when towed, or whatever else that after this manner may hinder the ship's way when she sails, are called *drags*.

DRAG-SAIL. Any sail with its clues stopped so as when veered away over the quarter to make a stop-water when veering in emergency. The drag-sail formed by the sprit-sail course was frequently used in former wars to retard the ship apparently running away until the enemy got within gun-shot.

DRAG-SAW. A cross-cut saw.

DRAG THE ANCHOR, To. The act of the anchors coming home.

DRAKE. An early piece of brass ordnance.

DRAKKAR. A Norman pirate boat of former times.

DRAUGHT, OR DRAFT. The depth of water a ship displaces, or of a body of fluid necessary to float a vessel; hence a ship is said to draw so many feet of water when she requires that depth to float her, which, to be more readily known, are marked on the stem and stern-post from the keel upwards. Also, the old name for a chart. Also, the delineation of a ship designed to be built, drawn on a given scale, generally a quarter-inch to the foot, for the builders. (*See* SHEER-DRAUGHT.)

DRAUGHT-HOOKS. Iron hooks fixed on the checks of a gun-carriage for dragging the gun along by *draught-ropes*.

DRAUGHTSMAN. The artist who draws plans or charts from instructions or surveys.

DRAW. A sail *draws* when it is filled by the wind. A ship *draws* so many feet of water.—*To let draw a jib* is to cease from flattening-in the sheet.—*Draw* is also a term for halliards in some of the northern fishing-boats.—*To draw*. To procure anything by official demand from a dock-yard, arsenal, or magazine.—*To draw up the courses*. To take in.—*To draw upon a ship* is to gain upon a vessel when in pursuit of her.

DRAWBACK. An abatement or reduction of duties allowed by the custom-house in certain cases; as for stores to naval officers in commission.

DRAW-BELLOWS. A northern term for *limber-holes* (which see).

DRAWING. The state of a sail when there is sufficient wind to inflate it, so as to advance the vessel in her course.

DRAWING UP. Adjusting a ship's station in the line; the converse of *dropping astern*.

DRAWING WATER. The number of feet depth which a ship submerges.

DRAWN BATTLE. A conflict in which both parties claim the victory, or retire upon equal terms.

DRAW-NET. Erroneously used for *drag-net*.

DRAWN FOR THE MILITIA. When men are selected by ballot for the defence of the country.

DRAW THE GUNS. To extract the charge of wad, shot, and cartridge from the guns.

DREDGE. An iron scraper-framed triangle, furnished with a bottom of hide and stout cord net above, used for taking oysters or specimens of shells from the bottom.

DREDGER-BOAT. One that uses the net so called, for turbots, soles, sandlings, &c.

DREDGING. Fishing by dragging the dredge.

DREDGING MACHINE. A large lighter, or other flat-bottomed vessel, equipped with a steam-engine and machinery for removing the mud and silt from the bottom, by the revolution of iron buckets in an endless chain.

DREDGY. The ghost of a drowned person.

DREINT. The old word used for drowned, from the Anglo-Saxon.

DRESS, To. To place a fleet in organized order; also, to arrange men properly in ranks; to present a true continuous line in front.—*To dress a ship.* To ornament her with a variety of colours, as ensigns, flags, pendants, &c., of various nations, displayed from different parts of her masts, rigging, &c., on a day of festivity.

DREW. A name in our northern isles for the *Fucus lorcus*, a narrow thong-shaped sea-weed.

DRIBBLE. Drizzling showers; light rain.

DRIES. A term opposed to *rains* on the west coast of Africa.

DRIFT. The altered position of a vessel by current or falling to leeward when hove-to or lying-to in a gale, when but little headway is made by the action of sails. In artillery, a priming-iron of modern introduction used to clear the vent of ordnance from burning particles after each discharge. Also, a term sometimes used for the constant deflection of a rifled projectile. (*See* DEFLECTION.)

DRIFTAGE The amount due to lee-way. (*See* DRIFT.)

DRIFT-BOLTS. Commonly made of steel, are used as long punches for driving out other bolts.

DRIFT-ICE. The debris of the main pack. (*See* ICE.)

DRIFTING-UP. Is used as relating to sands which are driven by the winds. As at Cape Blanco, on the coast of Africa, off the tail of the Desert of Zahara, where the houses and batteries have been thus obliterated.

DRIFT-MUD. Consisting chiefly of an argillaceous earth, brought down by the rivers, floated about, and successively deposited in banks; forming the alluvial and fertile European settlements of Guiana.

DRIFT-NET. A large net, with meshes of one inch, used in the pilchard fishery in August; also, for herrings and mackerel in March: used in drifting in the Chops of the Channel. Also, of strong gauze, for molluscs.

DRIFT-PIECES. Solid pieces fitted at the drifts, forming the scrolls on the drifts: they are commonly mitred into the gunwale.

DRIFTS. Detached masses of soil and underwood torn off the shore by floods and floating about, often mistaken for rocks and dangers. Also, in shipbuilding, those parts where the sheer is raised, and the rails are cut off, ending with a scroll; as the drift of the quarter-deck, poop-deck, and forecastle.

DRIFT-SAIL. A contrivance, by means of immersing a sail, to diminish the drift of a ship during a gale of wind. (*See* DRAG.)

DRIFT-WAY. Synonymous with *lee-way*.

DRILL. Systematized instruction in the practice of all military exercises.

DRILL-SHIPS. A recent establishment of vessels in which the volunteers composing the Royal Naval Reserve are drilled into practice.

DRINK-PENNY. Earnest money at rendezvous houses, &c.

DRIP-STONE. The name usually given to filters composed of porous stone.

DRIVE, To [from the Anglo-Saxon *dryfan*]. A ship drives when her anchor trips or will not hold. She drives to leeward when beyond control of sails or rudder; and if under bare poles, may drive before the wind. Also, to strike home bolts, tree-nails, &c.

DRIVER. A large sail formerly used with the wind aft or quartering. It was a square sail cut like a studding-sail, and set with a great yard on the end of the spanker-boom, across the taffrail. The name latterly has been officially applied to the spanker, both being the aftermost sails of a ship, the ring-tail being only an addition, as a studding or steering sail. (*See* STEERING SAIL.) Also, the foremost spur in the bilge-ways, the heel of which is fayed to the foreside of the foremost poppet, and the sides of it look fore and aft. Also, a sort of fishing-boat.

DRIVER-BOOM. The boom to which the driver is hauled out.

DRIVING A CHARGE. Ramming home the loading of a piece of ordnance.

DRIVING PILES. The motion of a ship bobbing in a head sea, compared to the vertical fall of monkeys on pile heads.

DROG. A Gaelic term, still in use, to express the agitation of the sea.

DROGHER. A small craft which goes round the bays of the West India Islands, to take off sugars, rum, &c., to the merchantmen.—*Lumber-drogher* is a vessel built solely for burden, and for transporting cotton and other articles coast-wise.

DROGHING. The carrying trade of the West India coasts.

DROITS OF ADMIRALTY. Rights, or rather perquisites, which flowed originally from the king by grant or usage, and now reserved to the crown by commission. They are of two kinds—viz. the civil, or those arising from wrecks of the sea, flotsam, jetsam, and lagan, royal fishes, derelicts, and deodands, ejectamenta maris, and the goods of pirates, traitors, felons, suicides, and fugitives within the admiralty jurisdiction; and the prize droits, or those accruing in the course of war, comprehending all ships and goods taken without commission, all vessels improperly captured before hostilities have been formally declared, or found or by accident brought within the admiralty, salvage for all ships rescued, and all ships seized, in any of the ports, creeks, or roads of the United Kingdom of Great Britain and Ireland before any declaration of war or reprisals by the sovereign.

DROM-FISH. A large fish taken and cured in quantities in the Portuguese harbours of South America, as well for ship's stores as for the times of fast.

DROMON. A Saracen term denoting the large king's ships from the ninth to the fifteenth century.

DROP, or Droop. When a line diverges from a parallel or a curve. It is also a name generally used to the courses, but sometimes given to the depth of the square sails in general; as, "Her main top-sail drops seventeen yards." The depth of a sail from head to foot amidships.—*To drop anchor* is simply to anchor:—underfoot, in calms, a kedge or stream is dropped to prevent drift.

DROP ASTERN, To. To slacken a ship's way, so as to suffer another one to pass beyond her. Also, distancing a competitor.

DROP DOWN A RIVER. Synonymous with *falling* (which see).

DROP-DRY. Completely water-tight.

DROPPING. An old mode of salute by lowering flags or uppermost sails.

DROPS. In ship-building, are small foliages of carved work in the stern munions and elsewhere. The term also means the fall or declivity of a deck, which is generally of several inches.

DROUD. A fish of the cod kind, frequenting the west coast of Scotland.

DROUGES. Quadrilateral pieces of board, sometimes attached to the harpoon line, for the purpose of checking in some degree the speed of the whale.

DROW. An old northern term for a severe gust of wind accompanied with rain.

DROWNED LAND. Extensive marshes or other water-covered districts which were once dry and sound land.

DROWNING. An early naval punishment; Richard I. enacted that whoever killed a man on shipboard, "he should be bound to the corpse, and thrown into the sea."

DROWNING-BRIDGE. A sluice-gate for overflowing meadows.

DROWNING THE MILLER. Adding too much water to wine or spirits; from the term when too much water has been put into a bowl of flour.

DRUB. To beat. (Captain's despatch.) "We have drubbed the enemy."

DRUDGE. A name truly applied to a cabin-boy.

DRUGGERS. Small vessels which formerly exported fish from Dieppe and other Channel ports, and brought back from the Levant spices and drugs.

DRUM. *See* Storm-drum.

DRUM-CAPSTAN. A contrivance for weighing heavy anchors, invented by Sir S. Morland, who died in 1695.

DRUMHEAD COURT-MARTIAL. Sudden court held in the field for the immediate trial of thefts or misconduct. (*See* Provost Martial.)

DRUMHEAD OF CAPSTAN. A broad cylindrical piece of elm, resembling a millstone, and fixed immediately above the barrel and whelps.
On its circumference a number of square holes are cut parallel to the
deck, to receive the bars.

DRUMLER. An ancient transport. (*See* DROMON.) Also, a small
piratical vessel of war.

DRUMMER. The marine who beats the drum, and whose pay is equivalent to that of a private of fourteen years' standing. Also, a singular fish
of the corvinas kind, which has the faculty of emitting musical noises,
whence it has acquired the name of *crocros*.

DRUXY. Timber in a state of decay, the condition of which is manifested
by veins or spots in it of a whitish tint.

DRY-BULB THERMOMETER. The readings of this instrument, when
compared with those of a wet-bulb thermometer, indicate the amount of
moisture in the air, and thence the probability of rain.

DRY DOCK. An artificial receptacle for examining and repairing vessels.
(*See* GRAVING DOCKS.)

DRY DUCKING. Suspending a person by a rope a few yards above the
surface of the water.

DRY FLOGGING. Punishing over the clothes of a culprit.

DRY GALES. Those storms which are accompanied with a clear sky, as
the *northers* of the Gulf of Mexico, the *harmattan* of Africa, &c.

DRY HOLY-STONING. *See* HOLYSTONE.

DRY-ROT. A disease destructive of timber, occasioned by a fungus, the
Merulius lachrymans, which softens wood and finally destroys it; it resembles a dry pithy cottony substance, whence the name dry-rot, though
when in a perfect state, its sinuses contain drops of clear water, which
have given rise to its specific Latin name. Free ventilation and cleanliness appear to be the best preservatives against this costly evil.

DRY ROWING. " Row dry." Not to dash the spray with the blade of
the oar in the faces of those in the stern-sheets.

D. S. Q. Means, in the complete book, discharged to sick quarters.

DUB. A northern term for a pool of deep and smooth water in a rapid
river.

DUBB, To. To smooth and cut off with an adze the superfluous wood.—
To dubb a vessel bright, is to remove the outer surface of the plank completely with an adze. Spotting to examine planks with the adze is also
dubbing.

DUBBAH, OR DUBBER. A coarse leathern vessel for holding liquids in
India.

DUBHE. A standard nautical star in the Great Bear.

DUCAT. A well-known coin in most parts of Europe; the average gold
ducat being nine shillings and sixpence, and the silver three shillings and
fourpence.

DUCATOON. A coin of the Dutch Oriental Isles, of seven shillings.
Also, a silver coin of Venice, value four shillings and eightpence.

DUCK, To. To dive, or immerse another under water; or to avoid a shot.

DUCK. The finest canvas (No. 8) for small sails, is sometimes so called; but it is really a lighter cloth than canvas, and is greatly used by seamen and soldiers on tropical stations for frocks and trousers.

DUCKING. A penalty which veteran sailors inflict on those who, for the first time, pass the tropics, the equator, or formerly even the Straits of Gibraltar; and is usually performed in the grog-tub or half-butt, with the assistance of a few buckets of water; the usual fine, however, always prevents the penalty being inflicted.

DUCKING AT THE YARD-ARM. A marine punishment unknown, except by name, in the British navy; but formerly inflicted by the French for grave offences, thus: the criminal was placed astride a short thick batten, fastened to the end of a rope which passed through a block hanging at the yard-arm. Thus fixed, he was hoisted suddenly up to the yard, and the rope being then slackened at once, he was plunged into the sea. This chastisement was repeated several times; conformable to the sentence, a gun advertised the other ships of the fleet thereof that their crews might become spectators. If the offence was very great, he was drawn underneath the keel of the ship, which was called keel-hauling. (*See* KEEL-HAULING.)

DUCKS. The general name for a sailor's dress in warm climates. Also, the military English of Bombay. *See also* JEMMY DUCKS, the keeper of the poultry on board ship. Dried herrings, or Digby ducks in N. S.

DUCK-UP! A term used by the steersman when the main-sail, fore-sail, or sprit-sail hinders his seeing to steer by a landmark, upon which he calls out, "Duck-up the clue-lines of those sails," that is, haul the sails out of the way. Also, when a shot is made by a chase-piece, if the clue of the sprit-sail hinders the sight, they call out, " Duck-up," &c.

DUDGEON. An old word for the box-handle of a dirk; it is mentioned by Shakspeare with the blade of the ideal dagger which Macbeth saw before him. It also means offence, anger.

DUDS. A cant term for clothes or personal property. The term is old, but still in common use, though usually applied to clothing of an inferior quality, and even rags and tatters.

DUEL. A single combat at a time and place appointed in consequence of a challenge; a practice which had its uses and abuses, now prohibited.

DUELLO. An Italian word expressive of duelling, long appropriated into our language.

DUFF. Pudding or dough.

DUFFERS. Low pedlars; also those women who assist smugglers. Also, cowardly fellows.

DUG-OUT. A canoe.

DUKE OF YORK. A nick-name for a particular storm try-sail used in the northern seas.

DULCE, DULSE, DELSE. *Iridea dulce,* one of the edible fuci. It is an article of trade in America and Holland, and is plentiful on the rocky coasts of Ireland and western England. It probably derived its name from being sweet and pleasant, not requiring cooking.

DULEDGE PLATES. An old name for the tyre-streaks or iron plates on the circumference of the wheel of a field-piece. Duledge was also used for dowel, the wooden pin connecting the felloes.

DULL'D. When said of the wind, fallen or moderated.

DULLISH. The Manx term for the marine eatable leaf *dillisk*.

DUMB-CHALDER. A metal cleat bolted to the back of the stern-post for one of the pintles to rest upon, to lessen both strain and friction. (*See* PINTLE.)

DUMB-CLEAT. Synonymous with *dumb-chalder* and *thumb-cleat*.

DUMB-CRAFT. Lighters, lumps, or punts, not having sails. Also, a name for the screws used for lifting a ship on a slip.

DUMB-PINTLE. A peculiar rudder-strap. (*See* PINTLE.)

DUMB-SCRAPING. Scraping wet decks with blunt scrapers.

DUMFOUNDER. To confuse or perplex.

DUMMY. A wood frame landing-place in front of a pier.

DUMP-BOLT. A short bolt driven in to the plank and timber as a partial security previous to the thorough fastenings being put in.

DUMPS. Nearly synonymous with *down in the mouth*.

DUN. A hill, an eminence.

DUNBAR MEDLAR. A salted herring.

DUNDERHEAD. A term used for the devil, as also for a stupid fellow.

DUN-DIVER. A name for the goosander (*Mergus merganser*) in immature plumage.

DUNES. An Anglo-Saxon word still in use, signifying mounds or ridges of drifted sands. (*See* DOWNS.)

DUN-FISH. A peculiar preparation of cod for the American market, by which it retains a dun or dark yellow colour. Dunning is extensively carried on in the spring at Portsmouth and other places in New Hampshire.

DUNGAREE-DUCK. A name given to a small dried fish in Bombay.

DUNGAREE-STUFF. A blue or striped cotton cloth much worn by the seafaring classes in India.

DUNGIYAH. A broad-beamed flat-bottomed Arabian coaster trading between the Red Sea, Gulf of Persia, and the Malabar coast.

DUN-HEAD. In east-country barges the after-planking which forms the cabin.

DUNKIRKS. The well-known name for pirates who sailed out of Dunkirk.

DUNLIN. The name of a species of sandpiper (*Tringa cinclus*).

DUNN, OR DUIN. A Gaelic word for a fort, a hill, a heap, or a knoll.

DUNNAGE. Loose wood or other substances, as horns, rattan, coir, &c., to stow amongst casks and other cargo to prevent their motion. A vessel dunnages below the dry cargo to keep it from bilge-water.

DUNNAGE BATTENS. An extra floor in a merchantman to preserve the cargo from wet in the event of leakage. They are also used in magazines and sail-rooms so as to form a vacant space beneath the powder-barrels and ceiling.

DUNNAGED. Goods or packages secured with dunnage.

DUNNAGE GRATINGS. Express gratings placed on a steamer's deck to place cargo upon, serving as dunnage.

DUNTER. A northern designation of the porpoise.

DUNTER-GOOSE. A name in the Orkneys for the *Somateria mollissima*, or eider-duck.

DUR-MAST. An inferior oak of more rapid growth than the true English.

DUST. The refuse of biscuit in the bread-room. Also used for money. This term probably got into use in India, where the boat hire on the Ganges was added to by the Ghât-Manjecs, in the way of "Dustooree." Moreover, a tumult or uproar.

DUTCH. Language, or rather gibberish, which cannot be understood by a listener. (*See* DOUBLE DUTCH.)

DUTCH-CAPER. A light-armed vessel of the seventeenth century, adapted for privateering, and much used by the Dutch.

DUTCH CONSOLATION. "Whatever ill befalls you, there's somebody that's worse;" or "It's very unfortunate; but thank God it's no worse."

DUTCH COURAGE. The excitement inspired by drinking spirits; false energy.

DUTCH EEL-SKUYT. A flat-bottomed somewhat cutter-rigged sea-boat, carrying lee-boards, fitted with two water-tight bulkheads, making a well for keeping live fish in, the water being admitted through perforated plates fastened on inside the ribs.

DUTCHIFYING. A term used for converting square sterns to round ones.

DUTCHMAN'S BREECHES. The patch of blue sky often seen when a gale is breaking, is said to be, however small, "enough to make a pair of breeches for a Dutchman." Others assign the habiliment to a Welshman, but give no authority for the assumption.

DUTCH PLAICE. The *Pleuronectes platessa*. When small, it is called fleak; when large, Dutch plaice.

DUTCH PUMP. A punishment so contrived that, if the prisoner would not pump hard, he was drowned.

DUTCH RECKONING. A bad day's work, all in the wrong.

DUTCH REDS. High-smoked herrings prepared in Holland.

DUTIES. Taxes levied by the custom-house upon goods exported or imported.

DUTTEES. Coarse brown calicoes of India.

DUTY. The exercise of those functions which belong to the service, and are carried out from the highest to the lowest.

DWANG-STAFF. This is otherwise the *wrain-staff* (which see).

DYCE. A langridge for the old hail-shot pieces.

DYCE, OR THYST, "VERY WELL DYCE." (*See* THUS.)

DYELLE. A kind of mud-drag used for cleaning rivers on our eastern coasts.

DYING MAN'S DINNER. A snatch of refreshment when the ship is in extreme danger.

DYKE. From the Anglo-Saxon *dic*, a mound or bank; yet in some parts of England the word means a ditch.

DYKE-CAM. A ditch-bank.

DYNAMOMETER. An instrument for measuring the amount of force, and used for indicating the thrust or force of a screw-propeller, or any other motor. There are many, varying in mode according to the express purpose of each, but all founded on the same principle as the name expresses—*power* and *measure*, so that a steel-yard is the simplest exponent.

E.

E. The second class of rating on Lloyd's books for the comparative excellence of merchant ships. (*See* A.)

EAGER. *See* EAGRE.

EAGLE. The insignia of the Romans, borrowed also by moderns, as Frederic of Prussia and Napoleon. Also, a gold coin of the United States, of the value of five dollars, or £1, 0s. 10d. sterling, at the average rate of exchange.

EAGLE, OR SPREAD-EAGLE. A punishment inflicted by *seizing* the offender by his arms and legs to the shrouds, and there leaving him for a specified time.

EAGRE, OR HYGRE. The reciprocation of the freshes of various rivers, as for instance the Severn, with the flowing tide, sometimes presenting a formidable surge. The name seems to be from the Anglo-Saxon *eágor*, water, or *Ægir*, the Scandinavian god of the sea. (*See* BORE and HYGRE.)

EAR. A west-country term for a place where hatches prevent the influx of the tide.

EARING-CRINGLE, AT THE HEAD OF A SAIL. In sailmaking it is an eye spliced in the bolt-rope, to which the much smaller head-rope is attached. The earings are hauled out, or lashed to cleats on the yards passing through the head corners or cringles of the sails.

EARINGS. Certain small ropes employed to fasten the upper corners of a sail to its yard, for which purpose one end of the earing is passed through itself, and the other end is passed five or six times round the yard-arm, and through the cringle; the two first turns, which are intended to stretch the head of the sail tight along the yard, are passed beyond the lift and rigging on the yard-arm, and are called outer turns, while the rest, which draw it close up to the yard, and are passed within the lift, &c., are called inner turns. Below the above are the *reef-earings*, which are used to reef the sail when the reef-tackles have stretched it to take off the strain.

EARNE. *See* ERNE.

EARNEST. A sum paid in advance to secure a seaman's service.

EARS. In artillery the lugs or ear-shaped rings fashioned on the larger bombs or mortar-shells for their convenient handling with shell-hooks. The irregularity of surface caused by the ears is intended to be modified in future construction by the substitution of *lewis-holes* (which see).

EAR-SHOT. The distance or range of hearing.

EARS OF A BOAT. The knee-pieces at the fore-part on the outside at the height of the gunwale.

EARS OF A PUMP. The support of the bolt for the handle or break.

EARTH. One of the primary planets, and the third in order from the sun.

EARTH-BAGS. *See* SAND-BAGS.

EAR-WIGGING. Feeding an officer's ear with scandal against an absent individual.

EASE, To STAND AT. To remain at rest.

EASE AWAY! To slacken out a rope or tackle-fall.

EASE HER! In a steamer, is the command to reduce the speed of the engine, preparatory to "stop her," or before reversing for "turn astern."

EASE OFF! EASE OFF HANDSOMELY, OR EASE AWAY THERE! To slacken out a rope or tackle-fall carefully.

EASE THE HELM! An order often given in a vessel close-hauled, to put the helm down a few spokes in a head sea, with the idea that if the ship's way be deadened by her coming close to the wind she will not strike the opposing sea with so much force. It is thought by some that extreme rolling as well as pitching are checked by shifting the helm quickly, thereby changing the direction of the ship's head, and what is technically called "giving her something else to do."

EASE UP, To. To come up handsomely with a tackle-fall.

EAST. From the Anglo-Saxon, *y'st*. One of the cardinal points of the compass. Where the sun rises due east, it makes equal days and nights, as on the equator.

EAST-COUNTRY. A term applied to the regions bordering on the Baltic.

EAST-COUNTRY SHIPS. The same as *easterlings*.

EASTERLINGS. Traders of the Baltic Sea. Also, natives of the Hanse Towns, or of the east country.

EASTERN AMPLITUDE. An arc of the horizon, intercepted between the point of the sun's rising and the east point of the magnetic compass.

EAST INDIA HOY. A sloop formerly expressly licensed for carrying stores to the E. I. Company's ships.

EASTING. The course made good, or gained, to the eastward.

EASTINTUS. From the Saxon, *east-tyn*, an easterly coast or country. *Leg. Edward I.*

EAST WIND. This, in the British seas, is generally attended with a hazy atmosphere, and is so ungenial as to countenance the couplet—

> "When the wind is in the east,
> 'Tis good for neither man nor beast."

EASY. Lower gently. A ship not labouring in a sea.—*Taking it easy.* Neglecting the duty. "Not so violent."

EASY DRAUGHT. The same as *light draught of water* (which see).

EASY ROLL. A vessel is said to "roll deep but easy" when she moves slowly, and not with quick jerks.

EATING THE WIND OUT OF A VESSEL. Applies to very keen seamanship, by which the vessel, from a close study of her capabilities, steals to windward of her opponent. This to be done effectually demands very peculiar trim to carry weather helm to a nicety.

EAVER. A provincial term for the direction of the wind. A quarter of the heavens.

EBB. The lineal descendant of the Anglo-Saxon *ep-flod*, meaning the falling reflux of the tide, or its return back from the highest of the flood, full sea, or high water. Also termed *sæ-æbbung*, sea-ebbing, by our progenitors.

EBB, Line of. The sea-line of beach left dry by the tide.

EBBER, or Ebber-shore. From the Anglo-Saxon signifying shallow.

EBB-TIDE. The receding or running out of the sea, in contradistinction to flood.

EBONY. A sobriquet for a negro.

ECHELON. [Fr.] Expressing the field-exercise of soldiers, when the divisions are placed in a situation resembling the steps of a ladder, whence the name.

ECHINUS. A word lugged in to signify the sweep of the tiller. (*See* Sea-egg.)

ECLIPSE. An obscuration of a heavenly body by the interposition of another, or during its passage through the shadow of a larger body. An *eclipse of the sun* is caused by the dark body of the moon passing between it and the earth. When the moon's diameter exceeds the sun's, and their centres nearly coincide, a *total eclipse* of the sun takes place; but if the moon's diameter be less, then the eclipse is *annular.*

ECLIPTIC. The great circle of the heavens which the sun appears to us to describe in the course of a year, in consequence of the earth's motion round that luminary. It is inclined to the equinoctial at an angle of nearly 23° 28', called the obliquity of the ecliptic, and cuts it in two points diametrically opposite to each other, called the equinoctial points. The time when the sun enters each of these points (which occurs about the 20th of March and 23d of September, respectively) is termed the equinox, day and night being then equal; at these periods, especially about the time of the vernal equinox, storms, called the equinoctial gales, are prevalent in many parts of the globe. The two points of the ecliptic, which are each 90° distant from the equinoctial points, are called the solstitial points. That great circle which passes through the equinoctial points and the poles of the earth, is called the equinoctial colure; and that which passes through the solstitial points and the poles of the earth, the solstitial colure.

ECLIPTIC CONJUNCTION. Is the moon in conjunction with the sun at the time of new moon, both luminaries having then the same longitude, or right ascension.

ECLIPTIC LIMITS. Certain limits of latitude within which eclipses take place, and beyond which they cannot occur.

ECONOMY. A term expressive of the system and internal arrangement pursued in a ship.

EDDY. Sometimes used for the dead-water under a ship's counter. Also, the water that by some interruption in its course, runs contrary to the direction of the tide or current, and appears like the motion of a whirlpool. Eddies in the sea not unfrequently extend their influence to a great distance, and are then merely regarded as contrary or revolving currents. It is the back-curl of the water to fill a space or vacuum formed sometimes by the faulty build of a vessel, having the after-body fuller than the fore, which therefore impedes her motion. It also occurs immediately after a tide passes a strait, where the volume of water spreads suddenly out, and curves back to the edges. The Chinese pilots call eddies, chow-chow water.

EDDY-TIDE. When the water runs back from some obstacle to the free passage of the stream.

EDDY-WIND. That which is beat back, or returns, from a sail, bluff hill, or anything which impedes its passage; in other words, whenever the edges or veins of two currents of air, coming from opposite directions, meet, they form an eddy, or *whirlwind* (which see). They are felt generally near high coasts intersected by ravines. The eddy-wind of a sail escaping, in a curve, makes the sail abaft shiver.

EDGE AWAY, To. To decline gradually from the course which the ship formerly steered, by sailing larger, or more off, or more away from before the wind than she had done before.

EDGE DOWN, To. To approach any object in an oblique direction.

EDGING OF PLANK. Sawing or hewing it narrower.

EDUCTION PIPE. A pipe leading from the bottom of a steam-cylinder to the upper part of the condenser in a steam-engine.

EEAST. The Erse term for a fish, still used in the Isle of Man.

EEKING. *See* EIKING.

EEL. A well-known fish (*Anguilla vulgaris*), of elongated form, common in rivers and estuaries, and esteemed for food.

EELER. An adept at knowing the haunts and habits of eels, and the methods of taking them.

EEL-FARES. A fry or brood of eels.

EEL-GRASS. A name for the sea-wrack (*Zostera marina*); it is thrown ashore by the sea in large quantities.

EEL-POUT. A name for the burbot (*Molva lota*), a fresh-water fish.

EEL-SKUYT. *See* Dutch Eel-skuyt.

EEL-SPEAR. A sort of trident with ten points for catching eels, called in Lincolnshire an *eel-stang*.

EFFECTIVE. Efficient, fit for service; it also means the being present and at duty.

EFFECTS. Personal property; sale of effects; or the auction of the property of deceased officers and seamen:

> "The *effects* of that sail
> Will be a sale of *effects*."

EFFLUENT, or Divergent, applied to any stream which runs out of a lake, or out of another river. All tributaries are affluents.

EGG, To. To instigate, incite, provoke, to urge on: from the Anglo-Saxon *eggion*.

EGGS. These nutritious articles of food might be used longer at sea than is usual. The shell of the egg abounds with small pores, through which the aqueous part of the albumen constantly exhales, and the egg in consequence daily becomes lighter, and approaches its decomposition. Reaumur varnished them all over, and thus preserved eggs fresh for two years; then carefully removing the varnish, he found that such eggs were still capable of producing chickens. Some employ, with the same intention, lard or other fatty substance for closing the pores, and others simply immerse the egg for an instant in boiling water, by which its albumen is in part coagulated, and the power of exhalation thereby checked. Eggs packed in lime-water suffered to drain, have after three years' absence in the West Indies been found good; this does not destroy vitality.

EGMONT, or Port Egmont Fowls. The large Antarctic gulls with dark-brown plumage, called *shoemakers*.

EGRESS. At a transit of an inferior planet over the sun, this term means the passing off of the planet from his disc.

EGYPTIAN HERRING. A northern coast name for the gowdanook, saury-pike, or *Scomberesox saurus*.

EIDER DUCK. The *Somateria mollissima*. A large species of duck, inhabiting the coasts of the northern seas. The down of the breast, with which it lines its nest, is particularly valuable on account of its softness and lightness.

EIGHEN. The index of the early quadrant.

EILET-HOLE [Fr. *œillet*]. *Refer to* Eyelet-hole.

EJECTAMENTA MARIS. Sea products thrown on the beach, whence they become droits of admiralty. (*See* Jetsom.)

EKE, To. [Anglo-Saxon *edcan*, to prolong.] To make anything go far by reduction and moderation, as in shortening the allowance of provisions on a voyage unexpectedly tedious.

EKEING. A piece of wood fitted, by scarphing or butting, to make good a deficiency in length, as the end of a knee and the like. The *ekeing* is also the carved work under the lower part of the quarter-piece, at the aft part of the quarter-gallery.

ELBOW. That part of a river where it suddenly changes its direction, forming a reach to the next angle or turn. Also, a promontory. Also, a communication in a steam-pipe.

ELBOW-GREASE. Hard labour with the arms.

ELBOW IN THE HAWSE. Two crosses in a hawse. When a ship, being moored in a tideway, swings twice the wrong way, thereby causing the cables to take half a round turn on each other. (*See* HAWSE.)

ELDEST. The old navy term for *first*, as applied to the senior lieutenant.

ELEMENTS. The first principles of any art or science.—The *elements of an orbit* are certain proportions which define the path of a heavenly body in space, and enable the astronomer to calculate its position for past or future times.

ELEPHANTER. A heavy periodical rain of Bombay.

ELEPHANT-FISH. The *Chimœra callorynchus*, named from the proboscis-like process on its nose. Though inferior to many other fish, it is yet palatable food.

ELEVATE! In great-gun exercise, the order which prepares for adjusting the quoin.

ELEVATED POLE. That terrestrial pole which is above the horizon of a spectator.

ELEVATION, IN SHIPBUILDING. A vertical and longitudinal view of a vessel, synonymous with *sheer-draught* and *sheer-plan*. In other words, it is the orthographic design whereon the heights and lengths are expressed.

ELEVATION, ANGLE OF. In gunnery, that which the axis of the bore makes with the plane of the horizon. It is attained by sinking the breech of the gun until its axis points above the object to be fired at, so that the shot may describe a curve somewhat similar to a parabola, counteracting the action of gravity during its flight, and alighting upon the mark.

ELGER. An eel-spear, *Promptorium Parvulorum*, yielding many together.

ELIGUGS. Aquatic birds of passage of the auk kind on our western coasts; called also razor-bills.

ELITE. The élite of naval or military forces is the choicest selection from them.

ELLECK. The trivial name of the *Trigla cuculus*.

ELLIOT-EYE. The Elliot-eye, introduced by the Hon. Admiral Elliot, secretary of the Admiralty, is an eye worked over an iron thimble in the end of a hempen bower-cable, to facilitate its being shackled to the chain for riding in very deep water.

ELLIPSE. In geometry, an oval figure, formed of the section of a cone by a plane cutting through both its sides obliquely.

ELMO'S FIRE, ST. *See* Compasant.

ELONGATION. The angular distance of a heavenly body from the sun eastward or westward.

ELVERS. The name of eels on the western coasts of England.

EMBARGO. A temporary injunction or arrest laid on ships or merchandise by public authority, sometimes general, to prevent all ships departing, and sometimes partial, as upon foreign ships only, or to prevent their coming in. A breach of embargo, under the knowledge of the insured, discharges the underwriters from liability.

EMBARK, To. To go on board, or to put on board a vessel.

EMBARKATION. Applies to the shipping of goods, troops, and stores. Also, the peculiar boats of a country. [Sp. *embarcation.*]

EMBARMENT. An old term, meaning an embargo.

EMBARRAS. An American term for places where the navigation of rivers or creeks is rendered difficult by the accumulation of drift-wood, trees, &c.

EMBATTLE. To arrange forces for conflict.

EMBATTLED. In buildings, crenellated or pierced with loop-holes.

EMBEDDED. Firmly fixed in the mud or sand.

EMBER-GOOSE (or Imber?). A name for the great northern diver or loon (*Colymbus glacialis*).

EMBEZZLEMENT, or simple theft, by persons belonging to a merchant ship, is not deemed a peril of the sea. But robbery violently committed by persons not belonging to the ship, is a peril for which the insurer is answerable.—*To embezzle* is to misappropriate by a breach of trust.

EMBOUCHURE. A French word adopted as signifying the mouth of a river, by which its waters are discharged, or by which it is entered. The term is now in general use.

EMBRASURES. The cut or opening made through the parapet of a battery for the muzzle of the gun and the passage of the shot.

EMERALDERS. A term for the natives of Ireland, from its evergreen verdure.

EMERGENCY. Imminent want in difficult circumstances.

EMERSION. The prismatic space or solid raised out on the weather side by the inclination of the ship. In astronomy it signifies the re-appearance of a celestial object after undergoing occultation or eclipse.

EMINENCE. A high or rising ground overlooking the country around.

EMISSARY. A culvert or drain.

EMPRISE. A hazardous attempt upon the enemy.

EMPTIONS. Stores purchased.

EMPTY. Cargo discharged.

EMPTY BASTION. In fortification is a bastion whereof the terreplein, or terrace in rear of the parapet, not having been carried farther to the rear than its regular distance, leaves a large space within it of a lower level.

EMPTY BOTTLE. *See* Marine Officer.

ENCAMPMENT. *See* CAMP.

ENCEINTE. [Fr.] A slightly bastioned wall or rampart line of defence, which sometimes surrounds the body of a place; when only flanked by turrets it is called a Roman wall.

ENCIRCLING REEFS. A name given to a form of coral reef, the architecture of myriads of zoophytes in tropical seas.

ENCOUNTER. The hostile meeting of two ships or squadrons; also, a conflict between troops.

ENDANGER, To. To expose to peril.

ENDECAGON. In geometry, a plane figure of eleven sides and angles.

ENDELONG. The old English word for lengthways.

END FOR END. Reversing cordage, casks, logs, spars, &c.—To shift a rope *end for end*, as in a tackle, the fall is made the standing part, and the standing part becomes the fall; or when a rope runs out all a block, and is unreeved; or in coming to an anchor, if the stoppers are not well put on, and the cable runs all out end for end. (*See* AN-END.)

END OF A TRENCH. The place where the trenches are opened.

END-ON. Said particularly of a ship when only her bows and head-sails are to be seen, but generally used in opposition to *broadside-on*.

ENEMY. The power or people against whom war is waged.

ENFIELD RIFLE. The name of the present regulation musket for infantry, as made at the government works at Enfield, on an improvement of the Minié principle; whether the breach-loading rifle, which it is intended to substitute for this arm, will acquire the same title, remains to be determined.

ENFILADE FIRE. Is that which sweeps a line of works or men from one end to the other; it is on land nearly the equivalent to "raking fire" at sea.

ENGAGEMENT. In a naval sense, implies a battle at sea, or an action of hostility between single ships, squadrons, or fleets of men-of-war. Also, a conflict between two contending armies.

ENGINE, MARINE. (*See* STEAM-ENGINE.) Engine was of old a military machine for warfare.

ENGINE-BEARERS. Sleepers, or pieces of timber placed between the keelson, in a steamer, and the boilers of the steam-engine, to form a proper seat for the boilers and machinery.

ENGINEER. A duly qualified officer appointed to plan and direct the attack or defence of a fortification, as well as the construction of fortified works. Engineers are also persons in charge of the machinery of steam-vessels. In government steamers they are in three classes, under warrant from the admiralty.

ENGINE-ROOM TELEGRAPH. A dial-contrivance by which the officer on deck can communicate with the engineer below.

ENGLAND EXPECTS EVERY MAN WILL DO HIS DUTY. This is introduced into a naval vocabulary, not as wanting explanation, but that in recording the most remarkable signal ever made to a fleet, we may remind the tyro, that these words of Nelson are admirably adapted for all the varying changes of sea-life, whether in times of war or peace.

ENGLISH. A term applied to the vessels and men of the whole empire, and its maritime population. "Indeed," says Burke in a letter to Admiral Keppel, "I am perfectly convinced that *Englishman* and *seaman* are names that must live and die together."

ENLARGE. The wind is said to enlarge when it veers from the side towards the stern.

ENLISTMENT. The engaging recruits for the army or marines.

ENNEAGON. A figure that has nine sides and as many angles.

ENNIS, or INNIS. A term for island on the west coast of Ireland and in some parts of Scotland.

ENROL, To. To enter the name on the roll of a corps.

ENSCONCE, To. To intrench; to protect by a slight fortification.

ENSENADA [Sp. bay]. This term is frequently used on the coasts of Chili and Peru.

ENSIGN. [From the Anglo-Saxon *segn.*] A large flag or banner, hoisted on a long pole erected over the stern, and called the ensign-staff. It is used to distinguish the ships of different nations from each other, as also to characterize the different squadrons of the navy; it was formerly written *ancient.* Ensign is in the army the title of the junior rank of subaltern officers of infantry; from amongst them are detailed the officers who carry the colours.

ENTERING at CUSTOM-HOUSE. The forms required of the master of a merchant ship before her cargo can be discharged.

ENTERING-LADDERS. Are of two sorts; one of them being used by the vessel's side in harbour or in fair weather, the other is made of ropes, with small staves for steps, and is hung out of the gallery to come aboard by, when the sea runs so high as to risk staving the boat if brought alongside; the latter are termed stern-ladders.

ENTERING-PORTS. Ports cut down on the middle gun-deck of three-deckers, to serve as door-ways for persons going in and out of the ship.

ENTERING-ROPES, or SIDE-ROPES. Three are sometimes used to aid in climbing the ship's side. They hang from the upper part on the right, left, and middle of the steps. (*See* GANGWAY.) The upper end of an entering-rope is rove through an eye in the iron stanchion at the gangway; it is walled, crowned, and otherwise ornamentally fitted.

ENTERPRISE. An undertaking of difficulty and danger.

ENTRANCE. A term for the bow of a vessel, or form of the *fore-body* under the load-water line; it expresses the figure of that which encounters the sea, and is the opposite of *run.* Also, the first appearance of a person on board after entry on the ship's books. Also, the forefoot of a ship. Also, the mouth of a harbour.

ENTRANCE MONEY. Payment on entering a mess.

ENTRY. In the ship's books; first putting down the appearance or day on which a man joins. Also, the forcing into an enemy's ship.

ENVELOPE. In astronomy, a band of light encircling the head of a comet on the side near the sun, and passing round it, so as to form the commencement of the tail.—In fortification, a work of single lines thrown up to inclose a weak ground; usually a mere earth-work.

EPAULE, OR SHOULDER. In fortification, that part of a bastion adjacent to the junction of a face with a flank. The actual meeting of these two lines forms the "angle of the shoulder."

EPAULEMENT. In fortification, a covering mass raised to protect from the fire of the enemy, but differing from a parapet in having no arrangement made for the convenient firing over it by defenders. It is usually adopted for side-passages to batteries and the like.

EPAULET. The bullion or mark of distinction worn on the shoulders by officers, now common to many grades, but till recently worn only by captains and commanders, whence the brackish poet—

> "Hail, magic power that fills an *epaulet*,
> No wonder hundreds for thee daily fret!"

the meaning of which is now pointless.

EPHEMERIS, OR NAUTICAL ALMANAC. This in its wide sense, and recognizing its value to navigators and astronomers, must be pronounced one of the most useful of publications. How Drake and Magellan got on is matter of marvel, for sailors were not especially administered to till 1675, when the *Kalendarium Nauticum*, by Henry Seaman, Mariner, appeared; it comprised the usual matter of annual almanacs, and was enriched with such precepts and rules in the practice of navigation and traffic as are in daily use. But in 1767 our nautical almanac, a tabular statement of the geocentric planetary positions, which may be said to have created a new era in voyaging, was published; and this book, with certain alterations, was in force up to 1830, when a commission of the Royal Society and astronomers established the present *Ephemeris*, now so much valued. It is published annually, but computed to four years in advance, to accommodate those proceeding on long voyages. Attempts have been made in other countries to publish *The Nautical Almanac*, improved and corrected, but they are mere copies, corrected by the errata furnished annually in advance.

EPICYCLOID. A geometrical curve generated by making a circle roll upon the circumference of another circle; it is found useful in determining the figure of the teeth of wheel-work, and other purposes in mechanics. If the generating circle proceeds along the convexity of the periphery, it is called an upper or exterior epicycloid; if along the concavity, a lower or interior epicycloid.

EPOCH. The time to which certain given numbers or quantities apply.

EPROUVETTE. A small piece of ordnance specially fitted for testing the projectile force of samples of gunpowder.

EQUATED ANOMALY. This is also called the true anomaly, and is the distance of the sun from the apogee, or a planet from its aphelion, seen from the sun.

EQUATION, Annual. *See* Annual Equation.

EQUATION OF EQUINOXES. The difference between the mean and apparent places of the equinox.

EQUATION OF THE CENTRE. The difference between the true and mean anomalies of a planet.

EQUATION OF TIME. The difference between mean and apparent time, or the acceleration or retardation of the sun's return to the meridian.

EQUATOR. Called also the equinoctial line, or simply the line, being an imaginary circle round the earth, dividing the globe into two equal parts, and equally distant from both poles. Extended to the heavens, it forms a circle called the celestial equator, which in like manner divides the heavens into two equal parts, the northern and southern hemispheres.

EQUATORIAL CURRENT. The set, chiefly westerly, so frequently met with near the equator, especially in the Atlantic Oceans.

EQUATORIAL DOLDRUMS. *See* Doldrums.

EQUATORIAL SECTOR. An instrument of large radius for finding the difference in the right ascension and declination of two heavenly bodies.

EQUATORIAL TELESCOPE. A glass so mounted that it enables the observer to follow the stars as they move equatorially.

EQUES AURATUS. An heraldic term for a knight.

EQUILATERAL TRIANGLE. A figure of three equal straight sides, and therefore of three equal angles.

EQUINOCTIAL. Synonymous with *equator* (which see).

EQUINOCTIAL GALES. Storms which are observed to prevail about the time of the sun's crossing the equator, at which time there is equal day and night throughout the world.

EQUINOCTIAL POINTS. *See* Ecliptic.

EQUINOXES. The two points of intersection of the ecliptic and the equator; so called, because on the sun's arrival at either of them, the night is everywhere equal in length to the day.

EQUIP, To. A term frequently applied to the business of fitting a ship for a trading voyage, or arming her for war. (*See* Fitting.)

EQUIPAGE. An admiral's retinue. Camp equipage consists of tents, furniture, cooking utensils, &c.

EQUIPMENT. The complete outfit of an officer.

EQUITABLE TITLE. Either this, or a legal claim, are absolutely necessary to establish an insurable interest in a ship or cargo. (*See* Qualified Property.)

ERIGONE. A name sometimes applied to the constellation Virgo.

ERNE. From the Anglo-Saxon *earne*, a vulture, a bird of the eagle kind. Now used to denote the sea-eagle.

ERRATIC WINDS. *See* Variable Winds.

ESCALADE. The forcing a way over a rampart or other defence, properly by means of ladders or other contrivances for climbing.

ESCAPE-VALVES. In marine engines. (*See* Cylinder Escape-valves.)

ESCARP. In fortification, that steep bank or wall immediately in front of and below the rampart, which is thus secured against being directly stormed by a superior force; it is generally the inner side of the ditch.

ESCHEATOR, The King's. An officer at the exchequer of very ancient establishment, under the lord-treasurer, whose business it is to inform of escheats and casual profits of the crown, and to seize them into the king's hands.

ESCORT. A guard of troops attending an individual by way of distinction. Also, a guard placed over prisoners on a march.

ESCUTCHEON. The compartment in the middle of the ship's stern, where her name is written. [Derived from *ex-scutum*.]

ESKIPPAMENTUM. An archaism for tackle or ship-furniture.

ESKIPPER. Anglo-Norman to ship, and *eskipped* was used for shipped.

ESKIPPESON. An old law term for a shipping or passage by sea.

ESNECCA. In the twelfth century, a royal yacht, though some deem it to have been a kind of transport.

ESPIALS. Night watches afloat, in dockyards and harbours; generally a boat named by the ordinary.

ESPLANADE. Generally that space of level ground kept vacant between the works of a fortress and neighbouring houses or other obstructions; though originally applied to the actual surface of the glacis.

ESQUIMAUX. A name derived from *esquimantsic*, in the Albinaquis language, *eaters of raw flesh*. Many tribes in the Arctic regions are still ignorant of the art of cookery.

ESSARA. The prickly heat.

ESTABLISHMENT. The regulated complement or quota of officers and men to a ship, either in time of war or peace. The equipment. The regulated dimensions of spars, cabin, rigging, &c.—*Establishment of a port.* An awkward phrase lately lugged in to denote the tide-hour of a port.

ESTIVAL. *See* Æstival.

ESTOC. A small stabbing sword.

ESTUARY. An inlet or shoaly arm of the sea into which a river or rivers empty, and subject to tidal influence.

ESTURE. An old word for the rise and fall of water.

ETESIAN WINDS. The *Etesiæ* of the ancients; winds which blow constantly every year during the time of the dog-days in the Levant.

ETIQUETTE. Naval or military observances, deemed to be law.

EUPHROE. *See* Uvrou.

EVACUATE. To withdraw from a town or fortress, in virtue of a treaty or capitulation; or in compliance with superior orders.

EVECTION. A term for the libration of the moon, or that apparent oscillatory inequality in her motion, caused by a change in the excentricity of her orbit, whereby her mean longitude is sometimes increased or diminished to the amount of 1° 20′, whereby we sometimes see a little further round one side than at others.

EVE-EEL. A northern name for the conger; from the Danish *hav-aal,* or sea-eel.

EVENING GUN. The warning-piece, after the firing of which the sentries challenge.

EVEN KEEL. When a ship is so trimmed as to sit evenly upon the water, drawing the same depth forward as aft. Some vessels sail best when brought by the head, others by the stern.

EVERY INCH OF THAT! An exclamation to belay a rope without rendering it.

EVERY MAN TO HIS STATION. *See* STATION.

EVERY ROPE AN END. The order to coil down the running rigging, or braces and bowlines, after tacking, or other evolution. Also, the order, when about to perform an evolution, to see that every rope is clear for running.

EVERY STITCH SET. All possible canvas spread.

EVOLUTION. The change of form and disposition during manœuvres, whether of men or ships; movements which should combine celerity with precision and regularity.

EWAGE. An old law term meaning the toll paid for water-passage.

EXALTATION. A planet being in that sign in which it is supposed to exert its utmost influence.

EXAMINATION. A searching by, or cognizance of, a magistrate, or other authorized officer. Now strict in navy and army.

EXCENTRIC. In a steam-engine, a wheel placed on the crank-shaft, having its centre on one side of the axis of the shaft, with a notch for the *gab-lever.*

EXCENTRIC ANOMALY. An auxiliary angle employed to abridge the calculations connected with the motion of a planet or comet in an elliptic orbit.

EXCENTRICITY. In astronomical parlance, implies the deviation of an elliptic orbit from a circle.

EXCENTRIC ROD, by its action on the gab-lever, which it catches either way, puts the engine into gear.

EXCHANGE. A term in the mercantile world, to denote the bills by which remittances are made from one country to another, without the transmission of money. The removal of officers from one ship to another. Also, a mutual agreement between contending powers for exchange of prisoners.

EXCHEQUERED. Seized by government officers as contraband. Marked with the broad arrow. It also refers to proceedings on the part of the crown against an individual in the Exchequer Court, where suits for debts or duties due to the crown are brought.

EXECUTION. The Lords of the Admiralty have a right to issue their warrant, and direct the time and manner, without any special warrant from the crown for that purpose.— *Military execution* is the ravaging and destroying of a country that refuses to pay contribution.

EXECUTIVE BRANCH. The commissioned and working officers of the ship, as distinguished from the civilian branch.

EXERCISE. The practice of all those motions, actions, and management of arms, whereby men are duly trained for service. Also, the practice of loosing, reefing, and furling sails.—*Exercise*, in naval tactics, may be applied to the forming a fleet into order of sailing, line of battle, &c. The French term is *évolutions* or *tactiques*, and may be defined as the execution of the movements which the different orders and disposition of fleets occasionally require, and which the several ships are directed to perform by means of signals. (*See* SIGNAL.)

EX LEX. An outlaw (a term of law).

EXPANSION-VALVE. In the marine engine, a valve which shuts off the steam in its passage to the slide-valves, when the piston has travelled a certain distance in the cylinder, leaving the remaining part of the stroke to be performed by the expansion of the steam.

EXPEDIENT. A stratagem in warfare.

EXPEDITION. An enterprise undertaken either by sea or land, or both, against an enemy; it should be conducted with secrecy and rapidity of movement.

EXPENDED. Used up, consumed, or asserted to be so.

EXPENSE BOOKS. Accounts of the expenditure of the warrant officer's stores, attested by the signing officers.

EXPLOITING. Transporting trees or timber by a river. Exploit was an old verb meaning to perform.

EXPLORATOR. An examiner of a country. A scout.

EXPORT, To. To send goods or commodities out of a country, for the purposes of traffic, under the general name of exports.

EXPORTATION. The act of sending exports to foreign parts.

EXPORTER. The person who sends the exports abroad.

EXPOSED ANCHORAGE. An open and dangerous place, by reason of the elements or the enemy.

EXTERIOR SIDE. The side of an imaginary polygon, upon which the plan of a fortification is constructed.

EXTERIOR SLOPE. In fortification, that slope of a work towards the country which is next outward beyond its superior slope.

EXTERNAL CONTACT. In a transit of Mercury or Venus over the sun's disc, this expression means the first touch of the planet's and sun's edges, before any part of the former is projected on the disc of the luminary.

EXTRAORDINARIES. Contingent expenses.

EXTREME BREADTH. The extent of the midships, or dead flat, with the thickness of the bottom plank included.

EXTREMITIES. The stem and stern posts of a ship.

EY. *See* EYGHT.

EYE. The circular loop of a shroud or stay where it goes over the mast. —*To eye*, to observe minutely.—*Flemish eye*, a phrase particularly applied to the eye of a stay, which is either formed at the making of the rope; or by dividing the yarns into two equal parts, knotting each pair separately, and pointing the whole over after parcelling. This eye stopped by the mouse forms the collar. It is not strong, soon rots, and seldom, if ever, used now where strength is of more importance than neatness.

EYE-BOLTS. Those which have an eye or opening in one end, for hooking tackles to, or fastening ropes.

EYELET-HOLES, are necessary in order to bend a sail to its yard or boom, or to reef it; they consist of round holes worked in a sail to admit a cringle or small rope through, chiefly the robans (or rope-bands), and the points of the reef-line. (*See* SAIL.)

EYE OF A BLOCK-STROP. That part by which it is fastened or suspended to any particular place upon the sails, masts, or rigging; the eye is sometimes formed by making two eye-splices, termed lashing eyes, on the ends of the strop, and then seizing them together with a small line, so as to bind both round a mast, yard, or boom, as is deemed necessary.

EYE OF AN ANCHOR. The hole in the shank wherein the ring is fixed.

EYE OF A STAY. That part of a stay which is formed into a sort of collar to go round the mast-head; the eye and mouse form the collar.

EYE OF THE WIND. The direction to windward from whence it blows. (*See* WIND'S-EYE.)

EYE-SHOT. Within sight.

EYES OF A MESSENGER. Eyes spliced in its ends to lash together.

EYES OF A SHIP. (*See* EYES OF HER.)

EYES OF HER. The foremost part of the bay, or in the bows of a ship. In olden times, and now in Spanish and Italian boats, as well as Chinese junks, an eye is painted on each bow. The hawse-holes also are deemed the "eyes of her."

EYE-SORE. Any disagreeable object.

EYE-SPLICE. (*See* SPLICED-EYE.) A kind of splice made by turning the end of a rope back, and the strands passed through the standing part.—*Eye of a splice*, the strand turned up, by the fid or marline spike, to receive the opposite strand.

EYGHT. An alluvian river-island, where osiers usually grow, called also *ait, ayt, ey, eyet,* or *eyot.* Also, the thickest part of a scule of herrings; when this is scattered by the fishermen, it is termed "breaking the ey."

F.

FACE. The edge of a sharp instrument. Also, the word of command to soldiers, marines, and small-arm men, to turn upon the heel a quarter or half a circle round in the direction ordered.

FACED. Turned up with facings on the cuffs and collars of uniforms and regimentals.

FACE OF A GUN. The surface of the metal at the extremity of the muzzle.

FACE-PIECE. A piece of elm tabled on to the knee of the head, in the fore-part, to assist the conversion of the main piece; and likewise to shorten the upper bolts, and prevent the cables from rubbing against them as the knee gets worn.

FACES OF A WORK. In fortification, are the two lines forming its most prominent salient angle.

FACHON. An Anglo-Norman term for a sword or falchion.

FACING. Letting one piece of timber into another with a rabbet to give additional strength or finish. Also, a movement for forming soldiers and small-arm men.—*Facings.* The front of regimentals and uniforms.

FACK. *See* FAKE.

FACTOR. A commercial superintendent, or agent residing beyond sea, commissioned by merchants to buy or sell goods on their account by a letter of attorney.

FACTORAGE. A certain percentage paid to the factor by the merchant on all he buys or sells.

FACTORY. A place where a considerable number of factors reside; as Lisbon, Leghorn, Calcutta, &c. Factory comprehends the business of a firm or company, as that of the India Company at Canton, or the Hudson's Bay Fur Company in North America.

FACULÆ. Luminous streaks upon the disc of the sun, among which the maculæ, or dark spots, usually appear.

FADOME. The old form used for *fathom* (which see).

FAFF, To. To blow in flaws.

FAG, To. To tire.—*A fag.* A deputy labouring-man, or one who works hard for another.

FAG-END. Is the end of any rope. This term is also applied to the end of a rope when it has become untwisted.

FAGGOTS. Men who used to be hired to answer to names on the books, when the crew were mustered by the clerk of the cheque. Such cheating was once still more prevalent in the army.

FAGOT. A billet for stowing casks. A *fascine* (which see).

FAG-OUT, To. To wear out the end of a rope or end of canvas.

FAIK, OR FALK. A name in the Hebrides for the sea-fowl razor-bill (*Alca torda*).

FAIR. A general term for the wind when favourable to a ship's course, in opposition to contrary or foul; *fair* is more comprehensive than *large*, since it includes about 16 points, whereas large is confined to the beam or quarter, that is, to a wind which crosses the keel at right angles, or obliquely from the stern, but never to one right astern. (*See* LARGE and SCANT.)—*Fair*, in shipbuilding, denotes the evenness or regularity of a curve or line.—*To fair*, means to clip the timbers fair.

FAIR-CURVE. In delineating ships, is a winding line whose shape is varied according to the part of the ship it is intended to describe. This curve is not answerable to any of the figures of conic sections, although it occasionally partakes of them all.

FAIRING. Sheering a ship in construction. Also, the draught of a ship. To run off a great number of different lines or curves, in order to ascertain the fairness in point of curvature of every part, and the beauty of the whole.

FAIR-LEAD. Is applied to ropes as suffering the least friction in a block, when they are said to lead fair.

FAIR-LEADER. A thimble or cringle to guide a rope. A strip of board with holes in it, for running-rigging to lead through, and be kept clear, so as to be easily distinguished at night.

FAIR-MAID. A west-country term for a dried pilchard.

FAIR-WAY. The navigable channel of a harbour for ships passing up or down; so that if any vessels are anchored therein, they are said to lie in the fair-way. (*See* PILOT'S FAIR-WAY.) Also, when the proper course is gained out of a channel.

FAIR-WEATHER. That to which a ship may carry the small sails.

FAKE. One of the circles or windings of a cable or hawser, as it lies disposed in a coil. (*See* COILING.) The fakes are greater or smaller in proportion to the space which a cable is allowed to occupy.

FALCON. In early times a small cannon, having a length of about 7 feet, a diameter of bore of 3 inches, and throwing a ball of nearly 3 lbs. weight, with a point-blank range of 130 paces, and a random one of 1500.

FALCONET. A primitive cannon smaller than the falcon; it threw a ball of $1\frac{1}{2}$ lb.

FALK. *See* FAKE.

FALL. A vertical descent of a river through a narrow rocky pass, or over a ledge, to the impediment of navigation. Also, the loose end of a tackle, or that part to which the power is applied in hoisting, and on which the people pull. Also, in shipbuilding, the descent of a deck from a fair-curve lengthwise, as frequently seen in merchantmen and yachts, to give height to the commander's cabin, and sometimes forward at the hawse-holes. Also, a large cutting down of timber. Also, North American English for autumn, when the navigation of northern inland waters is about to close till the succeeding spring.

FALL, To. A town or fortress is said to fall when it is compelled to surrender to besiegers.

FALL ABOARD OF, To. To strike another vessel, or have a collision with it. Usually applied to the motion of a disabled ship coming in contact with another.

FALL! A FALL! The cry to denote that the harpoon has been effectively delivered into the body of a whale.

FALL ASTERN, To. To lessen a ship's way so as to allow another to get ahead of her. To be driven backwards.

FALL BACK, To.   To recede from any position previously occupied.

FALL CALM, To.   Speaking of the weather, implies a total cessation of the wind.

FALL CLOUD.   *See* STRATUS.

FALL DOWN, To.   To sail, drift, or be towed to some lower part nearer a river's mouth or opening.

FALLEN-STAR.   A name for the jelly-fish or *medusa*, frequently thrown ashore in summer and autumn.

FALL FOUL OF, To.   To reprimand severely.   (*See* FALL ABOARD OF.)

FALL IN, To.   The order to form, or take assigned places in ranks.   (*See* ASSEMBLY.)

FALLING GLASS.   When the mercury of the barometer is sinking in the tube.

FALLING HOME.   When the top-sides are inclined within the perpendicular; opposite of *wall-sided*.   (*See* TUMBLING HOME.)

FALLING OFF.   The opposite of *griping*, or *coming up to the wind;* it is the movement or direction of the ship's head to leeward of the point whither it was lately directed, particularly when she sails near the wind, or lies by.   Also, the angle contained between her nearest approach to the direction of the wind, and her furthest declination from it when *trying*.

FALLING OUT.   When the top-sides project beyond a perpendicular, as in flairing.

FALLING STARS.   Meteors which have very much the appearance of real stars.   They were falsely regarded as foreboders of wind, as Seneca in *Hippolytus*, "Ocior cursum rapiente flamma stella cum ventis agitata longos porrigit ignes."   Some are earthy, others metallic.

FALLING TIDE, OR EBB OF TIDE.   This phrase, implying a previous flow of tide towards high-water, requires here only a partial explanation: the sea, after swelling for about six hours, and thus entering the mouths of rivers, and rising along the sea-shore more or less, according to the moon's age and other circumstances, rests for a quarter of an hour, and then retreats or ebbs during the next six hours.   After a similar pause the phenomenon recommences,—occupying altogether about twelve hours and fifty minutes.   A table of the daily time of high-water at each port is requisite for the shipping.   There are curious variations to this law, as when strong rivers rise and fall, and yet do not admit salt water.   Their currents, indeed, of fresh water, are found far off the land, as in the Tiber, and off several in the West Indies, South America, &c.   (*See* TIDES.)

FALL IN WITH, To.   To meet, when speaking of a ship; to discover, when speaking of the land.

FALL OF TIDE.   An ebb.

FALL OUT, To.   To increase in breadth.   Among soldiers and small-arm men, to quit the ranks of a company.

FALLS.   When a ship is not flush, this is the term given to those risings of some parts of her decks (which she may have) more than others.

FALL-WIND. A sudden gust.

FALMADAIR. An old word signifying rudder, or a pilot.

FALSE ALARM. *See* ALARM.

FALSE ATTACK. A feigned assault, made to induce a diversion or distraction of the enemy's forces, in order that the true object elsewhere may be carried.

FALSE COLOURS. To sail under false colours and chase is an allowable stratagem of war, but firing under them is not permitted by the maritime law of England.

FALSE FIRE, BLUE FLAMES. A composition of combustibles filled into a wooden tube, which, upon being set fire to, burns with a light blue flame from a half to several minutes. They are principally used as night-signals, but often to deceive an enemy.

FALSE KEEL. A kind of supplemental or additional keel secured under the main one, to protect it should the ship happen to strike the ground.

FALSE KELSON, OR KELSON RIDER. A piece of timber wrought longitudinally above the main kelson.

FALSE MUSTER. An incorrect statement of the crew on the ship's books, which if proved subjects the captain to cashiering.

FALSE PAPERS. Frequently carried by slavers and smugglers.

FALSE POST. *See* FALSE STERN-POST.

FALSE RAIL. A thin plank fayed at the head-rails as a strengthener.

FALSE STEM. A hard timber fayed to the fore-part of the main stem, its tail covering the fore-end of the keel. (*See* CUTWATER.)

FALSE STERN. An additional stern fixed on the main one, to increase the length and improve the appearance of a vessel.

FALSE STERN-POST. A piece bolted to the after-edge of the main stern-post to improve steerage, and protect it should the ship tail aground.

FAMILY-HEAD. When the stem was surmounted with several full-length figures, as was the custom many years ago.

FAMLAGH. The Erse or Manx term for oar or ore weed, wrack, or manure of sea-weed.

FANAL [Fr.] A lighthouse.

FANCY-LINE. A line rove through a block at the jaws of a gaff, used as a down-haul. Also, a line used for cross-hauling the lee topping-lift. Also, a cord laid up neatly for sashed cabin-windows. Sometimes used for *tracing-line*.

FANE. An old term for weather-cock : "a fayne of a schipe." (*See* VANE.)

FANG, To. To pour water into a pump in order to fetch it, when otherwise the boxes do not hold the water left on them.

FANGS. The valves of the pump-boxes.

FANIONS. Small flags used in surveying stations, named after the bannerets carried by horse brigades, and corrupted from the Italian word *gonfalone*, a standard.

FANNAG-VARRY. The Erse term for a shag or cormorant, still in use on our north-western shores, and in the Isle of Man.

FANNING. The technical phrase for breadthening the after-part of the tops. Also, widening in general.

FANNING-BREEZE. One so gentle that the sail alternately swells and collapses.

FANTODS. A name given to the fidgets of officers, who are styled jib-and-staysail Jacks.

FARDAGE. Dunnage; when a ship is laden in bulk.

FARE [Anglo-Saxon, *fara*]. A voyage or passage by water, or the money paid for such passage. Also, a fishing season for cod; and likewise the cargo of the fishing vessel. (*See* HOW FARE YE?)

FARE-CROFTS. The vessels that formerly plied between England and France.

FARRANE. The Erse term for a gentle breeze, still used on our north-western shores.

FARTHEL. An old word for furling sails. Also, a burden, according to Shakspeare in *Hamlet;* and a weight, agreeably to the depositions of the "Portingalls" before Sir Francis Drake, *in re* the great carrack's cargo in 1592; there were "ij^c fardells of synamon:" of this famous prize the queen reserved to herself the lion's share.

FASCINES. Faggots of brush or other small wood, varying according to the object in view and the material available, from about 6 to 9 inches in diameter, and from 6 to 18 feet in length, firmly bound with withes at about every 18 inches. They are of vast use in military field-engineering.

FASH. An irregular seam. The mark left by the moulds upon cast bullets. (Short for *fashion*—ship-fashion, soldier-fashion.)

FASHION-PIECES. The fashion of the after-part of a ship, in the plane of projection. They are the hindmost timbers in the run of a ship, which terminate the breadth, and form the shape of the stern; they are united to the stern-post, and to the end of the wing-transom by a rabbet.

FASKIDAR. A name of the *Cataractes parasiticus*, or Arctic gull.

FAST. A rope, cablet, or chain by which a vessel is secured to a wharf; and termed bow, head, breast, quarter, or stern fasts, as the case may be.

FAST AGROUND. Immovable, or high and dry.

FAST AND LOOSE. An uncertain and shuffling conduct.

FASTENINGS. "Let go the fasts!" throw off the ropes from the bollards or cleats. Also used for the bolts, &c., which hold together the different parts of a ship.

FASTNESS. A strong post, fortified by nature and art.

FAST SAILER. A ship which, in nautical parlance, "has legs."

FAST STAYING. Quick in going about.

FAT, OR BROAD. If the tressing in or tuck of a ship's quarter under water hangs deep, or is overfull, they say she has a *fat* quarter.

FATHER. The dockyard name given to the person who constructs a ship of the navy.

FATHER-LASHER. A name of the scorpius or scorpion, *Cottus scorpius,* a fish about 9 inches long, common near rocky coasts.

FATHOM [Anglo-Saxon, *fædm*].   The space of both arms extended. A measure of 6 feet, used in the length of cables, rigging, &c., and to divide the lead (or sounding) lines, for showing the depth of water.—*To fathom*, is to ascertain the depth of water by sounding.   To conjecture an intention.

FATHOM-WOOD.   Slab and other offal of timber, sold at the yards, by fathom lots : cubic measurement.

FATIGUE-PARTY.   A party of soldiers told off to any labour-duty not strictly professional.

FAULCON.   A small cannon.   (*See* FALCON.)

FAUN.   Anglo-Norman for a flood-gate or water-gate.

FAUSSEBRAYE.   In fortification, a kind of counter-gard or low rampart, intended to protect the lower part of the main escarp behind it from being breached, but considered in modern times to do more harm than good to the defence.

FAVOUR, To.   To be careful of; also to be fair for.—"*Favour her*" is purely a seaman's term; as when it blows in squalls, and the vessel is going rap-full, with a stiff weather-helm and bow-seas, "favour her boy" is "ease the helm, let the sails lift, and head the sea."   So, in hauling in a rope, *favour* means to trust to the men's force and elasticity, and not part the rope by taking a turn on a cleat, making a dead nip.   A thorough seaman "favours" his spars and rigging, and sails his ship economically as well as expeditiously.

FAY, To.   To fit any two pieces of wood, so as to join close and fair together; the plank is said to fay to the timbers, when it lies so close to them that there shall be no perceptible space between them.

FAY FENA.   A kind of Japanese galley, of 30 oars.

FEALTY.   Loyalty and due devotion to the queen's service.

FEARN.   A small windlass for a lighter.

FEAR-NOUGHT.   Stout felt woollen cloth, used for port-linings, hatch-way fire-screens, &c.   The same as *dread-nought*.

FEATHER.   (*See* SWINE'S or SWEDISH FEATHER.)   It is used variously. (*See also* FULL FEATHER and WHITE FEATHER.)

FEATHER, To Cut a.   When a ship has so sharp a bow that she makes the spray feather in cleaving it.

FEATHER AN OAR, To.   In rowing, is to turn the blade horizontally, with the top aft, as it comes out of the water.   This lessens the resistance of the air upon it.

FEATHER-EDGED.   A term used by shipwrights for such planks as are thicker on one edge than the other.

FEATHERING-PADDLES.   (Morgan's patent.)

FEATHER-SPRAY.   Such as is observed at the cutwater of fast steamers, forming a pair of wing feathers.

FEATHER-STAR.   The *Comatula rosacea,* one of the most beautiful of British star-fishes.

FEAZE, To.   To untwist, to unlay ropes; to teaze, to convert it into oakum.

FEAZINGS. The fagging out or unravelling of an unwhipped rope.

FECKET. A Guernsey frock.

FECKLESS. Weak and silly.

FEEDER. A small river falling into a large one, or into a dock or float. *Feeders*, in pilot slang, are the passing spurts of rain which feed a gale.

FEEDING-GALE. A storm which is on the increase, sometimes getting worse at each succeeding squall. When a gale freshens after rain, it is said to have fed the gale.

FEEDING-PART OF A TACKLE. That running through the sheaves, in opposition to the standing part.

FEED OF GRASS. A supply of any kind of vegetables.

FEED-PUMP. The contrivance by which the boilers of a steamer are supplied with water from the hot-well, while the engines are at work.

FEED-WATER. In steamers, the water which supplies the boiler.

FEEL THE HELM, To. To have good steerage way, carrying taut weather-helm, which gives command of steerage. Also said of a ship when she has gained headway after standing still, and begins to obey the helm.

FEINT. A mock assault, generally made to conceal a true one.

FELL, To. To cut down timber. To knock down by a heavy blow. *Fell* is the Anglo-Saxon for a skin or hide.

FELL-HEAD. The top of a mountain not distinguished by a peak.

FELL IN WITH. Met by chance.

FELLOES [from *felly*]. The arch-pieces which form the rim or circumference of the wheel, into which the spokes and handles are fitted.

FELLOW. A sailor's soubriquet for himself; he will ask if you "have anything for a fellow to do?"

FELLS. Upland levels and mountainous tracts.

FELT. Stuff made of wool and hair. Patent felt is saturated with tar, and used to place inside the doubling or sheathing of a vessel's bottom. Employed also in covering the boilers and cylinders of steam-engines.

FELUCCA. (*See* LUNTRA.) A little vessel with six or eight oars, frequent in the Mediterranean; its helm may be applied in the head or stern, as occasion requires. Also, a narrow decked galley-built vessel in great use there, of one or two masts, and some have a small mizen; they carry lateen sails.

FEN. Low tracts inundated by the tides, capable, when in a dry state, of bearing the weight of cattle grazing upon them; differing therein from bog or quagmire. When well drained, they form some of the best land in the country.

FENCE. A palisade. Also, the arm of the hammer-spring of a gun-lock.

FENCIBLES. Bodies of men raised for limited service, and for a definite period. In rank they are junior to the line and royal marines, but senior to yeomanry or volunteers.

FENCING. The art of using the small-sword with skill and address.

FEND. An aphæresis from defend; to ward off.

FEND or **FENDER BOLTS.** Made with long and thick heads, struck into the outermost bends or wales of a ship, to save her sides from hurts and bruises.

FENDER-PILES. In a dock, &c.

FENDERS. Two pieces of oak-plank fayed edgeways against the topsides, abreast the main hatchway, to prevent the sides being chafed by the hoisting of things on board. They are not wanted where the yard-tackles are constantly used. Also, pieces of old cable, or other materials, hung over the side to prevent it from chafing against a wharf; as also to preserve a small vessel from being damaged by a large one. The fenders of a boat are usually made of canvas, stuffed, and neatly painted.

FEND OFF, To. In order to avoid violent contact, is, by the application of a spar, junk, rattans, &c., to prevent one vessel running against another, or against a wharf, &c. Fend off, with the boat-hook or stretchers in a boat.—*Fend the boat*, keep her from beating against the ship's side.

FERNAN BAG. A small ditty-bag, often worn by sailors, for holding tobacco and other things. They have applied the term to the pouches in monkeys' cheeks, where they carry spare food.

FERRARA. A species of broad-sword, named after the famous Spanish sword-smith, Andrea Ferrara.

FERRIAGE. An old right of the admiralty over all rivers between the sea and the first bridges.

FERRY. A passage across a river or branch of the sea by boat.

FERRY-BOATS. Vessels or wherries duly licensed for conveying passengers across a river or creek.

FETCH, To. To reach, or arrive at; as, " we shall fetch to windward of the light-house this tack."

FETCH HEADWAY or **STERNWAY.** Said of a vessel gathering motion ahead or astern.

FETCHING THE PUMP. Pouring water into the upper part in order to expel the air contained between the lower box and that of the pump-spear. (*See* PUMP.)

FETCH OF A BAY or **GULF.** The whole stretch from head to head, or point to point.

FETCH WAY, To. Said of a gun, or anything which escapes from its place by the vessel's motion at sea.

FETTLE, To. To fit, repair, or put in order. Also, a threat.

FEU-DE-JOIE. A salute fired by musketry on occasions of public rejoicing, so that it should pass from man to man rapidly and steadily, down one rank and up the other, giving one long continuous sound.

FEZ. A red cloth skull-cap, worn by the people of Fez and Morocco, and in general use amongst Mediterranean sailors.

F. G. The initials on a powder cask, denote *fine grain*.

FICHANT. In fortification, said of flanking fire which impinges on the face it defends; that is, of a line of defence where the angle of defence is less than a right angle.

FID. A square bar of wood or iron, with a shoulder at one end, used to support the weight of the topmast when erected at the head of the lower mast, by passing through a mortise or hole at the lower end of the former, and resting its ends on the trestle-trees, which are sustained by the head of the latter; the fid, therefore, must be withdrawn every time the mast is lowered; the topgallant-mast is retained at the head of the topmast in the same manner. There is also a patent screw fid, which can be removed after hauling taut the mast rope, without having first to lift the mast. (*See* MAST.) A fid is also a conical pin of hard wood, of any size from 10 inches downwards, tapering to a point, used to open the strands of a rope in splicing: of these some are large, for splicing cables, and some small, for the bolt-ropes of sails, &c. Fid is improperly applied to metal of the same shape; they are then termed *marling-spikes* (called *stabbers* by sail-makers—which see). Also, the piece of oakum with which the vent of a gun is plugged. Some call it the *vent-plug* (which see). Also, colloquially used for a quid or chew of tobacco, or a small but thick piece of anything, as of meat in clumsy carving.

FIDDED. When a mast has been swayed high enough the fid is then inserted, and the mast-rope relieved of the weight.

FIDDLE. A contrivance to prevent things from rolling off the table in bad weather. It takes its name from its resemblance to a fiddle, being made of small cords passed through wooden bridges, and hauled very taut.

FIDDLE-BLOCK. A long shell, having one sheave over the other, and the lower smaller than the upper (*see* LONG-TACKLE BLOCKS), in contradistinction to double blocks, which also have two sheaves, but one abreast of the other. They lie flatter and more snugly to the yards, and are chiefly used for lower-yard tackles.

FIDDLE-FISH. A name of the king-crab (*Limulus polyphemus*), from its supposed resemblance to that instrument.

FIDDLE-HEAD. When there is no figure; this means that the termination of the head is formed by a scroll turning aft or inward like a violin: in contradistinction to the *scroll-head* (which see).

FIDE JUSSORS. Bail sureties in the instance court of the admiralty.

FIDLER. A small crab, with one large claw and a very small one. It burrows on drowned lands.

FIDLER'S GREEN. A sort of sensual Elysium, where sailors are represented as enjoying, for "a full due," those amenities for which Wapping, Castle Rag, and the back of Portsmouth Point were once noted.

FIELD. The country in which military operations are being carried on; the scene of a conflict.—*Taking the field*, quitting cantonments, and going on active service.

FIELD-ALLOWANCE. A small extra payment made to officers, and sometimes to privates, on active service in the field, to compensate partly the enhanced price of all necessaries.

FIELD-ARTILLERY. Light ordnance fitted for travel as to be applicable to the active operations of the field. The term generally includes the officers, men, and horses, also the service. According to the present excellent establishment of rifled field-guns for the British service, the Armstrong 12-pounder represents the average type.

FIELD-DAY. A day of exercise and evolutions.

FIELD-FORTIFICATION. Is the constructing of works intended to strengthen the position of forces operating in the field; works of that temporary and limited quality which may be easily formed with the means at hand.

FIELD-GLASS. A telescope, frequently so termed. Also, the binocular or opera-glass, used for field-work, night-work, and at races.

FIELD-GUN. *See* FIELD-ARTILLERY.

FIELD-ICE. A sheet of smooth frozen water of a general thickness, and of an extent too large for its boundaries to be seen over from a ship's mast-head. Field-ice may be all adrift, but yet pressed together, and when any masses detach, as they suddenly do, they are termed floes. They as suddenly become pressed home again and cause nips. (*See* NIP.)

FIELD-MARSHAL. The highest rank in the British army.

FIELD-OFFICERS. The colonel, lieutenant-colonels, and majors of a regiment; so called because, not having the common duties in quarters, they are mostly seen when the troops are in the field.

FIELD OF VIEW. That space which is visible in a telescope at one view, and which diminishes under augmenting eye-pieces.

FIELD-PIECES. Light guns proper to be taken into field operations; one or more of them is now carried by all ships of war for land service.

FIELD-WORKS. The constructions of field fortification (which see).

FIERY-FLAW, OR FIRE-FLAIRE. A northern designation of the sting-ray (*Raia pastinaca*).

FIFE-RAILS. Those forming the upper fence of the bulwarks on each side of the quarter-deck and poop in men-of-war. Also, the rail round the mainmast, and encircling both it and the pumps, furnished with belaying pins for the running rigging, though now obsolete under the iron rule.

FIFER AND FIDLER. Two very important aids in eliciting exact discipline; for hoisting, warping, and heaving at the capstan in proper time; rated a second-class petty officer styled "musician," pay £30, 8s. per annum.

FIG, OR FULL FIG. In best clothes. Full dress.

FIGALA. An East Indian craft with one mast, generally rowed with paddles.

FIGGER. The soubriquet of a Smyrna trader.

FIGGIE-DOWDIE. A west-country pudding, made with raisins, and much in vogue at sea among the Cornish and Devon men. Cant west-country term for plum-pudding—figs and dough.

FIGHT, SEA. *See* BATTLE, ENGAGEMENT, EXERCISE, &c.

FIGHTING-LANTERNS. Kept in their respective fire-buckets at quarters, in readiness for night action only. There is usually one attached to each gun; the bucket is fragile, but intended to screen the light, and furnished with a fire-lanyard.

FIGHTING-SAILS. Those to which a ship is reduced when going into action; formerly implying the courses and topsails only.

FIGHTING-WATER. Casks filled and placed on the decks, expressly for use in action. When the head was broken in, vinegar was added to prevent too much being taken by one man.

FIGHTS. Waste-cloths formerly hung about a ship, to conceal the men from the enemy. Shakspeare, who knew everything, makes Pistol bombastically exclaim—

"Clap on more sails: pursue, up with your fights."

Close fights, synonymous with *close quarters.*

FIGURE. The principal piece of carved work or ornament at the head of a ship, whether scroll, billet, or figure-head.

FIGURE-HEAD. A carved bust or full-length figure over the cut-water of a ship; the remains of an ancient superstition. The Carthaginians carried small images to sea to protect their ships, as the Roman Catholics do still. The sign or head of St. Paul's ship was Castor and Pollux.

FIGURE OF EIGHT. A knot made by passing the end of a rope over and round the standing part, up over its own part, and down through the bight.

FIGURE OF THE EARTH. The form of our globe, which is that of an oblate spheroid with an ellipticity of about $\frac{1}{305}$.

FIKE. *See* FYKE.

FILADIERE. A small flat-bottomed boat of the Garonne.

FILE. Originally a string of soldiers one behind the other, though in the present formation of British troops, the length of the string has been reduced to two.

FILE. *An old file.* A somewhat contemptuous epithet for a deep and cunning, but humorous person.

FILE OFF, To. To march off to a flank by files, or with a very small front.

FILL. To. To brace the yards so that the wind strikes the after side of the sails, and advances the ship in her course, after the sails had been shivering, or braced aback. A ship may be forced backward or forward, or made to remain in her place, with the same wind, by "backing, filling," or shivering the sails. (*See* BRACE, BACK, and SHIVER.) Colliers generally *tide it,* "backing and filling" down the Thames until they gain the reaches, where there is room for tacking, or the wind is fair enough for them to lay their course.—An idle skulker, a fellow who loiters, trying to avoid being seen by the officer of the watch, is said to be "backing and filling;" otherwise, doing nothing creditably.

FILL AND STAND ON. A signal made after "lying by" to direct the fleet to resume their course.

FILLER. A filling piece in a made mast.

FILLET. An ornamental moulding. Rings on the muzzle and cascabel of guns.

FILLET-HORSE.   The horse employed in the shafts of the limbers.

FILLING.   In ship-carpentry, wood fitted on a timber or elsewhere to make up a defect in the moulding way.   This name is sometimes given to a *chock.*

FILLING A SHIP'S BOTTOM.   Implies covering the bottom of a ship with broad-headed nails, so as to give her a sheathing of iron, to prevent the worms getting into the wood; sheathing with copper is found superior, but the former plan is still used for piles in salt-water.

FILLING IN.   The replacing a ship's vacant planks opened for ventilation, when preparing her, from ordinary, for sea.

FILLING POWDER.   Taking gunpowder from the casks to fill cartridges, when lights and fires should be extinguished.

FILLING ROOM.   Formerly a small place parted off and lined with lead, in a man-of-war magazine, wherein powder may be started loosely, in order to fill cartridges.

FILLINGS.   Fir fayed in between the cheeks of the head, and wherever solidity is required, as making the curve fair for the mouldings between the edges of the fish-front and the sides of the mast, or making the spaces between the ribs and timbers of a vessel's frame solid.

FILLING-TIMBERS.   Blocks of wood introduced in all well-built vessels between the frames, where the bilge-water may wash.

FILLING-TRANSOM, is just above the deck-transom, securing the ends of the gun-deck plank and lower-transoms.

FILL THE MAIN-YARD.   An order well understood to mean, fill the main-topsail, after it has been aback, or the ship hove-to.

FILTER.   A strainer to free water from its impurities, usually termed by seamen *dripstone* (which see).

FILUM AQUÆ.   The thread or middle of any river or stream which divides countries, manors, &c.—*File du mer,* the high tide of the sea.

FIMBLE HEMP; *female hemp,* is that which is chiefly used for domestic purposes, and therefore falls to the care of the women, as *carl* or *male hemp,* which produces the flower, does to the maker of cordage.

> "Wife, pluck fro thy seed hemp, the *fimble hemp* clean,
> This looketh more yellow, the other more green;
> Use this one for thy spinning, leave Michael the t'other,
> For shoe-thread and halter, for rope and such other."—*Tusser.*

FIN [Anglo-Saxon, *Finn*].   A native of Finland; those are *Fins* who live by fishing.   We use the whole for a part, and thus lose the clue which the Fin affords of a race of fishermen.

FIN-BACK.   *See* FINNER.

FIND, To.   To provide with or furnish.

FINDING.   The verdict of a court-martial.

FINDON HADDOCK.   The Finnan Haddie, a species of haddock cured by smoke-drying at Montrose and Aberdeen.

FINE.   A term of comparison, as fine ship, &c., or *lean* (which see).   Also, *see* FYEN.

FINE BREEZES. Said of the wind, when the flying-kites may be carried, but requiring a sharp look-out.

FINISHINGS. The carved ornaments of the quarter-galleries: *upper* and *lower*, as above or below the stools.

FINNER. Whales of the genus *Balænoptera* are so termed, being distinguished from the right whales by the possession of a small triangular adipose dorsal fin. There are several species, some of which grow to a greater length than any other animals of the order, viz. 80 or perhaps 90 feet. They are very active and difficult to harpoon, yield comparatively little oil, and their baleen, or "whalebone," is almost worthless; consequently, they suffer much less than the right whales from the persecutions of the whalers. The finner, or great black fish, is feared by whalers in general. It is vicious, and can only be attacked by large boats in shallow water, as at the Bermudas, where the whale-boats are about 50 or 60 feet long, and 12 feet beam. The fish yields one barrel of oil for every foot in length beyond thirty. (*See* RAZOR-BACK and RORQUAL.)

FINNIE. A northern name for salmon under a year old.

FINNOCK. A white kind of small salmon taken on the west coast of Scotland.

FINTRUM SPELDIN. A small dried haddock.

FIN-WHALE. *See* FINNER.

FIORD. A Norwegian pilot term for good channels among islets, and deep inlets of the sea.

FIRBOME. An old term for a beacon, and appears thus in the *Promptorium Parvulorum.*

FIR-BUILT. Constructed of fir.

FIRE! The order to put the match to the priming, or pull the trigger of a cannon or other fire-arm so as to discharge it. The act of discharging ordnance.

FIRE, Loss BY. Is within the policy of insurance, whether it be by accident, or by the fault of the master or mariners. Also, if a ship be ordered by a state to be burnt to prevent infection, or if she be burnt to prevent her falling into the hands of the enemy.

FIRE-AND-LIGHTS. Nickname of the master-at-arms.

FIRE-ARMS. Every description of arms that discharge missiles by gunpowder, from the heaviest cannon to a pistol.

FIRE-ARROWS. Missiles in olden times carrying combustibles; much used in the sea-fights of the middle ages.

FIRE-AWAY. Go on with your remarks.

FIRE-BALL. In meteorology, a beautiful phenomenon seen at times, the origin of which is as yet imperfectly accounted for. It is also the popular name for aërolites in general, because in their descent they appear to be burning.

FIRE-BALLS. Are used for destroying vessels run aground, and firing buildings. They are made of a composition of meal-powder, sulphur, saltpetre, and pitch, moulded into a mass with suet and tow.

FIRE-BARE. An old term from the Anglo-Saxon for *beacon*.

FIRE-BARS. The range fronting a steam-boiler.

FIRE-BILL. The distribution of the officers and crew in case of the alarm of fire, a calamity requiring judicious conduct.

FIRE-BOOMS. Long spars swung out from a ship's side to prevent the approach of fire-ships, fire-stages, or vessels accidentally on fire.

FIRE-BOX. A space crossing the whole front of the boiler over the furnace doors, opposite the smoke-box.

FIRE-BUCKETS. Canvas, leather, or wood buckets for quarters, each fitted with a sinnett laniard of regulated length, for reaching the water from the lower yards. (*See* FIRE-MEN.)

FIRE-DOOR. An access to the fire-place of an engine.

FIRE-DRAKE. A meteor, or the Corpo Santo. Also, a peculiar fire-work, which Shakspeare in *Henry VIII.* thus mentions: "That fire-drake did I hit three times on the head, and three times was his nose discharged against me; he stands there like a mortar-piece to blow us."

FIRE-EATER. One notoriously fond of being in action; much humbled by iron-clads.

FIRE-FLAUGHTS. The *aurora borealis*, or northern lights.

FIRE-HEARTH. The security base of the galley-range and all its conveniences.

FIRE-HEARTH-CARLINE. The timber let in under the beams on which the fire-hearth stands, with pillars underneath, and chocks thereon.

FIRE-HOOPS. A combustible invented by the knights of Malta to throw among their besiegers, and afterwards used in boarding Turkish galleys.

FIRE-LOCK. Formerly the common name for a musket; the fire-arm carried by a foot-soldier, marine, or small-arm man, until the general introduction of rifles. It carried a ball of about an ounce in weight.

FIREMEN. A first and second man is stationed to each gun, in readiness for active duty. The firemen, when called with the first and second division of boarders, were an effective force. If for duty aloft, each bucket had a lanyard which reached from the main-yard to the sea, so as to keep the lower sails well wet. The ship's engine was also manned by the second division of boarders, while the first division and carpenters cut away obstacles. (For firemen in a steamer, see STOKER.)

FIRE-RAFTS. Timber constructions bearing combustible matters, used by the Chinese to destroy an enemy's vessel.

FIRE-RAILS. *See* RAILS.

FIRE-ROLL. A peculiar beat of the drum to order people to their stations on an alarm of fire. Summons to quarters.

FIRE-SCREENS. Pieces of fear-nought, a thick woollen felt put round the hatchways in action.

FIRE-SHIP. A vessel filled with combustible materials, and fitted with grappling-irons, to hook and set fire to the enemy's ships. Notwithstanding what is said respecting the siege of Tyre, perhaps the practice of using regular fire-ships ought to be dated from the destruction of the fleet of Basilicus by the victorious Genseric near Carthage.

FIRE-SWAB. The bunch of rope-yarns sometimes secured to the tompion, saturated with water to cool the gun in action, and swab up any grains of powder.

FIRE-WORKS. *See* PYROTECHNY.

FIRING-PARTY. A detachment of soldiers, marines, or small-arm men selected to fire over the grave of an individual buried with military honours.

FIRMAUN. A Turkish passport.

FIRST. The appellation of the senior lieutenant; also, senior lieutenant of marines, and first captain of a gun.

FIRST FUTTOCKS. Timbers in the frame of a ship which come down between the floor-timbers almost to the keel on each side.

FIRST POINT OF ARIES. *See* ARIES.

FIRST QUARTER OF THE MOON. *See* QUARTER.

FIRST WATCH. The men on deck-duty from 8 P.M. till midnight.

FIRTH. A corruption of *frith*, in Scotland applied to arms of the sea, and estuaries of various extent; also given to several channels amongst the Orkneys.

FISH, OR FISH-PIECE. A long piece of hard wood, convex on one side and concave on the other; two are bound opposite to each other to strengthen the lower masts or the yards when they are sprung, to effect which they are well secured by bolts and hoops, or stout rope called woolding. Also, colloquially, an epithet given to persons, as a *prime* fish, a *queer* fish, a *shy* fish, a *loose* fish, &c. *As mute as a fish*, when a man is very silent. Also, *fish* among whalers is expressly applied to whales. At the cry of "Fish! fish!" all the boats are instantly manned.

FISH, ROYAL. Whale and sturgeon, to which the sovereign is entitled when either thrown on shore or caught near the coasts.

FISH-DAVIT. (*See* DAVIT.) That which steps into a shoe in the fore-chains, and is used for fishing an anchor.

FISHER-BOYS. The apprentices in fishing vessels.

FISHER-FISH. A species of *Remora*, said to be trained by the Chinese to catch turtle. When a turtle is perceived basking on the surface of the sea, the men, avoiding all noise, slip one of their remoras overboard, tied to a long and fine cord. As soon as the fish perceives the floating reptile he swims towards it, and fixes himself on it so firmly that the fishermen easily pull in both together.

FISHERMAN'S BEND. A knot, for simplicity called the king of all knots. Its main use is for bending studding-halliards to the yard, by taking two turns round the yard, passing the end between them and the yard, and half hitching it round the standing part. (*See* STUDDING-SAIL BEND.)

FISHERMAN'S WALK. An extremely confined space; "three steps and overboard," is often said of what river yachtsmen term their quarter-decks.

FISH-FAG. A woman who fags under heavy fish-baskets, but is applied also in opprobrium to slatterns.

FISH-FLAKE. A stage covered with light spars for the purpose of drying fish in Newfoundland.

FISH-FRONT. The strengthening slab on a made mast.

FISH-GARTH. The water shut in by a dam or weir by the side of a river for securing fish.

FISH-GIG. A staff with three, four, or more barbed prongs of steel at one end, and a line fastened to the other; used for striking fish at sea. Now more generally called *grains*.

FISH-HACK. A name of the *Gobius niger*.

FISHICK. An Orkney name for the brown whistle-fish, *Gadus mustela*.

FISHING. In taking celestial observations, means the sweeping to find a star or other object when near its approximate place.

FISHING-BOAT. A stout fishing-vessel with two lug-sails.

FISHING-FROG. A name of the *Lophius piscatorius*, angler or devil-fish, eaten in the Mediterranean.

FISHING-GROUND. Any bank or shoal frequented by fish.

FISHING-SMACK. A sloop having in the hold a well wherein to preserve the fish, particularly lobsters, alive.

FISHING-TAUM. A northern designation of an angling line, or angling gear.

FISHING-VESSELS. A general term for those employed in the fisheries, from the catching of sprats to the taking of whales.

FISH-LEEP. An old term for a fish-basket.

FISH-ROOM. A space parted off by bulkheads in the after-hold, now used for waste stores, but formerly used for stowing salt fish—an article of food long discontinued. In line-of-battle ships, a small store-room near the bread-room, in which spirits or wine, and sometimes coals, were stowed, with the stock-fish.

FISH-SPEAR. An instrument with barbed spikes.

FISH-TACKLE. A tackle employed to hook and draw up the flukes of a ship's anchor towards the top of the bow, after catting, in order to stow it; formerly composed of four parts, viz. the pendant, the block, the hook, and the tackle, for which see DAVIT.

FISH THE ANCHOR, To. To turn up the flukes of an anchor to the gunwale for stowage, after being catted.—*Other fish to fry*, a common colloquialism, expressing that a person has other occupation demanding his attention.

FISH-WIFE, OR FISH-WOMAN. A female carrier and vendor of fish in our northern cities.

FIST, To. To handle a rope or sail promptly; thus *fisting* a thing is readily getting hold of it.

FIT FOR DUTY. In an effective state for service.

FIT RIGGING, To. To cut or fit the standing and running rigging to the masts, &c.

FIT-ROD. A small iron rod with a hook at the end, which is put into the holes made in a vessel's side, to ascertain the length of the bolts or treenails required to be driven in.

FITTED FURNITURE. Rudder-chocks, bucklers, hawse-plugs, dead-lights, pump-boxes, and other articles of spare supply, sent from the dockyard.

FITTERS. Persons in the north who vend and load coals, fitting ships with cargoes, &c.

FITTING OUT A SHIP. The act of providing a ship with sufficient masts, sails, yards, ammunition, artillery, cordage, anchors, provisions, stores, and men, so that she is in proper condition for the voyage or pur-pose to which she is appointed.

FIUMARA. A term common to the Italian coasts for a mountain torrent.

FIVE-FINGERS. The name given to the *Asterias*, or star-fish, found on our shore. Cocker in 1724 describes it thus : "*Five-fingers*, a fish like a spur-rowel, destructive to oysters, to be destroyed by the admiralty law." They destroy the spat of oysters.

FIVE-SHARE MEN. In vessels, as whalers, where the men enter on the chances of success, &c., in shares.

FIX BAYONETS! Ship them ready for use.

FIXED AMMUNITION. Is, complete in each round, the cartridge being attached to the projectile, to facilitate simultaneous loading. In the British service it is only used for small mountain-pieces, but in the French for field-artillery in general. It does not stow conveniently.

FIXED BLOCKS. Solid pieces of oak let through the sides of the ship, and fitted with sheaves, to lead the tacks, sheets, &c., of the courses inboard.

FIXED STAR. *See* STARS (FIXED).

FIZZ. The burning of priming.

FLABBERGAST, To. To throw a person aback by a confounding asser-tion; to produce a state of extreme surprise.

FLADDERMUS. A base silver German coin of four kreutzers' value.

FLAG. A general name for the distinguishing colours of any nation. Also, a certain banner by which an admiral is distinguished at sea from the inferior ships of his squadron. The flags of the British navy were severally on a red, white, or blue field, and were displayed from the top of the royal pole of the main, fore, or mizen mast, according to the rank of the admiral, thus indicating nine degrees. This diversity of colour has now been long done away with. The white field, with the red St. George's cross, and the sinister upper corner occupied by the union, is now alone used in the British navy—the blue being assigned to the reserve, and the red to the mercantile navy. An admiral still displays his flag exclusively at the main truck; a vice-admiral at the fore; a rear-admiral at the mizen. The first flag in importance is the royal standard of Great Britain and Ireland, hoisted only when the king or queen is on board; the second is the anchor of hope, for the lord high-admiral, or the lords-commissioners of the admiralty; and the third is the union flag, for the admiral of the fleet, who is the next officer under the lord high-admiral. The various other departments, such as the navy board, custom-house, &c., have each their respective flags. Besides the national flag, merchant ships are permitted to bear lesser flags on any mast, with the arms or design of the firm to which they belong, but they "must not resemble or be mistaken for any of the flags or signals used by the royal navy," under certain penalties. When a council of war is held at sea, if it be on board the admiral's ship, a flag is hung on the main-shrouds; if the vice-admiral's, on the fore-shrouds; and if the rear-admiral's, on the mizen-shrouds. The flags borne on the mizen were particularly called gallants. There are also smaller flags used for signals. The word *flag* is often familiarly used to denote the admiral himself. Also, the reply from the boat if an admiral is on board—Flag!

FLAG-OFFICER. A term synonymous with *admiral*.

FLAG OF TRUCE. A white flag, hoisted to denote a wish to parley between the belligerent parties, but so frequently abused, with the design of obtaining intelligence, or to cover stratagems, &c., that officers are very strict in its admission. It is held sacred by civilized nations.

FLAG-SHARE. The admiral's share (one-eighth) in all captures made by any vessels within the limits of his command, even if under the orders of another admiral; but in cases of pirates, he has no claim unless he participates in the action.

FLAG-SHIP. A ship bearing an admiral's flag.

FLAG-SIDE of a SPLIT FISH. The side without the bone.

FLAG-STAFF. In contradistinction to mast-head, is the staff on a battery, or on a ship's stern, where the colours are displayed. (*See* FLARE.)

FLAKE. A small shifting stage, hung over a ship's side to caulk or repair a breach. (*See* FISH-FLAKE.)

FLAM. Wedge-shaped. Also, a sudden puff of wind. Also, a shallow.

FLAM-FEW. The brilliant reflection of the moon on the water.

FLAN. An old word, equivalent to a flaw, or sudden gust of wind from the land.

FLANCHING. The bellying out; synonymous with *flaring*.

FLANGE. In steamers, is the projecting rim at the end of two iron pipes for uniting them. (*See* PORT-FLANGE.)

FLANK, To. To defend that part; incorrectly used sometimes for firing upon a flank.

FLANK OF AN ARMY. The right or left side or end, as distinguished from the front and rear—a vulnerable point. Also, the force composing or covering that side. In fortification, a work constructed to afford flank defence.

FLANK-COMPANIES. The extreme right and left companies of a battalion, formerly called the grenadiers and light infantry, and wearing distinctive marks in their dress; now the title, dress, and duties of all the companies of a battalion are the same.

FLANK-DEFENCE. A line of fire parallel, or nearly so, to the front of another work or position.

FLANKED ANGLE. In fortification, a salient angle formed by two lines of flank defence.

FLAP. The cover of a cartridge-box or scupper.

FLAPPING. The agitation of a sail with sheet or tack carried away, or the sudden jerk of the sails in light winds and a heavy swell on.

FLARE. In shipbuilding, is flanching outwards, as at the bows of American ships, to throw off the bow-seas; it is in opposition to tumbling home and wall-sided.

FLARE. A name for the skate, *Raia batis.*

FLARE, To. To rake back, as of a fashion-piece or knuckle-timber.

FLASH. The laminæ and grain-marks in timber, when cut into planks. Also, a pool. Also, in the west, a river with a large bay, which is again separated from the outer sea by a reef of rocks.—*To make a flash,* is to let boats down through a lock; to flash loose powder at night to show position.

FLASHING-BOARD. To raise or set off.

FLASHING-SIGNALS. By Captain Colomb's plan, the lime light being used on shore, and a plain white light at sea, is capable of transmitting messages by the relative positions of long and short dashes of light by night, and of collapsing cones by day.

FLASH IN THE PAN. An expressive metaphor, borrowed from the false fire of a musket, meaning to fail of success after presumption.

FLASH RIM. In carronades, a cup-shaped enlargement of the bore at the muzzle, which facilitates the loading, and protects the ports or rigging of the vessel from the flash of explosion.

FLASH VESSELS. All paint outside, and no order within.

FLASK. A horn or other implement for carrying priming-powder. Smaller ones for fire-arms are usually furnished with a measure of the charge for the piece on the top.

FLAT. In shipbuilding, a straight part in a curve. In hydrography, a shallow over which the tide flows, and over the whole extent of which there is little or no variation of soundings. If less than three fathoms, it is called *shoal* or *shallow.*

FLAT-ABACK. When all the sails are blown with their after-surface against the mast, so as to give stern-way.

FLAT-AFT. The sheets of fore-and-aft sails may be hauled flat-aft, as the jib-sheet to pay her head off, the driver or try-sail sheets to bring her head to the wind; hence, "flatten in the head-sheets."

FLAT-BOTTOMED. When a vessel's lower frame has but little upward inclination.

FLAT CALM. When there is no perceptible wind at sea.

FLAT-FISH. The *Pleuronectidœ,* a family of fishes containing the soles, flounders, turbots, &c., remarkable for having the body greatly compressed laterally; they habitually lie on one side, which is white, the uppermost being coloured, and having both the eyes placed on it.

FLAT-NAILS. Small sharp-pointed nails with flat thin heads, longer than tacks, for nailing the scarphs of moulds and the like.

FLATS. All the floor-timbers that have no bevellings in mid-ships, or pertaining to the *dead-flat* (which see). Also, lighters used in river navigation, and very flat-floored boats for landing troops.

FLAT SEAM. The two edges or selvedges of canvas laid over each other and sewed down.

FLAT SEIZING. This is passed on a rope, the same as a round seizing, but it has no riding turns.

FLATTEN IN, To. The action of hauling in the aftmost clue of a sail to give it greater power of turning the vessel; thus, if the mizen or after sails are flatted in, it is to carry the stern to leeward, and the head to windward; and if, on the contrary, the head-sails are flatted in, the intention is to make the ship fall off when, by design or accident, she has come so near as to make the sails shiver; hence *flatten in forward* is the order to haul in the jib and foretopmast-staysail-sheets towards the middle of the ship, and haul forward the fore-bowline; this operation is seldom necessary except when the helm has not sufficient government of the ship, as in variable winds or inattentive steerage.

FLAUT. *See* FLUTE.

FLAVER. An east-country term for froth or foam of surf.

FLAWS. Sudden gusts of wind, sometimes blowing with violence; whence Shakspeare in *Coriolanus:*

"Like a great sea-mark, standing every flaw."

But flaws also imply occasional fickle breezes in calm weather. *Flaw* is also used to express any crack in a gun or its carriage.

FLEACHES. Portions into which timber is cut by the saw.

FLEAK. *See* DUTCH PLAICE.

FLEAM. A northern name for a water-course.

FLEAT, OR FLEET. *See* FLEETING.

FLEATE, To. To skim fresh water off the sea, as practised at the mouths of the Rhone, the Nile, &c. The word is derived from the Dutch *vlieten*, to skim milk; it also means to float. (*See* FLEET.)

FLECHE. The simplest form of field-work, composed of two faces meeting in a salient angle, and open at the gorge. It differs from the redan only in having no ditch.

FLECHERRA. A swift-sailing South American despatch vessel.

FLECK. An east-country term for lightning.

FLEECH. An outside portion of timber cut by the saw.

FLEET [Teut. *flieffen*]. The old word for float: as "we fleeted down the river with our boats;" and Shakspeare makes Antony say,

"Our sever'd navy too
Have knit again, and fleet, threat'ning most sea-like."

Fleet is also an old term for an arm of the sea, or running water subject to the tide. Also, a bay where vessels can remain afloat. (*See* FLOAT.) A salt-water tide-creek.

FLEET. A general name given to the royal navy. Also, any number of ships, whether designed for war or commerce, keeping in company. A fleet of ships of war is usually divided into three squadrons, and these, if numerous, are again separated into subdivisions. The admiral commands the centre, the second in command superintends the vanguard, and the third directs the rear. The term in the navy was any number exceeding a squadron, or rear-admiral's command, composed of five sail-of-the-line, with any amount of smaller vessels.

FLEET-DYKE. From the Teut. *vliet,* a dyke for preventing inundation.

FLEETING. To *come up* a rope, so as to haul to more advantage; especially the act of changing the situation of a tackle when the blocks are drawn together; also, changing the position of the dead-eyes, when the shrouds are become too long, which is done by shortening the bend of the shroud and turning in the dead-eye again higher up; the use of fleeting is accordingly to regain the mechanical powers, when destroyed by the meeting of the blocks or dead-eyes.—*Fleet ho!* the order given at such times. (*See* Tackle.)

FLEET THE MESSENGER. When about to weigh, to shift the eyes of the messenger past the capstan for the heavy heave.

FLEET-WATER. Water which inundates.

FLEMISH, To. To coil down a rope concentrically in the direction of the sun, or coil of a watch-spring, beginning in the middle without riders; but if there must be riding fakes, they begin outside, and that is the true *French coil.*

FLEMISH ACCOUNT. A deficit in accounts.

FLEMISH EYE. A kind of eye-splice, in which the ends are scraped down, tapered, passed oppositely, marled, and served over with spun yarn. Often called a *made-eye.*

FLEMISH FAKE. A method of coiling a rope that runs freely when let go; differing from the French, and was used for the head-braces. Each bend is slipped under the last, and the whole rendered flat and solid to walk on.

FLEMISH HORSE, is the outer short foot-rope for the man at the earing; the outer end is spliced round a thimble on the goose-neck of the studding-sail boom-iron. The inner end is seized by its eye within the brace-block-strop and head-earing-cleat.

FLEMISHING. A forcing or scoring of the planks.

FLENCH-GUT. The blubber of a whale laid out in long slices.

FLENSE, To. To strip the fat off a flayed seal, or the blubber from a whale.

FLESHMENT. Being in the first battle; and "fleshing the sword" alludes to the first time the beginner draws blood with it.

FLESH-TRAFFIC. The slave-trade.

FLET. A name of the halibut.

FLETCH, To. To feather an arrow.

FLEUZ. A north-country term for the fagged end of a rope.

FLEXURE. The bending or curving of a line or figure.

FLIBOAT. *See* Fly-boat.

FLIBUSTIER [Fr.]   A freebooter, pirate, &c.

FLICKER, To.   To veer about.

FLIDDER.   A northern name for the limpet.

FLIGHERS.   An old law-term meaning masts of ships.

FLIGHT.   A Dutch vessel or passage-boat on canals.   In ship-building, a sudden rising, or a greater curve than sheer, at the cheeks, cat-heads, &c.

FLIGHT of a Shot.   The trajectory formed between the muzzle of the gun and the first graze.

FLIGHT of the Transoms.   As their ends gradually close downwards on approaching the keel, they describe a curve somewhat similar to the rising of the floors; whence the name.

FLINCH.   In ship-building.   (See Snape.)

FLINCH-GUT.   The whale's blubber; as well as the part of the hold into which it is thrown before being barrelled up.

FLINCHING, Flensing, or Flinsing.   See Flense.

FLINDERS.   An old word for splinters ; thus Walter Scott's Borderer—

> "The tough ash-spear, so stout and true,
> Into a thousand flinders flew."

FLINT.   The stone of a gun-lock, by which a spark was elicited for the discharge of the loaded piece.

FLIP.   A once celebrated sea-drink, composed of beer, spirits, and sugar, said to have been introduced by Sir Cloudesley Shovel.   Also, a smart blow.

FLIPPER.   The fin-like paw or paddle of marine mammalia; it is also applied to the hand, as when the boatswain's mate exulted in having "taken a lord by the flipper."

FLITCH.   The outside cut or slab of a tree.

FLITTER.   The Manx name for limpet.

FLITTERING.   An old English word for floating.

FLIZZING.   The passage of a splinter [from the Dutch *flissen*, to fly].

FLO.   An old English word for arrow, used by Chaucer.

FLOAT [Anglo-Saxon *fleot* or *fleet*].   A place where vessels float, as at Northfleet.   Also, the inner part of a ship-canal.   In wet-docks ships are kept afloat while loading and discharging cargo.   Two double gates, having a lock between them, allow the entry and departure of vessels without disturbing the inner level.   Also, a raft or quantity of timber fastened together, to be floated along a river by a tide or current.

FLOATAGE.   Synonymous with *flotsam* (which see).   Pieces of wreck floating about.

FLOAT-BOARDS.   The same as *floats* of a paddle-wheel.

FLOATING ANCHOR.   A simple machine consisting of a fourfold canvas, stretched by two cross-bars of iron, rivetted in the centre, and swifted at the ends.   It is made to hang perpendicularly at some distance below the surface, where it presents great resistance to being dragged through the water, diminishing a ship's leeward drift in a gale where there is no anchorage.

FLOATING BATTERY. A vessel expressly fitted for action in harbours or sheltered waters, having heavier offensive and defensive dispositions (generally including much iron-plating) than would be compatible with a sea-going character. Also, a vessel used as a battery to cover troops landing on an enemy's coast. Also, one expressly fitted for harbour defence.

FLOATING BETHEL. An old ship fitted up in a commercial port for the purpose of public Worship.

FLOATING BRIDGE. A passage formed across a river or creek by means of bridges of boats, as over the Douro, Rhine, &c.

FLOATING COFFIN. (*See* FRAPPING A SHIP.) A term for the old 10-gun brigs.

FLOATING DAM. A caisson used instead of gates for a dry-dock.

FLOATING DOCK. *See* CAISSON.

FLOATING GRAVING-DOCK. A modified *camel* (which see).

FLOATING LIGHT. A vessel moored off rocks or sand-banks, hoisting lights at night.

FLOATING PIER. As the stage at Liverpool.

FLOATING STAGE. For caulkers, painters, &c.

FLOATS. Large flat-bottomed boats, for carrying blocks of stone. Also, the 'thwart boards forming the circumference and force of the paddle-wheels of steamers.

FLOE. A field of floating ice of any extent, as beyond the range of vision, for notwithstanding its cracks the floes pressed together are assumed as one; hence, if ships make fast to the floe-edge, and it parts from the main body, sail is made, and the ship goes to the next available floe-edge.

FLOGGING THE GLASS. Where there is no ship time-piece the watches and half-hour bells are governed by a half-hour sand-glass. The run of the sand was supposed to be quickened by vibration, hence some weary soul towards the end of his watch was said to flog the glass.

FLOME. An old word for a river or flood.

FLOOD AND FLOOD-TIDE. The flux of the tide, or the time the water continues rising. When the water begins to rise, it is called a young flood, next it is quarter-flood, half-flood, and top of flood, or high water.

FLOOD-ANCHOR. That which the ship rides by during the flood-tide.

FLOOD-MARK. The line made by the tide upon the shore at its greatest height; it is also called high-water mark. This denotes the jurisdiction of the High Court of Admiralty, or vice-admirals of counties.

FLOOK, OR FLUCK. The flounder; but the name, which is of very old standing, is also applied to various other pleuronects or flat-fish.

FLOOR. The bottom of a vessel on each side of the kelson; but strictly taken, it is only so much of her bottom as she rests upon when aground. Such ships as have long and withal broad floors, lie on the ground with most security; whereas others which are narrow in the floor, fall over on their sides and break their timbers.

FLOOR-GUIDE. In ship-building, is a ribband placed between the floor and the keel.

FLOOR-HEAD. This, in marine architecture, is the third diagonal, terminating the length of the floors near the bilge of the ship, and bevellings are taken from it both forward and abaft. The upper extremities of a vessel's floor-timbers, plumb to the quarter-beam.

FLOOR-HOLLOW. The inflected curve of the floor, extending from the keel to the back of the floor-sweep, which the floor does not take.

FLOOR-PLANS. In naval architecture, are longitudinal sections, whereon are represented the water-lines and ribband-lines.

FLOOR-RIBBAND. This is an important fir-timber which runs round a little below the floor-heads, for the support of the floors.

FLOOR-RIDERS. Knees brought in from side to side over the floor ceiling and kelson, to support the bottom, if bilged or weak, for heavy cargo.

FLOORS, or FLOOR-TIMBERS. Those parts of the ship's timbers which are placed immediately across the keel, and upon which the bottom of the ship is framed; to these the upper parts of the timbers are united, being only a continuation of floor-timbers upwards.

FLOOR-SWEEPS. The radii that sweep the heads of the floors. The first in the builder's draught, which is limited by a line in the body-plan, perpendicular to the plane of elevation, a little above the keel; and the height of this line above the keel is called the *dead-rising*.

FLOP, To. To fall flat down: as " soused flop in the lee-scuppers."

FLORY-BOATS. A local term for boats employed in carrying passengers to and fro from steamers which cannot get alongside of a quay at low-water.

FLOSH. A swamp overgrown with weeds.

FLOSK. The *Sepia loligo*, sea-sleeve, or anker-fish.

FLOTA. A Spanish fleet. (*See* GALLEON.)

FLOTAGES. Things accidentally floating on seas or rivers.

FLOTA NAVIUM. An old statute term for a fleet of ships.

FLOTE. An old English term for wave: thus Ariel tells Prospero that the dispersed ships—

> " All have met again,
> And are upon the Mediterranean flote."

FLOTE-BOTE. An old term for a yawl—a rough-built river boat.

FLOTERY. Floating, used by Chaucer and others.

FLOTILLA. A fleet or squadron of small vessels.

FLOT-MANN. A very early term for sailor.

FLOTSAM. In legal phraseology, is the place where shipwrecked goods continue to float and become derelict property. Sometimes spelled *flotson*.

FLOUNDER. A well-known pleuronect, better to fish for than to eat. Called also *floun-dab*.

FLOW. In tideology, the rising of the tide; the opposite of ebb. Also, the course or direction of running waters.

FLOWER OF THE WINDS. The mariner's compass on maps and charts.

FLOWERING. The phenomenon observed usually in connection with the spawning of fish, at the distance of four leagues from shore. The water appears to be saturated with a thick jelly, filled with the ova of fish, which is known by its adhering to the ropes that the cobles anchor with while fishing, for they find the first six or seven fathom of rope free from spawn, the next ten or twelve covered with slimy matter, and the remainder again free to the bottom; this gelatinous material may supply the new-born fry with food, and protect them by clouding the water.

FLOWING-HOPE. *See* FORLORN HOPE.

FLOWING-SHEET. In sailing free or large, is the position of the sheets or lower clues of the principal sails when they are eased off to the wind, so as to receive it more nearly perpendicular than when they are close-hauled, although more obliquely than when going before the wind; a ship is therefore said to have a flowing-sheet, when the wind crosses the line of her course nearly at right angles; that is to say, a ship steering due north with the wind at east, or directly on her side, will have a flowing-sheet; whereas, if the sheets were hauled close aft, she would sail two points nearer the wind—viz. N.N.E. This explanation will probably be better understood by considering the yards as plane faces of wedges—the more oblique fore and aft, the less headway force is given, until 22° before the transverse line or beam. This is the swiftest line of sailing. As the wind draws aft of the beam the speed decreases (unless the wind increases), so that a vessel with the wind abeam, and every sail drawing, goes much faster than she would with the same wind before it.

FLUCTUATION OF THE TIDE. The rising and falling of the waters.

FLUE. *See* FLUKE OF ANCHOR.

FLUES. In a steamer's boiler, are a series of oblong passages from the furnaces for the issue of heated air. Their object being, that the air, before escaping, shall impart some of its heat to the water in the boiler, thereby economizing fuel.

FLUFFIT. The movement of fishes' fins.

FLUID COMPASS. That in which the card revolves in its bowl floated by alcohol, which prevents the needle from undue vibrations. The pin is downwards to prevent rising, as in the suspended compass-card. The body, or card, on which the points of the compass are marked, is constructed of two segments of a globe, having a diameter of 7 inches to the (double) depth of 1 inch at the poles.

FLUKES. The two parts which constitute the large triangular tail of the whale; from the power of these the phrase obtained among whalers of *fluking* or *all-a-fluking*, when running with a fresh free wind. Flukes, or palms, are also the broad triangular plates of iron on each arm of the anchor, inside the bills or extreme points, which having entered the ground, hold the ship. Seamen, by custom, drop the *k*, and pronounce the word *flue*.

FLUMMERY. A dish made of oat-meal, or oats soured, &c.

FLURRY. The convulsive movements of a dying whale. Also, a light breeze of wind shifting to different points, and causing a little ruffling on the sea. Also, hurry and confusion.

FLUSH. An old word for even or level. Anything of fair surface, or in continuous even lines. Colloquially the word means full of, or abounding in pay or prize-money.

FLUSH-DECK. A continued floor laid from the stem to the stern, upon one range, without any break.

FLUSHED. Excited by success; flushed with victory.

FLUSTERED. Performing duty in an agitated and confused manner. Also, stupefied by drink.

FLUTE, OR FLUYT. A pink-rigged fly-boat, the after-part of which is round-ribbed. Also, vessels only partly armed; as armed *en flute*.

FLUTTERING. Used in the same sense as *flapping*.

FLUVIAL, OR FLUVIATILE. Of or belonging to a river.

FLUVIAL LAGOONS. Contradistinguished from marine lagoons, in being formed by river deposits.

FLUX. The flowing in of the tide.

FLY OF A FLAG. The breadth from the staff to the extreme end that flutters loose in the wind. If an ensign, the part which extends from the union to the outer part; the vertical height, to the head-toggle of which the halliards are bent, or which is next to the staff, is called the *hoist;* the lower (which is a rope rove through the canvas heading, and into which the head-toggle is spliced) is the long tack; on this rope the whole strain is sustained.

FLY, OR COMPASS-CARD, placed on the magnetic-needle and supported by a pin, whereon it turns freely. (*See* COMPASS.)

FLY-AWAY. Fictitious resemblance of land; "Dutchman's cape," &c. (*See* CAPE FLY-AWAY.)

FLY-BLOCK. The block spliced into the topsail-tye; it is large and flat, and sometimes double.

FLY-BOAT. A large flat-bottomed Dutch vessel, whose burden is generally from 300 to 600 tons. It is distinguished by a remarkably high stern, resembling a Gothic turret, and by very broad buttocks below. Also, a swift canal passage-boat.

FLY-BY-NIGHT. A sort of square-sail, like a studding-sail, used in sloops when running before the wind; often a temporary spare jib set from the topmast-head to the yard-arm of the square-sail.

FLYER. A fast sailer; a clipper.

FLYING ABOUT. Synonymous with *chop-about* (which see).

FLYING COLUMN. A complete and mobile force kept much on the move, for the sake of covering the designs of its own army, distracting those of the enemy, or maintaining supremacy in a hostile or disaffected region.

FLYING DUTCHMAN. A famous marine spectre-ship, formerly supposed to haunt the Cape of Good Hope. The tradition of seamen was that a Dutch skipper, irritated with a foul wind, swore by *donner* and *blitzen*, that he would beat into Table Bay in spite of God or man, and that, foundering with the wicked oath on his lips, he has ever since been working off and on near the Cape. The term is now extended to false reports of vessels seen.

FLYING JIB. A light sail set before the jib, on the flying jib-boom. The third jib in large ships, as the inner jib, the jib, and the flying jib, set on the flying jib-boom. (*See* JIB.)

FLYING JIB-BOOM. A spar which is pointed through the iron at the jib-boom end. It lies beside it, and the heel steps into the bowsprit cap.

FLYING-KITES. The very lofty sails, which are only set in fine weather, such as sky-sails, royal studding-sails, and all above them.

FLYING-LIGHT. The state of a ship when she has little cargo, provisions, or water on board, and is very crank.

FLYING-TO. Is when a vessel, from sailing free or having tacked, and her head thrown much to leeward, is coming to the wind rapidly, the warning is given to the helmsman, "Look out, she is flying-to."

FLY THE SHEETS, To LET. To let them go suddenly.

FLY-UP. A sudden deviation upwards from a sheer line; the term is nearly synonymous with *flight.—To fly up in the wind*, is when a ship's head comes suddenly to windward, by carelessness of the helmsman.

FLY-WHEEL. The regulator of a machine.

FOAM [Anglo-Saxon, *feam*]. The white froth produced by the collision of the waves, or by the bow of a ship when acted on by the wind; and also by their striking against rocks, vessels, or other bodies.

FOCAL LENGTH. The distance between the object-glass and the eye-piece of a telescope.

FOCUS. A point where converging rays or lines meet.

FOEMAN. An enemy in war; now used only by poets. One of Falstaff's recruits, hight Shadow, presented no mark to the enemy: "The foeman may with as great aim level at the edge of a pen-knife."

FŒNUS NAUTICUM. Nautical usury, bottomry.

FOG. A mist at sea, consisting of the grosser vapours floating in the air near the surface of the sea. The fog of the great bank of Newfoundland is caused by the near proximity of warm and cold waters. The air over the Gulf Stream, being warmer than that over the banks of Newfoundland, is capable of keeping much more moisture in invisible suspension; and when this air comes in contact with that above the cold water, it parts with some of its moisture, or rather holds it in visible suspension. There are also dry fogs, which are dust held in suspension, as the so-called African dust, which often partially obscures the sun, and reddens the sails of ships as they pass through the north-east trades.

FOG-BANK. A dense haze, presenting the appearance of a thick cloud resting upon the horizon; it is known in high latitudes as the precursor of wind from the quarter in which it appears. From its frequent resemblance to land it has obtained the name of *Cape Fly-away*.

FOG-BOW. A beautiful natural phenomenon incidental to high latitudes. It appears opposite to the sun, and is usually broad and white, but sometimes assumes the prismatic colours. Indicative of clearing off of mists. (*See* FOG-EATER.)

FOG-DOGS. Those transient prismatic breaks which occur in thick mists, and considered good symptoms of the weather clearing.

FOG-EATER. A synonym of *fog-dog* and *fog-bow*. It may be explained as the clearing of the upper stratum, permitting the sun's rays to exhibit at the horizon prismatic colours; hence "sun-gall."

FOGEY. An old-fashioned or singular person; an invalid soldier or sailor. Often means a stupid but irascible fellow.

FOGGY. Not quite sober.

FOGRAM. Wine, beer, or spirits of indifferent quality; in fact, any kind of liquor.

FOG-SIGNALS. The naval code established by guns to keep a fleet together, to tack, wear, and perform sundry evolutions. Also, certain sounds made in fogs as warnings to other vessels, either with horns, bells, gongs, guns, or the improved fog-whistle.

FOIL. A blunt, elastic, sword-like implement used in fencing.—*To foil* means to disconcert or defeat an enemy's intention.

FOILLAN. The Manx or Erse term for a gull.

FOIN. A thrust with a pike or sword.

FOKE-SILL. Among old salts may be termed a curt or nicked form of *forecastle.*

FOLDER. The movable sight of a fire-arm.

FOLLIS. A net with very large meshes, principally for catching thornbacks.

FOLLOWERS. A certain number of men permitted by the regulations of the service to be taken by the captain when he removes from one ship to another. Also, the young gentlemen introduced into the service by the captain, and reared with a father's care, moving with him from ship to ship; a practice which produced most of our best officers formerly, but innovation has broken through it, to the serious detriment of the service and the country.

FOLLOWING, NORTH OR SOUTH. *See* QUADRANT OF DOUBLE-STARS.

FOMALHAUT. A standard nautical star, called also a *Piscis australis.*

FOOL. "He's no fool on a march," a phrase meaning that such a person is equal to what he undertakes.

FOOLEN. The space between the usual high-water mark in a river and the foot of the wall on its banks, built to prevent its occasionally overflowing the neighbouring lands.

FOOL-FISH. A name of the long-finned file-fish, and so called from its apparently whimsical manner of swimming.

FOOLISH GUILLEMOT. The web-footed diving-bird, *Uria troile,* common on our coasts.

FOOT. The lower end of a mast or sail. Also, the general name of in-

fantry soldiers. Also, the measure of 12 inches, or one-sixth of a fathom.
—*To foot.* To push with the feet; as, "foot the topsail out clear of the top-rim."

FOOT-BANK. Synonymous with *banquette* (which see).

FOOT-BOARD. The same as *gang-board*, but not so sailor-like. (*See* STRETCHER.)

FOOT-BOAT. A west-country term for a boat used solely to convey foot passengers.

FOOT-CLUE OF A HAMMOCK. *See* HAMMOCK.

FOOT-HOOKS. Synonymous with *futtocks*.

FOOTING. A fine paid by a youngster or landsman on first mounting the top. Also, a slight payment from new comers on crossing the line, passing through the Straits of Gibraltar, entering the Arctic Seas, &c.

FOOT IT IN. An order to stow the bunt of a sail snugly in furling, executed by the bunt-men dancing it in, holding on by the topsail-tye. Frequently when a bunt-jigger has parted men have fallen on deck.

FOOT-RAILS. Narrow mouldings raised on a vessel's stern.

FOOT-ROPE. The rope to which the lower edge of a sail is sewed. (*See* BOLT-ROPE.)

FOOT-ROPES. Those stretching under the yards and jib-booms for the men to stand on; they are the same with *horses of the yards* (which see).

FOOT-SPACE-RAIL. The rail that terminates the foot of the balcony, in which the balusters step, if there be no pedestal rail.

FOOT-VALVE. A flat plate of metal filling up the passage between the air-pump and condenser. The lower valve of a steam-engine situated anywhere between the bottom of the working barrel and that of the condenser.

FOOT-WALING. The inside planking or lining of a ship over the floor-timbers; it is intended to prevent any part of her ballast or cargo from falling between her floor-timbers.

FORAD. An old corruption of *foreward*—in the fore-part of the ship.

FORAGE. Food for horses and cattle belonging to an army. Also, the act of a military force in collecting or searching for such forage, or for subsistence or stores for the men; or, with ill-disciplined troops, for valuables in general. Land-piracy.

FORAGE-GUARD. A party detached to cover foragers, those wooding, watering, &c.

FORAY. A plundering incursion.

FOR-BY. Near to; adjacent.

FORCAT. A rest for a musket in olden times.

FORCE. A term which implies the sudden rush of water through a narrow rocky channel, and accompanied by a fall of the surface after the obstacle is passed. It is synonymous with *fall*. Also, the force of each ship stated agreeably to the old usage in the navy, according to the number of guns actually carried. In these days of iron-clads, turret-ships, and heavy guns, this does not give a true estimate of a ship's force. Also, the general force, ships, men, soldiers, &c., engaged in any expedition; as expeditionary force.—Also, *force of wind*, now described by numbers, 0 being calm, 12 the heaviest gale.—*To force*, is to take by storm; to force a passage by driving back the enemy.—Colloquially, no force—gently.

FORCED MARCH. One in which the marching power of the troops is forced or exerted beyond the ordinary limit.

FORCED MEN. Those serving in pirate vessels, but who refused to sign articles.

FORCER. The piston of a *forcing-pump.*

FORCES. The army collectively, or naval and military forces engaged.

FORCING-PUMP. Any pump used to force water beyond that force demanded to deliver at its level, as fire-engines, &c.

FORD. The shallow part of a river, where troops may pass without injuring their arms.

FORE. The distinguishing character of all that part of a ship's frame and machinery which lies near the stem, or in that direction, in opposition to *aft* or *after.* Boarders to the fore—advance!

FORE-AND-AFT. From head to stern throughout the ship's whole length, or from end to end; it also implies in a line with the keel; and is the opposite of *athwart-ships*, which is from side to side.

FORE-AND-AFTER. A cocked hat worn with the peak in front instead of athwart. Also, a very usual term for a schooner with only fore-and-aft sails, even when she has a crossjack-yard whereon to set a square sail when occasion requires.

FORE-AND-AFT SAILS. Jibs, staysails, and gaffsails; in fact, all sails which are not set to yards. They extend from the centre line to the lee side of a ship or boat, so set much flatter than square-sails.

FORE-BAY. A rising at a lock-gate flooring. Also, the galley or the sick-bay.

FORE-BODY. An imaginary figure of that part of the ship afore the midships or dead-flat, as seen from ahead.

FORE-BOWLINE. The bowline of the fore-sail.

FORE-BRACES. Ropes applied to the fore yard-arms to change the position of the fore-sail occasionally.

FORECAST. A storm warning, or reasonable prediction of a gale from the inferences of observed meteorological instruments and phenomena.

FORECASTLE. Once a short deck placed in the fore-part of a ship above the upper deck; it was usually terminated, both before and behind, in vessels of war by a breastwork, the foremost part forming the top of the beak-head, and the hind part, of the fore-chains. It is now applied in men-of-war to that part of the upper deck forward of the after fore-shroud, or maintack-block, and which is flush with the quarter-deck and gangways. Also, a forward part of a merchantman under the deck, where the seamen live on a platform. Some vessels have a short raised deck forward, which is called a *top-gallant forecastle;* it extends from the bow to abaft the foremast, which it includes.

FORECASTLE-DECK. The fore-part of the upper deck at a vessel's bows.

FORECASTLE-JOKES. Practical tricks played upon greenhorns.

FORECASTLE-MEN. Sailors who are stationed on the forecastle, and are generally, or ought to be, prime seamen.

FORECASTLE-NETTINGS. *See* HAMMOCK-NETTINGS.

FORECASTLE-RAIL. The rail extended on stanchions across the after-part of the forecastle-deck in some ships.

FORE CAT-HARPINGS. *See* CAT-HARPINGS.

FORE-COCKPIT. *See* COCKPIT.

FORE-COURSE. The *fore-sail* (which see).

FORE-DECK. That part from the fore-mast to the bows.

FORE-FINGER, OR INDEX-FINGER. The pointing finger, which was called shoot-finger by the Anglo-Saxons, from its use in archery, and is now the *trigger-finger* from its duty in gunnery. (*See* SHOOT-FINGER.)

FORE-FOOT. The foremost piece of the keel, or a timber which terminates the keel at the forward extremity, and forms a rest for the stem's lower end; it is connected by a scarph to the extremity of the keel, and the other end of it, which is incurvated upwards into a sort of knee, is attached to the lower end of the stem; it is also called a gripe. As the lower arm of the fore-foot lies on the same level with the keel, so the upper one coincides with the middle line of the stem; its breadth and thickness therefore correspond with the dimensions of those pieces, and the heel of the cut-water is scarphed to its upper end. Also, an imaginary line of the ship's course or direction.

FORE-GANGER OF THE CHAIN BOWER CABLES. Is a length of 15 fathoms of stouter chain, in consequence of greater wear and tear near the anchor, and exposure to weather. Fore-ganger is also the short piece of rope immediately connecting the line with the shank of the harpoon, when spanned for killing.

FORE-GOER. The same as *fore-ganger*.

FORE-GRIPE. *See* GRIPE.

FORE-GUY. A rope to the swinging-boom of the lower studding-sail.

FORE-HAMMER. The sledge-hammer which strikes the iron on the anvil first, if it be heavy work, but the hand-hammer keeps time.

FORE-HOLD. The part of the hold before the fore hatchway.

FORE-HOODS. The foremost of the outside and inside planks of a vessel.

FORE-HOOKS. The same as *breast-hooks* (which see).

FOREIGN. Of another country or society; a word used adjectively, being joined with divers substantives in several senses.

FOREIGN-GOING. The ships bound on oceanic voyages, as distinguished from home-traders and coasters.

FOREIGN JUDGMENT. *See* JUDGMENT.

FOREIGN REMITTANCE. *See* WAGES REMITTED FROM ABROAD.

FOREIGN REMOVE-TICKET. A document for discharging men from one ship to another on foreign stations: it is drawn up in the same form as the *sick-ticket* (which see).

FOREIGN SERVICE. Vessels or forces stationed in any part of the world out of the United Kingdom. The opposite of *home service.*

FORELAND. A cape or promontory projecting into the sea: as the North and South Forelands. It is nearly the same with *headland,* only that forelands usually form the extremes of certain lines of sea-coast. Also, a space left between the base of a canal bank, and an adjacent drainage cut or river, so as to favour the stability of the bank.

FORE-LIGHTROOM. *See* LIGHT-ROOM.

FORELOCK. A flat pointing wedge of iron, used to drive through a mortise hole in the end of a bolt, to retain it firmly in its place. The forelock is sometimes twisted round the bolt's point to prevent its drawing. Also, spring-forelock, which expands as it passes through.

FORELOCK-BOLTS. Those with an eye, into which an iron forelock is driven to retain them in place. When secured in this way, the bolt is said to be forelocked.

FORELOCKS. The pins by which the cap-squares of gun-carriages are secured.

FORE-MAGAZINE. *See* MAGAZINE.

FORE-MAN AFLOAT. The dockyard officer in charge of the ship-wrights working on board a ship not in dock.

FORE-MAST. The forward lower-mast in all vessels. (*See* MAST.)

FORE-MAST MAN. From "before the mast." A private seaman as distinguished from an officer of a ship.

FOREMOST. Anything which is nearer to the head of a ship than another.

FORE-NESS. An old term for a promontory.

FORE-PART OF A SHIP. The bay, or all before the fore-hatches.

FORE-PEAK. The contracted part of a vessel's hold, close to the bow; close forward under the lower deck.

FORE-RAKE. That part of the hull which rakes beyond the fore-end of the keel.

FORE-REACH, To. To shoot ahead, or go past another vessel, especially when going in stays: to sail faster, reach beyond, to gain upon.

FORERUNNER. A precursor, an avant-courier.

FORERUNNERS OF THE LOG-LINE. A small piece of red bunting laid into that line at a certain distance from the log, the space between them being called the stray-line, which is usually from 12 to 15 fathoms, and is an allowance for the log to be entirely out of the ship's dead-water before they begin to estimate the ship's velocity, consequently the knots begin from that point. (*See* LOG.)

FORE-SAIL. The principal sail set on the foremast. (*See* SAIL.)

FORE-SHEET HORSE. An iron bar fastened at its ends athwart the deck before the mast of a sloop, for the foresail-sheet to traverse upon from side to side.

FORE-SHEETS OF A BOAT. The inner part of the bows, opposite to stern-sheets, fitted with gratings on which the bow-man stands.

FORE-SHEET TRAVELLER. An iron ring which traverses along on the fore-sheet horse of a fore-and-aft rigged vessel.

FORE-SHIP. An archaic form of forecastle of a ship; it means the fore-part of a vessel.

FORE-SHROUDS. *See* SHROUDS.

FORE-STAFF. An instrument formerly used at sea for taking the altitudes of heavenly bodies. The fore-staff, called also *cross-staff*, takes its name hence, that the observer in using it turns his face towards the object, in contradistinction to the back-staff, where he turns his back to the object. The fore or cross staff consists of a straight square staff, graduated like a line of tangents, and four crosses or vanes which slide thereon. The first and shortest of these vanes is called the ten cross or vane, and belongs to that side of the instrument whereon the divisions begin at 3° and end at 10°. The next longer vane is called the thirty cross, belonging to that side of the staff on which the divisions begin at 10° and end at 30°, called the thirty scale. The next is called the sixty cross, and belongs to that side where the divisions begin at 20° and end at 60°. The last and longest, called the ninety cross, belongs to that side whereon the divisions begin at 30° and end at 90°.

FORE-STAGE. The old name for forecastle.

FORE-STAY. *See* STAY.

FORE-TACK. Weather tack of the fore-sail hauled to the fore-boomkin when on a wind.

FORE-TACKLE. A tackle on the fore-mast, similar to the *main-tackle* (which see). It is used for similar purposes, and also in stowing the anchor, &c.

FORE-THWART. The seat of the bow-man in a boat.

FORE-TOP. *See* TOP.

FORETOP-GALLANT-MAST. *See* TOPGALLANT-MAST, to which may be added its proper sail, yard, and studding-sail.

FORETOP-MAST. *See* TOP-MAST.

FORETOP-MEN. Men stationed in the fore-top in readiness to set or take in the smaller sails, and to keep the upper rigging in order.

FORE-TYE. *See* TYE.

FORE-YARD. (*See* YARD.) For the yards, sails, rigging, &c., of the *top-mast* and *topgallant-mast* see those two articles.

FORFEITURE. The effect or penalty of transgressing the laws.

FORGE. A portable forge is to be found in every ship which bears a rated armourer; and it can be used either on board or ashore.

FORGE AHEAD, To. To shoot ahead, as in coming to an anchor—a motion or moving forwards. A vessel forges ahead when hove-to, if the tide presses her to windward against her canvas.

FORGING OVER. The act of forcing a ship violently over a shoal, by the effort of a great quantity of sail, steam, or other manœuvre.

FORK-BEAMS. Short or half beams to support the deck where there is no framing, as in the intervention of hatchways. The *abeam arm fork* is a curved timber scarphed, tabled, and bolted for additional security where the openings are large.

FORKERS. Those who reside in seaports for the sake of stealing dock-yard stores, or buying them, knowing them to be stolen.

FORLORN HOPE. Officers and men detached on desperate service to make a first attack, or to be the first in mounting a breach, or foremost in storming a fortress, or first to receive the whole fire of the enemy. Forlorn-hopes was a term formerly applied to the videttes of the army. This ominous name (the *enfants perdus* of the French) is familiarized into a better one among soldiers, who call it the *flowing-hope*. Promotion is usually bestowed on the survivors.

FORMATION. The drawing up or arrangement of troops, or small-arm men, in certain orders prescribed as the basis of manœuvres in general. Also, the particulars of a ship's build.

FORMER. The gunner's term for a small cylindrical piece of wood, on which musket or pistol cartridge-cases are rolled and formed. The name is also applied to the flat piece of wood with a hole in the centre used for making wads, but which is properly *form*.

FORMICAS. Clusters of small rocks [from the Italian for ants]. Also, Hormigas [Sp.]

FORMING THE LINE. *See* LINE.

FORMING THE ORDER OF SAILING. *See* SAILING.

FORMS. The moulds for making wads by. (*See* FORMER.)

FORT. In fortification, an inclosed work of which every part is flanked by some other part; though the term is loosely applied to all places of strength surrounded by a rampart.

FORTALEZZA [Sp.] A fort on the coast of Brazil.

FORTALICE. A small fortress or fortlet; a bulwark or castle.

FORTH. An inlet of the sea.

FORTIFICATION. The art by which a place is so fortified that a given number of men occupying it may advantageously oppose a superior force. The same word also signifies the works that cover and defend a place. Fortification is *defensive* when surrounding a place so as to render it capable of defence against besiegers; and *offensive* when comprehending the various works for conducting a siege. It is *natural* when it opposes rocks, woods, marshes, ravines, &c., to impede the progress of an enemy; and *artificial*, when raised by human ingenuity to aid the advantages of the ground. The latter is again subdivided into *permanent* and *field* fortification: the one being constructed at leisure and of permanent materials, the other raised only for temporary purposes.

FORTIFYING. The strengthening a ship for especial emergency, by doubling planks, chocks, and additional timbers and knees, strongly secured.

FORT-MAJOR. An officer on the staff of a garrison or fortress, who has, under the commanding officer, general charge of the routine duties and of the works.

FORTUNE OF WAR. The usual consolation in reverses—" Fortune de la guerre," or the chances of war.

FORTY-THIEVES. A name given to forty line-of-battle ships ordered by the Admiralty at one fell swoop, to be built by contract, towards the end of the Napoleon war, and which turned out badly. The writer served in one, the *Rodney* 74, which fully exposed her weakness in the first gale she experienced, and was sent home, thereby weakening the blockading fleet. Many never went to sea as ships of the line, but were converted into good frigates.

FORWARD. In the fore-part of the ship; the same as *afore*. Also, the word of command when troops are to resume their march after a temporary interruption.

FORWARD THERE! The hail to the forecastle.

FOSSE [Ital.] Synonymous with *moat* or *ditch*.

FOTHER [Anglo-Saxon *foder*]. A burden; a weight of lead equal to 19½ cwts. Leaden pigs for ballast.

FOTHERING. Is usually practised to stop a leak at sea. A heavy sail, as the sprit-sail, is closely thrummed with yarn and oakum, and drawn under the bottom: the pressure of the water drives the thrumming into the apertures. If one does not succeed others are added, using all the sails rather than lose the ship.

FOUGADE, or FOUGASS. A small charged mine, from 6 to 8 feet under a post in danger of falling into the enemy's hands.

FOUL. Generally used in opposition to *clear*, and implies entangled, embarrassed, or contrary to: as " a ship ran foul of us," that is, entangled herself among our rigging. Also, to contaminate in any way.

FOUL AIR. May be generated by circumstances beyond control: decomposing fungi, timber injected with coal tar, hatches battened down, and ashes or coal washed about. Whole crews on the coast of Africa, and in the West Indies, have been thus swept away, despite every precaution. But generally it may be avoided by cleanliness.

FOUL ANCHOR. An anchor is said to be *foul*, or *fouled*, either when it hooks some impediment under water, or when the ship, by the wind shifting, entangles her slack cable a turn round the stock, or round the upper fluke thereof. The last, from its being avoidable by a sharp lookout, is termed the seaman's disgrace.

FOUL BERTH. When a ship anchors in the hawse of another she gives the latter a foul berth; or she may anchor on one tide so near as to swing foul on the change either of wind or tide.

FOUL BILL. *See* BILL OF HEALTH.

FOUL BOTTOM. A ship to which seaweed, shells, or other encumbrances adhere. Also, the bottom of the sea if rocky, or unsafe from wrecks, and thence a danger of fouling the anchor.

FOUL COAST. One beset with reefs and breakers, offering dangerous impediments to navigation.

FOUL FISH. Applied to salmon in the spawning state, or such as have not for the current year made their way to the sea for purification; shedders.

FOUL GROUND. Synonymous with *foul bottom*.

FOUL HAWSE. When a vessel is riding with two anchors out, and the cables are crossed round each other outside the stem by the swinging of the ship when moored in a tide-way. (*See* ELBOW and HAWSE.)

FOUL ROPE. A rope entangled or unfit for immediate use.

FOUL WEATHER. That which reduces a ship to snug-sail.

FOUL-WEATHER BREEDER. A name given to the Gulf Stream from such a volume of warm water occasioning great perturbations in the atmosphere while traversing the Atlantic Ocean.

FOUL-WEATHER FLAG. Denotes danger for boats leaving the shore; watermen's fares increase with these signals.

FOUL WIND. That which prevents a ship from laying her course.

FOUNDER. The fall of portions of cliff, as along the coasts of Hampshire and Dorsetshire, occasioned by land-springs.

FOUNDER, To. To fill with water and go down.

FOUR-CANT. A rope composed of four strands.

FOWAN. The Manx term for a dry scorching wind; it is also applied by the northern fishermen to a sudden blast.

FOX. The old English broadsword. Also, a fastening formed by twisting several rope-yarns together by hand and rubbing it with hard tarred canvas; it is used for a seizing, or to weave a paunch or mat, &c. (*See* SPANISH FOX.)

FOXEY. A defect in timber which is over-aged or has been indifferently seasoned, and gives the defective part a reddish hue. The word is very old, and meant tainted or incipient rot.

FOY. A local term for the charge made for the use of a boat.

FOYING. An employment of fishermen or seamen, who go off to ships with provisions, or to help them in distress.

FOYST. An old name for a brigantine. The early voyagers applied the name to some large barks of India, which were probably *grabs*.

FRACTURES. Defects in spars which run across the fibres, being short fractures marked by jagged lines. (*See* SPRUNG.)

FRAISES. Principally in field fortification, palisades placed horizontally, or nearly so, along the crest of the escarp, or sometimes of the counterscarp; being generally concealed from direct artillery fire they very materially increase the difficulty of either of those slopes to an assailant. They project some 5 feet above the surface, and are buried for about the same length in the ground.

FRAME. The outer frame timbers of a vessel consist of the keel, stem, stern-posts, and ribs, which when moulded and bolted form the frame. (*See* TIMBERS.)

FRAME OF THE MARINE STEAM-ENGINE, is the strong supporter of the paddle-shafts and intermediate shaft; it rests on columns, and is firmly bolted to the engine bottom.

FRAMES. The bends of timbers constituting the shape of the ship's body —when completed a ship is said to be *in frame.*

FRAME-TIMBERS. These consist of the floor-timbers, futtocks, and top-timbers; they are placed upon the keel at right angles to it, and form the bottom and sides of the ship.

FRAMING. The placing, scarphing, and bolting of the frame-timbers of a ship. (*See* WARPING.)

FRANC. A French silver coin of the value of $9\frac{1}{2}d.$, and consisting of 100 centimes. The 20-franc piece in gold, formerly called *Louis,* now *Napoleon,* is current for 15s. $10\frac{1}{2}d.$ English.

FRANCESCONI. The dollars of Tuscany, in value 4s. $5\frac{1}{4}d.$ sterling. They each consist of 10 paoli.

FRANK. The large fish-eating heron of our lakes and pools.

FRAP. A boat for shipping salt, used at Mayo, one of the Cape de Verde Islands.

FRAP, To. To bind tightly together. To pass lines round a sail to keep it from blowing loose. To secure the falls of a tackle together by means of spun yarn, rope yarn, or any lashing wound round them. To snap the finger and thumb; to beat.

FRAPPING. The act of crossing and drawing together the several parts of a tackle, or other complication of ropes, which had already been strained to a great extent; in this sense it exactly resembles the operation of bracing up a drum. The frapping increases tension, and consequently adds to the security acquired by the purchase; hence the cat-harpings were no other than frappings to the shrouds.

FRAPPING A SHIP. The act of passing four or five turns of a large cable-laid rope round a ship's hull when it is apprehended that she is not strong enough to resist the violence of the sea. This expedient is only made use of for very old ships, which their owners venture to send to sea as long as possible, insuring them deeply. Such are termed, not unaptly, floating coffins, as were also the old 10-gun brigs, or any vessel deemed doubtful as to sea-worthiness. St. Paul's ship was "undergirded" or frapped.

FRAPPING TURNS. In securing the booms at sea the several turns of the lashings are frapped in preparation for the succeeding turns; in emergency, nailed.

FRAUDS, ACT OF. A statute of Charles II., the object of which was to meet and prevent certain practices by which the navigation laws were eluded.

FREDERIC. A Prussian gold coin, value 16s. 6d. sterling.

FREE, To.—*To free a prisoner.* To restore him to liberty.—*To free a pump.* To disengage or clear it.—*To free a boat or ship.* To clear it of water.

FREE. A vessel is said to be *going free* when the bowlines are slacked and the sheets eased; beyond this is termed large. (*See* SAILING LARGE.)

FREE-BOARD. *See* PLANK-SHEER.

FREEING. The act of pumping, or otherwise throwing out the water which has leaked into a ship's bottom. When all the water is pumped or baled out, the vessel is said to be free. Said of the wind when it exceeds 67° 30′ from right-ahead.

FREE PORT. Ports open to all comers free of entry-dues, as places of call, not delivery.

FREE SHIP. A piratical term for one where it is agreed that every man shall have an equal share in all prizes.

FREE TRADER. Ships trading formerly under license to India independent of the old East India Company's charter. Also, a common woman.

FREEZE, To. To congeal water or any fluid. Thus sea-water freezes at 28° 5′ Fah.; fresh water at 32°; mercury at 39° 5′ below zero. All fluids change their degree of freezing in accordance with mixtures of alcohol or solutions of salt used for the purpose. Also, according to the atmospheric pressure; and by this law heights of mountains are measured by the boiling temperature of water.

FREIGHT. By former English maritime law it became the *mother of wages*, as the crew were obliged to moor the ship on her return in the docks or forfeit them. So severely was the axiom maintained, that if a ship was lost by misfortune, tempest, enemy, or fire, wages also were forfeited, because the freight out of which they were to arise had perished with it. This harsh measure was intended to augment the care of the seamen for the welfare of the ship, but no longer holds, for by the merchant shipping act it is enacted that no right of wages shall be dependent on the earning of freight; in cases of wreck, however, proof that a man has not done his utmost bars his claim. Also, for the burden or lading of a ship. (*See* DEAD-FREIGHT.) Also, a duty of 50 sols per ton formerly paid to the government of France by the masters of foreign vessels going in or out of the several ports of that kingdom. All vessels not built in France were accounted foreign unless two-thirds of the crew were French. The Dutch and the Hanse towns were exempted from this duty of freight. —*To freight a vessel*, means to employ her for the carriage of goods and passengers.

FREIGHT OF A SHIP. The hire, or part thereof, usually paid for the carriage and conveyance of goods by sea; or the sum agreed upon between the owner and the merchant for the hire and use of a vessel, at the rate of so much for the voyage, or by the month, or per ton.

FREIGHTER. The party who hires a vessel or part of a vessel for the carriage of goods.

FREIGHTING. A letting out of vessels on freight or hire; one of the principal practices in the trade of the Dutch.

FRENCH FAKE. A name for what is merely a modification of the Flemish coil, both being extremely good for the object, that is, when a rope has to be let go suddenly, and is required to run freely. *Fake*, in contradistinction to long coil is, run a rope backward and forward in one-fathom bends, beside each other, so that it may run free, as in rocket-lines, to communicate with stranded vessels. (*See* FLEMISH FAKE.)

FRENCH LAKE. A soubriquet for the Mediterranean.

FRENCH LEAVE. Being absent without permission.

FRENCHMAN. . Formerly a term among sailors for every stranger or outlandish man.

FRENCH SHROUD-KNOT. The shroud-knot with three strands single walled round the bights of the other three and the standing part. (*See* SHROUD-KNOT.)

FRENCH THE BALLAST. A term used for *freshen the ballast.*

FRESCA. Fresh water, or rain, and land floods; old term.

FRESH. When applied to the wind, signifies strong, but not violent; hence an increasing gale is said to freshen. (*See* WIND, FORCE OF.) Also used for sweet; as, fresh water. Also, bordering on intoxication; excited with drinking. Also, an overflowing or flood from rivers and torrents after heavy rains or the melting of mountain snows. Also, an increase of the stream in a river. Also, the stream of a river as it flows into the sea. The fresh sometimes extends out to sea for several miles, as off Surinam, and many other large rivers.

FRESH BREEZE. A brisk wind, to which a ship, according to its stability, carries double or treble or close-reefed topsails, &c. This is a very peculiar term, dependent on the stability of the ship, her management, and how she is affected by it, on a wind or before it. It is numbered 6. Thus, a ship running down the trades, with studding-sails set, had registered "moderate and fine;" she met with a superior officer, close-hauled under close-reefed topsails and courses, was compelled to shorten sail, and lower her boat; the log was then marked "fresh breezes."

FRESHEN, To. To relieve a rope of its strain, or danger of chafing, by shifting or removing its place of nip.

FRESHEN HAWSE, To. To relieve that part of the cable which has for some time been exposed to friction in one of the hawse-holes, when the ship rolls and pitches at anchor in a high sea; this is done by applying fresh service to the cable within board, and then veering it into the hawse. (*See* SERVICE, CACKLING, or ROUNDING.)

FRESHEN THE BALLAST. Divide or separate it, so as to alter its position.

FRESHEN THE NIP, To. To veer a small portion of cable through the hawse-hole, or heave a little in, in order to let another part of it bear the stress and friction. A common term with tipplers, especially after taking the meridian observation.

FRESHEN WAY. When the ship feels the increasing influence of a breeze. Also, when a man quickens his pace.

FRESHES. Imply the impetuosity of an ebb tide, increased by heavy rains, and flowing out into the sea, which it often discolours to a considerable distance from the shore, as with the Nile, the Congo, the Mississippi, the Indus, the Ganges, the Rhone, Surinam, &c.

FRESHET. A word long used for pools or ponds, when swollen after rain or temporary inundations. It is also applied to a pond supplied by a spring.

FRESH GALE. A more powerful wind than a *fresh breeze* (which see).

FRESH GRUB. The refreshments obtained in harbour.

FRESH HAND AT THE BELLOWS. Said when a gale freshens suddenly.

FRESH SHOT. A river swollen by rain or tributaries; it also signifies the falling down of any great river into the sea, by which fresh water is often to be found on the surface a good way from the mouth of the river.

FRESH SPELL. Men coming to relieve a gang at work.

FRESH WATER. Water fit to drink, in opposition to sea or salt water; now frequently obtained at sea by distillation. (*See* Ice.)

FRESH-WATER JACK. The same as *fresh-water sailor*.

FRESH-WATER SAILOR. An epithet for a green hand, of whom an old saying has it, "whose shippe was drowned in the playne of Salsbury."

FRESH-WATER SEAS. A name given to the extensive inland bodies of fresh water in the Canadas. Of these, Lake Superior is upwards of 1500 miles in circuit, with a depth of 70 fathoms near the shores, while Michigan and Huron are almost as prodigious; even Erie is 600 miles round, and Ontario near 500, and Nepigon, the head of the system geographically, though the least important at present commercially, but just now partially explored, is fully 400. Their magnitude, however, appears likely to be rivalled geographically by the lakes lately discovered in Central Africa, the Victoria Nyanza and the Albert Nyanza.

FRESH WAY. Increased speed through the water; a ship is said to "gather fresh way" when she has tacked, or hove-to, and then fills her sails.

FRET. A narrow strait of the sea, from *fretum*.

FRET, To. To chafe.

FRET of Wind. A squally flaw.

FRETTUM, or Frectum. The freight of a ship, or freight-money.

FRETUM BRITANNICUM. A term used in our ancient writings for the Straits of Dover.

FRIAR-SKATE. The *Raia oxyrinchus*, or sharp-nosed ray.

FRICTION-ROLLER. A cylinder of hard wood, or metal, with a concave surface, revolving on an axis, used to lessen the friction of a rope which is passed over it. Friction-rollers are a late improvement in the sheaves of blocks, &c., by which the pin is relieved of friction by three rollers in the coak, placed equilaterally.

FRICTION-TUBE. The means of firing a gun most in favour at present in the British service; ignition is caused by the friction on sudden withdrawal of a small horizontal metal bar from the detonating priming in the head of the tube.

FRIDAY. The *dies infaustus*, on which old seamen were desirous of not getting under weigh, as ill-omened.

FRIEZE-PANEL. The lower part of a gun-port.

FRIEZING. The ornamental carving or painting above the drift-rails, and likewise round the stern or the bow.

FRIGATE. In the Royal Navy, the next class vessel to a ship of the line; formerly a light nimble ship built for the purpose of sailing swiftly. The name was early known in the Mediterranean, and applied to a long kind of vessel, navigated in that sea, with sails and oars. The English were the first who appeared on the ocean with these ships, and equipped them for war as well as for commerce. These vessels mounted from 28 to 60 guns, and made excellent cruisers. Frigate is now apocryphal, being carried up to 7000 tons. The *donkey-frigate* was a late invention to serve patronage, and sprigs of certain houses were educated in them. They carried 28 guns, carronades, and were about 600 tons burden, commanded by captains who sometimes found a commander in a sloop which could blow him out of water.—*Frigate* is also the familiar name of the membranous zoophyte, *Physalis pelagica*, or Portuguese man-of-war.

FRIGATE-BIRD. *Tachypetes aquila*, a sea-bird generally seen in the tropics. It seems to live on the wing, is partially web-footed, and only visits the land at breeding time.

FRIGATE-BUILT. The disposition of the decks of such merchant ships as have a descent of some steps from the quarter-deck and forecastle into the waist, in contradistinction to those whose decks are on a continued line for the whole length of the ship, which are called galley-built. (*See* DECK.)

FRIGATOON. A Venetian vessel, commonly used in the Adriatic, built with a square stern, and with only a main-mast, jigger mizen-mast, and bowsprit. Also applied to a ship sloop-of-war.

FRINGING-REEFS. Narrow fringes of coral formation, at a greater or less distance from the shore, according to the slopes of the land.

FRISKING. The wind freshening.

FRITH. Derived from *fretum maris*, a narrow strait: an arm of the sea into which a river flows. Synonymous with *firth* (which see).

FRITTERS. Tendinous fibres of the whale's blubber, running in various directions, and connecting the cellular substance which contains the oil. They are what remains after the oil has been *tried* out, and are used as fuel to *try* out the next whale.

FROG. An old term for a seaman's coat or frock.

FROG-BELT. A *baldrick* (which see).

FROG-FISH. *See* FISHING-FROG.

FROG-LANDERS. Dutchmen in colloquial language.

FROG-PIKE. A female pike, so called from its period of spawning being late, contemporary with the frogs.

FRONT. The foremost rank of a battalion, squadron, file, or other body of men.—*To front*, to face.

FRONTAGE. The length or face of a wharf.

FRONTIER. The limits or borders of a country.

FRONT OF FORTIFICATION. The whole system of works included between the salient angles, or the capitals prolonged, of any two neighbouring bastions.

FROSTED STEEL. The damasked sword-blades.

FROST-FISH. A small fish, called also *tommy-cod ;* in North America they are taken in large quantities in the depth of winter by fishing through holes cut in the ice.

FROST-RIME. *See* FROST-SMOKE.

FROST-SMOKE. A thick mist in high latitudes, arising from the surface of the sea when exposed to a temperature much below freezing; when the vapours as they rise are condensed either into a thick fog, or, with the thermometer about zero, hug the water in eddying white wreaths. The latter beautiful form is called in North America a " barber," probably from its resemblance to soap-suds.

FROTH. *See* FOAM.

F.R.S. The siglæ denoting a Fellow of the Royal Society.

FRUMENTARIÆ. The ancient vessels which supplied the Roman markets with corn.

FRUSH. A northern term for wood that is apt to splinter and break.

FRY. Young fishes.

FUCUS MAXIMUS. An enormous sea-weed, growing abundantly round the coasts of Tristan d'Acunha, and perhaps the most exuberant of the vegetable tribe. Said to rise from a depth of many fathoms, and to spread over a surface of several hundred feet, it being very tenacious.

FUDDLED. Not quite drunk, but unfit for duty.

FUELL. An old nautical word signifying an opening between two headlands, having no bottom in sight.

FU-FU. A well-known sea-dish of barley and treacle, in merchant ships.

FUGITIVES OVER THE SEA. By old statutes, now obsolete, to depart this realm without the king's license incurred forfeiture of goods ; and masters of ships carrying such persons beyond seas, forfeited their vessels.

FUGLEMAN, or more properly **FLUGELMAN.** A corporal, or active adept, who exhibits the time for each motion at the word of command, to enable soldiers, marines, and small-arm men to act simultaneously.

FULCRUM. The prop or support of a lever in lifting or removing a heavy body.

FULL. The state of the sails when the wind fills them so as to carry the vessel ahead.

FULL AND BY. Sailing close-hauled on a wind; when a ship is as close as she will lie to the wind, without suffering the sails to shiver; hence *keep her full* is the order to the helmsman not to incline too much to windward, and thereby shake the sails, which would retard the ship's velocity.

FULL BASTION. In fortification, is a bastion whereof the terreplein, or terrace in rear of the parapet, is extended at nearly the same level over the whole of its interior space.

FULL-BOTTOMED. An epithet to signify such vessels as are designed to carry large cargoes.

FULL DRIVE. Fully direct; impetuous violence.

FULL DUE. For good; for ever; complete; belay.

FULLER. The fluting groove of a bayonet.

FULL FEATHER. Attired in best dress or full uniform.

FULL FOR STAYS! The order to keep the sails full to preserve the velocity, assisting the action of the rudder in tacking ship.

FULL MAN. A rating in coasters for one receiving whole pay, as being competent to all his duties; able seaman.

FULL MOON. When her whole illuminated surface is turned towards us; she is then in opposition, or diametrically opposite, to the sun.

FULL PAY. The stipend allowed when on actual service.

FULL RETREAT. When an army, or any body of men, retire with all expedition before a conquering enemy.

FULL REVETMENT. In fortification, that form of retaining wall which is carried right up to the top of the mass retained, leaving no exterior slope above it; the term is principally used with reference to the faces of ramparts.

FULL SAILS. The sails well set, and filled by the wind.

FULL SEA. High water.

FULL SPEED! A self-explanatory order to the engineer of a steamer to get his engine into full play.

FULL SPREAD. All sail set.

FULL SWING. Having full power delegated; complete control.

FULMAR. A web-footed sea-bird, *Procellaria glacialis*, of the petrel kind, larger than the common gull; its eggs are taken in great quantity at St. Kilda and in the Shetlands.

FUMADO. A commercial name of the pilchard, when garbaged, salted, smoked, pressed, and packed.

FUMBLE-FISTED. Awkward in catching a turn, or otherwise handling a rope.

FUMIGATE, To. To purify confined or infectious air by means of smoke, sulphuric acid, vinegar, and other correctives.

FUMIGATION-LAMP. An invention for purifying the air in hospital-ships and close places.

FUNERAL HONOURS. Obsequies with naval or military ceremonies.

FUNGI. An almost incalculably numerous order of plants growing on dead vegetable matter, and often produced on a ship's lining by long-continued damp.

FUNK. Touch-wood. Also nervousness, cowardice, or being frightened. —*To funk.* To blow the smoke of tobacco.

FUNNEL. An iron tube used where necessary for carrying off smoke. The cylindrical appendages to the furnaces of a steam-ship: the funnel is fastened on the top of the steam-chest, where the flues for both boilers meet. Also, the excavation formed by the explosion of a mine. Also, in artillery, a cup-shaped funnel of leather, with a copper spout, for filling powder into shells.

FUNNEL-STAYS. The ropes or chains by which the smoke-funnel is secured in a steam-ship.

FUNNY. A light, clinker-built, very narrow pleasure-boat for sculling, *i.e.* rowing a pair of sculls. The stem and stern are much alike, both curved. The dimensions are variable, from 20 to 30 feet in length, according to the boat being intended for racing purposes (for which they are mostly superseded by wager-boats), or for carrying one or more sitters.

FUR. The indurated sediment sometimes found in neglected ships' boilers. (*See* FURRING.)

FURL, To. To roll up and bind a sail neatly upon its respective yard or boom.

FURLING. Wrapping or rolling a sail close up to the yard, stay, or mast, to which it belongs, by hauling on the clue-lines and bunt-lines, and winding a gasket or cord about it, to fasten it thereto and secure it snugly.

FURLING IN A BODY. A method of rolling up a topsail only practised in harbour, by gathering all the loose part of the sail into the top, about the heel of the topmast, whereby the yard appears much thinner and lighter than when the sail is furled in the usual manner, which is sometimes termed, for distinction sake, furling in the *bunt*. It is often practised to point the yards, the earings and robins let go, and the whole sail bunted in the top, and covered with tarpaulins.

FURLING-LINE. Denotes a generally flat cord called a *gasket*. In bad weather, with a weak crew, the topsail is brought under control by passing the topmast studding-sail halliards round and round all, from the yard-arm to the bunt; then furling is less dangerous.

FURLOUGH. A granted leave of absence.

FURNACE. The fireplace of a marine boiler.

FURNITURE. The rigging, sails, spars, anchors, cables, boats, tackle, provisions, and every article with which a ship is fitted out. The insurance risk may continue on them when put on shore, during a repair.

FUROLE. The luminous appearance called the *corpo santo* (which see).

FURRENS. Fillings: those pieces supplying the deficiency of the timber in the moulding-way.

FURRING. Doubling planks on a ship. Also, a furring in the ship's frame.—*Furring the boilers*, in a steamer, cleaning off the incrustation or sediment which forms on their inner surfaces.

FURROW. The groove or rabbet of a screw; the breech-sight or notch cut on the base-ring of a gun, and also on the swell of the muzzle, by which the piece is laid.

FURTHER ORDERS. These are often *impedimenta* to active service.

FURTHER PROOF. In prize matters, a privilege, where the court is not satisfied with that originally produced, by which it is allowed to state circumstances affecting it.

FURUBE. A fish taken in the Japanese seas, and considered to be dangerously poisonous.

FURZE. Brushwood, prepared for breaming.

FUSIL. Formerly a light musket with which sergeants of infantry and some particular regiments were armed.

FUSILIERS. Originally those regiments armed with fusils, by whom, though the weapon is obsolete, the title is retained as a distinction.

FUST. A low but capacious armed vessel, propelled with sails and oars, which formerly attended upon galleys; a *scampavia*, barge, or pinnace.

FUSTICK. In commerce, a dye-wood brought principally from the West Indies and Spanish Main.

FUTTLING. A word meaning *foot-waling* (which see).

FUTTOCK-HEAD. In ship-building, is a name for the 5th, the 7th, and the 9th *diagonals*, the intervening bevellings being known as *sirmarks*.

FUTTOCK-HOLES. Places through the top-rim for the futtock-plates.

FUTTOCK-PLANK. The first plank of the ceiling next the kelson; the limber-strake.

FUTTOCK-PLATES. Iron plates with dead-eyes, crossing the sides of the top-rim perpendicularly. The dead-eyes of the topmast rigging are set up to their upper ends or dead-eyes, and the futtock-shrouds hook to their lower ends.

FUTTOCK-RIDERS. When a rider is lengthened by means of pieces batted or scarphed to it and each other, the first piece is termed the first futtock-rider, the next the second futtock-rider, and so on.

FUTTOCKS, or FOOT-HOOKS. The separate pieces of timber which compose the frame. There are four futtocks (component parts of the rib), and occasionally five, to a ship. The timbers that constitute her breadth—the middle division of a ship's timbers, or those parts which are situated between the floor and the top timbers—separate timbers which compose the frame. Those next the keel are called ground-futtocks or navel-timbers, and the rest upper futtocks.

FUTTOCK-SHROUDS, or FOOT-HOOK SHROUDS. Are short pieces of rope or chain which secure the lower dead-eyes and futtock-plates of topmast rigging to a band round a lower mast.

FUTTOCK-STAFF. A short piece of wood or iron, seized across the upper part of the shrouds at equal distances, to which the cat-harping legs are secured.

FUTTOCK-TIMBERS. *See* FUTTOCKS.

FUZE. Formerly called also *fuzee*. The adjunct employed with shells for igniting the bursting charge at the required moment. Time-fuzes, prepared with some composition burning at a known rate, are cut or set to a length proportionate to the time which the shell is destined to occupy in its flight; concussion and percussion fuzes ignite the charge on impact on the object: the former by the dislocation of some of its parts throwing open new passages for its flame, and the latter by the action of various mechanism on its inner priming of detonating composition. They are made either of wood or of metal, and of various form and size according to the kind of ordnance they are intended for. Time-fuzes of special manufacture are also applied to igniting the charges of mines, subaqueous blasts, &c.

FUZZY. Not firm or sound in substance.

FYKE. A large bow-net used on the American coasts for taking the shad; hence called *shad-fykes*. Also, the *Medusa cruciata*, or Medusa's head.

FYRDUNG [the Anglo-Saxon *fyrd ung*, military service]. This appears on our statutes for inflicting a penalty on those who evaded going to war at the king's command.

G.

GAB. A notch on the eccentric rod of a steam-engine for fitting a pin in the gab-lever to break the connection with the slide-valves. (*See* GABBE.)

GABARRE. Originally a river lighter; now a French store-ship.

GABART, or GABBERT. A flat vessel with a long hatchway, used in canals and rivers.

GABBE. An old but vulgar term for the mouth.—*Gift of the gab*, or *glib-gabbet*, facility and recklessness of assertion.

GABBOK. A voracious dog-fish which infests the herring fisheries in St. George's Channel.

GABELLE [Fr.] An excise tribute.

GABERDINE. An old name for a loose felt cloak or mantle.

GABERT. A Scotch lighter. (*See* GABART.)

GABIONADE. A parapet of gabions hastily thrown up.

GABIONS. Cylindrical baskets open at both ends, about 3 feet high and 2 feet in diameter, which, being placed on end and filled with earth, greatly facilitate the speedy formation of cover against an enemy's fire. They are much used for revetments in field-works generally.

GABLE, or GABULLE. A term in early voyagers for *cable*. Thus,

> "Softe, ser, seyd the gabulle-rope,
> Methinke gode ale is in your tope."

GABLICK, or GAFFLOCK. An old term for a crow-bar.

GABY. A conceited simpleton.

GACHUPINS. The name given in South America to European Spaniards.

GAD. A goad; the point of a spear or pike.

GAD-YANG. A coasting vessel of Cochin-China.

GAFF. A spar used in ships to extend the heads of fore-and-aft sails which are not set on stays. The foremost end of the gaff is termed the jaw, the outer part is called the peak. The jaw forms a semicircle, and is secured in its position by a jaw-rope passing round the mast; on it are strung several small wooden balls called *trucks*, to lessen the friction on the mast when the sail is hoisting or lowering.—*To blow the gaff*, said of the revealing a plot or giving convicting evidence.

GAFF-HALLIARDS. *See* HALLIARDS.

GAFF-HOOK. In fishing, a strong iron hook set on a handle, supplementing the powers of the line and fish-hook with heavy fish, in the same way that the landing-net does with those of moderate size.

GAFFLE. A lever or stirrup for bending a cross-bow.

GAFF-NET. A peculiar net for fishing.

GAFF-TOPSAIL. A light triangular or quadrilateral sail, the head being extended on a small gaff which hoists on the topmast, and the foot on the lower gaff.

GAGE. The quantity of water a ship draws, or the depth she is immersed.

GAGE, WEATHER. When one ship is to windward of another she is said to have the weather-gage of her; or if in the opposite position, the lee-gage.

GAGE-COCKS. These are for ascertaining the height of the water in the boiler, by means of three or more pipes, having a cock to each.

GAINED DAY. The twenty-four hours, or day and night, gained by circumnavigating the globe to the eastward. It is the result of sailing in the same direction as the earth revolves, which shortens each day by four minutes for every degree sailed. In the Royal Navy this run gives an additional day's pay to a ship's crew.

GAIN THE WIND, To. To arrive on the weather-side of some other vessel in sight, when both are plying to windward.

GAIR-FISH. A name on our northern coasts for the porpoise.

GAIR-FOWL. A name of the great auk, *Alca impennis*. (*See* AUK.)

GAIRG. A Gaelic name for the cormorant.

GALAXY. A name of the Milky Way. (*See* VIA LACTEA.)

GALEAS. *See* GALLIAS.

GALE OF WIND. Implies what on shore is called a storm, more particularly termed a *hard gale* or *strong gale;* number of force, 10.—*A stiff gale* is the diminutive of the preceding, but stronger than a breeze.—*A fresh gale* is a still further diminutive, and not too strong for a ship to carry single-reefed topsails when close-hauled.—*A top-gallant gale*, if a ship can carry her top-gallant sails.—*To gale away*, to go free.

GALEOPIS. An ancient war-ship with a prow resembling the beak of a sword-fish.

GALITA. *See* GUERITE.

GALL. *See* WINDGALL.

GALLANTS. All flags borne on the mizen-mast were so designated.

GALLAN WHALE. The largest whale which visits the Hebrides.

GALLED. The result of friction, to prevent which it is usual to cover, with skins, mats, or canvas, the places most exposed to it. (*See* SERVICE.)

GALLEON, or Galion. A name formerly given to ships of war furnished with three or four batteries of cannon. It is now retained only by the Spaniards, and applied to the largest size of their merchant ships employed in West India and Vera Cruz voyages. The Portuguese also have ships trading to India and the Brazils nearly resembing the galleons, and called caragues. (*See* CARACK.)

GALLEOT, or Galliot. A small galley designed only for chase, generally carrying but one mast, with sixteen or twenty oars. All the seamen on board act as soldiers, and each has a musket by him ready for use on quitting his oar. Also, a Dutch or Flemish vessel for cargoes, with very rounded ribs and flattish bottom, with a mizen-mast stept far aft, carrying a square-mainsail and main-topsail, a fore-stay to the main-mast (there being no fore-mast), with fore-staysail and jibs. Some also call the bomb-ketches galliots. (*See* SCAMPAVIA.)

GALLERY. A balcony projecting from the admiral's or captain's cabin; it is usually decorated with a balustrade, and extends from one side of the ship to the other; the roof is formed by a sort of vault termed a cove, which is frequently ornamented with carving. (*See* STERN; also QUARTER-GALLERY.)

GALLERY of a Mine. The passage of horizontal communication, as distinguished from the shaft or vertical descent, made underground by military miners to reach the required position for lodging the charge, &c.; it averages 4½ feet high by 3 feet wide.

GALLERY-LADDER. Synonymous with *stern-ladder*.

GALLEY. A low, flat-built vessel with one deck, and propelled by sails and oars, particularly in the Mediterranean. The largest sort, called galleasses, were formerly employed by the Venetians. They were about 160 feet long above, and 130 by the keel, 30 wide, and 20 length of stern-post. They were furnished with three masts and thirty banks of oars, each bank containing two oars, and every oar managed by half-a-dozen slaves, chained to them. There are also *half-galleys* and *quarter-galleys*, but found by experience to be of little utility except in fine weather. They generally hug the shore, only sometimes venturing out to sea for a summer cruise. Also, an open boat rowing six or eight oars, and used on the river Thames by custom-house officers, and formerly by press-gangs; hence the names "custom-house galley," "press-galley," &c. Also, a clincher-built fast rowing-boat, rather larger than a gig, appropriated in a man-of-war for the use of the captain. The *galley* or *gally* is also the name of the ship's hearth or kitchen, being the place where the grates are put up and the victuals cooked. In small merchant-men it is called the caboose; and is generally abaft the forecastle or fore-part of the ship.

GALLEY-ARCHES. Spacious and well-built structures in many of the Mediterranean ports for the reception and security of galleys.

GALLEY-FOIST or Fust. The lord-mayor's barge, and other vessels for holidays. (*See* FUSTE.)

GALLEY-GROWLERS. Idle grumblers and skulkers, from whom discontent and mutiny generally derive their origin. Hence, "galley-packets," news before the mail arrives.

GALLEY-NOSE. The figure-head.

GALLEY-PACKET. An unfounded rumour. (*See* GALLEY-GROWLERS.)

GALLEY-PEPPER. The soot or ashes which accidentally drop into victuals in cooking.

GALLEY-SLANG. The neological barbarisms foisted into sea-language.

GALLEY-SLAVE. A person condemned to work at the oar on board a galley, and chained to the deck.

GALLEY-STOKER. A lazy skulker.

GALLEY-TROUGH. *See* GERLETROCH.

GALLIAS. A heavy, low-built vessel of burden. Not to be confounded with galley, for even Shakspeare, in the *Taming of the Shrew*, makes Tranio say :—

> " My father hath no less
> Than three great argosies; besides two galeasses,
> And twelve tight galleys."

GALLIED. The state of a whale when he is seriously alarmed.

GALLIGASKINS. Wide hose or breeches formerly worn by seamen also called *petticoat-trousers*. P. Penilesse, in his *Sap to the Divell*, says : " Some gally gascoynes or shipman's hose, like the Anabaptists," &c.

GALLING-FIRE. A sustained discharge of cannon, or small arms, which by its execution greatly annoys the enemy.

GALLIVATS. Armed row-boats of India, smaller than a grab; generally 50 to 70 tons.

GALLOON. Gold lace. [Fr. *galon;* Sp. *galon*.]

GALLOPER. A small gun used by the Indians, easily drawn by one horse.

GALLOW-GLASSES. Formerly a heavy-armed body of foot; more recently applied to Irish infantry soldiers.

GALLOWS. The cross-pieces on the small bitts at the main and fore hatchways in flush-decked vessels, for stowing away the booms and spars over the boats; also termed *gallowses, gallows-tops, gallows-bitts*, and *gallows-stanchions*. The word is used colloquially for archness, as well as for notoriously bad characters.

GALLS. Veins of land through which the water oozes.

GALL-WIND. *See* WINDGALL.

GALLY-GUN. A kind of culverin.

GALOOT. An awkward soldier, from the Russian *golut*, or slave. A soubriquet for the young or "green" marine.

GALORE. Plenty, abundance.

GAMBISON. A quilted doublet formerly worn under armour, to prevent its chafing.

GAME-LEG. A lame limb, but not so bad as to unfit for duty.

GAMMON, To. To pass the lashings of the bowsprit.

GAMMONING. Seven or eight turns of a rope-lashing passed alternately over the bowsprit and through a large hole in the cut-water, the better to support the stays of the foremast; after all the turns are drawn as firm as possible, the two opposite are braced together under the bowsprit by a frapping. Gammoning lashing, fashion, &c., has a peculiar seaman-like meaning. The gammoning turns are passed from the standing part or bolt forward, over the bowsprit, aft through the knee forward, making a cross lashing. It was the essence of a seaman's ability, and only fore-castle men, under the boatswain, executed it. Now galvanized chain is more commonly used than rope for gammoning.

GAMMONING-HOLE. A mortise-opening cut through the knee of the head, between the cheeks, through which the gammoning is passed.

GAMMON-KNEE. A knee-timber fayed and bolted to the stem, a little below the bowsprit.

GAMMON-PLATE. An iron plate bolted to the stem of some vessels for the purpose of supporting the gammoning of the bowsprit.

GAMMON-SHACKLE. A sort of triangular ring formed on the end of a gammon-plate, for the gammoning lashing or chain to be made fast to.

GAND-FLOOK. A name of the saury-pike, *Scomberesox saurus.*

GANG. A detachment; being a selected number of a ship's crew appointed on any particular service, and commanded by an officer suitable to the occasion.

GANG-BOARD. The narrow platform within the side next the gunwale, connecting the quarter-deck to the forecastle. Also, a plank with several cleats or steps nailed to it to prevent slipping, for the convenience of walking into or out of a boat upon the shore, where the water is shallow.

GANG-CASKS. Small barrels used for bringing water on board in boats; somewhat larger than *breakers*, and usually containing 32 gallons.

GANGWAY. The platform on each side of the skid-beams leading from the quarter-deck to the forecastle, and peculiar to deep-waisted ships, for the convenience of walking expeditiously fore and aft; it is fenced on the outside by iron stanchions and ropes, or rails, and in vessels of war with a netting, in which part of the hammocks are stowed. In merchant ships it is frequently called the gang-board. Also, that part of a ship's side, and opening in her bulwarks, by which persons enter and depart, provided with a sufficient number of steps or cleats, nailed upon the ship's side, nearly as low as the surface of the water, and sometimes furnished with a railed accommodation-ladder projecting from the ship's side, and secured by iron braces. Also, narrow passages left in the hold, when a ship is laden, in order to enter any particular place as occasion may require, or stop a leak. Also, it implies a thoroughfare of any kind.— *To bring to the gangway,* to punish a seaman by seizing him up to a grating, there to undergo flogging.

GANNERET. A sort of gull.

GANNET. The *Sula bassana,* or solan goose: a large sea bird of the family *Pelecanidœ,* common on the Scottish coasts.

GANNY-WEDGE. A thick wooden wedge, used in splitting timber.

GANTAN. An Indian commercial measure, of which 17 make a baruth.

GANT-LINE. Synonymous with *girt-line* (which see).

GANT-LOPE, OR GAUNTLOPE (commonly pronounced *gantlet*). A *race* which a criminal was sentenced to *run*, in the navy or army, for any heinous offence. The ship's crew, or a certain division of soldiers, were disposed in two rows face to face, each provided with a knotted cord, or *knittle*, with which they severely struck the delinquent as he ran between them, stripped down to the waist. This was repeated according to the sentence, but seldom beyond three times, and constituted "*running the gauntlet.*"

GANTREE, OR GANTRIL. A wooden stand for a barrel.

GANZEE. Corrupted from Guernsey. (*See* JERSEY.)

GAP. A chasm in the land, which, when near, is useful as a landmark.

GAPE. The principal crevice or crack in shaken timber.—*The seams gape*, or let in water.

GARAVANCES. The old term for *calavances* (which see).

GARBEL. A word synonymous with *garboard* (which see).

GARBLING. The mixing of rubbish with a cargo stowed in bulk.

GARBOARD-STRAKE, OR SAND-STREAK. The first range of planks laid upon a ship's bottom, next the keel, into which it is rabbeted, and into the stem and stern-post at the ends.

GARDE-BRACE. Anglo-Norman for armour for the arm.

GARE. *See* GAIR-FOWL. Also, the Anglo-Saxon for *ready.* (*See* YARE.)

GARETTE. A watch-tower.

GARFANGLE. An archaic term for an eel-spear.

GAR-FISH. The *Belone vulgaris*, or bill-fish, the bones of which are green. Also called the guard-fish, but it is from the Anglo-Saxon *gar*, a weapon.

GARGANEY. The *Querquedula circia*, a small species of duck, allied to the teal.

GARLAND. A collar of ropes formerly wound round the head of the mast, to keep the shrouds from chafing. Also, a strap lashed to a spar when hoisting it in. Also, a large rope grommet, to place shot in on deck. Also, in shore-batteries, a band, whether of iron or stone, to retain shot together in their appointed place. Also, the ring in a target, in which the mark is set. Also, a wreath made by crossing three small hoops, and covering them with silk and ribbons, hoisted to the main-topgallant-stay of a ship on the day of the captain's wedding; but on a seaman's wedding, to the appropriate mast to which he is stationed. Also, a sort of cabbage-net, whose opening is extended by a hoop, and used by sailors to contain their day's provisions, being hung up to the beams within their berth, safe from cats, rats, ants, and cockroaches.

GARNET. A sort of purchase fixed to the mainstay of a merchant-ship, and used for hoisting the cargo in and out at the time of loading or delivering her. A whip.—*Clue-garnet.* (*See* CLUE and CLUE GARNET-BLOCK.)

GARNEY. A term in the fisheries for the fins, sounds, and tongues of the cod-fish.

GARNISH. Profuse decoration of a ship's head, stern, and quarters. Also, money which pressed men in tenders and receiving ships exacted from each other, according to priority.

GARR. An oozy vegetable substance which grows on ships' bottoms.

GARRET, OR GARITA. A watch-tower in a fortification; an old term.

GARRISON. A military force guarding a town or fortress; a term for the place itself; also for the state of guard there maintained.

GARRISON GUNS. These are more powerful than those intended for the field; and formerly nearly coincided with naval guns; but now, the introduction of armour-plating afloat leads to furnishing coast-batteries with the heaviest guns of all.

GARRISON ORDERS. Those given out by the commandant of a garrison.

GARROOKA. A fishing-craft of the Gulf of Persia.

GARTERS. A slang term for the ship's irons or bilboes.

GARTHMAN. One who plies at a *fish-garth*, but is prohibited by statute from destroying the fry of fish.

GARVIE. A name on our northern shores for the sprat.

GASKET. A cord, or piece of plaited stuff, to secure furled sails to the yard, by wrapping it three or four times round both, the turns being at a competent distance from each other.—*Bunt-gasket* ties up the bunt of the sail, and should consequently be the strongest; it is sometimes made in a peculiar net form. In some ships they have given place to beckets.—*Double gaskets.* Passing additional frapping-lines round the yards in very stormy weather.—*Quarter-gasket.* Used only for large sails, and is fastened about half-way out upon the yard, which part is called the quarter.—*Yard-arm gasket.* Used for smaller sails; the end is made fast to the yard-arm, and serves to bind the sail as far as the quarter-gasket on large yards, but extends quite into the bunt of small sails.

GAS-PIPE. A term jocularly applied to the newly-introduced breech-loading rifle.

GAT. A swash-way, or channel amongst shoals.

GATE. The old name for landing-places, as Dowgate and Billingsgate; also in cliffs, as Kingsgate, Margate, and Ramsgate; those in Greece and in Italy are called *scala.* Also, a flood, sluice, or water gate.

GATE, OR SEA-GATE. When two ships are thrown on board one another by a wave, they are said to be in a sea-gate.

GATHER AFT A SHEET, To. To pull it in, by hauling in slack.

GATHER WAY, To. To begin to feel the impulse of the wind on the sails, so as to obey the helm.

GATH-LINN. A name of the north polar star; two Gaelic words, signifying ray and moisture, in allusion to its subdued brightness.

GATT. A gate or channel, a term used on the Flemish coast and in the Baltic. The Hellegat of New York has become Hell Gate.

GAUB-LINE. A rope leading from the martingale inboard. The same as *back-rope*.

GAUGE. *See* GAGE.

GAUGE-COCKS. A neat apparatus for ascertaining the height of the water in a steamer's boiler.

GAUGNET. The *Sygnathus acus*, sea-needle, or pipe-fish.

GAUNTLET. (*See* GIRT-LINE.) Also, a rope round the ship to the lower yard-arms, for drying scrubbed hammocks. Of old the term denoted the armed knight's iron glove. (*See* GANTLOPE, for *running the gauntlet*.)

GAUNTREE. The stand for a water or beer cask.

GAUNTS. The great crested grebe in Lincolnshire.

GAUT, OR GHAUT. In the East Indies, a landing-place; and also a chain of hills, as the Western Gauts, on the Mysore coast.

GAVELOCK. An iron crow. Of old, a pike; thus in Arthur and Merlin—

> "Gavelokes also thicke flowe
> So gnattes, ichil avowe."

GAVER. A Cornish name for the sea cray-fish.

GAW. A southern term for a boat-pole.

GAWDNIE. The dragonet, or yellow gurnard; *Callionymus lyra*.

GAW-GAW. A lubberly simpleton.

GAWKY. A half-witted, awkward youth. Also, the shell called horse-cockle.

GAWLIN. A small sea-fowl which the natives of the Western Isles of Scotland trust in, as a prognosticator of the weather.

GAWN-TREE. *See* GANTREE.

GAWPUS. A stupid, idle fellow.

GAWRIE. A name for the red gurnard; *Trigla cuculus*.

GAZONS [Fr.] Sods of earth or turf, cut in wedge-shaped form, to line the parapet and face the outside of works.

GAZZETTA. The name of a small coin in the Adriatic and Levant. It was the price of the first Venetian newspaper, and thereby gave the name to those publications. In the Greek islands the word is used for ancient coins.

G.C.B. The initials for Grand Cross of the most honourable and Military Order of the Bath.

GEAR [the Anglo-Saxon *geara*, clothing]. A general name for the rigging of any particular spar or sail; and in or out of gear implies anything being fit or unfit for use.

GEARING. A complication of wheels and pinions, or of shafts and pulleys, &c.

GEARS. *See* JEERS.

GEE, To. To suit or fit; as, "that will just gee."

GELLYWATTE. An old term for a captain's boat, the original of *jolly-boat*. (*See* Captain Downton's voyage to India in 1614, where " she was sent to take soundings within the sands.")

GENERAL. The commander of an army: the military rank corresponding to the naval one of admiral. The title includes all officers above colonels, ascending with qualifying prefixes, as brigadier-general, major-general, lieutenant-general, to general, above which is nothing save the exceptional rank of field-marshal and of captain-general or commander-in-chief of the land forces of the United Kingdom.

GENERAL AVERAGE. A claim made upon the owners of a ship and her cargo, when the property of one or more has been sacrificed for the good of the whole.

GENERAL BREEZO. *See* BREEZO.

GENERALISSIMO. The supreme commander of a combined force, or of several armies in the field.

GENERAL OFFICERS. All those above the rank of a colonel.

GENERAL ORDERS. The orders issued by the commander-in-chief of the forces.

GENERAL SHIP. Where persons unconnected with each other load goods on board, in contradistinction to a *chartered* ship.

GENEVA PRINT. An allusion to the spirituous liquor so called,—

> " And if you meet
> An officer preaching of sobriety,
> Unless he read it in *Geneva print*,
> Lay him by the heels."—*Massinger.*

GENOUILLERE [Fr.] That part of a battery which remains above the platform, and under the gun after the opening of the embrasure. Of course a knee-step.

GENTLE. A maggot or grub used as a bait by anglers.

GENTLE GALE. In which a ship carries royals and flying-kites; force 4.

GENTLEMEN. The messmates of the gunroom or cockpit—as mates, midshipmen, clerks, and cadets.

GEOCENTRIC. As viewed from the centre of the earth.

GEO-GRAFFY. A beverage made by seamen of burnt biscuit boiled in water.

GEOGRAPHICAL POSITION. *See* POSITION.

GEORGIUM SIDUS. The planet discovered by Sir W. Herschel was so named at first; but astronomers adopted *Uranus* instead, as safer to keep in the neutral ground of mythology.

GERLETROCH. The *Salmo Alpinus*, red char, or galley-trough.

GERRACK. A coal-fish in its first year.

GERRET. A samlet or parr.

GERRICK. A Cornish name for a sea-pike.

GERRON. A cant name for the sea-trout.

GESERNE. Anglo-Norman for battle-axe.

GESTLING. A meeting of the members of the Cinque Ports at Romney.

GET AFLOAT. Pulling out a grounded boat.

GET-A-PULL. The order to haul in more of a rope or tackle.

GHAUT. *See* GAUT.

GHEE. The substitute for butter served out to ships' companies on the Indian station.

GHOST. A false image in the lens of an instrument.

GHRIME-SAIL. The old term for a smoke-sail.

GIB. A forelock.

GIBB. The beak, or hooked upper lip of a male salmon.

GIBBOUS. The form of a planet's disc exceeding a semicircle, but less than a circle.

GIB-FISH. A northern name for the male of the salmon.

GIBRALTAR GYN. Originally devised there for working guns under a low roof. (*See* GYN.)

GIDDACK. A name on our northern coasts for the sand-launce or sand-eel, *Ammodytes tobianus.*

GIFFOOT. A Jewish corruption of the Spanish spoken at Gibraltar and the sea-ports.

GIFT-ROPE [synonymous with *guest-rope*]. A rope for boats at the guest-warp boom.

GIG. A light narrow galley or ship's boat, clincher-built, and adapted for expedition either by rowing or sailing; the latter ticklish at times.

GILDEE. A name in the Scottish isles for the *Morhua barbata,* or whiting pout.

GILGUY. A guy for tracing up, or bearing a boom or derrick. Often applied to inefficient guys.

GILL. A ravine down the surface of a cliff; a rivulet through a ravine. The name is often applied also to the valley itself.

GILLER. A horse-hair fishing line.

GILLS. Small hackles for drying hemp.

GILPY. Between a man and boy.

GILSE. A common misnomer of *grilse* (which see).

GILT. A cant, but old term for money, on which Shakspeare (*Henry V.* act ii. scene 1) committed a well-known pun—

"Have for the gilt of France (O guilt indeed!)"

GILT-HEAD, OR GILT-POLL. The *Sparus aurata,* a fish of the European and American seas, with a golden mark between the eyes. (*See* SEDOW.)

GIMBALS. The two concentric brass rings, having their axles at right angles, by which a sea-compass is suspended in its box, so as to counter-act the effect of the ship's motion. (*See* COMPASS.) Also used for the chronometers.

GIMBLETING. The action of turning the anchor round on its fluke, so that the motion of the stock appears similar to that of the handle of a gimlet when it is employed to bore a hole. To turn anything round on its end.

GIMLET-EYE. A penetrating gaze, which sees through a deal plank.

GIMMART. *See* GYMMYRT.

GIMMEL. Any disposition of rings, as links, device of machinery. (*See* GIMBAL.)

GIN. A small iron cruciform frame, having a swivel-hook, furnished with an iron sheave, to serve as a pulley for the use of chain in discharging cargo and other purposes.

GINGADO. *See* JERGADO.

GINGAL. A long barrelled fire-arm, throwing a ball of from $\frac{1}{4}$ to $\frac{1}{2}$ lb., used throughout the East, especially in China; made to load at the breach with a movable chamber. (*See also* JINGAL.)

GINGERBREAD-HATCHES. Luxurious quarters—
"Gingerbread-hatches on shore."

GINGERBREAD WORK. Profusely carved decorations of a ship.

GINGERLY. Spruce and smart, but somewhat affected in movement.

GINNELIN. Catching fish by the hand; tickling them.

GINNERS, OR GINNLES. The gills of fish.

GINSENG. A Chinese root, formerly highly prized for its restorative virtues, and greatly valued among the items of a cargo. It is now almost out of the *Materia Medica*.

GIP, To. To take the entrails out of fishes.

GIRANDOLE. Any whirling firework.

GIRD, To. To bind; used formerly for striking a blow.

GIRDLE. An additional planking over the wales or bends. Also, a frapping for girding a ship.

GIRT. The situation of a ship which is moored so taut by her cables, extending from the hawse to two distant anchors, as to be prevented from swinging to the wind or tide. The ship thus circumstanced endeavours to swing, but her side bears upon one of the cables, which catches on her heel, and interrupts her in the act of traversing. In this position she must ride with her broadside or stern to the wind or current, till one or both of the cables are slackened, so as to sink under the keel; after which the ship will readily yield to the effort of the wind or current, and turn her head thither. (*See* RIDING.)

GIRT-LINE. A whip purchase, consisting of a rope passing through a single block on the head of a lower mast to hoist up the rigging thereof, and the persons employed to place it; the girt-line is therefore the first rope employed to rig a ship. (Sometimes mis-called *gantline*.)

GISARMS. An archaic term for a halbert or hand-axe.

GIVE A SPELL. To intermit or relieve work. (*See* SPELL-O!)

GIVE CHASE, To. To make sail in pursuit of a stranger.

GIVE HER SO AND SO. The direction of the officer of the watch to the midshipman, reporting the rate of sailing by the log, and which requires correction in the judgment of that officer, from winds, &c., before marking on the log-board.

GIVE HER SHEET. The order to ease off; give her rope.

GIVE WAY. The order to a boat's crew to renew rowing, or to increase their exertions if they were already rowing. To hang on the oars.

GIVE WAY TOGETHER. So that the oars may all dip and rise together, whereby the force is concentrated.

GIVE WAY WITH A WILL. Pull heartily together.

GIVING. The surging of a seizing; new rope stretching to the strain.

GLACIS. In fortification, that smooth earthen slope outside the ditch which descends to the country, affording a secure parapet to the covered way, and exposing always a convenient surface to the fire of the place.

GLADENE. A very early designation of the sea-onion.

GLAIRE. A broadsword or falchion fixed on a pike.

GLANCE. (*See* NORTHERN GLANCE.) Also, a name for anthracite coal.

GLASAG. The Gaelic name of an edible sea-weed of our northern isles.

GLASS. The usual appellation for a telescope (see the old sea song of Lord Howard's capture of Barton the pirate). Also, the familiar term for a barometer. *Glass* is also used in the plural to denote time-glass on the duration of any action; as, they fought yard-arm and yard-arm three glasses, *i.e.* three half-hours.—*To flog or sweat the half-hour glass.* To turn the sand-glass before the sand has quite run out, and thus gaining a few minutes in each half-hour, make the watch too short.—*Half-minute and quarter-minute glasses*, used to ascertain the rate of the ship's velocity measured by the log; they should be occasionally compared with a good stop watch.—*Night-glass.* A telescope adapted for viewing objects at night.

GLASS CLEAR? Is the sand out of the upper part? asked previously to turning it, on throwing the log.

GLASSOK. A coast name for the say, seath, or coal-fish.

GLAVE. A light hand-dart. Also, a sword-blade fixed on the end of a pole.

GLAYMORE. A two-handed sword. (*See* CLAYMORE.)

GLAZED POWDER. Gunpowder of which the grains, by friction against one another in a barrel worked for the purpose, have acquired a fine polish, sometimes promoted by a minute application of black-lead; reputed to be very slightly weaker than the original, and somewhat less liable to deterioration.

GLEN. An Anglo-Saxon term denoting a dale or deep valley; still in use for a ravine.

GLENT, To. To turn aside or quit the original direction, as a shot does from accidentally impinging on a hard substance.

GLIB-GABBET. Smooth and ready speech.

GLIM. A light; familiarly used for the eyes.—*Dowse the glim*, put out the light.

GLOAMING. The twilight. Also, a gloomy dull state of sky.

GLOBE RANGERS. A soubriquet for the royal marines.

GLOBULAR SAILING. A general designation for all the methods on which the rules of computation are founded, on the hypothesis that the earth is a sphere; including great circle sailing.

GLOG. The Manx or Erse term which denotes the swell or rolling of the sea after a storm.

GLOOM-STOVE. Formerly for drying powder, at a temperature of about

140°; being an iron vessel in a room heated from outside, but steam-pipes are now substituted.

GLOOT. *See* GALOOT.

GLOWER, To. To stare or look intently.

GLUE. *See* MARINE-GLUE.

GLUM. As applied to the weather, overcast and gloomy. Socially, it is a grievous look.

GLUT. A piece of wood applied as a fulcrum to a lever power. Also, a bit of canvas sewed into the centre of a sail near the head, with an eyelet-hole in the middle for the bunt-jigger or becket to go through. Glut used to prevent slipping, as sand and nippers glut the messenger; the fall of a tackle drawn across the sheaves, by which it is choked or glutted; junks of rope interposed between the messenger and the whelps of the capstan.

GLYN. A deep valley with convex sides. (*See* CWM.)

GNARLED. Knotty; said of timber.

GNARRE. An old term for a hard knot in a tree; hence Shakspeare's "unwedgeable and gnarled oak."

GNOLL. A round hillock. (*See* KNOLL.)

GNOMON. The hand; style of a dial.

GO! A word sometimes given when all is ready for the launch of a vessel from the stocks.

GO AHEAD! OR GO ON! The order to the engineer in a steamer.

GO ASHORE, To. To land on leave.

GO ASHORES. The seamen's best dress.

GOBARTO. A large and ravenous fish of our early voyagers, probably a shark.

GOBBAG. A Gaelic name for the dog-fish.

GOB-DOO. A Manx term for a mussel.

GOBISSON. *Gambesson;* quilted dress worn under the habergeon.

GOBLACHAN. A Gaelic name for the parr or samlet.

GOB-LINE. *See* GAUB-LINE.

GOBON. An old English name for the whiting.

GOB-STICK. A horn or wooden spoon.

GO BY. Stratagem.—*To give her the go by*, is to escape by deceiving.

GOBY. A name of the *gudgeon* (which see). It was erroneously applied to white-bait.

GOD. We retain the Anglo-Saxon word to designate the ALMIGHTY; signifying good, to do good, doing good, and to benefit; terms such as our classic borrowings cannot pretend to.

GODENDA. An offensive weapon of our early times, being a pole-axe with a spike at its end.

GO DOWN. The name given to store-houses and magazines in the East Indies.

GODSEND. An unexpected relief or prize; but wreckers denote by the term vessels and goods driven on shore.

GOE. A creek, smaller than a voe.

GOELETTE [Fr.] A schooner. Also, a sloop-of-war.

GOGAR. A serrated worm used in the north for fishing-bait.

GOGLET. An earthen vase or bottle for holding water.

GOILLEAR. The Gaelic for a sea-bird of the Hebrides, said to come ashore only in January.

GOING ABOUT. Tacking ship.

GOING FREE. When the bowlines are slackened, or sailing with the wind abeam.

GOING LARGE. Sailing off the wind.

GOING THROUGH THE FLEET. A cruel punishment, long happily abolished. The victim was sentenced to receive a certain portion of the flogging alongside the various ships, towed in a launch by a boat supplied from each vessel, the drummers beating the rogue's march.

GOLDENEY. A name for the yellow gurnard among the northern fishermen.

GOLD FISH. The trivial name of the *Cyprinus auratus*, one of the most superb of the finny tribe. It was originally brought from China, but is now generally naturalized in Europe.

GOLD MOHUR. A well known current coin in the East Indies, varying a little in value at each presidency, but averaging fifteen rupees, or thirty shillings.

GOLE. An old northern word for a stream or sluice.

GOLLETTE. The shirt of mail formerly worn by foot soldiers. Also, a French sloop-of-war, spelled goëlette.

GOMER. A particular form of chamber in ordnance, consisting in a conical narrowing of the bore towards its inner end. It was first devised for the service of mortars, and named after the inventor, Gomer, in the late wars.

GOMERE [Fr.] The cable of a galley.

GONDOLA. A light pleasure-barge universally used on the canals of Venice, generally propelled by one man standing on the stern with one powerful oar, though the larger kinds have more rowers. The middle-sized gondolas are upwards of 30 feet long and 4 broad, with a well furnished cabin amidships, though exclusively black as restricted by law. They always rise at each end to a very sharp point of about the height of a man's breast. The stem is always surmounted by the ferro, a bright iron beak or cleaver of one uniform shape, seemingly derived from the ancient Romans, being the "rostrique tridentibus" of Virgil, as may be seen in many of Hadrian's large brass medals. The form of the gondola in the water is traced back till its origin is lost in antiquity, yet (like that of the Turkish caïques) embodies the principles of the wave-line theory, the latest effort of modern ship-building science. Also, a passage-boat of six or eight oars, used on other parts of the coast of Italy.

GONDOLIER. A man who works or navigates a gondola.

GONE. Carried away. "The hawser or cable is *gone*," parted, broken.

GONE-GOOSE. A ship deserted or given up in despair (*in extremis*).

GONFANON [Fr.] Formerly a cavalry banneret; corrupted from the *gonfalone* of the Italians.

GONG. A kind of Chinese cymbal, with a powerful and sonorous tone produced by the vibrations of its metal, consisting mainly of copper and tutenag or zinc; it is used by some vessels instead of a bell. A companion of Sir James Lancaster in 1605 irreverently states that it makes "a most hellish sound."

GONGA. A general name for a river in India, whence comes Ganges.

GOOD-AT-ALL-POINTS. Practical in every particular.

GOOD-CONDUCT BADGE. Marked by a chevron on the lower part of the sleeve, granted by the admiralty, and carrying a slight increase of pay, to petty officers, seamen, and marines. One of a similar nature is in use in the army.

GOOD MEN. The designation of the able, hard-working, and willing seamen.

GOOD SHOALING. An approach to the shore by very gradual soundings.

GOOLE. An old term for a breach in a sea-bank.

GOOSANDER. The *Mergus merganser*, a northern sea-fowl, allied to the duck, with a straight, narrow, and serrated bill, hooked at the point.

GOOSE-NECK. A curved iron, fitted outside the after-chains to receive a spare spar, properly the swinging boom, a davit. Also, a sort of iron hook fitted on the inner end of a boom, and introduced into a clamp of iron or eye-bolt, which encircles the mast; or is fitted to some other place in the ship, so that it may be unhooked at pleasure. It is used for various purposes, especially for guest-warps and swinging booms of all descriptions.

GOOSE-WINGS OF A SAIL. The situation of a course when the bunt-lines and lee-clue are hauled up, and the weather-clue down. The clues, or lower corners of a ship's main-sail or fore-sail, when the middle part is furled or tied up to the yard. The term is also applied to the fore and main sails of a schooner or other two-masted fore-and-aft vessel; when running before the wind she has these sails set on opposite sides.

GOOSE WITHOUT GRAVY. A severe starting, so called because no blood followed its infliction.

GORAB. *See* GRAB.

GORD. An archaism denoting a deep hole in a river.

GORES. Angular pieces of plank inserted to fill up a vessel's planking at any part requiring it. Also, the angles at one or both ends of such cloths as increase the breadth or depth of a sail. (*See* GORING-CLOTH.)

GORGE. The upper and narrowest part of a transverse valley, usually containing the upper bed of a torrent. Also, in fortification, a line joining the inner extremities of a work.

GORGE-HOOK. Two hooks separated by a piece of lead, for the taking of pike or other voracious fish.

GORGET. In former times, and still amongst some foreign troops, a gilt badge of a crescent shape, suspended from the neck, and hanging on the breast, worn by officers on duty.

GORING, or GORING-CLOTH. That part of the skirts of a sail cut on the bias, where it gradually widens from the upper part down to the clues. (*See* SAIL.)

GORMAW. A coast name for the cormorant.

GORSE. Heath or furze for breaming a vessel's bottom.

GO SLOW. The order to the engineer to cut off steam without stopping the play of the engine.

GOSSOON. A silly awkward lout.

GOTE. *See* GUTTER.

GOUGING. In ship-building (*see* SNAIL-CREEPING). Also, a cruel practice in one or two American states, now extremely rare, in which a man's eye was squeezed out by his rival's thumb-nail, the fingers being entangled in the hair for the necessary purchase.

GOUGINGS. A synonym of *gudgeons* (which see).

GOUKMEY. One of the names in the north for the gray gurnard.

GOULET. Any narrow entrance to a creek or harbour, as the *goletta* at Tunis.

GOURIES. The garbage of salmon.

GOVERNMENT. Generally means the constitution of our country as exercised under the legislature of king or queen, lords, and commons.

GOVERNOR. An officer placed by royal commission in command of a fortress, town, or colony. Governors are also appointed to institutions, hospitals, and other establishments. Also, a revolving bifurcate pendulum, with two iron balls, whose centrifugal divergence equalizes the motion of the steam-engine.

GOW. An old northern term for the gull.

GOWDIE. The *Callionymus lyra*, dragonet, or chanticleer.

GOWK. The cuckoo; but also used for a stupid, good-natured fellow.

GOWK-STORM. Late vernal equinoctial gales contemporary with the gowk or cuckoo.

GOWT, or GOTE. A limited passage for water.

GOYLIR. A small sea-bird held to precede a storm; hence seamen call them *malifiges*. Arctic gull.

GRAB. The large coasting vessel of India, generally with two masts, and of 150 to 300 tons.—*To grab*. In familiar language, to catch or snatch at anything with violence.

GRABBLE, To. To endeavour to hook a sunk article. To catch fish by hand in a brook.

GRAB SERVICE. Country vessels first employed by the Bombay government against the pirates; afterwards erected into the Bombay Marine.

GRACE. *See* ACT OF GRACE.

GRADE. A degree of rank; a step in order or dignity.

GRAFTING. An ornamental weaving of fine yarns, &c., over the strop of a block; or applied to the tapered ends of the ropes, and termed pointing.

GRAIN OF TIMBER. In a transverse section of a tree, two different grains are seen: those running in a circular manner are called the *silver grain;* the others radiate, and are called *bastard grain.*—*Grain* is also a whirlwind not unfrequent in Normandy, mixed with rain, but seldom continues above a quarter of an hour. They may be foreseen, and while they last the sea is very turbulent; they may return several times in the same day, a dead calm succeeding.

GRAIN. In the *grain of,* is immediately preceding another ship in the same direction.—*Bad-grain,* a sea-lawyer; a nuisance.

GRAIN-CUT TIMBER. That which is cut athwart the grain when the grain of the wood does not partake of the shape required.

GRAINED POWDER. That corned or reduced into grains from the cakes, and distinguished from mealed powder, as employed in certain preparations.

GRAINS. A five-pronged fish-spear, grains signifying branches.

GRAIN UPSET. When a mast suffers by buccles, it is said to have its grain upset. A species of wrinkle on the soft outer grain which will be found corresponding to a defect on the other side. It is frequently produced by an injudicious setting up of the rigging.

GRAM. A species of pulse given to horses, sheep, and oxen in the East Indies, and supplied to ships for feeding live-stock.

GRAMPUS. A corruption of *gran pisce.* An animal of the cetacean or whale tribe, distinguished by the large pointed teeth with which both jaws are armed, and by the high falcate dorsal fin. It generally attains a length of 20 to 25 feet, and is very active and voracious.

GRAMPUS, Blowing the. Sluicing a person with water, especially practised on him who skulks or sleeps on his watch.

GRAND DIVISION. A division of a battalion composed of two companies, or ordinary divisions, in line.

GRANDSIRE. The name of a four-oared boat which belonged to Peter the Great, now carefully preserved at St. Petersburg as the origin of the Russian fleet.

GRANNY'S BEND. The slippery hitch made by a lubber.

GRANNY'S KNOT. This is a term of derision when a reef-knot is crossed the wrong way, so as to be insecure. It is the natural knot tied by women or landsmen, and derided by seamen because it cannot be untied when it is jammed.

GRAPESHOT. A missile from guns intermediate between case-shot and solid shot, having much of the destructive spread of the former with somewhat of the range and penetrative force of the latter. A round of grapeshot consists of three tiers of cast-iron balls arranged, generally three in a tier, between four parallel iron discs connected together by a central wrought-iron pin. For carronades, the grape, not being liable to such a violent dispersive shock, they are simply packed in canisters with wooden bottoms.

GRAPNEL, or Grapling. A sort of small anchor for boats, having a ring at one end, and four palmed claws at the other.—*Fire grapnel.*

Resembling the former, but its flukes are furnished with strong fish-hook barbs on their points, usually fixed by a chain on the yard-arms of a ship, to grapple any adversary whom she intends to board, and particularly requisite in fire-ships. Also, used to grapple ships on fire, in order to tow them away from injuring other vessels.

GRAPNEL-ROPE. That which is bent to the grapnel by which a boat rides, now substituted by chain.

GRAPPLE, To. To hook with a grapnel; to lay hold of. First used by Duillius to prevent the escape of the Carthaginians.

GRASP. The handle of a sword, and of an oar. Also, the small of the butt of a musket.

GRASS. A term applied to vegetables in general. (*See* FEED.)

GRASS-COMBERS. A galley-term for all those landsmen who enter the naval service from farming counties. Lord Exmouth found many of them learn their duties easily, and turn out valuable seamen.

GRATING-DECK. A light movable deck, similar to the hatch-deck, but with open gratings.

GRATINGS. An open wood-work of cross battens and ledges forming cover for the hatchways, serving to give light and air to the lower decks. In nautical phrase, he "who can't see a hole through a grating" is excessively drunk.

GRATINGS OF THE HEAD. *See* HEAD-GRATINGS.

GRATUITOUS MONEY. A term officially used for bounty granted to volunteers in Lord Exmouth's expedition against Algiers.

GRAVE, To. To clean a vessel's bottom, and pay it over.

GRAVELIN. A small migratory fish, commonly reputed to be the spawn of the salmon.

GRAVELLED. Vexed, mortified.

GRAVING. The act of cleaning a ship's bottom by burning off the impurities, and paying it over with tar or other substance, while she is laid aground during the recess of the tide. (*See* BREAMING.)

GRAVING BEACH OR SLIP. A portion of the dockyard where ships were landed for a tide.

GRAVING-DOCK. An artificial receptacle used for the inspecting, repairing, and cleaning a vessel's bottom. It is so contrived that after the ship is floated in, the water may run out with the fall of the tide, the shutting of the gates preventing its return.

GRAVITATION. The natural tendency or inclination of all bodies towards the centre of the earth; and which was established by Sir Isaac Newton, as the great law of nature.

GRAVITY, CENTRE OF. The centre of gravity of a ship is that point about which all parts of the body, in any situation, balance each other. (*See* SPECIFIC GRAVITY.)

GRAWLS. The young salmon, probably the same as *grilse*.

GRAY-FISH, AND GRAY-LORD. Two of the many names given to the *Gadus carbonarius* or coal-fish.

GRAYLE. Small sand. Also, an old term for thin gravel.

GRAYLING. A fresh-water fish of the Salmo tribe. (*See* UMBER.)

GRAYNING. A species of dace found on our northern coast.

GRAY-SCHOOL. A particular shoal of large salmon in the Solway about the middle of July.

GRAZE. The point at which a shot strikes and rebounds from earth or water.

GRAZING-FIRE. That which sweeps close to the surface it defends.

GREASY. Synonymous with dirty weather.

GREAT CIRCLE. One whose assumed plane passes through the centre of the sphere, dividing it equally.

GREAT-CIRCLE SAILING. Is a method for determining a series of points in an arc of a great circle between two points on the surface of the earth, for the purpose of directing a ship's course as nearly as possible on such arc; that is, on the curve of shortest distance between the place from which she sets out, and that at which she is to arrive.

GREAT GUN. The general sea-term for cannons, or officers of great repute.

GREAT GUNS AND SMALL-ARMS. The general armament of a ship. Also, a slang term for the blowing and raining of heavy weather.

GREAT-LINE FISHING. That carried on over the deeper banks of the ocean. (*See* LINE-FISHING.) It is more applicable to hand-fishing, as on the banks of Newfoundland, in depths over 60 fathoms.

GREAT OCEAN. The Pacific, so called from its superior extent.

GREAT SHAKES. *See* SHAKES.

GREAVES. Armour for the legs.

GRECALE. A north-eastern breeze off the coast of Sicily, *Greece* lying N.E.

GREEN. Raw and untutored; a metaphor from unripe fruit—thus Shakspeare makes Pandulp say:

"How green are you and fresh in this old world!"

GREEN-BONE. The trivial name of the viviparous blenny, or guffer, the backbone of which is green when boiled; also of the gar-fish.

GREEN-FISH. Cod, hake, haddock, herrings, &c., unsalted.

GREEN-HANDS. Those embarked for the first time, and consequently inexperienced.

GREEN-HORN. A lubberly, uninitiated fellow. A novice of marked gullibility.

GREENLAND DOVE. The puffinet; called *scraber* in the Hebrides; about the size of a pigeon.

GREENLAND WHALE. *See* RIGHT WHALE.

GREEN-MEN. The five supernumerary seamen who had not been before in the Arctic Seas, whom vessels in the whale-fishery were obliged to bear, to get the tonnage bounty.

GREEN SEA. A large body of water shipped on a vessel's deck; it derives its name from the green colour of a sheet of water between the eye and the light when its mass is too large to be broken up into spray.

GREEN-SLAKE. The sea-weed otherwise called *lettuce-laver* (which see).

GREEN TURTLE. The common name for the edible turtle, which does not yield tortoise-shell.

GREENWICH STARS. Those used for lunar computations in the nautical ephemeris.

GREEP. The old orthography of *gripe.*

GREGO. A coarse Levantine jacket, with a hood. A cant term for a rough great-coat.

GRENADE. Now restricted to hand grenade, weighing about 2 lbs., and the fuze being previously lit, is conveniently thrown by hand from the tops of ships on to an enemy's deck, from the parapet into the ditch, or generally against an enemy otherwise difficult to reach. A number of grenades, moreover, being quilted together with their fuzes outwards, called a "bouquet," is fired short distances with good effect from mortars in the latter stages of a siege.

GRENADIERS. Formerly the right company of each battalion, composed of the largest men, and originally equipped for using hand-grenades. Now-a-days the companies of a regiment are equalized in size and other matters; and the title in the British army remains only to the fine regiment of grenadier guards.

GRENADO. The old name for a live shell. Thuanus says that they were first used at the siege of Wacklindonck, near Gueldres; and that their inventor, in an experiment in Venice, occasioned the burning of two-thirds of that city.

GREVE. A low flat sandy shore; whence *graving* is derived.

GREY-FRIARS. A name given to the oxen of Tuscany, with which the Mediterranean fleet was supplied.

GREY-HEAD. A fish of the haddock kind, taken on the coast of Galloway.

GREYHOUND. A hammock with so little bedding as to be unfit for stowing in the nettings.

GRIAN. A Gaelic term for the bottom, whether of river, lake, or sea.

GRIBAN. A small two-masted vessel of Normandy.

GRID. The diminutive of *gridiron.*

GRIDIRON. A solid timber stage or frame, formed of cross-beams of wood, for receiving a ship with a falling tide, in order that her bottom may be examined. The Americans also use for a similar purpose an apparatus called a *screw-dock,* and another known as the *hydraulic-dock.*

GRIFFIN, OR GRIFF. A name given to Europeans during the first year of their arrival in India; it has become a general term for an inexperienced youngster.

GRIG. Small eels.

GRILL, To. To broil on the bars of the galley-range, as implied by its French derivation.

GRILSE. One of the salmon tribe, generally considered to be a young salmon on the return from its first sojourn at the sea; though by some still supposed to be a distinct fish.

GRIN AND BEAR IT.   The stoical resignation to unavoidable hardship, which, being heard on board ship by Lord Byron, produced the fine stanza in "Childe Harold," commencing " Existence might be borne."

GRIND.   A half kink in a hempen cable.

GRIP.   The Anglo-Saxon *grep*.   The handle of a sword; also a small ditch or drain.   To hold, as "the anchor grips."   Also, a peculiar groove in rifled ordnance.

GRIPE.   Is generally formed by the scarph of the stem and keel.   (*See* FOREFOOT.)   This is retained, or shaved away, according to the object of making the vessel hold a better wind, or have greater facility in wearing. —*To gripe.*   To carry too much weather-helm.   A vessel gripes when she tends to come up into the wind while sailing close-hauled.   She gripes according to her trim.   If it continues it is remedied by lightening forward, or making her draw deeper aft.

GRIPED-TO.   The situation of a boat when secured by gripes.

GRIPES.   A broad plait formed by an assemblage of ropes, woven and fitted with thimbles and laniards, used to steady the boats upon the deck of a ship at sea.   The gripes are fastened at their ends to ring-bolts in the deck, on each side of the boat; whence, passing over her middle and extremities, they are set up by means of the laniards.   Gripes for a quarter boat are similarly used.

GRITT.   An east-country term for the sea-crab.

GROATS.   An allowance for each man per mensem, assigned formerly to the chaplain for pay.

GROBMAN.   A west-country term for a sea-bream about two-thirds grown.

GRODAN.   A peculiar boat of the Orcades; also the Erse for a gurnard.

GROG.   A drink issued in the navy, consisting of one part of spirits diluted with three of water; introduced in 1740 by Admiral Vernon, as a check to intoxication by mere rum, and said to have been named from his grogram coat.   Pindar, however, alludes to the Cyclops diluting their beverage with ten waters.   As the water on board, in olden times, became very unwholesome, it was necessary to mix it with spirits, but iron tanks have partly remedied this.   The addition of sugar and lemon-juice now makes grog an agreeable anti-scorbutic.

GROG-BLOSSOM.   A red confluence on the nose and face of an excessive drinker of ardent spirits; though sometimes resulting from other causes.

GROG-GROG.   The soft cry of the solan goose.

GROGGY, OR GROGGIFIED.   Rendered stupid by drinking, or incapable of performing duty by illness; as also a ship when crank, and birds when crippled.

GROGRAM.   From *gros-grain*.   A coarse stuff of which boat-cloaks were made.   From one which Admiral Vernon wore, came the term *grog*.

GROINING.   A peculiar mode of submarine embankment; a quay run out transversely to the shore.

GROMAL.   An old word for gromet, or apprentice.

GROMET. A boy of the crew of the ships formerly furnished by the Cinque Ports (a diminutive from the Teutonic *grom*, a youth); his duty was to keep ship in harbour. Now applied to the ship's apprentices.

GROMMET, OR GRUMMET. A ring formed of a single strand of rope, laid in three times round; used to fasten the upper edge of a sail to its stay in different places, and by means of which the sail is hoisted or lowered. Iron or wooden hanks have now been substituted. (*See* HANKS.) Grommets are also used with pins for large boats' oars, instead of rowlocks, and for many other purposes.

GROMMET-WAD. A ring made of 1½ or 2 inch rope, having attached to it two cross-pieces or diameters of the same material; it acts by the ends of these pieces biting on the interior of the bore of the gun.

GROOVE-ROLLERS. These are fixed in a groove of the tiller-sweep in large ships, to aid the tiller-ropes, and prevent friction.

GROPERS. The ships stationed in the Channel and North Sea.

GROPING. An old mode of catching trout by tickling them with the hands under rocks or banks. Shakspeare makes the clown in " Measure for Measure " say that Claudio's offence was—

> " Groping for trouts in a peculiar river."

GROSETTA. A minute coin of Ragusa, somewhat less than a farthing.

GROUND, To. To take the bottom or shore; to be run aground through ignorance, violence, or accident.—*To strike ground.* To obtain soundings.

GROUNDAGE. A local duty charged on vessels coming to anchor in a port or standing in a roadstead, as *anchorage*.

GROUND-BAIT, OR GROUNDLING. A loach or loche.

GROUND-GRU. *See* ANCHOR-ICE.

GROUND-GUDGEON. A little fish, the *Cobitis barbatula*.

GROUND-ICE. *See* ANCHOR-ICE.

GROUNDING. The act of laying a ship on shore, in order to bream or repair her; it is also applied to runnings aground accidentally when under sail.

GROUND-PLOT. *See* ICHNOGRAPHY.

GROUND-SEA. The West Indian name for the swell called *rollers*, or in Jamaica the *north sea*. It occurs in a calm, and with no other indication of a previous gale; the sea rises in huge billows, dashes against the shore with roarings resembling thunder, probably due to the "northers," which suddenly rage off the capes of Virginia, round to the Gulf of Mexico, and drive off the sea from America, affecting the Bahama Banks, but not reaching to Jamaica or Cuba. The rollers set in terrifically in the Gulf of California, causing vessels to founder or strike in 7 fathoms, and devastating the coast-line. H.M.S. *Lily* foundered off Tristan d'Acunha in similar weather. In all the latter cases no satisfactory cause is yet assigned. (*See* ROLLERS.)

GROUND-STRAKE. A name sometimes used for *garboard-strake*.

GROUND-SWELL. A sudden swell preceding a gale, which rises along shore, often in fine weather, and when the sea beyond it is calm. (*See* ROLLERS.)

GROUND-TACKLE. A general name given to all sorts of ropes and furniture which belong to the anchors, or which are employed in securing a ship in a road or harbour.

GROUND-TIER. The lowest water-casks in the hold before the introduction of iron tanks. It also implies anything else stowed there.

GROUND-TIMBERS. Those which lie on the keel, and are fastened to it with bolts through the kelson.

GROUND-WAYS. The large blocks and thick planks which support the cradle on which a ship is launched. Also, the foundation whereon a vessel is built.

GROUP. A set of islands not ranged in a row so as to form a chain, and the word is often used synonymously with *cluster*.

GROUPER. A variety of the snapper, which forms a staple article of food in the Bermudas, and in the West Indies generally.

GROWEN. *See* GROWN-SEA.

GROWING. Implies the direction of the cable from the ship towards the anchors; as, the cable *grows* on the starboard-bow, *i.e.* stretches out forwards towards the starboard or right side.

GROWING PAY. That which succeeds the *dead-horse*, or pay in prospect.

GROWLERS. Smart, but sometimes all-jaw seamen, who have seen some service, but indulge in invectives against restrictive regulations, rendering them undesirable men. There are also too many "civil growlers" of the same kidney.

GROWN-SEA. When the waves have felt the full influence of a gale.

GRUANE. The Erse term for the gills of a fish.

GRUB. A coarse but common term for provisions in general—

"In other words they toss'd the grub
Out of their own provision tub."

GRUB-TRAP. A vulgarism for the mouth.

GRUFF-GOODS. An Indian return cargo consisting of raw materials—cotton, rice, pepper, sugar, hemp, saltpetre, &c.

GRUMBLER. A discontented yet often hard-working seaman. Also, the gurnard, a fish of the blenny kind, which makes a rumbling noise when struggling to disengage itself on reaching the surface.

GRUMMET. *See* GROMMET.

GRUNTER. A name of the *Pogonias* of Cuvier (a fish also termed the banded drum and young sheepskin); and several other fish.

GRYPHON. An archaic term for the meteorological phenomenon now called *typhoon*. (*See* TYPHOON.)

GUAGE. An instrument for measuring shot, wads, &c. For round shot there are two kinds, viz. the high guage, a cylinder through which the shot must pass; and the low guage, a ring through which it must not pass.

GUAGE-ROD. A graduated iron for sounding the pump-well.

GUANO. The excrement of sea-birds, a valuable manure found in thick beds on certain islets on the coast of Peru, indeed, in all tropical climates. The transport of it occupies a number of vessels, called *guaneros.* It is of a dingy yellow colour, and offensive ammoniacal effluvium. Captain Shelvocke mentions it in 1720, having taken a small bark laden with it.

GUARA. The singular and ingenious rudder by which the rafts or balzas of Peru are enabled to work to windward. It consists of long boards between the beams, which are raised or sunk according to the required evolution. A device not unlike the sliding-keels or centre-boards lately introduced.

GUARANTEE. An undertaking to secure the performance of articles stipulated between any two parties. Also, the individual who so undertakes.

GUARD. The duty performed by a body of men stationed to watch and protect any post against surprise. A division of marines appointed to take the duty for a stated portion of time. "Guard, turn out!" the order to the marines on the captain's approaching the ship. Also, the bow of a trigger and the hilt of a sword.

GUARDA-COSTA. Vessels of war of various sizes which formerly cruised against smugglers on the South American coasts.

GUARD-BOARDS. Synonymous with *chain-wales.*

GUARD-BOAT. A boat appointed to row the rounds amongst the ships of war in any harbour, &c., to observe that their officers keep a good look-out, calling to the guard-boat as she passes, and not suffering her crew to come on board without previously having communicated the watch-word of the night. Also, a boat employed to enforce the quarantine regulations.

GUARD-BOOK. Report of guard; a copy of which is delivered at the admiral's office by the officer of the last guard. Also, a full set of his accounts kept by a warrant-officer for the purpose of passing them.

GUARD-FISH. A corruption of the word *gar-fish.*

GUARDIAN of the Cinque Ports. Otherwise *lord-warden* (which see).

GUARD-IRONS. Curved bars of iron placed over the ornaments of a ship to defend them from damage.

GUARDO. A familiar term applied equally to a guard-ship or any person belonging to her. It implies "harbour-going;" an easy life.

GUARDO-MOVE. A trick upon a landsman, generally performed in a guard-ship.

GUARD-SHIP. A vessel of war appointed to superintend the marine affairs in a harbour, and to visit the ships which are not commissioned every night; she is also to receive seamen who are impressed in time of war. In the great ports she carries the flag of the commander-in-chief. Each ship takes the guard in turn at 9 A.M.; the vessel thus on duty hoists the union-jack at the mizen, and performs the duties afloat for twenty-four hours. The officer of the guard is accountable to the admiral for all transactions on the water during his guard.

GUBB, or Gubben. The Erse term for a young sea-gull.

GUBBER. One who gathers oakum, driftwood, &c., along a beach. The word also means black mud.

GUDDLE, To. To catch fish with the hands by groping along a stream's bank.

GUDGE, To. To poke or prod for fish under stones and banks of a river.

GUDGEON. The *Gobio fluviatilis*, a well-known river-fish, 6 or 7 inches in length.

GUDGEONS. The metal braces with eyes bolted upon the stern-post for the pintles of the rudder to work in, as upon hinges. Also, the notches made in the carrick-bitts for receiving the metal bushes wherein the spindle of a windlass works.

GUEBRES. Fire worshippers. (*See* PARSEES.)

GUERDON. A reward or recompense for good service.

GUERILLA. Originally an irregular warfare, but now used mostly for the irresponsible kind of partisan who carries it on.

GUERITE, OR GALITA. In fortification, a projecting turret on the top of the escarp, whence a sentry may observe the outside of the rampart.

GUERNSEY-FROCK. *See* JERSEY.

GUESS-WARP, OR GUEST-ROPE. A rope carried to a distant object, in order to warp a vessel towards it, or to make fast a boat. (*See* CHEST-ROPE.)

GUESTLINGS. The name of certain meetings held at the Cinque Ports.

GUEST-WARP BOOM. A swinging spar (lower studding-boom) rigged from the ship's side with a warp for boats to ride by.

GUFFER. A British sea-fish of the blenny tribe, common under stones at low-water mark, remarkable as being ovo-viviparous.

GUIDE. *See* FLOOR-GUIDE.

GUIDE-RODS. The regulators of the cross-head of an engine's air-pump.

GUIDES. Men supposed to know the country and its roads employed to direct a body of men on their march. The French and Belgians have "corps de guides."

GUIDON. The swallow-tailed silk flag in use by dragoon regiments, instead of a standard. Also, the sergeant bearing the same.

GUIDOR. A name in our old statutes synonymous with *condor* (which see).

GUILLEM. A sea-fowl. (*See* LAVY.)

GUILLEMOT. A web-footed diving sea-bird allied to the auks.

GUIMAD. A small fish of the river Dee.

GUINEA-BOAT. A fast-rowing galley, of former times, expressly built for smuggling gold across the Channel, in use at Deal.

GUINEA-MAN. A negro slave-ship.

GUINEA-PIGS. The younger midshipmen of an Indiaman.

GUIST. The same as *guess* or *guest* (which see).

GULDEN. A name for a water-fowl.

GULF, OR GULPH. A capacious bay, and sometimes taking the name of a sea when it is very extensive; such are the Euxine or Black Sea, otherwise called the Gulf of Constantinople; the Adriatic Sea, called also the Gulf of Venice; the Mediterranean is itself a prodigious specimen. A gulf is, strictly speaking, distinguished from a sea in being smaller, and from a bay in being larger and deeper than it is broad. It is observed that the sea is always most dangerous near gulfs, from the currents being penned up by the shores.

GULF-STREAM. Is especially referable to that of Mexico, the waters of which flow in a warm stream at various velocities over the banks between Cuba and America, past the Bermudas, touch the tail of the great bank of Newfoundland, and thence in a sweep to Europe, part going north, and the other southerly down to the tropics again.

GULF-WEED. The *Fucus natans*, considered to belong to the Gulf Stream, and found floating in the Sargasso Sea in the North Atlantic. Many small crustaceæ live amongst it, and assume its bright orange-yellow hue.

GUL-GUL. A sort of chunam or cement made of pounded sea-shells mixed with oil, which hardens like a stone, and is put over a ship's bottom in India, so that worms cannot penetrate even when the copper is off.

GULL. A well-known sea-bird of the genus *Larus;* there are many species. Also, a large trout in the north. The name is, moreover, familiarly used for a lout easily deceived or cheated; thus Butler in *Hudibras*—

> "The paltry story is untrue,
> And forg'd to cheat such gulls as you."

It is also applied to the washing away of earth by the violent flowing of water; the origin perhaps of the Kentish gull-stream.

GULLET. A small stream in a water-worn course.

GULL-SHARPER. One who preys upon Johnny Raws.

GULLY. The channels worn on the face of mountains by heavy rains. Also, a rivulet which empties itself into the sea.

GULLY SQUALL. Well known off tropical America in the Pacific, particularly abreast of the lakes of Leon, Nicaragua, &c. Monte Desolado gusts have dismantled many stout ships.

GULPIN. An awkward soldier; a weak credulous fellow [from the Gaelic *golben*, a novice].

GUM. "Shaking the gum out of a sail" is said of the effect of bad weather on new canvas.

GUMPUS. A fish, called also *numscull*, for allowing itself to be guddled.

GUN. The usual service name for a *cannon* (which see); it was originally called great gun, to distinguish it from the small or hand guns, muskets, blunderbusses, &c. The general construction for guns of cast metal is fairly represented by the old rule that the circumference at the breech ought to measure eleven calibres, at the trunnions nine, and at the muzzle seven, for iron; and in each instance two calibres less for brass guns. But the introduction of wrought-iron guns, built up with outer jackets of metal shrunk on one above another, is developing other names and proportions in the new artillery. (*See* BUILT-UP GUNS.) The weight of these latter, though differently disposed, and required not so much for strength as for modifying the recoil or shock to the carriage on discharge, is not very much less, proportionally, for heavy guns of full power, than that of the old ones, being about $1\frac{1}{4}$ cwt. of gun for every 1 lb. of shot; for light guns for field purposes it is about $\frac{3}{4}$ cwt. for every 1 lb. of shot. Guns are generally designated from the weight of the shot they discharge, though some few natures, introduced principally for firing shells, were distinguished by the diameter of their bore in inches; with the larger guns of the new system, in addition to this diameter, the weight in tons is also specified.—*Gun*, in north-country cant, meant a large flagon of ale, and *son of a gun* was a jovial toper: the term owed its derivation to lads born under the breast of the lower-deck guns in olden times, when women were allowed to accompany their husbands. Even in 1820 the best petty officers were allowed this indulgence, about one to every hundred men. Gunners also, who superintended the youngsters, took their wives, and many living admirals can revert to kindness experienced from them. These "sons of a gun" were tars, and no mistake.—*Morning gun*, a signal fired by an admiral or commodore at day-break every morning for the drums or bugles to sound the reveillé. A gun of like name and nature is generally in use in fortresses; as is also the *evening gun*, fired by an admiral or commodore at 9 P.M. in summer, and 8 P.M. in winter, every night, on which the drums or bugles sound the retreat.

GUN AND HEAD MONEY. Given to the captors of an enemy's ship of war destroyed, or deserted, in fight. It was formerly assumed to be about £1000 per gun.

GUNBOAT. A light-draught boat fitted to carry one or more cannon in the bow, so as to cannonade an enemy while she is end-on. They are principally useful in fine weather, to cover the landing of troops, or such other occasions. They were formerly impelled by sails and sweeps, but now by steam-power, which has generally increased their size, and much developed their importance. According to Froissart, cannon were fired from boats in the fourteenth century.

GUN-CHAMBERS. In early artillery, a movable chamber with a handle, like a paterero, used in loading at the breech. In more recent times the name has been used for the small portable mortars for firing salutes in the parks.

GUN-COTTON. An explosive compound, having some advantages over gunpowder, but so irregular hitherto in its action that it is at present used only for mining purposes. It consists of ordinary cotton treated with nitric and sulphuric acid and water, and has been named by chemists "pyroxylin," "nitro-cellulose," &c.

GUN-DECK. *See* DECK.

GUN-FIRE. The morning or evening guns, familiarly termed "the admiral falling down the hatchway."

GUN-GEAR. Everything pertaining to its handling.

GUN-HARPOON. *See* HARPOON.

GUN-LADLE. *See* LADLE.

GUN-LOD. A vessel filled with combustibles, but rather for explosion than as a fire-ship.

GUN-METAL. The alloy from which brass guns are cast consists of 100 parts of copper to 10 of tin, retaining much of the tenacity of the former, and much harder than either of the components; but the late improved working of wrought-iron and steel has nearly superseded its application to guns.

GUNNADE. A short 32-pounder gun of 6 feet, introduced in 1814; afterwards termed the shell-gun.

GUNNEL. *See* GUNWALE.

GUNNELL. A spotted ribbon-bodied fish, living under stones and among rocks.

GUNNER, OF A SHIP OF WAR. A warrant-officer appointed to take charge of the ammunition and artillery on board; to keep the latter properly fitted, and to instruct the sailors in the exercise of the cannon. The warrant of chief-gunner is now given to first-class gunners.—*Quarter-gunners.* Men formerly placed under the direction of the gunner, one quarter-gunner being allowed to every four guns. In the army, gunner is the proper title of a private soldier of the Royal Artillery, with the exception of those styled drivers.

GUNNER-FLOOK. A name among our northern fishermen for the *Pleuronectes maximus*, or turbot.

GUNNER'S DAUGHTER. The name of the gun to which boys were *married*, or lashed, to be punished.

GUNNER'S HANDSPIKE. Is shorter and flatter than the ordinary handspike, and is shod with iron at the point, so that it bites with greater certainty against the trucks of guns.

GUNNER'S MATE. A petty officer appointed to assist the gunner.

GUNNER'S PIECE. In destroying and bursting guns, means a fragment of the breech, which generally flies upward.

GUNNER'S QUADRANT. *See* QUADRANT.

GUNNER'S TAILOR. An old rating for the man who made the cartridge-bags.

GUNNER'S YEOMAN. *See* YEOMAN.

GUNNERY. The art of charging, pointing, firing, and managing artillery of all kinds.

GUNNERY-LIEUTENANT. "One who, having obtained a warrant from a gunnery ship, is eligible to large ships to assist specially in supervising the gunnery duties; he draws increased pay."

GUNNERY-SHIP. A ship fitted for training men in the practice of charging, pointing, and firing guns and mortars for the Royal Navy. (*See* SEAMEN GUNNERS.)

GUNNING. An old term for shooting; it is now adopted by the Americans. After the wreck of the *Wager*, on hearing the pistols fired at Cozens, "it was rainy weather, and not fit for gunning, so that we could not imagine the meaning of it."—*Gunning a ship.* Fitting her with ordnance.—*Gunning*, in mining, is when the blast explodes and does not rend the mass.—*Gunning*, signals enforced by guns.

GUNNING-BOAT, OR GUNNING-SHOUT. A light and narrow boat in which the fen-men pursue the flocks of wild-fowl.

GUNNY. Sackcloth or coarse canvas, made of fibres used in India, chiefly of jute.

GUNNY-BAGS. The sacks used on the India station for holding rice, biscuit, &c.; often as sand-bags in fortification.

GUN-PENDULUM. *See* BALLISTIC PENDULUM.

GUN-PORTS. *See* PORT-HOLES.

GUNPOWDER. The well-known explosive composition which, for its regularity of effect and convenience in manufacture and use, is still preferred for general purposes to all the new and more violent but more capricious agents. In England it is composed of 75 parts saltpetre to 10 sulphur and 15 charcoal; these proportions are varied slightly in different countries. The ingredients are mixed together with great mechanical nicety, and the compound is then pressed and granulated. On the application of fire it is converted into gas with vast explosive power, but subject to tolerably well-known laws.

GUN-ROOM. A compartment on the after-end of the lower gun-deck of large ships of war, partly occupied by the junior officers; but in smaller vessels it is below the gun-deck, and the mess-room of the lieutenants.

GUNROOM-PORTS. In frigates, stern-ports cut through the gun-room.

GUN-SEARCHER. An iron instrument with several sharp-pointed prongs and a wooden handle: it is used to find whether the bore is honey-combed.

GUN-SHOT. Formerly, the distance up to which a gun would throw a shot direct to its mark, without added elevation; as the "line of metal" (which see) was generally used in laying, this range was about 800 yards. But now that ranges are so greatly increased, with but slight additions to the elevation, the term will include the distances of ordinary "horizontal fire" (which see); as between ships, with rifled guns, it will not quite reach two miles: though when the mark is large, as a town or dockyard, it is still within long range at five miles' distance.

GUN-SIGHT. *See* DISPART, or SIGHTS.

GUN-SLINGS. Long rope grommets used for hoisting in and mounting them.

GUN-STONES. An old term for cannon-balls, from stones having been first supplied to the ordnance and used for that purpose. Shakspeare makes Henry V. tell the French ambassadors that their master's tennis-balls shall be changed to gun-stones. This term was retained for a bullet, after the introduction of iron shot.

GUN-TACKLE PURCHASE. A tackle composed of a rope rove through two single blocks, the standing part being made fast to the strop of one of the blocks. It multiplies the power applied threefold.

GUNTEN. A boat of burden in the Moluccas.

GUNTER'S LINE. Called also the *line of numbers*, and the *line of lines*, is placed upon scales and sectors, and named from its inventor, Edmund Gunter. It is a logarithmic scale of proportionals, wherein the distance between each division is equal to the number of mean proportionals contained between the two terms, in such parts as the distance between 1 and 10 is 10,000, &c.

GUNTER'S QUADRANT. A kind of stereographic projection on the plane of the equinoctial; the eye is supposed in one of the poles, so that the tropic, ecliptic, and horizon form the arches of the circles, but the hour-circles are all curves, drawn by means of several altitudes of the sun, for some particular latitude, for every day in the year. The use of this instrument is to find the hour of the day, the sun's azimuth, and other common problems of the globe; as also to take the altitude of an object in degrees.

GUNWALE, or GUNNEL. Nearly synonymous with *plank-sheer* (which see); but its strict application is that horizontal plank which covers the heads of the timbers between the main and fore drifts. The *gunwale of a boat* is a piece of timber going round the upper sheer-strake as a binder for its top-work.—*Gunwale-to.* Vessels heeling over, so that the gunwale is even with the water. When a boat sails with a free wind, and rolls each side, or gunwale, to the water's edge, she rolls gunwale-to.

GURGE. A gulf or whirlpool.

GURNARD. A fish of the genus *Trigla*, so called from its peculiar grunt when removed from the water. Falstaff uses the term "soused gurnet" in a most contemptuous view, owing to its poorness; and its head being all skin and bone gave rise to the saying that the flesh on a gurnard's head is rank poison.

GURNET-PENDANT. A rope, the thimble of which is hooked to the quarter-tackle of the main-yard; it is led through a hole in the deck, for the purpose of raising the breech of a gun, when hoisting in, to the level required to place it on its carriage.

GUSSOCK. An east-country term for a strong and sudden gust of wind.

GUST, or GUSH. A sudden violent wind experienced near mountainous lands; it is of short duration, and generally succeeded by fine breezes.

GUT. A somewhat coarse term for the main part of a strait or channel, as the Gut of Gibraltar, Gut of Canso.

GUTTER [Anglo-Saxon *géotan*, to pour out or shed]. A ditch, sluice, or gote.

GUTTER-LEDGE. A crossbar laid along the middle of a large hatchway in some vessels, to support the covers and enable them the better to sustain any weighty body.

GUY. A rope used to steady a weighty body from swinging against the ship's side while it is hoisting or lowering, particularly when there is a high sea. Also, a rope extended from the head of sheers, and made fast at a distance on each side to steady them. The jib-boom is supported by its guys. Also, the name of a tackle used to confine a boom forward, when a vessel is going large, and so prevent the sail from gybing, which would endanger the springing of the boom, or perhaps the upsetting of the vessel.

Also, a large slack rope, extending from the head of the main-mast to the head of the fore-mast, and sustaining a temporary tackle to load or unload a ship with.

GYBING.   Another form for *jibing* (which see).

GYE.   A west-country term for a salt-water ditch.

GYMMYRT.   The Erse or Manx for rowing with oars.

GYMNOTUS ELECTRICUS.   An eel from the Surinam river, several feet in length, which inflicts electrical shocks.

GYN.   A three-legged machine fitted with a windlass, heaving in the fall from a purchase-block at the summit, much used on shore for mounting and dismounting guns, driving piles, &c.   (*See* GIBRALTAR GYN.)

GYP.   A strong gasp for breath, like a fish just taken out of the water.

GYVER.   An old term for blocks or pulleys.

GYVES.   Fetters; the old word for handcuffs.

H.

HAAF.   Cod, ling, or tusk deep-sea fisheries of the Shetland and Orkney islanders.

HAAF-BOAT.   One fitted for deep-water fishing.

HAAFURES.   A northern term for fishermen's lines.

HAAK.   *See* HAKE.

HAAR.   A chill easterly wind on our northern coasts.   (*See* HARR.)

HABERDDEN.   Cod or stock-fish dried and cured on board; that cured at Aberdeen was the best.

HABERGEON.   A coat of mail for the head and shoulders.

HABILIMENTS OF WAR.   A statute term for arms and all provisions for maintaining war.

HABLE.   An Anglo-Norman term for a seaport or haven; it is used in statute 27 Henry VII. cap. 3.

HACKATEE.   A fresh-water tortoise in the West Indies; it has a long neck and flat feet, and weighs 10 to 15 lbs.

HACKBUSH.   A heavy hand-gun.   (*See* HAGBUT.)

HACKLE, HECKLE, OR HETCHEL.   A machine for teazing flax.   Also, a west-country name for the stickleback.

HACK-SAW.   Used for cutting off the heads of bolts; made of a scythe fresh serrated.

HACK-WATCH, OR JOB-WATCH (which see).

HACOT.   From the Anglo-Saxon *hacod*, a large sort of pike.

HADDIE.   A north-coast diminutive of haddock.

HADDO-BREEKS.   A northern term for the roe of the haddock.

HADDOCK. The *Gadus œgilfinus,* a species of cod fabled to bear the thumb-mark of St. Peter.

HÆVER. *See* EAVER.

HAFNE. An old word for haven, from the Danish.

HAFT. (*See* HEFT). The handle of a knife or tool.

HAG-BOAT. *See* HECK-BOAT.

HAGBUT. A wall-piece placed upon a tripod; the arquebuse.

HAGBUTAR. The bearer of a firearm formerly used; it was somewhat larger than a musket.

HAGG. An arquebuse with a bent butt. Also, a swampy moss.

HAG'S TEETH. (*See* HAKE'S TEETH.) Those parts of a matting or pointing interwoven with the rest in an irregular manner, so as to spoil the uniformity. (*See* POINTING.) In soundings, *see* HAKE'S TEETH.

HAIK. *See* HIKE UP.

HAIL, To. To hail "from a country," or claim it as a birthplace. A ship is said to *hail* from the port where she is registered, and therefore properly belongs to. When hailed at sea it is, "From whence do you come?" and "where bound?"—"Pass within hail," a special signal to approach and receive orders or intelligence, when boats cannot be lowered or time is precious. One vessel, the senior, lies to; the other passes the stern under the lee.—*Hail-fellows,* messmates well matched.

HAILING. To call to another vessel; the salutation or accosting of a ship at a distance.

HAILING-ALOFT. To call to men in the tops and at the masthead to "look out," too often an inconsistent bluster from the deck.

HAIL-SHOT. Small shot for cannon.

HAILSHOT-PIECE. A sort of gun supplied of old to our ships, with dice of iron as the missile.

HAIR. The cold nipping wind called *haar* in the north : as in Beaumont and Fletcher,

"Here all is cold as the hairs in winter."

HAIR-BRACKET. The moulding at the back of the figure-head.

HAIR-TRIGGER. A trigger to a gun-lock, so delicately adjusted that the slightest touch will discharge the piece.

HAKE. An old term for a hand-gun. Also, the fish *Gadus merlucius,* a well-known gregarious and voracious fish of the cod family, often termed sea-pike.

HAKE'S TEETH. A phrase applied to some part of the deep soundings in the British Channel; but it is a distinct shell-fish, being the *Dentalium,* the presence of which is a valuable guide to the Channel pilot in foggy weather.

HALBAZ. *See* KALBAZ.

HALBERT. A sort of spear formerly carried by sergeants of infantry, that they, standing in the ranks behind the officers or the colours, should afford additional defence at those important points.

HALCYON PISCATOR, OR KING-FISHER. This beautiful bird's floating nest was fabled to calm the winds and seas while the bird sat. This occurring in winter gave rise to the expression "halcyon days."

HALE. An old word for *haul* (which see).

HALF AN EYE, SEEING WITH. Discerning instantly and clearly.

HALF-BEAMS. Short timbers, from the side to the hatchways, to support the deck where there is no framing. (*See* FORK-BEAMS.)

HALF-BREADTH OF THE RISING. A ship-builder's term for a curve in the floor-plan, which limits the distances of the centres of the floor-sweeps from the middle line of the body-plan.

HALF-BREADTH PLAN. In ship-building, the same as *floor-plan*.

HALF-COCK. To go off at half-cock is an unexpected discharge of a fire-arm; hurried conduct without due preparation, and consequently failure.

HALF-DAVIT. Otherwise *fish-davit* (which see).

HALF-DECK. A space between the foremost bulkhead of the steerage and the fore-part of the quarter-deck. In the Northumberland colliers the steerage itself is called the *half-deck*, and is usually the habitation of the crew.

HALF-DROWNED LAND. Shores which are rather more elevated and bear more verdure than *drowned land* (which see).

HALF-FLOOD. *See* FLOOD.

HALF-GALLEY. *See* GALLEY.

HALF-HITCH. Pass the end of a rope round its standing part, and bring it up through the bight. (*See* THREE HALF-HITCHES.)

HALF-LAUGHS AND PURSER'S GRINS. Hypocritical and satirical sneers.

HALF-MAN. A landsman or boy in a coaster, undeserving the pay of a *full-man*.

HALF-MAST. The lowering a flag in respect for the death of an officer.

HALF-MINUTE GLASS. *See* GLASS.

HALF-MOON. An old form of outwork somewhat similar to the ravelin, originally placed before the salients of bastions.

HALF-PIKE. An iron spike fixed on a short ashen staff, used to repel the assault of boarders, and hence frequently termed a *boarding-pike*.

HALF-POINT. A subdivision of the compass card, equal to 5° 37' of the circle.

HALF-PORTS. A sort of one-inch deal shutter for the upper half of those ports which have no hanging lids; the lower half-port is solid and hinged, having a semicircle cut out for the gun when level, and falling down outwards when ready for action; the upper half-port fits loosely into rabbets, and is secured only by laniards.

HALF-SEA. The old term for mid-channel.

HALF SEAS OVER. Nearly intoxicated. This term was used by Swift.

HALF-SPEED! An order in steam navigation to reduce the speed. (*See* FULL-SPEED!)

HALF-TIDE ROCKS. Those showing their heads at half-ebb. (*See* TIDE.)

HALF-TIMBERS. The short timbers or futtocks in the cant-bodies, answering to the lower futtocks in the square-body; they are placed so as to give good shiftings.

HALF-TOP. The mode of making ships' tops in two pieces, which are afterwards secured as a whole by what are termed sleepers.

HALF-TOPSAILS, UNDER. Said of a chase about 12 miles distant, the rest being below the horizon.

HALF-TURN AHEAD! An order in steam navigation. (*See* TURN-AHEAD!)

HALF-WATCH TACKLE. A luff purchase. (*See* WATCH-TACKLE.)

HALIBUT. A large oceanic bank fish, *Hippoglossus vulgaris*, weighing from 300 to 500 lbs. particularly off Newfoundland; it resembles plaice, and is excellent food, nor does it easily putrefy.

HALLEY'S CHART. The name given to the protracted curves of the variation of the compass, known as the variation chart.

HALLIARDS, HALYARDS, OR HAULYARDS. The ropes or tackles usually employed to hoist or lower any sail upon its respective yards, gaffs, or stay, except the cross-jack and spritsail-yard, which are always slung; but in small craft the spritsail-yard also has halliards. (*See* JEERS.)

HALO. An extensive luminous ring including the sun or moon, whose light, passing through the intervening vapour, gives rise to the pheno-menon. Halos are called *lunar* or *solar*, according as they appear round the moon or sun. Prismatically coloured halos indicate the presence of watery vapour, whereas white ones show that the vapour is frozen.

HALSE, OR HALSER. Archaic spelling for *hawser*.

HALSTER. A west-country term for a man who draws a barge along by a rope.

HALT! The military word of command to stop marching, or any other evolution. A halt includes the period of such discontinuance.

HALVE-NET. A standing net used in the north to prevent fishes from returning with the falling tide.

HALYARDS. *See* HALLIARDS.

HAMACS. Columbus found that the inhabitants of the Bahama Islands had for beds nets of cotton suspended at each end, which they called *hamacs*, a name since adopted universally amongst seamen. (*See* HAM-MOCKS AND HAMMACS.)

HAMBER, OR HAMBRO'-LINE. Small line used for seizings, lashings, &c.

HAMMACOE. Beam battens. (*See* HAMMOCK-BATTENS.)

HAMMER. The shipwright's hammer is a well-known tool for driving nails and clenching bolts, differing from hammers in general.

HAMMER, OF A GUN-LOCK. Formerly the steel covering of the pan from which the flint of the cock struck sparks on to the priming; but now the cock itself, by its hammer action on the cap or other percussion priming, discharges the piece. Whether the hammer will be superseded by the needle remains to be determined.

HAMMER-HEADED SHARK. The *Zygœna malleus*, a strange, ugly shark. The eyes are situated at the extremities of the hammer-shaped head. They seldom take bait or annoy human beings. They are for the most part inert, live near the surf edge, and are frequently found washed up on sandy beaches. Chiefly found on the coasts of Barbary.

HAMMERING. A heavy cannonade at close quarters.

HAMMOCK. A swinging sea-bed, the undisputed invention of Alcibiades; but the modern name is derived from the Caribbs. (*See* HAMACS.) At present the hammock consists of a piece of canvas, 6 feet long and 4 feet wide, gathered together at the two ends by means of clews, formed by a grommet and knittles, whence the *head-clue* and *foot-clue:* the hammock is hung horizontally under the deck, and forms a receptacle for the bed on which the seamen sleep. There are usually allowed from 14 to 20 inches between hammock and hammock in a ship of war. In preparing for action, the hammocks, together with their contents, are all firmly corded, taken upon deck, and fixed in various nettings, so as to form a barricade against musket-balls. (*See* ENGAGEMENT.)

HAMMOCK BATTENS OR RACKS. Cleats or battens nailed to the sides of a vessel's beams, from which to suspend the seamen's hammocks.

HAMMOCK-BERTHING. Forecastle-men forward, and thence passing aft, foretop-men, maintop-men, mizentop-men, waisters, afterguard, and boys. Quartermasters in the tiers.

HAMMOCK-CLOTHS. To protect them from wet while stowed in the nettings on deck.

HAMMOCK GANT-LINES. Lines extended from the jib-boom end around the ship, triced up to the lower yard-arms, for drying scrubbed hammocks.

HAMMOCK-NETTINGS. Take their distinguishing names according to their location in the ship, as forecastle, waist, quarter-deck.

HAMMOCK-RACKS. *See* HAMMOCK-BATTENS.

HAMPER. Things which, though necessary, are in the way in times of gale or service. (*See* TOP-HAMPER.)

HAMPERED. Perplexed and troubled.

HAMRON. An archaic term, meaning the hold of a ship.

HANCES. Spandrels; the falls or descents of fife-rails. Also, the breakings of the rudder abaft. (*See* HAUNCH.)

HAND. A phrase often used for the word man, as, " a hand to the lead," " clap more hands on," &c.—*To hand a sail*, is to furl it.—*To lend a hand*, to assist.—*Bear a hand*, make haste.—*Hand in the leech*, a call in furling sails. To comprehend this it must be understood that the leech, or outer border of the sail, if left to belly or fill with wind, would set at naught all the powers of the men. It is therefore necessary, as Falconer has it, "the tempest to disarm;" so by handing in this leech-rope before the yard, the canvas is easily folded in, and the gasket passed round.

HAND-GRENADE. A small shell for throwing by hand. (*See* GRENADE.)

HAND-GUN. An old term for small arms in the times of Henry VII. and VIII.

HANDLASS. A west-country term for a small kind of windlass.

HANDLE. The title prefixed to a person's name.—*To handle a ship well*, is to work her in a seaman-like manner.

HAND-LEAD. A small lead used in the channels, or chains, when approaching land, and for sounding in rivers or harbours under 20 fathoms. (*See* LEAD.)

HANDLES OF A GUN. The dolphins.

HAND-LINE. A line bent to the hand-lead, measured at certain intervals with what are called *marks* and *deeps* from 2 and 3 fathoms to 20.

HAND MAST-PIECE. The smaller hand mast-spars.

HAND MAST-SPAR. A round mast; those from Riga are commonly over 70 feet long by 20 inches diameter.

HANDMAID. An old denomination for a tender; thus, in Drake's expedition to Cadiz, two of her Majesty's pinnaces were appointed to attend his squadron as handmaids.

HAND-OVER-HAND. Hauling rapidly upon any rope, by the men passing their hands alternately one before the other, or one above the other if they are hoisting. A sailor is said to go hand-over-hand if he lifts his own weight and ascends a single rope without the help of his legs. Hand-over-hand also implies rapidly; as, we are coming up with the chase hand-over-hand.

HAND-PUMP. The common movable pump for obtaining fresh water, &c., from tanks or casks.

HAND-SAW. The smallest of the saws used by shipwrights, and used by one hand.

HAND-SCREW. A handy kind of single jack-screw.

HANDSOMELY. Signifies steadily or leisurely; as, "lower away handsomely," when required to be done gradually and carefully. The term "handsomely" repeated, implies "have a care; not so fast; tenderly."

HAND-SPIKE. A lever made of tough ash, and used to heave round the windlass in order to draw up the anchor from the bottom, or move any heavy articles, particularly in merchant ships. The handle is round, but the other end is square, conforming to the shape of the holes in the windlass. (*See* GUNNER'S HAND-SPIKE.)

HANDS REEF TOPSAILS! The order to reef by all hands, instead of the watch, or watch and idlers.

HAND-TIGHT. A rope hauled as taut as it can be by hand only.

HAND-UNDER-HAND. Descending a rope by the converse of hand-over-hand ascent.

HANDY-BILLY. A small jigger purchase, used particularly in tops or the holds, for assisting in hoisting when weak-handed. A watch-tackle. (*See* JIGGERS.)

HANDY-SHIP. One that steers easily, and can be worked with the watch; or as some seamen would express it, "work herself."

HANG. In timber, opposed to *sny* (which see).—*To hang*. Said of a mast that inclines; *it hangs forward*, if too much stayed; *hangs aft*, if it requires staying.—*To hang the mast.* By some temporary means, until the mast-rope be fleeted.—*To hang on a rope or tackle-fall,* is to hold it fast without belaying; also to pull forcibly with the whole weight.—*To hang aback.* To be slack on duty.

HANGER. The old word for the Persian dagger, and latterly for a short curved sword.

HANG-FIRE. When the priming burns without igniting the cartridge, or the charge does not rapidly ignite after pulling the trigger. Figuratively, *to hang fire,* is to hesitate or flinch.

HANGING. A word expressive of anything declining in the middle part below a straight line, as the hanging of a deck or a sheer. Also, when a ship is difficult to be removed from the stocks, or in manœuvre.

HANGING-BLOCKS. These are sometimes fitted with a long and short leg, and lash over the eyes of the topmast rigging; when under, they are made fast to a strap. The topsail-tye reeves through these blocks, the tye-block on the yard, and the standing part is secured to the mast-head.

HANGING-CLAMP. A semicircular iron, with a foot at each end to receive nails, by which it is fixed to any part of the ship to hang stages to, &c.

HANGING-COMPASS. A compass so constructed as to hang with its face downwards, the point which supports the card being fixed in the centre of the glass, and the gimbals are attached to a beam over the observer's head. There is usually one hung in the cabin, that, by looking up to it, the ship's course may be observed at any moment; whence it is also termed a tell-tale.

HANGING HOOK-POTS. Tin utensils fitted for hanging to the bars before the galley-grate.

HANGING-KNEES. Those which are applied under the loding-knees, and are fayed vertically to the sides.

HANGING-STAGE. Any stage hung over the side, bows, or stern, for painting, caulking, or temporary repairs.

HANGING STANDARD-KNEE. A knee fayed vertically beneath a hold-beam, with one arm bolted on the lower side of the beam.

HANGING-STOVES. Used for ventilating or drying between decks.

HANGING THE RUDDER. So as to allow the pintles to fall into their corresponding braces, constantly in boats, and frequently also in whaling vessels, but seldom in other ships: the rudder after being shipped is generally secured by wood-locks to prevent its unshipping at sea.

HANG ON HER! In rowing, is the order to stretch out to the utmost to preserve or increase headway on the boat.

HANK FOR HANK. In beating against the wind each board is thus sometimes denoted. Also, expressive of two ships which tack simultaneously and make progress to windward together in racing, &c.

HANKS. Hoops or rings of rope, wood, or iron, fixed upon the stays, to seize the luff of fore-and-aft sails, and to confine the stay-sails thereto, at different distances. Those of wood are used in lieu of grommets, being much more convenient, and of a later invention. They are framed by the bending of a rough piece of wood into the form of a wreath, and fastened at the two ends by means of notches, thereby retaining their circular figure and elasticity; whereas the grommets which are formed of rope are apt to relax in warm weather, and adhere to the stays, so as to prevent the sails from being readily hoisted or lowered.—*Iron hanks* are more generally used now that stays are made of wire.—*Hank* is also a skein of line or twine.—*Getting into a hank,* irritated by jokes.

HANSE-TOWNS. Established in the 13th century, for the mutual protection of mercantile property. Now confined to Lubeck, Hamburg, and Bremen.

HAPPY-GO-LUCKY. A reckless indifference as to danger.

HAQUE. A little hand-gun of former times.

HAQUEBUT. A form of spelling *arquebuse.* A bigger sort of hand-gun than the *haque.*

HARASS, To. To torment and fatigue men with needless work.

HARBOUR. A general name given to any safe sea-port. The qualities requisite in a good harbour are, that it should afford security from the effects of the wind and sea; that the bottom be entirely free from rocks and shallows, but good holding ground; that the opening be of sufficient extent to admit the entrance or departure of large ships without difficulty; that it should have convenience to receive the shipping of different nations, especially those which are laden with merchandises; and that it possess establishments for refitting vessels. To render a harbour complete, there ought to be good defences, a good lighthouse, and a number of mooring and warping buoys; and finally, that it have plenty of fuel, water, provisions, and other materials for sea use. Such a harbour, if used as a place of commercial transactions, is called a port.

HARBOUR-DUES. *See* PORT-CHARGES.

HARBOUR-DUTY MEN. Riggers, leading men, and others, ordered to perform the dockyard or port duties, too often superannuated, or otherwise unfit.

HARBOUR-GASKETS. Broad, but short and well-blacked gaskets, placed at equal distances on the yard, for showing off a well-furled sail in port: there is generally one upon every other seam.

HARBOUR-GUARDS. Men detached from the ordinary, as a working party.

HARBOUR-LOG. That part of the log-book which consists solely of remarks, and relates only to transactions while the ship is in port.

HARBOUR-MASTER. An officer appointed to inspect the moorings, and to see that the ships are properly berthed, and the regulations of the harbour strictly observed by the different ships frequenting it.

HARBOUR-REACH. The reach or stretch of a winding river which leads direct to the harbour.

HARBOUR-WATCH. A division or subdivision of the watch kept on night-duty, when the ship rides at single anchor, to meet any emergency.

HARD. A road-path made through mud for landing at. (*See* ARD.)

HARD-A-LEE. The situation of the tiller when it brings the rudder hard over to windward. Strictly speaking, it only relates to a tiller which extends *forward* from the rudder-head; now many extend *aft*, in which case the *order* remains the same, but the tiller and rudder are both brought over to windward. Also, the order to put the tiller in this position.

HARD AND FAST. Said of a ship on shore.

HARD-A-PORT! The order so to place the tiller as to bring the rudder over to the starboard-side of the stern-post, whichever way the tiller leads. (*See* HARD-A-LEE.)

HARD-A-STARBOARD. The order so to place the tiller as to bring the rudder over to the port-side of the stern-post, whichever way the tiller leads. (*See* HARD-A-LEE.)

HARD-A-WEATHER! The order so to place the tiller as to bring the rudder on the lee-side of the stern-post, whichever way the tiller leads, in order to bear away; it is the position of the helm as opposed to hard-a-lee (which see). Also, a hardy seaman.

HARD BARGAIN. A useless fellow; a skulker.

HARD FISH. A term indiscriminately applied to cod, ling, haddock, torsk, &c., salted and dried.

HARD GALE. When the violence of the wind reduces a ship to be under her storm stay-sails, No. 10 force.

HARD-HEAD. The *Clupea menhaden*, or *Alosa tyrannus*, an oily fish taken in immense quantities on the American coasts, insomuch that they are used for manuring land. Also, on our coasts the father-lasher or sea-scorpion, *Cottus scorpius*, and in some parts the grey gurnard, are so called.

HARD-HORSE. A tyrannical officer.

HARDING. A light kind of duck canvas made in the north.

HARD UP. The tiller so placed as to carry the rudder close over to lee-ward of the stern-post. Also, used figuratively for being in great distress, or poverty-struck; obliged to bear up for Poverty Bay; cleared out.

HARD UP IN A CLINCH, AND NO KNIFE TO CUT THE SEIZING. Over-taken by misfortune, and no means of evading it.

HARDS. *See* ACUMBA.

HARLE. Mists or thick rolling fogs from the sea, so called in the north. Also, a name of the *goosander* (which see).

HARMATTAN. A Fantee name for a singular periodical easterly wind which prevails on the west coast of Africa, generally in December, January, and February; it is dry, though always accompanied by haze, the result of fine red dust suspended in the atmosphere and obscuring the sun; this wind is opposed to the sea-breeze, which would otherwise blow fresh from the west on to the land.

HARNESS. An old statute term for the tackling or furniture of a ship.

HARNESS-CASK. A large conical tub for containing the salt provisions intended for present consumption. Alluding to the junk, which is often called salt-horse, it has been described as the tub where the horse, and not the harness, is kept.

HARP-COCK. An old modification of the harpoon.

HARPENS. *See* HARPINGS.

HARPER-CRAB. *See* TOMMY HARPER.

HARPINGS, OR HARPENS. The fore-parts of the wales which encompass the bow of a ship, and are fastened to the stem, being thicker than the after-part of the wales, in order to strengthen the ship in that place where she sustains the greatest shock of resistance in plunging into the sea, or dividing it, under a great pressure of sail. Also, the pieces of oak, similar to ribbands, but trimmed and bolted to the shape of the body of the ship, which hold the fore and after cant bodies together, until the ship is planked. But this term is mostly applicable to those at the bow; hence arises the phrase " clean and full harpings." Harpings in the bow of a vessel are decried as rendering the ship uneasy.—*Cat harpings.* The legs which cross from futtock-staff to futtock-staff, below the tops, to girt in the rigging, and allow the lower yards to brace sharp up.

HARPOON, OR HARPAGO. A spear or javelin with a barbed point, used to strike whales and other fish. The harpoon is furnished with a long shank, and has at one end a broad and flat triangular head, sharpened at both edges so as to penetrate the whale with facility, but blunt behind to prevent its cutting out. To the other end a fore-ganger is bent, to which is fastened a long cord called the whale-line, which lies carefully coiled in the boat in such a manner as to run out without being interrupted or entangled. Several coils, each 130 fathoms of whale-line (soft laid and of clean silky fibre) are in readiness; the instant the whale is struck the men cant the oars, so that the roll may not immerse them in the water. The line, which has a turn round the bollard, flies like lightning, and is intensely watched. One man pours water on the smoking bollard, another is ready with a sharp axe to cut, and the others see that the lines run free. Seven or eight coils have been run out before the whale " sounds," or strikes bottom, when he rises again to breathe, and probably gets a similar dose.—*Gun harpoon.* A weapon used for the same purpose as the preceding, but it is fired out of a gun, instead of being thrown by hand; it is made entirely of steel, and has a chain or long shackle attached to it, to which the whale-line is fastened. Greener's harpoon-gun is a kind of wall-piece fixed in a crutch, which steps into the bow-bollard of the whale-boat. The harpoon projects about four inches beyond the muzzle. It consists of its barbed point attached to a long link, with a solid button at its opposite end to fit the gun; on one rod of this link is a ring which runs to the muzzle, and is there attached to the whale-line by a thong of seal or walrus hide, wet. The gun being fired, the harpoon is projected, the ring sliding up to the button, when the line follows. Some of these harpoons or other engines have grenades—glass globules with prussic acid or other chemicals— which sicken the whale instantly, and little trouble ensues.

HARPOONER, Harponeer, or Harpineer. The expert bowman in a whale-boat, whose duty it is to throw or fire the harpoon.

HARP-SEAL. The *Phoca grœnlandica*, a species of seal from the Arctic seas; so called from the form of a dark-brown mark upon its back.

HARQUEBUSS, or Arquebuss. Something larger than a musket. Sometimes called caliver. (*See* Arquebuss.)

HARR, or Harl. A sea-storm, from a northern term for snarling, in allusion to the noise. Also, a cold thick mist or fog in easterly winds; the *haar*.

HARRY-BANNINGS. A north-country name for sticklebacks.

HARRY-NET. A net with such small meshes, and so formed, as to take even the young and small fish.

HARVEST-MOON. The full moon nearest the autumnal equinox, when for several successive evenings she rises at the same hour; and this name is given in consequence of the supposed advantage of the additional length of moonlight to agriculture.

HASEGA. A corruption of *asseguay* (which see).

HASK. An archaism for a fish-basket.

HASLAR HAGS. The nurses of the naval hospital Haslar.

HASLAR HOSPITAL. A fine establishment near Gosport, for the reception and cure of the sick and wounded of the Royal Navy.

HASP. A semi-circular clamp turning in an eye-bolt in the stem-head of a sloop or boat, and fastened by a forelock in order to secure the bowsprit down to the bows. (*See* Span Shackle.)

HASTAN. The Manx or Erse term for a large eel or conger.

HASTY-PUDDING. A batter made of flour or oatmeal stirred in boiling water, and eaten with treacle or sugar at sea. This dish is not altogether to be despised in need, although Lord Dorset—the sailor poet—speaks of it disparagingly :

> " Sure hasty-pudding is thy chiefest dish,
>   With bullock's liver, or some stinking fish."

HATCH. A half-door. A contrivance for trapping salmon. (*See* Heck.)

HATCH-BARS. To secure the hatches; are padlocked and sealed.

HATCH-BOAT. A sort of small vessel known as a pilot-boat, having a deck composed almost entirely of hatches.

HATCH-DECK. Gun brigs had hatches instead of lower decks.

HATCHELLING. The combing and preparing hemp for rope-making.

HATCHES. Flood-gates set in a river to stop the current of water. Also, coverings of grating, or close hatches to seal the holds.—*To lie under hatches, stowed in the hold.* Terms used figuratively for being in distress and death.

HATCHET-FASHION. Cutting at the heads of antagonists, instead of thrusting.

HATCH-RINGS. Rings to lift the hatches by, or replace them.

HATCHWAY. A square or oblong opening in the middle of the deck of a ship, of which there are generally three—the fore, main, and after—affording passages up and down from one deck to another, and again descending into the hold. The coverings over these openings are called hatches. Goods of bulk are let down into the hold by the hatchways. To lay anything in the hatchway, is to put it so that the hatches cannot be approached or opened. The hatches of a smaller kind are distinguished by the name of *scuttles.*

HATCHWAY-NETTINGS. Nettings sometimes placed over the hatchways instead of gratings, for security and circulation of air. They arrest the fall of any one from a deck above.

HATCHWAY-SCREENS. Pieces of fear-nought, or thick woollen cloth, put round the hatchways of a man-of-war in time of action, to screen the passages to the magazine.

HATCHWAY-STOPPERS. Those for a hempen cable are fitted as a ring-stopper, only a larger rope. They are rove through a hole on each side of the coamings, in the corner of the hatchway; and both tails, made selvagee-fashion, are dogged along the cable. When a chain-cable is . used, the stopper works from a beam on the lower deck.

HAT-MONEY. A word sometimes used for *primage*, or the trifling payment received by the master of a ship for care of goods.

HAUBERK. *See* AUBERK.

HAUGH. Flat or marshy ground by the side of a river.

HAUL, To. An expression peculiar to seamen, implying to pull or bowse at a single rope, without the assistance of blocks or other mechanical powers upon it; as "haul in," "haul down," "haul up," "haul aft," "haul together." (*See* BOWSE, HOIST, and ROWSE.) A vessel *hauls her wind* by trimming the yards and sails so as to lie nearer to, or close to the wind, and by the power of the rudder shaping her course accordingly.

HAUL ABOARD THE FORE AND MAIN TACKS. This is to haul them forward, and down to the chess-trees on the weather-side.

HAUL AFT A SHEET. To pull it in more towards the stern, so as to trim the sail nearer to the wind.

HAULAGE. A traction-way.

HAUL-BOWLINGS. The old name for the able-bodied seamen.

HAUL HER WIND. Said of a vessel when she comes close upon the wind.—*Haul your wind,* or *haul to the wind,* signifies that the ship's head is to be brought nearer to the wind—a very usual phrase when she has been going free.

HAUL IN, To. To sail close to the wind, in order to approach nearer to an object.

HAULING DOWN VACANCY. The colloquialism expressive of the promotion of a flag-lieutenant and midshipman on an admiral's hauling down his flag.

HAULING-LINE. A line made fast to any object, to be hauled nearer or on board, as a hawser, a spar, &c.

HAULING SHARP. Going upon half allowance of food.

HAUL MY WIND. An expression when an individual is going upon a new line of action. To avoid a quarrel or difficulty.

HAUL OF ALL! An order to brace round all the yards at once—a manœuvre sometimes used in tacking, or on a sudden change of wind; it requires a strong crew.

HAUL OFF, To. To sail closer to the wind, in order to get further from any object.

HAUL OUT TO LEEWARD! In reefing topsails, the cry when the weather earing is passed.

HAUL ROUND. Said when the wind is gradually shifting towards any particular point of the compass. Edging round a danger.

HAULS AFT, OR VEERS AFT. Said of the wind when it draws astern.

HAULSER. The old orthography for hawser.

HAULS FORWARD. Said of the wind when it draws before the beam.

HAUL UNDER THE CHAINS. This is a phrase signifying a ship's working and straining on the masts and shrouds, so as to make the seams open and shut as she rolls.

HAUL-YARDS. See HALLIARDS.

HAUNCES. The breakings of the rudder abaft.

HAUNCH. A sudden fall or break, as from the drifts forward and aft to the waist. The same as hance.

HAVEN [Anglo-Saxon, hœfen]. A safe refuge from the violence of wind and sea; much the same as harbour, though of less importance. A good anchorage rather than place of perfect shelter. Milford Haven is an exception.

HAVENET. This word has appeared in vocabularies as a small haven.

HAVEN-SCREAMER. The sea-gull, called hœfen by the Anglo-Saxons.

HAVERSACK. A coarse linen bag with a strap fitting over the shoulder worn by soldiers or small-arm men in marching order, for carrying their provision, instead of the knapsack.

HAVILLER. See HUFFLER.

HAVOC. Formerly a war cry, and the signal for indiscriminate slaughter. Thus Shakspeare,

"Cry havoc! and let slip the dogs of war."

HAWK'S-BILL. Chelone imbricata, a well-known turtle frequenting the Atlantic and Indian Oceans, so named from having a small mouth like the beak of a hawk; it produces the tortoise-shell of commerce. The flesh is indifferent, but the eggs very good.

HAWSE. This is a term of great meaning. Strictly, it is that part of a vessel's bow where holes are cut for her cables to pass through. It is also generally understood to imply the situation of the cables before the ship's stem, when she is moored with two anchors out from forward, one on the starboard, and the other on the port bow. It also denotes any small distance between her head and the anchors employed to ride her, as "he has anchored in our hawse," "the brig fell athwart our hawse," &c. Also, said of a vessel a little in advance of the stem; as, she sails athwart *hawse,* or has anchored *in the hawse.* If a vessel drives at her anchors into the hawse of another she is said to *"foul the hawse"* of the vessel riding there; hence the threat of a man-of-war's-man, "If you foul my hawse, I'll cut your cable," no merchant vessel being allowed to approach a ship-of-war within certain limits, and never to make fast to the government buoys.—*A bold hawse* is when the holes are high above the water. "Freshen hawse," or "veer out more cable," is said when part of the cable that lies in the hawse is fretted or chafed, and more should be veered out, so that another part of it may rest in the hawse. "Freshen hawse" also means, clap a service on or round the cable in the hawses to prevent it from fretting; hemp cables only are rounded or cackled. Also, a dram after fatiguing duty. "Clearing hawse," is untwisting or disentangling two cables that come through different holes, and make a foul hawse.

HAWSE-BAGS. Canvas bags filled with oakum, used in heavy seas to stop the hawse-holes and prevent the water coming in.

HAWSE-BLOCKS. Bucklers, or pieces of wood made to fit over the hawse-holes when at sea, to back the hawse-plugs.

HAWSE-BOLSTERS. Planks above and below the hawse-holes. Also, pieces of canvas stuffed with oakum and roped round, for plugging when the cables are bent.

HAWSE-BOX, OR NAVAL HOOD. Pieces of plank bolted outside round each of the hawse-holes, to support the projecting part of the hawse-pipe.

HAWSE-BUCKLERS. Plugs of wood to fit the hawse-holes, and hatches to bolt over, to keep the sea from spurting in.

HAWSE-FALLEN. To ride hawse-fallen, is when the water breaks into the hawse in a rough sea, driving all before it.

HAWSE-FULL. Riding hawse-full; pitching bows under.

HAWSE-HOLES. Cylindrical holes cut through the bows of a ship on each side of the stem, through which the cables pass, in order to be drawn into or let out of the vessel, as occasion requires.

HAWSE-HOOK. A compass breast timber which crosses the hawse-timber above the ends of the upper-deck planking, and over the hawse-holes. (*See* BREAST-HOOKS.)

HAWSE-PIECES. The timbers which compose the bow of a vessel, and their sides look fore and aft; it is a name given to the foremost timbers of a ship, whose lower ends rest upon the knuckle-timbers. They are generally parallel to the stem, having their upper ends sometimes terminated by the lower part of the beak-head and otherwise by the top of the bow. Also, timbers through which the hawse-holes are cut.

HAWSE-PIPE. A cast-iron pipe in the hawse-holes to prevent the cable from cutting the wood.

HAWSE-PLUGS. Blocks of wood made to fit into the hawse-pipes, and put in from the outside to stop the hawses, and thereby prevent the water from washing into the manger. The plug, coated with old canvas, is first inserted, then a mat or swab, and over it the buckler or shield, which bolts upward and downward into the breast-hooks.

HAWSER. A large rope or cablet, which holds the middle degree between the cable and towline, being a size smaller than the former, and as much larger than the latter; curiously, it is not hawser but cable laid.

HAWSER-LAID ROPE. Is rope made in the usual way, being three or four strands of yarns laid up right-handed, or with the sun; it is used for small running rigging, as well as for standing rigging, shrouds, &c.; in the latter case it is generally tarred to keep out rain. It is supposed that this style of rope is stronger in proportion to the number of yarns than cable or water-laid rope, which is more tightly twisted, each strand being a small rope. This latter is more impervious to water, and therefore good for cables, hawsers, &c.; it is laid left-handed, or against the sun.

HAWSE-TIMBERS. The upright timbers in the bow, bolted on each side of the stem, in which the hawse-holes are cut.

HAWSE-WOOD. A general name for the hawse-timbers.

HAY. A straight rank of men drawn up exactly in a line.

HAYE. A peculiar ground-shark on the coast of Guinea.

HAYLER. An archaism for halliard.

HAZE. A grayish vapour, less dense than a fog, and therefore does not generally exclude objects from sight.

HAZE, To. To punish a man by making him do unnecessary work.

HEAD. The upper part or end of anything, as a mast-head, a timber-head. Also, an ornamental figure on a ship's stem expressive of her name, or emblematical of her object, &c. (*See* BILLET-HEAD, BUST-HEAD, FAMILY-HEAD, FIDDLE-HEAD, FIGURE-HEAD, SCROLL-HEAD, &c.) Also, in a more enlarged sense, the whole fore-part of a ship, including the bows on each side; the head therefore opens the column of water through which the ship passes when advancing; hence we say, *head-way, head-sails, head-sea,* &c. It is evident that the fore-part of a ship is called its head, from its analogy to that of a fish, or any animal while swimming. Also, in a confined sense, to that part on each side of the stem outside the bows proper which is appropriated to the use of the sailors for wringing swabs, or any wet jobs, for no wet is permitted inboard after the decks are dried. Also, hydrographically, the upper part of a gulf, bay, or creek.—*By the head,* the state of a ship which, by her lading, draws more water forward than aft. This may be remedied without reference to cargo in ships-of-war, by shifting shot, guns, &c. Vessels *by the head* are frequently uneasy, gripe and pitch more than when *by the stern.*

HEAD AND GUN-MONEY. An encouragement in the prize acts by which £5 a head is given to the captors for every person on board a captured vessel of war, or pirate.

HEAD-BOARDS. The berthing or close-boarding between the head-rails.

HEAD-CLUE OF A HAMMOCK. Where the head rests. (*See* HAMMOCK.)

HEAD-CRINGLES. Earing-cringles at the upper clues or corners of a sail.

HEAD-EARINGS. The laniards to haul out the earings. (*See* EARINGS.)

HEADER. The person in the Newfoundland fishing vessels who is engaged to cut open the fish, tear out the entrails, break off the head, and pass it over to the *splitter,* who sits opposite to him.

HEAD-FAST. A rope or chain employed to fasten the head of a ship or boat to a wharf or buoy, or to some other vessel alongside.—*Head-fast of a boat,* the tow-rope or painter.

HEAD-HOLES. The eyelet-holes where the rope-bands of a sail are fitted; they are worked button-hole fashion, over grommets of twine of several thicknesses; sometimes of cod-line.

HEADING. As to ships in company, one advancing by sail or steam faster than another heads her.

HEADING UP THE LAND WATER. When the flood-tide is backed by a wind, so that the ebb is retarded, causing an overflow.

HEAD-KNEES. Pieces of moulded compass timber fayed edgeways to the cut-water and stem, to steady the former. These are also called *cheek-knees.*

HEADLAND. Wherever the coast presents a high cliffy salient angle to the sea, without projecting far into it, it is called a head-land; but if the point be low, it is a spit, tongue, or point. (*See* BLUFF.)

HEADMOST. The situation of any ship or ships which are the most advanced in a fleet, or line of battle. The opposite of *sternmost.*

HEAD-NETTING. An ornamental netting used in merchant ships instead of the fayed planking to the *head-rails.*

HEAD OF A COMET. The brighter part of a comet, from which the tail proceeds.

HEAD OF A MAST, OR MAST-HEAD. The upper part of any mast, or that whereon the caps or trucks are fitted.

HEAD OF A WORK. In fortification, the part most advanced towards the enemy. In progressive works, such as siege-approaches and saps, it is the farthest point then attained.

HEAD OF WATER. Water kept to a height by winds, or by artificial dams and sluice-gates. The vertical column which dock-gates have to bear.

HEAD-PIECE. A term for the helmet.

HEAD-PUMP. A small pump fixed at the vessel's bow, its lower end communicating with the sea: it is mostly used for washing decks.

HEAD-QUARTERS. The place where the general, or commanding officer, takes up his quarters. Also, the man-of-war, or transport, which carries the staff of an expedition.

HEAD-RAILS. The short rails of the head, extending from the back of the figure to the cat-head: equally useful and ornamental. There are two on each side, one straight and the other curved. (*See* FALSE-RAIL.) Also, used familiarly for teeth.

HEAD-ROPE. That part of the bolt-rope which terminates any sail on the upper edge, and to which it is accordingly sewed. (*See* BOLT-ROPE.) Also, the small rope to which a flag is fastened, to hoist it to the mast-head, or head of the ensign-staff.

HEAD-SAILS. A general name for all those sails which may be set on the foremast and bowsprit, jib, and flying jib-boom, and employed to influence the fore-part of the ship.

HEAD-SEA. A name given to the waves when they oppose a ship's course, as the ship must rise over, or cut through each. Their effect depends upon their height, form, and speed; sometimes they are steep, quick, and irregular, so that a ship is caught by a second before she has recovered from the first; these render her wet and uneasy.

HEAD-SHEETS. Specially jibs and staysail sheets, before the foremast.

HEAD-STICK. A short round stick with a hole at each end, through which the head-rope of some triangular sails is thrust, before it is sewed on. Its use is to prevent the head of the sail from twisting.

HEAD TO WIND. The situation of a ship or boat when her head is pointed directly to windward. The term is particularly applied in the act of tacking, or while lying at anchor.

HEAD-WAY. A ship is said to gather headway when she passes any object thrown overboard at the bow, and it passes astern into her wake. A ship may also, by the action of swell, forge ahead.

HEAD-WIND. A breeze blowing from the direction of the ship's intended course. Thus, if a ship is bound N.E. a N.E. wind is a head-wind "dead on end," as seamen express it.—*The wind heads us,* that is, veers towards the direction of the ship's course.

HEALD. The *heel* over of a grounded ship.

HEALTH-GUARD. Officers appointed to superintend the due observance of the quarantine regulations.

HEART. A block of wood forming a peculiar sort of triangular dead-eye, somewhat resembling the shape of a heart; it is furnished with only one large hole in the middle, grooved for the rope instead of the three holes. It is principally used to the stays, as the dead-eyes are to the shrouds. (*See* DEAD-EYE.)

HEARTH. Applied to the ship's fire-place, coppers, and galley generally.

HEARTY. Open and free. "My hearties," a cheerful salute to ship-mates and seamen in general. "What cheer, my hearties?" how fare ye? what's your news?

HEART-YARNS. The centre yarns of a strand. Also, the heart-yarn or centre, on which four-stranded rope is formed.

HEATH. Various broom-stuffs used in breaming.

HEAVE, To. To throw anything overboard. To cast, as heaving the log or the lead. Also, to drag, prize, or purchase, as heaving up the anchor.

HEAVE ABOUT, To. To go upon the other tack suddenly.

HEAVE AND A-WASH. An encouraging call when the ring of the anchor rises to the surface, and the stock stirs the water.

HEAVE AND A-WEIGH. Signifies that the next effort will start the anchor from its bed, and make it *a-trip.* "Heave and a-weigh, sir," from the forecastle, denotes that the anchor is a-weigh; it inspirits the men to run it to the bows rapidly.

HEAVE AND IN SIGHT. A notice given by the boatswain to the crew when the anchor is drawn up so near the surface of the water as to be seen by its muddy water surrounding it.

HEAVE AND PAUL. Is the order to turn the capstan or windlass till the paul may be put in, by which it is prevented from coming up, and is something similar to *belay*, applied to a running rope.

HEAVE AND RALLY! An encouraging order to the men at the capstan to heave with spirit, with a rush, and thereby force the anchor out of the ground. When there is a rising sea "heave and rally" implies, "heave and stand to your bars," the pauls taking the strain, and the next wave probably lifting the anchor.

HEAVE AND SET. The ship's motion in rising and falling to the waves when at anchor.

HEAVE HANDSOMELY. Gently.

HEAVE HEARTY. Heave strong and with a will.

HEAVE OF THE SEA. The power that the swell of the sea exerts upon a ship in driving her out of, or faster on in, her course, and for which allowance must be made in the day's work. It is a similar, or the same action in force as in a head-sea.

HEAVE OUT THERE! The order to hasten men from their hammocks.

HEAVER. A wooden bar or staff, sometimes tapered at the ends; it is employed as a lever or purchase on many occasions, such as setting up the topmast shrouds, stropping large blocks, seizing the standing rigging, &c. Also, a name on the Kentish shores for the haviler crab.

HEAVE SHORT, To. To heave in on the cable until the vessel is nearly over her anchor, or sufficiently near it for sail being made before the anchor is tripped. Short, is when the fore-stay and cable are in line.

HEAVE THE LEAD. To take soundings with the hand lead-line. "Get a cast of the lead," with the deep-sea lead and line.

HEAVE THE LOG. Determine the ship's velocity by the log line and glass.

HEAVE-TO, To. To put a vessel in the position of *lying-to*, by adjusting her sails so as to counteract each other, and thereby check her way, or keep her perfectly still. In a gale, it implies to set merely enough sail to steady the ship; the aim being to keep the sea on the weather bow whilst the rudder has but little influence, the sail is chiefly set on the main and mizen-mast; as hove-to under a close-reefed main-topsail, or main-trysail, or driver. It is customary in a foul wind gale, and a last resource in a fair one.

HEAVING AHEAD. Is the act of advancing or drawing a ship forwards by heaving on a cable or rope made fast to some fixed point before her.

HEAVING AND SETTING. Riding hard, pitching and sending.

HEAVING ASTERN. Causing a ship to recede or go backwards, by heaving on a cable or other rope fastened to some fixed point behind her. This more immediately applies to drawing a vessel off a shoal.

HEAVING A STRAIN. Working at the windlass or capstan with more than usual exertion.

HEAVING DOWN. (*See* CAREENING.) The bringing one of a ship's sides down into the water, by means of purchases on the masts, in order to repair any injury which is below her water-line on the other.

HEAVING IN. Shortening in the cable. Also, the binding a block and hook by a seizing.

HEAVING IN STAYS. The act of tacking, when, the wind being ahead, great pressure is thrown upon the stays.

HEAVING KEEL OUT. The utmost effect to be produced by careening, viz. to raise the keel out of the water in order to repair or clean it. (*See* HEAVING DOWN.)

HEAVING OUT. The act of loosing or unfurling a sail; particularly applied to the staysails; or in the tops, footing the sail out of the top.

HEAVING TAUT. The act of turning the capstan, &c., till the rope applied thereto becomes straight and ready for action.

HEAVING THROUGH ALL. The surging or slipping of the cable when the nippers do not hold.

HEAVY DRIFT-ICE. Dense ice, which has a great depth in the water in proportion to its size, and is not in a state of decay, therefore dangerous to shipping.

HEAVY GALE. A strong wind, in which a ship is reduced to storm-staysails and close-reefed maintopsail. Force 10.

HEAVY METAL, OR HEAVY ORDNANCE. Ordnance of large calibre.

HEAVY SEA. High and strong waves.

HEBBER-MAN. An old name for a fisherman on the Thames below London Bridge, who took whitings, smelts, &c., commonly at ebbing-water.

HEBBING-WEIR. Contrivances for taking fish at ebbing-water.

HECK-BOAT. The old term for pinks. Latterly a clincher-built boat with covered fore-sheets, and one mast with a trysail.

HECKLE. Said to be from the Teutonic *heckelen*, to dress flax for rope-making. Also, an artificial fly for fishing.

HECKLE-BACK. A name of the fifteen-spined stickleback, *Gasterosteus spinachia*.

HEDA. An early term for a small haven, wharf, or landing-place.

HEDAGIUM. A toll or duty paid at the wharf for landing goods, &c.

HEDGEHOGS. A name formerly applied to vessels which rowed with many oars. Also, small stunted trees unfit for timber.

HEEL. The after end of a ship's keel, and the lower end of the stern-post to which it is connected. Also, the lower end of any mast, boom, bowsprit, or timber. Also, that part of the end of the butt of a musket which is uppermost when at the firing position.—*To heel.* To lie over, or incline to either side out of the perpendicular : usually applied to a ship when canted by the wind, or by being unequally ballasted. (*See* CRANK, STIFF, and TRIM.)

HEEL-BRACE. A piece of iron-work applicable to the lower part of a rudder, in case of casualty to the lower pintles.

HEELING GUNWALE TO. Pressing down sideways to her upper works, particularly applied to boats running before a heavy sea, when they may roll their weather gunwales to.

HEEL-KNEE. The compass-piece which connects the keel with the stern-post.

HEEL-LASHING. The rope which secures the inner part of a studding-sail-boom to the yard; also, that which secures the jib-boom.

HEEL OF A MAST. The lower end, which either fits into the step attached to the keel, or in topmasts is sustained by the fid upon the trestle-trees. Heeling is the square part of the spar through which the fid hole is cut.

HEEL-ROPE. That which hauls out the bowsprit in cutters, and the jib and studding-sail booms, or anything else where it passes through the heel of the spar, except in the case of top-masts and topgallant-masts, where it becomes a *mast-rope*.

HEELS. *Having the heels of a ship;* sailing faster.

HEEL-TACKLES. The luff purchases for the heels of each sheer previous to taking in masts, or otherwise using them.

HEEVIL. An old northern term for the conger.

HEFT. The Anglo-Saxon *hæft;* the handle of a dirk, knife, or any edge-tool; also, the handle of an oar.

HEIGHT. Synonymous with hill, and meaning generally any ground above the common level of the place. Our early navigators used the word as a synonym of latitude.

HEIGHT OF THE HOLD. Used for the depth of the hold.

HEIGHT OF BREADTH. In ship-building, is a delineation generally in two lines—upper and lower—determining the height of the broadest place of each timber.

HELIACAL. A star rises heliacally when it first becomes visible in the morning, after having been hidden in the sun's rays; and it sets helia-cally when it is first lost in the evening twilight, owing to the sun's proximity.

HELIER. A cavern into which the tide flows.

HELIOCENTRIC. As seen from, or having reference to, the centre of the sun.

HELIOMETER. An instrument designed for the accurate measurement of the diameters of the sun or planets.

HELIOSTAADT, or HELIOTROPE. This instrument reflects the sun's rays by a silvered disc, used in the great trigonometrical surveys. It has been visible at 100 miles' distance, from Cumberland to Ireland.

HELL-AFLOAT. A vessel with a bad name for tyranny.

HELM. Properly is the tiller, but sometimes used to express the rudder, and the means used for turning it, which, in small vessels and boats, is merely a tiller, but in larger vessels a wheel is added, which supplies the leverage for pulling the tiller either way; they are connected by ropes or chains.—*A-lee the helm,* or *Down with the helm!* So place the tiller that the rudder is brought on the weather side of the stern-post. These, and the following orders, were established when tillers extended forward from the rudder-head, but now they often extend aft, which requires the motion of the tiller to be reversed. With the latter style of tiller the order "down with the helm" is carried out by bringing the tiller *up* to the weather side of the ship; which being done, the order "Helm's a lee" follows.—*Bear up the helm.* That is, let the ship go more large before the wind.—*Ease the helm.* To let the helm come more amidships, when it has been put hard up or down.—It is common to ease the helm before a heavy sea takes the ship when close-hauled.—*Helm amidships,* or *right the helm.* That is, keep it even with the middle of the ship, in a line with the keel.—*Helm over.* The position of the tiller to enable a vessel steaming ahead to describe a curve.—*Port the helm.* Place the tiller so as to carry the rudder to starboard. (*See A-lee the helm.*)— *Shift the helm.* Put it from port to starboard, and *vice versa,* or it may be amidships.—*Starboard the helm.* Place the tiller so as to carry the rudder to port.—*Up with the helm.* Place the tiller so as to carry the rudder to leeward. (*See A-lee the helm.*)

HELMED. An old word for steered; it is metaphorically used by Shakspeare in *Measure for Measure.*

HELMET. A piece of defensive armour; a covering for the head.

HELM-PORT. The round hole or cavity in a ship's counter, through which the head of the rudder passes into the trunk.

HELM-PORT TRANSOM. The piece of timber placed across the lower counter, withinside the height of the helm-port, and bolted through every timber for the security of that part of the ship.

HELMSMAN. The timoneer, or person who guides the ship or boat by the management of the helm. The same as *steersman.*

HELM-WIND. A singular meteorological phenomenon which occurs in the north of England. Besides special places in Cumberland and Westmoreland, it suddenly rushes from an immense cloud that gathers round the summit of Cross-Fell, covering it like a helmet. Its effects reach the sea-board.

HELMY. Rainy [from an Anglo-Saxon phrase for rainy weather].

HELTER-SKELTER. Hurry and confusion. Defiance of good order. Privateerism.

HELVE. The handle of the carpenter's mauls, axes, and adzes; also of an oar, &c.

HELYER. *See* HELIER.

HEMISPHERE. Half the surface of a globe. The celestial equator divides the heavens into two hemispheres—the northern and the southern.

HEMP. *Cannabis sativa.* A manufactorial plant of equal antiquity with flax. The produce of hemp in fibre varies from three to six hundred weight per acre, and forms the best of all cordage and ropes. It is mixed with opium in the preparation of those rich drugs called *hashishe* in Cairo and Constantinople. Those who were in the constant use of them were called *hashishin* (herb-eaters); and being often by their stimulative properties excited almost to frenzy and to murder, the word "assassin" is said to have been derived by the crusaders from this source. While the French army was in Egypt, Napoleon I. was obliged to prohibit, under the severest penalties, the sale and use of these pernicious substances.

HENDECAGON. A right-lined figure with eleven sides; if it be regular, the sides and angles are all equal.

HEN-FRIGATE. A ship wherein the captain's wife interfered in the duty or regulations.

HEN'S-WARE. A name of the edible sea-weed *Fucus esculentus*.

HEP-PAH, or HIPPA. A New Zealand fort, or space surrounded with stout palisades; these rude defences have given our soldiers and sailors much trouble to reduce. (*See* PAH.)

HEPTAGON. A right-lined figure with seven sides; if it be regular, the sides and angles are all equal.

HERCULES. The large mass of iron by the blows of which anchors are welded.

HERE-AWAY. A term when a look-out man announces a rhumb or bearing of any object in this quarter.

HERE-FARE [Anglo-Saxon]. An expedition; going to warfare.

HERISSON. A balanced barrier to a passage in a fort, of the nature of a turnstile.

HERLING. A congener of the salmon species found in Scotland; it is small, and shaped like a sea-trout.

HERMAPHRODITE or BRIG SCHOONER, is square-rigged, but without a top forward, and schooner-rigged abaft; carrying only fore-and-aft sails on the mainmast; in other phrase, she is a vessel with a brig's foremast and a schooner's mainmast.

HERMIT-CRAB. A name applied to a group of crabs (family *Paguridæ*), of which the hinder part of the body is soft, and which habitually lodge themselves in the empty shell of some mollusc. Also called *soldier-crabs*.

HERMO. A Mediterranean term for the meteor called *corpo-santo*.

HERNE. A bight or corner, as Herne Bay, so called from lying in an angle.

HERNSHAW AND HERNE. Old words for the heron.

HERON. A large bird of the genus *Ardea*, which feeds on fish.

HERRING. A common fish—the *Clupea harengus;* Anglo-Saxon *hœring* and *hering*.

HERRING-BONING. A method of sewing up rents in a sail by small cross-stitches, by which the seam is kept flat.

HERRING-BUSS. A peculiar boat of 10 or 15 tons, for the herring fishery. (*See* BUSS.)

HERRING-COB.   A young herring.

HERRING-GUTTED.   *See* SHOTTEN HERRING.

HERRING-HOG.   A name for the porpoise.

HERRING-POND.   The Atlantic Ocean.

HETERODROMOUS LEVERS.   The windlass, capstan, crank, crane, &c.

HETEROPLON.   A kind of naval insurance, where the insurers only run the risk of the outward voyage; when both the going out and return of a vessel is insured, it is called amphoteroplon.

HETTLE.   A rocky fishing-ground in the Firth of Forth, which gives name to the fish called Hettle-codling.

HEUGH.   A craggy dry dell; a ravine without water.

HEXAGON.   A right-lined figure with six sides; if it be regular, the sides and angles are all equal.

HEYS-AND-HOW.   An ancient sea-cheer.

HI!   Often used for *hoy;* as, "Hi, you there!"   Also, the old term for *they,* as in Sir Ferumbras—

> "Costroye there was, the Admiral,
>   With vitaile great plente,
> And the standard of the sowdon royal,
>   Toward Mantrible ridden hi."

HIDDEN HARBOUR.   That of which the outer points so overlap as to cause the coast to appear to be continuous.

HIDE, To.   To beat; to rope's-end or drub.   Also, to secrete.

HIE, To.   To flow quickly in a tide-way.

HIE ALOFT.   Away aloft.

HIGH.   In gunnery, signifies tightly fitting the bore; said of shot, wads, &c.   Also, a gun is said to be laid high when too much elevated.

HIGH-AND-DRY.   The situation of a ship or other vessel which is aground, so as to be seen dry upon the strand when the tide ebbs from her.

HIGH ENOUGH.   Said in hoisting in goods, water, or masts.

HIGH FLOOD.   *See* FLOOD.

HIGH LATITUDES.   Those regions far removed from the equator towards the poles of the earth above the 50th degree.

HIGH TIDE, OR HIGH WATER.   Figuratively, a full purse.   Constance, in Shakspeare's *King John,* uses the term *high tides* as denoting the gold-letter days or holidays of the calendar.

HIGH-WATER.   The greatest height of the flood-tide.   (*See* TIDE.)

HIGH-WATER MARK.   The line made by the water upon the shore, when at its greatest height; it is also designated the *flood-mark* and *spring-tide mark.*   This constitutes the boundary line of admiralty jurisdiction as to the soil.

HIGH WIND.   *See* HEAVY GALE.

HIGRE.   *See* BORE and EAGRE.

HIKE.   A brief equivalent to "Be off," "Go away."   It is generally used in a contemptuous sense; as, he was "hiked off"—that is, dismissed at once, or in a hurry.   To swing.

HIKE UP, To. To kidnap; to carry off by force.

HILL. In use with the Anglo-Saxons. An insulated rise of the ground, usually applied to heights below 1000 feet, yet higher than a *hillock* or *hummock* (which see).

HILLOCK. A small coast-hill, differing from a *hummock* in having a peaked or pointed summit.

HILT. The handle and guard of a sword.

HIND-CASTLE. A word formerly used for the poop, as being opposed to *fore-castle.*

HIPPAGINES, OR HIPPAGOGÆ. Ancient transports for carrying cavalry.

HIPPER, OR HIPPING-STONES. Large stones placed for crossing a brook.

HIPPOCAMPUS. A small fish, so termed from the head resembling that of a horse. They live among reeds and long fuci, to which they cling with prehensile tails.

HIPPODAMES. An old word for sea-horses.

HIPSY. A drink compounded of wine, water, and brandy.

HIRE, To. To take vessel or men on service at a stipulated remuneration.

HIRECANO. An old word for hurricane.

HIRST. The roughest part of a river-ford. A bank.

HITCH. A species of knot by which one rope is connected with another, or to some object. They are various; as, clove-hitch, racking-hitch, timber-hitch (stopped), rolling-hitch, running-hitch, half-hitch, blackwall-hitch, magnus-hitch, marline-spike hitch, harness-hitch, &c. (*See* BEND and KNOT.) It also signifies motion by a jerk. Figuratively, it is applied to an impediment. A seaman often *hitches up* his trowsers, which "have no lifts or braces."—*To hitch* is to make fast a rope, &c., to catch with a hook. Thus of old, when a boat was to be hoisted in, they said—"Hitch the tackles into the rings of the boat."

HITCHER. An old term for a boat-hook.

HO! OR HAY! An exclamation derived from our Danish ancestors, and literally meaning *stop!*

HOAKY. A common petty oath—"By the hoaky!" by your hearth or fire.

HOAM. The dried fat of the cod-fish.

HOASTMEN. An ancient guild at Newcastle dealing in coals.

HOAY, OR HOY! a word frequently added to an exclamation bespeaking attention, as "Maintop, hoay!" and is chiefly used to persons aloft or without the ship.

HOB-A-NOB. To drink cosily; the act of touching glasses in pledging a health. An early and extensive custom falling into disuse.

HOBBLE. A perplexity or difficulty.—*Hobbles*, irons or fetters.

HOBBLER. A coast-man of Kent, a bit of a smuggler, and an unlicensed pilot, ever ready for a job in either of these occupations. Also, a man on land employed in towing a vessel by a rope. Also, a sentinel who kept watch at a beacon.

HOBITS. Small mortars of 6 or 8 inches bore mounted on gun-carriages; in use before the howitzer.

HOBRIN.   A northern designation of the blue shark, *Squalus glaucus.*

HOC.   The picked dog-fish, *Squalus acanthias.*

HOCK-SAW.   A fermented drink along the coasts of China, partaking more of the nature of beer than of spirit, and therefore less injurious than *sam-tsin.*

HOD.   A hole under a bank or rock, forming a retreat for fish.

HODDY-DODDY.   A west-country name for a revolving light.

HODMADODS.   The name among early navigators for Hottentots.

HODMANDODS.   *See* Dodman.

HODOMETRICAL.   A method of finding the longitude at sea by dead reckoning.

HOE.   *See* Howe.

HOE-MOTHER, or Homer.   The basking-shark, *Squalus maximus.*

HOE-TUSK.   *Squalus mustela,* smooth hound-fish of the Shetlanders.

HOG.   A kind of rough, flat scrubbing broom, serving to scrape a ship's bottom under water, particularly in the act of *boot-topping* (which see); formed by inclosing a multitude of short twigs of birch, or the like, between two pieces of plank, which are firmly attached to each other; the ends of the twigs are then cut off even, so as to form a brush of considerable extent.   To this is fitted a long staff, together with two ropes, the former of which is used to thrust the hog under the ship's bottom, and the latter to guide and pull it up again close to the planks, so as to rub off all the dirt.   This work is usually performed in the ship's boat.

HOG-BOAT.   *See* Heck-boat.

HOGGED.   A significant word derived from the animal; it implies that the two ends of a ship's decks droop lower than the midship part, consequently, that her keel and bottom are so strained as to curve upwards. The term is therefore in opposition to that of *sagging.*

HOG-IN-ARMOUR.   Soubriquet for an iron-clad ship.

HOGO.   From the French *haut-gout,* a disagreeable smell, but rather applied to ill-ventilated berths than to bilge-water.

HOISE.   The old word for hoist.

HOIST.   The perpendicular height of a sail or flag; in the latter it is opposed to the fly, which implies its breadth from the staff to the outer edge : or that part to which the halliards are bent.

HOIST, or Hoise, To.   To raise anything; but the term is specially applied to the operation of swaying up a body by the assistance of tackles. It is also invariably used for the hauling up the sails along the masts or stays, and the displaying of flags and pendants, though by the help of a single block only.   (*See* Swaying, Tracing-up, and Whipping.)

HOISTING-TACKLE.   A whip, a burton, or greater purchase, as yard-arm tackles, &c.

HOISTING THE FLAG.   An admiral assuming his command "hoists his flag," and is saluted with a definite number of guns by all vessels present.

HOISTING THE PENDANT.   Commissioning a ship.

HOLD. The whole interior cavity of a ship, or all that part comprehended between the floor and the lower deck throughout her length.—*The after-hold* lies abaft the main-mast, and is usually set apart for the provisions in ships of war.—*The fore-hold* is situated about the fore-hatchway, in continuation with the main-hold, and serves the same purposes.—*The main-hold* is just before the main-mast, and generally contains the fresh water and beer for the use of the ship's company.—*To rummage the hold* is to examine its contents.—*To stow the hold* is to arrange its contents in the most secure and commodious manner possible.—*To trim the hold* (*see* TRIM). Also, an Anglo-Saxon term for a fort, castle, or stronghold. —*Hold* is also generally understood of a ship with regard to the land or to another ship; hence we say, "Keep a good hold of the land," or "Keep the land well aboard," which are synonymous phrases, implying to keep near the land; when applied to a ship, we say, "She holds her own;" *i.e.* goes as fast as the other ship; holds her wind, or way.—*To hold.* To assemble for public business; as, to hold a court-martial, a survey, &c.— *Hold!* An authoritative way of separating combatants, according to the old military laws at tournaments, &c.; stand fast!

HOLD A GOOD WIND, To. To have weatherly qualities.

HOLD-ALL. A portable case for holding small articles required by soldiers, marines, and small-arm men on service.

HOLD-BEAMS. The lowest range of beams in a merchantman. In a man-of-war they support the orlop-deck. (*See* ORLOP-BEAMS.)

HOLDERS. The people employed in the hold duties of a ship.

HOLD-FAST. A rope; also the order to the people aloft, when shaking out reefs, &c., to suspend the operation. In ship-building, it means a bolt going down through the rough tree rail, and the fore or after part of each stanchion.

HOLDING ON. The act of pulling back the hind part of any rope.

HOLDING ON THE SLACK. Doing nothing. (*See* EYELIDS.)

HOLDING WATER. The act of checking the progress of a boat by holding the oar-blades in the water, and bearing the flat part strongly against the current alongside, so as to meet its resistance. (*See* BACK-ASTERN, OAR, and ROWING.)

HOLD OFF. The keeping the hove-in part of a cable or hawser clear of the capstan.

HOLD ON. Keep all you have got in pulling a rope.—*Hold on a minute.* Wait or stop.—*Hold on with your nails and eyelids.* A derisive injunction to a timid climber.

HOLD ON, GOOD STICKS! An apostrophe often made when the masts complain in a fresh squall, or are overpressed, and it is unadvisable to shorten sail.

HOLD-STANCHIONS. Those which support the hold-beams amidships, and rest on the kelson.

HOLD UP, To. In meteorological parlance, for the weather to clear up after a gale; to stop raining.

HOLE. A clear open space amongst ice in the Arctic seas.

HOLEBER. A kind of light horseman, who rode about from place to place in the night, to gain intelligence of the landing of boats, men, &c., on the Kentish coast.

HOLES, EYELET OR ŒILLET. The holes in sails for points and rope-bands which are fenced round by stitching the edge to a small log-line grommet. In the drum-head of a capstan, the holes receive the capstan-bars.

HOLIDAY. Any part left neglected or uncovered in paying or painting, blacking, or tarring.

HOLLANDS. The spirit principally distilled in Holland.

HOLLARDS. The dead branches and loppings of trees.

HOLLEBUT. A spelling of *halibut*.

HOLLOA, OR HOLLA. An answer to any person calling from a distance, to show they hear. Thus, if the master intends to give any order to the people in the main-top, he previously calls, "Main-top, hoay." It is also the first answer received when hailing a ship. (*See* HAILING and HOAY.)

HOLLOW. The bore of a rocket. In naval architecture, a name for the fifth or *top-timber-sweep* (which see). Also, hollow or curved leeches of sails, in contradistinction to straight.

HOLLOW BASTION. In fortification, a bastion of which the terre-plein or interior terrace is not continued beyond a certain distance to the rear of the parapet, and thus leaves a central area at a lower level.

HOLLOW-MOULD. The same as *floor-hollow* (which see).

HOLLOWS AND ROUNDS. Plane-tools used for making mouldings.

HOLLOW SEA. The undulation of the waves after a gale; long hollow-jawed sea; ground-swell.

HOLLOW SHOT. Introduced principally for naval use before the horizontal firing of shells from guns became general. Their weight was about two-thirds that of the solid shot; thus they required less charge of powder and weight of gun than the latter, whilst their smashing effect and first ranges were supposed to be greater. It is clear, however, that if filled with powder, their destructive effect must be immensely increased.

HOLLOW SQUARE. The square generally used by British infantry; a formation to resist cavalry. Each side is composed of four ranks of men, the two foremost kneeling with bayonets forming a fence breast high; the inclosed central space affords shelter to officers, colours, &c. With breech-loading muskets this defence will become less necessary. (*See also* RALLYING SQUARE.)

HOLM. (*See* CLETT.) A name both on the shores of Britain and Norway for a small uninhabited island used for pasture; yet in old writers it sometimes is applied to the sea, or a deep water. Also, an ill-defined name applied to a low islet in a river, as well as the flat land by the river side.

HOLOMETRUM GEOMETRICUM. A nautical instrument of brass, one of which, price £4, was supplied to Martin Frobisher in 1576.

HOLSOM. A term applied to a ship that rides without rolling or labouring.

HOLSTER. A case or cover for a pistol, worn at the saddle-bow.

HOLT [from the Anglo-Saxon]. A peaked hill covered with a wood.

HOLUS-BOLUS. Altogether; all at once.

HOLY-STONE. A sandstone for scrubbing decks, so called from being originally used for Sunday cleaning, or obtained by plundering church-yards of their tombstones, or because the seamen have to go on their knees to use it.

HOME. The proper situation of any object, when it retains its full force of action, or when it is properly lodged for convenience. In the former sense it is applied to the sails; in the latter it usually refers to the stowage of the hold. The anchor is said *to come home* when it loosens, or drags through the ground by the effort of the wind or current. (*See* ANCHOR.) —*Home* is the word given by the captain of the gun when, by the sense of his thumb on the touch-hole, he determines that the charge is home, and no air escapes by the touch-hole. It is the word given to denote the top-sail or other sheets being "home," or butting.—*Sheet home!* The order to extend the clues of sails to the yard-arms.—*The wind blows home.* When it sets continuously over the sea and land with equal velocity. When opposed by vertical or high land, the breeze loses its force as the land is neared: then it does not blow home, as about Gibraltar and Toulon.

HOME-SERVICE. The Channel service; any force, either naval or military, stationed in and about the United Kingdom.

HOME-TRADERS. The contradistinction of foreign-going ships.

HOMEWARD-BOUND. Said of a ship when returning from a voyage to the place whence she was fitted out; or the country to which she belongs.

HOMEWARD-BOUNDER. A ship on her course home.

HOMMELIN. The *Raia rubus*, or rough ray.

HONEST-POUNDS. Used in contradistinction to *"purser's pounds"* (which see).

HONEYCOMB. A spongy kind of flaw in the metal of ordnance, generally due to faulty casting.

HONG. Mercantile houses in China, with convenient warehouses adjoin-ing. Also, a society of the principal merchants of the place.

HONOURS OF WAR. Favourable terms granted to a capitulating enemy on evacuating a fortress; they vary in degree, according to circum-stances; generally understood to mean, to march out armed, colours flying, &c., but to pile arms at a given point, and leave them, and be sent home, or give parole not to serve until duly exchanged.

HOO. *See* HOWE.

HOOD. A covering for a companion-hatch, skylight, &c. Also, the piece of tarred or painted canvas which used to cover the eyes of rigging to prevent water from damaging them; now seldom used. Also, the name given to the upper part of the galley chimney, made to turn round with the wind, that the smoke may always go to leeward.—*Naval hoods or whood.* Large thick pieces of timber which encircle the hawse-holes.

HOOD-ENDS. The ends of the planks which fit into the rabbets of the stem and stern posts.

HOOD OF A PUMP. A frame covering the upper wheel of a chain-pump.

HOODS, or HOODINGS. The foremost and aftermost planks of the bottom, within and without. Also, coverings to shelter the mortar in bomb-vessels.

HOOK. There are several kinds used at sea, as boat-hooks, can-hooks, cat-hooks, fish-hooks, and the like. A name given to reaches, or angular points in rivers, such as Sandy Hook at New York.—*Laying-hook.* A winch used in rope-making.—*Loof-tackle hooks,* termed *luffs.* A tackle with two hooks, one to hitch into a cringle of the main or fore sail in the bolt-rope, and the other to hitch into a strap spliced to the chess-tree. They pull down the sail, and in a stiff gale help to hold it so that all the stress may not bear upon the tack.

HOOK AND BUTT. The scarphing or laying two ends of planks over each other. (*See* BUTT AND BUTT and HOOK-SCARPH.)

HOOK-BLOCK. Any block, of iron or wood, strapped with a hook.

HOOK-BOLTS. Those used to secure lower-deck ports.

HOOKER, or HOWKER. A coast or fishing vessel—a small hoy-built craft with one mast, intended for fishing. They are common on our coasts, and greatly used by pilots, especially off the Irish ports. Also, Jack's name for his vessel, the favourite "old hooker." Also, a term for a short pipe, probably derived from *hookah.*

HOOKEY. *See* HOAKY.

HOOKING. In ship-carpentry this is the act of working the edge of one plank into that of another, in such a manner that they cannot be drawn asunder.

HOOK OF THE DECKS. *See* BREAST-HOOKS.

HOOK-POTS. Tin cans fitted to hang on the bars of the galley range.

HOOK-ROPES. A rope 6 or 8 fathoms long, with a hook and thimble spliced at one end, and whipped at the other: it is used in coiling hempen cables in the tiers, dragging chain, &c.

HOOK-SCARPH. In ship-carpentry, the joining of two pieces of wood by a strong method of hook-butting, which mode of connecting is termed *hook and butt.*

HOOP. The principal hoops of different kinds used for nautical purposes, are noticed under their several names, as mast-hoops, clasp-hoops, &c. In wind-bound ships in former times the left hands of several boys were tied to a hoop, and their right armed with a nettle, they being naked down to the waist. On the boatswain giving one a cut with his cat, the boy struck the one before him, and each one did the same, beginning gently, but, becoming irritated, they at last laid on in earnest. Also, a nautical punishment for quarrelsome fighters was, that two offenders, similarly fastened, thrashed each other until one gave in. The craven was usually additionally punished by the commander.

HOOPS. The strong iron bindings of the anchor-stock to the shank, though square, are called hoops.

HOPE. A small bay; it was an early term for valley, and is still used in Kent for a brook, and gives name to the adjacent anchorages. Johnson defines it to be any sloping plain between two ridges of hills.

HOPPER-PUNT. A flat-floored lighter for carrying soil or mud, with a *hopper* or receptacle in its centre, to contain the lading.

HOPPO. The chief of the customs in China.

HOPPO-MEN. Chinese custom-house officers.

HORARY ANGLE. The apparent time by the sun, or the sidereal time of the moon, or planets, or stars, from the meridian.

HORARY MOTION. The march or movement of any heavenly body in the space of an hour.

HORARY TABLES. Tables for facilitating the determination of horary angles.

HORIE-GOOSE. A northern name for the *Anser bernicla*, or brent-goose.

HORIOLÆ. Small fishing-boats of the ancients.

HORIZON. The apparent or visible circle which bounds our vision at sea; it is that line which is described by the sky and water appearing to meet. This is designated as the *sensible* horizon; the *rational*, or *true* one, being a great circle of the heavens, parallel to the sensible horizon, but passing through the centre of the earth.

HORIZON-GLASSES. Two small speculums on one of the radii of a quadrant or sextant; the one half of the fore horizon-glass is silvered, while the other half is transparent, in order that an object may be seen directly through it: the back horizon-glass is silvered above and below, but in the middle there is a transparent stripe through which the horizon can be seen.

HORIZONTAL. A direction parallel to the horizon, or what is commonly termed lying flat. One of the greatest inconveniences navigators have to struggle with is the frequent want of a distinct sight of the horizon. To obviate this a *horizontal spinning speculum* was adopted by Mr. Lerson, who was lost in the *Victory* man-of-war, in which ship he was sent out to make trial of his instrument. This was afterwards improved by Smeaton, and consists of a well-polished metal speculum about $3\frac{1}{2}$ inches in diameter, inclosed within a circular rim of brass, so fitted that the centre of gravity of the whole shall fall near the point on which it spins. This is the end of a steel axis running through the centre of the speculum, above which it finishes in a square for the convenience of fitting a roller on it, bearing a piece of tape wound round it. The cup in which it spins is made of agate flint, or other hard substance. Sextants, with spirit-levels attached, have latterly been used, as well as Becher's horizon; but great dexterity is demanded for anything like an approximation to the truth; wherefore this continues to be a great desideratum in navigation.

HORIZONTAL FIRE. From artillery, is that in which the piece is laid either direct on the object, or with but small elevation above it, the limit on land being 10°, and afloat still less. It is the most telling under ordinary circumstances, and includes all other varieties, with the exception of vertical fire, which has elevations of from 30° and upwards; and, according to some few, curved fire, an intermediate kind, of limited application.

HORIZONTAL PARALLAX. *See* PARALLAX.

HORIZONTAL PLAN. In ship-building, the draught of a proposed ship, showing the whole as if seen from above.

HORIZONTAL RIBBAND LINES. A term given by ship-wrights to those lines, or occult ribbands, by which the cant-timbers are laid off, and truly bevelled.

HORN. The arm of a cleat or kevel.

HORN-CARD. Transparent graduated horn-plates to use on charts, either as protractors or for meteorological purposes, to represent the direction of the wind in a cyclone.

HORNED ANGLE. That which is made by a right line, whether tangent or secant, with the circumference of a circle.

HORNEL. A northern term for the largest species of sand-launce or sand-eel.

HORN-FISC. Anglo-Saxon for the sword-fish.

HORN-FISTED. Having hands inured to hauling ropes.

HORNING. In naval architecture, is the placing or proving anything to stand square from the middle line of the ship, by setting an equal distance thereon.

HORN-KECK. An old term for the *green-back* fish.

HORNOTINÆ. Ancient vessels which were built in a year.

HORNS. The points of the jaws of the booms. Also, the outer ends of the cross-trees. Also, two extreme points of land inclosing a bay.

HORNS OF THE MOON. The extremities of the lunar crescent, in which form she is said to be horned.

HORNS OF THE RUDDER. *See* RUDDER-HORNS.

HORNS OF THE TILLER. The pins at the extremity.

HORN-WORK. In fortification, a form of outwork having for its head a bastioned front, and for its sides two long straight faces, which are flanked by the guns of the body of the place. Sometimes it is a detached outwork.

HOROLOGIUM UNIVERSALE. An old brass nautical instrument, one of which was supplied to Martin Frobisher, at an expense of £2, 6s. 8d., when fitting out on his first voyage for the discovery of a north-west passage.

HORS DE COMBAT. A term adopted from the French, signifying so far disabled as to be incapable of taking farther share in the action.

HORSE. A foot-rope reaching from the opposite quarter of a yard to its arms or shoulders, and depending about two or three feet under the yard, for the sailors to tread on while they are loosing, reefing, or furling the sails, rigging out the studding-sail booms, &c. In order to keep the horse more parallel to the yard, it is usually attached thereto at proper distances, by certain ropes called stirrups, which have an eye spliced into their lower ends, through which the horse passes. (*See* STIRRUP and FOOT-ROPE.) Also, a rope formerly fast to the foremast fore-shrouds, with a dead-eye to receive the spritsail-sheet-pendant, and keep the spritsail-sheets clear of the flukes of the anchor. Also, the breast-rope which is made fast to the shrouds to protect the leadsman. Also, applied to any pendant and thimble through which running-rigging was led, now commonly called a lizard. Also, a thick rope, extending in a perpendicular direction near the fore or after side of a mast, for the purpose of hoisting some yard, or extending a sail thereon; when before the mast, it is used for the square-sail, whose yard is attached to the horse by means of a traveller or bull's-eye, which slides up and down. When it is abaft the mast, it is intended for the trysail of a snow; but is seldom used in this position, except in those sloops of war which occasionally assume the appearance of snows to deceive the enemy. Also, the name of the sawyer's frame or trestle. Also, the round iron bar formerly fixed to the main-rail at the head with stanchions; a fir rail is now used, and the head berthed up. Also, in cutters or schooners, one horse is a stout iron bar, with a large thimble, which spans the vessel from side to side close to the deck before the foremast. To this the forestaysail-sheet is hauled, and traverses. The other horse is a similar bar abaft, on which the main-boom sheet traverses. Also, cross-pieces on the tops of standards, on which the booms or spare-spars or boats are lashed between the fore and main masts. Horses are also termed jackstays, on which sails are hauled out, as gaff-sails. Horse is a term of derision where an officer assumes the grandioso, demanding honour where honour is not his due. Also, a strict disciplinarian, in nautical parlance. Also, tough salt beef—*salt horse*. — *Flemish horse* is the horse which has an iron thimble in one end, which goes over the iron point of the yard-arm before the studding-sail boom-iron is put on; in the other, a lashing eye, which is secured near the head earing of the topsail. It is intended for the men at the earing in reefing, or when setting the top-gallant-studding-sails.

HORSE-ARTILLERY. A branch of field artillery specially equipped to manœuvre with cavalry, having lighter guns, and all its gunners mounted on horseback. Its service demands a rare combination of soldierly qualities.

HORSE-BUCKETS. Covered buckets for carrying spirits or water in.

HORSE-BUCKIE. The great whelk.

HORSE-COCKLE. *See* GAWKY.

HORSE-FOOT. A name of the *Limulus polyphemus* of the shores of America, where from its shape it is called the horse-shoe or lantern crab.

HORSE-LATITUDES. A space between the westerly winds of higher latitudes and the trade-winds, notorious for tedious calms. The name arose from our old navigators often throwing the horses overboard which they were transporting to America and the West Indies.

HORSE-MACKEREL. A large and coarse member of the Scomber family, remarkably greedy, and therefore easily taken, but unwholesome.

HORSE-MARINE. An awkward lubberly person. One out of place.

HORSE-MUSSEL. *See* DUCK-MUSSEL.

HORSE-POTATOES. The old word for yams.

HORSE-POWER. A comparative estimate of the capacity of steam-engines, by assuming a certain average effective pressure of steam, and a certain average linear velocity of the piston. The pressure multiplied by the velocity gives the effective force of the engine exerted through a given number of feet per minute; and since the force called a horse-power means 33,000 lbs. acting thus one foot per minute, it follows that the nominal power of the engine will be found by dividing the effective force exerted by the piston, multiplied by the number of feet per minute through which it acts by 33,000.

HORSES. Blocks in whalers for cutting blubber on. (*See* WHITE-HORSES.)

HORSE-SHOE. In old fortification, a low work of this plan sometimes thrown up in ditches.

HORSE-SHOE CLAMP. The iron or copper straps so shaped, used as the fastenings which connect the gripe with the fore-foot at the scarph of the keel and stem.

HORSE-SHOE HINGES. Those by which side-scuttles or ventilators to the cabins are hung.

HORSE-SHOE RACK. A sweep curving from the bitt-heads abaft the mainmast carrying a set of nine-pin swivel-blocks as the fair leaders of the light running gear, staysail, halliards, &c.

HORSE-TONGUE. A name applied to a kind of sole.

HORSE-UP. *See* HORSING-IRON.

HORSING-IRON. An iron fixed in a withy handle, sometimes only lashed to a stick or tree-nail, and used with a beetle by caulkers.—*To horse-up*, or harden in the oakum of a vessel's seams.

HOSE (for watering, &c.) An elastic pipe.

HOSE-FISH. A name for a kind of cuttle-fish.

HOSPITAL. A place appointed for the reception of sick and wounded men, with a regular medical establishment. (*See* NAVAL HOSPITALS.)

HOSPITAL-SHIP. A vessel fitted to receive the sick, either remaining in port, or accompanying a fleet, as circumstance demands. She carries the chief surgeons, &c. The *Dreadnought*, off Greenwich, is a free hospital-ship for seamen of all nations.

HOSTAGE. A person given up to an enemy as a pledge or security for the performance of the articles of a treaty.

HOSTILE CHARACTER is legally constituted by having landed in an enemy's territory, and by residing there, temporary absence being immaterial; by permanent trade with an enemy; and by sailing under an enemy's flag.

HOST-MEN. An ancient guild or fraternity at Newcastle, to whom we are indebted for the valuable sea-coal trade. (*See* HOAST-MEN.)

HOT COPPERS. Dry fauces; morning thirst, but generally applied to those who were drinking hard over-night.

HOT-PRESS. When the press-gangs were instructed, on imminent emergency, to impress seamen, regardless of the protections.

HOT-SHOT. Balls made red-hot in a furnace. Amongst the savages in Bergou, the women are in the rear of the combatants, and they heat the heads of the spears, exchanging them for such as are cooled in the fight.

HOT-WELL. In a steamer, a reservoir from whence to feed the boiler with the warm water received out of the condenser; it also forms part of the discharge passage from the air-pump into the sea.

HOUND-FISH. The old Anglo-Saxon term for dog-fish—*hund-fisc.*

HOUNDS. Those projections at the mast-head serving as supports for the tressel-trees of large and rigging of smaller masts to rest upon. With lower masts they are termed *cheeks.*

HOUNSID. A rope bound round with service.

HOUR-ANGLE. The angular distance of a heavenly body east or west of the meridian.

HOUR-GLASS. The sand-glass: a measure of the hour.

HOUSE, To. To enter within board. To house a topgallant-mast, is to lower it so as to prevent the rigging resting or chafing on the cap, and securing its heel to the mast below it. This admits of double-reefed top-sails being set beneath.

HOUSE-BOAT. One with a cabin; a *coche d'eau.*

HOUSED. The situation of the great guns upon the lower gun-decks when they are run in clear of the port, and secured. The breech being let down, the muzzle rests against the side above the port; they are then secured by their tackles, muzzle-lashings, and breechings. Over the muzzle of every gun are two strong eye-bolts for the muzzle-lashings, which are $3\frac{1}{2}$-inch rope. When this operation is well performed, no accident is feared, as every act is one of mechanical skill. A gun is sometimes housed fore and aft to make room, as in the cabin, &c. Ships in ordinary, not in commission, are housed over by a substantial roofing.

HOUSEHOLD TROOPS. A designation of the horse and foot guards, who enjoy many immunities and privileges for attending the sovereign.

HOUSEWIFE. *See* HUZ-ZIF.

HOUSING, OR HOUSE-LINE. A small line formed of three fine strands, smaller than rope yarn; principally used for seizings of the block-strops, fastening the clues of sails to their bolt-ropes, and other purposes. (*See* MARLINE, THUMB-LINE, IRISH TWINE.)

HOUSING IN. After a ship in building is past the breadth of her bearing, and that she is brought in too narrow to her upper works, she is said to be *housed in,* or pinched. (*See* TUMBLING-HOME.)

HOUSING OF A LOWER MAST. That part of a mast which is below deck to the step in the kelson; of a bowsprit, the portion within the *knight-heads.*

HOUSING-RINGS. Ring-bolts over the lower deck-ports, through the beam-clamps, to which the muzzle-lashings of the guns are passed when housed.

HOUVARI. A strong land wind of the West Indies, accompanied with rain, thunder, and lightning.

HOUZING. A northern term for lading water.

HOVE DOWN, properly *hove out* or *careened.* The situation of a ship when heeled or placed thus for repairs.—*Hove off,* when removed from the ground.—*Hove up,* when brought into the slips or docks by cradles on the gridiron, &c.

HOVE-IN-SIGHT. The anchor in view. Also, a sail just discovered.

HOVE-IN-STAYS. The position of a ship in the act of going about.

HOVE KEEL OUT. Hove so completely over the beam-ends that the keel is above the water.

HOVELLERS. A Cinque-Port term for pilots and their boatmen; but colloquially, it is also applied to sturdy vagrants who infest the sea-coast in bad weather, in expectation of wreck and plunder.

HOVERING, AND HOVERING ACTS. Said of smugglers of old.

HOVE-SHORT. The ship with her cable hove taut towards her anchor, when the sails are usually loosed and braced for canting; sheeted home. —*Hove well short,* the position of the ship when she is drawn by the capstan nearly over her anchor.

HOVE-TO. From the act of heaving-to; the motion of the ship stopped. It is curious to observe that seamen have retained an old word which has otherwise been long disused. It occurs in Grafton's *Chronicle,* where the mayor and aldermen of London, in 1256, understanding that Henry III. was coming to Westminster from Windsor, went to Knightsbridge, "and *hoved* there to salute the king."

HOW. An ancient term for the carina or hold of a ship.

HOW, HOE, OR HOO. A knoll, mound, or elevated hillock.

HOW FARE YE? Are you all hearty? are you working together? a good old sea phrase not yet lost.

HOWITZER. A piece of ordnance specially designed for the horizontal firing of shells, being shorter and much lighter than any gun of the same calibre. The rifled gun, however, throwing a shell of the same capacity from a smaller bore, and with much greater power, is superseding it for general purposes.

HOWKER. *See* HOOKER.

HOWLE. An old English word for the hold of a ship. When the foothooks or futtocks of a ship are scarphed into the ground-timbers and bolted, and the plank laid up to the orlop-deck, then they say, "the ship begins to howle."

HOY. A call to a man. Also, a small vessel, usually rigged as a sloop, and employed in carrying passengers and goods, particularly in short distances on the sea-coast; it acquired its name from stopping when called to from the shore, to take up goods or passengers. In Holland the hoy has two masts, in England but one, where the mainsail is sometimes extended by a boom, and sometimes without it. In the naval service there are *gun-hoy, powder-hoy, provision-hoy, anchor-hoy,* all rigged sloop-fashion.

HOYSE. The old word for hoist.

HUBBLE-BUBBLE. An eastern pipe for smoking tobacco through water, which makes a bubbling noise.

HUDDOCK. The cabin of a keel or coal-barge.

> "'Twas between Ebbron and Yarrow,
> There cam on a varry strong gale;
> The skipper luicked out o' th' huddock,
> Crying, 'Smash, man, lower the sail!'"

HUDDUM. The old northern term for a kind of whale.

HUER. A man posted on an elevation near the sea, who, by concerted signals, directs the fishermen when a shoal of fish is in sight. Synonymous with *conder* (which see). Also, the hot fountains in the sea near Iceland, where many of them issue from the land.

HUFFED. Chagrined, offended, often needlessly.

HUFFLER. One who carries off fresh provisions to a ship; a Kentish term.

HUG, To.—*To hug the land,* to sail as near it as possible, the land however being to windward.—*To hug the wind,* to keep the ship as close-hauled to the wind as possible.

HUGGER-MUGGER. In its Shakspearian bearing may have meant secretly, or in a clandestine manner, but its nautical application is to express anything out of order or done in a slovenly way.

HUISSIERS. The flat-bottomed transports in which horses were embarked in the Crusades.

HULCOCK. A northern name for the *Squalus galeus,* or smooth hound-fish.

HULK. Is generally applied to a vessel condemned as unfit for the risks of the sea, and used as a store-vessel and housing for crews while refitting the vessels they belong to. There are also hulks for convicts, and for masting, as *sheer-hulk.* (*See* SHEERS.)

HULL. The Gothic *hulga* meant a husk or external covering, and hence the body of a ship, independent of masts, yards, sails, rigging, and other furniture, is so called.—*To hull,* signifies to hit with shot; to drive to and fro without rudder, sail, or oar; as Milton—

> "He looked and saw the ark hull on the flood."

—*To strike hull* in a storm, is to take in her sails and lash the helm on the lee side of the ship, which is termed *to lie a-hull.*

HULL-DOWN. Is said of a ship when at such a distance that, from the convexity of the globe, only her masts and sails are to be seen.

HULLING. Lying in wait at sea without any sails set. Also, to hit with shot.

HULLOCK OF A SAIL. A small part lowered in a gale.

HULL-TO. The situation of a ship when she is lying a-hull, or with all her sails furled.

HULLY. A long wicker-trap used for catching eels.

HUMBER-KEEL. A particular clincher-built craft used on the Humber.

HUMLA-BAND. A northern term for the grommet to an oar-pin or thole.

HUMMOCK. A hill with a rounded summit or conical eminence on the sea-coast. When in pairs they are termed *paps* by navigators (which see).

HUMMOCKS OF ICE. Protuberant lumps of ice thrown up by some pressure upon a *field* or *floe*, or any other frozen plane. The pieces which rise when large fragments come in contact, and bits of pack are frozen together and covered with snow.

HUMMUMS. From the Arabic word *hammam*, a bagnio or bath.

HUMP-BACKED WHALE. A species of whalebone whale, the *Megaptera longimana*, which attains to 45 or 50 feet in length, and is distinguished by its low rounded dorsal fin.

HURD. The strand of a rope.

HURDICES. Ramparts, scaffolds, fortifications, &c.

HURDIGERS. Particular artificers employed in constructing the castles in our early ships.

HURLEBLAST. An archaic term for *hurricane*.

HURRICANE. *See* Typhoon.

HURRICANE-DECK. A light deck over the saloon of some steamers.

HURRICANE-HOUSE. Any building run up for temporary purposes; the name is occasionally given to the round-house on a vessel's deck.

HURRICANO. Shakspeare evidently makes King Lear use this word as a waterspout.

HURRY. A staith or wharf where coals are shipped in the north.

HURST. Anglo-Saxon to express a wood.

HURT. A wound or injury for which a compensation can be claimed.

HURTLE, To. To send bodily on by a swell or wind.

HUSBAND, or Ship's Husband. An agent appointed by deed, executed by all the owners, with power to advance and lend, to make all payments, to receive the prices of freights, and to retain all claims. But this office gives him no authority to insure or to borrow money; and he is to render a full account to his employers.

HUSH. A name of the lump-fish, denoting the female.

HUSSAR, or Huzzar. A Hungarian term signifying "twentieth," as the first hussars were formed by selecting from various regiments the ablest man in every twenty; now generally a light-cavalry soldier equipped somewhat after the original Hungarian fashion.

HUT. The same as *barrack* (which see).

HUTT, The breech-pin of a gun.

HUZZA! This was originally the *hudsa*, or cry, of the Hungarian light horse, but is now also the national shout of the English in joy and triumph.

HUZ-ZIF. A general corruption of *housewife*. A very useful contrivance for holding needles and thread, and the like.

HYDRAULIC DOCK. *See* CAISSON.

HYDRAULIC PRESS. The simple yet powerful water-press invented by Bramah, without which it would have been a puzzle to float the enormous *Great Eastern.*

HYDRAULIC PURCHASE. A machine for drawing up vessels on a slip, in which the pumping of water is used to multiply the force applied.

HYDRAULICS. *See* HYDROLOGY.

HYDROGRAPHER. One who surveys coasts, &c., and constructs true maps and charts founded on astronomical observations. The hydrographer to the admiralty presides over the hydrographical office.

HYDROGRAPHICAL CHARTS OR MAPS. Usually called *sea-charts,* are projections of some part of the sea and its neighbouring coast for the use of navigation, and therefore the depth of water and nature of the bottom are minutely noted.

HYDROGRAPHICAL OFFICE. A department of the admiralty where the labours of the marine surveyors of the Royal Navy are collected and published.

HYDROGRAPHY. The science of marine surveying, requiring the principal points to be astronomically fixed.

HYDROLOGY. That part of physics which explains the properties of water, and is usually divided into hydrostatics and hydraulics. The former treats of weighing water and fluids in general, and of ascertaining their specific gravities; the latter shows the manner of conveying water from one place to another.

HYDROMETER. An instrument constructed to measure the specific gravities of fluids. That used at sea for testing the amount of salt in the water is a glass tube containing a scale, the bottom of the tube swelling out into two bulbs, of which the lower is laden with shot, which causes the instrument to float perpendicularly, and as it displaces its own weight of water, of course it sinks deeper as the water is lighter, which is recorded by the scale.

HYGRE. (*See* BORE and EAGRE.) An effect of counter-currents.

HYGROMETER. An instrument for ascertaining the quantity of moisture in the atmosphere.

HYPERBOLA. One of the conic sections formed by cutting a cone by a plane which is so inclined to the axis, that when produced it cuts also the opposite cone, or the cone which is the continuation of the former, on the opposite side of the vertex.

HYPOTHECA. A mortgage. In the civil law, was where the thing pledged remained with the debtor.

HYPOTHECATION. An authority to the master, amounting almost to a power of the absolute disposal of the ship in a foreign country; he may hypothecate not only the hull, but his freight and cargo, for necessary and urgent repairs.

HYTHE. A pier or wharf to lade or unlade wares at [from the Anglo-Saxon *hyd,* coast or haven].

I.

I.   The third class of rating on Lloyd's books, for the comparative excellence of merchant ships. (*See* A.)

ICE-ANCHOR.   A bar of round iron tapered to a point, and bent as a pot-hook; a hole is cut in the ice, the point entered, and the hawser bent to the shorter hook; by this vessels ride safely till any motion of the ice capsizes it, and then it is hauled in.   The ice is usually entered by a lance, which cuts its hole easily.

ICE-BEAMS.   Strengtheners for whalers.   (*See* FORTIFYING.)

ICEBERG.   An insulated mountain of ice, whether on Arctic lands or floating in the sea.   Some have been known to be aground in 120 fathoms water, and rise to the height of 150 feet above it.   Cook's obtaining fresh water from floating icebergs was not a new discovery.   The Hudson's Bay ships had long made use of it; and in July, 1585, Captain Davis met with ice "which melted into very good fresh water."

ICE-BIRDS.   Small sea-fowl in the polar regions.

ICE-BLINK.   A streak or stratum of lucid whiteness which appears over the ice in that part of the atmosphere adjoining the horizon, and proceeds from an extensive aggregation of ice reflecting the rays of light into the circumambient air.

ICE-BOAT. ·   A peculiar track-schuyt for the Dutch canals in winter.

ICE-BOUND.   A vessel so surrounded by ice as to be prevented from proceeding on her voyage.

ICE-CHISEL.   A large socket-chisel into which a pole is inserted, used to cut holes in the ice.

ICE-CLAWS.   A flat claw with two prongs spread like a can-hook; the same as a single span or claw-dog.

ICE-FENDERS.   Fenders of any kind, used to protect a vessel from injury by ice; usually broken spars hanging vertically where the strain is expected.

ICE LANE OR VEIN.   A narrow temporary channel of water in the packs or other large collections of ice.

ICE-MASTER.   A pilot, or man of experience, for the Arctic Sea.

ICE-PLANK.   *See* SPIKE-PLANK.

ICE-QUAKE.   The rending crash which accompanies the breaking of floes of ice.

ICE-SAW.   A huge saw for cutting through ice; it is made of ¾ to ⅜ inch plates of iron, and varies in length from 10 to 24 feet.

ICE-SLUDGE.   Small comminuted ice, or bay-ice broken up by the wind.

ICE-TONGUE.   *See* TONGUE OF ICE.

ICHNOGRAPHY.   A ground plot or plan of a fortification, showing the details of the construction as if cut horizontally through.

ICK.   An Erse or Manx term for a creek or gullet.

IDLER.   A general designation for all those on board a ship-of-war, who, from being liable to constant day duty, are not subjected to keep the night-watch, but must go on deck if all hands are called during the night. Surgeons, marine-officers, pay-masters, and the civil department, are also thus denominated.

IDOLEERS. The name by which the Dutch authorities are known in their oriental colonies, the designation being a corruption of *edle herren.*

IGNORANCE. If a loss happen through the ignorance of the master of a ship, it is not considered as a peril of the sea; consequently the assurers are not liable. Nor is his ignorance of admiralty-law admissible as an excuse.

IGUANA. A large lizard used for food in tropical climates.

ILAND. The Saxon *ealand.* (*See* ISLAND.)

ILDE, AND ILE. Archaic terms for *island.*

ILET. Lacing holes. (*See* EYELET.)

ILLEGAL VOYAGE. (*See* VOYAGE.)

IMMER. A water-fowl (*see* EMBER-GOOSE). The *Colymbus immer* of Linn., the great plunger of Buffon.

IMMERSION. The prismatic solid carried under water on the lee-side of a ship by its inclination.—*Centre of immersion,* the mean centre of the part immersed. (*See* CENTRE OF CAVITY.) Astronomically, immersion means the disappearance of a heavenly body when undergoing eclipse.

IMP. One length of twisted hair in a fishing-line.

IMPEDIMENTA. The ancient term for the baggage of an army.

IMPORT, IMPORTATION, AND IMPORTER, being exactly the reverse of *export, exportation,* and *exporter,* refer to those terms, and take the opposite meaning. To import is therefore to bring commodities into a country for the purpose of traffic.

IMPOSSIBLE. A hateful word, generally supplanted among good seamen by "we'll try." A thing which is impossible in law, is pronounced to be all one with a thing impossible in nature.

IMPOST. The tax received for such foreign merchandises as are brought into any haven within a prince's dominions.

IMPREGNABLE. Said of a fortress or position supposed to be proof against any attack.

IMPRESS, To. To compel to serve.

IMPRESSION. The effect produced upon any ship, place, or body of troops, by a hostile attack.

IMPRESSMENT. The system and act of pressing seamen, and compelling them—under plea of state necessity—to serve in our men-of-war.

IMPREST. Charge on the pay of an officer.

IMPREST-MONEY. That paid on the enlistment of soldiers.

IN. The state of any sails in a ship when they are furled or stowed, in opposition to *out,* which implies that they are set, or extended to assist the ship's course. Hence, *in* is also used as an order to shorten sail, as "In topgallant-sails." It was moreover an old word for embanking and inclosing; thus Sir Nicholas L'Estrange (*Harleian*

MS. 6395) speaks of him who had "the patent for *inning* the salt marshes."

IN AND OUT. A term sometimes used for the scantling of timbers, the moulding way, and particularly for those bolts that are driven into the hanging and lodging knees, drawn through the ship's sides, and termed *in-and-out bolts.*

IN-BOARD. Within the ship; the opposite of *out-board.*

IN-BOATS! The order to hoist the boats in-board.

IN-BOW! The order to the bow-man to throw in his oar, and prepare his boat-hook, previous to getting alongside.

INCH. The smallest lineal measure to which a name is given; but it has many sub-divisions. Also, a general name for a small coast islet on the northern shores, from the old Gaelic word.

INCIDENCE, ANGLE OF. That which the direction of a ray of light, &c., makes at the point where it strikes with a line drawn perpendicularly to the surface of that body.

INCLINATION. In geometry, is the mutual tendency of two lines or planes towards each other, so as to form an angle.

INCLINATION OF AN ORBIT. The angle which the path of a comet or planet makes with the plane of the ecliptic.

INCLINATORY NEEDLE. An old term for the *dipping-needle* (which see).

INCLINOMETER. An invention by Wales in Cook's second voyage, where particulars are given.

INCOMPETENCY, OR INSUFFICIENCY, OF A MERCHANTMAN'S CREW. A bar to any claim on warrantry; as it is an implied condition in the seaworthiness of a ship, that at sailing she must have a master of competent skill, and a crew sufficient to navigate her on the voyage.

INDEMNIFICATION. A stipulated compensation for damage done.

INDEMNITY. Amnesty; security against punishment.

INDENTED LINE. In fortification, a connected line of works composed of faces which offer a continued series of alternate salient and re-entering angles. It is conveniently applied on the banks of a river entering a town, and was to be seen on the James river in Virginia, near Richmond, in 1864.

INDENTED PARAPET. One of which the interior slope is indented with a series of vertical cavities, enabling the men stationed within them to fire across the proper front.

INDENTING FOR STORES. An indispensable duty to show that every article has been actually received.

INDENTURES, PAIR OF. A term for *charter-party.*

INDEX. The flat bar which carries the nonius scale and index-glass of a quadrant, octant, quintant, or sextant.

INDEX-ERROR. The reading of the verniers of the above-named instruments. It is the correction to be applied to the + or — reading of a vernier when the horizon and index-glasses are parallel.

INDEX-GLASS. A plane speculum, or mirror of quick-silvered glass, which moves with the index, and is designed to reflect the image of the sun or other object upon the horizon glass, whence it is again reflected to the eye of the observer.

INDEX-ROD. A graduated indicator.

INDIAMAN. A term occasionally applied to any ship in the East India trade, but in strict parlance the large ships formerly officered by the East India Company for that trade, and generally armed.

INDIAN INK. Properly Chinese; compounded of a peculiar lamp-black and gum.

INDIAN OCEAN. The great Oriental Ocean.

INDRAUGHT. A particular flowing of the ocean towards any contracting part of a coast or coasts, as that which sets from the Atlantic into the Straits of Gibraltar, and on other coasts of Europe and Africa. It usually applies to a strong current, apt to engender a sort of vortex.

INDUCED MAGNETISM. The magnetic action of the earth, whereby every particle of soft iron in certain positions is converted into a magnet.

INDULTO. The duty formerly exacted by the crown of Spain upon colonial commodities.

INEQUALITY, SECULAR. A small irregularity in the motions of planets, which becomes important only after a long lapse of years. The *great inequality* of Jupiter and Saturn is a variation of their orbital positions, caused by the disturbing action of one planet on the other.

INERTIA. The passive principle by which bodies persist in a state of motion or rest, and resist as much as they are resisted. (*See* VIS INERTIÆ.)

INFANTRY. Foot soldiers of the regular army; so called throughout Europe after the original Spanish " infanteria," or troops of the infanta or queen of Spain, who first developed on a large scale the importance of the arm.

INFERIOR CONJUNCTION. Mercury or Venus is said to be in inferior conjunction, when it is situated in the same longitude as the sun, and between that luminary and the earth.

INFERIOR PLANETS. This name, the opposite of superior, is applied to Mercury and Venus, because they revolve in orbits interior to the earth's path.

INFORMATION. In admiralty courts, implies a clause introduced into a citation, intimating that in the event of a party cited not appearing, the court will proceed in his absence.

INGS. An old word said to be left here by the Danes; it signifies low grounds or springy meadows near a river, or creek, liable to occasional overflowings.

IN-HAULER. The rope used for hauling in the clue of a boom-sail, or jib-traveller: it is the reverse of *out-hauler*.

INITIAL VELOCITY. The velocity of a projectile at the moment of discharge from a gun.

INJECTION-PIPE. This is fixed in the interior of a marine steam-engine,

is fitted with a cock, and communicates with the water outside: it is for
the purpose of playing into the condenser while the engine is working,
and creating a vacuum.

INLAND SEA. Mediterranean. Implies a very large gulf surrounded
by land, except at the communication with the ocean, as the Baltic, Red,
and Mediterranean Seas.

INLAND TRADE. That which is wholly managed at home, and the
term is in contradistinction to commerce. In China it is applied to
canal-trade.

INLET. A term in some cases synonymous with *cove* and *creek* (which
see), in contradistinction to outlet, when speaking of the supply and discharge of lakes and broad waters, or an opening in the land, forming a
passage to any inclosed water.

INNER AND OUTER TURNS. Terms applied to the passing of the
reef-earings, besides its over and under turns.

INNER JIB-STAY. A temporary stay lashed half-way in, on the jib-
boom; it sets up with lashing-eyes at the fore top-mast head.

INNER POST, or INNER STERN-POST. The post on which the transoms
are seated. An oak timber brought on and fayed at the fore-edge of the
main-post, and generally continued as high as the wing-transom, to seat
the other transoms upon, and strengthen the whole. (*See* STERN-POST.)
It applies to the main stern-post in steamers, the screw acting between
it and the outer, on which the rudder is hung.

INNINGS. Coast lands recovered from the sea by draining.

INNIS. An old Gaelic term for an island, still in use.

INQUIRY, COURT OF, is assembled by order of a commanding officer
to inquire into matters of an intricate nature, for his information; but
has no power of adjudication whatever: but too like the Star Chamber.

INSHORE. The opposite of *offing.—Inshore tack.* Standing in from
seaward when working to windward on a coast.

INSHORED. Come to shore.

INSIDE MUSTER-PAPER. A description of paper supplied from the
dock-yards, ruled and headed, for making ships' books.

INSPECTION. The mode of working up the dead-reckoning by computed
nautical tables. Also, a general examination or survey of all parts of a
sea or land force by an officer of competent authority.

INSTALMENT. A partial payment.

INSTANCE COURT. A department of the admiralty court, governed
by the civil law, the laws of Oleron, and the customs of the admiralty,
modified by statute law.

INSTITUTION. An establishment founded partly with a view to instruction; as the Royal United Service Institution in London.

INSTRUCTIONS. *See* PRINTED INSTRUCTIONS.

INSTRUMENT. A term of extensive application among tools and weapons; but it is here introduced as an official conveyance of some right, or
the record of some fact.

INSUFFICIENCY of a Merchantman's Crew.   This bars the owner's claim on the sea-worthy warrant.   (*See* Incompetency.)

INSURANCE.   *See* Marine Insurance.

INSURED.   The party who obtains the policy and pays the premium.

INSURER.   The party taking the risk of a policy.   (*See* Underwriters.)

INTACT.   Unhurt; undamaged.

INTENSITY OF LIGHT.   The degree of brightness of a planet or comet, expressed as a number varying with the distance of the body from the sun and earth.

INTERCALARY.   Any period of time interpolated in the calendar for the purpose of accommodating the mode of reckoning with the course of the sun.

INTEREST POLICY.   *See* Policy.

INTERLOPER.   A smuggling or forced trade vessel.   As a nautical phrase it was generally applied to the "letters of marque" on the coasts of South America, or a cruiser off her admiral's limits (poaching).

INTERMEDIATE SHAFT.   In a steamer, is the iron crank common to both engines.

INTERNAL CONTACT.   This, in a transit of Mercury or Venus across the solar disc, occurs when the planet is just within the sun's margin.

INTERNAL PLANKING.   This is termed *ceiling* of the ship.

INTERNAL SAFETY-VALVE.   A valve opening from the outside of a steamer's boiler, in order to allow air to enter the boiler when the pressure becomes too weak within.

INTERROGATORIES.   The practice in the prize court is, on the breaking out of a war, to prepare standing commissions for the examination of witnesses, to which certain interrogatories are annexed; to these the examination is confined.   Private interrogatories are inadmissible as evidence.

INTERSECTION.   The point in which one line crosses another.

INTERTROPICAL.   The space included between the tropics on each side of the equator, making a zone of nearly 47°.

INTERVAL.   In military affairs, the lateral space between works or bodies of troops, as distinguished from distance, which is the depth or measurement in a direction from front to rear.

IN THE WIND.   The state of a vessel when thrown with her head into the wind, but not quite *all in the wind* (*see* All).   It is figuratively used for being nearly intoxicated.

INTRENCHMENT.   Any work made to fortify a post against an enemy, but usually implying a ditch or trench, with a parapet.

INUNDATIONS.   In ancient Egypt officers estimated the case of sufferers from the inundations of the Nile.   The changes of property in Bengal, by alluvion, are equally attended to.   *Inundation* is also a method of impeding the approach of an enemy, by damming up the course of a brook or river, so as to intercept the water, and set the neighbourhood afloat.   In Egypt the plan was diametrically opposite; for by flooding Lake Mareotis, our gun-boats were enabled greatly to annoy the French garrison at Alexandria.

INVALID.   A maimed or sick soldier or sailor.—*To invalid* is to cause to retire from active service from inability.

INVER.   A Gaelic name, still retained in Scotland, for the mouth of a river.

INVESTMENT.   The first process of a siege, in taking measures to seize all the avenues, blocking up the garrison, and preventing relief getting into the place before the arrival of the main army with the siege-train.

INVINCIBLE.   A name boastfully applied both to naval and military forces, which have nevertheless been utterly vanquished.

INVOICE.   An account from a merchant to his factor, containing the particulars and prices of each parcel of goods in the cargo, with the amount of the freight, duties, and other charges thereon.

INWARD.   The opposite of *outward* (which see).

INWARD CHARGES.   Pilotage and other expenses incurred in entering any port.

IODINE.   A substance chiefly obtained from kelp or sea-weed, extensively employed in medicine and the arts.   Its vapour has a beautiful violet colour.

IRIS EARS.   A name applied to the shells of the Haliotis—a univalve mollusc found clinging like limpets to rocks; very abundant in Guernsey.

IRISH HORSE.   Old salt beef: hence the sailor's address to his salt beef—

> " Salt horse, salt horse, what brought you here?
> You've carried turf for many a year.
> From Dublin quay to Ballyack
> You've carried turf upon your back," &c.

IRISH PENNANTS.   Rope-yarns hanging about on the rigging.   Loose reef-points or gaskets flying about, or fag-ends of ropes.

IRON-BOUND.   A coast where the shores are composed of rocks which mostly rise perpendicularly from the sea, and have no anchorage near to them, therefore dangerous for vessels to borrow upon.

IRON-BOUND BLOCKS.   Those which are fitted with iron strops.

IRON-CLAD, CASED, COATED, or PLATED VESSEL.   One covered entirely, or in special parts, with iron plates intended to resist ordinary missiles.   Where parts only are so protected, of course it may be done more effectually.

IRON GARTERS.   A cant word for bilboes, or fetters.

IRON-HORSE.   The iron rail of the head; the horse of the fore-sheet or boom-sheet traveller.

IRON-PLATED SHIPS.   *See* ARMOUR-CLAD.

IRONS.   A ship is said to be in irons when, by mismanagement, she is permitted to come up in the wind and lose her *way;* so that, having no steerage, she must either be boxed off on the former tack, or fall off on the other; for she will not cast one way or the other, without bracing in the yards. Also, *bilboes* (which see). Also, the tools used by the caulkers for driving oakum into the seams. (*See also* BOOM-IRONS.)

IRON-SICK. The condition of vessels when the iron work becomes loose in the timbers from corrosion by gallic acid, and the speeks or sheathing nails are eaten away by rust.

IRON-SIDES. Formerly a sobriquet for favourite veteran men-of-war, but latterly applied to iron and iron-clad ships.

IRON WEDGES. Tapered iron wedges on the well-known mechanical principle, for splitting out blocks and for other similar purposes.

IRON-WORK. A general name for all pieces of iron, of whatever figure or size, which are used in the construction and equipment of ships.

IRREGULAR BASTION. One whose opposite faces or flanks do not correspond; this, as well as the constant irregularity of most real fortification, is generally the result of the local features of the neighbourhood.

ISLAND. May be simply described as a tract of land entirely surrounded with water; but the whole continuous land of the Old World forms one island, and the New World another; while canals across the isthmuses of Suez and Panama would make each into two. The term properly only applies to smaller portions of land; and Australia, Madagascar, Borneo, and Britain are among the larger examples. Their materials and form are equally various, and so is their origin; some having evidently been upheaved by volcanic eruption, others are the result of accretion, and still more revealing by their strata that they were formerly attached to a neighbouring land. The sudden emergence of Sabrina, in the Atlantic, has occasioned wonder in our own day. So has that of Graham's Island, near the south coast of Sicily; and the Archipelago is daily at work.

ISLAND HARBOUR. That which is protected from the violence of the sea by one or more islands or islets screening its mouth.

ISLAND OF ICE. A name given to a great quantity of ice collected into one solid mass and floating upon the sea; they are often met with on the coasts of Spitzbergen, to the great danger of the shipping employed in the Greenland fishery.

ISLE. A colloquial abbreviation of *island*.

ISLE OF WIGHT PARSON. A cormorant.

ISLET, OR ISLOT. Smaller than an island, yet larger than a key; an insular spot about a couple of miles in circuit.

ISOSCELES. A triangle with only two of its sides equal.

ISSUE. The act of dispensing slops, tobacco, beds, &c., to the ship's company; a distribution.

ISSUE-BOOK. That which contains the record of issues to the crew, and the charges made against them.

ISTHMUS. A narrow neck of land which joins a peninsula to its continent, or two islands together, or two peninsulas, without reference to size. The Isthmus of Suez alone prevents Africa from being an island, as that of Darien connects the two Americas.

IURRAM. A Gaelic word signifying a boat-song, intended to regulate the strokes of the oars. Also, a song sung during any kind of work.

IVIGAR. A name in our northern isles for the sea-urchin, *Echinus marinus*.

IVORY GULL, or SNOW-BIRD. The *Larus eburneus* of Arctic seas. It has a yellowish beak, jet black legs, and plumage of a dazzling white.

J.

JAB, To. To pierce fish by prodding.

JABART. A northern term for a fish out of season.

JABB. A peculiar net used for catching the fry of the coal-fish.

JACK. In the British navy the jack is a small union flag, formed by the intersection of St. George's and St. Andrew's crosses (which see), usually displayed from a staff erected on the outer end of a ship's bow-sprit. In merchant ships the union is bordered with white or red. (*See* UNION-JACK.) Also, a common term for the jack or cross-trees. Also, a young male pike, *Esox lucius*, under a foot in length. Also, a drinking vessel of half-pint contents. (*See* BLACK-JACK.)—*Jack*, or *Jack Tar*, a familiar term for a sailor. A fore-mast man and an able seaman. It was an early term for short coats, jackets, and a sort of coat-of-mail or defensive lorica, or upper garment.

JACK ADAMS. A stubborn fool.

JACK AFLOAT. A sailor. Euripides used almost the same term in *floater*, for a seaman.

JACKASSES. Heavy rough boats used in Newfoundland.

JACKASS PENGUIN. A bird, apt while on shore to throw its head backwards, and make a strange noise, somewhat resembling the braying of an ass.

JACK-BARREL. A minnow.

JACK-BLOCK. A block occasionally attached to the topgallant-tie, and through which the top-gallant top-rope is rove, to sway up or strike the yard.

JACK-BOOTS. Large coverings for the feet and legs, outside all, worn by fishermen.

JACK CROSS-TREES. Single iron cross-trees at the head of long top-gallant masts, to support royal and skysail masts.

JACKEE-JA. A Greenland canoe.

JACKET. A doublet; any kind of outer coat.—*Cork jacket*, is lined with cork in pieces, in order to give it buoyancy, and yet a degree of flexibility, that the activity of the wearer may not be impeded in swimming.

JACKETS. The casings of the passages by which steam is delivered into the cylinders of steam-engines. They are non-conductors of heat to check its escape.

JACKETTING. A starting, or infliction of the rope's-end.

JACK-HERN. A name on our southern coasts for the heron.

JACKING. Taking the skin off a seal.

JACK IN OFFICE. An insolent fellow in authority.

JACK IN THE BASKET. A sort of wooden cap or basket on the top of a pole, to mark a sand-bank or hidden danger.

JACK IN THE BOX. A very handy engine, consisting of a large wooden male screw turning in a female one, which forms the upper part of a strong wooden box, shaped like the frustum of a pyramid. It is used by means of levers passing through holes in it as a press in packing, and for other purposes.

JACK IN THE BREAD-ROOM, OR JACK IN THE DUST. The purser's steward's assistant in the bread and steward's room.

JACK-KNIFE. A horn-handled clasp-knife with a laniard, worn by seamen.

JACKMAN. A musketeer of former times, wearing a short mail jack or jacket.

JACK NASTY-FACE. A cook's assistant.

JACK OF DOVER. An old sea-dish, the composition of which is now lost. Chaucer's host in rallying the cook exclaims,

> "And many a *Jack of Dover* hast thou sold,
> That hath been twies hot and twies cold."

JACK O' LANTERN. The *corpo santo*, or St. Elmo's light, is sometimes so called.

JACK-PINS. A name applied to the fife-rail pins, also called *Tackspins*.

JACK ROBINSON.—*Before you could say Jack Robinson*, is a very old expression for a short time,—

> "A warke it ys as easie to be doone,
> As tys to saye Jacke Robyson."

JACK'S ALIVE. A once popular sea-port dance.

JACK-SCREW. A small machine used to cant or lift weighty substances, and in stowing cotton or other elastic goods. It consists of a wooden frame containing cogged iron wheels of increasing powers. The outer one, which moves the rest, is put in motion by a winch on the outside, and is called either single or double, according to its increasing force. The pinions act upon an iron bar called the *spear*.

JACK-SHARK. A common sobriquet of the *Squalus* tribe.

JACK-SHARP. A small fresh-water fish, otherwise known as *prickly-back*.

JACK'S QUARTER-DECK. The deck elevation forward in some vessels, often called a top-gallant forecastle.

JACK-STAFF. A short staff raised at the bowsprit-cap, upon which the union-jack is hoisted.

JACK-STAYS. Ropes, battens, or iron bars placed on a yard or spar and set taut, either for bending the head of a sail to, or acting as a traveller. Frequently resorted to for the staystails, square-sail yard, &c.

JACOB'S LADDER. The assemblage of shakes and short fractures, rising one above another, in a defective single-tree spar. Also, short ladders made with wooden steps and rope sides for ascending the rigging.

JACOB'S STAFF, or Cross-staff. A mathematical instrument to take altitudes, consisting of a brass circle, divided into four equal parts by two lines cutting each other in the centre; at each extremity of either line is fixed a sight perpendicularly over the lines, with holes below each slit for the better discovery of distant objects. The cross is mounted on a staff or stand for use. Sometimes, instead of four sights, there are eight.

JACULATOR. A fish whose chief sustenance is flies, which it secures by shooting a drop of water at them from its mouth.

JAG, To. To notch an edge irregularly.—*Jagged*, a term applied to denti-culated edges, as in jagged bolts to prevent their coming out.

JAGARA, or Joggaree. A coarse brown sugar of India.

JAGS. Splinters to a shot-hole.

JAIL-BIRD. One who has been confined in prison, from the old term of *cage* for a prison; a felon absurdly (and injuriously to the country) sen-tenced to serve in the navy.

JALIAS. Small craft on the Arracan and Pegu coasts.

JAM, To. Anything being confined, so that it cannot be freed without trouble and force; the term is also applied to the act of confining it. To squeeze, to wedge, to press against. (*See* JAMBING.)

JAMAICA DISCIPLINE. The buccaneer regulations respecting prize shares, insisting that all prizes be divided among the captors.

JAMBEAUX. Armour to protect the legs.

JAMBING, or Jamming. The act of inclosing any object between two bodies, so as to render it immovable while they continue in that position; usually applied to a running rope, when, from pressure, it cannot travel in the blocks; the opposite of *rendering* (which see).

JAMBS. Door-posts in general; but in particular thick broad pieces of oak, fixed up endways, between which the lights of the powder magazine are fitted.

JAMMED IN A CLINCH. The same as *hard up in a clinch* (which see).—*Jammed in a clinch like Jackson*, involved in difficulty of a secondary degree, as when Jackson, after feeding for a week in the bread-room, could not escape through the scuttle.

JANGADA. A sort of fishing float, or rather raft, composed of three or four long pieces of wood lashed together, used on the coasts of Peru and Brazil. The owner is called a *jangadeira*, but the term is evidently an application of *jergado* (which see).

JANGAR. A kind of pontoon constructed of two boats with a platform laid across them, used by the natives in the East Indies to convey horses, cattle, &c., across rivers.

JANISSARY. A term derived from *jeni cheri*, meaning *new soldiers*, in the Turkish service.

JANTOOK, OR CHUNTOCK. A Chinese officer with vice-regal powers: he of Canton was called *John Tuck* by our seamen.

JANTY, OR JAUNTY. A vessel in showy condition; dressed in flags.

JAPANESE WHALE-BOAT. A long, open, and sharp rowing-boat of Japan.

JARGANEE. A Manx term for small worms on the sea-shore, and used as bait.

JARRING. The vibrations and tremblings occasioned in some steam-vessels by the machinery.

JAVA POT. A kind of sponge of the species *Alcyonum.*

JAVELS. An old term for dirty, idle fellows, wandering about quays and docks.

JAW. The inner, hollowed, semicircular end of a gaff or boom, which presses against the mast; the points of the jaw are called *horns.* Also, coarse and often petulant loquacity.—*Long-jawed* applies to a rope or cable, when by great strain it untwists, and exhibits one revolution where four were before; similar to long and short threads of the screw.

JAW-BREAKERS. Hard and infrequent words.

JAWING-TACKS. When a person speaks with vociferous fluency, he is said to have hauled his jawing-tacks on board.

JAW-ME-DOWN. An arrogant, overbearing, and unsound loud arguer.

JAW OF A BLOCK. The space in the shell where the sheave revolves.

JAW-ROPE. A line attached to the horns of the jaws to prevent the gaff from coming off the mast. It is usually furnished with bull's eyes (perforated balls) to make it shift easily up or down the mast.

JAYLS. The cracks and fissures of timber in seasoning.

JEER-BITTS. Those to which the jeers are fastened and belayed.

JEER-BLOCKS. Are twofold or threefold blocks, through which the jeer-falls are rove, and applied to hoist, suspend, or lower the main and fore yards.

JEER-CAPSTAN. One placed between the fore and main masts, serving to stretch a rope, heave upon the jeers, and take the viol to. Very seldom used. It is indeed deemed the spare capstan, and is frequently housed in by sheep-pens and fowl-racks.

JEERS. Answer the same purpose to the mainsail, foresail, and mizen, as halliards do to all inferior sails. The tye, a sort of runner, or thick rope, is the upper part of the jeers. Also, an assemblage of strong tackles by which the lower yards are hoisted up along the mast, or lowered down, as occasion requires; the former of which operations is called *swaying*, and the latter *striking* (both of which see).

JEFFERY'S GLUE. *See* MARINE GLUE.

JELBA. A large coasting-boat of the Red Sea.

JELLY-FISH. A common name for the *Medusæ*, soft gelatinous marine animals, belonging to the class *Acalephæ.*

JEMMY. A finical fellow in the usual sense, but adopted as a nautical term by the mutineers of '97, to express the *nobs*, or *heads* of officers. Also, a handy crow-bar or lever.

JEMMY DUCKS. The ship's poulterer. A sobriquet which has universally obtained in a man-of-war.

JERBE. *See* JELBA.

JERGADO, OR GINGADO. An early term for a light skiff (*circa* 1550).

JERK. A sudden snatch or drawing pull; particularly applied to that given to the trigger of a lock. (*See* SACCADE.)

JERKED BEEF. Charqui. Meat cured by drying in the open air, with or without salt. Also, the name of an American coin.

JERKIN. An old name for a coatee, or skirted jacket.

JERKING. A quick break in a heavy roll of the sea.

JEROME. A trading vessel of Egypt.

JERQUER. A customs officer, whose duty is to examine the landwaiters' books, and check them.

JERQUING A VESSEL. A search performed by the jerquer of the customs, after a vessel is unloaded, to see that no unentered goods have been concealed.

JERSEY. Fine wool, formerly called gearnsey, ganzee, or guernsey. —*Jersey frocks*, woollen frocks supplied to seamen.

JETSAM, OR JETSON. In legal parlance, is the place where goods thrown overboard sink, and remain under water. Also, the goods cast into the sea.

JETTISON, OR JETSEN. The act of throwing goods overboard to lighten a ship in stress of weather. The loss forms a subject for general average.

JETTY, JETTEE, OR JUTTY. A name given in the royal dockyards to that part of a wharf which projects beyond the rest, but more particularly the front of a wharf, the side of which forms one of the cheeks of a dry or wet dock. Such a projection, whether of wood or stone, from the outer end of a wharf, is called a *jetty-head*.

JEW-BALANCE. A Mediterranean name of the *Zygœna malleus*, or hammer-headed shark.

JEWEL. The starting of a wooden bridge. Also, the pivot of a watch-wheel.

JEWEL-BLOCKS. Are attached to eye-bolts on those yards where studding-sails are hoisted, and carry these sails to the extreme ends of the yards. When these jewel-blocks are removed, it is understood that there is no intention to proceed to sea, and *vice versa*. The halliards, by which the studding-sails are hoisted, are passed through the jewel-block, whence, communicating with a block on the several mast-heads, they lead downwards to the top or decks, where they may be conveniently hoisted. (*See* SAIL.)

JEWELS. *See* JOCALIA.

JEW'S-HARP. The shackle for joining a chain-cable to the anchor-ring.

JIB. A large triangular sail, set on a stay, forward. It extends from the outer end of the jib-boom towards the fore top-mast head; in cutters and sloops it is on the bowsprit, and extends towards the lower mast-head. (*See* SAIL.) The jib is a sail of great command with any side wind, in turning her head to leeward.   There are other jibs, as inner jib, standing-jib, flying-jib, spindle-jib, jib of jibs, jib-topsails, &c.—*Jib* is also used for the expression of the face, as the *cut of his jib*.   Also, the arm of a crane. —*To jib*, is when, before the wind, the sail takes over to the opposite quarter; dangerous in strong breezes.   (*See* GYBE.)—*Clear away the jib!* The order to loose it, preparatory to its being set.—*Flying-jib*.   A sail set upon the flying jib-boom.—*Middle or inner jib*.   A sail sometimes set on a stay secured to the middle of the jib-boom.

JIB AND STAYSAIL JACK.   A designation of inexperienced officers, who are troublesome to the watch by constantly calling it unnecessarily to trim, make, or shorten sail.

JIBBER THE KIBBER.   A cant term for a diabolical trick for decoying vessels on shore for plunder, by tying a lantern to a horse's neck, one of whose legs is checked; so that at night the motion has somewhat the appearance of a ship's light.—*Jib* or *jibber* means a horse that starts or shrinks; and Shakspeare uses it in the sense of a worn-out horse.

JIB-BOOM.   A continuation of the bowsprit forward, being a spar run out from the extremity in a similar manner to a topmast on a lower-mast, and serving to extend the foot of the jib and the stay of the fore-top-gallant mast, the tack of the jib being lashed to it.   It is usually attached to the bowsprit by means of the cap and the saddle, where a strong lashing confines it.—*Flying jib-boom*.   A boom extended beyond the preceding, to which it is secured by a boom-iron and heel-lashing; to the outer end of this boom the tack of the flying-jib is hauled out, and the fore-royal-stay passes through it.

JIB-FORESAIL.   In cutters, schooners, &c., it is the stay-foresail.

JIB-GUYS.   Stout ropes which act as backstays do to a mast, by support-ing the jib-boom against the pressure of its sail and the ship's motion.

JIBING, OR GYBING.   A corruption of *jibbing*.   The act of shifting over the boom of a fore-and-aft sail from one side of the vessel to the other. By a boom-sail is meant any sail the bottom of which is extended by a boom, which has its fore-end jawed or hooked to its respective mast, so as to swing occasionally on either side of the vessel, describing an arc, of which the mast will be the centre.   As the wind or the course changes, the boom and its sail are jibed to the other side of the vessel, as a door turns on its hinges.

JIB OF JIBS.   A sixth jib on the bowsprit, only known to flying-kite-men: the sequence being—storm, inner, outer, flying, spindle, jib of jibs.

JIB-STAY.   The stay on which the jib is set.

JIB-TOPSAIL.   A light sail set on the topmost stay of a fore-and-aft rigged vessel.

JIB-TRAVELLER.   An iron ring fitted to run out and in on the jib-boom, for the purpose of bringing outwards or inwards the tack, or the outer corner of the sail; to this traveller the jib-guys are lashed.

JIB-TYE. A rope rove through a sheave or block on the fore-topmast head, for hoisting the jib.

JIFFY. A short space of time, a moment. "In a jiffy," in an instant; equivalent with crack, trice, &c.

JIG. The weight furnished with hooks, used in *jigging* (which see).

JIGGAMAREE. A mongrel makeshift manœuvre. Any absurd attempt to substitute a bad contrivance for what the custom of the sea may be.

JIGGER. A light tackle used to hold on the cable when it is heaved into the ship. (*See* HOLDING ON.) Also, a small sail rigged out on a mast and boom from the stern of a cutter, boat, &c.—*Fleet-jigger.* A term used by the man who holds on the jigger, when by its distance from the windlass it becomes necessary to *fleet,* or replace it in a proper state for action. When the man gives the above notice, another at the windlass immediately fixes his handspike between the deck and the cable, so as to jam the latter to the windlass, and prevent it from running out till the jigger is replaced on the cable near the windlass.

JIGGER, CHIGRE. A very teazing sand-flea, which penetrates and breeds under the skin of the feet, but particularly at the toes. It must be removed, or it occasions dreadful sores. The operation is effected by a needle; but the sac which contains the brood must not be broken, or the whole foot would be infected, if any remained in it.

JIGGERED-UP. Done up; tired out.

JIGGER-MAST. In large vessels it is an additional aftermost mast; thus any sail set on the ensign-staff would be a jigger.

JIGGER-TACKLE. A small tackle consisting of a double and a single block, and used by seamen on sundry occasions about the decks or aloft.

JIGGING. A mode of catching fish by dropping a weighted line with several hooks set back to back amongst them, and jerking it suddenly upwards; the weight is frequently cast in the form of a small fish. Also, short pulls at a tackle fall.

JILALO. A large passage-boat of Manilla, fitted with outriggers.

JILL. A fourth part of a pint measure; a seaman's daily allowance of rum, which formerly was half a pint.

JIMMAL, OR JIMBLE. *See* GIMBAL.

JINGAL. A kind of long heavy musket supported about the centre of its length on a pivot, carrying a ball of from a quarter to half a pound, and generally fired by a matchlock; much used in China' and the Indies. It is charged by a separate chamber, dropped into the breech and keyed.

JINNY-SPINNER. One of the names for the cockroach.

JIRK, To. To cut or score the flesh of the wild hog on the inner surface, as practised by the Maroons. It is then smoked and otherwise prepared in a manner that gives the meat a fine flavour.

JOB. A stipulated work.

JOBATION. A private but severe lecture and reprimand.

JOB CAPTAIN. One who gets a temporary appointment to a ship, whose regular commander is a member of parliament, &c.

JOB-WATCH, or HACK-WATCH, for taking astronomical sights, which saves taking the chronometer on deck or on shore to note the time.

JOCALIA. An Anglo-Norman law-term signifying jewels, which, with gold and silver, were exempted in our smuggling enactments.

JOCKS. Scotch seamen.

JOG. The shoulder or step of the rudder.

JOGGING. A protuberance on the surface of sawn wood.

JOGGLE. The cubic joints of stones on piers, quays, and docks. Also, notches at the ends of paddle-beam iron-knees outside, to act as a stop to the diagonal iron-stay, which is extended between the arms of each knee. (*See* JUGLE.)

JOG-THE-LOO! A command in small vessels to work the pump-brake, or to pump briskly.

JOHN. A name given to dried fish. (*See* POOR JOHN.)

JOHN BULL. The origin of this nickname is traced to a satire written in the reign of Queen Anne, by Dr. Arbuthnot, to throw ridicule on the politics of the Spanish succession.

JOHN COMPANY. The former board of directors for East India affairs.

JOHN DORY. A corruption of *jaune doré*, which is the colour of this fish. It is one of the Scomberidæ, *Zeus faber*. John Dory was also the name of a celebrated French pirate.

JOHNNY RAW, or JOHNNY NEWCOME. An inexperienced youngster commencing his career; also applied to landsmen in general. (*See* RAW.)

JOHNNY SHARK. A common sobriquet of the Squalus tribe.

JOHN-O'-GROAT'S BUCKIE. A northern name for the *Cypræa pediculus*, a small shell found on our sea-coasts.

JOHN TUCK. The galley corruption of *chantuck*, or *jantook*, a Chinese viceroy, specially meaning the viceroy of Canton.

JOIN, To. To repair to a ship, and personally to enter on an official position on board her. So also the junction of one or more ships with each other.

JOINER. One who is a cabinet-maker, and performs neat work as captain's joiner.

JOINT. The place where any two pieces of timber or plank are united. It is also used to express the lines which are laid down in the mould-loft for shaping the timbers.

JOLLY. This term is usually applied to a comely and corpulent person, but afloat it is a familiar name for a soldier.—*Tame jolly*, a militiaman; *royal jolly*, a marine.

JOLLY-BOAT. A smaller boat than the cutter, but likewise clincher-built. It is generally a hack boat for small work, being about 4 feet beam to 12 feet length, with a bluff bow and very wide transom; a kind of washing-tub. (*See* GELLYWATTE and CUTTER.)

JOLLY JUMPERS. Sails above the moon-rakers.

JOLLY ROGER. A pirate's flag; a white skull in a black field.

JONATHAN. A name often applied to Americans in general, but really appropriate to the Quakers in America, being a corruption of John Nathan.

JONK. *See* JUNK.

JORUM, OF GROG, &c. A full bowl or jug.

JOURNAL. Synonymous at sea with *log-book;* it is a daily register of the ship's course and distance, the winds and weather, and a general account of whatever is of importance. In sea-journals, the day, or twenty-four hours, used to terminate at noon, because the ship's position is then generally determined by observation; but the shore account of time is now adopted afloat. In machinery, *journal* is the bearing part of a shaft, upon which it rests on its Y's or bearings.

JOURNEY-WORK. Work performed by the day.

JOVIALL. Relating to the system of the planet Jupiter.

JOVICENTRIC. As seen from, or having relation to, the centre of Jupiter.

JOWDER. A term on our western coasts to denote a retail dealer in fish.

JOWL. The head of a fish. (Also, *see* BLOCK.)—*Cheek by jowl.* Close together.

JUAN-MOOAR. The Manx and Erse term for the black-backed gull.

JUBALTARE. The early English word for Gibraltar.

JUDGE-ADVOCATE OF THE FLEET, OR TO THE FORCES. A legal officer whose duty it is to investigate offences previous to determining on sending them before a court-martial, and then to report on the sentence awarded. He has civil deputies in Great Britain; but officers (generally secretaries to admirals, or pursers) are appointed by the courts abroad.

JUDGE-ADVOCATE, DEPUTY. An officer appointed to assist the court upon some general courts-martial for the trial of officers, seamen, and marines, accused of a breach of the articles of war.

JUDGMENT. In prize matters, the sentences of foreign courts, even though such decisions be manifestly unjust, are conclusive in ours by comity. The tribunals of France are not so complacent.

JUFFER. *See* UPHER.

JUGGLE-MEER. A west-country word for a coast quagmire.

JUGLE, OR JOGGLE. In ship-building, a notch in the edge of a plank to admit the narrow butt of another, as of the narrow end of a steeling-strake.

JULIAN PERIOD. A period of 7980 years, dating from B.C. 4713; being the product of the numbers 15, 19, and 28 multiplied into each other, they being respectively the lengths, in Julian years, of the Indiction, Metonic Cycle, and Solar Cycle. The Julian year was a period of 365¼ days, which was adopted as the length of the year after the reformation of the calendar by Julius Cæsar.

JULIO. An Italian coin, worth about sixpence.

JUMPERS. The short external duck-frock worn by sail-makers, artificers, riggers, &c., to preserve the clothing beneath.

JUMP-JOINTED. When the plates of an iron vessel are flush, as in those that are carvel-built.

JUNCO. *See* PURR.

JUNGADA. A balza, or simple kind of raft, of several logs of wood, fitted with a tilt, and used on the coasts of Peru. It has a mast and sails, and by means of a rudder, not unlike a sliding keel in principle, is capable of working to windward. (*See* GUARA.)

JUNGLE. A wilderness of wood; in Bengal the word is also applied to a tract covered with long grass, which grows to an extraordinary height. Jungles are dreaded for the fevers they engender.

JUNK. The Chinese junk is the largest vessel built by that nation, and at one period exceeding in tonnage any war-vessels then possessed by England. The extreme beam is one-third from the stern; it shows no stem, it being chamfered off. The bow on deck is square, over which the anchors slide fore and aft. Having no keel, and being very full at the stern, a huge rudder is suspended, which at sea is lowered below the depth of the bottom. The masts are immense, in one piece. The cane sails are lug and heavy. The hull is divided into water-tight compartments, like tanks.—*Junk* is also any remnants or pieces of old cable, or condemned rope, cut into small portions for the purpose of making *points, mats, swabs, gaskets, sinnot, oakum,* and the like (which see). Also, a dense cellular tissue in the head of the sperm-whale, infiltrated with spermaceti. Also, salt beef, as tough to the teeth as bits of rope, whence the epithet.

JUNKET. A long basket for catching fish.—*Junketting,* good cheer and hearty jollification.

JUPITER. The longest known of the superior planets, and the largest in the solar system; it is accompanied by four satellites.

JURATORY CAUTION. A process in the instance court of the admiralty, to which a party is discretionally admitted on making oath that he is unable to find sureties.

JUREBASSO. A rating in former times given to a handy man, who was partly interpreter and partly purchaser of stock.

JURISDICTION. Right, power, or authority which magistrates or courts have to administer justice.—*Within jurisdiction of civil powers,* as regards naval matters, is within a line drawn from headland to headland in sight of each other, and forming part of the same county. The admiralty jurisdiction is confined to three miles from the coast in civil matters, but exists wherever the flag flies at sea in criminal.

JURY-MAST. A temporary or occasional mast erected in a ship in the place of one which has been carried away in a gale, battle, &c. Jury-masts are sometimes erected in a new ship to navigate her down a river, or to a neighbouring port, where her proper masts are prepared for her. Such jury-masts are simply less in dimension for a light-trimmed vessel; as a frigate would have a brig's spars.

JURY-RUDDER. A contrivance, of which there are several kinds, for supplying a vessel with the means of steering when an accident has befallen the rudder.

JUS PISCANDI.   The right of fishing.

JUWAUR.   The spring-flood of the Ganges and adjacent rivers.

K.

KAAG.   A Manx or Gaelic term for a forelock, stopper, or linch-pin.

KABBELOW.   Codfish which has been salted and hung for a few days,
but not thoroughly dried.   Also, a dish of cod mashed.

KABOZIR.   A chief or governor on the African coast.

KABURNS.   The old name for nippers.

KAFILA.   A well-known Eastern word, meaning a party with camels
travelling or sojourning; but it was also applied by our early voyagers to
convoys of merchant ships.

KAIA.   An old term for a quay or wharf.

KAIQUE.   See CAIQUE.

KALBAZ, OR HALBAZ.   Pronounced *kalva;* one of the best Turkish
delicacies, composed of honey, must, and almonds, beat up together.

KALENDAR.   Time accommodated to the uses of life.   (*See* ALMANAC.)

KALI.   *Salsola kali,* a marine plant, generally burned to supply soda
for the glass manufactories.   Sub-carbonate of potass.

KAMSIN.   A south-westerly wind which blows over Egypt in March and
April, generally not more than three successive days at a time.   Its
name signifies the wind of fifty days, not as blowing for such a period,
but because it only occurs during fifty days of March and April.

KANJIA.   A passage-boat of the Nile.

KANNA.   A name for *ginseng* (which see).

KARAVALLA.   *See* CARAVEL.

KARBATZ.   A common boat of Lapland.

KAT.   A timber vessel used on the northern coasts of England.

KATABATHRA.   Subterraneous passages in certain mountains in Greece,
through which the superfluous waters are discharged.

KATAN.   A Japanese sword, otherwise *cattan.*

KATTAN.   A corruption of *yataghan* (which see).

KATTY.   *See* CATTY.

KAULE.   A license for trade, given by the authorities in India to our
early voyagers.

KAVA.   A beverage, in the South Sea Islands, made by steeping the
Piper inebrians in water.

KAVER.   A word used in the Hebrides for a gentle breeze.

KAY, OR KEY [probably from the Dutch *kaayen,* to haul].   A place to
which ships are hauled.   Knoll or head of a shoal—*kaya,* Malay.

KAYAK.   A fishing-boat in all the north polar countries; most likely a
corrupted form of the eastern *kaique* by our early voyagers.

KAYNARD. A term of reproach amongst our early voyagers, probably from *canis*.

KAYU-PUTIH, OR CAJEPUTI OIL. From the Malay words *kayu*, wood; and *putih*, oil; the useful oil obtained from the *Melaleuca leucadendron*.

KAZIE. A Shetland fishing-boat.

K.C.B. Siglæ of Knight Commander of the most honourable military order of the Bath.

KEAVIE. A coast name for a species of crab that devours cuttle-fish greedily.

KEAVIE-CLEEK. In the north a crooked piece of iron for catching crabs.

KECKLING, OR CACKLING. Is covering a cable spirally (in opposition to *rounding*, which is close) with three-inch old rope to protect it from chafe in the hawse-hole.

KEDELS. *See* KIDDLES.

KEDGE, OR KEDGER. A small anchor used to keep a ship steady and clear from her bower-anchor while she rides in harbour, particularly at the turn of the tide. The kedge-anchors are also used to warp a ship from one part of a harbour to another. They are generally furnished with an iron stock, which is easily displaced for the convenience of stowing. The old English word *kedge* signified brisk, and they are generally run in to a quick step. (*See* ANCHOR, WARP.)—*To kedge.* To warp a ship a-head, though the tide be contrary, by means of the kedge-anchor and hawser.

KEDGER. A mean fellow, more properly *cadger;* one in everybody's mess, but in no one's watch. An old term for a fisherman.

KEDGE-ROPE. The rope which belongs to the kedge-anchor, and restrains the vessel from driving over her bower-anchor.

KEDGING. The operation of tide-working in a narrow channel or river, by kedge-hauling.

KEEL. The lowest and principal timber of a ship, running fore and aft its whole length, and supporting the frame like the backbone in quadrupeds; it is usually first laid on the blocks in building, being the base of the superstructure. Accordingly, the stem and stern-posts are, in some measure, a continuation of the keel, and serve to connect the extremities of the sides by transoms, as the keel forms and unites the bottom by timbers. The keel is generally composed of several thick pieces placed lengthways, which, after being scarphed together, are bolted and clinched upon the upper side. In iron vessels the keel is formed of one or more plates of iron, having a concave curve, or limber channel, along its upper surface.—*To give the keel,* is to careen.—*Keel* formerly meant a vessel; so many " keels struck the sands." Also, a low flat-bottomed vessel used on the Tyne to carry coals (21 tons 4 cwt.) down from Newcastle for loading the colliers; hence the latter are said to carry so many keels of coals. [Anglo-Saxon *ceol*, a small bark.]—*False keel.* A fir keel-piece bolted to the bottom of the keel, to assist stability and make a ship hold a better wind. It is temporary, being pinned by stake-bolts with spear-points; so when a vessel grounds, this frequently, being of fir or Canada elm, floats and comes up alongside.—*Rabbets of the keel.* The furrow, which is continued up stem and stern-post, into which the garboard and other streaks fay. The butts take into the gripe ahead, or after-deadwood and stern-post abaft.—*Rank keel.* A very deep keel, one calculated to keep the ship from rolling heavily.—*Upon an even keel.* The position of a ship when her keel is parallel to the plane of the horizon, so that she is equally deep in the water at both ends.

KEELAGE. A local duty charged on all vessels coming into a harbour.

KEEL-BLOCKS. Short log ends of timbers on which the keel of a vessel rests while building or repairing, affording access to work beneath.

KEEL-DEETERS. The wives and daughters of keel-men, who sweep and clean the keels, having the sweepings of small coal for their trouble.

KEEL-HAULING. A severe punishment formerly inflicted for various offences, especially in the Dutch navy. The culprit was suspended by a rope from one fore-yardarm attached to his back, with a weight upon his legs, and having another rope fastened to him, leading under the ship's bottom, and through a block at its opposite yard-arm; he was then let fall into the sea, when, passing under the ship's bottom, he was hoisted up on the opposite side of the vessel to the other yardarm. Aptly described as "under-going a great hard-ship."

KEELING. Rolling on her keel. Also, a sort of cod-fish; some restrict the term to the *Gadus morhua*, or large cod.

KEEL LEG or HOOK. Means any anchor; as, "she has come to a keelock."

KEELMEN. A rough and hardy body of men, who work the *keels* of Newcastle. Sometimes termed keel-bullies. They are recognized as mariners in various statutes.

KEEL-PIECES. The parts of the keel which are of large timber.

KEEL-RAKE. Synonymous with *keel-haul.* See KEEL-HAULING.

KEEL-ROPE. A coarse rope formerly used for cleaning the limber-holes.

KEELS. An old British name for long vessels—formerly written *ceol* and *cyulis.* Verstegan informs us that the Saxons came over in three large ships, styled by themselves *keeles.*

KEELSON, or KELSON. An internal keel, laid upon the middle of the floor-timbers, immediately over the keel, and serving to bind all together by means of long bolts driven from without, and clinched on the upper side of the keelson. The main keelson, in order to fit with more security upon the floor-timbers, is notched opposite to each of them, and there secured by spike-nails. The pieces of which it is formed are usually less in breadth and thickness than those of the keel.

KEELSON-RIDER. See FALSE KELSON.

KEEL-STAPLES. Generally made of copper, from six to twelve inches long, with a jagged hook to each end. They are driven into the sides of the main and false keels to fasten them.

KEEP. A strong donjon or tower in the middle of a castle, usually the last resort of its garrison in a siege. Also, a reservoir for fish by the side of a river.—*To keep*, a term used on several occasions in navigation; as, "*Keep her away*," alter the ship's course to leeward, by sailing further off the wind. The reverse is, "*Keep your wind, keep your luff*," close to the wind.

KEEP A GOOD HOLD OF THE LAND. Is to hug it as near as it can safely be done.

KEEP HER OWN. Not to fall off; not driven back by tide.

KEEPING A GOOD OFFING. To keep well off shore while under sail, so as to be clear of danger should the wind suddenly shift and blow towards the shore.

KEEPING A WATCH. To have charge of the deck. Also, the act of being on watch-duty.

KEEPING FULL FOR STAYS. A necessary precaution to give the sails full force, in aid of the rudder when going about.

KEEPING HER WAY. The force of steady motion through the water, continued after the power which gave it has varied or diminished.

KEEPING THE SEA. The term formerly used when orders were issued for the array of the inhabitants of the sea-coasts.

KEEP OFF. To fall to a distance from the shore, or a ship, &c. (*See* OFFING.)

KEEP THE LAND ABOARD. Is to sail along it, or within sight, as much as possible, or as close as danger will permit.

KEEP YOUR LUFF. An order to the helmsman to keep the ship close to the wind, *i.e.* sailing with a course as near as possible to the direction from which the wind is coming. (*See* CLOSE-HAULED.)

KEG. A small cask, of no fixed contents. Used familiarly for taking offence, as *to keg*, is to irritate.—*To carry the keg*. To continue; originally a smuggler's phrase.

KEGGED. Feeling affronted or jeered at.

KELDS. The still parts of a river, which have an oily smoothness while the rest of the water is ruffled.

KELF. The incision made in a tree by the axe when felling it.

KELING. A large kind of cod. Thus in Havelok:—

> "Keling he tok, and tumberel,
> Hering, and the makerel."

KELKS. The milt or roe of fish.

KELLAGH. The Erse term for a wooden anchor with a stone in it, but in later times is applied to any grapnel or small anchor.

KELP. *Salsola kali;* the ashes produced by the combustion of various marine algæ, and used in obtaining iodine, soda, &c.

KELPIE. A mischievous sea-sprite, supposed to haunt the fords and ferries of the northern coasts of Great Britain, especially in storms.

KELT. A salmon that has been spawning; a foul fish.

KELTER. Ships and men are said to be in primo kelter when in fine order and well-rigged.

KEMP. An old term for a soldier, camper, or camp man. Also a kind of eel.

KEMSTOCK. An old term for capstan.

KEN, To. Ang.-Sax. descrying, as Shakspeare in *Henry VI.:*—

"And far as I could ken thy chalky cliffs."

—*Ken*, a speck, a striking object or mark.

KENNETS. Large cleats. (*See* KEVELS.) Also, a coarse Welsh cloth of commerce; see statute 33, Henry VIII. c. 3.

KENNING BY KENNING. A mode of increasing wages formerly, according to whaling law, by seeing how a man performed his duty.

KENNING-GLASS. A hand spy-glass or telescope.

KEN-SPECKLED. Conspicuous; having distinct marks.

KENTLEDGE. Pigs of iron cast for permanent ballast, laid over the kelson-plates, or if in the limbers, then called limber-kentledge.

KENTLEDGE GOODS. In lieu of ballast.

KENT-PURCHASE. A misspelling of *cant*-purchase, or one used to turn a whale round during the operation of *flensing.*

KEPLER'S LAWS. Three famous laws of nature detected by Kepler early in the seventeenth century:—1. The primary planets revolve about the sun in ellipses, having that luminary in one of the foci. 2. The planets describe about the sun equal areas in equal times. 3. The squares of the periodic times of the planets are to each other as the cubes of their mean distances from the sun.

KEPLING. *See* CAPLIN.

KERFE. The furrow or slit made by the saw in dividing timber.

KERLANGUISHES. The swift-sailing boats of the Bosphorus. The name signifies swallows.

KERMES. A little red gall, occasioned by the puncture of the coccus ilicis on the leaves of the Quercus coccifera, or Kermes oak ; an article of commerce from Spain, used in dyeing.

KERNEL. Corrupted from *crenelle;* the holes in a battlement made for the purpose of shooting arrows and small shot.

KERNES. Light-armed Irish foot soldiers of low degree, who cleared the way for the heavy *gallow-glasses.*

KERS. An Anglo-Saxon word for water-cresses.

KERT. An old spelling for *chart.*

KERVEL. *See* CARVEL.

KETCH. A vessel of the galliot order, equipped with two masts—viz. the main and mizen masts—usually from 100 to 250 tons burden. Ketches were principally used as yachts for conveying great personages from one place to another. The peculiarity of this rig, affording so much space before the main-mast, and at the greatest beam, caused them to be used for mortar-vessels, hence—*Bomb-ketches*, which are built remarkably strong, with a greater number of riders than any other vessel of war, as requisite to sustain the violent shock produced by the discharge of their mortars. (*See* BOMB-VESSEL, MORTAR, and SHELL.)

KETERINS. Marauders who formerly infested the Irish coast and channel.

KETOS, or Cetus. An ancient ship of large dimensions.

KETTLE. The brass or metal box of a compass.

KETTLE-BOTTOM. A name applied to a ship with a flat floor.

KETTLE-NET. A net used in taking mackerel.

KETTLE OF FISH. To have made a pretty kettle of fish of it, implies a perplexity in judgment.

KEVEL-HEADS. The ends of the top timbers, which, rising above the gunwale, serve to belay the ropes, or to be used as kevels.

KEVELING. A coast name for the skate.

KEVELS, or Cavils. Large cleats, or also pieces of oak passing through a mortice in the rail, and answer the purpose of timber-heads for belaying ropes to.

KEY. In ship-building, means a dry piece of oak or elm, cut tapering, to drive into scarphs that have hook-butts, to wedge deck-planks, or to join any pieces of wood tightly to each other. Iron forelocks.

KEY, or Cay [derived from the Spanish *cayos*, rocks]. What in later years have been so termed will be found in the old Spanish charts as cayos. The term was introduced to us by the buccaneers as small insular spots with a scant vegetation; without the latter they are merely termed sandbanks. Key is especially used in the West Indies, and often applied to the smaller coral shoals produced by zoophytes.

KEY, or Quay. A long wharf, usually built of stone, by the side of a harbour, and having posts and rings, cranes, and storehouses, for the convenience of merchant ships.

KEYAGE, or Quayage. Money paid for landing goods at a key or quay. The same as *wharfage*.

KEYLE. (*See* Keel.) The vessel of that name.

KEY-MODEL. In ship-building, a model formed by pieces of board laid on each other horizontally. These boards, being all shaped from the lines on the paper, when put together and fairly adjusted, present the true form of the proposed ship.

KEY OF THE RUDDER. (*See* Woodlock.) In machinery, applies to wedges, forelocks, &c.

KHALISHEES. Native Indian sailors.

KHAVIAR. *See* Caviare.

KHIZR. The patron deity of the sea in the East Indies, to whom small boats, called *beera*, are annually sacrificed on the shores and rivers.

KIBE. A flaw produced in the bore of a gun by a shot striking against it.

KIBLINGS. Parts of a small fish used for bait on the banks of Newfoundland.

KICK. The springing back of a musket when fired. Also, the violent recoil by which a carronade is often thrown off the slide of its carriage. A comparison of excellence or novelty; the very kick.

KICKSHAW. Applied to French cookery, or unsubstantial trifles.

KICK THE BUCKET, To.   To expire; an inconsiderate phrase for dying.

KICK UP A DUST, To.   To create a row or disturbance.

KID.   A presuming man.—*Kiddy fellow*, neat in his dress.   Also, a compartment in some fishing-vessels, wherein the fish are thrown as they are caught.   Also, a small wooden tub for grog, with two ears; or generally for a mess utensil of that kind.   (*See* KIT.)

KIDDLES.   Stakes whereby the free passage of boats and vessels is hindered.   Also, temporary open weirs for catching fish.

KIDLEYWINK.   A low beershop in our western ports.

KIDNAP, To.   To crimp or carry off by artifice.

KIDNEY.   Men of the same kidney, *i.e.* of a similar disposition.

KIFTIS.   The large passage-boats of India, fitted with cabins on each side from stem to stern.

KIHAIA.   An officer of Turkish ports in superintendence of customs, &c.; often deputy-governor.

KILDERKIN.   A vessel containing the eighth part of a hogshead.

KILE.   *See* KYLE.

KILL.   A channel or stream, as Cats-kill, Schuylkill, &c.

KILL-DEVIL.   New rum, from its pernicious effects.

KILLER.   A name for the grampus, *Orca gladiator*, given on account of the ferocity with which it attacks and destroys whales, seals, and other marine animals.   (*See* GRAMPUS.)

KILLESE.   The groove in a cross-bow.

KILLING-OFF.   Striking the names of dead officers from the navy list by a *coup de plume*.

KILLOCK.   A small anchor.   Flue of an anchor.   (*See* KELLAGH.)

KILLY-LEEPIE.   A name on our northern shores for the *Tringa hypoleucos* or common sand-piper.

KILN.   The dockyard building wherein planks are steamed for the purpose of bending them to round the extremities of a ship.

KIN.   *See* KINN.

KING ARTHUR.   A game played on board ship in warm climates, in which a person, grotesquely personating King Arthur, is drenched with buckets of water until he can, by making one of his persecutors smile or laugh, change places with him.

KING-CRAB.   The *Limulus polyphemus* of the West Indies.

KING-FISH.   The *Zeus luna*.   Carteret took one at Masafuero $5\frac{1}{2}$ feet long, and weighing 87 lbs.   Also, the *Scomber maximus* of the West Indies.

KING-FISHER.   The *Alcedo ispida;* a small bird of brilliant plumage frequenting rivers and brooks, and feeding upon fish, which it catches with great dexterity.   (*See* HALCYON.)

KING JOHN'S MEN.   The Adullamites of the navy.

KING'S BARGAIN: GOOD OR BAD; said of a seaman according to his activity and merit, or sloth and demerit.

KING'S BENCHER. The busiest of the galley orators; also galley-skulkers.

KING'S HARD BARGAIN. A useless fellow, who is not worth his hire.

KING'S LETTER MEN. An extinct class of officers, of similar rank with midshipmen. The royal letter was a kind of promise that if they conducted themselves well, they should be promoted to the rank of lieutenant.

KING'S OWN. All the articles supplied from the royal magazines, and marked with the broad arrow. Salt beef or junk.

KING'S PARADE. A name given to the quarter-deck of a man-of-war, which is customarily saluted by touching the hat when stepping on it.

KINK. An accidental curling, twist, or doubling turn in a cable or rope, occasioned by its being very stiff, or close laid, or by being drawn too hastily out of the coil or tier in which it was coiled. (*See* COILING.)— *To kink.* To twist.

KINKLINGS. A coast name for periwinkles.

KINN. From the Gaelic word for head; meaning, in local names, a hill or promontory.

KINTLE. A dozen of anything. Remotely corrupted from *quintal*.

KINTLIDGE. A term for iron-ballast. (*See* KENTLEDGE.)

KIOCK, OR BLUE-BACK. An alosa fish, used by the American and other fishermen as a bait for mackerel.

KIOSK. A pavilion on the poop of some Turkish vessels.

KIPLIN. The more perishable parts of the cod-fish, cured separately from the body.

KIPPAGE. An old term for equipage, or ship's company.

KIPPER. Salmon in the act of spawning; also, the male fish, and especially beaked fish. Kipper is also applied to salmon which has undergone the process of *kippering* (which see).

KIPPERING. A method of curing fish in which salt is little used, but mainly sugar, pepper, and drying in the sun, and occasionally some smoke. Salmon thus treated is considered a dainty, though the cure is far less lasting than with salt.

KIPPER-TIME. The time during which the statutes prohibit the taking of salmon.

KISMISSES. The raisins issued in India, resembling the sultanas of the Levant. The word is derived from the Turkish. They seldom have seeds.

KIST. A word still in use in the north for chest.

KIT. A small wooden pail or bucket, wherewith boats are baled out; generally with an ear. (*See* KID.) Also, a contemptuous term for total; as, the whole kit of them.

KITT, OR KIT. An officer's outfit. Also, a term among soldiers and marines to express the complement of regimental necessaries, which they are obliged to keep in repair. Also, a seaman's *wardrobe*.

KITTIWAKE. A species of gull of the northern seas; so called from its peculiar cry: the *Larus tridactylus*.

KITTY-WITCH. A small kind of crab on the east coast.

KLEG. The fish *Gadus barbatus.*

KLEPTES. The pirates of the Archipelago; literally the Greek for robbers.

KLICK-HOOKS. Large hooks for catching salmon in the daytime.

KLINKER. A flat-bottomed lighter or praam of Sweden and Denmark.

KLINKETS. Small grating-gates, made through palisades for sallies.

KLIPPEN. The German for cliffs; in use in the Baltic.—*Blinde Klippen,* reefs of rocks under water.

KLOSH. Seamen of Denmark, Norway, and Sweden.

KNAGGY. Crochetty; sour-tempered.

KNAGS. Points of rocks. Also, hard knots in wood.

KNAP [from the Anglo-Saxon *cnæp,* a protuberance]. The top of a hill. Also, a blow or correction, as "you'll knap it," for some misdeed.

KNAPSACK. A light waterproof case fitted to the back, in which the foot-soldier carries his necessaries on a march.

KNARRS. Knots in spars. (*See* GNARRE.)

KNECK. The twisting of rope or cable as it is veering out.

KNEE. Naturally grown timber, or bars of iron, bent to a right angle, or to fit the surfaces, and to secure bodies firmly together, as hanging knees secure the deck-beams to the sides. They are divided into hanging-knees, diagonal hanging-knees, lodging-knees or deck-beam knees, transom-knees, helm-post transom-knees, wing transom-knees (which see).

KNEE OF THE HEAD. A large flat piece of timber, fixed edgeways, and fayed upon the fore-part of a ship's stem, supporting the ornamental figure. (*See* HEAD.) Besides which, this piece is otherwise useful as serving to secure the boom or bumkin, by which the fore-tack is extended to windward, and by its great breadth preventing the ship from falling to leeward, when close-hauled, so much as she would otherwise be liable to do. It also affords security to the bowsprit by increasing the angle of the bobstay, so as to make it act more perpendicularly on the bowsprit. The *knee of the head* is a phrase peculiar to shipwrights; by seamen it is called the *cut-water* (which see).

KNEES. *Dagger-knees* are those which are fixed rather obliquely to avoid an adjacent gun-port, or where, from the vicinity of the next beam, there is not space for the arms of two lodging-knees.—*Lodging-knees* are fixed horizontally in the ship's frame, having one arm bolted to the beam, and the other across two or three of the timbers.—*Standard-knees* are those which, being upon a deck, have one arm bolted down to it, and the other pointing upwards secured to the ship's side; such also, are the bits and channels.

KNEE-TIMBER. That sort of crooked timber which forms at its back or elbow an angle of from 24° to 45°; but the more acute this angle is, the more valuable is the timber on that account. Used for knees, rising floors, and crutches. Same as *raking-knees.*

KNETTAR. A string used to tie the mouth of a sack.

KNIFE. An old name for a dagger: thus Lady Macbeth—

"That my keen knife see not the wound it makes."

KNIGHT-HEADS. Two large oak timbers, one on each side of the stem, rising up sufficiently above it to support the bowsprit, which is fixed between them. The term is synonymous with *bollard timbers.*—*Knight-heads* also formerly denoted in many merchant ships, two strong frames of timber fixed on the main-deck, a little behind the fore-mast, which supported the ends of the windlass. They were frequently called the *bitts*, and then their upper parts only were denominated the knight-heads, from having been embellished with a carved head. (*See* WINDLASS.) Also, a name formerly given to the lower jear-blocks, which were then no other than bitts, containing several sheaves, and nearly resembling our present topsail-sheet bitts.

KNIGHTHOOD. An institution by princes, either for the defence of religion, or as marks of honour on officers who have distinguished themselves by their valour and address. This dignity being personal, dies with the individual so honoured. The initials of our own orders are:— K.G., Knight of the Garter; K.T., Knight of the Thistle; K.S.P., Knight of St. Patrick; G.C.B., Grand Cross of the Bath; K.C.B., Knight Commander of the Bath; G.C.H., Knight Grand Cross of the Hanoverian Guelphic Order; K.H., Knight of the Hanoverian Guelphic Order; G.C.M.G., Grand Cross of St. Michael and George; E.S.I., Most Exalted Star of India. The principal foreign orders worn by our navy are those of Hanover, St. Ferdinand and Merit, the Tower and Sword, Legion of Honour, Maria Theresa, St. Bento d'Avis, Cross of Charles III., San Fernando, St. Louis, St. Vladimir, St. Anne of Russia, Red Eagle of Prussia, Redeemer of Greece, Medjidie of Turkey, Leopold of Austria, Iron Crown of Austria, William of the Netherlands.

KNIGHTS. Two short thick pieces of wood, formerly carved like a man's head, having four sheaves in each, one of them abaft the foremast, called *fore-knight*, and the other abaft the main-mast, called *main-knight*.

KNITTLE. *See* NETTLE.

KNOB, OR KNOBBE. An officer; perhaps from the Scotch term *knabbie*, the lower class of gentry.

KNOCKER. A peculiar and fetid species of West Indian cockroach, so called on account of the knocking noise they make in the night.

KNOCK OFF WORK AND CARRY DEALS. A term used to deride the idea of any work, however light, being relaxation; just as giving up taking in heavy beams of timber and being set to carry deals, is not really knocking off work.

KNOLL. The top of a rounded hill; the head of a bank, or the most elevated part of a submarine shoal. [Perhaps derived from *nowl*, a provincialism for head.]

KNOPP. *See* KNAP.

KNOT. A large knob formed on the extremity of a rope, generally by untwisting its ends, and interweaving them regularly among each other; of these there are several sorts, differing in form, size, and name, as diamond knot, kop knot, overhand knot, reef knot, shroud knot, stopper knot, single wall knot, double wall knot. The bowline knot is so firmly made, and fastened to the cringles of the sails, that they must break, or the sails split, before it will slip. (*See* RUNNING BOWLINE.) The sheep-shank knot serves to shorten a rope without cutting it, and may be presently loosened. The wall-knot is so made with the lays of a rope that it cannot slip, and serves for sheets, tacks, and stoppers. Knots are generally used to act as a button, in preventing the end of a rope from slipping through the hole of a dead-eye, or through the turns of a laniard, by which they are sometimes made fast to other ropes.—*Knot* also implies a division on the log line, bearing a similar proportion to a mile, which half a minute does to an hour; that is, it is $\frac{1}{120}$ of a mile; hence we say, the ship was going 8 knots, signifying 8 miles per hour. Indeed, in nautical parlance, the words knot and mile are synonyms, alluding to the geographical mile of 60' to a degree of latitude.

KNOWL. A term commonly given to the summits of elevated lands in the west of England, therefore probably the same as *knoll*.

KNOWLEDGE. In admiralty law, opposed to ignorance, and the want of which is liable to heavy penalty.

KNUCKLE. A sudden angle made on some timbers by a quick reverse of shape, such as the knuckles of the counter-timbers.

KNUCKLE-RAILS. Those mouldings which are placed at the knuckles of the stern timbers.

KNUCKLE-TIMBERS. The top-timbers in the fore-body, the heads of which stand perpendicular, and form an angle with the flair or hollow of the topside.

KNUCKLE-UNDER. Obey your superior's order; give way to circumstances.

KNURRT. Stunted; not freely grown.

KOFF. A large Dutch coasting trader, fitted with two masts, and sails set with sprits.

KOMETA. A captain formerly elected in the Spanish navy by twelve experienced navigators.

KOOLIE, OR COOLIE. An Indian day-labourer and porter.

KOOND. A large cistern at a watering-place in India.

KOPEK. A Russian copper coin, 100 of which make a rouble; in value nearly a halfpenny, and named from *kopea*, a spear, because formerly stamped with St. George spearing the dragon.

KOROCORA. A broad-beamed Molucca vessel, with high stem and stern, and an outrigger. It is common among the Malay islands.

KOTA. An excellent turpentine procured in India.

KOUPANG. A gold coin of Japan and the Moluccas, of various value, from 25 to 44 shillings.

KOWDIE. The New Zealand pine spars.

KRABLA. A Russian vessel, usually from Archangel, fitted for killing the whale, walrus, and other Arctic quarry.

KRAKEN. The fictitious sea-monster of Norway.

KRANG. The body of a whale when divested of its blubber, and therefore abandoned by the whalers.

KRAYER. A small vessel, but perhaps larger than the cogge, being thus mentioned in the *Morte Arthure*—

> "Be thanne cogge appone cogge, krayers and other."

KREE, To. A north country word: to beat, or bruise.

KREEL. A framework of timber for the catching of fish, especially salmon. Also a crab-pot, made of osiers, on the principal of a wire mouse-trap. Also, a sportsman's fishing basket.

KRENNEL. The smaller cringle for bowline bridles, &c.

KRINGLE, To. To dry and shrivel up. Also a form of *cringle* (which see).

KRIS. The formidable dagger used by the Malays.

KROO-MEN, OR CREW-MEN. Fishmen. A tribe of African negroes inhabiting Cape Palmas, Krou-settra, and Settra-krou, subjects of Great Britain, and cannot be made slaves; they are specially employed in wooding and watering where hazardous to European constitutions.

KUB-HOUSE, OR CUBBOOS. *See* CABOOSE.

KYAR. Cordage made in India from the fibres which envelope the cocoa nut, and having the advantage of elasticity and buoyancy, makes capital cables for country ships. (*See* COIR.)

KYDLE. A dam in a river for taking fish—

> "Fishes love soote smell; also it is trewe
> Thei love not old kydles as thei doe the newe."

KYLE. A bay, or arm of the sea, on our northern shores, as the Kyles of Bute, &c.

KYNTALL. An old form of *quintal* (which see).

L.

L. The three L's were formerly vaunted by seamen who despised the use of nautical astronomy; viz. lead, latitude, and look-out, all of them admirable in their way. Dr. or Captain Halley added the fourth L—the greatly desired longitude.

LAAS. An obsolete term for an illegal net or snare.

LABARUM. A standard in early days.

LABBER, To. To struggle in water, as a fish when caught. To splash.

LABOUR. In the relative mechanical efforts of the human body labouring in various posture, $682\frac{1}{3}$ have been given for the rowing effort, 476 for the effort at a winch, and $209\frac{1}{3}$ for the effort at a pump.

LABOURING. The act of a ship's working, pitching, or rolling heavily, in a turbulent sea, by which the masts, and even the hull, are greatly endangered.

LABOURSOME. Said of a ship which is subject to roll and pitch violently in a heavy sea, either from some defect in her construction, or improper stowage of her hold.

LACE, To. To apply a bonnet by lacing it to a sail. Also, to beat or punish with a rattan or rope's-end. Also, the trimmings of uniforms.

LACHES. In law, loose practice, or where parties let matters sleep for above seven years, when by applying to the admiralty court they might have compelled the production of an account.

LACING. Rope or cord used to lace a sail to a gaff, or a bonnet to a sail. Also, one of the principal pieces that compose the knee of the head, running up as high as the top of the hair-bracket. Also, a piece of compass or knee timber, fayed to the back of the figure-head and the knee of the head, and bolted to each.

LACUSTRINE. Belonging or referring to a lake.

LADDER. The *accommodation ladder* is a sort of light staircase occasionally fixed on the gangway. It is furnished with rails and man-ropes; the lower end of it is kept at a proper distance from the ship's side by iron bars or braces to render it more convenient. (*See* GANGWAY.)—*Forecastle-ladder* and *hold-ladder*, for getting into or out of those parts of a ship.—*Jacob's ladder*, abaft top-gallant masts, where no ratlines are provided.—*Quarter* or *stern ladders.* Two ladders of rope, suspended from the right and left side of a ship's stern, whereby to get into the boats which are moored astern.

LADDER-WAYS. The hatchways, scuttles, or other openings in the decks, wherein the ladders are placed.

LADE. Anglo-Saxon *lædan*, to pour out. The mouth of a channel or drain. To *lade* a boat, is to throw water out.

LADE-GORN, or LADE-PAIL. A bucket with a long handle to lade water with.

LADEN. The state of a ship when charged with materials equal to her capacity. If the goods be heavy, her burden is determined by weight; but if light, she carries as much as she can conveniently stow. A ton in measure is estimated at 2000 lbs. in weight; a vessel of 200 tons ought therefore to carry a weight equal to 400,000 lbs; but if she cannot float high enough with as great a quantity of it as her hold will contain, then a diminution of it becomes necessary. Vessels carry heavy goods by the ton of 20 cwt., but lighter goods by a ton of cubic feet, which varies according to the custom of the port; in London it is 40, in India from 50 to 52, depending on the goods. Vessels can carry (not safely) twice their tonnage.

LADEN IN BULK. A cargo neither in casks, bales, nor cases, but lying loose in the hold, only defended from wet by mats and dunnage. Such are usually cargoes of salt, corn, &c.

LADIA. An unwieldy boat in Russia, for transporting the produce of the interior.

LADIE'S LADDER. Shrouds rattled too closely.

LADING. A vessel's cargo.

LADLE, FOR A GUN. An instrument for charging with loose powder; formed of a cylindrical sheet of copper-tube fitted to the end of a long staff.—*Paying-ladle.* An iron ladle with a long channelled spout opposite to the handle; it is used to pour melted pitch into the seams.

LADRON. A term for thief, adopted from the Spanish.

LADRONE SHIP. Literally a pirate, but it is the usual epithet applied by the Chinese to a man-of-war.

LADY OF THE GUN-ROOM. A gunner's mate, who takes charge of the after-scuttle, where gunners' stores are kept.

LAGAN, OR LAGAM. Anglo-Saxon *liggan.* A term in derelict law for goods which are sunk, with a buoy attached, that they may be recovered. Also, things found at the bottom of the sea. Ponderous articles which sink with the ship in wreck.

LAGGERS. On canals, men who lie on their backs on the top of the lading, and pushing against the bridges and tunnels pass the boats through. Also, a transported convict; a lazy fellow.—*To lag.* To loiter.

LAGGIN. The end of the stave outside a cask or tub.

LAGOON. An inland broad expanse of salt water, usually shallow, and connected with the sea by one or more channels, or washes over the reef.

LAGOON ISLANDS. Those produced by coral animals; they are of various shapes, belted with coral, frequently with channels by which ships may enter, and lie safely inside. They are often studded with the cocoa-nut palm. (*See* ATOLLS.)

LAGUNES. The shallows which extend round Venice; their depth between the city and the mainland is 3 to 6 feet in general; they are occasioned by the quantities of sand carried down by the rivers which descend from the Alps, and fall into the Adriatic along its north-western shores.

LAG-WOOD. The larger sticks from the head of an oak-tree when felled.

LAID. A fisherman's name for the pollack. Also, a term in rope-making, the twist being the lay; single-laid, is one strand; hawser-laid, three strands twisted into a rope; cablet-laid, three ropes laid together; this is also termed water-laid.

LAID ABACK. *See* ABACK.

LAID TO. A term used sometimes for *hove to,* but when a vessel lays to the sails are kept full. As in a gale of wind, under staysails, or close reefs, &c.

LAID UP. A vessel dismantled and moored in a harbour, either for want of employment, or as unfit for further service.

LAKE. A large inland expanse of water, with or without communication with the sea. A lake, strictly considered, has no visible affluent or effluent; but many of the loughs of Ireland, and lochs of Scotland, partake of the nature of havens or gulfs. Moreover, some lakes have affluents without outlets, and others have an outlet without any visible affluent; therein differing from lagoons and ponds. The water of lakes entirely encompassed by land is sometimes *salt;* that communicating with the sea by means of rivers is fresh.

LAKE-LAWYER. A voracious fish in the lakes of America, called also the *mud-fish.*

LAMANTIN. A name used by the early voyagers for the manatee.

LAMB'S-WOOL SKY. A collection of white orbicular masses of cloud.

LAMBUSTING. A starting with a rope's-end.

LAMPER-EEL. A common corruption of *lamprey.*

LAMPREY. An eel-like cyclostomous fish, belonging to the genus *Petromyzon.* There are several species, some marine, others fluviatile.

LAMPRON. The old name for the lamprey.

LAMP-SHELLS. A name applied to the *Terebratulæ* of zoologists.

LANCE-KNIGHT. A foot-soldier of old.

LANCEPESADO. From Ital. *lancia spezzata,* or broken lance; originally a soldier who, having broken his lance on the enemy, and lost his horse in fight, was entertained as a volunteer till he could remount himself; hence *lance-corporal,* one doing corporal's duty, on the pay of a private.

LANCHANG. A Malay proa, carrying twenty-five or thirty men.

LAND. In a general sense denotes *terra firma,* as distinguished from sea; but, also, *land-laid,* or to *lay the land,* is just to lose sight of it.—*Land-locked* is when land lies all round the ship.—*Land is shut in,* signifies that another point of land hides that from which the ship came.—*The ship lies land to,* implies so far from shore that it can only just be discerned. —*To set the land,* is to see by compass how it bears.—*To make the land.* To sight it after an absence.—*To land on deck.* A nautical anomaly, meaning to lower casks or weighty goods on deck from the tackles.

LAND-BLINK. On Arctic voyages, a peculiar atmospheric brightness on approaching land covered with snow; usually more yellow than *ice-blink.*

LAND-BREEZE. A current of air which, in the temperate zones, and still more within the tropics, regularly sets from the land towards the sea during the night, and this even on opposite points of the coast. It results from land losing its heat quicker than water; hence the air above it becomes heavier, and rushes towards the sea to establish equilibrium.

LANDES. The heathy track between Bordeaux and the Basses Pyrénées; but also denoting uncultivated or unreclaimable spots.

LAND-FALL. Making the land. "A good land-fall" signifies making the land at or near the place to which the course was intended, while "a bad land-fall" implies the contrary.

LAND-FEATHER. A sea-cove.

LAND HO! The cry when land is first seen.

LAND-ICE. Flat ice connected with the shore, within which there is no channel.

LANDING-STRAKE. In boats, the upper strake of plank but one.

LANDING-SURVEYOR. The custom-house officer who appoints and superintends the landing-waiters.

LANDING-WAITERS. Persons appointed from the custom-house to inspect goods discharged from foreign parts.

LAND-LOUPER. [Dutch.] Meaning he who flies from this country for crime or debt, but not to be confounded with *land-lubber* (which see).

LAND-LUBBER. A useless long-shorer; a vagrant stroller. Applied by sailors to the mass of landsmen, especially those without employment.

LANDMARK. Any steeple, tree, windmill, or other object, serving to guide the seaman into port, or through a channel.

LAND-SHARKS. Crimps, pettifogging attorneys, slopmongers, and the canaille infesting the slums of seaport towns.

LAND-SLIP. The fall of a quantity of land from a cliff or declivity; the land sliding away so as often to carry trees with it still standing upright.

LANDSMEN. The rating formerly of those on board a ship who had never been at sea, and who were usually stationed among the waisters or after-guard. Some of those used to small craft are more ready about the decks than in going aloft. The rating is now Second-class Ordinary.

LAND-TURN. A wind that blows in the night, at certain times, in most hot countries.

LAND-WAITERS. *See* LANDING-WAITERS.

LANE. "Make a lane there!" An order for men to open a passage and allow a person to pass through.

LANE OR VEIN OF ICE. A narrow channel between two fields. Any open cracks or separations of floe offering navigation.

LANGREL, OR LANGRAGE. A villanous kind of shot, consisting of various fragments of iron bound together, so as to fit the bore of the cannon from which it is to be discharged. It is seldom used but by privateers.

LANGUET. A small slip of metal on the hilt of a sword, which overhangs the scabbard; the ear of a sword.

LANIARD, OR LANNIERS. A short piece of rope or line made fast to anything to secure it, or as a handle. Such are the laniards of the gun-locks, of the gun-ports, of the buoy, of the cat-hook, &c. The principal laniards are those which secure the shrouds and stays, termed laniards of lower, topmast, or other rigging. (*See* DEAD-EYE and HEART.)

LANTCHA. A large Malay craft of the Indian Archipelago.

LANTERN. Ships of war had formerly three poop-lanterns, and one in the main-top, to designate the admiral's ship; also deck-lanterns, fighting-lanterns, magazine-lanterns, &c. The signal-lanterns are peculiar. The great ship lantern, hanging to the poop, appears on the Trajan Column.

LANTERN-BRACES. Iron bars to secure the lanterns.

LANTERN-FISH. A west-country name for the smooth sole.

LANTIONE. A Chinese rowing-boat.

LANYARDS. *See* LANIARD.

LAP-JOINTED. The plates of an iron vessel overlapping each other, as in *clincher work.*

LAPLAND WITCHES. People in Lapland who profess to sell fair winds, thus retaining a remnant of ancient classical superstition.

LAP OVER OR UPON. The mast carlings are said to lap upon the beams by reason of their great depth, and head-ledges at the ends lap over the coamings.

LAPPELLE, OR LAPEL. The facing of uniform coats. Until the introduction of epaulettes in 1812, the *white lapelle* was used as synonymous with lieutenant's commission. Hence the brackish poet, in the craven midshipman's lament—

> "If I had in my country staid,
> I then had learnt some useful trade,
> And scorned the white lapelle."

LAPPING. The undulations occasioned in the waves by the paddle-wheels of a steam-boat. In the polar seas, lapping applies to the young or thin ice, one plate overlapping another, so dangerous to boats and their crews. Also, the overlaying of plank edges in working.

LAPS. The remaining part of the ends of carlings, &c., which are to bear a great weight or pressure; such, for instance, as the capstan-step.

LAP'S COURSE. One of the oldest and most savoury of the regular forecastle dishes. (*See* LOBS-SCOUSE.)

LARBOARD. The left side of a ship, when the spectator's face is towards the bow. The Italians derive starboard from *questa borda*, "this side," and larboard from *quella borda*, "that side;" abbreviated into *sta borda* and *la borda*. Their resemblance caused so many mistakes that, by order of the admiralty, larboard is now thrown overboard, and *port* substituted. "Port the helm" is even mentioned in Arthur Pit's voyage in 1580.

LARBOARD-WATCH. The old term for port-watch. The division of a ship's company called for duty, while the other, the starboard, is relieved from it. (*See* WATCH.)

LARBOLINS, OR LARBOLIANS. A cant term implying the larboard-watch, the opposite of starboard :—

> "Larbolins stout, you must turn out,
> And sleep no more within;
> For if you do, we'll cut your clue,
> And let starbolins in."

LARGE. Sailing large : going with the wind free when studding-sails will draw.

LARK. A small boat. Also, frolicsome merriment. (*See* SKYLARKING.)

LARRUP, To. An old word meaning to beat with a rope's-end, strap, or colt.

LASCAR. A native sailor in the East Indies ; also, in a military sense, natives of India employed in pitching tents, or dragging artillery, as gun-lascars.

LASH. A string, or small cord, forming the boatswain's cat.—*To lash* or *lace*. To bind anything with a rope or line.

LASH AND CARRY. The order given by the boatswain and his mates on piping up the hammocks, to accelerate the duty.

LASH AWAY. A phrase to hasten the lashing of hammocks.

LASHER. *See* FATHER LASHER.

LASHER BULL-HEAD. A name for the fish *Cottus scorpius.*

LASHING. A rope used to fasten any movable body in a ship, or about her masts, sails, and rigging.

LASHING-EYES. Fittings for lower stays, block-strops, &c., by loops made in the ends of ropes, for a lashing to be rove through to secure them.

LASK, To. To go large.—*Lasking along.* Sailing away with a quartering wind.

LASKETS. Small lines like hoops, sewed to the bonnets and drablers of a sail, to secure the bonnets to the courses, or the drablers to the bonnets.

LAST. A dry measure containing 80 bushels of corn. A cargo. A weight of 4000 lbs. A last of cod or white herrings is 12 barrels. Last, or ship-last, a Swedish weight of 2 tons.

LASTAGE. This is a commercial term for the general lading of a ship. It is also applied to that custom which is paid for wares sold by the last, as herrings, pitch, &c.

LASTER. The coming in of the tide.

LAST QUARTER. *See* QUARTER, LAST.

LATCH. An old term for a cross-bow; temp. Henry VII.—*Lee-latch.* Dropping to leeward of the course.

LATCHES. The same as *laskets* (which see; also *keys*).

LATCHINGS KEYS. Loops on the head-rope of a bonnet, by which it is laced to the foot of the sail.

LATEEN SAIL AND YARD. A long triangular sail, bent by its foremost leech to a lateen yard, which hoists obliquely to the mast; it is mostly used by xebecs, feluccas, &c., in the Mediterranean. A gaff-topsail, if triangular and set on a yard, is lateen. The term *lateen-rigged*, where sails have short tacks, is wrong. These latter are nothing more or less than clumsy lugs or quadrilaterals. The lateen tack is the yard-arm bowsed amidships.

LATHE. A term for a sort of a cross-bow once used in the fleet.

LATHER, To. To beat or drub soundly.

LATITUDE. In wide terms, the extent of the earth from one pole to the other; but strictly it is the distance of any place from the equator in degrees and their parts; or an arc of the meridian intercepted between the zenith of the place and the equinoctial. Geographical latitude is either northern or southern, according as the place spoken of is on this or that side of the equator. Geocentric latitude is the angular distance of a place from the equator, as corrected for the oblateness of the earth's form; in other words, it is the geographical latitude diminished by the angle of the vertical.

LATITUDE BY ACCOUNT. That estimated by the log-board, and the last determined by observation.

LATITUDE BY OBSERVATION. The latitude determined by observations of the sun, star, or moon, by meridional, as also by double altitudes.

LATITUDE OF A CELESTIAL OBJECT. An arc of a circle of longitude between the centre of that object and the ecliptic, and is north or south according to its position.

LAUNCE. A term when the pump sucks—from the Danish *læns*, exhausted. Also, a west-country term for the sand-eel, a capital bait for mackerel.

LAUNCE-GAY. An offensive weapon used of old, but prohibited by statute so far back as 7 Richard II. c. 13.

LAUNCH. The largest or long boat of a ship of war. Others of greater size for gun-boats are used by the French, Spaniards, Italians, &c., in the Mediterranean. A launch being proportionably longer, lower, and more flat-bottomed than the merchantman's long-boat, is in consequence less fit for sailing, but better calculated for rowing and approaching a flat shore. Its principal superiority consists in being much fitter to under-run the cable, lay out anchors, &c., which is a very necessary employment in the harbours of the Levant, where the cables of different ships are fastened across each other, and frequently render such operations necessary.

LAUNCH, To. To send a ship, craft, or boat off the slip on shore into the water, "her native element," as newspapers say. Also, to move things; as, *launch forward*, or *launch aft*. *Launch* is also the movement by which the ship or boat descends into the water.

LAUNCH-HO! The order to let go the top-rope after the top-mast has been swayed up and fidded. It is literally "high enough." So in pumping, when the spear sucks, this term is "Cease."

LAUNCHING-WAYS. In ship-building, the bed of timber placed on the incline under the bottom of a ship; otherwise called *bilgeways*. On this the cradles, which are movable vertical shores, to keep the ship upright, slide. Sometimes also termed *bilgeways*.

LAVEER, To. An old sea-term for beating a ship to windward; to tack.

LAVER. An edible sea-weed — the *Ulva lactuca*, anciently *lhavan*. From this a food is made, called *laver-bread*, on the shores of S. Wales.

LAVY. A sea-bird nearly as large as a duck, held by the people of the Hebrides as a prognosticator of weather.

LAW OF NATIONS. It was originally merely the necessary law of nature applied to nations, as in the instance of receiving distressed ships with humanity. By various conventional compacts, the Law of Nations became positive; thus flags of truce are respected, and prisoners are not put to death. One independent state is declared incompetent to prescribe to another, so long as that state is innoxious to its neighbours. The Law of Nations consists of those principles and regulations, founded in reason and general convenience, by which the mutual intercourse between independent states is everywhere conducted.

LAX. A term for salmon when ascending a river, on the north coast of Scotland.

LAX-FISHER. A taker of salmon in their passage from the sea.

LAY, By the. When a man is paid in proportion to the success of the voyage, instead of by the month. This is common in whalers.

LAY, To. To come or go; as, *lay aloft, lay forward, lay aft, lay out.* This is not the neuter verb *lie* mispronounced, but the active verb *lay.* (*See* Lie out.)

LAY A GUN, To. So to direct it as that its shot may be expected to strike a given object; for which purpose its axis must be pointed above the latter, at an angle of elevation increasing according to its distance.

LAY-DAYS. The time allowed for shipping or discharging a cargo; and if not done within the term, fair weather permitting, the vessel comes on demurrage. Thus Captain Cuttle—

> " A rough hardy seaman, unus'd to shore ways,
> Knew little of ladies, but much of lay-days."

LAY HER COURSE, To. To be able to sail in the direction wished for, however barely the wind permits it.

LAY IN. The opposite of *lay out.* The order for men to come in from the yards after reefing or furling. It also applies to manning, or *laying in*, to the capstan-bars.

LAYING or Lying out on a yard. To go out towards the yard-arms.

LAYING or LYING ALONG. Pressed down sideways by a stiff gale.

LAYING A ROPE. Arranging the yarns for the strands, and then the strands for making a rope, or cable.

LAYING DOWN, or Laying off. The act of delineating the various lines of a ship to the full size on the mould-loft floor, from the draught given.

LAYINGS. A sort of pavement of culch, on the mud of estuaries, for forming a bed for oysters.

LAYING-TOP. A conical piece of wood, having three or four scores or notches on its surface, used in rope-making to guide the lay.

LAY IN SEA-STOCK, To. To make provision for the voyage.

LAY IN THE OARS. Unship them from the rowlocks, and place them fore and aft in the boat.

LAY LORDS. The civil members of the admiralty board.

LAY OF A ROPE. The direction in which its strands are twisted; hawser is right-handed; cablet left-handed.

LAY or LIE ON YOUR OARS! The order to desist rowing, without laying the oars in.—*Lay out on your oars!* is the order to give way, or pull with greater force.

LAY OUT. *See* Lie out.

LAY THE LAND, To. Barely to lose sight of it.

LAY-TO. To bring the weather-bow to the sea, with one sail set, and the helm lashed a-lee. (*See* Lie-to.)

LAY UP A SHIP, To. To dismantle her.

LAZARETTO. A building or vessel appointed for the performance of quarantine, in which all persons are confined coming from places infected with the plague or other infectious diseases. Also, a place parted off at the fore part of the 'tween decks, in some merchantmen, for stowing provisions and stores in.

LAZARUS. The game at cards, called also *blind-hookey* and *snogo*.

LAZY GUY. A small tackle or rope to prevent the spanker-boom from swaying about in fine weather.

LAZY PAINTER. A small temporary rope to hold a boat in fine weather.

LEAD, SOUNDING. An instrument for discovering the depth of water; it is a tapered cylinder of lead, of 7, 14, or 28 lbs. weight, and attached, by means of a strop, to the lead-line, which is marked at certain distances to ascertain the fathoms. (*See* HAND LEAD-LINE.)—*Deep-sea lead.* A lead of a larger size, being from 28 to 56 lbs. in weight, and attached to a much longer line. (*See* DEEP-SEA LEAD-LINE.)—*To heave the lead.* To throw it into the sea as far ahead as possible, if the ship is under way.

LEAD. The direction in which running ropes lead fair, and come down to the deck. Also, in Arctic seas, a channel through the ice; synonymous with *lane*. To lead into battle, or into harbour.

LEADER. A chief. Also, the conducting ship, boat, or man in an enterprise. Also, the guide in firing rockets.

LEADING-BLOCKS. The several blocks used for guiding the direction of any purchase, as hook, snatch, or tail blocks.

LEADING-MARKS. Those objects which, kept in line or in transit, guide the pilot while working into port, as trees, spires, buoys, &c.

LEADING-PART. The rope of a tackle which runs between the fall and the standing part. Generally confused with the fall. It is that part of the fall which is to be hauled on, or over-hauled, to ease the purchase.

LEADING-STRINGS. The yoke-lines for steering a boat.

LEADING-WIND. Wind abeam or quartering; more particularly a free or fair wind, and is used in contradistinction to a scant wind. (*See* WIND.)

LEAD-LINE. A line attached to the upper end of the sounding-lead. (*See* HAND-LINE and DEEP-SEA LINE.)

LEAD-NAILS. Small round-headed composition nails for nailing lead.

LEADSMAN. The man who heaves the hand-lead in the channels. In Calcutta the young gentlemen learning to be pilots are called leadsmen.

LEAF. The side of a lock-gate.

LEAGUE. A confederacy; an alliance. Also, a measure of length consisting of three nautical miles, much used in estimating sea-distances; = 3041 fathoms.

LEAGUER. An old term for a camp. Also, *leaguers*, the longest water-casks, stowed next the kelson, of 159 English imperial gallons each. Before the invention of water-tanks, leaguers composed the whole ground tier of casks in men-of-war.

LEAK [Anglo-Saxon *leccinc*]. A chink in the deck, sides, or bottom of a ship, through which the water gets into her hull. When a leak begins, a vessel is said to have *sprung* a leak.

LEAKAGE. Loss by the act of leaking out of a cask. Also, an allowance of 12 per cent., to merchants importing wine, by the customs.

LEAKIES. Certain irregularities of tide in the Firth of Forth.

LEAKY. The state of a ship admitting water, and a cask or other vessel letting out its contents.

LEAN. Used in the same sense as *clean* or *sharp*; the reverse of *full* or bluff in the form of a ship.

LEAN-BOW. Having a sharp entrance; a thin narrow bow being opposed to bold bow. *Fine forward*, very fine is *lean as a lizard*.

LEAP. The sudden fall of a river in one sheet. Also, a weel, made of twigs, to catch fish in.

LEAPER. *See* LIPPER.

LEAT. A canal leading from a pool to a mill-course.

LEATHAG. A Celtic name for the plaice or flounder.

LEATHER. *See* LATHER.

LEATHER-JACKET. A tropical fish with a very thick skin.

LEAVE. Permission to be absent from the ship for the day. (*See* ABSENCE, LIBERTY.)—*French leave.* Going on shore without permission.— *Long leave.* Permission to be absent for a number of days.

LEAVE-BREAKING. A liberty man not being back to his time.

LEAVE-TICKET. *See* LIBERTY TICKET.

LEAX. *See* LEX.

LEDGE. A compact line of rocks running parallel to the coast, and which is not unfrequent opposite sandy beaches. The north coast of Africa, between the Nile and the Lesser Syrtis, is replete with them.

LEDGES. The 'thwart-ship pieces from the waste-trees to the roof-trees in the framing of the decks, let into the carlings, to bear gratings, &c. Any cross-pieces of fir or scantling.

LEDO. A barbarous Latin law-term (*ledo -onis*) for the rising water, or increase of the sea.

LEE. From the Scandinavian word *læ* or *laa*, the sea; it is the side opposite to that from which the wind is blowing; as, if a vessel has the wind on her port side, that side will be the weather, and the starboard will be the lee side.—*Under the lee*, expresses the situation of a vessel anchored or sailing near the weather-shore, where there is always smoother water than at a great distance from it.—*To lay a ship by the lee*, or *to come up by the lee*, is to let her run off until the wind is brought on the lee-quarter, so that all her sails lie flat against the masts and shrouds.

LEE-ANCHOR. The leeward one, if under weigh; or that to leeward to which a ship, when moored, is riding.

LEE-BEAM. On the lee-side of the ship, at right angles with the keel.

LEE-BOARDS. Wooden wings or strong frames of plank affixed to the sides of flat-bottomed vessels, such as Dutch schuyts, &c.; these traversing on a stout bolt, by being let down into the water, when the vessel is close-hauled, decrease her drifting to leeward.

LEECHES. The borders or edges of a sail, which are either sloping or perpendicular; those of the square sails are denominated from the ship's side, as the starboard-leech of the mainsail, &c.; but the sails which are fixed obliquely on the masts have their leeches named from their situation with regard to the ship's length, as the hoist or luff, or fore-leech of the mizen, the after-leech of the jib, &c.

LEECH-LINES. Ropes fastened to the leeches of the mainsail, foresail, and cross-jack, communicating with blocks under the tops, and serving to truss those sails up to the yards. (*See* BRAILS.)—*Harbour leech-lines.* Ropes made fast at the middle of the topsail-yards, then passing round the leeches of the topsails, and through blocks upon the topsail-tye, serving to truss the sails very close up to the yard, previous to their being furled in a body.

LEECH-ROPE. A name given to that vertical part of the bolt-rope to which the border or edge of a sail is sewed. In all sails whose opposite leeches are of the same length, it is terminated above by the earing, and below by the clue. (*See* BOLT-ROPE, CLUE, and EARING.)

LEE-FANG. A rope rove through the cringle of a sail, for hauling in, so as to lace on a bonnet.

LEE-FANGE. The iron bar upon which the sheets of fore-and-aft sails traverse, in small vessels. (*See* HORSE.)

LEE-GUAGE. Implies being farther from the point whence the wind blows, than another vessel in company.

LEE-GUNWALE UNDER. A colloquial phrase for being sorely over-pressed, by canvas or other cause.

LEE-HATCH, TAKE CARE OF THE! A word of caution to the helmsman, not to let the ship fall to leeward of her course.

LEE-HITCH. The helmsman getting to leeward of the course.

LEE-LURCHES. The sudden and violent rolls which a ship often takes to leeward when a large wave strikes her on the weather-side.

LEE-SHORE. A ship is said to be on a lee-shore, when she is near it, with the wind blowing right on to it.

LEE-SIDE. All that part of a ship or boat which lies between the mast and the side farthest from the wind, the other half being the weather-side.

LEE-SIDE OF THE QUARTER-DECK. Colloquially called the midshipman's parade.

LEE-TIDE. A tide running in the same direction as the wind, and forcing a ship to leeward of the line upon which she appears to sail.

LEEWARD. The lee-side. (*See* LEE.) The opposite of *lee* is *weather*, and of *leeward*, *windward*.

LEEWARDLY. Said of a ship or vessel which presents so little resistance to the water, when on a wind, as to bag away to leeward. It is the contrary to *weatherly*.

LEE-WAY. What a vessel loses by drifting to leeward in her course. When she is sailing close-hauled in a smooth sea with all sail set, she should make little or no lee-way; but a proportionate allowance must be made under every reduction of sail or increase of sea, the amount depending on the seaman's skill, and his knowledge of the vessel's qualities.

LEE-WHEEL. The assistant to the helmsman.

LEG. The run made on a single tack. Long and short legs (*see* TACK and HALF-TACK).

LEG ALONG. Ropes laid on end, ready for manning.

LEG-BAIL. Dishonest desertion from duty. The phrase is not confined to its nautical bearing.

LEGGERS. *See* LEAGUERS.

LEGS. (*See* ANGLE.) A fast-sailing vessel is said to have legs.—*Legs* are used in cutters, yachts, &c., to shore them up in dry harbours when the tide leaves them. The leech-line cringles have also been called legs. Also, the parts of a point which hang on each side of the sail.

LEGS OF THE MARTINETS. Small lines through the bolt-ropes of the courses, above a foot in length, and spliced at either end into themselves, making a small eye into which the martinets are hitched.

LEGS AND WINGS. *See* OVERMASTED.

LEISTER. A three-pronged dart for striking fish, used in the north of England.

LEIT. A northern term for a snood or link of horse-hair for a fishing-line.

LEITH. A channel on the coast of Sweden, like that round the point of Landfoort to Stockholm.

LEMBUS. A light undecked vessel, used by ancient pirates.

LEMING-STAR. An old name for a comet.

LEMON-ROB. The inspissated juice of limes or lemons, a powerful antiscorbutic.

LEND A FIST OR A HAND. A request to another to help.

LEND US YOUR POUND HERE! A phrase demanding assistance in man-weight; alluding to the daily allowance of beef.

LENGTHENING. The operation of cutting a ship down across the middle, and adding a certain portion to her length. This is done by sawing her planks asunder in different parts of her length, on each side of the midship-frame, to prevent her from being weakened too much in one place. One end is then drawn apart to the required distance. An intermediate piece of timber is next added to the keel, and the vacancy filled up. The two parts of the keelson are afterwards united. Finally, the planks of the side are prolonged, so as to unite with each other, and those of the ceiling re-fitted.

LENGTHENING-PIECE. The same as *short top-timber* (which see).

LENS. The glass of a telescope, or of a microscope, with curved surfaces like a lentil, whence the name.

LENT. The spring fast, during which butchers were prohibited to kill flesh unless for victualling ships, except by special license.

LENTRIÆ. Ancient small vessels, used on rivers.

LENUNCULI. Ancient fishing-boats.

LEO. The fifth sign of the zodiac, which the sun enters about the 22d of July. It is one of the ancient constellations.

LEPPO. A sort of chunam, used on the China station, for paying vessels.

LERRICK. A name of the water-bird also called sand-lark or sand-piper.

LESSER CIRCLE. One whose plane does not pass through the centre of the sphere, and therefore divides it unequally. (*See* GREAT CIRCLE.)

LET DRAW! The order to let the wind take the after-leeches of the jibs, &c., over to the lee-side, while tacking.

LET DRIVE, To To slip or let fly. To discharge, as a shot from a gun.

LET FALL! The order to drop a sail loosed from its gaskets, in order to set it.

LET FLY, To. To let go a rope at once, suddenly.

LET GO AND HAUL! or AFORE HAUL! The order to haul the head-yards round by the braces when the ship casts on the other tack. "Let go," alluding to the fore-bowline and lee head-braces.

LET GO UNDER FOOT. *See* ANCHOR UNDER FOOT.

LET IN, To. To fix or fit a diminished part of one plank or piece of timber into a score formed in another to receive it, as the ends of the carlings into the beams.

LET OUT, OR SHAKE OUT, A REEF, To. To increase the dimensions of a sail, by untying the points confining a reef in it.

LET-PASS. Permission given by superior authority to a vessel, to be shown to ships of war, to allow it to proceed on its voyage.

LET RUN, OR LET GO BY THE RUN. Cast off at once.

LETTER-BOARD. Another term for *name-board* (which see).

LETTER-BOOK. A book wherein is preserved a copy of all letters and orders written by the captain of a ship on public service.

LETTER MEN. *See* KING'S LETTER MEN.

LETTERS. *See* CIRCULARS and OFFICIAL LETTERS.

LETTERS OF MART OR MARQUE. A commission formerly granted by the lords of the admiralty, or by the admiral of any distant station, to a merchant-ship or privateer, to cruize against and make prizes of the enemy's ships. The ship so commissioned is also called a *letter of marque.* The act of parliament requires that on granting letters of marque and reprisal, the captain and two sureties shall appear and give security. In 1778 it was decided that all the ships taken from France by vessels having letters of marque only against the Americans, became droits of admiralty. This commission was forfeitable for acts of cruelty or mis-conduct.

LETTERS OF REPRISAL. The same as *letters of marque.*

LETTUCE-LAVER. The edible sea-weed *Ulva lactuca.*

LEVANT. A wind coming from the east, which freshens as the sun rises, and subsides as it declines—*To levant*, to desert.

LEVANTER. A strong and raw easterly wind in the Mediterranean.

LEVANTS. Land-springs on the coasts of Sussex and Hampshire.

LEVEE. A French word for a mole or causeway, adopted of late for river embankments of magnitude, as those of the Po, the Thames, and the Mississippi.

LEVEL-ERROR. The microscopic deviation of the axis of a transit instrument from the horizontal position.

LEVELING. The art of finding how much higher or lower horizontally any given point on the earth's surface is, than another point on the same; practised in various ways.

LEVELLED OUT. Any line continued out from a given point, or intersection of an angle, in a horizontal direction.

LEVEL-LINES. Lines determining the shape of a ship's body horizontally, or square from the middle line of the ship.

LEVELS. Horizontal lines; or as a base square to a perpendicular bob.

LEVER. In the marine steam-engine, the lever and counter-balance weight are fixed upon the wiper-shaft, to form an equipoise to the valves. There is one on each side of the cylinder. (*See* SPANNER.)—Also, an inflexible bar of iron or wood to raise weights, which takes rank as the first and most simple of the mechanical powers.—*To lever.* An old word for unloading a ship.

LEVERAGE. The amount of a lever power.

LEVES. Very light open boats of the ancients.

LEVET. The blast of a trumpet or horn.

LEVIN. The old term for lightning.

LEVY. An enrolment or conscription.—*To levy.* To raise recruits.

LEWER. A provincialism for hand-spike; a corrupt form of *lever.*

LEWIS-HOLES. Two holes in the surface of a mortar, superseding ears.

LEWTH [from the Anglo-Saxon *lywd*]. A place of shelter from the wind.

LEX, or LEAX. The Anglo-Saxon term for salmon.

L. G. These uncials on a powder-barrel mean large-grain powder.

LIBERA PISCARIA. A law-term denoting a fishery free to any one.

LIBERTY. Permission to go on shore or ship-visiting.

LIBERTY-DAY. A day announced for permitting a part of the crew to go ashore.

LIBERTY-LIQUOR. Spirits formerly allowed to be purchased when seamen had visitors; now forbidden.

LIBERTY-MEN. Those on leave of absence.

LIBERTY-TICKET. A document specifying the date and extent of the leave granted to a seaman or marine proceeding on his private affairs.

LIBRA. The seventh sign of the zodiac, which the sun enters about the 21st of September; the commencement of this constellation, where the equator intersects the ecliptic, is called the *autumnal equinox*, from night and day being equal.

LIBRATION OF THE MOON. *See* EVECTION.

LIBURNA, or LIBURNICA. Light ancient galliots, both for sails and oars; of the latter from one rank to five; so called from the Liburni, pirates of the Adriatic.

LICENSE. An official permission from the Board of Trade, to such persons as it thinks fit to supply seamen or apprentices for merchant-ships in the United Kingdom. (*See* RUNNER, LICENSED.)

LICK. In common parlance is a blow. To do anything partially, is to *give it a lick and a promise*, as in painting or blacking.—*To lick*, to surpass a rival, or excel him in anything.—*Lick of the tar-brush*, a seaman.

LICORN. An old name for the howitzer of the last century, then but a kind of mortar fitted on a field-carriage to fire shells at low angles.

LIDO. A borrowed term signifying the shore or margin of the sea.

LIE A HULL. Synonymous with *hull to*, or *hulling*.

LIE ALONG, To. (*See* ALONG.) A ship is said to lie along when she leans over with a side wind.—*To lie along the land*, is to keep a course parallel with it.

LIE ATHWART, To. When the tide slackens, and the wind is across tide, it makes a vessel ride athwart.

LIE BY, To. Dodging under small sail under the land.

LIE IN! The order to come in from the yards when reefing, furling, or other duty is performed.

LIEN. A claim to property, and a consequent right of retention. But ships cannot be the subjects of a specific lien to the creditors who supply them with necessaries, because a lien presumes possession by the creditor, and therein the power of holding it till his demands are satisfied. To prevent manifest impediment to commerce, the law of England rejects almost wholly the doctrine of lien as regards ships.

LIE OFF! An order given to a boat to remain off on her oars till permission is given for her to come alongside.

LIE OUT! The order to the men aloft to distribute themselves on the yards for loosing, reefing, or furling sails.

LIE OVER. A ship heeling to it with the wind abeam.

LIESTER. *See* LISTER.

LIE THE COURSE, To. When the vessel's head is in the direction wished.

LIE TO, To. To cause a vessel to keep her head steady as regards a gale, so that a heavy sea may not tumble into her. She has perhaps a main-topsail or trysails, and comes up to within six points, and falls off to wind abeam, forging rather ahead, but should not altogether fall too much to leeward.

LIE UNDER ARMS, To. To remain in a state of preparation for immediate action.

LIEUTENANT, IN THE ROYAL NAVY. The officer next in rank and power below the commander. There are several lieutenants in a large ship, and they take precedence according to the dates of their commissions. The senior lieutenant, during the absence of the commander, is charged with the command of the ship, as also with the execution of whatever orders he may have received from the commander relating to the queen's service; holding another's place, as the name implies in French.—*Lieutenant in the army.* The subaltern officer next in rank below the captain.

LIEUTENANT-AT-ARMS. Formerly the junior lieutenant, who, with the master-at-arms, was charged with the drilling of the small-arm men.

LIEUTENANT-COLONEL. The next below the colonel, generally having the active command in the regiment, whether in cavalry, infantry, or artillery, the full colonels being mostly on staff employ, or even in retirement.

LIEUTENANT-GENERAL. The officer taking the next place to a general, ranking with vice-admiral.

LIEUTENANT'S STORE-ROOM. More commonly called the *wardroom storeroom* (which see).

LIFE-BELT. An india-rubber or cork girdle round a person's waist to buoy him up in the water.

LIFE-BOAT. One of such peculiar construction that it cannot sink or be swamped. It is equipped for attending wherever a wreck may happen, and saving the lives of the crew: really one of the greatest blessings conferred by civilization and humanity on mariners. Life-boats were invented by Admiral Samuel Graves, who died in 1787. The Royal National Life-boat Institution has saved by its boats, or by special exertions for which it has granted rewards, 14,980 lives, from the year of its establishment, 1824, to the end of 1865.

LIFE-BUOYS. Are of various descriptions. A very useful one, patented by Cook, is supplied to all Her Majesty's ships. It is composed of two copper cylinders, and has a balanced stem carrying a fuse, burning twenty minutes. It is kept suspended on the quarter, can be let go, and ignited instantaneously, and will support two men for a considerable time.

LIFE-GUARDS. A greatly-privileged body of cavalry, specially assigned to the guarding of the sovereign's person.

LIFE-KITE. A contrivance for saving the lives of shipwrecked persons by forming a communication between the wreck and a lee-shore.

LIFE-LINES. Stretched from gun to gun, and about the upper deck in bad weather, to prevent the men being washed away. The life-lines aloft are stretched from the lifts to the masts to enable seamen to stand securely when manning yards, as in a salute to admirals, &c.

LIFE-PRESERVER. An air-tight apparatus for saving people in cases of wreck.

LIFT. A term applied to the sails when the wind catches them on the leeches and causes them to ruffle slightly. Also implies help in work in hand, as "give us a lift."

LIFT AN ANCHOR, To. Either by the purchase; or a ship if she has not sufficient cable on a steep bank *lifts*, or shoulders, her anchor.

LIFTED. Promoted somewhat unexpectedly.

LIFTER. *See* WIPER.

LIFTING. The rising of fog or haze from the surface of the water.

LIFTING-JACK. A portable machine for lifting heavy objects, acting by the power either of the lever, the tooth and pinion, or the screw.

LIFTS. Ropes which reach from each mast-head to their respective yard-arms to steady and suspend the ends. Their use is to keep the yard in equilibrium, or to raise one of its extremities higher than the other if necessary, but particularly to support the weight when a number of men are employed on it, furling or reefing the sail. The yards are said to be squared by the lifts when they hang at right angles with the masts. —*Topping lifts.* (*See* TOPPING.)

LIG. A fish-hook, with lead cast round its upper part in order to sink it.

LIGAN. *See* LAGAN.

LIGGER. A line with a float and bait, used for catching pike. A night-hook laid for a pike or eel.

LIGHT, To. To move or lift anything along; as "light over to windward," the cry for helping the man at the weather-earing when taking in a reef. Each man holding by a reef-point helps it over, as the lee-earing cannot be passed until the man to windward calls out, "Haul out to leeward."

LIGHT AIRS. Unsteady and faint flaws of wind.

LIGHT ALONG! Lend assistance in hauling cables, hawsers, or large ropes along, and lifting some parts in a required direction.

LIGHT-BALLS. Are thrown from mortars at night to discover the enemy's working parties, &c. They are composed of saltpetre, sulphur, resin, and linseed-oil, and burn with great brilliancy. The *parachute light-ball*, which suspends itself in the air by the action of the heated gas from the light against the parachute, is most convenient.

LIGHT BOBS. The old soubriquet for *light infantry* (which see).

LIGHT BREEZES. When light airs have become steady.

LIGHTEN, To. To throw ballast, stores, cargo, or other things, overboard in stress of weather, to render the vessel more buoyant.

LIGHTER. A large, open, flat-bottomed boat, with heavy bearings, employed to carry goods to or from ships.—*Ballast lighter.* A vessel fitted up to raise ballast from the bottom of a harbour.—*Covered or close lighter.* One furnished with a deck throughout her whole length, in order to secure such merchandise as might be damaged by wet, and to prevent pillage.

LIGHTERAGE. The charge made for the hire of a lighter.

LIGHTERMAN. A man employed in a lighter.

LIGHT-HANDED. Short of the complement of men.

LIGHT-HORSE. A name formerly given to all mounted men who were not encumbered with armour.

LIGHT-HORSEMAN. An old name for the light boat, since called a gig. (*See* WALLMIA.)

LIGHTHOUSE. A sort of tower, erected upon a headland, islet, or rock, whose lights may be seen at a great distance from the land to warn shipping of their approach to these dangers.—A *floating light*, or *light vessel*, strongly moored, is used to mark dangers under water. Lights are variously distinguished, as by the number, colour, and continuity of their lights, whether flashing, revolving, &c.

LIGHT ICE. That which has but little depth in the water; it is not considered dangerous to shipping, as not being heavy.

LIGHT INFANTRY. Troops specially trained to the extended and rapid movements necessary to cover the manœuvres of the main body.

LIGHTNING-CONDUCTOR. The lightning-conductor (introduced by Sir Snow Harris) is a plate connected from the royal mast-head down to the deck, thence by the beams to the ship's copper into the sea. Another kind is a copper-wire chain or rope hoisted to the truck, then passing down by the backstays over the channels into the sea.

LIGHT-PORT. A scuttle made for showing a light through. Also, a port in timber ships kept open until brought deep by cargo. It is then secured and caulked in. (*See* RAFT-PORT.)

LIGHT-ROOM. In a ship-of-war, a small space parted off from the magazine, having double-glass windows for more safely transmitting the light by which the gunner and his assistants fill their cartridges. Large ships generally have two light-rooms, the after and the fore.

LIGHTS. In men-of-war, all the seamen's lights are extinguished by 8 P.M., the officers' at 10, unless the commanding officer gives his permission, through the master-at-arms, for a longer time, as occasion may require.

LIGHT SAILS. All above the topgallant-sails; also the studding-sails and flying jib. Men-of-war carry topgallant-sails over double reef.

LIGHT SHIP. In contradistinction to laden; a ship is said to be light when she has no cargo, or merely in ballast. When very crank, she is said to be *flying light*. Also, a vessel bearing a light as a guide to navigators.

LIGHT WATER-DRAUGHT. The depth of water which a vessel draws when she is empty, or nearly so.

LIGHT WATER-LINE. The line showing the depression of the ship's body in the water when just launched, or quite unladen. (*See* WATER-LINE.)

LIGNAMINA. Timber fit for building.

LIGNUM VITÆ. *Guaiacum officinale.* A West Indian tree, of the wood of which sheaves of blocks are made. It was allowed to be imported free of all duties.

LIMB. The graduated arc of an astronomical or surveying instrument. In astronomy, it is the edge or border of the disc of the sun, moon, or one of the planets; in which sense we say the upper limb, the lower limb, the sun or moon's nearest limb, &c.

LIMBER. In artillery, the two-wheeled carriage to which the trail of a field gun-carriage is attached for travel.—*Limber-boxes* are the chests fitted above the axletree of the limber for ammunition.—*Limber up!* is the command so to raise and attach.

LIMBER BOARDS OR PLATES. Short movable pieces of plank; a part of the lining of a ship's floor, close to the keelson, and immediately above the limbers. They are occasionally removed to clear them of any rubbish by which they may be clogged, so as to interrupt the passage of water to the pump-well.

LIMBER-BOX. Synonymous with *limber-trunk.*

LIMBER-CLEARER. A small chain rove fore-and-aft through the limber passage to clear it when necessary, by hauling backwards and forwards.

LIMBER-PASSAGE. The line of limber-holes throughout the whole length of the floor, on each side of the keelson, for the water to have free access to the pumps.

LIMBER-PLATES. *See* LIMBER-BOARDS.

LIMBER-STREAK. The streak of foot-waling nearest the keelson, wrought over the lower ends of the first futtocks.

LIMBO. Restraint, durance, confinement under arrest, or in the bilboes. Dante uses this term for a division of the infernal regions.

LIMB-TANGENT. The accurate touch of the edge of a celestial body to the horizon.

LIME OR LEMON JUICE. A valuable anti-scorbutic, included by act of parliament in the scale of provisions for seamen. It has latterly been so much adulterated that scurvy has increased threefold in a few years.

LIME-POTS. Formerly supplied among the munitions of war to ships.

LIMITING PARALLELS. The parallels of latitude upon the earth's surface, within which occultations of stars or planets by the moon are possible. They are given in the *Nautical Almanac* for each occultation.

LIMMER. The side-rope to a poop or other ladder.

LIMPET. A well-known shell-fish, giving rise to the brackish proverb, "Sticking fast like a limpet to a rock."

LINCH OR LINS PIN. The iron pin which keeps the trucks of a gun-carriage confined to the axle-tree.

LINE, To. To cover one piece with another. Also, to mark out the work on a floor for determining the shape of a vessel's body.—*To line a ship*, is to strike off with a batten, or otherwise, the directional lines for painting her. (*See* TOE A LINE.)

LINE. The general appellation of a number of small ropes in a ship, as buntlines, cluelines, bowlines, &c. Also, the term in common parlance for the equator. Also, in the army, distinguishes the regular numbered regiments of cavalry and infantry from the artillery and guards, to whom exceptional functions are assigned. In fortification, it means a trench, approaches, &c. In a geometrical sense, it signifies length without breadth; and in military parlance, it is drawing up a front of soldiers. —*Concluding line.* A small rope, which is hitched to the middle of every step of a stern-ladder. *Deep-sea line.* A long line, marked at every five fathoms with small strands of line, knotted, and used with the deep-sea lead. The first 20 fathoms are marked as follows: 2 and 3 fathoms with black leather; 5 with white bunting; 7 with red; 10 with leather and a hole in it. Then 13, 15, and 17 repeat the previous marks of 3, 5, and 7. Two knots indicate 20, three knots 30, four knots 40 fathoms, and so on, with an additional knot for every ten. Meanwhile a single knot indicates the intermediate fives. Besides this system some pilots prefer their own marks, as in the Hooghly, where they always measure the line for themselves. The term "deep-sea line" must not now be confined to the use of the lead for the ordinary purposes of safe navigation; deep-sea soundings for scientific purposes are recorded in thousands of fathoms, in which case the line is sometimes made of silk, the object being to obtain the largest amount of strength with a small weight.—*Fishing-lines.* Particular kinds of lines, generally used for fishing snood, mackerel, whiting, cod, albacore, &c.—*Hand-line.* A line about 20 fathoms long, marked like the first 20 fathoms of the deep-sea line. It is made fast to a hand-lead of from 7 to 14 lbs., and used to determine the depth of water in going in or out of a harbour, river, channel, &c.— *Hauling-line.* Any rope let down out of a top, &c., to haul up some light body by hand.—*Knave-line.* A rope fastened to the cross-trees, under the main or fore top, whence it comes down by the ties to the ram-head, and there it is rove through a piece of wood about 2 feet long, and so is brought to the ship's side, and there hauled up taut to the rails.—*Life-line.* A rope occasionally extended in several situations for persons to lay hold of, to prevent their falling.—*Mar-line.* A particular kind of small line, composed of two strands very little twisted; there is both tarred and white mar-line. That supplied for the gunner and for bending light sails is untarred.— *Navel-line.* A rope depending from the heads of the main and fore masts, and passed round to the bight of the truss to keep it up, whilst the yard is being swayed up, or when the truss, in bracing sharp up, is overhauled to the full.—*Spilling-lines.* Ropes fixed occasionally to the square sails, particularly the main and fore courses in bad weather, for reefing or furling them more conveniently; they are rove through blocks upon the yard, whence leading round the sail they are fastened abaft the yard, so that the sail is very closely confined.—*White-line.* That which has not been tarred, in contradistinction to *tarred line.*

LINE-BREADTH. *See* BREADTH-LINE.

LINE OF BATTLE. A disposition of the fleet at the moment of engagement, by signal or previous order, on which occasion the vessels are usually drawn up as much as possible in a specified bearing, as well to gain and keep the advantage of the wind, as to run the same board, about 1 cable, or 100 fathoms distant from each other. The line-of-battle in sea-fights occurs both in Plutarch (*Themistocles*) and Froissart.

LINE-OF-BATTLE SHIPS. Formerly those of 74 guns and upwards; or in these iron days, any vessel capable of giving and taking the tremendous blows of the larger ordnance.

LINE OF BEARING. A previously determined bearing given out by a commander-in-chief, as well as line-of-battle. "From line of battle form line of bearing," or reverse. The line of bearing must be that point of the compass on which the ships bear from each other, and from which the line of battle can readily be formed without losing speed or ground.

LINE OF COLLIMATION. *See* COLLIMATION, LINE OF.

LINE OF DEFENCE. In fortification, the face of a work receiving flank defence, together with its prolongation to the flanking work.

LINE OF DEMARCATION. A line which is drawn by consent, to ascertain the limits of territories belonging to different powers.

LINE OF LINE. *See* GUNTER'S LINE.

LINE-OF-METAL ELEVATION. That which the axis of a gun has above the object when its line of metal is pointed on the latter; it averages $1\frac{1}{2}°$ in guns of the old construction.

LINE OF NODES. The imaginary line joining the ascending and descending nodes of the orbit of a planet or comet.

LINE OF OPERATIONS. In strategy, the line an army follows to attain its objective point.

LINE OUT STUFF. To mark timber for dressing to shape.

LINERS. Line-of-battle ships. Also, a designation of such packet or passenger ships as trade periodically and regularly to and from ports beyond sea, in contradistinction to chance vessels. Also, a term applied by seamen to men-of-war and to their crews.

LINES. With shipwrights, are the various plans for determining the shape and form of the ship's body on the mould-loft floor. Also, a species of field-works, consisting of a series of fronts, constructed in order to cover the front and form the immediate defence of an army or the frontiers of a state.

LINES OF FLOTATION. Those horizontal marks supposed to be described by the surface of the water on the bottom of a ship, and which are exhibited at certain depths upon the sheer-draught. (*See* LIGHT WATER-LINE, and LOAD WATER-LINE.)

LING. A brush-wood useful in breaming. Also, a fish, the *Lota molva;* it invariably inhabits the deep valleys of the sea, while the cod is always found on the banks. When sun-dried it is called stock-fish.

LINGET. Small langridge; slugs.

LINGO. A very old word for tongue or dialect, rather than language or speech.

LININGS. The reef-bands, leech and top linings, bunt-line cloths, and other applied pieces, to prevent the chafing of the sails. In ship-building, the term means thin dressed board nailed over any rough surface to give it a finish

LINKISTER. An interpreter; linguist.

LINKS. A northern phrase for the windings of a river; also for flat sands on the sea-shore, and low lands overflowed at spring tides.

LINK WORMING. Guarding a cable from friction, by worming it with chains.

LINNE. A Gaelic term for pool, pond, lake, or sea.

LINSEY-WOLSEY. A stuff in extensive use commercially; it is a mixture of flax and wool.

LINSTOCK. In olden times it was a staff about 3 feet long, having a sharp point at the foot to stick in the deck, and a forked head to hold a lighted match. It gave way to the less dangerous match-tub, and since that to gun-locks, friction tubes, &c. Shakspeare in *Henry V.* says:

> " And the nimble gunner
> With *linstock* now the devilish cannon touches,
> And down goes all before them."

LINTRES. Ancient canoes capable of carrying three lintrarii.

LIP. Insolence and bounce.

LIPPER. A sea which washes over the weather chess-tree, perhaps *leaper*. Also, the spray from small waves breaking against a ship's bows.

LIPPING. Making notches on the edge of a cutlass or sword.

LIPS OF SCARPHS. The substance left at the ends, which would otherwise become sharp, and be liable to split.

LIQUORS. A term applicable to all fluids, but at sea it is expressly applied to alcoholic spirits.

LIRA. An Italian coin. A silver coin of about tenpence sterling.

LISBONINE. A national denomination for the moidore.

LISSOM. Active, supple.

LIST, To. To incline to one side; as "the ship has a list to port," *i.e.* leans over to that side.

LIST. A roll of names, as the army and navy lists; but usually at sea it means the doctor's list. Also, the abbreviation for *enlist*. "Why did you list?" said when a man is grumbling who has entered a service voluntarily.

LIST AND RECEIPT. The official document sent with officers or men of any description, discharged from one ship to another; it merely states the names and qualities, with the date of discharge.

LISTER. A sort of three-pronged harpoon used in the salmon fisheries; also, a light spear for killing fish in general.

LISTING. A narrow strip cut off the edge of a plank, in order to expose for examination, and get at, a vessel's timbers.

LITTER. A sort of hurdle bed, on which to carry wounded men from the field to the boats.

LITTORAL. Relating to a coast; often used as synonymous with seaboard.

LITTORARIÆ. Ancient coasting vessels.

LIVE, To. To be able to withstand the fury of the elements; said of a boat or ship, &c.

LIVE-LUMBER. Passengers, *ladies*, landsmen, cattle, sheep, pigs, and poultry.

LIVELY. To lift lightly to the sea; as a boat, &c.

LIVER-FACED. Mean and cowardly, independent of complexion.

LIVERY-ARROW. A missile formerly supplied to our ships of war.

LIVE-SHELL. One filled with its charge of powder or other combustible. It is also called a *loaded shell*.

LIVID SKY. That blackish red and blue which pervade the sky, previous to an easterly gale, at sea :—

> "Deep midnight now involves the livid skies
> Where eastern breezes, yet enervate, rise."--*Falconer.*

LIZARD. A piece of rope, sometimes with two legs, and one or more iron thimbles spliced into it. It is used for various purposes; one is often made fast to the topsail-tye, for the bunt-lines to reeve through, to confine them to the centre of the yard. A lizard with a tail and thimble is used as a fair lead, to lead out where the lift runs in a line with the object. The lower boom topping-lift is thus helped by carrying the lizard out to the fore-brace block. In yards sent aloft ready for crossing, the lizard confines the yard rope until the order is given, "Sway across," when, letting the lizard run, all cross simultaneously.

LIZIERE. In fortification, a word sometimes used for *berm* (which see). A narrow bank of earth supporting the parapet when deformed by fire.

LLANOS [Sp. *plains*]. Immense plains in S. America, with alternate arid patches and verdure.

LLOYD'S. An establishment which, from a subscription coffee-house, has grown to a society which has transacted the bulk of the British insurance business regularly since 1601; and even before that period assurers had met there "time out of mind." A register is kept of every ship, whether foreign or English, with the place where it was built, the materials used in its construction, its age, state of repair, and general character.

LLOYD'S AGENTS. Persons appointed in all parts of the commercial world, to forward accounts of the arrivals and departures of vessels, or any information interesting to the underwriters.

LLOYD'S LIST. A gazette, published formerly twice a week, but latterly daily, under the superintendence of a committee chosen by the subscribers, and transmitted over the whole world.

LLOYD'S REGISTER. An annual list of British and foreign shipping, ranked by letter and number in different classes.

LLOYD'S SURVEYORS. Practical persons specially appointed in London, and most of the outports of the United Kingdom, to investigate the state and condition of merchant-ships for the underwriters.

LOADED-SHELL. A shell filled with lead, to be thrown from a mortar. The term is also used for *live-shells*.

LOADING-CHAMBER. The paterero, or inserting piece in breech-loading.

LOADING OF A SHIP. *See* Cargo and Lading.

LOADSMAN. A pilot, or person who conducts into or out of harbours.

LOADSTONE. *See* Magnet and Dipping-needle.

LOAD WATER-LINE. The draught of water exhibited when the ship is properly loaded; in a word, her proper displacement, not always sufficiently considered.

LOAD WATER-SECTION. A horizontal section at the load water-line in the shipbuilder's draught.

LOAFER. One who hangs about a dock, ready for every job except a hard one.

LOATH TO DEPART. Probably the first line of some favourite song; formerly the air was sounded in men-of-war, when going foreign, for the women and children to quit the ship.

LOB. A sluggish booby; whence *lubber*. Also, that part of a tree where it first divides into branches.

LOBBY. A name sometimes given to an apartment close before the great cabin bulkhead.

LOB-COCK. A lubber; an old term of utter contempt.

LOBLOLLY. A name formerly applied to pottage, burgoo, or gruel.

LOBLOLLY-BOY. A man who attended the surgeon and his assistants, to summon the sick, and attend on them. A man is now stationed in the bay, under the designation of *sick-berth attendant.*

LOBSCOUSE. An olla-podrida of salt-meat, biscuit, potatoes, onions, spices, &c., minced small and stewed together. (*See* LAPS-COURSE.)

LOBSTER. A well-known marine crustacean, *Astacus marinus.* Also, red-coats of old; whence *lobster-box,* a colloquialism for barracks.

LOBSTER-BOAT. A bluff, clincher-built vessel, fitted with a well, to preserve the lobsters alive.

LOBSTER-TOAD. *See* DEEP-SEA CRAB.

LOB-TAILING. The act of the sperm whale in violently beating the water with its tail.

LOB-WORM. A worm found at low-water in sand, esteemed for bait.

LOCAL ATTRACTION. The effect of the iron in a ship on her compasses; it varies with the position of a compass in a ship, also with that of a ship on the earth's surface, and with the direction of the ship's head. In iron ships it is affected by the line of direction in which they are built. Its detection and remedies are amongst the most important studies of navigators of iron ships and steamers.

LOCAL MARINE-BOARD. *See* MARINE BOARDS.

LOCH. Gaelic for lake, in Scotland and Ireland. In Scotland also an arm of the sea, where the tides ebb and flow; on the east coast called a *firth,* though on the west mostly termed a *loch.*

LOCHABER AXE. A formidable weapon once used by the Highlanders.

LOCK. The striking instrument by which fire is produced for the discharge of a gun, containing the cock, the hammer, the pan, &c. It was first introduced in naval ordnance by Sir Charles Douglas, and has now given way to the *detonating hammer* and friction tube, as the old match and the salamander did to the lock.

LOCK. A spelling of *loch* (which see). Also, the general name for any works made to confine or raise the water of a river; a canal inclosed between the sluice-gate above and the flood-gate below.

LOCK, To. To entangle the lower yards when tacking.

LOCKAGE. The cost of passing vessels through canal-locks.

LOCKER. Divisions in cabins and store-rooms.—*Boatswain's locker.* A chest in small craft wherein material for working upon rigging is kept. —*Chain-locker* or *chain-well,* where the chain-cables are kept; best abreast the main-mast, as central weight, but often before the fore-mast.—*Davy Jones' locker.* The bottom of the sea, where nothing is lost, because you know where it is.—*Shot-lockers,* near the pump-well in the hold.. Also, the receptacle round the coamings of hatchways.

LOCKET. The chape of a sword-scabbard.

LOCK-FAST. A modified principle in the breech-loading of fire-arms.

LOCKING-IN. The alternate clues and bodies of the hammocks when hung up.

LOCK, STOCK, AND BARREL. An expression derived from fire-arms, and meaning the whole.

LOC-MEN, OR LOCO-MEN. An old term for pilots.

LOCOMOTIVE-POWER. The force of sails and wind, or steam.

LODE-MANAGE, OR LODEMANSHIP. The hire of a pilot. It also meant both pilotage and seamanship; whence Chaucer—

> "His herborough, his moone, and his lodemanage,
> There was none such from Hull to Cartage."

LODE-MEREGE. In the laws of Oleron, seems identical with *lode-manage.*

LODE-SHIP. A pilot boat, which was also employed in fishing ; it is mentioned in statute 31 Edward III. c. 2.

LODESMEN. An Anglo-Saxon word for pilots.

LODE-STAR. The north star. But Spenser alludes to any star as a guide to mariners :—

> "Like as a ship, whose lode-star, suddenly
> Cover'd with clouds, her pilot hath dismay'd."

Shakspeare coincides with this, in comparing Hermia's eyes to lode-stars.

LODGE ARMS. The word of command to an armed party preparatory to their breaking off.

LODGEMENT. In fortification, an established footing, such as a besieger makes by throwing up hasty cover, against the fire of the defenders, on any freshly gained post.

LODGING KNEES, OR DECK-BEAM KNEES. Those riding on the hanging or dagger-knees, and fixed horizontally in the ship's frame.

LODIA. A large trading boat of the White Sea.

LOE, OR LAWE. An eminence, whether natural or artificial.

LOFTY SHIPS. Once a general name for square-rigged vessels :—

> "A mackerel sky and mares' tails
> Make lofty ships carry low sails."

LOG-BOARD. Two boards shutting together like a book, and divided into several columns, in which to record, through the hours of the day and night, the direction of the wind and the course of the ship, with all the material occurrences, together with the latitude by observation. From this table the officers work the ship's way, and compile their journals. The whole being written by the mate of the watch with chalk, is rubbed out every day at noon. Now a slate is more generally used.

LOG-BOOK. Mostly called the log, is a journal into which the log-board is daily transcribed, together with any other circumstance deserving notice. The intermediate divisions or watches are usually signed by the commanding officer. It is also divided into *harbour-log* and *sea-log.*

LOG-CANOE. One hollowed out of a single log. (*See* CANOE.)

LOGGED. Entered in the log. A very serious punishment, not long disused, as a mark of disgrace, by recording the omissions of an officer. It may yet be demanded if arrest ensues.

LOGGED. When a ship is on her beam ends, or in that state in which she is unmanageable at sea. (*See* WATER-LOGGED.)

LOGGERHEAD, OR LOGGER-HEAT. A round ball of iron attached to a long handle with a hook at the end of it. It heats tar by being made hot in the fire, and then plunged into the tar-bucket. It was also used to pound cocoa before chocolate was supplied. Also, an upright rounded piece of wood, near the stern of a whale-boat, for catching a turn of the line to. Also, a name given to a well-known turtle, *Chelonia caouana*, from its having a great head; it is sometimes called the *whooper* or *whapper*. (*See* TURTLE.)

LOG-GLASS. The sand-glass used at heaving the log to obtain the rate of sailing. It is a 28 seconds glass for slow sailing, and 14 seconds for fast sailing.

LOG-LINE AND LOG-SHIP. A small line about 100 fathoms long, fastened to the log-ship by means of two legs, one of which passes through a hole at the corner, and is knotted on the opposite side, while the other leg is attached by a pin fixed into another hole so as to draw out when *stop* is called, *i.e.* when the glass has run out. This line, from the distance of 10, 12, or 15 fathoms of the log-ship, has certain knots or divisions, which ought to be 47 feet 4 inches from each other, though it was the common practice at sea not to have them above 42 feet. The estimate of the ship's way or distance run is done by observing the length of the line unwound whilst the glass is running; for so many knots as run out in that time, so many miles the ship sails in an hour.—*To heave the log* is to throw it into the water on the lee-side, well out of the wake, letting it run until it gets beyond the eddies, then a person holding the glass turns it up just as the first mark, or stray-line, goes out, from which the knots begin to be reckoned. The log is, however, at best, a precarious way of computing, and must be corrected by experience. The inventor of it is not known, and no mention is made of it till the year 1607, in an East India voyage, published by Purchas. The mode before, and even now in some colliers, and in native craft in the East Indies, is to throw a *log* or chip overboard at the foremost channel-plate, and to walk aft, keeping up with it until it passes the stern, thus estimating (and closely too by practice) the rate of motion. Other methods have been invented by various people, but *Massey's Patent Log* gives the most accurate measurement. The same principle is also applied to the deep-sea sounding-lead.

LOGWOOD. Dyewood, *Hæmatoxylon campechianum*. It occurs on both sides of the American coasts near the Isthmus of Darien, and is a great article of trade, varying from £5 to £10 per ton. Recent discoveries of the products of coal have reduced the price.

LOICH. A statute term, comprehending the fishes lobbe, ling, and cod.

LONDAGE. An old term for landing from a boat.

LONDON WAGGON. The tender which carried the impressed men from off the tower to the receiving-ship at the Nore.

LONGÆ. Roman row-boats built to carry a large number of men.

LONG AND SHORT BOARDS. *See* TACK and HALF-TACK.

LONG BALLS. Engaging beyond the reach of carronades.

LONG BOAT. Is carvel-built, full, flat, and high, and is usually the largest boat belonging to a ship, furnished with spars and sails, and may be armed and equipped for cruizing short distances ; her principal employ, however, is to bring heavy stores on board, and also to go up small rivers to fetch water, wood, &c. At sea it is stowed between the fore and main masts. Not used in the navy. (*See* LAUNCH.)

LONG-BOW. A noted weapon formerly supplied to our men-of-war.

LONG CHALKS. Great strides. (*See* CHALK.)

LONGER. Each row of casks in the hold, athwart. Also, the fore and aft space allotted to a hammock; the longers reckoned similarly to last.

LONG-GASKETS. Those used for sea service; the opposite of *harbour gaskets* (which see).

LONGIE. A name of the foolish guillemot, *Uria troile*, in the north.

LONGITUDE. Is an arc of the equator, or any parallel of latitude, contained between the meridian of a place and that of Greenwich, or any other first meridian. These arcs being similar, are expressed by the same number of degrees and miles, though the absolute distance on the earth's surface decreases as the latitude increases, for which see DEPARTURE. East longitude extends 180 degrees to the right, when looking north, and west longitude as many to the left of the first meridian.

LONGITUDE, GEOCENTRIC. The angular distance of a heavenly body from the first point of Aries, measured upon the ecliptic, as viewed from the earth.

LONGITUDE, HELIOCENTRIC. The angular distance of a body from the first point of Aries, measured upon the ecliptic, as viewed from the sun.

LONGITUDE BY ACCOUNT. The distance east and west, as computed from the ship's course and distance run, carried forward from the last astronomical determination.

LONGITUDE BY CHRONOMETER. Is estimated by the difference between the time at the place, and the time indicated by chronometer.

LONGITUDE BY LUNAR OBSERVATION. The longitude calculated by observing the moon's angular distance from the sun or a fixed star. It is the only check on chronometers, and very valuable in long voyages, though now much neglected, since the establishment of compulsory examination in the merchant service, which does not require lunars.

LONGITUDE OF A CELESTIAL BODY. An arc of the ecliptic, contained between the first point of Aries and a circle of longitude passing through the centre of the body.

LONGITUDINAL SECTION. In ship-building, a line which cuts the draught of a vessel lengthwise.

LONG-JAWED. The state of rope when its strands are straightened by being much strained and untwisted, and from its pliability will coil both ways.

LONG-LEAVE. Permission to visit friends at a distance.

LONG-LEGGED. Said of a vessel drawing much water.—*Long leggers*, lean schooners. Longer than ordinary proportion to breadth. Swift.

LONG OYSTER. A name of the sea cray-fish.

LONG-SERVICE. A cable properly served to prevent chafing under particular use.

'LONG-SHORE. A word used rather contemptuously for *along-shore;* land usage.—*'Long-shore fellows*, landsmen pretenders.—*'Long-shore owners*, those merchants who become notorious for sending their ships to sea scantily provided with stores and provisions.

LONG-SHOT. A distant range. It is also used to express a long way; a far-fetched explanation; something incredible.

LONG STERN-TIMBERS. *See* STERN-TIMBERS.

LONG STROKE. The order to a boat's crew to stretch out and hang on her.

LONG-TACKLES. Those overhauled down for hoisting up topsails to be bent. Long-tackle blocks have two sheaves of different sizes placed one above the other, as in fiddle-blocks.

LONG-TAILS. A sobriquet for the Chinese.

LONG TIMBERS, or LONG TOP-TIMBERS. Synonymous with *double futtocks*. Timbers in the cant-bodies, reaching from the dead-wood to the head of the second futtock, and forming a floor.

LONG TOGS. Landsman's clothes.

LONG TOM, or LONG TOM TURKS. Pieces of lengthy ordnance for chasers, &c.

LONG VOYAGE. One in which the Atlantic Ocean is crossed.

LONG-WINDED WHISTLERS. Chase-guns.

LOO, or LOE. A little round hill or heap of stones.—*Under the loo*, is shelter from the wind; to leeward.

LOOF. The after part of a ship's bow, before the chess-tree, or that where the planks begin to be incurvated as they approach the stem. Hence, the guns which lie here are called *loof-pieces*.

LOOF. Usually pronounced and spelled *luff* (which see).

LOOK, To. The bearing or direction, as, *she looks up*, is approaching her course.—*A plank looks fore and aft*, means, is placed in that direction.

LOOK-OUT. Watchful attention; there is always a look-out kept from the forecastle, foretopsail-yard, or above, to watch for any dangerous object lying near a ship's track, for any strange sail heaving in sight, &c.; the officer of the watch accordingly calls frequently from the quarter-deck to the masthead-man appointed for this service, "Look out afore there."

LOOK OUT FOR SQUALLS. Beware; cautionary.

LOOM. The handle of an oar. Also, the track of a fish.

LOOM, To. An indistinct enlarged appearance of any distant object in light fogs, as the coast, ships, &c.; "that land looms high," "that ship looms large." The effect of refraction.

LOOM-GALE. An easy gale of wind, in which a ship can carry her whole topsails atrip.

LOON, or LUNDE. The great northern diver, *Colymbus glacialis*. A bird about the size of a goose, which frequents the northern seas, where "as straight as a loon's leg," is a common comparison.

LOOP. A bight or bend. The winding of a river.

LOOP-HOLES. Small openings made in the walls of a castle, or a fortication, for musketry to fire through. Also, certain apertures formed in the bulk-heads, hatches, and other parts of a merchant-ship, through which small arms might be fired on an enemy who boarded her, and for close fight. They were formerly called *meurtrières*, and were introduced in British slave-vessels.

LOOPS OF A GUN-CARRIAGE. The iron eye-bolts to which the tackles are hooked.

LOOSE, To. To unfurl or cast loose any sail, in order to its being set, or dried after rain.

LOOSE A ROPE, To. To cast it off, or let it go.

LOOSE FALL. The losing of a whale after an apparently good opportunity for striking it.

LOOSE ICE. A number of pieces near each other, but through which the ship can make her way.

LOOSERS. Men appointed to loose the sails.

LOOSING FOR SEA. Weighing the anchor.

LOOT. Plunder, or pillage; a term adopted from China.

LOOVERED BATTENS. The battens that inclose the upper part of the well. (*See* LOOVER-WAYS.)

LOOVER-WAYS. Battens or boards placed at a certain angle, so as to admit air, but not wet; a kind of Venetian-blind.

LOP AND TOP. The top and branches of a felled tree.

LOP-SIDED. Uneven; one side larger than the other.

LORCHA. A swift Chinese sailing vessel carrying guns.

LORD OF MISRULE. *See* MASTER OF MISRULE.

LORDS COMMISSIONERS. *See* COMMISSIONERS.

LORD WARDEN OF THE CINQUE PORTS. A magistrate who has the jurisdiction of the ports or havens so called. Generally held by one high in office, or an old minister.

LORICA. A defensive coat-armour made of leather; when iron plates were applied, it became a *jack*.

LORN. A northern name for the crested cormorant, *Phalacrocorax cristatus*.

LORRELL. An old term for a lubberly fellow.

LOSE WAY, To. When a ship slackens her progress in the water.

LOSING THE NUMBER OF THE MESS. Dead, drowned, or killed. (*See* NUMBER.)

LOSING GROUND. Dropping to leeward while working; the driftage.

LOSS. Total loss is the insurance recovered under peril, according to the

LOSSAN —— LOWER-HOPE   457

invoice price of the goods when embarked, together with the premium of insurance. Partial loss upon either ship or goods, is that proportion of the prime cost which is equal to the diminution in value occasioned by the damage. (*See* INSURANCE.)

LOSSAN. A Manx or Erse term for the luminosity of the sea.

LOST. The state of being foundered or cast away; said of a ship when she has either sunk, or been beat to pieces by the violence of the sea.

LOST DAY. The day which is lost in circumnavigating the globe to the westward, by making each day a little more than twenty-four hours long. (*See* GAINED DAY.)

LOST HER WAY. When the buoy is streamed, and all is ready for dropping the anchor.

LOST! LOST! When a whale *flukes, dives,* or takes tail up to "*running,*" and the boats have no chance in chasing.

LOST OR NOT LOST. A phrase originally inserted in English policies of insurance, in cases where a loss was already apprehended. It is now continued by usage, and is held not to make the contract a wager, nor more hazardous.

LOT. The abbreviation of allotment, or allowance to wife or mother. (*See* ALLOTMENT.)

LOTMAN. An old term for pirate.

LOUGH. *See* LOCH.

LOUND. Calm, out of wind.

LOW. An old term for a small hill or eminence.

LOW AND ALOFT. Sail from deck to truck: "every stitch on her."

LOWE. A flame, blaze. The torch used in the north by fish-poachers.

LOWER, To. The atmosphere to become cloudy. Also, to ease down gradually, expressed of some weighty body suspended by tackles or ropes, which, being slackened, suffer the said body to descend as slowly, or expeditiously, as occasion requires.

LOWER-BREADTH-SWEEP. The second on the builder's draught, representing the lower height of breadth, on which line is set off the main half-breadth of the ship at its corresponding timber.

LOWER COUNTER. The counter between the upper counter and the rail under the lights.

LOWER-DECKERS. The heaviest armament, usually on the lower deck.

LOWER-FINISHING. *See* FINISHINGS.

LOWER HANDSOMELY, LOWER CHEERLY. Are opposed to each other; the former being the order to lower gradually, and the latter to lower expeditiously.

LOWER-HEIGHT. *See* MAIN-BREADTH.

LOWER-HOLD. The space for cargo in a merchant-vessel, fitted with 'tween-decks.

LOWER-HOLD-BEAMS. The lowest range of beams in a merchantman.

LOWER-HOPE. A well-known reach in the Thames where ships wait for the turn of the tide.

LOWER-LIFTS. The lifts of the fore, main, and cross-jack yards.

LOWER MASTS. *See* MASTS.

LOWER TRANSIT. The opposite to the upper transit of a circumpolar star: the passage *sub polo.*

LOW LATITUDES. Those regions far removed from the poles of the earth towards the equator, 10° south or north of it.

LOW SAILS. The courses and close-reefed topsails.

LOW WATER. The lowest point to which the tide ebbs. (*See* TIDE.) Also, used figuratively for being in distress, without money.

LOXODROMIC. The line of a ship's way when sailing oblique to the meridian.

LOXODRONIUS. The *traverse table.*

LOZENGE. The diamond-cut figure. (*See* RHOMBUS.)

LUBBER, OR LUBBART. An awkward unseamanlike fellow; from a northern word implying a clownish dolt. A boatswain defined them as "fellows fitted with teeth longer than their hair," alluding to their appetites.

LUBBER-LAND. A kind of El Dorado in sea-story, or country of pleasure without work, all sharing alike.

LUBBER'S HOLE. The vacant space between the head of a lower-mast and the edge of the top, so termed from timid climbers preferring that as an easier way for getting into the top than trusting themselves to the futtock-shrouds. The term has been used for any cowardly evasion of duty.

LUBBER'S POINT. A black vertical line or mark in the compass-bowl in the direction of the ship's head, by which the angle between the magnetic meridian and the ship's line of course is shown.

LUBRICATOR. The oil or similar material applied to the bearings of machinery to obviate friction. Also, special preparations of the same included in cartridges for rifled firearms, to prevent the fouling from the burnt powder adhering to the interior of the bore.

LUCE. The old word for a full-grown pike or jack, immortalized by Shakspeare.

LUCIDA. The bright star or *a* of each constellation.

LUCKEN. An unsplit haddock half-dry.

LUCKY MINIE'S LINES. The long stems of the sea-plant *Chorda filum.*

LUCKY-PROACH. A northern term for father-lasher, *Cottus scorpius.*

LUFF, OR LOOFE. The order to the helmsman, so as to bring the ship's head up more to windward. Sometimes called springing a luff. Also, the air or wind. Also, an old familiar term for lieutenant. Also, the fullest or roundest part of a ship's bows. Also, the weather-leech of a sail.

LUFF AND LIE. A very old sea-term for hugging the wind closely.

LUFF AND TOUCH HER! Try how near the wind she will come. (*See* TOUCH.)

LUFF INTO A HARBOUR, To. To sail into it, shooting head to wind,

gradually. A ship is accordingly said to spring her luff when she yields
to the effort of the helm, by sailing nearer to the wind, or coming to, and
does not shake the wind out of her sails until, by shortening all, she
reaches her anchorage.

LUFF ROUND, or LUFF A-LEE. The extreme of the movement, by
which it is intended to throw the ship's head up suddenly into the wind,
in order to go about, or to lessen her way to avoid danger.

LUFF TACKLE. A purchase composed of a double and single block, the
standing end of the rope being fast to the single block, and the fall coming
from the double. This name is given to any large tackle not destined for
any particular place, but to be variously used as occasion may require.
It is larger than the jigger-tackle, but smaller than the fore and main
yard-tackles or the stay-tackles. (*See* LUFF UPON LUFF.)

LUFF UPON LUFF. One luff-tackle applied to the fall of another, to
afford an increase of purchase.

LUG. The *Arenicola piscatorum*, a sand-worm much used for bait. Also,
of old, the term for a perch or rod used in land-measuring, containing
16½ feet, and which may have originated the word *log*.

LUGAR [Sp.] A name for watering-places on the Spanish coast.

LUG-BOAT. The fine Deal boats which brave the severest weather; they
are rigged as luggers, and dip the yards in tacking. They really constitute a large description of life-boat.

LUGGER. A small vessel with quadrilateral or four-cornered cut sails, set
fore-and-aft, and may have two or three masts. French coasters usually
rig thus, and are called *chasse marées;* but with us it is confined to fishing
craft and ships' boats; some carry topsails. During the war of 1810 to
1814 French luggers, as well as Guernsey privateers, were as large as 300
tons, and carried 18 guns. One captured inside the Needles in 1814,
carried a mizen-topsail. The *Long Bet* of Plymouth, a well-known
smuggler, long defied the Channel gropers, but was taken in 1816.

LUGS. The ears of a bombshell, to which the hooks are applied in lifting it.

LUG-SAIL. A sail used in boats and small vessels. It is in form like
a gaff-sail, but depends entirely on the rope of the luff for its stability.
The yard is two-thirds of the breadth at foot, and is slung at one-fourth
from the luff. On the mast is an iron hoop or traveller, to which it is
hoisted. The tack may be to windward, or at the heel of the mast amidships. It is powerful, but has the inconvenience of requiring to be
lowered and shifted on the mast at every tack, unless the tack be secured
amidships. Much used in the barca-longa, navigated by the Spaniards.

LULL. The brief interval of moderate weather between the gusts of wind
in a gale. Also, an abatement in the violence of surf.

LULL-BAG. A wide canvas hose in whalers for conducting blubber into
the casks, as it is "made off."

LUMBER. Logs as they arrive at the mills. Also, timber of any size,
sawed or split for use. Also, things stowed without order.

LUMBERER. One who cuts timber (generally in gangs) in the forests of North America during the winter, and, on the melting of the snow, navigates it, first by stream-driving the separate logs down the spring torrents, then in bays or small rafts down the wider streams, and finally in rafts of thousands of square yards of surface down the navigable rivers, to the mills or to the port of shipment.

LUMIERE CENDREE. A term adopted from the French to signify the ash-coloured faint illumination of the dark part of the moon's surface about the time of new moon, caused by sunlight reflected from the earth.

LUMP. A stout heavy lighter used in our dockyards for carrying anchors, chains, or heavy stores to or from vessels. Also, the trivial name of the baggety, an ugly fish, likewise called the sea-owl, *Cyclopterus lumpus.* Also, undertaking any work by the lump or whole.—*By the lump,* a sudden fall out of the slings or out of a top; altogether.

LUMPERS. So named from labouring at lump or task work. Labourers employed to load and unload a merchant ship when in harbour. In the north the term is applied to those who furnish ballast to ships.

LUMP SUM. A full payment of arrears, and not by periodical instalments of money.

LUNAR. The brief epithet for the method of finding the longitude by the moon and sun or moon and stars. (*See* WORKING A LUNAR.)

LUNAR DAY. The interval between a departure and return of the moon to the meridian.

LUNAR DISTANCES. An important element in finding the longitude at sea, by what is termed nautical astronomy. It is effected by measuring the apparent distance of the moon from the sun, planet, or certain bright stars, and comparing it with that given in the nautical almanac, for every third hour of Greenwich time.

LUNAR INEQUALITY. *See* VARIATION OF THE MOON.

LUNAR OBSERVATIONS. The method of observing the apparent distances between given celestial objects, and then clearing the angles from the effects of parallax and refraction.

LUNAR TABLES. The tabulated logarithmic aid for correcting the apparent distance, and facilitating the reduction of the observations.

LUNATION. The period in which the moon goes through every variety of phase; that is, one synodical revolution.

LUNETTE. In fortification, a work composed of two faces meeting in a salient angle, from the inner extremities of which two short flanks run towards the rear, leaving an open gorge; it is generally applied only in connection with other works. Prize-masters will recollect that *lunette* is also the French name for a spy-glass or telescope.

LUNGE [a corruption of *allonge*]. A pass or thrust with a sword; a shove with a boarding-pike.

LUNI-SOLAR. A chronological term; it is the moon's cycle multiplied into that of the sun.

LUNI-SOLAR PRECESSION. *See* PRECESSION.

LUNT. A match-cord to fire great guns—a match for a linstock.

LUNTRA. *See* FELUCCA.

LURCA. An old term for a small Mediterranean coaster.

LURCH. A heavy roll, weather or lee, as occasioned by a sea suddenly striking or receding from the weather-bilge of the vessel.—*To be left in the lurch* is to be left behind in a case where others make their escape.

LUSH. Intoxicating fluids of any kind. Also, a northern term for splashing in water.

LUSORIÆ. Ancient vessels of observation or pleasure.

LUST. An archaism of *list.* (*See* LIST.)

LUTE-STERN. Synonymous with *pink-stern.*

LUTINGS. The dough stoppages to the seams of the coppers, &c., when distilling sea water.

LYING. The situation of a whale when favourable for sticking—the "lie" usually occurs after feeding.

LYING ALONG. *See* LAYING ALONG.

LYING ON HIS OARS. Taking a rest; at ease.

LYING-TO. *See* LIE-TO.

LYM. From the Celtic *leim,* a port; as Lyme and Lymington.

LYMPHAD. The heraldic term for an old-fashioned ship or galley.

LYNCH-LAW. A word recently imported into our parlance from America, signifying illegal and revengeful execution at the wish of a tumultuous mob.

LYRA. One of the ancient northern constellations. Also, a name of the gray gurnard, or *crooner* (which see).

LYRIE. The name in the Firth of Forth for the *Cottus cataphractus,* or armed bull-head.

LYTER. The old orthography for *lighter* (which see).

LYTHE. A name for the pollack, *Gadus pollachius.* Also, the coal-fish in its fourth year.

M.

MAASH. A large trading vessel of the Nile.

MACE. A war-club of old.

MACHICOULIS. A projecting gallery over gateways, or walls insufficiently flanked: being open at the bottom between its supporting corbels, it allows of defending the foot of the wall.

MACKEREL. The *Scomber vulgaris,* a well-known sea-fish.

MACKEREL-BOAT. A stout clinch-worked vessel, with a large foresail, spritsail, and mizen.

MACKEREL-SKY. *See* CIRRO-CUMULUS.

MACKEREL-STURE. A northern name for the tunny, *Scomber thynnus.*

MACULÆ. Dark temporary spots which are very frequently observed upon the sun's disc: they are of various forms, surrounded by a lighter shade or penumbra.

MAD. The state of a compass needle, the polarity of which has been injured.

MADDY, OR MADDIE. A large species of mussel abundant among the rocks of the western islands of Scotland and Wales.

MADE. A professional term for having obtained a commission, or being promoted. Also, in some points synonymous with *built.* (*See* MASTS, &c.)

MADE-EYE. Synonymous with *flemish-eye* (which see).

MADE MASTS. The large masts made in several pieces. A ship's lower mast is a made spar; her topmast is a whole spar.—*Made block* is one having its shell composed of different pieces.

MADRIERS. Long and broad planks, used for supporting the earth in mining. Also, an old term for sheathing.

MAGAZINE. A place built for the safe-keeping of ammunition; afloat it is confined to a close room, in the fore or after part, or both, of a ship's hold, as low down as possible; it is lighted occasionally by means of candles fixed in the light-room adjoining it, and no person is allowed to enter it with a lamp or candle. (*See* LIGHT-ROOM.)

MAGELLANIC CLOUDS. A popular term for the two *Nebiculæ*, or great cloudy-looking spots in the southern heavens, which are found to consist of a vast number of nebulæ and clusters of stars.

MAGELLAN JACKET. A name given to a watch-coat with a hood, worn in high latitudes—first used by Cook's people.

MAGGED. Worn, fretted, and stretched rope, as a magged brace. Also, reproved.

MAGNET. *See* COMPASS.

MAGNETIC AMPLITUDE. The angle between the east or west point of a compass and any heavenly body at its rising or setting.

MAGNETIC AZIMUTH. An arc of the horizon intercepted between the azimuth circle of a celestial object and the magnetic meridian.

MAGNETIC COMPENSATOR. An iron plate fixed near the compass, to neutralize the effect of local attraction upon the needle.

MAGNETIC NEEDLE. Applied to theodolites, ships' compasses, &c. A balanced needle, highly magnetized, which points to the magnetic pole, when not influenced by the local attraction of neighbouring iron. The magnetism may be discharged by blows, or a fall; hence, after an action at sea, the needles are often found to be useless, until re-magnetized.

MAGNETIC STORM. An extraordinary magnetic action indicated by delicate magnetometers in a magnetic observatory, not perceptible on ordinary magnets.

MAGNETIC TELEGRAPH. An instrument for communicating messages by means of magnetism.

MAGNITUDE OF AN ECLIPSE. The proportion which the eclipsed part of the surface of the sun or moon bears to the diameter; it is some-times expressed in digits, but more frequently as a decimal, the diameter being taken as unity.

MAGNITUDES OF STARS. The relative degrees of apparent size in which the fixed stars are arranged, and classed according to the intensity of their light. The first six classes, designated by Greek letters, include all those which are distinctly visible to the naked eye.

MAHONE, Mahonna, or Maon. A former Turkish flat-bottomed vessel of burden, mentioned among the ships of Soliman Pasha, in the siege of Diu.

MAID. A coast name of the skate.

MAIDEN. A fortress which has never been taken.

MAIL. A coat of armour. Also, a number of rings interwoven net-wise, and used for rubbing off the loose hemp from white cordage after it is made.

MAIL-SHELL. A name for the chiton.

MAIN. A continent or mainland. Also, figuratively, the ocean.

MAIN-BODY. The body of troops that marches between the advance-guard and the rear-guard of an army.

MAIN-BOOM. The spar which stretches the foot of the boom-mainsail in a fore-and-aft rigged vessel.

MAIN-BRACE. A purchase attached to the main-yard for trimming it to the wind.

MAIN-BREADTH. The broadest part of a ship at any particular timber or frame, distinguished by upper and lower heights of breadth lines.

MAIN-CAPSTAN. The after one, as distinguished from the jeer-capstan.

MAIN-COURSE. The main-sail.

MAIN-GUARD. The principal guard of a garrison town, usually posted in the place-of-arms, or the market-place.

MAIN-HOLD. That part of a ship's hold which lies near the main-hatch.

MAIN-ICE. A body of impenetrable ice apparently detached from the land, but immovable; between which and the land are lanes of water.

MAIN-JEERS. Jeers for swaying up the main-yard.

MAIN-KEEL. The principal keel, as distinguished from the false-keel and the keelson.

MAIN-PIECE. The strong horizontal beam of the windlass, supported at the ends by iron spindles in the *windlass-bitts.*

MAIN-PIECE of the Rudder. The *rudder-stock*, or piece which is connected by the *rudder-bands* to the stern-post.

MAIN-POST. The stern-post, as distinguished from the false-post and inner-post.

MAIN ROYAL-MAST. That above the main topgallant-mast.

MAIN-SAIL. This, in a square-rigged vessel, is distinguished by the so-termed *square main-sail;* in a fore-and-aft rigged vessel it obtains the name of *boom main-sail.* Brigs carry both.

MAINSAIL HAUL! The order given to haul the after-yards round when the ship is nearly head to wind in tacking.

MAIN-SHAFT. The principal shaft in machinery.

MAINSHEET-HORSE. A kind of iron dog fixed at the middle of a wooden beam, stretching across a craft's stern, from one quarter stanchion to the other; on it the mainsheet-block travels.

MAIN-SPRING. The source of continuous motion in a time-keeper. Also, that part of a musket-lock which is sunk into the stock.

MAIN-STAYSAIL. A storm-sail set between the fore and main masts.

MAIN-TACK BLOCK. A block forming part of the purchase used for hauling the main-tack down to.

MAIN-TACKLE. A large and strong tackle, hooked occasionally upon the main pendant, and used for various purposes, particularly in securing the mast, by setting up the rigging, stays, &c.

MAIN-TACKLE PENDANT. A stout piece of rope with a hook in one end, and a thimble in the other, sometimes used for hauling the main-tackle down.

MAIN-TOP BOWLINE. The bowline of the main-topsail. It is used to haul the weather-leech forward when on a wind, which makes the sail stand better.

MAIN-TOPSAIL HAUL! The order used instead of *mainsail haul,* when the mainsail is not set.

MAIN-TRANSOM. A term often applied to the *wing-transom* (which see).

MAIN-WALES. The lower wales, which are generally placed on the lower breadth, and so that the main-deck knee-bolts may come into them.

MAIN-YARD MEN. Those in the doctor's list.

MAISTER. *See* MASTER.

MAIZE. Indian corn, an article of extensive commerce in many countries. In Italy it is called *Turkey grain* and *grano d'India;* in America simply *corn,* all other grains retaining their distinctive names.

MAJOR. The next rank below that of lieutenant-colonel; the junior field-officer.

MAJOR AXIS. In the orbit of a planet, means the line joining its aphelion and perihelion.

MAJOR-GENERAL. The next in rank below the lieutenant-general.

MAJOR OF BRIGADE. *See* BRIGADE-MAJOR.

MAKE, To. Is variously applied in sea-language.

MAKE A GOOD BOARD. *See* BOARD.

MAKE A LANE THERE! The order of the boatswain for the crew to separate at muster, to facilitate the approach of any one whose name is called. (*See* LANE.)

MAKE BAD WEATHER, To. A ship rolling, pitching, or leaking violently in a gale.

MAKE FAST. A word generally used for tying or securing ropes. To fasten.

MAKE FREE WITH THE LAND, To. To approach the shore closely.

MAKE HEADWAY. A ship makes headway when she advances through the water.

MAKE IT SO. The order of a commander to confirm the time, sunrise, noon, or sunset, reported to him by the officer of the watch.

MAKE LEEWAY, To. To drift to leeward of the course.

MAKE READY! Be prepared.

MAKES. This expresses coming on; as, the tide makes, &c.

MAKE SAIL, To. To increase the quantity of sail already set, either by letting out reefs, or by setting additional sails.

MAKE STERNWAY, To. To retreat, or move stern foremost.

MAKE THE LAND, To. To see it from a distance after a voyage.

MAKE WATER, To. Usually signifies the act of a ship leaking, unless the epithet *foul* be added. (*See* FOUL WATER.)

MAKING IRON. One of the caulker's tools; it has a groove in it, and is used after the caulking iron to finish off the seam. (*See* MEAKING.)

MAKING OFF. Cutting the flensed blubber of a whale into pieces, fitted to pass in at the bilge-holes of the butts which receive it.

MALA FIDES. In admiralty law, not to be presumed, even under concealment of letters, or deviation from truth in formal papers.

MALDUCK. One of the names given to the fulmar, *Procellaria glacialis*.

MALKIN. A joint-staff sponge, for cleaning out a piece of ordnance.

MALINGERER [Fr. *malingre*]. One who counterfeits illness for the purpose of avoiding duty.

MALLARD. The male of the wild duck (*Anas boschas*).

MALLEMAK, OR MOLLYMAUK. A sea-bird; the *Procellaria glacialis*, called also *fulmar* (which see).

MALLEMAROKING. The visiting and carousing of seamen in the Greenland ships.

MALLET. A wooden hammer, of which there are several sorts.—*A caulking mallet* is employed to drive the oakum into the seams of a ship. The head of this mallet is long, cylindrical, and hooped with iron.— *Serving mallet.* A cylindrical piece of wood with a groove on one side and a handle on the other. It is used in serving the rigging, binding the spun yarn more firmly about it than could be done by hand.

MALLOW. A northern name for the sea-plant *Zostera marina*.

MALTHA. Mineral pitch.

MAN. A ship is frequently spoken of as *man;* as man-of-war, merchantman, Guineaman, East or West Indiaman, Greenlandman, &c.

MAN, To. To provide a competent number of hands for working and fighting a ship; to place people for duty, as "Man the barge;" "Man the capstan;" "Man the yards," &c.

MAN, ISLE OF, BATTERY. A name given to the three guns mounted on ships' turrets.

MANACLE. A handcuff.

MANARVEL, To. To pilfer small stores.

MANATEE, MANATI, OR SEA-COW (*Manatus americanus*). A herbivorous aquatic animal of the order *Sirenia*, found in the West Indies and South American rivers. Another species (*Manatus senegalensis*) inhabits the west coast of Africa.

MAN-BOUND. Detained in port in consequence of being short of complement.

MAN-BROKER. Synonymous with *crimp* (which see).

MANBY'S MORTAR. An efficient apparatus for throwing a shell with a line and chain attached to it, over a stranded vessel, and thereby opening a communication between the wreck and the shore.

MANCHE OF MANGALORE. A flat-bottomed boat of burden, about 25 to 35 feet long, 6 or 7 feet broad, and 4 or 5 feet deep, for landing the cargoes of the *patamirs*, which are discharged and loaded at the mouth of the river. These boats are sewed together like the Masulah boats of Madras.—The *Manché of Calicut* is very similar to the foregoing, with the exception of a raking stem for the purpose of taking the beach.

MANCHINEEL. *Hippomane mancinella*, a tree which grows to a vast size on the coasts of the Caribbee Isles and neighbouring continent. The fruit and sap are highly poisonous; but sleeping beneath the branches does not cause death, as was erroneously supposed.

MANDARIN. A Portuguese word derived from *mandare*, " to command." It is unknown to the Chinese and Tonquinese, who style their dignitaries "quahn."

MANDILION. A loose boat-cloak of former times.

MANDRIL. A wooden cylinder for forming paper cartridges.

MANGER. A small berthing in the bows, extending athwart the deck of a ship-of-war immediately within the hawse-holes, and separated on the after-part from the rest of the deck by the *manger-board*, a strong coaming rather higher than the hawse-holes, serving to prevent the ingress of the sea when the cables are bent; this water is returned to the sea through the manger-scuppers, which are made large for that purpose.

MANGONEL. An ancient military engine in the form of a gigantic crossbow, discharging large darts and stones, used in battering fortified places: a kind of balista.

MANGONIZE, To. To traffic in slaves.

MAN-HANDLE, To. To move by force of men, without levers or tackles.

MAN-HOLE. The aperture, secured by a door, in the upper part of a steam-boiler, which allows a person to enter for repairing it or removing the deposit or crust of salt.

MAN-HUNTING. The impress service.

MANIFEST. An official inventory of the cargo of a merchant ship, specifying the name and tonnage of the vessel, the description of goods, the names of shippers and consignees, and the marks of each package.

MANILLA ROPE. A valuable cordage made in the Philippines, which, not being subject to rot, does not require to be tarred.

MANIPLE. A small armed party; a term derived from the subdivision of a Roman cohort.

MANŒUVRE. A dexterous management of anything connected with the ship.

MAN-OF-WAR. Any vessel in the royal navy.

MAN-OF-WAR BIRD, OR FRIGATE BIRD. *Frigata aquila*, a sea-bird of the family *Pelicanidæ*, found in the tropics, remarkable for the length of its wings and rapidity of its flight.

MAN-OF-WAR FASHION. A state of order, tidiness, and good discipline.

MAN-OF-WAR'S MAN. A seaman belonging to the royal navy.

MANOMETER. A steam-gauge.

MAN OVERBOARD! A cry which excites greater activity in a ship than any other, from the anxious desire to render assistance.

MAN SHIP! Is to range the people on the yards and rigging in readiness to give three cheers, as a salute on meeting, parting company, or other occasions; a good old custom now slackening. In war, as instanced by the *Nymphe* and *Cleopatra*, the meeting of enemies was truly chivalrous; though there was a case where the response was so moderated as to be laughed at as "a cheer with the chill on."

MANSIONS OF THE MOON. *See* LUNAR MANSIONS.

MANTILLIS. A kind of shield anciently fixed upon the tops of ships as a cover for archers.

MANTLETS. Large movable musket-proof blinds used by besiegers at the head of a sap, now mostly fitted to embrasures to protect the gunners from sharpshooters: they are best when made of plaited rope.

MANUAL-EXERCISE. The regulated series of motions for handling and carrying the musket, except what is connected with firing it.

MANUBALIST. A stout cross-bow.

MANXMAN. A seaman or native of the Isle of Man.

MANZERA. A vessel used in the Adriatic for carrying cattle.

MAON. *See* MAHONE, PORT OF.

MAR. Latin *mare*, the sea: a prefix, as Margate, the sea-way, &c.

MARABUT. A sail which galleys hoisted in bad weather. Also, small edifices on Barbary headlands, occupied by a priest.

MARCHES. Borders or confines of a country, as the marches of Ancona, &c.

MARCHING ORDER. A soldier fully equipped with arms, ammunition, and a portion of his kit, carries from 30 to 35 lbs. In *service marching* order, by the addition of provisions and some campaigning necessaries, he carries nearly 50 lbs. But *heavy marching* order, which was yet heavier, is now happily abolished.

MARCO-BANCO. An imaginary coin of Hamburg commerce, equal to 1*s.* 5¾*d.* sterling.

MARE'S TAILS. A peculiar modification of the cirrus, indicating wind.

MARGIN LINE. A line or edge parallel to the upper side of the wing transom, and just below it, where the butts of the after bottom planks terminate.

MARINARIUS.   An old statute term for a mariner or seaman.

MARINATE, To.   To salt fish, and afterwards preserve it in oil or vinegar.

MARINE.   Belonging to the sea.   It is a general name for the royal or mercantile navy of any state; also the whole economy of nautical affairs.

MARINE BAROMETER.   A barometer, the tube of which is contracted in one part to prevent the sudden oscillations of the mercury by the ship's motion.

MARINE BOARDS.   Establishments at our different ports for carrying into effect the provisions of the Merchant Shipping Act.

MARINE BUILDINGS.   Those constructed for making or preserving ships, as docks, arsenals, store-houses, &c.

MARINE CLOTHING-ROOM.   A compartment of the after-platform, to receive the clothes and stores of the royal marines.

MARINE ENGINES.   Those steam engines which are used to propel ships, whether on the ocean or in rivers, in contradistinction to locomotives on shore.

MARINE GLUE, or JEFFREY'S GLUE.   A well-known adhesive composition of great importance in ship carpentry, and in various nautical uses. The substance is said to consist of caoutchouc, gum, and mineral oil.

MARINE INSURANCE.   A contract by which an individual or a company agree to indemnify the losses or damages happening to a ship or cargo during a voyage.   For this agreement the shipowner pays a sum in advance, called the premium, which falls to the insurer in case the ship arrives safe in a specified harbour.   If the ship or cargo, however, be lost by default of the person insured, the insurer shall not be accountable. Among the Romans, the state made good losses by shipwreck, which occasioned many frauds.   It is mentioned in the laws of Oleron, but was regulated under its present bearings in England in 1601.

MARINE LAGOON.   A lake or inlet formed by the encroachments of the sea, and the deposits of fluviatile action.

MARINE O●FICER.   An officer of the Royal Marines.   Jocularly and witlessly applied to an empty bottle, as being "useless;" but better rendered as having "done its duty, and ready to do it again."

MARINER.   One who obtains his living on the sea, in whatever rank. But with our old voyagers mariners were able seamen, and sailors only *ordinary* seamen.   Thus, Middleton's ship sailed from Bantam in 1605, leaving 18 men behind, "of whom 5 were mariners, and 13 sailors."

MARINE RAILWAY.   A term which has been applied to a slip for hauling vessels on to repair.

MARINER'S COMPASS.   *See* COMPASS.

MARINER'S NEEDLE.   The magnetized bar of a mariner's compass.

MARINES, THE ROYAL.   A body of officers and soldiers raised to serve on board men-of-war, and trained to fight either at sea or on shore:

their chosen body of artillery was esteemed one of the best under the crown. (*See* ARTILLERY.) "Tell that to the marines" was a common rejoinder to any improbable assertion, when those fine fellows had not acquired their present high estimation.

MARINE STORES. A general term for the ironwork, cordage, sails, provisions, and other outfit, with which a vessel is supplied.

MARITIMA ANGLIÆ. The profit and emolument formerly arising to the king from the sea, but which was afterwards granted to the lord high admiral.

MARITIME. Pertaining to sea affairs: all but synonymous with *marine* (which see.)

MARITIME COUNTRY. A country which has its shores washed by the sea.

MARITIME INTEREST. *See* BOTTOMRY.

MARITIME LAW. That branch of international law, or the law of nations, which consists of general principles, chiefly derived from ancient codes of law, and admitted by civilized nations, as to commercial inter-course with enemies and neutrals.

MARITIME LIEN. A privileged claim in respect of service done to, or injury caused by, a ship, to be carried into effect by legal process.

MARITIME POSITIONS. The intersection of the geographical co-ordi-nates of the latitudes and longitudes of places on the globe.

MARITIME POWERS. Those states which possess harbours, &c., on the coasts, and a powerful navy to defend them.

MARK. A certain regulated length for Spanish sword-blades, under penalty of fine, and the weapon to seizure. Also, any object serving for the guidance of ships, as sea-marks, land-marks, leading-marks, &c. Also, a piece of twine on a running rope, as a brace, &c., to show when, by being near the belaying pin or the bitts, it has been sufficiently hauled in. "Mark of the fore-brace down, sir;"—answer, "Belay, oh."

MARKAB. The lucida, or chief star, in the ancient constellation *Pegasus*.

MARKS AND DEEPS. Marks are the measured notifications on the hand lead-line, with white, blue, and red bunting, leather, and knots; deeps are the estimated fathoms between these marks. They are thus noted: mark 2 leather; mark 3 blue; deep 4; mark 5 white; deep 6; mark 7 red; deep 8; deep 9; mark 10 leather; deep 11; deep 12; mark 13 blue; deep 14; mark 15 white; deep 16; mark 17 red; deep 18; deep 19; mark 20 two knots.

MARL, To. To souse fish in vinegar to be eaten cold. *See* SOUSE.

MARLE, To. To wind marline, spun-yarn, twine, &c., about a rope, so that every turn is secured by a kind of knot, and remains fixed, in case the rest should be cut through by friction. It is commonly used to fasten slips of canvas, called parsling, upon the surface of a rope, to prevent its being galled, or to attach the foot of a sail to its bolt-rope, &c., with marling hitches, instead of sewing it.

MARLINE. *See* LINE.

MARLINE-HOLES. Holes made for marling, or lacing the foot-rope and clues in courses and topsails.

MARLINE-SPIKE. An iron pin tapering to a point, and principally used to separate the strands of a rope, in order to introduce the ends of some other through the intervals in the act of knotting or splicing; it is also used as a lever in marling, fixing seizings, &c. (*See* FID.)

MARLINE-SPIKE HITCH. A peculiar hitch in marling, made by laying the marline-spike upon the seizing stuff, and then bringing the end of that seizing over the standing part, so as to form a jamming bight.

MARMIT. A pot fitted with a hook for hanging it to the bars of the galley-range.

MAROON. A name for a bright light of that colour used for signals; and also for an explosive ball of prepared paste-board.

MAROONING. A custom among former pirates, of putting an offender on shore on some desolate cape or island, with a gun, a few shot, a flask of powder, and a bottle of water.

MARQUE. *See* LETTERS OF MARQUE.

MARQUEE. An officer's oblong tent; has two poles, and curtains all round; it is often assigned to various staff purposes.

MARROT. A name for the guillemot.

MARRY, To, THE ROPES, BRACES, OR FALLS. To hold both together, and by pressure haul in both equally. Also so to join the ends of two ropes, that they will pass through a block.

MARS. One of the ancient superior planets, the next to the earth in order of distance from the sun.

MARSH [Anglo-Saxon *mersc*, a fen]. Low land often under water, and producing aquatic vegetation. Those levels near the sea coast are usually saturated with salt water.

MARSILIANA. A Venetian ship of burden, square-sterned.

MART. A commercial market. Also a colloquialism for marque, as a letter of *mart* or *marque.*

MARTELLO TOWER. So named from a tower in the Bay of Mortella, in Corsica, which, in 1794, maintained a very determined resistance against the English. A martello tower at the entrance of the bay of Gaeta beat off H.M.S. *Pompée,* of 80 guns. A martello is built circular, and thus difficult to hit, with walls of vast thickness, pierced by loop-holes, and the bomb-proof roof is armed with one heavy traversing gun. They are 30 to 40 feet high, surrounded by a dry fosse, and the entrance is by a ladder at a door several feet from the ground.

MARTIAL LAW. The law of war, obtaining between hostile forces, or proclaimed in rebellious districts; it rests mainly on necessity, custom in like cases, and the will of the commander of the forces; thus differing from *military law* (which see). Martial law is proclaimed when the civil law is found to be insufficient to preserve the peace; in the case of insur-rection, mutiny, &c., the will and judgment of the officer in command becomes law.

MARTIN. A cat-sized creature with a valuable fur imported from Hudson's Bay and Canada in prodigious numbers.—"*My eye and Betty Martin,*" is a common expression implying disbelief; a corruption of the Romish *mihi, beate Martine!*

MARTINET. A rigid disciplinarian; but one who, in matters of inferior moment, harasses all under him.

MARTINGALE. A rope extending downwards from the jib-boom end to a kind of short gaff-shaped spar, fixed perpendicularly under the cap of the bowsprit; its use is to guy the jib-boom down in the same manner as the bobstays retain the bowsprit. The spar is usually termed the *dolphinstriker*, from its handy position whence to strike fish.

MARTNETS. The leech-lines of a sail—they were said to be *topped* when the leech was hauled by them close to the yard.

MARYN [Anglo-Nor.] The sea-coast.

MARYNAL. An ancient term for mariner.

MASCARET. A peculiar movement of the sea near Bordeaux in summer, at low water.

MASK. A cruive or crib for catching fish. A battery is said to be masked when its external appearance misleads the enemy.

MAST [Anglo-Saxon *mæst*, also meant chief or greatest]. A long cylindrical piece of timber elevated perpendicularly upon the keel of a ship, to which are attached the yards, the rigging, and the sails. It is either formed of one piece, and called a pole-mast, or composed of several pieces joined together and termed a made mast. A lower mast is fixed in the ship by *sheers* (which see), and the foot or keel of it rests in a block of timber called the step, which is fixed upon the keelson.—*Expending a mast*, or carrying it away, is said, when it is broken by foul weather.—*Fore-mast.* That which stands near the stem, and is next in size to the main-mast.—*Jury-mast. (See* JURY.)—*Main-mast.* The largest mast in a ship.—*Mizen-mast.* The smallest mast, standing between the main-mast and the stern. —*Over-masted,* or *taunt-masted.* The state of a ship whose masts are too tall or too heavy.—*Rough-mast,* or *rough-tree.* A spar fit for making a mast. *(See* BOWSPRIT and JIB-BOOM.)—*Springing a mast.* When it is cracked horizontally in any place.—*Top-mast.* A top-mast is raised at the head or top of the lower-mast through a cap, and supported by the trestle-trees.—*Topgallant-mast.* A mast smaller than the preceding, raised and secured to its head in the same manner.—*Royal-mast.* A yet smaller mast, elevated through irons at the head of the topgallant-mast; but more generally the two are formed of one spar.—*Under-masted* or *low-masted ships.* Vessels whose masts are small and short for their size.— *To mast a ship.* The act of placing a ship's masts.

MAST-CARLINGS. Those large carlings which are placed at the sides of the masts from beam to beam, to frame the partners and give support.

MAST-COAT. A conical canvas fitted over the wedges round the mast, to prevent water oozing down from the decks.

MASTER. The epithet for the captain or commander of a merchant vessel. When England first became a maritime power, ships with sailors, and a master to navigate, were furnished by the Cinque Ports, &c., and the fighting part of the men was composed of soldiers sent on board, commanded by generals, &c. Among the early voyagers there was a distinction between *master* and *maister*, the latter being the office; as, "we spoke the *Dragon*, whereof Master Ivie was maister," in Welsh's *Voyage to Benin*, A.D. 1590. In most applications, *master* denotes chief; as master boat-builder, master caulker, master sailmaker, &c.

MASTER OF A SHIP-OF-WAR. An officer appointed by the commissioners of the navy to attend to the navigating a ship under the direction of the captain, the working of a ship into her station in the order of battle, and in other circumstances of danger, but he reports to the first lieutenant, who carries out any necessary evolution. It is likewise his duty, in concert with lieutenants on surveys, to examine and report on the provisions. He is moreover charged with their stowage. For the performance of these services he is allowed several assistants, who are termed second-masters, master's assistants, &c. This officer's station has been termed the meridional altitude of the lower order of midshipmen, but it is requisite that he be both a good officer and a seaman. He ranks after lieutenants according to date, but is subordinate in command to all lieutenants.

MASTER AND COMMANDER. A title which, in 1814, was simplified to commander, the next degree above lieutenant; he ranks with, but after, a lieutenant-colonel.

MASTER-AT-ARMS. In former times was an officer appointed to command the police-duty of a ship, to teach the crew the exercise of small arms, to confine by order of superiors any prisoners, and to superintend their confinement. Also, to take care that fires and lights were put out at the proper hour, and no spirituous liquors brought on board. He was assisted by *ship's corporals*, who also attended the gangway with the sentinels. Until 1816, the junior lieutenant was nominally lieutenant-at-arms, and drilled the seamen, assisted by the serjeant of marines.

MASTER-ATTENDANT. An officer in the royal dockyards appointed to assist in the fitting or dismantling, removing or securing vessels of war, &c., at the port where he resides; to inspect the moorings in the harbour, to visit all the ships in ordinary, and to attend at the general musters in the dockyard, taking care that all the individuals registered in the navy-book are present at their duty.

MASTER MARINER. Shipmaster or captain of a merchant vessel.

MASTER OF MISRULE. An officer of an hour or two, when the hands were piped "to mischief." The lord or abbot of misrule on shore has immemorially been a person selected to superintend the diversions of Christmas. In these larks, however, malicious mischief was unknown.

MASTER OF THE FLEET. A master on board the commander-in-chief's ship, who has a general superintendence of the stores issued to the fleet, and reports to the flag-captain any deviations from rule which he may observe.

MASTER-SHIPWRIGHT. The chief superintendent in the building and repairing of ships in the royal dockyards.

MAST-HEAD. The upper part of a mast above the rigging.

MAST-HEADING. A well-known marine punishment, said to give midshipmen the best time for reading. A court-martial, as a substitute, punishes the parents as well as the thoughtless youth.

MAST-HEAD MEN. The men stationed aloft to keep a look-out.

MAST-HEAD PENDANTS. *See* PENDANT.

MAST-HIGH. A figurative expression of height.

MAST-HOLES. The apertures in the deck-partners for stepping the masts.

MAST-HOOPS. The iron hoops on made or built masts.

MAST-HOUSE. In dockyards, where masts are made.

MASTIC. An excellent cement latterly introduced into ship-building, instead of putty and other appliances, to protect the heads of bolts.

MAST-ROPE [Anglo-Saxon *mœst-ràp*]. That which is used for sending masts up or down.

MASULAH OR MASSOOLAH BOATS. Madras boats, of which the planks are sewed together with coir yarn, crossing the stitches over a wadding of coir or straw, which presses on the joints, and prevents much leakage. The vessel is thus rendered pliable, and yields to the shock on taking the ground in the surf, which at times runs from 10 to 16 feet high. They are rowed by twelve men, in double banks, with oars formed by an oval piece of board lashed to the end of a rough piece of wood. They are guided by one man with a long steer-oar, who stamps and yells with excitement as he urges the men to pull when a rolling surf is coming up astern. These boats are from 30 to 35 feet in length, 10 to 11 feet in breadth, and 7 to 8 feet in depth.

MAT. To prevent chafing, a thick mat is woven from strands of old rope, spun yarn, or foxes, containing each a greater or lesser number of rope-yarns, in proportion to the intended mat to be made. The largest and strongest kinds are called *paunch-mats*. The *thrum-mat* is precisely similar to the present cocoa-nut fibre door-mats. Where it is possible, rounding is now used instead of mats, it being neater and holding less water.

MATCH. A wager of emulation by rowing, sailing, manœuvring, &c. (*See* QUICK MATCH.)—*Slow match*, used by artillerymen, is a very loose rope steeped in a solution of nitre, and burns at the rate of about one inch an hour, and is either used alone, or for lighting the port-fires, by which guns are yet fired for salutes on shore.

MATCHLOCK. A musket fired with a match fixed on the cock opening the pan; long out of use, except in China and some parts of India.

MATCH-TUBS. Conical tubs about 18 inches in height, which have a sunken head perforated with holes, to admit the slow match to hang with the lighted end downwards.

MATE. Generally implies adjunct or assistant.

MATE OF A MERCHANT-SHIP. The officer who commands in the absence of the master, and shares the duty with him at sea. (*See* CHIEF MATE or OFFICER.) There are first, second, third, and fourth mates.

MATE OF A WATCH. The senior or passed midshipman is responsible to the officer of the watch. He heaves the log, inserts on the log-board all incidents occurring during his watch, musters the men of the watch, and reports to the officer in charge, who, when he is relieved, writes his initials on the log-board.

MATE OF THE LOWER-DECK. An officer of considerable importance in former times in ships of the line; he was responsible for the state and condition of the lower deck, and the residents there.

MATE OF THE MAIN-DECK. The officer appointed to superintend all the duties to be executed upon the main-deck during the day.

MATERIAL MEN. The persons who furnish all tackles and stores, &c., to repair or fit out ships. The high court of Admiralty allows material men to sue against remaining proceeds in the registry, notwithstanding past prohibitions.

MATERIEL. A French word that has been naturalized in speaking of naval or military stores.

MATHEMATICS. The science which treats of every kind of quantity that can be numbered or measured.

MATIES, OR MATEYS. Dockyard artificers, shipwrights, carpenters, &c.

MATO. A shell formerly of some commercial value on the west coast of Africa.

MATRASS. The square head of an arrow called *quarril.* In chemistry it is the Florence oil flask used for evaporation. From its thinness it will stand great gradual heat.

MATROSS. Formerly an assistant gunner in the artillery.

MATTHEW WALKER. A knot, so termed from the originator. It is formed by a half hitch on each strand in the direction of the lay, so that the rope can be continued after the knot is formed, which shows as a transverse collar of three strands. It is the knot used on the end of the laniards of rigging, where dead-eyes are employed.

MAUD. A salmon-net fixed in a square form by four stakes.

MAUL. A heavy iron hammer, used for driving trenails or bolts; it has one end faced, and the opposite pointed, whence it is often called a pin-maul.—*Top-maul* is distinguished by having an iron handle, with an eye at the end, by which it is tied fast to the mast-head. It is kept aloft for driving the iron fid in or out of the topmast.

MAUND. An Indian weight, which varies in amount depending on the part of the country. Also, a basket used by fishermen; a measure of small fish.

MAUNJEE. The native boatmen of the river Hooghly.

MAVIS-SKATE. The sharp-nosed ray. (*See* FRIAR-SKATE.)

MAW, OR SEA-MAW. The common gull, *Larus canus.*

MAY. *See* VENDABALES.

MAYHEM, OR MAHIM. The law-term for maim.

MAZE. In the herring trade, 500 fishes.

MAZOLET. An Indian bark boat, caulked with moss.

MEAKER. A west-country term for a minnow.

MEAKING IRON. The tool used by caulkers to run old oakum out of the seams before inserting new.

MEALED. Mixed or compounded.—*Mealed powder*, gunpowder pulverized by treating with spirits of wine.

MEALES, OR MIOLS. Immense sandbanks thrown up by the sea on the coasts of Norfolk, Lancashire, &c.

MEAN. As a general term implies the medium, but a mean of bad observations can never make a good one.

MEAN ANOMALY. *See* ANOMALY.

MEAN DISTANCE. The average distance of a planet from the sun; it is equal to half the longer axis of the ellipse, and hence is frequently termed the semi-axis-major.

MEAN EQUINOX. The position of the equinox independent of the effects of nutation.

MEAN MOTION. The rate at which a body moving in an elliptic orbit would proceed at an equal velocity throughout.

MEAN NOON. The noon of a mean day supposing the year to be divided into days of equal length. It differs from *apparent noon* by the amount of the equation of time for that date.

MEAN OBLIQUITY. The obliquity of the ecliptic, unaffected with nutation.

MEAN PLACE OF A STAR. Its position at a given time, independent of aberration and nutation.

MEAN SUN. *See* TIME.

MEAN TIME. *See* TIME.

MEASURE. A comprehensive term including length, surface, time, weight, solidity, capacity, and force of gravity.

MEASURING LINE. The old term for the first meridian reckoned off from a ship's longitude. Also, the five-fathom line used by the boatswain.

MECHANICS. The science which explains the properties of moving bodies, and of the machines from which they receive their impetus. The mechanical powers consist of six primary instruments, the lever, the balance, the pulley, the wheel, the screw, and the wedge: to which is sometimes added the inclined plane; and of some, or all of these, every compound machine consists.

MECK. A notched staff in a whale-boat on which the harpoon rests.

MEDICAL BOARD. A number of medical officers convened to examine sick and wounded officers and men, for invaliding or discharge.

MEDICINE-CHEST. A large chest containing the medical necessaries that may be required for 100 men during the cruize. Several chests are thus fitted and supplied in proportion to the ship's crew, ready for detached service.

MEDICINES. Merchantmen are legally bound to carry medicines in proportion to their crew, with instructions for their use if there be no surgeon on board.

MEDICO. A familiar appellation for the ship's surgeon.

MEDITERRANEAN or **INLAND SEA.** A term applied to a sea surrounded on all sides, except its immediate entrance, by land; as the Mediterranean, so styled *par excellence;* also, the Baltic, the Red Sea, &c.

MEDITERRANEAN PASS. A document formerly granted by the Lords of the Admiralty to registered vessels, which was valuable when the Barbary powers were unchecked. (*See* PASS.)

MEDIUM. *See* RESISTING MEDIUM.

MEERMAID. A name given by our northern fishermen to the *Lophius piscatorius*, or frog-fish, without reference to the *mermaid* (which see).

MEER-SWINE. The porpoise [from the German *meerschwein*].

MEET HER! The order to adjust the helm, so as to check any further movement of the ship's head in a given direction.

MEGANESE [Gr.] A large portion of land, inferior in extent to a continent, but which, though insular, is too large to be termed an island, as New Holland.

MEMORIAL. An official petition on account of services performed.

MEN. The ship's company in general.

MEND SAILS, To. To loose and skin them afresh on the yards.

MEND THE SERVICE. Put on more service to the cable, or any part of the rigging chafed.

MERCANTILE MARINE. *See* MARINE.

MERCANTILE MARINE FUND. A public fund accumulated by fees payable to the Board of Trade on account of the merchant shipping.

MERCATOR'S CHART or **PROJECTION.** Introduced by Gerard Mercator, *circa* 1556 : it is a projection of the surface of the earth in the plane, with all the meridians made parallel with each other, consequently the degrees of longitude all equal, the degrees of latitude increasing in a corresponding ratio towards the poles. This is the chart most commonly used in navigation; and its use appears to have obtained quickly, for in 1576, among the items of Martin Frobisher's outfit, we find, "For a greate Mappe Universall of Mercator, in prente, £1, 6s. 8d."

MERCATOR'S SAILING. Performed loxodromically, by means of Mercator's charts.

MERCHANTMAN. A trading vessel employed in importing and exporting goods to and from any quarter of the globe.

MERCHANT SERVICE. The mercantile marine.

MERCHANT-VENTURERS. A company of merchants who traded with Russia, Turkey, and other distant parts. In the *Affectionate Shepheard,* 1594, we find—

> "Well is he tearm'd a merchant venturer,
>   Since he doth venter lands, and goods, and all;
> When he doth travell for his traffique far,
>   Little he knowes what fortune may befall."

MERCURIAL GAUGE. A curved tube partly filled with mercury, to show the pressure of steam in an engine.

MERCURY. One of the ancient inferior planets, and the nearest to the sun, as far as we yet know. (*See* Transit of.) Also, a name for quicksilver; the fluid metal so useful in the construction of the marine barometer, thermometer, and artificial horizon.

MERE. An Anglo-Saxon word still in use, sometimes meaning a lake, and generally the sea itself.

MERIDIAN, of the Earth. Is an imaginary great circle passing through the zenith and the poles, and cutting the equator at right angles. When the sun is on the meridian of any place, it is mid-day there, and at all places situated under the same meridian.—*First meridian* is that from which the longitude is reckoned. Magnetic meridian is not a great circle but a wavy line uniting those poles. In common acceptation, a meridian is any line supposed to be drawn from the north to the south pole; therefore a place being under the same meridian as another place, is either due north or south of it.—*Plane of the meridian* is the plane of this great circle, and its intersection with the sensible horizon is called the *meridian line.*—The *meridian transit* of a heavenly body is the act of passing over the said plane, when it is either due north or south of the spectator.— *Ante meridiem,* or A.M., before noon.—*Post meridiem,* or P.M., after noon.

MERIDIAN ERROR. The deviation of a transit-instrument from the plane of the meridian at the horizon; it is also termed the *azimuthal error.*

MERLON. That part of the parapet of a battery between two adjacent embrasures, 15 or 20 feet long in general.

MERMAID. A fabulous sea-creature of which the upper half was said to resemble a woman, the lower half a fish.

MERMAID'S GLOVE. The name of a peculiar sponge, *Spongia palmata,* abundant at Bermuda.

MERMAID'S PURSE. The oblong · horny cases with long filiform appendages developed from each of the four corners, found on the seashore, being the outer covering of the eggs of several species of rays and sharks. Also, the hollow root of the sea-weed *Fucus polyschides.*

MERRY DANCERS. The glancings and coruscations of the aurora borealis, or northern lights.

MERRY MEN OF MAY. Dangerous currents formed by the ebb-tides.

MESON. A very old form of spelling *mizen.*

MESS. Any company of the officers or crew of a ship, who eat, drink, and associate together. (*See* Number.) Also, the state of a ship in a sudden squall, when everything is let go and flying, and nothing hauled in.

MESS-DECK. The place where a ship's crew mess.

MESSENGER. A large cable-laid rope, used to unmoor or heave up the anchor of a ship, by the aid of the capstan. This is done by binding a part of the messenger to the cable by which the ship rides, in several places, with pliant nippers, and by winding another part of it about the capstan. The messenger has an eye-splice at each end, through which several turns of a strong lashing are passed, forming an endless rope. So that by putting on fresh nippers forward, and taking them off as they are hove aft, the capstan may be kept constantly going, and the cable is walked in without stopping. (*See* VIOL.) A superior plan is now adopted, in which the messenger, consisting of a pitch chain which has a double and single link alternately, works in iron spurs fastened above the lower rim of the capstan. This avoids the trouble of shifting or fleeting the messenger while heaving in. Again, the cable itself is commonly brought to the capstan.—*Light forward the messenger!* is the order to pull the slack of it towards the hawse holes, on the slack or opposite side, so as to be ready to fasten upon the cable which is being hove in, as it comes off the manger-roller at the bows.

MESSENGERS. Boys appointed to carry orders from the quarter-deck. In some ships they wore winged caps of the Mercury type.

MESS-KID. A wooden tub for holding cooked victuals or cocoa.

MESSMATE. A companion of the same mess-table, hence comrades in many ways; whence the *saw:* "Messmate before a shipmate, shipmate before a stranger, stranger before a dog."

MESS-TRAPS. The kids, crockery, bowls, spoons, and other articles of mess service.

META-CENTRE. That point in a ship where a vertical line drawn from the centre of cavity cuts a line perpendicular to the keel, passing through the centre of gravity. As this depends upon the situation of the centre of cavity, the meta-centre is often called the *shifting centre.* Safety requires this point to be above the centre of gravity.

METAL. A word comprehending the great guns, or ordnance generally, of a ship or battery.

METEINGS. The measurement and estimate of timber.

METEOR. *See* COMPASANT, WATERSPOUT, &c.

METEORITES. Meteoric stones which fall from the atmosphere, composed of earthy and metallic substances, in which iron, nickel, &c., enter largely.

METEOROLOGIC TELEGRAPHY. The sending of telegrams to various stations at home and abroad, with the object of improving the science of meteorology, and issuing storm warnings, &c.

METONIC CYCLE. A cycle of 19 years, which contains 235 lunations, and results in a correspondence of the solar and lunar years. The discovery of this astronomical period may be safely assigned to Meton in 432 B.C.

MEW [Anglo-Saxon *mæw*]. A name for the sea-gull.

MIASMA. An impure effluvium in the air—proceeding from marshes or moist ground acted upon by solar heat—by which malaria fevers, particularly intermittents, are produced.

MICROMETER. An instrument used to measure small angles, diameters, and distances of heavenly bodies.

MID. The intermediate or middle part of anything. Also, *per contractionem*, a midshipman.

MID-CHANNEL. Implies half way across any river, channel, &c.

MIDDLE BAND. One of the bands of a sail, to give additional strength.

MIDDLE-LATITUDE SAILING. A method of converting departure in difference of longitude, and *vice versa*, by using the middle latitude instead of the meridional parts, as in Mercator's sailing.

MIDDLE-TIMBER. That timber in the stern which is placed amidships.

MIDDLE-TOPSAIL. A deep-roached sail, set in some schooners and sloops on the heel of their topmasts between the top and the cap. A modification of this, under the name of a lower topsail, is now very common in double-topsail-yarded ships. (Cunningham's topsails.)

MIDDLE-WALES. The three or four thick strakes worked along each side between the lower and middle-deck-ports in three-deckers.

MIDDLE-WATCH. The portion of the crew on deck-duty from midnight to 4 A.M.

MIDDLE-WATCHER. The slight meal snatched by officers of the middle-watch about five bells (or 2·30 A.M.)

MIDDLING A SAIL. Arranging it for bending to the yard.

MIDDY. An abbreviation for the younger midshipmen, synonymous with *mid*.

MIDRIB. A narrow canal or culvert.

MIDSHIPMAN. A naval cadet appointed by the admiralty, with the exception of one in each ship appointed by the captain. No person can be appointed midshipman until he has served one year, and passed his examinations; nor a lieutenant without having previously served six years in the royal navy as midshipman, and having further passed two severe examinations—one in seamanship and one in gunnery. A midshipman is then the station in which a young volunteer is trained in the several exercises necessary to attain a knowledge of steam, machinery, discipline, the general movements and operations of a ship, and qualify him to command.

MIDSHIPMAN'S NUTS. Broken pieces of biscuit as dessert.

MIDSHIPMAN'S ROLL. A slovenly method of rolling up a hammock transversely, and lashing it endways by one clue.

MIDSHIPS. The middle part of the vessel, either with regard to her length or breadth. (*See* AMIDSHIPS.)

MILDERNIX. A strong canvas of which courses were formerly made; it appears in old statutes.

MILE. The statute mile is 5280 feet; but that used at sea, termed the mean nautic mile, consists of 6075·6 feet, or 60 to a degree.

MILITARY EXECUTION. The levying contributions from a country by military occupation and force.

MILITARY LAW. That under which soldiers and sailors are governed, founded on the acts of parliament passed to that end.

MILITIA. A military force raised by ballot.

MILKY WAY. *See* VIA LACTEA.

MILL. A boxing match, whether standing up or nailed to a chest.

MILLAR'S SIGHT. General Millar's simple dispart—a sliding pillar bearing a scale graduated to tangents of degrees for setting the gun by.

MILLED LEAD. Sheet lead.

MILLER, To DROWN THE. To put an overdose of water to grog.

MILLER'S THUMB. A freshwater fish, the *Cottus cataphractus.*

MILT. The soft roe, or spermatic part, of the male fish.

MINE. A passage made under ground, with a chamber at the end, under the place intended to be blown up; it is entered by the shaft, which leads through the gallery to the chamber.

MINERAL OIL. *See* PETROLEUM.

MINIE RIFLE. This has acquired a great name, though not yet in general use.

MINION. An old four-pounder gun about 7 feet long. Its point-blank range was 120 paces, with a random one of 1500. Bourne, in 1578, mentions the minion as requiring shot 3 inches in diameter.

MINISTER. A minister, though termed plenipotentiary, has no power to grant protection to vessels or cargoes otherwise subject to the operations and laws of hostilities.

MINNIS. An old British word for a rock or piece of rising ground.

MINNOW. A small fresh-water fish—the *Leuciscus phoxinus.* The term was used in contempt by Shakspeare and the elders.

MINOR AXIS. In a planetary orbit, signifies the line perpendicular to the major axis, and passing through the centre of the ellipse.

MINOR PLANETS. *See* ASTEROIDS.

MINUTE MILE. The sixtieth part of a degree of longitude or latitude: in the latter case it is the sixtieth part of a degree of a great circle, in the former it decreases in length as the latitude increases.

MINUTE AND HALF-MINUTE GLASSES. *See* GLASS.

MINUTE-GUNS. Fired at intervals of a minute each during the progress of important funerals.

MINUTES. Short notices taken in writing of any important proceedings.

MIRA. A remarkable variable star in Cetus.

MIRACH. One of the bright stars in Andromeda.

MIRAGE, OR LOOM. A word, which has crept into use since the French expedition to Egypt, to express the extraordinary refraction which light undergoes when strata of air, of different densities, extend above each other. The mirage, reflecting objects at a great height, inverts and doubles the image.

MIRE-BUMPER AND MIRE-DRUM. North-country names of the bittern.

MIRKLES. The radicle leaves of the *Fucus esculentus,* a sea-weed eaten on our northern coasts.

MIRROR. The speculum of a quadrant, or any silvered or polished reflecting surface.

MISCHIEF. *See* MASTER OF MISCHIEF.

MISREPRESENTATION to the Underwriters, of any fact or circumstance material to the risk of insuring, whether by the insured or his agent, and whether fraudulent or innocent, renders the contract null and void. (*See* Representation.)

MISSILES. Projectiles of every kind propelled by force.

MISSING. If a vessel is not heard of within six months after her departure (or after the last intelligence of her) from any port in Europe, and within twelve months from other parts of the world, she is deemed to be lost. Presumptive proof will suffice if none of her crew appear.

MISSING STAYS. To fail in going about from one tack to another; when, after a ship gets her head to the wind, she comes to a stand, and begins to fall off on the same tack.

MIST [Anglo-Saxon]. A thin vapour, between a *fog* and *haze*, and is generally wet.

MISTICO. Equivalent to our *hermaphrodite*, being a small Mediterranean vessel, between a xebec and a felucca. (*See* Xebec.)

MISTRAL. A cold N.W. wind experienced on the Mediterranean shores of France. [Corrupted from *maestrale*.]

MITTS. A protection for the hand, covering the thumb in one space and the fingers in another, so that men wearing them can still handle ropes.

MIXED MATHEMATICS. Pure mathematics when applied to practical subjects, as astronomy, optics, hydrography, gunnery, engineering, and the like.

MIZAR. The star ζ in Ursa Major; the middle one in the tail.

MIZEN. The spanker or driver is often so named.

MIZEN-MAST. The aftermost mast of a ship (*see* Shroud, Stay, Yard, &c.), observing only that the epithet of fore, main, or mizen, is added to each term, to distinguish them from each other. (*See* Bonaventure.)

MIZEN MAST-HEAD. Rear-admirals carry their flag at their mizen.

MIZEN STAY-SAIL. A fore-and-aft sail of various shapes set on the mizen stay.

MOAT. Synonymous with *ditch* (which see).

MOBILIZATION. The organizing a body of men for active service. Also, a term in naval tactics, applied to the movement of fleets.

MOCCASSIN. A slipper made of green hide, and worn in cases of necessity; a term derived from the North American Indians.

MODERATE BREEZE. When all the flying kites may be pleasantly carried.

MODERATE GALE. In which a ship carries double reefs in her topsails.

MOHUR. A gold coin in the East Indies, value 30s. to 32s.

MOIDORE. A Portuguese gold coin, the sterling value of which is £1, 7s.

MOINEAU. A little flat bastion formerly raised before a curtain, otherwise too long.

MOIST DAUGHTERS. Spenser's term for the Hyades, a group of seven stars in the head of the Bull.

MOKES. The meshes of a fishing-net.

MOLE. A long pier of massy masonry, covering the entrance of a harbour. Also applied to the harbours formed by them, as those of Genoa, Marseilles, Naples, &c.

MOLLY-MAWK. A bird which follows in the wake of a ship rounding the Cape. It is a small kind of albatross.

MOMENTUM. Is the product of a weight multiplied by its velocity; that is, in marine dynamics, by its distance from a point determined as the centre of momentum; or from a line called the axis of the momentum.

MONERES, OR MONOCRATA. Galleys with only one rank of oars.

MONEY-BOUND. A phrase expressive of such passengers as are detained on board till a remittance arrives for paying the passage made.

MONGER. A trader. (*See* MONKEY.)

MONITION. Legal notice or warning.

MONITOR. A very shallow, semi-submerged, heavily-armoured steamer, carrying on her open deck either one or two plated revolving turrets, each containing either one or two enormous guns: originally designed by Ericson in the United States during the recent war, to combine the maximum of gun power with the minimum of exposure; they have been very formidable in sheltered and intricate waters, but it remains yet to be shown that they would be effective on the open sea.

MONKEY. A machine composed of a long pig of iron, traversing in a groove, which is raised by a pulley, and let fall suddenly on the head of large bolts for driving them. A larger kind is used in *pile-driving*. Also, a kind of wooden kid for grog. Also, in Queen Elizabeth's reign, a small trading vessel. Also, passion; as a man's "monkey is up." Also, a machine with which the *hercules* facilitates the welding of anchors.

MONKEY-BLOCK. A small single block strapped with a swivel. Also, those nailed on the topsail-yards of some merchantmen, to lead the buntlines through.

MONKEY-BOAT. A half-decked boat above-bridge on the Thames.

MONKEY-JACKET. A warm jacket for night-watches, &c.

MONKEY-PUMP. Straws or quills for sucking the liquid from a cask, through a gimlet-hole made for the purpose—a practice as old as the time of Xenophon, who describes this mode of drinking from the prize jars of Armenia.

MONKEY-SPARS. Reduced masts and yards for a vessel devoted to the instruction and exercise of boys.

MONKEY-TAIL. A lever for training a carronade.

MONK-FISH. The *Squatina angelus*. (*See* DEVIL-FISH.)

MONK'S SEAM. That made after sewing the edges of sails together, one over the other, by stitching through the centre of the seam. Also, the fash left at the junction of the moulds when a ball is cast.

MONMOUTH CAP. A flat worsted cap formerly worn by soldiers and sailors. In the old play *Eastward Ho*, it is said, "Hurl away a dozen of Monmouth caps or so, in sea ceremony to your bon voyage."

MONOXYLON [Gr.] Boats in the Ionian Isles propelled with one oar.

MONSOON [from the Persian *monsum*, season]. The periodical winds in certain latitudes of India and the Indian Ocean. They continue five or six months from one direction, and then alter their course, and blow (after the tempestuous tumult of their shifting has subsided) during an equal space of time from an opposite point of the compass, with the same uniformity. They are caused by the unequal heating of land and water, and occur in the tropics, where the "trade" would constantly blow if it were not for the presence of land. (*See* WIND). The south-west monsoon is called by the Arabs *khumseen*, denoting fifty, as they suppose it to precede the overflowing of the Nile by fifty days. (*See* KAMSIN.)

MONTE PAGNOTE. In former days an eminence out of cannon shot of operations, where spectators were not exposed to danger.

MONTERO. A military cap and hood formerly worn in camp.

MONTHLY ALLOWANCE. A sum paid monthly to warrant and petty officers not allowed to draw bills; and to seamen, marines, and boys serving on board. Wages are now paid regularly.

MONTHLY NOTES. *See* ALLOTMENT.

MOON. Our satellite; she performs her revolution in 27 days, 7 hours, 43 minutes. (*See* FULL MOON and NEW MOON.) A hazy or pale colour of the moon, revealing the state of our atmosphere, is supposed to forebode rain, and a red or copper colour to forebode wind.

MOON-BLINK. A temporary evening blindness occasioned by sleeping in the moonshine in tropical climates; it is technically designated *nyctalopia*.

MOON-CULMINATORS. Certain stars near the same parallel of declination as the moon, and not differing greatly from her in right ascension, given in the Ephemeris as proper objects for comparison with her, to determine the longitudes of places.

MOONEY. Not quite intoxicated, but unfitted for duty.

MOON IN DISTANCE. When the angle between her and the sun, or a star, admits of measurement for lunar observation.

MOONISH. Variable, as with Shakspeare's Rosalind.

MOON-RAKERS. Sails above the sky-sails. They are usually designated moon-sails.

MOON-SHEERED. A ship the upper works of which rise very high, fore and aft.

MOONSHINE. Illicit hollands, schiedam, and indeed smuggling in general; excused as a *matter of moonshine*. A mere nothing.

MOON-STRUCK. An influence imputed to the moon in the tropics, by which fish, particularly of the *Scomber* class, though recently taken, become intenerated, and even spoiled; while some attribute poisonous qualities to them in this state. Human beings are also said to be injured by sleeping in the moon's rays.

MOOR. An upland swamp, boggy, with fresh water. Also, an open common.

MOOR, To. To secure a ship with anchors, or to confine her in a particular station by two chains or cables, either fastened to the mooring chains or to the bottom; a ship is moored when she rides by two anchors.

MOOR A CABLE EACH WAY, To. Is dropping one anchor, veering out two cables' lengths, and letting go another anchor from the opposite bow; the first is then hove in to one cable, or less according to circumstances, while the latter is veered out as much, whereby the ship rides between the two anchors, equally distant from both. This is usually practised in a tide-way, in such manner that the ship rides by one during the flood, and by the other during the ebb.

MOOR ACROSS, To. To lay out one of the anchors across stream.

MOOR ALONG, To. To anchor in a river with a hawser on shore to steady her.

MOOR-GALLOP. A west-country term for a sudden squall coming across the moors.

MOORING-BRIDLE. The fasts attached to moorings, one taken into each hawse-hole, or bridle-port.

MOORING-CHOCKS. Large pieces of hard wood with a hole in the centre, shod with iron collars, and fastened between two stanchions in large ships, for the moorings to pass through.

MOORING POSTS OR PALLS. Strong upright posts fixed into the ground, for securing vessels to the landing-place by hawsers or chains. Also, strong pieces of oak inserted into the deck of a large ship for fastening the moorings to when alongside a quay.

MOORING-RINGS. Iron swivel rings fixed on piers or buoys, &c., for securing vessels to.

MOORINGS. Indicated by buoys to which ships are fastened; they are attached by bridles to heavy anchors and cables laid down in the most convenient parts of rivers and harbours. They are termed "*swinging*," or "all fours," depending on whether the ship is secured by the bow only, or by bow and stern. By their means many more ships are secured in a certain space than would be possible if they used their own anchors.

MOOR QUARTER-SHOT, To. To moor quartering, between the two ways of across and along.

MOOR THE BOAT, To. To fasten her with two ropes, so that the one shall counteract the other, and keep her in a steady position.

MOOR WITH A SPRING ON THE CABLE, To. *See* SPRING.

MOOTER. A spike, bolt, treenail.

MOOTING. In ship-building, making a treenail exactly cylindrical to a given size or diameter, called the *moot*.

MOP. A young whiting.

MOPPAT. An early name for the sponge of a cannon.

MOPUSSES. A cant term for money in general.

MORASS. Nearly the same thing as a marsh or swamp. In tropical regions they are often overflowed with salt water, yet covered with mangrove and many aquatic plants.

MORGLAY. A great sword, alluded to formerly.

MORION. An ancient steel casque or helmet, without beaver or visor. According to Chaucer it was of more uses than one:—

"Their beef they often in their morion stewed."

MORNING GUN. The gun fired from the admiral's or senior officer's ship, to announce daybreak, which is answered by the muskets of the sentries in the other ships.

MORNING STAR. An offensive weapon of the mediæval times, consisting of a staff, to which was attached an iron ball covered with spikes. Also, the planet which is near the meridian at day-dawn.

MORNING WATCH. Those of the crew on watch from 4 to 8 A.M.

MORRA. An ancient game still played in Italy with extraordinary zest, by two persons raising the right hand, and suddenly and contemporaneously throwing it down with only some of the fingers extended, when the aim is to guess what they unitedly amount to. Also, a term for a headland or promontory on the coasts of Chili and Peru. Also, a round tower or fort, as at Havana [from the Spanish *morro*, round].

MORRIS-PIKE. A formidable Moorish weapon, the precursor of the boarding-pike.

MORSE. *See* WALRUS.

MORSING POWDER. An old term for priming powder.

MORTAR. A short piece of ordnance used for throwing shells, so that they may fall nearly vertical; they thus acquire force for breaking through roofs, decks, &c. It is fired at a fixed angle of elevation, generally at 45°, the charge of powder varying according to the range required.

MORTAR-BED AND BED-BEAMS. *See* BOMB-BED, &c.

MORTAR-VESSEL. *See* BOMB-VESSEL.

MORTGAGE. A registered ship, or share therein, which has been made a security for a money-loan, or other valuable consideration, is termed a mortgage in the Merchant Shipping Act.

MORTICE. A morticed block is one made out of a single block of wood, chiselled for one or more sheaves; in distinction from a *made block*. The chisel used for morticing is peculiar to that purpose.

MORUACH. A peculiar seal, which has been frequently mistaken on our northern shores for a mermaid.

MOSES. A flat-bottomed boat used in the West Indies for bringing off hogsheads of sugar; it is termed single or double, according to its size.

MOSES' LAW. The term among pirates for inflicting thirty-nine lashes on the bare back—forty save one.

MOSQUITO. A term applied to a gnat-like species of stinging insects, found chiefly in low marshy places and the neighbourhood of rivers.

MOSQUITO FLEET. An assemblage of small craft.

MOSQUITO NET. A light curtain spread over a cot or bed in warm climates, to protect the sleeper from mosquitoes.

MOSS-BONKER. The name given by American fishermen to the *hard-head* (which see).

MOTHER CARY'S CHICKEN. The stormy petrel, *Procellaria pelagica*.

MOTHER CARY'S GOOSE. The name given by Captain Cook's people to an oceanic brown bird, *Procellaria gigantea*, which Pernety calls *Quebranta-huessos* (bone-breaker).

MOTHER-OF-PEARL. The iridescent nacreous inner layer of several species of shells, especially the "pearl-oyster" (*Meleagrina margaritifera*).

MOTHERY [probably from the Dutch *mœder*, mud]. Thick and mouldy; generally applied to decomposing liquors.

MOTION. Change of place; it is termed *direct*, in the sky, when it is in the direction of the earth's annual revolution; *retrograde*, when it proceeds contrary to these conditions; by *sidereal* is meant the motion of a body with respect to the fixed stars.—*Tropical motion* is the movement of a body in respect to the equinox or tropic, which has itself a slow motion among the stars, as shown under precession. (*See* PROPER MOTION.) —*Motion*, in mechanics, is either simple or compound, as one or more powers are used. The momentum of a moving body, or quantity of motion, arises from its velocity multiplied into the quantity of matter it contains.

MOTION, CENTRE OF. That point of a body which remains at rest whilst all the other parts are in motion about it : as the mathematical centre of a revolving sphere.

MOTOR. The prime mover in machinery.

MOULDED. The size of the timber, the way the mould is laid; cut to the mould.

MOULDED BREADTH. The measure of beam from outside to outside of the timbers, without the thickness of the plank.

MOULDING DIMENSION. In ship-building, implies the depth or thickness of any piece of timber.

MOULDING EDGE. That edge of a timber to which, in shaping it, the mould is applied.

MOULDINGS OF A GUN. The several rings and ornaments.

MOULD-LOFT. A long building, on the floor of which the intended vessel is laid off from the several draughts in full dimensions.

MOULDS. In naval architecture, are thin flexible pieces of board used on the mould-loft floors as patterns.

MOUNT, OR MOUNTAIN. An Anglo-Saxon term still in use, usually held to mean eminences above 1000 feet in height. In a fort it means the *cavalier* (which see).

MOUNT, TO. When said of a ship-of-war, implies the number of guns she carries.—*To mount*, in a military sense, is also to furnish with horses.

MOUNT A GUN, TO. To place it on its carriage.

MOUNT AREEVO! [Sp. *montar arriba*]. Mount aloft; jump up quickly.

MOUNTEBANK. The *Gammarus arcticus*, or arctic shrimp.

MOURNING. A ship is in mourning with her ensign and pennant half-mast, her yards topped awry, or apeek, or alternately topped an-end. If the sides are painted blue instead of white, it denotes deep mourning;

this latter, however, is only done on the ship where the admiral or captain was borne, and in the case of merchant ships on the death of the owner.

MOUSE. A kind of ball or knob, wrought on the collars of stays by means of spun-yarn, higher parcelling, &c. The mouse prevents the running eye from slipping. (*See* PUDDENING.) Also, a match used in firing a mine. Also, a mark made upon braces and other ropes, to show their squaring or tallying home.—*To mouse a hook*, to put a turn or two of rope-yarn round the point of a tackle-hook and its neck to prevent its unhooking.—*To raise a mouse*, to strike a blow which produces a lump.

MOUTH [the Anglo-Saxon *muda*]. The embouchure opening of a port or outlet of a river, as Yarmouth, Tynemouth, Exmouth, &c.

MOVE OFF, To. To defile.

MOVER. Synonymous with *motor*.

MOVING SANDS. Synonymous with *quicksands*.

MOWELL. The old English name for *mullet*.

MOYAN. A species of early artillery.

MOYLE, To. To defile; an old term.

MUCK. *See* AMOCK.

MUD-DRAGS. Implements and machines for clearing rivers and docks.

MUD OR BALLAST DREDGER. A vessel of 300 tons or more, fitted with steam-engine beams and metal buckets. By this powerful machine for cutting or scraping, loose gravel banks, &c., are removed from the entrances to docks and rivers.

MUD-FISH. The *Lepidosiren*, a very remarkable fish of the Gambia and other African rivers.

MUD-HOLE. An orifice with steam-tight doors in a marine engine, through which the deposit is removed from the boilers.

'MUDIAN, 'MUGIAN, OR BERMUDIAN. A boat special to the Bermuda Islands, usually decked, with the exception of a hatch; from two to twenty tons burden; it is short, of good beam, and great draft of water abaft, the stem and keel forming a curved line. It carries an immense quantity of iron, or even lead, ballast. Besides a long main and short jib-boom, it has a long, tapering, raking mast, stepped just over the forefoot, generally unsupported by shrouds or stays; on it a jib-headed mainsail is hoisted to a height of twice, and sometimes three times, the length of the keel. This sail is triangular, stretched at its foot by a long boom. The only other sail is a small foresail or jib. They claim to be the fastest craft in the world for working to windward in smooth water, it being recorded of one that she made five miles dead to windward in the hour during a race; and though they may be laid over until they fill with water, they will not capsize.

MUD-LANDS. The extensive marshes left dry by the retiring tide in estuaries and river mouths.

MUD-LARKS. People who grovel about bays and harbours at low water for anything they can find.

MUD-LIGHTER. Large heavy punts which receive the mud or other matter from a dredging vessel. It is the *Marie Salope* of the French. (*See* HOPPER-PUNT.)

MUD-PATTENS. Broad clogs used for crossing mud-lands in the south of England by those who take sea-fowl.

MUD-SHORES. Are not unfrequent on an open coast. The most remarkable instance, perhaps, is that of the Guiyana; the mud brought down by the river being thrown up by the current, and silted, with belts of mangroves in patches.

MUFFLED DRUM. The sound is thus damped at funerals: passing the spare cord, which is made of drummer's plait (to carry the drum over the shoulder), twice through the snares or cords which cross the lower diameter of the drum.

MUFFLE THE OARS, To. To put some matting or canvas round the loom when rowing, to prevent its making a noise against the tholes, or in the rowlocks. For this service thole-pins are best. In war time, rowing guard near the ships or batteries of the enemy, or cutting out, many a pea-jacket has been sacrificed for this purpose. Whale-boats have their oars muffled to prevent frightening the whales.

MUFTI. Plain clothes. The civilian dress of a naval or military officer when off duty. This, though not quite commendable, is better than the half and half system, for a good officer should be either in uniform or out of it.

MUGGY. Half intoxicated. A sheet in the wind. Also used to express damp, oppressive weather.

MULCT. A fine in money for some fault or misdemeanour. Also, fines formerly laid on ships by a trading company, to raise money for the maintenance of consuls, &c.

MULET. A Portuguese craft, with three lateen sails.

MULL. Derived from the Gaelic *mullach*, a promontory or island; as Mull of Galloway, Mull of Cantyre, Isle of Mull. Also, when things are mismanaged; "we have made a mull of it."

MULLET. A well-known fish, of which there are several species. The gray mullet, *Mugil capito*, and the red mullet, *Mullus surmuletus*, are the most common on the British coast.

MULLS. The nickname of the English in Madras, from mulligatawney having been a standard dish amongst them.

MULREIN. A name in the Firth of Forth for the frog-fish, *Lophius piscatorius*.

MULTIPLE STARS. When several stars appear in close proximity to each other, they are spoken of, collectively, as a multiple star.

MUMBO JUMBO. A strange minister of so-called justice on the Gold Coast, who is usually dressed up for the purpose of frightening women and children. He is the arbiter of domestic strife.

MUNDUC. A sailor employed at the pearl-fishery, to haul up the diver and oysters.

MUNDUNGUS [from the Spanish *mondongo*, refuse, offal]. Bad, rank, and dirty tobacco.

MUN-FISH. Rotten fish, used in Cornwall for manure.

MUNITION BREAD. Contract or commissariat bread; *Brown George*.

MUNITIONS. Provisions; naval and military stores.

MUNITION SHIPS. Those which carry the naval stores for a fleet, as distinguished from the victuallers.

MUNJAK. A kind of pitch used in the Bay of Honduras for vessels' bottoms.

MUNNIONS, OR MUNTINS. The divisional pieces of the stern-lights; the pieces that separate the lights in the galleries.

MURÆNA. An eel-like fish, very highly esteemed by the ancient Romans.

MURDERER. The name formerly used for large blunderbusses, as well as for those small pieces of ordnance which were loaded by shifting metal chambers placed in the breech.

MURLOCH. The young pickled dog-fish.

MURRE. The Cornish name for the razor-bill, *Alca torda*.

MURROCH. A term for shell-fish in general on the west coast of Scotland.

MUSKET. The regulation fire-arm for infantry and small-arm men. That of the English service, when a smooth bore, threw its bullet of about an ounce 250 yards with good effect; now, rifling has trebled its range, whilst breech-loading has done at least as much by its rapidity of fire.

MUSKET-ARROWS. Used in our early fleets, and for conveying notices in 1815.

MUSKETEERS. An early name for those soldiers who were armed with muskets.

MUSKETOON. A short kind of blunderbuss with a large bore, to carry several musket or pistol bullets; it was much used on boat service. They were mounted on swivel crutches, and termed top-pieces; quarter pieces in barges and pinnaces, where timbers were especially fitted for them.

MUSKET-PROOF. Any bulk-head, parapet, or substance which effectually resists the force of a musket-ball.

MUSKET-SHOT. Was the computed distance of 400 yards, now undergoing change.

MUSLIN, OR DIMITY. The flying kites of a ship. "Give her the muslin," or "Spare not the dimity," frequently used in tropical chase of slavers.

MUSTER, To. To assemble in order that the state and condition of the men may be seen, and also at times to inspect their arms and clothing.

MUSTER-BOOK. A copy of a ship of war's open list, drawn up for the use of the clerk of the check, in calling over the crew. A copy of the muster-book is to be transmitted every two months to the admiralty.

MUSTER-PAPER. A description of paper supplied from the dockyards, ruled and headed, for making ships' books.

MUSTER-ROLL. A document kept by the master of every British vessel, specifying the name, age, quality, and country of every person of the ship's company; even neutrals are compelled to produce such a paper in time of war.

MUSTER THE WATCH. A duty performed nightly at 8 P.M., and repeated when the watch is relieved up to 4 A.M.

MUTCHKIN. A pint measure.

MUTILATION. The crime of self-maiming to avoid serving.

MUTINOUS. Showing symptoms of sedition.

MUTINY. Revolt or determined disobedience of regular authority by soldiers or sailors, and punishable with death. Shakspeare makes Hamlet sleep

> "Worse than the *mutines* in the bilboes."

MUTINY-ACT. On this document the Articles of War are founded.

MUTTON-SNAPPER. A large fish of the *Mesoprion* genus, frequenting tropical seas, and prized in the Jamaica markets. (*See* SNAPPER.)

MUZZLE OF A PIECE OF ORDNANCE. The forward extremity of the cylinder, and the metal which surrounds it, extending back to the neck, where it meets the chase, marked by a moulded ring in old guns.

MUZZLE-LASHINGS. The ropes which confine the muzzles of lower-deck guns to the housing bolts.

MUZZLE-RING. That which encompassed and strengthened the muzzle or mouth of a cannon; now disused.

MUZZLE TO THE RIGHT, OR MUZZLE TO THE LEFT! The order given to trim the gun to the object.

MUZZY. Half-drunk.

MYLKERE. The old English name for the milt of a fish.

MYOPARA. An ancient corsair's vessel.

MYRMIDON [from *mur-medon*, a sea-captain]. The Myrmidons were a people of Thessaly, said to have first constructed ships.

MYSERECORD. A thin-bladed dagger with which a grievously wounded warrior was despatched as an act of mercy.

MYTH. Obelisk, tower, land, or anything for directing the course by sight.

N.

NAB. The bolt-toe, or cock of a gun-lock.

NABB. A cant term for the head. Also, a protuberance on the rocky summit of a hill; a rocky ledge below water.

NACA, OR NACELLE. A French boat without mast or sail, used as early as the twelfth century.

NACRE. The mother-of-pearl which lines some shells, both univalve and bivalve.

NACTA. A small transport vessel of early times.

NADIR. The lower pole of the rational horizon, the other being the zenith.

NAID. A northern term for a lamprey, or large eel.

NAIL, To. Is colloquially used for binding a person to a bargain. In weighing articles of food, a nail is 8 lbs.

NAILING A GUN. Synonymous with *cloying* or *spiking*. When necessary to abandon cannon, or when the enemy's artillery, though seized, cannot be taken away, it is proper to spike it, which is done by driving a steel or other spike into the vent. The best method sometimes to render a gun serviceable again is to drill a new vent. (*See* SPIKE.)

NAILS OF SORTS. Nails used in carpentry under the denominations of 4, 6, 8, 10, 24, 30, and 40 penny-nails, all of different lengths.

NAKE! The old word to unsheath swords, or make them naked.

NAKED. State of a ship's bottom without sheathing, Also, a place without means of defence.

NAKHADAH, OR NACODAH. An Arab sea-captain.

NAME. The name of a merchant ship, as well as the port to which she belongs, must be painted in a conspicuous manner on her stern. If changed, she must be registered *de novo*, and the old certificate cancelled.

NAME-BOARD. The arch-board, or part whereon the ship's name and port are painted.

NAME-BOOK. The Anglo-Saxon *nom-bóc*, a mustering list.

NANCY. An east-country term for a small lobster.

NANCY DAWSON. A popular air by which seamen were summoned to grog.

NANKIN. A light fawn-coloured or white cotton cloth, almost exclusively worn at one time in our ships on the India station. It was supplied from China, but is now manufactured in England, Malta, and the United States.

NANT. A brook, or small river, on the coasts of Wales.

NAPHTHA. A very inflammable, fiercely burning fluid, which oozes from the ground or rock in many different localities, and may be obtained by the distillation of coal, cannel, and other substances. It is nearly related to petroleum (which see), and is used for lighting, combustible, and various other purposes.

NAPIER'S BONES. Small rods, arranged by Lord Napier to expedite arithmetical calculations. In *Hudibras:*

> "A moon-dial, with Napier's bones,
> And several constellation stones."

NARKE. A ray of very wonderful electric powers.

NARROWING OF THE FLOOR-SWEEP. For this peculiar curve, *see* RISING HALF-BREADTH.

NARROWS. The most confined part of a channel between two lands, or any contracted part of a navigable river.

NARWHAL. The *Monodon monoceros*, an animal of the cetacean order, found in the Arctic seas, and distinguished by the single long pointed tusk projecting straight forward from its upper jaw, whence it is also termed sea-unicorn.

NATURAL FORTIFICATION. Those obstacles, in the form or nature of the country, which impede the approaches of an enemy.

NATURAL MOTION. A term applied to the descending parabolic curve of a shot or shell in falling.

NAUFRAGIATE, To. An old expression, meaning to suffer shipwreck. It occurs in Lithgow's *Pilgrime's Farewell*, 1618.

NAULAGE. A freight or fare.

NAUMACHIA. An artificial piece of water whereon the ancient Romans represented a sea-fight, supposed to have originated in the first Punic war.

NAUROPOMETER. An instrument for measuring the amount of a ship's heel or inclination at sea.

NAUSCOPY. The tact of discovering ships or land at considerable distances.

NAUTICAL. Relating to navigation, sailors, or maritime affairs in general.

NAUTICAL ALMANAC. A book of the first necessity to navigators. (*See* EPHEMERIS.)

NAUTICAL ASSESSORS. Persons of nautical experience appointed to assist the judge of the admiralty and other courts in technical difficulties.

NAUTICAL ASTRONOMY. That part of the celestial science which treats of the planets and stars so far as relates to the purposes of navigation.

NAUTICAL DAY. This day commences at noon, twelve hours before the civil day, and ends at noon of the day following. (*See* DAY.)

NAUTICAL MILE (MEAN) = 6075·6 feet.

NAUTICAL STARS. About 72 of the brightest, which have been selected for determining the latitude or the longitude, by lunar distances, and inserted, corrected to the year, in the Nautical Ephemeris.

NAUTICAL TABLES. Those especially computed for resolution of matters dependent on nautical astronomy, and navigation generally.

NAUTICUM FŒNUS. Marine usury; bottomry.

NAUTILUS. The pearly nautilus, *N. pompilius*, is a marine animal, belonging to the same class (*Cephalopoda*) as the cuttle-fish, but protected by a beautiful, chambered, discoid shell. The paper-nautilus (*Argonauta argo*) belongs to a different family of the same class, and has a simple, delicate, boat-like shell.

NAVAL. Of or belonging to a ship, or, as now commonly adopted, to the royal navy; hence, naval stores, naval officers, &c.

NAVAL ARCHITECTURE. The construction, or art and science, of building ships.

NAVAL ARMAMENT. A fleet or squadron of ships of war, fitted out for a particular service.

NAVAL CADET. *See* CADET.

NAVAL HOSPITALS. Greenwich is styled by eminence *the Royal Hospital*, yet the naval medical establishments in England and the colonies are all royal. At home they are Haslar, Plymouth, Yarmouth, Haul-bowline, Chatham, and Woolwich ; abroad, Malta, Jamaica, Halifax, Bermuda, Cape of Good Hope, and Hong Kong. Besides these useful hospitals, there are other stations of relief around the coasts.

NAVAL OFFICER. One belonging to the royal navy. Also, the person in charge of the stores in a royal dockyard abroad.

NAVAL RESERVE. A body of volunteers, consisting of coasters and able merchant seamen, who are drilled for serving on board our ships of war in case of need. They receive a fixed rate of compensation, become entitled to a pension, and enjoy other privileges. They are largely officered from their own body.

NAVAL SCIENCE. A knowledge of the theory of ship-building, seaman-ship, navigation, nautical astronomy, and tactics.

NAVAL STORES. All those particulars which are made use of, not only in the royal navy, but in every other kind of navigation. There are various statutes against stealing or embezzling them.

NAVAL STORE-SHIP. A government vessel, appropriated to carrying stores and munitions of war to different stations.

NAVAL TACTICS. The warlike evolutions of fleets, including such manœuvres as may be judged most suitable for attack, defence, or retreat, with precision. The science of tactics happens never to have proceeded from naval men. Thus Père la Hoste among the French, and a lawyer among the English, are the prime authorities. Moreover, it is a fact well known to those who served half a century back, when Lord Keith, Sir P. Durham, Sir P. Malcolm, and B. Hallowell practised their squadrons, that questions remained in dispute and undecided for at least sixteen years.

NAVE-HOLE. The hole in the centre of a gun-truck for receiving the end of the axle-tree.

NAVEL HOODS. Those hoods wrought above and below the hawse-holes, outside a ship, where there are no cheeks to support a bolster.

NAVEL LAVER. The sea-weed *Ulva umbilicus.*

NAVEL LINE. *See* LINE.

NAVIGABLE. Any channel capable of being passed by ships or boats.

NAVIGANT. An old word for sailor.

NAVIGATION. The art of conducting vessels on the sea, not only by the peculiar knowledge of seamanship in all its intricate details, but also by such a knowledge of the higher branches of nautical astronomy as enables the commander to hit his port, after a long succession of bad weather, and an absence of three or four months from all land. Any man without science may navigate the entire canals of Great Britain, but may be unable to pass from Plymouth to Guernsey.

NAVIGATION ACTS. Various statutes by which the legislature of Great Britain has in a certain degree restricted the intercourse of foreign vessels with her own ports, or those of her dependent possessions; the object being to promote the increase of British shipping.

NAVIGATOR. A person skilled in the art of navigation. In old times, the ship's *artist*. Also, one who plies merely on canals. Also, the *navvy* who works on embankments, cuttings, &c.

NAVITHALAMUS. A word in Law-Latin signifying a yacht.

NAVVIES. The vigorous labourers employed in cutting canals, railroads, or river works in temporary gangs.

NAVY. Any assembly of ships, whether for commerce or war. More particularly the vessels of war which, belonging to the government of any state, constitute its maritime force. The Royal Navy of Great Britain is conducted under the direction of the lords-commissioners for executing the office of lord high-admiral, and by the following principal officers under them:—the controller of the navy, controlling dockyards, building, &c., with his staff; the accountant-general, store-keeper general, and controller of victualling. These several lords meet as a board at Somerset House on special days to give the affairs the force of the board of admiralty.

NAVY AGENTS. Selected mercantile houses, about fourteen, who manage the affairs of officers' pay, prizes, &c., for which the law authorizes a certain percentage. They hold powers of attorney to watch the interests of their clients.

NAVY BILLS. Bills of removal, transfer, &c., are not negotiable, nor can they be made other use of.

NAVY BOARD. The commissioners of the navy collectively considered, but long since abolished.

NAVY TRANSPORT. *See* TRANSPORT.

NAVY-YARD. A royal arsenal for the navy.

NAY-WORD. The old term for the watchword, parole, or counter-sign.

NAZE. *See* NESS.

NEALED. *See* ARMING.

NEALED-TO. A shore, with deep soundings close in.

NEAPED. The situation of a ship which, within a bar-harbour, is left aground on the spring-tides so that she cannot go to sea or be floated off till the return of the next spring-tides.

NEAP-TIDES. A term from the Ang.-Sax. *nepflods.* They are but medium tides, in respect to their opposites, the springs, being neither so high, so low, nor so rapid. The phenomenon is owing to the attractions of the sun and moon then partly counteracting each other.

NEAR, AND NO NEAR. Synonymous terms used as a warning to the helmsman when too near the wind, not to come closer to it, but to keep the weather-helm in hand.

NEAT. *See* NET, as commercial weight.

NEB. This word, the Ang.-Sax. *nebb,* face as well as nose, is sometimes used for *ness* (which see). Also, a bird's beak.

NEBULA. An old term for a cluster of stars looking like a cloudy spot till separated by telescopic power; but the term is also now correctly applied to masses of nebulous matter only.

NECESSARIES. Minor articles of clothing or equipment, prescribed by regulation, but provided by the men out of their own pay.

NECESSARY MONEY. An extra allowance formerly allowed to pursers for the coals, wood, turnery-ware, candles, and other necessaries provided by them.

NECESSITY. If a ship be compelled by necessity to change the order of the places to which she is insured, this is not deemed deviation, and the underwriters are still liable.

NECK. The elbow or part connecting the blade and socket of a bayonet. *Goose-neck*, at the ends of booms, to connect them with the sides, or at the yard-arm for the studding-sail boom-iron.

NECK OF A GUN. The narrow part where the chase meets the swell of the muzzle.

NECKED. Treenails are said to be necked where they are cracked, bent, or nipped between the outside skin and the timbers of a vessel, whether from bad driving or severe straining.

NECKING. A small neat moulding at the foot of the taffrail over the light.

NECKLACE. A ring of wads placed round a gun, as sometimes practised, for readiness and stowage. Also, a strop round a lower mast carrying leading-blocks. Also, the chain necklace, to which the futtock-shrouds are secured in some vessels.

NECK OF LAND. Dividing two portions of water, or it may be the neck of a peninsula.

NECK OF THE CASCABLE. The part between the swell of the breech of a gun and the button. Its narrowest part within the button.

NECKUR. A Scandinavian sea-sprite, whence some derive our "Old Nick" in preference to St. Nicholas, the modern patron of sailors.

NEEDLE. The Ang.-Sax. *nœdl*. (*See also* MAGNETIC NEEDLE.)

NEEDLE-FISH. The shorter pipe-fish, stang, or sting, *Sygnathus acus*.

NEEDLE-GUN. One wherein the ignition for the cartridge is produced by the penetration of the detonating priming by a steel spike working in the lock. It is the Prussian musket.

NEEDLES. Used by sailmakers, are *seaming*, *bolt-rope*, or *roping* needles, all three-sided, and of very fine steel.—The *Needles* of the Isle of Wight are the result of cracks in the rocks, through which the sea has worn its way, as also at Old Harry, Swanage Bay. As the chalk formation stretches westward, the structure changes in hardness until at Portland we meet with Portland stone. In California many of the needle rocks are of volcanic origin; others again are basaltic columns.

NEGLECT. A charge not exceeding £3, from the wages of a seaman, in the Complete Book, for any part of the ship's stores lost overboard, or damaged, from his gross carelessness.

NEGLIGENCE. If agent or broker engages to do an act for another, and he either wholly neglects it, or does it unskilfully, an action on the case will lie against him.

NEGOTIATE, To. The duty of a diplomatist; the last resource and best argument being now 12-ton guns.

NEGRO-BOAT. *See* ALMODIE.

NEGROHEAD. Hard-rolled tobacco.

NEGRO-HEADS. The brown loaves issued to ships in ordinary.

NELLY. *Diomedea spadicea,* a sea-bird of the family *Procellaridæ,* which follows in the wake of a ship when rounding the Cape of Good Hope: it is very voracious of fat blubber.

NEPTUNE. A superior planet, recently discovered; it is the most distant member of the solar system yet known, and was revealed by the effect which its attraction had produced upon the movements of Uranus; this was one of the most admirable solutions in modern mathematical science. Neptune, so far as is yet known, has no satellites.

NEPTUNES. Large brass pans used in the Bight of Biafra for obtaining salt.

NEPTUNE'S GOBLETS. The large cup-shaped sponges found in the eastern seas; *Raphyrus patera.*

NEPTUNE'S SHEEP. Waves breaking into foam, called white horses.

NESS [Ang. Sax. *næs*]. A projection of land, as Dungeness, Sheerness, &c. It is common in other European languages, as the French *nez,* Italian *naso,* Russian *noss,* Norwegian *naze,* &c. Our Dunnose is an example.

NEST. *See* CROW'S NEST.

NET. In commerce, is the weight of a commodity alone, without the package.

NET AND COBLE. The means by which sassine or flood-gates are allowed in fishings on navigable rivers.

NETTING. Network of rope or small line for the purpose of securing hammocks, sails, &c.—*Boarding netting.* A stout netting formerly extended fore and aft from the gunwale to a proper height up the rigging. Its use was to prevent an enemy from jumping on board.—*Splinter netting.* Is stretched from the main-mast aft to the mizen-mast, in a horizontal position, about 12 feet above the quarter-deck. It secures those engaged there from injury by the fall of any objects from the mast-heads during an action:

> "And has saved the lives of many men
> Who have fallen from aloft."

NETTLES. Small line used for seizings, and for hammock-clues. (*See* KNITTLE.)—*To nettle,* is to provoke.

NEUTRALS. Those who do not by treaty owe anything to either party in war; for if they do they are confederates. They are not to interfere between contending powers; and the right of security justifies a belligerent in enforcing the conditions. They are not allowed to trade from one port of the enemy to another, nor to be habitually employed in his coasting trade. Indeed the simple conveyance of any article to the opponent of the blockading squadron, at once settles the non-admission, or even hovering.

NEVER SAY DIE! An expressive phrase, meaning do not despair, there is hope yet.—*Nil desperandum!* As Cowper says,

"Beware of desperate steps. The darkest day,
Wait till to-morrow, will have passed away."

NEW ACT. The going on shore without leave, and which though thus termed new, is an old trick.

NEWCOME. An officer commencing his career. Any stranger or fresh hand newly arrived.

NEWELL. An upright piece of timber to receive the tenon of the rails that lead from the breast-hook to the gangway.

NEWGATE BIRDS. The men sent on board ship from prisons; but the term has also been immemorially used, as applied to some of the *Dragon's* men in the voyage of Sir Thomas Roe to Surat, 1615.

NEW MOON. The moon is said to be new when she is in conjunction with the sun, or between that luminary and the earth.

NEWS. "Do you hear the news?" A formula used in turning up the relief watch.

NICE STEERAGE. That which is required in tideways and intricate channels, chasing or chased.

NIDGET. A coward. A term used in old times for those who refused to join the royal standard.

NIGHT-CAP. Warm grog taken just before turning in.

NIGHTINGALES. *See* SPITHEAD-NIGHTINGALES.

NIGHT ORDER-BOOK. A document of some moment, as it contains the captain's behests about change of course, &c., and ought to be legibly written.

NIGHT-WALKER. A fish of a reddish colour, about the size of a haddock, so named by Cook's people from the greatest number being caught in the night; probably red-snapper.

NIGHT WARD. The night-watch.

NILL. Scales of hot iron at the armourer's forge. Also, the stars of rockets.

NIMBUS. Ragged and hanging clouds resolving into rain. (*See* CUMULO-CIRRO-STRATUS.)

NINE-PIN BLOCK. A block in that form, mostly used for a *fair-leader* under the cross-pieces of the forecastle and quarter-deck bitts.

NINES, To THE. An expression to denote complete.

NINGIM. A corruption of *ginseng* (which see).

NIP. A short turn in a rope. Also, a fishing term for a bite. In Arctic parlance, a nip is when two floes in motion crush by their opposite edges a vessel unhappily entrapped. Also, the parts of a rope at the place bound by the seizing, or caught by jambing. Also, *Nip in the hawse;* hence "freshen the nip," by veering a few feet of the service into the hawse.

NIPCHEESE. The sailor's name for a purser's steward.

NIPPER. The armourer's pincers or tongs. Also, a hammock with so little bedding as to be unfit for stowing in the nettings.

NIPPERING. Fastening nippers by taking turns crosswise between the parts to jam them; and sometimes with a round turn before each cross. These are called racking turns.

NIPPER-MEN. Foretop-men employed to bind the nippers about the cables and messenger, and to whom the boys return them when they are taken off.

NIPPERS. Are formed of clean, unchafed yarns, drawn from condemned rope, unlaid. The yarns are stretched either over two bolts, or cleats, and a fair strain brought on each part. They are then "marled" from end to end, and used in various ways, viz. to bind the messenger to the cable, and to form slings for wet spars, &c. The nipper is passed at the manger-board, the fore-end pressing itself against the cable; after passing it round cable and messenger spirally, the end is passed twice round the messenger, and a foretop-man holds the end until it reaches the fore-hatchway, when a maintop-man takes it up, and at the main-hatchway it is taken off, a boy carrying it forward ready coiled for further use.—*Selvagee nippers* are used when from a very great strain the common nippers are not found sufficiently secure; selvagees are then put on, and held fast by means of tree-nails. (*See* SELVAGEE and TREE-NAILS.)—*Buoy and nipper.* Burt's patent for sounding. By this contrivance any amount of line is loosely veered. So long as the lead descends, the line runs through the nipper attached to a canvas inflated buoy. The instant it is checked or the lead touches bottom, the back strain nips the line, and indicates the vertical depth that the lead has descended.

NIPPLE. In ship-building. Another name for *knuckle* (which see). Also, the nipple of a gun or musket lock; the perforated projection which receives the percussion-cap.

NISSAK. The Shetland name for a small porpoise.

NITRE. *Potassæ nitras*, a salt formed by the union of nitric acid with potash; the main agent in gunpowder.

NITTY. A troublesome noise; a squabble.

NOAH'S ARK. Certain clouds elliptically parted, considered a sign of fine weather after rain.

NOB. The head; therefore applied to a person in a high station of life. (*See* KNOB.)

NOCK. The forward upper end of a sail that sets with a boom. Also, a term used for *notch*.

NOCTURNAL, NOCTURLABIUM. An instrument chiefly used at sea, to take the altitude or depression of some of the stars about the pole, in order to find the latitude and the hour of the night.

NOCTURNAL ARC. That part of a circle, parallel to the equator, which is described by a celestial object, between its setting and rising.

NODDY. The *Sterna solida*, a dark web-footed sea-bird, common about the West Indies. Also, a simpleton; so used by Shakspeare in the *Two Gentlemen of Verona*.

NODES. Those points in the orbit of a planet or comet where it intersects the ecliptic. The ascending node is the point where it passes from the south to the north side of the ecliptic; the descending node is the opposite point, where the latitude changes from north to south. (*See* LINE OF NODES.)

NOG. A tree-nail driven through the heels of the shores, to secure them.

NOGGIN. A small cup or spirit-measure, holding about ¼ of a pint.

NOGGING. The act of securing the shores by tree-nails. Also, warming beer at the galley-fire.

NO HIGHER! *See* NEAR.

NO-HOWISH. Qualmy; feeling an approaching ailment without being able to describe the symptoms.

NO-MAN'S LAND. A space in mid-ships between the after-part of the belfry and the fore-part of a boat when it is stowed upon the booms, as is often done in a deep-waisted vessel; this space is used to contain any blocks, ropes, tackles, &c., which may be necessary on the forecastle, and probably derives its name from being neither on the starboard nor port side, neither in the waist, nor on the forecastle.

NONAGESIMAL DEGREE. The point of the ecliptic which is at the greatest altitude above the horizon.

NON-COMBATANTS. A term applied erroneously to the purser, master surgeon, &c., of a man-of-war, for all men on board may be called on, more or less, to fight.

NON-COMMISSIONED OFFICERS. In familiar parlance, *non-coms.* are the sergeants, corporals, and others, appointed under special regulations, by the orders of the commanding officer.

NON-CONDENSING ENGINE. A high-pressure steam-engine.

NONIUS SCALE, OR VERNIER. That fixed to the oblong opening near the lower end of the index-bar of a sextant or quadrant; it divides degrees into minutes, and these again into parts of seconds.

NO! NO! The answer to the night-hail by which it is known that a midshipman or warrant officer is in the boat hailed.

NON-RECOIL. This was effected by securing the breeching while the gun was run out: often practised in small vessels.

NOOK. A small indentation of the land; a little cove in the inner parts of bays and harbours.

NOOK-SHOTTEN. A Shakspearian expression for a coast indented with bays; as in *Henry V.* Bourbon speaks contemptuously of "that nook-shotten isle of Albion."

NOON. Mid-day.

NOOSE. A slip or running knot.

NORE. The old word for north. Also, a canal or channel.

NORIE'S EPITOME. A treatise on navigation not to be easily cast aside.

NORLAND. Of, or belonging to, the north land.

NORMAL LEVEL OF A BAROMETER. A term reckoned synonymous with *par-line* (which see).

NORMAN. A short wooden bar thrust into one of the holes of the windlass or capstan in a merchantman, whereon to veer a rope or fasten the cable, if there be little strain upon it.   Also fixed through the head of the rudder, in some ships, to prevent the loss of the rudder.   Also, a pin placed in the bitt-cross-piece to confine the cable from falling off.

NORRIE, AND TAMMIE NORRIE.   The Scotch name for the puffin.

NORTH.   From the Anglo-Saxon *nord*.

NORTH-AWAY YAWL.   The old term for *Norway yawl* (which see).

NORTH-EAST PASSAGE.   To the Pacific, or round the north of Europe, has been divided into three parts, thus : 1. From Archangel to the river Lena; 2. from the Lena, round Tschukotskoi-ness to Kamtschatka; and 3. from Kamtschatka to Japan.   They have been accomplished at various times, but not successively.

NORTHERN DIVER.   The *Colymbus glacialis*, a large diving-bird.

NORTHERN-GLANCE.   The old sea-name of the *aurora borealis* (which see).

NORTHERN LIGHTS.   *See* NORTHERN-GLANCE.

NORTHERS.   Those winds so well known to all seamen who have fre-quented the West Indies, and which are preceded by the appearance of a vast quantity of fine cobwebs or gossamer in the atmosphere, which clings to all parts of a vessel's rigging, thus serving as a warning of an approach-ing gale.   Northers alternate with the seasons in the Gulf of Mexico, the Florida Channel, Jamaica, Cuba, &c.   Their cold is intense.

NORTH FOLLOWING.   For this and *north preceding, see* QUADRANT.

NORTH PASSAGE TO THE INDIES.   The grand object of our maritime expeditions at a remote period, prosecuted with a boldness, dexterity, and perseverance which, although since equalled in the same pursuit, have not yet been surpassed:—

> "I will undertake
> To find the north passage to the Indies sooner,
> Than plough with your proud heifer."—*Massinger.*

NORTH SEA.   The Jamaica name for the north swell.   (*See* GROUND-SEA.)

NORTH-WESTER.   This wind in India usually commences or terminates with a violent gust from that quarter, with loud thunder and vivid light-ning.   Also, gales which blow from the eastern coast of North America in the Atlantic during the autumn and winter.

NORTH-WEST PASSAGE.   By Hudson's Bay into the Pacific Ocean has been more than once attempted of late years, but hitherto without success.   Some greatly doubted the practicability of such an enterprise; but the north-west passage, as far as relates to the flow of the sea beneath the ice, was satisfactorily solved by H.M.S. *Investigator*, Sir R. Maclure, reaching the western end of Barrow's Straits.   The former question, up to Melville Island, which Sir R. Maclure reached and left his notice at in 1852, having been already thoroughly established by Sir E. Parry in 1820.

NORTH WIND.   This wind in the British seas is dry and cold, and generally ushers in fair weather and clear skies. The barometer rises with the wind at north, and is highest at N.N.E.; the air forming this wind comes from colder latitudes, and has therefore lost most of its moisture.

NORWAY SKIFF. A particularly light and buoyant boat, which is both swift and safe in the worst weather.

NORWAY YAWL. This, of all small boats, is said to be the best calculated for a high sea; it is often met with at a distance from land, when a stout ship can hardly carry any sail. The parent of the *peter-boat*.

NOSE. Often used to denote the stem of a ship. Also, a neck of land: *naes*, or *ness*.

NOTARY. The person legally empowered to attest deeds, protests, or other documents, in order to render them binding.

NOTCH. The gaffle of a cross-bow.

NOTCH-BLOCK. *See* SNATCH-BLOCK.

NOTCH-SIGHT OF A GUN. A sight having a V-shaped notch, wherein the eye easily finds the lowest or central point.

NOTHING OFF! A term used by the man at the conn to the steersman, directing him to keep her close to the wind; or "nothing off, and very well thus!" (*See* THUS.)

NOTIONS. An American sea-term for a cargo in sorts; thus a notion-vessel on the west coast of America is a perfect bazaar; but one, which sold a mixture—logwood, bad claret, and sugar—to the priests for sacrament wine had to run for it.

NOUD. A term in the north for fishes that are accounted of little value.

NOUP. A round-headed eminence.

NOUS. An old and very general term for intelligent perception, evidently from the Greek.

NOUST. A landing-place or indent into the shore for a boat to be moored in; a term of the Orkney Isles.

NOZZLE-FACES. Square plates of brass raised upon the cylinder; one round each of the steam-ports, for the valve-plates to slide upon.

NOZZLES. In steamers, the same as steam-ports; they are oblong passages from the nozzle-faces to the inside of the cylinder; by them the steam enters and returns above and below the piston. Also pump nozzles.

NUBECULÆ, MAJOR AND MINOR. The *Magellanic clouds* (which see).

NUCLEUS OF A COMET. The condensed or star-like part of the head.

NUDDEE. A Hindostanee word for a river.

NUGGAR. A term in the East Indies for a fort, and also for an alligator.

NULLAH. A ravine or creek of a stream in India.

NUMBER. The number on the ship's books is marked on the clothing of seamen; that on a man's hammock or bag corresponds with his number on the watch and station bill. The ships of the royal navy are denoted by flags expressing letters, and when passing or nearing each other the names are exchanged by signals.—*Losing the number of the mess*, is a phrase for dying suddenly; being killed or drowned.

NUMERARY or MARRYAT'S SIGNALS.   A useful code used by
the mercantile marine, by an arrangement of flags from a cypher to units,
and thence to thousands. (*See* SIGNALS.)

NUN-BUOY.   A buoy made of staves, somewhat in the form of a double
cone; large in the middle, and tapering rapidly to the ends; the slinging
of which is a good specimen of practical rigging tact.

NURAVEE YAWL.   A corruption of *Norway yawl* (which see).

NURSE.   An able first lieutenant, who in former times had charge of a
young boy-captain of interest, but possessing no knowledge for command.
Also, a small kind of shark with a very rough skin; a dog-fish.

NUT.   A small piece of iron with a female screw cut through the middle
· of it, for screwing on to the end of a bolt.

NUTATION.   An oscillatory motion of the earth's axis, due chiefly to the
action of the moon upon the spheroidal figure of our globe.

NUTS OF AN ANCHOR.   Two projections either raised or welded on the
square part of the shank, for securing the stock to its place.

NYCTALOPIA.   *See* MOON-BLINK.

O.

O.   The fourth class of rating on Lloyd's books for the comparative excellence of merchant ships.   But insured vessels are rarely so low
(*See* A.)

O! or Ho!   An interjection commanding attention or possibly the cessation of any action.

OAK.   *Quercus*, the valuable monarch of the woods.   "Hearts of oak are
our ships," as the old song says.

OAKUM [from the Anglo-Saxon *œcumbe*].   The state into which old ropes
are reduced when they are untwisted and picked to pieces.   It is principally used in caulking the seams, for stopping leaks, and for making
into twice-laid ropes.   Very well known in workhouses.—*White Oakum.*
That which is formed from untarred ropes.

OAKUM-BOY.   The caulker's apprentice, who attends to bring oakum,
pitch, &c.

OAR.   A slender piece of timber used as a lever to propel a boat through
the water.   The blade is dipped into the water, while the other end
within board, termed the loom, is small enough to be grasped by the
rower.   The *silver oar* is a badge of office, similar to the staff of a peace-
officer, which on presentation, enables a person intrusted with a warrant
to serve it on board any ship he may set foot upon.—*To boat the oars*, is
to cease rowing and lay the oars in the boat.—*Get your oars to pass!*
The order to prepare them for rowing, or shipping them.

OAR, To SHOVE IN AN. To intermeddle, or give an opinion unasked.

OAR-PROPULSION. The earliest motive power for vessels; it may be by the broadside in rowlocks abeam, by sweeps on the quarters fore and aft, or by sculling with one oar in the notch of the transom amidships. (*See* STERN-OAR.)

OARS! The order to cease rowing, by lifting the oars from the water, and poising them on their looms horizontally in their rowlocks.—*Look to your oars!* Passing any object or among sea-weed.—*Double-banked oars* (which see).

OASIS. A fertile spot in the midst of a sandy desert.

OATH. A solemn affirmation or denial of anything, 'before a person authorized to administer the same, for discovery of truth and right. (*See* CORPORAL OATH.) Hesiod ascribes the invention of oaths to discord. The oath of supremacy and of the Protestant faith was formerly taken by an officer before he could hold a commission in the royal navy.

OAZE. Synonymous with the Ang.-Sax. *wase* when applied to mud. (*See* OOZE.)

OBEY. A word forming the fulcrum of naval discipline.

OBI. A horrible sorcery practised among the negroes in the West Indies, the infliction of which by a threat from the juggler is sufficient to lead the denounced victim to mental disease, despondency, and death. · Still the wretched trash gathered together for the obi-spell is not more ridiculous than the amulets of civilized Europe.

OBLATE. Compressed or flattened.

OBLIGATION. A bond containing a penalty, with a condition annexed for payment of money or performance of covenants.

OBLIMATION. The deposit of mud and silt by water.

OBLIQUE-ANGLED TRIANGLE. Any other than a right-angled triangle.

OBLIQUE ASCENSION. An arc between the first point of Aries and that point of the equator which comes to the horizon with a star, or other heavenly body, reckoned according to the order of signs. It is the sum or difference of the right ascension and ascensional difference.

OBLIQUE BEARINGS. Consist in determining the position of a ship, by observing with a compass the bearings of two or more objects on the shore whose places are given on a chart, and drawing lines from those places, so as to make angles with their meridians equal to the observed bearings; the intersection of the line gives on the chart the position of the ship. This is sometimes called the method of cross-bearings.

OBLIQUE SAILING. Is the reduction of the position of the ship from the various courses made good, oblique to the meridian or parallel of latitude. If a vessel sails north or south, it is simply a distance on the meridian. If east or west, on the parallel, and refers to parallel sailing. If oblique, it is solved by middle latitude, or Mercator sailing.

OBLIQUE STEP. A movement in marching, in which the men, while advancing, gradually take ground to the right or left.

OBLIQUITY OF THE ECLIPTIC. The angle between the planes of the ecliptic and the equator, or the inclination of the earth's equator to the plane of her annual path, upon which the seasons depend: this amounts at present to about 23° 27'.

OBLONG SQUARE. A name improperly given to a parallelogram. (*See* THREE SQUARE.)

OBSERVATION. In nautical astronomy, denotes the taking the sun, moon, or stars' altitude with a quadrant or sextant, in order thereby to find the latitude or time; also, the lunar distances.

OBSERVE, To. To take a bearing or a celestial observation.

OBSIDIONAL CROWN. The highest ancient Roman military honour; the decoration of the chief who raised a siege.

OBSTACLES. Chains, booms, abattis, snags, palisades, or anything placed to impede an enemy's progress. Unforeseen hindrances.

OBTURATOR. A cover or valve in steam machinery.

OBTUSE ANGLE. One measuring above 90°, and therefore beyond a right angle; called by shipwrights *standing bevellings*.

OBTUSE-ANGLED TRIANGLE. That which has one obtuse angle.

OCCIDENT. The west.

OCCULTATION. One heavenly body eclipsing another; but in nautical astronomy it is particularly used to denote the eclipses of stars and planets by the moon.

OCCUPY, To. To take military possession.

OCEAN. This term, in its largest sense, is the whole body of salt water which encompasses the globe, except the collection of inland seas, lakes, and rivers: in a word, that glorious type of omnipotent power, whether in calm or tempest:—

> " Dark, heaving, boundless, endless, and sublime,
> The image of Eternity."

In a more limited sense it is divided into—1. The Atlantic Ocean. 2. The Pacific Ocean. 3. The Indian Ocean. 4. The Southern Ocean.

OCEAN-GOING SHIP. In contradistinction to a coaster.

OCHRAS. A Gaelic term for the gills of a fish.

OCTAGON. A geometrical figure which has eight equal sides and angles.

ODHARAG. The name of the young cormorant in our northern isles.

OE. An island [from the Ang.-Sax.] *Oes* are violent whirlwinds off the Ferroe Islands, said at times to raise the water in syphons.

OFERLANDERS. Small vessels on the Rhine and the Meuse.

OFF. The opposite to *near*. Also applied to a ship sailing from the shore into the open sea. Also, implies abreast of, or near, as "We were off Cape Finisterre."—*Nothing off!* The order to the helmsman not to suffer the ship to fall off from the wind.

OFFAL. Slabs, chips, and refuse of timber, sold in fathom lots at the dockyards.

OFF AND ON. When a ship beating to windward approaches the shore by one board, and recedes from it when on the other. Also used to denote an undecided person. Dodging off a port.

OFF AT A TANGENT. Going in a hurry, or in a testy humour.

OFF DUTY. An officer, marine, or seaman in his watch below, &c. An officer is sometimes put "off duty" as a punishment.

OFFENCES. Crimes which are not capital, but by the custom of the service come under the articles of war.

OFFICER. A person having some command. A term applied both in the royal and mercantile navies to any one of a ship's company who ranks above the foremast-men.

OFFICER OF THE DAY. A military officer whose immediate duty is to attend to the interior economy of the corps to which he belongs, or of those with which he may be doing duty.

OFFICER OF THE WATCH. The lieutenant or other officer who has charge of, and commands, the watch.

OFFICERS' EFFECTS. The effects of officers who die on board are not generally sold; but should they be submitted to auction, the sale is to be confined entirely amongst the officers.

OFFICIAL LETTERS. All official letters which are intended to be laid before the commander-in-chief, must be signed by the officers themselves, specifying their rank under their signatures. All applications from petty officers, seamen, and marines, relative to transfer, discharge, or other subjects of a similar nature, are to be made through the captain or commanding officer. They ought to be written on foolscap paper, leaving a margin, to the left hand, of one-fourth of the breadth, and superscribed on the cover "On H. M. Service."

OFFING. Implies to seaward; beyond anchoring ground.—*To keep a good offing,* is to keep well off the land, while under sail.

OFF-RECKONING. A proportion of the full pay of troops retained from them, in special cases, until the period of final settlement, to cover various expected charges (for ship-rations and the like).

OFF SHE GOES! Means run away with the purchase fall. Move to the tune of the fifer. The first move when a vessel is launched.

OFF THE REEL. At once; without stopping. In allusion to the way in which the log-line flies off the reel when a ship is sailing fast.

OFFWARD. The situation of a ship which lies aground and leans from the shore; "the ship heels offward," and "the ship lies with her stern to the offward," is when her stern is towards the sea.

OGEE. In old-pattern guns, the doubly curved moulding added, by way of finish, to several of the rings.

OGGIDENT. Jack's corruption of *aguardiente* [Sp.], a fiery and very unwholesome spirit.

OIL-BUTT. A name for the black whale.

OILLETS, OR ŒILLETS. Apertures for firing through, in the walls of a fort.

OITER. A Gaelic word still in use for a sand-bank.

OJANCO SNAPPER. A tropical fish of the Mesoprion family, frequenting the deep-water banks of the West Indies.

OKE. A Levant weight of $2\frac{3}{4}$ lbs., common in Mediterranean commerce.

OLD COUNTRY. A very general designation for Great Britain among the Americans. The term is never applied to any part of the continent of Europe.

OLD HAND. A knowing and expert person.

OLD HORSE. Tough salt-beef.

OLD ICE. In polar parlance, that of previous seasons.

OLD-STAGER. One well initiated in anything.

OLD-STAGERISM. An adherence to established customs; sea conservatism.

OLDSTERS. In the old days of cock-pit tyranny, mids of four years' standing, and master's-mates, &c., who sadly bullied the youngsters.

OLD WIFE. A fish about 2 feet long, and 9 inches high in the back, having a small mouth, a large eye, a broad dorsal fin, and a blue body. Also, the brown long-tailed duck of Pennant.

OLD WOMAN'S TOOTH. A peculiar chisel for stub morticing.

OLERON CODE. A celebrated collection of maritime laws, compiled and promulgated by Richard Cœur-de-Lion, at the island of Oleron, near the coast of Poitou, the inhabitants of which have been deemed able mariners ever since. It is reckoned the best code of sea-laws in the world, and is recorded in the black book of the admiralty.

OLICK. The torsk or tusk, *Gadus callaris*.

OLIVER. A west-country term for a young eel.

OLPIS. A classic term for one who, from a shore eminence, watched the course which shoals of fish took, and communicated the result to the fishers. (*See* CONDOR.)

OMBRE. A fish, more commonly called grayling, or *umber*.

ON. The sea is said to be "on" when boisterous; as, there is a high sea on.

ON A BOWLINE. Close to the wind, when the sail will not stand without hauling the bowlines.

ONAGER. An offensive weapon of the middle ages.

ON A WIND. Synonymous with *on a bowline*.

ON BOARD. Within a ship; the same as *aboard*.

ONCIA. A gold coin of Sicily; value three ducats, or 10*s*. 10*d*. sterling.

ONCIN. An offensive weapon of mediæval times, consisting of a staff with a hooked iron head.

ON DECK THERE! The cry to call attention from aloft or below.

ONE-AND-ALL. A mutinous sea-cry used in the Dutch wars. Also, a rallying call to put the whole collective force on together.

ON EITHER TACK. Any way or every way; a colloquialism.

ON END. The same as *an-end* (which see). Top-masts and topgallant-masts are on end, when they are in their places, and sail can be set on them.

ONE O'CLOCK. *Like one o'clock*. With speed; rapidly.

ONERARIÆ. Ancient ships of burden, with both sails and oars.

ONE, TWO, THREE! The song with which the seamen bowse out the bowlines; the last haul being completed by belay O!

ONION-FISH. The *Cepola rubescens*, whose body peels into flakes like that vegetable. It is of a pale red colour.

ON SERVICE. On duty.

ON-SHORE WINDS. Those which blow from the offing, and render bays uncomfortable and insecure.

ON THE BEAM. Implies any distance from a ship on a line with her beams, or at right angles with the keel.

ON THE BOW. At any angle on either side of the stem up to 45°; then it is either four points on the bow, or four points before the beam.

ON THE QUARTER. Being in that position with regard to a ship, as to be included in the angles which diverge from right astern, to four points towards either quarter.

OOMIAK. A light seal-skin Greenland boat, generally worked in fine weather by the women, but in bad weather by the men.

OPEN. The situation of a place which is exposed to the wind and sea. Also, applied in meteorology, to mild weather. Also, open to attack, not protected. Also, said of any distant visible object.

OPEN HAWSE. When a vessel rides by two anchors, without any cross in her cables.

OPEN ICE. Fragments of ice sufficiently separate to admit of a ship forcing or boring through them under sail.

OPENING TRENCHES. The first breaking of ground by besiegers, in order to carry on their approaches towards a besieged place.

OPEN LIST. One of a ship's books, which contains the whole of the names of the actual officers and crew, in order to regulate their victualling. The crew are mustered by the open list.

OPEN LOWER DECKERS, To. To fire the lower tier of guns. Also said of a person using violent language.

OPEN ORDER. Any distance ordered to be preserved among ships, exceeding a cable's length.

OPEN PACK. A body of drift ice, the pieces of which, though very near each other, do not generally touch. It is opposed to close pack.

OPEN POLICY. Where the amount of the interest of the insured is not fixed by the policy, but is left to be ascertained by the insured, in case a loss shall happen.

OPEN ROADSTEAD. A place of hazard, as affording no protection either from sea or wind.

OPERATIONS. Field movements, whether offensive or defensive.

OPHIUCHUS. One of the ancient constellations, of which the lucida is *Ras-al-ague*, one of the selected nautical objects at Greenwich. This asterism is sometimes called *Serpentarius*, its Latin name, instead of its Greek.

OPINION. An experienced witness, who never saw the ship, yet may legally prove that from the description of her by another witness she was not sea-worthy.

OPOSSUM-SHRIMP. A crustacean, so named from its young being

carried about in a sort of pouch for some little time after being hatched; the *Mysis flexuosus* of naturalists.

OPPIGNORATION. The pawning of part of the cargo to get money for the payment of the duty on the remainder.

OPPOSITE TACKS. Making contrary boards. Also, a colloquialism for cross purposes.

OPPOSITION. A celestial body is said to be in opposition to the sun when their longitudes differ 180°, or half the circumference of the heavens.

OPTICK. An old term for a magnifying-glass.

ORAGIOUS. An old term for stormy or tempestuous weather:—

> "The storme was so outrageous,
> And with rumlings oragious,
> That I did feare."

ORAMBY. A sort of state-barge used in the Moluccas; some of them are rowed by 40, 80, or even, it is said, 100 paddles each.

ORARIÆ. Ancient coasting vessels.

ORB. The circular figure made by a body of troops.

ORBIT. The path described by a planet or comet round the sun.

ORBITAL. Relating to the orbit of a heavenly body.

ORC. Wrack or sea-weed, used as manure on some of the coasts of England.

ORCA. A classical name for a large voracious sea-animal, probably a grampus. Anglicized as ork or orc; thus in the second song of Drayton's strange *Polyolbion*—

> "The ugly orks, that for their lord the ocean woo."

And Milton afterwards introduces them—

> "An island salt and bare,
> The haunt of seals and orcs, and sea-mews clang."

ORDER ARMS! The word of command, with muskets or carbines, to bring the butt to the ground, the piece vertical against the right side, trigger-guard to the front.—*Open order* and *close order*, are terms for keeping the fleet prepared for any particular manœuvre.

ORDER-BOOK. A book kept for the purpose of copying such occasional successive orders as the admiral, or senior officer, may find it necessary to give.

ORDERLY. The bearer of official messages, and appointed to wait upon superior officers with communications.

ORDERLY OFFICER. In the army. *See* OFFICER OF THE DAY.

ORDER OF BATTLE. The arranging of ships or troops so as to engage the enemy to the best advantage.

ORDER OF SAILING. *See* SAILING.

ORDERS. Societies of knights. (*See* KNIGHTHOOD.)

ORDERS IN COUNCIL. Decrees given by the privy council, signed by the sovereign, for important state necessities, independently of any act of parliament; but covered by an act of indemnity when it is assembled.

ORDINARY. The establishment of the persons formerly employed to take charge of the ships of war which are laid up in ordinary at several harbours adjacent to the royal dock-yards. These duties are now under the superintendent of the dockyard. Also, the state of such men-of-war and vessels as are out of commission and laid up.

ORDINARY SEAMAN. The rating for one who can make himself useful on board, even to going aloft, and taking his part on a top-sail or topgallant-yard, but is not a complete sailor, the latter being termed an able seaman. It would be well if our merchant seamen consisted of apprentices and A.B.'s.

ORDINARY STEP. The common march of 110 paces in a minute.

ORDNANCE. A general name for all sorts of great guns which are used in war. Also, all that relates to the artillery and engineer service.

ORDNANCE-HOY. A sloop expressly fitted for transporting ordnance stores to ships, and from port to port.

OREILLET. The ear-piece of a helmet.

OREMBI. A small *korocora* (which see).

ORGUES. Long-pointed beams shod with iron, hanging vertically over a gateway, to answer as a portcullis in emergency.

ORIENT. The east point of the compass.

ORIFLAMME. The banner of St. Dennis; but the term is often applied to the flags of any French commander-in-chief.

ORIGIN. Merchant ships claiming benefit for importation, must obtain and produce certificates of *origin*, in respect to the goods they claim for. (*See* PRODUCTION.)

ORIGINAL ENTRY. The date at which men enter for the navy, and repair on board a guardship, or tender, where bedding or slops may be supplied to them, and are forwarded with them to their proper ships.

ORILLON. In fortification, a curved projection formed by the face of a bastion overlapping the end of the flank; intended to protect the latter from oblique fire; modern ricochet fire renders it of little consequence.

ORION. One of the ancient constellations, of which the lucida is the well-known nautical star *Betelgeuze*.

ORISONT. The horizon; thus spelled by our early navigators.

ORLOP. The lowest deck, formerly called "over-lop," consisting of a platform laid over the beams in the hold of ships of war, whereon the cables were usually coiled, and containing some cabins as well as the chief store-rooms. In trading vessels it is often a temporary deck.

ORLOP-BEAMS, OR HOLD-BEAMS. Those which support the orlop-deck, but are chiefly intended to fortify the hold.

ORNAMENTS. The carvings of the head, stern, and quarters of the old ships.

ORNITHÆ. An ancient term for the periodical winds by which migratory birds were transported.

ORTHODROMIC. The course which lies on a meridian or parallel.

ORTHOGRAPHIC PROJECTION. The profile, or representation of a vertical section, of a work in fortification.

ORTIVE AMPLITUDE. The eastern one.

OSCILLATING MARINE-ENGINE. A steam-engine where the top of the piston-rod is coupled with the crank, and the piston-rod moves backward and forward in the direction of the axis of the cylinder, while its extremity revolves in a circle with the crank.

OSCILLATING PUMP-SPEAR. A contrivance by which the pumps of a large vessel are worked, connected with a crank-shaft and fly-wheel, driven by handles in the same way as a winch.

OSMOND. The old term for pig-iron; a great article of lading.

OSNABURG. In commerce, a coarse linen cloth manufactured in Scotland, but resembling that made at Osnaburg in Germany.

OSPREY. The fish-hawk, *Pandion haliœtus;* Shakspeare, in *Coriolanus,* says—

> "I think he'll be to Rome
> As is the osprey to the fish."

OS SEPIÆ. The commercial term for the sepia, or cuttle-fish bones.

OSTMEN. A corrupted form of *Hoastmen.*

OTSEGO BASS. *Corregonus otsego,* a fish of the American lakes.

OTTER-PIKE. The lesser weever, *Trachinus draco;* also called sea-stranger.

OTTOMITES. An old term for Turks. See Shakspeare in *Othello.*

OUNDING. Resembling or imitating waves; used by Chaucer and others.

OUSTER LE MER. The legal term for excuse, when a man did not appear in court on summons, for that he was then beyond the seas.

OUT-AND-OUTER. An old phrase signifying thorough excellence; a man up to his duty, and able to perform it in style.

OUT-BOARD. The outside of the ship: the reverse of *in-board.*

OUT-BOATS. The order to hoist out the boats.

OUT-EARING CLEAT. This is placed on the upper side of the gaff, to pass the outer earing round from the cringle.

OUTER-JIB. In sloops, where the head-sails are termed foresail-jib and outer-jib, if set from the foremast-head. It is now very common for *ships* to set two standing jibs, the stay and tack of the inner one being secured at the middle of the jib-boom.

OUTER TURNS AND INNER TURNS. The *outer turns* of the earing serve to extend the sail outwards along its yard. The *inner turns* are employed to bind the sail close to the yard.

OUT-FIT. The stores with which a merchant vessel is fitted out for any voyage. Also, the providing an individual with clothes, &c.

OUT-FLANK, To. By a longer front, to overlap the enemy's opposite line, and thus gain a chance to turn his flank.

OUT-HAUL, OR OUT-HAULER. A rope used for hauling out the tack of a jib lower studding-sail, or the clue of a boom-sail. The reverse of *in-haul.*

OUT-HOLLING. Clearing tide-ports, canals, and channels of mud.

OUTLANDISH. Foreign; but means with Jack a place where he does not feel at home, or a language which he does not understand.

OUT-LET. The effluent or stream by which a lake discharges its water. Also applied to the spot where the efflux commences.

OUT-LICKER. A corruption of *out-rigger* (which see).

OUT-LIER. A word which has been often used for *out-rigger*, but applies to out-lying rocks, visible above water.

OUT-OARS. The order to take to rowing when the sails give but little way on a boat.

OUT OF COMMISSION. A ship where officers and men are paid off, and pennant hauled down.

OUT OF TRIM. A ship not properly balanced for fast sailing, which may be by a defect in the rigging or in the stowage of the hold.

OUT OF WINDING. Said of a plank or piece of timber which has a fair and even surface without any twists: the opposite of *winding*.

OUT OR DOWN. An exclamation of the boatswain, &c., in ordering men out of their hammocks, *i.e.* turn out, or your laniard will be cut.

OUT-PENSIONERS. Those entitled to pensions from Greenwich Hospital, but not admitted to "the house."

OUT-PORTS. Those commercial harbours which lie on the coasts; all ports in the United Kingdom out of London. (*See* CLOSE-PORTS.)

OUTREGANS. Canals or ditches navigable by boats.

OUT-RIGGER. A strong beam, of which there are several, passed through the ports of a ship, and firmly lashed at the gunwale, also assisted by guys from bolts at the water-line, to secure the masts in the act of careening, by counteracting the strain they suffer from the tackles on the opposite side. Also, any boom rigged out from a vessel to hang boats by, clear of the ship, when at anchor. Also, any spar, as the boomkin, for the fore-tack, or the jigger abaft to haul out the mizen-sheet, or extend the leading blocks of the main braces. Also, a small spar used in the tops and cross-trees, to thrust out and spread the breast back-stays to windward. Also, a counterpoising log of wood, rigged out from the side of a narrow boat or canoe, to prevent it from being upset.

OUT-SAIL, To. To sail faster than another ship, or to make a particular voyage with greater despatch.

OUTSIDE MUSTER-PAPER. A paper with the outer part blank, but the inner portion ruled and headed; supplied from the dock yards to form the cover of ships' books.

OUTSIDE PLANKING. Such are the wales, the plank-sheer, the garboard-strakes, and the like.

OUTWARD. A vessel is said to be entered outwards or inwards according as she is entered at the custom-house to depart for, or as having arrived from, foreign parts.

OUTWARD CHARGES. Pilotage and other dues incurred from any port: the reverse of *inward charges*.

OUTWORKS. Works included in the scheme of defence of a place, but outside the main rampart; if "detached," they are moreover outside the glacis.

OUVRE L'ŒIL. A mark on French charts over supposed dangers.

OVER and UNDER TURNS. Terms applied to the passing of an earing, besides its inner and outer turns.

OVER-ANENT. Opposite to.

OVER-BEAR. One ship overbears another if she can carry more sail in a fresh wind.

OVERBOARD. The state of any person or thing in the sea which had been in a ship.—*Thrown overboard* also means cast adrift by the captain; withdrawal of countenance and support.

OVER-BOYED. Said of a ship when the captain and majority of the quarter-deck officers are very young.

OVERFALL. A rippling or race in the sea, where, by the peculiarities of bottom, the water is propelled with immense force, especially when the wind and tide, or current, set strongly together. (*See* RIPPS.)

OVER-GUNNED. Where the weight of metal is disproportioned to the ship, and the quarters insufficient for the guns being duly worked.

OVERHAND KNOT. Is made by passing the end of a rope over its standing part, and through the bight.

OVERHAUL. Has many applications. A tackle when released is overhauled. To get a fresh purchase, ropes are overhauled. To reach an object, or take off strain, weather-braces are overhauled. A ship overhauls another in chase when she evidently gains upon her. Also, overhauls a stranger and examines her papers. Also, is overhauled, or examined, to determine the refit demanded.

OVER-INSURANCE. *See* RE-INSURANCE, and DOUBLE INSURANCE.

OVERLAP. A designation of the hatches of a ship ; planks in clinch-built boats. Points of land *overlap* a harbour's mouth at a particular bearing. —*To overlap*, to fay upon.

OVERLAY DAYS. Days for which demurrage can be charged.

OVER-LOFT. An old term for the upper deck of a ship.

OVER-LOOKER. Generally an old master appointed by owners of ships to look after everything connected with the fitting out of their vessels when in harbour in England.

OVER-MASTED. The state of a ship whose masts are too high or too heavy for her weight to counterbalance.

OVER-PRESS, To. To carry too much sail on a ship.

OVER-RAKE. When a ship rides at anchor in a head-sea, the waves of which frequently break in upon her, they are said to over-rake her.

OVER-RIGGED. A ship with more and heavier gear than necessary, so as to be top-hampered.

OVER-RISEN. When a ship is too high out of the water for her length and breadth, so as to make a trouble of lee-lurches and weather-rolls. Such were our 80-gun three-deckers and 44's on two decks, happily now no more.

OVER-RUNNING. (*See* UNDER-RUN.) Applied to ice, when the young ice overlaps, and is driven over.

OVER-SEA VESSELS. Ships from foreign parts, as distinguished from coasters.

OVER-SETTING. The state of a ship turning upside down, either by carrying too much sail or by grounding, so that she falls on one side. (*See* UPSET.)

OVERSHOOT, To. To give a ship too much way.

OVERSLAUGH.. From the Dutch *overslag*, meaning the bar of a river or port. Also, in military parlance, the being passed over in the roaster for some recurring duty without being assigned to it in turn.

OVER-SWACK. An old word, signifying the reflux of the waves by the force of the wind.

OVERWHELM. A comprehensive word derived from the Ang.-Saxon *wylm*, a wave. Thus the old song—

"Lash'd to the helm, should seas o'erwhelm."

OWLER. An old term on our southern coast for smuggler. Particularly persons who carried wool by night, in order to ship it contrary to law.

OWN, To. To be a proprietor in a ship.

OWNERS. The proprietors of ships. They are bound to perform contracts made by their masters, who are legally their agents.

OXBOWS. Bends or reaches of a river.

OX-EYE. A small cloud, or weather-gall, seen on the coast of Africa, which presages a severe storm. It appears at first in the form of an ox-eye, but soon overspreads the whole hemisphere, accompanied by a violent wind which scatters ships in all directions, and many are sunk downright. Also, a water-fowl. Also, the smaller glass bull's eyes.

OXYGON. A triangle which has three sharp or acute angles.

OXYRHINCUS. A large species of the skate family.

OYSE. An inlet of the sea, among the Shetlands and Orkneys.

OYSTER-BED. A "laying" of culch, that is, stones, old shells, or other hard substances, so as to form a bed for oysters, which would be choked in soft mud.

OYSTER-CATCHER, OR SEA-PYE. The black and white coast-bird, *Hæmatopus ostralegus.*

OZELLA. A Venetian coin both in gold and silver; the former being £1, 17s. 4d., and the latter 1s. 7d., in sterling value.

P.

PACE. A measure, often used for reconnoitring objects. The common pace is 2½ feet, or half the geometrical pace. The pace is also often roughly assumed as a yard.

PACIFIC OCEAN. A name given by the Spaniards to the "Great Ocean," from the fine weather they experienced on the coast of Peru.   Other parts, however, prove this a misnomer.

PACK-ICE.   A large collection of broken floe huddled together, but constantly varying its position; said to be open when the fragments do not touch, and close when the pieces are in contact.

PACKING-BOXES.   Recesses in the casing of a steamer, directly facing the steam-ports, filled with hemp-packing and tallow, in order to form steam-tight partitions.

PACKS.   Heavy thunder clouds.

PAD, or Pad-piece.   In ship-building, a piece of timber placed on the top of a beam at its middle part, in order to make up the curve or round of the deck.

PADDLE.   A kind of oar, used by the natives of India, Africa, America, and by most savages; it is shorter and broader in the blade than the common oar.—To paddle, is to propel a boat more purely by hand, that is, without a fulcrum or rowlock.

PADDLE-BEAMS.   Two large beams projecting over the sides of a steamer, between which the paddle-wheels revolve.   (See Sponsons.)

PADDLE-BOX.   The frame of wood which encircles the upper part of the paddle-wheel.

PADDLE-BOX BOATS.   Boats made to fit the paddle-box rim, stowed bottom upwards on each box.

PADDLE-SHAFT.   The stout iron axis carrying the paddle-wheels, which revolves with them when keyed.

PADDLE-STEAMER.   A steam-ship propelled through the water by paddle-wheels.

PADDLE-WHEELS.   The wheels on each side of a steamer, suspended externally by a shaft, and driven by steam, to propel her by the action of the floats.

PADDY, or Padi.   Rice in the husk, so called by the Malays, from whose language the word has found its way to all the coasts of India.

PADDY-BOATS.   A peculiar Ceylon boat, for the conveyance of rice and other necessaries.

PADDY'S HURRICANE.   Not wind enough to float the pennant.

PADRONE.   (See Patron or Master.)   This word is not used in larger vessels than coasters.

PADUAN.   A small Malay vessel, armed with two guns, one aft and the other forward, for piratical purposes.

PAGODA.   Tall tapering buildings erected by the Chinese and other eastern nations, to note certain events, or as places for worship, of which the great pagoda of Pekin may be taken as an example.   They are rather numerous on the banks of the Canton River.   (See Star-pagoda.)

PAH.   A New Zealand stronghold.   (See Hep-pah.)

PAHI.   The large war-canoe of the Society Islands.

PAID OFF.   See Paying-off.

PAINTER.   A rope attached to the bows of a boat, used for making her fast: it is spliced with a thimble to a ring-bolt inside the stem. "Cut your painter," make off.

PAIR-OAR. A name of the London wherry of a larger size than the scull.

PAIXHAN GUN. Introduced by the French General Paixhan about 1830, for the horizontal firing of heavy shells; having much greater calibre, but proportionally less metal, than the then current solid-shot guns.

PALABRAS. Sp. words; hence *palaver* amongst natives of new countries where the Spaniards have landed.

PALADIN. A knight-errant.

PALANQUIN. The covered litter of India.

PALAVER. *See* PALABRAS.

PALES AND CROSS-PALES. The interior shores by which the timbers of a ship are kept to the proper breadth while in frame.

PALISADES. [Sp.] Palings for defensive purposes, formed of timber or stout stakes fixed vertically and sharpened at the head.

PALLET. A ballast-locker formerly used, to give room in the hold for other stowage.

PALLETTING. A slight platform made above the bottom of the magazines, to keep the powder from moisture.

PALM. The triangular face of the fluke of an anchor. Also, a shield-thimble used in sewing canvas, rope, &c. It consists of a flat thimble to receive the head of the needle, and is fixed upon a piece of canvas or leather, across the *palm* of the hand, hence the name.

PALMAIR. An old northern word for rudder. Also, a pilot.

PALMETTO. One of the palm tribe, from the sheath of which sennit is worked for seamen's (straw) hats.

PALM-WINE. A sub-acid and pleasant fermented tropical drink. (*See* TODDY.)

PAMBAN MANCHE, OR SNAKE-BOAT OF COCHIN. A canoe used on the numerous rivers and back-waters, from 30 to 60 feet 1 ng, and cut out of the solid tree. The largest are paddled by about twenty men, double-banked, and, when pressed, they will go as much as 12 miles an hour.

PAMPAS. The Savannah plains of South America, so extensive that, as Humboldt observes, whilst their northern extremity is bounded by palm-trees, their southern limits are the eternal snows of the Magellanic straits.

PAMPERO. A violent squall of wind from the S.W., attended with rain, thunder, and lightning, over the immense plains or pampas of the Rio de la Plata, where it rages like a hurricane.

PAN. In fire-arms, is a small iron cavity of the old flint lock, adjacent to the touch-hole of the barrel, to contain the priming powder.

PANCAKES. Thin floating rounded spots of snow ice, in the Arctic seas, and reckoned the first indication of the approach of winter, in August.

PANDEL. A Kentish name for the shrimp.

PANDOOR. A northern name for a large oyster, usually taken at the entrance of the pans.

PANGAIA. A country vessel of East Africa, like a barge, with one mat-sail of cocoa-nut leaves, the planks being pinned with wooden pins, and sewed with twine.

PANNIKIN. A small tin pot.

PANNYAR. Kidnapping negroes on the coast of Africa.

PANSHWAY. A fast-pulling passenger-boat used on the Hooghly.

PANTOGRAPH. An instrument to copy or reduce drawings.

PANTOMETER. An instrument for taking angles and elevations, and measuring distances.

PAOLO. A Papal silver coin, value $5\frac{1}{4}$d.; ten paoli make a crown.

PAPS. Coast hills, with rounded or conical summits; the lofty paps of Jura are three in number.

PAR, or PARR. In ichthyology, the samlet, brannock, or branling. Also, a commercial term of exchange, where the moneys are equalized.

PARA. A small Turkish coin of 3 aspers, $1\frac{1}{2}$ farthing.

PARABOLA. A geometrical figure formed by the section of a cone when cut by a plane parallel to its side.

PARADE. An assembling of troops in due military order. Also, the open space where they parade or are paraded. The quarter-deck of a man-of-war is often termed the sovereign's parade.

PARALLACTIC ANGLE. The angle made at a star by arcs passing through the zenith and pole respectively.

PARALLAX. An apparent change in the position of an object, arising from a change of the observer's station, and which diminishes with the altitude of an object in the vertical circle. Its effect is greatest in the horizon, where it is termed the *horizontal parallax*, and vanishes entirely in the zenith. The positions of the planets and comets, as viewed from the surface of the earth, differ from those they would occupy if observed from its centre by the amount of parallax, the due application of which is an important element. The stars are so distant that their positions are the same from whatever part of the earth they are seen; but attempts have been made to detect the amount of variation in their places, when observed from opposite points of the earth's orbit, the minute result of which is termed the *annual parallax;* and the former effect, due to the observer's station on our globe, is called the *diurnal parallax.*

PARALLEL. A term for those lines that preserve an equal distance from each other. It is sometimes used instead of latitude, as, "Our orders were to cruise in the parallel of Madeira." More definitely, they are imaginary circles parallel with the equator, ninety in the northern, and ninety in the southern hemispheres.

PARALLEL-BAR. In the marine steam-engine, forms a connection with the pump-rods and studs along the centre line of the levers.

PARALLEL OF LATITUDE. Is a circle parallel to the equator passing through any place. *Almucantar* is the Arabic name.

PARALLELOGRAM. A right-lined quadrilateral figure, the opposite sides of which are parallel and equal.

PARALLELOPIPED. A prism or solid figure contained under six parallelograms, the opposite sides of which are equal and parallel.

PARALLELS. The trenches or lines made by a besieger parallel to the general defence of a place, for the purpose of connecting and supporting his several approaches.

PARALLEL SAILING. Sailing nearly on a given parallel of latitude.

PARALLELS OF DECLINATION. Secondary circles parallel to the celestial equator.

PARANZELLO. A small Mediterranean vessel, pink-sterned, with a lateen mainsail and mizen, and a large jib.

PARAPET. A breast-high defence against missiles; its top is usually sloped away to the front, that the defenders may conveniently fire over it; and it is preferred of earth, of a thickness proportionate to the kind of fire it is intended to resist; its height also is often much increased.

PARASANG. A Persian military measure, sometimes assumed as a league, but equal to about 4 English miles.

PARBUCKLE. A method of hauling up or lowering down a cask, or any cylindrical object, where there is no crane or tackle; the middle of a rope is passed round a post, the two ends are then passed under the two quarters of the cask, bringing the ends back again over it, and they being both hauled or slackened together, either raise or lower the cask, &c., as may be required. The parbuckle is frequently used in public-house vaults. Guns are parbuckled up steep cliffs without their carriages, and spars in timber-yards are so dealt with.

PARCEL, To. To wind tarred canvas round a rope.

PARCELLING. Narrow strips of old canvas daubed with tar and frequently wound about a rope like bandages, previous to its being served.

PARCLOSE. A name of the limber-hole.

PARDON. The gazetted amnesty or remission of penalty for deserters who return to their duty; the same as *act of grace.*

PARGOS. A fish resembling a large bream, from which the crews of Quiros and Cook suffered violent pains and bad effects. The porgy of Africa and the West Indies.

PARHELION. A mock or false sun; sometimes more than one.

PARIAH. The low-caste people of Hindustan; outcasts.—*Pariah-dogs;* also outcasts of no known breed.

PARK. A piece of ground (other than a battery) appointed for the ranging of guns or of ordnance stores.

PARLEY. That beat of drum by which a conference with the enemy is desired. Synonymous with chamade.—*To parley.* To bandy words.

PARLIAMENT-HEEL. The situation of a ship when careened by shift of ballast, &c.; or the causing her to incline a little on one side, so as to clean the side turned out of water, and cover it with fresh composition, termed *boot-topping* (which see).

PAR-LINE. A term signifying the normal level of a barometer for a given station, or the mean pressure between 32° and the sea-level, to which last the observations are all to be corrected and reduced.

PAROLE. The word of honour given by a prisoner of war until exchanged. Also, synonymous with *word* (which see).

PAROLE-EVIDENCE. In insurance cases it is a general rule, that the policy alone shall be conclusive evidence of the contract, and that no parole-evidence shall be received to vary the terms of it.

PARRALS, or PARRELS. Those bands of rope, or sometimes iron collars, by which the centres of yards are fastened at the slings to the masts, so as to slide up and down freely when requisite.

PARREL-ROPE. Is formed of a single rope well served, and fitted with an eye at each end; this being passed round the yard is seized fast on, the two ends are then passed round the after-part of the mast, and one of them being brought under, and the other over the yard, the two eyes are lashed together; this is seldom used but for the top-gallant and smaller yards.

PARREL WITH RIBS AND TRUCKS, or JAW PARRELS. This is formed by passing the two parts of the parrel-rope through the two holes in the ribs, observing that between every two ribs is strung a truck on each part of the rope. (*See* RIB and TRUCK.) The ends of the parrel-rope are made fast with seizings; these were chiefly used on the top-sail-yards.

PARREL WITH TRUCKS. Is composed of a single rope passing through a number of bull's-eye trucks, sufficient to embrace the mast; these are principally used for the cheeks of a gaff.

PARSEES. The great native merchants of Bombay, &c., and a very useful class as merchants and shopkeepers all along the Malabar coast. They are the remains of the ancient Persians, and are Guebres, or fire-worshippers.

PART, To. To break a rope. To part from an anchor is in consequence of the cable parting.

PARTAN. A name on our northern coasts for the common sea-crab.

PARTING. The state of being driven from the anchors by breaking the cables. The rupture or stranding of any tackle-fall or hawser.

PARTIZAN, or PERTUISAN. A halbert formerly much used. Thus in Shakspeare (*Antony and Cleopatra*), "I had as lief have a reed that will do me no service, as a partizan I could not heave." Also, a useful stirring man, fit for all sorts of desultory duties.

PARTIZAN WARFARE. Insurrectionary, factional, and irregular hostilities.

PARTNERS. A frame-work of thick plank, fitted round the several scuttles or holes in a ship's decks, through which the masts, capstans, &c., pass; but particularly to support it when the mast leans against it.

PARTNERSHIP with a neutral cannot legalize commerce with a belligerent.

PART OWNERS. Unlike any other partnership, they may be imposed upon each other without mutual consent, whence arises a frequent appeal to both civil and common law. (*See* SHIPOWNER.)

PARTRIDGES. Grenades thrown from a mortar.

PARTY. The detachment of marines serving on board a man-of-war. Also, a gang of hands sent away on particular duties.

PASHA. Viceroy. A Turkish title of honour and command.

PASS. A geographical term abbreviated from passage, and applied to any defile for crossing a mountain chain. Also, any difficult strait which commands the entrance into a country. Also, a certificate of leave of absence for a short period only. Also, a thrust with a sword.

PASS, OR PASSPORT. A permission granted by any state to a vessel, to navigate in some particular sea without molestation; it contains all particulars concerning her, and is binding on all persons at peace with that state. It is also a letter of licence given by authority, granting permission to enter, travel in, and quit certain territories.

PASS, To. To give from one to another, and also to take certain turns of a rope round a yard, &c., as "Pass the line along;" "pass the gasket;" "pass a seizing;" "pass the word there," &c.

PASSAGE. A voyage is generally supposed to comprise the outward and homeward passages. Also, a west country term for ferry. (*See* VOYAGE.)

PASSAGE-BOAT. A small vessel employed in carrying persons or luggage from one port to another. Also, a ferry-boat.

PASSAGE-BROKER. One who is licensed to act in the procuring of passages by ships from one port to another.

PASSAGE-MONEY. The allowance made for carrying official personages in a royal ship. Also, the charge made for the conveyance of passengers in a packet or merchant-vessel.

PASSAGES. Cuts in the parapet of the covered way to continue the communication throughout.

PASSANDEAU. An ancient 8-pounder gun of 15 feet.

PASSAREE, OR PASSARADO. A rope in use when before the wind with lower studding-sail-booms out, to haul out the clues of the fore-sail to tail-blocks on the booms, so as to full-spread the foot of that sail.

PASSED. The having undergone a regular examination for preferment.

PASSED BOYS. Those who have gone through the round of instruction given in a training-ship.

PASSE-VOLANT. A name applied by the French to a *Quaker* or wooden gun on board ship; but it was adopted by our early voyagers as also expressing a movable piece of ordnance.

PASSPORT. *See* PASS.

PASS-WORD. The countersign for answering the sentinels.

PATACHE. A Portuguese tender, from 200 to 300 tons, for carrying treasure: well armed and swift.

PATACOON. A Spanish piece of eight, worth 4*s*. 6*d*.

PATALLAH. A large and clumsy Indian boat, for baggage, cattle, &c.

PATAMAR. An excellent old class of advice-boats in India, especially on the Bombay coast, both swift and roomy. They are grab-built, that is, with a prow-stern, about 76 feet long, 21 feet broad, 11 feet deep, and 200 tons burden. They are navigated with much skill by men of the Mopila caste and other Mussulmans.

PATAMOMETER. An instrument for measuring the force of currents.

PATAXOS. A small vessel formerly used by the Spaniards as an advice-boat.

PATCH. The envelope used with the bullet in old rifles.—*Muzzle-patch* is a projection on the top of the muzzle of some guns, doing away with the effect of dispart in laying.

PATELLA. The limpet, of which there are 250 known species.

PATERERO. A kind of small mortar sometimes fired for salutes or rejoicing, especially in Roman Catholic countries on holidays.

PATERNOSTER-WORK. The framing of a chain-pump.

PATH. The trajectory of a shell.

PATOO-PATOO. A formidable weapon with sharp edges, used by the Polynesian Islanders and New Zealanders as a sort of battle-axe to cleave the skulls of their enemies.

PATROL. The night-rounds, to see that all is right, and to insure regularity and order.

PATRON, or PADRONE. The master of a merchant vessel or coaster in the Mediterranean. Also, a cartridge-box, *temp.* Elizabeth.

PAUL BITT. A strong timber fixed perpendicularly at the back of the windlass in the middle, serving to support the system of pauls which are pinned into it, as well as to add security to the machine.

PAULER, THAT IS A. A closer or stopper; an unanswerable or puzzling decision.

PAUL RIM. A notched cast-iron capstan-ring let into the ship's deck for the pauls to act on.

PAULS, or PAWLS. A stout but short set of bars of iron fixed close to the capstan-whelps, or windlass of a ship, to prevent them from recoiling and overpowering the men. Iron or wood brackets suspended to the paul-bitts of a windlass, and dropping into appropriate scores, act as a security to the purchase. To the windlass it is vertical; for capstans, horizontal, bolted to the whelps, and butting to the deck-rim.

PAUL THERE, MY HEARTY. Tell us no more of that. Discontinue your discourse.

PAUNCH-MAT. A thick and strong mat formed by interweaving sinnet or strands of rope as close as possible; it is fastened on the outside of the yards or rigging, to prevent their chafing.

PAVILION. A state tent.

PAVILLON [Fr.] Colours; flag; standard.

PAVISER. Formerly a soldier who was armed with a pavise or buckler.

PAWK. A young lobster.

PAWL. *See* PAUL.

PAY. A buccaneering principle of hire, under the notion of plunder and sharing in prizes, was, *no purchase no pay.*

PAY, To [from Fr. *poix*, pitch]. To pay a seam is to pour hot pitch and tar into it after caulking, to defend the oakum from the wet. Also, to beat or drub a person, a sense known to Shakspeare as well as to seamen.

PAY A MAST OR YARD, To. To anoint it with tar, turpentine, rosin, tallow, or varnish; tallow is particularly useful for those masts upon which the sails are frequently hoisted and lowered, such as topmasts and the lower masts of sloops, schooners, &c.

PAY A VESSEL'S BOTTOM, To. To cover it with tallow, sulphur, rosin, &c. (*See* BREAMING.)

PAY AWAY. The same as *paying out* (which see). To pass out the slack of a cable or rope.—*Pay down.* Send chests or heavy articles below.

PAYING OFF. The movement by which a ship's head falls off from the wind, and drops to leeward. Also, the paying off the ship's officers and crew, and the removal of the ship from active service to ordinary.

PAYING OUT. The act of slackening a cable or rope, so as to let it run freely. When a man talks grandiloquently, he is said to be "paying it out."

PAY-MASTER. The present designation of the station formerly held by the purser; the officer superintending the provisioning and making payments to the crew.

PAY ROUND, To. To turn the ship's head.

PAY-SERJEANT, IN THE ARMY. A steady non-commissioned officer, selected by the captain of each company, to pay the subsistence daily to the men, after the proper deductions.

PEA-BALLAST. A coarse fresh-water sand used by ships in the China trade for stowing tea-chests upon.

PEA OR P.-JACKET. A skirtless loose rough coat, made of Flushing or pilot cloth.

PEAK. The more or less conical summit of a mountain whether isolated or forming part of a chain. Also, the upper outer corner of those sails which are extended by a gaff.

PEAK, To. To raise a gaff or lateen yard more obliquely to the mast. *To stay peak,* or *ride a short stay peak,* is when the cable and fore-stay form a line: a long peak is when the cable is in line with the main-stay.

PEAK DOWNHAUL. A rope rove through a block at the outer end of the gaff to haul it down by.

PEAK HALLIARDS. The ropes or tackles by which the outer end of a gaff is hoisted, as opposed to the *throat-halliards* (which see).

PEAK OF AN ANCHOR. The bill or extremity of the palm, which, as seamen by custom drop the *k*, is pronounced pea; it is tapered nearly to a point in order to penetrate the bottom.

PEAK PURCHASE. A purchase fitted in cutters to the standing peak-halliards to sway it up taut.

PEARL. A beautiful concretion found in the interior of the shells of many species of mollusca, resulting from the deposit of nacreous substance round some nucleus, mostly of foreign origin. The *Meleagrina margaritifera*, or pearl oyster of the Indian seas, yields the most numerous and finest specimens.

PECTORAL FINS. The pair situated behind the gills of fishes, corresponding homologically to the fore limbs of quadrupeds and the wings of birds.

PEDESTAL-BLOCKS. Synonymous with *plumber-blocks* (which see).

PEDESTAL-RAIL. A rail about two inches thick, wrought over the foot-space rail, and in which there is a groove to steady the heel of the balusters of the galleries.

PEDRO. An early gun of large calibre for throwing stone-balls.

PEDRO-A-PIED [*Pedro-pee*]. The balance on one leg in walking a plank as a proof of sobriety. A man placed one foot on a seam and flourished the other before and behind, singing, "How can a man be drunk when he can dance Pedro-pee," at which word he placed the foot precisely before the other on the seam, till he proved at least he had not lost his equilibrium. This was an old custom.

PEECE. An old term for a fortified position.

PEEGAGH. The Manx or Erse term for a large skate.

PEEK. *See* PEAK.

PEEL. A stronghold of earth and timber for defence. Also, the wash of an oar.

PEGASUS. One of the ancient northern constellations, of which the lucida is Markab.

PEKUL. A Chinese commercial weight of about 130 or 132 lbs.

PELAGIANS. Fishes of the open sea.

PELICAN. A well-known water-bird. Also, the old six-pounder culverin.

PELL [from the British *pwll*]. A deep hole of water, generally beneath a cataract or any abrupt waterfall. Also, a large pond.

PELLET. An old word for shot or bullet.

PELLET-POWDER. Has its grains much larger and smoother, and is intended to act more gradually than service gunpowder, but by the English it is at present considered rather weak.

PELTA. An ancient shield or buckler, formed of scales sewed on skins.

PEMBLICO. A small bird whose cry was deemed ominous at sea as presaging wind.

PEMMICAN. Condensed venison, or beef, used by the hunters around Hudson's Bay, and largely provided for the Arctic voyages, as containing much nutriment in a small compass. Thin slices of lean meat are dried over the smoke of wood fires; they are then pounded and mixed with an equal weight of their own fat. It is generally boiled and eaten hot where fire is available.

PEN. A cape or conical summit. Also, the Creole name for houses and plantations in the country. Also, an inclosure for fishing on the coast.

PENA, or PENON. High rocks on the Spanish coasts.

PENANG LAWYER. A cane, with the administration of which debts were wont to be settled at Pulo-Penang.

PENCEL. A small streamer or pennon.

PENDANT. *See* PENNANT.

PENDANT. A strop or short piece of rope fixed on each side, under the shrouds, upon the heads of the main and fore masts, from which it hangs as low as the cat-harpings, having an iron thimble spliced into an eye at the lower end to receive the hooks of the main and fore tackles. There are besides many other pendants, single or double ropes, to the lower extremity of which is attached a block or tackle; such are the fish-pendant, stay-tackle-pendant, brace-pendant, yard-tackle-pendant, reef-tackle-pendant, &c., all of which are employed to transmit the efforts of their respective tackles to some distant object.—*Rudder-pendants.* Strong ropes made fast to a rudder by means of chains. Their use is to prevent the loss of the rudder if by any accident it should get unshipped.

PENDULUM. A gravitating instrument for measuring the motion of a ship and thereby assisting the accuracy of her gunnery in regulating horizontal fire.

PENGUIN. A web-footed bird, of the genus *Aptenodytes*, unable to fly on account of the small size of its wings, but with great powers of swimming and diving: generally met with in high southern latitudes.

PENINSULA. A tract of land joined to a continent by a comparatively narrow neck termed an isthmus.

PENINSULAR WAR. A designation assigned to the Duke of Wellington's campaigns in Portugal and Spain.

PENKNIFE ICE. A name given by Parry to ice, the surface of which is composed of numberless irregular vertical crystals, nearly close together, from five to ten inches long, about half an inch broad, and pointed at both ends. Supposed to be produced by heavy drops of rain piercing their way through the ice rather than by any peculiar crystallization while freezing.

PENNANT. A long narrow banner with St. George's cross in the head, and hoisted at the main. It is the badge of a ship-of-war. Signal pennants are 9 feet long, tapering from 2 feet at the mast to 1 foot. They denote the vessels of a fleet; there are ten pennants, which can be varied beyond any number of ships present. When the pennant is half mast, it denotes the death of the captain. When hauled down the ship is out of commission. Broad pennant denotes a commodore, and is a swallow-tailed flag, the tails tapering, and would meet, if the exterior lines were prolonged; those of a cornet could not.

PENNANT-SHIP. Generally means the commodore, and vessels in the employ of government. It is also an authority delegated by the commander of convoy to some smart merchant ship to assist in the charge, and collect stragglers.

PENNOCK. A little bridge thrown over a water-course.

PENNY-WIDDIE. A haddock dried without being split.

PENSIONERS. Disabled soldiers or sailors received into the superb institutions of Chelsea and Greenwich, or, "recently if they choose," receiving out-pensions.

PENSTOCK. A flood-gate to a mill-pond. Also used in fortification, for the purpose of inundating certain works.

PENTAGON. A right-lined figure of five equal sides and angles.

PENUMBRA. The lighter shade which surrounds the dark shadow of the earth in an eclipse of the moon. Also, the light shade which usually encircles the black spots upon the sun's disc.

PEON-WOOD. *See* POON-WOOD.

PEOTTA. A craft of the Adriatic, of light burden, propelled by oars and canvas.

PEPPER-DULSE. *Halymenia edulis;* a pungent sea-weed, which, as well as *H. palmata*, common dulse, is eaten in Scotland.

PER-CENTAGE. A proportional sum by which insurance, brokerage, freight, del credere, &c., are paid.

PERCER. A rapier; a short sword.

PERCH. A pole stuck up on a shoal as a beacon; or a spar erected on or projected from a cliff whence to watch fish.

PERCUSSION. The striking of one body by another.

PERDEWS. A corruption from *enfans perdus*, to designate those soldiers who are selected for the *forlorn hope* (which see).

PERIGEE. That point in the moon's orbit where she is nearest to the earth; or the point in the earth's orbit where we are nearest to the sun.

PERIHELION. That point in the orbit of a planet or comet which is nearest to the sun.

PERIKO. An undecked boat of burden in Bengal.

PERIL, OR PERIL OF THE SEA. Does not mean danger or hazard, but comprises such accidents as arise from the elements, and which could not be prevented by any care or skill of the master and crew. (*See* ACT OF GOD.)

PERIMETER. The sum of all the sides of a geometrical figure taken together.

PERIODICAL WINDS. *See* MONSOONS and TRADE-WINDS.

PERIODIC INEQUALITIES. Those disturbances in the planetary motions, caused by their reciprocal attraction in definite periods.

PERIODIC TIME. The interval of time which elapses from the moment when a planet or comet leaves any point in its orbit, until it returns to it again.

PERIPHERY. The circumference of any curved figure.

PERISHABLE MONITION. The public notice by the court of admiralty for the sale of a ship in a perishable condition, whose owners have proved contumacious.

PERMANENT MAGNETISM. The property of attraction and repulsion belonging to magnetized iron. (*See* INDUCED MAGNETISM.)

PERMANENT RANK. That given by commission, and which does not cease with any particular service.

PERMIT. A license to sell goods that have paid the duties or excise.

PERPENDICLE. The plumb-line of the old quadrant.

PERPENDICULAR. A right line falling from or standing upon another vertically, and making the angle of 90° on both sides.

PERRIWINKLE. The *win-wincle* of the Ang.-Sax., a favourite little shell-fish, the pin-patch, or *Turbo littoreus.*

PERRY. An old term for a sudden squall.

PERSONNEL. A word adopted from the French, and expressive of all the officers and men, civil and military, composing an army or a naval force.

PERSPECTIVE. The old term for a hand telescope. Also, the science by which objects are delineated according to their natural appearance and situation.

PERSUADER. A rattan, colt, or rope's end in the hands of a boatswain's mate. Also, a revolver.

PERTURBATIONS. The effects of the attractions of the heavenly bodies upon each other, whereby they are sometimes drawn out of their elliptic paths about the central body, as instanced by the wondrous discovery of Neptune.

PESAGE. A custom or duty paid for weighing merchandise, or other goods.

PESETA, or Pistoreen. A Spanish silver coin: one-fifth of a piastre.

PESSURABLE, or Pestarable, of our old statutes, implied such merchandise as take up much room in a ship.

PETARD. A hat-shaped metal machine, holding from 6 to 9 lbs of gunpowder; it is firmly fixed to a stout plank, and being applied to a gate or barricade, is fired by a fuse, to break or blow it open. (*See* Powder-Bags.)

PETARDIER. The man who fixes and fires a petard, a service of great danger.

PET-COCK. A tap, or valve on a pump.

PETER. *See* Blue Peter.

PETER-BOAT. A fishing-boat of the Thames and Medway, so named after St. Peter, as the patron of fishermen, whose cross-keys form part of the armorial bearings of the Fishmongers' Company of London. These boats were first brought from Norway and the Baltic; they are generally short, shallow, and sharp at both ends, with a well for fish in the centre, 25 feet over all, and 6 feet beam, yet in such craft boys were wont to serve out seven years' apprenticeship, scarcely ever going on shore.

PETER-MAN, or Peterer. A fisherman. Also, the Dutch fishing vessels that frequented our eastern coast.

PETITORY SUITS. Causes of property, formerly cognizable in the admiralty court.

PETREL. The *Cypselli* of the ancients, and *Mother Cary's chickens* of sailors; of the genus *Procellaria.* They collect in numbers at the approach of a gale, running along the waves in the wake of a ship; whence the name *peterel*, in reference to St. Peter's attempt to walk on the water. They are seen in all parts of the ocean. The largest of the petrels, *Procellaria fuliginosa*, is known by seamen as Mother Cary's goose.

PETROLEUM. Called also rock, mineral, or coal, oil. A natural oil widely distributed over the globe, consisting of carbon and hydrogen, in the proportion of about 88 and 12 per cent. It burns fiercely with a thick black smoke; and attempts, not yet successful, have been made to adapt it as a fuel for steamers.

PETRONEL. An old term for a horse-pistol; also for a kind of carbine.

PETTAH. A town adjoining the esplanade of a fort.

PETTICOAT TROWSERS. A kind of kilt formerly worn by seamen in general, but latterly principally by fishermen. (*See* GALLIGASKINS.)

PETTY AVERAGE. Small charges borne partly by a ship, and partly by a cargo, such as expenses of towing, &c.

PETTY OFFICER. A divisional seaman of the first class, ranking with a sergeant or corporal.

PHALANX. An ancient Macedonian legion of varying numbers, formed into a square compact body of pikemen with their shields joined.

PHARONOLOGY. Denotes the study of, and acquaintance with, light-houses.

PHAROS. A lighthouse; a watch-tower.

PHASELUS. An ancient small vessel, equipped with sails and oars.

PHASES. The varying appearances of the moon's disc during a lunation; also those of the inferior planets Venus and Mercury, as they revolve round the sun.

PHILADELPHIA LAWYER. "Enough to puzzle a Philadelphia lawyer" is a common nautical phrase for an inconsistent story.

PHINAK. A species of trout. (*See* FINNOCK.)

PHYSICAL ASTRONOMY. That department of the science which treats of the causes of the motions of the heavenly bodies.

PHYSICAL DOUBLE-STAR. *See* DOUBLE-STAR and BINARY SYSTEM.

PIASTRE. A Spanish silver coin, value 4s. 3d. sterling. Also, a Turkish coin of 40 paras, or 1s. 7d.

PICARD. A boat of burden on the Severn, mentioned in our old statutes.

PICCANINNY. A negro or mulatto infant.

PICCAROON. A swindler or thief. Also, a piratical vessel.

PICCARY. Piratical theft on a small scale.

PICKERIE. An old word for stealing; under which name the crime was punishable by severe duckings.

PICKET. A pointed staff or stake driven into the ground for various military purposes, as the marking out plans of works, the securing horses to, &c. (*See also* PIQUET, an outguard.)

PICKETS. Two pointers for a mortar, showing the direction of the object to be fired at, though it be invisible from the piece.

PICKLE-HARIN. A sea-sprite, borrowed from the Teutonic.

PICKLING. A mode of salting naval timber in our dockyards, to insure its durability. (*See* BURNETIZE.)

PICK UP A WIND, To. Traverses made by oceanic voyagers; to run from one trade or prevalent wind to another, with as little intervening calm as possible.

PICTARNIE. A name on our northern coasts for the *Sterna hirundo*, the tern, or sea-swallow.

PICUL. *See* PEKUL.

PIE. The beam or pole that is erected to support the *gun* for loading and unloading timber. Also called *pie-tree*.

PIECE OF EIGHT. The early name for the coin of the value of 8 reals, the well-known Spanish dollar.

PIER. A quay; also a strong mound projecting into the sea, to break the violence of the waves.

PIERCER. Used by sailmakers to form eyelet-holes.

PIGGIN. A little pail having a long stave for a handle; used to bale water out of a boat.

PIG-IRON. (*See* Sow.) An oblong mass of cast-iron used for ballast; there are also pigs of lead.

> " A nodding beam or pig of lead
> May hurt the very ablest head."

PIG-TAIL. The common twisted tobacco for chewing.

PIG-YOKE. The name given to the old Davis quadrant.

PIKE. (*See* HALF-PIKE.) A long, slender, round staff, armed at the end with iron. (*See* BOARDING-PIKE and PYKE.) Formerly in general use, but which gave way to the bayonet. Also, the peak of a hill. Also, a fish, the *Esox lucius*, nicknamed the freshwater-shark.

PIKE-TURN. *See* CHEVAUX DE FRISE.

PIL, OR PYLL. A creek subject to the tide.

PILCHARD. The *Clupea pilcardus*, a fish allied to the herring, which appears in vast shoals off the Cornish coast about July.

PILE. A pyramid of shot or shell.—*To pile arms*, is to plant three fire-locks together, and unite the ramrods, to steady the outspread butt-ends of the pieces resting on the ground. A pile is also a beam of wood driven into the ground to form by a number a solid foundation for building upon. A *sheeting-pile* has more breadth than thickness, and is much used in constructing coffer-dams.

PILE-DRIVER. A machine adapted for driving piles. Also, applied to a ship given to pitch heavily in a sea-way.

PILGER. An east-country term for a fish-spear.

PILING ICE. In Arctic parlance, where from pressure the ice is raised, slab over slab, into a high mass, which consolidates, and is often mistaken for a berg.

PILL. (*See* PIL.) A term on the western coast for a draining rivulet, as well as the creek into which it falls.

PILLAGE. Wanton and mostly iniquitous plunder. But an allowed ancient practice, both in this and other countries, as shown by the sea ordinances of France, and our black book of the admiralty.

PILLAN. A northern coast name for the shear-crab.

PILLAR OF THE HOLD. A main stanchion with notches for descent.

PILLAW. A dish composed at sea of junk, rice, onions, and fowls; it figured at the marriage feast of Commodore Trunnion. It is derived from the Levantine *pillaf.*

PILLOW. A block of timber whereon the inner end of the bowsprit is supported.

PILMER. The fine small rain so frequent on our western coasts.

PILOT. An experienced person charged with the ship's course near the coasts, into roads, rivers, &c., and through all intricate channels, in his own particular district.—*Branch pilot.* One who is duly authorized by the Trinity board to pilot ships of the largest draft.

PILOTAGE. The money paid to a pilot for taking a ship in or out of port, &c.

PILOT CUTTER. A very handy sharp built sea-boat used by pilots.

PILOT-FISH. *Naucrates ductor,* a member of the Scomber family, the attendant on the shark.

PILOT'S-ANCHOR. A kedge used for dropping a vessel in a stream or tide-way.

PILOT'S FAIRWAY, or PILOT'S WATER. A channel wherein, according to usage, a pilot must be employed.

PINCH-GUT. A miserly purser.

PINCH-GUT PAY. The short allowance money.

PINE. A genus of lofty coniferous trees, abounding in temperate climates, and valuable for its timber and resin. The masts and yards of ships are generally of pine. (*See* PITCH-PINE.)—*Pine* is also a northern term for drying fish by exposure to the weather.

PING. The whistle of a shot, especially the rifle-bullets in their flight.

PINGLE. A small north-country coaster.

PINK. A ship with a very narrow stern, having a small square part above. The shape is of old date, but continued, especially by the Danes, for the advantage of the quarter-guns, by the ship's being contracted abaft. Also, one of the many names for the minnow.—*To pink*, to stab, as, between casks, to detect men stowed away.

PINKSTERN. A very narrow boat on the Severn.

PIN-MAUL. *See* MAUL.

PINNACE. A small vessel propelled with oars and sails, of two, and even three masts, schooner-rigged. In size, as a ship's boat, smaller than the barge, and, like it, carvel-built. The armed pinnace of the French coasts was of 60 or 80 tons burden, carrying one long 24-pounder and 100 men. In *Henry VI.* Shakspeare makes the pinnace an independent vessel, though Falstaff uses it as a small vessel attending on a larger. Also, metaphorically, an indifferent character.

PINNOLD. A term on our southern shores for a small bridge.

PINS.—*Belaying pins.* Short cylindrical pieces of wood or iron fixed into the fife-rail and other parts of a vessel, for making fast the running-rigging.

PINTADOS. Coloured or printed chintzes, formerly in great demand from India, and among the fine goods of a cargo.

PIN-TAIL. The *Anas acuta*, a species of duck with a long pointed tail. Also, in artillery, the iron pin on the axletree of the limber, to which the trail-eye of the gun-carriage is attached for travel.

PINTLES. The rudder is hung on to a ship by pintles and braces. The braces are secured firmly to the stern-post by jaws, which spread and are bolted on each side. The pintles are hooks which enter the braces, and the rudder is then wood-locked; a dumb pintle on the heel finally takes the strain off the hinging portions.

PIONEERS. A proportion of troops specially assigned to the clearing (from natural impediments) the way for the main body; hence, used generally in the works of an army, its scavenging, &c. Labourers of the country also are sometimes so used.

PIPE. A measure of wine containing two hogsheads, or 125 gallons, equal to half a tun. Also, a peculiar whistle for summoning the men to duty, and directing their attention by its varied sounds. (*See* CALL.)

PIPE-CLAY. Known to the ancients under the name of *paretonium;* formerly indispensable to soldiers as well as the jolly marines.

PIPE DOWN! The order to dismiss the men from the deck when a duty has been performed on board ship.

PIPE-FISH. A fish of the genus *Syngnathus*, with an elongated slender body and long tubular mouth.

PIPER. A half-dried haddock. Also, the shell *Echinus cidaris*. Also, the fish *Trigla lyra.*

PIQUET. A proportion of a force set apart and kept on the alert for the security of the whole.—The *outlying piquet*, some distance from the main body, watches all hostile approach.—The *inlying piquet* is ready to act in case of internal disorder, or of alarm.

PIRACY. Depredation without authority, or transgression of authority given, by despoiling beyond its warrant. Fixed domain, public revenue, and a certain form of government, are exempt from that character, therefore the Barbary States were not treated by Europe as such. The Court of Admiralty is empowered to grant warrants to commit any person for piracy, only on regular information upon oath. By common law, piracy consists in committing those acts of robbery and depredation upon the high seas, which, if committed on land, would have amounted to felony, and the pirate is deemed *hostis humani generis.*

PIRAGUA [Sp. *per agua*]. *See* PIROGUE.

PIRATE. A sea-robber, yet the word *pirata* has been formerly taken for a sea-captain. Also, an armed ship that roams the seas without any legal commission, and seizes or plunders every vessel she meets; their colours are said to be a black field with a skull, a battle-axe, and an hour-glass. (*See* PRAHU.)

PIRIE.   An old term for a sudden gust of wind.

PIRLE.   An archaic word signifying a brook or stream.

PIROGUE, OR PIRAGUA.   A canoe formed from the trunk of a large tree, generally cedar or balsa wood.   It was the native vessel which the Spaniards found in the Gulf of Mexico, and on the west coasts of South America; called also a dug-boat in North America.

PISCARY.   A legal term for a fishery.   Also, a right of fishing in the waters belonging to another person.

PISCES.   The twelfth sign of the zodiac, which the sun enters about the 21st of February.

PISCIS AUSTRALIS.   One of the ancient southern constellations, the lucida of which is Fomalhaut.

PISTOL.   An old word for a swaggering rogue; hence Shakspeare's character in *Henry V.*

PISTOLA.   A Papal gold coin of the sterling value of 13s. 11d.

PISTOLE.   A Spanish gold coin, value 16s. 6d. sterling.

PISTOLET.   This name was applied both to a small pistol and a Spanish pistole.

PISTOLIERS.   A name for the heavy cavalry, temp. Jac. I.

PISTOL-PROOF.   A term for the point of courage for which a man was elected captain by pirates.

PISTON.   In the marine steam-engine, a metal disc fitting the bore of the cylinder, and made to slide up and down within it easily, in order, by its reciprocating movement, to communicate motion to the engine.

PISTON-ROD.   A rod which is firmly fixed in the piston by a key driven through both.

PIT.   In the dockyards.   *See* SAW-PIT.

PITCH.   Tar and coarse resin boiled to a fluid yet tenacious consistence. It is used in a hot state with oakum in caulking the ship to fill the chinks or intervals between her planks.   Also, in steam navigation, the distance between two contiguous threads of the screw-propeller, is termed the *pitch.* Also, in gunnery, the throw of the shot.—*To pitch*, to plant or set, as tents, pavements, pitched battles, &c.

PITCH-BOAT.   A vessel fitted for boiling pitch in, which should be veered astern of the one being caulked.

PITCHED.   A word formerly used for *stepped,* as of a mast, and also for *thrown.*

PITCH-HOUSE.   A place set apart for the boiling of pitch for the seams and bottoms of vessels.

PITCH IN, To.   To set to work earnestly; to beat a person violently.   (A colloquialism.)

PITCHING.   The plunging of a ship's head in a sea-way; the vertical vibration which her length makes about her centre of gravity; a very straining motion.

PITCH-KETTLE. That in which the pitch is heated, or in which it is carried from the *pitch-pot.*

PITCH-LADLE. Is used for paying decks and horizontal work.

PITCH-MOP. The implement with which the hot pitch is laid on to ships' sides and perpendicular work.

PITCH-PINE. *Pinus resinosa,* commonly called Norway or red pine. (*See* PINE.)

PITH. Well known as the medullary part of the stem of a plant; but figuratively, it is used to express strength and courage.

PIT-PAN. A flat-bottomed, trough-like canoe, used in the Spanish Main and in the West Indies.

PIT-POWDER. That made with charcoal which has been burned in pits, not in cylinders.

PIVOT. A cylinder of iron or other metal, that may turn easily in a socket. Also, in a column of troops, that flank by which the dressing and distance are regulated; in a line, that on which it wheels.

PIVOT-GUN. Mounted on a frame carriage which can be turned radially, so as to point the piece in any direction.

PIVOT-SHIP. In certain fleet evolutions, the sternmost ship remains stationary, as a pivot upon which the other vessels are to form the line anew.

PLACE. A fortress, especially its main body.

PLACE FOR EVERYTHING, AND EVERYTHING IN ITS PLACE. One of the golden maxims of propriety on board ship.

PLACE OF ARMS. In fortification, a space contrived for the convenient assembling of troops for ulterior purposes; the most usual are those at the salient and re-entering angles of the covered-way.

PLACER. A Spanish nautical term for shoal or deposit. Also, for deposits of precious minerals.

PLACES OF CALL. Merchantmen must here attend to two general rules:—If these places of call are enumerated in the charter-party, then such must be taken in the order laid down; but if leave be given to call at all, or any, then they must be taken in their geographical sequence.

PLAGES [Lat.] An old word for the divisions of the globe; as, *plages of the north,* the northern regions.

PLAIN. A term used in contradistinction to mountain, though far from implying a level surface, and it may be either elevated or low.

PLAN. The area or imaginary surface defined by, or within any described lines. In ship-building, the *plan of elevation,* commonly called the *sheer-draught,* is a side-plan of the ship. (*See* HORIZONTAL PLAN and BODY-PLAN, or plan of projection.)

PLANE. In a general sense, a perfectly level surface; but it is a term used by shipwrights, implying the area or imaginary surface contained within any particular outlines, as the plane of elevation, or sheer-draught, &c.

PLANE-CHART. One constructed on the supposition of the earth's being an extended plane, and therefore but little in request.

PLANE OF THE MERIDIAN. *See* MERIDIAN.

PLANE-SAILING.   That part of navigation which treats a ship's course as an angle, and the distance, difference of latitude, and easting or westing, as the sides of a right-angled triangle.   The easting or westing is called departure.   To convert this into difference of longitude, parallel, middle latitude, or Mercator's sailing is needed, depending on circumstances.   Plane-sailing is so simple that it is colloquially used to express anything so easy that it is impossible to make a mistake.

PLANE TRIANGLE.   One contained by three right lines.

PLANETS, PRIMARY.   Those beautiful opaque bodies which revolve about the sun as a centre, in nearly circular orbits.   (*See* INFERIOR, MINOR, and SUPERIOR.)

PLANETS, SECONDARY.   The satellites, or moons, revolving about some of the primary planets—the moon being our satellite.

PLANIMETRY.   The mensuration of plane surfaces.

PLANK.   Thick boards, 18 feet long at least, from 1½ to 4 inches thick, and 9 or 10 inches broad; of less dimensions, it is called *board* or *deal* (which see), the latter being 8 or 9 inches wide, by 14 feet long.

PLANKING.   The outside and inside casing of the vessel.

PLANK IT, To.   To sleep on the bare decks, choosing, as the galley saying has it, the softest plank.

PLANK-SHEER.   Pieces of plank covering the timber-heads round the ship; also, the gunwale or covering-board.   The space between this and the line of flotation has latterly been termed the free-board.

PLAN OF THE TRANSOMS.   The horizontal appearance of them, to which the moulds are made, and the bevellings taken.

PLANT.   A stock of tools, &c.   Also, the fixtures, machinery, &c., required to carry on a business.

PLANTER.   In Newfoundland it means a person engaged in the fishery; and in the United States the naked trunk of a tree, which, imbedded in a river, becomes one of the very dangerous snag tribe.

PLASH, To.   To wattle or interweave branches.

PLASTRON.   A pad used by fencers.   Also, the shield on the under surface of a turtle.

PLATE.   In marine law, refers to jewels, plate, or treasure, for which freight is due.   Thus, *plate-ship* is a galleon so laden.

PLATE.   *Backstay-plate.*   A piece of iron used instead of a chain to confine the dead-eye of the backstay to the after-channel.—*Foot-hook or futtock plates.*   Iron bands fitted to the lower dead-eyes of the topmast-shrouds, which, passing through holes in the rim of the top, are attached to the upper ends of the futtock-shrouds.

PLATE-ARMOUR.   Thick coverings or coatings for ships on the new principle, to render them impervious to shot and shell, if kept just outside of *breaking-plate* distance.

PLATEAU.   An upland flat-topped elevation.

PLATFORM.   A kind of deck for any temporary or particular purpose: the orlop-deck, having store-rooms and cabins forward and aft, and the middle part allotted to the stowage of cables. Also, the flooring elevation of stone or timber on which the carriage of a gun is placed for action. Hence, in early voyages, a fort or battery, with well-mounted ordnance, is called "the platform."

PLATOON. Originally a small square body or subdivision of musketeers; hence, *platoon exercise*, that which relates to the loading and firing of muskets in the ranks; and *platoon firing, i.e.* by subdivisions.

PLAY. Motion in the frame, masts, &c. Also said of the marine steam-engine when it is in action or in play. Also, in long voyages or tedious blockades, play-acting may be encouraged with benefit; for the excitement and employment thus afforded are not only good anti-scorbutics, but also promoters of content and good fellowship: in such—

> "Jack is not bound by critics' crabbed laws,
> But gives to all his unreserved applause:
> He laughs aloud when jokes his fancy please—
> Such are the honest manners of the seas.
> And never—never may he ape those fools
> Who, lost to reason, laugh or cry by rules."

PLAYTE. An old term for a river-boat.

PLEDGET. The string of oakum used in caulking. Also, in surgery, a small plug of lint.

PLEIADES. The celebrated cluster of stars in Taurus, of which seven or eight are visible to the naked eye; the assisted vision numbers over 200.

PLENY TIDES. Full tides.

PLICATILES. Ancient vessels built of wood and leather, which could be taken to pieces and carried by land.

PLONKETS. Coarse woollen cloths of former commerce. (*See* statute 1 R. III. c. 8.)

PLOT, or PLOTT. A plan or chart. (*See* ICHNOGRAPHY.)

PLOTTING. The making of the plan after an actual survey of the place has been obtained.

PLOUGH. An instrument formerly used for taking the sun's altitude, and possessed of large graduations. When a ship cuts briskly through the sea she is said to plough it.

PLUCKER. The fishing frog, *Lophius piscatorius.*

PLUG. A conical piece of wood to let in or keep out water, when fitted to a hole in the bottom of a boat.—*Hawse-plugs.* To stop the hawse-holes when the cables are unbent, and the ship plunges in a head-sea.—*Shot-plugs.* Covered with oakum and tallow, to stop shot-holes in the sides of a ship near the water-line; being conical, they adapt themselves to any sized shot-holes.

PLUMB. Right up and down, opposed to parallel.—*To plumb.* To form the vertical line. Also, to sound the depth of water.

PLUMBER-BLOCKS. These, in a marine steam-engine, are Y's, wherein are fixed the bushes, in which the shafts or pinions revolve.

PLUMMET. A name sometimes given to the hand-lead, or any lead or iron weight suspended by a string, as used by carpenters, &c.

PLUNDER. A name given to the effects of the officers and crew of a prize, when pillaged by the captors, though the act directs that "nothing shall be taken out of a prize-ship till condemned." (*See* PILLAGE.)

PLUNGING FIRE. A pitching discharge of shot from a higher level, at such an angle that the shot do not ricochet.

PLUNGING SPLASH. The descent of the anchor into the water when let go.

PLUSH [evidently from *plus*]. The overplus of the grog, arising from being distributed in a smaller measure than the true one, and assigned to the cook of each mess, becomes a cause of irregularity. (*See* TOT.)

PLUVIOMETER, OR RAIN-GAUGE. A measurer of the quantity of rain which falls on a square foot. There are various kinds.

PLY, To. To carry cargoes or passengers for short trips. Also, *to work to windward*, to beat. Also, *to ply an oar*, to use it in pulling.

PLYMOUTH CLIMATE.

> "The west wind always brings wet weather,
> The east wind wet and cold together;
> The south wind surely brings us rain,
> The north wind blows it back again."

PLYMOUTH CLOAK. An old term for a cane or walking stick.

P.M. [Lat. *post meridiem*.] Post meridian, or after mid-day.

P.O. Mark for a petty officer.

POCHARD. A kind of wild duck.

POCKET. A commercial quantity of wool, containing half a sack. Also, the frog of a belt.

POD. A company of seals or sea-elephants.

POGGE. The miller's thumb, *Cottus cataphractus*.

POHAGEN. A fish of the herring kind, called also *hard-head* (which see).

POINT. A low spit of land projecting from the main into the sea, almost synonymous with promontory or head. Also, the rhumb the winds blow from.

POINT A GUN, To. To direct it on a given object.

POINT A SAIL, To. To affix points through the eyelet-holes of the reefs. (*See* POINTS.)

POINT-BEACHER. A low woman of Portsmouth.

POINT-BLANK. Direct on the object; "blank" being the old word for the mark on the practice-butt.

POINT-BLANK FIRING. That wherein no elevation is given to the gun, its axis being pointed for the object.

POINT-BLANK RANGE. The distance to which a shot was reckoned to range straight, without appreciable drooping from the force of gravity. It varied from 300 to 400 yards, according to the nature of gun; and was measured by the first graze of the shot fired horizontally from a gun on its carriage on a horizontal plane. The finer practice of rifled guns is much abating the use of the term, minute elevations being added to the point-blank direction for even the very smallest ranges.

POINT BRASS OR IRON. A large sort of plumb for the nice adjustment of perpendicularity for a given line.

POINT-DE-GALLE CANOE. Consists of a single stem of *Dúp* wood, 18 to 30 feet long, from 1½ to 2½ feet broad, and from 2 to 3 feet deep. It is fitted with a balance log at the ends of two bamboo outriggers, having the mast, yard, and sail secured together; and, when sailing, is managed in a similar way to the catamaran. They sail very well in strong winds, and are also used by the natives of the Eastern Archipelago, especially at the Feejee group, where they are very large.

POINTER. The index or indicator of an instrument.—*Station pointer.* A brass graduated circle with one fixed and two radial legs; by placing them at two adjoining angles taken by a sextant between three known objects, the position of the observer is fixed on the chart.

POINTER-BOARD. A simple contrivance for duly training a ship's guns.

POINTERS. Stout props, placed obliquely to the timbers of whalers, to sustain the shock of icebergs. All braces placed diagonally across the hold of any vessel, to support the bilge and prevent loose-working, are called pointers. Also, the general designation for the stars α and β in the Great Bear, a line through which points nearly upon the pole-star.

POINT-HOLES. The eyelet-holes for the points.

POINTING. The operation of unlaying and tapering the end of a rope, and weaving some of its yarns about the diminished part, which is very neat to the eye, prevents it from being fagged out, and makes it handy for reeving in a block, &c.

POINT OF THE COMPASS. The 32d part of the circumference, or 11° 15′.

POINTS. *See* REEF-POINTS.—*Armed at all points,* is when a man is defended by armour cap-à-pie.

POINTS OF SERVICE. The principal details of duty, which ought to be executed with zeal and alacrity.

POLACRE. A ship or brig of the Mediterranean; the masts are commonly formed of one spar from truck to heel, so that they have neither tops nor cross-trees, neither have they any foot-ropes to their upper yards, because the men stand upon the topsail-yards to loose and furl the top-gallant sails, and upon the lower yards to loose, reef, or furl the topsails, all the yards being lowered sufficiently for that purpose.

POLANS. Knee-pieces in armour.

POLAR CIRCLES. The Arctic and the Antarctic; 23° 28′ from either pole.

POLAR COMPRESSION. *See* COMPRESSION OF THE POLES.

POLAR DISTANCE. The complement of the *declination.* The angular distance of a heavenly body from one of the poles, counted on from 0° to 180°.

POLARIS. *See* POLE-STAR.

POLAR REGIONS. Those parts of the world which lie within the Arctic and Antarctic circles.

POLDAVIS, OR POLDAVY. A canvas from Dantzic, formerly much used in our navy. A kind of sail-cloth thus named was also manufactured in

Lancashire from about the year 1500, and regulated by statute 1 Jac. cap. 24.

POLE. The upper end of the highest masts, when they rise above the rigging.

POLEAXE, or POLLAX. A sort of hatchet, resembling a battle-axe, which was used on board ship to cut away the rigging of an adversary. Also in boarding an enemy whose hull was more lofty than that of the boarders, by driving the points of several into her side, one above another, and thus forming a kind of scaling-ladder; hence were called boarding-axes.

POLEMARCH. The commander-in-chief of an ancient Greek army.

POLE-MASTS. Single spar masts, also applied where the top-gallant and royal masts are in one. (See MASTS.)

POLES. Two points on the surface of the earth, each 90° distant from all parts of the equator, forming the extremities of the imaginary line called the earth's axis. The term applies also to those points in the heavens towards which the terrestrial axis is always directed.—*Under bare poles.* The situation of a ship at sea when all her sails are furled. (See SCUDDING and TRYING.)

POLE-STAR. *a Ursæ minoris.* This most useful star is the lucida of the Little Bear, round which the other components of the constellation and the rest of the heavens appear to revolve in the course of the astronomical day.

POLICY. A written contract, by which the insurers oblige themselves to indemnify sea-risks under various conditions. An *interest* policy, is where the insurer has a real assignable interest in the thing insured; a *wager* policy, is where the insurer has no substantial interest in the thing insured; an *open* policy, is where the amount of interest is not fixed, but left to be ascertained in case of loss; a *valued* policy, is where an actual value has been set on the ship or goods.

POLLACK. The *Merlangus pollachius,* a well-known member of the cod family.

POLLUX. *β Geminorum.* A bright and well-known star in the ancient constellation Gemini, of which it is the second in brightness.

POLRON. That part of the armour which covered the neck and shoulders.

POLTROON. Not known in the navy.

POLYGON. A geometrical figure of any number of sides more than four; regular or irregular. In fortification the term is applied to the plan of a piece of ground fortified or about to be fortified; and hence, in some countries, to a fort appropriated as an artillery and engineering school.

POLYMETER. An instrument for measuring angles.

POLYNESIA. A group of islands: a name generally applied to the islands of the Pacific Ocean collectively, whether in clusters or straggling.

POMELO, or PUMELO. *Citrus decumana.* A large fruit known by this name in the East Indies, but in the West by that of shaddock, after Captain Shaddock, who introduced it there.

POMFRET. A delicate sea-fish, taken in great quantities in Bombay and Madras.

POMMELION. A name given by seamen to the cascable or hindmost knob on the breech of a cannon.

PONCHES. Small bulk-heads made in the hold to stow corn, goods, &c.

PONCHO. A blanket with a hole in the centre, large enough for the head to pass through, worn by natives of South and Western America.

POND. A word often used for a small lagoon, but improperly, for ponds are formed exclusively from springs and surface-drainage, and have no affluent. Also, a cant name for the Mediterranean. Also, the summit-level of a canal.

PONENT. Western.

PONIARD. A short dagger with a sharp edge.

PONTAGE. A duty or toll collected for the repair and keeping of bridges.

PONTONES. Ancient square-built ferry-boats for passing rivers, as described by Cæsar and Aulus Gellius.

PONTOON. A large low flat vessel resembling a barge of burden, and furnished with cranes, capstans, tackles, and other machinery necessary for careening ships; they are principally used in the Mediterranean. Also, a kind of portable boat specially adapted for the formation of the floating bridges required by armies: they are constructed of various figures, and of wood, metal, or prepared canvas (the latter being most in favour at present), and have the necessary superstructure and gear packed with them for transport.

POO. A small crab on the Scottish coast.

POOD. A Russian commercial weight, equal to 36 lbs. English.

POODLE. An old Cornish name for the English Channel. Also, a slang term for the aide-de-camp of a garrison general.

POOL. Is distinguished from a *pond*, in being filled by springs or running water. Also, a *pwll* or port.

POOP. [From the Latin *puppis*.] The aftermost and highest part of a large ship's hull. Also, a deck raised over the after-part of a spar-deck, some-times called the *round-house*. A frigate has no poop, but is said to be pooped when a wave strikes the stern and washes on board.

POOPING, or being Pooped. The breaking of a heavy sea over the stern or quarter of a boat or vessel when she scuds before the wind in a gale, which is extremely dangerous, especially if deeply laden.

POOP-LANTERN. A light carried by admirals to denote the flag-ship by night.

POOP-NETTING. *See* Hammock-netting.

POOP-RAILS. The stanchions and rail-work in front of the poop. (*See* Breast-work and Fife-rails.)

POOP-ROYAL. A short deck or platform placed over the aftmost part of the poop in the largest of the French and Spanish men-of-war, and serving as a cabin for their masters and pilots. This is the topgallant-poop of our ship-wrights, and the former round-house cabin of our merchant vessels.

POOR JOHN. Hake-fish salted and dried, as well as dried stock-fish, and bad *baccalao*, or cod, equally cheap and coarse. Shakspeare mentions it in *Romeo and Juliet*.

POPLAR. The tree which furnishes charcoal for the manufacture of gun-powder.

POPLER. An old name for a sea-gull.

POPPETS. Upright pieces of stout square timber, mostly fir, between the bottom and bilge-ways, at the run and entrance of a ship about to be launched, for giving her further support. Also, poppets on the gunwale of a boat support the wash-strake, and form the rowlocks.

POPPLING SEA. Waves in irregular agitation.

PORBEAGLE. A kind of shark.

PORPESSE, PORPOISE, OR PORPUSS. The *Phocæna communis*. One of the smallest of the cetacean or whale order, common in the British seas.

PORT. An old Anglo-Saxon word still in full use. It strictly means a place of resort for vessels, adjacent to an emporium of commerce, where cargoes are bought and sold, or laid up in warehouses, and where there are docks for shipping. It is not quite a synonym of *harbour*, since the latter does not imply traffic. Vessels hail from the port they have quitted, but they are compelled to have the name of the vessel and of the port to which they belong painted on the bow or stern.—*Port* is also in a legal sense a refuge more or less protected by points and headlands, marked out by limits, and may be resorted to as a place of safety, though there are many ports but rarely entered. The left side of the ship is called *port*, by admiralty order, in preference to *larboard*, as less mistakeable in sound for starboard.—*To port the helm.* So to move the tiller as to carry the rudder to the starboard side of the stern-post.—*Bar-port.* One which can only be entered when the tide rises sufficiently to afford depth over a bar; this in many cases only occurs at spring-tides.—*Close-port.* One within the body of a city, as that of Rhodes, Venice, Amsterdam, &c.—*Free-port.* One open and free of all duties for merchants of all nations to load and unload their vessels, as the ports of Genoa and Leghorn. Also, a term used for a total exemption of duties which any set of merchants enjoy, for goods imported into a state, or those exported of the growth of the country. Such was the privilege the English enjoyed for several years after their discovery of the port of Archangel, and which was taken from them on account of the regicide in 1648.

PORTABLE SOUP, and other preparations of meat. Of late years a very valuable part of naval provision.

PORTAGE. Tonnage. Also, the land carriage between two harbours, often high and difficult for transport. Also, in Canadian river navigation means the carrying canoes or boats and their cargo across the land, where the stream is interrupted by rocks or rapids.

PORT ARMS! The military word of command to bring the firelock across the front of the body, muzzle slanting upwards; a motion preparatory for the "charge bayonets!" or for inspecting the condition of the locks.

PORT-BARS. Strong pieces of oak, furnished with two laniards, by which the ports are secured from flying open in a gale of wind, the bars resting against the inside of the ship; the port is first tightly closed by its hooks and ring-bolts.

PORT-CHARGES, OR HARBOUR-DUES. Charges levied on vessels resorting to a port.

PORTCULLIS. A heavy frame of wooden or iron bars, sliding in vertical grooves within the masonry over the gateway of a fortified town, to be lowered for barring the passage. When hastily made, it was termed a sarrazine.

PORTE. *See* SUBLIME PORTE.

PORT-FIRE. A stick of composition, generally burning an inch a minute, used to convey fire from the slow-match or the like to the priming of ordnance, though superseded with most guns by locks or friction-tubes. With a slightly altered composition it is used for signals; also for firing charges of mines.

PORT-FLANGE. In ship-carpentry, is a batten of wood fixed on the ship's side over a port, to prevent water or dirt going into the port.

PORT-GLAIVE. A sword-bearer.

PORT-LAST, OR PORTOISE. Synonymous with *gunwale.*

PORT-MEN. A name in old times for the inhabitants of the Cinque Ports; the burgesses of Ipswich are also so called.

PORT-MOTE. A court held in haven towns or ports.

PORT-NAILS. These are classed double and single: they are similar to clamp-nails, and like them are used for fastening iron work.

PORT-PENDANTS. Ropes spliced into rings on the outside of the port-lids, and rove through leaden pipes in the ship's sides, to work the port-lids up or down by the tackles.

PORT-PIECE. An ancient piece of ordnance used in our early fleets.

PORT-PIECE CHAMBER. A paterero for loading a port-piece at the breech.

PORT-REEVE. A magistrate of certain seaport towns in olden times.

PORT-ROPES. Those by which the ports are hauled up and suspended.

PORTS, OR PORT-HOLES. The square apertures in the sides of a ship through which to point and fire the ordnance. Also, aft and forward, as the *bridle-port* in the bows, the *quarter-port* in round-stern vessels, and *stern-ports* between the stern-timbers. Also, square holes cut in the sides, bow, or stem of a merchant ship, for taking in and discharging timber cargoes, and for other purposes.—*Gunroom-ports.* Are situated in the ship's counter, and are used for stern-chasers, and also for passing a small cable or a hawser out, either to moor head and stern, or to spring upon the cable, &c. (*See* MOOR and SPRING.)—*Half-port.* A kind of shutter which hinges on the lower side of a port, and falls down outside when clear for action; when closed it half covers the port to the line of metal of the gun, and is firmly secured by iron hooks. The upper half-port is temporary and loose, will not stand a heavy sea, and is merely secured by two light inch-rope laniards.

PORT-SALE. A public sale of fish on its arrival in the harbour.

PORT-SASHES. Half-ports fitted with glass for the admission of light into cabins.

PORT-SHACKLES. The rings to the ports.

PORT-SILLS. In ship-building, pieces of timber put horizontally between the framing to form the top and bottom of a port.

PORT-TACKLES. Those falls which haul up and suspend the lower-deck ports, so that since the admiralty order for using the word *port* instead of *larboard*, we have *port port-tackle falls.*

PORTUGUESE. A gold coin, value £1, 16s., called also *moiadobras.*

PORTUGUESE MAN-OF-WAR. A beautiful floating acalephan of the tropical seas; the *Physalis pelagica.*

POSITION. Ground (or water) occupied, or that may be advantageously occupied, in fighting order.

POSITION, GEOGRAPHICAL, of any place on the surface of the earth, is the determination of its latitude and longitude, and its height above the level of the sea.

POSSESSORY. A suit entered in the admiralty court by owners for the seizing of their ship.

POST. Any ground, fortified or not, where a body of men can be in a condition for defence, or fighting an enemy. Also, the limits of a sentinel's charge.

POST-CAPTAIN. Formerly a captain of three years' standing, now simply captain, but equal to colonel in the army, by date of commission.

POSTED. Promoted from commander to captain in the navy; a word no longer officially used.

POSTERN. A small passage constructed through some retired part of a bastion, or other portion of a work, for the garrison's minor communications with the town, unperceived by the enemy.

POSTING. Placing people for special duty. Also, publicly handing out a bad character.

POST OF HONOUR. The advance, and the right of the lines of any army.

POUCH. A case of strong leather for carrying ammunition, used by soldiers, marines, and small-arm men. Also, the crop of a shark.

POUCHES. Wooden bulk-heads across the hold of cargo vessels, to prevent grain or light shingle from shifting.

POULDRON. A shoulder-piece in armour. Corrupted from *epauldron.*

POULTERER. Called "Jemmy Ducks" on board ship; he assists the butcher in the feeding and care of the live stock, &c.

POUND. A lagoon, or space of water, surrounded by reefs and shoals, wherein fish are kept, as at Bermuda.

POUND-AND-PINT-IDLER. A sobriquet applied to the purser.

POUNDER. A denomination applied to guns according to the weight of the shot they carry; at present everything larger than the 100 pounder is described by the diameter of its bore, coupled with its total weight.

POW. A name on the Scotch shores for a small creek. Also, a mole.

POWDER. *See* GUNPOWDER.

POWDER, To. To salt meat slightly; as Falstaff says, "If thou embowel me to-day, I'll give you leave to powder me, and eat me too, to-morrow." —*Powdering-tub.* A vessel used for pickling beef, pork, &c.

POWDER-BAGS. Leathern bags containing from 20 to 40 lbs. of powder; substituted for petards at the instance of Lord Cochrane, as being more easily placed. They have lately been called Ghuznee bags.

POWDER-HOY. An ordnance vessel expressly fitted to convey powder from the land magazine to a ship; it invariably carries a red distinguishing flag, and warns the ship for which the powder is intended, to put out all fires before she comes alongside.

POWDER-MAGAZINE. The prepared space allotted for the powder on board ship.

POWDER-MONKEY. Formerly the boy of the gun, who had charge of the cartridge; now powder-man.

POWDER-VESSEL. A ship used as a floating magazine.

POWER. Mechanical force; in the steam-engine it is esteemed effective, expansive, or full. (*See* HORSE-POWER.)

POZZOLANA. Volcanic ashes, used in cement, especially if required under water.

PRACTICABLE. Said of a breach in a rampart when its slope offers a fair means of ascent to an assaulting column.

PRACTICAL ASTRONOMY. A branch of science which includes the determination of the magnitude, distance, and phenomena of the heavenly bodies; the ready reduction of observations for tangible use in navigation and geography; and the expert manipulation of astronomical instruments.

PRÆCURSORIÆ. Ancient vessels which led or preceded the fleets.

PRÆDATORIÆ, OR PRÆDATICÆ. Long, swift, light ancient pirates.

PRAHU. [Malay for boat.] The larger war-vessels among the Malays, range from 55 to 156 feet in length, and carry 76 to 96 rowers, with about 40 to 60 fighting men. The guns range from 2 inches to 6 inches bore, are of brass, and mounted on stock-pieces, four to ten being the average. These boats are remarkable for their swiftness.

PRAIA [Sp. *playa*]. The beach or strand on Portuguese coasts.

PRAIRIE. The natural meadows or tracts of gently undulating, wonderfully fertile land, occupying so vast an extent of the great river-basins of North America.

PRAM, OR PRAAM. A lighter used in Holland, and the ports of the Baltic, for loading and unloading merchant ships. Some were fitted by the French with heavy guns, for defending the smaller ports.

PRANKLE. A Channel term for the *prawn*.

PRATIQUE. A Mediterranean term, implying the license to trade and communicate with any place after having performed the required quarantine, or upon the production of a clean bill of health.

PRAWN. A marine crustacean larger than a shrimp, much esteemed as an article of food.

PRAYER-BOOK. A smaller hand-stone than that which sailors call "bible;" it is used to scrub in narrow crevices where a large holy-stone cannot be used. (*See* HOLY-STONE.)

PRECEDENCE. The order and degree of rank among officers of the two services. (*See* RANK.)

PRECESSION OF THE EQUINOXES. A slow motion of the equinoctial points in the heavens, whereby the longitudes of the fixed stars are increased at the present rate of about $50\frac{1}{4}''$ annually, the equinox having a retrograde motion to this amount. This effect is produced by the attraction of the sun, moon, and planets upon the spheroidal figure of the earth; the luni-solar precession is the joint effect of the sun and moon only.

PREDY, OR PRIDDY. A word formerly used in our ships for "get ready;" as, "Predy the main-deck," or get it clear.

PRE-EMPTION. A right of purchasing necessary cargoes upon reasonable compensation to the individual whose property is thus diverted. This claim is usually restricted to neutrals avowedly bound to the enemy's ports, and is a mitigation of the former practice of seizing them. (*See* COMMEATUS.)

PREMIUM. Simply a reward; but in commerce it implies the sum of money paid to the underwriters on ship or cargo, or parts thereof, as the price of the insurance risk.

PREROGATIVE. A word of large extent. By the constitution of England the sovereign alone has the power of declaring war and peace. The crown is not precluded by the Prize Act from superseding prize proceedings by directing restitution of property seized, before adjudication, and against the will of the captors.

PRESENT! The military word of command to raise the musket, take aim, and fire.

PRESENT ARMS! The military word of command to salute with the musket.

PRESENT USE. Stores to be immediately applied in the fitting of a ship, as distinguished from the supply for future sea use.

PRESERVED MEAT AND VEGETABLES. The occasional use of such food and lime-juice at sea, is not only a great luxury, but in many cases essential to the health of the crew, as especially instanced by the increase of scurvy in ships where this precaution is neglected.

PRESIDENT. At a general court-martial it is usual for the authority ordering it to name the president, and the office usually falls upon the second in command.

PRESS, TO. To reduce an enemy to straits. (*See* IMPRESSMENT.)

PRESS-GANG. A party of seamen who (under the command of a lieutenant) were formerly empowered, in time of war, to take any seafaring men—on shore or afloat—and compel them to serve on board men-of-war. Those who were thus taken were called *pressed men.*

PRESS OF SAIL. As much sail as the state of the wind, &c., will permit a ship to carry.

PRESSURE-GAUGE. The manometer of a steam-engine.

PREST. Formerly signified quick or ready, and a *prest man* was one willing to enlist for a stipulated sum—the very reverse of the *pressed man* of later times. (*See* PRESS-GANG.)

PRESTER. An old name for a meteor.

PRESUMPTIVE EVIDENCE. Is such as by a fair and reasonable interpretation is deducible from the facts of a case.

PREVENTER. Applied to ropes, &c., when used as additional securities to aid other ropes in supporting spars, &c., during a strong gale; as preventer-backstays, braces, shrouds, stays, &c.

PREVENTER-PLATES. Stout plates of iron for securing the chains to the ship's side; one end is on the chain-plate bolt, the other is bolted to the ship's side below it.

PREVENTER-STOPPERS. Short pieces of rope, knotted at each end, for securing the clues of sails or rigging during action, or when strained.

PREVENTIVE SERVICE. The establishment of coast-guards at numerous stations along the shores of the United Kingdom for the prevention of smuggling.

PRICKER. A small marline-spike for making and stretching the holes for points and rope-bands in sails. Also, the priming-wire of a gun. Also, a northern name for the basking-shark.

PRICKING A SAIL. The running a middle seam between the two seams which unite every cloth of a sail to the next adjoining. This is rarely done till the sails have been worn some time, or in the case of heavy canvas, storm-sails, &c. It is also called middle-stitching.

PRICKING FOR A SOFT PLANK. Selecting a place on the deck for sleeping upon.

PRICKING HER OFF. Marking a ship's position upon a chart by the help of a scale and compasses, so as to show her situation as to latitude, longitude, and bearings of the place bound to.

PRIDE OF THE MORNING. A misty dew at sunrise; a light shower; the end of the land breeze followed by a dead calm in the tropics.

PRIEST'S-CAP. An outwork which has three salient angles at the head and two inwards.

PRIMAGE. Premium of insurance. Also, a small allowance at the water side to master and mariner for each pack or bale of cargo landed by them: otherwise called *hat-money*.

PRIMARY PLANET. (*See* PLANETS, PRIMARY.)

PRIME. The fore part of the artificial day; that is, the first quarter after sunrise.

PRIME, To. To make ready a gun, mine, &c., for instantaneous firing. Also, to pierce the cartridge with the priming-wire, and apply the quill-tube in readiness for firing the cannon.—*To prime a fire-ship.* To lay the train for being set on fire.—*To prime a match.* Put a little wet bruised powder made into the paste called devil, upon the end of the rope slow-match, with a piece of paper wrapped round it.

PRIME VERTICAL. That great circle which passes through the zenith and the east and west points of the horizon.

PRIMING-IRONS. Consist of a pointed wire used through the vent to prick the cartridge when it is "home," and of a flat-headed one similarly inserted after discharge to insure its not retaining any ignited particles.

PRIMING-VALVES. The same with escape-valves.

PRINTED INSTRUCTIONS. The name of the volume formerly issued by the admiralty to all commanders of ships and vessels for their guidance; now superseded by Queen's Regulations.

PRISE, To. To raise, or slue, weighty bodies by means of a lever purchase or power. (*See* PRIZING.)

PRISE-BOLTS. Knobs of iron on the cheeks of a gun-carriage to keep the handspike from slipping when prising up the breech.

PRISM. In dioptrics, is a geometrical solid bounded by three parallelograms, whose bases are equal triangles.

PRISMATIC COMPASS. One so fitted with a glass prism for reading by reflection, that the eye can simultaneously observe an object and read its compass bearing.

PRISONER AT LARGE. Free to take exercise within bounds.

PRISONERS OF WAR. Men who are captured after an engagement, who are deprived of their liberty until regularly exchanged, or dismissed on their parole.

PRISONER UNDER RESTRAINT. Suspended from duty; deprived of command.

PRISON-SHIP. One fitted up for receiving and detaining prisoners of war.

PRITCH. A dentated weapon for striking and holding eels.

PRIVATE. The proper designation of a soldier serving in the ranks of the army, holding no special position.

PRIVATEER PRACTICE, OR PRIVATEERISM. Disorderly conduct, or anything out of man-of-war rules.

PRIVATEERS, or men-of-war equipped by individuals for cruising against the enemy; their commission (*see* LETTERS OF MARQUE) is given by the admiralty, and revocable by the same authority. They have no property in any prize until it is legally condemned by a competent court. The admiral on the station is entitled to a tenth of their booty. This infamous species of warfare is unhappily not yet abolished among civilized nations.

PRIVATE PROPERTY. Commissions of privateers do not extend to the capture of private property on land; a right not even granted to men-of-war. Private armed ships are not within the terms of a capitulation protecting private property generally.

PRIVATE SIGNAL. Understood by captains having the key, but totally incomprehensible to other persons.

PRIVY-COAT. A light coat or defence of mail, concealed under the ordinary dress.

PRIZE. A vessel captured at sea from the enemies of a state, or from pirates, either by a man-of-war or privateer. Vessels are also looked upon as *prize*, if they fight under any other standard than that of the state from which they have their commission, if they have no charter-party, and if loaded with effects belonging to the enemy, or with contraband goods. In ships of war, the prizes are to be divided among the officers, seamen, &c., according to the act; but in privateers, according to the agreement between the owners. By statute 13 Geo. II. c. 4, judges and officers failing in their duty in respect to the condemnation of prizes, forfeit £500, with full costs of suit, one moiety to the crown, and the other to the informer. Prize, according to jurists, is altogether a creature of the crown; and no man can have any interest but what he takes as the mere gift of the crown. Partial interest has been granted away at different times, but the statute of Queen Anne (A.D. 1708) is the first which gave to the captors the whole of the benefit.

PRIZE ACT OF 1793. Ordained that the officers and sailors on board every ship and vessel of war shall have the sole property in all captures, being first adjudged lawful prize, to be divided in such proportions and manner as his Majesty should order by proclamation. In 1746 a man, though involuntarily kept abroad above three years in the service of his country, was deemed to have forfeited his share to Greenwich.

PRIZE-ACTS. Though expiring with each war, are usually revived nearly in the same form.

PRIZEAGE. The tenth share belonging to the crown out of a lawful prize taken at sea.

PRIZE-COURT. A department of the admiralty court; (*oyer et terminer*) to hear and determine according to the law of nations.

PRIZE-GOODS. Those taken upon the high seas, *jure belli*, from the enemy.

PRIZE-LIST. A return of all the persons on board, whether belonging to the ship, or supernumeraries, at the time a capture is made; those who may be absent on duty are included.

PRIZE-MASTER. The officer to whom a prize is given in charge to carry her into port.

PRIZE-MONEY. The profits arising from the sale of prizes. It was divided equally by chart. 5 Hen. IV.

PRIZING. The application of a lever to lift or move any weighty body. Also, the act of pressing or squeezing an article into its package, so that its size may be reduced in stowage.

PROA, OR FLYING PROW. *See* PRAHU.

PROBATION. The noviciate period of cadets, midshipmen, apprentices, &c.

PROBE. A surgical sounder.—*To probe.* To inquire thoroughly into a matter.

PROCEEDS. The product or produce of prizes, &c.

PROCESSION. A march in official order. At a naval or military funeral, the officers are classed according to seniority, the chiefs last.

PROCURATION, LETTERS OF. Are required to be exhibited in the purchase of ships by agents in the enemy's country.

PROCYON. a *Canis minoris*, the principal star of the Lesser Dog.

PROD. A poke or slight thrust; as in *persuading* with a bayonet.

PRODD. A cross-bow for throwing bullets, temp. Hen. VII.

PRODUCTION. For obtaining the benefits of trading with our colonies, it is necessary that the goods be accompanied by a "certificate of production" in the manner required by marine law. (*See* ORIGIN.)

PROFILE DRAUGHTS. In naval architecture, a name applied to two drawings from the sheer draught: one represents the entire construction and disposition of the ship; the other, her whole interior work and fittings.

PROFILE OF A FORT. *See* ORTHOGRAPHY.

PROG. A quaint word for victuals. Swift says, "In town you may find better prog." It is also a spike.

PROGRESSION. *See* ARC OF DIRECTION.

PROJECTILES. Bodies which are driven by any one effort of force from the spot where it was applied.

PROJECTION. A method of representing geometrically on a plane surface varied points, lines, and surfaces not lying in any one plane: used in charts and maps, where it is of various kinds, as globular, orthographic, Mercator's, &c. In ship-building, an elevation taken amidship. (*See* BODY-PLAN.)

PROKING-SPIT. A long Spanish rapier.

PROMISCUI USUS. A law term for those articles which are equally applicable to peace or war.

PROMONTORY. A high point of land or rock projecting into a sea or lake, tapering into a neck inland, and the extremity of which, towards the water, is called a cape, or headland, as Gibraltar, Ceuta, Actium, &c.

PROMOVENT. The plaintiff in the instance-court of the admiralty.

PRONG. Synonymous with *beam-arm* or *crowfoot* (which see).

PROOF. The trial of the quality of arms, ammunition, &c., before their reception for service. Guns are proved by various examinations, and by the firing of prescribed charges; powder by examinations, and by carefully measured firings from each batch.

PROOFS OF PROPERTY. Attestations, letters of advice, invoices, to show that a ship really belongs to the subjects of a neutral state.

PROOF TIMBER. In naval architecture, an imaginary timber, expressed by vertical lines in the sheer-draught, to prove the fairness of the body.

PROPELLER. This term generally alludes to the Archimedean screw, or screw-propeller.

PROPER MOTION OF THE STARS. A movement which some stars are found to possess, independent of the apparent change of place due to the precession of the equinoxes, the accounting for which is as yet only ingenious conjecture.

PROPORTION. In naval architecture, the length, breadth, and height of a vessel, having a due consideration to her rate, and the object she is intended for.

PROPPETS. Those shores that stand nearly vertical.

PROSPECTIVE, OR PROSPECT GLASS. An old term for a deck or hand telescope, with a terrestrial eye-piece. (*See* SPY-GLASS.)

PROTECTIONS, ON PAPER, against impressment, were but little regarded. Yet seafaring men above 55, and under 18, were by statute exempted, as were all for the first two years of their going to sea, foreigners serving in merchant ships or privateers, and all apprentices for three years.

PROTEST. A formal declaration drawn up in writing, and attested before a notary-public, a justice of the peace, or a consul in foreign parts, by the master of a merchant-ship, his mate, and a part of the ship's crew, after the expiration of a voyage in which the ship has suffered in her hull, rigging, or cargo, to show that such damage did not happen through neglect or misconduct on their part.

PROTRACTOR. An instrument for laying off angles on paper, having an open mark at the centre of the circle, with a radial leg, and vernier, which is divided into degrees (generally 90).

PROVE, To. To test the soundness of fire-arms, by trying them with greater charges than those used on service.

PROVEDORE [Sp.] One who provided victuals for ships.

PROVENDER. Though strictly forage, is often applied to provisions in general.

PROVISIONS. All sorts of food necessary for the subsistence of the army and navy. Those shipped on board for the officers and crew of any vessel, including merchant-ships, are held in a policy of insurance, as part of her outfit.

PROVISO. A stern-fast or hawser carried to the shore to steady by. A ship with one anchor down and a shore-fast is moored *a proviso*. Also, a saving clause in a contract.

PROVOST-MARSHAL. The head of the military police. An officer appointed to take charge of prisoners at a court-martial, and to carry the sentences into execution. The executive and summary police in war.

PROW. Generally means the foremost end of a vessel. Also, a name for the beak of a xebec or felucca.

PUCKA. A word in frequent use amongst the English in the East Indies, signifying sterling, of good quality.

PUCKER. A wrinkled seam in sail-making. Also, anything in a state of confusion.

PUDDENING, OR PUDDING. A thick wreath of yarns, matting, or oakum (called a *dolphin*), tapering from the middle towards the ends, grafted all over, and fastened about the main or fore masts of a ship, directly below the trusses, to prevent the yards from falling down, in case of the ropes by which they are suspended being shot away. Puddings are also placed on a boat's stem as a kind of fender; and also laid round the rings of anchors to prevent hempen cables or hawsers from chafing.

PUDDING AND DOLPHIN. A larger and lesser pad, made of ropes, and put round the masts under the lower yards.

PUDDLE-DOCK. An ancient pool of the Thames, the dirtiness of which afforded Jack some pointed sarcasms.

PUDDLING. A technical term for working clay to a plastic state in an inclosed space, until it is of the requisite consistence for arresting the flow of water. A term in iron furnace work.

PUFF. A sudden gust of wind. A whistle of steam.

PUFFIN. The *Fratercula arctica*, a sea-bird with a singular bill, formerly supposed to be a bird in show, but a fish in substance, in consequence of which notion the pope permitted its being eaten in Lent.

PULAS. An excellent twine, made by the Malays from the *kaluwi*, a species of nettle.

PULL-AWAY-BOYS. A name given on the West Coast of Africa to the native Kroomen, who are engaged by the shipping to row boats and do other work not suited to Europeans in that climate.

PULL FOOT, To. To hasten along; to run.

PULLING. The act of rowing with oars; as, "Pull the starboard oars," "Pull together."

PULL-OVER. An east country term for a carriage-way.

PULO. The Malay word for island, and frequently met with in the islands of the Eastern seas.

PULWAR. A commodious kind of passage-boat on the Ganges.

PUMMEL. The hilt of a sword, the end of a gun, &c.—*To pummel.* To drub or beat.

PUMP. A well-known machine used for drawing water from the sea, or discharging it from the ship's pump-well.—*Chain-pump*, consists of a long chain, equipped with a sufficient number of metal discs armed with leather, fitting the cylinders closely, and placed at proper distances, which, working upon two wheels, one above deck and the other below, in the bottom of the hold, passes downward through a copper or wooden tube, and returning upward through another, continuously lifts portions of water. It is worked by a long winch-handle, at which several men may be employed at once; and it thus discharges more water in a given time than the common pump, and with less labour.—*Main pumps.* The largest pumps in a ship, close to the mainmast, in contradistinction to *bilge pumps*, which are smaller, and intended to raise the water from the bilges when a ship is laying over so that it cannot run to the main pump-well.—*Hand-pump*, is the distinctive appellation of the common small pump. Superseded by Downton and others.

PUMP-BARREL. The wooden tube which forms the body of the machine, and wherein the piston moves.

PUMP-BOLTS. Saucer-headed bolts to attach the brake to the pump-standard and pump-spear.

PUMP-BRAKE. The handle or lever of the old and simplest form of pump.

PUMP-CARLINES. The framing or partners on the upper deck, between which the pumps pass into the wells.

PUMP-CHAINS. The chains to which the discs, &c., are attached in the chain-pump.

PUMP-CISTERNS. Are used to prevent chips and other matters getting to, and fouling the action of, the chain-pumps.

PUMP-COAT. A piece of stout canvas nailed to the pump-partners where it enters the upper deck, and lashed to the pump, to prevent the water from running down when washing decks, &c.

PUMP-DALES. Pipes or long wooden spouts extending from the chain-pumps across the ship, and through each side, serving to discharge the water without wetting the decks.

PUMP-FOOT. The lower part, or well-end, of a pump.

PUMP-GEAR. A term implying any materials requisite for fitting or repairing the pumps, as boxes, leather, &c.

PUMP-HOOK. An iron rod with an eye and a hook, used for drawing out the lower pump-box when requisite.

PUMPKIN, OR POMPION. *Cucurbita pepo*, a useful vegetable for sea use.

PUMP SHIP! The order to the crew to work the pumps to clear the hold of water.

PUMP-SPEAR. The rod of iron to which the upper box is attached—and to the upper end of which the brake is pinned—whereby the pump is put in motion.

PUMP SUCKS. The *pump sucks* is said when, all the water being drawn out of the well, and air admitted, there comes up nothing but froth and wind, with a whistling noise, which is music to the fagged seaman.

PUMP-TACKS. Small iron or copper tacks, used for nailing the leather on the pump-boxes.

PUNCH. An iron implement for starting bolts in a little, or for driving them out, called a *starting* or *teeming punch*. Also, a well-known sea-drink, now adopted in all countries. It was introduced from the East Indies, and is said to derive its name from *panch*, the Hindostanee word for *five*, in allusion to the number of its ingredients. (*See* BOULEPONGES.)

PUNISHMENT. The execution of the sentence against an offender, as awarded by a court-martial, or adjudged by a superior officer.

PUNISHMENT DRILL. Fatiguing exercise or extra drill for petty delinquencies.

PUNK. The interior of an excrescence on the oak-tree; used as tinder, and better known as touch-wood. (*See* SPUNK.)

PUNT. An Anglo-Saxon term still in use for a flat-bottomed boat, used by fishermen, or for ballast lumps, &c.

PUOYS. Spiked poles used in propelling barges or keels.

PURCHASE. Any mechanical power which increases the force applied. It is of large importance to nautical men in the combinations of pulleys, as whip, gun-tackle, luff-tackle, jeer, viol, luff upon luff, runner, double-runner, capstan, windlass, &c.

PURCHASE A COMMISSION, To. A practice in our army, which has been aptly termed the "buying of fetters;" it is the obtaining preferment at regulated prices. At present the total value of a commission in a regiment of infantry of the line ranges from £450 for an ensigncy, up to £4540 for a lieutenant-colonelcy, and higher in the other branches of the service.

PURCHASE-BLOCKS. All blocks virtually deserve this name, but it is distinctively given to those used in moving heavy weights.

PURCHASE-FALLS. The rope rove through purchase-blocks.

PURRE. A name for the dunlin, *Tringa alpina*, a species of sand-piper frequenting our shores and the banks of rivers in winter.

PURSE-NET. A peculiar landing-net in fishing. It is used in the seine and trawl to bewilder the fish, and prevent their swimming out when fairly inside; like a wire mouse-trap.

PURSER. An officer appointed by the lords of the admiralty to take charge of the provisions and slops of a ship of war, and to see that they were carefully distributed to the officers and crew, according to the printed naval instruction. He had very little to do with money matters beyond paying for short allowance. He was allowed one-eighth for waste on all provisions embarked, and additional on all provisions saved; for which he paid the crew. The designation is now discarded for that of *pay-master*.

PURSER'S DIP. The smallest dip-candle.

PURSER'S GRINS. Sneers.

PURSER'S NAME. An assumed one. During the war, when pressed men caught at every opportunity to desert, they adopted *aliases* to avoid discovery if retaken, which alias was handed to the purser for entry upon the ship's books.

PURSER'S POUND. The weight formerly used in the navy, by which the purser retained an eighth for waste, and the men received only seven-eighths of what was supplied by government. One of the complaints of the mutiny was, having the purser's instead of an honest pound. This allowance was reduced to one-tenth.

PURSER'S SHIRT. "Like a purser's shirt on a hand-spike;" a comparison for clothes fitting loosely.

PURSER'S STEWARD. The official who superintended and noted down the exact quantity and species of provisions issued to the respective messes both of officers and men.

PURSER'S STOCKING. A slop article, which stretched to any amount put into it. (*See* SHEW A LEG.)

PURSUE, To. To make all sail in chase.

PUSH, To. To move a vessel by poles.

PUSHING FOR A PORT. Carrying all sail to arrive quickly.

PUT ABOUT. Go on the other tack.

PUT BACK, To. To return to port—generally the last left.

PUTHAG. A name on the Scottish shores for the porpoise; it is a Gaelic word signifying *the blower*.

PUT INTO PORT, To.   To enter an intermediate or any port in the course of a voyage, usually from stress of weather.

PUT OFF! or Push off.   The order to boats to quit the ship or the shore.

PUTTING A SHIP IN COMMISSION.   The formal ceremony of hoisting the pennant on the ship to be fitted.   This act brought the crew under martial law.

PUTTING A STEAM-ENGINE IN GEAR.   This is said when the gab of the eccentric rod is allowed to fall upon its stud on the gab-lever.

PUTTOCK.   A cormorant; a ravenous fellow.

PUTTOCK-SHROUDS.   Synonymous with *futtock;* a word in use, but not warranted.

PUT TO SEA, To.   To quit a port or roadstead, and proceed to the destination.

PYKAR.   A herring-boat, or small vessel, treated of in statute 31 Edward III. c. 2.

PYKE, To.   A old word signifying to haul on a wind.

PYKE-MAW.   The great tern, *Larus ridibundus;* a species of sea-gull.

PYKE OFF, To.   To go away silently.

PYPERI.   A sort of vessel made of several pieces of wood merely lashed together; hardly superior to a raft, but sharp forward to cut the water.

PYRAMID.   A solid, the base of which is any right-lined plane figure, and its sides are triangles, having their vertices meeting in one point, named its vertex.

PYROTECHNY.   The science of artificial fire-works, including not only such as are used in war, but also those intended for amusement.

Q.

QUADE.   An old word for unsteady.—*Quade wind,* a veering one.

QUADRANT.   A reflecting instrument used to take the altitude above the horizon of the sun, moon, or stars at sea, and thereby to determine the latitude and longitude of the place, &c. &c.   It was invented by Hadley.   Also, in speaking of double stars, or of two objects near each other, the position of one component in reference to the other is indicated by the terms, *north following, north preceding, south following,* or *south preceding,* the word quadrant being understood.—*A gunner's quadrant,* for determining the gun's angle of *elevation.*   The long arm is inserted into the bore, while the short one remains outside, with a graduated arc and plummet, showing the inclination.   For *depression,* on the contrary, the long arm must be applied to the face of the piece.   Also, a graduated arc on the carriage showing, by an index on the trunnion, the gun's elevation above the plane of its platform; first applied by the gallant Captain Broke.—The *mural quadrant,* was framed and fitted with telescope, divisions, and plumb-line, firmly attached to the side of a wall built in the plane of the meridian; only used in large observatories.—*Senical quadrant,* consists of several concentric quadratic arcs, divided into eight equal parts by radii, with parallel right lines crossing each other at right angles. It was made of brass, or wood, with lines drawn from each side intersecting one another, and an index divided by sines also, with 90° on the limb, and two sights on the edge, to take the altitude of the sun. Sometimes, instead of sines, they were divided into equal parts. It was in great use among the French navigators, from its solving the problems of plane sailing.

QUADRATE, To. To trim a gun on its carriage and its trucks; to adjust it for firing on a level range.

QUADRATURE. The moon is said to be in quadrature at the first and last quarter, when her longitude differs 90° from that of the sun.

QUADROON [from L. *quatuor,* four]. The offspring of a mulatto woman and a white man.

QUAGMIRE. A marsh in which, from its concave and impermeable bottom, the waters remain stagnant, rendering the surface a quaking bog.

QUAKER. A false or wooden gun; so called in allusion to the "Friends" not fighting.

QUALIFIED PROPERTY. Not only those who have an absolute property in ships and goods, but those also who have but a qualified property therein, may insure them. (*See* EQUITABLE TITLE.)

QUALITIES. The register of the ship's trim, sailing, stowage, &c., all of which are necessary to her *behaviour.*

QUAMINO. A negro.

QUANT. An old term for a long pole used by the bargemen on our east coast; it is capped to prevent the immerged end from sticking in the mud.

QUARANTINE. Is, at most, a seclusion of forty days, from a free communication with the inhabitants of any country, in order to prevent the importation of the plague, or any other infectious disorder, either by persons or goods. The quarantine laws originated in the Council of Health at Venice in the fourteenth or fifteenth century. (*See* LAZARETTO.)

QUARRIL. The short dart or arrow shot from a cross-bow; or the bricolle of the middle ages.

QUARRY. The prey taken by whalers; a term borrowed from falconers.

QUARTE. In sword defence was one of the four guards, and also a position in fencing.

QUARTER. This term literally implies one quarter of the ship, but in common parlance applies to 45° abaft the beam. Thus the log is hove over the lee-quarter; quarter boats hang abaft the mizen-mast, &c. Again, the quarters apply to the divisional batteries, as forward, main, middle, or lower-decks, forecastle, and quarter-deck, and yet these comprise both sides. Close-quarters may be on any point, and the seaman rather delights in the bow attack, using the bowsprit as his bridge.— *Giving quarter.* The custom of asking and giving quarter in warfare originated, it is said, between the Dutch and Spaniards, that the ransom of an officer or soldier should be a *quarter* of his year's pay. No quarter is given to pirates, but it is always given to a vanquished honourable opponent.—*On the quarter,* 45° abaft the beam.

QUARTER, FIRST. When the moon appears exactly as a half-moon, 90° from the sun towards the east, she is in the first quarter, with her western half illuminated.

QUARTER, LAST. When the moon appears exactly as a half-moon, and her angular distance from the sun 90°, but towards the west, she is said to be in the last quarter, with her eastern half illuminated.

QUARTER-BADGE. Artificial galleries; a carved ornament near the stern of those vessels which have no quarter-galleries.

QUARTER-BILL. A list containing the different stations to which the officers and crew are quartered in time of action, with their names.

QUARTER-BLOCKS. Blocks fitted under the quarters of a yard, on each side the slings, for the topsail-sheets, topsail-cluelines, and topgallant-sheets to reeve through.

QUARTER-BOAT. Any boat is thus designated which is hung to davits over the ship's quarter.

QUARTER-CASK. One-half of a hogshead, or 28 imperial gallons.

QUARTER-CLOTHS. Long pieces of painted canvas, extended on the outside of the quarter-netting, from the upper part of the gallery to the gangway.

QUARTER-DAVITS. Pieces of iron or timber with sheaves or blocks at their outer ends, projecting from a vessel's quarters, to hoist boats up to.

QUARTER-DECK. That part of the upper deck which is abaft the main-mast. (*See* DECK, and JACK'S QUARTER-DECK.)

QUARTER-DECKERS. Those officers more remarkable for etiquette than for a knowledge of seamanship.

QUARTER-DECKISH. Punctilious, severe.

QUARTER-DECK NETTINGS. *See* NETTINGS.

QUARTER-DECK OFFICERS. A term implying the executive in general; officers whose places in action are there, in command.

QUARTER-FAST. *See* FAST.

QUARTER-FLOOD. *See* FLOOD.

QUARTER-GALLERY. A sort of balcony with windows on the quarters of large ships. (*See* GALLERY.)

QUARTER-GALLEY. A Barbary cruiser.

QUARTER-GUARD. A small guard posted in front of each battalion in camp.

QUARTER-GUNNER. *See* GUNNER.

QUARTER-LADDER. From the quarter-deck to the poop.

QUARTERLY ACCOUNT OF PROVISIONS. A return sent to the Admiral and Victualling Board, at the expiration of every three months.

QUARTERLY BILL. The document by which officers draw three months' personal pay.

QUARTERLY RETURNS. Those made every three months to the admiral, or senior officer, of the offences and punishments, the officers serving on board, &c.

QUARTER-MAN. A dockyard officer employed to superintend a certain number of workmen.

QUARTER-MASTER. A petty officer, appointed to assist the master and mates in their several duties, as stowing the hold, coiling the cables, attending the binnacle and steerage, keeping time by the watch-glasses, assisting in hoisting the signals, and keeping his eye on general quarter-deck movements. In the army, a commissioned officer, ranking with subalterns, charged with the more immediate supervision of quarters, camps, and the issue of arms, ammunition, rations, stores, &c., for his own regiment.

QUARTER-MASTER GENERAL. Is the head of that department of the army which has charge of the quartering, encamping, embarking, and moving of troops, and of the supply of stores connected therewith.

QUARTER-NETTINGS. The places allotted on the quarters for the stowage of hammocks, which, in action, serve to arrest musket-balls.

QUARTER-PIECES. Projections at the after-part of the quarter, forming the boundaries of the galleries.

QUARTER-POINT. A subdivision of the compass-card, equal to $2° 48' 45''$ of the circle.

QUARTER-PORTS. Those made in the after side-timbers, and especially in round-stern vessels. They are inconvenient for warping, and generally fitted with rollers.

QUARTER-RAILS. Narrow moulded planks, reaching from the stern to the gangway, and serving as a fence to the quarter-deck, where there are no ports or bulwarks.

QUARTERS. The several stations where the officers and crew of a ship of war are posted in time of action. (*See* BATTLE, ENGAGEMENT, &c.) But this term differs in the army, for the soldier's quarters are his place of rest. (*See* HEAD-QUARTERS, WINTER-QUARTERS, &c.)

QUARTER-SIGHTS. The engraved index on the base-rings of cannon in quarter degrees from point-blank to two or three degrees of elevation.

QUARTER-SLINGS. Are supports attached to a yard or other spar at one or both sides of (but not in) its centre.

QUARTERS OF THE YARDS. The space comprehended between the slings, or middle and half-way out on the yard-arms.

QUARTER-STANCHIONS. Strong iron stanchions in a square-sterned vessel, connecting the main-rail with the taff-rail; used for ridge-ropes to extend the awnings.

QUARTER-TACKLE. A strong tackle fixed occasionally upon the quarter of the main-yard, to hoist heavy bodies in or out of the ship.

QUARTER-TIMBERS. The framing timbers in a vessel's quarter.

QUARTER-WATCH. A division of one-fourth of the crew into watches, which in light winds and well-conducted ships is enough; but the officers are in three, and they must not be found nodding.

QUARTER-WIND. Blowing upon a vessel's quarter, abaft the main-shrouds.

QUASHEE. The familiar designation of a West India negro.

QUATUOR MARIA, or British Seas, are those four which surround Great Britain.

QUAY. *See* KEY.

QUEBRADA. From the Spanish for ravine, or broken ground.

QUEBRANTA HUESOS [Sp.] Literally, *bone-breaker.* The great petrel, *Procellaria gigantea.*

QUECHE. A small Portuguese smack.

QUEEN ANNE'S FREE GIFT. A sum of money formerly granted to surgeons annually, in addition to their monthly twopences from each man, or as often as they passed their accounts.

QUEEN'S COCKPIT. A mess of dissolute mates and midshipmen of the old *Queen,* 98, who held a sort of examination of ribaldry for a rank below that of gentleman.

QUEEN'S OWN. Sea provision (when a queen reigns); similar to *king's own.*

QUEEN'S PARADE. The quarter-deck.

QUERCITRON. *Quercus tinctoria,* the name of a North American oak, which affords a valuable yellow dye.

QUERIMAN. A mullet of Guiana, found in turbid waters, where it lives by suction.

QUERPO [Sp. *cuerpo,* body]. A close short jacket :

"Long-quartered pumps, with trowsers blue,
And querpo jacket, which last was new.".

QUICKEN, To. In ship-building, to give anything a greater curve; as, *to quicken the sheer,* opposed to straightening it.

QUICKLIME. That which is unslacked, good for cleaning and white-washing ships' holds.

QUICK-MARCH, OR QUICK-STEP. The ordinary pace is $3\frac{1}{4}$ miles to the hour, or 110 paces (275) feet to the minute.

QUICKMATCH. Used as a train to any charge to be fired rapidly, is made of cotton threads treated with a composition of gunpowder, gum, and water; and burns nearly as would a train of loose powder.

QUICK RELIEF. One who turns out speedily to relieve the watch before the sound is out of the bell.

QUICK-SAND. A fine-grained loose sand, into which a ship sinks by her own weight as soon as the water retreats from her bottom.

QUICK SAVER. A span formerly used to prevent the courses from bellying too much when off the wind.

QUICK-STEP. *See* QUICK-MARCH.

QUICK-WORK. Generally signifies all that part of a ship which is under water when she is laden; it is also applied to that part of the inner upper-works of a ship above the covering board. Also, the short planks worked inside between the ports. In ship-building the term strictly applies to that part of a vessel's side which is above the chain-wales and decks, as well as to the strakes which shut in between the spirkettings and clamps. In general parlance quick-work is synonymous with *spirketting*.

QUID. The chaw or dose of tobacco put into the mouth at a time. *Quid est hoc?* asked one, tapping the swelled cheek of his messmate; *Hoc est quid*, promptly replied the other.

QUIETUS. A severe blow, a settler.

QUIHI. The sobriquet of the English stationed or resident in Bengal, the literal meaning being, "Who is there?" It is the customary call for a servant; one always being in attendance, though not in the room.

QUILKIN. A west-country term for a frog.

QUILL-DRIVER. Captain's clerk, purser's secretary, *et hoc genus omne*.

QUILL-TUBES. Those in use with port-fires for firing guns before the introduction of detonating and friction tubes. (*See* TUBES.)

QUILTING. A kind of coating formed of sinnet, strands of rope, &c., outside any vessel containing water. Also, the giving a man a beating with a rope's end.

QUINCUNX. Forming a body of men chequerwise. A method of surveying a coast by five vessels in quincunx was proposed by A. Dalrymple to the admiralty, when that board would not have allowed of the employment of one.

QUINK. A name in the Orkneys for the golden-eyed duck, *Anas clangula*.

QUINTAL. A commercial weight of a hundred pounds.

QUINTANE. An early military sport, to try the agility of our country youth.

QUINTE. The fifth guard in fencing.

QUISCHENS. The old term for *cuisses*, the pieces of armour which protected the thighs.

QUITTANCE. A release or discharge in writing for a sum of money or other duty, which ought to be paid or done on the ship's account.

QUOD. Durance, prison.

QUOIN. A wooden wedge adjusted to support the breech of a gun, so as to give the muzzle the required elevation or depression. Also, one of the mechanical powers.

QUOINS. Are employed to wedge off casks of liquids from each other, and steady them, in order that their bilges may not rub at sea, and occasion leaks.

QUOST. The old spelling of *coast*. See Eliot's *Dictionarie*, 1559.

QUOTA-MEN. Those raised for the navy at enormous expense by Pitt's quota-bill, in 1795, under bounties of from £20 to £60.

R.

R. In the muster-book means *run*, and is placed against those who have deserted, or missed three musters.

R.A. *See* RIGHT ASCENSION.

RABANET, OR RABINET. A small slender piece of ordnance, formerly used for ships' barricadoes. It had a one-inch bore, which carried about a half-pound ball.

RABBET, OR REBATE. An angular incision cut longitudinally in a piece of timber, to receive the ends of a number of planks, to be securely fastened therein. Thus the ends of the lower planks of a ship's bottom terminate upon the stem afore, and on the stern-post abaft. The surface of the garboard streak, whose edge is let into the keel, is in the same manner level with the side of the keel at the extremities of the vessel. They are therefore termed stem, stern, or keel rabbets.

RACE. Strong currents producing overfalls, dangerous to small craft. They may be produced by narrow channels, crossing of tides, or uneven bottoms. Such are the races of Portland, Alderney, &c. Also, a mill-race, or tail-course.

RACE, To. Applies to marking timber with the race-tool.

RACE-HORSE. (*Alca ?*) A duck of the South Seas; thus named, says Cook, for "the great swiftness with which they run on the water." Now called a steamer.

RACK. The superior stratum of clouds, or that moving rapidly above the scud. The line in which the clouds are driven by the wind, is called the rack of the weather. In Shakspeare's beautiful thirty-third sonnet the sun rises in splendour, but—

> " Anon permits the basest clouds to ride
> With ugly rack on his celestial face,
> And from the forlorn world his visage hide,
> Stealing unseen to west with this disgrace."

Also, a frame of timber containing several sheaves, as a fair leader. Also, various rails for belaying pins.—*To rack.* To seize two ropes together, with racking or cross-turns.

RACK-BAR. A billet of wood used for twisting the bight of a swifter round, in order to bind a raft firmly together.

RACK-BLOCK. A range of sheaves cut in one piece of wood, for running ropes to lead through.

RACK-HURRY. The tram-way on which coal-waggons run to a *hurry*.

RACKING. Spun-yarn or other stuff used to rack two parts of a rope together.

RACKING A TACKLE OR LANNIARD. The fastening two running parts together with a seizing, so as to prevent it from rendering through the blocks.

RACKING-TURNS. *See* NIPPERING.

RACK-RIDER. The name of the samlet in northern fisheries, so called because it generally appears in bad weather.

RADDLE, To. To interlace; as in making boats' gripes and flat gaskets.

RADE [Fr.] An old spelling of the sea-term *road*. (*See* ROAD.)

RADIUS. The semi-diameter of a circle, limb of a sextant, &c.

RADIUS-BAR OF PARALLEL MOTION. An intervening lever for guiding the side-rods of a steam-engine.

RADIUS-VECTOR. An imaginary line joining the centres of the sun and a planet or comet in any point of its orbit.

RADUS. A term used for the constellation Eridanus.

RAFT. A sort of float formed by an assemblage of casks, planks, or pieces of timber, fastened together with swifters and raft-dogs side by side, as well as tier upon tier. The timber and plank with which merchant ships are laden in the different ports of the Baltic, are attached together in this manner, in order to float them off to the shipping; but the rafts of North America are the most gigantic in the world. Also, a kind of floating bridge of easy construction for the passage of rivers by troops, &c.

RAFT-DOG. A broad flat piece of iron, having a sharp point at each end, with the extremities bent at right angles. There are also *dog-hooks*, having the shoulder bent into a hook, by which the raft-chains are secured, or suddenly thrown off and released.

RAFTING. Conveying goods by floating, as by raft-chains, lashings, &c.

RAFT-PORT. A large square hole, framed and cut through the buttocks of some ships, immediately under the counter—or forward between the breast-hooks of the bow—to load or unload timber.

RAG-BOLTS. Those which are jagged or barbed, to prevent working in their holes, and to make them hold more securely. The same as *barb-bolts*.

RAILS. Narrow pieces of wood, with mouldings as ornaments, mortised into the heads of stanchions, or nailed for ornament on several parts of a ship's upper works.

RAILS OF THE HEAD. Curved pieces of timber extending from the bows on each side to the continuation of the ship's stem, to support the knee of the head, &c.

RAILS OF THE STERN. (*See* STERN-RAILS.)

RAINBOW.

> " A rainbow towards night,
> Fair weather in sight.
> Rainbow at night,
> Sailor's delight;
> Rainbow in morning,
> Sailors, take warning."

RAIN-CLOUD. *See* NIMBUS.

RAINS. Belts or zones of calms, where heavy rain prevails; they exist between the north-east and south-east trade-winds, changing their latitude several degrees, depending on the sun's declination. In India "the rains" come in with the S.W. monsoon.

RAISE, To. To make an object subtend a larger angle by approaching it, which is the foundation of perspective, and an effect increased by the sphericity of our globe: the opposite of *laying* (which see).

RAISE A SIEGE, To. To abandon or cause the abandonment of a siege.

RAISED UPON. When a vessel is heightened in her upper works.

RAISE-NET. A kind of staked net on our northern shores, so called from rising and falling with the tide.

RAISE or RISE TACKS AND SHEETS. The lifting the clues of the courses, previously to bracing round the yards in tacking or wearing.

RAISE THE METAL, To. To elevate the breech, and depress thereby the muzzle of a gun.

RAISE THE WIND, To. To make an exertion; to cast about for funds.

RAISING A MOUSE. The process of making a lump on a stay. (*See* MOUSE.)

RAISING A PURCHASE. The act of disposing certain machines, so that, by their mutual effects, they may produce sufficient force to overcome the weight or resistance of the object to which this machinery is applied.

RAKE. The projection of the upper parts of a ship, at both ends, beyond the extremities of the keel. Also, the deviation of the masts from the *vertical line of position*, reckoned from the keel forward or aft.

RAKING. Cannonading a ship, so that the shot shall range in the direction of her whole length between decks, called a raking fire; and is similar to military enfilading.

RAKISH. Said of a ship when she has the appearance of force and fast sailing.

RALLYING SQUARE. That formed by skirmishers or dispersed troops when suddenly menaced by cavalry, each man as he runs in successively placing himself with his back close against those already formed.

RAM. A long spar, iron-hooped at the ends, used for driving out blocks from beneath a vessel's keel, and for driving planks an end while only wedged to the ship's side. Also, a new rating in the navy. (*See* STEAM-RAM.)

RAMBADE. The elevated platform built across the prow of a galley, for boarding, &c.

RAMED. The state of a ship on the stocks, when all the frames are set upon the keel, the stem and stern-post put up, and the whole adjusted by the ram-line.

RAM-HEAD. An old word for halliard-block.

RAM HOME, To. To drive home the ammunition in a gun.

RAMMER. A cylindrical block of wood nearly fitting the bore of a cannon, and fastened on a wooden staff; used in loading to drive home the charge of a cannon.

RAMP. An oblique or sloping interior road to mount the *terre-plein* of the rampart.

RAMPART. An artificial embankment surrounding a fortified place, capable of covering the buildings from view, and of resisting the cannon of an enemy. Generally having a parapet on its top, and a wall for its front.

RAMPER-EEL. A name of the *lamprey, Petromyzon marinus.*

RAM-REEL. Synonymous with *bull-dance.*

RAMROD. In muzzle-loading, is the implement used in charging a piece, to drive home the powder and shot.

RAMSHACKLE. Out of repair and ungainly; disorderly.

RAN. Yarns coiled on a spun-yarn winch.

RANCE. The strut or support of a Congreve rocket.

RANDAN. A mode of rowing with alternate long and short oars.

RANDOM SHOT. A shot, or *coup perdu*, made when the muzzle is highly elevated; the utmost range may be at an angle of 45°, which is supposed to carry about ten times as far as the point blank; but improved gunnery has now put the term out of use.

RANGE. Placed in a line or row; a term hydrographically applied to hills, as "the coast-range." Also, *galley-range*, or fire-grate.

RANGE, To. To sail in a parallel direction, and near to; as "we ranged the coast;" "the enemy came ranging up alongside of us."

RANGE-HEADS. The *windlass-bitts* (which see).

RANGE OF A GUN. The horizontal distance which it will send a shot, at a stated elevation, to the point of its first graze. Also, a place where gun-practice is carried on. Also, a *level range* implies the gun lying horizontal. The various positions between this and 45° are called *intermediate ranges.*

RANGE OF CABLE. A sufficient quantity of cable left slack to allow the anchor to reach the ground before the cable is checked by the double turns round the bitts, the object being to let the anchor hook the bottom quickly, and to prevent the heavy shock which would be caused if its weight were suddenly brought upon the bitts.

RANGES, Horned. Pieces of timber containing belaying pins, inside a ship. Also, pieces of oak placed round the hatchways to contain shot.

RANK. Degree of dignity; officers of the navy rank with those of the army according to the following table :—

1. The Admirals of the Fleet	rank with	Field-marshals.
2. Admirals	,,	Generals.
3. Vice-admirals	,,	Lieutenant-generals.
4. Rear-admirals	,,	Major-generals.
5. Captains of the Fleet } 6. Commodores	,,	Brigadier-generals.
7. Captains of 3 years	,,	Colonels.
8. Captains under 3 years	,,	Lieutenant-colonels.
9. Commanders	next to	Do.
10. Lieutenants, 8 years	rank with	Majors.
11. Lieutenants, under 8 years	,,	Captains.
12. Sub-lieutenants	,,	Lieutenants.
13. Midshipmen	,,	Ensigns.

Also, the order or straight line made by men drawn up side by side.

RANK AND FILE. This word includes corporals as well as privates, all below sergeants. (*See* FILE.)

RANSACK, To. To pillage; but to ransack the hold is merely to overhaul its contents.

RANSOM. Money paid for the liberty of a war-prisoner, a city, or for the restoration of a captured vessel: formerly much practised at sea. It then fell into disuse, but was revived for a time in the seventeenth century. At length the greater maritime powers prohibited the offering or accepting such ransoms. By English law, all such securities shall be absolutely void; and he who enters into any such contract shall forfeit £500 on conviction. A privateer taking ransom forfeits her letters of marque, and her commander is punishable with a heavy penalty and imprisonment.

RAPER. An old term for a rope-maker.

RAP-FULL. Applies to a ship on a wind, when "keep her rap full!" means, do not come too close to the wind, or lift a wrinkle of the sail.

RAPID. A slope, down which water runs with more than ordinary rapidity, but not enough to be called a "fall;" and sometimes navigable by boats.

RAPPAREE. A smuggler, or one who lives on forced hospitality.

RASE. An archaism for a channel of the sea, and not a mispronunciation of *race* (which see).

RASEE. A line-of-battle ship with her upper works taken off, or reduced a deck, to lighten her; some of the old contract-built ships of the line, yclept "Forty Thieves," were thus converted into heavy frigates, as the *Duncan, America, Warspite*, &c.

RASH. A disease which attacks trees that have ceased to grow.

RASING. Marking timber by the *rasing-knife*, which has a peculiar blade hooked at its point, as well as a centre-pin to describe circles.

RASING-IRON. A tool for clearing the pitch and oakum out of the seams, previous to their being caulked afresh.

RAT. A term for one who changes his party for interest: from rats deserting vessels about to sink. These mischievous vermin are said to have increased after the economical expulsion of cats from our dockyards. Thus, in the petition from the ships-in-ordinary, to be allowed to go to sea, even to carry passengers, we read :——

> "Tho' it was hemigrants or sodgers—
> Anything afore them rats,
> Which now they is our only lodgers;
> For weil they knows, the artful dodgers,
> The Board won't stand th' expense of cats."

Injury done by rats is not included in a policy of insurance. Also, a rapid stream or race, derived from sharp rocks beneath, which injure the cable.

RATCHER. An old term for a rock.

RATCHET. A saw-toothed wheel in machinery, as the winch, windlass, &c., in which the paul catches.

RATE. A tariff or customs roll. Also, the six orders into which the ships of war were divided in the navy, according to their force and magnitude.

Thus the *first rate* comprehended all ships of 110 guns and upwards, having 42-pounders on the lower deck, diminishing to 6-pounders on the quarter-deck and forecastle. They were manned with 850 to 875 men, including officers, seamen, marines, servants, &c.—*Second rate.* Ships carrying from 90 to 100 guns.—*Third rate.* Ships from 80 to 84 guns.—*Fourth rate.* Ships from 60 to 74 guns; these were comprehended under the general names of frigates, and never appeared in the line of battle.—*Fifth rate.* Mounting from 32 to 40, or even 60 guns.—And *Sixth rate.* Mounting from any number, or no guns, if commanded by captains; those commanded by commanders were deemed sloops. Since the late introduction of massive iron, a captain may command but one gun.

RATE A CHRONOMETER, To. To determine its daily gaining or losing rate on mean time.

RATED SHIP. Synonymous with *post-ship* in former times; the term *ship* alone now infers that it is a captain's command, whilst *sloop* means a commander's.

RATH. A Gaelic term in use for *raft*—a timber raft; it is also an ancient earthen fort.

RATING. The station a person holds on the ship's books.

RATION. Each man's daily allowance of provisions; including, in the army, fuel and forage to man and horse.

RATIONAL HORIZON. *See* Horizon.

RATLINES, or Ratlings. Small lines which traverse the shrouds of a ship (at distances of 15 or 16 inches) horizontally from the deck upwards, and are made firm by jamming clove-hitches; they form a series of steps, like the rounds of a ladder.

RAT'S-TAIL. The tapering end of a rope. Also, the round tapered file for enlarging holes in metal.

RATTAN [Malay, *rotan*]. One of the genus *Calamus*, used for wicker-work, seats of chairs, &c. In the eastern seas they constitute the chief cables, even to 42 inches circumference, infinitely stronger than hemp, light, and not easily chafed by rocks; very useful also to seamen for brooms, hoops, hanks for sails, &c.

RATTLE DOWN RIGGING, To; or, To Rattle the Shrouds. To fix the ratlines in a line parallel to the vessel's set on the water.

RAUN. An old Manx term for a seal. In the north it implies the roe of salmon, used as a bait.

RAUNER. A northern term for the female salmon, as having the raun or roe.

RAVE-HOOK. In ship carpentry, a hooked iron tool used when enlarging the butts for receiving a sufficient quantity of oakum.

RAVELIN. In fortification, an outwork consisting of two long faces meeting in a salient angle, covering the curtain, and, generally, the shoulders of the bastions; it affords a powerful defence to the ground in front of the latter, which may rarely be approached till after the fall of the ravelin.

RAVINE. A deep chasm through which the rains are carried off elevated lands.

RAY. A line of sight. Also, a flat rhomboidal fish with a rough skin; genus, *Raia*.

RAZE, To. To level or demolish (applicable to works or buildings).

RAZED. Fortifications are said to be razed when totally demolished.

RAZOR-BACK. The fin-whale (*Balænoptera*), so called from its prominent dorsal fin. It usually attains the length of 70 feet.

RAZOR-BILL. A sea-fowl allied to the auks, *Alca torda*.

REACH, or RATCH. A straight part of a navigable river; the distance between any two elbows on the banks, wherein the current flows in uninterrupted course.

REACHING. Sometimes used for standing off and on: a vessel is also said to be on a reach, when she is sailing by the wind upon any tack. A vessel also *reaches* ahead of her adversary.

READY ABOUT! or READY OH! The order to prepare for tacking, each man to his station. (*See* ABOUT.)

READY WITH THE LEAD! A caution when the vessel is luffed up to deaden her way, followed by " heave."

REAL. A silver coin of Spain, value 5d. sterling. One-eighth of a dollar.

REALILLO. A small Spanish silver coin, value half a real.

REAM or REEM OUT, To. To enlarge the bore of a cannon with a special tool, so that it may take a larger projectile.

REAMING. Fishing vessels shifting their quarters while fishing. This word is often used for *reeming* (which see).

REAR. An epithet for anything situated behind another, as the hindmost portion of a fleet or army. (*See* DIVISION.) To *rear* an object in view, is to *rise* or approach it.

REAR-ADMIRAL. The officer in command of the third division of a fleet, whose flag is at the mizen.

REAR-GUARD.. That part of the army which brings up and protects the rear.

REARING. The upper-works tumbling home, or being wall-sided.

REAR-RANK. The last rank of a body of men drawn up in simple line.

REAR-SHIP. The sternmost ship of a fleet.

RE-ASSEMBLE. To gather together a fleet, or convoy, after having been scattered.

REASTY. Rancid or rusty pork or butter, &c.

REAVEL, or RAFFLE. To entangle; to knot confusedly together.

REBALLING. The catching of eels with earth-worms attached to a ball of lead suspended by a string from a pole.

REBATE. *See* DISCOUNT.

REBATES. The grooves formed on each side of the keel, stem, or stern-post, to receive the planks. (*See* RABBET.)

REBELS. Revolters and mutineers; in admiralty law the same as enemies.

RECEIVERS of Droits of Admiralty. Now termed *receivers of wreck* (which see).

RECEIVERS OF WRECK. Persons specially charged with wrecked property for the benefit of the shipping interests.

RECEIVING-SHIP. At any port, to receive supernumerary seamen, or entered or impressed men for the royal navy.

RECIPROCATE. The alternate motion balancing a steam-engine.

RECIPROCITY. The enlarging or contracting particular admiralty statutes, to meet the usages of foreign powers.

RECKONING, Ship's. The ship's position resulting from the courses steered, and distances run by log, brought up from the last astronomical observations. If unaccompanied by corrections for longitude by chronometer, and for latitude, it is termed only the dead reckoning.

RECOIL. The running in of a gun when discharged, which backward motion is caused by the force of the fire.

RECONNAISSANCE. A word adopted from the French, as meaning a military or nautical examination of a place.

RECONNOITRING. Sailing within gunshot of an enemy's port to ascertain his strength and capabilities for offence and defence. Also, a rapid examination of coasts and countries, for correcting the defects of many previous maps and charts.

RECREANT. This term was for him who had yielded in single combat.

RECTA PRISA REGIS. In law, the sovereign's right to prisage, or one pipe of wine before, and another behind the masts, as customary in every cargo of wine.

RECTIFIER. An instrument used for determining the variation of the compass, in order to rectify the ship's course, &c. It consists of two circles, either laid upon or let into one another, and so fastened together in their centres that they represent two compasses, the one fixed, the other movable; each is divided into 32 points of the compass, and 360°, and numbered both ways from the north and the south, ending at the east and west in 90°. The fixed compass represents the horizon, in which the north and all the other points are liable to variation.

REDAN. The simplest form of regular fortification, consisting of two faces meeting in a salient angle; generally applied in connection with other works.

REDD. The spawn of fish. Also, the burrow scooped out by salmon in which to deposit their ova.

REDD-FISH. A northern general term for fishes in the spawning state, but particularly applied to salmon.

REDEMPTIONER. One who purchases his release from obligation to the master of a ship, by his services; or one whose services are sold to pay the expenses of his passage to America or elsewhere.

REDHIBITION. An action to annul or set aside a contract of sale.

RED-HOT BALLS. Shot made red-hot in a furnace, and in that state discharged at the enemy. The loading is managed with wet wads.

REDOUBT. An inclosed work, differing from a fort, in that its parts do not flank one another.

RED PINE. *Pinus rubra*, the red spruce; the timber of which is preferred throughout the United States for yards, and imported for that purpose into Liverpool from Nova Scotia.

REDUCE, To. To degrade to a lower rank; or to shorten the allowance of water or provisions.

REDUCE A CHARGE, To. To diminish the contents of a cartridge, sometimes requisite during heavy firing.

REDUCE A PLACE, To. To compel its commander to surrender, or vacate it by capitulation.

REDUCTION OF CELESTIAL OBSERVATIONS. The process of calculation, by which observations are rendered subservient to utility.

REEF. A certain portion of a sail comprehended between the head of a sail and any of the reef-bands. The intention of each reef is to reduce the sail in proportion to the increase of the wind; there are also reefs parallel to the foot or bottom of large sails, extended upon booms.— *Close-reefed* is when all the reefs of the top-sails are taken in.—*Reef* is also a group or continuous chain of rocks, sufficiently near the surface of the water to occasion its breaking over them. (*See* FRINGING-REEFS and BARRIER-REEFS.)

REEF-BAND. A narrow band of canvas sewed on the reef-line to support the strain of the reef-points. It is pierced with eyelet-holes, through which the points are passed each way with a running eye.

REEF-CRINGLES. *See* CRINGLES.

REEF-EARINGS. *See* EARINGS.

REEFED TOPMAST. When a topmast is sprung in or near the cap, the lower piece is cut off, and a new fid-hole cut, by which the mast is reefed or shortened.

REEFERS. A familiar term for midshipmen, because they have to attend in the tops during the operation of taking in reefs.

REEF-KNOT. Is one in which the ends fall always in a line with the outer parts; in fact, two loops, easy to untie, never jamming. That with the second tie across, is termed a granny's knot.

REEF-LINE. Casual aids in bad weather to help the men at the earings. When the vessel was going free, and the sail could not be "spilled," the men were, if blowing hard, often aided by passing the studding-sail halyards loosely round the sail, clewed up spirally from yard-arm to bunt.

REEF-PENDANT. A rope going through a cringle in the after-leech of a boom mainsail, and through a check sheave-hole in the boom, with a tackle attached to its end to bowse the after-leech down to the boom by which the sail is held reefed. On the lower yards it is a pendant for a similar purpose as the reef-tackle.

REEF-POINTS. Small flat pieces of plaited cordage or soft rope, tapering from the middle towards each end, whose length is nearly double the circumference of the yard, and used for the purpose of tying up the sail in the act of reefing; they are made fast by their eyes on each side of the eyelet-holes.

REEF-TACKLES, are indeed pendants and tackles. The pendant is rove through the sister-block, then a sheave in the yard-arm, and secured to a strong cringle beneath the close reef, sometimes through a block, and the end secured to the yard-arm. Within the sister-block it becomes a gun-tackle purchase, with the fall leading on deck. The reef-tackles are hauled out, and the other aids complete, before the men are sent aloft.

REEF-TACKLE SPAN. Two cringles in the bolt-rope, about a couple of feet apart, when a block is used.

REELS. Well-known wheels moving round an axis, and serving to wind various lines upon, as the log-reel for the log-line, deep-sea reel (which contains the deep-sea line, amounting to 150 or 200 fathoms), spun-yarn reel, &c. "She went 10 knots off the reel"—*i.e.* by the log-line.

REEMING. A term used by caulkers for opening the seams of the plank with reeming-irons, that the oakum may be more readily admitted. This may be a corruption of *rimer*, for opening circular holes in metal.

REEMING-BEETLE. A caulker's largest mallet.

REEMING-IRON. The larger iron used by caulkers in opening the seams.

RE-ENTERING ANGLE. In fortification, is an angle whose vertex points inward, or towards the place.

REEVE, To. To pass the end of a rope through any cavity or aperture, as the channel of a block; to *unreeve* is the opposite.

REEVING. In polar voyaging, following up serpentine channels in the ice, till the vessel reaches open water, or *reeves the pack*.

REFITTING. Repairing any damages which a ship may have sustained.

REFLECTING CIRCLE. An instrument used instead of a sextant, quintant, or quadrant; but the quintant embraces as much—viz. 152 degrees. The instrument reflects a celestial or any distant object so as to bring the image into contact with any object seen direct, by which their angular distance is measured, as in lunar distances.

REFLECTION, ANGLE OF. Whether the instance be a ray of light or a cannon-ball, the angle of reflection will always be found equal to the angle of incidence.

REFLUX. The ebbing of the tide, or reflow of the waters, which have been pressed back.

REFORMADES. The sons of the nobility and gentry who served in the navy under letters from Charles II., and were allowed table-money and other encouragements to raise the character of the service.

REFRACTING TELESCOPE. That through which objects are seen directly through its double object-glass.

REFRACTION. An inflection of the rays of light: that property of the atmosphere which bends the rays of light in their passage to the eye from a different density, and causes the altitude of heavenly bodies to appear greater than it really is, especially near the horizon. (*See* TERRESTRIAL REFRACTION.)

REFUSAL OF A PILE. Its stoppage or obstruction, when it cannot be driven further in.

REGAL FISHES. In statute law, these are whales and sturgeons.

REGARDERS. Inspectors of the felling of timber.

REGATTA. A rowing-match formerly peculiar to the republic of Venice; but now the term is applied to yacht and boat races in general.

REGIMENT. A body of men commanded by a colonel, complete in its own organization, and divided into companies of infantry or troops of cavalry.

REGIMENTAL ORDERS. Such as the commanding officer may deem it necessary to issue for the discipline of the regiment.

REGIMENTALS. The regulation dress for the individuals of a regiment.

REGIMENTAL STAFF-OFFICERS. The surgeon, adjutant, paymaster, assistant-surgeon, and quarter-master of each regiment.

REGION. Any large tract of land or water on the earth's surface, having some feature common to every part of itself, and different from what exists elsewhere; as northern, southern, or intertropical region; mountainous region; region of perpetual congelation, &c.

REGISTER. A purchaser has no title to a ship, either at law or in equity, unless he be mentioned in the register. If a vessel, not duly registered, exercise any of the privileges of a British ship, she is liable to forfeiture.

REGISTER ANEW. When any registered ship is so altered as not to correspond with the "particulars" relating to the description in her register-book, either a new certificate of registry, or an official indorsement of the old one, is necessary.

REGISTER OF VICE-ADMIRALTY COURT. Not responsible for money transmitted under proper precautions, and in the usual course of business, but afterwards lost by the failure of the consignee.

REGISTER SHIP. A Spanish plate-ship or galleon.

REGISTRY OF SEAMEN. A record of merchant seamen kept by the registrar-general of seamen.

REGNI POPULI. An old law-term given to the people of Surrey and Sussex, and on the sea-coasts of Hampshire.

REGULATOR. A name for the governor of a steam-engine. Also, a valve-cock. The *regulator* of a clock is the shortening or lengthening pendulum or escapement.

REGULUS. α Leonis; the principal star in the old constellation Leo.

REIGNING WINDS. The prevalent winds on any particular coast or region. (*See* WIND.)

REIN. A crack or vein in a musket-barrel.

REINFORCE, To. To strengthen a fleet, squadron, army, or detachment, by additional means and munitions.

REINFORCE. In artillery, that increase, beyond its general conical outline, of the metal towards the breech, which was marked on old pattern guns by rings. They are generally in cast guns omitted now, though the principle of the reinforce remains, yet less defined in nature and number, in the recent wrought and built-up guns.

RE-INSURANCE. To insure the same property a second time by other underwriters. If an underwriter find that he has incautiously bound himself to a greater amount than he can discharge, he may shift it, or part of it, from himself to others, by a reinsurance policy made on the same risk.

REIS. Small coins of Portugal, of which 4800 go to the moidore.

RELIEF. The change of watches. Also, the person relieving a particular station. Also, a fresh detachment of troops, ordered to replace those already on duty. In fortification, the total height of the crest of the parapet above the bottom of the ditch.

RELIEVE, To. To put fresh men or ships upon a stipulated duty.

RELIEVING TACKLES. Those which are occasionally hooked to the tiller, in order to steer by in bad weather or in action, when any accident has happened to the wheel or tiller-rope.

REMA, or Reume. The tide.

REMAIN. The quantity of stores left on charge for survey, after a voyage.

REMARK-BOOK. This contains hydrographical observations of every port visited, and is sent annually to the admiralty, together with any charts, plans, or views which have been taken. Often a very dull miscellany, though kept by intelligent masters.

REMBERGE. A long narrow rowing vessel of war, formerly used by the English. Its name is derived from *remo* and *barca*, and it seems to have been the precursor of the Deal luggers.

REMBLAI. The mass of earth requisite for the construction of the rampart. An embankment.

REMORA. The *sucker-fish*. It has a long oval plate on the top of the head, by which, having exhausted the air in it, it clings to a ship's bottom, to the sides of a shark, or to turtle.

REMOVAL FROM THE LIST. Dismission, or dropping an officer out of the service.

RENDERING. The act of yielding to any force applied. For instance, the rope of a laniard or tackle is said to render when, by pulling upon one part, each other part takes its share of the strain. Any rope, hawser, or cable is "rendered" by easing it round the bitts, particularly in riding with a strain to freshen the nip.

RENDEZVOUS. The port or place of destination where the several ships of a fleet are appointed to join company.

REPEATING FIRE-ARM. One by which a number of charges, previously inserted, may be fired off in rapid succession, or after various pauses. The principle is very old, but the effective working of it is new.

REPEAT SIGNALS, To. Is to make the same signal exhibited by the admiral, in order to its being more readily distinguished at a distance, or through smoke, &c. Frigates and small vessels out of the line were deemed repeating ships, and enforced signals by guns. The *repeat* from a superior intended to convey rebuke for inattention, is usually accompanied by one gun, or several.

REPLENISH, To. To obtain supplies of water and provisions up to the original amount.

REPORT OF GUARD. The document rendered in by the guard-boat, of every vessel boarded during her hours of duty, with their arrivals, sailings, and other occurrences.

REPORT OF SURVEY. The opinion of surveys officially signed by surveying officers.

REPORT ONE'S SELF, To. When an officer returns on board from duty, or from leave of absence.

REPRESENTATION. A collateral statement of such facts not inserted on the policy of insurance, as may give the underwriters a just estimate of the risk of the adventure. (*See* WARRANTY.)

REPRIMAND. A formal reproof for error or misconduct, conveyed sometimes publicly, sometimes confidentially, sometimes by sentence of court-martial, or on the judgment, mature or otherwise, of a superior.

REPRISAL. The taking one thing in satisfaction for another, as the seizing of ships and goods for injury inflicted; a right exerted, though no actual war be commenced. It is authorized by the law of nations if justice has been solemnly called for and denied. The word is synonymous with *marque* in our admiralty courts.

REPRISE, OR REPRISAL. Is the retaking a vessel from the enemy before she has arrived in any neutral or hostile port. If a vessel thus retaken has been 24 hours in the possession of an enemy, she is deemed a lawful recapture; but if within that time, she is merely *detenu*, and must be wholly restored to the owner. An amount of salvage is sometimes awarded to the re-captors. Also, if a vessel has from any cause been abandoned by the enemy, before he has taken her into any port, she is to be restored to the original proprietor. (*See* SALVAGE.)

REQUISITION. An official demand for stores, &c.

RESCUE. Any vessel recovered by the insurrection of prisoners on board of her, or by her being forced by stress of weather into our ports, she is restored on *salvage*. There is no rule prescribed by the law of England in the case of foreign property rescued; with British subjects the court usually adopts the proportion of re-capture. In respect to foreigners the only guide is that of "quantum meruit."

RESERVE. A portion drawn out from the main body, and stationed in the rear for a special object.

RE-SHIP. To ship again, or ship goods that have been imported or conveyed by water.

RESIDENT. A British subject residing in an enemy's country may trade generally with the natives, but not in contraband.

RESISTING MEDIUM. An assumed thin ethereal fluid, which, from the retardation of Encke's comet, may be supposed to pervade the planetary space—perhaps the *spiritus subtilissimus* of Newton—in virtue of which periodical comets seem to have their velocity diminished, and their orbits contracted at every revolution.

RESOLVE, To. To reduce a traverse, or day's work, to its exact limits.

RESOURCE. Expedient. A good seaman is ever a man of resources.

RESPONDENTIA. A loan made upon goods laden in a ship, for which the borrower is personally responsible; differing therein from bottomry, where the ship and tackle are liable. In bottomry the lender runs no risk, though the goods should be lost; and upon respondentia the lender must be paid his principal and interest, though the ship perish, provided the goods be safe.

RESPONSIBILITY. Often a wholesome restraint; but the bugbear of an inefficient officer.

REST. A pole with an iron fork at the top for the support of the old heavy musket.

RET, To. To soak in water, as in seasoning timber, hemp, &c.

RETINUE. Applied strictly to the admiral's suite or followers, though it means an accompanying train in general.

RETIRE. The old war-term for retreat. Thus Shakspeare makes Richard Plantagenet exclaim—

> " Ne'er may he live to see a sunshine day,
> That cries Retire, if Warwick bid him stay."

RETIRED LIST. A roll whereon deserving officers are placed whose health, age, or want of interest justifies their retirement from active service.

RETIRED PAY. A graduated pension for retired officers; but the term is nearly synonymous with *half pay.*

RETRACTUS AQUÆ. An old law-term for the ebb or return of tide.

RETREAT. The order in which a fleet or squadron declines engagement. Or the retrograde movement of any body of men who retire from a hostile force. Also, that beat of drum about sunset which orders the guards and piquets to take up their night duties.

RETRENCHMENT. A defence with a ditch and breastwork behind another post or defence, whereby the besieger, on forcing the original work, is confronted by a fresh one.

RETROGRADATION. An apparent motion of the planets contrary to the order of the signs, and to their orbital march. The arc of retrogradation is the angular distance thus apparently traversed. Mars may be watched as an instance.

RETROGRADE MOTION. *See* MOTION.

RETURN. A ship on a return voyage is not generally liable; but if she sailed on the outward voyage under false papers, the liability to confiscation continues.

RETURN A SALUTE, To. Admirals are saluted, but return two guns less for each rank that the saluting officer is below the admiral.

RETURNS. All the various reports and statements required by officers in command to be made periodically. (*See* SUPPLIES AND RETURNS.)

REVEILLE. The beat of drum at break of day, when night duties cease.

REVENUE. In cases of revenue proceedings, the law harshly provides that the *onus probandi* is to be on the claimant, however injured.

REVENUE-CUTTERS. Sharp-built single-masted vessels armed, for the purpose of preventing smuggling, and enforcing the custom-house regulations. They are usually styled *revenue-cruisers.*

REVERSE. A change; a vicissitude. Also, the flank at the other extremity from the pivot of a division is termed the reverse flank.

REVETMENT. A sloping wall of brick-work, or any other attainable material, supporting the outer face of the rampart, and lining the side of the ditch.

REVIEW. The inspection of a fleet or army, or of any body of men under arms.

REVOLUTION, Time of. In relation to a planet or comet, this is the time occupied in completing a circuit round the sun, and is synonymous with *periodic time.*

RHE. A very old word signifying an overflow of water.

RHILAND-ROD. A Dutch measure of 12 English feet, formerly in use with us: it is more properly *Rhine-land rod.*

RHODIAN LAWS. A maritime code, asserted, but without sufficient proof, to be the basis of the Roman sea-laws. The code published by Leunclavius and others, as a body of Rhodian laws, is a mere forgery of modern times.

RHODINGS. The brass cleats on which the axles of the pumps work.

RHOMBOID. An oblique parallelogram, having its opposite sides equal and parallel, but its angles not right angles.

RHOMBUS. A lozenge-shaped figure, having four equal sides, but its angles not right angles.

RHUMB, or Rhomb. A vertical circle of any given place, or the intersection of a part of such a circle with the horizon. Rhumbs, therefore, coincide with points of the world, or of the horizon; and hence seamen distinguish the rhumbs by the same names as the points and winds, as marked on the fly or card of the compass. The *rhumb-line,* therefore, is a line prolonged from any point of the compass in a nautical chart, except the four cardinal points; or it is a line which a ship, keeping in the same collateral point or rhumb, describes throughout its whole course.

RHYDAL [from the Celtic *rhydle*]. A ford or channel joining lakes or broad waters.

RIBADOQUIN. A powerful cross-bow for throwing long darts. Also, an old piece of ordnance throwing a ball of one or two pounds.

RIBBANDS. In naval architecture, long narrow flexible pieces of fir nailed upon the outside of the ribs, from the stem to the stern-post of a ship, so as to encompass the body lengthways, and hold the timbers together while in frame.

RIBBING-NAILS. Similar to deck-nails, but not so fine; they have large round heads with rings, so as to prevent their heads from splitting the timbers, or being drawn through.

RIBBONS. The painted mouldings along a ship's side. Also, the tatters of a sail in blowing away.

RIBS. The frame timbers which rise from the bottom to the top of a ship's hull: the hull being as the body, the keel as the backbone, and the planking as the skin.

RIBS AND TRUCKS. Used figuratively for fragments.

RIBS OF A PARREL. An old species of parrel having alternate ribs and bull's-eyes; the ribs were pieces of wood, each about one foot in length, having two holes in them through which the two parts of the parrel-rope are reeved with a bull's-eye between; the inner smooth edge of the rib rests against, and slides readily up and down, the mast.

RICKERS. Lengths of stout poles cut up for the purpose of stowing flax, hemp, and the like. Spars supplied for boats' masts and yards, boat-hook staves, &c.

RICOCHET. The bound of a shot. *Ricochet fire*, that whereby, a less charge and a greater elevation being used, the shot or shell is made to just clear a parapet, and bound along the interior of a work.

RIDDLE. A sort of weir in rivers.—*To riddle.* To fire through and through a vessel, and reduce her to a sieve-like condition.

RIDE, To. To ride at anchor. A vessel rides easily, apeak, athwart, head to wind, out a gale, open hawse, to the tide, to the wind, &c. A rope rides, as when round the capstan or windlass the strain part overlies and jams the preceding turn.—*To ride between wind and tide.* Said of a ship at anchor when she is acted upon by wind and tide from different directions, and takes up a position which is the result of both forces.

RIDEAU. A rising ground running along a plain, nearly parallel to the works of a place, and therefore prejudicial.

RIDERS. Timbers laid as required, reaching from the keelson to the orlop-beams, to bind a ship and give additional strength. They are variously termed, as *lower futtock-riders* and *middle futtock-riders.* When a vessel is weak, or has broken her floors or timbers, riders are introduced to secure the ship, and enable her to reach a port where she can be properly repaired. Stringers are also used, but these run horizontally.—*Riders* are also upper tiers of casks, or any stowed above the ground tier in the hold.

RIDING A PORT-LAST. With lower yards on the gunwales.

RIDING-BITTS. Those to which the cable is made fast.

RIDING-DOWN. The act of the men who throw their weight on the head of a sail to stretch it. Also, of the man who comes down a stay, &c., to tar it; or foots the bunt in.

RIDGE. Hydrographically means a long narrow stretch of shingle or rocks, near the surface of the sea. (*See* REEF and SHALLOW.) Geographically, the intersection of two opposite slopes, or a range of hills, or the highest line of mountains.

RIDGE-ROPES, are of various kinds. Thus the centre-rope of an awning, and those along the rigging to which it is stretched, the man-ropes to the bowsprit, safety lines from gun to gun in bad weather—all obtain this name.

RIFE. An old provincial term for a salt-water pond.

RIFLED ORDNANCE. That which is provided with spiral grooves in the interior of the bore, to give rotatory motion to the projectile, thereby much increasing its accuracy of flight, and permitting the use of elongated shot and shell.

RIFLE-PIT. Cover hastily thrown up by one or two skirmishers, but contributing, when a line of them is joined together, to form works sometimes of much importance.

RIG. Colloquially, mischievous frolic not carried to excess.

RIG, To. To fit the shrouds, stays, braces, and running-rigging to their respective masts, yards, and sails. Colloquially, it means to dress.—*To rig in a boom*, is to draw it in.—*To rig out a boom*, is to run it out from a yard, in order to extend the foot of a sail upon it, as with studding-sail booms, &c.

RIGEL. β *Orionis*, one of the bright stars in Orion.

RIGGED. Completely equipped.

RIGGERS. Men employed on board ships to fit the standing and running rigging, or to dismantle them. The riggers in the naval yards, who rig ships previous to their being commissioned, are under the master-attendant, and perform all anchor, mooring, and harbour duties also.

RIGGING. A general name given to all the ropes or chains employed to support the masts, and arrange the sails according to the direction of the wind. Those are termed "standing" which are comparative fixtures, and support the masts, &c.; and those "running," which are in constant use, to trim the yards, and make or shorten sail, &c.

RIGGING-LOFT. A long room or gallery in a dockyard, where rigging is fitted by stretching, serving, splicing, seizing, &c., to be in readiness for the ship.

RIGGING-MATS. Those which are seized upon a vessel's standing rigging, to prevent its being chafed.

RIGGING OUT. A term for outfitting. Also, a word used familiarly to express clothing of ship or tar.

RIGGING-STOPPER. *See* STOPPERS.

RIGHT. As to direction, fully or directly; thus, right ahead, or right away, &c.

RIGHT ANGLE. An angle formed by a line rising or falling perpendicularly upon another, and measuring 90°, or the quadrant of a circle.

RIGHT-ANGLED TRIANGLE. That which has one right angle.

RIGHT ASCENSION. An arc of the equator between the first point of Aries, and the hour circle which passes through any planet or star; or that point of the equinoctial, which comes to the meridian with any heavenly object, and is therefore similar to terrestrial longitude.

RIGHT ATHWART. Square, or at right angles with the keel.

RIGHT AWAY! It is a habit of seamen answering when a sail is discovered from the mast-head; "Right away on the beam, sir," or "on the bow," &c.

RIGHT-HAND ROPE. That which is laid up and twisted with the sun, that is to the right hand; the term is opposed to *water-laid rope*, which is left-handed.

RIGHTING. The act of a ship recovering her upright position after she has been laid upon a careen, which is effected by casting loose the careening tackles, and, if necessary, heaving upon the relieving tackles. A ship is also said *to right* at sea, when she rises with her masts erect, after having been listed over on one side by grounding, or force of wind.

RIGHT THE HELM! The order to put it amidships, that is, in a line with the keel.

RIGHT ON END. In a continuous line; as the masts should be.

RIGHT SAILING. Running a course on one of the four cardinal points, so as to alter only a ship's latitude, or longitude.

RIGHT UP AND DOWN. Said in a dead calm, when the wind is no way at all. Or, in anchor work, when the cable is in that condition, the boatswain calls, "Up and down, sir," whereupon "Thick and dry (nippers) for weighing" are ordered.

RIGHT WAY. When the ship's head casts in the desired direction. Also, when she swings clear at single anchor.

RIGHT WHALE. A name applied to the whale with a very large head and no dorsal fin, which yields the whalebone and train-oil of commerce, in opposition to the finbacks or rorquals, which are scarcely worth catching. There are several species found both in the Arctic and Southern seas, but never within the tropics.

RIG OF A SHIP. The disposition of the masts, cut of sails, &c., whether square or fore-and-aft rigs. In fact, the rig denotes the character of the vessel.

RIG THE CAPSTAN, To. To fix the bars in the drum-head in readiness for heaving; not forgetting to pin and swift. (*See* CAPSTAN.)

RIG THE GRATINGS. Prepare them for punishment.

RILE. An old corruption of *rail*. To ruffle the temper; to vex.

RILL. A very small run of fresh water, less than a rivulet.

RIM, OR BRIM. A name given to the circular edge of a top. (*See* TOP.)

RIM-BASE. The shoulder on the stock of a musket.

RIME. Hoar-frost; condensed vapour.

RIMER. A palisade in fortification; but for its naval application, *see* REEMER. Also, a tool for enlarging holes in metal plates, &c.

RIMS. Those pieces which form the quarter-galleries between the stools. Also, the cast-iron frame in which the dropping pauls of a capstan traverse, and bring up the capstan.

RING. A commercial measure of staves, or wood prepared for casks, and containing four shocks. Also, the iron ring to which the cable is bent to the anchor in the summit of the shank.

RING-BOLT. An iron bolt with an eye at one end, wherein is fitted a circular ring. They are more particularly used for managing cannon, and are for this purpose fixed on each side of the port-holes. They are driven through the plank and the corresponding timber, and retained in this position by a clinching ring.

RING-DOGS. Iron implements for hauling timber along: made by connecting two common dogs by a ring through the eyes. When united with cordage they form a *sling-dog* (which see).

RING-ROPES. Ropes rove through the ring of the anchor, to haul the cable through it, in order to bend or make it fast in bad weather; they are first rove through the ring, and then through the hawse-holes, when the end of the cable is secured to them.

RINGS. The annual circular layers in timber. Also, grommets, or circles of metal for lifting things by hand, or securing the points of bolts, &c., as hatch or port rings.

RING-STOPPER. A long piece of rope secured to an after ring-bolt, and the loop embracing the cable through the next, and others in succession nip the cable home to each ring-bolt in succession. It is a precaution in veering cable in bad weather.

RING-TAIL. A kind of studding-sail hoisted beyond the after edge of those sails which are extended by a gaff and a boom over the stern. The two lower corners of this sail are stretched to a boom, called a *ring-tail boom*, which rigs in and out upon the main or driver boom.

RINK. A space of ice devoted to certain recreations, as a skating or a curling rink: generally roofed in from the snow in Canada.

RIONNACK. A name of the horse-mackerel among the Scottish islands.

RIP. A pannier or basket used for carrying fish.—*To rip*, to strip off a ship's planks.

RIPARIA. A law-term for the water running between the banks of a river.

RIPARY. Inhabiting the sea-shore.

RIPE [from the Latin, *ripa*]. The banks of a tide-river, and the sea-shore: a term in use on our southern coasts.

RIPPERS, or RIPIERS. Men from the sea-shores, who sell fish to the inland towns and villages.

RIPPING-IRON. A caulker's tool for tearing oakum out of a seam, or stripping copper or sheathing from a ship's bottom. (*See* REEMER.)

RIPPLE. The small waves raised on the surface of the water by the passage of a slight breeze, or current, caused by foul bottom.

RIPPLE-MARKS. The ripply appearance left at low water on the flat part of a sandy beach.

RIPPS. *See* TIDE-RIPPS. Also, strange overfalls, the waves of which, even in calm weather, will throw their crests over the bulwarks.

RISBERM. Fascines placed to oppose the violence of the surf.

RISING-FLOORS. The floor-timbers, which rise gradually from the plane of the midship floor, so as to sharpen the form of a vessel towards the bow and stern.

RISINGS OF BOATS. A narrow strake of board fastened withinside to support the thwarts.

RISING-SQUARE. In ship-carpentry, a square used in the whole mould-ing, upon which is marked the height of the rising line above the keel.

RISK A RUN, To. To take chance without convoy.

RISKS. The casualties against which insurances are made on ships and cargoes.

RITTOCH. An Orkney name for the tern, *Sterna hirnudo.*

RIVAGE. An old term, from the French, for a coast or shore of the sea, or a river.

RIVAGIUM. A law-term for a duty paid to the sovereign on some rivers for the passage of boats or vessels.

RIVAILE. An Anglo-Norman term for a harbour.

RIVE. The sea-shore. Also, as a verb, to split wood.

RIVER-BOATS. Wherries, and the like, which ply in harbours and rivers for the conveyance of passengers.

RIVER-HARBOUR. That which is situated in the channel of a river, especially such as are at the embouchure with a bar in front.

RIVER-LAKES. Large pools of water occupying a portion of the valleys or hollows through which the courses of rivers lie.

RIVER-RISK. A policy of insurance from the docks to the sea, at any port.

RIVET. The roe of a fish. Also, a hinge-pin, or any piece of riveted work. The soft iron pin by which the ends of a cask hoop, or the plates of a boiler, &c., are secured by clinching.

RIVIERA. An Italian term for a coast, as the *Riviera di Genoa.*

RIX-DOLLAR. A silver coin common in northern Europe, of the aver-age value of 4s. 6d.

ROACH. The hollow curvature of the lower parts of upper square-sails, to clear the stays when the yards are braced up.

ROAD, or ROADSTEAD. An off-shore well-known anchorage, where ships may await orders, as St. Helen's at Portsmouth, Cowes, Leith, Basque Roads, Saugor, and others, where a well-found vessel may ride out a gale.

ROADSTER, or ROADER. Applied chiefly to those vessels which work by tides, and seek some known road to await turn of tide or change of wind. If a vessel under sail strike against any roader and damage her, the former is obliged by law to make good the damages.

ROAST-BEEF DRESS. Full uniform; probably from its resemblance to that of the royal beef-eaters.

ROAST BEEF OF OLD ENGLAND. A popular air, by which officers are summoned to the dinner-table.

ROBANDS, or ROBBENS. (*See* ROPE-BANDS.)

ROBINET. An ancient military machine for throwing darts and stones; now the name of some useful cocks in the steam-engine, as for gauge, brine, trial, and steam-regulator.

ROCK. An extensive geological term, but limited in hydrographical par-lance to hard and solid masses of the earth's surface; when these rise in insulated masses nearly to the surface of the sea, they render navigation especially dangerous.—*Half-tide rock.* A rock which appears above water at half-ebb.

ROCK-COD. A species of cod found on a rocky bottom.

ROCKET. The well-known pyrotechnical preparation, but modified to suit various purposes. A cylindrical case charged with a fiercely burning composition, the gases of which, rushing out from the after-end against the resisting atmosphere, propel the whole forward at a rate continually increasing, until the composition be expended. It is generally kept in balance by a long light stick or tail attached. The case is made of metal or paper, and variously headed to the amount of 32 lbs. if its purpose be war (*see* CONGREVE ROCKETS); life-saving (by conveying a line over a stranded vessel); even the killing of whales, when reduced to 1, 2, or 3 lbs.; or, lastly, signals, for which it is fired straight upwards.

ROCKET-BOAT. Flat-bottomed boats, fitted with rocket-frames to fire Congreve rockets from, in naval bombardment.

ROCKET-BRIGADE. A body of horse-artillery assigned to rocket service.

ROCKET-FRAME. The stand from which Congreve rockets are fired.

ROCK-HIND. A large fish of tropical regions, *Serranus catus.*

ROCK-SCORPION. A name applied to persons born at Gibraltar.

ROD. The connecting and coupling bars of the steam-engine. (*See* SOUNDING-ROD.)

RODD. A sort of cross-bow formerly in use in our navy.

RODDEN-FLEUK. A northern name for the turbot.

RODDING TIME. The season for fish-spawning.

RODE OF ALL. Improperly so written for *rowed of all* (which see). The order to throw in and boat the oars.

RODGERS' ANCHOR. The excellent small-palmed, very strong and good-holding anchor. It is the result of many years' study and experiment by Lieutenant Rodgers, R.N.

RODMAN GUN. One cast on the excellent method of Captain Rodman, formerly of the United States Ordnance—viz. on a core artificially kept cool; whereby the outer metal, cooling last, shrinks on to and compresses the inner, instead of drawing outwards and weakening it, as it must do when cooled first in a solid casting.

ROGER. The black flag hoisted by pirates. (*See* JOLLY ROGER.)

ROGER'S BLAST. A provincialism denoting a sudden and local motion of the air, resembling a miniature whirlwind.

ROGUE'S MARCH. The tune appropriated to drumming a bad character out of a ship or out of a regiment.

ROGUE'S YARN. A yarn twisted the contrary way to the rest of a rope, for detecting theft or embezzlement. Being tarred if in a white rope, but white in a tarred rope, it is easily discovered. It is placed in the middle of each strand in all the cordage made for the royal navy. Lately the rogue's yarn has been superseded by a thread of worsted: a different coloured worsted being used in each dockyard, so that any defective rope may be traced to the place where it was made.

ROLE D'EQUIPAGE. An important document in admiralty law. (*See* MUSTER-ROLL.)

ROLL. A uniform beat of the drum, without variation, for a considerable time. The divisions are summoned by roll of drum, one roll for each. (*See* MUSTER-ROLL.)

ROLLER. A mighty oceanic swell said to precurse the northers of the Atlantic, and felt in great violence at Tristan d'Acunha, where H.M.S. *Lily* foundered with all hands in consequence, and several vessels at St. Helena have been driven from their anchors and wrecked. These waves roll in from the north, and do not break till they reach soundings, when they evince terrific power, rising from 5 to 15 feet above the usual level of the waters. A connection with volcanoes has been suggested as a cause.

ROLLERS. Cylindrical pieces of timber, fixed either horizontally or vertically in different parts of a ship above the deck, so as to revolve on an axis, and prevent the cables, hawsers, and running rigging from being chafed, by lessening their friction. The same as *friction roller*. Also, movable pieces of wood of the same figure, which are occasionally placed under boats, pieces of heavy timber, &c.

ROLLING. That oscillatory motion by which the waves rock a ship from side to side. The larger part of this disturbance is owing to the depth of the centre of gravity below the centre of figure, the former exercising a violent re-action when disturbed from its rest by passing seas; therefore it is diminished by raising the weights, and must by no means be confounded with heeling.

ROLLING-CHOCK, OR JAW-PIECE. Similar to that of a gaff, fastened to the middle of an upper yard, to steady it.

ROLLING-CLEAT. Synonymous with *rolling-chock*.

ROLLING DOWN TO ST. HELENA. Running with a flowing sheet by the trade-wind.

ROLLING-HITCH. Pass the end of a rope round a spar or rope; take it round a second time, riding the standing part; then carry it across, and up through the bight.

ROLLING-SWELL. That heaving of the sea where the waves are very distant, forming deep troughs between.

ROLLING-TACKLES. Used to prevent the yards from swaying to and fro under heavy rolling motion.

ROLLSTER, OR ROSTER. A rotation list of officers.

ROLL UP A SAIL, To. To hand it quickly.

ROMAN CEMENT. A cement which hardens under water; used for piers, docks, &c., as pozzolana, Aberthaw limestone, &c.

ROMBOWLINE, OR RUMBOWLINE. Condemned canvas, rope, and the like. Also the coarse rope used to secure new coils.

RONDEL. An old term for a light, round shield.

RONE. A northern term for the roe of a fish.

RONNAL. A northern term for a female fish, as kipper is for the male.

ROOBLE. A Russian coin. (*See* RUBLE.)

ROOD-GOOSE. A name for the brent-goose.

ROOF-TREE. *See* ROUGH-TREE.

ROOKE, OR ROUKE. A mist, dampness, or fog.

ROOM. A name given to some reserved apartment in a ship, as—*The bread-room.* In the aftermost part of the hold: properly lined to receive the bread, and keep it dry.—*The cook-room.* (*See* GALLEY.)—*The gun-room.* On the after gun-deck of ships of the line, or steerage of frigates; devoted to the gun-room officers.—*Light-room.* Attached to the magazine.—*Sail-rooms,* devoted to the sails, are on the orlop deck, and are inclosed for the reception of the spare sails.—*Slop-room.* Devoted to slop-clothing.—*Spirit-room.* A secure space in the after-part of a ship's hold, for the stores of wine, brandy, &c.—*Steward's-room.* The office devoted to the purser's steward of former times, now paymaster's steward, whence he issues most of the light provisions to the ship's company.—*Ward-room.* A room over the gun-room in ships of the line, where the lieutenants and other principal officers sleep and mess. The term *sea-room* is applied when a ship obtains a good offing, is clear of the coast dangers, and is free to stand on a long course without nearing danger.

ROOM, ROOMER, OR GOING ROOM. The old term for going large, or from the wind. (*See* LASK and LARGE.) It is mentioned by Bourne in 1578.

ROOMING. An old word to signify running to leeward.—*To go room.* To bear down.

ROOST. A phrase applied to races of strong and furious tides, which set in between the Orkney and Shetland Islands, as those of Sumburgh and the Start.

ROPE. Is composed of hemp, hide, wire, or other stuff, spun into yarns and strands, which twisted together forms the desired cordage. The word is very old, being the actual representative of the Anglo-Saxon *ráp.—To rope a sail.* To sew the bolt-rope round its edges, to strengthen it and prevent it from rending.

ROPE-BANDS. Small plaited lines rove through the eyelet holes with a running eye, by which the head of a sail, after the earings are secured, is brought to the yard or jackstay.

ROPE-HOUSE. A long building in a dock-yard, where ropes are made.

ROPE-LADDER. Such as hangs over the stern, to enable men to go into boats, &c.

ROPE-MAKER. A first-class petty officer in the navy.

ROPE OF SAND. A term borrowed from a Greek proverb signifying attempting impossibilities; without cohesion. Said of people who ought, but will not combine to effect a necessary object.

ROPES. A general name given to all the cordage above one inch in circumference used in rigging a ship; but the name is severally applied to the awning, bell, boat, bolt, breast, bucket, buoy, davit, entering, grapnel, guest or guist, guy, heel, keel, man, parral, passing, ring, rudder, slip, swab, tiller, top, and yard: all which see under their respective heads. Ropes are of several descriptions, viz.:—*Cable-laid,* consists of three strands of already formed hawser-laid or twisted left-hand, laid up into one opposite making nine strands.—*Hawser-laid*, is merely three strands of simple yarns twisted right, but laid up left.—*Four-strand* is similarly laid with four strands, and a core scarcely twisted.—*Sash-line* is plaited and used for signal halliards.—*Rope-yarn* is understood to be the selected serviceable yarns from condemned rope, and is worked into twice-laid. The refuse, again, into rumbowline for temporary purposes, not demanding strength.

ROPES, HIGH. *On the high ropes.* To be ceremonious, upstart, invested with brief authority.

ROPE'S END. The termination of a fall, and should be pointed or whipped. Formerly much used for illegal punishment.

ROPE-YARN. The smallest and simplest part of any rope, being one of the large threads of hemp or other stuff, several of which being twisted together form a strand.

ROPING-NEEDLES. Those used for roping, being strong accordingly.

RORQUAL, OR FURROWED WHALE. A name of Scandinavian origin applied to the finback whales, distinguished from the right whales by the small size of their heads, shortness of their whalebone, the presence of a dorsal fin, and of a series of conspicuous longitudinal folds or furrows in the skin of the throat and chest.

ROSE, OR STRAINER. A plate of copper or lead perforated with small holes, placed on the heel of a pump to prevent choking substances from being sucked in. Roses are also nailed, for the like purpose, upon the holes which are made on a steamer's bottom for the admission of water to the boilers and condensers.

ROSE-LASHING. This lashing is middled, and passed opposite ways; when finished, the ends appear as if coiled round the crossings.

ROSINA. A Tuscan gold coin, value 17s. 1d. sterling.

ROSS. A term from the Celtic, signifying a promontory.

ROSTER, OR ROLLSTER. A list for routine on any particular duty. (*See* ROLLSTER.)

ROSTRAL-CROWN. The naval crown anciently awarded to the individual who first boarded an enemy's ship.

ROSTRUM. A prow; also a stand for a public speaker.

ROTATION. The motion of a body about its axis.

ROTHER. This lineal descendant of the Anglo-Saxon *róter* is still in use for *rudder* (which see).

ROTTEN ROW. A line of old ships-in-ordinary in *routine* order.

ROUBLE. *See* RUBLE.

ROUGH BOOKS. Those in which the warrant officers make their immediate entries of expenditure.

ROUGH-KNOTS, OR ROUGH NAUTS. Unsophisticated seamen.

ROUGH MUSIC. Rolling shot about on the lower deck, and other discordant noises, when seamen are discontented, but without being mutinous.

ROUGH-SPARS. Cut timber before being worked into masts, &c.

ROUGH-TREE. An unfinished spar: also a name given in merchant ships to any mast, or other spar above the ship's side; it is, however, with more propriety applied to any mast, &c., which, remaining rough and unfinished, is placed in that situation.

ROUGH-TREE TIMBER. Upright pieces of timber placed at intervals along the side of a vessel, to support the rough-tree. They are also called stanchions.

ROUND. *To bear round up.* To go before the wind.—*To round a point*, is to steer clear of and go round it.

ROUND-AFT. The outward curve or segment of a circle, that the stern partakes of from the wing transom upwards.

ROUND AND GRAPE. A phrase used when a gun is charged at close quarters with round shot, grape, and canister; termed a belly-full.

ROUND DOZEN. A punishment term for thirteen lashes.

ROUND-HOUSE. A name given in East Indiamen and other large merchant ships, to square cabins built on the after-part of the quarter-deck, and having the poop for its roof; such an apartment is frequently called the *coach* in ships of war. Round, because one can walk round it. In some trading vessels the round-house is built on the deck, generally abaft the main-mast.

ROUND-IN, To. To haul in on a fall; the act of pulling upon any slack rope which passes through one or more blocks in a direction nearly horizontal, and is particularly applied to the braces, as "Round-in the weather-braces." It is apparently derived from the circular motion of the rope about the sheave or pulley, through which it passes.

ROUNDING. A service wrapped round a spar or hawser. Also, old ropes wound firmly and closely about the layers of that part of a cable which lies in the hawse, or athwart the stem, &c. It is used to prevent the cable from being chafed. (*See* KECKLING and SERVICE.)

ROUNDING-UP. Is to haul through the slack of a tackle which hangs in a perpendicular direction, without sustaining or hoisting any weighty body.

ROUNDLY. Quickly.

ROUND-RIBBED. A vessel of burden with very little run, and a flattish bottom, the ribs sometimes almost joining the keel horizontally.

ROUND ROBBIN [from the French *ruban rond*]. A mode of signing names in a circular form, after a complaint or remonstrance, so that no one can tell who signed first.

ROUNDS. General discharges of the guns. Cartridges are usually reckoned by rounds, including all the artillery to be used; as, fifty rounds of ammunition. Also, going round to inspect sentinels. The general visiting of the decks made by officers, to see that all is going on right. Also, the steps of a ladder.

ROUND SEAM. The edges or selvedges sewed together, without lapping.

ROUND SEIZING. This is made by a series of turns, with the end passed through the riders, and made fast snugly.

ROUND SEIZING.   In applying this the rope does not cross, but both parts are brought close together, and the seizing crossed.

ROUND SHOT.   The cast-iron balls fitting the bores of their respective guns, as distinguished from grape or other shot.

ROUNDS OF THE GALLEY.   The opposite of what is termed Coventry; for it is figurative of a man incurring the expressed scorn of his shipmates.

ROUND SPLICE.   One which hardly shows itself, from the neatness of the rope and the skill of the splicer.   Properly a long splice.

ROUND STERN.   The *segmental stern*, the bottom and wales of which are wrought quite aft, and unite in the stern-post: it is now used in our navy, thus securing an after battery for the ship.   It had long obtained in the Danish marine.

ROUND THE FLEET.   A diabolical punishment, by which a man, lashed to a frame on a long-boat, was towed alongside of every ship in a fleet, to receive a certain number of lashes by sentence of court-martial.

ROUND-TO, To.   To bring to, or haul to the wind by means of the helm. To go round, is to tack or wear.

ROUND-TOP.   A name which has obtained for modern tops, from the shape of the ancient ones.   (*See* TOP.)

ROUND-TURN IN THE HAWSE.   A term implying the situation of the two cables of a ship, which, when moored, has swung the wrong way three times successively; if after this she come round till her head is directed the same way as at first, this makes a *round turn and elbow*.   A round turn is also the passing a rope completely round a timber-head, or any proper thing, in order to hold on.   (*See* HOLDING ON.)   Also, to pass a rope over a belaying pin.   Also, the bending of any timber or plank upwards, but especially the beams which support the deck, and curve upwards towards the middle of the deck.   This is for the purpose of strength, and for the convenience of the run of water to the scuppers.— *To round up* a fall or tackle, is to gather in the slack; the reverse of overhaul.

ROUND UP OF THE TRANSOMS.   That segment of a circle to which they are sided, or of beams to which they are moulded.

ROUNDURE.   An old English word for circle.

ROUSE, To.   To man-handle.   "Rouse in the cable," haul it in, and make it taut.

ROUSE AND BIT.   The order to turn out of the hammocks.

ROUST.   A word used in the north of Scotland to signify a tumultuous current or tide, occasioned by the meeting of rapid waters.   (*See* ROOST.)

ROUT.   The confusion and disorder created in any body of men when defeated and dispersed.

ROUTE.   The order for the movement of a body of men, specifying its various stages and dates of march.

ROUTINE.   Unchanging adherence to official system, which, if carried too far in matters of service, often bars celerity, spirit, and consequently success.

ROVE. A rope when passed through a block or sheeve-hole.

ROVENS. A corruption of *rope-bands* (which see). Also, the ravellings of canvas or buntin.

ROVER. A pirate or freebooter. (*See* PIRATE.) Also, a kind of piratical galley of the Barbary States.

ROVING COMMISSION. An authority granted by the Admiralty to a select officer in command of a vessel, to cruise wherever he may see fit. [From the Anglo-Saxon *rówen*.]

ROW, To. To propel a boat or vessel by oars or sweeps, which are managed in a direction nearly horizontal. (*See* OAR.)

ROW DRY! The order to those who row, not to splash water into the boat.

ROWED OF ALL! The orders for the rowers to cease, and toss their oars into the boat simultaneously, in naval style.

ROW IN THE SAME BOAT, To. To be of similar principles.

ROWL. The iron or wooden shiver, or wheel, for a whip-tackle.

ROWLE. A light crane, formerly much used in clearing boats and holds.

ROWLOCKS. Those spaces in the gunwale, or upper edge of a boat's side, wherein the oars work in the act of rowing.

ROW-PORTS. Certain scuttles or square holes, formerly cut through the sides of the smaller vessels of war, near the surface of the water, for the purpose of rowing them along in a calm or light wind, by heavy sweeps, each worked by several men. (*See* SWEEP.)

ROYAL. The name of a light sail spread immediately next above the top-gallant sail, to whose yard-arms the lower corners of it are attached; it used to be termed top-gallant royal, and is never used but in fine weather. Also, the name of a small mortar.

ROYAL FISH. Whales, porpoises, sturgeons, &c., which, when driven on shore, become droits of admiralty.

ROYAL MARINE ARTILLERY. Originally selected from the royal marines, now specially enlisted. (*See* ARTILLERY, ROYAL MARINE.)

ROYAL MARINES. *See* MARINES.

ROYAL MERCHANT. A title of the Mediterranean traders of the thirteenth century, when the Venetians were masters of the sea.

ROYAL MORTAR. A brass one of 5½ inches diameter of bore, and 150 lbs. weight, throwing a 24-pounder shell up to 600 yards; most convenient for advanced trenches and boat work.

ROYAL NAVAL RESERVE. *See* NAVAL RESERVE.

ROYALS. A familiar appellation for the marines since the mutiny of 1797, when they were so distinguished for the loyalty and steadiness they displayed. Also called *royal jollys*. (*See* JOLLY.)

ROYAL STANDARD. *See* STANDARD.

ROYAL YACHT. A vessel built and equipped expressly for the use of the sovereign.

ROYAL YACHT CLUB. A very useful and honourable association. (*See* YACHT CLUB.)

ROYAL YARD. The fourth yard from the deck, on which the royal is set.

ROYNES. An archaic term for streams, currents, or other usual passages of rivers and running waters.

RUBBER. A small instrument used to rub or flatten down the seams of a sail, in sail-making.

RUBBLE-WORK. A mass of masonry, formed of irregular stones and pebbles imbedded in mortar. It is used in the interior of docks, piers, and other erections, and is opposed to ashlar-work.

RUBLE. A Russian silver coin of 100 kopeks, in value about 3*s*. 2*d*. sterling, so called from *rubli*, a notch; derived from the time when bars of silver, marked with notches at different distances to represent different values, were used in Russia instead of coin, portions of the bar being cut off as required.

RUDDER. The appendage attached by pintles and braces to the stern-post of a vessel, by which its course through the water is governed. It is formed of several pieces of timber, of which the main one is generally of oak, extending the whole length. Tiphys is said to have been its inventor. The Anglo-Saxon name was *steor-roper*.

RUDDER BANDS or BRACES. The iron or composition hinges on which a rudder turns.

RUDDER-CASE. The same as *rudder-trunk* (which see).

RUDDER-CHAINS. Strong copper chains connected with the aft side of the rudder by a span clamp and shackles. They are about 6 feet in length; a hempen pendant is then spliced into the outer link, and allowing for slack to permit the rudder free motion, they are stopped to eye-bolts along the stern-moulding, terminating on the fore-side of the stools of the quarter galleries. They are, when the rudder or tiller is damaged, worked by tackles hooked to the after-channel bolts. But their principal use in later times is to save the rudder if unshipped by striking on a reef or shoal.

RUDDER-CHALDER. The same as *gudgeon* (which see) and *chalder*.

RUDDER-CHOCKS. *See* CHOCKS.

RUDDER-COAT. A canvas coat affixed to the rudder, encasing the opening in the counter, to prevent the sea from rushing in through the tiller-hole.

RUDDER-GUDGEON. Those secured to a ship are termed braces; gudgeon is more applicable to boats or small vessels.

RUDDER-HEAD. The upper end of the rudder-stock. Also, the flat surface of the trunk, which in cabins and ward-rooms forms a very convenient table.

RUDDER-HORN. A kind of iron crutch bolted to the back of the rudder, for attaching the rudder chains to in case of necessity.

RUDDER-HOUSE. Synonymous with *wheel-house*.

RUDDER-IRONS. The pintles, gudgeons, and braces of the rudder are frequently so called, though they were usually of copper.

RUDDER-PENDANTS. *(See* RUDDER-CHAINS.) Hempen pendants fastened to the rudder-chains, for steering in cases of accident, and towing the rudder to prevent its being lost if it gets unshipped.

RUDDER-PINTLES. The hooks attached to the rudder, which enter the braces, and hang it.

RUDDER-RAKE. The aftermost part of the rudder.

RUDDER-STOCK. The main piece of a rudder.

RUDDER-TACKLES. Attached to the rudder-pendants.

RUDDER-TRUNK. A casing of wood fitted or boxed firmly into a cavity in the vessel's counter, called the helm-port, through which the rudder-stock is introduced.

RUFFLE. A low vibrating sound of the drum, continuous like the roll, but not so loud: it is used in complimenting officers of rank.

RUFFLERS. Certain fellows who begged about formerly, under pretext of having served in the wars.

RULE OF THUMB. That rule suggested by a practical rather than a scientific knowledge. In common matters it means to estimate by guess, not by weight or measure.

RULES OF THE SEA. Certain practices and regulations as to steerage, which are recognized by seamen as well as by law, in order to prevent the collision of ships, or to determine who has contravened them; precedents in one sense, custom in another.

RULE-STAFF. A lath about 4 inches in breadth, used for curves in ship-building.

RUMBELOW. A very favourite burden to an old sea-song, of which vestiges still remain.

RUMBO. Rope stolen from a royal dockyard.

RUM-GAGGER. A cheat who tells wonderful stories of his sufferings at sea to obtain money.

RUMMAGE. The search by custom-house officers for smuggled goods.

RUN. The distance sailed by a ship. Also, used among sailors to imply the agreement to work a single passage from one place to another, as from Jamaica to England, and so forth.—*To make a run.* To sway with alacrity.

RUN, CLEAN. When the after part of a ship's form exhibits a long clean curvature approaching to a wedge—*Full run.* When it is otherwise.

RUN OF THE ICE. In Arctic parlance, implies that the ice is suddenly impelled by a rushing motion, arising from currents at a distance.

RUN, To LOWER BY THE. To let go altogether, instead of lowering with a turn on a cleat or bitt-head.

RUN ATHWART A SHIP'S COURSE, To. To cross her path.

RUN AWAY WITH HER ANCHOR. Said of a ship when she drags or "shoulders" her anchor; drifting away owing to the anchor not holding, for want, perhaps, of sufficient range of cable.

RUN AWAY WITH IT! The order to men on a tackle fall, when light goods are being hoisted in, or in hoisting topsails, jib, or studding-sails.

RUNDLE. That part of a capstan round which the messenger is wound, including the drum-head. (*See* WHELPS.)

RUN DOWN A COAST, To. To sail along it, keeping parallel to or skirting its dangers.

RUN DOWN A VESSEL, To. To pass over, into, or foul her by running against her end-on, so as to jeopardize her.

RUNE [from the Teutonic *rennen*, to flow]. A water-course.

RUNGS. The same as the floor or ground timbers, and whose ends are the rung-heads. Also, a spoke, and the step or round of a ladder.

RUNLET. A measure of wine, oil, &c., containing eighteen gallons and a half.

RUN-MONEY. The money paid for apprehending a deserter, and charged against his wages. Also, the sum given to seamen for bringing a ship home from the West Indies, or other places, in time of war. Coasters are sometimes paid by the run instead of by the month.

RUNNER-PURCHASE. The addition of a tackle to a single rope, then termed a pendant, passing through a block applied to the object to be moved; as it might be the laniard of a shroud, the end of the runner-pendant being fast to some secure fixed object; as in backstays, &c.

RUNNERS. Ships which risk every impediment as to privateers or blockade, to get a profitable market.

RUNNERS OF FOREIGN GOODS. Organized smugglers.

RUNNING AGREEMENT. In the case of foreign-going ships making voyages averaging less than six months in duration, running agreements can legally be made with the crew to extend over two or more voyages.

RUNNING-BLOCKS. Those which are made fast to the running rigging or tackles.

RUNNING-BOWLINE-KNOT. Is made by taking the end round the standing part, and making a bowline upon its own part.

RUNNING BOWSPRIT. One which is used in revenue cutters and smacks; it can be reefed by sliding in, and has fid holes for that purpose. (*See* SLOOP.)

RUNNING-DOWN CLAUSE. A special admission into policies of marine insurance, to include the risk of loss or damage in consequence of the collision of the ship insured with other vessels.

RUNNING-DOWN THE PORT. A method practised in the ruder state of navigation, when the longitude was very doubtful, by sailing into its parallel of latitude, and then working for it on its parallel.

RUNNING FOUL. A vessel, by accident or bad steerage, falling in contact with another under sail. (*See* ATHWART HAWSE.) The law and custom of the sea requires that the ship on the port tack shall bear up and give way to that on the starboard tack. Foreigners observe this general custom. Steamers however are always bound to give way to vessels under canvas, having the power to alter course without altering sails, or endangering the vessel.

RUNNING GOODS. Landing a cargo of contraband articles.

RUNNING OUT, AND RUNNING IN, THE LOWER DECK GUNS. The old practice of morning and evening evolutions in a line-of-battle ship, wind and weather permitting.

RUNNING PART OF A TACKLE. Synonymous with the fall, or that part on which the man power is applied to produce the intended effect.

RUNNING THE GANTLET. *See* GANT-LOPE (pronounced *gantlet*).

RUN OUT A WARP, To. To carry a hawser out from the ship by a boat, and fasten it to some distant place to remove the ship towards that place, or to keep her steady whilst her anchors are lifted, &c.

RUPEE. The well-known coin of the East Indies. There are gold rupees of nearly 30 shillings in value; but the current rupee is of silver, varying a little from 2 shillings, according to its being named Bombay, Arcot, or Sicca.

RUSPONE. A gold Tuscan coin of the value of £1, 8*s*. 7*d*. sterling.

RUT OF THE SEA. The point of impact where it dashes against anything.

RUT OF THE SHORE. The sea breaking along the coast.

RUTTER, OR ROUTIER. The old word for an outline chart for ships' tracks [from *route*]. It was also applied to a journal or log-book; or to a set of sailing instructions, as a directory.

RYDE. A small stream.

RYNE. An Anglo-Saxon word still in use for a water-course, or streamlet which rises high with floods.

S.

S. A bent iron, called a crooked catch, or pot-hook, in anchors, &c.

SABANDER. The familiar of *shah-bander*, an eastern title for captain or governor of a port.

SABATINES. Steel coverings for the feet; sometimes slippers or clogs.

SABRE. A sword with a broad and rather heavy blade, thick at the back, and curved towards the point, intended for cutting more than for thrusting.

SABRETACHE. A flat leathern case or pocket suspended at the left side of a cavalry officer's sword-belt.

SACCADE. The sudden jerk of the sails in light winds and a heavy swell.

SACCOLEVA, OR SACOLEGE. A Levantine small craft of great sheer, carrying a sail with an enormous sprit, so called.

SACK, To [from the Anglo-Saxon *sæc*]. To pillage a place which has been taken by storm.

SACKS OF COALS. The seaman's name for the black *Magellanic clouds*, or patches of deep blue sky in the milky-way near the south pole.

SADDLE HILL.   A high land visible from the coast, having a centre less
elevated than its ends, somewhat like a riding-saddle.

SADDLES.   Chocks of notched wood embracing spars, to support others attached to them; thus we have a saddle-crutch for the main or driver boom
on the taffarel; another on the bowsprit to support the heel of the jib-boom.

SAFE-CONDUCT.   A security passport granted to an enemy for his safe
entry and passage through the realm.

SAFEGUARD.   Protection given to secure a people from oppression in
time of trouble.

SAFETY-KEEL.   A construction of keel for further security, by Oliver
Lang.

SAFETY-PIN.   To secure the head of the capstan bar.

SAFETY-VALVE.   A conical valve on the top of the steam-chest, communicating with the boiler of a steam-engine, and opening outwardly; it
is so adapted and loaded, that when the steam in the boiler exceeds its
proper pressure, it raises the valve, and escapes by a pipe called the waste
steam-pipe.

SAGG, To.   To bend or give way from heavy weight; to press down
towards the middle; the opposite of *hogging*.   In Macbeth the word is
figuratively applied—

> " The mind I sway by, and the heart I bear,
> Shall never sagg with doubt, nor shake with fear."

SAGGING TO LEEWARD.   To drift off bodily to leeward.   The movement by which a ship makes a considerable leeway.

SAGITTA.   One of the ancient northern constellations.

SAGITTARII.   The name in our records for some small vessels with oars
and sails, used in the twelfth century.

SAGITTARIUS.   The ninth sign of the zodiac, which the sun enters
about the 21st of November.

SAGUM.   An ancient military cloak.

SAIC.   A sort of Greek ketch, which has no top-gallant nor mizen sails,
but still spreads much canvas.

SAIL.   The terms applicable to the parts of a sail comprise:—Seaming the
cloths together; cutting the gores; tabling and sewing on the reef, belly,
lining, and buntline bands, roping, and marling on the clues and foot-rope.
The *square sails* comprise courses, topsails, topgallant sails, royals, skysails
on each mast.   The *fore and aft*, are jibs, staysails, trysails, boom mainsails
and foresails, gaff topsails, to which may be added the studding-sails and
the flying kites.   Also, a distant ship is called a sail.

SAIL BURTON.   A purchase extending from topmast-head to deck, for
sending sails aloft ready for bending; it usually consists of two single blocks,
having thimbles and a hook; a leading block on the slings through which
the fall leads to bear the topsail clear of the top-rim.

SAIL HO!   The exclamation used when a strange ship is first discerned
at sea—either from the deck or from the mast-head.

SAIL-HOOK. A small hook used for holding the seams of a sail while in the act of sewing.

SAILING. The movement of a vessel by means of her sails along the surface of the water. *Sailing*, or the *sailings*, is a term applied to the different ways in which the path of a ship at sea, and the variations of its geographical position, are represented on paper, all which are explained under the various heads of great circle sailing, Mercator's sailing, middle latitude sailing, oblique sailing, parallel sailing, plane sailing.

SAILING, ORDER OF. The general disposition of a fleet of ships when proceeding on a voyage or an expedition. It is generally found most convenient for fleets of ships of war to be formed in three parallel lines or columns. But squadrons of less than ten sail of the line are placed in two lines.

SAILING CAPTAIN. An officer in some navies, whose duties are similar to those of our masters in the royal navy.

SAILING DIRECTIONS. Works supplied by the admiralty to Her Majesty's ships, which advise the navigator as to the pilotage of coasts and islands throughout the world.

SAILING ICE. A number of loose pieces floating at a sufficient distance from each other, for a ship to be able to pick her way among them. Otherwise termed *open ice;* when she forces her way, pushing the ice aside, it is termed boring.

SAILING LARGE. With a quartering wind. (*See* LARGE.)

SAILING ORDERS. Written instructions for the performance of any proposed duty.

SAIL-LOFT. A large apartment in dockyards where the sails are cut out and made.

SAIL-LOOSERS. Men specially appointed to loose the sails when getting under weigh, or loosing them to dry.

SAIL-MAKER. A qualified person who (with his mates) is employed on board ship in making, repairing, or altering the sails; whence he usually derives the familiar sobriquet of *sails*.

SAIL-NETTING. The fore-topmast staysail, main-topmast staysail, and main staysail are generally stowed in the nettings.

SAILOR. A man trained in managing a ship, either at sea or in harbour. A thorough sailor is the same with mariner and seaman, but as every one of the crew is dubbed a sailor, there is much difference in the absolute meaning of the term. (*See* MARINER and SEAMAN.)

SAILORS' HOME. A house built by subscription, for the accommodation of seamen on moderate terms, and to rescue them from swindlers, crimps, &c. Sailors' homes are a great boon also to shipwrecked mariners. Homes for married seamen and their families are now contemplated, and it is hoped that the admiralty will set the example, by building them for the royal navy, and letting them at moderate rents.

SAILOR'S PLEASURE. A rather hyperbolic phrase for a sailor's overhauling his ditty-bag at a leisure moment, and restowing his little hoard.

SAILS, To Loose. To unfurl them, and let them hang loose to dry; or
the movement preparatory to "making sail."—*To make sail*, to spread
the sails to the wind in order to begin the action of sailing, or to increase
a ship's speed.—*To shorten sail*, to take in part of or all the sails, either
by reefing or furling, or both.—*To strike sail*, to lower the upper sails.
A gracious mode of salute on passing a foreigner at sea, especially a
superior.

SAINT CUTHBERT'S DUCK. The *Anas mollissima;* the eider, or
great black and white duck of the Feroe Islands.

SAINT ELMO'S LIGHT. *See* Compasant.

SAINT SWITHIN. The old notion is, that if it should rain on this
bishop's day, the 6th of July, not one of forty days following will be
without a shower.

SAKER. A very old gun, 8 or 9 feet long, and of about 5 lbs. calibre:
immortalized in Hudibras:—

> "The cannon, blunderbuss, and saker,
> He was th' inventer of, and maker."

The name is thought to have been derived from the French oath *sacre*.

SALADE. An Anglo-Norman term for a light helmet or head-piece.

SALADIN. The first coat-of-arms; so called because the crusaders assumed
it in imitation of the Saracens, whose chief at that time was the redoubt-
able Saladin.

SALAM, To. To salute a superior; a very common term, borrowed from
India. Overdoing it does not please Jack, for he dislikes to see his commander "salamming like a captured Frenchman."

SALAMANDER. The heated iron formerly used for firing guns, especially
in salutes, as it ensures regularity.

SALE OF COMMISSIONS. The regulated disposal of full-pay, unattached, retired, and half-pay commissions in the army.

SALE OF EFFECTS. *See* Effects, of dead men sold by auction "at the
mast."

SALIENT ANGLE. In fortification, one of which the point projects
outwards.

SALINAS, or Salines. Salt-ponds, natural or artificial, near the sea-coast.

SALINOMETER. A brine-gauge for indicating the density of brine in
the boilers of marine steam-engines, to show when it is necessary to
blow off.

SALLY. A sudden expedition out of a besieged place against the besiegers
or some part of their works; also called a *sortie.—To sally.* To move
a body by jerks or rushes; a sudden heave or set. Thus, when a vessel
grounds by the bow or stern, and the hawsers are severely taut, the sally
is practised. This is done by collecting all hands at the point aground,
and then by a simultaneous rush reaching the part afloat.

SALLY-PORT. An opening cut in the glacis of a place to afford free
egress to the troops in case of a sortie. Also, a large port on each quarter

of a fire-ship, out of which the officers and crew make their escape into the boats as soon as the train is fired. Also, a place at Portsmouth exclusively set apart for the use of men-of-war's boats. Also, the entering port of a three-decker.

SALMAGUNDI. A savoury sea dish, made of slices of cured fish and onions.

SALMON. The well-known fish, *Salmo salar*. It is partly oceanic and partly fluviatile, ascending rivers in the breeding season.

SALMON-LADDER. A short trough placed suitably in any fall where the water is tolerably deep, leaving a narrow trough at intervals for the fish to pass through, with barriers to break the force of the water.

SALOON. A name for the main cabin of a steamer or passenger ship.

SALT, or Old Salt. A weather-beaten sailor. One of the old seamen who not only have known but have felt what war was.

SALT-BOX. A case for keeping a temporary supply of cartridges for the immediate use of the great guns; it is under the charge of the cabin-door sentry.

SALT-EEL. A rope's-end cut from the piece for starting the *homo delinquens*.

SALT-JUNK. Navy salt beef. (*See* JUNK.)

SALTPETRE. The neutral salt; also called *nitre* (which see).

SALT-PITS. Reservoirs to contain sea-water for the purpose of making salt.

SALUTE. A discharge of cannon or small arms, display of flags, or cheering of men, in deference, by the ships of one nation to those of another, or by ships of the same nation to a superior or an equal. Also, the proper compliment paid by troops, on similar occasions, whether with the sword, musket, or hand.

SALVAGE. Originally meant the thing or goods saved from wreck, fire, or enemies. It now signifies an allowance made to those by whose means the ship or goods have been saved. These cases, when fairly made out, are received with the most liberal encouragement. Goods of British subjects, retaken from the enemy, are restored to the owners, paying for salvage one-eighth of the value to ships-of-war; one-sixth to privateers. When a ship is in danger of being stranded, justices of the peace are to command the constables to assemble as many persons as are necessary to preserve it; and on its being thus preserved, the persons assisting therein shall, in thirty days after, be paid a reasonable reward for the salvage; otherwise the ship or goods shall remain in the custody of the officers of the customs as a security for the same.

SALVAGE LOSS. A term in marine insurance implying that the underwriters are liable to pay the amount insured on the property lost in the ship, but taking credit for what is saved.

SALVAGER. One employed on the sea-coast to look to the rights of salvage, wreck, or waif.

SALVO. A discharge from several pieces simultaneously, as a salute.

SALVOR. The person claiming and receiving salvage for having saved a ship and cargo, or any part thereof, from impending peril, or recovered after actual loss.

SAMAKEEN.   A Turkish coasting trader.

SAMBUCCO.   A pinnace common among the Arabs on the east coast of Africa, as at Mombaze, Melinda, &c.   The name is remarkable, as Athenæus describes the musical instrument *sambuca* as resembling a ship with a ladder placed over it.

SAMPAAN, or SAMPAN.   A neatly-adjusted kind of hatch-boat, used by the Chinese for passengers, and also as a dwelling for Tartar families, with a comfortable cabin.

SAMPHIRE.   *Crithmum maritimum*, a plant found on sea-shores and salt marshes, which forms an excellent anti-scorbutic pickle.

SAMS-CHOO.   A Chinese spirit distilled from rice; it is fiery, fetid, and very injurious to European health.

SAMSON'S POST.   A movable pillar which rests on its upper shoulder against a beam, with the lower tenons into the deck, and standing at an angle of 15° forward.   To this post, at 4 feet above the deck, a leading or snatch-block is hooked, and any fore-and-aft purchase is led by it across the deck to one similar, so that, from the starboard bow to the starboard aft Samson-post, across to the port-post and forward, the whole crew can apply their force for catting and fishing the anchor, or hoisting in or out boats; top-tackle falls, &c., are usually so treated.

SANDAL.   A long narrow Barbary boat, of from 15 to 50 tons; open, and fitted with two masts.

SAND-BAGS.   Small square cushions made of canvas and painted, for boats' ballast.   Also, bags containing about a cubical foot of earth or sand, used for raising a parapet in haste, and making temporary loop-holes for musketry; also, to repair any part beaten down or damaged by the enemy's fire.

SAND and CORAL BANK.   An accumulation of sand and fragments of coral above the surface of the sea, without any vegetation; when it becomes verdant it is called a *key* (which see).

SAND-DRIFTS.   Hillocks of shifting sands, as on the deserts of Sahara, &c.

SANDERLING.   A small wading bird, *Calidris arenaria*.

SAND-HILLS.   Mounds of sand thrown up on the sea-shore by winds and eddies.   They are mostly destitute of verdure.

SAND-HOPPER.   A small creature (*Talitra*), resembling a shrimp, which abounds on some beaches.

SAND-LAUNCE.   *Ammodytes tobianus*, a small eel-like fish, which buries itself in the sand.

SAND-PIPER.   A name applied to many species of small wading birds found on the sea-shore and banks of lakes and rivers, feeding on insects, crustaceans, and worms.

SAND-SHOT.   Those cast in moulds of sand, when economy is of more importance than form or hardness; the small balls used in case, grape, &c., are thus produced.

SAND-STRAKE. A name sometimes given to the garboard-strake.

SAND-WARPT. Left by the tide on a shoal. Also, striking on a shoal at half-flood.

SANGAREE. A well known beverage in both the Indies, composed of port or madeira, water, lime-juice, sugar, and nutmeg, with an occasional corrective of spirits. The name is derived from its being blood-red. Also, arrack-punch.

SANGIAC. A Turkish governor; the name is also applied to the banner which he is authorized to display, and has been mistaken for St. Jacques.

SAP. That peculiar method by which a besieger's zig-zag approaches are continuously advanced in spite of the musketry of the defenders; gabions are successively placed in position, filled, and covered with earth, by men working from behind the last completed portion of the trench, the head of which is protected by a moving defence called a *sap-roller*. Its progress is necessarily slow and arduous. There is also the *flying sap*, used at greater distances, and by night, when a line of gabions is planted and filled by a line of men working simultaneously; and the *double sap*, used when zig-zags are no longer efficient, consisting of two contiguous single saps, back to back, carried direct towards the place, with frequent returns, which form traverses against enfilade; the *half-double sap* has its reverse side less complete than the last.

SARABAND. A forecastle dance, borrowed from the Moors of Africa.

SARACEN. A term applied in the middle ages indiscriminately to all Pagans and Mahometans.

SARDINE. *Engraulus maletta*, a fish closely allied to the anchovy; found in the Mediterranean and Atlantic.

SARGASSO. *Fucus natans*, or gulf-weed, the sea-weed always to be found floating in large quantities in that part of the Atlantic south of the Azores, which is not subject to currents, and which is called the Sargasso Sea.

SARKELLUS. An unlawful net or engine for destroying fish. (*Inquisit. Justic. anno* 1254.)

SAROS. *See* CYCLE OF ECLIPSES.

SARRAZINE. A rough portcullis.

SARRE. An early name for a long gun, but of smaller dimensions than a bombard.

SASH. A useful mark of distinction worn by infantry and marine officers; it is made of crimson silk, and intended as a waist-band, but latterly thrown over the left shoulder and across the body. Also, now worn by the naval equerries to the queen. Serjeants of infantry wear it of the same colour in cotton.

SASSE. A kind of weir with flood-gate, or a navigable sluice.

SATELLITES. Secondary planets or moons, which revolve about some of the primary planets. The moon is a satellite to the earth.

SATURN. One of the ancient superior planets remarkable for the luminous rings with which his globe is surrounded, and for his being accompanied by no fewer than eight moons.

SAUCER, or Spindle of the Capstan. A socket of iron let into a wooden stock or standard, called the step, resting upon, and bolted to, the beams. Its use is to receive the spindle or foot on which the capstan rests and turns round.

SAUCER-HEADED BOLTS. Those with very flat heads.

SAUCISSON, or Saucisse. A word formerly used for the *powder-hose*, a linen tube containing the train of powder to a mine or fire-ship, the slow match being attached to the extremity to afford time for the parties to reach positions of safety.

SAUCISSONS. Faggots, differing from fascines only in that they are longer, and made of stouter branches of trees or underwood.

SAUVE-TETE. *See* Splinter-netting.

SAVANNAH [Sp. *Sabana*]. A name given to the wonderfully fertile natural meadows of tropical America; the vast plains clear of wood, and covered in general with waving herbage, in the interior of North America, are called *prairies* (which see).

SAVE-ALL, or Water-sail. A small sail sometimes set under the foot of a lower studding-sail.

SAW-BILL. A name for the goosander, *Mergus merganser*.

SAW-BONES. A sobriquet for the surgeon and his assistants.

SAW-FISH. A species of shark (*Pritis antiquorum*) with the bones of the face produced into a long flat rostrum, with a row of pointed teeth placed along each edge.

SAY-NAY. A Lancashire name for a lamprey.

SAYTH. A coal-fish in its third year.

SCAFFLING. A northern term for an eel.

SCALA. Ports and landing-places in the Levant, so named from the old custom of placing a ladder to a boat to land from. Gang-boards are now used for that purpose.

SCALDINGS! Notice to get out of the way; it is used when a man with a load wishes to pass, and would lead those in his way to think that he was carrying hot water.

SCALE. An old word for commercial emporium, derived from *scala*. Also, the graduated divisions by which the proportions of a chart or plan are regulated. Also, the common measures of the sheer-draught, &c. (*See* Gunter's Scale.)

SCALENE TRIANGLE. That which has all three sides unequal.

SCALING. The act of cleaning the inside of a ship's cannon by the explosion of a reduced quantity of powder. Also, attacking a place by getting over its defences.

SCALING-LADDERS. Those made in lengths which may be carried easily, and quickly fitted together to any length required.

SCAMPAVIA. A fast rowing war boat of Naples and Sicily; in 1814–15 they ranged to 150 feet, pulled by forty sweeps or oars, each man having his bunk under his sweep. They were rigged with one huge lateen at one-third from the stem; no forward bulwark or stem above deck; a long brass 6-pounder gun worked before the mast, only two feet above water; the jib, set on a gaff-like boom, veered abeam when firing the gun. Abaft a lateen mizen with topsail, &c.

SCANT. A term applied to the wind when it heads a ship off, so that she will barely lay her course when the yards are very sharp up.

SCANTLING. The dimensions of a timber when reduced to its standard size.

SCAR. In hydrography applies to a cliff; whence are derived the names Scarborough, Scarnose, &c. Also, to rocks bare only at low water, as on the coasts of Lancashire. Also, beds of gravel or stone in estuaries.

SCARBRO' WARNING. Letting anything go by the run, without due notice. Heywood in his account of Stafford's surprise of Scarborough castle, in 1557, says:—

> "This term *Scarborow warning* grew (some say),
> By hasty hanging for rank robbery theare,
> Who that was met, but suspected in that way,
> Straight he was truss't, whatever he were."

SCARFED. An old word for "decorated with flags."

SCARP. A precipitous steep; as either the escarp or counterscarp of a fort: but a bank or the face of a hill may also be *scarped*.

SCARPH, OR SCARFING. Is the junction of wood or metal by sloping off the edges, and maintaining the same thickness throughout the joint. The stem and stern posts are scarfed to the keel.

SCARPHS OF THE KEEL. The joints, when a keel is made of several pieces. (*See* SCARPH.)

SCARRAG. Manx or Erse for a skate or ray-fish.

SCAT. A west of England term for a passing shower.

SCAUR. *See* SCAR.

SCAW. A promontory or isthmus.

SCAWBERK. An archaism for scabbard.

SCEITHMAN. An old statute term signifying *pirate*.

'SCENDING [from *ascend*]. The contrary motion to pitching. (*See* SEND).

SCHEDAR. The lucida of the ancient constellation Cassiopæa, and one of the nautical stars.

SCHEMER. One who has charge of the hold of a North Sea ship.

SCHENOGRAPHY. Representation of ships or forts in some kind of perspective.

SCHNAPS. An ardent spirit, like Schiedam hollands, impregnated with narcotic ingredients; a destructive drink in common use along the shores of the northern seas.

SCHOCK. A commercial measure of 60 cask staves. (*See* RING.)

SCHOOL. A term applied to a shoal of any of the cetacean animals.

SCHOONER. Strictly, a small craft with two masts and no tops, but the name is also applied to fore-and-aft vessels of various classes. There are two-topsail schooners both fore and aft, main-topsail schooners, with two square topsails; fore-topsail schooners with one square topsail. Ballahou schooners, whose foremast rakes forward; and we also have three-masted vessels called schooners.

SCHOUT. A water-bailiff in many northern European ports, who superintends the police for seamen.

SCHRIVAN. An old term for a ship's clerk.

SCHULL. *See* SCHOOL.

SCHUYT. A Dutch vessel, galliot rigged, used in the river trade of Holland.

SCIMETAR. An eastern sabre, with a broad, very re-curved blade.

SCOBS. The scoria made at the armourer's forge.

SCONCE. A petty fort. Also, the head; whence Shakspeare's pun in making Dromio talk of having his sconce ensconced. Also, the Anglo-Saxon for a dangerous candle-holder, made to let into the sides or posts in a ship's hold. Also, *sconce of the magazine*, a close safe lantern.

SCOODYN. An old word to express the burring which forms on vessels' bottoms, when foul.

SCOOP. A long spoon-shaped piece of wood to throw water, when washing a ship's sides in the morning. *Scooping* is the same as *baling* a boat.

SCOPE. The riding scope of a vessel's cable should be at least three times the depth of water under her, but it must vary with the amount of wind and nature of the bottom.

SCORE. Twenty; commercially, in the case of certain articles, six score went to the hundred—a usage thus regulated:

"Five score's a hundred of men, money, and pins:
Six score's a hundred of all other things."

Also an angular piece cut out of a solid. Also, an account or reckoning.

SCORE OF A BLOCK, OR OF A DEAD EYE. The groove round which the rope passes.

SCORPIO. The eighth sign of the zodiac, which the sun enters about the 22d of October. a Scorpii, *Antares;* a nautical star.

SCOT, OR SHOT. Anglo-Saxon *sceat.* A share of anything; a contribution in fair proportion.

SCOTCHMAN. A piece of stiff hide, or batten of wood, placed over the backstays fore-swifter of the shrouds, &c., so as to secure the standing rigging from being chafed. Perhaps so called from the skotch or notch where the seizing is passed.

SCOTCH MIST. Mizzle, or small soaking rain.

SCOTCH PRIZE. A mistake; worse than no prize, or one liable to hamper the captors with heavy law expenses.

SCOTIA. Carved mouldings and grooves.

SCOUR A BEACH, To, To pour a quick flanking fire along it, in order to dislodge an enemy.

SCOURER, OR SCOURING-STICK. Spring-searcher. An implement to clean the interior of musket barrels.

SCOURGE. A name of the boatswain's cat.

SCOUR THE SEAS, To. To infest the ocean as a pirate.

SCOUSE. A dish made of pounded biscuit and salt beef cut into small pieces, boiled up with seasoning. (*See* LOB-SCOUSE.)

SCOUTS. Small vessels of war for especial service. (*See* SKOUTS.) Also, intelligent men sent in advance to discover the enemy, and give an account of his force.

SCOW. A large flat-bottomed boat, used either as a lighter, or for ferrying.

SCOW-BANKER. A manager of a scow. Also, a contemptuous term for a lubberly fellow.

SCOWRING. The cleansing and clearing a harbour by back-water, or otherwise. Also an old term for tropical flux or dysentery.

SCRABBLE. A badly written log. This term is used by the translators of the Bible at David's feigned madness, when he "scrabbled on the doors of the gate."

SCRABER. The puffinet, *Colymbus grille.* (*See* GREENLAND DOVE.)

SCRAPER [from the Anglo-Saxon *screope*]. A small triangular iron instrument, having two or three sharp edges. It is used to scrape the ship's side or decks after caulking, or to clean the top-masts, &c. This is usually followed by a varnish of turpentine, or a mixture of tar and oil, to protect the wood from the weather. Also, metaphorically, a cocked hat, whether shipped fore-and-aft or worn athwart-ships.

SCRATCH-RACE. A boat-race where the crews are drawn by lot.

SCRAWL. The young of the dog-crab, or a poor sort of crab itself.

SCREEN-BERTH. Pieces of canvas temporarily hung round a berth, for warmth and privacy. (*See* BERTH.)

SCREW-DOCK. *See* GRIDIRON.

SCREW-GAMMONING FOR THE BOWSPRIT. A chain or plate fastened by a screw, to secure a vessel's bowsprit to the stem-head, allowing for the tricing up of the bowsprit when required.

SCREW-PROPELLER. A valuable substitute for the cumbersome paddle-wheels as a motive-power for steam-vessels: the Archimedean screw plying under water, and hidden by the counter, communicates motion in the direction of its axis to a vessel, by working against the resisting medium of water. (*See* TWIN-SCREW.)

SCREWS. Powerful machines for lifting large bodies. (*See* BED, BARREL, and JACK SCREWS.)

SCREW-WELL. A hollow trunk over the screw of a steamer, for allowing the propeller to be disconnected and lifted when required.

SCRIMP. Scant. A word used in the north; as, a scrimp wind, a very light breeze.

SCRIVANO. A clerk or writer; a name adopted in our early ships from the *Portuguese* or *Spanish.*

SCROLL-HEAD. A slightly curved piece of timber bolted to the knees of the head, in place of a figure: finished off by a volute turning outwards, contrary to the *fiddle-head.*

SCROVIES. An old name given to the worthless men picked up by crimps, and sent on board as A.B's.

SCRUFF. The matter adhering to the bottoms of foul vessels.

SCUD. The low misty cloud. It appears to fly faster than others because it is very near the earth's surface. When scud is abundant, showers may be expected.—*To scud.* To run before a gale under canvas enough to keep the vessel ahead of the sea: as, for instance, a close-reefed main topsail and foresail; without canvas she is said to scud under *bare poles,* and is very likely to be pooped. When a vessel makes a sudden and precipitate flight, she is said to scud away.—*Scud like a 'Mudian.* Be off in a hurry.

SCUDO. A coin of Italy, varying in value in the different provinces.

SCUFFLE. A confused and disorderly contention—

> "Then friends and foes to battle they goes;
> But what they all fights about—nobody knows."

SCULL. A short oar of such length that a pair of them, one on each side, are conveniently managed by a single rower sitting in the middle of the boat. Also, a light metal-helmet worn in our early fleet.—*To scull.* To row a boat with a pair of sculls. Also, to propel a boat by a particular method of managing a single oar over the boat's stern, and reversing the blade each time. It is in fact the half-stroke of the screw rapidly reversed, and closely resembles the propelling power of the horizontal tail of the whale.

SCULPTURES. The carved decorations of the head, stern, and quarter of an old ship-of-war. Also, the copper plates which "adorned" the former books of voyages and travels.

SCUM OF THE SEA. The refuse seen on the line of tidal change; the drift sent off by the ebbing tide. Or (in the neighbourhood of the rains), the fresh water running on the surface of the salt and carrying with it a line of foam bearing numerous sickly gelatinous marine animals, and physaliæ, commonly called Portuguese men-of-war, affected by the fresh water and other small things often met with on the surface sea.

SCUM-O'-THE-SKY. Thin atmospheric vapours.

SCUPPER-HOSE. A canvas leathern pipe or tube nailed round the outside of the scuppers of the lower decks, which prevents the water from discolouring the ship's sides.

SCUPPER-LEATHER. A flap-valve nailed over a scupper-hole, serving to keep water from getting in, yet letting it out.

SCUPPER-NAILS. Short nails with very broad flat heads, used to nail the flaps of the scuppers, so as to retain the hose under them: they are also used for battening tarpaulins and other general purposes.

SCUPPER-PLUGS. Are used to close the scuppers inboard.

SCUPPERS. Round apertures cut through the water ways and sides of a ship at proper distances, and lined with metal, in order to carry the water off the deck into the sea.

SCUPPER-SHOOTS. Metal or wooden tubes which carry the water from the decks of frigates to the sea-level.

SCURRY. Perhaps from the Anglo-Saxon *scur*, a heavy shower, a sudden squall. It now means a hurried movement; it is more especially applied to seals or penguins taking to the water in fright.

SCUTTLE. A small hole or port cut either in the deck or side of a ship, generally for ventilation. That in the deck is a small hatch-way.

SCUTTLE, To. To cut or bore holes through part of a ship when she is stranded or overset, and continues to float, in order to save any part of her contents. Also, a trick too often practised by boring holes below water, to sink a ship, where fictitious cargo is embarked and the vessel insured beyond her value. (*See* BARRATRY.)

SCUTTLE or SCUTTLED BUTT. A cask having a square piece sawn out of its bilge and lashed in a convenient place to hold water for present use.

SCUTTLE-HATCH. A lid or hatch for covering and closing the scuttles when necessary.

SEA. Strictly speaking, *sea* is the next large division of water after *ocean*, but in its special sense signifies only any large portion of the great mass of waters almost surrounded by land, as the Black, the White, the Baltic, the China, and the Mediterranean seas, and in a general sense in contra-distinction to land. By sailors the word is also variously applied. Thus they say—"We shipped a heavy sea." "There is a great sea on in the offing." "The sea sets to the southward," &c. Hence a ship is said to head the sea when her course is opposed to the direction of the waves.—*A long sea* implies a uniform motion of long waves, the result of a steady continuance of the wind from nearly the same quarter.—*A short sea* is a confused motion of the waves when they run irregularly so as frequently to break over a vessel, caused by sudden changes of wind. The law claims for the crown wherever the sea flows to, and there the admiralty has jurisdiction; accordingly, no act can be done, no bridge can span a river so circumstanced without the sanction of the admiralty. It claims the fore-shore unless specially granted by charter otherwise, and the court of vice-admiralty has jurisdiction as to flotsom and jetsom on the fore-shore. But all crimes are subject to the laws, and are tried by the ordinary courts as within the body of a county, comprehended by the chord between two headlands where the distance does not exceed three miles from the shore. Beyond that limit is "the sea, where high court of admiralty has jurisdiction, but where civil process cannot follow."

SEA-ADDER. The west-country term for the pipe-fish *Syngnathus*. The name is also given to the nest-making stickle-back.

SEA-ANCHOR. That which lies towards the offing when a ship is moored.

SEA-ATTORNEY. The ordinary brown and rapacious shark.

SEA-BANK. A work so important that our statutes make it felony, without benefit of clergy, maliciously to cut down any sea-bank whereby lands may be overflowed.

SEA-BEANS. Pods of the acacia tribe shed into the rivers about the

Gulf of Mexico, and borne by the stream to the coasts of Great Britain, and even further north.

SEA-BEAR. A name applied to several species of large seals of the genus *Otaria*, found both in the northern and southern hemispheres. They differ from the true seals, especially in the mode in which they use their hind limbs in walking on land.

SEA-BOARD. The line along which the land and water meet, indicating the limit common to both.

SEA-BOAT. A good sea-boat implies any vessel adapted to bear the sea firmly and lively without labouring heavily or straining her masts or rigging. The contrary is called *a bad sea-boat*.

SEA-BORNE. Arrived from a voyage: said of freighted ships also afloat.

SEA-BOTTLE. The pod or vesicle of some species of *sea-wrack* or *Fucus gigantea* of Cape Horn and the Straits of Magellan.

SEA-BREEZE. A wind from the sea towards the land. In tropical climates (and sometimes during summer in the temperate zone) as the day advances the land becomes extremely heated by the sun, which causes an ascending current of air, and a wind from the sea rushes in to restore equilibrium. Above the sea-breeze is a counter current, which was clearly shown in Madras, where an æronaut waited until the sea-breeze had set in to make his ascent, expecting to be blown inland, but after rising to a certain height found himself going out to sea, and in his haste to descend he disordered the machinery, and could not close the valve which allowed the gas to escape, so fell into the sea about three miles from the land, but clung to his balloon and was saved. Also, a cool sea drink.

SEA-BRIEF. A specification of the nature and quantity of the cargo of a ship, the place whence it comes, and its destination. (*See* PASSPORT.)

SEA-CALF. A seal, *Phoca vitulina*.

SEA-CAP. The white drift or breaks of a wave. *White horses* of trades.

SEA-CARDS. The old name for charts.

SEA-CAT. A name of the wolf-fish, *Anarrhicas lupus*.

SEA-CATGUT. The *Fucus filum*, or sea-thread.

SEA-COAST, OR SEA-BORD. The shore of àny country, or that part which is washed by the sea.

SEA COCOA-NUT, OR DOUBLE COCOA-NUT. The fruit of the *Lodoicea Seychellarum*, a handsome palm growing in the Seychelles Islands. It was once supposed to be produced by a sea-weed, because so often found floating on the sea around.

SEA-COULTER. The puffin or coulter-neb, *Fratercula arctica*.

SEA-COW. One of the names given to the *manatee* (which see).

SEA-CRAFTS. In ship-building, a term for the scarphed strakes otherwise called *clamps*. For boats, *see* THWART-CLAMPS.

SEA-CROW. A name on our southern coast for the cormorant.

SEA-CUCKOO. The *Trigla cuculus*, or red gurnard, so called from the unmusical grunt which it emits.

SEA-CUNNY. A steersman in vessels manned with lascars in the East India country trade.

SEA-DEVIL. A name for the *Lophius piscatorius*, or angler, a fish with a large head and thick short body.

SEA-DOG. A name of the common seal.

SEA-DOGG. The meteor called also *stubb* (which see).

SEA-DRAGON. An early designation of the *stinging-weever*.

SEA-EAGLE. A large ray-fish with a pair of enormous fins stretching out from either side of the body, and a long switch tail, armed with a barbed bone, which forms a dangerous weapon. *Manta* of the Spaniards.

SEA-EDGE. The boundary between the icy regions of the "north water" and the unfrozen portion of the Arctic Sea.

SEA-EEL. The *conger* (which see).

SEA-EGG. A general name for the *echinus*, better known to seamen as the *sea-urchin* (which see).

SEA-FARDINGER. An archaic expression for a seafaring man.

SEA-FISHER. An officer in the household of Edward III.

SEA-FRET. A word used on our northern coasts for the thick heavy mist generated on the ocean, and rolled by the wind upon the land.

SEA-FROG. A name for the *Lophius piscatorius*, or angler.

SEA GATE or GAIT. A long rolling swell: when two ships are thrown aboard one another by its means, they are said to be in a sea-gate.

SEA-GAUGE. An instrument used by Drs. Hale and Desaguliers to investigate the depth of the sea, by the pressure of air into a tube prepared for the purpose, showing by a mark left by a thin surface of treacle carried on mercury forced up it during the descent into what space the whole air is compressed, and, consequently, the depth of water by which its weight produced that compression. It is, however, an uncertain and difficult instrument, and superseded by Ericson's patent, working on the same principle, but passing over into another tube the volume of water thus forced in. (*See* WATER-BOTTLE.)

SEA-GOING. Fit for sea-service abroad.

SEA-GREEN. The colour which in ancient chivalry denoted inconstancy.

SEA-GROCER. A sobriquet for the purser.

SEA-GULL. A well-known bird. When they come in numbers to shore, and make a noise about the coast, or when at sea they alight on ships, sailors consider it a prognostic of a storm. This is an old idea; see Virg. Georg. lib. i., and Plin. lib. xviii. c. 35.

SEA-HARE. *Aplysia*, a molluscous animal.

SEA-HEN. A name of the fish *Trigla lyra*, or *crooner* (which see).

SEA-HOG. A common name for the porpoise, *Phocœna communis*.

SEA-HORSE. A name for the walrus, *Trichecus rosmarus*. Also, the *hippocampus* (which see).

SEA-ICE. Ice within which there is a separation from the land.

SEAL [from the Anglo-Saxon *seolh*]. The well-known marine piscivorous animal.

SEA-LAKE. Synonymous with *lagoon* (which see).

SEA-LAWS. The codes relating to the sea; as, the laws of Rhodes, Oleron, Wisboy, &c.

SEA-LAWYER. An idle litigious 'long-shorer, more given to question orders than to obey them. One of the pests of the navy as well as of the mercantile marine. Also, a name given to the tiger-shark.

SEALED ORDERS. Secret and sealed until the circumstances arise which authorize their being opened and acted on. Often given to prevent officers from divulging the point to which they are ordered.

SEA-LEGS. Implies the power to walk steadily on a ship's decks, notwithstanding her pitching or rolling.

SEA-LETTER. *See* PASSPORT.

SEA-LION. A large seal of the genus *Otaria*, distinguished from the sea-bear, to which it otherwise has a great resemblance, by the shaggy mane on its neck and shoulders.

SEA-LOG. That part of the log-book relating to whatever happens while the ship is at sea.

SEA-LUMP. *See* LUMP.

SEAM. The sewing together of two edges of canvas, which should have about 110 stitches in every yard of length. Also, the identical Anglo-Saxon word for a horse-load of 8 bushels, and much looked to in carrying fresh fish from the coast. Also, the opening between the edges of the planks in the decks and sides of a ship; these are filled with a quantity of oakum and pitch, to prevent the entrance of water. (*See* CAULKING.)

SEA-MALL. A name for a sea-gull.

SEAMAN. This is a term seldom bestowed among seafaring men upon their associates, unless they are known to be pre-eminent in every duty of the thorough-paced tar; one who never issues a command which he is not competent to execute himself, and is deemed an authority on every matter relating to sea-craft.—The *able seaman* is the seafaring man who knows all the duties of common seamanship, as to rig, steer, reef, furl, take the lead, and implicitly carry out the orders given, in a seamanlike manner. His rating is A.B.; pay in the navy, 24s. to 27s. per month.—The *ordinary seaman* is less qualified; does not take the weather-helm, the earing, or lead; pay about 21s. to 23s. per month.—The *landsman* is still less qualified.

SEAMAN'S DISGRACE. A foul anchor.

SEAMANSHIP. The noble practical art of rigging and working a ship, and performing with effect all her various evolutions at sea.

SEAMAN'S WAGES. A proper object of the admiralty jurisdiction.

SEA-MARK. A point or object distinguishable at sea, as promontories, steeples, rivers, trees, &c., forming important beacons, and noted on charts. By keeping two in a line, channels can be entered with safety, and thus the errors of steerage, effect of tide, &c., obviated. These erections are a branch of the royal prerogative, and by statute 8 Eliz. cap. 13, the corporation of the Trinity House are empowered to set up any beacons or sea-marks wherever they shall think them necessary; and, if any person shall destroy them, he shall forfeit £100, or, in case of inability to pay, he shall be, *ipso facto*, outlawed.

SEAMEN-GUNNERS. Men who have been trained in a gunnery ship, and thereby become qualified to instruct others in that duty.

SEA-MEW. A sea-gull.

SEA-MOUSE. The *Aphrodita aculeata*, a marine annelid, remarkable for the brilliant iridescence of the long silky hairs with which its sides are covered.

SEA-NETTLE. An immemorial name of several zoophytes and marine creatures of the class *Acalephœ*, which have the power of stinging, particularly the *Medusœ*.

SEA-OWL. A name of the lump-fish, *Cyclopterus lumpus*.

SEA-PAY. That due for actual service in a duly-commissioned ship.

SEA-PERIL. Synonymous with *sea-risk*.

SEA-PIE. The pied oyster-catcher, *Hœmatopus ostralegus*. Also, a favourite sea-dish in rough weather, consisting of an olla of fish, meat, and vegetables, in layers between crusts, the number of which denominate it a two or three decker.

SEA-PINCUSHION. The name among northern fishermen for a kind of star-fish of the genus *Goniaster*.

SEA-POACHER. A name of the pogge, *Cataphractus schonveldii*.

SEA-PORCUPINE. Several fish of the genera *Diodon* and *Tetraodon*, beset with sharp spines, which they can erect by inflating themselves with air.

SEA-PORK. The flesh of young whales in the western isles of Scotland; the whale-beef of the Bermudas, &c. It is also called sea-beef.

SEA-PORT. A haven near the sea, not situated up a river.

SEA-PURSE. *See* MERMAID'S PURSE.

SEA-QUADRANT. The old name of Jacob's cross-staff.

SEA-QUAKE. The tremulous motion and shock of an earthquake felt through the waves.

SEA-RATE. The going of a chronometer as established on board, instead of that supplied from the shore. This may be done by lunars. From motion and other causes their rates after embarkation are frequently useless, and rates for their new ever-changing position are indispensable. This rate is sometimes *loosely* deduced between two ports; but as the meridian distances are never satisfactorily known, even as to the spots of observation, they cannot be relied on but as comparative.

SEARCH. If the act of submitting to search is to subject neutral vessels to confiscation by the enemy, the parties must look to that enemy whose the injustice is for redress, but they are not to shelter themselves by committing a fraud upon the undoubted rights of the other country.

SEARCH, RIGHT OF. *See* VISITATION.

SEARCHER. A custom-house officer employed in taking an account of goods to be exported. Also, (*see* GUN-SEARCHER).

SEA-REACH. The straight course or reach of a winding river which stretches out to sea-ward.

SEA-RISK. Liability to losses by *perils of the sea* (which see).

SEA-ROKE. A cold fog or mist which suddenly approaches from the sea, and rapidly spreads over the vicinity of our eastern shores, to a distance of 8 or 10 miles inland.

SEA-ROOM. Implies a sufficient distance from land, rocks, or shoals wherein a ship may drive or scud without danger.

SEA-ROVERS. Pirates and robbers at sea.

SEA-SERGEANTS. A society of gentlemen, belonging to the four maritime counties of South Wales, holding their anniversaries at sea-port towns, or one within the reach of tidal influence. It was a secret association of early date, revived in 1726, and dissolved about 1765.

SEA-SLATER. The *Ligia oceanica*, a small crustacean.

SEA-SLEEVE. A name of the flosk or squid, *Loligo vulgaris*.

SEA-SLETCH. *See* SLETCH.

SEA-SLUG. The Holothuria. An animal of the class *Echinodermata*, with elongated body, and flexible outer covering.

SEASONED TIMBER. Such as has been cut down, squared, and stocked for one season at least.

SEASONING. The keeping a vessel standing a certain time after she is completely framed, and dubbed out for planking. A great prince of this maritime country in passing a dockyard, inquired what those *basket-ships* were for!

SEA-SPOUT. The jetting of sea-water over the adjacent lands, when forced through a perforation in a rocky shore; both its egress and ingress are attended with a rumbling noise, and the spray is often very injurious to the surrounding vegetation.

SEA-STAR. A common rayed or star-like animal, belonging to the class *Echinodermata*. Also called *star-fish* (*Asteria*).

SEA-STREAM. In polar parlance, is when a collection of bay-ice is exposed on one side to the ocean, and affords shelter from the sea to whatever is within it.

SEA-SWABBER. A reproachful term for an idle sailor.

SEA-SWALLOW. The tern, a bird resembling the gull, but more slender and swift.

SEA-SWINE. The porpoise.

SEAT. A term often applied to the peculiar summit of a mountain, as the Queen of Spain's Seat near Gibraltar, the Bibi of Mahratta's Seat near Bombay, Arthur's Seat at Edinburgh, &c.

SEA-TANG. Tangle, a sea-weed.

SEAT-LOCKERS. Accommodations fitted in the cabins of merchantmen for sitting upon, and stowing cabin-stores in.

SEAT OF WATER. Applies to the line on which a vessel sits.

SEA-TRANSOM. That which is bolted to the counter-timbers, above the upper, at the height of the port-sills.

SEA-TURN. A tack into the offing.

SEA-URCHIN. The *Echinus*, an animal of the class *Echinodermata*, of globular form, and a hard calcareous outer covering, beset with movable spines, on the ends of which it crawls about.

SEA-WALLS. Elevations of stones, stakes, and other material, to prevent inundations.

SEA-WARD. Towards the sea, or offing.

SEA-WARE. The sea-weed thrown up by surges on a beach.

SEA-WATER. "The quantity of solid matter varies considerably in different seas, but we may assume that the average quantity of saline matter is 3½ per cent., and the density about 1·0274 " (*Pereira*). The composition of the water of the English Channel according to Schweitzer is—

	Grains.
Water .	964·74372
Chloride of Sodium .	27·05948
,, Potassium	0·76552
,, Magnesium	3·66658
Bromide of Magnesium	0·02929
Sulphate of Magnesia	2·29578
,, Lime	1·40662
Carbonate of Lime	0·03301
	1000·00000

SEA-WAY. The progress of a ship through the waves. Also, said when a vessel is in an open place where the sea is rolling heavily.

SEA-WAY MEASURER. A kind of self-registering log invented by Smeaton, the architect of the Eddystone lighthouse.

SEA-WEASEL. An old name of the lamprey.

SEA-WOLF. The wolf-fish, *Anarrhicas lupus.*

SEA-WOLVES. A name for privateers.

SEA-WORTHY. The state of a ship in everyway fitted for her voyage. It is the first stipulation in every policy of insurance, or other contract, connected with a vessel: "for she shall be tight, staunch, and strong, sufficiently manned, and her commander competent to his duty." (*See* OPINION.)

SEA-WRACK GRASS. *Zostera marina;* used in Sweden and Holland for manuring land. At Yarmouth it is thrown on shore in such abundance that mounds are made with it to arrest the encroachments of the sea. It is also used as thatch.

SECANT. A line drawn from the centre of a circle to the extremity of the tangent.

SECCA. A shoal on Italian shores and charts.

SECOND. The sixtieth part of a minute. A division of a degree of a circle. A term applied both to time and to space. Also, second in a duel; a very important part to play, since many a life may be saved without implicating honour.

SECONDARY PLANET. *See* SATELLITE.

SECOND-CAPTAIN. Commanders under captains in the navy, of late.

SECOND-COUNTER. *See* COUNTER.

SECOND-FUTTOCKS. The frame-timbers scarphed on the end of the futtock-timbers.

SECOND-HAND. A term in fishing-boats to distinguish the second in charge.

SECOND OFFICER. Second mate in merchantmen.

SECOND-RATE. Vessels of seventy-four guns (on the old scale).

SECTION. A draught or figure representing the internal parts of a ship cut by a plane at any particular place athwart ships or logitudinally.

SECTOR. *See* DIP-SECTOR.

SECULAR ACCELERATION. *See* ACCELERATION OF THE MOON.

SECULAR INEQUALITY. *See* INEQUALITY.

SECURE ARMS! Place them under the left arm, to guard the lock from the weather or rain.

SEDITION. Mutinous commotion against the constituted authorities, especially dangerous at sea.

SEDOW. The old English name for the fish called gilt-head; *Sparus auratus.*

SEDUCE, To. To inveigle a man to desertion.

SEELING. A sudden heeling over, and quick return.

SEER. The tumbler of a gun-lock.

SEE-SAW. Reciprocating motion.

SEGE. An old law-term for the seat or berth in which a ship lies.

SEGMENT. In geometry, any part of a circle which is bounded by an arc and its chord, or so much of the circle as is cut off by that chord.

SEGMENTAL STERN. *See* ROUND STERN.

SEGMENT-SHELL. For use with rifled guns; an elongated iron shell having very thin sides, and built up internally with segment-shaped pieces of iron, which, offering the resistance of an arch against pressure from without, are easily separated by the very slight bursting charge within; thereby retaining most of their original direction and velocity after explosion.

SEIN, OR SEINE. The name of a large fishing-net. Also, a flat seam.

SEIN-FISH. By statute (3 Jac. I. c. 12) includes that sort taken with a sein.

SEIZING. Fastening any two ropes, or different parts of one rope together, with turns of small stuff.

SEIZINGS. The cords with which the act of seizing is performed; they vary in size in proportion to the rope on which they are used.

SEIZLING. A young carp.

SEIZURE. The right of naval officers to seize anywhere afloat, is legally established: a ship, therefore, although incapable of cruising, may still make a seizure in port,

SELCHIE. The northern name for the seal, *Phoca vitulina.*

SELENOCENTRIC. Having relation to the centre of the moon.

SELENOGRAPHY. The delineation of the moon's surface.

SELLING OUT. An officer in the army wishing to retire from the service, may do so by disposing of his commission.

SELLOCK. *See* SILLUK.

SELVAGE. The woven edge of canvas formed by web and woof. See *Boke of Curtasye* (14th century):—

"The overnape shal doubulle be layde,
To the utter side the selvage brade."

SELVAGEE. A strong and pliant hank, or untwisted skein of rope-yarn marled together, and used as a strap to fasten round a shroud or stay, or slings to which to hook a tackle to hoist in any heavy articles.

SEMAPHORE. An expeditious mode of communication by signal; it consists of upright posts and movable arms, now chiefly used for railway signals, electric telegraphs being found better for great distances.

SEMEBOLE. An old term for a pipe, or half a tun of wine.

SEMI-AXIS MAJOR. *See* MEAN DISTANCE.

SEMICIRCLE. A figure comprehended between the diameter of a circle and half the circumference.

SEMI-DIAMETER. The angle subtended by half the diameter of a heavenly body; in the cases of the sun and moon it is much used in navigation.

SEMI-DIURNAL ARC. Half the arc described by a heavenly body between its rising and setting.

SEMI-ISLET. An old term for *bridge-islet* (which see).

SEND, To. To rise after pitching heavily and suddenly between two waves, or out of the trough of the sea.

SENDING, OR 'SCENDING. The act of being thrown about violently when adrift.

SENIORITY. The difference of rank, or standing in priority, according to dates of commissions; or if on the same day, the order in which they stand on the official printed lists.

SENIOR OFFICER. The commanding officer for the time being.

SENNIT. A flat cordage formed by plaiting five or seven rope-yarns together. Straw, plaited in the same way for hats, is called plat-sennit; it is made by sailors in India from the leaf of the palm, for that well-known straw-hat, adorned with flowing ribbons, which formerly distinguished the man-of-war's man.

SENSIBLE HORIZON. *See* HORIZON.

SENTINEL, OR SENTRY. A soldier, marine, or seaman placed upon any post, to watch and enforce any specific order with which he may be intrusted.

SENTRY GO! The order to the new sentry to proceed to the relief of the previous one.

SEQUIN. A Turkish and Venetian gold coin of the current value of 6s. 11d.

SERANG. A boatswain of Lascars.

SERASKIER. A Turkish general.

SERGEANT. The senior non-commissioned rank in the army and marines.

SERGEANT-MAJOR. The senior sergeant in a regiment, or first non-commissioned officer; usually a zealous and thorough soldier.

SERON. A commercial package of Spanish America, made of green bullock's-hide with the hair on.

SERPENTARIUS. See OPHIUCHUS.

SERPENTIN. An ancient 24-pounder gun, the dolphins of which represented serpents; it was 13 feet long, and weighed 4360 lbs.

SERPENTINE POWDER. An old term for a peculiar granulated gunpowder.

SERRATED. Notched like the edge of a saw.

SERVE, To. To supply the gun with powder and shot. Also, to handle it through all the changes of station.

SERVE THE VENT, To. To stop it with the thumb.

SERVICE. The profession; as a general term, expresses every kind of duty which a naval or military man can be called upon to perform. Also, implying any bold exploit.—*To see service*, is a common expression, which implies actual contest with the enemy.—*Service*, of served rope, is the spun-yarn wound round a rope by means of a *serving-board* or *mallet*.

SERVICEABLE. Both as respects men and stores, capable of or fit for duty.

SERVING-BOARD. A flattened piece of hard wood with a handle, for passing service on the smaller ropes.

SERVING-MALLET. The mallet, grooved on the under side, with which spun-yarn, or other small stuff, is wrapped tightly round a rope.

SERVING OUT SLOPS. Distributing clothing, &c. Also, a cant term to denote punishment at the gangway.

SET. The direction in which a current flows, or of the wind. (*See* DIRECTION.)—*To set*, is to observe the bearings of any distant object by the compass. (*See* BEARING.) Also applied to the direction of the tide, as "the tide setting to the south," is opposed to a swelling sea setting to the north-west. Also, when applied to sails, implies the loosing and spreading them, so as to force the ship through the water on weighing. When in chase, or other emergency, the term is sometimes used as synonymous with *make sail*.

SET-BOLTS. Used in drifting out bolts from their position. Also employed for forcing the planks and other works, bringing them close to one another, as Blake's bringing-to bolts, with wood screws, eyes, and rings.

SET FLYING. Sails that do not remain aloft when taken in, but are hauled on deck or stowed in the tops, as skysails, studding-sails, &c.

SET IN. Said when the sea-breeze or weather appears to be steady.

SET ON! The order to set the engine going on board a steamer.

SETT. A kind of shipwright's power, composed of two ring-bolts and a wrain-staff, with cleats and lashings. Also, the particular spot in a river or frith, where stationary nets are fixed.

SETTEE. A single-decked Mediterranean vessel with a long and sharp prow, without topmasts, and carrying lateen sails. They were mostly used as transports to galleys.

SET THE CHASE, To. To mark well the position of the vessel chased by bearing, so that by standing away from her on one tack, she may be cut off on the other.

SETTING. The operation of moving a boat or raft by means of poles. Also, arranging the sights of a gun, or pointing it.

SETTING POLE. A pole, generally pointed with iron, forced into the mud, by which boats and barges are moored in shallow water.

SETTING THE WATCH. The military night guard or watch at the evening gun-fire. Naval watches are not interfered with by time.

SETTING-UP. Raising a ship from her blocks, shores, &c., by wedges driven between the heels of the shore and the dock foundation.

SETTLE. Now termed the *stern-sheets* [derived from the Anglo-Saxon *settl*, a seat].—*To settle*. To lower; also to sink, as "the deck has settled;" "we settled the land." (*See* LAYING.) "Settle the main topsail halliards," *i.e.* ease them off a little, so as to lower the yard, as on shaking out a reef.

SETTLING. Sinking in the water.

SET UP. Soldiers, mariners, and small-arm men, well drilled, and instructed to be upright and soldierlike in their carriage, are "well set up."

SET UP RIGGING, To. To take in the slack of the shrouds, stays, and backstays, to bring the same strain as before, and thus secure the masts.

SEVERALTY. The denomination under which disagreements respecting accounts amongst the part-owners of a ship are referred, either to equity courts, or the common law.

SEVERE. Effectual; as, a *severe* turn in belaying a rope.

SEW, OR SUE. Pronounced *sue*. (*See* SEWED.)

SEWANT. A north-country name for the plaice.

SEWARD, OR SEA-WARD. An early name for the *custos maris*, or he who guards the sea-coast.

SEWED. A ship resting upon the ground, where the water has fallen, so as to afford no hope of floating until lightened, or the return tide floats her, is said to be sewed, by as much as the difference between the surface of the water, and the ship's floating-mark. If not left quite dry, she sews to such a point; if the water leaves her a couple of feet, she is sewed two feet.

SEWIN. A white kind of salmon taken on the coast of Wales. Sometimes this word is used for the dish called *sowens*.

SEXAGESIMAL DIVISIONS. The circumference of the circle is divided into 360 degrees, each degree into 60 minutes, and each minute into 60 seconds. The Americans afterwards used 60 thirds, but European astronomers prefer decimals.

SEXTANT. A mathematical instrument for taking altitudes of, and measuring the angular distances between, the heavenly bodies. It is constructed on a principle similar to Hadley's quadrant; but the arc contains a sixth part of a circle, and measures angles up to 120°.

SHACKLE [from the Anglo-Saxon *sceacul*]. A span with two eyes and a bolt, attached to open links in a chain-cable, at every 15 fathoms; they are fitted with a movable bolt, so that the chain can there be separated or coupled, as circumstances require. Also, an iron loop-hooked bolt moving on a pin, used for fastening the lower-deck port-bars.

SHACKLE-BREECHING. Two shackles are turned into the breeching, by which it is instantly disconnected from the port-ringbolts. Also, the lug of the cascable is cut open to admit of the bight of the breeching falling into it, thus obviating the loss of time by unreeving.

SHACKLE-CROW. A bar of iron slightly bent at one end like the common crow, but with a shackle instead of a claw at the bent end. It is used for drawing bolts or deck-nails. (*See also* SPAN-SHACKLES.)

SHACKLE-NET. The northern term for flue-net.

SHACKLES. Semicircular clumps of iron sliding upon a round bar, in which the legs of prisoners are occasionally confined to the deck. *Manacles* when applied to the wrists. (*See* BILBOES.)

SHAD. The *Clupea alosa*, a well-known fish, of very disputed culinary merit, owing perhaps to its own dietetic habits.

SHADES. Coloured glasses for quadrants, sextants, and circles. (*See* DARK GLASSES, or SCREENS.)

SHAFT OF A MINE. The narrow perpendicular pit by which the gallery is entered, and from which the branches of the mine diverge.

SHAG. A small species of cormorant, *Phalacrocorax graculus*.

SHAG-BUSH. An old term for a harquebus, or hand-gun.

SHAKE, To. To cast off fastenings, as—*To shake out a reef.* To let out a reef, and enlarge the sail.—*To shake off a bonnet* of a fore-and-aft sail. —*To shake a cask.* To take it to pieces, and pack up the parts, then termed "shakes." Thus the term expressing little value, "No great shakes."

SHAKE IN THE WIND, To. To bring a vessel's head so near the wind, when close-hauled, as to shiver the sails.

SHAKES. A name given by shipwrights to the cracks or rents in any piece of timber, occasioned by the sun or weather. The same as *rends* or *shans* (which see).

SHAKING A CLOTH IN THE WIND. In galley parlance, expresses the being slightly intoxicated.

SHAKINGS. Refuse of cordage, canvas, &c., used for making oakum, paper, &c.

SHALLOP, SHALLOOP, OR SLOOP. A small light fishing vessel, with only a small mainmast and foremast for lug-sails. They are commonly good sailers, and are therefore often used as tenders to men-of-war. Also, a large heavy undecked boat, with one mast, fore-and-aft mainsail, and jib-foresail. The gun-boats on the French coasts were frequently termed chaloupes, and carried one heavy gun, with a crew of 40 men. Also, a small boat rowed by one or two men.

SHALLOWS. A continuation of shoal water.

SHALLOW-WAISTED. Flush-decked vessels are thus termed, in contradistinction to the deep-waisted.

SHAN. A defect in spars, most commonly from bad collared knots; an
injurious compression of fibres in timber: the turning out of the cortical
layers when the plank has been sawed obliquely to the central axis of the
tree.

SHANK. An arrangement of deep-water fishing lines. Also, a handle or
shaft. Also the bar or shaft of an anchor, constituting its main piece, at
one end of which the stock is fixed, and at the other the arms.

SHANK-PAINTER. The stopper which confines the shank of the anchor
to the ship's side, and prevents the flukes from flying off the bill-board.
Where the bill-board is not used, it bears the weight of the fluke end of
the anchor.

SHANTY. A small hut on or near a beach.

SHAPE. The lines and form of a vessel.—*To shape a course.* To assign
the route to be steered in order to prosecute a voyage.

SHARE AND SHARE ALIKE. The golden rule of all messes at sea.

SHARK. A name applied to many species of large cartilaginous fish of
the family *Squalidæ.* Their ferocity and voracity are proverbial. Also,
applied to crimps, sharpers, and low attorneys.

SHARP. Prompt and attentive.—*Be sharp!* Make haste.—*Look sharp!*
Lose no time. Also, an old term for a sword.

SHARP BOTTOM. Synonymous with a sharp floor; used in contradistinction to a flat floor: the epithet denotes vessels intended for quick
sailing.

SHARP LOOK-OUT BEFORE! The hail for the forecastle look-out
men to be extremely vigilant.

SHARP UP. Trimmed as near as possible to the wind, with the yards
braced up nearly fore and aft.

SHAVE. A close run; a narrow escape from a collision.

SHEAF. A bundle of arrows, as formerly supplied to our royal ships.

SHEAL. A northern term for a fisherman's hut, whence several of them
together became *sheals* or *shields.*

SHEAR. An iron spear, of three or more points, for catching eels.

SHEAR-HOOKS. A kind of sickle formerly applied to the yard-arms,
for cutting the rigging of a vessel running on board.

SHEARS. *See* SHEERS.

SHEAR-WATER. A sea-fowl, *Puffinus anglorum.*

SHEATHING. Thin boards formerly placed between the ship's body and
the sheets of copper, to protect the planks from the pernicious effects of
the worm. Tar and hair, or brown paper dipped in tar and oil, is laid
between the sheathing and the bottom. In 1613 a junk of 800 or 1000
tons was seen in Japan all sheeted with iron; and yet it was not
attempted in Europe till more than a hundred years afterwards. But by
1783 ships of every class were coppered.

SHEATHING-NAILS. These are used to fasten wood-sheathing, and prevent the filling-nails from tearing it too much. Those used for copper-sheathing are of mixed metal, cast in moulds about one inch and a quarter long. The heads are flat on the upper side, and counter-sunk below, with the upper side polished to prevent the adhesion of weeds.

SHEAVE. The wheel on which the rope works in a block; it is generally formed of lignum vitæ, sometimes of brass, and frequently of both; the interior part, or that which sustains the friction against the pin, being of brass, let into the exterior, which is of lignum vitæ, and is then termed a sheave with a brass coak, *bouche*, or bush. The name also applies to a cylindrical wheel made of hard wood, movable round a stout pin as its axis; it is let through the side and chess-trees for leading the tacks and sheets. Also, the number of tiers in coiling cables and hawsers.

SHEAVE-HOLE. A channel cut in masts, yards, or timber, in which to fix a sheave, and answering the place of a block. It is also the groove cut in a block for the ropes to reeve through.

SHEBEEN. A low public-house, yet a sort of sailor trap.

SHED. A pent-house or cover for the ship's artificers to work under.

SHEDDE. An archaic term for the slope of a hill.

SHEDDERS. Female salmon. (*See* Foul Fish.)

SHEDELE. A channel of water.

SHEEN-NET. A large drag-net.

SHEEPSHANK. A hitch or bend made on a rope to shorten it temporarily; and particularly used on runners, to prevent the tackle from coming block and block. It consists in making two long bights in a rope, which shall overlay one another; then taking a half hitch over the end of each bight, with the standing part, which is next to it.

SHEER. The longitudinal curve of a ship's decks or sides; the hanging of the vessel's side in a fore-and-aft direction. Also, a fishing-spear in use on the south coast. (*See* Shear.) Also, the position in which a ship is sometimes kept when at single anchor, in order to keep her clear of it [evidently from the Erse *sheebh*, to drift].

SHEER, To Break. To deviate from that position, and thereby risk fouling the anchor. Thus a vessel riding with short scope of cable breaks her sheer, and bringing the force of the whole length of the ship at right angles, tears the anchor out of the ground, and drifts into deep water.

SHEER-BATTEN. A batten stretched horizontally along the shrouds, and seized firmly above each of their dead-eyes, serving to prevent the dead-eyes from turning at that part. This is also termed a *stretcher*.

SHEER-DRAUGHT. In ship-building, a section supposed to be cut by a plane passing through the middle line of the keel, the stem, and the stern-post: it is also called the *plan of elevation*, and it exhibits the outboard works, as the wales, sheer-rails, ports, drifts, height of water-line, &c.

SHEERED. Built with a curved sheer. (*See* Moon-sheered.)

SHEER-HULK. An old ship fitted with sheers, &c., and used for taking out and putting in the masts of other vessels.

SHEERING. The act of deviating from the line of the course, so as to form a crooked and irregular path through the water; this may be occasioned by the ship's being difficult to steer, but more frequently arises from the negligence or incapacity of the helmsman. For *sheering* or *shearing* in polar seas, *see* LAPPING.

SHEER-LASHING. Middle the rope, and pass a good turn round both legs at the cross. Then take one end up and the other down, around and over the cross, until half of the lashing is thus expended; then ride both ends back again on their own parts, and knot them in the middle. Frap the first and riding turns together on each side with sennit.

SHEER-MAST. The peculiar rig of the rafts on the Guayaquil river; also of the piratical prahus of the eastern seas, and which might be imitated in some of our small craft with advantage: having a pair of sheers (instead of a single mast) within which the fore-and-aft mainsail works, or is hoisted or slung.

SHEER-MOULD. Synonymous with *ram-line* (which see).

SHEER OFF, To. To move to a greater distance, or to steer so as to keep clear of a vessel or other object.

SHEER-PLAN. The draught of the side of a proposed ship, showing the length, depth, rake, water-lines, &c.

SHEER-RAIL. The wrought-rail generally placed well with the sheer or top-timber line; the narrow ornamental moulding along the topside, parallel to the sheer.

SHEERS. Two or more spars, raised at angles, lashed together near their upper ends, and supported by guys; used for raising or taking in heavy weights. Also, to hoist in or get out the lower masts of a ship; they are either placed on the side of a quay or wharf, on board of an old ship cut down (*see* SHEER-HULK), or erected in the vessel wherein the mast is to be planted or displaced, the lower ends of the props resting on the opposite sides of the deck, and the upper parts being fastened together across, from which a tackle depends; this sort of sheers is secured by stages extending to the stem and stern of the vessel.

SHEER-SAIL. A drift-sail.

SHEER TO THE ANCHOR, To. To direct the ship's bows by the helm to the place where the anchor lies, while the cable is being hove in.

SHEER UP ALONGSIDE, To. To approach a ship or other object in an oblique direction.

SHEER-WALES. Strakes of thick stuff in the topsides of three-decked ships, between the middle and upper deck-ports. Synonymous with *middle-wales.*

SHEET. A rope or chain fastened to one or both the lower corners of a sail, to extend and retain the clue down to its place. When a ship sails with a side wind, the lower corners of the main and fore sails are fastened by a tack and a sheet, the former being to windward, and the latter to leeward; the tack is, however, only disused with a stern wind, whereas the sail is never spread without the assistance of one or both of the sheets; the stay-sails and studding-sails have only one tack and one sheet each; the staysail-tacks are fastened forward, and the sheets drawn aft; but the studding-sail tacks draw to the extremity of the boom, while the sheet is employed to extend the inner corner.

SHEET-ANCHOR. One of four bower anchors supplied, two at the bows, and one at either chest-tree abaft the fore-rigging; one is termed the sheet, the other the spare anchor; usually got ready in a gale to let go on the parting of a bower. To a sheet anchor a stout hempen cable is generally bent, as lightening the strain at the bow, and being more elastic.

SHEET-BEND. A sort of double hitch, made by passing the end of one rope through the bight of another, round both parts of the other, and under its own part.

SHEET-CABLE. A hempen cable used when riding in deep water, where the weight of a chain cable would oppress a ship.

SHEET-COPPER. Copper rolled out into sheets, for the sheathing of ships' bottoms, &c.

SHEET-FISH. The *Silurus glanis*, a large fish found in many European rivers and lakes.

SHEET HOME! The order, after the sails are loosed, to extend the sheets to the outer extremities of the yards, till the clue is close to the sheet-block. Also, when driving anything home, as a blow, &c.

SHEET IN THE WIND. Half intoxicated; as the sail trembles and is unsteady, so is a drunken man.

SHELDRAKE. The *Anas tadorna*, a large species of wild duck.

SHELF. A dangerous beach bounded by a ledge of flat rocks awash. In icy regions, (*see* TONGUE).

SHELF-PIECES. Strakes of plank running internally in a line with the decks, for the purpose of receiving the ends of the beams. They are also called *stringers*.

SHELKY. A name for the seal in the Shetland Isles.

SHELL. In artillery, a hollow iron shot containing explosive materials, whether spherical, elongated, eccentric, &c., and destined to burst at the required instant by the action of its fuse (which see).—*Common shells* are filled with powder only, those fired from mortars being spherical, and having a thickness of about one-sixth of their diameter. (*See* also SEG-MENT-SHELL and SHRAPNEL-SHELL.) Also, the hard calcareous external covering of the mollusca, crustacea, and echinoderms.

SHELL-FISH. A general term applied to aquatic animals having a hard external covering or shell, as whelks, oysters, lobsters, &c. These are not, however, properly speaking, fish.

SHELLING. The act of bombarding a fort, town, or position.

SHELL OF A BLOCK. The outer frame or case wherein the sheave or wheel is contained and traverses about its axis.

SHELL-ROOM. An important compartment in ships of war, fitted up with strong shelves to receive the shells when charged.

SHELL, SHRAPNEL. *See* SHRAPNEL-SHELL.

SHELVES. A general name given to any dangerous shallows, sand-banks, or rocks, lying immediately under the surface of the water.

SHELVING. A term expressive of step-like rocks lying in nearly horizontal strata, or inclining very gradually; as a "shelving bottom," or a "shelving land." Applied to the shore, it means that it ascends from the sea, and passes under it at an extremely low angle, so that vessels of draught cannot approach.

SHERE. An archaic sea-term for running aground.

SHEVO. An entertainment, thought by some to be derived from the gaiety of the chevaux, or horse-guards; more probably from *chez-vous*.

SHIBAH. A small Indian vessel.

SHIELD-SHIP. A vessel fitted with one or more massive iron shields, each protecting a heavy gun or guns. The name was applied to an improvement on the "cupola-ship," before the latter was perfected into the "turret-ship."

SHIELD TOWER or TURRET. A revolving armoured cover for guns.

SHIEVE, To. To have head-way. To row the wrong way, in order to assist the steersman in a narrow channel.

SHIFT. In ship-building, when one butt of a piece of timber or plank overlaunches the butt of another, without either being reduced in length, for the purpose of strength and stability.—*To shift* [thought to be from the Anglo-Saxon *scyftan*, to divide]. To change or alter the position of; as, to shift a sail, top-mast, or spar; to shift the helm, &c. Also, to change one's clothes.

SHIFT A BERTH, To. To move from one anchorage to another.

SHIFTED. The state of a ship's ballast or cargo when it is shaken from one side to the other, either by the violence of her rolling, or by her too great inclination to one side under a great press of sail; this accident, however, rarely happens, unless the cargo is stowed in bulk, as corn, salt, &c.

SHIFTER. A person formerly appointed to assist the ship's cook in washing, steeping, and shifting the salt provisions; so called from having to change the water in the steep-tub.

SHIFTING A TACKLE. The act of removing the blocks of a tackle to a greater distance from each other, in order to extend their purchase; this operation is otherwise called *fleeting* (which see).

SHIFTING BACKSTAYS, also Preventer. Those which can be changed from one side of a ship to the other, as the occasion demands.

SHIFTING BALLAST. Pigs of iron, bags of sand, &c., used for ballast, and capable of being moved to trim the vessel. Also, a term applied to messengers, soldiers, and live-stock.

SHIFTING-BOARDS. One or more wooden bulk-heads in a vessel's hold, put up fore-and-aft, and firmly supported, for preventing a cargo which is stowed in bulk from shifting.

SHIFTING-CENTRE. *See* Meta-centre.

SHIFTING SAND. A bank, of which the sand, being incoherent, is subject to removal or being driven about by the violence of the sea or the power of under-currents. Very accurate experiments have proved that the sands at the mouths of rivers are differently acted on during every hour of tide (or wind together); hence sands shift, and even stop up or render some channels unsafe.

SHIFTING THE MESSENGER. Changing its position on the capstan from right to left, or *vice versâ*.

SHIFTING-WINDS. Variable breezes, mostly light.

SHIFT OF WIND. Implies that it varies, or has changed in its direction.

SHIFT THE HELM! The order for an alteration of its position, by moving it towards the opposite side of the ship; that is, from port to starboard, or *vice versâ*.

SHIMAL. A severe gale of wind from the N.W. in the Gulf of Persia and its vicinity; it is accompanied by a cloudless sky, thus differing from the *shurgee*.

SHINDY. A kind of dance among seamen; but also a row. Apparently modernized from the old Erse *sheean*, clamour.

SHINE. *To take the shine out of.* To excel another vessel in a manœuvre. To surpass in any way.

SHINER. The familiar name for a lighthouse. Also, a name for the *dace* (which see). Also, money; Jack's "shiners in my sack."

SHINGLE. Coarse gravel, or stones rounded by the action of water; it is used as ballast.

SHINGLES. Thin slips of wood, used principally in America, in lieu of slate or tiles in roofing. In very old times a planked vessel was termed a "shyngled or clap-boarded ship."

SHINGLE-TRAMPER. A coast-guard man.

SHIN UP, To. To climb up a rope or spar without the aid of any kind of steps.

SHIP [from the Anglo-Saxon *scip*]. Any craft intended for the purposes of navigation; but in a nautical sense it is a general term for all large square-rigged vessels carrying three masts and a bowsprit—the masts being composed of a lower-mast, top-mast, and topgallant-mast, each of these being provided with tops and yards.—*Flag-ship.* The ship in which the admiral hoists his flag; whatever the rank of the commander be; all the lieutenants take rank before their class in other ships.—*Line-of-battle ship.* Carrying upwards of 74 guns.—*Ship of war.* One which, being duly commissioned under a commissioned officer by the admiralty, wears a pendant. The authority of a gun-boat, no superior being present, is equal to that of an admiral.—*Receiving ship.* The port, guard, or admiral's flag-ship, stationed at any place to receive volunteers, and bear them *pro. tem.* in readiness to join any ship of war which may want hands.—*Store-ship.* A vessel employed to carry stores, artillery, and provisions, for the use of a fleet, fortress, or garrison.—*Troop-ship.* One appointed to carry troops, formerly called a transport.—*Hospital-ship.* A vessel fitted up to attend a fleet, and receive the sick and wounded. Scuttles are cut in the sides for ventilation. The sick are under the charge of an experienced surgeon, aided by a staff of assistant-surgeons, a proportional number of assistants, cook, baker, and nurses.—*Merchant ship.*—A vessel employed in commerce to carry commodities of various sorts from one port to another. (*See* MERCHANT.)—*Private ship of war.* (*See* PRIVATEER, and LETTERS OF MARQUE.)—*Slaver,* or *slave-ship.* A vessel employed in carrying negro slaves.—*To ship.* To embark men or merchandise. It also implies to fix anything in its place, as "Ship the oars," *i.e.* place them in their rowlocks; "Ship capstan-bars." Also, to enter on board, or engage to join a ship.—*To ship a sea.* A wave breaking over all in a gale. Hence the old saying—

> " Sometimes we ship a sea,
> Sometimes we see a ship."

To ship a swab. A colloquialism for mounting an epaulette, or receiving a commission.

SHIP-BOY. Boys apprenticed to learn their sea-duties, but generally appointed as servants.

SHIP-BREAKER. A person who purchases old vessels to break them to pieces for sale.

SHIP-BROKER. One who manages business matters between ship-owners and merchants, in procuring cargoes, &c., for vessels.

SHIP-BUILDER. Synonymous with naval constructor.

SHIP-BUILDING, OR NAVAL ARCHITECTURE. The art of constructing a ship so as to answer a particular purpose either for war or commerce. It is now expanding into a science.

SHIP-CHANDLER. A tradesman who supplies ships with their miscel-laneous marine stores. (*See* MATERIAL MEN.)

SHIP-CONTRACTOR. The charterer or freighter of a vessel.

SHIP-CRAFT. Nearly the same as the Anglo-Saxon *scyp-cræft,* an early word for navigation.

SHIP CUT DOWN. One which has had a deck cut off from her, whereby a three-decker is converted into a two-decker, and a two-decker becomes a frigate. They are then termed razées.

SHIP-GUNS. Those cast expressly for sea-service.

SHIP-KEEPER. An officer not much given to going on shore. Also, the man who has charge of a ship whilst she is without any part of her crew.

SHIP-LANGUAGE. The shibboleth of nautic diction, as *tau'sle, fok'sle,* for topsail, forecastle, and the like.

SHIP-LAST. *See* LAST.

SHIP-LAUNCH. *See* LAUNCH.

SHIP-LOAD. The estimated lading or cargo of a vessel.

SHIP-LOG. *See* LOG.

SHIP-LORD. A once recognized term for the owner of a ship.

SHIP-MAN [Anglo-Saxon *scyp-mann*]. The master of a barge, who in

the days of Chaucer had but "litel Latin in his mawe," and who, though
" of nice conscience toke he no kepe," was certainly a good fellow.

SHIPMAN'S CARD.   A chart; thus Shakspeare's first witch in *Macbeth*
had winds—

> " And the very ports they blow,
> All the quarters that they know
> I' the shipman's card."

SHIP-MASTER.   The captain, commander, or padrone of a vessel.   (*See*
MASTER.)

SHIP-MATE.   A term once dearer than brother, but the habit of short
cruises is weakening it.

SHIPMENT.   The act of shipping goods, or any other thing, on board a
ship or vessel.

SHIP-MONEY.   An imposition charged throughout this realm in the time
of Charles I., but which was declared illegal.

SHIP-OWNER.   A person who has a right of property in a ship.   The
interest of part-owners is quite distinct, so that one cannot dispose of the
share of the other, or effect any insurance for him, without special
authority.

SHIPPER.   He who embarks goods; also mentioned in some of our
statutes as the master of a ship.   (*See* SCHIPPER.)

SHIPPING AFFAIRS.   All business of a maritime bearing.

SHIPPING GOODS.   Receiving and stowing them on board.

SHIPPING GREEN SEAS.   When heavy seas tumble over the gunwale
either to windward or leeward; sometimes resulting from bad steerage and
seamanship, or overpressing the vessel.

SHIPPING MANIFEST.   *See* MANIFEST.

SHIPPING MASTERS.   Persons officially appointed and licensed to
attend to the entering and discharging of merchant seamen.

SHIP-PROPELLER.   *See* SCREW-PROPELLER.

SHIP RAISED UPON.   One of which the upper works have been
heightened by additional timbers.   About the year 1816 several credit-
able corvettes of 600 tons were constructed; after three had been tried,
the mistaken order was issued to make them into frigates.   Hence the
term donkey and jackass frigates, *Athol* and *Niemen* to wit.

SHIP'S BOOKS.   The roll of the crew, containing every particular in
relation to entry, former ships, &c.

SHIP-SHAPE.   In colloquial phrase implies, in a seamanlike manner; as,
"That mast is not rigged ship-shape;" "Put her about ship-shape," &c.
(*See* BRISTOL-FASHION.)

SHIP'S HUSBAND.   The agent or broker who manages her accounts
with regard to work performed, repairs, &c., under refit or loading.

SHIP-SLOOP.   Commanders were appointed to 24-gun sloops, but when
the same sloops were commanded by captains, they were rated ships.

SHIP'S LUNGS.   Dr. Hall's name for the bellows with which he forced
the foul air out of ships.

SHIP'S PAPERS. Documents descriptive of a vessel, her owners, cargo, destination, and other particulars necessary for the instance court. Also, those documents required for a neutral ship to prove her such.

SHIP'S REGISTRY AND CERTIFICATE. An official record of a ship's size, the bills of lading, ownership, &c.

SHIP'S STEWARD. The person who manages the victualling or mess departments. In the navy, paymaster's steward.

SHIP-STAR. The Anglo-Saxon *scyp-steora*, an early name for the pole-star, once of the utmost importance in navigation.

SHIP-TIMBER. Contraband in time of war.

SHIPWRECK. The destruction of a vessel by her beating against rocks, the shore, &c.—too often including loss of life. In early times the seizure of goods, and even the murder of the mariners, was apt to be the consequence.

SHIPWRIGHT. A builder of ships. The art of bending planks by fire is attributed to Pyrrhon, the Lydian, who made boats of several configurations.

SHIPYARD. Synonymous with *dockyard*.

SHIVER. Synonymous with *sheave*.

SHIVERING. To trim a ship's yards so that the wind strikes on the edges or leaches of the sails, making them flutter in the wind. The same effect may be intentionally produced by means of the helm.

SHOAL. A danger formed by sunken rocks, on which the sea does not break; but generally applied to every place where the water is shallow, whatever be the ground. (*See* FLAT SHOAL, SHOLE, or SCHOLE.) Also, denotes a great quantity of fishes swimming in company—*squamosæ cohortes*. Also, a vessel is said to shoalen, or shoal her water, when she comes from a greater into a less depth.

SHOALED-HARBOUR. That which is secured from the violence of the sea, by banks, bars, or shoals to seaward.

SHOD, OR SHODE. An anchor is said to be shod when, in breaking it from its bed, a quantity of clayey or oozy soil adheres to the fluke and shank.

SHOE. The iron arming to a handspike, polar-pile, &c.

SHOE OF THE ANCHOR. A flat block of hard wood, convex on the back, and having a hole sufficiently large to contain the bill of the anchor-fluke on the fore-side; used to prevent the anchor from tearing the planks on the ship's bow when fishing it, for which purpose the shoe slides up and down along the bow. Where vessels ease the anchor down to "a cock-bill," it is also sometimes used.—*To shoe or clamp an anchor.* To cover the palms with broad triangular pieces of thick plank, secured by iron hoops and nails. Its use is to give the anchor a greater resisting surface when the mud is very soft. Also, for transporting on shore.

SHOE OF THE FOREFOOT. *See* FOREFOOT, GRIPE, HORSE.

SHOE-PIECE. A board placed under the heel of a spar, or other weighty mass, to save the deck. In some cases intended to slip with it.

SHOLES. *See* SOLES.

SHOOT, To.   To move suddenly; as "the ballast shoots on one side."   Also, a ship shoots ahead in stays.   Also, to push off in a boat from the shore into a current; to descend a rapid.   The term is well used thus amongst the powerful rivers of N. America, of which perhaps the finest example is given by the St. Lawrence at La Chine, there reported to rush in spring-time at the rate of 40 miles an hour.   Thus the shooting Old London Bridge was the cause of many deaths, and gave occasion to the admirable description in the *Loves of the Triangles* (anti-Jacobin), when all were agreed:

> "'Shoot we the bridge,' the vent'rous boatmen cry;
> 'Shoot we the bridge,' th' exulting fare reply."

SHOOT-FINGER.   This was a term in use with the Anglo-Saxons from its necessity in archery, and is now called the trigger-finger from its equal importance in modern firearms.   The mutilation of this member was always a most punishable offence; for which the laws of King Alfred in-flicted a penalty of fifteen shillings, which at that time probably was a sum beyond the bowman's means.

SHOOTING-GLOVES.   These were furnished to the navy when cross-bows, long-bows, and slur-bows were used.

SHOOTING OF NETS.   The running out of nets in the water, as seins, drift-nets, herring-nets, &c.; but it does not apply to trawls.

SHOOTS, or SHUTS.   A large pipe or channel to lead away water, dirt, ballast, shot, &c., is called a shoot.   The overfalls of a river, where the stream is narrowed by its banks, whether naturally or artificially, especi-ally the arches of a bridge, constitute a shoot.

SHOOT THE COMPASS, To.   To shoot wide of the mark.

SHOOT THE SUN, To.   To take its meridional altitude; literally aim-ing at the reflected sun through the telescope of the instrument.   "Have you obtained a shot?" applied to altitudes of the meridian, as for time, lunar distances, &c.

SHORE.   A prop fixed under a ship's sides or bottom, to support her when laid aground or on the stocks.   Shores are also termed *legs* when used by a cutter or yacht, to keep the vessel upright when the water leaves her. (*See* Legs.)   Also, the general name for the littoral of any country against which the waves impinge, while the word *coast* is applied to that part of the land which only lies contiguous to the sea.—*Bold shore*.   A coast which is steep-to, permitting the near approach of shipping without danger; it is used in contradistinction to a *shelving-shore*.

SHORE-ANCHOR.   That which lies between the shore and the ship when moored.

SHORE-BOATS.   Small boats or wherries plying for hire at seaports.

SHORE-CLEATS.   Heavy cleats bolted on to the sides of vessels to sup-port the shore-head, and sustain the ship upright.

SHORE-FAST.   A hawser carried out to secure a vessel to a quay, mole, or anchor buried on shore.

SHORE-REEF.   The same as fringing-reef.

SHORT, SHORT STAY, SHORT APEEK. "Heave short," means to heave in the cable till it is nearly up and down, and would hold the vessel securely until she had set all common sail, and would not drag or upset the anchor. If, however, the wind be free, and the making sail unimportant, *short* would probably be *short apeek*, or up and down, the last move of weighing awaiting perhaps signal or permission to part.

SHORT ALLOWANCE. When the provisions will not last the period expected, they may be reduced in part, as two-thirds, half-allowance, &c., and thus *short-allowance money* becomes due, which is the nominal value of the provisions stopped, and paid in compensation.

SHORT BOARDS. Frequent tacking, where there is not room for long boards, or from some other cause, as weather or tide, it is required to work to windward on short tacks in a narrow space.

SHORTEN, To. Said of a ship's sails when requisite to reduce those that are set. And *shorten in*, when alluding to the anchor, by heaving in cable.

SHORT-HANDED. A deficient complement of men, or short-handed by many being on the sick-list.

SHORT-LINKED CHAIN. A cable without studs, and therefore with shorter links than those of stud-chains; such are slings and chains generally used in rigging bobstays, anchor-work, &c. Cables only have studs.

SHORT-SEA. A confused cross sea where the waves assume a jerking rippling action, and set home to the bows or sides; especially tiresome to boats, hampering the oars, and tumbling in-board. Also, a race.

SHORT-SERVICE. Chafing geer put on a hemp cable for a short range.

SHORT-SHEETS. Belong to shifting sails, such as studding-sails, &c.

SHORT-TACKS. *See* SHORT BOARDS.

SHORT-TIME OR SAND GLASS. One of 14 seconds, used in heaving the log when the ship is going fast.

SHOT. All sorts of missiles to be discharged from firearms, those for great guns being mainly of iron; for small-arms, of lead. When used without prefix, the term generally means the solid shot only, as fired for a heavy blow, or for penetration. Also, a synonym of *scot*, a reckoning at an inn, and has immemorially been thus understood. Ben Jonson's rules are

"As the fund of our pleasure, let each pay his shot."

Also, a lot or quantity. Also, the particular spot where fishermen take a draught with their nets, and also the draught of fishes made by a net. Also, the sternmost division of a fishing-boat. Also, arrows, darts, or anything that was shot. Also, a kind of trout. Also, a foot-soldier who carried a fire-lock.—*To be shot of*, signifies to get rid of, turned out.—*To shot the guns*. In active service the guns were generally loaded, but not shotted, as, from corrosion, it was found difficult to draw the shot; and the working and concussion not unfrequently started it, and consequently, if the gun was fired before re-driving it "home," it was in danger of bursting.

SHOT-LOCKER. A compartment built up in the hold to contain the shot.

SHOT-NET. A mackerel-net.

SHOT-PLUGS. Tapered cones to stop any sized shot-hole.

SHOT-RACKS. Wooden frames fixed at convenient distances to contain shot. There are also, of recent introduction, iron rods so fitted as to confine the shot.

SHOTTEN-HERRING. A gutted herring dried for keeping. Metaphorically, a term of contempt for a lean lazy fellow.

SHOULDER of a Bastion. The part of it adjacent to the junction of a face with a flank. The *angle of the shoulder* is that formed by these two lines.

SHOULDER ARMS! The military word of command to carry the musket vertically at the side of the body, and resting against the hollow of the shoulder; on the left side with the long rifle, on the right with the short.

SHOULDER-OF-MUTTON SAIL. A kind of triangular sail of peculiar form, used mostly in boats. It is very handy and safe, particularly as a mizen. It is the Bermuda or 'Mugian rig.

SHOULDER THE ANCHOR. When a seaman forgets his craft, and gives his ship too little cable to ride by, she may be thrown across tide, lift or shoulder her anchor, and drift off.

SHOUT. A light and nearly flat-bottomed boat used in our eastern fens for shooting wild-duck. (*See* Gunning-boat.)

SHOUTE-MEN. The old name for the lightermen of the Thames.

SHOVEL. A copper implement for removing a cartridge from a gun without injuring it. Formerly used, and as late as 1816 by the Turks, to convey the powder into the chamber without using cartridges: also used to withdraw shot where windage was large. (*See* Ladle.)

SHOVELL, or Shoveller. *Spathulea clypeata*, a species of duck with a broad bill. Formerly written *schevelard*. Also applied to a hoverer or smuggler.

SHOVE OFF! The order to the bowman to put the boat's head off with his boat-hook.

SHOW A LEG! An exclamation from the boatswain's mate, or master-at-arms, for people to show that they are awake on being called. Often "Show a leg, and turn out."

SHRAB. A vile drugged drink prepared for seamen who frequent the filthy purlieus of Calcutta. (*See* Doasta.)

SHRAPNEL SHELL. Invented by General Shrapnel to produce, at a long range, the effect of common case; whence they have been also called *spherical case*. They have a thickness of only one-tenth of their diameter; so that, on the action of the fuse, they are opened by a very small bursting charge, and allow the bullets with which they are filled to proceed with much the same direction and velocity that the shell had at the moment of explosion. They require, however, extremely nice management.

SHRIMP. The small crustacean *Crangon vulgaris*, well known as an article of food.

SHROUD-KNOT. *See* KNOT.

SHROUD-LAID. The combination in the larger cordage, also known as hawser-laid.

SHROUD-ROPE. A finer quality of hawser-laid rope than is commonly used for other purposes. It is also termed purchase-rope; but four-stranded rope is frequently used for standing rigging. All the strands are finer, of better hemp, and pass the gauge. Thus the patent shroud-laid rope, made from clean Petersburgh hemp, was found to break at a strain between $6\frac{3}{4}$ and $7\frac{1}{4}$ cwt. per inch of girth in inches squared. Thus a patent rope of 5 inches would require 175 cwt. Common rope, 25 threads in each strand, broke with 5 cwt. per inch, and fell off at 130 threads to 4 cwt. per inch. Thus,

	cwt.	qrs.	lbs.
A common 10-inch cable weighed per 100 fathoms,	19	0	21
A superior ,, ,,	21	0	3

SHROUDS. The lower and upper standing-rigging. They are always divided into pairs or couples; that is to say, one piece of rope is doubled, and the parts fastened together at a small distance from the middle, so as to leave a sort of noose or collar to fix upon the mast-head; the ends have each a dead-eye turned in, by which they are set up by laniards to the channel. (*See* CHANNEL and DEAD-EYES.)—*Bentinck shrouds.* Strong ropes fixed on the futtock-staves of the lower rigging, and extending to the opposite channels, where they are set up by means of dead-eyes and laniards, or gun-tackle runner purchases, in the same manner as the other shrouds. Their use is to support the masts when the ship rolls.—*Bowsprit shrouds* are now generally made of chain. They support the bowsprit in the same way that other shrouds support the masts.—*Bumkin or boomkin shrouds.* Strong chains fixed as stays to the bumkin ends, to support the strain exerted by the fore-tacks upon them.—*Futtock or foot-hook shrouds.* Portions of rigging (now sometimes chain) communicating with the futtock-plates above the top, and the cat-harpings below, and forming ladders, whereby the sailors climb over the top-brim. *Top-gallant shrouds* extend to the cross-trees, where, passing through holes in the ends, they continue over the futtock-staves of the topmast rigging, and descending almost to the top, are set up by laniards passing through thimbles instead of dead-eyes.—*Topmast shrouds* extend from the topmast head to the edges of the tops, and are set up to the futtock dead-eyes.

SHROUD-STOPPER. A stout rope-stopper made fast above and below a part of the shroud which has been damaged by an enemy's shot, or otherwise.

SHROUD-TRUCKS. Small pieces of wood with holes in them, but no sheaves; they are seized on the standing-rigging as fair leaders for the running-rigging. (*See* BULL'S-EYES.)

SHUNT. A term recently introduced among engineers and gunners; but traceable back to the year 931, a "zunte-stone" being placed on a spot where the road deviated.

SHURQEE. A prevailing S.E. wind in the Gulf of Persia; it is usually preceded by a heavy dew, which is quite the reverse with the *shimal*.

SHUT IN, To. Said of landmarks or points of land, when one is brought to transit and overlap the other, or intercept the view of it.

SHUTTING ON. Joining the arms of an anchor to its shank. Also, welding one piece of iron to another to lengthen it.

SICK-BAY. A portion of the fore-part of the main-deck, reserved for the accommodation of the sick and wounded; any other place set apart for invalids is called the *sick-berth*.

SICK-BERTH ATTENDANT. *See* LOBLOLLY-BOY.

SICK-BOOK. An account of such officers and men as are on the sick list on board, or are sent to an hospital, hospital-ship, or sick-quarters.

SICK-FLAG. The yellow quarantine flag, hoisted to prevent communication; whence the term of the yellow flag, and yellow admirals. There are two others—one with a black ball, the other with a square in the centre—denoting plague, or actual diseases.

SICK-MESS. A table for those on the doctor's list. When seamen are thus placed, their provisions are turned over to the surgeon, who accounts for their re-purchase by government, if not consumed, and the proceeds are applied to purchase comforts beyond those allowed by the service.

SICK-TICKET. A document given to an officer, seaman, or marine, when sent to an hospital, certified by the signing officer and the surgeon, stating the entry, rank, rating, &c., together with other particulars.

SIDE. All that part of a ship which extends from stem to stern in length, and from the upper edge of the gunwale above, to the lower edge of the mainwale, below which the *bottom* commences.

SIDE-BOYS, OR SIDE-MEN. Those appointed to attend the gangways when boats come alongside, and offer the man-ropes to the officer ascending.

SIDE COUNTER-TIMBER. The stern timber which partakes of the shape of the topside, and heels upon the end of the wing-transom.

SIDE-KEELSONS. A name for sister-keelsons. First used in mortar-vessels to support the bomb-beds; later they have crept in to support the engines in steamers, and furnish a free flow beneath their flooring for the water, as well as for ventilation.

SIDE-LADDER, OR ACCOMMODATION-LADDER. A complete staircase structure used in harbour by most large ships.

SIDE-LEVER. A lever on each side of the cylinder of a marine steam-engine, resembling the beam of the ordinary land-engine. (*See* LEVER.)

SIDE OUT FOR A BEND, To. The old well-known term to draw the bight of a hempen cable towards the opposite side, in order to make room for the bight being twined to coil it in the tier. The most expert and powerful seamen were selected for this duty, now rare.

SIDE-PIECES. Parts of a made mast.

SIDEREAL ASTRONOMY. That branch of the science which relates to the fixed stars.

SIDEREAL DAY. The interval between the departure and return of a star to the meridian; in other words, its two successive transits.

SIDEREAL PERIOD. *See* REVOLUTION.

SIDEREAL TIME. The time shown by a clock regulated by the fixed stars, and compensated to accelerate upon mean time by the daily amount of 3 minutes 56·56 seconds.

SIDE-RODS. Rods hanging from each of the cross-heads, one on each side of the cylinder of a steam-engine, and connected to the pins of the side-levers below; their duty is to cause a simultaneous movement.

SIDE-SCALE. A simple graduation, adopted by Sir Philip Broke in the *Shannon*, for the quick elevation or depression of the guns.

SIDE-STEPS. Pieces of wood bolted to the side of a ship for the convenience of ascending; in smaller vessels they have a ladder made of rope with wooden thwarts, which hooks to the gangway.

SIDING OR SIDED. The dimensions or size of timber, the contrary way to which the mould side is placed; one side sided smooth, to work from or to fit.

SIDING DIMENSION. The breadth of any piece of timber.

SIEGE. A continued endeavour, by systematic military means, such as batteries, trenches, mines, &c., to overpower the defences of a place and take possession of it.

SIEGE-ARTILLERY. The ordnance (guns, mortars, howitzers, &c.) used for overpowering the fire and destroying the defences of a fortified place; their weight and power, limited mainly by the kind of transport at hand, seldom exceed those of the light 100-pounder rifled gun, and are mostly above those of *guns of position*, such as the old 18-pounder, or the 40-pounder rifle.

SIEGE-TRAIN. Properly, the whole of the material, with its transport, required for carrying on a siege; but more frequently used for the necessary *siege artillery*, together with its ammunition, carriages, machines, and appliances of all kinds.

SIESTA. The hour of the afternoon in hot climates, when Spaniards, Italians, &c., retire to repose during the heat of the day.

SIGHTING THE LAND. Running in to catch a view.

SIGHTS. The fixed marks on fire-arms, by which their direction is regulated in aiming: generally, two small fittings of brass or iron, that near the breech having a notched head, and that towards the muzzle a pointed one. (*See* DISPART.)—*Astronomical sights.* Observations taken to determine the time or latitude, as well as for chronometer rates.

SIGHT THE ANCHOR, To. To heave it up in sight, in order to prove that it is clear, when, from the ship having gone over it, there is suspicion that it may be fouled by the slack cable.

SIGHT-VANES. *See* VANES.

SIGNALIZE, To. To distinguish one's self; a word also degraded to the meaning of communicating intelligence by means of signals or telegraph.

SIGNAL-MAN. The yeoman of the signals; a first-class petty officer in the navy.

SIGNAL OF DISTRESS. When a ship is in imminent danger, she hoists her national flag upside down, and, if she is armed, fires minute guns; also lets fly top-gallant sheets, &c.; indeed does anything to attract observation.

SIGNAL-OFFICER. In a repeating frigate, a signal-midshipman; in a flag-ship, a flag-lieutenant.

SIGNALS. Codes of signals have been used for centuries and changed frequently. Their use is too well known to need explanation. They are conveyed by flags, semaphores, balls, guns, lights, rockets, bells, horns, whistles, &c., and half a century since were carried on with incredible ability. It may be also observed that signal officers of those days became subsequently the elite of the navy; *signal-officer* being then a proud term of distinction.—*Fog-signals*, certain operations which emit sound.—*Night-signals*, either lanterns disposed in certain figures, flashes, or false fires, &c.

SIGNIFER. The zodiac.

SIGNING OFFICERS. The captain, senior lieutenant, master, and purser (now paymaster); but where the document relates to the stores in charge of any stated officer, that officer is to sign it instead of the purser.

SIGNS OF THE ZODIAC. The emblems of the twelve divisions, into which the ancients divided the zodiac.

SILL. A northern term for the young of a herring.

SILLOCK. The podling, or young of the coal-fish, affording food and oil on the Scottish coasts; they are grayish, and are taken when somewhat less than a herring.

SILL OF A DOCK. The timber at the base against which the gates shut; and the depth of water which will float a vessel in or out of it, is measured from it to the surface.

SILLON. An old word for envelope. In fortification, formerly, a counter-guard.

SILLS. The upper and lower parts of the framing of the ports. The bottom pieces of any ports, docks, scuttles, or hatches.

SILT. Sediment; ooze in a harbour, or at a lock-gate.

SILT-GROUNDS. Deep-water banks off Jamaica, where *silt-snappers* are fished for.

SILT-UP, To. To be choked with mud or sand, so as to obstruct vessels.

SILVER-CÆDUA. A statute term for wood under twenty years' growth.

SILVER-OAR. One of the badges of the civil court afloat, conferring the power to arrest for debt if not less than £20.

SILVER-THAW. The term for ice falling in large flakes from the sails and rigging, consequent on a frost followed suddenly by a thaw.

SIMOOM. The Arabian name for the *sirocco* (which see). The simoom, sirocco, samiel, and klamsin, seem to be modifications of the same wind from the desert.

SIMULATION. The vice of counterfeiting illness or defect, for the purpose of being invalided.

SINE. A right sine in geometry, is a right line drawn from one end of an arc perpendicularly upon the radius from the centre to the other end of the arc; or it is half the chord of twice the arc.

SINET. An old Chaucerian term for zenith.

SINGING. The chaunt by which the leadsman in the chains proclaims his soundings at each cast:—

> "To heave the lead the seaman sprung,
> And to the pilot cheerly sung,
> By the deep—nine."

SINGLE, To. To unreeve the running part of topsail sheets, &c., to let them run freely, or for harbour duty.

SINGLE-ACTION ENGINE. *See* ATMOSPHERIC STEAM-ENGINE.

SINGLE ANCHOR. A ship unmoored, having hove up one bower, rides by the other.

SING SMALL. To make a bullying boaster *sing small*, by lowering his arrogance.

SINICAL QUADRANT. *See* QUADRANT.

SINNET. *See* SENNIT.

SIR. Once a scholastic title applied to priests and curates; now to knights. "Aye, aye, sir," is the well-known answer from seamen, denoting 'cuteness, combined with good humour and obedience.

SIRIUS. The principal star, *a*, of the constellation Canis Major, and the brightest in the heavens; the dog-star.

SIROCCO. An oppressively hot parching wind from the deserts of Africa, which in the southern part of Italy and Sicily comes from the south-east; it sometimes commences faintly about the summer solstice.

SISERARA, OR SURSERARA. A tremendous blow; or a violent rebuke.

SISSOO. An Indian timber much used in the construction of country ships.

SISTER OR CISTERN BLOCK. A turned cylindrical block having two sheave-holes, one above the other. It fits in between the first pair of topmast shrouds on each side, and is secured by seizings below the cat-harpings. The topsail-lift reeves through the lower, and the reef-tackle pendant through the upper.

SISTER KEELSONS. Square timbers extending along the floors, by the main keelson, leaving sufficient space on each side for the limbers. (*See* SIDE KEELS.)

SISTROID ANGLE. One like a sistrum, the Egyptian musical instrument.

SITCH. A little current of water, generally dry in summer.

SIX-UPON-FOUR. Reduced allowance; four rations allotted to six men.

SIX-WATER GROG. Given as a punishment for neglect or drunkenness, instead of the usual *four-water*, which is one part rum, and four parts water, lime-juice, and sugar.

SIZE, To. To range soldiers, marines, and small-arm men, so that the tallest may be on the flanks of a party.

SIZE-FISH. A whale, of which the whale-bone blades are six feet or upwards in length; the harpooner gets a bonus for striking a "size-fish."

SIZES. A corruption for *six-upon-four* (which see).

SKARKALLA. An old machine for catching fish.

SKART. A name of the cormorant in the Hebrides.

SKATE. A well-known cartilaginous fish of the ray family, *Raia batis*.

SKATE-LURKER. A cant word for a begging impostor dressed as a sailor.

SKEDADDLE, To. To stray wilfully from a watering or a working party. An archaism retained by the Americans.

SKEDDAN. The Manx or Erse term for herrings.

SKEEL. A cylindrical wooden bucket. A large water-kid.

SKEER, or SCAR. A place where cockles are gathered. (*See* SCAR.)

SKEET. A long scoop used to wet the sides of the ship, to prevent their splitting by the heat of the sun. It is also employed in small vessels for wetting the sails, to render them more efficacious in light breezes; this in large ships is done by the fire engine.

SKEE-TACK. A northern name for the cuttle-fish.

SKEGG. A small and slender part of the keel of a ship, cut slanting, and left a little without the stern-post; not much used now, owing to its catching hawsers, and occasioning dead water. The after-part of the keel itself is also called the skegg.

SKEGG-SHORES. Stout pieces of plank put up end-ways under the skegg of the ship, to steady the after-part when in the act of being launched.

SKELDRYKE. An old term for a small passage-boat in the north.

SKELETON OF A REGIMENT. Its principal officers and staff.

SKELLY. The *Leuciscus cephalus*, or chub. In the northern lakes it is often called the fresh-water herring.

SKELP, To. To slap with the open hand: an old word, said to have been imported from Iceland:—

> "I canno' tell a';
> Some gat a skelp, and some gat a claw."

SKENE, or SKAIN. A crooked sword formerly used by the Irish.

SKENY. A northern term to express an insulated rock.

SKER, or SKERRY. A flat insulated rock, but not subject to the overflowing of the sea: thus we have "the Skerries" in Wales, the Channel Islands, &c.

SKEW. Awry, oblique; as a skew bridge, skew angle, &c. Also, in Cornwall, drizzling rain. Also, a rude-fashioned boat.

SKEWER-PIECES. When the salt meat is cut up on board ship by the petty officers, the captain and lieutenants are permitted to select *whole* pieces of 8 or 16 lbs., for which they are charged 2 or 4 lbs. extra. The meat being then divided into messes, the remnants are cut into small pieces termed skewer-pieces, and being free from bone, are charged *ad lib.* to those who take them.

SKID-BEAMS. Raised stanchions in men-of-war over the main-deck, parallel to the quarter-deck and forecastle beams, for stowing the boats and booms upon.

SKIDDY-COCK. A west-country term for the water-rail.

SKIDER. A northern term for the skate.

SKIDS. Massive fenders; they consist of long compassing pieces of timber, formed to answer the vertical curve of a ship's side, in order to preserve it when weighty bodies are hoisted in or lowered against it. They are mostly used in whalers. Boats are fitted with permanent fenders, to prevent chafing and fretting. Also, beams resting on blocks, on which small craft are built. Also, pieces of plank put under a vessel's bottom, for launching her off when she has been hauled up or driven ashore.

SKIFF. A familiar term for any small boat; but in particular, one resembling a yawl, which is usually employed for passing rivers. Also, a sailing vessel, with fore-and-aft mainsail, jib foresail, and jib: differing from a sloop in setting the jib on a stay, which is eased in by travellers. They have no topmast, and the mainsail hauls out to the taffrail, and traverses on a traveller iron horse like a cutter's foresail.

SKILLET. A small pitch-pot or boiler with feet.

SKILLY. Poor broth, served to prisoners in hulks. Oatmeal and water in which meat has been boiled. Hence, *skillygalee,* or burgoo, the drink made with oatmeal and sugar, and served to seamen in lieu of cocoa as late as 1814.

SKIN. This term is frequently used for the inside planking of a vessel, the outside being the *case.*

SKIN OF A SAIL. The outside part when a sail is furled. To furl in a clean skin, is the habit of a good seaman.—*To skin up a sail in the bunt.* To make that part of the canvas which covers the sail, next the mast when furled, smooth and neat, by turning the sail well up on the yard.

SKIP-JACK. A dandified trifling officer; an upstart. Also, the merry-thought of a fowl. Also, a small fish of the boneta kind, which frequently jumps out of the water. A name applied also to small porpoises.

SKIPPAGE. An archaism for tackle or ship furniture.

SKIPPER. The master of a merchant vessel. Also, a man-of-war's man's constant appellation for his own captain. Also, the gandanock, or saury-pike, *Esox saurus.*

SKIRLING. A fish taken on the Welsh coasts, and supposed to be the fry of salmon.

SKIRMISH. An engagement of a light and irregular character, generally for the purpose of gaining information or time, or of clearing the way for more serious operations.

SKIRTS. The extreme edges of a plain, forest, shoal, &c.

SKIS-THURSDAY. "The Lady-day in Lent" of the Society of Ship-wrights at Newcastle, instituted in 1630.

SKIT. An aspersive inuendo or for fun.

SKIVER. A dirk to stab with.

SKOODRA. A Shetland name for the ling.

SKOOL. The cry along the coast when the herrings appear first for the season : a corruption of *school*.

SKOORIE. A northern term for a full-grown coal-fish.

SKOTTEFER [Anglo-Sax. *scot*, an arrow or dart]. Formerly, an archer.

SKOUTHER. A northern name for the stinging jelly-fish.

SKOUTS. Guillemots or auks, so called in our northern islands from their wary habits.

SKOW. A flat-bottomed boat of the northern German rivers.

SKRAE-FISH. Fish dried in the sun without being salted.

SKUA. A kind of sea-gull.

SKUNK-HEAD. An American coast-name for the pied duck.

SKURRIE. The shag, *Phalacrocorax graculus*. Applied to frightened seals, &c.

SKY-GAZER. The ugly hare-lipped *Uranoscopus*, whose eyes are on the crown of its head; the Italians call him *pesce-prete*, or priest-fish. Also, a sail of very light duck, over which un-nameable sails have been set, which defy classification.

SKY-LARKING. In olden times meant mounting to the mast-heads, and sliding down the royal-stays or back-stays for amusement; but of late the term has denoted frolicsome mischief, which is not confined to boys, unless three score and ten includes them.—*Skying* is an old word for shying or throwing.

SKYLIGHT. A framework in the deck to admit light vertically into the cabin and gun-room.

SKYSAIL. A small light sail above the royal.

SKYSAIL-MAST. The pole or upper portion of a royal mast, when long enough to serve for setting a skysail; otherwise a skysail-mast is a sepa-rate spar, as *sliding gunter* (which see).

SKY-SCRAPER. A triangular sail set above the skysail; if square it would be a moonsail, and if set above that, a star-gazer, &c.

SLAB. The outer cut of a tree when sawn up into planks. (Alburnum.)

SLAB-LINES. Small ropes passing up abaft a ship's mainsail or foresail, led through blocks attached to the trestle-trees, and thence transmitted, each in two branches, to the foot of the sail, where they are fastened. They are used to truss up the slack sail, after it has been "disarmed" by the leech and bunt-lines.

SLACK. The part of a rope or sail that hangs loose.—*To slack*, is to de-crease in tension or velocity; as, "Slack the laniard of our main-stay ;" or "The tide slackens."

SLACK HELM. If the ship is too much by the stern, she will carry her helm too much *a-lee*.

SLACK IN STAYS. Slow in going about. Also applied to a lazy man.

SLACK OFF, OR SLACKEN! The order to ease away the rope or tackle by which anything is held fast; as, "Slack up the hawser."

SLACK WATER. The interval between the flux and reflux of the tide, as between the last of the ebb and first of the flood, or *vice versa*, during which the water remains apparently quiescent.

SLADE [the Anglo-Saxon *slæd*]. A valley or open tract of country.

SLAKE. An accumulation of mud or ooze in the bed of a river.

SLANT OF WIND. An air of which advantage may be taken.

SLANT TACK. That which is most favourable to the course when working to windward.

SLAVER. A vessel employed in the odious slave-trade.

SLED. The rough kind of sleigh in North America, used for carrying produce, too heavy for amusement.

SLEE. A sort of cradle placed under a ship's bottom in Holland, for drawing her up for repairs.

SLEECH. A word on our southern coasts for mud or sea-sand used in agriculture.

SLEEP. A sail sleeps when, steadily filled with wind, it bellies to the breeze.

SLEEPERS. Timbers lying fore and aft in the bottom of the ship, now generally applied to the knees which connect the transoms to the after timbers on the ship's quarter. They are particularly used in Greenland ships, to strengthen the bows and stern-frame, to enable them to resist the shocks of the ice. Also, any wooden beams used as supports. Also, ground tier casks.

SLEEVE. The word formerly used to denote the narrows of a channel, and particularly applied to the Strait of Dover, still called *La Manche* by the French. When Napoleon was threatening to invade England, he was represented trying to get into a coat, but one of the sleeves utterly baffled him, whence the point: "*Il ne peut pas passer La Manche.*"

SLEEVE-FISH. A name for the calamary, *Loligo vulgaris*, an animal allied to the cuttle-fish.

SLICE. A bar of iron with a flat, sharp, spear-shaped end, used in stripping off sheathing, ceiling, and the like. The *whaler's slice* is a slender chisel about four inches wide, used to cut into, and flinch the fish.

SLICES. Tapering wedges of plank used to drive under the false keel, and between the bilge-ways, preparatory to launching a vessel.

SLICK. Smooth. This is usually called an Americanism, but is a very old sea-term. In the *Book for Boys and Girls*, 1686, it is aptly illustrated:

> "The mole's a creature very smooth and slick,
> She digs i' th' dirt, but 'twill not on her stick."

SLIDE-VALVE CASING. A casing on one side of the cylinder of an engine, which covers the nozzles or steam-ports, and confines the slide-valves.

SLIDE-VALVE ROD. A rod connecting the slide-valves of an engine, to both of which it is joined; it passes through the casing cover, the opening of which is kept steam-tight.

SLIDE-VALVES.   The adaptations used in a marine-engine to change the admission of the steam into, and its eduction from, the cylinder, by the upper and lower steam-ports alternately.

SLIDING BAULKS, OR SLIDING-PLANKS.   Those timbers fitted under the bottom of a ship, to descend with her upon the bilge-ways when launched.

SLIDING BILGE-BLOCKS.   Those logs made to slide under the bilge of a ship in order to support her.

SLIDING GUNTERS.   Masts fitted for getting up and down with facility abaft the mast; generally used for *kites*, as royals, skysails, and the like.

SLIDING-KEEL.   A contrivance to prevent vessels from being driven to leeward by a side-wind; it is composed of planks of various breadths, erected vertically, so as to slide up and down, through the keel.

SLING, To.   To pass the top-chains round the yards when going into action.   Also, to set any large article, in ropes, so as to put a tackle on, and hoist or lower it.   When the clues are attached to a cot or hammock, it is said to be slung; also water-kegs, buoys, &c., are slung.

SLING-DOGS.   In timber lifting, a dog is an iron implement with a fang at one end, and an eye at the other, in which a rope may be made fast for hauling anything along.   Two of these fastened together by a shackle through the eyes are called sling-dogs. (*See* SPAN-DOGS.)   Also, an ancient piece of ordnance. (*See* SLYNG.)

SLING-HOOP.   That which suspends the yard from the mast, by which it is hoisted and lowered.

SLINGS.   A rope fitted to encircle any large article, and suspend it while hoisting and lowering.   Also, leather straps made fast to both ends of a musket, serving for the men to hang them by on their shoulders, that both hands may be free.—*Boat-slings*.   Strong ropes, furnished with hooks and iron thimbles, whereby to hook the tackles to keel, stem, and stern bolts, in order to hoist the boats in or out of the ship.—*Buoy-slings* are special fittings adopted in order that a buoy may securely ride on the wave, and mark the position of the anchor, the buoy-rope being attached to an eye in the slings.—*Butt-slings* are those used in slinging casks; they may be described as a running eye over one end, and a similar one made with two half hitches over the standing part on the other; all of which jam close home when the strain is brought on the bight.—*Yard-slings*. The rope or chain used to support a yard which does not travel up and down a mast.   The slings of a yard also imply that part on which the slings are placed.—*Slings* is also a term on the American coast for drams, or a drink of spirits and water; the custom of *slinging* prevails there extensively, even where intoxication is despised.

SLIP.   An inclined plane by the water side, on which a ship may be built. There are also slips up which vessels may be drawn for receiving repairs.

Also, a short memorandum of the proposed insurance of a ship, which is sometimes offered to the underwriters for subscription, previous to the effecting of a policy. Also, in steam navigation, the difference between the pitch of the propelling screw, and the space through which the screw actually progresses in the water, during one revolution.—*To slip*, is to let go the cable with a buoy on the end, and quit the position, from any sudden requirement, instead of weighing the anchor.—*To slip by the board.* To slip down by the ship's side.

SLIP-BEND. When a man makes a false step, and slips down a hatchway, or overboard.

SLIP-KNOT, OR SLIPPERY-HITCH. One which will not bear any strain, but will either become untied, or will traverse along the other part of the rope.

SLIP-ROPE. A rope passed through anything in such a manner that it will render or may be slipped instantaneously, as in canting to make sail, &c.

SLIP-SHACKLE. A shackle with a lever-bolt, for letting go suddenly; yet, when ringed, is sufficient to secure the ship.

SLIVE, OR SLIVER. An old term for a sluice. Also, any thin piece of split wood used as a filling. Also, a short slop wrapper, formerly called a *sliving.*

SLOOP. In general parlance is a vessel similar to a cutter; the bowsprit, however, is not running, and the jib is set on a standing stay with hanks. In North America the sloop proper sets only a mainsail and foresail, the latter jib-shaped, on a short standing bowsprit, and has no topmast. The rig is greatly used for yachts there, and is most effective in moderate weather. Sloop in the royal navy is a term depending on the rank of the officer in command. Thus, the donkey frigate *Blossom* was one cruise rated a *ship*, when commanded by a captain—the next, a *sloop*, because only commanded by a commander.

SLOP-BOOK. A register of the slop clothing, soap, and tobacco, issued to the men; also of the religious books supplied.

SLOPE OF WIND. A breeze favouring a long tack near to the required course, and which may be expected to veer to fair.

SLOP-ROOM. The place appointed to keep the slops in, for the ship's company; generally well aft and dry.

SLOPS. A name given to ready-made clothes, and other furnishings, for seamen, by Maydman, in 1691. In Chaucer's time, *sloppe* meant a sort of breeches. In a MS. account of the wardrobe of Queen Elizabeth, is an order to John Fortescue for the delivery of some Naples fustian for "Sloppe for Jack Greene, our Foole."

SLOP-SHOP. A place where ready-made clothing for seamen is sold, not at all advantageously to Jack.

SLOT. An archaic term for a castle or fort. Also, a groove or hole where a pin traverses.

SLOT-HOOP. The same as *truss-hoops.*

SLOW HER! In steam navigation, the same as "Ease her!"

SLOW MATCH. *See* MATCH.

SLOW TIME. In marching, means 75 paces to a minute.

SLUDGE. A wet deposit formed by streams. Also, a stratum of young ice in rough seas. Also, in polar parlance, comminuted fragments of brash ice.

SLUDGE-HOLES. Adaptations at the ends of the water-passages between the flues of a steamer's boilers, by which the deposits can be raked out.

SLUE, To. To turn anything round or over *in situ:* especially expressing the movement of a gun, cask, or ship; or when a mast, boom, or spar is turned about in its cap or boom iron.

SLUED. When a man staggers under drink; unable to walk steadily.

SLUE-ROPE. A rope peculiarly applied for turning a spar or other object in a required direction.

SLUR-BOW. A species of cross-bow formerly used for discharging fire arrows.

SLUSH. The fat of the boiled meat in the coppers, formerly the perquisite of the ship's cook. Also applied to anything like plashy ground, but most commonly to snow in a thaw. Any wet dirt.

SLUSH-BUCKET. A bucket kept in the tops, to grease the masts, sheets, &c., to make all run smoothly.

SLUSH-ICE. The first layer which forms when the surface is freezing.

SLY-GOOSE. A northern term for the sheldrake, *Tadorna vulpanser.*

SLYNG. An ancient piece of sea-ordnance: there were also *di-slyngs.*

SMACK. A vessel, sometimes like a cutter, used for mercantile purposes, or for carrying passengers; the largest of which, the Leith smacks, attained the size of 200 tons.

SMACK-SMOOTH. Level with the surface; said of a mast which has gone by the board.

SMALL. The narrow part of the tail of a whale, in front of the flukes. Also, that part of the anchor-shank which is immediately under the stock.

SMALL-ARM MEN. Those of the crew selected and trained to the use of small-arms. When they have effected their boarding, they seldom retain more than their pistol and cutlass.

SMALL-ARMS. The muskets, pistols, cutlasses, tomahawks, and boarding-pikes, in charge of the gunner, on board ship.

SMALL-HELM. One of the principal results of sound seamanship is the proper trim of the vessel and the sail carried; by which means the action of the rudder is reduced to a minimum, not requiring the tiller to be moved either hard up or hard down. Also used to denote that a turbulent jaw-me-down bully has been brought to his senses by a more vigorous mind.

SMALL SAILS. Topgallant-studding-sails and the *kites.*

SMALL STUFF. The term for spun-yarn, marline, and the smallest kinds of rope, even for yarns.

SMART. Ready, active, and intelligent.

SMART-MONEY. A pension given to a wounded man, according to the extent of the injury and his rank. Thus a lieutenant gets £91, 5s. for the loss of a leg, and a captain £300.

SMART-TICKET. The certificate from a captain and surgeon, by which only the smart-money is obtainable.

SMASHERS. Anything large or powerful. Also, pieces of ordnance of large calibre, in form between the gun and the carronade. Also, a very general epithet for north-country seamen.

SMELT [Anglo-Saxon, *smylt*]. The fry of salmon, samlet, or *Salmo eperlanus*.

SMEW. The white-headed goosander, *Mergus albellus*.

SMITER. An archaism for a scimitar. In the legend of Captain Jones, 1659, we are told:

> "His fatal *smiter* thrice aloft he shakes,
> And frowns; the sea, and ship, and canvas quakes."

SMITING-LINE. A line by which a yarn-stoppered sail is loosed, without sending men aloft. If well executed, marks the seaman.

SMOKE-BALLS. A pyrotechnical preparation, thrown to short distances from mortars, to choke men out of mines, to conceal movements, &c. They continue to smoke densely from 25 to 30 minutes.

SMOKE-BOX. A part which crosses the whole front of a marine boiler, over the furnace doors; or that part between the end of tubes furthest from the fire-place and bottom of the funnel.

SMOKES. Dense exhalations, mixed with the finer particles of sand, on the Calabar shores and borders of the Great Zahara desert, which prevail in autumn. Also, the indications of inhabitants when coasting new lands. For its meaning in Arctic voyages, *see* VAPOUR.

SMOKE-SAIL. A small sail hoisted against the foremast when a ship rides head to wind, to give the smoke of the galley an opportunity of rising, and to prevent its being blown aft on to the quarter-deck.

SMOOTH. A Cornish term applied when the surf abates its fury for a short space. Also, the lee of a ship or of a rock.

SMUG-BOATS. Contraband traders on the coast of China; opium boats.

SMUGGLING. Defrauding the public revenue by importing or exporting goods without paying the customs dues chargeable upon them.

SMURLIN. A bivalve mollusc, *Mya truncata*, used as food in the Shetland Islands.

SNAGGLE, To. To angle for geese with a hook and line properly baited.

SNAGS. The old word for lopped branches and sharp protuberances, but now chiefly applied to sunken obstructions in the American rivers.

SNAIL-CREEPING. Gouging out the surfaces of timbers in crooked channels, to promote a circulation of air.

SNAKE-PIECES. *See* POINTERS.

SNAKING. The passing of small stuff across a seizing, with marline hitches at the outer turns; or the winding small ropes spirally round a large one, the former lying in the intervals between the strands of the latter. (*See* WORMING.) The stays and back-stays, when the *Shannon* engaged the *Chesapeake*, were snaked with half-inch rope from fathom to fathom, to prevent their falling if shot away. Also, the finishing touch to neat seizings, to prevent the parts from separating when becoming slack by drying.

SNAPE, To. In ship-carpentry, is to hance or bevel the end of anything, so as to fay upon an inclined plane: it is also designated *flinch.*

SNAP-HAUNCE. An old word for a fire-lock or musket; a spring-lock for fire-arms.

SNAPING-POLE. An old term for a fishing-rod.

SNAPPER. A well-known fish of the Mesoprion tribe, highly valued as food in the West Indies and tropics generally.

SNAPPING-TURTLE. A well-known freshwater tortoise of the rivers in the United States; *Chelydra serpentina.*

SNARES. The cords which pass across the diameter of one hoop at the end of a drum.

SNARLEY-YOW. A discontented, litigious grumbler. An old guard-ship authority who knows when to play the courtier.

SNARL-KNOT. A northern expression for a knot that cannot be drawn loose.

SNATCH. Any open lead for a rope: if not furnished with a sheave, it is termed a *dumb snatch*, as on the bows and quarters for hawsers.

SNATCH-BLOCK. A single iron-bound block, with an opening in one side above the sheave, in which the bight of a rope may be laid, instead of reeving the end through, which in some circumstances would be very inconvenient, as when warps are led to the capstan, &c. The same as *notch-block.*

SNEER. To "make all sneer again" is to carry canvas to such an extent as to strain the ropes and spars to the utmost.

SNEEZER. A stiff gale of wind.

SNIFTING-VALVE. In the marine engine (*see* TAIL-VALVE).

SNIGGLING. A peculiar mode of catching eels in small streams and ponds, described by Izaak Walton.

SNIKKER-SNEE. A combat with knives; also, a large clasp-knife.

SNOGO. A cock-pit game at cards, called also *blind hookey*, apparently affording equal chances, but easily managed to his own advantage by a knavish adept.

SNOOD [Anglo-Saxon, *snod*]. A short hair-line or wire to which hooks are fastened below the lead in angling. Or the link of hair uniting the hook and fishing-line.

SNOOK. A fish of the family *Scomberidæ, Thyrsites atun*, abundant in Table Bay, whence it is exported, when salted, to the Mauritius.

SNOTTER. The lower support of the *sprit* (which see).

SNOW. A vessel formerly much in use. It differs slightly from a brig. It has two masts similar to the main and fore masts of a ship, and close abaft the main-mast a trysail-mast. Snows differ only from brigs in that the boom-mainsail is hooped to the main-mast in the brig, and traverses on the trysail-mast in the snow.

SNUBBING HER. Bringing a ship up suddenly with an anchor, and short range of cable, yet without jerking. [Said to be from the Icelandic *snubba*.]

SNUG. Under proper sail to meet a gale.

SNY. A gentle bend in timber, curving upwards: when it curves downwards, it is said to *hang*.

SO! An order to desist temporarily from hauling upon a rope, when it has come to its right position.

SOAK AND SEND! The order to pass wet swabs along.

SOAM. The dried air-bladder of herrings.

SOCKETS. The holes in which swivel-pintles, or the capstan or windlass spindles move.

SOD-BANK. A peculiar effect of refraction sometimes seen in calm weather, showing all objects on the water multiplied or magnified. A poor name for a fine phenomenon.

SOFT-LAES. A term on our northern coast for the small coves and bays formed by the waves on the more friable parts of cliffs.

SOFT-PLANK. Picking a soft plank in the deck, is choosing an easy berth. (*See* PLANK IT.)

SOFT TOMMY, OR SOFT TACK. Loaves of bread served out instead of biscuit.

SOLAN-GOOSE. The gannet, *Sula bassana*, a well-known sea fowl, frequenting the coasts of many countries in the northern hemisphere in the summer to lay its eggs, and then migrating.

SOLANO. An oppressive wind, blowing from Africa into the Mediterranean; synonymous with *sirocco*.

SOLAR DAY. Is the interval which elapses between two successive meridian transits of the sun, and is the unit of time in common use.

SOLAR SPECTRUM. The coloured image of the sun produced by refraction through a prism.

SOLAR SPOTS. *See* MACULÆ.

SOLAR SYSTEM. The sun, planets, and comets, which are assumed to form a system, independent of the surrounding fixed stars.

SOLDIER. One that has enlisted to serve his government in peace or war; receiving pay, and subject to the Mutiny Act and Articles of War.

SOLDIER-CRAB. A name for the *hermit-crab* (which see).

SOLDIER'S WIND. One which serves either way; allowing a passage to be made without much nautical ability.

SOLE. A common flat-fish, *Solea vulgaris*. Also, the decks of the cabin and forecastle in some ships, respectively called the *cabin* and *forecastle soles*. Also, the lining of the bilgeways, rudder, and the like.

SOLENT SEA. The old name of the narrow strait between Hampshire and the Isle of Wight.

SOLE OF A GUN-PORT. The lower part of it, more properly called *port-sill.*

SOLE OF THE RUDDER. A piece of timber attached to its lower part to render it nearly level with the false keel.

SOLLERETS. Pieces of steel which formed part of the armour for the feet.

SOLSTICES. The epochs when the sun passes through the solstitial points.

SOLSTITIAL COLURE. A great circle passing through the poles and solstitial points.

SOLSTITIAL POINTS. The two points where the tropics meet the ecliptic, in longitude 90° and 270°.

SOMA. A Japan junk of burden.

SONG. The call of soundings by the leadsman in the channels. Songs are also used to aid the men in keeping time when pulling on a rope, where a fife is not available. They are very common in merchant ships. The whalers have an improvised song when cutting docks in the ice in Arctic seas.

SON OF A GUN. An epithet conveying contempt in a slight degree, and originally applied to boys born afloat, when women were permitted to accompany their husbands to sea; one admiral declared he literally was thus cradled, under the breast of a gun-carriage.

SOPS. A northern term for small detached clouds, hanging about the sides of a mountain.

SORT. "That's your sort," means approval of a deed.

SORTIE. *See* SALLY.

SOUGH. An old northern term for the distant surging of the sea; a hollow murmur or howling, or the moaning of the wind before a gale.

SOUND [Anglo-Saxon, *sund*]. An arm of the sea over the whole extent of which soundings may be obtained, as on the coasts of Norway and America. Also, any deep bay formed and connected by reefs and sandbanks. On the shores of Scotland it means a narrow channel or strait. Also, the air-bladder of the cod, and generally the swimming-bladder or "soundes of any fysshes." Also, a cuttle-fish.

SOUND, VELOCITY OF. May be freely assumed at nearly 1142 feet in a second of time, when not affected by the temperature or wind; subject to corrections when great accuracy is required.

SOUND DUES. A toll formerly levied by the Danes on all merchant vessels passing the sound or strait between the North Sea and the Baltic.

SOUNDING. The operation of ascertaining the depth of the sea, and the quality of the ground, by means of a lead and line, sunk from a ship to the bottom, where some of the ooze or sand adheres to the tallow in the hollow base of the lead. Also, the vertical diving of a whale when struck. It is supposed to strike the bottom, and will take 3 or 4 coils of whale-line, equal to 2000 feet.

SOUNDING-LEAD. *See* LEAD.

SOUNDING-LINE. This line, with a plummet, is mentioned by Lucilius; and was the *sund-gyrd* of the Anglo-Saxons.

SOUNDING-ROD. A slight rod of iron marked with feet and inches, which being let down by a line in a groove of the side of the pump, indicates what water there is in the well, and consequently whether the ship requires pumping out or not.

SOUNDINGS. To be in soundings implies being so near the land that a deep-sea lead will reach the bottom, which is seldom practicable in the ocean. As soundings may, however, be obtained at enormous depths, and at great distances from the land, the term is limited in common parlance to parts not far from the shore, and where the depth is about 80 or 100 fathoms. Also, a name given to the specimen of the ground brought up adhering to the tallow stuck upon the base of the deep-sea lead, and distinguishing the nature of the bottom, as sand, shells, ooze, &c.

SOUNDLESS. Places assumed formerly to be bottomless, but thousands of fathoms are now measured. Our elders little thought of a submarine telegraph across the Atlantic Ocean!

SOURCE. The spring or origin of a stream or river, or at least one of the tributaries of supply.

SOURS. An old word for a rise, or rapid ascent.

SOUSE. A method of pickling fish by immersing them in vinegar after being boiled. (*See* MARL.)

SOUSED GURNET. Best expressed by Falstaff's—"If I be not ashamed of my soldiers, I am a souse, gurnet."

SOUTHERN CROSS. The popular name of a group of stars near the South Pole, which are somewhat in the figure of a cross.

SOUTHERN-LIGHTS. *See* AURORA AUSTRALIS.

SOUTHING. In navigation, implies the distance made good towards the south: the opposite of *northing*.

SOUTHING OF THE MOON. The time at which the moon passes the meridian of any particular place. Popularly the term is used to denote the meridian transit of any heavenly body south of the observer.

SOUTH SEA. *See* PACIFIC OCEAN.

SOUTH-WESTER. A useful water-proof hat for bad weather.

SOUTH-WIND. A mild wind in the British seas with frequent fogs; it generally brings rain or damp weather.

SOW. The receptacle into which the molten iron is poured in a gun-foundry. The liquid iron poured from it is termed *pig*, whence the term pig-ballast.

SPADE. In open speaking, to call a spade a spade is to give a man his real character. The phrase is old and still in use.

SPADO, OR SPADROON. A cut-and-thrust sword [from the Spanish].

SPAKE-NET. A peculiar net for catching crabs.

SPALDING-KNIFE. A knife used for splitting fish in Newfoundland.

SPALDINGS. A north-country name for whitings and other small fish, split and dried.

SPALES. In naval architecture, internal strengthening by cross artificial beams. (*See* CROSS SPALES.)

SPAN. A rope with both ends made fast, so that a purchase may be hooked to its bight. Also, a small line or cord, the middle of which is usually attached to a stay, whence the two ends branch outwards to the right and left, having either a block or thimble attached to their extremities. It is used to confine some ropes which pass through the corresponding blocks or thimbles as a fair leader.

SPAN-BLOCKS. Blocks seized into each bight of a strap, long enough to go across a cap, and allow the blocks to hang clear on each side, as main-lifts, topmast studding-sail, halliards, blocks, &c.

SPAN IN THE RIGGING, To. To draw the upper parts of the shrouds together by tackles, in order to seize on the cat-harping legs. The rigging is also "spanned in" when it has been found to stretch considerably on first putting to sea, but cannot be set up until it moderates.

SPANISH-BURN. A specious method of hiding defects in timber, by chopping it in pieces.

SPANISH-BURTON. The *single* is rove with three single blocks, or two single blocks and a hook in the bight of one of the running parts. The *double* Spanish-burton is furnished with one double and two single blocks.

SPANISH DISTURBANCE. An epithet given to the sudden armament on the Nootka Sound affair, in 1797, an epoch from which many of our seamen dated their service in the late wars.

SPANISH MACKEREL. An old Cornish name for the tunny, or a scomber, larger than the horse-mackerel.

SPANISH REEF. The yards lowered on the cap. Also, a knot tied in the head of the jib.

SPANISH WINDLASS. A wooden roller, or heaver, having a rope wound about it, through the bight of which an iron bolt is inserted as a lever for heaving it round. This is a handy tool for turning in rigging, heaving in seizings, &c.

SPANKER. A fore-and-aft sail, setting with a boom and gaff, frequently called the *driver* (which see). It is the aftermost sail of a ship or bark.

SPANKER-EEL. A northern term for the lamprey.

SPANKING. Going along with a fresh breeze when the spanker tells, as the aft well-boomed out-sail. The word is also used to denote strength, spruceness, and size, as a *spanking breeze*, a *spanking frigate*, &c.

SPANNER. An instrument by which the wheel-lock guns and pistols were wound up; also used to screw up the nuts of the plummer boxes. Also, an important balance in forming the radius of parallel motion in a steam-engine, since it reconciles the curved sweep which the side-levers describe with the perpendicular movement of the piston-rod, by means of which they are driven.

SPANNING A HARPOON. Fixing the line which connects the harpoon and its staff. The harpoon iron is a socketed tool, tapering 3 feet to the barb-heads; on that iron socket a becket is worked; the staff fits in loosely. The harpoon line reeves upwards from the socket through this becket, and through another on the staff, so that on striking the whale the staff leaps out of the socket and does not interfere with the iron, which otherwise might be wrenched out.

SPAN OF RIGGING. The length of shrouds from the dead-eyes on one side, over the masthead, to the dead-eyes on the other side of the ship.

SPAN-SHACKLE. A large bolt running through the forecastle and spar-deck beams, and forelocked before each beam, with a large triangular shackle at the head, formerly used for the purpose of receiving the end of the davit. Also, a bolt similarly driven through the deck-beam, for securing the booms, boats, anchors, &c.

SPAR. The general term for any mast, yard, boom, gaff, &c. In shipbuilding, the name is applied to small firs used in making staging.

SPAR-DECK. This term is loosely applied, though properly it signifies a temporary deck laid in any part of a vessel, and the beams whereon it rests obtain the name of skid-beams in the navy. It also means the quarter-deck, gangways, and forecastle of a deep-waisted vessel; and, rather strangely, is applied to the upper entire deck of a double-banked vessel, without an open waist.

SPARE. An epithet applied to any part of a ship's equipage that lies in reserve, to supply the place of such as may be lost or rendered incapable of service; hence we say, spare tiller, spare topmasts, &c.

SPARE ANCHOR. An additional anchor the size of a bower.

SPARE SAILS. An obvious term. They should be pointed before stowing them away in the sail-room.

SPARLING. A name on the Lancashire coasts for the smelt (*Osmerus eperlanus*).

SPARTHE. An Anglo-Saxon term for a halbert or battle-axe.

SPAT. The spawn or ova of the oyster.

SPEAK A VESSEL, To. To pass within hail of her for that purpose.

SPECIFIC GRAVITY. The comparative weights of equal bulks of different bodies, water being generally represented as unity.

SPECK-BLOCKS. *See* FLENSING.

SPECK-FALLS, or PURCHASE. Ropes rove through two large purchaseblocks at the mast-head of a whaler, and made fast to the *blubber-guy*, for hoisting the blubber from a whale.

SPECKTIONEER. The chief harpooner in a Greenland ship. He also directs the cutting operations in clearing the whale of its blubber and bones.

SPECTRUM. The variously coloured image into which a ray of light is divided on being passed through a prism.

SPEED-INDICATOR. A modification of Massey's log.

SPELL. The period wherein one or more sailors are employed in particular duties demanding continuous exertion. Such are the spells to the hand-lead in sounding, to working the pumps, to look out on the masthead, &c., and to steer the ship, which last is generally called the "trick at the wheel." *Spel-ian*, Anglo-Saxon, "to supply another's room." Thus, *Spell ho!* is the call for relief.

SPENCER. The fore-and-main trysails; fore-and-aft sails set with gaffs, introduced instead of main-topmast and mizen staysails.

SPENT. From *expend:* said of a mast broken by accident, in contradistinction to one shot away.

SPENT SHOT. A shot that has lost its penetrative velocity, yet capable of inflicting grave injury as long as it travels.

SPERM WHALE. Otherwise known as the cachalot, *Physeter macrocephalus.* A large cetacean, belonging to the division of delphinoid or toothed whales. It is found in nearly all tropical and temperate seas, and is much hunted for the valuable sperm-oil and spermaceti which it yields. When full grown, it may attain the length of 60 feet, of which the head occupies nearly one-third.

SPERONARA. A Mediterranean boat of stouter build than the scampavia, yet rowed with speed: in use in the south of Italy and Malta.

SPHERA NAUTICA. An old navigation instrument. In 1576 Martin Frobisher was supplied with a brass one, at the cost of £4, 6s. 8d.

SPHERE. The figure formed by the rotation of a circle. A term singularly, but very often, misapplied in parlance for orbit.

SPHERICAL CASE-SHOT. *See* SHRAPNEL SHELL.

SPHERICAL TRIANGLE. That contained under three arcs of great circles of a sphere.

SPHEROID. The figure formed by the rotation of an ellipse, differing little from a circle.

SPICA, OR α VIRGINIS. The lucida of Virgo, a standard nautical star.

SPIDER. An iron outrigger to keep a block clear of the ship's side.

SPIDER-HOOP. The hoop round a mast to secure the shackles to which the futtock-shrouds are attached. Also, an iron encircling hoop, fitted with belaying pins round the mast.

SPIDER-LINES. A most ingenious substitution of a spider's long threads for wires in micrometer scales, intended for delicate astronomical observations.

SPIKE-NAILS. *See* DECK-NAILS.

SPIKE-PLANK. (*Speak-plank ?*) In Polar voyages, a platform projecting across the vessel before the mizen-mast, to enable the ice-master to cross over, and see ahead, and so pilot her clear of the ice. It corresponds with the bridge in steamers.

SPIKE-TACKLE AND CANT-FALLS. The ropes and blocks used in whalers to sling their prey to the side of the ship.

SPIKE-TUB. A vessel in which the fat of bears, seals, and minor quarry is set aside till a "making off" gives an opportunity for adding it to the blubber in the hold.

SPIKING A GUN. Driving a large nail or iron spike into the vent, which will render the cannon unserviceable until removed. (*See* CLOY.)

SPILE. A stake or piece of wood formed like the frustum of a cone. A vent-peg in a cask of liquor. Small wooden pins which are driven into nail-holes to prevent leaking.

SPILINGS. In carpentry and ship-building, the dimensions taken from a straight line, a mould's edge, or rule-staff, to any given sny or curve of a plank's edge.

SPILL, To. Whether for safety or facility, it is advisable to shiver the wind out of a sail before furling or reefing it. This is done either by collecting the sail together, or by bracing it bye, so that the wind may strike its leech and shiver it. A very effeminate captain was accustomed to order, "Sheevar the meezen taus'le, and let the fore-topmast staysail lie dormant in the brails !"

SPILLING LINES. Ropes contrived to keep the sails from blowing away when they are clued up, being rove before the sails like the bunt-lines so as to disarm the gale, in contradistinction to clue-lines, &c., which cause the sails to belly full.

SPIN A TWIST or A YARN, To. To tell a long story; much prized in a dreary watch, if not tedious.

SPINDLE. The vertical iron pin upon which the capstan moves. (*See* Capstan.) Also, a piece of timber forming the diameter of a made mast. Also, the long-pin on which anything revolves. A windlass turns on horizontal spindles at each extremity.

SPINGARD. A kind of small cannon.

SPIRE-VAPOUR. A name suggested to Captain Parry for certain little vertical streams of vapour rising from the sea or open water in the Arctic regions, resembling the *barber* in North America (which see).

SPIRIT-ROOM. A place or compartment abaft the after-hold, to contain the ship's company's spirits.

SPIRKITTING. That strake of planks which is wrought, anchor-stock fashion, between the water-way and the lower sill of the gun-ports withinside of a ship of war.—*Spirkitting* is also used to denote the strake of ceiling between the upper-deck and the plank-sheer of a merchantman; otherwise known as *quick-work.*

SPIT. A bank, or small sandy projection, with shallow water on it, generally running out from a point of land. Also, meteorologically, very slight rain.

SPITFIRE-JIB. In cutters, a small storm-jib of very heavy canvas.

SPITHEAD NIGHTINGALES. Boatswains and boatswains' mates, when winding their calls, especially when piping to dinner.

SPLA-BOARDS. Planks fixed at an obtuse angle, to reflect light into a magazine.

SPLICE. The joining of two ropes together. Familiarly, two persons joined in wedlock.—*To splice.* To join the two untwisted ends of a rope together. There are several methods of making a splice, according to the services for which it is intended; as:—*The long rolling splice* is chiefly used in lead-lines, log-lines, and fishing-lines, where the short splice would be liable to separation, as being frequently loosened by the water.—*The long splice* occupies a great extent of rope, but by the three joinings being fixed at a distance from each other, the increase of bulk is divided; hence it resembles a continuous lay, and is adapted to run through the sheave-hole of a block, &c., for which use it is generally intended.—*The short splice* is used upon cables, slings, block-strops, and, in general, all ropes which are not intended to run through blocks.—*Spliced eye* forms a sort of eye or circle at the end of a rope, and is used for splicing in thimbles, bull's-eyes, &c., and generally on the end of lashing block-strops. (*See* Eye-splice.)

SPLICE THE MAIN BRACE. In nautical parlance, to serve out an extra allowance of grog in bad weather or after severe exertion.

SPLICING FID. A tapered wooden pin for opening the strands when splicing large ropes; it is sometimes driven by a large wooden mallet called a *commander.*

SPLINTER-NETTING. A cross-barred net formed of half-inch rope lashed at every rectangular crossing, and spread from rigging to rigging between the main and mizen masts, to prevent wreck from aloft, in action, from wounding the men at the upper-deck guns. They are frequently used at the open hatchways to prevent accidents.

SPLITTER. A man engaged in the Newfoundland fisheries to receive the fish from the *header,* and, with a sharp knife, dexterously to lay it open.

SPLITTING OUT. To remove the blocks on which a vessel rests in a dock, or at launching, when the pressure is too great for them to be driven, but by splitting.

SPLITTING THE BOOKS. The making of a new complete-book after payment, in which the dead, run, or discharged men are omitted; but the numbers which stood against the men's names in the first list must be continued.

SPOKES. The handles of the wheel, not the radii.—*To put a spoke in a man's wheel,* is to say something of him to his advantage, or otherwise.

SPOKE-SHAVE. That useful instrument similar to the carpenter's drawing-knife, for smoothing rounds or hollows.

SPOLIATION OF A SHIP'S PAPERS. An act which, by the maritime law of every court in Europe, not only excludes further proof, but does, *per se,* infer condemnation. Our own code has so far relaxed that this circumstance shall not be damnatory. The suppression of ships' papers, however, is regarded in the admiralty courts with great suspicion.

SPONSON. The curve of the timbers and planking towards the outer part of the *wing,* before and abaft each of the paddle-boxes of a steamer.

SPONSON-RIM. The same as *wing-wale* (which see).

SPONTOON. A light halbert.

SPOOM, To. An old word frequently found in Dryden, who thus uses it,

"When virtue *spooms* before a prosp'rous gale,
My heaving wishes help to fill the sail."

SPOON-DRIFT. A showery sprinkling of the water swept from the tops of the waves in a brisk gale. Driving snow is also sometimes termed spoon-drift.

SPOONING, or Spooming. Driving under a heavy gale, such as forces a ship to run before it without any canvas set.

SPOON-WAYS. In slave-ships, stowing the poor wretches so closely locked together, that it is difficult to move without treading upon them.

SPOTS ON THE SUN. *See* Maculæ.

SPOUT. A term applied to the blowing or breathing of whales and other cetaceans. The expired air, highly charged with moisture from the lungs, has frequently been mistaken for a stream of water. (*See also* Water-spout.)

SPOUTER. A whaling term for a South Sea whale.

SPRAT WEATHER. The dark days of November and December, so called from that being the most favourable season for catching sprats.

SPREAD A FLEET, To. To keep more open order.

SPREAD EAGLE. A person seized in the rigging; generally a passenger thus made to pay his entrance forfeit.

SPREE. Uproarious jollity, sport, and merriment.

SPRING. A crack running obliquely through any part of a mast or yard, which renders it unsafe to carry the usual sail thereon, and the spar is then said to be sprung. Also, a hawser laid out to some fixed object to slue a vessel proceeding to sea. (*See* Warp.)—*To spring.* To split or break.—*To spring a butt.* To start the end of a plank on the outside of a ship's bottom. (*See* Butt.)—*To spring a leak*, is when a vessel is suddenly discovered to leak.—*To spring the luff*, easing the helm down to receive a breeze; to bring a vessel's head closer to the wind in sailing. Thus a vessel coming up sharply to the wind under full way shoots, and may run much to windward of her course, until met by a contrary helm. —*To spring a mine.* To fire its charge.

SPRING-BEAM. In a steamer, a fore-and-aft beam for connecting the two paddle-beams, and supporting the outer end of the paddle-shaft.

SPRING-FORELOCK. One jagged or split at the point, thereby forming springs to prevent its drawing.

SPRING-SEARCHER. A steel-pronged tool to search for defects in the bore of a gun.

SPRING-STAYS. Are rather smaller than the stays, and are placed above them, being intended as substitutes should the main one be shot away.

SPRING-TIDE. The periodical excess of the elevation and depression of the tide, which occurs when both the sun and moon act in the same direction.

SPRIT [Anglo-Saxon, *spreotas*]. A small boom which crosses the sail of a boat diagonally from the mast to the upper aftmost corner: the lower end of the sprit rests in a sort of becket called the snotter, which encircles the mast at that place. These sails are accordingly called sprit-sails. Also, in a sheer-hulk, a spur or spar for keeping the sheers out to the required distance, so that their head should plumb with the centre of the ship when taking out or putting in masts.

SPRIT-SAIL. A sail formerly attached to a yard which hung under the bowsprit, and of importance in naval actions of old.

SPRIT-SAIL SHEET KNOT. May be crowned and walled, or double-walled, and is often used as a stopper-knot.

SPRIT-SAIL TOP-SAIL. A sail extended above the sprit-sail by a yard, which hung under the jib-boom.—*Top-gallant sprit-sail* was set upon the flying jib-boom in the same manner that the sprit-sail was set upon the inner jib-boom. The sprit-sail course, top-sail, and topgallant-sail were similar in effect to those on the foremast, and in former times, when the bowsprit stood more erect, it was indeed the bowsprit or mast.

SPRIT-SAIL YARD. A yard slung across the bowsprit, lashed to the knight-heads, and used to spread the guys of the jib and flying jib-boom. To this yard the sprit-sail was formerly bent.

SPRIT-SAIL YARDING. A cruelty in which some fishermen wreak vengeance on sharks, dog-fish, &c., that encroach on their baits, and foul their nets. They thrust a piece of wood through the gills of the unconscious offender, and in that condition turn it adrift upon the ocean.

SPROKET-WHEEL. That at the upper extremities of the chain-pump-tubes, worked by crank-handles.

SPRUNG. Damaged in various ways. Also, the ship slued round by means of guys. In ship-building, it indicates that a plank is strained so as to crack or fly open.

SPUEING THE OAKUM. When the ship's labouring forces the caulking out of her seams.

SPUN. The being turned back or rejected, on being examined touching qualifications.

SPUNGE. A cylindrical block of wood covered with sheepskin, used to clean the interior of a gun after firing, and to extinguish any sparks that may remain behind. The *rope-sponge*, fixed on a strong rope instead of a staff, has a rammer-head on its opposite end: it is used for service with lower-deck guns in bad weather when the ports cannot be opened except at moments for firing.

SPUNK. A fungus (*Polyporus fomentarius* and others) growing on the trunks of trees, from which tinder is made.

SPUN-YARN. A small line, formed of two, three, or more old rope-yarns not laid, but twisted together by hand or winch. Spun-yarn is used for various purposes, as seizing and serving ropes, weaving mats, &c.

SPUR. A projecting portion of a cliff. In fortification, spurs are walls that cross a part of the rampart and join to the town-wall. Also, in a sheer-hulk, the same as *sprit* (which see).

SPURKETS, or SPIRKETS. The spaces between the timbers along a ship's side betwixt the upper and lower futtocks, or betwixt the rungs fore and aft.

SPURLING-LINE. The line which formed the communication between the wheel and the tell-tale: it went round a small barrel, abaft the barrel of the wheel, and made the pointer show the position of the tiller.

Also, a line with thimbles as fair-leaders for running rigging. Now out of use.

SPURN-WATER. A channel left above the ends of a deck, to prevent water from coming any further. The water-ways.

SPURS, or SPUR-SHORES. Large pieces of timber in launching, the lower ends of which are fixed to the bilge-ways, and the upper ends fayed and bolted to the ship's bottom for additional security.

SPURS OF THE BEAMS. Curved pieces of timber, serving as half-beams, to support the decks, where a whole one cannot be placed, on account of the hatchways.

SPURS OF THE BITTS. The same as *standards* (which see).

SQUAD. A diminutive of *squadron*. Also, a small party of soldiers assembled for drill or inspection.

SQUADRON. A division of a fleet, as van, centre, and rear squadrons. A flying squadron may be commanded by a rear-admiral, and consist of any class of vessels. Also, a body of cavalry consisting of two troops, or from 80 to 150 men. Squadron is the ordinary unit in reckoning the cavalry force of an army.

SQUALL. A sudden gust of wind, frequently occasioned by the interruption and reverberation of the wind from high mountains. These are very frequent in the Mediterranean, particularly in the Levant.—*A black squall.* One attended with a dark cloud and generally heavy rain.—*A white squall.* This furious and dangerous gust occurs in clear weather, without any other warning than the white foam it occasions on the surface of the sea, and a very thin haze. When this squall reaches a ship, copious rain attends it. It is very destructive to the flying-kite school, and many lives have been sacrificed by it.

SQUARE. An instrument formed by a stock and a tongue fixed at right angles. Also, in the army, a formation of infantry devised to resist cavalry. (*See* HOLLOW SQUARE and RALLYING SQUARE.) Also, a term peculiarly appropriated to the yards and their sails. Thus, when the yards hang at right angles with the mast they are said to be "square by the lifts;" when perpendicular to the ship's length, they are "square by the braces;" but when they lie in a direction perpendicular to the plane of the keel, they are "square by the lifts and braces." The yards are said to be very square when they are of extraordinary length, and the same epithet is applied to their sails with respect to their breadth. Also, a figure composed of four equal sides and four right angles, is the square of geometry.

SQUARE-BUTTED. The yard-arms of small shipping so made that a sheave-hole can be cut through without weakening the yard.

SQUARE-FRAMES. In marine architecture, implies those frames which are square with the line of the keel, having no bevelling upon them.

SQUARE IN THE HEAD. Very bluff and broad in the fore-body.

SQUARE-KNOT. The same as *reef-knot.*

SQUARE MAINSAIL. *See* MAINSAIL.

SQUARE or SQUARING MARKS. Marks placed upon the lifts and braces.

SQUARE RIBBONS. A synonym of *horizontal lines*, or *horizontal ribbons*.

SQUARE-RIGGED. Ships having chiefly square sails; a term used in contradistinction to all vessels which do not use them. It is also applied to vessels with unusually long yards. The term is also familiarly used to denote a person's being full-dressed.

SQUARE-SAIL. The flying sail, set on the fore-yard of a schooner, or the spread-yard of a cutter or sloop.

SQUARE-SAIL BOOM. A boom hooked on to an eye-bolt in the fore-part of the foremast of a fore-and-aft vessel, to boom out the square-sail.

SQUARE-SAILS. Colloquially applied to the courses; but the term may be used for any four-cornered sail extended to a yard suspended by the middle.

SQUARE-STERNED. Implies a stern where the wing-transom is at right angles with the stern-post. (*See* PINK and ROUND STERN.)

SQUARE-STERNED AND BRITISH BUILT. A phrase to express the peculiar excellence of our first-class merchantmen.

SQUARE TIMBERS. Those timbers which stand square with, or perpendicular to, the keel.

SQUARE-TOPSAIL SLOOP. Sloops which carry standing yards.

SQUARE TUCK. The after-part of a ship's bottom, when terminated in the same direction up and down as the wing-transom.

SQUARE YARDS! The order to attend to the lifts and braces, for going before the wind.—*To square a yard.* In working ship, means to bring it in square by the marks on the braces. Figuratively, to settle accounts.

SQUARING THE DEAD-EYES. Bringing them to a line parallel to the sheer of the ship.

SQUARING THE RATLINES. Seeing that all are horizontal and ship-shape.

SQUATTER. The flutter of sea-birds along the water. Also, one who settles, without a title. The hybrid but expressive Americanism *absquatulate*, means to clear off; the reverse of to *squat*.

SQUAW. A woman of the North American Indians.

SQUEEGEE. An effective swabbing implement, having a plate of gutta-percha fitted at the end of a broom handle.

SQUETEE. The Yankee name of a labrus, very common in the waters of Long Island Sound and adjacent bays, but never found in rivers.

SQUID. An animal allied to the cuttle-fish, belonging to the class *Cephalopoda;* the calamary or *Loligo* of naturalists.

SQUILGEE, or SQUILLAGEE. A small swab made of untwisted yarns. Figuratively, a lazy mean fellow.

SQUIRM. A wriggling motion like that of an eel. Also, a twist in a rope.

STABBER. A pegging awl; the same as *pricker*.

STABILITY. A quality implying a ship's capacity to bear every motion of the sea.

STACK. A precipitous rock rising out of the sea, in northern hydrography.

STACKEN CLOUD. The same as *cumulus* (which see).

STADE. The Anglo-Saxon *stæde*, still in use. A station for ships. From stade is derived *staith* (which see).

STAFF. A light pole erected in different parts of a ship, whereon to hoist and display the colours; as, *the ensign-staff*, reared immediately over the stern; *the jack-staff*, fixed on the bowsprit-cap. In military affairs, the staff includes all officials not having direct and specific military command, as the adjutant-general, quartermaster-general, majors of brigade, aides-de-camp, &c. This term has been unaccountably pilfered by the admiralty lately from the army, as a prefix to a naval title.

STAFF-CAPTAIN. A designation conferred in 1863 upon masters of the fleet.

STAFF-COMMANDERS. A designation conferred in 1863 on masters of fifteen years' seniority.

STAFF-OFFICER. On the general staff of the army, or of a combined force. *See* STAFF.

STAG. A name given to a rock that should be watched for, as off the Lizard, Castlehaven, &c.

STAGE. Planks let over the ship's sides by ropes, whereon the people may stand when repairing, &c.—*A floating stage* is one which does not need the support of ropes.—*Stage-gangway* (*see* BROW).

STAGER. A resident or practised person. *See* OLD-STAGER.

STAGGERING UNDER IT. A ship's labouring under as much canvas as she can bear.

STAGNES. A statute term for pools of standing water.

STAITH [Anglo-Saxon *stæde*]. An embankment on the river bank whence to load vessels. Also, a large wooden wharf, with a timber frame of either shoots or drops, according to circumstances.

STAKES. A *weir* (which see) for taking fish, as black-stakes, &c.

STAL-BOAT. A peculiar fishing-boat, mentioned in statute 27 Eliz. c. 21.

STALKERS. Certain fishing-nets mentioned in old statutes.

STAMMAREEN. The after or helmsman's seat in a Shetland fishing-boat.

STAMP AND GO! The order to step out at the capstan, or with hawsers, topsail-haliards, &c., generally to the fife or fiddle.

STANCH. *See* STAUNCH.

STANCHIONS. Any fixed upright support. Also, those posts of wood or iron which, being placed pillar-wise, support the waist-trees and guns.

STANCHIONS OF THE NETTINGS. Slender bars of iron or wood, the lower ends of which are fixed in iron sockets at proper distances.

STAND, To. The movement by which a ship advances towards a certain object, or departs from it; as, "The enemy stands in shore;" "We saw three sail standing to the southward." "That ship has not a mast standing," implies that she has lost all her masts.

STANDARD. Formerly, in ship-building, was an inverted knee, placed upon the deck instead of beneath it, and having its vertical branch pointed upwards from that which lay horizontally.—*Royal standard.* A flag in which the imperial ensigns of England, Scotland, and Ireland are quartered. It is never hoisted on board a ship unless when visited by the royal family, and then it is displayed at the mast-head allotted to the rank; at the main only for the sovereign.

STANDARD-DEALS. Those planks of the pine or fir above 7 inches wide and 6 feet long: under that length they are known as *deal-ends.*

STANDARD-KNEES. *See* DECK STANDARD-KNEES.

STAND BY! The order to be prepared; to look out to fire when directed. —To *stand by* a rope, is to take hold of it; *the anchor,* prepare to let go.

STAND CLEAR OF THE CABLE! A precautionary order when about to let go the anchor, that nothing may obstruct it in running out of the hawse-holes. Also, a warning when idlers obstruct quarter-deck duty.

STANDEL. In our statutes, is a young store oak-tree.

STAND FROM UNDER! A notice given to those below to keep out of the way of anything being lowered down, or let fall from above.

STANDING BACKSTAYS. The rigging proper. (*See* BACKSTAYS.)

STANDING BEVELLING. The alteration made obtuse or outside a square, in hewing timber, as opposed to acute, or *under-bevelling,* which is within a square.

STANDING BOWSPRIT. One that is fixed permanently in its place, not the *running-in bowsprit* of a cutter.

STANDING-JIB. The jib, as distinguished from the other jibs.

STANDING-LIFTS. Ropes from the mast-heads to the ends of the upper yards, to keep them square and steady when the sail is not set.

STANDING ORDERS. Special regulations remaining constant for some particular branch of service.

STANDING PART OF A HOOK. That part which is attached to a block, chain, or anything which is to heave the hook up, with a weight hanging to it; the part opposite to the point.

STANDING PART OF A SHEET. That part which is secured to a ring at the ship's bow, quarter, side, &c.

STANDING PART OF A TACKLE OR ROPE. The part which is made fast to the mast, deck, or block, in contradistinction to that which is pulled upon, and is called the fall, or running part.

STANDING PULL. One with the face towards the tackle, being about 2 feet each pull.

STANDING RIGGING. That part which is made fast, and not hauled upon; being the shrouds, backstays, and stays for the support of the masts.

STANDING UP. A ship in good trim, and well attended to, is said *to stand well up to her canvas.*

STANDING WARRANTS. Those officers who remain with a ship in ordinary, or on the stocks, as the gunner, carpenter, boatswain, and cook, and till 1814 the purser.

STANDING WATER. Water where there is no current or tide.

STAND IN SHORE, To. To sail directly for the land.

STAND OF ARMS. A complete set for one man; now-a-days, simply a musket and bayonet. Also, an arm-stand holding the muskets and cutlasses on the quarter-deck—ornamental, and ready for salute or service.

STAND RIGHT UNDER! Jocularly, " Get out of the way."

STAND SQUARE, To. To stand or be at right angles relatively to some object.

STANGS. Poles put across a river. Also, eel-spears.

STANK. An old statute term for *staunch* (which see).

STAPLE. *Merchants of the staple* formerly meant those who exported the staple wares of the country.

STAPLE-KNEES, OR STAPLE-LODGING KNEES. The same as *deck standard-knees* (which see).

STAR, DOUBLE. *See* DOUBLE STAR.

STAR, TEMPORARY. *See* TEMPORARY STAR.

STAR, VARIABLE. *See* VARIABLE STAR.

STARBOARD. The opposite of *larboard* or *port;* the distinguishing term for the right side of a ship when looking forward [from the Anglo-Saxon *stéora-bórd*].

STARBOARD THE HELM! So place the helm that the rudder is brought on the port side of the stern-post. (*See* HARD-A-STARBOARD.)

STAR-BOLINS. The old familiar term for the men of the starboard watch, as larbolin was for the larboard or port watch.

STAR-FISHES. *See* SEA-STAR.

STAR-FORTS. Those traced in the form of a star, with alternate salient and re-entering angles. They are not in much favour, being expensive in construction, of small interior space, and having much dead space in their ditches.

STAR-GLINT. A meteorite.

STAR-PAGODA. A gold coin of the East Indies. In Madras its value is 7s. 6d.

STARS, FIXED. Those innumerable bodies bespangling the heavens from pole to pole, distinguishable from the planets by their apparent fixity; it is, however, certain that many of them move through space at a rate vastly greater than that of the earth in her orbit, though, from their enormous distance, we can with difficulty perceive it.

START. A long handle or tail; whence, by analogy, "start point." But sometimes applied by navigators to any point from which a departure is taken. Also, the expected place of a struck whale's rising, after having plunged or sounded.—*To start*, applied to liquids, is to empty; but if to any weight, as the anchor, &c., implies to move.—*To start bread.* To turn it out of bags or casks, and stow it in bulk.—*To start a butt-end.* When a plank has loosened or sprung at the butt-end, by the ship's labouring, or other cause.—*To start a tack or sheet.* To slack it off, as in tacking or manœuvring, "raise tacks and sheets."

STARTING. An irregular and arbitrary mode of punishment with canes or ropes' ends, long since illegal in the British navy.

STARTING-BOLT, or Drift-bolt. A bolt used to drive out another; it is usually a trifle smaller.

STASH IT THERE! An old order to cease or be quiet.

STATE-ROOM. A sleeping cabin, or small berth, detached from the main cabin of merchantmen or saloon of passenger vessels.

STATION. The allotted places of the duties of each person on board. In most merchantmen the cry of "Every man to his station, and the cook to the fore-sheet," is calling the hands and the idlers.

STATIONARIÆ. Those vessels of a Roman fleet ordered to remain at anchor.

STATIONARY POINTS. Those points in a planet's orbit in which, as viewed from the earth, it appears to have no motion amongst the stars.

STATION-BILL. A list containing the appointed posts of the crew when performing any evolution but action.

STATIONER. One who has had experience, or who has been some time on a particular station.

STATIONING A SHIP'S COMPANY. Arranging the crew for the ready execution of the evolutionary duties of a ship.

STATION-POINTER. A circular instrument furnished with one standard radius, and two movable. By laying off two observed angles right and left from a central object, and laying the instrument over the objects on a chart, the position of the observer is instantly fixed.

STATIONS FOR STAYS! Repair to your posts to tack ship.

STAUNCH. A flood-gate crossing a river to keep up a head of water, and, by producing a rush in dry weather, floating the lighters over the adjacent shallows.

STAVE, To. To break a hole in any vessel. Also, to drive in the head of a cask, as of spirits, to prevent the crew from misusing it in case of wreck.—*To stave off.* To boom off; to push anything off with a pole.

STAVES. Wood prepared for the component parts of a cask. In 1781, staves were ruled not to be a naval store, unless it were shown that the French at Brest were in some peculiar want of casks. Also, the wood of lances, formerly an object of great care, insomuch that Shakspeare makes Richard III. say :—

> "Look that my staves be sound, and not too heavy."

STAY. A large strong rope extending from the upper end of each mast towards the stem of the ship, as the shrouds are extended on each side. The object of both is to prevent the masts from springing, when the ship is pitching deep. Thus stays are fore and aft; those which are led down to the vessel's side are *back-stays.*—*The fore-stay* is that which reaches from the foremast-head towards the bowsprit end.—*The main-stay* is that which extends to the ship's stem.—*The mizen-stay* is that which is stretched to a collar on the main-mast, immediately above the quarter-deck.—*The fore-topmast stay* is that which comes to the end of the bow-sprit, a little beyond the fore-stay, on which the fore-topmast staysail runs on hanks.—*The main-topmast stay* is attached to the hounds of the fore-mast, or comes on deck.—*The mizen-topmast stay* is that which comes to the hounds of the main-mast. The top-gallant, royal, or any other masts, have each a stay, named after their respective masts.—*Spring-stay* is a kind of substitute nearly parallel to the principal stay, and intended to help the principal stay to support its mast.—*Stay of a steamer.* An iron bar between the two knees which secure the paddle-beams. (*See* FUNNEL-STAYS.)—*To stay.* To tack, to bring the ship's head up to the wind for going about; hence to *miss stays*, is to fail in the attempt to go about.— *In stays*, or *hove in stays*, is the situation of a vessel when she is staying, or in the act of going about; a vessel in bad trim, or lubberly handled, is sure to be *slack in stays*, and *refuses stays*, when she has to wear.

STAY APEEK. When the cable and fore-stay form a line. (*See* APEEK.)

STAY-BARS, OR STAY-RODS. Strong malleable iron bars for supporting the framings of the marine steam-engine.

STAYED FORWARD. This term is applied to masts when they incline forward out of the vertical line; the opposite of *rake* (which see.)

STAYSAIL. A triangular sail hoisted upon a stay.

STAYSAIL-NETTING. *See* BOWSPRIT-NETTING.

STAYSAIL-STAY. The stay on which a staysail is set.

STAY-TACKLES, FORE AND MAIN. Special movable purchases for hoisting in and out boats, anchors, &c. They plumb the fore and main hatchways, working in conjunction with fore and main yard tackles.

STEADY! The order given to the steersman, in a fair wind, to steer the ship on her course without deviating; to which he answers, *Steady it is, sir.*

STEADY-FAST. A hawser carried out to some fixed object to keep a vessel steady in a tide-way, or in preparation for making sail from a fast.

STEADY GALE. A fresh breeze pretty uniform in force and direction.

STEALING. The gaining of a rat-line or two in height while waiting on the lower part of the rigging for the order to go aloft. Also, a vessel is said *to steal ahead* when she moves with the lightest breath of air.

STEAM-CHEST. The reservoir for steam above the water of the boiler; sometimes termed *steam-chamber.*

STEAM-CRANE. A crane worked by means of a steam-engine.

STEAM-CYLINDER. *See* CYLINDER.

STEAM-FRIGATE. A large armed steamer commanded by a captain in the navy.

STEAM-HOIST. A machine in dockyards for driving piles, working pumps, &c.

STEAM NAVIGATION. The management of vessels propelled by steam-power.

STEAM-PACKET. A steamer employed in trading regularly between two places with goods and passengers.

STEAM-PIPE. *See* WASTE-STEAM PIPE.

STEAM-PORTS. Oblong passages leading from the nozzle-faces to the inside of the cylinder; by them the steam enters and returns, above and below the piston.

STEAM-RAM. A new order of war-vessel, fitted for running prow on against an enemy's ship, to stave her in by crushing.

STEAM SLOOP-OF-WAR. One commanded by a commander.

STEAM-TUG. A vessel fitted with a marine steam-engine, and expressly employed for towing ships.

STEAM-WINCH. A machine for hoisting out cargo or working a ship's pumps.

STEATÆ. Broad low vessels used by the ancient pirates.

STEELER, OR STEALER. The foremost and aftermost plank in a strake, which drops short of the stem or stern-post.

STEEP-TO. [Anglo-Saxon *stéap*.] Said of a bold shore, admitting of the largest vessels coming very close to the cliffs without touching the bottom. (*See* BOLD SHORE.)

STEEP-TUB. A large tub in which salt provisions are soaked previous to being cooked.

STEERAGE. The act of steering. (*See* NICE STEERAGE.) Also, that part of the ship next below the quarter-deck, immediately before the bulkhead of the great cabin in most ships of war. The portion of the 'tween-decks just before the gun-room bulkhead. In some ships the second-class passengers are called *steerage passengers*. The admiral's cabin on the middle deck of three-deckers has been called the *steerage*.

STEERAGE-WAY. When a vessel has sufficient motion in the water to admit of the helm being effective.

STEER HER COURSE, To. Going with the wind fair enough to lay her course.

STEERING [Anglo-Saxon *stéoran*]. The perfection of steering consists in a vigilant attention to the motion of the ship's head, so as to check every deviation from the line of her course in the first instant of its commencement, and in applying as little of the power of the helm as possible, for the action of the rudder checks a ship's speed.

STEERING-SAIL. An incorrect name for a studding-sail.

STEER LARGE, To. To go free, off the wind. Also, to steer loosely.

STEER SMALL, To. To steer well and within small compass, not dragging the tiller over from side to side.

STEERSMAN. The helmsman or timoneer; the latter from the French *timon*, helm.

STEEVING. Implies the bowsprit's angle from the horizon : formerly it stood at an angle of 70 to 80 degrees, and was indeed almost a bow mast or sprit. Also, the stowing of cotton, wool, or other cargo, in a merchantman's hold with a jack-screw.

STEM. The foremost piece uniting the bows of a ship; its lower end scarphs into the keel, and the bowsprit rests upon its upper end. The outside of the stem is usually marked with a scale of feet and inches, answering to a perpendicular from the keel, in order to ascertain the ship's draught of water forward.—*False stem.* When a ship's stem is too flat, so that she cannot keep a wind well, a false stem, or gripe, is fayed on before the right one, which enables her to hold a better wind.—*From stem to stern*, from one end of the ship to the other.—*To stem*, to make way against any obstacle. "She does not stem the tide," that is, she cannot make head against it for want of wind.

STEM-KNEE. In ship-building, the compass-timber which connects the keel with the stem. (*See* DEADWOOD-KNEE.)

STEMSON. An arching piece of compass-timber, worked within the apron to reinforce the scarph thereof, in the same manner as the apron supports that of the stem. The upper end is carried as high as the upper deck, the lower being scarphed on to the kelson.

STEP. A large clamp of timber fixed on the kelson, and fitted to receive the tenoned heel of a mast. The steps of the main and fore masts of every ship rest upon the kelson; that of the mizen-mast sometimes rests upon the lower-deck beams.—*To step a boat's mast.* To erect and secure it in its step in readiness for setting sail.

STEP OF THE CAPSTAN. A solid block of wood fixed between two of the ship's beams to receive the iron spindle and heel of the capstan.

STEP OUT, To. To move along simultaneously and cheerfully with a tackle-fall, &c.

STEPPES. The specific application is to the vast level plains of South-east and Asiatic Russia, resembling the Landes of France. (*See* LANDES.)

STEPPING. The sinking a rabbet in the dead-wood, wherein the heels of the timbers rest. (*See* BEARDING-LINE.)

STEPS OF THE SIDE. Pieces of quartering nailed to the sides amidships, from the wale upwards; for the people ascending or descending the ship.

STERE'S-MAN. A pilot or steerer, from the Anglo-Saxon *stéora.*

STERE-TRE. An archaic word for rudder.

STERN. The after-part of a ship, ending in the taffarel above and the counters below.—*By the stern.* The condition of a vessel which draws more water abaft than forward.

STERNAGE. The after-part of a ship, and therefore Shakspeare's term is simple enough for any but commentators. Henry V.'s fleet is sailing away:—

> "O, do but think,
> You stand upon the rivage, and behold
> A city on the inconstant billows dancing;
> For so appears this fleet majestical,
> Holding due course to Harfleur. Follow, follow!
> Grapple your minds to sternage of this navy."

STERN-ALL. A term amongst whalers, meaning to pull the boat stern foremost, to back off after having entered an iron (*harpoon*).

STERN-BOARD. This term is familiarly known to seamen as tacking by misadventure in stays; or purposely, as a seamanlike measure, to effect the object. Thus a ship in a narrow channel is allowed to fly up head to wind until her stem nearly touches a weather danger; the head-yards are then quickly braced abox, and the helm shifted. Thus she makes stern-way until all the sails are full, when she is again skilfully brought to the wind before touching the danger under her lee. Generally speaking, however, it refers to bad seamanship.

STERN-CHASERS. The guns which fire directly aft.

STERN-DAVITS. Pieces of iron or timber projecting from the stern, with sheaves or blocks at their outer ends, for hoisting boats up to.

STERN-FAST. A rope used to confine the stern of a vessel to a wharf, &c.

STERN-FRAME. That strong and ornamental union based on the stern-post, transom, and fashion-pieces.

STERN-KNEE. Synonymous with *stern-son* (which see).

STERN-LADDER. Made of ropes with wooden steps, for getting in and out of the boats astern.

STERNMOST. Implies anything in the rear, or farthest astern, as opposed to headmost.

STERN-PORTS. The ports made between the stern-timbers.

STERN-POST. The opposite to the *stem;* scarphed into the keel, and suspending the rudder. In steam-ships, where a screw is fitted, it works between this and an after stern-post which carries the rudder.

STERN-SHEETS. That part of a boat between the stern and the aft-most thwart, furnished with seats for passengers.

STERN-SON. A knee-piece of oak-timber, worked on the after dead-wood; the fore-end is scarphed into the kelson, and the after-side fayed into the throats of the transoms.

STERN-WALK. The old galleries formerly used to line-of-battle ships.

STERN-WAY. The movement by which a ship goes stern foremost. The opposite of *head-way.*

STEVEDORE, or STIVADORE. A stower; one employed in the hold in loading and unloading merchant vessels.

STEWARD. There are several persons under this appellation in most ships, according to their size, appointed to the charge of the sea-stores of the various grades. The paymaster's steward has most to do, having to serve the crew, and therefore has assistants, distinguished by the sobriquet of Jack-o'-the-dust, &c. In large passenger ships which do not carry a purser, part of his duties devolves upon the captain's steward. In smaller merchant ships the special duties of the steward are not heavy, so that he assists in the working of the ship, and in tacking; his station is, *ex officio,* the main-sheet.

STICHLING. A grown perch, thus described by old Palsgrave: "Stycke-lyng, a maner of fysshe."

STICKLEBACK. A very small fish, armed with sharp spines on its back.

STICKS. A familiar phrase for masts.

STIFF. Stable or steady; the opposite to *crank;* a quality by which a ship stands up to her canvas, and carries enough sail without heeling over too much.

STIFF BOTTOM. A clayey bottom.

STIFF BREEZE. One in which a ship may carry a press of sail, when a little more would endanger the spars.

STIFFENING ORDER. A custom-house warrant for making a provision in the shipping of goods, before the whole inward cargo is discharged, to prevent the vessel getting too light.

STILL WATER. Another name for *slack-tide;* it is also used for water under the lee of headlands, or where there is neither tide nor current.

STING-RAY. A fish, *Trygon pastinaca,* which wounds with a serrate bone, lying in a sheath on the upper side of its tail; the wound is painful, as all fish-wounds are, but not truly poisonous, and the smart is limited by superstition to the next tide.

STINK-BALLS. A pyrotechnical preparation of pitch, rosin, nitre, gunpowder, colophony, assafœtida, and other offensive and suffocating ingredients, formerly used for throwing on to an enemy's decks at close quarters, and still in use with Eastern pirates, in earthen jars or stink-pots.

STIPULATION. A process in the instance-court of the admiralty, which is conventional when it regards a vessel or cargo, but prætorian and judicial in proceedings against a person.

STIREMANNUS. The term in *Domesday Book* for the pilot of a ship or steersman.

STIRRUP. An iron or copper plate that turns upwards on each side of a ship's keel and dead-wood at the fore-foot, or at her skegg, and bolts through all: it is a strengthener, but not always necessary.

STIRRUPS. Ropes with eyes at their ends, through which the foot-ropes are rove, and by which they are supported; the ends are nailed to the yards, and steady the men when reefing or furling sails.

STIVER. A very small Dutch coin. "Not worth a stiver" is a colloquialism to express a person's poverty.

STOACH-WAY. The streamlet or channel which runs through the silt or sand at low-water in tidal ports; a term principally used on our southern shores.

STOAKED. The limber holes impeded or choked, so that the water cannot come to the pump-well.

STOCADO. A neat thrust in fencing.

STOCCADE. A defensive work, constructed of stout timber or trunks of trees securely planted together. Originally written *stockade.*

STOCKADE. Now spelled *stoccade.*

STOCK AND FLUKE. The whole of anything.

STOCK-FISH. Ling and haddock when sun-dried, without salt, were called stock-fish, and used in the navy, but are now discontinued, from being thought to promote the scurvy.

STOCK OF AN ANCHOR. A cross-beam of wood, or bar of iron, secured to the upper end of the shank at right angles with the flukes; by its means the anchor is canted with one fluke down, and made to hook the ground.—*Stock of a gun, musket, or pistol,* is the wooden part to which the barrel is fitted, for the convenience of handling and firing it. *Stock* is also applied to stores laid in for a voyage, as sea-stock, live-stock, &c. —*To stock to,* in stowing an anchor, is, by means of a tackle upon the upper end of the stock, to bowse it into a perpendicular direction, which tackle is hence denominated the stock-tackle.

STOCKS. A frame of blocks and shores whereon to build shipping. It has a gradual declivity towards the water.

STOER-MACKEREL. A name for the young tunny-fish.

STOITING. An east-country term for the jumping of fishes above the surface of the water.

STOKE, To. To frequent the galley in a man-of-war, or to trim fires.

STOKE-HOLE. A scuttle in the deck of a steamer to admit fuel for the engine. Also, the space for the men to stand in, to feed and trim the fires.

STOKER, or FIREMAN. The man who attends to feed and trim the fires for the boilers in a steam-vessel.

STOMACH-PIECE. *See* APRON.

STONACRE. A sloop-rigged boat employed to carry stone on the Severn.

STONE. The old term for a gun-flint.

STONE-BOW. A cross-bow for shooting stones.

STOOL. A minor channel abaft the main channels, for the dead-eyes of the backstays. (*See* BACKSTAY-STOOLS.)

STOOLS. Chocks introduced under the lowest transoms of a ship's stern-frame, to which the lower ends of the fashion-pieces are fastened; they form the securities of the quarter-galleries. Also, the thick pieces of plank, fayed together edgeways, and bolted to the sides of the ship for backstays. Also, the ornamental block for the poop-lantern to stand upon.

STOP. A small projection on the outside of the cheeks of a lower mast, at the upper parts of the hounds. Also, the word given by him who holds the glass in heaving the log, to check the line and determine how fast she is going.—*To stop.* To tie up with small stuff; as a sail is *stopped* when sending it aloft to prevent the wind from blowing it away; a flag is *stopped* to make a wheft, &c.

STOP HER! An order to check the cable in being payed out. Also, a self-explanatory phrase to direct the engineer of a steamer to stop the action of the engines.

STOPPAGE in TRANSITU. A valuable privilege under which an unpaid consigner or broker may stop or countermand his goods upon their passage to the consignee on the insolvency of the vendee.

STOPPER of the ANCHOR. A strong rope attached to the cat-head, which, passing through the anchor-ring, is afterwards fastened to a timber-head, thereby securing the anchor on the bow.

STOPPER of the CABLE. Commonly called a deck-stopper. A piece of rope having a large knot at one end, and hooked or lashed to a ring-bolt in the deck by the other; it is attached to the cable by a laniard, which is passed securely round both, by several turns passed behind the knot, or round the neck of the stopper, by which means the cable is restrained from running out of the ship when she rides, and is an additional security to the bitted cable.—*Dog-stopper.* A strong rope clenched round the mainmast, and used on particular occasions to relieve and assist the preceding when the ship rides in a heavy sea, or otherwise veering with a strain on the cable.—*Wing-stoppers.* Similar pieces of rope clenched round one of the beams near the ship's side, and serving the same purpose as the preceding.—*Rigging-stoppers* have a knot and a laniard at each end; they are used when the shrouds, stays, or backstays are stranded in action, or in a gale; they are then lashed above and below, in the same manner as those of the cables, to the wounded parts of the shroud, &c., which are thereby strengthened, so as to be fit for service. Other rigging-stoppers have dead-eyes and tails, so that by securing one dead-eye above and the other below the injury, they can be set up by their laniard, and brought to an even strain with the other shrouds. Stoppers are also pieces of rope used to prevent the running-rigging from coming up whilst being belayed. Sometimes they have a knot at one end, and a hook at the other, for various purposes about the decks.

STOPPERING. The act of checking or holding fast any rope or cable by means of a stopper.

STOPPER-KNOT. Single and double wall, without crowning, and the ends stopped together.

STOP THE VENT, To. To close it hermetically by pressing the thumb to it.

STOP-WATER. Anything tending to impede the sailing of a ship, by towing overboard. Also, a name for particular tree-nails.

STORE-KEEPER. An officer in the royal dockyards, invested with the general charge of naval stores, as the sails, anchors, cordage, &c.

STORES. A general term for the arms, clothing, ropes, sails, provisions, and other outfit, with which a ship is supplied.

STORE-SHIP. A government vessel appropriated for carrying munitions and stores.

STORM, To. To take by vigorous assault, in spite of the resistance of the defenders.

STORM-BREEDERS. Heavy cumulo-stratus clouds.

STORM-DRUM. A canvas cylinder 3 feet in length, expanded at each end by a strong wooden hoop 3 feet in diameter. Fitzroy's is painted black, and presents, when suspended, the appearance of a black square of 3 feet, from all points of view.

STORM-FINCH. The petrel, or Mother Cary's chicken.

STORM-JIB. In cutters, the fifth or sixth size: the inner jib of square-rigged ships.

STORM-KITE. A contrivance for sending a hawser from a stranded vessel to the shore.

STORMS [from the Anglo-Saxon *steorm*]. Tempests, or *gales of wind* in nautic language, are of various kinds, and will be found under their respective designations. But that is a storm which reduces a ship to her storm stay-sails, or to her bare poles.

STORM-SAIL. A sail made of stout No. 1 canvas, of reduced dimensions, for use in a gale.

STORM-SIGNAL. The hoisting of a danger-flag. Also, Fitzroy's drum and cone, which show the direction of the expected gale.

STORM-TRYSAIL. A fore-and-aft sail, hoisted by a gaff, but having no boom at its foot, and only used in foul weather.

STORM-WARNING. *See* FORECAST.

STORM-WAVE. A wave which tumbles home without being accompanied by wind. Sometimes the result of a gale elsewhere.

STORMY PETREL. A small dark coloured sea-bird, *Procellaria pelagica.*

STOVE. Broken in; thus, when violent damage is done to the upper part of a ship's hull, she is said to be *stove;* when on any portion of her bottom, she is *bilged.*—*A stove*, is a kind of kiln for warping timber in.—*Hanging stoves* are also used on board ship for airing the 'tween decks.

STOWAGE. An important art more practised than understood, for the stower seldom consults the specialities of the vessel's construction; it is the general disposition of the ballast, cargo, &c., contained in a ship's hold, with regard to their shape, size, or solidity, agreeably to the form of the vessel, and its probable centre of gravity. A badly stowed vessel cannot be properly handled, and is indeed dangerous to the lives of all on board. Owners and masters are legally liable to the losses by bad stowage or deficient dunnage. (*See* WET.)

STOWAGE GOODS. Those which usually pay freight according to bulk.

STOWED IN BULK. *See* BULK.

STOWING HAMMOCKS. Placing them in a neat and symmetrical order in the hammock-netting.

STOWING-STRAKE. *See* STEELER.

STRAGGLING-MONEY. If a man be absent from his duty without leave, but not absent long enough to be logged as *run*, and is brought on board, a deduction is to be made from his wages at the discretion of the captain; not, however, to exceed the sum of £1.

STRAIGHT OF BREADTH. The space before and abaft the dead-flat, in which the ship is of the same uniform breadth as at the dead-flat.

STRAIN-BANDS. Bands of canvas sustaining the strain on the belly of the sails, and reinforced by the linings, &c.

STRAIT, OR STRAIGHT. A passage connecting one part of a sea with another; as, the Straits of Gibraltar, of Sunda, of Dover, &c. This word is often written in the plural, but without competent reason.

STRAIT GULF. An arm of the sea running into the land through a narrow entrance channel, as the Gulf of Venice. The Mediterranean itself is but a vast strait gulf.

STRAKE. One breadth of plank in a ship, either within or without board, wrought from the stem to the stern-post.—*Garboard-strake.* The lowest range of planks, faying into the keel-rabbets.—*Wash-strake* guards spray.

STRAND. A number of rope-yarns twisted together; one of the twists or divisions of which a rope is composed. The part which passes through to form the eye of a splice. Also, a sea-margin; the portion alternately left and covered by tides. Synonymous with *beach.* It is not altered from the original Anglo-Saxon.

STRANDED. A rope is stranded when one of its strands is broken by chafing, or by a strain. A vessel is stranded when driven on shore, in which case the justices of the peace may call in assistance. The term "stranded on the beach," is not so incorrect as has been asserted; and comes under the usual exception in charter-parties and bills of lading, of "all and every dangers of the seas, rivers, and navigation of whatsoever nature or kind;" and in all policies of insurance it falls under the general words of "all other perils, losses, or misfortunes," against the risk of which the insurance is made.

STRANGE SAIL. A vessel heaving in sight, of which the particulars are unknown.

STRAPS OF THE RUDDER. *See* PINTLE.

STRATAGEM. A plan devised to throw dust into the eyes of an enemy, in order to deceive him.

STRATEGY. The science of the naval and military combinations which compel movements and battles, or the contrary, but not including the operations of actual battle, which belong to *tactics.*

STRATUS. A low cloud which forms a horizontal line. The higher cloud of the same shape is called *cirro-stratus.*

STRAW! A word of command, now obsolete, formerly given to dismiss soldiers who were to remain in readiness to fall in again at a moment's notice.

STRAY LINE OF THE LOG. About 10 or 12 fathoms of line left unmarked next the log-ship, in order that it may get out of the eddy of the ship's wake before the measuring begins, or the glass is turned.

STRAY-MARK. The mark at the junction of the stray and log lines.

STREAM. Anglo-Saxon for *flowing water*, meaning especially the middle or most rapid part of a tide or current.

STREAM-ANCHOR. A smaller one by two-thirds than the bowers, and larger than the kedges, used to ride steady, or moor with occasionally. In certain cases it is used for warping.

STREAM-CABLE. A hawser smaller than the lower cables, and used with the stream-anchor to moor the ship in a sheltered river or haven; it is now more generally a small chain.

STREAMER. Formerly described thus:—" A streamer shall stand in the toppe of a shippe, or in the forecastle, and therein be putt no armes, but a man's conceit or device, and may be of the length of 20, 30, 40, or 60 yardes."

STREAM-ICE. A collection of pieces of drift or bay ice, joining each other in a ridge following in the line of current. (*See* SEA-STREAM.)

STREAM-LAKE. One which communicates with the sea by means of a river.

STREAM THE BUOY, To. To let the buoy fall from the after-part of the ship's side into the water, preparatory to letting go the anchor, that it may not foul the buoy-rope as it sinks to the bottom.

STREMES. An old English word for "the rays of the sun."

STRENGTH. In naval architecture, means giving the various pieces of a ship their proper figures, so that by their combination and disposition they may be united into a firm and compact frame. In regimental affairs it implies merely the number of men actually serving.

STRENGTH OF THE TIDE. Where it runs strongest, which in serpentine courses will be found in the hollow curves.

STRESS. Hard pressure by weather or other causes. Stress of weather often compels a ship to put back to the port whence she sailed.

STRETCH. A word frequently used instead of tack; as, "We shall make a good stretch."—*To stretch.* To sail by the wind under a crowd of canvas.

STRETCH ALONG A BRACE, To. To lay it along the decks in readiness for the men to lay hold of; called *manning it.*

STRETCHER. *See* SHEER-POLE.

STRETCHERS. Narrow pieces of wood placed athwart the bottom of a boat, for the rowers to place their feet against, that they may communicate greater effort to their oars. Also, cross-pieces placed between a boat's sides to keep them apart when hoisted up and griped. Colloquially, a *stretcher* means a lie exaggerated to absurdity.

STRETCH OUT! In rowing, is the order to pull strong; to bend forward to the utmost.

STRICTLAND. An archaic term for an isthmus.

STRIKE, To. A ship strikes when she in any way touches the bottom. Also, to lower anything, as the ensign or topsail in saluting, or as the yards, topgallant-masts, and topmasts in a gale. It is also particularly used to express the lowering of the colours in token of surrender to a victorious enemy.

STRIKE DOWN! The order to lower casks, &c., into the hold.

STRIKERS. Men furnished with harpoons or grains to attack fish; hence the term *dolphin-striker* (which see), where these men place themselves.

STRIKE SOUNDINGS, To. To gain bottom, or the first soundings, by the deep-sea lead, on coming in from sea.

STRING [Anglo-Saxon *stræng*]. In ship-building, a strake within side, constituting the highest range of planks in a ship's ceiling, and it answers to the sheer-strake outside, to the scarphs of which it gives strength.

STRINGERS. A name sometimes applied to *shelf-pieces* (which see). Also, heavy timber similarly carried round a ship to fortify her for special heavy service, as whaling, &c.

STRIPPED TO THE GIRT-LINE. All the standing-rigging and furniture having been cleared off the masts in the course of dismantling.

STRIPPING. An inconvenient fault of many lead-coated projectiles—the throwing off portions of their coating on discharge from the gun.

STRIP THE MASTS, To. To clear the masts of their rigging.

STROKE. A pull or single sweep of the oars in rowing; hence the order, "Row a long stroke," which is intended to move the boat forward more steadily.

STROKE-OAR. The aftermost oar in a boat, from which the others take their time.

STROKE OF THE SEA. The shock occasioned to a vessel by a heavy sea striking her.

STROKE-SIDE OF A BOAT. That in which the after starboard rowlock is placed, or where the after oar is rowed if single-banked.

STROKESMAN. The man who rows the aftmost oar in a boat.

STROM. An archaism of storm or tempest.

STROMBOLO. Bits of ampelite or cannel-coal found on our southern coasts, charged with bitumen, sulphur, and salt. The name is referred to the Island of Stromboli, but the Brighton people insist that it is from the Flemish *strom-bollen*, meaning stream or tide balls.

STRONG-BACK. The same with *Samson's post* (which see). Also, an adaptation of a strong piece of wood over the windlass, to lift the turns of a chain-cable clear of it.

STRONG BREEZE. That which reduces a ship to double-reefed topsails, jib, and spanker.

STRONG GALE. That strength of wind under which close-reefed topsails and storm-staysails are usually carried when close-hauled.

STROP, OR STRAP. A piece of rope, spliced generally into a circular wreath, and used to surround the body of a block, so that the latter may be hung to any particular situation about the masts, yards, or rigging. Strops are also used occasionally to fasten upon any large rope for the purpose of hooking a tackle to the eye or double part of the strop, in order to extend or pull with redoubled effort upon the same rope; as in setting up the rigging, where one hook of the tackle is fixed in a strop applied to the particular shroud, and the other to its laniard.

STROP-BOUND BLOCK. A single block used in the clue of square-sails for the clue-lines to lead through; it has a shoulder left on each side to prevent the strop from chafing.—*Iron-strop*, a hoop of iron, in lieu of rope, round the shell of a block.

STRUCK BY A SEA. Said of a ship when a high rolling wave breaks on board of her.

STRUT. A stanchion or sustaining prop to the lower beams.

STUBB, OR DOGG. The lower part of a rainbow visible towards the horizon, and betokening squally weather: it is fainter than the wind-gall. On the banks of Newfoundland they are considered precursors of clearer wearer, and termed fog-dogs.

STUD, OR BAR. A small piece of cast-iron introduced across the middle of each link of the larger chain-cables, where, acting as a strengthener, it prevents collapse, and keeps the links endways to each other.

STUDDING-SAIL BOOM. A spar rigged out for the purpose of setting a studding-sail, and taking its name from the sail it belongs to.

STUDDING-SAILS. Fine-weather sails set outside the square-sails; the term "scudding-sails" was formerly used.—*Topmast and top-gallant studding-sails.* Those which are set outside the top-sails and topgallant-sails. They have yards at the head, and are spread at the foot by booms, which slide out on the extremities of the lower and topsail yards, and their heads or yards are hoisted up to the topsail and top-gallant yard-arms.

STUDDING-SAIL YARD. The spar to which the head of the studding-sail is extended.

STUFF. A *coat of stuff*, a term used for any composition laid on to ships' spars, bottom, &c. Also, square timber of different thicknesses.

STUFFING-BOX. A contrivance on the top of a steam cylinder-cover, packed with hemp, and kept well soaked with tallow, to prevent steam from passing through while the piston-rod is working.

STUMP. A derogatory but well-known name in navigating our eastern coasts for the beautiful tower of Boston church. (*See* SNAG.)

STUMP TOPGALLANT-MASTS. Those without a royal pole.

STUN-SAILS. A corruption of *studding-sails* (which see).

STURGEON. *Acipenser sturio*, a large fish; it has a cartilaginous skeleton, with a small circular and tubular mouth. It is found in the European seas and larger rivers. The roes are made into *caviare*, and the sounds and muscular parts into isinglass. It is a royal fish in England.

STURRE-MANNE. An old name for a sea-captain.

SUBALTERNS. All commissioned army officers ranking below captains.

SUB-LIEUTENANT. A rank lately reproduced, to which a midshipman is entitled on passing for lieutenant; formerly styled mate.

SUBMARINE BANK. An extensive sandy plateau with deep water over it.

SUBMARINE TELEGRAPH. Consists of a steel wire-rope, containing a heart of gutta-percha and other soft materials, in which are inclosed the copper wires through which the communication by electricity is conveyed. Rapid progress has been made in the art of making and handling this rope, as is proved by the existence of two cables between Ireland and America, one of which was recovered from the deep sea by creeping.

SUBMARINE THERMOMETER. An instrument for trying the temperature of the sea at different depths. It consists of a hollow weighted cylinder in which a Six's thermometer is placed; the cylinder being provided with a valve at each end, opening upwards, so that as it sinks the valves open, allowing a free course of water through the cylinder: when it reaches the required depth the line is checked and the valves close; it is then hauled gently in, and the thermometer reaches the surface surrounded by water of the required depth, indicating its temperature.

SUBSIDY. A stipulated sum of money paid by one ruler to another, in pursuance of a treaty of alliance for offensive and defensive war. Also, a sum allowed for the conveyance of mails.

SUBSISTENCE. The amount to be issued to troops as daily pay, after making the regulated deductions for rations, necessaries, &c.

SUCCADES. Sweetmeats entered at the custom-house; formerly a large part of the cargo of Spanish West Indiamen.

SUCCOUR. An enterprise undertaken to relieve a place besieged or blockaded, by either forcing the enemy from before it, or throwing in supplies.

SUCKING. The action of the pump when the well is nearly dry, or at least so low at the pump-foot as to admit air.

SUCK-STONE. An archaic name for the remora.

SUCK THE MONKEY, To. To rob the grog-can. (*See* MONKEY.)

SUCTION. The rising of a fluid by the pressure of the atmosphere into a space where a vacuum has been created.

SUFFERANCE. A permission on the custom-house *transire* (which see.)

SUFFERANCE WHARF. *See* WHARF.

SUFFOLK BANG. A very poor and hard kind of cheese, which was indignantly refused in our North Sea fleet. It was, as farmer's boy Bloomfield admitted, "too hard to bite."

SUGAR-LOAF. A term applied to conical hills along a sea-coast.

SUGAR-LOAF SEA. High turbulent waves with little wind.

SUGG, To. To move or rock heavily on a bank or reef.

SUIT OF SAILS. The whole of the sails required to be bent for a vessel.

SULLAGE. The deposition of mud and silt by water.

SULLIT. A broad Dutch fishing-boat.

SULPHUR. A mineral which forms a principal ingredient in the manufacture of gunpowder, and greatly increases the rapidity of its combustion.

SUMMER-BLINK. A transient gleam of sunshine in bad weather.

SUMMER COUTS. A northern name for the aurora borealis.

SUMMER SOLSTICE. *See* CANCER.

SUMP. A bog or swamp. Also, a patent fuse used in mining.

SUMPIT. An arrow blown from the sumpitan, in Borneo. The sumpitan is about 7 feet long; the arrow has been driven with some force at 130 yards. Some suppose it to be poisoned.

SUN. The central body of our planetary system, and the source of light and heat; it is 850,000 miles in diameter.—*With the sun, i.e.* from left to right.—*Against the sun,* from right to left.

SUN AND MOON IN DISTANCE. When the angle between those bodies admits of measurement for lunars (about 130°).

SUNDAY. Ought to be a day of rest at sea as well as on shore, when religious services might generally be performed. Though called the negro's holiday, it often brings but little cessation from work in some merchantmen; they sail on a Sunday, not because of exigency, but because it is otherwise a leisure day, and thereby gained to the owners.

SUN-FISH. The *Orthagoriscus mola*, a whimsical-looking creature, like the head of a large fish severed from its body. Also, a name in the south for the basking shark, from its habit of lying in the sunshine.

SUNKEN ROCK. That which lies beneath the surface of the sea, and is dangerous to navigation.

SUNK LAND. Shallows and swamps.

SUN-STAR. The *Solaster paposa*, one of the largest and handsomest of our radiated star-fishes.

SUPERANNUATED. Applied to such as have permission to retire from the service on a stated pension, on account of age or infirmity.

SUPER-CARGO. A person charged with the accounts and disposal of the cargo, and all other commercial affairs in the merchant-ship in which he sails.

SUPER-HEATED. Said of steam, the heat of which has been raised after being generated.

SUPER-HEATER. A contrivance for increasing the temperature of the steam to the extent that it would lose on its way from the boiler, until exhausted from the cylinder.

SUPERIOR CONJUNCTION. When an inferior planet is situated in the same longitude as the sun, and has that luminary between it and the earth, it is said to be in superior conjunction.

SUPERIOR PLANETS. Those which revolve about the sun as a centre, outside the earth's orbit; the opposite of *inferior.*

SUPERIOR SLOPE. The inclined upper surface of a parapet.

SUPERNATANT PART OF A SHIP. That part which, when afloat, is above the water. This was formerly expressed by the name *dead-work.*

SUPERNUMERARIES. Men over and above the established complement of a ship, who are entered on a separate list in the ship's books for victuals and wages.

SUPPLEMENT OF LONGITUDE. The term usually applied to its complement, or what it wants of 180°.

SUPPORT A FRIEND, To. To make every exertion to assist a vessel in distress, from whatever cause. Neglect of this incurs punishment.

SUPPORTERS. Circular knee-timbers placed under the cat-heads for their support and security.

SURA. The drink otherwise called *toddy* (which see).

SURDINY. An old name for the fish *sardine.*

SURE, or SHORE. *See* SHORE.

SURES. Peculiar southerly winds which blow on the coasts of Chili, Peru, and Mexico, accompanied by a fog or vapour, called *sures pardos.*

SURF. The swell and foam of the sea, which breaks upon the shore, or any rock lying near the surface. The most violent surfs are those which break upon a flat shore, as on the Coromandel and African coasts.

SURFACE CURRENT. A current which does not extend more than 8 or 10 feet below the surface. Also, fresh water running over salt at the mouths of great rivers.

SURF-BOAT. A peculiar kind of flat-bottomed boat, varying according to local exigencies, for landing men, or goods, in surf. (*See* MASSOOLAH-BOAT.)

SURGE. A large swelling wave. Also, the tapered part of the whelps between the chocks of the capstan, upon which the messenger is readily surged.—*To surge*, is to slacken up suddenly a portion of a rope where it renders round a pin, windlass, or capstan; as, "Surge the messenger." A ship is said *to surge* on a reef when she rises and falls with the heave of the sea, so as to strike heavily.

SURGE HO! The notice given when a rope or cable is to be surged.

SURGEON. A competent medical officer, appointed to attend the sick and wounded on board a ship of war, for which purpose he has, according to the rate of the ship, from one to two assistants, once called surgeon's mates, but latterly *assistant-surgeons* (which see).

SURGE THE CAPSTAN, To. To slacken the rope heaved round upon its barrel, to prevent its parts from riding or getting foul.

SURINGER. An archaism for surgeon.

SURMARKS. In ship-building, the points on the moulds where the bevellings are to be applied to the timbers.

SURROGATES. Those substituted or appointed in the room of others; as naval captains formerly acting for judges in Newfoundland.

SURVEY. An inspection or examination made by several practical officers into the condition of any stores belonging to a ship. Also, those important astronomical observations, soundings, and other data, collected by officers who are employed in constructing charts and plans of seas, shoals, rocks, harbours, &c.

SURVEYING VESSELS. Those equipped for examining coasts, dangers, &c.; their utility is unquestionable. Some of the smaller vessels of war on every station might be profitably employed in thus examining all reported dangers.

SURVEYORS AT LLOYD'S. *See* LLOYD'S SURVEYORS.

SURVEYORS OF THE NAVY. Two officers who formerly sat at the navy board, being invested with the charge of building and repairing the royal ships at the different dockyards of the kingdom; for which they were trained to the theory and practice of ship-building.

SUSPENSION OF ARMS. A short truce agreed upon by contending forces, for a special object of importance.

SUTILES. Ancient cobles made of strong staves sewed together, and covered with leather or skins.

SUTLER. A victualler who follows the camp to sell provisions to the troops. In garrisons and garrison-towns there are also sutlers who provide victuals of every kind; but Drayton's sutlers must have been very petty traders, as, when at Agincourt, Isambert's "rascals" were noted—

> "For setting on those with the luggage left,
> A few poor sutlers with the campe that went,
> They basely fell to pillage and to theft."

SWAB. A sort of long mop, formed of rope-yarns of old junk, used for cleaning and drying the decks and cabins of a ship. Also, a sobriquet for a sot. Also, for an epaulette.—*Hand-swab*. A small swab for wiping dry the stern-sheets of a boat, washing plates and dishes, &c.

SWABBER. Formerly a petty officer on board ships of war, whose employment was to see that the decks were kept clean. Also, a man formerly appointed to use the swabs in drying up the decks. He was sometimes called ship's sweeper; more commonly captain of swabbers.

SWAB-ROPE. A line bent to the eye of a swab for dipping it overboard in washing it.

SWAB-WASHER. The principal swab-washer, or captain of the head, in large ships.

SWAB-WRINGERS. People appointed to wash the swabs and wring them out, ready for use.

SWAD, OR SWADKIN. A newly raised soldier. Also, a fish-basket.

SWADDIE. A discharged soldier.

SWAGG, To. To sink down by its own weight; to move heavily or bend. Synonymous with *sagg*. Also, the bellying of a heavy rope.

SWAKE. A provincial term for a pump-handle.

SWALLOW. The score of a block.

SWALLOW'S TAIL. In fortification, an old form of outwork, having its front broken into a re-entering angle, and its two long flanks converging towards the rear.

SWALLOW-TAILS. The points of a burgee. Also, the tails of a coat.

SWAMP. A tract of land or bog on which, from its impermeable bottom, the collected fresh water remains stagnant.

SWAPE. A wooden support for a small light. Also, a pump-handle; a lever. Also, a long oar used in working a coal-keel in the north.

SWART-BACK. The *Larus marinus*, or great black and white gull.

SWARTS. A name formerly applied by voyagers to Indians and negroes.

SWASH. A sudden surge of the sea. Also, a shoal in a tide-way or mouth of a river, over which the water flows, and the tide ripples in ebbing or flowing.

SWASHWAY. A channel across a bank, or among shoals, as the noted instance between the Goodwin Sands.

SWATHE. The entire length of a sea-wave.

SWAY, To, OR SWAY AWAY. To hoist simultaneously; particularly applied to the lower yards and topmasts, and topgallant-masts and yards.—*To sway away on all top-ropes*. To go great lengths (colloquially).

SWAY UP, To. To apply a strain on a mast-rope in order to lift the spar upwards, so that the fid may be taken out, previous to lowering the mast. Or sway yards aloft ready for crossing.

SWEARING. A vulgar and most irrational vice, which happily is fast going out. Habitual swearing was usually typical of a bad officer. It may have originated in the custom too often demanded by law, of solemn asseverations on frivolous subjects.

SWEATING THE PURSER. Wasting his stores. Burning his candles, &c.

SWEEP. The trending or inclination of a coast to a crescent. Also, that part of the mould of a ship, where she begins to compass in the rungheads. Also, a large kind of oar.—*To sweep a coast.* To sail along at a reasonable distance with a vigilant inspection.

SWEEPING. The act of dragging the bight or loose part of a small rope along the ground, in a harbour or roadstead, in order to recover a sunk anchor or wreck. The two ends of the rope are fastened to two boats, a weight being suspended to the middle, to sink it to the ground, so that, as the boats row ahead, it may drag along the bottom. Also, a term used for rapidly scrutinizing a certain portion of the heavens in quest of planets, comets, &c.

SWEEP OF THE TILLER. A semi-circular frame on which the tiller traverses in large ships; it is fixed under the beams near the fore-end of the tiller, which it supports.

SWEEP-PIECE. A block at the bottom of the port-sill for receiving the chock of the gun-carriage, and to aid in training the gun.

SWEEPS. Large oars used on board ships of war in a calm, either to assist the rudder in turning them round, or to propel them ahead when chasing in light winds. Brigs of 386 tons have been swept at 3 knots or more.

SWEETENING COCK. A wholesome contrivance for preventing fetid effluvia in ships' holds, by inserting a pipe through the ship's side, with a cock at its inner end, for admitting water to neutralize the accumulated bilge-water, as also to supply the wash-deck pump.

SWELCHIE. A rapid current formed by the tide of the Pentland Firth against the Isle of Stroma. Also, a seal in those parts.

SWELL. A rolling wave which seldom breaks unless it meets resistance, generally denoting a continuous heaving, which remains for some time after the wind which caused it has subsided. Also, the gradual thickening of the muzzle of a gun, hounds of a mast, &c.

SWIFT. When the lower rigging becomes slack at sea, single blocks are placed on each shroud about 8 feet above the deck, a hawser rove through them, and the rigging swifted in, to bring a fair strain. The bars of the capstan are swifted, by passing a rope-swifter over all their ends, and bowsing it well taut. The rigging is also swifted down preparatory to replacing the ratlines truly horizontal after setting up.

SWIFTER. A strong rope, sometimes encircling a boat, about 9 inches below her gunwale, both to strengthen her and protect her in cases of collision. (*See* FENDER.)

SWIFTERS. A pair of shrouds, fixed on the starboard and port sides of the lower mast, above the pendants, and before all the other shrouds: they are never confined to the cat-harpings.

SWIFTING A SHIP. Either bringing her aground or upon a careen; also passing cables round her bottom and upperworks, to help to keep her from straining—the "undergirding" mentioned by St. Paul in his shipwreck.

SWIG OFF, To. To pull at the bight of a rope by jerks, having its lower end fast; or to gain on a rope by jumping a man's weight down, instead of hauling regularly.

SWILKER, To. A provincialism for splashing about.

SWILL. A wicker fish-basket. The air-bladder of a fish.—*To swill.* To drink greedily.

SWIM, To [from the Anglo-Saxon *swymm*]. To move along the surface of the water by means of the simultaneous movement of the hands and feet. With the Romans this useful art was an essential part of education.

SWIMS. The flat extremities of east-country barges.

SWINE-FISH. A northern name of the wolf-fish, *Anarhichas lupus.*

SWINE'S FEATHER. The spike or tuck on the top of a musket-rest [corrupted from *sweyn*, a boar's bristle].

SWING, To. A ship is said to swing to the wind or tide, when they change their direction while she is lying at anchor.—*To swing ship for local attraction and adjustment of compasses.* This is done by taking the bearings of a very distant object at each point of the compass to which her head is brought; also, by using a theodolite on shore, and taking its bearing from the ship, and the observer's head from the theodolite.

SWINGING-BOOM. The spar which stretches the foot of a lower studding-sail; in large ships they have goose-necks in one end which hook to the foremost part of the fore-chains to iron strops fitted for the purpose. In port they are hooked to bolts at the bends, which, by bringing them lower down, enables the boats to ride easier by them as guest-warp booms.

SWIPES. The weak beer supplied to ships on the home station. A swipe is an implement for drawing water for a brewery, the name of which has thus been transferred to the beer.

SWIRL. An eddying blast of wind; a whirling wavy motion. Also, a knot in timber.

SWISH. An old term for the light driving spray of the sea.

SWIVEL. A pivot working freely round in a socket. They are fitted in boats' bows, ships' tops and bulwarks, &c., for bearing small cannon of ½ lb. or 1 lb. calibre, which are worked by hand, and called swivels. Also, a strong link of iron used in mooring chains, &c., which permits the bridles to be turned repeatedly round, as occasion requires. Also, a swivel-link in chain-cables, made so as to turn upon an axis, and keep the turns out of the chain.

SWONA WELLS. Whirlpools much dreaded by the sailors of the Pentland Firth. They seem to be caused by the rapidity of the tide and the position of Swona, which exactly crosses the stream.

SWORD-FISH. A large fish of the family *Scomberidœ*, remarkable for the prolongation of the nose into a straight, pointed, sword-like weapon. The European species, common in the Mediterranean, is the *Xiphias gladius* of naturalists.

SWORD-MAT. A mat made with shoulders to protect the laniards of the lower rigging, boats' gripes, &c., and worked by a piece of wood somewhat resembling a sword in shape, to drive home the roving threads.

SYKE [from the Anglo-Saxon *sych*]. A streamlet of water that flows in winter and dries up in summer.

SYMPIESOMETER, OR OIL-BAROMETER. A convenient portable instrument for measuring the weight of the atmosphere by the compression of a gaseous column; capital for small cabins.

SYNODICAL MONTH. The period in which the moon goes through every variety of phase, as from one conjunction to another.

SYNODICAL PERIOD OR REVOLUTION. If the interval of periodic time of a planet, or comet, be taken in reference to its passages through either of the nodes, its circuit is called synodical.

SYPHERED. One edge of a plank overlapping that of another, so that both planks shall make a plane surface with their bevelled edges, though not a flat or square joint.

SYSTEM. The method of disposing the correlative parts of a fortification, proposed variously by many eminent engineers.

SYSTEM OF THE UNIVERSE. *See* COPERNICAN SYSTEM.

SYZIGEE. Either conjunction or opposition, in reference to the orbit of the moon.

T.

TAB. The arming of an archer's gauntlet or glove.

TABERIN. A species of shark greatly dreaded by the pearl-fishers of Ceylon.

TABERNACLE. A strong trunk on the deck of river barges, forming a kind of hinge to enable them to lower the mast when going under bridges. Also, used to elongate the mast of any boat by stepping it in a tabernacle.

TABLE-CLOTH. A fleecy-looking cloud which sometimes covers the "table" or flat top of Table Mountain, at the Cape of Good Hope; it is the forerunner of a south-easter, being the condensation of moisture in the sea-air as it ascends the mountain side.

TABLE-LAND. Land which is flat-topped, however it may be raised more or less above the ordinary level of the vicinity.

TABLE-MONEY. An allowance to admirals and senior officers, in addition to their pay, to meet the expenses of their official guests.

TABLES. *See* ASTRONOMICAL TABLES, and NAUTICAL TABLES.

TABLE-SHORE. A low level shore.

TABLET. *See* TRAPEZOID. Also, a flat coping stone placed at the top of the revêtement of the escarp, to protect the masonry from the weather.

TABLING. A broad hem on the edges of a ship's sails, to strengthen them in that part which is sewed to the bolt-rope. Also, letting one piece of timber into another, similar to the *hooking* of planks, so that they cannot be pulled asunder.

TACES. *See* TAISHES.

TACK. A rope to confine the weather lower corners of the courses and staysails when the wind crosses the ship's course obliquely. Also, the rope employed to haul out the lower outer clue of a studding-sail to the boom-end. With jibs and fore-and-aft sails, the tack confines them amidships. A ship is said to be *on the tack* of the side from which the wind comes: even if it be on the quarter.—*To tack.* To go about, to change the course from one board to another from the starboard to the port tack, or *vice versâ.* It is done by turning the ship's head suddenly to the wind, whereby her head-sails are thrown aback, and cause her to fall off from the wind to the other tack. The opposite to *wearing.*

TACK AND HALF-TACK. Working to windward, or along shore, by long and short boards, or legs, alternately.

TACKLE. A purchase formed by the connection of a fall, or rope, with two or more blocks. When a power sustains a weight by a rope over a fixed sheave, the weight and power will be equal; but if one end of the rope be fixed, and the sheave be movable with the weight, then the power will be but half the weight; but in a combination of sheaves, or pulleys, the power will be to the weight as 1 to the numbers of parts of the fall.—*Ground-tackle.* Anchors, cables, &c.—*Tack-tackle.* A small tackle used to pull down the tacks of the principal sails to their respective stations, and particularly attached to the mainsails of brigs, sloops, cutters, and schooners.

TACKLE-FALL. The part hauled upon in any tackle, simple or compound.

TACK OR SHEET. A man's saying that he will not start tack or sheet implies resolution.

TACK-PINS. The belaying pins of the fife-rail; called also Jack-pins.

TACTICS. The art of disposing and applying naval or military forces in action with the enemy, in whose presence strategy gives place to tactics.

TAFFIA. A bad spirit, made and sold at Mauritius.

TAFFRAIL, OR TAFFAREL. The upper part of a ship's stern, a curved railing, the ends of which unite to the quarter-pieces.

TAIL. A rope spliced into the strop or round of any block, leaving a long end for making fast to rigging, spars, &c.—*To tail on to a bank.* To be aground abaft only.—*To tail up* or *down a stream.* When at anchor in a river, is as a ship's stern swings.

TAIL-BLOCK. A rope-stropped block, having an end of rope attached to it as a tail, by which it may be fastened to any object at pleasure.

TAIL OF A GALE. The latter part of a gale, when its violence is dying out.

TAIL ON, OR TALLY ON. The order to clap on to a rope.

TAIL-RACE. The water which leaves the paddles of a steam-boat. Also, the water-course of a mill beyond the water-wheel.

TAIL-TACKLE. A luff-tackle purchase, with a hook in the end of the single block, and a tail to the upper end of the double block. Synonymous with *watch-tackle.*

TAIL UP. When a whale dives perpendicularly. In this case whalers expect the fish to rise near the same spot. Also termed *fluking.*

TAIL-VALVE. A valve in the air-pump at the opposite side from the condenser, and connected with the latter by a pipe under the air-pump: it opens when pressed by steam entering the condenser by the blow-through valve, but the weight of the atmosphere is sufficient to keep it shut so long as there is a vacuum in the condenser.

TAINT. By admiralty law, the taint of contraband extends to all property on board belonging to the owners of detected contraband articles.

TAISHES. Armour for the thighs.

TAISTE. A northern name for the black guillemot.

TAJASO. The jerked beef supplied to ships on some parts of the coast of America.

TAKE. The draught of fishes in a single drag of the net. Also, *to take,* in a military sense, to take or adopt any particular formation, as to take open order, or to take ground to the right or the left.—To *take* an astronomical observation, so to ascertain the position of a celestial body as to learn from it the place of the ship.

TAKEL [Anglo-Saxon]. The arrows which used to be supplied to the fleet; the *takill* of Chaucer.

TAKEN AFT. Complained of on the quarter-deck.

TAKE-UP. The part between the smoke-box and the bottom of the funnel in a marine boiler. Also, a seaman *takes up slops* when he applies to the purser for articles of ready-made clothes, to be charged against his wages. Also, an officer *takes up the gauntlet* when he accepts a challenge, though no longer in the form of a glove.

TAKE WATER ON BOARD, To. To ship a sea.

TAKING A DEPARTURE. Determining the place of a ship by means of the bearing and distance of a known object, and assuming it as the point to be calculated from.

TAKING IN. The act of brailing up and furling sails at sea; generally used in opposition to setting. (*See* FURL and SHORTEN.) Also said of a ship when loading.

TAKING OFF. Said of tides, when decreasing from the spring-tides.

TALARO. A silver coin of Ragusa, value 3s. sterling: also of Venice, value 4s. 2d.

TALE [from Anglo-Saxon *tael,* number]. Taylor thus expressed it in 1630—

> " Goods in and out, which daily ships doe fraight
> By guesse, by tale, by measure, and by weight."

TALLANT. The upper hance, or break of the rudder abaft.

TALL SHIP. A phrase among the early voyagers for square-rigged vessels having topmasts.

TALLY, To. To haul the sheets aft; as used by Falconer—

> " And while the lee clue-garnet's lower'd away,
> Taut aft the sheet they tally, and belay."

TALUS. The old word in fortification for slope.

TAMBOUR. A projecting kind of stockade, attached to ill-flanked walls, &c.

TAN and TANNED SAILS. Those steeped in oak-bark.

TANG, or TANGLE. *Fucus digitata*, and other sea-weed, which are used as manure.

TANGENT. A right line raised perpendicularly on the extremity of a radius, touching the circle without cutting it.

TANGENT-SCALE. Fitted to the breech of a gun for admeasuring its elevation; it is a sliding pillar marked with degrees and their subdivisions (according to the distance between the sights on the gun), and bears a notch or other sight on its head. With rifled guns a vernier, reading the minutes, is generally added.

TANGENT-SCREW. A screw acting tangentially to a circle, by means of which a slow motion may be given to the vernier of any instrument.

TANG-FISH. A northern name for the seal.

TANK. A piece of deep water, natural as well as artificial. Also, an iron cistern for containing fresh water—a great improvement on wooden casks for keeping water sweet.

TANKA. A covered Chinese shore-boat for conveying passengers to ships; worked by women only.

TANTARA. An old word for the noise of a drum.

TAPERED. A term applied to ropes which decrease in size towards one end, as tacks and sheets. Also termed *rat-tailed*.

TAPERED CLEAT. A piece of wood bolted under the beams, to support them when pillars are not used.

TAPPING A BUOY. Clearing it of the water which has entered it by leakage, and would otherwise prevent its watching.

TAP THE ADMIRAL. Opprobriously applied to those who would "drink anything;" from the tale of the drunkard who stole spirits from the cask in which a dead admiral was being conveyed to England.

TAR [Anglo-Saxon *tare*]. A kind of turpentine which is drained from pines and fir-trees, and is used to preserve standing rigging, canvas, &c., from the effects of weather, by rendering them water-proof. Also, a perfect sailor; one who knows his duty thoroughly. (*See* JACK TAR.) —*Coal* or *gas tar.* A fluid extracted from coal during the operation of making gas, &c.; chiefly used on wood and iron, in the place of paint.

TARBET, or TARBERT. Applied to low necks of land in Scotland that divide the lakes from the sea. It literally means boat-carrying, and is analogous to the Canadian "portage."

TARBRUSH, Touch of the. A nautical term applied to those who are slightly darkened by mixed blood.

TARGET [Anglo-Saxon *targe*]. A leathern shield. A mark to aim at.

TARGIA. An archaic term for a vessel, since called a *tartan*.

TARI. A coin of Italy, value 8d. sterling.

TARIFF. List of duties payable upon exported and imported goods.

TARITA. An ancient term for a ship of burden.

TARN. A small mountain lake [probably from the Icelandic *tiaurn*].

TARPAULIN. Canvas well covered with tar or paint to render it waterproof. Also, the foul-weather hats and jackets of seamen; often applied to the men themselves. Properly *paulin* when paint is used.

TARRED WITH THE SAME BRUSH. Equivalent to "birds of a feather."

TARRING AND FEATHERING. A punishment now obsolete,—inflicted by stripping the delinquent, then smearing him with tar, covering him with flocks and feathers, and towing him ashore. It was ordered in the naval enactments of Richard I. for theft.

TARROCK. The kittiwake, *Larus tridactylus*, a small species of gull.

TARRY-BREEKS. A north-country name for a sailor.

TARTAN. A small coasting vessel of the Mediterranean, with one mast and a bowsprit, lateen-rigged.

TARTAR. A domineering commanding officer.—*To catch a Tartar.* Said of a vessel which mistakes her enemy's force, and is obliged to yield.

TASKING. Examining a vessel to see whether her timbers are sound.

TASTING TIMBER. Chipping it with an adze, and boring it with an augur, to ascertain its quality.

TATOOING. The Burmese, South Sea Islanders, and others, puncture the skin until it bleeds, and then rub in fine soot and other colouring matter. The practice has become common amongst sailors.

TATTIES. Mats hung before doors and windows in India, on which water is thrown, to cool the air inside by evaporation.

TATTOO. The evening sound of drum or trumpet, after which the roll is called, and all soldiers not on leave of absence should be in their quarters.

TAUNT. High or tall, commonly applied to very long masts.—*All a taunto* is a ship having all her light and long spars aloft.

TAURUS. The second sign of the zodiac, which the sun enters about the 20th of April.

TAUT [from the Anglo-Saxon *tought*]. Tight.

TAUT BOWLINE. A ship sailing close-hauled is "on a taut bowline."

TAUT HAND. A strict disciplinarian.

TAUT HELM, or Taut Weather-helm. A ship with a side wind is said to carry a taut weather-helm, when the water presses heavily on the lee side of the rudder; often the result of her being too much by the head.

TAUT LEECH. A sail well set on a wind, and well filled.

TEACH, To. In marine architecture, is applied to the direction which any line or curve seems to point out.

TEAGLE. A northern word for a crane for lifting goods.

TEAK. *Tectona grandis*, a stately tree, the pride of Indian and Burmese forests, used extensively in ship-building; having the valuable property of not shrinking, and, by means of its essential oil, preserving the iron bolts driven into it from rusting.

TEAL. A small species of wild duck, *Querquedula crecca*.

TEAM. Ships blockading a port, being generally formed in a line, are said to be "in the team."

TEAM-BOAT. A ferry-boat worked with horses by paddle-wheel propulsion.

TEA-WAGGON. A name given to the old East India Company's ships on account of their cargo.

TEAZED OAKUM. Oakum worked out for caulking. (Tow).

TE DEUM. A hymn sung in thanksgiving for victory obtained. In many cases the causes of war are such that chanting the Te Deum is rank blasphemy.

TEE-IRON. An instrument for drawing the lower box in the barrel of a pump. T-shaped clamp, knee, or other piece of iron-work.

TEETH. A name for the guns in a ship.

TEE-TOTALLER. A very old and general amplification of *totally*, recently borrowed from sea diction to mark a class who wholly abstain from alcoholic drinks.

TELEGRAPH, To. To convey intelligence to a distance, through the medium of signals.

TELESCOPIC OBJECTS. All those which are not visible to the unassisted eye.

TELL OFF, To. To divide a body of men into divisions and subdivisions, preparatory to a special service.

TELL-TALE. A compass hanging face downwards from the beams in the cabin, showing the position of the vessel's head. Also, an index in front of the wheel to show the position of the tiller.

TELL-TALE SHAKE. The shake of a rope from aloft to denote that it wants letting go.

TELL THAT TO THE MARINES! A sailor's exclamation when an improbable story is related to him.

TEMOINS. *See* WITNESSES.

TEMPEST. A word not much used by seamen. It is, however, synonymous with *storm*, *gales*, &c. (*See* STORMS.)

TEMPORARY RANK. That owing to an acting commission, or to local circumstances, ceasing with a particular service.

TEMPORARY STARS. Those which have suddenly become visible, and after attaining considerable brightness, have as suddenly vanished : that seen by Tycho in 1572 is a notable instance.

TENAILLE. In fortification, a long low outwork traced on the inward prolongation of the faces of the bastions. It covers the curtain, and conveniently defends the interior of the ravelin and its redoubt.

TENAILLON. In fortification, a low outwork of two faces meeting in a salient angle, sometimes attached to ravelins to afford nearer flanking fire.

TENCH. *Tinca vulgaris*, a well-known fresh-water fish.

TEND, To. To watch a vessel at anchor on the turn of a tide, and cast her by the helm, and some sail if necessary, so as to keep the cable clear of the anchor or turns out of her cables when moored.

TENDER. A small vessel duly commanded, and employed to attend a larger one, to supply her with stores, to carry intelligence or volunteers and impressed men to receiving ships, &c. An enemy's ship captured by cutters or boats fitted out as tenders by men-of-war, but without any commission or authority from the admiralty, will not insure a prize to the benefit of the ship. The condemnation will be as a droit of admiralty, on the principle that an officer does not retain his commission for the purposes of prize on board another ship; but if captured by one of her boats, and brought to the ship, she is good prize, as with slaves. *Tender* is also a synonym of *crank;* thus, a spar may be *tender.*

TENDING. The movement by which a ship turns or swings round when at single anchor, or moored by the head, at every change of tide or wind.

TENON. The square heel of a mast, cut for fitting into the step. Also, the end of any piece of timber which is fashioned to enter into a mortise in another piece; they are then said to be tenoned together; as, for instance, the stern-post is tenoned into the keel.

TEN-POUNDER. A name given to a bony mullet-shaped fish of the West Indies.

TENSILE STRAIN. The greatest effort to extend, stretch, or draw asunder, as in proving bars of iron, chain-cables, &c.

TENT. A canvas shelter pitched upon a pole or poles, and stayed with cords and pegs. Also, a roll of lint, or other material, used in searching a wound. Also, a small piece of iron which kept up the cock of a gunlock.

TEREDO NAVALIS. A worm which, furnished with a peculiar augur adaptation at its head, bores into timber, forming a shell as it progresses. They attain the length of three feet or more, with a diameter of one inch or less. Even if the ship be destroyed by them, the loss is not within the policy of insurance.

TERMINAL VELOCITY of any given Body. The greatest velocity it can acquire by falling freely through the air; the limit being arrived at when the increase of the atmospheric resistance becomes equal to the increase of the force of gravity.

TERMINATOR. The line separating the illuminated from the dark portion of the moon's disc.

TERM-PIECES, or Terms. Pieces of carved work on each side of the taffrail upon the side stern-timber, and extending down as low as the foot-rail of the balcony.

TERN, or Sea-swallow. A species of sea-bird, allied to the gulls, but of smaller and lighter make, and with longer and more pointed wings and tail; genus *Sterna*.

TERNARY SYSTEM.   Three stars in close proximity, and found to be in physical connection, as, for instance, ζ Cancri.

TERRADA.   An Indian boat, otherwise called *tonee*.   A large 'long-shore boat of the Gulf of Persia.

TERRAPIN (contracted by sailors into *turpin* and *tenopen*).   A fresh-water tortoise, plentiful in America, and much esteemed for food.

TERREPLEIN.   In fortification, the horizontal surface of the rampart in rear of the parapet.

TERRESTRIAL REFRACTION.   The property of the atmosphere by which objects appear to be higher than they really are, and in certain cases producing the effect called *deceptio visus*, and *fata morgana*.

TERRITORY.   The protection of neutral territory operates to the resti-tution of enemy's property captured within its limits.   Since the intro-duction of fire-arms that distance has usually been recognized to be almost three English miles.

TERTIATE, To.   To examine whether a piece of ordnance is truly bored and has its due proportion of metal in every part, especially at the vent, the trunnions, and the muzzle.

TESTING A CHAIN-CABLE.   Trying its strength by the hydraulic machine, which strains it beyond what it is likely to undergo when in use.

TESTONE.   A silver Papal coin, value 1s. 3d.   A testone is also a current coin in Portugal, consisting of 100 reis.

TETE DE PONT.   A work covering the farther end of a bridge from assault from the country beyond.

TEW, To.   To beat hemp.

THAUGHTS (properly ATHWARTS).   *See* THWARTS.

THEODOLITE.   The theodolite, as used in land-surveying, levelling, &c., is well known.   But the great theodolite, with its vertical circle and telescope adapted to the observation of the heavenly bodies, as used by nautical astronomers, commonly called an alt-azimuth instrument, is almost an observatory *per se*.   By this alone, within three hours on each side of noon, the longitude, latitude, and magnetic variation of a position may be determined.

THERE!   A word added in hailing any part of a ship; as, "Forecastle there!" "Mast-head there!"

THERE AWAY!   A phrase accompanied by pointing on a bearing, or to an object in sight.   Thereabout, in that quarter.

THERMOMETER.   An instrument to measure the amount of heat by the expansion of a fluid (generally quicksilver) contained in a glass bulb, in connection with which is a hermetically closed tube, up which the fluid rises as the heat increases.   This tube is graduated differently in different countries.

THERMOMETRIC SAILING.   A scheme for detecting the approach to shoal water by the diminution of temperature, and found to be useful in some places, such as the Agulhas and Newfoundland Banks; in the latter a difference of 20° has been observed, on quitting the Gulf Stream and gaining soundings in 100 fathoms.

THICK-AND-DRY FOR WEIGHING! To clap on nippers closely, just at starting the anchor from the ground.

THICK AND THIN BLOCK, OR FIDDLE-BLOCK. A block having one sheave larger than the other, sometimes used for quarter-blocks.

THICK STUFF. Sided timber, or naval planks, under one foot, and above 4 inches in thickness.

THIEVES' CAT. A cat-o'-nine-tails having knots upon it, and only used for the punishment of theft.

THIMBLE. An iron ring with a concave outer surface to contain snugly in the cavity a rope, which is spliced about it. Its use is to defend the rope which surrounds it from being injured by another rope, or the hook or a tackle which passes through it.

THIMBLE-EYES. Are thimble-shaped apertures in iron-plates where sheaves are not required; frequently used instead of dead-eyes for the topmast-rigging, futtock-plates, and backstays in the channels.

THODS. An old northern term for sudden gusts of wind.

THOKES. Fish with broken bellies, which are prohibited to be mixed or packed with tale fish.

THOLE, THOLE-PIN, OR THOWEL [from the Anglo-Saxon *thol*]. Certain pins in the gunwale of a boat, instead of the rowlock-poppets, and serving to retain the oars in position when pulling; generally there is only one pin to each oar, which is retained upon the pin by a grommet, or a cleat with a hole through it, nailed on the side of the oar. The principal use is to allow the oar, in case of action, suddenly to lie fore-and-aft over the side, and take care of itself. This was superseded by the swinging thowel, or metal crutch, in 1819, and by admiralty order at Portsmouth Yard in 1830.

THORN-BACK. A well-known fish of the ray kind, *Raia clavata*.

THOROUGH-PUTS, OR THOROUGH-FOOTS, are kinks or tangles in a rope; or parts of a tackle not leading fair by reason of one of the blocks having been passed round part of the fall, and so *getting a turn*.

THOUGHT. An old spelling of *thwart*.

THRASHER, OR THRESHER. A species of shark with a long tail, *Carcharias vulpes*. Also applied to a kind of grampus, which was supposed to attack the whale by leaping out of the water and inflicting blows with its powerful tail.

THREAD [Ang.-Sax. *thréd*]. The middle of a river or stream.—*To thread*. To run a ship through narrow and intricate channels among islands.

THREE-COCKED HAT. A silly article of sea-wear now happily passing away, retained only by coachmen, lord-mayor's men, and parish beadles.

THREE-DECKERS. Ships with three full batteries.

THREE HALF-HITCHES ARE MORE THAN A KING'S YACHT WANTS. An exclamatory remark to a green hand, meaning that two are enough.

THREE SHEETS IN THE WIND. Unsteady from drink.

THREE SISTERS. Formerly the badge of office of boatswains' mates and masters-at-arms, made of three rattans bound together with waxed twine.

THREE-SQUARE. An odd word applied to staysails, or anything triangular, as was the oblong square to a parallelogram.

THRIFT. *Armeria*, a genus of handsome plants growing on the sea-coast.

THROAT. The widened and hollowed end of a gaff next the mast; opposed to *peak*, the outer end. Also, the midship portion of the floor-timbers and transoms. The contrary of *breech*.

THROAT-BOLTS. Eye-bolts fixed in the lower part of tops, and the jaw-ends of gaffs, for hooking the throat-halliards to.

THROAT-BRAILS. Those which are attached to the gaff for trussing up the sail close to the gaff as well as the mast. (*See* BRAILS, and TOPMAST-STAYSAILS.) Falconer says :—

> "For he who strives the tempest to disarm,
> Will never first embrail the lee yard-arm."

Brail thus applies to leech-lines, clue-lines, &c.

THROAT-HALLIARDS. Ropes or tackles applied to hoist the inner part of the gaff, and its portion of the sail, and hook on to the throat-bolts, as above.

THROAT-SEIZING. In blocks, confines the hook and thimble in the strop home to the scores. Also, in turning in rigging, the throat-seizing is passed with riding turns, through which the end is hove taut, and being turned up sharply, is well seized to the standing part of the rigging, making it a severe cross nip, which cannot render or slip.

THROT. That part of the mizen-yard close to the mast.

THROTTLE-VALVE. A valve in the steam-pipe of an engine for preventing the escape of steam, or regulating the velocity of its passage from the boiler to the cylinder.

THROUGH ALL. Carrying canvas in heavy squalls without starting a stitch. It demands not only courage, but seamanlike judgment. Also applied to the cable, or any purchase where, by reason of its slipperiness, the purchase does not nip; she is then said to be "heaving through all." "Fresh nippers, thick and dry, for weighing," are then called for, and sand applied to overcome the slipping.

THROUGH FASTENINGS. Applied to bolts and treenails driven through both the timber and plank of the sides.

THROUGH-PIECES. *See* GRAVING-PIECES.

THROUGH THE FLEET. A seaman's being sentenced by court-martial to be towed by a boat from every ship through the fleet, and receive alongside each a proportion of the lashes to be inflicted. But this was only awarded where the offence deserved a less punishment than death, and is now discontinued, solitary confinement or penal servitude being substituted.

THROW. A cast of the hand-lead.

THROWING a Steam-engine out of Gear. Disconnecting the eccentric rod from the gab-lever.

THRUM. Any coarse woollen or hempen yarn. It is used for mops, &c., in the cabins; also for mats, which are worked on canvas with a large bolt-rope needle.—*To thrum.* A vessel, when leaky, is thrummed by working some heavy spare sail, as the spritsail, into a thrummed mat, greasing and tarring it well, passing it under the bottom, and heaving all parts tight. The pressure forces the tarred oakum into the openings, and thus, in part, arrests the ingress of water.

THRUMMED MAT. A small mat faced with rope-yarn or spun yarn, which is used in a vessel's rigging to prevent chafing.

THRUST. The effort of a screw-propeller.

THUD. The sound of a bullet on hitting the intended object.

THULE [Gaelic *thuath*]. An extreme object to the north.

THUMB-CLEAT. In shape resembling a thumb. They arrest the topsail-reef-earings from slipping, and are also lashed to the rigging with a hollow, cut out to act as a hook, to suspend the bight of a rope, as the truss-pendants on the lower masts.

THUNDERING. A sailor's emphatic word for anything choice, large, fine, or powerful.

THUNDER SQUALL. This is similar to the black squall, only that it is always preceded and attended by lightning and thunder, and accompanied by extremely heavy rain.

THUNNY. *See* Tunny.

THUS, Very well Thus, or Dyce. The order to the helmsman to keep the ship in her present direction, when sailing close-hauled. This truly sailor's motto was adopted by the Earl St. Vincent.

THWART CLAMPS or KNEES. Those which secure the after, main, and fore thwarts to the rising and gunwales, and which support the masts.

THWART-MARKS, to a Harbour. Two objects on the land, which, brought into line with each other, mark the safe course between shoals, as those on Southsea Common act for the Needles, Swashways, &c.

THWARTS (properly Athwarts). The seats or benches athwart a boat whereon the rowers sit to manage their oars.

THWART-SHIPS. Across the ship, or from one side to the other. (*See* Athwart.)

TIBRIC. An old name for the coal-fish.

TIBURON [Sp.] The shark.

TICKET. An official warrant of discharge, so that a heavy penalty attaches to the loss of any of the blank ones in the captain's charge. It is always used in counterparts, which are ordered to be perfect duplicates of each other.

TICKET-BOOK. A register for accounting for all tickets and certificates received and used.

TICKLING OF FISH. The same as *gennelin*. (*See* Groping.)

TIDAL WAVE. The wave caused by the combined action of the sun and moon: its greatest influence is felt some time after the moon has passed the meridian of any place.

TIDE. A regular periodical current of waters, setting alternately in a flux and reflux; it is owing to the attraction of the sun and moon, but chiefly to the latter. The highest as well as most rapid, perhaps, are in the Gulf of Fundy and the river Wye; and on the contrary the lowest, as well as feeblest, are in the Mediterranean generally.—*To tide*, is to work up or down a river or harbour, with a fair tide in a head wind or a calm; coming to anchor when the tide turns.

TIDE or TIDAL HARBOUR. A port which can only be entered at a certain time of flood.

TIDE AND HALF-TIDE. Those roadsteads affected by several rivers or channels leading into them; as, for instance, Spithead.

TIDE-BALL. A ball hoisted to denote when the depth of water permits vessels to enter a bar-harbour, or to take the bar outside, from the known depth within.

TIDE-GATE. A place where the tide runs strong.

TIDE-GAUGE. An instrument contrived for measuring the height of the tides.

TIDE, Ebb of. The falling tide.

TIDE-POOL. A sort of basin worn in seaside rocks.

TIDE-RIP. Those short ripplings which result from eddies, or the passage of the tide over uneven bottom; also observed in the ocean where two currents meet, but not appearing to affect a ship's course.

TIDE-RODE. The situation of a vessel at anchor when she swings by the force of the tide. In opposition to *wind-rode*.

TIDE'S WORK. The amount of progress a ship has made during a favourable tide. Also, a period of necessary labour on a ship during the ebbing and slack water of a tide. That is when the sea has left the vessel aground between two tides, so as to enable workmen to repair defects down to a certain depth, laid bare by the receding tide.

TIDE-WAY. The mid-stream; or a passage or channel through which the tide sets, and runs strongly.

TIE-FOR-TYE. Mutual obligation and no favour; as in the case of the *tie-mate*, the comrade who, in the days of long hair, performed the tie for tie on the tails. (*See* Tye.)

TIER. A regular row of anything. Also, a range in the hold; hence the terms, ground tier, second and upper tier, &c., of casks or goods stowed there.—*Cable-tier.* The space in a ship where hempen cables were coiled.

TIERCE. Is specially applied to provision casks, and is the third of a pipe; but the beef-tierce contains 280 lbs., or 28 galls., whilst that of pork only contains 260 lbs., or 26 galls. Now the beef-tierce often contains 336 lbs., and the pork 300 lbs.

TIERERS. Men formerly stationed in the tiers for coiling away the cables, where strength, activity, and ability shone conspicuously.

TIER-SHOT. That kind of grape-shot which is secured in tiers by parallel iron discs.

TIES. An old name for mooring bridles. Also, stops to a sail. (*See* TYE.)

TIGHT. Close, free from leaks. Hence a ship is said to be tight when no water leaks in; and a cask is called tight when none of the liquid leaks out. Applied to ropes or chains this word becomes *taut*.

TILLER. A straight-grained timber beam, or iron bar, fitted into or round the head of the rudder, by means of which the latter is moved. (*See* HELM.)

TILLER-HEAD. The extremity of the tiller, to which the tiller-ropes are attached.

TILLER-ROPES. The ropes which form a communication between the end of the tiller and the barrel of the wheel; they are frequently made of untarred rope, though hide is much better; and iron chains are also used. By these the tiller is worked and the vessel steered.

TILLER-SWEEP. *See* SWEEP OF THE TILLER.

TILT. A small canopy extended over the stern-sheets of a boat, supported by iron or wood work, to keep off rain, as an awning is used to keep off the sun.—*To tilt.* To lift up a little on one side or end of anything.

TILT-BOAT. One expressly fitted like a tilt-waggon, to preserve powder or other fragile stores from the weather.

TIMBER [Anglo-Saxon]. All large pieces of wood used in ship-building, as *floor-timbers, cross-pieces, futtocks, frames,* and the like (all which see).

TIMBER AND ROOM, is the distance between two adjoining timbers, which always contain the breadth of two timbers, and two or three inches besides. The same as *room and space,* or *berth and space.*

TIMBER-CONVERTER. A dock-yard official who has the charge of converting timber for its different purposes in ship-building.

TIMBER-HEADS. The heads of the timbers that rise above the decks, and are used for belaying hawsers, large ropes, &c. (*See* KEVEL-HEADS.) These being such important parts of a ship, men of acknowledged talent in the royal navy are styled "the *timber-heads* of the profession."

TIMBER-HITCH, is made by taking the end of a rope round a spar, and after leading it under and over the standing part, passing two or three turns round its own part, making in fact a running but self-jamming eye.

TIMBERS. The incurvated ribs of a ship which branch outwards from the keel in a vertical direction, so as to give strength, figure, and solidity to the whole fabric. One timber is composed of several pieces. (*See* FRAME.)—*Cant or square timbers,* are those which are placed obliquely on the keel towards the extremities of a ship, forming the dead solid wood of the gripe, and of the after heel.—*Filling timbers.* Those which are put up between the frames. One mould serves for two timbers, the fore-side of the one being supposed to unite with the after-side of the one before it, and so make only one line.—*Knuckle-timbers* are the foremost cant-timbers on a ship's bow: the hindmost on the quarter are termed *fashion-pieces.*

TIMBER-TASTER. One appointed to examine and pronounce upon the fitness of timber.

TIME, MEAN, OR MEAN SOLAR TIME. That shown by a clock or watch when compensated for the unequal progress of the sun in the ecliptic, and which thence forms an equable measure of time.—*To take time* is for an assistant to note the time by a chronometer at each instant that the observer calls "stop," on effecting his astronomical observation for altitude of a heavenly body, or for contact with the sun and moon, or moon and star.

TIME-KEEPER, TIME-PIECE, OR CHRONOMETER. An instrument adapted for measuring mean time. The result of many years of study and experiment by our best horologists. (*See* LONGITUDE.)

TIMENOGUY. Formerly a rope carried taut between different parts of a vessel, to prevent the sheet or tack of a course from getting foul in working ship; specially from the fore-rigging to the anchor-stock, to prevent the fouling of the fore-sheet.

TIMONEER [derived from the French]. The helmsman. Also, one on the look-out, who directs the helmsman.

TIMONOGY. This term properly belongs to steering, and is derived from *timon*, the tiller, and the twiddling-lines, which worked in olden times on a gauge in front of the poop, in ships of the line, by which the position of the helm was easily read even from the forecastle.

TINDAL. A Lascar boatswain's-mate.

TINKER. A small mortar formerly used on the end of a staff, now superseded by the Coehorn. Also, a small mackerel.

TINKERMEN. Fishermen who destroyed the fry of fish on the Thames by nets, and other unlawful contrivances, till suppressed by the mayor and corporation of London.

TIN-POTTER. A galley skulker, shamming Abraham.

TIPPET. A snood for a fishing-line.

TIPPING ALL NINES, OR TIPPED THE NINES. Foundering from press of sail.

TIPPING THE GRAMPUS. Ducking a skulker for being asleep on his watch. (*See* BLOWING THE GRAMPUS.)

TIRE. Synonymous with *tier*.

TITIVATE, TO; OR TITIVATE OFF TO THE NINES. To freshen the paint-work; to put into the highest kelter.

TOAD-FISH. The *Lophius piscatorius*, or fishing-frog.

TOBACCO. Has been supplied for the use of the ships' companies in the royal navy from the 1st January, 1799.

TOBACCO-CHARTS. The worthless charts formerly sold by ship-chandlers.

TOD-BOAT. A broad flat Dutch fishing-boat.

TODDY. The sura or juice extracted from various kinds of palm, and often called palm-wine. A mixture of spirits, water, and sugar is also called toddy. (*See* ARRACK.)

TOE A LINE! The order to stand in a row.

TOGGLE. A strong pin of wood, sometimes used instead of a hook in fixing a tackle, or it is put through the bight or eye of a rope, bolt, or block-strop, to keep it in its place. In ships of war it is usual to fix toggles upon the running parts of the topsail-sheets, the jears, &c., when preparing for action, so that if the rope is shot away below, the toggle may stop the yard from coming down. The toggle is used in masting operations, in securing the standing part of fore and main sheets, but especially in whaling operations, cutting in, flensing, &c., a hole is cut in the blubber, the eye of the purchase strop passed through and toggled. In cold weather especially it is preferred to the hook, which at low temperatures is apt to snap suddenly, and is, moreover, heavier to handle. The term is also used for putting the bights of the sheets in the beckets. (*See* BECKET.)

TOGGLE-BOLT. This bolt is used to confine the ensign-staff, and the like, into its place by means of a strap; it has a flat head, and a mortice through it, that receives a toggle or pin.

TOGS. A very old term for clothes.—*Togged to the nines*, in full dress.—*Sunday togs*, the best clothes.

TOISE. The French fathom, nearly approaching to ours: the proportion of the English yard to the French demi-toise being as 36 to 38·35. The toise is equal to 6·3946 English feet.

TOKE. A drink made from honey in Madagascar; very dangerous to Europeans.

TOKO FOR YAM. An expression peculiar to negroes for crying out before being hurt.

TOLEDO. An esteemed Spanish sword, so called from the place of manufacture.

TOLL. A demand, &c., at the Sound; hence the epithet of *Sound dues*.

TOM. A pet bow-chaser, a 9 or 12-pounder. (*See* LONG TOM.)

TOMAHAWK. A weapon somewhat resembling a hand pole-axe, much used in boarding an enemy, as it is not only effective in combat, but useful in holding on, and in cutting away fasts and rigging when required. The name is derived from the hatchet of the North American Indians.

TOM ASTONERS. Dashing fellows; from astound or "astony," to terrify.

TOM COX'S TRAVERSE. Up one hatchway and down another: others say three turns round the long boat, and a pull at the scuttle. It means the work of an artful dodger, all jaw, and no good in him.

TOMMY COD. A very small variety of the *Gadus morrhua*, which mostly appears in the winter months; whence it is also called frost-fish at Halifax and in Newfoundland.

TOM NORIE. A name of the puffin, *Fratercula arctica*.

TOM PEPPER. A term for a liar; he having, according to nautic tradition, been kicked out of the nether regions for indulging in falsehood.

TOMPION. A circular plug of wood, used to stop the muzzle of a gun, and thereby keep out the wet at sea. The tompions are carefully encircled with tallow or putty for the same purpose. Also, the stopper fitted to go between the powder and shell in a mortar. This name is often pronounced as well as written *tompkin*.

TOM-TOM. A small drum, made from the stem of a hollowed tree, generally of the palm-tribe, as the centre is pithy and the skin flinty. It is covered by the skin of a lizard or shark, and beaten with the fingers. It is used throughout the tropics, and produces a hollow monotonous sound. In the East Indies it is used to proclaim public notices, and to draw attention to conjurors, snake-charmers, &c.

TON, or Tun [from the Anglo-Saxon *tunne*]. In commerce, 20 cwt., or 2240 lbs., but in the cubical contents of a ship it is the weight of water equal to 2000 lbs., by the general standard for liquids. A tun of wine or oil contains 4 hogsheads. A ton or load of timber is a measure of 40 cubic feet in the rough, and of 50 when sawn: 42 cubic feet of articles equal one ton in shipment.

TONEE. A canoe of some burden, made of the hollowed trunk of a tree in early use on the Malabar coast. (*See* TERRADA.)

TON FOR TON AND MAN FOR MAN. A phrase implying that ships sailing as consorts, ought fairly to divide whatever prize they take.

TONGUE [Anglo-Saxon *tunga*]. The long tapered end of one piece of timber made to fay into a scarph at the end of another piece, to gain length. Also, a low salient point of land. Also, a dangerous mass of ice projecting under water from an iceberg or floe, nearly horizontally; it was on one of these shelves that the *Guardian* frigate struck.

TONGUE OF A BEVEL. The movable part of the instrument by which the angles or bevellings are taken.

TONNAGE. A custom or impost formerly granted to the crown for merchandise imported or exported. Also, the admeasurement of a ship, and thence to ascertain her cubical contents converted into tons. (*See* BURDEN.)

TOP. A sort of platform placed over the head of the lower mast, from which it projects like a scaffold. The principal intention of the top is to extend the topmast-shrouds, so as to form a greater angle with the mast, and thereby give it additional support. It is sustained by certain timbers bolted fore-and-aft on the bibs or shoulders of the mast, and called the trestle-trees; athwart these are the cross-trees. In ships of war it is used as a kind of redoubt, and is fortified accordingly. It is also very convenient for containing the materials for setting the small sails, fixing and repairing the rigging, &c. The tops are named after their respective masts. This top was formerly fenced on the after-side by a rail about three feet high, between the stanchions of which a netting was usually constructed, and stowed in action with hammocks. This was covered with red baize, or canvas painted red, and called the top-armour. Top-armours were in use with the Spaniards in 1810.

TOP-ARMINGS. Hammocks stowed inside the rigging for the protection of riflemen.

TOP A YARD OR BOOM, To. To raise up one end of it by hoisting on the lift, as the spanker-boom is lifted before setting the sail.

TOP-BLOCK. A large single block with an iron strop and hook, by which it is hooked into an eye-bolt under the lower cap, and is used for the top-pendant to reeve through in swaying up or lowering down the topmasts.

TOP BURTON-TACKLE. *See* Burton.

TOP-CASTLES. Castellated ledgings surrounding the mast-heads of our early ships, in which the pages to the officers were stationed to annoy the enemy with darts, &c.

TOP-CHAIN. A chain to sling the yards in time of battle, in case of the ropes by which they are hung being shot away.

TOPE. A small-sized Chinese junk. Also, the *Galeus vulgaris*, a kind of shark. Also, a small grove of trees in India.

TOP-GALLANT. In the Cotton MSS. this word appears as "top-gar-land."

TOPGALLANT-FORECASTLE. A short deck forward above the upper deck, mostly used as a galley, but in some merchantmen a berthing place for their crews, though generally very wet and uncomfortable for want of a few necessary fittings. Also, it facilitates working the head-sails.—In several of the ironclad frigates, chase-guns are fitted there.

TOPGALLANT-MAST. The third mast above the deck; the uppermost before the days of royals and flying kites.

TOP-GALLANT QUARTER-BOARDS, or Top-gallant Bulwarks. *See* Quarter-boards.

TOPGALLANT-SAILS. The third sails above the decks: they are set above the topsail-yards, in the same manner as the topsails above the lower yards.

TOP-HAMPER. Any unnecessary weight either on a ship's decks or about her tops and rigging. Also, applied to flying-kites and their gear. Also, to an officer overclothing himself.

TOP-LANTERN, or Top-light. A large signal-lantern placed in the after-part of a top, in ships where an admiral's flag or commodore's pen-dant flies.

TOP-LINING. A lining on the after-part of sails, to prevent their chafing against the top-rim. Also, a platform of thin board nailed upon the upper part of the cross-trees on a vessel's top.

TOP-MAST. The second division of a mast above the deck. (*See* Mast.)

TOP-MAUL. A large hammer used to start the topmast fid, and to beat down the top, when setting up topmast-rigging.

TOP-MEN. Selected smart seamen stationed in the several tops, to attend the taking in or setting of the upper sails.

TOP-NETTINGS. *See* Top.

TOPPING. Pretentious; as, topping the officer; also, fine, gallant, &c.

TOPPING-LIFTS. Those lifts which support a spar, davit, &c.

TOP-RAIL. A rail supported on stanchions across the after-part of each of a ship's tops.

TOP-RIDERS. *See* UPPER FUTTOCK-RIDERS.

TOP RIM OR BRIM. The circular sweep of the fore part of a vessel's top, and covering in the ends of the cross-trees and trestle-trees, to prevent their chafing the topsail.

TOP-ROPE. The mast-rope employed to sway up a topmast or topgallant-mast, in order to fix it in its place, or lower it. The top-rope is rove through a block which is hooked on one side of the cap, and passing through the sheave-hole of the mast, is brought upwards on the opposite side, and fastened to an eyebolt in the foremost part of the cap. To the lower end of the topmast top-rope a tackle is fixed. (*See* TOP-TACKLE.) "Swaying on all top-ropes;" figuratively, "going the whole hog" in joviality or any trickery.

TOPSAIL HAUL! OR MAIN-TOPSAIL HAUL! When the mainsail is not set, this is the order given to haul the after-yards round when the ship is nearly head to wind in tacking.

TOP-SAILS. The second sails above the decks, extending across the topmasts, by the topsail-yards above, and by the lower yards beneath, being fastened to the former by earings and robands, and to the latter by the topsail-sheets, which, passing through two great blocks or cheeks fixed on its extremities, and thence to two other blocks fixed on the inner part of the yard close by the mast, lead downwards to the deck.—*Paying debts with flying topsails*, or *with a flying fore-topsail*, is leaving them unpaid. Vessels not having topsail-yards rigged aloft, set topsails flying, as cutters yachts, schooners, &c.

TOPSAIL-SCHOONER. Is full schooner-rigged, but carries a square-topsail on the foremast; the foresail not bent, but set as a square-sail. She may also carry a main-topsail, and is then termed a two-topsail schooner.

TOPSAIL-SHEET BITTS. Standing bitt-heads through which the topsail-sheets lead, and to which they are belayed.

TOP-SAWYER. The leading man in any undertaking. One who excels; inasmuch as the man of most intellect guides the saw, and No. 2 gets the sawdust in his face.

TOP-SIDE. All that part of a ship's side which is above the main-wales: that is, those strakes between the sheer-strake and upper black-strake.

TOP-SWIVEL. Once a favourite arm for ships' tops, but from the confined space and elevation rather an encumbrance than a useful addition.

TOP-TACKLE. A large tackle, or properly pendant, hooked to the lower end of the topmast top-rope, and to the deck, in order to increase the mechanical power in lifting the topmast in order to fid it. It is composed of two strong iron-bound double or triple blocks, the hooks of which work on a swivel.

TOP-TACKLE PENDANT. The pendant used with the above. The topmast is swayed up by a top-rope or hawser. The pendant, which is of better material, and hawser-laid, has an eye and thimble spliced in one end, and is pointed at the other. This pendant is barely long enough to lower the topmast temporarily in bad weather, and when the topmast is high enough for fidding, the purchase is block and block, and cannot lift it higher. (*See* TOP-ROPE.)

TOP THE GLIM, To. To snuff the candle.

TOP THE OFFICER, To. To arrogate superiority.

TOP-TIMBER BREADTH. The distance between the upper part of the same timber and the middle line.

TOP-TIMBER HOLLOW. A name sometimes given to the back sweep which forms the upper part of the top-timber.

TOP-TIMBERS. The first general tier which reach the top are called long top-timbers, and those below short top-timbers.

TOP YOUR BOOM. *See* BOOM.

TOR. A high rock or peak: also a tower, thus retaining the same meaning it had, as *torr*, with the Anglo-Saxons.

TORMENTER. The large two-pronged iron fork used by the ship's cook, to fish out the cooked meat from the copper.

TORMENTUM. A pistol; a gun; a piece of ordnance.

TORNADO. A peculiar squall, accompanied with rain and lightning, similar in suddenness to the white squall of the West Indies, and experienced off the equatorial region of the west coast of Africa between December and June. It appears first as a small black spot in the east, and barely affords time to put the ship before the wind and clue up all. The wind veers round the compass, and lasts a very short time.

TORPEDO. A cartilaginous fish allied to the rays, furnished with electrical organs, by means of which it is able to give powerful shocks. Also, a contrivance for blowing up ships of war by means of a submerged apparatus.

TORRENT. A land flood rushing from mountainous tracts, often with destructive effect. It is produced by an accumulation of water from rains or the melting of snows.

TORSE. A coarse kind of hemp, better known as cordilla in commerce.

TORSION OF CABLES. All ropes formed by twisting have a contrary turn, and a disposition to kink from torsion.

TORSK. *See* TUSK.

TORTS. Private wrongs either to persons or property afloat. They are cognizable by the admiralty court, according to locality.

TORTUE DE MER. A turtle. Also a French gabare, troop, or store ship, with very high 'tween decks.

TOSHING. A cant word for stealing copper sheathing from vessels' bottoms, or from dock-yard stores.

TOSS IN YOUR OARS! The order to desist rowing, and throw the oars in out of the rowlocks.

TOSS THE OARS UP! Throw them up out of the rowlocks, and raise them perpendicularly an-end; the act is intended as a compliment to a superior officer rowing by. Also, the order to a boat's crew to get the oars ready for rowing, and to salute the officer on his entering the boat.

TOSS UP THE BUNT, To.   In furling a sail, to make its final package
at the centre of the yard when in its skin.

TOT, or Tott.   A drinking-cup somewhat smaller than the regulation
half-pint, by which a surplus is left in the distribution of the regular
allowance of grog, and awarded to the cook of each mess, for the day, for
his trouble.

TOTAL LOSS.   A term in marine insurance, implying that the underwriters are to pay the amount insured without salvage.

TOTE.   An abbreviation of total.—*To tote.*   To watch, to spy, or to carry,
whence the very singular fish on the southern coasts of America, which
carries small pebbles on its little sharp horns for making a *nest* is called
the *stone-toter.*

TOTTY-LAND.   Certain heights on the side of a hill [probably derived
from the Anglo-Saxon *totian,* to elevate].

TOUCH.   In ship-building, the broadest part of a plank worked top-and-
butt.   Also, the angles of the stern-timbers at the counters.   Also, *keep
ing touch* is fulfilling the terms of an agreement—speaking of the faith
between seamen and their employers.

TOUCH-AND-GO.   Said of anything within an ace of ruin; as in rounding a ship very narrowly to escape rocks, &c., or when, under sail, she
rubs against the ground with her keel, without much diminution of her
velocity.

TOUCH-AND-TAKE.   An old proverb which Nelson applied to a ship
about to encounter her opponent.   A Nelsonian maxim.

TOUCH-BOX.   The receptacle for lighted tinder when match-locks were
used.

TOUCH-HOLE.   The small aperture at the end of a musket or pistol, by
which the fire of the priming was communicated to the charge.   In guns,
called the vent.

TOUCHING.   The state of a ship's sails when they first begin to lift or
shiver with their edges in the direction of the wind.   It is occasioned
either by a change in the wind or in the ship's course.   (*See* FULL AND
BY.)—*Luff and touch her !* is the order to the helmsman to bring the
vessel up, and see how near she will come to the wind, or to give facility
for taking in a reef when about to lower the topsails, or for deadening
the ship's way.

TOUCHING AT.   Stopping or anchoring at some intermediate port in the
course of a voyage.

TOUCH OF THE TAR-BRUSH.   A nautical phrase expressive of those
officers who are seamen as well as *quarter-deckers.*   Also said of a white
person in whose ancestry there has been some admixture of one of the
dark races.

TOUCH UP IN THE BUNT, To.   To mend the sail on the yard;
figuratively, to goad or remind forcibly.

TOUCH-WOOD.   *See* PUNK.

TOURNIQUET.   Screw-bandages used for stopping the flow of blood.

They are distributed about the quarters before action, and a number of men are taught to apply them. A handkerchief and toggle, or stick of any kind, is sometimes substituted.

TOUT, To. An old term for looking out, or keeping a prying watch; whence the revenue cruisers and the customs officers were called touters. The name is also given to crimps.

TOW, To. To draw or drag a ship or boat by means of a rope attached to another vessel or boat, which advances by steam-power, rowing, or sailing. The Roman method, as appears by the triumphal arch at Orange, was by a rope fastened to a pulley at the top of the mast. They also fastened a rope to the head of a boat, and led it over men's shoulders, as practised on our canals at the present day.

TOWAGE. The towing of a vessel through the water. Also, the money given for being towed. Vessels thus relieved give claim for salvage service.

TOW-BLOWEN. A term on our eastern coasts for a blown herring.

TOWEL. A word very absurdly introduced into marine law. "If a mariner," says Molloy, "shall commit a fault, and the master shall lift up the towel three times before any mariner, and he shall not submit, the master at the next place of land may discharge him." Some think that this refers to an oaken stick, but it is no doubt corrupted from the *oster la touaille*, or turning a delinquent out of his mess, of the laws of Oleron.

TOWING-BRIDLE. A stout chain with a hook at each end for attaching a tow-rope to; also, a large *towing-hook* in the bight of the chain.

TOWING-HOOK. *See* TOWING-BRIDLE.

TOWING OVERBOARD. Drawing anything after a ship or boat when she is sailing or rowing. As a manœuvre to deceive an enemy, and induce him to chase, it was common to tow a sail astern by a hawser, at the same time keeping the three masts in line, so as to deceive the chaser as to distance.

TOWING-PATH. The hauling-way along a canal or artificial harbour.

TOWING-POST. A substantial timber fixed through the deck of a steam-tug for making the tow-rope fast to. Also, a similar post in canal barges to keep the tow-line up clear of the path.

TOW-LINE [Anglo-Saxon *toh-line*]. A small hawser or warp used to move a ship from one part of a harbour or road to another by means of boats, steamers, kedges, &c.'

TOWN-MAJOR. An officer in a garrison specially supervising the detail of the guards, and of other local current duties.

T-PLATES. Iron plates in the form of the letter T placed under the channels to add strength.

TRABACCOLO. An Adriatic trading craft.

TRABALEO. Ancient coasting vessels.

TRABARIÆ. Ancient canoes, made of hollowed trees, capable of carrying two or three men.

TRACE. In fortification, the horizontal disposition of the works; also, a plan of the same.

TRACK-BOAT [from the Dutch *treck-schuyt*]. A vessel used on a canal or narrow stream.

TRACKING. Hauling any vessel or floating body along a canal or river by a rope dragged along the bank by men or horses.

TRACK OF A SHIP. The line of a ship's course through the water. (*See* WAKE.)

TRADE. Implies the constant destination of any particular merchant vessels, as the Lisbon trade, West India trade, &c.

TRADER. A vessel employed regularly in any particular branch of commerce, whether sea-borne or coasting, British or foreign.

TRADE-ROOM. A part of the steerage of a Yankee notion-trader where light goods and samples of the cargo are kept for general business.

TRADE-WINDS. Currents of air moving from about the 30th degree of latitude towards the equator. The diurnal motion of the earth makes them incline from the eastward, so that in the northern hemisphere they are from the N.E., and in the southern hemisphere from the S.E. Their geographical position in latitude varies with the declination of the sun. In some parts of the world, as the Bay of Bengal and China Sea, the action of the sun on the neighbouring land has the power of reversing the trades; the winds are there called *monsoons*.

TRADING-VESSEL. *See* TRADER.

TRAIL A PIKE, To. To hold the spear end in the right hand, and the butt trailed behind the bearer.

TRAIL-BOARDS. A carved board on each side of the stem, reaching from it to the figure, or to the brackets. The carved work between the cheek-knees of the head at the heel of the figure.

TRAIN or TRAIL OF ARTILLERY. A certain number of pieces of ordnance, completely mounted and fitted with appurtenances and retinue of attendants, ready to follow in rear of an army, &c. (*See* BATTERING GUNS.) Also, the hinder part of a gun-carriage.—*Train* also signifies a line of gunpowder or other combustible material forming a communication with any body intended to be set on fire or exploded.

TRAINING-LEVEL. A gravitating instrument for the same purpose as the training-pendulum.

TRAINING-PENDULUM. An improved pendulum to facilitate the accurate elevation and depression of guns on board ship, by means of coloured spirits or quicksilver confined in a tube.

TRAINING-SHIP FOR THE MERCHANT SERVICE. A vessel properly equipped with instructors and means to rear able-bodied lads for the merchant service.

TRAINING-SHIP FOR NAVAL CADETS. H.M.S. *Britannia*, commanded by a captain and complement of officers for the primary training of naval cadets. They are nominated by the first lord, examined as to ability and constitution, and entered on trial. If they pass a pretty rigid examination, they are nominated to ships; but if they fail, they are not admitted into the navy. Great interest is required for a nomination.

TRAIN-TACKLE. A tackle which is during action hooked to an eye-bolt in the train of a gun-carriage, and to a ring-bolt in the deck; its use is to prevent the gun from running out of the port whilst loading, and for running it in when fired.

TRAJECTORY. An astronomical term for the orbital curve described by a planet or comet, now seldom used in that science, but generally employed for the path described by a shot or shell.

TRAMMEL. A large drag-net for the cod fishery.

TRAMONTANA. The north wind in general in the Mediterranean, but also denoting a peculiar cold and blighting wind, very hurtful in the Archipelago.

TRAN. A Norwegian word for fish-oil, adopted in our northern fisheries.

TRANKEH, or TRANKIES. A large boat of the Gulf of Persia.

TRANSFER. There can be no legal transfer of property captured at sea, without a legal condemnation in the admiralty court, and therefore the sale or occupancy of vessels and goods by pirates does not alter or extinguish the loser's right of property. Transfer is the legal state of a registered ship, or shares in her, to persons qualified to be owners of British ships. Also, the turning over men or companies from one ship to another.

TRANSHIPMENT OF TREASURE. Ships on a distant station receiving treasure for conveyance to some other man-of-war about to proceed to England, from another port on the same station. Both captains partake of the freight, relatively as to distance and deposit.

TRANSIRE. A custom-house document specifying the goods shipped by a coasting vessel, docketted with a sufferance for their discharge on arriving at the place of destination.

TRANSIT. The precise culmination of a heavenly body over the meridian of a place.

TRANSIT OF MERCURY OR VENUS. These planets being situated between the sun and the earth, occasionally appear to us to pass over his disc, from east to west.

TRANSIT INSTRUMENT. A telescope fitted with vertical wires, and revolving on an axis in the plane of the meridian, with which the time may be obtained by observing the passage of the stars and planets compared with their computed time.

TRANSITU. Goods of an enemy's colony surrendering between the time of sailing and capture do not change their hostile character in *transitu;* though the owners may have become British subjects by capitulation, upon the principle that the national character cannot be altered in transitu. (*See* STOPPAGE IN TRANSITU.)

TRANSMISSION. The property in a merchantman, or a share therein, transmitted in consequence of the authenticated death, bankruptcy, or insolvency of any registered owner.

TRANSOM. The vane of a cross-staff, made to slide along it by means of a square socket; it may be set to any of the graduations.

TRANSOM OF A GUN-CARRIAGE. A cross piece of timber uniting the cheeks; generally between the trunnion-holes and the fore axle-tree.

TRANSOM-KNEES. Curved timbers, or pieces of iron, which bind and connect the ship's quarter to the transoms, being bolted to the latter, and to the after timbers. Knees which have one arm applied to either end of a transom, and the other running diagonally along, and bolted to the ship's side.

TRANSOMS. 'Thwartship pieces forming the buttocks of a ship, extended across the stern-post, to which they are bolted, and give her after-part the figure most suitable to the service for which she is intended.— *Deck-transom.* That on which all the lower deck planks are rabbeted. The first, second, third transoms, &c., are respectively below the preceding.—*Helm-post transom.* That which is at the head of the stern-post, and forms the upper part of the gun-room ports.—*Wing-transom.* The next below, and forming the lower part.

TRANSPORT. A private ship hired by government for carrying troops, stores, and munitions of war. The proportion of tonnage for troops embarked in transports is two tons per man.

TRANSPORTING. Moving a ship by means of hawsers only, from one part of a harbour to another.

TRANSPORTING-BLOCKS. Two snatch-blocks, fitted one on each side above the taffrail, to admit a hawser, when transporting a ship.

TRANSPORT OFFICE. Formerly a department under government directed by commissioners, who chartered vessels and appointed officers for conveying troops to or from this country: they were also to provide accommodation and provision for all prisoners of war, as well as to regulate their exchange by cartel, &c. Now under a naval director of transport.

TRANS-SHIP, To. To remove a cargo from one ship to another.

TRANSVERSE AXIS. The first or principal diameter of an ellipse; that which crosses it lengthwise. (*See* MAJOR AXIS.)

TRANSVERSE SECTION. A 'thwartship view of any part of a ship when cut by a plane at right angles to the keel.

TRANTER. One who carries fish for sale.

TRAP-CREEL. A basket for catching lobsters.

TRAPEZIUM. A quadrilateral figure that has only two of its four sides parallel.

TRAPEZOID, OR **TABLET.** Has all its four sides and angles unequal, and no sides parallel.

TRAVADO, OR **TRAVAT** [from *tornado*]. A heavy squall, with sudden gusts of wind, lightning, and rain, on the coast of North America; like the African tornado, it commences with a black cloud in calm weather and a clear sky.

TRAVEL, To. For a thimble, block, &c., to run along on beams or ropes.

TRAVELLER. One or more iron thimbles with a rope spliced round them, sometimes forming a kind of tail, but more generally a species of grummet.—*Traveller of boat's masts, jib-boom,* &c. An iron ring fitted so as to slip up and down a spar, to run in and out on a boom or gaff, for the purpose of extending or drawing in the outer corner or tack of the sail.

TRAVELLER-IRON. To a cutter's foresail, boom-mainsail, or spanker-boom; generally termed traveller horse. (*See* HORSE.)

TRAVELLING-BACKSTAYS, are generally the breast backstays, which set up with a runner purchase in the channels on the weather side; that to leeward is let go in stays. The traveller is a strong parrel-strop which passes round the mast, and through two thimbles of which the breast backstays reeve. As the yard is hoisted this slips up, but when a reef is taken in it is rode down by the feet of two men close to the tye block, and thus supports the mast from the toprim to the parrel.

TRAVELLING-GUYS. The jib traveller guys are seized on to the traveller, and are shortened in and set up when the jib is eased in.

TRAVELLING-MARTINGALE. A similar contrivance adapted to a martingale to support the jib-boom in that particular part where the jib-tack is fixed. (*See* MARTINGALE.)

TRAVERSE. Denotes the several courses a ship makes under the changes of wind or manœuvres. It is self-evident that if she steered a course there would be no traverse. But her course being north, and the wind from the north, it is evident she could have but two courses open to her, E.N.E., or W.N.W. The reduction of the distances run on each course, corrected for variation and leeway, constitutes the traverse table, from which the reckoning is deduced each day up to noon. From this zig-zag set of lines we have the term *Tom Cox's traverse* (which see). Also, in fortification, a mound, often of parapet form, raised to cover from enfilade or reverse fire. Also, to traverse a gun or mortar. To alter its direction from right to left, or *vice versâ*, with handspikes, tackles, &c.

TRAVERSE A YARD, To. To get it fore and aft.

TRAVERSE-BOARD. A thin circular piece of board, marked with all the points of the compass, and having eight holes bored in each, and eight small pegs hanging from the centre of the board. It is used to determine the different courses run by a ship during a watch, by sticking one peg into the point on which the ship has run each half hour. It is useful in light and variable winds.

TRAVERSE-HORSE. *See* JACKSTAYS.

TRAVERSE QUESTIONS. Cross examinations at a court-martial.

TRAVERSE SAILING. Resolving a traverse is merely a general term for the determination of a single course equivalent to a series of successive courses steered, whatever be the manner of finding the lengths of the lines forming the triangles.

TRAVERSE-TABLE. A table which gives the difference of latitude and departure corresponding to a certain course and distance, and *vice-versâ*. It is generally calculated to every quarter of a point or degree, and up to a distance of 300 miles.

TRAVERSE-WIND. A wind which sets right in to any harbour, and prevents the departure of vessels.

TRAVERSIER. A small fishing vessel on the coast of Rochelle.

TRAVERSUM. A archaic term for a ferry.

TRAWL. A strong net or bag dragged along the bottom of fishing-banks, by means of a rope, a beam, and a pair of iron trawl-heads.

TRAYERES. An archaic term for a sort of long-boat.

TREADING A SEAM, OR DANCING PEDRO-PEE. *See* PEDRO-A-PIED.

TREAD OF A SHIP OR KEEL. The length of her keel.

TREAD WATER, To. The practice in swimming by which the body is sustained upright, and the head kept above the surface.

TREBLE-BLOCK. One fitted with three sheaves or rollers.

TREBLING. Planking thrice around a whaler's bows in order the more effectually to withstand the pressure of the ice.

TREBUCHET. An engine of old to cast stones and batter walls.

TRECK-SCHUYT. A canal boat in Holland for carrying goods and passengers.

TREEING. In the Arctic regions, refraction sometimes causes the ice to resemble a huge wall, which is considered an indication of open water in that quarter.

TREE-NAILS. Long cylindrical oak or other hard wood pins, driven through the planks and timbers of a vessel to connect her various parts.

TREE-NAIL WEDGE. A cross is cut in the tree-nail end, and wedges driven in, caulked; or sometimes a wedge is driven into its inner end, and the tree-nail is thus secured.

TREES OF A SHIP. The chess-trees, the cross-trees, the rough-trees, the trestle-trees, and the waste-trees.

TRELAWNEY. A poor mess composed of barley-meal, water, and salt.

TRENCHES. The earthworks by which a besieger approaches a fortified place; generally half sunk in the ground, the other half formed by the excavated earth thrown, as a parapet, to the front.

TRENCHMAN. *See* TRUGMAN.

TRENCH THE BALLAST, To. To divide the ballast in a ship's hold to get at a leak, or to trim and stow it.

TREND, To. To bend or incline, speaking of a coast; as, "The land trends to the south-west." Also, the course of a current or stream.

TREND OF AN ANCHOR. The lower end of the shank, where it thickens towards the arms, usually at one-third from the crown. In round terms, it is the same distance on the shank from the throat that the arm measures from the throat to the bill.

TRENNEL. *See* TREE-NAILS.

TREPANG. An eastern name for the *Holothuria*, or *bêche-de-mer*, frequently called the sea-slug; used as an article of food by the Chinese.

TRESTLE-TREES. Two strong bars of timber fixed horizontally fore-and-aft on each side of the lower masthead, to support the topmast, the lower cross-trees, and top; smaller trestle-trees are fitted on a topmast-head to support the topgallant-mast and topmast cross-trees.

TRIANGLE, or TRIGON. A geometrical figure consisting of three sides and as many angles. Also, a machine formed by spars for lifting weights, water-casks, &c. Also, a stage hung round a mast, to scrape, paint, or grease it.

TRIANGULUM. One of the ancient northern constellations.

TRIATIC STAY. A rope secured at each end of the heads of the fore and main masts, with thimbles spliced in its bight to hook the stay-tackles to. This term applies also to the jumper-stay, extending in schooners from the mainmast-head to the foremast-head, clearing the end of the fore gaff.

TRIBUTARY. Any stream, large or small, which directly or indirectly joins another stream.

TRICE, To. To haul or lift up by means of a lashing or line.

TRICE UP—LIE OUT! The order to lift the studding-sail boom-ends while the topmen move out on the yards, preparatory to reefing or furling.

TRICING BATTENS. Those used for the hammocks, or tricing up the bags between the beams on the lower-deck.

TRICING-LINE. A small cord, generally passing through a block or thimble, and used to hoist up any object to render it less inconvenient; such are the tricing-lines of the yard-tackle, &c.

TRICK. The time allotted to a man on duty at the helm. The same a spell.

TRICKER. An old spelling for the trigger of a gun.

TRIE. An old word for trim.—Out of trie, crank.

TRIGGER. In ship-building, is the letting fall the paul of the cradle by which the dog-shore falls flush, and offers no further obstruction to the ship gliding down the ways into her absurdly termed "native element." Also, a small catch under the lock of fire-arms, by drawing which back, when the piece is cocked, it is discharged.

TRIGGER-FINGER. See FORE-FINGER.

TRIGGER-LINE. A line by which the gun is fired.

TRIG-MEAT. A western term for any kind of shell-fish picked up at low water.

TRIGON. See TRIANGLE.

TRIGONOMETRY. The science which deals with measuring triangles, or determining their unknown sides and angles, plane or spherical.

TRIM. The set of a ship on the water, whether by the head or the stern, or on an even keel. It is by the disposition of the ballast, cargo, masts, and other weight which she carries, that a vessel is best adapted for navigation. Also, the working or finishing of any piece of timber or plank to its proper shape or form.—In trim, is neat and regular.—To trim, is to arrange the sails so that they may receive the full advantage of the wind.

TRIM OF THE HOLD. The arrangement of the cargo, &c., by which a vessel carries sail well, and becomes under control as well as seaworthy.

TRIMMED. Sails properly set, and yards well braced after tacking.

TRIMMED SHARP. The arrangement of a ship's sails in a slant wind, so that she may keep as close as possible to the breeze.

TRIMMING A JACKET. Rope's-ending the wearer.

TRIMONIER. A corruption of *timoneer*, but formerly a rating on ships' books.

TRIM THE BOAT! The order to sit in the boat in such a manner as that she shall float upright. Also, to edge aft, so that her steerage becomes easier, and she does not ship heavy seas.

TRINK. An old contrivance for catching fish. (Statute 2 Hen. VI. c. 15.)

TRIP. An outward-bound passage or short voyage, particularly in the coasting trade. It also denotes a single board in plying to windward. Also, the movement by which an anchor is loosened from its bed and raised clear of the bottom, either by its cable or buoy-rope.—*The anchor's a-trip*, *i.e.* no longer holds.

TRIPLE STAR. Three stars situated in close proximity, but apparently only optically connected. (*See* TERNARY SYSTEM.)

TRIPPING. Giving a yard the necessary cant by a tripping-line. Also, the lifting an upper mast to withdraw its fid, in order that it may be lowered by means of the mast-rope.

TRIPPING-LINE. A small rope serving to unrig the lower top-gallant yard-arm of its lift and brace, when in the act of sending it down on deck. Also, the line used for tripping an upper mast.

TROACHER, or TROAKER. A dealer in smuggled goods.

TROCHOID, or CYCLOID. A geometrical curve, resulting from a circle being made to run along a right line, whence the French designate it *roulette*. But if a circle be made to roll along the circumference of another circle, it becomes an *epicycloid* (which see).

TROITE. An archaism for the cuttle-fish.

TROLLING. Drawing the bait along the water to imitate the swimming of a real fish; this is generally done by a long line attached to the stern of a sailing-boat. The word of old signified sauntering or idling about.

TROMBONE. A species of blunderbuss for boat service, taking its name from its unseemly trumpet mouth.

TRONA. An article of export from Tripoli and Egypt; the *natron* of commerce, and *over munnoo* of the East Indies. Sesqui-carb. of soda mixed with salt and sulphate of soda.

TROOP. A company of cavalry, commanded by a captain, generally from forty to sixty strong. Also, an assembling beat of the drum.—*Trooping the guard*, or *the colours*, are special military ceremonies connected with guard-mounting.—*Troop the guard*. A ceremony daily practised in large ships by the marines at morning muster.

TROOP-BOATS. Are built with great flatness of floor, with extreme breadth, carried well forward and aft, and possessing the utmost buoyancy, as well as capacity for stowage. They were carried as paddle-box boats (inverted), and thus protected the paddles as well as being ready for use.

TROOP-SHIPS. A class of vessel of excellent account, during war, in the hands of government; far preferable to hired transports for the purpose of conveying soldiers, especially cavalry and their horses. They were usually, in the last French war, 50's and 64's; and with the lower-deck guns taken out, were roomy and airy.

TROPHY. Anything captured from an enemy and shown or treasured as a token of victory.

TROPICAL MOTION. *See* MOTION.

TROPICAL REVOLUTION. If the periodic time of a circuit round the sun be taken in reference to the equinoxes or tropics, it is called a tropical revolution.

TROPIC-BIRD. *Phaeton ætherius*, a well-known sea-bird, distinguished by two very long feathers in its tail; also termed *boatswain-bird*, from the tail feathers resembling a marline-spike.

TROPICS. Two imaginary lines upon the globe, or lesser circles of the sphere, parallel to the equator, and at 23½° distance on each side of it; they touch the ecliptic at its greatest distances from the equator, and from the boundaries of the sun's declination, north and south.

TROUGH [from the Anglo-Saxon *troh*]. A small boat broad at both ends. Also, the hollow or interval between two waves, which resembles a broad and deep trench perpetually fluctuating. As the set of the sea is produced by the wind, the waves and the trough are at right angles with it; hence a ship rolls heaviest when she is in the trough of the sea.

TROUL. The action of silt being rolled along by a tide.

TROUNCE, To. To beat or punish. An old word; in Mathew's translation of the Bible, 1537, we find, "The Lord trounced Sisera."

TROUNCER. An old word for a waister.

TROUS DE LOUP. Holes dug in the form of an inverted cone, with a sharp picket or stake in each, to break the march of an enemy's column when advancing to the attack.

TROW. A clinker-built, flat-floored barge used on the Severn, &c. Also, a sort of double boat with an interval between, and closed at the ends; it is used on the Tyne for salmon-fishing, the fisherman standing across the opening, leister in hand, ready to strike the quarry which passes.

TRUCE. The exhibition of a flag of truce has been religiously respected amongst civilized nations. It is a request by signal to desist from farther warfare, until the object of the truce requested has been acceded to or rejected.

TRUCHMAN. *See* TRUGMAN.

TRUCK. A Cornish word for the trough between two surfs. Also, exchange, as fish for grog, &c.

TRUCKLE. A Welsh coracle.

TRUCKS. Pieces of wood of various forms, though mostly round; they are for different purposes, as wheels on which the gun-carriages run.—*Trucks of the flagstaves or at the masthead.* Circular caps on the upper mastheads; they are generally furnished with two or more small sheaves, through which the signal halliards are rove.—*Trucks of the parrels.*

Spherical pieces of wood, termed bull's-eyes, having a hole through them, in which is inserted the rope of the parrel. (*See* PARREL.)—*Trucks for fair leaders*, are similar to bull's eyes, but are scored to fit the shrouds to which they are seized. The ropes are thus kept from getting jammed between the yards and the rigging; they are also useful, especially at night, as guides to particular ropes.

TRUE ANOMALY. *See* ANOMALY.

TRUE-BLUE. A metaphorical term for an honest and hearty sailor: "true to his uniform, and uniformly true."

TRUE-HORIZON. *See* HORIZON.

TRUE TIDE. Opposed to *cross-tide* (which see).

TRUE WATER. The exact depth of soundings.

TRUFF. A west-country name for a trout.

TRUG. A rough basket for carrying chips of timber.

TRUGMAN. An early word for interpreter, being a corruption of dragoman; also called *trench-man*, but not *trencher-man*, as a worthy Mediterranean consul wrote it.

TRUMPETER. A petty officer and musician stationed on the poop, to sound salutes and various evolutionary orders.

TRUNCHEON. A field-marshal's baton; also a constable's.

TRUNDLE-HEAD. The lower drum-head of a capstern, when it is double, and worked on one shaft both on an upper and lower deck.

TRUNDLE-SHOT. An iron bolt 16 or 18 inches long, with sharp points, and a ball of lead just inside each head.

TRUNK. (*See* RUDDER-TRUNK.) Also, a large species of turtle. Also, a place for keeping fish in. Also, an iron hoop with a bag, used to catch crabs and lobsters.—*Fire-trunks*. Funnels fixed in fire-ships under the shrouds, to convey the flames to the masts, rigging, and sails.

TRUNK-ENGINE. A direct-acting steam-engine, in which the end of the connecting-rod is attached to the bottom of a hollow trunk, passing steam-tight through the cylinder cover.

TRUNK-FISH. A name of the *Ostracion*, a fish remarkable for having its body encased in an inflexible armour of hard octagonal plates, the fins, mouth, and gill-openings passing through holes in this casing.

TRUNNION-RING. The ring round a cannon next before the trunnions, now disused.

TRUNNIONS. The arms, or two pieces of metal projecting from the opposite sides of a gun, by which it rests and swings upon its carriage, acting as an axis of elevation or depression. Also, pieces of well-seasoned wood, used in securing the ship's timbers.

TRUSS. The trusses or parrels of the lower yards serve to bind them to their masts and are bowsed taut when the yards are trimmed, in order to arrest motion and friction. But the introduction of an iron goose-neck, centering and securing the yard well free of the mast, very much supersedes the use of trusses.

TRUSS-HOOPS. Synonymous with clasp-hoops for masts or spars; they are open iron hoops, so made that their ends, being let into each other, may be well fastened by means of iron wedges or forelock keys.

TRUSS-PARREL. That part of a rope-truss which goes round the yard.

TRUSS-PENDANT. That part of a rope-truss into which the truss-tackle blocks are seized.

TRUSS-PIECES. The fillings in between the frame compartments of the riders, in diagonal trussing.

TRUSS-TACKLE. A gun-tackle purchase applied to the ends of the truss-pendants, to bowse them taut home to the mast.

TRUSS UP, To. To brail up a sail suddenly; to toss up a bunt.

TRY, To, or Lie-to, in a Gale, is, by a judicious balance of canvas, to keep a ship's bow to the sea, and, with as much as she can safely show, prevent her rolling to windward in the trough of a sea. Close-hauled under all sail, a vessel gains headway within six points of the wind; but in *trying* she may come up to five and fall off to seven: so that a vessel does not hold her own. If the vessel be in proper trim, or properly stowed, she will naturally keep to the wind; but custom, and deficiency of seamanlike ability, have induced the lazy habit of lashing the helm alee.

TRY BACK FOR A BEND, To. To pay back some of the bight of a cable, in order to have sufficient to form the bend.

TRY DOWN, To. To boil out the oil from blubber at sea in whalers.

TRYING THE RANGE. A lubberly mode of estimating the distance of an enemy's ship or fort by firing a shot at it.

TRYSAIL. A reduced sail used by small craft in lieu of their mainsail during a storm. Also, a fore-and-aft sail, set with a boom and gaff, in ships, synonymous with the spencers of brigs and schooners, and the spanker or driver of ships. (*See* Storm Trysail.)

TRYSAIL-MAST. A spar abaft the fore and main mast, for hoisting the trysail.

TRY-WORKS. Large copper boilers, for boiling the blubber in whalers.

TUB, Grog. A half-cask, set apart for mixing the daily allowance of spirit with water, lime-juce, and sugar, prior to its being served out to the ship's company.

TUB, Match. A conical tub used to guard the slow match in action. They were formerly about five-gallon capacity, the head being sunk about two inches, and four holes bored to insert slow matches. They are now almost disused, except to keep a light ready for signal purposes, as rockets, blue lights, &c., by night.

TUBES. *See* Chain-pump.

TUBES, for Guns. A kind of portable priming, for insertion into the vent,—of various patterns. (*See* Friction-tube, Quill-tubes, &c.)

TUBS, Topsail-Halliard. Circular framed racks in which the topsail-halliards are coiled clear for running, and are prevented from fouling by being sent adrift in a gale.

TUBULAR BOILERS. Those in which the flame and hot gases, after leaving the furnaces, pass through a great number of small iron or brass tubes surrounded by water, by which means these gases are made to impart some of their heat to the water before they escape; thus fuel is economized.

TUCK. The after-part of a ship, immediately under the stern or counter, where the ends of the bottom planks are collected and terminate by the tuck-rail. Thus the fir frigates of 1812–14 had flat, square transoms similar to boats, or heart-shaped. Hence our square-tucked frigates, brigs, &c.

TUG. A vessel for towing in and out of harbours and the like. (*See* STEAM TUG.)

TUG, To [from the Anglo-Saxon *teogan*, to pull]. It now signifies to hang on the oars, and get but little or nothing ahead.

TUGG. A heavy sort of wain or cart, on which the ship-timber for naval arsenals was formerly conveyed from Sussex.

TUMBLE IN. *See* TUMBLING HOME.

TUMBLER. One of the numerous names for the porpoise, *Phocœna communis*. Also, a contrivance to avoid the necessity of having copper nailed on the mast to prevent a gaff from chafing it.

TUMBLE UP! A requisition of the boatswain's mates, &c., to quicken the hands after being piped up. The cry is well understood, though so contrary to the known tendency of gravitation.

TUMBLING-HOME. The opposite of wall-sided, or flaring out. That part of a ship's side which curves inwardly above the extreme breadth. In all old sea-books this narrowing of a ship from the extreme breadth upwards is called housing in. (*See* UPPER-WORKS.)

TUMBLING SEA. The increased rolling before a gale.

TUMBRIL. A covered cart for conveying ammunition and pioneers' tools.

TUM-TUM. A West India dish, consisting of boiled plantain beat into a paste and fried.

TUNGULA. A small boat in the Moluccas and Borneo.

TUNNY. A well-known large fish of the family *Scomberidœ*. It forms an important branch of Mediterranean commerce.

TURBONADA. A roaring squall, or short hurricane, of frequent occurrence in the Pacific Ocean [a mimo-phonetic term adopted from the Spaniards].

TURBOT. The *Pleuronectes maximus*, a flat fish in the highest esteem with all icthyophagi.

TURKEY-GRAIN. A name for maize.

TURK'S HEAD. An ornamental knot, so called from resembling a turban, used on side-ropes, &c.; it is worked with a piece of small line by following the lead till it is formed with three parts to each cross.

TURN, To TAKE OR CATCH A. To pass a rope once or twice round a cleat, pin, kevel, or any other thing, to keep it fast.

TURN AHEAD! A self-explanatory order to the engineer, in regulating the movement of a steamer.

TURN A TURTLE, To. To take the animal by seizing a flipper, and throwing him on his back, which renders him quite helpless. Also applied to a vessel capsizing; or throwing a person suddenly out of his hammock.

TURN IN, To. To go to bed.—*To turn out.* To get up.

TURN IN A DEAD-EYE or HEART, To. To seize the end of a shroud or stay, &c., securely round it.

TURNING IN RIGGING. The end of a vessel's shrouds carried round the dead-eyes, laid back and secured by seizings.

TURNING-ROOM. Space in a narrow channel for a ship to work in.

TURN IN THE HAWSE. Two crosses in a cable.

TURN OF THE TIDE. The change from ebb to flood, or the contrary.

TURN OUT THE GUARD! The order for the marines of the guard to fall in, on the quarter-deck, in order to receive a superior officer on board.

TURN OVER MEN, To. To discharge them out of one ship into another.

TURN THE GLASS. The order in throwing the log when the stray line is payed out.

TURN THE HANDS UP, To. To summon the entire crew on deck.

TURN TO WINDWARD, To. To gain on the wind by alternate tacking. It is when a ship endeavours to make progress against the wind by a compound course inclined to the place of her destination; otherwise called plying or beating to windward.

TURNPIKE-SAILORS. Rascals who go about dressed as sailors pretending that they have been shipwrecked, and soliciting charity.

TURPIS CAUSA. An unsustainable suit for wages, on the part of a British pilot, for navigating a foreign ship to an enemy's port.

TURRET-SHIP. A vessel, more or less armoured, fitted with one or more heavily plated revolving turrets, each carrying one or more guns of the heaviest class, which look out above the deck; the whole worked by steam-power. It represents the present improvement on the inventions of the cupola-ship, shield-ship, and monitor.

TURTLE. The well-known marine reptile described by early navigators as "reasonable toothsom meate." The horny covering of the shell of some species furnishes the substance commonly known as *tortoise-shell.*

TURTLE-CRAWL. A shallow lagoon, wherein turtles are kept.

TURTLE-PEG. A socketed pointed iron on a staff; it is slightly barbed, and is a special tool for sticking turtle.

TUSK. The *Brosmus vulgaris*, a savoury fish taken in the northern seas, about the size of the ling, but with a broader tail.

'TWEEN or 'TWIXT DECKS. The one under the gun deck, where sailors usually mess.

TWICE-LAID. Rope made from a selection of the best yarns of old rope. Also, a sea-dish made of the salt-fish left from yesterday's dinner, and beaten up with potatoes or yams.

TWIDDLING-LINE. A piece of small rope ornamentally fitted and used for steadying the steering-wheel when required: no longer used.

TWIG, To. To pull upon a bowline. Also, in familiar phrase, to understand or observe.

TWIG-AIT. A river islet where osiers grow.

TWINE. A kind of strong thread used in sailmaking; it is of two kinds: extra, for sewing the seams; and ordinary, for the bolt-ropes. (*See* WHIP-PING-TWINE.) Irish twine or thumb-line, like nettles, is worked by the fingers from fine yarns drawn from bolt-rope.

TWIN-SCREW. A steamer fitted with two propellers and independent engines, to enable her to turn rapidly on her own axis. The twin-screw principle is not new, but latterly it has been so perfected that speed in turning is no longer a matter of doubt.

TWO-BLOCKS. The same as *chock-a-block* (which see).

TWO-HANDED FELLOWS. Those who are both seamen and soldiers, or artificers; as the marines and, specially, marine artillerymen.

TWO-HANDED SAW. A very useful instrument in ship-carpentry; it is much longer than the hand-saw, and requires two men to use it.

TWO-MONTHLY BOOK. A book kept by the captain's clerk, to be forwarded every two months, when possible, in order to prevent frauds; and in the event of a ship being lost, to have the accounts to the nearest period.

TWO MONTHS' ADVANCE. *See* ADVANCE MONEY.

TWO-PENCES. A deduction from each man, per mensem, formerly assigned to the surgeon for wages.

TWO-TOPSAIL-SCHOONER. *See* TOPSAIL-SCHOONER.

TWY. A meteor squall on the coasts of Wiltshire, Hampshire, &c.

TYE. A runner of thick rope or chain, which forms part of the purchase used for hoisting the topsail and top-gallant yards.

TYE-BLOCK. The block on the yard through which the tye is rove, and passes on to be secured at the mast-head. The block secured to the lower end of the tye is the fly-block.

TYMOOM. A Chinese river craft.

TYNDARIDES. The ancient name of the meteor called *corposanto*.

TYPHOON, TY-FONG, OR TAI-PHON. The Chinese word for a *great wind*, applied to hurricanes or cyclones. They are revolving storms of immense force, occurring most frequently in those parts of the world which are subject to monsoons, and take place at those seasons when the monsoons are changing. They seem to be eddies formed by the meeting of opposing currents of air—for instance, the westerly winds near the equator and the easterly winds of higher latitudes—which accounts for the important fact that these storms revolve in opposite directions in the two hemispheres—in the southern with, in the northern against, the hands of a watch; but the circular tendency in both supports the name of cyclone.

U.

UGLY. A term applied to a threatening heavy atmosphere, also to a head-sea. Also, to an ugly craft, as a mischievous foe, or a pirate.

ULCUS. An old term for the hulk of a ship of burden (*leg*. Ethelred).

ULIGINOUS CHANNELS. Those connecting the branches of rivers, by cuts through the soil.

ULLAGE. The remainder in a cask or package which has leaked or been partially used.—*Ullaged* is used for damaged, short of contents.

ULTIMATUM. The final conditions upon which any proposition or treaty with an enemy can be ratified.

ULTRA MARE. Beyond seas—a naval law term.

ULTRA VIRES. Beyond the power of might or right to interfere.

ULTRA-ZODIACAL. Beyond the limits of the zodiac; applied to those asteroids that revolve outside the ancient zodiac.

UMBRA. The dark shadow of the moon, earth, or any other planet.

UMBRELLA-WARPING. A contrivance similar to an umbrella, by which ships in a calm can be warped ahead.

UNATTACHED. In military phraseology, an officer not belonging to any one company or regiment, or on half-pay.

UNBEND, To. To cast off or untie; to remove the sails from their yards and stays; to cast loose the cables from their anchors, or to untie one rope from another.

UNBITT, To. To remove the turns of a cable from off the bitts. (*See* BITTS.)

UNCLAIMED, AS DERELICT. Vessels found at sea without a human being, or a domestic animal, on board are good prizes, if not claimed within 366 days. If so claimed, full salvage, or half her value, is assigned to the salvors.

UNDECAGON. A geometrical figure of eleven equal sides and angles.

UNDER BARE POLES. The condition of a ship under no canvas, or when the wind is too violent to allow of any sail being set on her.

UNDER-BEVELLING. The alteration made inside a square in hewing timber, as opposed to standing-bevelling.

UNDER-BRIGHT. A meteorological term for the strong light which sometimes appears below clouds near the horizon.

UNDER CANVAS. Synonymous with *under sail*.

UNDER-CURRENT. A stream which sets beneath the surface-water of the sea whilst that is either in a quiescent state or moving in a contrary direction. Swift rivers may run out at top whilst the flood-tide runs in below.

UNDER DECK. The floor of a cabin, or 'tween decks.

UNDER FOOT. Under the ship's bottom; said of an anchor which is dropped while she has headway. An anchor is often dropped under foot when calm prevails and the drift would be towards danger.—*To drop an anchor under foot*, is to let it go and veer a little of the riding cable when the coming home, or parting of the one by which she is riding, is feared.

UNDER LEVEL. *See* BEVELLING.

UNDER-MANNED. When a ship has an insufficient complement, or is short-handed.

UNDER-MASTED. When the masts are either too small or too short, so that a ship cannot spread the sail necessary to give her proper speed.

UNDER METAL. The condition of a gun when the muzzle is depressed, and the metal, *i.e.* the breech, raised; the proper position when not in use, to prevent moisture collecting in the chamber.

UNDER-RUN A HAWSER OR **WARP, To.** To haul a boat along underneath it, in order to clear it, if any part happens to be foul. *To under-run a tackle*, is to separate the several parts of which it is composed, and range them in order, so that the general effort may not be interrupted when it is put in motion by the parts crossing, or by thorough-foots.

UNDER SAIL. The state of a ship when she is in motion from the action of wind on her sails.

UNDER-SET. Wherever the wind impels the surface-water directly upon the shore of a bay, the water below restores equilibrium by taking a direction contrary to the wind. The *resaca*, or underset, is particularly dangerous on those beaches where heavy surf prevails.

UNDER-SHORE, To. To support or raise a thing by putting a spar or prop under it, as a ship is shored up in dock.

UNDER-SKINKER. Assistant to the purser's steward.

UNDER THE LEE. Sheltered from the wind by some intervening object, as a ship under the lee of the land.

UNDER THE SEA. A ship lying-to in a heavy gale, and making bad weather of it.

UNDER THE WIND. So situated to leeward of something as not to feel the wind.

UNDER-TOW. An under current especially noticed at the mouths of great rivers, or where tide and half-tides prevail, completely hampering the sails even with a good breeze. (*See* UNDER-CURRENT.)

UNDER WAY. A ship beginning to move under her canvas after her anchor is started. Some have written this *under weigh*, but improperly. A ship is *under weigh* when she has *weighed* her anchor: she may be with or without canvas, or hove-to. As soon as she gathers way she is *under way*. This a moot point with old seamen.

UNDERWRITERS. The parties who take upon themselves the risk of insurance, and so called from subscribing their names at the foot of the policy. They are legally presumed to be acquainted with every custom of the trade whereon they enter a policy.

UNICORN. The old name for the howitzer, as improved from the licorn, borrowed from the Turks during the last century by the Russians, and from the latter by Europe generally.

UNICORN-FISH, OR SEA-UNICORN. A name for the *narwhal* (which see).

UNIFORM. The dress prescribed by regulation for officers and men of the army, navy, marines, &c.

UNION. The national flag of Great Britain, on shore or afloat. It is a composition of the crosses of St. George of England, St. Andrew of Scotland, and St. Patrick of Ireland, the last having been brought in in 1801. It was formerly inscribed, "For the Protestant Religion and for the Liberty of England." It is in the upper canton of all British ensigns. At the main it is the proper flag of an admiral of the fleet; and was thus flown by Lord Howe at the battle of June 1, 1794.

UNION DOWN. When a ship hoists her ensign upside down it is a signal of distress or of mourning.

UNION-JACK. The union flag used separately; in the merchant service it must have a broad white border.

UNLIMBER, To. With a gun on a travelling-carriage, to release it from the limber, by lifting the trail off the pintail and placing it on the ground, thus bringing it to the position for action.

UNLIVERY. Expenses of unlivery and appraisement are a charge in the first instance against the captors of a prize, to be afterwards apportioned by them ratably against the cargo.

UNMANAGEABLE. When a vessel refuses to answer her helm, has lost her rudder, or is crippled in masts or sails.

UNMOORED. Having one anchor weighed; lying at single anchor.

UNREEVING. The act of withdrawing a rope from any block, thimble, dead-eye, &c., through which it had formerly passed. (*See* REEVE.)

UNRIG, To. To dismantle a ship of her standing and running rigging. —*To unrig the capstan* is to take out the bars.

UNROOMAGED. An antiquated sea term, which, from its application by Sir W. Raleigh, in his account of Sir R. Granville's action, may mean "out of trim."

UNROVE HIS LIFE-LINE. Departed this life.

UNSERVICEABLE TICKET. This is made out in the same manner, and requires the same notations, as a *sick-ticket* (which see), only that no inventory of clothes and other effects is necessary.

UNSHIP, To. The opposite of *to ship.* To remove any piece of timber from its situation in which it is generally used, as "unship the oars," lay them in the boat from the rowlocks; "unship the capstan bars, &c.

UNWHOLESOME SHIP. One that will neither hull, try, nor ride, without labouring heavily in a sea. Also applied to a sugar ship diverted from her former trade, and not properly cleansed, even before taking in a cargo of timber.

UP ALONG. Sailing from the mouth of the channel upwards.

UP ANCHOR. Pipe to weigh; every man to his station.

UP AND DOWN. The situation of the cable when it has been hove in sufficiently to bring the ship directly over the anchor. (*See* RIGHT UP AND DOWN.)

UP-AND-DOWN TACKLE. A purchase used in bowsing down the eyes of the lower rigging over the mast-heads; lifting objects from the hold; getting anchors over the side, &c.

UP BOATS! The order to hoist the boats to the stern and quarter davits.

UP COURSES! The order to haul them up by the clue-garnets, &c.

UPHAND-SLEDGE. A large sledge-hammer used in blacksmith's work, and lifted with both hands, in contradistinction to the short stroke by the master smith.

UPHROE. See UVROU.

UPMAKING. Pieces of plank or timber piled on each other as filling-up in building, more especially those placed between the bilge-ways and ship's bottom preparatory to launching.

UPPER COUNTER. The counter between the wing transom and the rail. (See COUNTER.)

UPPER DECK. The highest of those decks which are continued throughout the whole length of a ship without falls or interruptions, as the quarter-deck, waist, and forecastle of frigates, &c.

UPPER FINISHING. See FINISHINGS.

UPPER MASTS. The top-mast, topgallant-mast, and royal-mast; any spars above these are termed poles. (See POLE-MASTS.)

UPPER STRAKE OR WASH OF BOATS. A strake thicker than those of the bottom, wrought round the gunwales, and lined within the poppets.

UPPER OR TOP-RIDER FUTTOCKS. These timbers stand nearly the same as breadth-riders, and very much strengthen the topside.

UPPER TRANSIT. The passage of a circumpolar star over the meridian above the pole; the opposite of the lower transit.

UPPER-WORKS. That part of a ship which rises from the water's surface when she is properly trimmed for a voyage.

UP SCREW! The order in steamers to lift the screw on making sail.

UP WITH THE HELM. Put it a-weather; that is, over to the windward side, or (whichever way the tiller is shipped) so as to carry the rudder to leeward of the stern-post.

URANOGRAPHY. The delineation of constellations, nebulæ, &c., on celestial charts or globes.

URANOSCOPUS. See SKY-GAZER.

URANUS. A superior planet discovered by the elder Herschel in 1781; it has four known satellites, but possibly six, according to the impression of the discoverer.

URCA. An armed Spanish fly-boat.

URSA MAJOR. One of the ancient northern constellations.

URSA MINOR. An ancient northern constellation, in which the north polar star is situated.

USAGES. Besides the general laws of merchants, there are certain commercial and seafaring usages which prevail in particular countries with the force of law. Underwriters are bound by usages; and they are legal precedents, binding in courts-martial.

USHANT TEAM. The sobriquet given to that portion of the Channel fleet which blockaded Brest.

UTLAGHE. An outlaw; whence by corruption *laggers*, people transported by sentence of law.

UVROU. The circular piece of wood, with holes in it, by which the legs of a crowfoot are extended for suspending an awning.

V

VACUUM. A space utterly empty, even of air or vapour.

VADMEL. Coarse woollen manufacture of the Orkneys. (*See* WAD-MAREL.)

VAIL, To. An old word signifying to lower, to bend in token of submission; as, "Vail their top-gallants." Thus in the old play *George a-Green*, "Let me alone, my lord; I'll make them vail their plumes."

VAKKA. A large canoe of the Friendly Islands, with an outrigger.

VALE, or DALE (which see). Also, gunwale.—*To vale*, was an old term for "dropping down," as in a river.

VALUATION. In cases of restitution after property has been sold, and account of sales cannot be obtained, it may be taken at the invoice price, and 10 per cent profit; but this mode of estimating it does not include freight, even though the ship and cargo belong to the same person.

VALUED POLICY. Is where a value has been set upon the ships or goods insured, and this value inserted in the policy in nature of liquidated damages, to save the necessity of proving it, in case of a total loss.

VALVES. See under their respective particular names.

VAMBRACE. Armour for the front of the arm.

VAN [formerly *vant*, contracted from *avant*]. That part of a fleet, army, or body of men, which is advanced in the first line or front.—*Vanguard*. The advanced division.

VANE. A piece of buntin extended on a wooden stock, which turns upon a spindle at the mast-head; it shows the direction of the wind.—*A distinguishing vane*, denotes the division of a fleet to which a ship of the line belongs, according to the mast on which it is borne.—*Dog-vane*. A small light vane, formed of thin slips of cork, stuck round with feathers, and strung upon a piece of twine. It is usually fastened to the top of a half-pike, and placed on the weather side of the quarter-deck, in order to show the helmsman the direction of the wind.

VANES. The sights of cross-staffs, fore-staffs, quadrants, &c., are pieces of brass standing perpendicularly to the plane of the instrument; the one opposite to the fore horizon-glass is the foresight-vane, the other the back-sight-vane.

VANE-SPINDLE. The pivot on which the masthead-vane turns; it should never be made of metal, lest it attract lightning, unless the masts be fitted with Sir W. Snow Harris's conductors.

VANFOSSE. A wet ditch at the outer foot of the glacis.

VANG. A rope leading from the end of the gaff to the rail, one on each side, so that the two form guys attached to the outer ends of the gaffs to steady them, and when the sails are not set keep them amidships.

VANGEE. A contrivance for working the pumps of a vessel by means of a barrel and crank-breaks.

VAPOUR, OR SMOKE. In polar parlance, a peculiar but natural result of the conversion of water into ice, which is too often supposed to indicate open water.

VARIABLES. Those parts of the sea where a steady wind is not ex-pected.

VARIABLE STARS. Those which are found to exhibit periodical fluc-tuations of brightness; of which Algol and Mira Ceti are notable ex-amples.

VARIATION. A term applied to the deviation of the magnetic needle or compass, from the true north point towards either east or west; called also the *declination*. The variation of the needle is properly defined as the angle which a magnetic needle suspended at liberty makes with the meridian line on a horizontal plane; or an arc of the horizon, compre-hended between the true and the magnetic meridian. (*See* ANNUAL VARIATION.)

VARIATION CHART. The well-known chart produced by Halley, whereon a number of curved lines show the variation of the compass in the places they pass through. The admiralty variation chart has been brought to great perfection.

VARIATION OF THE MOON. An inequality in the movement of our satellite, amounting at certain times to 37' in longitude: it was the first lunar inequality explained by Newton on the principles of gravita-tion.

VARIATION OF THE VARIATION. Is the change in the declina-tion of the needle observed at different times in the same place.

VEDETTE. One or two cavalry soldiers stationed on the look-out.

VEER, To. To let out, to pay out, to turn or change. Also, to veer or wear, in contradistinction from tacking. In tacking it is a necessary condition that the ship be brought up to the wind as close-hauled, and put round against the wind on the opposite tack. But in veering or wearing, especially when strong gales render it dangerous, unseamanlike, or impossible, the head of the vessel is put away from the wind, and turned round 20 points of the compass instead of 12, and, without strain or danger, is brought to the wind on the opposite tack. Many deep-thinking seamen, and Lords St. Vincent, Exmouth, and Sir E. Owen, issued orders to wear instead of tacking, when not inconvenient, deeming the accidents and wear and tear of tacking, detrimental to the sails, spars, and rigging.

VEER A BUOY IN A SHIP'S WAKE, To. To slack out a rope to which a buoy has been attached, and let it go astern, for the purpose of bringing up a boat, or picking up a man who may have fallen overboard.

VEER AND HAUL, To. To gently tauten and then slacken a rope three times before giving a heavy pull, the object being to concentrate the force of several men. The wind is said to veer and haul when it alters its direction; thus it is said, to veer aft, and haul forward.

VEER AWAY THE CABLE, To. To slack and let it run out.

VEERING CABLE, The. That cable which is veered out in unmooring, and not unspliced or unshackled in clearing hawse.

VEGA. α Lyræ. The bright lucida of the old northern constellation Lyra.

VEIN. The clear water between the openings of floes of ice. The same as *ice-lane*. Also, a very limited current of wind—a cat's-paw.

VELOCITY. In naval architecture, designing for velocity is giving that form to a ship's body by which she will pass through the water in the quickest space of time.

VELOCITY OF TIDE or CURRENT, depends on several circumstances. First, the tide varies with the state of the moon, running strongest at the springs, and the force of the ebb is much increased by rains, land freshes, &c. The currents also vary, especially when wind and tide combine to accelerate their action.

VENDAVAL [Sp. south wind, *tiempo di vendavales*]. A stormy time on the coast of Mexico, in the autumn, with violent thunder, lightning, and rain.

VENDUE MASTER. A commercial and marine auctioneer.

VENE-SEANDES. The old commercial term for Venetian sequins.

VENT. In artillery, the small aperture near the breech by which the fire of the priming is communicated to the charge.

VENT-BIT. A peculiar augur or screw gimlet used for clearing the vent of a gun when obstructed.

VENT-FIELD OF A GUN. The raised tablet in the metal near the breech in which the vent is bored.

VENTILATOR. The name of various machines contrived to expel the foul air from the store-rooms and hold, and introduce fresh in its stead.

VENT-PIECE. The movable fitment which closes the breech and contains the vent in Armstrong breech-loading guns.

VENT-PLUG. A fid or stopple made of leather or oakum fitting in the vent of a piece to stop it against weather, &c.

VENTRAL FIN. The posterior pair of fins under the body of fishes, corresponding to the hind legs of terrestrial quadrupeds.

VENUS. One of the inferior planets, and the second in order of distance from the sun. (*See* TRANSIT OF VENUS).

VERIFICATION OF SHIP'S PAPERS. In this necessary process it is declared that papers of themselves prove nothing, and require to be supported by the oaths of persons in a situation to give them validity.

VERITAS. A register of shipping established in Paris, on the principle of Lloyd's List.

VERNAL EQUINOX. The point where the sun crosses the equator, going north. It is opposite the place of the autumnal equinox. (*See* EQUINOXES.)

VERNIER, OR NONIUS. A graduated scale for the measurement of minute divisions, especially on the arcs of astronomical instruments, sextants, &c. The thousandth part of a degree can be taken by the naked eye; the ten thousandth by a microscope.

VERSED SINE. In geometry, is the part of the radius intercepted between the arc and its sine.

VERTEX. The zenith, the point overhead; the apex of a conical mountain.

VERTICAL ANGLES. Opposite angles made by two lines cutting or crossing each other, and are always equal. (*See* ANGLE OF THE VERTICAL.)

VERTICAL CIRCLES. Great circles of the sphere intercepting each other in the zenith and nadir, and cutting the horizon at right angles.

VERTICAL FIRE. In artillery, that directed upward at such an angle as that it will fall vertically, or nearly so, to its destination. It includes all elevations above 30°, though the most usual is 45°. It is very effective with shells; but with small balls, as proposed by Carnot and others, who have ill reckoned the retardation by the atmosphere, it is insignificant.

VERTICAL FORCE. The centre of displacement is also that of the centre of vertical force that the water exerts to support the immersed vessel. Also, the dip of the magnetic needle, measured by vibrations of the dipping needle over certain arcs, and referable to some fixed position, as Greenwich, where corresponding observations with the same needle have been previously, as well as subsequently, made.

VERTICAL PLAN. *See* ORTHOGRAPHY.

VERTICITY. The tendency of the loadstone to point towards the magnetic north and south.

VESSEL. A general name for all the different sorts of ships, boats, &c., navigated on the ocean or on rivers and canals.

VETAYLE. An archaism for victuals.

VIA LACTEA. That well-known irregular luminous band, stretching across the sky from horizon to horizon: it consists of myriads of small stars, and has passed under the names of Milky Way, Galaxy, Jacob's Ladder, Watling-strete, &c.

VICE-ADMIRAL. The rank in the fleet next to that of an admiral; he carries his flag at the fore.

VICE-ADMIRALTY COURTS. Branches of the High Court of Admiralty, instituted for carrying on the like duties in several of our colonies, prize-courts, &c. (*See* ADMIRALTY, HIGH COURT OF.)

VICE-CONSUL. An officer appointed in seaports to aid the consul in affairs relating to merchant vessels. If there be a resident consul, the vice-consul is appointed and paid by him. Vice-consuls wait on commanders, consuls on captains, captains on consuls-general—the naval authority providing boats.

VICE-NAIL. A screw.

VICTUALLER. A vessel which carries provisions. In the early age of the navy, each man-of-war had a victualler especially attached to her; as, in Henry VIII.'s reign, we find the *Nicholas Draper*, of 140 tons and 40 men, was victualler to the *Trinity Sovereign;* the *Barbara* of Greenwich to the *Gabriel Royal*, and so on.

VICTUALLING-BILL. A custom-house document, warranting the shipment of such bonded stores as the master of an outward-bound merchantman may require for his intended voyage.

VICTUALLING-BOOK. A counterpart of the ship's open list, which is kept by the purser, to enable him to make the necessary entries in it.

VICTUALLING-YARDS FOR THE ROYAL NAVY. Large magazines where provisions and similar stores are deposited, conveniently contiguous to the royal dockyards. The establishments in England and Ireland are at Deptford, Gosport, Plymouth, and Cork; and abroad at Malta, Gibraltar, Cape of Good Hope, Jamaica, Halifax, Trincomalee, and Hongkong.

VIDETTE. *See* VEDETTE.

VI ET ARMIS. With force of arms.

VIGIA [Sp. look-out]. A hydrographical warning on a chart to denote that the pinnacle of a rock, or a shoal, may exist thereabout.

VINTINER [from *vigintinarius*]. An officer in our early fleet who commanded a company of twenty men.

VIOL, OR VOYOL. A large messenger formerly used to assist in weighing an anchor by the capstan.

VIOL OR VOYOL BLOCK. A large single-sheaved block through which the messenger passed when the anchor was weighed by the fore or jeer capstan; its block was usually lashed to the main-mast. This voyol-purchase was afterwards improved thus: the voyol-block was securely lashed to the cable at the manger-board, the jeer-fall rove through it, and brought to the jeer-capstan, and the standing part belayed to the bitts; thus a direct runner purchase instead of a dead nip was obtained. It was only used when other means failed, and, after the introduction of Phillipps' patent capstan, was disused.

VIOLENCE. The question in tort, as to the amount of liability incurred by the owners for outrages and irregularities committed by the master.

VIRE. The arrow shot from a cross-bow; also called a quarril.

VIRGILIÆ. A denomination of the Pleiades.

VIRGO. The sixth sign of the zodiac, which the sun enters about the 21st August. Spica, *a* Virginis, is a star of the first magnitude.

VIS INERTIÆ. That physical property in all bodies by which they resist a power that endeavours to put them in motion, or to change any motion they are possessed of; it is in proportion to their weight.

VIS INSITA. The innate force of matter; another name for *vis inertiæ*. It is that by which a vessel "keeps her way."

VISITATION AND SEARCH. The law of nations gives to every belligerent cruiser the right of visitation and search of all merchant ships; wherefore, resistance to such search amounts to a forfeiture of neutrality.

VISNE. A neighbouring place; a term often used in law in actions of marine replevin.

VIS VIVA. The whole effective force or power of acting which resides in a given moving body.

VITRY. A light and durable canvas.

VITTORY. A fine canvas, of which the waistcloths were formerly made.

VIVANDIERE. A kind of female sutler. In the French army they are attached to regiments, which they accompany, sometimes even into the skirts of action.

VIVIER. A French fishing-boat, the same as the *well-boats* of the English coasts, in having a well amidships in which to keep the fish alive until arrival in port.

VIZY, or Vize. An old name for the muzzle-sight on a musket.

VOCABULARY. The system of naval signals based on Sir Home Popham's improvements.

VOES. Arms or inlets of the sea, or sounds, in the Shetland and Orkney Isles. Also applied to creeks and bays.

VOGOVANS. From *voguer* and *avant*, chief rowers in the galleys.

VOLANT. A piece of steel on a helmet, presenting an acute angle to the front.

VOLCANO. A burning mountain or vent for subterranean fire; also applied to one which vomits only mud and water.

VOLLEY. The simultaneous discharge of a number of firearms.

VOLLIGUE. A small boat used on the shores of Asia Minor.

VOLUME. The contents of the globe of a planet, usually given in its proportion to that of the earth; or any named mass, solid, fluid, or vaporous.

VOLUNTARY CHARGE. A document delivered with the purser's accounts respecting provisions.

VOLUNTARY STRANDING. The beaching or running a vessel purposely aground to escape greater danger; this act is treated as particular average loss, and not a damage to be made good by general contribution.

VOLUNTEER. One who freely offers himself for a particular service. Formerly, in the army, a gentleman who, without any certain post or employment, served in the hope of earning preferment, or from patriotism. Latterly, also a civilian who has enrolled himself in a corps of volunteers, for organization and training for the defence of the country.

VOLUNTEERING from a Merchantman into the Navy. Any seaman can leave his ship for the purpose of forthwith entering into the royal navy; and thus leaving his ship does not render him liable to any forfeiture whatever.

VOLUTE. *See* Scroll-head.

VOLVELLE. The contrivance of revolving graduated circles, for making calculations, in old scientific works.

VORTEX. A whirlwind, or sudden, rapid, or violent motion of air or water in gyres or circles.

VOUCHER. A written document or proof, upon which any account or public charge is established.

VOYAGE. A journey by sea. It usually includes the outward and homeward trips, which are called passages.

VOYOL. *See* VIOL.

VRACH. Sea-weed used as a manure in the Channel Islands. Also, a Manx term for the mackerel.

VULFE. A rapid whirlpool or race on the coast of Norway.

W.

WABBLE, To [from the Teutonic *wabelen*]. To reel confusedly, as waves on a windy day in a tide-way. It is a well-known term among mechanics to express the irregular motion of engines or turning-lathes when loose in their bearings, or otherwise out of order. A badly stitched seam in a sail is wabbled. It is also applied to the undulation of the compass-card when the motion of the vessel is considerable and irregular.

WAD. A kind of plug, closely fitting the bore of a gun, which is rammed home over the shot to confine it to its place, and sometimes also between the shot and the cartridge: generally made of coiled junk, otherwise a rope grommet, &c.

WADE, To. An Anglo-Saxon word, meaning to pass through water without swimming. In the north, the sun was said to wade when covered by a dense atmosphere.

WAD-HOOK. An iron tool shaped like a double cork-screw on the end of a long staff, for withdrawing wads or charges from guns; called also a *worm*.

WADMAREL. A hairy, coarse, dark-coloured stuff of the north, once in great demand for making pea-jackets, pilot-coats, and the like.

WAFT [said to be from the Anglo-Saxon *weft*], more correctly written *wheft*. It is any flag or ensign, stopped together at the head and middle portions, slightly rolled up lengthwise, and hoisted at different positions at the after-part of a ship. Thus, at the ensign-staff, it signifies that a man has fallen overboard; if no ensign-staff exists, then half-way up the peak. At the peak, it signifies a wish to speak; at the mast-head, recals boats; or as the commander-in-chief or particular captain may direct.

WAFTORS. Certain officers formerly appointed to guard our coast fisheries. Also, swords blunted to exercise with.

WAGER POLICY. An engagement upon interest or no interest; the performance of the voyage in a reasonable time and manner, and not the bare existence of the ship or cargo, is the object of insurance.

WAGES or PAY of the Royal Navy is settled by act of parliament. In the merchant service seamen are paid by the month, and receive their wages at the end of the voyage.

WAGES REMITTED FROM ABROAD. When a ship on a foreign station has been commissioned twelve calendar months, every petty officer, seaman, and marine serving on board, may remit the half of the pay due to them to a wife, father, mother, grandfather, grandmother, brother, or sister.

WAGGON. A place amidships, on the upper deck of guard-ships, assigned for the supernumeraries' hammocks.

WAGGONER. A name applied to an atlas of charts, from a work of this nature published at Leyden in 1583, by Jans Waghenaer.

WAIF. Goods found and not claimed; derelict. Also used for *waft*.

WAIST. That portion of the main deck of a ship of war, contained between the fore and main hatchways, or between the half-deck and galley.

WAIST-ANCHOR. An additional or spare anchor stowed before the chess-tree. (*See* Spare Anchor.)

WAIST-BOARDS. The berthing made to fit into a vessel's gangway on either side.

WAIST-CLOTHS. The painted canvas coverings of the hammocks which are stowed in the waist-nettings.

WAISTERS. Green hands, or worn seamen, in former times stationed in the waist in working the ship, as they had little else of duty but hoisting and swabbing the decks.

WAIST-NETTINGS. The hammock-nettings between the quarter-deck and forecastle.

WAIST-RAIL. The channel-rail or moulding of the ship's side.

WAIST-TREE. Another name for *rough-tree* (which see).

WAIVE, To. To give up the right to demand a court-martial, or to enforce forfeitures, by allowing people who have deserted, &c., to return to their duties.

WAIVING. The action of dispensing with salutes—by signal, by motion of the hand to guards, &c., and to vessels, which may be, in accordance with old custom, passing under the lee to be hailed and examined.

WAIVING AMAIN. A salutation of defiance, as by brandishing weapons, &c.

WAKE. The transient, generally smooth, track impressed on the surface-water by a ship's progress. Its bearing is usually observed by the compass to discover the angle of lee-way. A ship is said to be in the wake of another, when she follows her upon the same track. Two distant objects observed at sea are termed in the wake of each other, when the view of the farthest off is intercepted by the one that is nearer. (*See* Crossing a Ship's Wake.)

WALE-REARED. Synonymous with *wall-sided*.

WALES. The thickest strakes of wrought stuff in a vessel. Strong planks extending all along the outward timbers on a ship's side, a little above her water-line; they are synonymous with *bends* (which see). The channel-wale is below the lower-deck ports, and the main-wale between the top of those ports and the sills of the upper-deck ports.

WALK AWAY! The order to step out briskly with a tackle fall, as in hoisting boats.

WALK BACK! A method in cases where a purchase must not be lowered by a round turn, as "Walk back the capstan;" the men controlling it by the bars and walking back as demanded.

WALKER'S KNOT. *See* Matthew Walker.

WALKING A PLANK. An obsolete method of destroying people in mutiny and piracy, under a plea of avoiding the penalty of murder. The victim is compelled to walk, pinioned and blindfolded, along a plank projecting over the ship's side, which, canting when overbalanced, heaves him into the sea. Also, for detecting whether a man is drunk, he is made to walk along a quarter-deck plank.

WALKING AWAY WITH THE ANCHOR. Said of a ship which is dragging, or *shouldering*, her anchor; or when, from fouling the stock or upper fluke, she trips the anchor out of the ground.

WALKING SPEAKING-TRUMPET. A midshipman repeating quarter-deck orders.

WALK SPANISH, To. To quit duty without leave; to desert.

WALK THE QUARTER-DECK, To. A phrase signifying to take the rank of an officer.

WALK THE WEATHER GANGWAY NETTING. A night punishment in a man-of-war for those of the watch who have missed their muster.

WALL. A bank of earth to restrain the current and overflowing of water. (*See* Sea-bank.)

WALL-KNOT, or Wale-knot. A particular sort of large knot raised upon the end of a rope, by untwisting the strands, and passing them among each other.

WALL-PIECE. A very heavy powerful musket, for use in fortified places.

WALL-SIDED. The sides of a ship continuing nearly perpendicular down to the surface of the water, like a wall. It is the mean between *tumbling home* and *flairing out*.

WALRUS [Dan. *hval-ros*]. The *Trichecus rosmarus*, a large amphibious marine animal, allied to the seals, found in the Arctic regions. Its upper canines are developed into large descending tusks, of considerable value as ivory. It is also called morse, sea-horse, and sea-cow. This animal furnished Cook, as well as our latest Arctic voyagers, with

Arctic beef. The skin is of the utmost importance to the Esquimaux, as well as to the Russians of Siberia, &c.

WALT. An old word, synonymous with *crank;* or tottering, like a sprung spar.

WANE. In timber, an imperfection implying a want of squareness at one or more of its corners; under this deficiency it is termed *wane-wood.*

WANE-CLOUD. *See* CIRRO-STRATUS.!

WANGAN. A boat, in Maine, for carrying provisions.

WANY. Said of timber when spoiled by wet.

WAPP, OR WHAP. A name formerly given to any short pendant and thimble, through which running-rigging was led. Also, a rope where-with rigging was set taut with wall-knots, one end being fast to the shroud, and the other brought to the laniard. But any shroud-stopper is a *wapp.*

WAR. A contest between princes or states, which, not being determinable otherwise, is referred to the decision of the sword. It may exist without a declaration on either side, and is either *civil, defensive,* or *offensive.*

WAR-CAPERER. A privateer.

WARDEN. *See* LORD-WARDEN.

WARD-ROOM. The commissioned officers' mess-cabin, on the main-deck in ships of the line.

WARD-ROOM OFFICERS. Those who mess in the ward-room, namely: the commander, lieutenants, master, chaplain, surgeon, paymaster, marine-officers, and assistant-surgeons.

WARE, To. *See* VEER.

WAREHOUSING SYSTEM. The use of bonding places under charge of officers of the customs, in which goods may be deposited, without any duty upon them being exacted, until they be cleared for home use, or for exportation.

WAR ESTABLISHMENT. Increased force of men and means.

WARM-SIDED. Mounting heavy metal, whether a ship or a fort.

WARNER. A sentinel formerly posted on the heights near sea-ports to give notice of the approach of vessels. Also, beacons, posts, buoys, lights, &c., warning vessels of danger by day as well as by night.

WARNING-SIGNAL. Hoisted to warn vessels not to pass a bar. Also, to warrant higher pay to watermen plying between Portsmouth and Spithead, &c., according to severity of weather.

WARP. A rope or light hawser, employed occasionally to transport a ship from one place to another in a port, road, or river. Also, an east-coast term for four herrings. Also, land between the sea-banks and the sea.— *Warp of lower rigging.* A term used in the rigging-loft, as, before cutting out a gang of rigging, it is warped. Also, to form the warp of spun-yarn in making sword-mats for the rigging-gripes, slings, &c.—*To warp.* To move a vessel from one place to another by warps, which are attached to buoys, to other ships, to anchors, or to certain fixed objects on shore. Also, to flood the lands near rivers in Yorkshire.

WARPING AND FRAMING THE TIMBERS. Putting in the beam-knees, coamings, &c., and dividing the spaces between the beams for fitting the carlines.

WARPING-BLOCK. A block made of ash or elm, used in rope-making for warping off yarn.

WARRANT. A writ of authority, inferior to a commission; in former days it was the name given to the deed conferring power on those officers appointed by the navy board, while those granted by the admiralty were styled commissions. Also, a document, under proper authority, for the assembling of a court-martial, punishment, execution, &c. Also, a tabulated regulation for cutting standing and running rigging, as well as for supply of general stores, as warranted by the admiralty.—*Brown-paper warrants.* Those given by a captain, and which he can cancel.

WARRANT-OFFICER. Generally one holding his situation from particular boards, or persons authorized by the sovereign to grant it. In the royal navy it was an officer holding a warrant from the navy board, as the master, surgeon, purser, boatswain, gunner, carpenter, &c. In the year 1831, when the commissioners of the navy, or navy board, were abolished, all these powers reverted to the admiralty, but the commissions and warrants remain in effect the same.

WARRANTY. The contract of marine insurance, expressing a certain condition on the part of the insured, upon which the contract is to take effect; it is always a part of the written policy, and must appear on the face of it. In this it differs from *representation* (which see).

WARREN-HEAD. A northern term for a dam across a river.

WAR-SCOT. A contribution for the supply of arms and armour, in the time of the Saxons.

WAR-SHIP. Any ship equipped for offence and defence; whereas *man-of-war* generally signifies a vessel belonging to the royal navy.

WARTAKE. An archaic term for a rope-fast, or spring. In that early sea-song (*temp.* Henry VI.) which is in the library of Trinity College, Cambridge, the skipper of the ship carrying a cargo of "pylgryms" exclaims, "Hale in the wartake!"

WARTH. An old word signifying a ford. Also, a flat meadow close to a stream.

WASH. An accumulation of silt in estuaries. Also, a surface covered by floods. Also, a shallow inlet or gulf: the east-country term for the sea-shore. Also, the blade of an oar. Also, a wooden measure of two-thirds of a bushel, by which small shell-fish are sold at Billingsgate, equal to ten strikes of oysters.—*Wash,* or *a-wash.* Even with the water's edge.

WASH-BOARD, or WASH-STRAKE. A movable upper strake which is attached by stud-pins on the gunwales of boats to keep out the spray. Wash-boards are also fitted on the sills of the lower-deck ports for the same purpose.

WASH-BOARDS. A term for the white facings of the old naval uniform.

WASHERMAN. A station formerly for an old or otherwise not very useful person on board a man-of-war.

WASHERS. Leather, copper, lead, or iron rings interposed at the end of spindles, before a forelock or linch-pin, to prevent friction, or galling the wood, as of a gun-truck. Also used in pump-gear.

WASHING-PLACE. In 1865, baths and suitable washing-places were fitted for personal use in the ships of the royal navy. Both hot and cold water are supplied. Shades of Drake, Frobisher, and Raleigh, think of that!

WASHING THE HAND. A common hint on leaving a ship disliked.

WASH-WATER. A ford.

WATCH. The division of the ship's company into two parties, one called the starboard, and the other the larboard or port watch, alluding to the situation of their hammocks when hung up; these two watches are, however, separated into two others, a first and second part of each, making four in all. The crew can also be divided into three watches. The officers are divided into three watches, in order to lighten their duty; but it is to be borne in mind that the watch may sleep when their services are not demanded, whereas it is a crime, liable to death, for an officer to sleep on his watch. In a ship of war the watch is generally commanded by a lieutenant, and in merchant ships by one of the mates. The word is also applied to the *time* during which the watch remains on deck, usually four hours, with the exception of the dog-watches.—*Anchor-watch.* A quarter watch kept on deck while the ship rides at single anchor, or remains temporarily in port.—*Dog-watches.* The two reliefs which take place between 4 and 8 o'clock P.M., each of which continues only two hours, the intention being to change the turn of the night-watch every twenty-four hours.—*First watch.* From 8 P.M. till midnight.—*Middle-watch.* From midnight till 4 A.M.—*Morning-watch.* From 4 to 8 A.M. —*Watch* is also a word used in throwing the deep-sea lead, when each man, on letting go the last turn of line in his hand, calls to the next abaft him, "Watch, there, watch!" A buoy is said to *watch* when it floats on the surface of the water.

WATCH AND WATCH. The arrangement of the crew in two watches.

WATCH-BILL. The pocket "watch and station bill," which each officer is expected to produce if required, and instantly muster the watch, or the men stationed to any specific duty.

WATCHET. A light blue, or sky-coloured cloth worn formerly by English sailors, especially by the boats' crews of men-of-war.

WATCH-GLASSES. The half-hour glasses employed to measure the periods of the watch, so that the several stations therein may be regularly kept and relieved, as at the helm, pump, look-out, &c. (*See* GLASS.)

WATCHING A SMOOTH. Looking for a temporary subsidence of the waves of a head-sea, previous to easing down the helm, in tacking ship.

WATCH-SETTING. In the army, retreat, or the time for mounting the night-guards.

WATCH-TACKLE. A small luff purchase with a short fall, the double block having a tail to it, and the single one a hook. Used for various purposes about the decks, by which the watch can perform a duty without demanding additional men.

WATER, To. To fill the casks or tanks; to complete water.

WATERAGE. The charge for using shore-boats.

WATER-BAILIFF. An officer in sea-port towns for the searching of vessels.

WATER-BALLAST. Water when used to stiffen a ship, whether carried in casks, tanks, bags, or otherwise. The iron screw-colliers of the present day have immense tanks constructed in their floors, on the upper part of which the coals rest; when they are discharged, the tanks are allowed to fill with water, which acts as ballast for the return voyage, and is pumped out by the engine as the coals are taken in.

WATER-BARK. A small decked vessel or tank, used by the Dutch for carrying fresh water.

WATER-BATTERY. One nearly on a level with the water—*à fleur d'eau;* a position of much power when vessels cannot get close to it.

WATER-BEWITCHED. Bad tea, *geograffy*, 5-water grog, and the like greatly diluted drinks.

WATER-BORNE. When a ship just floats clear of the ground. Also, goods carried by sea, or on a river.

WATER-CROW. The lesser cormorant, or shag.

WATER-DOG. *See* WATER-GALL.

WATER-FLEAS. The groups of crustaceous organisms classed as *Entomostraca*.

WATER-GAGE. A sea wall or bank. Also, an instrument to measure the depth of inundations.

WATER-GALL. A name of the *wind-gall* (which see). Shakspeare, in the *Rape of Lucrece*, uses the term thus:—

> "And round about her tear-distained eye
> Blue circles stream'd, like rainbows in the sky.
> These water-galls in her dim element
> Foretell new storms to those already spent."

WATER-GAVEL. A rent paid for fishing in some river, or other benefit derived therefrom.

WATER-GUARD. Custom-house officers employed to prevent fraud on the revenue in vessels arriving at, or departing from, a port.

WATER HIS HOLE. A saying used when the cable is up and down, to encourage the men to heave heartily, and raise the shank of the anchor so that the water may get down by the shank, and relieve the anchor of the superincumbent mud.

WATER-HORSE. Cod-fish stacked up in a pile to drain, under the process of cure.

WATER-LAID ROPE. The same as *cablet;* it coils against the sun, or to the left hand.

WATER-LINE. In former ships of war, a fine white painted line or bend, representing the deep line of flotation, on the coppered edge.—*Load-water line.* That which the surface of the water describes on a ship when she is loaded or ready for sea.

WATER-LINE MODEL. The same as *key-model* (which see).

WATER-LOGGED. The state of a ship full of water, having such a buoyant cargo that she does not sink. In this dangerous and unmanageable situation there is no resource for the crew except to free her by the pumps, or to abandon her by taking to the boats; for the centre of gravity being no longer fixed, the ship entirely loses her stability, and is almost totally deprived of the use of her sails, which may only operate to accelerate her destruction by oversetting her, or pressing her head under water. Timber-laden vessels, water-logged, frequently float for a very long period.

WATER-PADS. Fellows who rob ships and vessels in harbours and rivers.

WATER-PLOUGH. A machine formerly used for taking mud and silt out of docks and rivers.

WATER-SAIL. A *save-all*, or small sail, set occasionally under the lower studding-sail or driver-boom, in a fair wind and smooth sea.

WATER-SCAPE. A culvert, aqueduct, or passage for water.

WATER-SHED. A term introduced into geography to denote the dividing ridges in a hilly country. In geology, it implies that the water is shed thence naturally, by the inclination, to the valley base. As regards nautical men in search of water, it is therefore expedient to look for the depressed side of the strata.

WATER-SHOT, or QUARTER-SHOT. When a ship is moored, neither across the tide, nor right up and down, but quartering between both.

WATER-SHUT. An old name for a flood-gate.

WATER-SKY. In Arctic seas, a dark and dull leaden appearance of the atmosphere, the reflected blue of the sea indicating clear water in that direction, and forming a strong contrast to the pale *blink* over land or ice.

WATER-SNAKES. A group of snakes (*Hydrophis*), whose habitat is the sea. Some of them are finely coloured, and generally very like land-snakes, except that their tails are broader, so as to scull or propel them through the water.

WATER-SPACE. The intervening part between the flues of a steamer's boiler.

WATER-SPOUT. A large mass of water collected in a vertical column, and moving rapidly along the surface of the sea. As contact with one has been supposed dangerous, it has been suggested to fire cannon at them, to break the continuity by aërial concussion. In this phenomenon, heat and electricity seem to take an active part, but their cause is not fully explained, and any facts respecting them by observers favourably placed will help towards further researches into their nature. (*See* WHIRL-WIND.)

WATER-STANG. A spar or pole fixed across a stream.

WATER-STEAD. An old name for the bed of a river.

WATER-STOUP. A northern name for the common periwinkle.

WATER-TAKING. A pond, the water of which is potable.

WATER-TANKS. *See* TANKS.

WATER-TIGHT. Well caulked, and so compact as to prevent the admission of water. The reverse of *leaky*.

WATER-WAYS. Certain deck-planks which are wrought next to the timbers; they serve to connect the sides of a ship to her decks, and form a channel to carry off any water by means of scuppers.

WATER-WAR. A name for the bore or hygre of the Severn.

WATER-WITCH. A name of the dipper.

WATER-WRAITH. Supposed water-spirits, prognosticating evil, in the Shetland Islands.

WATH. A passage or ford through a river.

WATTLES. A kind of hair or small bristles near the mouth and nostrils of certain fish. Also, hurdles made by weaving twigs together.

WAVE [from the Anglo-Saxon *wæg*]. A volume of water rising in surges above the general level, and elevated in proportion to the wind.

WAVESON. Such goods as after shipwreck appear floating on the waves. (*See* FLOTSAM.)

WAVING. Signals made by arm or otherwise to a vessel to come near or keep off.

WAY. Is sometimes the same as the ship's *rake* or *run*, forward or backward, but is most commonly understood of her sailing. *Way* is often used for *wake*. Thus when she begins her motion she is said to be *under way;* and when that motion increases, to have *fresh-way* through the water. Hence, also, she is said to have *head-way* or *stern-way*, to *gather way* or to *lose way*, &c. (*See* WIND'S-WAY.)—*Gangway*, means a clear space to pass. The gangway is the side space between the forecastle and quarter-deck.

'WAY ALOFT! OR 'WAY UP! The command when the crew are required aloft to loose, reef, furl sails, or man yards, &c.

WAY-GATE. The tail-race of a mill.

WAYS. Balks laid down for rolling weights along.—*Launching-ways*. Two parallel platforms of solid timber, one on each side of the keel of a vessel while building, and on which her cradle slides on launching.

WEAL. A wicker basket used for catching eels.

WEAR. *See* WEIR.—*To wear*. (*See* VEER.)

WEAR AND TEAR. The decay and deterioration of the hull, spars, sails, ropes, and other stores of a ship in the course of a voyage.

WEATHER [from the Anglo-Saxon *wæder*, the temperature of the air]. The state of the atmosphere with regard to the degree of wind, to heat and cold, or to dryness and moisture, but particularly to the first. It is a word also applied to everything lying to windward of a particular situation, hence a ship is said to have the weather-gage of another when further to windward. Thus also, when a ship under sail presents either of her sides to the wind, it is then called the *weather-side*, and all the rigging situated thereon is distinguished by the same epithet. It is the opposite of *lee*. To weather anything is to go to windward of it. The land to windward, is a weather shore.

WEATHER-ANCHOR. That lying to windward, by which a ship rides when moored.

WEATHER-BEAM. A direction at right angles with the keel, on the weather side of the ship.

WEATHER-BITT. Is that which holds the weather-cable when the ship is moored.

WEATHER-BOARD. That side of the ship which is to windward.

WEATHER-BOARDS. Pieces of plank placed in the ports of a ship when laid up in ordinary; they are in an inclined position, so as to turn off the rain without preventing the circulation of air.

WEATHER-BORNE. Pressed by wind and sea.

WEATHER-BOUND. Detained by foul winds; our forefathers used the term *wæder fæst*.

WEATHER-BREEDERS. Certain appearances in the heavens which indicate a gale, as wind-galls, fog-dogs, &c.

WEATHER-CLOTHS. Coverings of painted canvas or tarpaulin, used to preserve the hammocks when stowed, from injury by weather.

WEATHER-COIL. When a ship has her head brought about, so as to lie that way which her stern did before, as by the veering of the wind; or the motion of the helm, the sails remaining trimmed.

WEATHER-COILING. A ship resuming her course after being taken aback; rounding off by a stern-board, and coming up to it again.

WEATHER-EYE. "Keep your weather-eye open," be on your guard; look out for squalls.

WEATHER-GAGE. A vessel has the weather-gage of another when she is to windward of her. Metaphorically, to get the weather-gage of a person, is to get the better of him.

WEATHER-GALL:—

> "A weather-gall at morn,
> Fine weather all gone."

(*See* WIND-GALL.)

WEATHER-GLASS. A familiar term for the barometer.

WEATHER-GLEAM. A peculiar clear sky near the horizon, with great refraction.

WEATHER-GO. The end of a rainbow, as seen in the morning in showery weather.

WEATHER-HEAD. The secondary rainbow.

WEATHER-HELM. A ship is said to carry a weather-helm when she is inclined to gripe, or come too near the wind, and therefore requires the helm to be kept constantly a little to windward.

WEATHER-LURCH. A heavy roll to windward.

WEATHERLY. Said of a well-trimmed ship with a clean bottom, when she holds a good wind, and presents such lateral resistance to the water, that she makes but little lee-way while sailing close-hauled.

WEATHER ONE'S DIFFICULTIES, To. A colloquial phrase meaning to contend with and surmount troubles.

WEATHER-ROLLS. Those inclinations, so inviting to coming waves, which a ship makes to windward in a heavy sea; the sudden rolls which she makes to leeward being termed lee-lurches.

WEATHER-ROPES. An early term for those which were tarred.

WEATHER-SHEETS. Those fast to the weather-clues of the sails.— "Haul over the weather-sheets forward," applies to the jib when a vessel has got too close to the wind and refuses to answer her helm.

WEATHER-SHORE. The shore which lies to windward of a ship.

WEATHER-SIDE. That side of a ship on which the wind blows; it is the promenade for superior officers. (See also its synonym WINDWARD.)

WEATHER THE CAPE, To. To become experienced; as it implies sailing round Cape Horn, or the Cape of Good Hope.

WEATHER-TIDE. The reverse of *lee-tide*. That which, running contrary to the direction of the wind, by setting against a ship's lee-side while under sail, forces her up to windward.

WEATHER-WARNING. The telegraphic cautionary warning given by hoisting the storm-drum on receiving the forecast.

WEATHER-WHEEL. The position of the man who steers a large ship, from his standing on the weather-side of the wheel.

WEAVER. One of the popular names of the fish *Trachinus vipera*.

WEDGE [from the Anglo-Saxon *wege*]. A simple but effective mechanical force; a triangular solid on which a ship rests previous to launching. Many of the wedges used in the building and repairing of vessels are called *sett-wedges*.

WEDGE-FIDS. For top and top-gallant masts; in two parts, lifting by shores and sett-wedges. (*See* SETTING-UP.)

WEDGE-SHAPED GULF. One which is wide at its entrance, and gradually narrows towards its termination, as that of California.

WEDGING UP. Gaining security by driving wedges.

WEED, To. To clear the rigging of stops, rope-yarns, and pieces of oakum.

WEEKLY ACCOUNT. A correct return of the whole complement made every week when in harbour to the senior officer. Also, a sobriquet for the white patch on a midshipman's collar.

WEEL. A kind of trap-basket, or snare, to catch fish, made of twigs and baited; contrived similarly to a mouse-trap, so that fish have a ready admittance, but cannot get out again.

WEEPING. The oozing of water in small quantities through the seams of a ship.

WEEVIL [from the Anglo-Saxon *weft*]. *Curculio*, a coleopterous insect which perforates and destroys biscuit, wood, &c.

WEFT. *See* WAFT.

WEIGH, To [from the Anglo-Saxon *woeg*]. To move or carry. Applied to heaving up the anchor of a ship about to sail, but also to the raising any great weight, as a sunken ship, &c.

WEIGHAGE. The charge made for weighing goods at a dock.

WEIGH-SHAFT. In the marine-engine, the same as *wiper-shaft*.

WEIGHT-NAILS. Somewhat similar to deck-nails, but not so fine, and with square heads; for fastening cleats and the like.

WEIGHT OF METAL. The weight of iron which the whole of the guns are capable of projecting at one round from both sides when single-shotted. (*See* BROADSIDE-WEIGHT.)

WEIR. An old word for sea-weed. Also, a fishing inclosure; and again, a dam, or strong erection across a river, to divert its course.

WELD, To. To join pieces of iron or other metal by placing in contact the parts heated almost to fusion, and hammering them into one mass.

WELKIN [from the Anglo-Saxon *weal can*]. The visible firmament.

"One cheer more to make the welkin ring."

WELL [from the Anglo-Saxon *wyll*]. A bulk-headed inclosure in the middle of a ship's hold, defending the pumps from the bottom up to the lower deck from damage, by preventing the entrance of ballast or other obstructions, which would choke the boxes or valves in a short time, and render the pumps useless. By means of this inclosure the artificers may likewise more readily descend into the hold, to examine or repair the pumps, as occasion requires.

WELL, OR TRUNK OF A FISHING-VESSEL. A strong compartment in the middle of the hold, open to the deck, but lined with lead on every side, and having the bottom perforated with small holes through the floor, so that the water may pass in freely, and thus preserve the fish alive which are put into it. Lobster-boats are thus fitted.

WELL-CABINS. Those in brigs and small vessels, which have no after-windows or thorough draught.

WELL-END. *See* PUMP-FOOT.

WELL FARE YE, MY LADS! An exclamation of approbation to the men at a hard heave or haul.

WELL FOUND. Fully equipped.

WELL-GROWN. A term implying that the grain of the wood follows the shape required, as in knee-timber and the like.

WELL OFF, To. A mode of shutting off a leak by surrounding it by timbers screwed home through the lining to the timbers, and carrying up this trunk, like a log-hut, above the water-line.

WELL-ROOM OF A BOAT. The place in the bottom where the water lies, between the ceiling and the platform of the stern-sheets, from whence it is baled into the sea.

WELL THERE, BELAY! Synonymous with *that will do*.

WELSHMAN'S BREECHES. *See* DUTCHMAN'S BREECHES.

WEND A COURSE, To. To sail steadily on a given direction.

WENDING. Bringing the ship's head to an opposite course. Turning as a ship does to the tide.

WENTLE. An old term signifying to roll over.

WENTLE-TRAP. The *Scalaria pretiosa*, a very elegant univalve shell, much valued by collectors.

WEST-COUNTRY PARSON. A fish, the hake (*Gadus marlucius*), is so called, from a black streak on its back, and from its abundance along our western coast.

WESTER, or WASTER. A kind of trident used for striking salmon in the north.

WESTING. This term in navigation means the distance made by course or traverses to the westward; or the sun after crossing the meridian.

WESTWARD [Anglo-Saxon *weste-wearde*].—*Westward-hoe.* To the west! It was one of the cries of the Thames watermen.

WEST WIND. This and its collateral, the S.W., prevail nearly three-fourths of the year in the British seas, and though boisterous at times, are very genial on the whole.

WET. The owners and master of a ship are liable for all damage by wet. (*See* STOWAGE.)

WET-BULB THERMOMETER. One of which the bulb is kept moist by the capillary attraction of cotton fibres from an attached reservoir.

WET-DOCK. A term used for *float* (which see), and also *dock.*

WETHERS. The flukes or hands of a harpoon.

WETTING A COMMISSION. Giving an entertainment to shipmates on receiving promotion.

WHALE. A general term for various marine animals of the order *Cetacea*, including the most colossal of all animated beings. From their general form and mode of life they are frequently confounded with fish, from which, however, they differ essentially in their organization, as they are warm-blooded, ascend to the surface to breathe air, produce their young alive, and suckle them, as do the land mammalia. The cetacea are divided into two sections:—1. Those having horny plates, called baleen, or "whalebone," growing from the palate instead of teeth, and including the right whales and rorquals, or finners and hump-backs (see these terms). 2. Those having true teeth and no whalebone. To this group belong the sperm-whale, and the various forms of bottle-noses,' black-fish, grampuses, narwhals, dolphins, porpoises, &c. To the larger species of many of these the term "whale" is often applied.

WHALE-BIRD. A beautiful little bird seen hovering in flocks over the Southern Ocean, in search of the small crustaceans which constitute their food.

WHALE-BOAT. A boat varying from 26 to 56 feet in length, and from 4 to 10 feet beam, sharp at both ends, and admirably adapted to the intended purpose, combining swiftness of motion, buoyancy, and stability.

WHALE-CALF. The young whale.

WHALE-FISHERIES. The places at which the capture of whales, or "whale-fishery," is carried on. The principal are the coasts of Greenland and Davis Straits, for the northern right whale; Bermuda, for humpbacks; the Cape of Good Hope and the Australian seas, for the southern right whale; the North Pacific, for the Japanese right whale; and various places in the intertropical and southern seas, for the sperm-whale. But the constant persecution to which these animals are subjected causes a frequent change in their habitats. They have been nearly exterminated, or rendered so scarce as not to be worth following, in many districts where they formerly most abounded, and in order to make the trade remunerative, new grounds have to be continually sought. Maury's "whale charts" give much valuable information on this subject.

WHALER. A name for a vessel employed in the whale-fisheries.

WHALE'S FOOD. The name given in the North Sea to the *Clio borealis*, a well-known mollusk, on which whales feed.

WHANGERS, or COD-WHANGERS. Fish-curers of Newfoundland. An old term for a large sword.

WHAPPER. The largest of the turtle kind, attaining 7 or 8 cwts., off Ascension. [The name is supposed to be derived from *guapa*, Sp., grand or fine.] (*See* LOGGERHEAD.)

WHARF, or QUAY. An erection of wood or stone raised on the shore of a road or harbour for the convenience of loading or discharging vessels by cranes or other means. A wharf is of course built stronger or slighter in proportion to the effort of the tide or sea which it is intended to resist, and the size of vessels using it.— *Wharf*, in hydrography, is a scar, a rocky or gravelly concretion, or frequently a sand-bank, as Mad Wharf in Lancashire, where the tides throw up dangerous ripples and overfalls.

WHARFAGE DUES. The dues for landing or shipping goods at a wharf; customs charges in particular. Thus for goods not liable to duty, and forcibly taken for examination, wharfage charges are demanded even from a ship of war!

WHARFINGER. He who owns or keeps a wharf and takes account of all the articles landed thereon or removed from it, for which he receives a certain fee.

WHARF-STEAD. A ford in a river.

WHAT CHEER, HO? Equivalent among seamen to, *How fare ye?*

WHAT SHIP IS THAT? A question often put when a *jaw-breaking* word has been intrusively uttered by *savants*.

WHAT WATER HAVE YOU? The question to the man sounding, as to the depth of water which the lead-line gives.

WHAUP. The larger curlew, *Numenius arcuatus*.

WHEAT. An excellent article for sea-diet; boiled with a proportion of molasses, it makes a most nutritious breakfast. As it stows well, and would even yield nearly the same weight in bread, it should be made an article of allowance.

WHEEL. A general name for the helm, by which the tiller and rudder are worked in steering the ship; it has a barrel, round which the tiller-ropes or chains wind, and a wheel with spokes to assist in moving it.

WHEEL AND AXLE. A well-known mechanical power, to which belong all turning or wheel machines, as cranes, capstans, windlasses, cranks, &c.

WHEEL-HOUSE. A small round-house erected in some ships over the steering-wheel for the shelter of the helmsman.

WHEEL-LOCK. A small machine attached to the old musket for producing sparks of fire.

WHEEL-ROPES. Ropes rove through a block on each side of the deck, and led round the barrel of the steering-wheel. Chains are also used for this purpose.

WHEELS. *See* TRUCKS.

WHEFT. More commonly written *waft* (which see). Although *wheft* is given in the official signal-book, bibliophilists ignore the term.

WHELK. A well-known shell-fish, *Buccinum undatum.*

WHELPS. The brackets or projecting parts which rise out of the barrel or main body of the capstan, like buttresses, to enlarge the sweep, so that a greater portion of the cable, or whatever rope encircles the barrel, may be wound about it at one turn without adding much to the weight of the capstan. The whelps reach downwards from the lower part of the drum-head to the deck. The pieces of wood bolted on the main-piece of a windlass, or on a winch, for firm holding, and to prevent chafing, are also called whelps.

WHERE AWAY? In what bearing? a question to the man at the mast-head to designate in what direction a strange sail lies.

WHERRY. A name descended from the Roman *horia,* the *oare* of our early writers. It is now given to a sharp, light, and shallow boat used in rivers and harbours for passengers. The wherries allowed to ply about London are either scullers worked by one man with two sculls, or by two men, each pulling an oar. Also, a decked vessel used in fishing in different parts of Great Britain and Ireland: numbers of them were notorious smugglers.

WHETHER OR NO, TOM COLLINS. A phrase equivalent to, "Whether you will or not, such is my determination, not to be gainsaid."

WHICH WAY DOES THE WIND LIE? What is the matter?

WHIFF. The *Rhombus cardina,* a passable fish of the pleuronect genus. Also, a slight fitful breeze or transient puff of wind.

WHIFFING. Catching mackerel with a hook and line from a boat going pretty fast through the water.

WHIFFLERS. The old term for fifers, preceding the body of archers who cleared the way, but more recently applied to very trifling fellows. Smollett named Captain Whiffle in contempt.

WHIMBREL. The smaller species of curlew, *Numenius phœpus.*

WHIMSEY. A small crane for hoisting goods to the upper stories of warehouses.

WHINYARD. A sort of hanger, serving both as a weapon and a knife. An archaism for a cutlass. See the Gentleman in the *Cobler of Canterburie*, 1590:—

> "His cloake grew large and sid,
> And a faire winniard by his side."

WHIP. A single rope rove through a single block to hoist in light articles. Where greater and steadier power is demanded, a block is added, and the standing part is made fast near the upper block. Thus it becomes *a double whip.—To whip.* To hoist by a whip. Also to tie twine, whipping fashion, round the end of a rope to prevent its untwisting.

WHIP, OR WHIP-STAFF. A strong staff fastened into the helm for the steersman to move the rudder thereby.

WHIP-JACK. An old term, equivalent to fresh-water sailor, or a sham-shipwrecked tar. (*See* TURNPIKE-SAILORS.)

WHIPPERS. Men who deliver the cargoes of colliers in the river Thames into lighters.

WHIPPING-TWINE. Used to whip the ends of ropes.

WHIP-RAY. A ray with a long tail ending in a very fine point. It is armed with a dangerous serrated spine, jagged like a harpoon. Called also *sting-ray* and *stingaree.*

WHIP-SAW. The largest of that class of useful instruments, being that generally used at the saw-pit.

WHIP UPON WHIP. A sort of easy purchase, much used in colliers. It consists of one whip applied to the falls of another.

WHIRL, OR ROPE-WINCH. Small hooks fastened into cylindrical pieces of wood which communicate by a leather strap with a spoke-wheel, whereby three of them are set in motion at once. Used for spinning yarn for ropes. Now more commonly made of iron.

WHIRLER, OR TROUGHTON'S TOP. An ingenious instrument invented by Troughton, and intended to serve as an artificial horizon at sea; but it was found that its centrifugal force was incapable of counteracting the ordinary motion of a ship.

WHIRLPOOL. An eddy or vortex where the waters are continually rushing round. In rivers they are very common, from various accidents, and are usually of little consequence. In the sea they are more dangerous, as the classical Charybdis, and the celebrated Mäelstrom and Saltenstrom, both on the coast of Norway.

WHIRLWIND. A revolving current of wind of small diameter that rises suddenly, but is soon spent.

WHISKERS. Two booms, half-yards, or iron spars projecting on each side before the cat-heads; they are for spreading the guys of the jib-boom instead of having a spritsail-yard across. In many vessels the sprit-sail (then termed spread-yard) is lashed across the forecastle so as to rest before the cat-heads on the gunwale, and the guys rove through holes bored in it, and set up in the fore-channels.

WHISTLE. From the Ang.-Sax. *wistl.* (*See* BOATSWAIN'S CALL.)

WHISTLE FOR THE WIND, To. A superstitious practice among old seamen, who are equally scrupulous to avoid whistling during a heavy gale.—*To wet one's whistle.* To take a drink. Thus Chaucer tells us that the miller of Trumpington's lady had

"Hir joly whistle wel ywette."

WHISTLING PSALMS TO THE TAFFRAIL. Expending advice to no purpose.

WHITE BAIT OR BITE. The *Clupea alba,* a well-known fish caught in the Thames, but strictly a sea-fish, erroneously held to be mere fry till 1828, when Yarrell raised it to the rank of a perfect fish.

WHITE BOOT-TOP. A painted white line carried fore and aft on the hammock-netting base. It gives a longer appearance to a ship.

WHITE CAPS. Waves with breaking crests, specially between the east end of Jamaica and Kingston; but obtaining generally when the sea-breeze, coming fresh over the waves, and travelling faster, turns their tops: termed also *white-horses.*

WHITE FEATHER. The figurative symbol of cowardice : a white feather in a cock's tail being considered a proof of cross-breeding.

WHITE-FISH. A fish of the salmon family, found in the lakes of North America; also a name of the *hard-head* (which see). It is a general name for ling, cod, tusk, haddock, halibut, and the like, and for roach, dace, &c., from the use of their scales to form artificial pearls. Also applied to the beluga or white whale (*Beluga leucas*), a cetacean found in the Arctic seas and the Gulf of St. Lawrence. It is from 12 to 15 feet long.

WHITE-HERRING. A pickled herring in the north, but in other parts a fresh herring is so called.

WHITE-HORSE. A name of the *Raia fullonica.* (*See also* WHITE CAPS.)

WHITE-LAPPELLE. A sobriquet for a lieutenant, in allusion to his former uniform. (*See* LAPPELLE.)

WHITE-ROPE. Rope which has not been tarred. Manilla, coir, and some other ropes, do not require tarring.

WHITE SQUALL. A tropical wind said to give no warning; it sweeps the surface with spoon-drift.

WHITE-TAPE. A term amongst smugglers for hollands or gin.

WHITE-WATER. That which is seen over extensive sandy patches, where, owing to the limpidity and shallowness of the sea, the light of the sky is reflected.

WHITING. The name given in Cumberland to the *Salmo albus,* or white salmon. Also the *Gadus merlangus,* both split or dried.

WHITTLE [from the Anglo-Saxon *hwytel*]. A knife; also used for a sword, but contemptuously.—*To whittle.* To cut sticks.

WHITWORTH GUN. A piece rifled by having a twisted hexagonal bore, and throwing a more elongated shot with a sharper twist than the Armstrong gun, with results experimentally more beautiful, but not yet so practically useful.

WHO COMES THERE? The night challenge of a sentry on his post.

WHOLE-MOULDING. The old method of forming the principal part of a vessel. Boats are now the only vessels in which this method is practised.

WHOLESOME SHIP. One that will try, hull, and ride well, without heavy labouring in the sea.

WHOODINGS. Those ends of planks which are let into the rabbets of the stem, the stern-posts, &c. (*See* RABBET and HOOD-ENDS.)

WHO SAYS AMEN? Who will clap on with a will?

WHO SHALL HAVE THIS? An impartial sea method of distributing the shares of short commons. One person turns his back on the portions, and names some one, when he is asked, "*Who shall have this?*"

WICH. A port, as Harwich, Greenwich, &c.

WICK [Anglo-Saxon *wyc*]. A creek, bay, or village, by the side of a river.

WICKET. A small door in the gate of a fortress, for use by foot-passengers when the gate is closed.

WIDDERSHINS. A northern term signifying a motion contrary to the course of the sun. The Orkney fishermen consider themselves in imminent danger at sea, if, by accident, their vessel is turned *against the sun.*

WIDE-GAB. A name of the *Lophius piscatorius*, toad-fish, or fishing-frog.

WIDOWS' MEN. Imaginary sailors, formerly borne on the books as A.B.'s for wages in every ship in commission; they ceased with the consolidated pay at the close of the war. The institution was dated 24 Geo. II. to meet widows' pensions; the amount of pay and provisions for two men in each hundred was paid over by the paymaster-general of the navy to the widows' fund.

WILD. A ship's motion when she steers badly, or is badly steered. A *wild roadstead* implies one that is exposed to the wind and sea.

WILDFIRE. A pyrotechnical preparation burning with great fierceness, whether under water or not; it is analogous to the ancient Greek fire, and is composed mainly of sulphur, naphtha, and pitch.

WILD-WIND. An old term for *whirlwind.*

WILL, WITH A. With all zeal and energy.

WILL. A term on our northern shores for a sea-gull.

WILLICK. A northern name for the *Fratercula arctica*, or puffin.

WILLIE-POURIT. A northern name for the seal.

WILLIWAW. A sort of whirlwind, occurring in Tierra del Fuego.

WILLOCK. A name for the guillemot, *Uria troile.*

WIMBLE. The borer of a carpenter's centre-bit.

WINCH [from the Anglo-Saxon *wince*]. A purchase formed by a shaft whose extremities rest in two channels placed horizontally or perpendicularly, and furnished with cranks, or clicks, and pauls. It is employed as a purchase by which a rope or tackle-fall may be more powerfully applied than when used singly. A small one with a fly-wheel is used for making ropes and spun-yarn. Also, a support to the windlass ends. Also, the name of long iron handles by which the chain-pumps are worked. Also, a small cylindrical machine attached to masts or bitts in vessels, for the purpose of hoisting anything out of the hold, warping, &c.

WINCH-BITTS. The supports near their ends.

WIND [precisely the Anglo-Saxon word]. A stream or current of air which may be felt. The horizon being divided into 32 points (see COMPASS), the wind which blows from any of them has an assignable name.

WINDAGE. The vacant space left between a shot and the bore of the piece to which it belongs, generally expressed by the difference of their diameters; it is for facility of loading, but the smaller it is the better will be the performance of the gun.

WIND AND WATER LINE. That part of a ship lying at the surface of the water which is alternately wet and dry by the motion of the waves.

WIND A SHIP OR BOAT, To. To change her position by bringing her stern round to the place where the head was. (See WENDING.)

WIND AWAY, To. To steer through narrow channels.

WIND-BANDS. Long clouds supposed to indicate bad weather.

WIND-BOUND. Detained at an achorage by contrary winds.

WIND-FALL. A violent gust of wind rushing from coast-ranges and mountains to the sea. Also, some piece of good luck, a turtle, fish, vegetables, or a prize.

WIND-GAGE. See ANEMOMETER.

WIND-GALL. A luminous halo on the edge of a distant cloud, where there is rain, usually seen in the wind's eye, and looked upon as a sure precursor of stormy weather. Also, an atmospheric effect of prismatic colours, said likewise to indicate bad weather if seen to leeward.

WINDING A CALL. The act of blowing or piping on a boatswain's whistle, to communicate the necessary orders. (See CALL.)

WINDING-TACKLE. A tackle formed of one fixed triple three-sheaved block, and one double or triple movable block. It is principally used to hoist any weighty materials, as the cannon, into or out of a ship.

WINDING-TACKLE PENDANT. A strong rope made fast to the lower mast-head, and forming the support of the winding-tackle.

WIND IN THE TEETH. Dead against a ship.

WINDLASS [from the Ang.-Sax. windles]. A machine erected in the fore-part of a ship which serves to ride by, as well as heave in the cable. It is composed of the carrick-heads or windlass-heads, which are secured to all the deck-beams beneath, and backed by long sleeper knees on deck. The main-piece is whelped like the capstan, and suspended at its ends by powerful spindles falling into metal bearings in the carrick or windlass heads. Amidships it is supported by chocks, where it is also furnished with a course of windlass-pawls, four taking at separate angles on a main ratchet, and bearing on one quadrant of the circumference. The cables have three turns round this main-piece (one cable on each side): holes are cut for the windlass-bars in each eighth of the squared sides. The windlass may be said also to be supported or reinforced by the pawl-bitts, two powerful bitt-heads at the centre.—Spanish windlass. A machine formed of a handspike and a small lever, usually a tree-nail, or a tree-nail and a marline-spike, to set up the top-gallant rigging, heave in seizings, or for any other short steady purchase.

WINDLASS-BITTS. *See* CARRICK-BITTS.

WINDLASS-CHOCKS. Those pieces of oak or elm fastened inside the bows of small craft, to support the ends of the windlass.

WINDLASS-ENDS. Two pieces which continue the windlass outside the bitt-heads.

WINDLASS-LINING. Pieces of hard wood fitted round the main-piece of a windlass to prevent chafing, and also to enable the cable to hold on more firmly.

WINDLESTRAY. A sort of bent or seaside grass.

WINDLIPPER. The first effects of a breeze of wind on smooth water, before waves are raised.

WIND-RODE. A ship is wind-rode when the wind overcomes an opposite tidal force, and she rides head to wind.

WINDS. *Local* or *peculiar.*—*Trade-winds* occur within and beyond the tropical parallels. They are pretty regular in the North Atlantic, as far as 5° N., where calms may be expected, or the south-east trade may reach across, depending on the season; but when near land they yield to the *land and sea breezes.* Thus at 10° N. the land-breeze will be at E. from 11 P.M. until 6 A.M., then calm intervenes up to 10 A.M., when the sea-breeze sets in, probably W., and blows home fresh. Yet at 20 miles off shore the trade-wind may blow pretty strong from N.E. or E.N.E.—The *harmattan* is a sudden dry wind blowing off the coast of Africa, so charged with almost impalpable dust that the sun is obscured. It sucks up all moisture, cracks furniture and earthenware, and prostrates animal nature. The rigging of vessels becomes a dirty brown, and the dust adhering to the blacking cannot be removed.—The *tornado* lasts for a short time, but is of great force during its continuance.—The *northers* in the Gulf of Mexico, or off the Heads of Virginia, are not only very heavy gales, but are attended with severe cold. On a December day, off Galveston, the temperature in a calm was at sunset 86°. The norther came on about midnight, and at 8 A.M. the temperature had fallen to 12°, and icicles were hanging from the eaves of the houses. The *Tiempo di Vendavales,* or southers of Western America, is an opposite, blowing heavily home to the coast. The *taifung* of China, or typhoon of the Indian seas, is indeed precisely similar to the hurricane of the West Indies.

WIND-SAIL. A funnel of canvas employed to ventilate a ship by conveying a stream of fresh air down to the lower decks. It is suspended by a whip through the hatchways, and kept open by means of hoops; the upper part is also open on one side, and guyed to the wind. Ships of war in hot climates have generally three or four of these wind-sails.

WIND-TAUT. A vessel at anchor, heeling over to the force of the wind.

WIND-TIGHT. A cask or vessel to contain water is said to be windtight and water-tight.

WINDWARD. The weather-side; that on which the wind blows; the opposite of *leeward* (which see). Old sailors exhort their neophytes to throw nothing over the weather-side except ashes or hot water: a hint not mistakable.

WINDWARD SAILING, OR TURNING TO WINDWARD. That mode of navigating a ship in which she endeavours to gain a position situated in the direction whence the wind is blowing. In this case progress is made by frequent tacking, and trimming sail as near as possible to the wind.

WINDWARD SET. The reverse of *leeward set.*

WINDWARD TIDE. *See* WEATHER-TIDE.

WINE OF HEIGHT. A former perquisite of seamen on getting safely through a particular navigation.

WING. The projecting part of a steamer's deck before and abaft each of the paddle-boxes, bounded by the *wing-wale.*

WING-AND-WING. A ship coming before the wind with studding-sails on both sides; also said of fore-and-aft vessels, when they are going with the wind right aft, the foresail boomed out on one side, and the mainsail on the other.

WINGERS. Small casks stowed close to the side in a ship's hold, where the large casks would cause too great a rising in that part of the tier.

WINGS. Those parts of the hold and orlop-deck which are nearest to the sides. This term is particularly used in the stowage of the several materials contained in the hold, and between the cable-tiers and the ship's sides. In ships of war they are usually kept clear, that the carpenter and his crew may have access round the ship to stop shot-holes in time of action. Also, the skirts or extremities of a fleet, when ranged in a line abreast, or when forming two sides of a triangle. It is usual to extend the wings of a fleet in the daytime, in order to discover any enemy that may fall in their track; they are, however, generally summoned by signal to form close order before night. In military parlance, the right and left divisions of a force, whether these leave a centre division between them or not.—*Wing-transom.* The uppermost transom in the stern-frame, to which the heels of the counter-timbers are let on and bolted.

WING UP BALLAST, To. To carry the dead weight from the bottom as high as consistent with the stability of a ship, in order to ease her quick motion in rolling.

WING-WALE. A thick plank extending from the extremity of a steamer's paddle-beam to her side; it is also designated the *sponson-rim.*

WINNOLD-WEATHER. An eastern-county term for stormy March weather.

WINTER-FISH. This term generally alludes to cured cod and ling.

WINTER-QUARTERS. The towns or posts occupied during the winter by troops who quit the campaign for the season. Also, the harbour to which a blockading fleet retires in wintry gales. In Arctic parlance, the spot where ships are to remain housed during the winter months—from the 1st October to the 1st July or August.

WINTER-SOLSTICE. *See* CAPRICORNUS.

WIPER. A cogged contrivance in machinery by which a rotatory motion is converted into a reciprocating motion.

WIPER-SHAFT. An application to the valve equipoise of a marine-engine: their journals or bearings lie in bushes, which are fixed upon the frame of the engine.

WIRE-MICROMETER. An instrument necessary for delicate astronomical measurements. It contains vertical and horizontal wires, or spider-lines, acting in front of a comb or scale for distances, and on a graduated circle on the screw-head for positions.

WIRE-ROPE. Rigging made of iron wire galvanized, and laid up like common cordage.

WISBUY LAWS. A maritime code which, though framed at a town in the now obscure island of Gothland, in the Baltic, was submissively adopted by Europe.

WISHES [from the British *usk*, water]. Low lands liable to be overflowed.

WISHY-WASHY. Any beverage too weak. Over-watered spirits.

> " His food the land-crab, lizard, or the frog;
> His drink a wish-wash of six-water grog."

WITH. An iron instrument fitted to the end of a boom or mast, with a ring to it, through which another boom or mast is rigged out and secured. Also, in mechanics, the elastic withe handles of cold chisels, set-tools, &c., which prevent a jar to the assistant's wrist.

WITH A WILL. Pull all together.

WITHERSHINS. *See* WIDDERSHINS.

WITHEYS. Any low places near rivers where willows grow.

WITHIN-BOARD. Inside a ship.

WITHOUT. Outside, as, studding-sail without studding-sail; or, *without board*, outside a ship.

WITH THE SUN. Ropes coiled from the left hand towards the right; but where the sun passes the meridian north of the observer, it is of course the reverse.

WITNESSES, or TEMOINS, are certain piles of earth left in digging docks, or other foundations, to judge how many cubic feet of earth have been removed.

WITTEE-WITTEE. The ingeniously-constructed fish-hook of the Pacific islanders, made of mother-of-pearl, with hair tufts, serving at once both as hook and bait.

WOARE. An old term for sea-weed. Also, the shore margin or beach.

WOBBLE, To. In mechanics, to sway or roll from side to side. (*See* WABBLE.)

WOLD. An extensive plain, covered with grass and herbs, but bare of trees.

WOLF. A kind of fishing-net.

WOLF-FISH. *Anarrichas lupus*, also called cat-fish. A fish of the northern seas, from 2 to 3 feet long, with formidable teeth, with which it crushes the shells of the crustaceans and mollusks on which it feeds.

WOLYING. The old way of spelling *woolding*.

WONDER-CHONE. An old term, mentioned by Blount as a contrivance for catching fish.

WONGS. A term on our east coast, synonymous with low lands or *wishes* (which see).

WOOD, To. A gun is said to wood when it takes the portsills or port-sides, or the trucks the waterways.—*To wood*. When wooding-parties are sent out to cut or procure wood for a ship.

WOOD AND WOOD. When two pieces of timber are so let into each other as to join close. Also, when a tree-nail is driven through, its point being even with the inside surface.

WOODEN BUOYS. Buoyant constructions of wood of various shapes, with a ring-bolt at each end, to which vessels can make fast for a time. (*See* DOLPHIN.)

WOOD-ENDS. See HOOD-ENDS.

WOODEN WALLS. A term signifying the fleet, and though thought to be peculiarly English, was used by the Delphic oracle, when applied to by the Athenians on the Persian invasion: "Defend yourselves by wooden walls."

WOODEN-WINGS. The lee-boards, for keeping barges to windward.

WOOD-LOCKS OF THE RUDDER. Pieces of timber sheathed with copper, in coppered ships, placed in the throating or scores of the stern-post, to prevent the rudder from rising or unshipping.

WOOD-MULLS. Large thick hose worn by the men in coasters and fish-ing-boats.

WOOD-SHEATHING. All plank applied to strengthen a vessel. (*See* DOUBLE.)

WOOF. A northern name of the gray gurnard.

WOOLDERS. Bandages. The bolt of a Spanish windlass is called a woolder.

WOOLDING. The act of winding a piece of rope about a mast or yard, to support it where it is fished, or when it is composed of several pieces. Also, the rope employed in this service.

WOOL-PACKS. In meteorology, light clouds in a blue sky.

WORD. The watchword; the parole and countersign, which, being issued to the authorized persons at guard-mounting, become a test whereby spies or strangers are detected.

WORK, To. Said of a ship when she strains in a tempestuous sea, so as to loosen her joints.

WORK ABACK. This is said of a steam-engine if reversed, to propel the vessel astern.

WORK A SHIP, To. To adapt the sails to the force and direction of the wind.

WORK DOUBLE TIDES, To. Implying that the work of three days is done in two, or at least two tides' work in twenty-four hours.

WORKING A DAY'S WORK. Reducing the dead-reckoning and meridian altitudes to noon of each day.

WORKING A LUNAR. Reducing the observations of the sun and moon, or moon and stars, in order to find the longitude. Also, a phrase used when a man sleeps during a conversation.

WORKING AN OBSERVATION. Reducing the altitudes or distances of heavenly bodies by calculation.

WORKING PARTIES. Gangs of hands employed on special duties out of the ship or dockyard.

WORKING TO WINDWARD. Sailing against the wind by alternate tacks. (*See* BEATING.)

WORKING UP. The keeping men at work on needless matters, beyond the usual hours, for punishment.

WORKS. All fortificational constructions, whether permanent, field, or makeshifts of the moment; from the most solid bastion to the rudest rifle-pit.

WORK UP JUNK, To. To draw yarns from old cables, &c., and therewith to make foxes, points, gaskets, sinnit, or spun-yarn.

WORM. An iron tool shaped like a double corkscrew on the end of a long staff, for withdrawing charges, ignited remains of cartridges, &c., from fire-arms. Called also a wad-hook in artillery. (*See also* TEREDO NAVALIS.)
—*To worm.* The act of passing a rope spirally between the lays of a cable; a smaller rope is wormed with spun-yarn. Worming is generally resorted to as a preparative for serving. (*See* LINK-WORMING.)

WORM-EATEN, OR WORMED. The state of a plank or of a ship's bottom when perforated by a particular kind of boring mollusk, *Teredo navalis*, which abounds in the tropics.

WORMS. Timber is preserved against worms by several coats of common whale-oil, or by the patents of Payne, Sir W. Burnett, Kyan, and others.

WRACK. The English name for the fucus; the sea-weed used for the manufacture of kelp, and in some places artificially grown for that purpose.

WRACK-RIDER. A species of brandling faintly barred on both sides.

WRAIN-BOLT. A ring-bolt with two or more forelock-holes in it, occasionally to belay or make fast towards the middle. It is used, with the wrain-staff in the ring, for *setting-to* the planks.

WRAIN-STAFF. A stout billet of tough wood, tapered at its ends, so as to go into the ring of the wrain-bolt, to make the necessary setts for bringing-to the planks or thick stuff to the timber.

WRASSE. The *Crenilabrus tinca*, a sea-fish, sometimes called old-wife.

WRECK. The destruction of a ship by stress of weather, rocks, &c.; also the ruins of the ship after such accidents; also the goods and fragments which drive on shore after a ship is stranded. It is said that the term is derived from the sea-weed called *wrack*, denoting all that the sea washes on shore as it does this weed. A ship cast on shore is no wreck, in law, when any domestic animal has escaped with life in her. The custody of the cargo or goods belongs to the deputy of the vice-admiral, and they are restored to the proprietors without any fees or salvage, but what the labour of those who saved them may reasonably deserve.

WRECKAGE. Spars, rigging, or goods floating about after a wreck.

WRECKERS. A name which includes both meritorious salvors of ships in distress, and the felonious brutes who merely hasten to wrecks for plunder. One of our British colonies deemed it so entirely a legal procedure to make a wreck of or cripple a vessel on the reef, that a naval officer was threatened with legal proceedings by a lawyer whom he prevented from carrying out his practice afloat.

WRECK-FREE. Is to be exempt from the forfeiture of shipwrecked goods and vessels: a privilege which Edward I. granted by charter to the barons of the Cinque Ports.

WRIGHT'S SAILING. Synonymous with *Mercator's sailing.*

WRING A MAST, To. To bend, cripple, or strain it out of its natural position by setting the shrouds up too taut. The phrase, *to wring,* is also applied to a capstan when by an undue strain the component parts of the wood become deranged, and are thereby disunited. The head of a mast is frequently wrung by bracing up the lower yards beyond the dictates of sound judgment.

WRONG, To. To outsail a vessel by becalming her sails is said to wrong her.

WRONG WAY. When the ship casts in the opposite direction to that desired. Also, a ship swinging in a tide's way, out of the direction which would keep her hawse clear.

WRUNG-HEADS. An old term for that part of a ship near the floor-heads and second futtock-heels, which, when she lies aground, bears the greatest strain.

X.

XEBEC, or ZEBEC. A small three-masted vessel of the Mediterranean, distinguished from all other European vessels by the great projection of her bow and overhanging of her stern. Being generally equipped as a corsair, the xebec was constructed with a narrow floor, for speed, and of great breadth, to enable her to carry a great press of sail. On the Barbary coast the xebec rig was deemed to vary from the felucca, which in hull is the same, by having the foremast square-rigged.

XERAFEEM. A Malabar coin of the value of 1s. 4d. sterling.

XEROONITZ. A Russian coin of two roubles, or 9s. sterling.

XERO-POTAMO. A term common on the coasts of Greece for fiumare, or torrents, which are dry at certain seasons.

XUGIA. The second bank of rowers in an ancient trireme.

XYLOSTROMA. Oak-leather, a peculiar fungus found within growing oaks.

Y.

YACHT. A vessel of state or pleasure: the former is usually employed to convey great personages. One of the designs of a yacht being accommodation, they are usually fitted up with great comfort; their propulsion is by sails or steam. Small yachts, rigged as sloops, were formerly used by the commissioners of the navy; they were originally royal yachts, and one at Chatham was renowned as the yacht of Queen Elizabeth, the same plate being in use in her up to a very late date. Private pleasure-boats, when sufficiently large for a sea voyage, are also termed yachts. (*See* ROYAL YACHT.)

YACHT CLUB, ROYAL. An institution embodied by a number of noblemen and gentlemen about the year 1820, to which certain privileges are attached. It was originally established at Cowes, but several ports, as well as the Thames, have their special clubs, and similar privileges.

YAM. The tubers of the *Dioscorea sativa*, and others; a valuable vegetable on long voyages. *D. aculeata* frequently produces tubers 3 feet long, and weighing 30 lbs. Also, the West India word for food; "Toko for yam," the negro's punishment—blows but no food.

YANKEE. An appellation often erroneously given to North Americans in general, whereas it is strictly applicable to those of the New England states only; it is not used complimentarily in the back settlements.

YARD. A measure of length, consisting of 3 feet.

YARD [Anglo-Saxon *gyrde*]. A long cylindrical timber suspended upon the mast of a vessel to spread a sail. They are termed square, lateen, or lug: the first are suspended across the masts at right angles, and the two latter obliquely. The square yards taper from the middle, which is called the slings, towards the extremities, which are termed the yard-arms; and the distance between is divided by the artificers into quarters, called the first, second, third quarters, and yard-arms. The middle quarters are formed into eight sides, and each of the end parts is figured like the frustum of a cone: on the alternate sides of the octagon, in large spars, oak battens are brought on and hooped, so as to strengthen, and yet not greatly increase, the weight.—*To brace the yards.* To traverse them about the masts, so as to form greater or lesser angles with the ship's length. (*See* BRACE.)—*To square the yards.* (*See* SQUARE.)

YARD-ARM. That part of a yard outside the quarter, which is on either side of the mast beyond the battens, when it lies athwart the ship. It generally means the extremity of the yard, and it is fitted with sheave-holes for reeving sheets through.

YARD-ARM AND YARD-ARM. The situation of two ships lying

alongside one another, so near that their yard-arms nearly touch each other, or even cross. The term implies close action and no mistake.

YARD-ARM CLEATS. Wooden wedges fixed on the yards at those points where they support the lifts and braces, and where the head-earings are secured. The reef-cleats on the topsail-yards are beyond the lifts and braces.

YARD-ARM PIECE. An octagonal piece of timber supplied to replace a yard-arm if shot away. It is one-third the length of the main-yard.

YARD-ROPE. Is only used for temporary purposes; the most usual application of the term is that by which a yard is hoisted for crossing, or sent down. Also, rove for execution. The yard-rope of the lighter yards is the halliards, which, when the yard is crossed, is made into tie and halliards by a peculiar mode of toggling on the halliard purchase, as in the order, "Toggle the halliards!"

YARDS. *See* DOCKYARDS.

YARDS APEEK. When they are topped, so as to resemble St. Andrew's cross; it is done as a token of mourning, or for convenience when vessels lie alongside of each other, as in the docks.

YARD-TACKLES. Tackles attached to the fore and main yards of a ship, whereby, with the assistance of the stay-tackles, the boats and other weights are hoisted in and out. Yard-tackles are sometimes hooked to a pendant, which is secured to the top-mast head, and hauled out to the yard-arm by means of a small tackle, until the yard-tackle plumbs the spot where it is wished to work.

YARE [Ang.-Sax. for dexterous or quick]. It was formerly a favourite nautical phrase, as "Be yare at the helm;" and is used by Shakspeare's boatswain in the *Tempest*.

YAREMLEK. A silver Turkish coin of 20 paras, or 9d. sterling.

YARMOUTH CAPON. A red herring; a bloater.

YARMOUTH HERRING-BOAT. A clincher-built vessel with lug-sails, similar to the drift or mackerel boats.

YARN. One of the threads of which ropes are composed. A number of these are twisted together to form a strand, in proportion to the size of the proposed rope. Three strands are then twisted into one another, which completes the process of ordinary rope-making; but cables, hawsers, and other ground tackling, are composed of three strands, each of which is formed of three lesser ones. (*See* CABLE, HAWSER, &c.)—*A tough yarn.* A long story, or tale, hard to be believed.

YARN-SPINNING. A figurative expression for telling a story.

YATAGHAN. A crooked sabre used in the Levant. Also, the knife-swords of India.

YAUGH. An archaic term for a little bark, pinnace, or yacht.

YAW. The quick movement by which a ship deviates from the direct line of her course towards the right or left, from unsteady steering.

YAWL. A man-of-war's boat, resembling the pinnace, but rather smaller; it is carvel-built, and generally rowed with twelve oars. The yawl in the

Customs Act is a carvel-built vessel of the cutter class, but having a
jigger or mizen lug, the boom-mainsail being curtailed, so that its boom
traverses clear of the mizen-mast : used also by yachts.   Also, a small
fishing-vessel.

YAW-SIGHTED.   A nautical term for those who squint.

YAW-YAW.   A nickname for the seamen of the shores of the Baltic.

YEAR.   The duration of the earth's revolution round the sun, or of the
apparent revolution of the sun in the ecliptic.

YELL.   An old sea-term to express a rolling motion.

YELLOW ADMIRAL.   A retired post-captain, who, not having served
his time in that rank, is not entitled to his promotion to the active flag.

YELLOW-BELLY.   A name given to a person born in the fens along
our eastern shores: also occasionally to half-castes, &c.

YELLOW FEVER.   A cant term for drunkenness at Greenwich Hospital;
the sailors when punished wearing a parti-coloured coat, in which yellow
predominates.

YELLOW-FLAG.   The signal of quarantine.

YELLOWING.   The passing over of captains at a flag promotion.

YELLOW-TAIL.   A well-known tropical fish, often in company with
whip-rays; it is about 4 feet long, with a great head, large eyes, and
many fins.   *Leiostomas.*

YEO-HEAVE-YEOING.   The chant or noise made at the windlass and
purchase-falls in a merchantman, to cheer and lighten labour, but not
permitted in a man-of-war.

YEOMAN.   An experienced hand placed in charge of a store-room, who
should be able to keep the accounts of supply and expenditure.

YESTY [from the Anglo-Saxon *gist*].   A foaming breaking sea.   Shakspeare in *Macbeth* gives great power to this state of the waters :—

> "Though the yesty waves
> Confound, and swallow navigation up."

YOKE.   A transverse board or metal bar, a substitute for the tiller, which
crosses the head of a boat's rudder, and having two lines extending from its
opposite extremities to the stern-sheets of the boat, whereby she is steered.

YOKE-LINES.   The ropes by which the boat's steerage is managed.

YOUNG.   A word often used for uninitiated.— *Young gentlemen*, a general
designation for midshipmen, whatever their age.

YOUNG FLOOD.   *See* FLOOD.

YOUNG ICE.   Nearly the same as bay-ice, except that it is only applied
to ice very recently formed, or of the present season.

YOUNGSTER, OR YOUNKER [an old term; from the Anglo-Saxon *junker*].
A volunteer of the first-class, and a general epithet for a stripling in the
service.

YOUNG WIND.   The commencement of the land or sea breeze.

YOU, SIR !   The irritating mode in which some officers address the seamen.
The late Lord Collingwood never permitted it.

YOW-YOW. A smaller kind of Chinese sampan.

Y'S OF AN INSTRUMENT. The Y-shaped bearings for the telescope axis, on the precision of which the value of an astronomical observation much depends: similar to the bearings of steam-engines, &c.

Z.

ZAFAR. A coil of Spanish rope.

ZAMBO. A term on the Spanish Main for a race produced by the union of the negro and the Indian; it literally means *bow-legged*.

ZEAL. A quality essentially requisite in forming the character of an efficient officer, since it comprehends ardour for the service, prompt obedience to orders, cheerful disposition, and a studious application to professional science.

ZECCHINO [from *zecca*, a mint]. A gold coin of Italy; average value, 9s. 6d.

ZECHIN. A Turkish coin. (*See* SEQUIN.)

ZENITH. The pole of the horizon, or that point in the heavens directly overhead, as nadir is that which is directly under our feet.

ZENITH-DISTANCE. The angular distance of any celestial object from the zenith at the time of observation. In navigation the meridional zenith-distance of a heavenly body is much used for finding the latitude.

ZEPHYR. The west wind, but generally considered to apply to any light pleasant breeze.

ZERO. The cypher or nought at the beginning of a graduated arc.

ZETETIC. The analytic method of investigating a mathematical problem.

ZIG-ZAG. The winding trench of approach of a besieger, directed by short turns alternately right and left of the defences of the place, to avoid being enfiladed by them. Called also a *boyau*.

ZIG-ZAG COURSE. Working to windward by very short tacks or angular turning boards.

ZODIAC. A broad zone or belt of the heavens, the middle of which is the ecliptic, extending 9° on either side of it. It is divided into twelve signs, each measuring 30° along the ecliptic.

ZODIACAL LIGHT. A pyramidal cone of light, apparently emanating from the rising and setting sun, commonly seen in the tropics; in higher latitudes most visible about the time of the equinoxes.

ZOLL, OR SAUL. An Indian timber, much used in the construction of country vessels.

ZONE. *See* BELT.

ZONE OF DECLINATION. A belt of the heavens included between certain parallels of declination.

ZONES, IN GEOGRAPHY, are longitudinal belts into which the surface of the earth is divided, according to their various relation to the sun's apparent motion. They are—the *torrid* or *equatorial zone*, bounded by the two tropics (which see), to every part of which, at some time or other, the sun is vertical; the *frigid zones*, from the poles to the polar circles, to every part of which in succession, periodically, the sun is at mid-day below the horizon; and the *temperate zones*, intermediate between the two former, to all of which the sun rises every day in the year.

ZOOPHYTE. A term compounded of two Greek words, signifying animal-plant, vaguely applied to various low forms of animal organizations, as the sea-anemones and coral animals, which present a certain superficial resemblance to plants.

ZOPISSA. Tar or pitch scraped off the bottoms of old ships, and thought to be astringent and good for ulcers. Also, a highly preservative varnish in use by the ancients for ships' bottoms, sarcophagi, &c.

ZUHN. A species of Indian rush, from which an inferior kind of cordage and canvas is made.

ZUMBRA. A Spanish skiff or yawl.

Grafica Veneta S.p.A.
via Padova 2, 35010 Trebaseleghe (PD)
Printed in China